INTRODUCTION TO LEGAL STUDIES

SECOND EDITION

edited by

THE DEPARTMENT OF LAW CASEBOOK GROUP

Carleton University

B. WRIGHT
B. DAWSON
N. SARGENT
A. BARTHOLOMEW
D. FRASER
P. SWAN
A. HUNT
R. MOHR
P. FITZGERALD

CANADIAN LEGAL STUDIES SERIES

CAPTUS PRESS

Canadian Legal Studies Series
Introduction to Legal Studies, Second Edition

Canadian Cataloguing in Publication Data
Main entry under title:

Introduction to legal studies

(Canadian legal studies series)
2nd ed.
Includes bibliographical references.

ISBN 1–895712–71–8

1. Law — Canada   2.   Sociological jurisprudence.
I. Wright, Barry, 1957–   II. Series.

KE442.I57 1995   349.71   C95–932136–5
KF385.ZA2I57 1995

First Captus Press edition, 1990
Revised edition, 1991

Captus Press Inc.
York University Campus
4700 Keele Street
North York, Ontario
M3J 1P3   Canada
Phone   (416) 736–5537
FAX   (416) 736–5793
EMail   captpres@io.org

0 9 8 7 6 5
Printed and bound in Canada

Editors' Note

These materials are the collective product of the Department of Law Casebook Group. *Introduction to Legal Studies* is designed as a reader for students enroled in the first year course of Carleton University's undergraduate-level studies programme. The materials are intended to situate the study of legal rules, institutions and processes in their social context. Particular attention has been given to selecting materials which reflect different theoretical and methodological approaches to questions about the social significance of law and the relationship between law and social change.

While the materials are intended for use by Carleton students, we hope that this reader will also prove relevant for students enroled in undergraduate legal studies programmes elsewhere in Canada. Please note that some articles have had their footnotes or endnotes removed. These can be found by going to the original work.

Acknowledgement

The original edition of these materials could not have been put together without the energy and enthusiasm of our research assistant Laura Landry, who acted as a catalyst in prompting suggestions from the various editors in respect to different selections of the materials. We would like to express our appreciation for her assistance.

Table of Contents

3 Language, Law and Power

4 Legal Method and Social Inquiry

7 Dispute Resolution

8 People in the Legal Process: Access to "Justice"

9 People in the Legal Process: The Personnel of Law

10 Law and Social Transformation

A. The Institutional Framework of Law Reform

B. Social Movements and Rights Struggles

A Pound of Flesh[†]

Shylock: We trifle time; I pray thee, pursue sentence.

Portia: A pound of that same merchant's flesh is thine;
The court awards it and the law doth give it.

Shylock: Most rightful judge!

Portia: And you must cut this flesh from off his breast;
The law allows it and the court awards it.

Shylock: Most learned judge!

Portia: Tarry a little; there is something
This bond doth give thee here not a jot of blood;
The words expressly are 'a pound of flesh';
Take then they bond, take thou thy pound of flesh;
But in cutting, if thou dost shed
One drop of Christian blood, thy lands and goods
Are, by the laws of Venice, confiscate
Unto the state of Venice.

Questions

1. Reconstruct the rule which saves Antonio, the merchant of Venice, from Shylock's knife.

2. State the mechanism of the application of the rule which saves Antonio.

3. The application of legal rules in this manner is often referred to as an example of "legalism". What is "legalism"?

---

† Excerpt from Shakespeare, William, *The Merchant of Venice*, Act IV, Scene 1, lines 312–28.

The Legal Terrain

A. Law in Social Life

The Functions of Law[†]
E.A. Hoebel

LAW performs certain functions essential to the maintenance of all but the most simple societies.

The first is to define relationships among the members of a society, to assert what activities are permitted and what are ruled out, so as to maintain at least minimal integration between the activities of individuals and groups within the society.

The second is derived from the necessity of taming naked force and directing force to the maintenance of order. It is the allocation of authority and the determination of who may exercise physical coercion as a socially recognized privilege-right, along with the selection of the most effective forms of physical sanction to achieve the social ends that the law serves.

The third is the disposition of trouble cases as they arise.

The fourth is to redefine relations between individuals and groups as the conditions of life change. It is to maintain adaptability.[1]

Purposive definition of personal relations is the primary law-job. Other aspects of culture likewise work to this end, and, indeed, the law derives its working principles (jural postulates) from postulates previously developed in the nonlegal spheres of action. However, the law's important contribution to the basic organization of society as a whole is that the law specifically and explicitly defines relations. It sets the expectancies of man to man and group to group so that each knows the focus and the limitations of its demand-rights on others, its duties to others, its privilege-rights and powers as against others, and its immunities and liabilities to the contemplated or attempted acts of others.[2] This is the "bare-bones job", as Karl Llewellyn likes to call it. It is the ordering of the fundamentals of living together.

No culture has a specific starting point in time; yet in the operation of the first function it is as though men were getting together and saying to each other. "Look here! Let's have a little organization here or we'll never get anywhere with this mess! Let's have a clear understanding of who's who, what we are to do, and how we are going to do it!" In its essence it is what the social-contract theorists recognized as the foundation of social order.

The second function of the law — the allocation of authority to exercise coercive physical force — is something almost peculiar to things legal.

Custom has regularity, and so does law. Custom defines relationships, and so does law. Custom is sanctioned, and so is law. But the sanctions of law may involve physical coercion. Law is distinguished from mere customs in that it endows certain selected individuals with the privilege-right of applying the sanction of physical coercion, if need be. The legal, let it be repeated, has teeth that can bite. But the biting, if it is to be legal and not mere gangsterism, can be done only by those persons to whom the law has allocated the privilege-right for the affair at hand.[3]

We have seen that in primitive law authority is a shifting, temporary thing. Authority to enforce a norm resides (for private wrongs) with the wronged individual and his immediate kinsmen — but only for the duration of time necessary to follow through the procedural steps that lead to redress or punishment of the culprit. In primitive

†   Hoebel, Edward Adamson, "The Functions of Law" in *The Law of Primitive Man* (Cambridge, Mass.: Harvard University Press, 1954), 275–84, 287. Copyright © 1954 by the President and Fellows of Harvard College; Copyright © renewed 1982 by Edward Adamson Hoebel. Reprinted by permission of Harvard University Press. Acknowledgement also to artist, John Fowler.

law the tendency is to allocate authority to the party who is directly injured. This is done in part out of convenience, for it is easier to let the wronged party assume the responsibility of legal action. It is also done because the primitive kinship group, having a more vital sense of entity, is naturally charged with a heavier emotional effect. In any event, when the community qua community acknowledges the exercise of force by a wronged person or his kinship group as correct and proper in a given situation, and so restrains the wrongdoer from striking back, then law prevails and order triumphs over violence.

We have also found in our studies of primitive societies that in a limited number of situations authority is directly exercised by the community on its own behalf. It takes the form of lynch law in some instances where clear procedures have not been set up in advance, as in the Comanche treatment of excessive sorcery and Shoshone treatment of cannibalism. Lynch law among primitives, however, is not a backsliding from, or detouring around, established formal law as it is with us. It is a first fitful step toward the emergence of criminal law in a situation in which the exercise of legal power has not yet been refined and allocated to specific persons. It is a blunt crude tool wielded by the gang hand of an outraged public.

Yet lynch law is rare among primitives. Even the simplest of them have crystallized standards as to what constitutes criminal behaviour, and the exercise of public authority is delegated to official functionaries — the chieftain, the council of chiefs, and the council of elders.

Power may sometimes be personal, as is the power of the bully in the society of small boys, and as was to some extent the power of William the Conqueror. But personal tyranny is a rare thing among primitives. Brute force of the individual does not prevail. Chiefs must have followers. Followers always impose limitations on their leaders. Enduring power is always institutionalized power. It is *transpersonalized*. It resides in the office, in the social status, rather than in the man. The constitutional structures of the several tribes examined in this book have all clearly revealed how political and legal authority are in each instance delimited and circumscribed.

This point is emphasized only to dispel any residue of the hoary political philosophies that assumed without basis in fact that primitive societies existed under the rule of fang and claw.

However, the personal still obtrudes. An "office" although culturally defined is, after all, exercised by an individual. And who that individual is at any moment certainly makes a difference. There is leeway in the exercise or non-exercise of power just as there are limits. A man may be skilled in finding the evidence and the truth in the cases he must judge and in formulating the norms to fit the case in hand — or he may be all thumbs. He may be one who thirsts for power and who will wield all he can while grasping for more. Or he may shrink from it.

Power defined through allocation of legal authority is by its nature trans-personalized, yet by the nature of men it can never be wholly depersonalized. A Franklin Roosevelt is not a Warren Harding...

The third function of law calls for little additional comment.... Some trouble cases pose absolutely new problems for solution. In these cases the first and second functions may predominate. Yet this is not the situation in the instance of most legal clashes in which the problem is not the formulation of law to cover a new situation but rather the application of pre-existing law. These cases are disposed of in accordance with legal norms already set before the issue in question arises. The job is to clean the case up, to suppress or penalize the illegal behaviour and to bring the relations of the disputants back into balance, so that life may resume its normal course. This type of law-work has frequently been compared to work of the medical practitioner. It is family doctor stuff, essential to keeping the social body on its feet. In more homely terms, Llewellyn has called it, "garage-repair work on the general order of the group when that general order misses fire, or grinds gears, or even threatens a total breakdown."[4] It is not ordinarily concerned with grand design, as is the first law-job. Nor is it concerned with redesign as is the fourth. It works to clean up all the little social messes (and the occasional big ones) that recurrently arise between the members of the society from day to day.

Most of the trouble cases do not, in a civilized society, of themselves loom large on the social scene, although in a small community even one can lead directly to a social explosion if not successfully cleaned up. Indeed, in a primitive society the individual case always holds the threat of a little civil war if procedure breaks down, for from its inception it sets kin group against kin group — and if it comes to fighting, the number of kinsmen who will be involved is almost always immediately enlarged. The fight may engulf a large part of the tribe in internecine throat-cutting. Relatively speaking, each run-of-the-mill trouble case in primitive law imposes a more pressing demand for settlement upon the legal system than is the case with us.

While system and integration are essential, flexibility and constant revision are no less so. Law is a dynamic process in which few solutions can be permanent. Hence, the fourth function of law: the redefinition of relations and the reorientation of expectancies.

Initiatives with scope to work means new problems for the law. New inventions, new ideas, new behaviours keep creeping in. Especially do new behaviours creep in, nay, sweep in, when two unlike societies come newly into close contact. Then the law is called upon to decide what principles shall be applied to conflicts of claims rooted in disparate cultures. Do the new claims fit comfortably to the old postulates?[5] Must the new realized ways of behaving be wholly rejected and legally suppressed because they are out of harmony with the old values? Or can they be modified here and altered there to gain legal acceptance? Or can the more difficult operations of altering or even junking old postulates to accommodate a new way be faced? Or can fictions be framed that can lull the mind into acceptance of the disparate new without the wrench of acknowledged junking of the old? What *is* that is wanted? The known and habitual, or the promise of the new and untested? Men may neglect to turn the law to the answer of each questions. But they do not for long. Trouble cases generated by the new keep marching in. And the fourth law-job presses for attention.

Recapitulation of just one Cheyenne case will throw the process into focus. The acquisition of horses greatly altered all Plains Indian cultures. One important Cheyenne basic postulate ran,[6] "Except for land and tribal fetishes, all material goods are private property, but they should be generously shared with others." When it came to horses, this led some men to expect that they could freely borrow horses without even the courtesy of asking. For horse owners this got to the point of becoming a serious nuisance, as in the cases of Pawnee and Wolf Lies Down.[7] Wolf Lies Down put his trouble case to the members of the Elk Soldier Society. They got his horse back for him with a handsome free-will offering of additional "damages" from the defendant to boot. The trouble case was neatly disposed of. But the Elk Soldiers did not stop there. There was some preventive channeling of future behaviour to be done. Hence the "Now we shall make a new rule.[8] There shall be no more borrowing of horses without asking. If any man takes another's goods without asking, we will go over and get them back for him. More than that, if the taker tries to keep them, we will give him a whipping." Here was the fourth function of law being performed. The lines for future conduct re horses were made clear.

Work under Function IV[9] represents social planning brought into focus by the case of the instant and with an eye to the future.

The problem of reorienting conduct and redirecting it through the law when new issues emerge is always tied to the bare-bones demand of basic organization and the minimal maintenance of order and regularity. It may also shade over into work colored by a greater or lesser desire to achieve more than a minimum of smoothness in social relations. When this becomes an important aspect of law-work, a special aspect of law-ways activity may be recognized: the creation of techniques that efficiently and effectively solve the problems posed to all the other law-jobs so that the basic values of the society are realized through the law and not frustrated by it.

The doing of it has been called by Llewellyn "Juristic Method".[10] It is the method not only of getting the law-jobs done but doing them with a sure touch for the net effect that results in smoothness in the doing and a harmonious wedding of what is aspired to by men and what

is achieved through the law. It is the work not just of the craftsman but of the master craftsman...

. . . .

The very fact that the bulk of the substance and procedure of primitive law emerges through case action involving claim and counterclaim, pleading and counterpleading, tends to keep legal behaviour relatively close to the prevailing social values. Which way a new issue will go will depend not alone upon the facts but also upon the skill of the litigants in framing the issue and arguing the relevance of their respective positions to the prevailing social ideas of right conduct and group well-being — or upon persuasiveness in argument that a new orientation of values is in order to meet changed conditions, even though the tough man and his kinsman, though "wrong," may sometimes makes his position stick with naked force. Thus, the wise claimant argues his case not in terms of "this is good for me" but rather by maintaining "this is what we all want and should do". If he is a primitive advocate, it is more likely than not that he will also insist, if he can, that this is the way it has been from time immemorial. But the past certainly has no inflexible grip on primitive law.

Fiction[11] is one of the great devices of juristic method by means of which men fit new legal norms into old principles so as to reorient conduct without the need to junk long-standing postulates. Except for the universal practice of adoption, whereby outsiders are identified as *if* they are actually kinsmen, primitive men do not have to rely too heavily on the subterfuge of fiction to achieve legal change. Nevertheless, when the need is there many tribes have had recourse to its use.

An outstanding example may be found in adoptive marriage among the patrilineal groups of Indonesia. The important value for these people is to maintain the unbroken continuity of the paternal lineage. To do this, a family without sons adopts their daughter's husband as a "son" with the effect that her children remain within their clan and their inheritance will remain within their line.[12]

. . . .

When the law-jobs get done, these norms inevitably become the common denominator of legal culture. But the functions of law, whatever the norms they may give rise to in any particular society, are what constitute the crucial universal elements of the law. Any one or half-hundred societies may select one rule of law and not another — the range is wide — but none can ignore the law-jobs. In the last analysis, that the law-jobs get done is more important than how they are done. Their minimal doing is an imperative of social existence. Their doing with juristic finesse is an achievement of high skill.[13]

Endnotes

1. *Cf.* K.N. Llewellyn. "The Normative, the Legal, and the Law-Jobs: The Problem of Juristic Method," *Yale Law Journal*, 49:1355–1400 (1940). See also Llewellyn and Hoebel, *The Cheyenne Way*, Chap. xi. [*Cf. ante*, 762.]

2. [Hoebel is following Hohfeld's terminology; *cf. ante*, 541. The use of contemporary technical terms when describing primitive societies is criticized by Sawer, as this in itself tends to give tribal law the appearance of a degree of definition which it does not have, and thereby begs the very question to be decided, i.e., to what extent legal institutions and concepts in our sense are reproduced in undeveloped forms of society; see G. Sawer, *Law in Society*, pp. 43–47.]

3. [On the relationship between law and custom, *cf. ante*, 877.]

4. Llewellyn, "The Normative, the Legal, and the Law-Jobs", p. 1375. [And see *ante*, 762.]

5. [This refers to the basic jural postulates of the particular society: *cf. ante*, 568.]

6. [As formulated by Hoebel. Hoebel is not explicit about his technique of identifying these principles and about his method of selection. See Moore, "Law and Anthropology," in *Biennial Review of Anthropology* (1969), p. 263.]

7. [See pp. 146–49 of Hoebel's book.]

8. [Llewellyn and Hoebel, *The Cheyenne Way* (1941), p. 128, admit this promulgation of a "new law" is truly a "rare occurrence."]

9. [See *ante*, 898.]

10. [*Cf. ante*, 775.]

11. "Any assumption which conceals, or affects to conceal, the fact that a rule of law has undergone alteration, its letter remaining unchanged, its operation being modified." Maine, *Ancient Law*, p. 25 [and see *post*, 1230].

12. Ter Haar, *Adat Law in Indonesia*, pp. 175–76.

13. [For an assessment of Hoebel's contribution to the anthropology of law see Pospisil (1973) 7 *Law and Soc. Rev.* 537. His greatest and more lasting impact on the discipline is said to be his introduction into the discipline of the "case method" of study. It is however a restricted view not readily applicable in "trouble-less" cases. It places an over-emphasis on conflict and suffers from similar defects as Realism, from which it was taken. See Holleman (1973) 7 *Law and Soc. Rev.* 611. He remarks "one cannot even record what law does without recording what law is" (p. 616). Hoebel recognized this: legal rules were "guides for action, and more often than not the real norms of behaviour coincide with them" (*The Law of Primitive Man*, p. 30).]

The Cheyenne Way[†]
K.N. Llewellyn and E.A. Hoebel

A war party of eight Cheyennes, on its way south to take horses from the Kiowas, Comanches, or Apaches, was stopping at a large Arapaho camp. At the same time some Apaches came to visit Bull, an Arapaho leader. The Apaches told their host that the Kiowas and Comanches were seeking peace with the Arapahoes and Cheyennes. Bull took the opportunity to bring the eight Cheyennes together with the Apaches in his tipi; he filled his pipe and offered the smoke. The Cheyennes declined, Seven Bulls, the leader of the war party saying, "Friend, you know that we are not chiefs. We cannot smoke with these men, nor make peace with them. We have no authority; we can only carry the message. I have listened to what you say and tomorrow with my party I will start back [He has authority to call off his own raid.] to our Cheyenne village, and I will carry this word to the chiefs. It is for them to decide what must be done. We are young men and cannot say anything, but we will take your message back to the chiefs."

When Seven Bulls reached the Cheyenne camp with his companions, he told of the Kiowa-Comanche proposition. That night a crier went about the camp calling for the chiefs to convene the next day. The big double-sized chiefs' lodge was pitched and early the next morning the chiefs all gathered there. Seven Bulls and his companions were sent for to deliver their message officially. The proposal was then on the floor.

After the first speakers had sat down, it was evident that there was no ready agreement at hand within the Council, so the proposition was made and accepted that the Dog Soldier Society should be asked to render a decision to the Council on the question.

High Backed Wolf, who was the directing head chief of the Council, sent one of the door-servants to bring in White Antelope and Little Old Man, the bravest chiefs of the Dog Soldier Society. When these two had been greeted in the chiefs' lodge, High Backed Wolf told them about the order of business, describing to them the state of opinion in the Council. "Now, my friends," he

---

[†] Llewellyn, K.N., and Hoebel, Edward Adamson, *The Cheyenne Way: Conflict and Case Law in Primitive Jurisprudence* (Oklahoma: University of Oklahoma Press, 1941), 91–94, 127–28. Copyright © 1941 by the University of Oklahoma Press. Reprinted by permission of the publisher.

concluded, "you go and assemble your Dog Soldiers. Tell them about this matter and talk it over among them. Let us know what you think of it. Tell us what you think is best to be done."

When the Dog Soldiers had assembled, White Antelope laid the problem before them. "The chiefs are leaving this matter to us," he told his followers, "because we are the strongest of the military groups. It is my own thought that our chiefs are in favor of making peace. What do you all think about it?"

Said another of the Dog Soldier chiefs, "I think it best to leave the decision to you two, White Antelope and Little Old Man. Whatever you say will please us all." All the Dogs agreed to this with one assent.

The two men accepted it and declared for peace. Leaving their troop, they went back to where the Council was waiting for them, to tell the Council that they would make peace with the enemies. The chiefs all stood up at this and gladly said, "Thank you, thank you, Dog Soldiers."[1]

The procedure which has just been described is a typical handling of an important situation in the Cheyenne manner. The proposition, the reader will realize, was no simple one. The Cheyenne had become dependent upon the horse, and any warrior's path to glory and wealth lay most easily and quickly in raids upon the rich horse herders of the south, these same Kiowas and Comanches. Acceptance of the proposal meant that the young men would be blocked in one of their main and favorite avenues of activity. Hostility with the Kiowas and Comanches had been unceasing for at least half a century. The alternative values to the Cheyennes are not clear to us, unless they lay in some scheme for trading horses, on which we lack information. The soldier interest in the case is obvious; no less obvious is the fact that it had the favorable aspect of coinciding with the interests of the whole Cheyenne tribe. In the light of this one understands the diplomatic reluctance of the Council of Forty-Four to reach a decision by themselves. So smooth a delegation of an important decision, inverting the pyramid without any bickering, yet with the machinery at all points for the sensing of opinion in widening representative groups, is an act of social beauty. From the Council to the Dog Men, from the Dog Men to their two most outstanding warriors, to a momentous decision binding on the entire tribe! Nevertheless, the Council at no time gave up its authority; the decision, be it noted, was reported for announcement back to the Council, which then discharged the Dog Soldiers with thanks. This is also a superb face-producing, as well as face-saving, procedure. The actual announcement of the decision for peace was made to the camp at large by the head priest-chief himself.

Such interaction between the Council and the military societies was not unusual; rather, whenever there was an important problem of tribal policy (new policy in general or in particular) to be decided, it was the ordinary thing to see the chiefs' and the soldiers' messengers moving back and forth between the meeting lodges, sensing, reporting, and subtly influencing the state of both "expert" and "lay" opinion until the decision was accomplished. In this way, the legislative knot was cut without resort to dictatorship or friction.

But what happened when there was an irreconcilable opposition within the body politic? Then the governmental authority could act with force. It acted also with tact. It moved sometimes in involution. Power was present, form was not always achieved. Note, however, the Cheyenne drive for form, if repetition of situation makes it possible, if time serves, if dramatic urge finds — even for a sole occasion — an inventive voice. Seven Bulls was called on for an "official" presentation of a proposal the camp had buzzed with for a night. Little Wolf was "required" to be present. Compare the careful staging of Pawnee's rehabilitation. It is not too much to argue that *drama* is a vital *line* of reconciliation hit on by the Cheyennes, between their urge toward form (pattern, ritual) and their urge toward individualizing self-glorification. If this be sound, it suggests a relation between aesthetic balance and soundness of working institution, or of the individual's work in and with an institution, which deserves inquiry.

. . . .

While Wolf Lies Down was away, a friend took one of his horses to ride to war. This man had brought his bow and arrow and left them in the lodge of the horse's owner. When Wolf Lies Down returned, he knew by this token security who had his horse, so he said nothing.

A year passed without the horse's return, and then Wolf Lies Down invited the Elk Soldier chiefs to his lodge, because he was in their society. "There is this thing," he told them. "My friend borrowed my horse, leaving his bow and arrow; there they are yet. Now I want to know what to do. I want you to tell me the right thing. Will you go over and ask him his intentions?"

The borrower was in another camp well distant, yet the chiefs agreed. "We'll send a man to bring him in, get his word, or receive his presents," they promised.

The camp moved while the messenger was gone, but he knew of course where it would be on his return. The soldier returned with the borrower, who was leading two horses, "one spotted, one ear-tipped." He called for the four Elk chiefs on his arrival. The chiefs laid before him the story told by Wolf Lies Down.

"That is true," the man assented. "My friend is right. I left my bow and arrow here. I intended to return his horse, but I was gone longer than I expected. I have had good luck with that horse, though. I have treated it better than my own. However, when I got back to camp I found my folks there. Our camps were far apart and I just could not get away. I was waiting for his camp and mine to come together. Now, I always intended to do the right thing. I have brought two good horses with me. My friend can have his choice. In addition I give his own horse back, and further, I am leaving my bow and arrow."

Then up spoke Wolf Lies Down, "I am glad to hear my friend say these things. Now I feel better. I shall take one of those horses, but I am giving him that one he borrowed to keep. From now on we shall be bosom friends."

The chiefs declared, "Now we have settled this thing. Our man is a bosom friend of this man. Let it be that way among all of us. Our society and his shall be comrades. Whenever one of us has a present to give, we shall give it to a member of his soldier society.

"Now we shall make a new rule. There shall be no more borrowing of horses without asking. If any man takes another's goods without asking, we will go over and get them back for him. More than that, if the taker tries to keep them, we will give him a whipping."

Thus was a situation fraught with possible friction brought to an amicable close through the good offices of the chiefs of the society of an aggrieved member.

Far more important, however, was the crystallization of a new social policy, the formulation of a law making it a crime henceforth to borrow an owner's horse without his expressed permission. The old custom of free utilization of another's goods, providing one left an identifying "security," was apparently creating friction as it came to be applied to horses. What between good friends could develop into a tense situation — as evidenced here by the resort to soldier chiefs as spokesmen of inquiry — could become immediately and actively disruptive if the concept "friend" were loosely interpreted by a borrower, or the horse not cared for, or if the unnotified borrowing broke in upon the owner's plans, or one owner became the recipient of too many such evidences of friendship. Pawnee's case of horse "borrowing" and its punishment (CASE 2) shows the degree of social irresponsibility which the older practice, left unguarded, could engender. Black Wolf stated that the soldiers, and even the tribal chiefs, had been for some time talking about means of putting a stop to the practice. The Elk Soldier chiefs on this occasion took the opportunity to make the step. After declaring the case at hand settled, they moved into general policy. They did not mix the two. Note also, as a soldier society moves into the very unfamiliar matter of legislation, their sound technical attention to what they shall do, if...

Endnote

1.   This version of the peace decision which was made by the Cheyennes in 1840 is adapted from Grinnell's detailed history of the event. Mr. Grinnell's account continues with a vivid description of the ensuing meeting of the Cheyennes with the allied Kiowas and Comanches for the formal dedication of the peace, a peace which was never broken from that date forward. See Grinnell, *The Fighting Cheyennes*, 60–66.

The Spectacle of the Scaffold[†]
M. Foucault

OF all the reasons why punishment that was not in the least ashamed of being 'atrocious' was replaced by punishment that was to claim the honour of being 'humane' there is one that must be analysed at once, for it is internal to the public execution itself: at once an element of its functioning and the principle of its perpetual disorder.

In the ceremonies of the public execution, the main character was the people, whose real and immediate presence was required for the performance. An execution that was known to be taking place, but which did so in secret, would scarcely have had any meaning. The aim was to make an example, not only by making people aware that the slightest offence was likely to be punished, but by arousing feelings of terror by the spectacle of power letting its anger fall upon the guilty person: 'In criminal matters, the most difficult point is the imposition of the penalty; it is the aim and the end of the procedure, and its only fruit, by example and terror, when it is well applied to the guilty person' (Bruneau, unnumbered preface to the first part).

But, in this scene of terror, the role of the people was an ambiguous one. People were summoned as spectators: they were assembled to observe public exhibitions and *amendes honorables*; pillories, gallows and scaffolds were erected in public squares or by the roadside; sometimes the corpses of the executed persons were displayed for several days near the scenes of their crimes. Not only must people know, they must see with their own eyes. Because they must be made to be afraid; but also because they must be the witnesses, the guarantors, of the punishment, and because they must to a certain extent take part in it. The right to be witnesses was one that they possessed and claimed; a hidden execution was a privileged execution, and in such cases it was often suspected that it had not taken place with all its customary severity. There were protests when at the last moment the victim was taken away out of sight. The senior postal official who had been put on public exhibition for killing his wife was later taken away from the crowd. 'He was put into a hired coach; it was thought that if he had not been well escorted, it would have been difficult to protect him from being ill-treated by the populace, who yelled and jeered at him' (Hardy, I, 328). When the woman Lescombat was hanged, care was taken to hide her face; she had 'a kerchief over her neck and head, which made the public murmur and say that it was not Lescombat' (Anchel, 70–71). The people claimed the right to observe the execution and to see who was being executed. The first time the guillotine was used the *Chronique de Paris* reported that people complained that they could not see anything and chanted, 'Give us back our gallows' (Lawrence, 71ff). The people also had a right to take part. The condemned man, carried in procession, exhibited, humiliated, with the horror of his crime recalled in innumerable ways, was offered to the insults, sometimes to the attacks of the spectators. The vengeance of the people was called upon to become an unobtrusive part of the vengeance of the sovereign. Not that it was in any way fundamental, or that the king had to express in his own way the people's revenge; it was rather that the people had to bring its assistance to the king when the king undertook 'to be avenged on his enemies', especially when those enemies were to be found among the people. It was rather like a 'scaffold service' that the people owed the king's vengeance. This 'service' had been specified in the old ordinances; the edict of 1347 concerning blasphemers stipulated that they would be exhibited at the pillory 'from the hour of prime, to that of their deaths. And mud and other refuse, though no stone or anything injurious, could be thrown at their faces.... The second time, in case of relapse, it is our will that he be put in the pillory on a solemn market day, and that his upper lip be split so that the teeth appear.' No doubt, at the classical period, this form of participation in the torture was no more than tolerated and attempts were made to limit it: because of the barbarities that it gave rise to and the usurpation it involved of the power to punish. But it belonged too closely to the general economy of the public execution for it to be eliminated altogether. Even in the eighteenth century, there were scenes like the one that accompanied the execution of Montigny in 1737; as the executioner was carrying out the execution, the local fish-wives walked in procession, holding aloft an effigy of the condemned man, and then cut off its head (Anchel, 63). And very often, as they moved slowly in procession through it, criminals had to be 'protected' from the crowd — both as an example and as a target, a possible threat and a 'prey', promised but also forbidden. In calling on the crowd to manifest its power, the sovereign tolerated for a moment acts of violence, which he accepted as a sign of allegiance, but which were strictly limited by the sovereign's own privileges.

Now it was on this point that the people, drawn to the spectacle intended to terrorize it, could express its rejection of the punitive power and sometimes revolt. Preventing an execution that was regarded as unjust, snatching a condemned man from the hands of the executioner, obtaining his pardon by force, possibly pursuing and assaulting the executioners, in any case abusing the judges and causing an uproar against the sentence — all this formed part of the popular practices that invested, traversed and often overturned the ritual of the public execution. This often happened, of course, in the case of those condemned for rioting: there were the disturbances that followed a famous case of child abduction, when the crowd wanted to prevent the execution of three supposed rioters, who were to be hanged at the cemetery of Saint-Jean, 'because there were fewer entrances and processions to guard'; the terrified executioner cut down one of the condemned men; the archers let fly their arrows. It occurred again after the corn riots of 1775; and again in 1786, when the day-labourers marched on Versailles and set about freeing their arrested comrades. But apart from these cases, when the process of agitation had been triggered off previously and for reasons that did not concern some measure of penal justice, one finds many examples when the agitation was provoked directly by a verdict and an execution: small, but innumerable 'disturbances around the scaffold'.

In their most elementary forms, these disturbances began with the shouts of encouragement, sometimes the cheering, that accompanied the condemned man to his execution. Throughout the long procession, he was sustained by 'the compassion of the meek and tenderhearted, and with the applause, admiration and envy of all the bold and hardened' (Fielding, 449). If the crowd gathered round the scaffold, it was not simply to witness the sufferings of the condemned man or to excite the anger of the executioner: it was also to hear an individual who had nothing more to lose curse the judges, the laws, the government and religion. The public execution allowed the luxury of these momentary saturnalia, when nothing remained to prohibit or to punish. Under the protection of imminent death, the criminal could say everything and the crowd cheered. 'If there were annals in which the last words of the tortured and executed were scrupulously recorded, and if one had the courage to read through them, even if one did no more than question the vile populace that gathers around the scaffolds out of cruel curiosity, one would be told that no one who had died on the wheel did not accuse heaven for the misery that brought him to the crime, reproach his judges for their barbarity, curse the minister of the altars who accompanies them and blaspheme against the God whose organ he is' (Boucher d'Argis, 128–29). In these executions, which ought to show only the terrorizing power of the prince, there was a whole aspect of the carnival, in which rules were inverted, authority mocked and criminals transformed into heroes, The shame was turned round; the courage, like the tears and the cries of the condemned, caused offence only to the law. Fielding notes with regret: 'To unite the ideas of death and shame is not so easy as may be imagined... I will appeal to any man who hath seen an execution, or a procession to an execution; let him tell me. When he hath beheld a poor wretch, bound in a cart, just on the verge of eternity, all pale and trembling with his approaching fate, whether the idea of shame hath ever intruded on his mind? Much less will the bold daring rogue, who glories in his present condition, inspire the beholder with any such sensation' (Fielding, 450). For the people who are there and observe, there is always, even in the most extreme vengeance of the sovereign a pretext for revenge.

This was especially the case if the conviction was regarded as unjust — or if one saw a man of the people put to death, for a crime that would have merited, for someone better born or richer, a comparatively light penalty. It would seem that certain practices of penal justice were no longer supported in the eighteenth century — and perhaps for longer — by the lower strata of the population. This would explain why executions could easily lead to the beginnings of social disturbances. Since the poorest — it was a magistrate who made the observation (Dupaty, 1786, 247) — could not be heard in the courts of law, it was where the law was manifested publicly, where they were called upon to act as witnesses and almost as co-adjutors of this law, that they could intervene, physically: enter by force into the punitive mechanism and redistribute

its effects; take up in another sense the violence of the punitive rituals. There was agitation against the difference in penalties according to social class: in 1781, the parish priest of Champré had been killed by the lord of the manor, and an attempt was made to declare the murderer insane; 'the peasants, who were extremely attached to their pastor, were furious and had at first seemed ready to lay violent hands upon their lord and to set fire to the castle.... Everyone protested, and rightly, against the indulgence of the minister who deprived justice of the means of punishing so abominable a crime' (Hardy, IV, 394). There was agitation, too, against the excessive sentences passed on certain common offenses that were not regarded as serious (such as house-breaking); or against punishments for certain offenses connected with social conditions such as petty larceny; the death penalty for this crime aroused a great deal of discontent, because there were many domestic servants in a single household and it was difficult for them, in such a case, to prove their innocence, and also because they could easily be victims of their employers' spite and because the indulgence of certain masters who shut their eyes to such behaviour made the fate of servants accused, condemned and hanged even more iniquitous. The execution of such servants often gave rise to protests (*cf.* Hardy, I, 319; III, 227–28; IV, 180). There was a small riot in Paris in 1761 in favour of a servant woman who had stolen a piece of cloth from her master. Despite the fact that the woman admitted her guilt, handed back the material and begged for mercy, the master refused to withdraw his complaint; on the day of the execution, the local people prevented the hanging, invaded the merchant's shop and looted it; in the end, the servant was pardoned, but a woman, who attempted, unsuccessfully, to stick a needle into the wicked master, was banished for three years (Anchel, 226).

One remembers the great legal affairs of the eighteenth century, when enlightened opinion intervened in the persons of the *philosophes* and certain magistrates: Calas, Sirven and the Chevalier de La Barre, for instance. But less attention is given to the popular agitations caused by punitive practice. Indeed, they seldom spread beyond town, or even a district. Yet they did have a real importance. Sometimes these movements, which originated from below, spread and attracted the attention of more highly placed persons who, taking them up, gave them a new dimension (in the years preceding the Revolution, the affair of Catherine Espinas, falsely convicted of parricide in 1785, or the case of the three men of Chaumont, condemned to the wheel, for whom Dupaty, in 1786, wrote his celebrated memoir, or that of Marie Françoise Salmon, whom the parlement or Rouen in 1782 had condemned to the stake, for poisoning, but who in 1786 had still not been executed). More usually, those disturbances had maintained around penal justice and its manifestations, which ought to have been exemplary, a state of permanent unrest.

How often had it proved necessary, in order to ensure order around the scaffolds, to take steps that were 'distressing to the people' and 'humiliating for the authorities' (Argenson, 241)? It was evident that the great spectacle of punishment ran the risk of being rejected by the very people to whom it was addressed. In fact, the terror of the public execution created centres of illegality: on execution days, work stopped, the taverns were full, the authorities were abused, insults or stones were thrown at the executioner, the guards and the soldiers; attempts were made to seize the condemned man, either to save him or to kill him more surely; fights broke out, and there was no better prey for thieves than the curious throng around the scaffold, (Hardy recounts a number of cases like the important theft that was committed in the very house in which the police magistrate was lodging — IV, 56.) But above all — and this was why these disadvantages became a political danger — the people never felt closer to those who paid the penalty than in those rituals intended to show the horror of the crime and the invincibility of power: never did the people feel more threatened, like them, by a legal violence exercised without moderation or restraint. The solidarity of whole sections of the population with those we would call petty offenders — vagrants, false beggars, the indigent poor, pickpockets, receivers and dealers in stolen goods — was constantly expressed: resistance to police searches, the pursuit of informers, attacks on the watch or inspectors provide abundant evidence of this (*cf.* Richet, 118–19). And it was the breaking up of this solidarity that was becoming the aim of penal and police repression. Yet out of the ceremony of the public executing, out to that uncertain festival in which violence was instantaneously reversible, it was this solidarity much more than the sovereign power that was likely to emerge with redoubled strength, The reformers of the eighteenth and nineteenth centuries were not to forget that, in the last resort, the executions did not, in fact, frighten the people. One of their first cries was to demand their abolition.

To clarify the political problem posed by the intervention of the people in the spectacle of the executions, one need only cite two events. The first took place at Avignon at the end of the seventeenth century. It contained all the principal elements of the theatre of horror: the physical confrontation between the executioner and the condemned man, the reversal of the duel, the executioner pursed by the people, the condemned man saved by the ensuing riot and the violent inversion of the penal machinery. A murderer by the name of Pierre du Fort was to be hanged; several times he 'had caught his feet in the steps' and had not been able to swing freely. 'Seeing this, the executioner had pulled his jerkin up over his face and struck him below the knees, on the stomach and on the belly. When the people saw that the executioner was causing him too much pain, and even believing that he was killing him down there with a bayonet...moved by compassion for the patient

and fury at the executioner, they threw stones at the scaffold just as the executioner knocked away the two ladders and threw the patient down and leaped on to his shoulders and kicked him, while the wife of the said executioner pulled at his feet from under the gallows. In doing so, they made blood come from his mouth. But the hail of stones came thicker — one stone even struck the hanged man on the head — which forced the executioner to dash to the ladder, which he descended so rapidly that half-way down he fell from it, and struck his head on the ground. Then a crowd of people fell upon him. He got to his feet, bayonet in hand, threatening to kill anyone who came near him; after falling several times, he finally got to his feet, only to be beaten by the crowd, rolled in the mud and nearly drowned in the stream, then dragged by the Cordeliers Cemetery. His servant was also beaten and, with bruises on his head and body, was taken to the hospital where he died some days later. However, some strangers and unknown people mounted the ladder and cut the rope while others caught the hanged man from below after he had been hanging there longer than it took to say a full Miserere. The crowd then smashed the gallows and broke the executioner's ladder into pieces.... Children carried off the gallows and threw it into the Rhône.' The condemned man was then taken to a cemetery 'so that he should not be recaptured by the law and from there to the church of Sainte-Antoine'. The archbishop gave him his pardon, had him taken to the hospital and asked that particular care be taken of him. Lastly, adds the writer of the account, 'we had a new suit, two pairs of stockings and shoes made for him. We dressed him in new clothes from head to toe. Our colleagues gave him shirts, breeches and a wig' (Duhamel, 5–6; scenes of this kind were still taking place in the nineteenth century — *cf.* Lawrence, 56 and 195–98).

The other event took place in Paris, a century later. It was in 1775, shortly after the corn riot. Because of the state of extreme tension among the people, the authorities wanted the execution to take place without interruption. Between the scaffold and the public, kept at a safe distance, two ranks of soldiers stood on guard, one facing the execution that was about to take place, the other facing the people in case of riot. Contact was broken: it was a public execution, but one in which the element of spectacle was neutralized, or rather reduced to abstract intimidation. Protected by force of arms, on an empty square, justice quietly did its work. If it showed the death that it had dealt, it was from high and far: 'The two gallows, which were eighteen feet high, no doubt by way of an example, were not set up until three o'clock in the afternoon. From two o'clock, the Place de Grève and all the surrounding streets had been filled with detachments of different troops, some on foot, some on horse; the Swiss and the French guards continued to patrol the adjacent streets. No one was allowed on to the Grève during the execution, and all around one could see a double row of soldiers, bayonets at the ready, standing back to back, so that some looked outwards and some into the square; the two wretches...cried out all the way that they were innocent and continued to protest in like manner as they mounted the ladder' (Hardy, III, 67).

Whatever the part played by feelings of humanity for the condemned in the abandonment of the liturgy of the public executions, there was, in any case, on the part of the state power, a political fear of the effects of these ambiguous rituals.

B. Connecting Law and Society

Law and the Behavioural Sciences[†]
L. Friedman and S. Macaulay

LAW is assumed to make a difference to the people and groups who are subject to it. Obviously, law as a whole does make a difference, and so, too, do particular laws and particular activities of legal officials. But the effect is not necessarily one which is deducible from a reading of the *words* of statutes and case-law. There are stringent laws in the States against sale and possession of marijuana, but more people seem to smoke marijuana all the time. Prohibition is another example of a classic problem often referred to as the "limits of legal action". The problem is classic, but so far there are no classic answers or even serious attempts at one...

That legal systems, on the other hand, reflect the larger society is undeniable. But this statement by itself is far too general to be very meaningful. Here too, the problem is classic and the solutions imperfect. What people or groups influence what kinds of legal action and by what means? The reflection of society in the legal system is not easy to trace. Influences travel devious and myriad routes.

There are respects, too, in which it is useful to look at the legal system in isolation — not in the dogmatic, rule-bound isolation of conceptual jurisprudence — but as a little world in itself, a social system which demands responses, role-players, and moving parts. All systems are alike in some general characteristics. Their structures, if comparable, generate comparable internal pressures which drive them to behaviour of this or that kind. People working within a system, for example, will tend to try to make their tasks manageable and personally rewarding. What can one meaningfully say about the legal system as a system?

This does not mean that there are not properties unique to a legal system, compared to other social systems. Legal tasks are different from those undertaken by business corporations, the family or a university. Some of the properties and values of the legal system are of crucial importance to society as a whole. For example, the American legal system is, in part, organized around a set of values for which the phrase "due process" is a shorthand expression. Due process, in turn, has an important impact on American society, both in terms of actual results and as a value that percolates into other parts of the social order. What these consequences are is an important empirical question.

. . . .

...We are convinced for a variety of reasons that an integration of the study of law with social science methods and concepts is both inevitable and desirable. Classical legal research and education thought of itself as "scientific," but it took law to be a deductive science. It did not have much propensity to go out and look at the world. When this idea died (slowly), it was replaced by a new justification: the old materials were preserved, but now they were defended on the grounds that they were just the thing for the inculcation of legal method, that is, skills and habits of thought which a lawyer ought to have.... It ought to be (if one dares use the word) more *relevant* to social problems. It ought to be more empirical. There is now a good deal of emphasis on social science and empirical methods, and the trend is clearly in this direction. But elementary teaching materials for an introductory course in law and social science are badly needed.

Second, we are equally convinced that the social sciences need to study law more closely. It is a social phenomenon of great importance, and it has been unduly neglected, partly because of the insularity of legal scholarship, partly because of the insularity of the social sciences. Here too, the trend is clear: sociology of law, behavioral political science, anthropology of law, psychology and psychiatry and law, and legal economics have all received new infusions of persons and enthusiasm in the last generation. But how does the social science student enter into the legal thickets? It is possible for him to go to law school, or to take particular law school courses, but this is a wasteful method for those who do not intend to practise and who are interested only in certain aspects of the law. Again, the solution is elementary teaching materials and an introductory course in law and social science.

[†]   Friedman, Lawrence, and Macaulay, Stewart, *Law and the Behavioural Sciences*, 2nd ed. (Indianapolis: Bobbs-Merrill, 1977), xiii, xiv. Reprinted by permission of the authors.

11

Laws and the Behavioral Sciences: Is There any There There?[†]
S. Macaulay

AS recently as fifteen years ago, when Lawrence Friedman and I (1969) were trying to fashion the first edition of our teaching materials, social science and law was largely unexplored territory. There were a few classic articles known to and cited by all. There was no *Law & Society Review, Law & Policy* or *Journal of Legal Studies*. Law reviews occasionally did print articles with some description of the legal system in operation, but they were hard to find since they were buried among the endless variations on conventional legal themes.

The volume of work in law and social science exploded during the late 1960s and 1970s. The decades of reform and counterreform provoked much of the work. Both reformers and researchers assumed, or hoped, that social science would support their causes. Evaluation research, however, often was disappointing. Again and again, it showed a gap between the promise and performance of the American legal system, although it seldom tried to explain why laws remained on the books but were not put into action. In spite of the disappointing results, the river of policy-related research flowed on, getting wider and wider. Today political leaders of all persuasions cite research useful to their causes. Social scientists from all the major departments in most universities turn some attention to the legal system, and it would be a most primitive law school that allowed its graduates to pass through without ever hearing of police discretion, plea bargaining, and the games played by insurance adjusters and plaintiffs' lawyers.

Any list would be arbitrary. However, I think anyone reviewing the accomplishments of the past few decades would conclude that we are far more aware of many or most of the following ideas:

1. *Law is not free.* There are barriers to access to the legal system which some people can jump far more easily than others. Most simply, few can afford to invest the substantial sums needed to hire lawyers, investigators and experts, run risks of retaliation and injuries to reputation, become emotionally involved in a cause, and diverted from alternative uses of their time to participate in a process where they may lose totally or recover what so often are inadequate remedies. Moreover, some people can afford to run up the costs of participation to run poorer opponents out of the game, and the threat that this may happen deters many from entering the contest. Thus, many people are left to lump it, whatever their legal rights. When we turn to social regulation, we find that it involves costs which some can pass along to others. It usually is fruitful to ask who benefits from and who pays for any type of legal action. Often we will find that regulation operates as a kind of regressive taxation, burdening the have-nots far more than the haves.

2. *Law is delivered by actors with limited resources and interests of their own in settings where they have discretion.* "Street-level bureaucrats" such as police, assistant prosecuting attorneys, case workers, clerks of court, those handling intake at administrative agencies and many more, have discretion although no one planned it that way. This is true for a number of reasons. Policies conflict and the rules may be unclear. As a result, those who deal with the public may have a choice of goals to pursue or rationalizations for whatever they want to do to serve the public or their own self interest. Those who do the day-to-day work of a legal agency often are hard to supervise because they control the official version of events by writing reports in the files. Resource constraints often make it impossible to "go by the book" since officials cannot do everything mandated. If those enforcing a law cannot carry out all their duties, they must choose which of them under what circumstances they will attempt to implement. Those choices of "street-level bureaucrats" are unlikely to be random or neutral in their impact. They will be affected by folk wisdom or bias, reward and punishment structures, and self-interest.

3. *Many of the functions usually thought of as legal are performed by alternative institutions, and there is a great deal of interpretation between what we call public and private sectors.* We live in a world of "legal pluralism" where rules are made and interpreted and sanctions imposed by many public and private governments which are only loosely coordinated. Some conduct is entirely within the jurisdiction of one government or another; sometimes units are complementary and support each other; often they are rivals and compete for influence. Examples of private governments range from the Mafia to the American Arbitration Association. Trade associations, sports leagues, church groups, neighborhood organizations and many other "private" units such as business corporations exercise what are, effectively, legal powers. They make rules by constitutions, charters and standard contracts; they interpret them in their day-to-day operations; they offer benefits on certain conditions; and they

---

† Macaulay, Stewart, "Laws and the Behavioral Sciences: Is There any There There?" (1984), 6 *Law and Policy* 149 at 149, 152. Reprinted by permission of Basil Blackwell, Ltd., Oxford, U.K.

may suspend or expel members, associates or employees as a sanction. Indeed, in many instances these sanctions may be more powerful than any the law has to offer. Also, those who regularly interact in valued long-term relationships usually form semi-autonomous social fields (Moore, 1973) which regulate a great deal of behaviour. For example, both business people who deal regularly and those plaintiffs' and defendants' lawyers who specialize in personal injury work in a community are subject to the rules and sanctions of their social fields. Moreover, at all levels of society, public government tends to exist at the margins of long-term continuing relations, usually affecting but seldom controlling behaviour. Indeed, distinctions between public and private arenas tend to disappear in practice. Police, prosecutors, clerks of the court, judges, field officers of administrative agencies, mayors, governors, legislators and other public officials and their assistants often are enmeshed in long-term valued relationships with those they purport to regulate. Problems are transformed, filtered and channelled into and out of the public legal system and systems of private regulation as part of complicated processes. Lawyers and others often play critical roles in assigning problems to the jurisdiction of one or another norm-defining-and-sanctioning system. One cannot understand legal action without understanding the collaborating and rival institutions in a society.

4. *People, acting alone and in groups, cope with law and cannot be expected to comply passively.* Many people are able to ignore most legal commands, or redefine them to serve self-interest or "common sense", and live with a vague and often inaccurate sense of the nature of law and legal process — all without encountering serious problems. There is great opportunity for evasion in a society that values privacy, civil liberties, and limited investment in government. Coping with the law can become a game that offsets any sense of obligation. Many participants in social fields and networks pass along techniques of evasion, legitimate breaking the law, honor the crafty, and even sanction those who would comply. The law is frequently uncertain and plausible arguments can be fashioned to rationalize much of what many people want to do. This means that there is great opportunity for bargaining in the shadow of the law or in the shadow of questionable assumptions about the law. Thus, people's views of the likely legal consequences of action at best affect but do not determine their behaviour. Sometimes, however, the command of the law rings loud and clear and has direct impact on behaviour. In short, the role of law is not something that can be assumed but must be established in every case.

5. *Lawyers play many roles other than adversary in a courtroom.* Lawyer self-interest, and their view of what is best for a client, often dictates that litigation should

be avoided, and lawyers seek other ways to provide service to clients. They tend to know who makes decisions and what kinds of appeals, legal and other types, are likely to be effective. They know how to bargain and how to manipulate situations so that accommodations can be reached. Often they serve as coercive mediators, acting in settings where their profession itself is a tacit threat of trouble if people do not behave reasonably. Instead of pursuing only their client's immediate interest, lawyers often act as what Justice Brandeis called "counsel for the situation", seeking what they see as the best long-term solution for all concerned. Often lawyers, with more or less success, seek to transform clients' perceptions about what is just, or at least tolerable. Often they deal with bruised egos and manage public relations far more than they vindicate clients' rights. As Marc Galanter observes, these professional practices tend to breed distinct bargaining arenas where veteran players know the going rate for, say, breaking and entering with one prior offense, a whiplash injury in a rear end collision, and the like. The "hired gun" battling for a client to the limits of law and ethics is found only in a limited set of situations. The development of these less adversarial roles explains why we find those aggrieved being offered a deal more often than we see rights being vindicated. This may be of concern if we think that rights ought to be clarified and vindicated to serve social purposes. Also, the wide variety of roles played by lawyers is a factor in making the functioning of social institutions far more complex than formal descriptions assume. For example, many lawyers' stock in trade includes their contacts with officials, knowledge of acceptable rhetoric, and awareness of mutually advantageous possibilities. Thus, they are able to cut through formal channels and get things done. When this happens regularly, behaviour in a corporation or a public agency no longer follows official procedures. If we think those procedures serve certain functions, this activity by lawyers, or others playing similar roles, will undercut them.

6. *Our society deals with conflict in many ways, but avoidance and evasion are important ones.* At times we mobilize social institutions in the service of values and interests: we fought a civil war; the army has enforced civil rights laws; the FBI has suppressed what its leaders saw as radical causes; and the criminal process has jailed people who challenged the safety and privileges of those who count. More often, however, we honor principled behaviour in words but practise accommodation. We may pass symbolic laws declaring the good, the true and the beautiful, but we leave enforcement to local option. We find social consensus at a high level of abstraction and so keep our doctrines ambiguous or contradictory. This avoids the costs of definition and of deciding that some interpretations of values are right while others are wrong. Thus, a simple means-and-ends view of law should be

suspect. Moreover, while some may be fooled by the gap between law's announced promises and the system's performance, others are well aware of what is going on. Whether law is supposed to solve social problems is always something to establish rather than something that can be assumed.

7. *While law matters in American society, its influence tends to be indirect, subtle and ambiguous.* It is easy to find gaps between the promise and performance of our law. Americans are selectively law abiding: some refuse to register for the draft as a matter of principle; some cheat on their taxes or redefine their obligations under those laws in questionable fashion; many drive while intoxicated, Businesses pollute the environment, distribute dangerously defective products, and bribe public officials. Nonetheless, law matters in a number of ways. For example, many ideas that are part of our common normative vocabulary are crystallized in law, and they both help rationalize action and affect our expectations about the social world. Indeed, even the sports pages of our newspapers more and more resemble law reviews as a legal vocabulary is appropriated to explain players' relations with teams, teams' relations with cities, and the like. While the ability of the legal system to prompt social change that is unwanted by a large or powerful minority may be limited, often law can add gasoline to an already burning fire. The struggle to gain legal rights can be the focus of a social movement, forcing reformers to define goals and to select means to obtain them. Even failed reform efforts may influence the behaviour of both proponents and opponents. Moreover, law can restrain power in many situations. For many reasons, those with power hesitate to exercise it too crudely. The effort to cloak an exercise of power with a mantle of right or to cover up abuses are costly exercises which, at times, deter action. Law and lawyers have helped gain accommodations for some of the less powerful by using legal symbols and procedures. In this culture even the counter-attacks by the powerful have to be rationalized in legal rhetoric. This effort may affect both the form and substance of the way such battles are fought and resolved.

The picture formed by connecting these seven points cannot be ignored by a reformer or theorist who wants to act through or think about law in this society. While fanta-

sies may be lovely things if they are recognized for what they are, romanticized views of social life are not always innocent.For example, consider all the proposals to "solve the crime problem" by simple solutions such as easing the rules concerning search and seizure; curbing the insanity defense; increasing sentences for those convicted; and ending plea bargaining. Whatever else one can say for such proposals, they appear to be cheap. If crime were caused by words in a Supreme Court opinion or a statute, then crime could be ended by paying a printer to set new text. No new taxes would be imposed. No extra services would be required. All that would be needed would be to muzzle lawyers and judges. However, few conversant with law and society literature see these kinds of proposal for fighting crime as much more than the wares of one more snake oil salesman.

Similarly, Marc Galanter (1983) criticizes the frequent assertions that our legal institutions are overwhelmed by a flood of litigation prompted by the excessive litigiousness of Americans provoked by greedy lawyers. He finds instead that there is little persuasive evidence of a litigation explosion and that modern patterns of disputing are a conservative adaptation to changing conditions. The argument that there has been a serious problem created by increasing litigation "displays the weakness of contemporary legal scholarship and policy analysis" as "theories were put forward without serious consideration of whether they fit the facts."

Much the same can be said for theoretical literature that attempts to explain rules of law in terms of promoting efficiency without considering how, if at all, those rules are implemented. This kind of writing may have value as a study of ideology, but sometimes it seems to have a kinship with W.C. Fields conning a mark. Writers in this camp often neglect their own teachings. They fail to consider the costs of moving from what they view as a messy and inefficient welfare state to the brave new competitive world. Since they are not interested in distributional questions, they can ignore those left behind. Perhaps the trip *is* worth the price, but the true price must be assessed before this judgement can be made. We always must ask who benefits and who pays how much to reach any utopia; the social study of law should make it clear that such questions must be asked of any reformer or revolutionary.

The New Legal Scholarship: Problems and Prospects[†]
J. Hagan

DEFINING THE FIELD

Legal scholarship has changed dramatically in this century. Early in this century, legal scholarship found form and coherence in a method of study and teaching often referred to as the doctrinal approach. This approach placed its emphasis on the determination of rules, principles and procedures through the detailed analysis of cases — a method that goes back at least as far as Langdell's reforms at the Harvard Law School. There can be little debate as to the professional success of this approach to legal scholarship. It provided a method for teaching and for the writing of legal treatises and law review articles that endures to this day.

Yet if there was a purity to this methodological emphasis on "law in the books", there was also an incompleteness that led others to call for research on the "law in action". Often known as the legal realist movement, and best documented in its emergence at the Yale Law School, this approach to legal scholarship called attention to gaps between doctrine and practice. It is interesting to note that both the traditional doctrinal approach and legal realism were eager to claim the mantle of science. In doing so, the doctrinal approach focused on recorded cases as its units for observation and analysis, while the realists moved beyond these official accounts to examine the way the law actually was applied and affected people's lives. The realist's point was that the law often only affected social life indirectly and that doctrine frequently affected society in uncertain and unanticipated ways.

Today, few scholars conceive of themselves as legal realists *per se*. This is probably because there are now few legal scholars who see the "gap" between the law and the contexts in which it is applied as being as clear cut as the realists seemed once to imply. Rather, legal doctrine and the society out of which it grows are seen as intimately interconnected. That is, we now recognize that the meaning of legal rules resides not only in the internal relations of the principles and value they contain, but also in the ways rules are distributed, achieved and changed — through their career in the real world of claims, counter-claims, negotiations, arbitrations, etc. In these and other ways (made explicit below), we have entered a world of post-doctrinal scholarship that now takes the law and the contexts in which it develops as the combined focus for research.

Two distinguishable streams of work characterize post-doctrinal legal scholarship. The first stream consists of what we will call normative interpretative legal studies, and is most provocatively represented by the critical legal studies movement in prominent American law schools. This work is often historical and sometimes comparative in form, and is most frequently distinguished by the interpretative reanalysis of case law doctrine in the format of contextualized critiques. It is interesting to note that the case law base and library setting of much critical legal study marks a continuation of traditional doctrinal methods. However, the critical and contextualized form of this work makes it radically different from the older doctrinal approach.

The second stream of post-doctrinal legal scholarship has taken on many names but here will be called empirical behavioral legal studies. These studies are not explicitly concerned with either the justification or criticism of case law doctrine, but instead strive to be value neutral. An explicit goal of this approach is to frame legal issues as empirical questions that can be answered without consideration of value preferences. For example, "the gap problem" that so concerned the legal realists is not taken here as inherently good or bad, or as something to be reduced; rather, in empirical behavioral legal studies the gap is taken as something to be explained, as in Stewart Macaulay's classic study of non-contractual relations in business. That is, the purpose is not to find the doctrinal principle that will reestablish legal order, thereby, for example, making all business relations contractual. The purpose instead is to make explicit the discontinuity between law and everyday practice and then to explain this discontinuity, so that what happens on each side of it can be better understood. The emphasis here is on casual and functional explanations, with the explanations made testable by the articulation of propositions that are predictive, and therefore assessable through comparisons of theoretically derived expectations with empirically generated observations. This work can be experimental as well as non-experimental, cross-sectional, longitudinal and comparative as well as historical and critical.

There is increasing reason to believe that the two streams of post-doctrinal scholarship we have described can be joined by a pragmatic tradition of empirical legal scholarship. It is therefore worthwhile taking note of what this new legal scholarship offers, and of what the obstacles to this new tradition might be. We consider the possibilities first, and the obstacles second.

---

†   Hagan, John, "The New Legal Scholarship: Problems and Prospects" (1986), 1 *Revue canadienne droit et société/Canadian Journal of Law and Society* 35–37. Reprinted by permission of the publisher.

In the most general terms, the new legal scholarship offers a more inclusive look at the interrelationships between law and the surrounding society. It does this first by shifting our attention outward and downward from "law at the top". This means moving our focus from the highly publicized and recognized importance of decisions made, for example, in appellate and trial courts, away from the professionals who "make" these cases, down to the law's users and consumers. Law at the bottom becomes as important and as interesting, and therefore as much in need of explanation, as law at the top. Among other things, we begin to seek explanations of the movement of legal activity up and down this hierarchy.

The downward thrust of the new legal scholarship extends attention simultaneously to less formal manifestations of law. Among the most central of these manifestations is the negotiated outcome. Bargaining is a pervasive feature of law more broadly conceived. Galanter writes that, "[t]he negotiated outcome in the shadow of the law turns out to be the master pattern of disputing..." What might otherwise be seen as adjudicative processes are now seen as negotiative ones, with authoritative decision makers now cast in the roles of arbitrators and mediators. Legal rules and principles surely still apply, but their role is less determinative, and now understood as less definitive.

The parties to the negotiated outcomes are also more broadly conceived, as are the settings in which they act. The actors in these larger social dramas include legally recognized authorities, users and consumers of law and their authorized and unauthorized agents, other interested parties, and the broader social audience that must be considered in shaping negotiated outcomes. These actors are seen and heard not only in more formal and heavily monitored legal settings, but in a plurality of other places. Private governments, semi-autonomous social and professional fields, indigenous law and other forms of regulation

are related to law in ways that depend on one another for mutual effect. Governmental law is intimately interrelated with other kinds of law and social institutions in which regulators and regulatees conduct their everyday business. Law is seen here as plural, not singular.

The influence of law is also understood in symbolic as much as or more than in instrumental terms. Indeed, scarcity of legal resources requires that this must be so, for the cost of direct law enforcement sharply curtails the range over which the law can be applied. However, when law is conceived as symbolic information flows, apart from the direct and instrumental exercise of force, the broad impact of law, albeit indirect and often with unintended effects, is more easily grasped. For example, general deterrence, legal socialization and bargaining in the shadow of the law are all seen as broader manifestations of the law as it symbolically affects people's everyday lives.

In all of these ways, the new legal scholarship has dramatically increased what we know about the way law actually works — about plea bargaining, negotiated settlements, selective prosecution, litigants' strategies, the working routines of courts and judges; about the practice of law, client-lawyer relationships, the structure and politics of the bar; about legal education and the public consumption of law. Journals such as *Law & Society Review*, the *Journal of Legal Studies*, the *Journal of Law & Economics*, the *Journal of Legal Education*, *Law & Human Behaviour* and the *American Bar Association Research Journal* are alive with the emerging products of this work. An increasing number of monographs and texts are also available. All of this reflects an accumulation of empirical legal study that is impressive compared to the dearth of such material available less than a generation ago.

. . . .

The Possibilities and Perils of Legal Studies[†]
N.C. Sargent

THE PEDAGOGIC CHALLENGE

Roger Cotterrell (1986) points out that one of the defining characteristics of any discipline or knowledge-field lies in the fact that its intellectual frame of reference (its object of inquiry, the conceptual and methodological tools relied

upon and the manner in which the autonomy of the field of inquiry is established) tends to be autonomous and self-validating. Consequently, one of the problems inherent in any attempt to challenge the intellectual hegemony of any discipline or paradigm lies in establishing the intellectual space from which to mount such a challenge.

† Sargent, Neil C., "The Possibilities and Perils of Legal Studies" (1990), 8 *Law in Context*, forthcoming at 4–14.

Cotterrell's insight has particular relevance in relation to the difficulties inherent in developing an interdisciplinary approach to legal studies which is capable of challenging the dominant legal positivist tradition within legal education. This is because the intellectual hegemony of the legal positivist tradition is intimately connected with the professionalization of legal education and the institutional autonomy of the professional law school. This is no accident. The development of legal positivism as a closed form of knowledge-formation, with its own internal canons of enquiry, has played an important role in raising the status of law to that of a 'learned' profession (Arthurs, 1987). Moreover, the focus of legal positivism on the substantive content of legal texts and on internal conventions of reasoning and analysis reflects precisely those areas of knowledge and expertise over which legal professionals have traditionally exercised a monopoly.

The strength of this intellectual tradition lies in the way it colonizes the imagination of legal scholars. As such it imposes a powerful intellectual brake upon their research and teaching agendas, which is all the more insidious for being largely invisible. Legal positivism involves epistemological assumptions about the nature of law as an object of inquiry which reinforce the insularity of legal scholarship from the academic concerns of scholars in other disciplines. At its heart is a conceptualization of law as a normatively closed form of knowledge and system of inquiry which have few, if any, necessary reference points to the social, political or economic environment in which law operates (Cotterrell, 1986). Despite the recent burgeoning of critical perspectives on law which seek to challenge many of the tenets of the dominant positivist tradition, such as the Critical Legal Studies Movement, in one important respect little seems to have changed. The focus of enquiry of most contemporary legal scholarship remains defined by its concern with legal doctrine, notwithstanding the explicitly political agenda of much of the new critical scholarship. Moreover, the modes of inquiry relied upon even by critical legal scholars are still oriented around textual analysis and deconstruction, even if the claimed rationality and objectivity of traditional modes of legal interpretation have become increasingly contested with the new critical scholarship.

Consequently, there is still no obvious mandate for travel outside these conventional boundaries in search of empirical evidence about the impact of law in practice. Nor is there any need to investigate the role of legal institutions or legal actors other than as sources of authoritative texts for analysis or interpretation. In this respect, Supreme Court justices are necessarily more important as authors of legal texts than trial court justices, notwithstanding the claims of the Legal Realists to the contrary. Similarly, the role of the court as a trier of fact and in processing disputes is less significant to most legal schol-

ars than its role as a source of texts for interpretation and analysis.

By contrast, the assumption that legal texts can be read independently from their social, cultural, economic or political environment tends to be viewed by many social scientists with a considerable degree of skepticism, bordering at times on disbelief. Those issues which are of marginal concern to legal scholars in their search for authoritative texts are precisely the issues about the workings of the legal system, the behaviour of legal actors, the effectiveness of legal rules and decision-making processes, that are likely to be of interest to social science researchers. Consequently, the sources of data, the methods of enquiry and the conceptual frameworks utilised by social science researchers in their investigations of law are based on very different foundations than those which inform most conventional legal scholarship (Friedman, 1986; Hagan, 1986).

One of the major problems inherent in attempting to develop an interdisciplinary approach to legal studies which is able to draw from both these disciplinary traditions lies in the fact that they appear to be mutually exclusive of one another. This is borne out by the history of the law-and-society movement in the United States, which despite its promising beginnings and its relatively lengthy history, has largely failed to penetrate the mainstream of American legal scholarship (Friedman, 1986).

As a result, there is sometimes a tendency on the part of social science researchers to regard the disciplinary claims made by legal academics as something of a contradiction in terms. Legal scholarship tends to be dismissed by many social scientists on the grounds that it lacks theoretical or methodological coherence. The question is often asked whether there is anything sufficiently distinctive about legal being treated as a separate disciplinary field (Friedman, 1986; Cotterrell, 1986). From this perspective, law is frequently seen as a proper object of inquiry only within the confines of another disciplinary tradition, such as sociology, political science, history, psychology or philosophy.

Why not then simply abandon the legal academics to their search for authoritative texts while the social scientists get on with the work of investigating the way in which law operates as a social phenomenon and impacts upon people's lives? The answer that I would give to this question is two-fold. First, that law is too important a social institution to be left only to lawyers. This implies that the language of law and content of legal doctrine should not be regarded as simply the dry, technical preserve of lawyers. Law plays a crucial ideological role in shaping popular understandings about the nature of power relations and the structure of social ordering within liberal democratic societies. Consequently, the entire terrain of law, which includes the role of legal education, the nature and form of legal reasoning, the hierarchical structure of legal authority, as well as the content of legal rules, needs to be studied as a complex social phenomenon that can only be fully understood through the use of social science concepts and methods of inquiry.

Closely related to this first point is a further observation concerning the limits of empirical enquiry as a means of understanding the social significance of law. Law as a social phenomenon is more than just a set of empirically observable relations or activities that can be examined according to well-established canons of enquiry to produce empirically-testable hypotheses about the behaviour or significance of law or legal institutions in practice. Here I clearly part company with many in the socio-legal studies movement in Britain and Australia and in the law-and-society movement in the United States and Canada. It follows from the point made above that legal discourse and doctrine must also become part of the province of social science enquiry, even if not readily amenable to empirical methods of investigation.

Given the significance of law as a source of contested meanings about the nature of social relations, a crucial question for investigation becomes what are the limits of law as an agency of social or political change? To what extent, for example, is the language of legal rights capable of redressing situations of substantive social, economic or political inequality? Or is the discourse of legal rights so closely wedded to liberal notions of abstract individualism and formal equality that it has the effect of channelling progressive political struggles into narrowly circumscribed legal issues? These are not questions which can be answered solely by reference to internal canons of interpretation and precedent,

such as legal academics are used to. Rather, what is at issue are fundamental questions about the relationship between legal concepts and the structure of social, economic and political ordering within Canadian society.

What this translates to in practice is the need to insert questions of theory and method into the design of any legal studies curriculum in a way that is central to the pedagogic enterprise. This implies that conventional legal methods of inquiry are inadequate alone to generate meaningful hypotheses about the nature of law or the connection between legal relations and social relations. It also implies a significant degree of skepticism about the ability of empirical enquiry alone to produce any more meaningful responses to these questions unless explicitly informed by an awareness of wider theoretical issues.

Consequently, the prescription offered is for a legal studies approach which claims law as an appropriate field of inquiry, but which rejects any conception of law as a unitary mode of discourse that can be investigated by reliance on internal canons of inquiry alone. Rather, the focus should be on exploring the multi-faceted character of law as a complex social phenomenon, and the manner in which different theoretical and methodological perspectives give rise to different types of questions about the role and functions of law and the relationship between legal and social change (*cf.* Hunt, 1986; Boyd, 1989). Perhaps it should come as no great surprise that this also reflects the intellectual trajectory followed in the development of the Carleton law program.

Further Reading

Lawrence Friedman, "The Law and Society Movement" (1986), 38 *Stanford Law Review* 763.

C. Campbell, "Legal Thought and Juristic Values" (1974), 1 *British Journal of Law and Society* 13.

Roger Cotterrell, "Law and Sociology: Notes on the Constitution and Confrontation of Disciplines" (1986), 13 *Journal of Law and Society* 9.

Richard Abel, "Law Books and Books About Law" (1973), 26 *Stanford Law Review* 175.

David Nelkin, "The 'Gap Problem' in the Sociology of Law: A Theoretical Review" (1981), 1 *Windsor Yearbook of Access to Justice* 35–61.

Law and Morality

R. v. Dudley & Stephens[†]

INDICTMENT for the murder of Richard Parker on the high seas within the jurisdiction of the Admiralty.

At the trial before Huddleston, B., at the Devon and Cornwall Winter Assizes, November 7, 1884, the jury at the suggestion of the learned judge, found the facts of the case in a special verdict which stated "that on July 5, 1884, the prisoners, Thomas Dudley and Edward Stephens, with one Brooks, all able-bodied English seamen, and the deceased also an English boy, between seventeen and eighteen years of age, the crew of an English yacht, a registered English vessel, were cast away in a storm on the high seas 1,600 miles from the Cape of Good Hope, and were compelled to put into an open boat belonging to the said yacht. That in this boat they had no supply of water and no supply of food, except two 1 lb. tins of turnips, and for three days they had nothing else to subsist upon. That on the fourth day they caught a small turtle, upon which they subsisted for a few days, and this was the only food they had up to the twentieth day when the act now in question was committed. That on the twelfth day the remains of the turtle were entirely consumed, and for the next eight days they had nothing to eat. That they had no fresh water, except such rain as they from time to time caught in their oilskin capes. That the boat was drifting on the ocean, and was probably more than 1000 miles away from land. That on the eighteenth day, when they had been seven days without food and five without water, the prisoners spoke to Brooks as to what should be done if no succour came, and suggested that some one should be sacrificed to save the rest, but Brooks dissented, and the boy, to whom they were understood to refer, was not consulted. That on the 24th of July, the day before the act now in question, the prisoner Dudley proposed to Stephens and Brooks that lots should

be cast who should be put to death to save the rest, but Brooks refused to consent, and it was not put to the boy, and in point of fact there was no drawing of lots. That on that day the prisoners spoke of their having families, and suggested it would be better to kill the boy that their lives should be saved, and Dudley proposed that if there was no vessel in sight by the morrow morning the boy should be killed. That next day, the 25th of July, no vessel appearing, Dudley told Brooks that he had better go and have a sleep, and made signs to Stephens and Brooks that the boy had better be killed. The prisoner Stephens agreed to the act, but Brooks dissented from it. That the boy was then lying at the bottom of the boat quite helpless, and extremely weakened by famine and by drinking sea water, and unable to make any resistance nor did he ever assent to his being killed. The prisoner Dudley offered a prayer asking forgiveness for them all if either of them should be tempted to commit a rash act, and that their souls might be saved. That Dudley, with the assent of Stephens, went to the boy, and telling him that his time was come, put a knife into his throat and killed him then and there; that the three men fed upon the body and blood of the boy for four days; that on the fourth day after the act had been committed the boat was picked up by a passing vessel, and the prisoners were rescued, still alive, but in the lowest state of prostration. That they were carried to the port of Falmouth, and committed for trial at Exeter. That if the men had not fed upon the body of the boy they would probably not have survived to be so picked up and rescued, but would within the four days have died of famine. That the boy, being in a much weaker condition, was likely to have died before them. That at the time of the act in question there was no sail in sight, nor any reasonable prospect of

† *R. v. Dudley & Stephens* (1884), 14 Q.B.D. 273; 54 L.J.M.C. 32; 52 L.T. 107; 1 T.L.R. 118; 15 Cox C.C. 624; 49 J.P. 69; 33 W.R. 347. Queen's Bench.

relief. That under these circumstances there appeared to the prisoners every probability that unless they then fed or very soon fed upon the boy or one of themselves they would die of starvation. That there was no appreciable chance of saving life except by killing some one for the others to eat. That assuming any necessity to kill anybody, there was no greater necessity for killing the boy than any of the other three men. But whether upon the whole matter by the jurors found the killing of Richard Parker by Dudley and Stephens be felony and murder the jurors are ignorant, and pray the advice of the Court thereupon, and if upon the whole matter the Court shall be of opinion that the killing of Richard Parker be felony and murder, then the jurors say that Dudley and Stephens were each guilty of felony and murder as alleged in the indictment."

LORD COLERIDGE C.J.: — From these facts, stated with the cold precision of a special verdict, it appears sufficiently that the prisoners were subject to terrible temptation, to sufferings which might break down the bodily power of the strongest man, and try the conscience of the best. Other details yet more harrowing, facts still more loathsome and appalling, were presented to the jury, and are to be found recorded in my learned Brother's notes. But nevertheless this is clear, that the prisoners put to death a weak and unoffending boy upon the chance of preserving their own lives by feeding upon his flesh and blood after he was killed, and with the certainty of depriving *him* of any possible chance of survival. The verdict finds in terms that "if the men had not fed upon the body of the boy they would *probably* not have survived," and that "the boy being in a much weaker condition was *likely* to have died before them." They might possibly have been picked up next day by a passing ship; they might possibly not have been picked up at all; in either case it is obvious that the killing of the boy would have been an unnecessary and profitless act. It is found by the verdict that the boy was incapable of resistance, and, in fact, made none; and it is not even suggested that his death was due to any violence on his part attempted against, or even so much as feared by, those who killed him. Under these circumstances the jury say that they are ignorant whether those who killed him were guilty of murder, and have referred it to this Court to determine what is the legal consequence which follows from the facts which they have found.

There remains to be considered the real question in the case — whether killing under the circumstances set forth in the verdict be or be not murder. The contention that it could be anything else was, to the minds of us all, both new and strange, and we stopped the Attorney General in his negative argument in order that we might hear what could be said in support of a proposition which appeared to us to be at once dangerous, immoral, and opposed to all legal principle and analogy. All, no doubt, that can be said has been urged before us, and we are now

to consider and determine what it amounts to. First it is said that it follows from various definitions of murder in books of authority, which definitions imply, if they do not state, the doctrine that in order to save your own life you may lawfully take away the life of another, when that other is neither attempting nor threatening yours, nor is guilty of any illegal act whatever towards you or any one else. But if these definitions be looked at they will not be found to sustain this contention. The earliest in point of date is the passage cited to us from Bracton, who lived in the reign of Henry III.

But in the very passage as to necessity, on which reliance has been placed, it is clear that Bracton is speaking of necessity in the ordinary sense — the repelling by violence, violence justified so far as it was necessary for the object, any illegal violence used towards oneself.

It is, if possible, yet clearer that the doctrine contended for receives no support from the great authority of Lord Hale. For in the chapter in which he deals with the exemption created by compulsion or necessity he thus expresses himself: — "If a man be desperately assaulted and in peril of death, and cannot otherwise escape unless, to satisfy his assailant's fury, he will kill an innocent person then present, the fear and factual force will not acquit him of the crime and punishment of murder, if he commit the fact, for he ought rather to die himself than kill an innocent; but if he cannot otherwise save his own life the law permits him in his own defence to kill the assailant, for by the violence of the assault, and the offence committed upon him by the assailant himself, the law of nature, and necessity, hath made him his own protector *cum debito moderamino inculpatae tutelae*." (*Hale's Please of the Crown*, vol. 1, 51.)

But, further still, Lord Hale in the following chapter deals with the position asserted by the casuists, and sanctioned, as he says, by Grotius and Puffendorf, that in a case of extreme necessity, either of hunger or clothing; "theft is no theft, or at least not punishable as theft, as some even of our own lawyers have asserted the same." "But," says Lord Hale, "I take it that here in England, that rule, at least by the laws of England, is false; and therefore, if a person being under necessity for want of victuals or clothes, shall upon that account clandestinely and *anima furandi* steal another man's goods, it is felony, and a crime by the laws of England punishable with death." (*Hale, Please of the Crown*, i, 54). If, therefore, Lord Hale is clear — as he is — that extreme necessity of hunger does not justify larceny, what would he have said to the doctrine that it justified murder?

Is there, then, any authority for the proposition which has been presented to us? Decided cases there are none. The American case cited by my Brother Stephen in his Digest, from Wharton on Homicide, in which it was decided, correctly indeed, that sailors had no right to throw passengers overboard to save themselves, but on the somewhat strange ground that the proper mode of determining who was to be sacrificed was to vote upon the subject by ballot, can hardly, as my Brother Stephen says, be an authority satisfactory to a court in this country.

The one real authority of former time is Lord Bacon, who, in his commentary on the maxim, "*necessitas inducit privilegium quoad jura privata*," lays down the law as follows: — "Necessity carrieth a privilege in itself. Necessity is of three sorts — necessity of conservation of life, necessity of obedience, and necessity of the act of God or of a stranger. First of conservation of life, if a man steal viands to satisfy his present hunger, this is no felony nor larceny. So if divers be in danger of drowning by the casting away of some boat or barge, and one of them get to some plank, or on the boat's side to keep himself above water, and another to save his life thrust him from it, whereby he is drowned, this is neither *se defendendo* nor by misadventure, but justifiable." On this it is to be observed that Lord Bacon's proposition that stealing to satisfy hunger is no larceny is hardly supported by Staundforde, whom he cites for it, and is expressly contradicted by Lord Hale in the passage already cited. And for the proposition as to the plank or boat, it is said to be derived from the canonists. At any rate he cites no authority for it, and it must stand upon his own. Lord Bacon was great even as a lawyer; but it is permissible to much smaller men, relying upon principle and on the authority of others, the equals and even the superiors of Lord Bacon as lawyers, to question the soundness of his dictum. There are many conceivable states of things in which it might possibly be true, but if Lord Bacon meant to lay down the broad proposition that a man may save his life by killing, if necessary, an innocent and unoffending neighbour, it certainly is not law at the present day.

Now, except for the purpose of testing how far the conservation of a man's own life is in all cases and under all circumstances, an absolute, unqualified, and paramount duty, we exclude from our consideration all the incidents of war. We are dealing with a case of private homicide, not one imposed upon men in the service of their Sovereign and in the defence of their country. Now it is admitted that the deliberate killing of this unoffending and unresisting boy was clearly murder, unless the killing can be justified by some well-recognised excuse admitted by the law. It is further admitted that there was in this case no such excuse, unless the killing was justified by what has been called "necessity." But the temptation to the act which existed here was not what the law has ever called necessity. Nor is this to be regretted. Though law and morality are not the same, and many things may be immoral which are not necessarily illegal, yet the absolute divorce of law from morality would be of fatal consequence; and such divorce would follow if the temptation to murder in this case were to be held by law an absolute

defence of it. It is not so. To preserve one's life is generally speaking a duty, but it may be the plainest and the highest duty to sacrifice it. War is full of instances in which it is a man's duty not to live, but to die. The duty in case of shipwreck, of a captain to his crew, of the crew to the passengers, of soldiers to women and children, as in the noble case of the *Birkenhead*; these duties impose on men and moral necessity, not of the preservation, but of the sacrifice of their lives for others, from which in no country, least of all, it is to be hoped, in England, will men ever shrink, as indeed, they have not shrunk. It is not correct, therefore, to say that there is any absolute or unqualified necessity to preserve one's life. "*Necesse est ut eam, no at vivam*," is a saying of a Roman officer quoted by Lord Bacon himself with high eulogy in the very chapter on necessity to which so much reference has been made. It would be a very easy and cheap display of commonplace learning to quote from Greek and Latin authors, from Horace, from Juvenal, from Cicero, from Euripides, passage after passage, in which the duty of dying for others has been laid down in glowing and emphatic language as resulting from the principles of heathen ethics; it is enough in a Christian country to remind ourselves of the Great Example whom we profess to follow. It is not needful to point out the awful danger of admitting the principle which has been contended for. Who is to be the judge of this sort of necessity? By what measure is the comparative value of lives to be measured? Is it to be strength, or intellect, or what? It is plain that the principle leaves to him who is to profit by it to determine the necessity which will justify him in deliberately taking another's life to save his own. In this case the weakest, the youngest, the most unresisting, was chosen. Was it more necessary to kill him than one of the grown men? The answer must be "No" —

So spake the Fiend, and with necessity,
The tyrant's plea, excused his devilish deeds.

It is not suggested that in this particular case the deeds were "devilish," but it is quite plain that such a principle once admitted might be made the legal cloak for unbridled passion and atrocious crime. There is no safe path for judges to tread but to ascertain the law to the best of their ability and to declare it according to their judgment; and if in any case the law appears to be too severe on individuals, to leave it to the Sovereign to exercise that prerogative of mercy which the Constitution has intrusted to the hands fittest to dispense it.

It must not be supposed that in refusing to admit temptation to be an excuse for crime it is forgotten how terrible the temptation was; how awful the suffering; how hard in such trials to keep the judgment straight and the conduct pure. We are often compelled to set up standards we cannot reach ourselves, and to lay down rules which we could not ourselves satisfy. But a man has no right to declare temptation to be an excuse, though he might himself have yielded to it, nor allow compassion for the criminal to change or weaken in any manner the legal definition of the crime. It is therefore our duty to declare that the prisoners' act in this case was wilful murder, that the facts as stated in the verdict are no legal justification of the homicide; and to say that in our unanimous opinion the prisoners are upon this special verdict guilty of murder.

The Court then proceeded to pass sentence of death upon the prisoners.

This sentence was afterwards commuted by the Crown to six months' imprisonment.

Tragic Choices†
P.J. Fitzgerald

"YOU can't win 'em all," we say to console ourselves when things go wrong. What if they go so wrong that winning is impossible? What if life really puts us on the spot and confronts us with a tragic choice? Let's look at the following examples.

A pilot named Marten Hartwell crashed in the Northwest Territories in the early 70's. He was the only survivor. To stay alive until he was rescued he had to eat. His only source of food was the dead body of his companion, a young nurse. What should he have done — become a cannibal or starved to death? He chose to live.

In another case, some years ago, an international expedition set out to climb Mount Everest. One of the team, a man called Harsh, slipped and fell. He came to rest suspended upside down over an icefield. To get to him his companions would have had to venture across the extremely dangerous ice; and when they reached him there was no guarantee that they could bring him back alive. What should they have done — risked their lives with little hope of saving Harsh, or let him die? They let him die.

There are even worse situations. Two mountaineers were climbing in the Alps, roped together. On an isolated peak, one slipped and fell. Unable to move, he lay dangling at the end of the rope. The other climber couldn't lift his companion back up, nor could he himself move on without cutting the rope. What should he have done — cut the rope and sent his companion to his death, or stayed where he was till both died of exposure? He cut the rope.

1. What would you have done in Hartwell's place?
2. Do you think the Everest climbers ought to have risked their lives to save Harsh?
3. If you had been the climber in the Alps, would you have cut the rope?

4. Which would you put first — self-preservation or the maintenance of another human life?
5. Do you think the law should have the answers to these questions?

THE ONLY WAY

Sometimes the law is forced to deal with these tragic choices, as it did in the following nineteenth century English case. The case concerned three shipwrecked sailors and a cabin boy. The story as a grisly one. The facts were not in dispute. The only question was: had the law been broken? To answer this, the judges had to decide what the law was. And their decision, given almost a hundred years ago in England, still contains the law for Canada today.

For over twenty days three sailors and a cabin boy had drifted in an open boat a thousand miles from land. Their only food was two tins of turnips and a turtle they had caught, their only drink the rain collected in their oilskin capes. When this gave out, they stayed seven days without food and five without water. They couldn't have lived many more days unless they took the only course remaining. That course, said one of them, Captain Dudley, was to sacrifice one life to save the rest — kill one for the other three to eat.

Which one? The captain, who proposed this course? The sailor, Stephens, who agreed with him? The other sailor, Brooks, who disagreed? Or the seventeen-year-old cabin boy, prostrate from famine and drinking seawater? Which one should be the sacrificial victim?

1. Even if there is only one course, would they be right to take it?
2. If so, who should be the victim?
3. And how should they decide on the victim?

---

† Fitzgerald, P.J., "Tragic Choices" in *This Law of Ours* (Toronto: Prentice-Hall of Canada, Ltd.) 40–49, 333–45. Reprinted by permission of the author.

THE AGONY AND THE ARGUMENT

"If no help comes," said Dudley and Stephens, "We'll have to sacrifice one to save the rest." Brooks knew they meant the boy and didn't agree.

"Let's do it this way," said the captain the next day; "let's all draw lots to see which one to kill." It was the twentieth day when he made this suggestion to Brooks and Stephens. He never made it to the boy himself. But Brooks would not agree and lots were never drawn.

"We have families," said Dudley and Stephens, "and the boy has no one dependent on him. Better to kill him to save the rest of us. If no help comes tomorrow, we'll have to kill the boy."

Next day no help came. No ship appeared. The captain motioned to Stephens and to Brooks that they had better kill the boy, who lay helpless at the bottom of the boat. He would have died anyway before the other three. Once again Brooks would have no part of it.

1. Three possibilities of setting the question emerge from what the captain said. What are they?
2. Which is the best?
3. Who should decide?

THE ULTIMATE SOLUTION

The captain, a religious man, offered a prayer. He asked forgiveness for them all. Then he and Stephens told the boy his time had come. They put a knife to his throat and killed him.

For four days afterwards the three men fed upon his body and his blood. Had they not done so, they would all have died. On the fourth day a passing ship picked them up. All three were in the lowest state of prostration. Their rescuers brought them home to England, where the law took over.

The authorities investigated the incident and then launched a murder prosecution against two of the survivors —Dudley and Stephens. Brooks was never charged, but was a witness at the trial.

The trial took place before a jury which gave a special verdict. Instead of pronouncing the defendants guilty or not guilty, they merely decided what had happened. They decided that Dudley and Stephens had killed the boy, and that they had had no other chance of survival. They left it to the judge to say whether this was murder or not.

1. Do you think the sailors were justified in killing the cabin boy?
2. Can you think of any circumstances where killing is justified?
3. Do you think the case should have come to trial at all?
4. Was it fair that Brooks wasn't charged?

5. Only very exceptionally does a jury refuse to say "guilty" or "not guilty." Why do you think they did so in this case?
6. If you had been on the jury, would you have wanted to refuse to give a verdict?

THE JUDGES' VERDICT

Was the act of Dudley and Stephens justified? The jury left it to the judges to determine. This is what the judges said:

There remains to be considered the real question in the case — whether killing under the circumstances set forth in the verdict be or be not murder.

Now except for the purpose of testing how far the conservation of a man's own life is in all cases and under all circumstances, an absolute, unqualified, and paramount duty, we exclude from our consideration all the incidents of war. We are dealing with a case of private homicide, not one imposed upon men in the service of their Sovereign and in the defence of the country. Now it is admitted that the deliberate killing of this unoffending and unresisting boy was clearly murder, unless the killing can be justified by some well-recognized excuse admitted by the law. It is further admitted that there was in this case no such excuse, unless the killing was justified by what has been called "necessity." But the temptation to the act which existed here was not what the law has ever called necessity. Nor is this to be regretted. Though law and morality are not the same, and many things may be immoral which are not necessarily illegal, yet the absolute divorce of law from morality would be of fatal consequence; and such divorce would follow if the temptation to murder in this case were to be held by law an absolute defense of it. It is not so. To preserve one's life is generally speaking a duty, but it may be the plainest and the highest duty to sacrifice it. War is full of instances in which it is a man's duty not to live, but to die. The duty, in case of shipwreck, of a captain to his crew, of the crew to the passengers, of soldiers to women and children, these duties impose on men and moral necessity, not of the preservation, but of the sacrifice of their lives for others, from which in no country, least of all, it is to be hoped, in England, will men ever shrink, as indeed they have not shrunk. It is not correct, therefore, to say that there is any absolute or unqualified necessity to preserve one's life.

23

It is not needful to point out the awful danger of admitting the principle which has been contended for. Who is to be the judge of this sort of necessity? By what measure is the comparative value of lives to be measured? Is it to be strength, or intellect, or what? It is plain that the principle leaves to him who is to profit by it to determine the necessity which will justify him in deliberately taking another's life to save his own. In this case the weakest, the youngest, the most unresisting, was chosen. Was it more necessary to kill him than one of the grown men? The answer must be "No."

It is not suggested that in this particular case the deeds were "devilish," but it is quite plain that such a principle once admitted might be made the legal cloak for unbridled passion and atrocious crime. There is no safe path for judges to tread but to ascertain the law to the best of their ability and to declare it according to their judgment; and if in any case the law appears to be too severe on individuals, to leave it to the Sovereign to exercise that prerogative of mercy which the Constitution has entrusted to the hands fittest to dispense it.

It must not be supposed that in refusing to admit temptation to be an excuse for crime it is forgotten how terrible that temptation was; how awful the suffering; how hard in such trials to keep the judgment straight and the conduct pure. We are often compelled to set up standards we cannot reach ourselves, and to lay down rules which we could not ourselves satisfy. But a man has no right to declare temptation to be an excuse, though he might himself have yielded to it, nor allow compassion for the criminal to change or weaken in any manner the legal definition of the crime. It is therefore our duty to declare that the prisoners' act in this case was wilful murder, that the facts as stated in the verdict are no legal justification of the homicide; and to say that in our unanimous opinion the prisoners are upon this special verdict guilty of murder. (*R. v. Dudley & Stephens*, 1884)

1. What is the argument put forward by the defence?
2. Why did the judges say it wasn't necessary to kill the cabin boy? Do you agree with them?
3. What did the judges say would be the consequences of accepting the argument put forward by the defence? Do you agree?
4. Do you think it was easier for the judges than it was for the jury to decide whether Dudley and Stephens were guilty? If so, why?

5. What do you think the consequence would have been if the judges, like the jury, had been unable to decide?

THE SENTENCE OF THE COURT

What Dudley and Stephens did was murder, said the judges. And murder was a capital offence in England at that time. The Lord Chief Justice sentenced them as follows:

The sentence of the court upon you is that you be taken from this place to a lawful prison and thence to a place of execution, and that you there suffer death by hanging; and that your body be afterwards buried within the precincts of the prison in which you shall have been confined before your execution. And may the Lord have mercy on your souls. (*R. v. Dudley & Stephens*, 1884)

1. Was the death penalty justified in this case?
2. Is it ever justified? Does this alter your views on the sanctity of human life?
3. If they had had to decide, do you think the jury would have decided any differently than the judges did?

THE PUNISHMENT

Dudley and Stephens were sentenced to death, but they were given a reprieve: the *royal prerogative of mercy* was exercised in their favor and the death sentence was commuted to one of life imprisonment. But this was not the end of it. The authorities exercised their discretion and released the prisoners after six months.

1. Should there be a royal prerogative of mercy? Why or why not?
2. Should the government be able to alter the sentences passed by the judges?
3. Should the law fix the sentence the judges must pass (as it does in murder cases)? Why not leave sentencing to the judges' discretion?
4. Do you think it was their knowledge of the penalty for murder that prevented the jury from saying Dudley and Stephens were guilty? If so, do you think the jury should have allowed that knowledge to prevent them?

THE MORAL DILEMMA

Murder, says the law, is intentionally killing a person without lawful justification. This is common sense, because in general we believe it is wrong to kill. However, we think it is justified in exceptional cases. When is it justified? The difficulty of this question can be seen from the following example, well known to legal textbook writers.

Two sailors, X and Y, are shipwrecked. Neither can swim. X reaches a floating plank and climbs onto it. Y reaches the plank and tries to climb onto it. The plank will hold only one person, so X prevents Y from getting onto it and Y drowns.

1. Is this situation exceptional enough to make X's act morally justified?
2. Suppose Y had climbed onto the plank and pushed X off, would Y's act have been morally justified?
3. Suppose the survivor in 1 or 2 had been charged in front of Dudley's and Stephens's judges with murder. What verdict do you think would have been given?
4. Suppose Y climbed onto the plank and X remained on it, and they both drowned. Would each have been justified in staying on the plank?

JETTISONING THE CARGO

"Necessity knows no law," it is often said. In other words, you can't be held legally liable for an act you had to do. From this point of view Dudley and Stephens would not be guilty of the murder of the cabin boy because their act was one which was necessary for their survival. But the judges in their case rejected the defendants' plea of necessity. As a result, it has been said that there is no defence of necessity in common law.

This is not true. Necessity can be a good defence, as in the 1608 *Mouse's* case.

A ship carrying a cargo of goods was overtaken by a storm. The captain feared that it would sink and that all aboard would be drowned, because it was already dangerously low in the water. To stop it from sinking further he ordered the crew to throw the cargo overboard. This lightened the vessel and enabled her to keep afloat, survive the storm, and come to safety.

The captain, so the court held at this trial, was within his rights in throwing the cargo overboard. He had to sacrifice the cargo for the greater good of saving human life.

1. Suppose the cargo had been a human one. Would the captain's act have been justified?
2. Suppose the open boat with the three men and the cabin boy had been sinking. Would Captain Dudley have been entitled to throw one of the passengers overboard to save the rest? If so, which one? If not, can you think of any circumstances where a captain might be morally justified in throwing a passenger overboard?
3. Saving human life is obviously more important than saving cargo. In Dudley's and Stephens's case was it

equally obvious that saving the lives of the three sailors was more important than saving the cabin boy's life?
4. In such a case do three lives have three times the importance of one life?
5. Because the cabin boy would have died before they were rescued, was it more important to save the sailors' lives?
6. Do you think Dudley and Stephens would have been well-advised to put forward such arguments? Would they have answered the judges' points?
7. What light does this case throw on the notion of necessity? What do we mean by saying it was necessary for the captain to throw the cargo overboard? What did Dudley mean by saying it was necessary to kill the cabin boy?
8. There is a well-known story about Oscar Wilde in which a beggar, trying to convince Wilde to give him some money, says, "Man must live." Wilde answers, "I don't see the necessity." What point is Wilde making? Strictly speaking, is anything ever really necessary?

MOTHER AND CHILD

Fortunately, necessity cases such as that involving Dudley and Stephens are rare. Much more common is another situation where necessity may be raised as a defence — the situation of abortion.

Abortion means trying to bring about a woman's miscarriage so as to stop her from giving birth. It was a crime at common law and it is a crime in Canada under the Criminal Code. A pregnant woman who tries to bring about her own abortion commits an offence punishable with two years' imprisonment. Any other person who tries to procure a woman's abortion — whether she is pregnant or not — commits an offence punishable with life imprisonment.

Here we see the law underlining the sanctity of human life. Not only does it prohibit killing people already born, it also prohibits any intervention with the foetus which will prevent its live birth. Life in the womb enjoys the law's protection too.

But what about the mother? How much say should she have in the matter? What if she doesn't want to bear the child? Should she and not the law have control over her body? What if the birth could harm the mother? Can she take the foetus's life to save her own?

Canadian law, like that of many other countries, provides a compromise on these questions. Basically, abortion is illegal. In exceptional circumstances, however, it is allowed. It is allowed if it is performed by a doctor in an approved hospital and if the special abortion committee for that hospital certifies that the woman's life or health is endangered by the continuation of the pregnancy.

What about abortions performed otherwise than in accordance with that procedure? That was the problem raised by Dr. Henry Morgentaler.

A twenty-six-year-old female student who came to Canada on a student visa in 1972 became pregnant in July 1973. She was ineligible for medicare, so a hospital abortion would have cost her more than she could pay.

Meanwhile her pregnancy made her anxious, unable to eat or sleep properly, prone to vomiting, and very depressed. She was referred to Dr. Morgentaler who later explained he feared she might do something foolish unless her condition was relieved. He therefore performed an abortion on her in August 1973.

Charged with performing an illegal abortion, he argued, among other things, that he acted out of necessity. The jury *acquitted* him.

The Crown, however, appealed. The Quebec Court of Appeal reversed the decision and entered a conviction. They held that there was no room for a defence of necessity because there was no evidence of urgent need for an abortion.

Dr. Morgentaler appealed and his case came before the Supreme Court of Canada. The court was divided in its views. A minority, including Chief Justice Laskin, held that there was sufficient evidence for a defence of necessity — the pregnancy was harmful to the woman's health and the doctor was afraid it might lead her to do something foolish.

The majority of the judges, however, took the opposite view. They held that there wasn't sufficient evidence of necessity — Dr. Morgentaler had done nothing to find out why the woman couldn't have done this. They therefore upheld the conviction, and as they were the majority of the court, the conviction stood. Dr. Morgentaler went to prison.

1. What is abortion?
2. What arguments can you advance for making abortion a crime?
3. What counter arguments are there?
4. What is the compromise on abortion contained in Canadian law?
5. Why didn't the abortion performed by Dr. Morgentaler come within the lawful exception?
6. On what grounds could Dr. Morgentaler be said to have a defence of necessity?
7. Why did the Supreme Court of Canada reject this argument?

ENEMIES IN WAR

Dr. Morgentaler's case, like Dudley's and Stephens's, occurred in times of peace. Wartime gives rise to different principles. A soldier killing the enemy on the battlefield is not guilty of murder in the eyes of the law. Such killing is justified in law. It is also justified, many would argue, according to our ordinary notions of right and wrong. How far should the justification extend? Consider the following case.

During the Second World War a British bomber pilot was shot down over Germany and taken prisoner. He escaped and on his way through Germany to neutral territory, he carried on his own private war effort: each day he killed one German soldier. Back in England, he resumed his flying duties and ended the war with high rank and honors.

1. Do you think such killings are justified?
2. Are there any moral limits to the right to kill the enemy in war?
3. If Dudley and Stephens had been survivors of a warship torpedoed by the enemy, and the boy a survivor of the enemy submarine, would they have been justified in killing him simply as an enemy?
4. Would they have been justified in killing him for food?

THE ROMAN SOLDIER'S WAY OUT

So far we've discussed the taking of other people's lives. What about taking one's own life? Suicide has often been seen as an honorable way out. The Roman solider, if defeated, preferred death to dishonor. Rather than surrender and allow himself to be captured he would fall upon his sword and kill himself. We see this in the story of Brutus.

Law and Morality[†]
Lord P. Devlin

THE relationship between law and morals has recently, in England and in the United States and also in Canada, received quite a considerable degree of interest. Of course, if one wants to go back to the very beginning, one must begin with John Stuart Mill in 1859 and the publication of his essay *On Liberty*, and his announcement of the famous principle which should govern, in his view, all law-making in relation to all subjects. That principle is, he said:

> ...the sole end for which mankind are warranted, individually or collectively, in interfering in the liberty of action of any of their number, is self-protection. That the only purpose for which power can be rightfully exercised over any member of a civilized community, against his will, is to prevent harm to others. His own good, either physical or moral, is not a sufficient warrant. He cannot rightfully be compelled to do or forbear because it will be better for him to do so, because it will make him happier, because in the opinions of others, to do so would be wise, or even right.

This principle was attacked by Mr. Justice Stephen in the celebrated book, *Liberty, Equality, Fraternity*, which he wrote in the 1870's. I think it is fair to say that the principle never got beyond academic discussion; nor had it ever been translated into practice. However, it was resurrected and translated into practice in 1957 in the report of the committee that was presided over by Sir John Wolfenden on the amendment of the laws on homosexuality and prostitution. There the principle was stated in this way:

> There must remain a realm of private morality and immorality which is, in brief and crude terms, not the law's business.

. . . .

The attraction of the doctrine, for undoubtedly it is attractive, to me lies in this: that it seems to be a logical extension from freedom of religion. We have now achieved, not without a great struggle, the sort of society in which a man's religion is his own affair. Ought not his morals to be his own affair too? Is there any greater need, we may ask ourselves, for a common morality than there is for a common religion? However, there is a distinction. The ordinary free thinker has no religion. He can doubt the existence of God as he does the existence of the Devil, and if society can accommodate people who have no personal religion and yet reckon them as good citizens, as so many of them are, then there is no need for a common religion. But it is one thing to doubt the existence of God and the Devil and another thing to doubt the existence of good and evil. God and the Devil is what religion is about; good and evil is what morals are about. Whether good and evil are properly personified in God and the Devil is a theological question upon which the man of faith, and the free thinker, can disagree, but there will be no disagreement, and can be no disagreement about whether good and evil exist.

Thus, while Mill, in common with most free thinkers, both of his century and of the present one, had no personal religion, and would deny the need for a common religion, he had a personal morality and he accepted the need for a common morality. Indeed, his opinion of what was virtuous did not substantially differ from that of his contemporaries, but no one, he felt, could be sure. In a free society, full scope must be given to individuality as one of the elements of well-being, and the individual must be free to question, to challenge, and to experiment. "The liberty of the individual", he wrote:

> must be thus far limited; he must not make himself a nuisance to other people. But if he refrains from molesting others in what concerns them, and merely acts according to his own inclination and judgment in things which concern himself, the same reasons which show that opinion should be free, prove also that he should be allowed, without molestation, to carry his opinions into practice at his own cost. That mankind is not infallible; that his truths, for the most part, are only half-truths; that unity of opinion, unless resulting from the fullest and freest comparison of opposite opinions, is not desirable, and diversity not an evil, but a good; until mankind is much more capable than at present of recognizing all sides of the truth, are principles applicable to men's modes of action, not less than to their opinions. As it is useful that while mankind is imperfect there should be different opinions, so it is that there should be different experiments of living; that free scope should be given to varieties

†   Devlin, Lord Patrick, "Law and Morality" (1964), 3 *Manitoba Law School Journal* at 243, 248–54. (Based on material in *The Enforcement of Morals* published by O.U.P., 1965). Reprinted by permission of Oxford University Press.

of character, short of injury to others; and that the worth of different modes of life should be proved practically, when anyone thinks fit to try them.

You see, it is with freedom of opinion and discussion that Mill is primarily concerned. Freedom of action follows naturally on that. Men must be allowed to do what they are allowed to talk about doing. Evidently, what Mill visualizes is a number of people doing things he himself would disapprove of but doing them earnestly and openly after thought and discussion in an endeavour to find a way of life best suited to them as individuals.

This seems to me on the whole to be an idealistic picture. It has happened to some extent, say in the last couple of generations in the growth of free love outside marriage. Although for many it is just the indulgence of the flesh, for some it is a serious decision to break the constraint of chastity outside marriage. But in the area of morals that is touched by the law I find it difficult to think of any other example of high-mindedness. A man does not, as a rule, commit bigamy because he wants to experiment with two wives instead of one. He does not, as a rule, lie with his daughter or sister because he thinks that an incestuous relationship can be a good one, but because he finds in it a way of satisfying his lust in the home. He does not keep a brothel so as to prove the value of promiscuity, but so as to make money. There must be some homosexuals who believe theirs to be a good way of life, but many more who would like to get free of it if only they could. And certainly no one in his senses can think that habitual drunkenness or drugging leads to any good at all. But Mill believed, you see, that diversity in morals and the removal of restraint on what was traditionally held to be immorality (and held by him to be immorality) would liberate men to prove what they thought to be good. He would have been the last man to have advocated the removal of restraint so as to permit self-indulgence. He conceived of old morality being replaced by a new and perhaps better morality. He would not have approved of those who did not care whether there is any morality at all, but he never really grappled with the fact that along the paths that depart from traditional morals, pimps leading the weak astray far outnumber spiritual explorers at the head of the strong.

But let me return to the distinction I was drawing between freedom of religion and freedom in morals. The abolition of established religion is a relatively recent development. It is a feature of modern thought. It came with the Reformation, which is comparatively late in the history of civilization. Before that it would have been thought that a society could not exist without a common religion. The pluralist society in which we now live was not achieved without the complete destruction of medieval thought, and it involved a change of civilization which was comparable with the triumphs of Christianity over paganism. Mill

records how the Emperor Marcus Aurelius, whom he considered to be one of the greatest of world rulers — tender, enlightened and humane — persecuted Christianity because existing society, as he saw it, was held together by belief in and reverence of the received divinities. The struggle more recently between received religion and freedom of conscience was of the same order, and entailed as much suffering.

But the removal of religion from the structure of society does not mean that a society can exist without faith. There is faith in moral belief as well as in religious belief, and although it is less precise and less demanding, moral belief is not necessarily less intense. In our society we believe in the advance of man towards a goal, and this belief is the mainspring of our morals. We believe that at some time in the history of mankind, whether on a sudden by divine stroke, or imperceptibly in evolutionary millennia, there was extracted from the chaos of the primeval mind, concepts of justice, benevolence, mercy, continence and others, that we call virtues. The distinction between virtue and vice, between good and evil as it affects our actions, is what morals is about. A common religious faith means that there is common agreement about the end of man; a common moral faith means that there is common agreement about the way he should go. A band of travellers can go forward together without knowing what they will find at the end of the journey, but they cannot keep in company if they do not journey in the same direction.

Keeping in company is what society is about.

Diversity in moral belief and practice would be no more injurious to a society which had no common morality than the like diversity in religious matters is to a society without a common religion. However, as I have said, Mill and his disciples do not conceive of a society without a common morality. If they did, if they wanted a society in which morality is as free as religion, they would indeed be faint-hearted in what they preached. They could not then sensibly permit the law, as they do, to punish the corruption of youth or public acts of indecency. Where there is freedom of religion the conversion of a youth is not thought of as corruption. Men would have thought of it as that in the Middle Ages, just as we now think of the introduction of a youth to homosexual practices as corruption and not as conversion. Where there is true freedom of religion it would be thought intolerant to object to a religious ceremony in a public place on the ground that it was offensive to have brought to one's attention the exhibition of a faith which one thought false and pernicious. Why, then, do we object to the public exhibition of a false morality and call it indecency? If we thought that unrestricted indulgence in the sexual passions was as good a life as any other for those who liked it we should find nothing indecent in the practice of it either in public or in private. It would become no more indecent than kissing in public. Decency as an objective depends on the belief in continence as a virtue, a virtue which requires sexual activity to be kept within prescribed bounds.

These reflections show the gulf which separates the religious toleration we have achieved from the moral toleration that Mill wanted. The former is practicable, because while each man believes that his own religion, or the lack of it, is the truth or nearest to the truth, he looks upon the alternatives as lesser good and not as evil. What Mill demands is that we must tolerate what we know to be evil and what no one asserts to be good. He does not ask that in particular cases we should extend tolerance out of pity. He demands that we should cede it forever as a right. Because it is evil we can protect youth from corruption by it, but save for that we must allow it to spread unhindered by the law and infect the minds of those who are not strong enough to resist it. Why do ninety-nine of us have to grant this license to the other one? Because, the answer is, we are fallible; are all quite convinced that what we call vice is evil, but we may be mistaken. True it is that if the waters of toleration are poured upon the muck, bad men will wallow in the bog, but it may be (how can we tell otherwise?) that it is only in such a bog that seed may flourish that some day some good man may bring to fruit, and that otherwise the world would lose and be the poorer for it. That is the kernel of Mill's freedom; that is why we must not suppress vice. It is not because it is not evil; Mill thought that it was. It is not because legal suppression would be futile; some of Mill's followers advanced this argument, but he did not. Nor is it because Mill thought that virtue would be bound to triumph over vice without the aid of the law; in some cogent passages he refuted that argument. When all this is stripped away, the kernel of Mill is just this: that he beseeches us to think it possible that we may be mistaken. Because of this possibility he demands almost absolute freedom for the individual to go his own way, the only function of society being to provide for him an ordered framework within which he might experiment in thought, and in action, secure from physical harm.

There is here, I believe, a flaw. Even assuming that we accept Mill's ideal, it is unacceptable to the lawmaker as a basis for action because it fails to distinguish sufficiently between freedom of thought and freedom of action. It may be a good thing for the man to keep an open mind about all his beliefs so that he will never claim for them absolute certainty and never dismiss entirely from his mind the thought that he may be wrong. But where there is a call for action he must act on what he believes to be true. The lawyer, who in this respect stands somewhere midway between the philosopher and the man of action, requires to be satisfied beyond a reasonable doubt. If he is so satisfied, he would then think it right to punish a man for breach of the law while acknowledging the possibility that he may be mistaken. Is there any difference, so far as the freedom of the individual is concerned, between pun-

ishing a man for an act which admittedly he did, and which we believe, perhaps erroneously, to be wrong, he denying that it is wrong; and punishing him for an act that is admittedly wrong, and which we honestly but perhaps erroneously believe that he did, he denying that he did it? Suppose you prosecute a man for bigamy. His defence might be, "I honestly believed that my first wife was dead". If that defense is rejected, it is rejected because there is no reasonable doubt in the minds of the jury that he did not honestly believe it. And yet they must say, "We might be mistaken; we are not required to have absolute certainty, but we must act on what we reasonably believe to be true". Well, then, if his defence were simply that: "I admit I married a second time but I honestly believe that bigamy is a good thing", must we not act in the same way? We must say, "Well, we have no reasonable doubt that bigamy is a bad thing; we can't be certain, we may be mistaken, but we must act upon our belief". Philosophers, after all, may philosophize under the shadow of perpetual doubt, but the governors of society cannot do their duty if they are not permitted to act upon what they believe.

I might now usefully return to what Mill said about Marcus Aurelius. He cited him as an example of the fallibility of even the best and wisest of men. Marcus Aurelius thought Christianity wholly unbelievable, and could see in it only a force that would cause the society he governed to fall into pieces. Mill certainly did not regard Christianity as an unmixed blessing, but it might have been a different thing, he thought, if it had been adopted under Marcus Aurelius instead of under Constantine. So, Mill urged, unless a man flatters himself that he is wiser than Marcus Aurelius, let him abstain from that assumption of joint infallibility of himself and the multitude which the great man made with such unfortunate results. The example is a perfectly fair one on the point of fallibility. If we were to be confronted with the creed today which taught that constraint was the only vice and the unlimited indulgence of the appetites of all sorts the only virtue worth cultivating, we should look at it without any comprehension at all. But I dare say that our contempt would not be greater than that of Marcus Aurelius for Christianity, or that of a medieval philosopher for the notion that heresy was something to be tolerated. The example is also a fair one on the point I am making. What else, one may ask, did Mill expect Marcus Aurelius to do? It is idle to lament that he did not forestall Constantine in accepting Christianity, for he could not accept what he disbelieved. In Mill's view, and probably in that of most of his disciples, Marcus Aurelius was right in rejecting the claims of Christianity. On this view the Emperor's mistake lay in his failure to realize that if he permitted the destruction of his society through the agency of a religion which he rightly concluded to be false, the successor civilization would be an improvement upon him. To put Mill's question again in another context, can any man, putting himself in the position of the great Emperor, flatter himself that he would have acted more wisely?

It is not feasible to require of any society that it should permit its own destruction by that which, whether rightly or wrongly, it honestly believes to be in error in case it may be mistaken. To admit that we are not infallible is not to admit that we are always wrong. What we believe to be evil may indeed be evil, and we cannot forever condemn ourselves to inactivity against evil because of the chance that we may by mistake destroy good.

For better or for worse, the lawmaker must act according to his lights, and he cannot, therefore, accept Mill's doctrine as practicable even if, as an ideal, he thought it desirable. But I must say that for my part I do not accept it even as an ideal. I accept it as an inspiration. What Mill taught about the value of freedom of inquiry and the dangers of intolerance has placed all free men forever in his

debt. His admonitions were addressed to a society that was secure and strong and hidebound. Their repetition today is to a society much less solid. As a tract of the times, what Mill wrote was superb, but as dogma it has lost much of its appeal. I say dogma, for Mill's doctrine is just as dogmatic as any of those he repudiates. It is dogmatic to say that if only we were allowed to behave just as we liked so long as we did not injure each other the world would become a better place for all of us. There is no more evidence for this sort of utopia than there is evidence of the existence of heaven, and there is nothing to show that the one is any more easily attained than the other. We must not be bemused by words. If we are not entitled to call our society free unless we pursue freedom to an extremity that would make society intolerable for most of us, then let us stop short of the extreme and be content with some other name. The result may not be freedom unalloyed, but there are alloys which strengthen without corrupting.

The Appeal of Natural Law[†]
R. Cotterrell

IT might seem that analytical jurisprudence has made redundant the ideas and perspectives of classical common law thought with which Chapter 2 was concerned. But this book's discussion of the development of English analytical jurisprudence in the writings of Bentham, Austin and Hart and the associated development reflected in Kelsen's work has tried to show that normative legal theory does not necessarily progress through a straightforward superseding of inadequate theory by better theory addressing the same concerns. Rather, it sometimes shows important shifts of emphasis and *altered* concerns. These, in turn, may be the result of felt political or professional necessities. Analytical jurisprudence can be understood in part as reflecting a demand for a systematic, rational legal science to underpin modern legal professionalism and to accommodate the political idea of law as a technical instrument of government in modern western states. Classical common law thought flourished in a different era with different preoccupations. Nevertheless, analytical jurisprudence has not necessarily provided a fully adequate perspective from which to view contemporary Anglo-American law. The modern so-called "natural law" theory to be considered in this chapter can be viewed as, in part, an attempt to push the methods of analytical jurisprudence

to conclusions more satisfactory in various ways than those the analytical jurists themselves typically reach. At the same time it can be seen as, in part, a means of recovering certain themes in classical common law thought which analytical jurisprudence seems to have largely relegated to the sidelines of theoretical concern.

LEGAL POSITIVISM AND NATURAL LAW

One aspect of the aspiration towards a "science" of law reflected in the work of such different writers as Bentham, Austin, Hart and Kelsen is the insistence on an analytical separation of law from morality. In no case does this imply that morality is unimportant. But it does entail the claim that clear thinking about the nature of law and its analytical structure necessitates treating it as a distinct phenomenon capable of being analysed without invoking moral judgements. Hence, as Austin explains in a famous passage: "The existence of law is one thing; its merit or demerit is another. Whether it be or be not is one enquiry; whether it be or be not conformable to an assumed standard, is a different enquiry. A law, which actually exists, is a law,

[†]   Cotterrell, Roger, "The Appeal of Natural Law" in *The Politics of Jurisprudence* (London: Butterworths, 1989), 118 at 118–38. Reprinted by permission of the author.

though we happen to dislike it... This truth, when formally announced as an abstract proposition, is so simple and glaring that it seems idle to insist upon it. But simple and glaring as it is...the enumeration of the instances in which it has been forgotten would fill a volume" (Austin 1832: 184).

So Austin, like Bentham before him, criticises Blackstone for continually confusing legal and moral analysis in his *Commentaries*; for treating as law what he thought *ought* to be law; for declaring that human laws are invalid if contrary to the laws of God; for asserting that all human laws derive validity only from God's superior law (*cf.* Blackstone 1809 I: 41). The invocation of moral precepts — whether or not linked to a supra-human authority such as the will or law of God — as part of the criteria of the validity of man-made law seemed to Bentham and Austin to be dangerous. It prevented an objective, "scientific" analysis of the nature of law as human creation, and a clear set of indisputably objective criteria for determining which regulations should be recognised as possessing the authority of law. It left such matters to ethical speculation. Since ethical views vary, the way is opened for anyone to claim the right to "second guess" the authority of law and state. Danger lies also in another direction, according to Bentham. To confuse legal and moral authority allows reactionaries to claim "this is the law; therefore it must be right;" existing law is assumed to possess not only authority as law but also moral authority. Blackstone's primary failing in Bentham's eyes was, thus, his tendency to merge legal and moral authority, which went along with a complacency implying that English law as expounded in the *Commentaries* was the best of all law for the best of all possible worlds (Bentham 1977: 498–9; Hart 1958: 53).

This chapter is concerned with the claim of the major analytical jurists that law and morality should be clearly separated for purposes of analysis, and with some important challenges to that claim. Since the term analytical jurisprudence refers only to an aspiration and effort to analyse systematically law's conceptual structures, on the basis that they are worthy of study in their own right as distinct objects of analysis, it does not *necessarily* demand this law-morality separation. So, although writers who have considered themselves or been considered to be analytical jurists have typically subscribed to the separation of law and morality, it is convenient to use a more specific term to refer to the adoption of this analytical separation. As has been seen, Austin treated positive law as the appropriate focus of legal science and distinguished it from all moral rules or principles not specifically "set down" (posited) or legislated in some form but merely accepted, as well as from (religious) rules or principles attributed to some supra-human authority. Thus, the term now generally used to refer to insistence on the separation of law and morality is *legal positivism*. It is sometimes used imprecisely to refer also to a number of actual or supposed

characteristics of analytical jurisprudence (*cf.* Hart 1958: 57–8). In this chapter, however, legal positivism will be taken to mean specifically the insistence by Bentham, Austin, Hart, Kelsen and many other jurists on the necessity of analytically separating normative legal theory's inquiries into the nature of law from inquiries into its moral worth.

In contrast to legal positivism stands a tradition of thought adopting an apparently diametrically opposed position — that law cannot be properly understood except in moral terms; that it is fundamentally a moral phenomenon; that questions of law's nature and existence cannot be isolated from questions about its moral worth. This tradition is usually termed *natural law theory*. Its history extends through at least 2,500 years of Western philosophy. One of its most powerful themes (though an ambiguous one, as will appear) is expressed in the declaration that *lex iniusta non est lex* — an unjust law is no law at all. It may well be that statements like this in the history of natural law theory have never meant what they seem, at face value, to mean (Finnis 1980: 363–6). Nevertheless, they do suggest the persistent claim that questions about the nature of law and the conditions of its existence as an authoritative normative order cannot be treated in isolation from questions about its moral foundations. Thus typically, in many different ways throughout its long history, natural law theory has postulated the existence of moral principles having a validity and authority independent of human enactment, and which can be thought of as "higher" or more fundamental law against which the worth or authority of human law can be judged. This fundamental "natural law" is variously seen as derived from human nature, the natural conditions of existence of humanity, the natural order of the universe, or the eternal law of God. The method of discovering it is usually claimed to be human reason. Natural law thus requires no human legislator. Yet it stands in judgment on the law created by human legislators.

Natural Law and Classical Common Law Thought

Why might this dispute about the relations of law and morality bear on the question of whether any of the perspectives or concerns of classical common law thought survive their displacement by positivist analytical jurisprudence, from Bentham onwards? As was seen in Chapter 2, classical common law thought assumed various sources of law's authority. Law was seen as rooted in immemorial custom, or community life; in a transcendent reason, or the accumulation of ancient wisdom greater than that of any individual. By contrast, Bentham's and Austin's writings ground law's authority in the existence of habitual obedience to a sovereign, a purportedly objective "test" to distinguish law from non-law and identify legal authority. Hart and Kelsen focus on the fact of social acceptance of a rule of recognition or a basic norm as the fundamental prerequisite for a determination of legal authority. Positivist theories attempt to provide criteria of the "legal" and of law's authority in specific formal conditions which avoid vague ideas of the nature of the community or of social organisation, or of some transcendent reason. Because common law thought identified the source of legal authority, not in the state or sovereign or in rule-governed procedures of legal enactment but in reason or community, it allowed at various times, as has been seen, for the possibility that — in theory, at least — some legislation or judicial decisions could be void either as abuses of legal authority or as misstatements of the law.

Given this facet of classical common law thought it is unsurprising that at times it related closely to natural law ideas (Gough 1955: ch 3; Haines 1930: ch 2), which also claimed the possibility of evaluating law's authority before the tribunal of reason. The notion of common law as something not residing in rules but in more fundamental principles expressing a transcendent reason or ancient wisdom had close affinities with natural law doctrines asserting the existence of some higher (moral) law governing and providing ultimate authority for the ordinary rules of human (positive) law. On the other hand, natural law theory was always a two-edged sword. In English history it was used to defend the divine right of the monarch, as expressed in prerogatives, against the claims of common law (Pocock 1957: 55). Equally, it could be used to assert limits on, or a limiting interpretation of, the powers of Parliament, as in Coke's famous pronouncements in *Calvin's Case* (1608) (Gough 1955: 44–5). But appeals to natural law as a set of principles which could control the substance of human law ceased to be practically significant in England once parliamentary sovereignty was recognised. As classical common law thought had to accommodate and eventually give way to a view of law as created by political authority, so natural law thought gave way to legal positivism.

In the United States, natural law ideas proved important in the formative era of judicial interpretation of the Constitution, since, the temptation to fill out the meaning of a written fundamental constitutional document by appealing to an unwritten fundamental natural law proved irresistible to the courts. Constitutional adjudication entrusted to a Supreme Court which assumed the authority to pronounce on the constitutional validity of legislation[1] raised special issues. Indeed, this may be one consideration which has made legal positivism somewhat less secure in modern American legal philosophy (as exemplified by Lon Fuller's work discussed later in this chapter, and the literature considered in Chapter 6) than it has been in England (but *cf.* Fuller 1940: 116–21).

Today, in the Anglo-American context, the fate of common law thought is not unconnected with that of natu-

ral law thought (although, outside the Anglo-American context, natural law's history must necessarily be understood in different terms). Common law thought has had to find a place, if at all, in an environment dominated by conceptions of law as posited by sovereign law-makers of various kinds or their delegates or agencies. Equally, natural law theory, insofar as it has survived at all in the Anglo-American legal world, has tended to locate itself in the interstices of legal positivism, accepting much of positivist analytical jurisprudence and seeking to supplement or correct, rather than dismiss out of hand, many of the ideas which have been the concern of Chapters 3 and 4.

IS NATURAL LAW DEAD?

Our concern is not with the long history of natural law theory in Western civilization but with its particular appearances in the modern Anglo-American legal context. In this perspective the decline of natural law theory can be dated conveniently from Bentham's attack on natural law ideas in Blackstone's *Commentaries*. Bentham's view that natural law was a "formidable non-entity," and natural law reasoning a "labyrinth of confusion" (Bentham 1977: 17, 20) based on moral prejudices, or unprovable speculations about human nature, went along with a profound political distrust of resonant phrases about the "rights of man" enshrined in constitutional documents such as those inspired by the French Revolution of 1789. In a single line of positivist legal thinking in England, running from Bentham to A.V. Dicey's late nineteenth century work on *The Law of the Constitution*, specific positive rules of law providing clearly defined rights enforceable in the ordinary courts are contrasted favourably with "practically worthless" (Dicey 1959: 256) broad declarations of the rights of man grounded in natural law conceptions but unenforced in practice. The rise of legal positivism is often associated with the nineteenth century prestige of "science" in general and the aspiration to produce a specific legal science which has been noted in previous chapters. But more is at stake than that. It is not a change in attitudes to science, morality or religion which should be held primarily accountable for the decline of natural law thinking and the rise of modern legal positivism but a change in the nature of law itself and its political and professional environment.

Insofar as law became seen as an instrument of state policy — and in the utilitarian view an instrument of progress, if used with caution — it was revealed as an amoral and infinitely plastic device of government. Insofar as it regulated increasingly complex and differentiated Western societies it could be seen as, above all, a means of controlling the interplay of conflicting interests. The social theorist Max Weber, writing of nineteenth century developments, noted that: "In consequence of both juridical rationalism and modern intellectual scepticism in general, the axioms of natural law have lost all capacity to provide the fundamental basis of a legal system... The disappearance of the old natural law conceptions has destroyed all possibility of providing the law with a metaphysical dignity by virtue of its immanent qualities. In the great majority of its most important provisions, it has been unmasked all too visibly, indeed, as the product or the technical means of a compromise between conflicting interests" (Weber 1978: 874–5). Such an interpretation of law as a compromise (above all, of economic interests) could be offered even for constitutions, such as that of the United States, which expressed principles purportedly grounded the ideas of "natural rights" — truths declared to be self-evident because founded in the nature of mankind or of human society (see e.g., Levy 1987).

Classical natural law theory (broadly, that developed before the nineteenth century) sought a grounding for human law in unchanging principle, derived from "nature" in some sense — the natural order of things, and usually held to be discoverable by reason. But two legal developments in Western societies have made it especially hard to accept any such approach to understanding the general character of law. One is legal doctrine's ever-increasing technicality and complexity. This is partly the result of law's methods of compromise between conflicting interests being extended to cover more and more sectors of social life, and being invoked in support of more, and more diverse, interests within the regulated populations. The other development is the deliberate use of law as a steering mechanism in society. This presupposes that law can change rapidly and continuously but also that it does so not as a reflection of enduring principle but as a mechanism aimed at *creating* principles of social order. These principles are, however, time-bound; pragmatic principles for the moment and the context, quite unlike timeless principles of natural law. As the social theorist Niklas Luhmann has written, "it is increasingly questionable whether principles and ultimate perspectives [such as those of natural law] withdrawn from all variation and relativity" can "provide an apt instrument for stabilisation and control" in modern societies (Luhmann 1982: 103).

Thus, the issue is not exactly that of being unable to agree about ultimate values; or that it is impossible any longer to accept that reason can discover universal "truths" about human nature, or God's plan, or the hidden order of the universe or any such postulated foundation of natural law. The fact that agreement is difficult to reach does not show that principles of natural law are non-existent (*cf.* Finnis 1980: 24). As the political philosopher Leo Strauss remarks, "by proving that there is no principle of justice that has not been denied somewhere or at some time, one has not yet proved that any given denial was justified or reasonable" (Strauss 1953: 9). The problem is that even if there *are* universal principles of natural law

they may not offer a convincing guide or grounding for complex, highly technical and ever-changing modern law. After all, legal positivism does not deny that the substance of law can be subject to moral criticism.[2] The issue is not whether law can be morally evaluated but whether its *essential character* must be explained in moral terms. As an effort to provide such an explanation, natural law ideas are, in the view of many writers, "devoid of any and every convincing theoretical justification" (Habermas 1974: 113).

NATURAL LAW AND LEGAL AUTHORITY

None of this should necessarily lead to the conclusion that the problems which natural law theory addressed in the past have disappeared. Different kinds of classical natural law theory confronted a variety of issues. Among the most important are the following: what is the ultimate source of authority or legitimacy of human law and of human lawmakers; assuming this authority to be in essence a moral one is it limited and, if so, what are the limits and whence do they derive; by what criteria is it possible to evaluate the moral worth and authority of laws; how should one view laws created by abuse of lawmaking authority; in what circumstances, if any, do governments and laws cease to command moral authority with the result that any obligation to obey them ceases? If the word "moral" is replaced in these questions with the word "legal", all of them are ones which positivist analytical jurists have sought to answer in various ways. The concern which links positivist analytical jurisprudence and natural law theory is a concern with the nature of legal *authority*; with identifying its sources and its limits.

In positivist theory this concern is treated as raising technical issues. It is, above all, a matter of adequately conceptualising the highest authority of a legal system — for example, in terms of sovereignty, rule(s) of recognition, or basic norm — and determining the logical or practical relations between this authority concept and the other conceptual components of legal analysis and legal practice. For natural lawyers, however, the issues raised are moral ones. Almost inevitably, however, they turn into — or serve as cloaks for — political issues. This is because, while moral reasoning as applied to matters of private conscience may produce a coherent ethics to govern an individual's life, moral reasoning applied to such a social and public matter as legal regulation will typically produce prescriptions as to how the power of the state should be exercised or limited in controlling citizens' actions. Natural law theory, when taken seriously, becomes a force in political struggle — usually in defence of existing legal and political systems (by demonstrating their legitimacy grounded in "reason" or "nature"), but occasionally as a weapon of rebellion or revolution (*cf.* Kelsen 1945: 416–7).

As regards law's authority, therefore, the primary difference between positivist theory and natural law theory is not a polar opposition but a difference as to how far inquiries about law's ultimate authority should be taken, insofar as positivists are prepared to admit that law's authority over the individual can be evaluated in moral terms and natural lawyers are prepared to recognise political authorities (such as the state) as having general, inherent law-making authority. The medieval theologian St. Thomas Aquinas, whose writings are one of the primary sources of natural law theory, recognised the state's authority to legislate on numerous morally neutral matters about which natural law — the part of God's eternal law which can be grasped by mankind's unaided reason — would have nothing directly to say. The moral significance of this legislation would be only as part of the state's overall system of regulation which must, in Aquinas' view, serve the common good in order to conform with natural law.

Even as regards exercises of state authority which transgress dictates of natural law, issue is not necessarily clearly joined between classical natural law theory and legal positivism. Aquinas does not declare that all such laws lack validity or force. The philosopher John Finnis has argued that the "central tradition of natural law theorising" — essentially that grounded in Aquinas' ideas and their antecedents — recognises the *legal* validity of unjust laws. That is, it recognises them as laws according to criteria (such as Hartian rules of recognition) that positivist theorists would emphasise (Finnis 1980: 364–5). Certainly, where laws represent an abuse of the authority indicated by natural law (as where they are not created for the common good but for the vain whim of the lawmaker) one should, in Aquinas' view, obey God rather than the human lawmaker. But where laws are unjust merely because they do not conform to the established norms of human welfare (for example, because they impose an unjust distribution of burdens on those subject to the law) he suggests that it might be better to obey. Even if the laws do not bind in conscience one should avoid the corrupting example and civil disorder attendant on law-breaking (*cf.* Finnis 1980: 360).

This apparent hedging of bets on the moral obligation to obey unjust laws can be understood as an attempt to work out realistically the idea that the authority of a legal system as a whole is founded on its dedication to the "common good". Hence even where some laws are unjust, obligation to the system as a whole may remain insofar as it is of sufficient worth to justify its being protected against adverse effects arising from the corrupting example and disorder of law-breaking. The conflict between natural law and positivism thus tends to become a dispute as to whether the authority of a legal system as a whole can

only be understood and judged in relation to some specific moral *purpose* (such as promotion of the common good) for which all legal systems exist. In general, the answer of natural lawyers is yes, and of positivists, no.

THE "REBIRTH" OF NATURAL LAW

The key to the debate around natural law is thus the issue of the nature of legal authority. Natural law theory seems to become significant in debate at times when political and legal authority are under challenge. In times of stability positivist criteria of legal authority typically seem sufficient. In times of political turmoil or rapid political change they frequently seem inadequate; legal understanding seems to demand not merely technical guidance about the nature of valid law but moral or political theory. Questions as to what rules are valid as law become elements of ideological struggle; a matter of winning hearts and minds for or against established regimes. Some of the material in Chapter 4 hinted at this dimension of the determination of legal validity. Kelsen's efforts to establish a pure theory of law are, in part, an attempt to protect law from politicisation; an attempt made in full awareness of the difficulties of doing so "when in great and important countries, under the rule of party dictatorships, some of the most prominent representatives of jurisprudence know no higher task than to serve — with their 'science' — the political power of the moment" (Kelsen 1945: xvii). Indeed, Kelsen recognises that acceptance of a positivist science of law, such as his own, may be possible only "in a period of social equilibrium" (1945: xvii).

Thus, it is tempting to suggest that the enduring appeal of natural law arises precisely from its willingness to confront directly the moral-political issues of legality which arise in times of disorder and conflict, while positivist analytical jurisprudence presupposes a political stability which it cannot, itself, explain or even consider as a subject within the concerns of legal philosophy. However, the situation is more complex than that because modern versions of natural law theory have been developed in relatively stable societies such as those of twentieth century Britain and the United States. This suggests that legal positivism is seen by natural law writers as inadequate even where political authority is not being seriously challenged. Perhaps the best way to understand the matter is to recognise that a degree of "instability" as regards law-making authority is actually built into the structure of stable legal systems as portrayed by positivist analytical jurisprudence. This is because key questions about how law changes remain apparently impossible to address in modern positivist theory. This has been seen in Chapter 4 where it was noted that judicial law-making is, for Hart, the exercise of "discretion", which his normative legal theory cannot really analyse, and is, for Kelsen, explicitly a matter of politics outside the compass of the pure theory of law.

Certain processes of law-making are, therefore, "unstable" in the sense that what determines their outcome is a matter which positivist theory cannot subject to rational legal analysis. Given this state of affairs it is not surprising that natural law began to become a focus of attention again precisely at the time when modern legal positivism might be thought to have consolidated its victories. In 1911, the American jurist Roscoe Pound wrote "It is not an accident that something very like a resurrection of natural law is going on the world over" (Pound 1911: 162; *cf.* Pound 1921: 82) and Charles Grove Haines, analysing this twentieth century rebirth, saw, as an important reason for it, the felt need to elaborate principles of "higher law" to guide the actions of judges in developing law (Haines 1930: 323–30). In the common law world where, traditionally, the role of the judge has seemed central within the legal system this matter is, no doubt, of special importance. It returns us to the link noted earlier, between common law thought and natural law theory.

Nevertheless, part of the motivation for rethinking the relative virtues of legal positivism and natural law theory has come from twentieth century experience of tyranny and political instability, and especially from *ex post facto* reflection by jurists on the legal history of the German Third Reich (1933–45). Here issues of the ultimate authority of law are thrown into sharp relief and the theme of the Rule of Law, which was identified in Chapter 4 as an important political preoccupation informing modern analytical jurisprudence, is highlighted in a new form. In this context, the Rule of Law appears not just as a matter of protecting the autonomy of legal structures, processes and professional knowledge against politicisation by overweening state direction, but as a defence against uncontrolled terror and arbitrary violence. In the light of the Nazi experience, professional legal knowledge founded on a separation of law and morals — the positivist science of law — can be portrayed in a natural law perspective as, itself, a weapon of tyranny. This is precisely because it refuses to confront ultimate questions about the necessary *moral* criteria which state regulation must conform to in order to possess authority which a lawyer, or any other citizen, must recognise. The debate between positivists and natural lawyers, in this context, becomes a debate about the meaning of the Rule of Law. Should it be understood as the positivist aspiration to remove political and moral choices as far as possible from the determination of rights and duties; or should it be seen as the natural lawyer's insistence that morally acceptable purposes must govern the unavoidably political decisions as to what rights and duties will be held to exist?

ANGLO-AMERICAN LESSONS FROM THE NAZI ERA

The historical legacy of the Nazi era has explicitly influenced modern Anglo-American debates between legal positivists and natural lawyers. One of the most direct confrontations, between the positivist H.L.A. Hart and the American natural lawyer Lon Fuller, centred in part on discussion of the way in which post-war German courts were apparently evaluating the legality of acts done during the Nazi period and which were claimed to be lawful on the basis of Nazi law (Hart 1958; Fuller 1958). More generally, the influence of emigré scholars, who fled from Germany during the 1930s and, in many cases, settled eventually in the United States, helped to feed into Anglo-American legal and political consciousness insights and dilemmas about the nature and authority of legal regulation which experience of Nazi practices and policies inspired (e.g., Neumann 1944: Neumann 1986; Kirchheimer 1961). In addition, reflection on the character of war crimes trials and their basis of legitimacy and on the ultimate foundation of the principles applied to judge guilt in them, undoubtedly made the issue of the nature and authority of Nazi regulation a matter of direct concern in the Anglo-American world and, at the same time, informed wider speculation about legal methods and reasoning (e.g., Shklar 1964: Part 2) and the adequacy of legal positivism (Paulson 1975).

The 1958 Hart-Fuller debate is a good starting point in considering the recent confrontation of legal positivism and modern natural law in the Anglo-American context, and especially as an introduction to Fuller's influential ideas which will be the concern of much of the remainder of this chapter. At the time of his exchange with Hart, Fuller was professor of jurisprudence at Harvard University, where he taught, with a break during the 1940s, for more than thirty years until his retirement in 1972. As his biographer notes, he is "unquestionably the leading secular natural lawyer of the twentieth century in the English-speaking world" (Summers 1984: 151).

Hart argues that the positivists' analytical separation of law and morality is an aid to clear thinking; it avoids confusing legal and moral obligation. To say that a rule is a valid law (judged by such positivist criteria as its being the sovereign's command, authorised by a rule of recognition or imputed from a basic norm) merely asserts the existence of *legal* obligation. Whether one ought *morally* to disobey an unjust law is a matter about which positivist analytical jurisprudence can remain uncommitted, for moral issues are not within its province. For Fuller, however, such a view is both unrealistic and dangerous. It oversimplifies problems of obligation under a manifestly unjust regime and it sets up an unreal opposition — a legal obligation to obey as against a moral obligation to disobey; as if one can keep them separate. It assumes that there can be order in a legal system without any moral content in it. For Fuller, the legal obligation to obey laws does not automatically follow from their enactment by a recognised, formal procedure. It depends on the legal system's claim, and ability to command, what Fuller calls *fidelity to law*. When certain minimum moral qualities cease to exist in a legal system, it ceases to command fidelity; that is, it ceases to have a claim to citizens' obedience. The order and coherence of a legal system (its ability simply to go on functioning) depend on a minimum moral content. Without this it ceases to be a legal system at all.

It is not very clear what is involved in this last claim. It seems to relate to the question of the definition or specification law; to what it is to be able to say that law *exists*. In terms of normative legal theory's concerns, therefore, the claim is that a general concept of law necessarily entails moral elements of some sort. If, however, the criticism is raised that — as suggested earlier in this chapter — much of modern regulation is technical and conventional (for example, a requirement that a will must be attested by two witnesses to be valid; or the rule that in England one must drive on the left hand side of the road) rather than the expression of moral values — Fuller's answer is that law's existence depends on its authority (its capacity to demand fidelity) and this authority ultimately depends on certain elements of moral worth. Again, however, a positivist critic could deny that *legal* authority requires any moral component. As Austin noted: "The most pernicious laws, and therefore those which are most opposed to the will of God, have been and are continually enforced as laws by judicial tribunals... An exception, demurrer, or plea, founded on the law of God was never heard in a Court of Justice..." (Austin 1832: 185). Must we say, therefore, that the positivist view offers hard-headed realism about the way legal systems actually function (with no necessary direct dependence on moral principle), whereas Fuller's thesis is merely wishful thinking about values which *ought to be*, but are not necessarily, built into law?

In this 1958 paper, as in earlier writings (1940: 101, 110; 1946), Fuller distances his thinking from classical natural law theory. As has been noted, this classical theory was generally vulnerable to the positivist criticism that modern law — in Weber's terms, a technical means of compromising or managing conflicting interests — is no longer usefully analysed in terms of moral absolutes and requires a "science" explicitly recognising its human origins and instrumental political character. Fuller's strategy is to emphasise that the necessary morality of law is a *procedural* one, relating to the way law is created, expressed, interpreted and applied, rather than to any particular substantive content of legal rules. Looked at this way, even purely technical rules, such as the one requiring two witness attestations for a valid will, have a moral dimension. Everything depends on how the rule operates, *how* it comes into being, is expressed, interpreted or enforced.

The historical example of Nazi Germany provides material to illustrate Fuller's thesis. To assume, as Hart does, that the only difference between Nazi law and English law was that the Nazis used their laws to achieve purposes odious to English people is, Fuller argues, to ignore the much more fundamental moral differences between the two legal regimes. Nazi law made frequent and pervasive use of methods which show, in terms of Anglo-American standards, a most serious perversion of procedural regularity. For example, frequent use was made of retroactive statutes to cure irregularities. A notorious example occurred after the Roehm purge of June 30th and July 1st 1934 when, on Adolf Hitler's orders, more than seventy members of the Nazi party were shot. On July 3rd, a law was passed ratifying the massacre as a series of lawful executions. Hitler apparently later declared that at the time of the purge "the supreme court of the German people consisted of myself" (Fuller 1958: 650). Secondly, Fuller notes "repeated rumours" of secret laws and regulations making it impossible for most people even to discover the rules upon which officials were supposed to act. More generally, however, since "unpublished instructions to those administering the law could destroy the letter of any published law by imposing on it an outrageous interpretation, there was a sense in which the meaning of every law was 'secret'" (Fuller 1958: 652). Thirdly, when legal formalities and procedures became inconvenient to the Nazi regime they could be bypassed by means of Nazi gangs taking action "on the street" and achieving the required objective by violence. Fourthly, "the Nazi-dominated courts were always ready to disregard any statute, even those enacted by the Nazis themselves, if this suited their convenience or if they feared that a lawyer-like interpretation might incur displeasure 'above'" (Fuller 1958: 652).

Assuming this picture of Nazi law in action is correct, what should be said of a legal system like this? The first point is that it seems less like a system of legal order than of discretions in policy-implementation organised around the furtherance of political aims of the regime in power (*cf.* Kirchheimer 1941). Not only is it inefficient, as a functioning system of *rules*, but it lacks all procedural fairness and propriety. These latter deficiencies point to a decline in what Fuller terms the *internal morality* of law. Thus, for him, they involve not just issues of efficiency but moral issues. We should be prepared to say (irrespective of the substantive content of Nazi laws) that the way the laws were applied was not merely procedurally inefficient but manifestly unjust. Fuller argues (1958: 642) that the authority of law (its capacity to demand fidelity) derives from a moral understanding[3] between rulers and ruled, such that citizens accord moral respect to the constitution which governs them as "necessary, right, and good". In the 1958 paper this is inadequately analysed because there is no clear indication of the criteria to be satisfied to ensure this recognition by citizens.

The best way to support Fuller's argument about a link between the moral authority of law and its procedural proprieties would be to suggest that a gross and cynical discarding of formal and predictable procedure constitutes a kind of "fraud" on those who must obey. There can be no moral understanding between rulers and ruled in such circumstances. The ruled have no chance to orient themselves to the dictates of the ruler's authority. Although they must obey, they are not given a reasonable chance to do so in an orderly and rational manner. This is not, however, spelled out in Fuller's 1958 paper, though related arguments appear in his later writings (*cf.* Fuller 1969a: 153, 159–62). Instead he claims, without any real justification, that a decline in the moral aims or purposes of law, which he calls law's "external" morality and which determine the authority and respect attaching to the legal system, is likely to be accompanied by a decline in the (procedural) internal morality, and *vice versa* (Fuller 1958: 645).

THE IDEAL OF LEGALITY AND THE EXISTENCE OF LAW

However, the important point being made from the Nazi example is that the stable forms and procedures of law and the nature of its authority are linked and Fuller is specific in his claims about the consequence of disintegration of these forms and procedures in practice in Nazi Germany. He suggests that the decline in procedural propriety, in the internal morality of law, was so serious that a legal system, as such, *ceased to exist* in Germany during the Nazi period. Hence post-war courts should not recognise Nazi law. Matters of legality in the Nazi period should be clarified, where necessary, by retroactive legislation. This claim about the non-existence of law in Nazi Germany is, indeed, one which other writers had already made, and on the basis of similar arguments about the effects of the procedural arbitrariness of the Nazi regime. Franz Neumann, a distinguished jurist who practiced law in Germany during the years leading to the Nazi accession to power in 1933, wrote, observing Nazi Germany from exile in America, that "there is no realm of law in Germany, although there are thousands of technical rules that are calculable" (Neumann 1944: 468). Another eminent German scholar, Otto Kirchheimer, wrote to similar effect: "With the access to power of National Socialism the common legal bond of a generally applicable civil law disappeared more and more..." (Kirchheimer 1941: 89).

Obviously a specific definition of the word "law" is involved here and Nazi regulation is being tested against it. But, in Fuller's 1958 essay, no such definition is made explicit. In Kirchheimer's and especially Neumann's writings, however, the concept of law employed is elaborated. Indeed Neumann used it in major writings of the 1930s and 1940s as the criterion for assessing general changes in the character of twentieth century regulation and as the organising concept for the most detailed historical analysis available in English of the notion of the Rule of Law (Neumann 1986).

Neumann writes bluntly: "the National Socialist legal system is nothing but a technique of mass manipulation by terror" (1944: 458). If law is merely the sovereign's command such a system must be recognised as legal. But if law "must be rational either in form or in content" Nazi regulation definitely does not deserve the name of law. For Neumann, law is both *voluntas* (the expression of sovereign power) and *ratio* (the expression of reason, or rational principle grounded in general ethical postulates) and the legal history of Western civilization is a history of the attempt to reconcile these typically incompatible yet essential components of legality (Neumann 1986: 45–6; 1944: 451–2). The component of *ratio* insists that law be a matter of general rules, not special individualised commands. It requires also that these general rules be clear and predictable in application, not vague general norms providing broad authority for virtually free official discretion. Hence, although Nazi regulation made considerable use of technical rules, it lacked the character of law.

Kirchheimer elaborates similar arguments. He sees Nazi regulation as guided wholly by policy demands. These necessitated technically rational norms of a purely provisional character which could be changed quickly to meet the needs of the moment, without notice and, if necessary, retrospectively. Such requirements precluded the existence of a stable body of general laws which could only hamper governmental freedom to shape, adjust and implement policy. The aim of adjudication and rule application in such a regime is not to maximise legal stability but to execute given commands "so as to have the maximum effect in the shortest possible time" (Kirchheimer 1941: 99). Thus, the legal regime of contract is largely replaced by a system of private command and administrative order; that of family law becomes a regime of policy regarding population development and social organisation. Even the idea of the state, as the abstract source or structure of regulation, is discarded in favour of the ultimate "total and all-embracing" personal authority of the leader (Krausnik et al. 1968: 128; Neumann 1944: 467–70)

For Fuller, the point of referring to evidence from a grossly pathological regulatory system is to try to show that legality is a more complex notion than legal positivism understands it to be. For rules to be "legal" it is not enough that they conform to the legal criteria expressed in a rule of recognition, or can be imputed from some basic norm of the legal system. Legality is a matter also of the way rules operate, of how they are drafted, promulgated, applied, interpreted and enforced. Neumann and Kirchheimer had already offered a broadly similar message. Neumann, however, rejects natural law theory in his writings as a mystification usually adopted to justify the *status quo*. He is concerned only to confront positivist analytical jurisprudence with political and social realities and to demonstrate its descriptive inadequacy in failing to take account of them. Fuller, by contrast, eventually chooses the terrain of natural law on which to fight (*cf.* Fuller 1969a: 96–7). The message of Nazi experience for him is that legal positivism cannot appreciate the moral conditions under which legality is possible. Legal order must be "good order" so as to create conditions for fidelity to law. Good order demands conformity, at least a minimum extent, with the internal morality of law. Legality, for Fuller, is thus a special kind of morality.

Before considering Fuller's ideas expressed in other writings it is appropriate to take stock, in a preliminary way, of this critique of legal positivism, since it remains substantially unchanged in his later work.[4] A familiar positivist reaction to Fuller is to express approval of all the procedural proprieties upon which he insists while denying their moral character, and denying also that Fuller's conception of legality in any way invalidates positivist analyses of law. The positivist claim is that the theoretical relationships between legal rules (in Hart's concept of law) and legal norms (in Kelsen's theory) are not invalidated by procedural impropriety. They exist even if denied in practice. Indeed, as has been seen, part of Kelsen's objective is to defend a rational legal science (as professional legal reasoning) in the face of political manipulation of law. The proper framing, application and interpretation of law are thus not moral matters for Kelsen and Hart, but consequences of adherence to a coherent positivist view of a legal system and of the necessary relationships between its doctrinal elements.

Fuller's claims are symptomatic of an impatience with legal positivism's *silences* — with what it refuses to say about law — rather than with its explicit tenets. In Chapter 4 it was noted that modern analytical jurisprudence contributes to lawyers' professional concerns by attempting to establish a coherent concept (Hart) or science (Kelsen) of law which adequately reflects the normative view of rules or norms held by legal "insiders"; in other words, above all, by lawyers. At the same time, a political dimension to these theories was noted. They suggest an image of the Rule of Law as somehow inbuilt in the very concept of law or legal system, because of their portrayal of law as a self-regulating system. But Fuller's procedural natural law theory seeks to show the inadequacy of this formal Rule of Law conception. Legality is typically reduced in the implicit positivist conception to a professional understanding of the doctrinal consequences of a logically integrated systems of rules. The actual operation of rules is ignored and, indeed, is largely irrelevant to this conception. Fuller, however, passionate about the evils of Nazism

(Summers 1984: 7,152), insists on the inadequacy of any such abstract and formal view of legality and the Rule of Law and emphasises the need to examine the practical conditions of the making and application of rules.

Nevertheless, if the legal professional concern for a coherent portrayal of doctrine in its logical relationships is the concern which analytical jurisprudence as a type of normative legal theory is attempting to meet, its failure to address wider political and ethical dimensions of law in action is not necessarily inimical to the achievement of its objectives. Its silences on the moral issues of Nazi law do not, in themselves, invalidate its theses or render them incoherent. On this view, Fuller's natural law approach merely strains at the limits of normative legal theory as a rationalisation of legal professional knowledge; it asserts a need to infuse a more profound political awareness into normative legal theory. As will appear later, even legal positivists have realized that this might be desirable.

A PURPOSIVE VIEW OF LAW

Fuller's other writings make it clear, however, that his main concerns about law's morality are not with such questions of legal pathology as whether Nazi law was too evil to be law, but with constructive issues as to how to infuse the highest legal virtues into systems, such as those of Anglo-American law, which he would regard as far from pathological. The principles of internal morality of law — the procedural criteria by which Nazi legal tyranny is measured in the 1958 essay — are discussed in Fuller's most influential book *The Morality of Law*, first published in 1964, as criteria also of possible legal excellence.

In *The Morality of Law* Fuller distinguishes between two kinds of morality or moral judgement. The morality of duty refers to the basic moral demands of order without which mere existence (whether of a society or of a legal system) becomes impossible. The morality of aspiration, by contrast, refers not to a moral minimum, but a maximum. "It is the morality of the Good Life, of excellence, of the fullest realisation of human powers" (1969a: 5). Duty and aspiration constitute the ends of a moral scale rising from the bare moral necessities for any human achievement, through to the highest moral ideals. Moral demands can be pitched at various points on this scale. For example, a judgment about the morality of gambling could stress that extensive gambling directly harms society, the individual and the individual's family in economic, psychological and other ways. These "duty" considerations might suggest that gambling should be legally prohibited. On the other hand , gambling on a small scale and for low stakes might not seem harmful in these basic ways but only a matter for regret that the individual can find no better use of time and energy. The aspiration that people should live "good lives" is not something to which they should be compelled. We assume that law should require the moral minimum, not try to force citizens to become saints.

This idea of a moral scale enables Fuller to pose, as a fundamental problem of all legal regulation, that of deciding where the pressures of duty stop and the excellences of aspiration begin. Law's impositions must be sufficient to sustain duty but they become tyrannous if they seek to impose excellence. Hence one of the most important arts of law-making is that of judging for each issue, each law each activity or situation, what level of moral demands law should operate with. But the demand for legality is itself a moral demand. Therefore, it is necessary to decide how far it relates to the morality of duty and how far to that of aspiration. Where on the moral scale is the internal morality of law to be located? In *The Morality of Law* law's internal morality is first presented negatively as "eight ways to fail to make law". These are:

(i) a failure to achieve rules at all, so that every issue must be decided on an *ad hoc* basis;
(ii) a failure to publicise the rules to be observed;
(iii) the abuse of retroactive legislation "which not only cannot itself guide action, but undercuts the integrity of rules prospective in effect, since it puts them under the threat of retrospective change";
(iv) a failure to make rules understandable;
(v) enactment of contradictory rules or
(vi) rules requiring conduct beyond the powers of the affected party;
(vii) introducing such frequent changes in the rules that those addressed cannot orient their conduct by them; and
(viii) a failure of congruence between the rules and their actual administration (Fuller 1969a: 39).

Total failure in any one of these directions, or a pervasive general failure in them (as with Nazi regulation) would, for Fuller, result in the non-existence of a legal system (1969a: 39). At this basic level, therefore, the internal morality of law provides a minimum morality of duty without which the existence of a legal system is impossible.

Beyond such rare pathological cases, however, the internal morality of law is primarily a morality of aspiration; the aspiration to maximise legality, to make legal order as good an order as can be. The internal morality can then be expressed as eight excellences which are the reverse of the "eight ways to fail to make": government always by rules, which are always publicised, prospective, understandable, non-contradictory, etc. Yet Fuller stresses that it would be counterproductive to try to realise fully all eight excellences in a working legal system. No system of rules could function on such a basis but would collapse in chaos or paralysis. For example, retroactive laws are sometimes inevitable, not all legal disputes can be solved by existing rules, and rules cannot achieve perfect clarity in advance of all applications of them. Thus, the achievement of legality is not merely the acceptance of a set of moral principles. It is a matter of judging the point on the moral scale between duty and aspiration where each component of legality, as related to each concrete problem of legal regulation in the particular legal system concerned, should be set. And the point on the scale will vary with circumstance and time. The achievement of legality is, thus, a task requiring all the skills of legislator and jurist. It is the heart of "the enterprise of subjecting human conduct to the governance of rules" (1969a: 91, 96).

The use of this last mentioned phrase is the closest Fuller comes to defining law (*cf.* 1969a: 106), but the definition, such as it is, is instructive. It emphasises that law is a purposive activity (not merely rules or norms which are the product of the activity). Equally Fuller's definition reflects his view (readily acceptable to many legal sociologists but sometimes less so to lawyers and legal philosophers) that the term "law" need not be limited to refer only to rules enforced by state agencies. Fuller's purposive concept of law allow it to be applied to rule structures governing numerous social institutions — such as schools, hospitals or business corporations — and social groups. The internal morality of law provides criteria of legality by which rule systems of many kinds can be judged. Indeed, this concept of legality has been used in sociological studies in such fields as industrial relations (Selznick 1969) and policing (Skolnick 1975).

There is much of value in these ideas. Nevertheless, it is clear that we have moved on to different terrain from that of positivist analytical jurisprudence. What is now offered by Fuller no longer appears as a direct critique of legal positivism but as a different enterprise concerned with the examination of law in purposive terms. Although Fuller presents his ideas as an attack on legal positivism, they cannot be defended as a critique of the logic of positivist analytical jurisprudence but only of the inappropriateness, narrowness or political and social irrelevance of its projects. His claims are strong ones. But they amount to saying: you should have devoted your researches to this rather than that. And the positivist can still reply: maybe so, but your arguments are no criticism of what I have done in seeking to rationalise the legal knowledge which is important to lawyers.

Endnotes

1.   *Marbury v. Madison* (1803), 1 Cranch 137.

2.   Although for Kelsen, it would be not the law as such but the content of its norms which could be re-evaluated from a moral perspective: *cf.* Kelsen 1945: 374–75.

3.   In later writings Fuller refers to this, following the social philosopher Georg Simmel, as a 'kind of reciprocity': see Fuller 1969a: 39.
4.   And see generally the extensive criticisms of positivism in Fuller 1940.

The Minneapolis Ordinance: Feminist Law Making[†]
S.G. Cole

Anew American legal approach to pornography has met with some uproarious opposition in some unlikely places. The proposed law, known as the Minneapolis Ordinance, was drafted by feminists yet some of its most vituperative opposition has come from feminist quarters. At this writing most major feminist publications in the U.S. have given considerable coverage to the controversy, in which the battle lines have been drawn so bizarrely that women calling themselves feminists have taken the major step of speaking out against the Ordinance in the pages of *Penthouse* magazine. The situation is a very perplexing one for Canadian observers, many of whom are not accustomed to such public infighting within the women's movement.

For those readers in need of more background, the Minneapolis Ordinance was drafted by Catharine MacKinnon and Andrea Dworkin while the people of Minneapolis were trying to cope with an expanding pornography industry in their midst. Whereas the City Council was proposing zoning restrictions to control where pornography could be sold, Dworkin and MacKinnon convinced council members that there was another way to address the matter. They drafted an ordinance which defines the practice of pornography as an act of sex discrimination and which gives women the right to sue pornographers for the harm pornographers have done to them. The ordinance defines pornography as the sexually explicit subordination of women in pictures and in words and which has one or more of nine characteristics (for a copy of the complete law, see *Ms*, April 1984, p. 46).[1] The law makes actionable four activities associated with pornography: coercion into pornographic performance; forcing pornography on a person; assaults caused by specific pornography; and trafficking pornography. The City Council of Minneapolis passed the Ordinance twice but the mayor vetoed it both times. Eventually, the city of Indianapolis, after engaging MacKinnon as a consultant, passed a version of the law, only to have it challenged immediately by the American Booksellers Association as unconstitutional and a violation of

the first amendment of the U.S. constitution. The American Booksellers have won both the district court case and the ensuing appeal (*American Booksellers Association Inc. v. Hudnut*, 598 F. Supp. 1316 (S.D. Ind., 1984) affirmed August 27, 1985).

In the course of my own work, I have found that looking at pornography as if it were just pictures undermines attempts women make to describe what pornography is and does. The pictures don't do the violence, argue pornography's apologists and defenders, people do, and so it is a mistake to blame the pictures. Some feminists have tried to counter this defence by comparing the activities of pornographers with the activities of advertisers. Advertisers use pictures to galvanize sales of a particular product; pornographers use pictures to turn consumers on to a particular kind of sex, sex which makes the subordination of women by men sexual, if not inevitable. It is what goes on in the making of the pornography and what happens to the women around the consumers of it that count here. Pornography is thus a practice, not a picture, a practice which is harmful and for which practitioners ought to be held accountable. The Minneapolis Ordinance puts this view into law, describing pornography as a practice of sex discrimination. It takes the onus off the pictures and places it where it belongs, on the actions of real people.

I should say that ever since I heard of the Ordinance I have been impressed with its potential, especially as it could develop here in Canada. After years exploring the harm pornography is and does, I tried for a while to gloss over the excesses made by censor boards and the courts when coming to decisions on obscenity. I had hoped that maybe the law could work for women, but I came to a personal impasse: although pornography is bad, so is censorship. But the Minneapolis Ordinance is not really censorship at all. It contains no provisions for prior restraint like the ones sanctioned by some provincial *Theatres Acts*. Only if a woman has suffered injury in the production of pornographic materials can the pictures be prevented from

†   Cole, Susan G., "The Minneapolis Ordinance: Feminist Law Making" in *Women in the Criminal Justice System: Resources for Feminist Research* (Toronto: Ontario Institute for Studies in Education, 1985–86), vol. 14, 30–32. Reprinted by permission of the author and the publisher.

being shown; no new powers are granted to police. In fact the law is drafted as a civil ordinance and not a criminal law for a specific reason. Instead of relying on police the authors of the Ordinance wanted women, who are much better situated to know the harm pornography is, to be empowered to lay a complaint and to seek financial compensation. This is one of the law's essential attractions. Instead of filling government coffers with fines, as if pornography does harm to the state, women will be compensated directly for harm done to them through the practice of pornography. A complainant would, however, have to prove that an injury occurred, that the materials involved were actually pornography, and that they subordinated her. Conceivably the ordinance could introduce a whole new legal lexicon.

Still, American opponents of the law see it as censorship. Many of the law's critics use words that create an immediate panic among traditional defenders of civil liberties: "ban" is a favourite, "restrictions" is another. Some of them, living in a political culture where speech has been protected assiduously for over two hundred years, understand the difference between the Ordinance and state censorship, but still they blanche at the thought of any mechanism existing to curtail someone's freedom of expression — even when the "expression" is found harmful. Either way, it is doubtful whether Canadians experience the same terror. Some people interpret the Canadian apathetic stance to state control as part of a collective willingness to concede authority in a regulation-oriented political climate. They have a point. In fact if I were to crystallize the American response to pornographic excess, I would automatically utter the words "freedom of speech". If I were to crystallize the Canadian response I would say something like "form a government committee to figure out a way to take control".

In light of this Canadian inclination, the Ordinance grows even more appealing. In the midst of the "censor everything" mentality, and in the wake of the Fraser reports which endorse at least some form of government control, The Minneapolis Ordinance provides rich opportunities. And whereas Americans, some of them feminists, might anticipate abuse of the law, casting us forever into the future tense, Canadians might consider the ordinance a welcome alternative to the real censorship we experience right here in the present.

In the meantime, some American feminists and lesbians continue to attack the ordinance as dangerous and inimical to feminism itself. The law is too vague, they say, and it might eventually put feminist erotica in legal jeopardy. But the law is actually concrete. No person can breeze into a Human Rights panel and argue that pro-Lesbian sexual materials, for example, are offensive. To begin with, the materials must be pornography. They must be sexually explicit, which *is* a meaningful term with a body of law behind it (accordingly, the question, "what about the Bible's description of Sodom and Gemorrah, to say

nothing of Harlequin Romances and *Lolita*," which is posed by many critics of the law is a red herring designed to throw us off course: none of these is sexually explicit). Second, the materials must have one or more of the nine characteristics enumerated in the law (it is worth noting that these nine features were included in the definition through the simple process of looking at the pornography and describing it). Third, a complainant who refers to pornography as "offensive" will make little headway using this law: she must prove that the materials sexually subordinated her. This would not be easy to prove. In fact, it is likely that it would be more difficult to prove an injury than it would be to abuse this law. And finally, according to the proposed law, an item is not pornographic just because it depicts gay sex. In fact, there is nothing in the ordinance's definitions that target gay materials *per se*.

Contrast this to existing obscenity law. According to Section 159 of the *Canadian Criminal Code*, the distribution of obscene materials is against the law, obscene being defined as the undue exploitation of sex based on Canadian community standards (American law addresses "prurient interest" and applies a community standard as well). *This* is a law that worries about offending sensibilities. *This* is a law that makes gay materials vulnerable: in a homophobic society, same sex sexually explicit materials are bound to violate community standards. *This* is a law that is dangerously vague. How do we define a contemporary Canadian community standard in a country so diverse? A censor board in Saskatchewan, using its standards, has been known to ban a film that the Ontario board just clips and that the Quebec board leaves untouched. Canadian community standards are desperately elusive. Not so the standard applied by the Ordinance; and there is only one, the standard of the equality of the sexes, a standard consistently vexed by the presence of pornography in our lives. Yet, it is the Ordinance that comes under attack, leaving obscenity on the books to be used and abused by police and prosecutors.

Proponents of the Ordinance are accused of making disturbing political connections with the American Moral Majority and this alliance has come under sharp criticism. This criticism imagines that nothing can be done about pornography without the decency contingent being in on the activity.

In Minneapolis, the law was supported by grass roots feminists who provided the City Council with much evidence on the harm caused by pornography. In Suffolk County, New York, right-wingers tried to develop a strategy of civil suits against pornography, changing the Minneapolis Ordinance to suit moral majority standards. They failed. Dworkin, MacKinnon, and the supporters of the Ordinance had nothing to do with the initiative. To call them pawns of the right wing because right wingers tried to abuse the Ordinance is akin to calling the framers of the Canadian Charter of Rights anti-choice because Joe

Borowski used the articles in the Charters in his attempts to protect the rights of the fetus.

The Ordinance was introduced to the Indianapolis City Council by Beulah Coughenour, an anti-ERA activist, who had hired Catharine MacKinnon as a consultant on pornography problems. Here finally is a real, though tenuous, connection with a member of conservative forces. But Coughenour is an individual, not a group, and her support of the Ordinance hardly constitutes a coalition between feminism and the moral majority. It is true that many feminists in Indianapolis opposed the Ordinance, including members of the National Organization of Women (NOW). But that betokens feminist opposition, not right-wing support, and in any event, former NOW President Karen De Crow's article in the May 1985 *Penthouse* criticizing the law leads me to wonder at what point, especially ensconced in a pornographic magazine, such opposition no longer becomes feminist at all.

Critics of the Ordinance assess the political situation in the U.S. and they do not like what they see: rollbacks in sex education initiatives, lost ground in the battle for reproductive freedom, Reaganism rolling over the poor and disenfranchised. This shift to the right is real, but in deeming it so, liberals, some of them feminists, have made the mistake of assuming that all legal initiatives, especially touching the area of sexual "expression", must also be an expression of Reaganism. The state, especially one under Ronald Reagan's sway, is hostile to sexuality, they argue, and this law gives the state leeway that will come back to haunt us. What they fail to note is that the obscenity doctrine, with all of its vagueness, has provided the state with ample ammunition to wipe out the pornography and sex industries. But this has not happened. In fact, the industries have burgeoned instead. As for the Ordinance and the potential for Reaganites to embrace it as their own, it is instructive to point out that Sarah Evans Barker, the judge who struck down the Ordinance in the District Court in Indiana, is a Reagan appointee. So is Judge Easterbrook, who affirmed that decision in the Court of Appeal. Taking this into account, the claim that ordinance proponents are collaborating with right-wingers and the Reagan administration loses a good deal of credibility.

Here in Canada, the Canadians for Decency are not happy with the Ordinance. In part, their antipathy grows out of impatience with having to listen to feminists who seldom support an ordinance-like approach without providing a sharp critique of obscenity. Actually, the forces of repression are more interested in strengthening the authority of police than they are in empowering women to use the courts to redress the harms done to them. For its part, the government is not about to use the Ordinance's definition of pornography to redefine obscenity, because police and judges are not happy with the prospect of having to dispense with what they perceive as a finely tuned body of law. They think they know their standards and that changing them would be a dreadful inconvenience.

In essence, the criticisms launched by Americans at the Ordinance barely hold up in the U.S. and they are almost entirely inappropriate in the Canadian context. Perhaps the ultimate irony is that while U.S. feminists (and non feminists) worry that the Ordinance will do too much, conservatives here are concerned that civil suits will *debilitate* police initiatives against pornography, and feminists fear that the Ordinance will do too little. Whatever the case, and however influential we allow American opinion to be, it is crucial that we examine the potential of the Ordinance with Canadian eyes and values. While Americans continue to talk themselves out of any way to do anything about pornography, we might find that the Ordinance could transform Canadian legal discourse on a practice that hurts women. We might even change some women's lives.

Endnotes

1. The nine characteristics are stated in the Ordinance: "*Pornography* is the graphic sexually explicit subordination of women through pictures and/or words that also includes one or more of the following: (i) women are presented dehumanized as sexual objects, things, or commodities: or (ii) women are presented as sexual objects who enjoy pain or humiliation; or (iii) women are presented as sexual objects who experience sexual pleasure in being raped; or (iv) women are presented as sexual objects tied up or cut up or mutilated or bruised or physically hurt; or (v) women are presented in postures or positions of sexual submission, servility, or display; or (vi) women's body parts-including but not limited to vaginas, breasts, or buttocks-are exhibited such that women are reduced to those parts; or (vii) women are presented as whores by nature; or (viii) women are presented being penetrated by objects or animals; or (ix) women are presented in scenarios of degradation, injury, torture, shown as filthy or inferior, bleeding, bruised, or hurt in a context that makes these conditions sexual."

Censorship and Law Reform: Will Changing the Laws Mean a Change for the Better?[†]

Judge L. King

MUCH pornography is abhorrent. No one denies that. So is chauvinism, patriarchy and misogyny. The challenge is how to rid society of these evils. Law reform in the guise of tightened censorship laws, expanded human rights codes, a redrafted *Criminal Code* and new civil suits has become the latest panacea for abolishing pornography. But law reform in this area is no answer. Legislation, if carefully drafted, is and will continue to be useful in many ways in improving women's rights in the realm of family law, equal pay and other areas. But when dealing with images — which ones should go and which ones can stay — no amount of tinkering with words can guarantee women a just law.

First of all, pornography is a telling symptom of a patriarchal society and censoring pornography is like using an Aspirin to cure cancer: it might ease the pain, but does not eliminate the disease, and may well have serious side effects. Second, freedom of expression is a fundamental right only tentatively secured and ought not to be dismissed lightly, especially for at best a doubtful result. In fact, censorship in all its forms has historically been used against women — remember that it was not long ago that any public advocacy of birth control was forbidden, even illegal.

As a feminist, a lawyer and someone who has worked in the area of women's concerns for many years, it is my belief that focusing our efforts on law reform in an attempt to abolish pornography is fraught with danger. In this chapter I want to illustrate the traps in present and proposed antipornography laws in the hope that women will be more cautious before adopting this tactic. It is not my intention here to examine in detail the censorship laws of every province, or the other laws, such as the *Criminal Code*, that control means of expression. Rather I will explore how certain laws have been and will be applied — an exercise that will serve to demonstrate the futility of the antipornography law reform measures currently being proposed.

Censorship exists in a variety of forms in Canada: customs regulations, sections of the *Criminal Code*, local retail bylaws. But most notorious are the provincial laws that empower censor boards to cut or ban films and videos prior to their release. Such schemes were implemented in the early 1900s, with the advent of films, and have changed little to this day. Basically, they require that any film or video, before being shown publicly, must be approved by a province's censor board. It does not matter what the content of the film is — it can be anything from a travelogue to a thriller. Nor does it matter whether it is for

screening at a Famous Players theatre or a women's meeting in a church hall; if the public can attend, prior approval of the film by the censor board is necessary.

All provinces and territories except the Yukon classify films, dictating which audiences can see them; all but Manitoba and the Yukon also have the power to demand cuts or ban films outright. A fee, sometimes considerable, is almost always charged for this "service," and the process of submitting films for approval can be a lengthy and bureaucratic one. These factors alone effectively censor the activities of those who lack funds, time or the knack of dealing with bureaucracies.

In recent years, the Ontario Board of Censors has become the most influential — and infamous — of the provincial bodies. It has been challenged more often in the courts than any other board in the country and has been the subject of the greatest amount of scrutiny and criticism from both filmmakers and the public. And its power does not stop at the Ontario border. Because many films are first released in Toronto, and hence vetted by the Ontario board, distributors often incorporate cuts demanded by the board in prints destined for distribution in other provinces. Consequently, Ontario is an interesting laboratory for testing the efficacy of law reforms aimed at eliminating pornography.

In 1984, Dr. Robert Elgie, the Minister for Consumer and Corporate Relations, under whose jurisdiction the censor board falls, stated: "The government [of Ontario] has always been concerned about violence, degrading and often violent pornography." Yet when one looks at what guidelines the Ontario Board of Censors uses and what works it actually cuts and bans, the discrepancy between the high-sounding words of elected officials and the day-to-day practice of bureaucrats is obvious — and it is the day-to-day practice that counts. The board identifies as its areas of concern "indignity to the human body; explicit scenes of defecation, urination or vomiturition; blasphemous or sacrilegious presentations." The guidelines that the board has established for itself also identify the types of scenes it believes should be eliminated from films: "Explicit portrayal of sexual activity; sexual exploitation of children; undue and prolonged scenes of violence, torture, bloodletting; ill-treatment of animals; undue and prolonged emphasis on genitalia." Such broad statements leave immense discretion to the board.

Obviously, those who think that the censor board is in operation primarily to curtail degrading images of

---

† King, Judge Lynn, "Censorship and Law Reform: Will Changing the Laws Mean a Change for the Better?" in ed. Varda Burstyn, *Women Against Censorship* (Vancouver: Douglas & McIntyre (Educational) Ltd., 1985), 79–82, 86–88. Reprinted by permission of the author.

women have chosen the wrong protector. The board's concern lies not with eliminating misogynist images but mainly in ensuring that explicit sexuality is avoided and traditional values upheld. Indeed, Mary Brown, the current head of the board, has said that "many films now ridicule the values most families live by, promoting promiscuity at an early age, attacking parental and school authority and demeaning religious faith." In her view, *Breaking Away* and *Coming Home* should have been banned, the former for debasing parental authority and the latter for promoting extramarital affairs. She has not yet banned these films, but there is nothing in the law to stop her. More important, though, her statement gives an indication of the values the censor board wants to protect — hardly feminist values.

It is not surprising that in 1981 the board did ban *Beau Pere*, directed by Bertrand Bleir, whose *Get Out Your Handkerchiefs* had won an Oscar for best foreign film three years before. *Beau Pere* is a gently comic and ironic film about a 14-year-old girl dealing with the death of her mother and her relationship during the crisis with her dead mother's boyfriend. The sexual scenes between the girl and man are discreet; in the board's view, however, "the sexual relationship between the girl and her stepfather is quite explicit." Worse, the board believed that "the affair is condoned as a means of helping the man through an emotional and psychological crisis — it tends to 'normalize' incestuous relationships with a minor."

Do we really want a censor board writing film reviews for us and deciding what we can and cannot see? If the question becomes whether a film condones or normalizes an action, where does censorship stop? By the same logic, *Reds* should be banned for condoning or normalizing communism and *Terms of Endearment* for condoning or normalizing extramarital sex.

The board's concern with the contravention of traditional heterosexual values makes films that treat homosexuality as an acceptable, even positive, aspect of social life particularly vulnerable. One, at least, has been banned outright: *Taxi to the Loo*, a nonviolent, nonexploitive film dealing with homosexuality and the importance of integrating sexuality with emotional involvement and personal growth. In 1984, the board initially ordered cuts in the militantly feminist and prolesbian *Born in Flames* and only retreated after a public outcry. In fact, many distributors of films about gays or with gay content will not send their films to Ontario.

The power of the board does not stop with determining what films can be viewed, in what form they appear and by whom they can be seen. It also dictates where films are shown, and these decisions, too, leave no doubt about the board's views and values. In 1981, *Rameau's Nephew*, directed by the internationally renowned artist Michael Snow, was ordered cut because it contained an explicit scene of penetration and another of urination. (Neither of these scenes was in any sense "pornographic," just

graphic.) When Snow refused to make the cuts, the board gave permission for the film to be shown at the prestigious Art Gallery of Ontario in Toronto, but turned down a simultaneous request from The Funnel, a Toronto experimental film theatre. When asked to justify this discrimination, the board cited the art gallery's "tradition and stature in the community" and the Funnel's obscurity. Similar elitism has characterized the board's decisions about where the National Film Board's documentary on pornography, *Not a Love Story*, can be shown. The board has allowed it to be screened in an "environment of concern" like the posh St. Lawrence Centre in Toronto, but not at regular movie theatres frequented by ordinary, everyday people. The message seems to be that sexual representation, whether "art" or "porn," will not adversely affect upper-class or educated people but will harm everyone else. In 1981 it even threatened to withhold approval of *Trace*, a 20-second experimental film, because the board found the film's structure unacceptable: "It has no beginning or end. All it was was a lot of flashing symbols on the screen," it declared...

. . . .

Once a law or regulation is on the books, it is the personnel of the state — its bureaucrats, its judiciary — who enforce it. Feminists may think that a particular law looks good as written and may be assured repeatedly that it will be used to stamp out misogynist pornography and nothing else. But feminists do not control the censors who demand the cuts; feminists do not control the attorney-general or the police who initiate the prosecution; feminists do not control the courts that decide the fate of the accused — nor will we for a long time to come.

I doubt whether feminists would have wanted Al Razutis's *A Message from Our Sponsor*, an experimental film that was very critical of the exploitation of women in advertising, censored. Yet the censor board demanded cuts and, when Razutis refused, it became illegal to publicly show the film in Ontario. I doubt whether feminists really wanted Canadian Images, a Peterborough, Ontario, film festival that consistently programs feminist films, to be prosecuted under the *Theatres Act* for screening *A Message from Our Sponsor*, and yet this is precisely what happened in 1981, at great expense to the state — yes, it's your tax dollars — and the accused. And I doubt whether feminists really wanted the conviction that ultimately resulted.

The vast and complex body of the state is not neutral, but works along clearly patriarchal lines. It is therefore irrational to expect that same state to adopt feminist principles when dealing with sexual representation. The censor boards of a male-dominated state will never view films through a feminist's eye; the logic of sexism will even find positive what many feminists deplore. For example, one of the very mainstays of the present retail system is the use of women's bodies to sell everything from candies to cars, a situation feminists find offensive; the Ontario Board of Censors, however, ruled that Razutis's film critique of this system could not be shown. The board does not stand apart from the way power and privilege work in our society but is part of this system and reflects its values every day. Those values are not feminists' values.

These problems are not peculiar to the area of film censorship. Another method of state control is the *Criminal Code* sections dealing with "Offences Tending to Corrupt Morals," which include publishing or distributing obscene material; exhibiting a disgusting object or indecent show; presenting an immoral, indecent or obscene performance; and mailing anything that is obscene, indecent, immoral or scurrilous. (At present any work whose dominant characteristic is found to be undue exploitation of sex, or sex and crime, horror, cruelty or violence is considered obscene.) There are even more provisions, but these examples serve to show how all-encompassing the attempts to control all forms of expression, including books, paintings and movies, are.

It is obvious that these laws are not intended to prohibit degrading images of women but rather to impose and uphold the sexist values and morals of the state. It is no accident that *The Body Politic*, a Toronto gay journal, has been prosecuted repeatedly under this section of the code, nor that a Toronto gay bookstore, Glad Day Books, has been frequently harassed under the same section. Even though it is not illegal for consenting homosexuals to engage in sex, the state still harasses gays by prosecuting depictions of their sexuality and will continue to do so as long as there are anti-porn laws allowing it to.

One of the factors that enables such state action is the present concept of "community standards." When an obscenity case is heard, the court must determine whether the work on trial exceeds the accepted standards of tolerance in the "contemporary Canadian community" — that is, whether the "exploitation" is "undue." Some feminists have naively endorsed this concept, believing that through the application of this test, those materials they find unacceptable would be judged illegal. But such a system has dangerous implications, for "community," in the court's view, must encompass everyone, including those who oppose abortion, premarital sex and birth control. Even if a book or movie is for and about women, everyone, including the most chauvinistic of men, is taken into account when the community's standard of tolerance is determined. Furthermore, the Crown is not even required to call expert evidence as to what contemporary community standards are.

Ultimately it is the presiding judge who must endeavor to decide what he (almost invariably he), in the light of his experience, believes the community's standards to be. A recent example of how this concept can be applied was the 1983 case involving the interpretation of the *Customs Act*. Under this act, books, printed papers, drawings, paintings or representations of "an immoral or indecent character" are prohibited from entering Canada. When a Mr. Tom Luscher of British Columbia attempted to import one issue of a magazine for himself alone, he was prohibited from doing so by customs officials. Luscher appealed to the federal court and the judge found that the magazine in question was simply concerned with the sexual activity of a man and a woman from foreplay to orgasm. The judge ruled that these actions were in no way unnatural or unlawful and, indeed, that they were a common part of the lives of Canadian men and women; he also found that Luscher had no intention of circulating or selling the magazine; and only planned to use it in the privacy of his bedroom as a means of fantasy enhancement. Nonetheless, the judge found when measuring the magazine against *his* assessment of the current community standards of tolerance, that the customs officials had been correct in prohibiting the magazines as immoral or indecent.

In 1983, Ontario County Court Judge Stephen Borins pointed out the absurdity of attempting to interpret community standards when he was required to determine whether 25 videotapes were obscene (although, despite his reservations about the undertaking, he did uphold the charges for 11 of the tapes):

> This is a very difficult judgment to make in a community of 24,000,000 people who inhabit the second largest country in the world.... No doubt very different levels of tolerance exist in small communities such as Goose Bay in Labrador, Dawson in the Yukon, and Nobleton in Ontario, and the large metropolitan centres of Montreal, Toronto and Vancouver. As well, Canada is a pluralistic society and different parts of that society will have different points of view. Yet it remains the task of the trier of fact, who is assumed to have his finger on the "pornographic pulse" of the nation, to assess objectively whether or not the contemporary Canadian community will tolerate distribution of the motion pictures before the Court. There is some irony to this requirement. The Judge, who by the very institutional nature of his calling is required to distance himself or herself from society for the purposes of the application of the test of obscenity is expected to be a person for all seasons, familiar with and aware of the national level of tolerance. Thus the trial Judge (or jury) is required to rely upon his or her own experience and decide as best he or she can what most people in Canada would think about such material to arrive upon a measure of community tolerance of that material. Judge or jurors lacking experience in the field of pornography and the attitudes of others toward it

face a substantial challenge in making the findings demanded by the law.

Some feminists support an amendment to the *Criminal Code* introduced by former Justice Minister Mark McGuigan that would substitute the word "pornography" for "obscenity." Others, including the National Action Committee on the Status of Women, have endorsed changing "undue exploitation" to "degrading representations" or "coercive representations." However, these terms would still have to be interpreted first by the police, then by judges, in light of contemporary standards. It is easy to imagine the judge finding two lesbians making love a "degrading representation," perhaps even "coercive" ("How else could it have happened?") There is no reason to believe that tinkering with the words of this section of the *Criminal Code* will alter the court's ingrained biases. Words do not change the system; they can simply mislead us into believing the system is responsive.

The 1984 experience of the Maximum Art Gallery in Toronto illustrates the perils of believing otherwise. The gallery had displayed in its front window a painting by Bill Stapleton that showed a Mayan woman being raped by Guatemalan soldiers, the artist's representation of an incident he had been told of while visiting a refugee camp in southern Mexico. Stapleton said of the painting: "It was a hard subject to do, and I considered the effect it would have on people, but that's what is happening down there.... It's just awful, and it's my responsibility as an artist to reveal what's happening."

But shortly after the picture went on display, the gallery's curators were told by police to remove it from the window or face obscenity charges under the *Criminal Code*. The police had apparently polled several people passing the gallery about their reactions to the painting and "every one of them said it was horrible, disgusting, obscene.... You're talking about a painting of a gang rape scene."

Many feminists concerned about the consequences of such measures as tightening film censorship laws and amending the *Criminal Code* have been drawn to another possibility: amending the hate propaganda laws. These forbid "the advocating or promoting of genocide of an identifiable group or inciting hatred against an identifiable group where such incitement is likely to lead to a breach of the peace." At present the identifiable groups protected are those distinguished by color, race, religion or ethnic origin; it has been proposed that gender be included in the list. I was drawn to this idea initially, as were a number of the other contributors to this book. But on consideration we realized this approach was as problematic as others discussed earlier.

First, although pornography is frequently misogynist, it is unlikely that the courts would conclude that it "advocates or promotes genocide of women." Similarly, it is unlikely that the present legal system, even if it acknowledged that pornography incites hatred of women, would consider such incitement is likely to lead to a breach of the peace. Nor is changing the wording of the hate laws the answer. One of the differences between pornography and hate propaganda directed against the groups currently included in the law is that pornography usually involves the depiction of sex in some way. Although this may be primarily sex based on hatred, introducing the concept of sex could lead to the stifling of sexual imagery that has nothing whatsoever to do with hatred. Margaret Laurence's beautiful and at times sexually explicit novel *The Diviners* was almost removed from the Grade 13 curriculum and school libraries in some Ontario areas several years ago because some book banners believed that her "aim in life is to destroy the home and family." They might have as erroneously said that she hated women, that destroying the home and family was tantamount to hatred of women and hence the incitement of harm against women.

A system whose very structure protects and perpetuates the privilege of men as a group will not — cannot — fulfil a feminist mandate in the area of image depiction. The idea that we can develop a "feminist jurisprudence" is appealing in the abstract, but in practice it involves a fundamental contradiction in terms that is never systematically resolved in women's favor. As proof we need only examine some of our other experiences with law reform, for by looking at areas other than censorship we can clearly see the problems inherent in relying on changing laws and can better put the censorship/sexual representation debate into perspective.

Further Reading

Dworkin, Ronald, "Lord Devlin and the Enforcement of Morals" (1965–66), 75 *Yale Law Journal* 986.

Hart, H.L.A., "Positivism and the Separation of Law and Morals" (1958), 71 *Harvard Law Review* 593.

Fuller, Lon, "Positivism and Fidelity to Law: A Reply to Professor Hart" (1958), 71 *Harvard Law Review* 630.

Mahoney, Kathleen E., "Obscenity, Morals and the Law: A Feminist Critique" (1984), 17 *Ottawa Law Review* 33.

Fuller, Lon, "The Problem of the Grudge Informer" in *The Morality of Law* (New Haven: Yale University Press, 1969), 245–53.

3 Language, Law and Power

A. Legal Reasoning and Legal Knowledge

Introduction to Legal Method[†]
J. Farrar and A. Dugdale

LEGAL REASONING AND LOGIC

Lawyers are often thought of as having logical minds. This gives the impression that legal reasoning itself is or should be governed by logic. Certainly logic plays an important role in legal reasoning but as we will see it is only part of the story.

When we refer to logic we are often thinking of the deductive form of argument known as *the syllogism*. It goes like this:

> All men are mortal — Major Premise
> Socrates is a man — Minor Premise
> Therefore Socrates is mortal — Conclusion.

A lawyer advising his client as to the application of a detailed statutory provision will employ this type of reasoning. The statute is a major premise, the lawyer identifies his case as falling within the statute and then deduces as the conclusion the way in which it applies to his client. Deductive logic is only applicable once a clear major premise has been established. If the source is not a statute but case law, no major premise is likely to be clear from just one case decision. Instead the lawyer will have to examine several cases to find a major premise which underlies them all. He will have to reason from particular case decisions to a general proposition. This form of reasoning is often referred to as inductive logic as opposed to deductive logic where the reasoning is from the general proposition to the particular conclusion in the case itself. Thus, a lawyer advising on the application of case law to a particular situation will employ first inductive reasoning to find a general proposition of law and then deductive reasoning to determine how it applies to the facts.

Judges too make use of inductive and deductive logic when deciding cases. Lord Diplock explained very fully how a court uses this form of reasoning in the case of *Dorset Yacht Co. v. The Home Office*[1] which concerned the question whether Borstal Officers owed a duty of care to the public to prevent escapes by those in their custody. He said that the court should proceed:

> ...by seeking first to identify the relevant characteristics that are common to the kinds of conduct and relationship between the parties which are involved in the case for decision and the kinds of conduct and relationships which have been held in previous decisions of the courts to give rise to a duty of care.
>
> The method adopted at this stage of the process is analytical and inductive. It starts with an analysis of the characteristics of the conduct and relationship involved in each of the decided cases. But the analyst must know what he is looking for, and this involves his approaching his analysis with some general conception of conduct and relationships which ought to give rise to duty of care. This analysis leads to a proposition which can be stated in the form;
>
> In all the decisions that have been analysed a duty of care has been held to exist wherever the

---

† Farrar, John, and Dugdale, Anthony, eds., *Introduction to Legal Method* (London: Sweet & Maxwell, 1984), 74–78. Reprinted by permission of Sweet & Maxwell Ltd.

conduct and the relationship possessed each of the characteristics A, B, C, D, etc., and has not so far been found to exist when any of these characteristics were absent.

For the second stage, which is deductive and analytical, that proposition is converted to: 'In all cases where the conduct and relationship possess each of the characteristics A, B, C, D, etc., a duty of care arises.' The conduct and relationship involved in the case for decision is then analysed to ascertain whether they possess each of these characteristics. If they do the conclusion follows that a duty of care does arise in the case for decision.

In this extract Lord Diplock adds one further element to the model of inductive and deductive reasoning, namely that at the inductive stage the analyst must have some idea of what he is looking for. In other words he must categorise the issue and decide which previous decisions are so closely analogous to the issue in question that this can be used as a basis for inducing the relevant proposition of law. Judges and legal advisers frequently use this form of reasoning, arguing that previous decisions are or are not sufficiently similar to be relevant to the issue in question. Analogical reasoning of this kind is not strictly logical. It is a looser form of reasoning which raises broader issues.

Lord Diplock went on to stress one further limitation upon logical reasoning in the following terms:

But since *ex hypothesi* the kind of case which we are now considering offers a choice whether or not to extend the kinds of conduct or relationships which give rise to a duty of care, the conduct or relationship which involved in it will lack at least one of the characteristics A, B, C or D, etc. And the choice is exercised by making a policy decision as to whether or not a duty of care ought to exist if the characteristic which is lacking were absent or redefined in terms broad enough to include the case under consideration.

Cases which involve a question of what law should be applied come before the court precisely because there is no purely logical answer to the question. Instead there is a choice which according to Lord Diplock, is exercised by making a policy decision. But how does the judge make this decision? Obviously he will be influenced by the rhetoric of the parties' counsel, by the way in which they have framed the issue and the analogies they have suggested.[2] He may have his own personal views, although on legal matters these are likely to have become "institutionalised" over the years of practice before the courts.[3] Perhaps the most important influence on his choice, is the

knowledge that he will have to justify his decision in a reasoned judgment. It is to this "justificatory" nature of legal reasoning that we now turn.

LEGAL REASONING AND JUSTIFICATION

How will a judge justify his decision? Obviously he will appeal to authority, to the sources of law, the past precedents, the statutory wording. Until the last 20 years or so, this might have been the limit of his expressed justification. Judgments were often written in such a way as to suggest that the authorities provided an obvious answer.[4] Nowadays the judges are more willing to recognise that the authorities present a choice and that their decision can be properly justified in other terms.

Professor Neil MacCormick, in his book *Legal Reasoning and Legal Theory*, suggests that two factors in particular may be considered by a judge when justifying his decision. The first is the extent to which a proposed decision will cohere with existing principles and authorities. The greater the inconsistency with the existing legal framework that will result from a proposed decision, the less likely it is to be adopted. The second concerns the broader consequences of the decision for potential litigants, the legal system and indeed the role of law in society. Will these consequences be acceptable in terms of justice or common sense? Other writers have made similar suggestions and if you examine the judgment of Lord Roskill in the *Veitchi* case which we have set out as an appendix to Chapter 8 you will see an example of a judge employing justificatory arguments of this kind. He discussed the existing trend of case law to show how his proposed decision would fit the pattern. He argued that an opposite decision would perpetuate artificial distinctions. He considered the consequences of his proposed decision, the possibility that it would release the "floodgates" of litigation but concluded that although this argument had its place it was overridden by the principle suggesting liability. When you have read this chapter you will understand more of the background to the case and the basis of the principle. Of course, the fact that Lord Roskill justified his decision in terms of coherence and consequence does not prove that he is right. The dissenting Law Lords employed just the same kind of arguments to the opposite effect. What it illustrates is simply the process of reasoned justification.

Other types of argument may be used as justification. Judges may refer to common sense, the supposed view of a reasonable man[5] or they may refer to notions of justice and fairness.[6] In Chapter 10 we describe the way in which the courts have interpreted the statutory phrase "intentionally homeless" and there you will see examples of the appeal to common sense and other factors to justify a particular decision. Professor John Wisdom, a philosopher, has summed up the nature of legal reasoning by saying that it is "not a chain of demonstrative reasoning. It is a presenting and representing of those features of the cases which severally co-operate in favour of the conclusion.... The reasons are like the legs of a chair not the links of a chain."[7] In this respect legal reasoning employs the process of practical reasoning we all use in everyday life. We tend to weigh a collection of reasons for or against a particular decision rather than think in terms of deductive logic. However, whilst in our own practical reasoning we can take into account anything within our own knowledge, it is important to realise that a judge can only properly take into account those considerations which can be adequately argued before a court of law...

Endnotes

1.   [1970] A.C. 1004.
2.   See the interesting description of the influence of counsel's arguments in Paterson, *The Law Lords*, pp. 49–65.
3.   The institutionalised views of a judge may still influence his decision. Whether the influence is desirable is debatable. See Griffiths, *The Politics of the Judiciary*; and Devlin, "Judges, Government and Politics," (1978) 41 *M.L.R.* 501.
4.   The reasons for this "formalist" approach of the judges prior to 1960 and for the subsequent change to a more open approach are explained in Stevens *Law and Politics*, esp. Chaps. 10 and 12.
5.   See, e.g., the judgment of Megarry V.C. in *Ross v. Caunters* [1980] Ch. 297.
6.   This was commonly the case in the judgments of the former Master of the Rolls, Lord Denning. He gives his own views on decision-making in his book *The Family Story*, section 7.
7.   *Philosophy and Psycho-Analysis*, p. 157.

A Bedtime Story[†]
J. Paul

IMAGINE you are twelve years old and your parents have left you with a babysitter. Your primary concern is that you be permitted to stay up until 11 o'clock so that you can watch a special two-hour episode of *Miami Vice* on television. (Note here that since this example will focus on achieving your own objectives, it is already once removed from the real world where a lawyer who represents herself has a fool for a client. Courses in your second and third years will particularly stress methods for learning your client's wishes, which you should thoroughly understand before doing anything.)

As you approach the sitter to discuss the situation, you might ask yourself a few questions. Perhaps most importantly, you would like to know what your parents told the sitter concerning your bedtime. (**Check the Rules**). Suppose you find a note on the table with detailed instructions telling the sitter that he should put you to bed at 11 P.M. (**Statutes**). You seem to be in luck and your chances of getting what you want have increased. Suppose instead that there is no note, but that this sitter has stayed with you a few times before and has always put you to bed at 11 P.M. (**Precedent**). You still seem to be in good shape.

Life, however, is seldom so simple. Suppose that most of the other times the sitter has stayed with you have been Saturday nights. Only once has he stayed with you on a weeknight. On that particular night he let you and your friend, who was sleeping over, stay up until a bit past eleven to watch the end of a World Series game in which your friend's favorite team was playing. You argue to the sitter that although it is a Tuesday night, you should be able to stay up late to see *Miami Vice*, just as you and your friend were permitted to stay up to see the World Series. You might start off by stressing that because the sitter let your friend stay up late to see something very special to her, it's only fair that you should get to stay up late to see something special to you. (**Like Cases Should Be Treated Alike**).

The sitter, of course, will try to explain to you that the previous occasion when you stayed up late is very different from tonight. He might say that when he let you and your friend stay up late to watch the World Series, there were several very unusual circumstances that caused him to depart from his general sentiment that 10 P.M. is a good weeknight bedtime for children your age. He claims that he was only willing to let you stay up late to see the

†   Paul, Jeremy, "A Bedtime Story" (1988), 74 *Virginia Law Review* 915 at 928–34. Reprinted by permission of Virginia Law Review and Fred B. Rothman & Co.

World Series, which occurs only once a year, on an evening when you had a friend staying over, also not an everyday event. It would be wrong to conclude from that, the sitter may argue, anything more than that the next time the World Series is on and you have a friend over, you may stay up to see the end again. (**Narrowing Precedential Holding**). You are not pleased by the sitter's view and would probably point out why. From your perspective, the sitter is being arbitrary. After all, the previous time you, and particularly your friend, were allowed to stay up late for a special television event. You say the rule should be that whenever there is a special event on TV, you may stay up until it's over. (**Broadening Precedential Holding**). Of course, even if the sitter agrees that you can stay up late for special events, you will still have to convince him that *Miami Vice* fits into that category. The sitter may ask what is so special about *Miami Vice*. It's on every week and if *Miami Vice* counts as special, won't you be able to stay up late whenever you can find something on TV you want to watch? (**Category Characterization**). You respond that, on the contrary, this *Miami Vice* is extremely unusual. First, *Miami Vice* normally runs one hour, and this is a *special* two-hour episode that gives the writers more time to develop a better plot. Second, *Miami Vice* is normally on Friday nights, so its appearance on Tuesday is *not likely to recur*. Moreover, because characters from one episode frequently show up later in the season, if you miss this one special premiere episode, you'll have greater difficulty understanding later episodes. (**Category Characterization**).

And this is only the beginning. So far we have mostly assumed that the sitter has been free to establish your bedtime without instructions from your parents. Suppose now that your parents have a standard note for all sitters, which says you are to go to sleep at 10 P.M. on weeknights and 11 P.M. on weekends. Today is Tuesday, so you're in trouble. Were you not a budding lawyer, you might just decide to settle for an *A Team* rerun. You remember, however, that school is starting two hours late tomorrow because of the annual teachers' meeting. You alert the sitter of your opportunity to sleep late and await a reaction.

The sitter, of course, may check his own school schedule and demonstrate that you have mistaken the date for the meeting, which will not be held until the following week. (**Wrong on the Facts**). More likely, the sitter may know nothing of the schedule and be faced with the difficult problem of deciding whether you are telling the truth about the meeting or indeed even about why you desire to stay up late. (**Probing the Proof Problem**). You persist, however, knowing that the sitter knows you to be generally trustworthy. You explain to the sitter that the normal bedtime rule should not apply tonight because it's clear that the reason you are supposed to go to bed early on weeknights is so that you will awaken early for school. (**Spotting a Gap in the Rule**). The sitter might try to argue

that the note says weeknights, and therefore, it means weeknights. (**Literalism**). You will insist, however, that the sitter should look to the reasons behind the rule when making a decision. (**Purposivism**).

If the sitter is particularly resourceful, he will attempt to engage you in a general discussion of his role. (**Institutional Competence**). He might say, listen here, you might be right about the purpose of this rule, but it's your parents' job to make the rules and my job to apply them. (**Judicial Deference**). How can I know for sure what the purpose is? All I can see is the word "weeknight." (**Ambiguity of Legislative Intent**). Indeed, if you force me to guess at purpose, it seems reasonable to conclude that by using the word "weeknight" your parents actually meant to exclude all other possibilities. (**Negative Implication**). Moreover, if we take your view, then next week a mean sitter who simply wants you out of her hair might make you go to bed at 10 P.M. on Friday because you have to wake up early for football practice. (**Dangers of Judicial Bias**). Not only that, but if your parents are unhappy, they can rewrite the rules, (**Encourage Legislative Clarity**), or buy you a video cassette recorder. (**Resort To Technology**).

You want to see Crockett and Tubbs, however, and so you reply that the sitter has a poor understanding of the importance of his job. (**Institutional Competence**). There is no point in applying the rules, you insist, unless the sitter is accomplishing what your parents want. (**Judicial Support**). The sitter cannot know for sure what your parents meant, but if he doesn't try to ascertain their meaning, you argue, he will be flouting their authority and ducking an issue he has to decide. (**Ambiguity of Legislative Langauge**). If a mean sitter furthers personal goals using reasoning based on the alleged purpose of your parents' instructions, you point out, your parents can always rewrite the rules then. (**Encourage Legislative Clarity**). In the meantime, you ask, how can you be sure that the sitter's refusal to let you watch *Miami Vice* doesn't stem from the sitter's own bias against prime time television? (**Dangers of Judicial Bias**).

Notice the incredible outpouring of debate once you identified what might be described as gaps in the bedtime rules. These gaps resulted either from the uncertain meaning of a previous decision or an arguable ambiguity in the bedtime instructions. Had it been a Sunday night, for example, you could argue both that it is a weeknight or a weekend, and arguments similar to those discussed above would ensue. Spotting gaps is therefore a key skill that we will repeatedly emphasize. Sometimes, however, there is no rule at all covering a particular topic, and you must address yourself to the decisionmaker of first impression, a legislature or, in some cases, an appellate court.

Suppose you had caught your parents on the way out the door and were trying to get them to write the instructions so that you could see *Miami Vice*. You might begin by asserting your independence, claiming you were old

50

enough to make your own decisions about when to go to bed. Letting the sitter decide would encourage dependence on your part, shackle your decisionmaking abilities, and interfere with your right of self-determination. (**Facilitation**). Your parents would counter by pointing to your lack of information concerning your health, your tendency to discount long-term risks, and the damage you might cause to yourself and others (parents who would have to stay home with you and pay for your doctor) by staying up late and getting sick. (**Paternalism**). Your parents might also stress the rights of the sitter to do his homework with you peacefully asleep, (**Rights as Security**), the fact that the sitter will charge less if you are awake fewer hours, and the good you can accomplish if you get a good night's sleep. (**Long-Run Cost-Benefit Analysis**). You might counter by asserting the right to move freely about in your own home. (**Rights as Freedom of Action**). You might also stress that you will be better able to make friends if you have watched *Miami Vice*, since all the kids will be talking about it. And you might say that the sitter will charge the same whether you have a fixed bedtime or not because he probably needs the job. (**Long-Run Cost-Benefit Analysis**). Finally, you might emphasize that when your parents have gone out in the past, they have never left instructions for the sitter. In the absence of instructions, you have always been able to convince the sitter to let you stay up until 11 P.M. and were expecting to do so again tonight. (**Expectations**). Indeed, you were so confident that you agreed to speak to your entire English class tomorrow about the program. (**Reliance**). Your parents, however, may be unmoved by this line of reasoning and tell you that if you had wanted to be sure you could stay up late, you should have asked them in advance. (**Source and Legitimacy of Expectations**).

If you are forced to agree to some limit on bedtime, you might suggest a more flexible approach. For example, the sitter might be told to put you to bed when you looked tired. (**Standard**). This would have some advantages to you since you might always be able to argue that you don't really look tired. (**Litigant Manipulability**). And you might perceive it as more consistent with the idea of having a bedtime imposed. (**Fairness**). On the other hand, you would fear that the sitter could say you looked tired anytime. (**Judicial Manipulability**). Also, it would be difficult for you to plan your TV watching since you would not know in advance when you would have to go to bed. (**Unpredictability**).

You might be willing to settle for a fixed bedtime of 10 P.M. on school nights and 11 P.M. on other nights, (**Rule**), with a special provision explaining that the 11 P.M. rule would apply in case there is a morning teachers' meeting the next day. (**Exception**). This has the advantage of being easier for the sitter than the "looking tired" test. (**Ease of Application**). It also makes it relatively easy for you to guide your activity. (**Predictability**). (**Ease of Application + Predictability = Formal Realizability**). But it has the danger from your perspective of forcing you to go to bed sometimes when you are not tired, (**Overinclusive**), and from your parents' perspective, of letting you stay up sometimes when you are exhausted. (**Underinclusive**). It also fails to account for the fact that your schedule at school is different every day, and thus you do not have a standard wake-up time. (**Rigidity of Rules**).

You might ask your parents to write in more exceptions so that you can stay up later when you don't have to get up early. The more your schedule varies, however, the more categories the rule must have and the more difficult it will become for the sitter. (**Exceptions Riddle the Rule**). If early morning French classes are on the third, seventh, and twelfth day of months with thirty days, the sitter might prefer rigidity to exceptions, while your parents might prefer to go back to the "looking tired" standard rather than have to chart your busy schedule for sitters. You might try suggesting an exception that would permit the sitter to let you stay up past the regular time if there is a good reason for doing so and otherwise not. This type of exception, however, will lose almost all the advantages of ease of application gained by a rule in the first place. (**Exception Swallows the Rule**). If you are going to go for the fixed bedtime, therefore, you will have to put up with some lack of precision.

You might never have guessed that so many different factors might be at stake in setting a bedtime. The ability to consider these various factors and, more importantly, to craft arguments for particular solutions to problems based on the kinds of considerations described in this story, however, precisely parallels crucial legal skills. The more systematic your ability to generate such arguments, the better lawyer you will be.

Law and Modern Society[†]

P. Atiyah

THE DOCTRINE OF PRECEDENT

There are, of course, rules about law-making by courts, rules laid down by the courts themselves. Not everything said by a judge makes law. In the first place, decisions on pure questions of fact clearly do not create precedents. The fact that X shot Y may make him guilty of murder but is of no relevance to another case in which Z is the accused. Even evaluative decisions, such as a decision that a certain piece of conduct constitutes negligence, are not regarded as decisions on points of law which can constitute precedents. To take a simple example, if a judge says that a defendant in a civil action was driving his car at 80 mph in a public street, and that he was therefore guilty of negligence, that is no precedent for holding that it is negligence for another driver in a subsequent case to have driven at the same speed (even on the same road). This is partly because (as is commonly said) evaluative decisions like this must depend on all the circumstances of the case, and so it is impossible to be sure that the relevant facts in the first decision were in all respects the same as in the second. But it also seems pretty clear that one reason why decisions of this kind are not treated as precedents is simply that the courts do not want to make their every decision suffocated under the weight of previous cases. If every case of this kind became a precedent, the volume of case law would become enormous, the argument of simple cases would become inordinately complicated, as each side would support its case with a mountainous pile of precedents, and judges would find it increasingly difficult to explain why and how decision Z was consistent with decisions A, B, C...in favour of one side, and not inconsistent with decisions M, N, O...in favour of the other side. So judicial decisions would inevitably appear inconsistent, and this is disliked by judges. Decisions on discretionary matters are also not decisions which can constitute precedents, although the guiding principles on which discretions are to be exercised are treated as questions of law.

The doctrine of precedent, then, is largely concerned with pure questions of law. A decision on a point of law constitutes a precedent which can in principle *bind* other courts to follow it. But before we can say that a decision constitutes a binding precedent two further qualifications need to be made. First, it must indeed be a *decision*, and not merely an *obiter dictum*, that is, a statement made by the way, an aside. In principle the distinction between the binding part of the decision (the *ratio decidendi*) and an *obiter dictum* is clear, but in practice it is not always easy to distinguish between them. Sometimes judges give several reasons for a decision: are they all binding, or is there one binding reason, the others being merely *dicta*? Or again, there may be several different judgements given in an appeal court, and the reasons given by all the judges may not wholly coincide, so what is the *ratio decidendi* then? In any event, the question of *ratio* or *dictum* may be less important than the weight of the remarks in their context, and the tribunal from which they emanate. Fully considered *dicta* in the House of Lords are usually treated as more weighty than the *ratio* of a judge at first instance in the High Court. So the whole distinction is more blurred than it might seem. Further, the distinction often does not matter at all. It does not matter basically when the second court agrees with the decision (or *dicta*) in the previous case, and would arrive at the same conclusion anyhow; it does not matter even when the second court might, if it were to go into the issue in depth, have doubts about the first decision (or *dicta*) but feel disinclined to reopen the issue for any one of a number of possible reasons. Nor does the distinction between *ratio* and *dicta* matter if the second court disagrees so strongly with what was said in the earlier case that it is not prepared to follow it, even if in theory some lawyers might regard the prior case as a binding precedent. Where this happens, the second court may 'distinguish' the first decision by finding some relevant fact to be decisive of the second case which was not present in the first. Every lawyer knows that fine distinctions are sometimes seized upon to justify departing from a prior decision without an apparent breach with the rules of binding precedent.

The second qualification that needs to be made to the binding nature of the doctrine of precedent is that the strictly binding feature of the doctrine depends on the relative status of the courts concerned. Decisions of the House of Lords bind all lower courts, and are normally treated as binding by the House itself. Since 1966 the House has claimed the right to overrule previous decisions in exceptional cases, but it has so far been very sparing in its willingness to exercise this power. Decisions of the Court of Appeal bind lower courts, and also in principle bind the Court of Appeal itself. But there is much controversy on this and practice varies. Lord Denning, who as Master of the Rolls presides over the Court of Appeal, has frequently expressed his belief that that court ought to have the same freedom to depart from its own prior decisions as the House of Lords now claims; some of his

[†] Atiyah, Patrick, "The Doctrine of Precedent", *Law and Modern Society* (New York: Oxford University Press, 1983), 134–37. Reprinted by permission of Oxford University Press.

colleagues appear to agree with him, but a majority do not. Furthermore, while most of those who agree with Lord Denning are generally prepared to accept the majority view that the Court of Appeal should remain bound by its own decisions, Lord Denning himself (and occasionally, it would seem, one or two others) are not. There are, in any event, a number of established exceptions to the rule that that court is bound by its own decisions, but their limits are somewhat ill-defined, so in practice it is really quite rare that the court must seriously face the question whether it is absolutely bound by one of its own decisions.

Decisions of Divisional Courts bind all lower courts, and even decisions of a single High Court judge are treated as binding on magistrates and tribunals, and generally by lawyers in the public service. Decisions of judges below the level of the High Court are not regarded as binding on anyone, and there is no systematic method of reporting such decisions.

The above account of the doctrine of precedent may well give a misleading impression of the importance of single binding decisions. Undoubtedly there are some situations where such decisions settle the law on a clear, simple point. In the interpretation of a statute, for instance, a simple ambiguity may be found which gives two alternative meanings to a section: the choice may be stark and straight-forward, even though the resolution of the ambiguity may be quite difficult. In such a case, a single decision may settle the issue, particularly if it is in the Court of Appeal or the House of Lords. But much more commonly, it is clusters of decisions which are important for the development of the law. Usually it is found that areas of doubt and uncertainty in the law, as well as newly developing areas, give rise to more litigation than other areas: this occurs for the obvious reason that lawyers are unable to advise their clients with the same degree of confidence in these areas, and the prospects of successful appeals may well be higher in such cases. So it quite often happens that a whole series of new cases arises in a relatively short period of time. When this happens, it also often becomes clear that new vistas are opening up, and, perhaps, that new problems, hitherto unsuspected, have been thrown up. Such a cluster of cases may well trigger off academic writing, which in turn may influence counsel in arguing subsequent cases. After a while matters may settle down again, and a new bit of law is, as it were, digested by the law and lawyers. This sort of development does not necessarily raise serious issues about the binding force of particular precedents, though such a development is occasionally triggered off by a loosening-up of the effect of an earlier series of precedents.

One recent illustration of this process, of some general interest, concerns the liability of barristers and solicitors for negligence in handling their clients' affairs. Until the early 1960s the law was taken to be settled that (1) a solicitor was liable for negligence on the same footing as any other professional adviser, but (2) that a barrister was not so liable because a barrister did not have a direct contract with his client — the client being compelled to approach the barrister through the solicitor with whom he contracted. Then in 1964 the House of Lords decided the famous *Hedley Byrne* case [1964] AC 465 which had nothing at all to do with the liability of barristers or solicitors, but which recognized for the first time that liability for negligent professional advice might arise *in tort*, that is, even between parties not in a contractual relationship. Barristers, of course, were quick to appreciate that their own traditional immunities might now be called in question, and in two subsequent decisions the House of Lords has begun to explore this possibility. These two decisions have laid down a new framework of law, much of which remains to be filled in by later decisions. Barristers remain immune from negligence liability in respect of the actual conduct of a case in court and in respect of advisory work which is so closely connected with the conduct of the case that it is in effect preparatory work for the trial, but they are no longer immune in respect of purely advisory work. Further, although none of these cases has so far actually involved the liability of a solicitor, it is pretty clear from *dicta* in them, that a solicitor's liability will now be equated with a barrister's, and he will share the barrister's immunity in respect of the actual conduct of a case in court — and cases in lower courts often are handled by solicitors. What is now likely to happen is that there will be a number of cases defining somewhat more clearly the line between purely advisory work and preparation for actual litigation.

This series of cases (and I have omitted some of the less significant) illustrates the way in which the common law can still develop, step by step, almost as though it were an organic growth. We now have a number of judgments in several cases, each of which offers arguments and opinions in favour of this or that development. Hypothetical examples may also be given, some of the arguments in one judgment may be rebutted in another judgment, and so on. Then for a while, the issues may move into the public domain, particularly where, as in this case, there is a public interest in the legal rules being developed. There may be academic articles and notes, media discussion, perhaps anecdotal evidence of past injustices, and possibly even a parliamentary debate. All this may indirectly feed into the next round of developments, and so the process continues.

The Bramble Bush†
K. Llewellyn

WE turn first to what I may call the orthodox doctrine of precedent, with which, in its essence, you are already familiar. Every case lays down a rule, the rule of the case. The express ratio decidendi is prima facie the rule of the case, since it is the ground upon which the court chose to rest its decision. But a later court can reexamine the case and can invoke the canon that no judge has power to decide what is not before him, can, through examination of the facts or of the procedural issue, narrow the picture of what was actually before the court and can hold that the ruling made requires to be understood as thus restricted. In the extreme form this results in what is known as expressly "confining the case to its particular facts." This rule holds only of redheaded Walpoles in pale magenta Buick cars. And when you find this said of a past case you know that in effect it has been overruled. Only a convention, a somewhat absurd convention, prevents flat overruling in such instances. It seems to be felt as definitely improper to state that the court in a prior case was wrong, peculiarly so if that case was in the same court which is speaking now. It seems to be felt that this would undermine the dogma of the infallibility of courts. So lip service is done to that dogma, while the rule which the prior court laid down is disembowelled. The execution proceeds with due respect, with mandarin courtesy.

Now this orthodox view of the authority of precedent — which I shall call the *strict* view — is but *one of two views* which seem to me wholly contradictory to each other. It is in practice the dogma which is applied to *unwelcome* precedents. It is the recognized, legitimate, honorable technique for whittling precedents away, for making the lawyer, in his argument, and the court, in its decision, free of them. It is a surgeon's knife.

It is orthodox, I think, because it has been more discussed than is the other. Consider the situation. It is not easy thus to carve a case to pieces. It takes thought, it takes conscious thought, it takes analysis. There is no great art and no great difficulty in merely looking at a case, reading its language, and then applying some sentence which is there expressly stated. But there is difficulty in going underneath what is said, in making a keen reexamination of the case that stood before the court, in showing that the language used was quite beside the point, as the point is revealed under the lens of leisured microscopic refinement. Hence the technique of distinguishing cases has given rise to the closest of scrutiny. The technique of arguing for a distinction has become systematized. And when men start talking of authority, or of the doctrine of precedent, they turn naturally to that part of their minds which has been *consciously* devoted to the problem; they call up the cases, the analyses, the arguments, which have been made under such conditions. They put this together, and call this "*the* doctrine". I suspect there is still another reason for the orthodoxy. That is that only finer minds, minds with sharp mental scalpels, can do this work, and that it is the finer minds — the minds with a sharp cutting edge — which write about it and which thus set up the tradition of the books. To them it must seem that what blunt minds can do as well as they is poor; but that which they alone can do is good. They hit in this on a truth in part: you can pass with ease from this strict doctrine of precedent to the other. If you can handle this, then you can handle both. Not vice versa. The strict doctrine, then, is the technique to be learned. *But not to be mistaken for the whole.*

For when you turn to the actual operations of the courts, or, indeed, to the arguments of lawyers, you will find a totally different view of precedent at work beside this first one. That I shall call, to give it a name, the *loose view* of precedent. That is the view that a court has decided, and decided authoritatively, *any* point or all points on which it chose to rest a case, or on which it chose, after due argument, to pass. No matter how broad the statement, no matter how unnecessary on the facts or the procedural issues, if that was the rule the court laid down, then that the court has held. Indeed, this view carries over often into dicta, and even into dicta which are grandly obiter. In its extreme form this results in thinking and arguing exclusively from *language* that is found in past opinions, and in citing and working with that language wholly without reference to the facts of the case which called the language forth.

Now it is obvious that this is a device not for cutting past opinions away from judges' feet, but for using them as a springboard when they are found convenient. This is a device for *capitalizing welcome precedents*. And both the lawyers and the judges use it so. And judged by the *practice* of the most respected courts, as of the courts of ordinary stature, this doctrine of precedent is like the other, recognized, legitimate, honorable.

What I wish to sink deep into your minds about the doctrine of precedent, therefore, is that it is two-headed. It is Janus-faced. That it is not one doctrine, nor one line of doctrine, but two, and two which, *applied at the same time to the same precedent, are contradictory of each other*. That there is one doctrine for getting rid of precedents deemed troublesome and one doctrine for making use of precedents that seem helpful. That these two doctrines exist side by

---

† Llewellyn, Karl, *The Bramble Bush* (New York: Oceana Publications, Inc., 1930), 66–69. Reprinted by permission of Oceana Publications, Inc.

side. That the same lawyer in the same brief, the same judge in the same opinion, may be using the one doctrine, the technically strict one, to cut down half the older cases that he deals with, and using the other doctrine, the loose one, for building with the other half. Until you realize this you do not see how it is possible for law to change and to develop, and yet to stand on the past. You do not see how it is possible to avoid the past mistakes of courts, and yet to make use of every happy insight for which a judge in writing may have found expression. Indeed it seems to me that here we may have part of the answer to the problem as to whether precedent is not as bad as good — supporting a weak judge with the labors of strong predecessors, but binding a strong judge by the errors of the weak. For look again at this matter of the *difficulty* of the doctrine. The strict view — that view that cuts the past away — is *hard* to use. An ignorant, an unskilful judge will find it hard to use: the past will bind him. But the skilful judge — he whom we would make free — *is* thus made free. He has the knife in hand; and he can free himself.

Nor, until you see this double aspect of the doctrine-in-action, do you appreciate how little, in detail, you can predict *out of the rules alone*; how much you must turn, for purposes of prediction, to the reactions of the judges to the facts and to the life around them. Think again in this connection of an English court, all the judges unanimous upon the conclusion, all the judges in disagreement as to what rule the outcome should be rested on.

Applying this two-faced doctrine of precedent to your work in a case class you get, it seems to me, some such result as this: You read each case from the angle of its *maximum* value as a precedent, at least from the angle of its maximum value as a precedent *of the first water*. You will recall that I recommended taking down the ratio decidendi in substantially the court's own words. You see now what I had in mind. Contrariwise, you will also read each case for its *minimum* value as a precedent, to set against the maximum. In doing this you have your eyes out for the narrow issue in the case, the narrower the better. The first question is, how much can this case fairly be made to stand for by a later court to whom the precedent is welcome? You may well add — though this will be slightly flawed authority — the dicta which appear to have been well considered. The second question is, how much is there in this case that cannot be got around, even by a later court that wishes to avoid it?

You have now the tools for arguing from that case as counsel on *either* side of a new case. You turn them to the problem of prediction. Which view will this same court, on a later case on slightly different facts, take: will it choose the narrow or the loose? Which use will be made of this case by one of the other courts whose opinions are before you? Here you will call to your aid the matter of attitude that I have been discussing. Here you will use all that you know of individual judges, or of the trends in specific courts, or, indeed, of the trend in the line of business, or in the situation, or in the times at large — in anything which you may expect to become apparent and important to the court in later cases. But always and always, you will bear in mind that each precedent has not one value, but two, and that the two are wide apart, and that whichever value a later court assigns to it, such assignment will be respectable, traditionally sound, dogmatically correct. Above all, as you turn this information to your own training you will, I hope, come to see that in most doubtful cases the precedents *must* speak ambiguously until the court has made up its mind whether each one of them is welcome or unwelcome. And that the job of persuasion which falls upon you will call, therefore, not only for providing a technical ladder to reach on authority the result that you contend for, but even more, if you are to have *your* use of the precedents made as *you* propose it, the job calls for you, on the facts, to persuade the court your case is sound.

People — and they are curiously many — who think that precedent produces or ever did produce a certainty that did not involve matters of judgment and of persuasion, or who think that what I have described involves improper equivocation by the courts or departure from the court — ways of some golden age — such people simply do not know our system of precedent in which they live.

The Politics of Law: A Progressive Critique†
D. Kairys

THE idealized model of the legal process discussed in the introduction is based on the notion that there is a distinctly legal mode of reasoning and analysis that leads to and determines "correct" rules, facts, and results in particular cases. The concept of legal reasoning is essential to the fundamental legitimizing claim of government by

---

† From David Kairys, ed. *The Politics of Law: A Progressive Critique* (New York: Pantheon Books, 1982), 11–17. Copyright © 1982 by David Kairys. Reprinted by permission.

law, not people; it purports to distinguish legal analysis and expertise from the variety of social, political, and economic considerations and modes of analysis that, in a democratic society, would be more appropriately debated and determined by the people, not judges.

This chapter focuses on one of the basic elements or mechanisms of legal reasoning, *stare decisis*, which embodies the notion of judicial subservience to prior decisions or precedents. The notion is that judges are bound by and defer to precedents, thereby restricting their domain to law rather than politics.

If legal reasoning has any real meaning, *stare decisis*, applied by a skilled and fair legal mind, should lead to and require particular results in specific cases. But anyone familiar with the legal system knows that some precedents are followed and some are not; thus, not all precedents are treated similarly or equally. Moreover, the meaning of a precedent and its significance to a new case are frequently unclear. The important questions, largely ignored by judges, law teachers, and commentators, are: How do courts decide which precedents to follow? How do they determine the significance of ambiguous precedents? Do precedents really matter at all? Why do lawyers spend so much time talking about them?

The Supreme Court's recent decisions concerning exercise of free-speech rights in privately owned shopping centers provide a good illustration (illustrations in private law areas are contained in other portions of this book). In *Amalgamated Food Employees Union Local 590 v. Logan Valley Plaza* (1968), the Court upheld the constitutional right of union members to picket a store involved in a labour dispute in the shopping center where it was located. The Court recognized that shopping centers have to a large extent replaced inner-city business districts. The best, and perhaps only, place to communicate with suburbanites is in shopping centers. Citing *Marsh v. Alabama* (1946), in which First Amendment freedoms were upheld applicable to a "company town," the Court ruled that the interest in free speech outweighed the private-property interests of shopping-center owners.

However, only four years later, in *Lloyd v. Tanner* (1972), the Court held that an antiwar activist had no right to distribute leaflets in a shopping center, even though this center regularly attracted political candidates by avowing that it provided the largest audience in the state. The majority opinion justified the decision by claiming to differentiate the facts involved from those in *Logan Valley* primarily on the grounds that speech concerning a labour dispute relates more closely to the activities of a shopping center than does antiwar speech. (In legal parlance, this is called distinguishing a precedent.)

Then, in *Hudgens v. NLRB* (1976), the Court announced that, contrary to explicit language in *Lloyd*, the Court had actually overruled *Logan Valley* in the *Lloyd* case. The Court said that to treat labour speech differently

from antiwar speech would violate the norm that First Amendment freedoms do not depend on the content of the speech, a result that surely was not intended in *Lloyd*. Having rewritten *Lloyd*, the *Hudgens* court went on to say that it was bound by *Lloyd* (as rewritten) and to hold that union members involved in a labour dispute with a store located in a shopping centre do not have a constitutional right to picket in that shopping center. The stated rationale for this complete turnabout, within only eight years, was *stare decisis*: "Our institutional duty is to follow until changed the law as it is now, not as some members of the Court might wish it to be."

The Court offered no explanation of what happened to this "institutional duty" in *Lloyd*, since the *Lloyd* court would seem to have been bound by *Logan Valley* (which the *Hudgens* court held had decided the same issue decided in *Lloyd*). Nor did the Court explain how its duty to "follow until changed the law as it now is" binds it in any real sense, since even within the system of *stare decisis* it is understood that the Court can change the law or overrule, ignore, or rewrite prior decisions. The Supreme Court is never really *bound* by a precedent. Finally, the majority opinion in *Hudgens* castigated the dissenting judges for deciding cases on the basis of what they "might wish [the law] to be," but there is no indication of how the majority's decision-making process is different. The majority simply outnumbered the minority.

There were ample precedents supporting each of the conflicting policies in *Hudgens*. Freedom of speech was favored over private property in *Marsh* (from an earlier period when First Amendment rights were being expanded) and in *Logan Valley* itself. Private property and the interests of suburbanites in isolation were favored in earlier cases and recently in *Lloyd*. This policy conflict clearly was not — and could not be — resolved by some objective or required application of *stare decisis* or any other legal principle.

Unstated and lost in the mire of contradictory precedents and justifications was the central point that none of these cases was or could be decided without ultimate reference to values and choices of a *political* nature. The various justifications and precedents emphasized in the opinions serve to mask these little-discussed but unavoidable social and political judgments. In 1968, a majority of the members of the Court resolved the conflict in favour of freedom of speech; in 1972, a majority retreated from that judgement; in 1976, a majority decided that property interests would prevail.

In short, these cases demonstrate a central deception of traditional jurisprudence: the majority claims for its social and political judgement not only the status of law (in the sense of binding authority), which it surely has, but also that its judgement is the product of distinctly legal reasoning, of a neutral, objective application of legal expertise. This latter claim, essential to the legitimacy and mystique of the courts, is false.

Stare decisis is so integral to legal thinking and education that it becomes internalized by people trained in the law, and its social role and ideological content become blurred and invisible. To see these aspects of and to understand *stare decisis*, it is helpful to separate the social role from the functional impact on the decision-making process.

Our legal norms are broadly and vaguely stated. They do not logically lead to particular results or rationales concerning most important or difficult issues. A wide variety of interpretations, distinctions, and justifications are available; and judges have the authority and power to choose the issues they will address and to ignore the constitutional provisions, statutes, and precedents, evidence, and the best legal arguments.

Moreover, there are prior decisions similar or related by analogy to both sides of almost any difficult or important issue. This should not be surprising, since issues are difficult or important largely because there are significant policies, rooted in social reality and/or legal doctrine, supporting both sides. Each such policy, or a closely related policy, will have been favored or given high priority in some context and/or during some period. Usually the various relevant precedents will provide some support for both sides rather than lead to a particular rule or result.

Indeed, often the same precedent will provide support for both sides. For example, suppose after *Hudgens* an antinuclear activist claimed the right to distribute leaflets and picket in a privately owned railroad terminal. The terminal's counsel would agree that *Hudgens* should be broadly construed as definitively resolving the issue of speech on private property that is open to the public. He or she would emphasize the physical and functional similarities of shopping centers and train terminals. On the other hand, the activist's counsel would urge that *Hudgens* be narrowly construed as applicable only to the particular problem of labour picketing and only to the shopping center involved in that case or, at most, to shopping centers generally. He or she would emphasize the differences between train terminals and shopping centers. Much of the legal education consists of training students to make arguments and distinctions of this kind. Both sides would argue that *Hudgens*, properly construed (a phrase likely to be found in both briefs), supports each of them. The judge would then decide the case, citing *Hudgens* as support for his or her decision regardless of which side won. There is no *legal* explanation in any of this; the law has provided a falsely legitimizing justification for a decision that is ultimately social and political.

Thus, *stare decisis* neither leads to nor requires any particular results or rationales in specific cases. A wide variety of precedents and a still wider variety of interpretations and distinctions are available from which to pick and choose. Social and political judgments about the substance, parties, and context of the case guide such choices, even when they are not the explicit or conscious basis of decision. In the shopping-center cases, justices who placed a preeminent value on freedom of speech found *Marsh* and *Logan Valley* precedents that should be followed, while justices who viewed property rights as more important placed considerable precedential weight on *Lloyd*.

Judicial decisions ultimately depend on judgments based on values and priorities that vary with particular judges (and even with the same judge, depending on the context) and are the result of a composite of social, political, institutional, experiential, and personal factors. The socially and legally important focus of judicial decision-making — hidden by *stare decisis* and the notion of legal reasoning, and largely ignored in law schools, opinions, and law review articles — should be on the content, origins, and development of these values and priorities.

This does not mean that judicial values and priorities, or the results in particular cases, are random or wholly unpredictable. The shared backgrounds, socialization, and experience of our judges, which include law school and usually law practice, yield definite patterns in the ways they categorize, approach, and resolve social and political conflicts. Moreover, some rules and results are relatively uncontroversial and predictable in a particular historical context, not based on *stare decisis* or any other legal principle but because of widely shared social and political assumptions characteristic of that context.

While seeming to limit discretion and to require objective and rational analysis, *stare decisis* in fact provides and serves to disguise enormous discretion. This discretion is somewhat broader in the higher courts, but it exists at all levels. Lower courts have an added institutional concern, since their decisions can be reviewed, but they also have added discretion stemming from their relatively larger control over the facts and the credibility of witnesses.

Functionally, *stare decisis* is not a process of decision making or a mechanism that ensues continuity, predictability, rationality, or objectivity. Precedents are largely reduced to rationalizations, not factors meaningfully contributing to the result; they support rather than determine the principles and outcomes adopted by judges.

There are, however, difficult and important cases where *stare decisis* or continuity seems to have considerable significance. For example, it is widely believed (and I will here assume) that a majority of the Supreme Court would decide *Miranda v. Arizona* differently now than it did in 1966, and yet the Court has not overruled *Miranda*. There are two major, alternative explanations.

First, if one regards *stare decisis* as a decision-making process and accepts traditional jurisprudence, the Court is bound by *Miranda*. I obviously reject this: the *Hudgens* court also should have been bound by *Logan Valley*, and there is no objective explanation for the difference based in legal reasoning.

Second, although a present majority may substantively favour overruling *Miranda*, based on a different social and political judgment concerning police conduct and the rights of criminal defendants, there is not a majority willing to do so for institutional and political reasons unrelated to the substance of the issue, to any "duty" to follow precedent, or to any legal decision-making process. Rather, their decision not to overrule is based on the likely public perception of and reaction to such a decision and the effect on the Court's power and legitimacy. Thus, hypothetically (and without consulting any law clerks), there may be six justices whose substantive judgment is to overrule *Miranda*, but perhaps two or more of these six will not so vote. The "constrained" justices are not and do not view themselves as substantively, analytically, or institutionally "bound"; their judgment is to overrule. However, if the Court overrules *Miranda*, a well-known symbol, the decision would be widely perceived as political — and therefore raises the spector of government by people, not law. In fact, such a decision would not be any more political than was *Miranda* itself (just a different politics and a different context). But the popular perception could create a serious crisis of legitimacy and undermine the Court's power.

Stare decisis is integral to the popular conception of the judicial process and an important component of the ideology with which judicial power is justified and legitimized. This ideological role is perhaps easiest to see if one looks at the historical development of *stare decisis*. Viewing *stare decisis* as a component of a neutral, objective of quasi-scientific discipline, one would expect a progressive development and a general tendency toward reliance on precedent, or at least toward concrete, rational standards for determining when precedent will not be followed. However, it is clear that *stare decisis* has not developed this way. The meaning and importance of *stare decisis* are not fixed by or independent of social and historical circumstances, and there has been no long-term tendency toward refinement. Rather, *stare decisis* has conveniently fallen by the wayside in periods where the legitimacy and power of the courts stood to be enhanced by openly rejecting continuity in favour of politically popular change.

For example, in the early 1800s, long-established legal principles of property, exchange, and relations among people clashed with an evolving social commitment to economic development. Widespread construction of mills and dams, for instance, was inconsistent with established rights of downstream and upstream landowners (based on the earlier conception of land as a source of enjoyment in its natural state rather than as a productive asset). In this context, *stare decisis* was explicitly rejected by the courts; rather, the law was seen as an active promoter of socially desirable goals and conduct (i.e., capitalist economic growth). After a basic substantive transformation was accomplished (circa 1850), the new legal values were consolidated and entrenched by limiting the effect of social concerns on the law and by the reemergence of legal formalism and *stare decisis*. However, the renewed deference to precedent, though often expressed in terms of principles derived from time immemorial, looked back only as far as the early 1800s to the recently transformed legal norms.

In sum, *stare decisis*, while integral to the language of legal discourse and the mystique of legal reasoning, serves a primarily ideological rather than functional role. Nor is there any more validity to the notion of legal reasoning when the source of law is a statutory or constitutional provision or the language of an agreement. Courts determine the meaning and applicability of the pertinent language; similar arguments and distinctions are available; and the ultimate basis is a social and political judgment. Indeed, even the facts relevant to a particular controversy (largely reduced to uncontroversial givens in law schools) are not capable of determination by any distinctly legal or nonpolitical methodology. Law is simply politics by other means.

In a broader sense, the ideological role of concepts like legal reasoning is but one aspect of a larger social phenomenon. In many areas of our lives, essentially social and political judgments gain legitimacy from notions of expertise and analysis that falsely purport to be objective, neutral, and quasi-scientific. For example, cost-benefit analyses have been used to lend a false scientific gloss to people-made judgments about workplace safety standards that place profits above human life. If religion is the opiate of the masses, it seems that objectivity, expertise, and science have become the tranquilizers.

Further Reading

James Boyd White, *Heracles' Bow: Essays on Rhetoric and Poetics of Law* (Madison, Wisconsin: University of Wisconsin Press, 1985), Chapter 4 ("The Invisible Discourse of the Law").

Margot Stubbs, "Feminism and Legal Positivism" (1986), 3 *Australian Journal of Law and Society* 63–91.

B. Standpoint and "Voice" in the Legal System

The Maleness of Legal Language[†]
K. Busby

INTRODUCTION

Language is one of the most important determinants of reality. Some would say that it is the primary means by which we construct reality,[1] but others would go further and say that language makes us what we are.[2] Since reality is not experienced in the same way by every person, different societies and groups within a given society have different registers that they use to express their respective concerns, ideas, interests and perspectives. A particular register (that is, a specific stratification within an actually existent language system such as English), will obviously share many features of that system but it will also have its own specialized vocabulary, grammar and style.

Language is not used uniformly by all people nor is it equally accessible to everyone, and not all discourses or language registers are valued in the same way. The most powerful registers such as those used by law, medicine and religion, are controlled by and are fully accessible to a select group of highly trained people. The kind of English spoken by some Black Americans in Harlem could also be described as a specific register: it too is only fully accessible to a select group of individuals, although most people would ascribe to it a very different value than, for example, the register used by lawyers. Rather, use within a particular registry is impressed with social ideology: the linguistic structure of a text reflects, affects and helps to maintain the roles, purposes and ideologies of its participants or subjects.[3] As well, these structures assume meanings that impliedly express social and political values.

Since Simone de Beauvoir said that men describe the world "from their own point of view which they confuse with the absolute truth,"[4] feminists in all disciplines have begun to show how male voices, perspectives, interests and ideas have prevailed in all thinking.[5] The task of determining how androcentric or "male as norm" thought has come to dominate is difficult because "...it is metaphysically nearly perfect. Its point of view is the standard for universality, its particularity the meaning of universality".[6] Can it be said that language, particularly the language of the legal register, shields a male subjectivity? Is the insidious message of the legal register, therefore, the superiority of the male and its politics, patriarchy?[7] These are two of the important questions that I will address in this article.

I will examine the thesis that grammatical features of the legal register such as pronouns, generics, lexicon, semantics and syntax trivialize, exclude and devalue women and characteristics associated with women. By analyzing the details of language as used in legal texts we can begin to see its preconstructions and preferred meanings and to understand its historical and social genesis.[8] My modest goal in this paper is to collect together and to examine some examples from the legal register in order to begin to see what connections can be made between language, gender and oppression in the context of the legal register.[9]

GENDER

It is necessary for me to touch on the issue of what is gender and the tension between simplistic reductive gender categorizations and the equally unacceptable assumption of no difference at all.[10] In this paper "gender" means the various psychological and social characteristics that are usually attributed to an individual according to biological sex. When a characteristic is described as "female" or "male", I mean that it is one usually attributed to women or to men respectively. Such attribution is not exclusive to one sex or the other as either sex may exhibit the gender characteristics of the other. I do not think that I am expressing preferences in this article for one set of characteristics over another although I think that the present legal system favours the male set over the female. Further, I would deny that there is anything deterministic or immutable about gender. But as long as gender has meaning, an analysis of the effect of gender categorizations will be necessary.

. . . .

[†] Busby, Karen, "The Maleness of Legal Language" (1989), 18 *Manitoba Law Journal* 191 at 191–93, 195–204, 206–08, 210–12. Reprinted by permission of the author.

PRONOUNS AND OTHER
FALSE GENERICS

The first issue to be discussed in any feminist analysis of language is the use of male pronouns when the referent is indefinite or inclusive of both women and men. This issue receives so much attention because of its pervasiveness and, more important, because it is one of the least subtle of sexist forms.[11] According to the masculist theory of marking, male pronouns can be marked or unmarked. The context is supposed to determine whether the referent is a male gender specific noun (marked) or a noun that includes men and women (unmarked).

Marking theory has not always been a "rule of grammar". It was the work of prescriptive grammarians from the 16th century onward to suppress the alternative use of "she" or "they". Ann Bodine has revealed that the authors of grammatical treatises appealed not to the laws of language but to the laws of nature. These authors stated that the generic masculine had the virtue of being first in the natural order and in propriety.[12] These men also said that the male pronoun was more comprehensive.

The connection between language, gender and the suppression of women is clear and present in the use of male pronouns. Use of the generic male pronoun perpetuates and conceals male domination at all levels of conceptualization and language.[13] I cannot assume that I have been included within the ambit of a particular passage; my presence is never a given. The subliminal message that I am not relevant or, even more alienating, that I am the "other" is constantly given and received. Take almost any legal text and count how often a male pronoun is used. You can begin then to realize how often I am told that maybe I am not included.

My personal experience is verified by sociological and psychological studies that reveal that the use of the male pronouns does not bring women into readers' minds. Men use and understand "he" more often in its marked or gender specific sense than its unmarked or generic sense. They are less likely to contemplate women as possible actors.[14] Women are more likely than men to use "he and she" or "they" rather than "he" thereby clarifying whether we have been included.[15] When "he" is used in connection with a neutral noun such as "person" or "clerk", the described individual will be perceived as a man.[16] It seems clear then that the use of male pronouns exerts important subliminal influences on people's perception of women as secondary or marginal.[17]

The problems that arise in connection with generic nouns are even more acute. Throughout the texts studied in the legal philosophy seminar there are of course many references simply to "men" to which I must ask whether it includes women; to "people" to which I ask whether women are truly included; and to "men and women" to which I must ask why there is a specific reference to women. The context rarely provides an answer to these questions. Consider the following examples of seemingly generic or unmarked nouns, most of which are from the materials used in the legal philosophy seminar.

Aristotle's "Just Man"

At first blush, it appears that this usage is generic. However, a passage on "household justice" found near the end of the excerpt[18] suggests that Aristotle does not contemplate women as political actors. Unless readers pick up this clue, they would be unaware of Aristotle's systematic exclusion of women and mistakenly assume that women are included within the concept of "just man".

Hart's "Ordinary Citizen"

In a discussion on the morality of acts performed privately and the indecency of acts performed publicly, H.L.A. Hart discusses recent amendments to English prostitution law and says that

> it has not made prostitution a crime but punished its public manifestations in order to protect the ordinary citizen who is an unwilling witness of it in the street from something offensive.[19]

The offensive act of which he speaks could refer to someone witnessing a prostitute and a customer bargaining over fees in a public place. If this is the case, Hart's ordinary citizen could refer to both women and men as both could witness the event. Alternatively, Hart could be speaking of the offence to a particular man who is solicited by a prostitute and who finds such solicitation unwanted. Since this law was not used to punish men who sought the services of a prostitute, Hart did not have in mind the offence to uninterested women who are solicited by men seeking to pay money to have sex. If this alternative describes what Hart was talking about, and his example is ambiguous, then his ordinary citizen is a man. Hart's perspective on solicitation is not surprising as the legal system has long perceived prostitutes and not their customers as being the cause of prostitution or money for sex.

Hart's ordinary citizen is an example of how language that appears to include the experience of both men and women may be seen on closer examination to exclude the experience of women. Apparently gender neutral language may conceal a possibly male exclusive perspective. Hart, like many men, fails to realize that women are subject to unwanted solicitation by men for sex for money. The failure to perceive problems from alternative perspectives is one of the reasons why men and women, or in this particular case, prostitutes and johns, are not treated in the same way by the legal system.

Rawls' "Rational Man"

In developing his theory of justice, John Rawls is concerned with the choices that rational men[20] would make in a hypothetical situation of equal liberty. To this end, he places his actors in an abstract, decontextualized void that he names the original position. He assumes that parties in the original position are rational and mutually disinterested; they are not concerned with one another's interests. The pursuit of individual liberty therefore is second only to the satisfaction of the most basic of human wants.[21] Social ties are useful only insofar as they further individual interests.

While the assumptions Rawls makes about the primacy of autonomy are accurate in relation to men, recent studies have shown that his assumptions about human nature are not accurate when applied to women.[22] Carol Gilligan and others[23] have shown that women have a more relational and affiliational concept of self. We are less likely than men to be disinterested in the situations of others and social ties are ends in themselves and not the means to individualistic ends. By virtue of his assumptions, it is clear that Rawls' "rational man" is a man. He fails to consider what women in the original position might choose. The very foundation of Rawl's legal theory is considerably weakened when it is realized that it has excluded the preferences of half the population.

"Reasonable Man"

The most important concept in law, its standard of the objective, excludes from its ambit women's conduct except in those instances where such conduct in a given situation would be the same as that of men. Dolores Donovan and Stephanie Wildman analyze the idea of the "reasonable man" in the criminal law context of self-defense and provocation.[24] They concluded that the standard of the "reasonable man" applies only to white middle class male techniques for self-defence and reactions to provocation. The standard fails to account, for example, for any behaviour that may be described as culturally female. Similarly, Leslie Bender reviews the standard of care required in tort negligence law, that of the "reasonable person".[25] She too concludes that this is another example of male naming and acceptance of the implicit male norm.

It should be clear that we cannot resolve the problem of androcentricity implicit in the notion of the reasonable man simply by changing the standard from that of the reasonable man to that of the reasonable person. This nominal change will not, by itself, make the concept more flexible and inclusive. While this is a necessary first step, there must also be a recognition by those using and applying the standard of the built-in bias of the present masculist reasonable man standard and an understanding that the new standard requires that we view situations from different perspectives.

The problems that have been noted in relation to the use of male pronouns and generics amount to much more than an annoying use of language. Such usage leads to serious ambiguities. Because the legal register prides itself on clarity and precision, this reason alone should be sufficient to radically reform the practice. But more insidiously, the use of "he" and "man" and other unmarked generic forms also conceals an inherent bias in favour of the "male as norm" while hiding under the guise of a neutral inquiry. Once this bias is revealed, as for example in the case of Rawls' "rational man", the very foundation of certain ideas becomes questionable. Or, as happens with the example of the "ordinary citizen" and the "reasonable man", the exclusion of women, in situations where it might be different from that of men, may pervert the formation of a legal principle such as the rules on prostitution or provocation.

Solutions to the problems of gender exclusivity and ambiguity arising in relation to pronouns and generics are not easy to find given both the pervasiveness of the problem and the unwillingness of many women and men to recognize that a problem exists.[26] But the starting point must be an identification and understanding of the sexist effects of a linguistic practice. This foundation helps us to recognize when a particular usage has sexist implications.

LEXICON AND SEMANTICS

Mary Daly has said that we have inherited a contaminated language.[27] Dale Spender states that every meaning is man-made and inevitably encodes a male point of view which is at odds with women's experiences.[28] In this part I will simply describe, by way of example, how the lexicon and semantics differentiate between men and women. In particular, I will consider the systematic devaluation of words associated with women, the use and effects of sexual stereotypes, how some metaphorical concepts personify or alienate women, the sexist etymology of some words and the need for new words to describe women's experiences. As will be seen, the observations of Daly and Spender have some truth in the context of the legal register.

Systematic Semantic Derogation

Consider the meanings associated with each word in these word dichotomies: bachelor/spinster; governor/governess; master/mistress; courtier/courtesan; king/queen; baron/dame; and sir/madame. Even the same words have different meanings depending on the sex of the referent: he is a professional/she is a professional; he is a tramp/she is a tramp. The idea of Holmes' "bad man"[29] takes on a different connotation if he becomes, instead, a "bad woman".[30] In *every* case, the female side of the dichotomy has an additional meaning that either has a negative sexual connotation or assumes female subservience. In the absence of the male counterpart, some of the words are best known in the devalued sense, for example, mistress and dame. I cannot think of any dichotomies in which the female word has not been assigned a devalued meaning; the same is not true of the male words.

It has often been said that male qualities include rationality, objectivity, detachment, abstraction, control, principles, aggressiveness, ambition, and autonomy. Notice that many of these words are also used to describe the desirable traits of the law.[31] Women, on the other hand, are emotional, subjective, attached, contextual, spontaneous, personal, passive, supportive and compassionate. Few of these words could be used to describe the law.

If a woman embodies male characteristics, a less valued or devalued word will be substituted for the more positive word used in relation to men: scheming, political, cold, conjectured, manipulative, aggressive, ambitious and selfish. (Note that words like aggressive and ambitious can have very different meanings depending on the sex of the referent.) Finally when female characteristics are attributed to a man the word used will not have a less valued connotation as happens when male characteristics are attributed to women. Rather, these words will often be positive: uninhibited, open minded, loyal, practical, easy going, contemplative, committed and considerate.

Perhaps it could be said that the examples offered so far express sexism through purely emotive meanings and while the prescription would involve a reassessment of usage, there is nothing of particular linguistic interest in the examples. I think such an observation would be incorrect for it would ignore that it is the *female* side which is systematically devalued. If it can be said that there is a "process of systematic semantic derogation of words associated with women,"[32] then sexism as reflected in language cuts much deeper than emotive meaning. Spender has observed that *all* words associated with women acquire negative connotations because there is a "fundamental semantic 'rule' in our society that constructs male supremacy."[33]

I think these examples raise several other questions, including: why has the male set of characteristics become personified in the law and the female side regarded as the opposite of what law ought to be? Is Fran Olsen correct in asserting that the law has a sex?[34] What are the implications of gendered character attribution on women in the profession of law?[35] While these are interesting and important questions, they are beyond the scope of this paper.

Stereotypes

Since virtually all the references to human beings in the texts used in legal philosophy seminars are to men, specific references to women attract special attention. Just how am I represented in the casebook? With the sole exception of

Kent Greenawalt's reference to a female law teacher and a female villager,[36] all the women in the materials are cultural stereotypes. (However, Greenawalt's women are given the suggestive names of Constance and Faith.) There are sex crime victims, wives (but few husbands[37]) and prostitutes. There is Oliver Holmes' Mrs. Quickly[38] who "would be sure to dwell upon [a client's white hat] along with the parcel gilt goblet and the sea-coal fire" rather than the contents of a contract. The implicit message is that women are silly. Next we have Greenawalt's beauty contestants[39] who are judged by men and juxtaposed against the example of "five experienced men". While the reference to the men is necessary because he is discussing Dworkin's reference[40] to the same class, the example of beauty contestants in this context makes the objectivication of women even more apparent. The implicit message is that women are to stand around being pretty while men work.

Ronald Dworkin provides the most examples of women in stereotyped roles. The child who needs to be bussed to school is a girl.[41] Does he use feminine pronouns when speaking of children to reinforce the idea of women as childlike? The archetype for his judge is the Greek hero, Hercules,[42] a curious choice given the more appropriate archetype, Athena, the Greek goddess of justice. Does he doubt the intellectual or rational capacity of women? While men are never afforded courtesy titles, "Mrs. MacPherson"[43] is never described simply as "MacPherson." What could be the possible relevance of her marital status in a legal text?

Finally Dworkin refers to "the timid lady on the streets of Chicago [who] is not entitled to just the degree of quiet that now obtains."[44] Why does he refer to her as "timid" when his style is otherwise free of gratuitous adjectives? Are we to assume that the gender specific reference is relevant and contributes to understanding? By referring to her as a "lady", a word which suggests a certain delicacy, and implying that her concerns are trivial (the noise), is he also commenting on the nature of women? This reference appears in a section on the enforcement of personal rights. Does he use a woman to describe the situations in which personal rights would not prevail because her sex facilitates somehow in understanding his point?

The stereotypes and linguistic structure that Dworkin uses reflects and expresses the roles, purposes and ideologies he ascribes to his subjects just as much as his more apparent content. According to Dworkin, we are childlike, dependent, passive and trite.

Undoubtedly there are stereotypical portraits of men in the seminar materials, but on the whole the range of characteristics attributed to the men represented is broader than the narrow range attributed to women. In a more equal world, the use of stereotypes would not threaten women because the assigned role would be recognized only for its usefulness in a particular context. But as matters now stand, sexual stereotypes reinforce the idea of the limited potential of women by describing them as unintelligent, dependent, passive objects. The systematic use of stereotypes conditions people to believe that women are not capable of doing things.

Metaphors

The use of metaphors, the experience of one thing in terms of another, is pervasive and affects not only how we speak but also how we think and act.[45] The purpose of metaphors is to facilitate understanding by describing those things that are unknown or difficult to describe in terms of things we know. The assumption is that the person receiving the information knows and understands the original reference in the same sense as the person communicating the information.

Consider for example, the metaphorical concept of WOMEN AS SEXUAL OBJECT as used in legal discourse: "piercing the corporate veil" and "raping the corporation". These notions have to do with control or dominance in the legal sense. The attribution of femaleness to the corporate body facilitates a male conceptualization of the action being described.[46] Rawls may have been using a variation of this metaphorical concept when he speaks of the "veil of ignorance" in developing his notion of the original position.[47] When covered by the veil and therefore on the female side, his subjects are unreal and unknowing; life only truly exists on the other side of the veil. In relying on these metaphorical concepts, the legal register perpetuates the idea of women as passive, submissive and ignorant.

George Lakoff gives a particularly frightening analysis of the relationship between our metaphors for anger and for lust and notes that these metaphors often overlap.[48] For example, ANGER IS HEAT (i.e., I was boiling with anger) and LUST IS HEAT (i.e., you are hot). He states that the connection between these two metaphors has important social consequences as that they enter our[49] reasoning: anger and lust come to be seen as the same thing. Lakoff concludes that these metaphors actually provide a rationale for rape.

Another metaphorical concept well known to the legal register is ARGUMENT AS WAR.[50] Consider the following examples:

  i)   her defence is weak
  ii) he attacked this argument
  iii) you can never beat them

The structure of the disagreements as created by the metaphorical concept also dictates the process or how those in the argument will act. Arguments, especially legal arguments, are seen as adversarial and often violent with clear victors and victims. Because women have been socialized

to avoid conflict and seek reconciliation and harmony,[51] the pervasive use of ARGUMENT AS WAR alienates women from participation in legal discourse and entrenches a patriarchal or male perspective on legal reasoning and method.

We could of course conceive of argument in a different way. Consider the metaphorical concept of ARGUMENT AS DANCE:

  i)   his argument does not jive
  ii) she never misses a beat
  iii) that leads me to

In my view, ARGUMENT AS DANCE creates a structure of agreement and cooperation and embraces the idea of a process that leads to a mutually satisfying conclusion.[52] In one legal philosophy seminar we consciously attempted to use ARGUMENT AS DANCE instead of ARGUMENT AS WAR in our discussion. Most people felt a real change in the dynamics of our interaction. We were less antagonistic and more willing to listen to each other. Tensions that had existed dissolved or at least were dealt with in a positive, constructive way.

Finally, I would like to consider the pervasive use of sport analogies in legal discourse. Llewellyn,[53] Dworkin[54] and Hart[55] liken law to a baseball game. This does not assist those who are unfamiliar with the rules of the game or those who are uncomfortable with participation in sports in understanding the ideas being discussed. The analogy of sport as law excludes many women (and some men) from participation in the discourse and thereby limits its utility. If you have trouble seeing this point, consider how you might feel if a common metaphorical concept in law was CONTRACT AS RECIPE.

We should not view metaphors as a matter of mere language. When we use a metaphor to describe something, the metaphor and the thing become one: woman becomes object, sex becomes anger, argument becomes war and law becomes a game. Each of these metaphors has the effect of oppressing women by objectifying or alienating us, by structuring and legitimating violent actions or by excluding us from the discourse.

Etymology and Word Creation

The study of etymology yields some interesting examples of the connection between language and gender. It was a Jewish custom (and remains an Arabic custom) for men to swear mutual oaths by placing a hand on each other's testicles. Words like testament, testify and testimony find their root in this custom.[56] Women would have been precluded from making such oaths. The word 'rape' once simply meant to steal or to plunder; the victim was not the raped woman but rather it was her father or husband who was thought to have lost something.[57] But while etymology reveals examples of practices that once clearly suppressed women, it may be difficult to prove that the root meanings of words continues to affect the discourse today. Therefore I simply offer these examples and leave it to someone else to discover whether these word histories have a deeper continuing significance.

A more serious problem arises in connection with those experiences for which no descriptive word exists. Without a word to describe an experience, it might be difficult to imagine that the experience has a basis in reality. For example, in her classic feminist work *The Feminine Mystique*,[58] Betty Friedan identifies "the problem that has no name." The problem, briefly, is the lack of utility attached to the work that homemakers do and the resulting frustration they feel. What word describes what homemakers do? When I refer to it as 'work' I am usually misunderstood. Friedan's problem is still unnamed.

The legal register "places great stress upon the legal signifier or legal word as an entity in itself."[59] Therefore, the birth of new words to describe experiences better known to women is important to recognition by the legal system of these experiences when appropriate. "Sexual harassment" and "sexism" are examples of words conceived by feminists[60] that have gradually received wider acceptance. These words have now been accepted into the legal register and have become legal entities with legal consequences. On the other hand, the legal register seems to have adopted the signifier "surrogate mother" to describe a woman who agrees to conceive and bear a child for its biological father. The word "surrogate" detracts from the fact that she is also the biological mother of the child by suggesting that she is external to the process.[61]

Of particular interest are the semantic implications of the expressions "domestic violence" and "wife battering". Why has the expression "domestic violence" prevailed in usage over "wife battering"? The former names neither the wife, nor by implication, the husband; it suggests that the problem is private (and therefore outside the realm of the law) and, as violence is a prevailing problem in our society anyway, there may be the suggestion that this is nothing special. "Wife battering" names the survivor, implicates the criminal and describes the crime that has been committed. The development of the term "domestic violence" itself was an important step in the broader societal recognition of the tragedy of men beating women in the home. Ultimately, however, the term is not strong enough to describe the true dynamics of most situations.

Feminists use the word 'survivor' to describe and empower those adults who have been subject to sexual abuse as children and who continue to bear the emotional and physical scars of that abuse.[62] This word is not, however, widely used outside feminist circles. Perhaps as information on the continuing effects of child sexual abuse is more widely available, the word 'survivor' will also become better known. Should this happen, perhaps this word will join 'sexual harassment' and 'sexism' in the legal register. Survivors might then be eligible for compensation for the abuse suffered. But without a discrete word such as 'survivor' to serve as the legal entity, it would seem less likely that the experience will be seen as one deserving legal redress.

The problems noted in relation to the lexicon and semantics are of a different sort than those that arise in connection with the use of male pronouns and false generics. They are less obvious as their offensiveness is not in isolated usage but rather in their systematic insidiousness. Further, whereas male pronouns and generics conceal an androcentric bias, the semantics of the legal register can be seen as more thoroughly misogynist. The words used to describe women construct an ideal of subservience or sexual usefulness. The roles we are ascribed and the language used to describe legal processes impliedly express accord with patriarchal political values. The consequence is the exclusion of women as actors in the legal system except in very narrowly prescribed roles.

. . . .

TOWARDS A CONCLUSION

Ever since I began studying law, I have had a growing uncomfortableness about what the language of legal discourse seems to say or imply about me as woman. But like most good women law students I avoided raising these issues because they did not seem to be quite on point: language was not a legal problem. When I returned to law school to do a master of law degree and had the opportunity to write a more theoretical paper rather than a paper on doctrine, language seemed an obvious choice. My original plan was to pull together a list of examples from the legal texts — a sort of glossary — and let their obviousness speak for itself.

The paper is well on its way to achieving its original plan, although that has now become its first goal. While the list of examples can be expanded and improved upon, I have said enough to show that the legal discourse systematically excludes, devalues, trivializes and ignores women. Obviously there will be disagreement with what I have and have not included. Hopefully, a dialogue will continue. For now, I will begin to formulate some conclusions.

Deborah Cameron has said that like a wolf whistle, a sexist remark has significance beyond the immediate offence it gives. Not only is it a manifestation of an unacceptable misogyny but it is also the mechanism by which misogyny is constructed and transmitted.[63] One can hope that the worst stereotypes are behind us now. This statement is probably too optimistic, however, as long as expressions like "raping the corporation" are current and if law professors continue to insist in classroom dialogues to refer to women only as wives or sex crime victims. This language so fundamentally alienates women that we cannot participate in the discourse without first denying ourselves.[64]

The original emphasis in writings on women and language focused on "non-sexist" language.[65] Simply stated, writers were to substitute sex-specific terms with generic terms. As was noted earlier,[66] the exclusive use of unmarked masculine pronouns and generics has the effect of excluding women from the readers' mental landscape. Such an exclusion leads to an androcentric view of the world: women are invisible and irrelevant.

By making the important switch to non-sexist language, women come into focus. This is an important first step. There is, however, a problem with thinking that if we use the pronouns "he" and "she" interchangeably and if we refer to policemen as police officers, no further change or analysis is required. Inherent in such a reformist theory is that we ought to reduce some forms of oppression and then, by implication, we legitimate the remaining forms. We must also refuse to accept stultifying stereotypes and alienating metaphors. We need to examine word choices for sexist semantic implications. Non-sexist language also requires that expressions used to describe women have a parallel meaning when used in reference to men. For example, if we speak of a "working mother" we should speak also of a "working father".

The obvious intent of these kinds of changes is to ensure that the content of legal discourse is changed to ensure the inclusion of women. I have stated in this paper that language contributes very significantly to androcentricity in law. We cannot assume that androcentricity is avoided by substituting "reasonable person" for "reasonable man". While the kinds of changes in language that I suggested help change how women are perceived in the legal system, law makers must then be willing to adopt new perspectives that come with that change. Otherwise the end effect will simply make women into honorary men. Analogical reasoning — the meta-metaphor[67] — will bind the law to androcentricity unless law-makers struggle against it.

There is a problem with stopping at a prescription for non-sexist language. If we use a generic term to describe a sex specific situation, another form of sexism is created. Thus, even if Rawls' "rational man" was styled as a "rational person," this character would still be a man. However, now that fact would be even less apparent. The language that we use must be sensitive to gender when the sex of the referent is a socially significant variable.

In this paper I have tried to show how finely sexist usage is woven into the fabric of legal language. Many of these problems can be redressed by using non-sexist language. However, some problems such as the problems associated with semantics and syntax, require a more heightened sensitivity to their oppressive effect because of the social construction of dominance by men. This sensitivity requires that we probe deeply into meaning. What is not being said? What actors are not named? What are readers being encouraged to imply? Is male dominance encouraged or assumed?

The elimination of sexist language is critical to the elimination of sexism. The first step is to understand how it is expressed in language. To paraphrase Richard Scrutton, each of us inherits in language the sexism of many generations. To rehabilitate this repository of human experience is to alter out most fundamental perceptions.[68] Finally, we must care about what we say and be willing always to challenge, monitor, and change our language.

Endnotes

1. See, e.g., D. Spender, *Man Made Language* (London: Routledge and Kegan Paul, 1980) at 139 wherein she outlines the theory of linguistic determinism and cites the best-known works.
2. See, e.g., D. Cameron, *Feminism and Linguistic Theory* (London: The MacMillan Press, 1985) chapters 5 and 6 for a review of the theories of structuralism. M. Ashe also discusses structuralism in "Mind's Opportunity: Birthing a Poststructuralist Feminist Jurisprudence" (1987), 38 *Syracuse L.R.* 1129.
3. See generally, P. Goodrich, "The Role of Linguistics in Legal Analysis", [1984] 47 *Mod.L.R.* 523 at 531.
4. S. de Beauvoir, *The Second Sex* (New York: Knopf, 1953) at 10.
5. The idea of "male as (unstated) norm" has been considered in many law review articles. See, e.g.: M. Minow, "Supreme Court Forward: Justice Engendered" (1987), 101 *Harv. L. Rev.* 10; A. Scales, "The Emergence of Feminist Jurisprudence: An Essay" (1986), 95 *Yale L.J.* 1373; and K. Lahey, "...Until Women Themselves Have Told All They Have to Tell..." (1985), 23 *Osg. Hall L.J.* 519.
6. C. MacKinnon, "Feminism, Marxism, Method and the State: Toward Feminist Jurisprudence" (1983), 8 *Signs* 635 at 638–39. S. Rowbotham in *Woman's Consciousness, Man's World* (Baltimore: Penguin Books, 1973) at 32–33 makes a similar point when she says that "the language of theory — removed language — only expresses a reality experienced by the oppressors. It speaks only for their world, from their point of view...language is part of the political and ideological powers of rulers".
7. I would define "patriarchy" as a political structure that values and rewards men more than women.
8. See P. Goodrich, *Legal Discourse: Studies in Linguistics, Rhetoric and Legal Analysis* (New York: St. Martins Press, 1987) at 204 for a more detailed explanation of this method of textual analysis.
9. Cameron, *supra*, note 2 at 7 suggests that the appropriate inquiry is as to the connections between language, gender and oppression and I will use this question throughout this article.
10. See generally: J. Flax, "Post Modernism and Gender Theory in Feminist Theory" (1987), 12 *Signs* 621; M.J. Frug, "Re-reading Contracts: A Feminist Analysis of a Contracts Casebook" 34 *Amer. U.L.R.* 1065, text accompanying notes 3–13.
11. See W. Martyna, "Beyond The He/Man Approach: The Case For Non-Sexist Language" (1980), 5 *Signs* 482 at 483.
12. A. Bodine, "Androcentrism in Prescriptive Grammar" (1974), 4 *Language in Society* 129.
13. K. De Jong, "On Equality and Language" (1985), 1 *Can. J. W. and L.* at 122. R. West in "Gender and Jurisprudence" (1988), 55 *U. of Chi. L.R.* 1 at 2 notes that liberal legalism and critical legal theory are "essentially and irretrievably masculine" and therefore that the "...increasing use of the female pronoun in liberal and critical legal theory, although well-intended, is empirically and experientially false". It is not clear from the text whether her comments are rhetorical or prescriptive.

While West's article is analytically illuminating, she seems to view 'male' and 'female' characteristics as exclusive to men and women respectively. As noted, I believe that members of either sex may exhibit the characteristics usually associated with the opposite sex. Hence the use of female pronouns is not necessarily experientially false. More importantly, the end effect of such a prescription, if that is in fact West's comment, is to polarize dialogue so thoroughly that communication between the sexes would be virtually impossible.

14. Martyna, *supra*, note 19 at 489.

15. *Ibid.*

16. Cameron, *supra*, note 2 at 69.

17. See Cameron, *supra*, note 2 at 79.

18. Aristotle, *The Nicomachean Ethics*, (ca. 336–322 B.C.) in Greenawalt, *supra*, note 12 at 418.

19. H.L.A. Hart, *Law, Liberty and Morality*, (1963) in Greenawalt, *supra*, note 12 at 622.

20. J. Rawls, *A Theory of Justice*, (1972) in Greenawalt, *supra*, note 12 at 514.

21. *Ibid.*

22. For an example of a more developed critique, see M. Matsuda, "Liberal Jurisprudence and Abstracted Visions of Human Nature: A Feminist Critique of Rawls' Theory of Justice" (1986), 16 *N. Mex. L.R.* 613. Robin West, *supra*, note 21, develops a rich analysis of the assumptions underlying what she describes as the masculine jurisprudence of liberal and critical legalism and cultural and radical feminism. She notes at 14 that

> Underlying both radical and cultural feminism is a conception of women's existential state that is grounded in women's potential for physical, material connection to human life, just as underlying both liberal and critical legalism is a conception of men's existential state that is grounded in the inevitability of men's physical separation from the species.

23. See, e.g.: C. Gilligan, *In a Different Voice: Psychological Theory and Women's Development* (Cambridge: Harvard University Press, 1982); N. Chodorow, *The Reproduction of Mothering: Psychoanalysis of the Sociology of Gender* (Berkeley: Univ. of California Press, 1978); and D. Dinnerstein, *The Mermaid and the Minotaur: Sexual Arrangements and Human Malaise* (New York: Harper and Row, 1976).

24. D. Donovan and S. Wildman, "Is the Reasonable Man Obsolete: A Critical Perspective on Self Defense and Provocation" (1981), *Loyola L.A.L. Rev.* 435.

25. L. Bender, "A Lawyer's Primer on Feminist Theory and Tort" (1988), 38 *J. of Legal Ed.* 3.

26. There are a number of sources on how to deal with difficult pronoun and generic problems. The best known of these is C. Miller and K. Swift, *The Handbook of Nonsexist Writing* (New York: Harper and Row, 1981).

27. M. Daly, *Gyn/Ecology: The Meta-Ethics of Radical Feminism* (Boston: Beacon Press, 1978) at 5. See also her *Webster's First Intergalactic Wickedary of the English Language* (Boston: Beacon Press, 1987).

28. Spender, *supra*, note 1 at 2.

29. O.W. Holmes, "The Path of Law" (1897) in Greenawalt, *supra*, note 12 at 3.

30. M.B. Hintikka and J. Hintikka, "How Can Language Be Sexist?" in ed. S. Harding and M. Hintikka, *Discovering Reality: Feminist Perspectives on Epistemology, Metaphysics, Methodology and Philosophy of Science* (Boston: D. Reidel Publishing Co., 1983) discuss whether "good man" and "good woman" mean the same thing. They conclude that they do not.

31. F. Olsen, "The Sex of Law" (unpublished manuscript on file with me, 1984). The lists of words used in this paragraph were suggested by Olsen or in one of the other articles cited in these notes.

32. Spender, *supra*, note 1 at 18.

33. *Ibid.*, at 18.

34. Olsen, *supra*, note 39.

35. See: C. Menkel Meadow, "Portia in a Different Voice: Speculations on Women's Lawyering Process" (1985), 1 *Berkeley Women's L.J.* 39 and "Excluded Voices: New Voices in The Legal Profession Making New Voices in Law" (1987), 42 *U. of Miami L.R.* 29.

36. K. Greenawalt, "Promise, Benefit and Need: Ties that Bind Us To The Law", (1984) in Greenawalt, *supra*, note 12 at 722.

37. The fathers that appear in the legal philosophy materials are fierce patriarchs. For example, H. Kelsen, "General Theory of Law and State", (1946) in Greenawalt, *supra*, note 12 at 184 uses the example of a mother telling her child to go to school "because your father has ordered it". He goes on to say that the general norm to be extracted from this statement is that "children ought to obey their father". The mother's authority is not considered.

38. Holmes, *supra*, note 37 at 2.

39. Greenawalt, "Discretion and Judicial Decision", (1977) in Greenawalt, *supra*, note 12 at 289.

40. R. Dworkin, "The Model of Rules" (1977) in Greenawalt, *supra*, note 12 at 247.

41. R. Dworkin, "Hard Cases" (1975) in Greenawalt, *supra*, note 12 at 319.

42. *Ibid.*, at 344.

43. *Ibid.*, at 358.

44. R. Dworkin, "Taking Rights Seriously" (1971) in Greenawalt, *supra*, note 12 at 792.

45. G. Lakoff and M. Johnson, *Metaphors We Live By* (Chicago: University of Chicago Press, 1980) at 38.

46. This analysis was suggested by Judy Greenberg as noted in K. Lahey and S. Salter, "Corporate Law in Legal Theory and Legal Scholarship: From Classicism to Feminism" (1985), 23 *Osg. H.L.J.* 543 at 555.

47. Rawls, *supra*, note 28. See also Matsuda, *supra*, note 30 at 616.

48. G. Lakoff, *Women, Fire and Dangerous Things: What Categories Reveal About The Mind* (Chicago: University of Chicago Press, 1987) at 409–413.

49. I would note that Lakoff does not comment on whether women use the same kind of metaphors as men do. The use of the pronoun "our" in this context therefore is ambiguous — does it refer to just men or to both men and women? More specifically, do both women and men reach the metaphorical conclusion of LUST AS ANGER?

50. Lakoff and Johnson, *supra*, note 59 at 4–5, and J. Penelope, "Language and the Transformation of Consciousness" (1984), 4 *Law and Inequality J.* 379.

51. See, e.g., Gilligan, *supra*, note 31 at 164, M. French, *Beyond Power: On Women, Men and Morals* (New York: Summit Books, 1985) at 482.

52. This conclusion is suggested by Penelope, *supra*, note 58.

53. K. Llewellyn, "The Bramble Bush" (1930) in Greenawalt, *supra*, note 12 at 41.

54. R. Dworkin, "The Model of Rules" in Greenawalt, *supra*, note 12 at 258.

55. H.L.A. Hart, "The Concept of Law" (1961) in Greenawalt, *supra*, note 12 at 80.

56. R. Brasch, *How Did Sex Begin?* (New York: David MacKay Co., 1973) at 152 as cited in B. Walker, *The Women's Encyclopedia of Myths and Secrets* (San Francisco: Harper Row, 1983) at 793–94.

57. S. Brownmiller, *Against Our Will: Men, Women and Rape* (New York: Bantam Books, 1976) at 8–22 and 422–424.

58. B. Friedan, *The Feminine Mystique* (New York: Norton, 1963).

59. Goodrich, *supra*, note 8 at 177–78.

60. See, e.g., C. Backhouse and L. Cohen, *The Secret Oppression: Sexual Harassment of the Working Women* (Toronto: MacMillan of Canada, 1978) and C. MacKinnon, *Sexual Harassment of Working Women: A Case of Sexual Discrimination* (New Haven: Yale University Press, 1979).

61. This example is from M. Eichler, "Foundation of Bias: Sexist Language and Sexist Thought" in S. Martin and K. Mahoney, eds., *Equality and Judicial Neutrality* (Toronto: Carswell, 1987) at 26–27.

62. One reader of an earlier draft of this paper asked why I considered child sexual assault to be a "gender issue". It has been estimated that 38% of girls and 10% of boys are sexually abused by a dominant male from the family unit. Obviously then, many more women than men will have problems in their adult life. Further, some of the effects of child sexual abuse are passivity and a sense of helplessness. Since girls are socialized to be passive and dependent, sexual abuse would reinforce this socialization. Boys are usually socialized to be active and independent and therefore may have other ways of coping with the sexual abuse.

Most importantly, child sexual abuse is a gender issue because in the vast majority of cases it is *men* who commit the offense. Feminism is concerned with the psychology and sociology of both men and women. See, generally, D. Russell, *The Secret Trauma: Incest in the Lives of Girls and Women* (New York: Basic Books, 1986).

63. Cameron, *supra*, note 2 at 7.

64. See Menkel Meadow, *Excluded Voices, supra*, note 43, wherein she discusses alienation and assimilation of voices, including the female voice, that are excluded from legal discourse.

65. See, e.g., Martyna, *supra*, note 19.

66. See text accompanying notes 19–25.

67. The expression "meta-metaphor" is from C. MacKinnon, *Feminism Unmodified: Discourses on Life and Law* (Cambridge: Harvard University Press, 1987) at 9.

68. Richard Scrutton's original sentence had of course a very different meaning as he was arguing for the use of "he" as a generic pronoun: "Each of us inherits in language the wisdom of many generations. To mutilate this repository of human experience is to alter our most fundamental perceptions." As quoted, in its original form in Cameron, *supra*, note 2 at 79.

Native Culture on Trial[†]
L. Mandell

INTRODUCTION

Several months ago, when I was talking to an Indian elder about the evidence he was to give in a hunting trial, I became concerned that court might be starting momentarily. I asked whether anyone knew the time and the old man replied: "It's almost summer."

The first task in advancing cases involving aboriginal rights through Canadian courts is to make the different world view of the Indian Nations visible.

Judges have a greater responsibility than other professionals to understand Indian world views and property definitions. This is especially so today because since the recent entrenchment of aboriginal and treaty rights in the Constitution[1] Indian Nations are looking to the courts for assistance in righting the wrongs of the past and in shaping their relationship with Canada. Yet in general, judges have no better knowledge than the general public and arguably, as a group, they suffer from a somewhat poorer exposure to the day-to-day life and struggle of the Indian Nations. It can therefore be expected that certain judges will fail to appreciate the history and aspirations of the Indian Nations.

A brief examination of several leading cases illustrates some of the central difficulties facing Indian Nations in their efforts to enforce recognition of their rights through the courts. The cases show the difficulty some judges have experienced in overcoming their learned biases. This paper will demonstrate this point by canvassing judicial reaction and decisions to legal questions of aboriginal title, definitions of aboriginal property rights, recognition of aboriginal religion, and the legal debate involving the extinguishment of aboriginal title.

JUDICIAL DECISIONS IN RELATION TO ABORIGINAL PROPERTY RIGHTS

The Supreme Court of Canada has placed the onus of proof on the Indian Nations in cases where the Nation asserts an existing title. The onus shifts to the Indians because of an initial assumption that the Crown's "discovery" of this continent (which had been occupied for thousands of years by the Indian Nations) gave it rights to the soil. Alternatively, the assertion is that the Crown conquered the Indian Nations by exercising jurisdiction over the territory. The result of this manifestly arrogant assertion of power is that the courts have said that the extent of Indian title depends upon the degree to which the Nation traditionally possessed their lands. In *Kruger v. R.*,[2] Mr. Justice Dickson said that proof of aboriginal title will be decided when title is directly in issue:[3]

> Interested parties should be afforded an opportunity to adduce evidence in detail bearing upon the resolution of the particular dispute. Claims to aboriginal title are woven with history, legend, politics and moral obligations. If the claim of any Band in respect of any particular land is to be decided as a justiciable issue and not a political issue, it should be so considered on the facts pertinent to that Band and to that land, and not on any global basis.

The Indian elders in British Columbia question why they must subject their relationship to the land to a non-Indian court's strict scrutiny: why they must explain their use of the land to obtain "rights" abstractly defined by others. They believe that the Indians have rights to their

---

† Mandell, Louise, "Native Culture on Trial" in eds. S. Martin and K. Mahoney, *Equality and Judicial Neutrality* (Toronto: Carswell, 1987), 358–65. Reprinted by permission of the editors, Sheilah L. Martin and Kathleen E. Mahoney, and Carswell — a division of Thomson Canada Limited.

land because their people go back with the land for thousands of years. What they do not understand is how the Crown acquired its "rights" to their land.

An example of the Indians' misunderstanding occurred during the course of taking commission evidence in a land claims case presently advancing through the courts in British Columbia. Lawyers for the Crown cross-examined an elder for many days on the extent of his hunting, fishing, trapping and berry-picking practices throughout his territory. The plaintiffs had originally advanced evidence to prove that an aboriginal title was established by these activities. The elder turned to the Crown's lawyers and asked whether the Queen had ever been questioned on whether she had ever shot a deer in his territory and if not, how does she claim her right to his land.

Notwithstanding the inherent problems with where the onus of proof is placed, many Nations, when trying to discharge this burden of proof, find that judges do not recognize their legitimate relationship to the land. In those cases the courts tend to evaluate traditional Indian customs against their own modern non-Indian values. This problem was fatal to the way of life of aborigines in Australia when a court would not give legal weight to Indian concepts of property. In the case of *Milirrpum v. Nabalco Party Ltd. and Commonwealth of Australia*[4] the Indians alleged that they had a legal property right in lands they traditionally used and occupied. The action was brought to stop a mining operation which threatened to harm traditional lands. The plaintiffs introduced complex evidence on their social rules and customs to establish that they had proprietary legal rights in the land. The judge described the Indians' relationships to the land as follows:[5]

As I understand it, the fundamental truth about the aboriginals' relationship to the land is that whatever else it is, it is a religious relationship... the physical and spiritual universes are not felt as distinct. There is an unquestioned scheme of things in which the spirit ancestors, the people of the clan, particular land and everything that exists on and in it, are organic parts of one indissoluble whole...it is not in dispute that each clan regards itself as a spiritual entity having a spiritual relationship to particular places or areas, and having a duty to care for and tend that land by means of ritual observances.

After examining this evidence the judge found it showed:[6]

A subtle and elaborate system highly adapted to the country in which the people lead their lives which provided a stable order of society and was remarkably free from the vagaries of personal whim or influence. If ever a system could be

called a "government of laws, and not of men", it is shown in the evidence before me.

Despite these observations the judge decided that the Indians had no proprietary interest in their lands. He concluded:[7]

In my view, the proper procedure is to bear in mind the concepts of "property" in our law, and in what I know of how other systems which have the concept, as well as my understanding permits, and look at the aboriginal system to find what there corresponds to or resembles "property".

In my opinion, therefore, there is so little resemblance between property, as our law, or what I know of any other law, understands that term, and the claims of the plaintiffs for their clans, that I must hold that these claims are not in the nature of proprietary interests.

The judge ruled against the Indian Nations because the Indian view of property was different from that of the colonizers. The result was their traditional lands could be mined, notwithstanding the destruction mining would bring to their way of life.

JUDICIAL REACTIONS TO ABORIGINAL RELIGIOUS VALUES

An example of bias in religious values in a Canadian court is the recent case of *Anderson Jack v. R.*,[8] where the Supreme Court of Canada displayed its incapacity to recognize and give legal force and effect to Indian religious beliefs and practices. The case involved two Indian men who were charged under a provincial Wildlife Act with hunting deer out of season. The hunting took place as part of an ancient traditional ceremony where food is burned for the benefit of deceased relatives. Dr. Barbara Lane, an anthropologist, explained the religious practice to the court:

Well, this is a very ancient traditional practice among all Coast Salish people and the essence of the ceremony is to provide food for deceased relatives by burning it and the essence of the food, as I understand it, is transmitted through the smoke to the essence of the deceased person.

Many witnesses told the court how this practice of burning expresses the world view of the Coast Salish people. These explanations were summarized by Judge Taggart of the Court of Appeal of British Columbia and repeated in the judgment of Mr. Justice Beetz of the Supreme Court of Canada:[9]

The religious ceremony was described by witnesses who were members of the Tsartlip Band and by Dr. Barbara Lane. Dr. Lane is an anthropologist who since 1948 has studied the Coast Salish people and especially their religious beliefs and practices. She said that the Coast Salish people were believed to have lived in British Columbia for about 20,000 years. The Coast Salish believe that members of their people who die do not go to another world but that their spirits remain close to where they lived. The belief is that the spirits have the same kinds of needs and desires as living people. Dr. Lane explained the belief in this way:

> They become lonely and want to visit their relatives, they become hungry and want to have the kind of foods that they had before, and they have desires for other things that they've left behind here, and they transmit these desires to their close relatives through dreams and other kinds of experiences, and these needs are satisfied and the desires of the deceased relatives are met by the living providing to them the things that they request....

> As I was attempting to suggest earlier, the entire world view of Coast Salish Indian people is quite different from that which those of us who are raised in the Judeo-Christian tradition have. Coast Salish Indian people perceive of the world as an intimately inter-related phenomenon in which the living and the dead animals and humans, all things are intimately connected and belong together in this place and do not leave it. And the function of burning food for the dead is to carry on the mutual responsibilities and respect that Indian people here try to accord to all of the other parts of the world as they see it. One of the things that always seems to be incomprehensible to Indian people is how the rest of us can pick ourselves up from one part of the world and move to another and abandon and cut ourselves off from our dead relatives because they perceive of themselves as being in continuous association with and having ongoing responsibilities to the dead.

The hunt took place to assist Elizabeth Jack, the wife of the defendant Anderson Jack and the sister of the defendant George Louie Charlie. Elizabeth Jack had conducted a burning at Christmas in 1977 for her dead great-grandfather. At that burning, she burnt potatoes, hamburger, Indian bread and clams. During the burning, her dead relative communicated through her father, a Shaman, Louie Charlie, that the great-grandfather wanted raw deer meat.

Elizabeth Jack became very sick. She believed her sickness was a reaction to her not having satisfied the wishes of her dead relative for raw deer meat. She went to Louie Charlie for assistance. The power to do the work done by Louie Charlie and perform burnings is handed down from one generation to another. Burnings are considered to be a sacred practice and each burning must be done at set times and by special people who are recognized as able to do the work.

Louie Charlie gave evidence that his instructions must be carried out and exercised precisely, otherwise the family doing the burning would continue to be troubled. Louie Charlie directed Elizabeth and the defendants to hunt deer at Pender Island, an old hunting place of the Saanich People. Elizabeth Jack gave evidence that the deer came forth to be burned for her great-grandfather:

> Then we saw one there, standing, and they wouldn't do anything about it, and I told them, "Well, there it is, it's just standing there, in the grass, like, you can see it clear." So I told them, "That's the one I want, I got to have it, because I want to feed my grandparents."...Then he looked at us, my brother looked at us, and then he aim, and he was still standing there, so he shot it, and it just dropped there...then we went back in the camp there, we cleaned it out and all that and I told him, "You have to bury the head", and all that, the guts and things like that. So they did.

Later that morning wildlife officers stopped the hunters, seized the deer, and charged the hunters with offences under the Wildlife Act.[10]

At trial, the Provincial Court judge accepted that the accused were sincere and that the burning practice had its roots in religious practice going back at least 20,000 years. However, he subjected the hunting to the rules of the Wildlife Act, finding that the policy of the Wildlife Act did not impair the defendants' status and capacity as Indians:[11]

> ...if Indians wish to exercise their historic religious practices there are ways within the bounds of the Provincial Statute in which to exercise those religious practices. They can, for example, retain a supply of deer meat in storage for such purposes...the purpose of the Act is what matters. This Act is being held to be and is, clearly I think, of general application and was certainly not aimed at preventing the Coast Salish from exercising any religious practice. The act of burning food as an offering to the spirit of an ancestor is not prohibited. If it is exercised within the limits of the general law it may be freely carried out by the Sannich people.

On Appeal, the County Court judge found against the accused on another footing. The court distinguished between religious belief and religious practice and said that although freedom of religion protects religious belief, religious practices must be exercised within the limits of law.[12] The British Columbia Court of Appeal divided on the question. The majority judgment agreed with the County Court and held that: "freedom of religion must be exercised within the limits permitted by validly enacted legislation...."[13] The court also said that the Wildlife Act must be directed against Indian religion in its policy in order for the courts to hold that it does not apply to Indians. The court refused to accept the argument that the *effect* of the Wildlife Act was to prevent and prohibit the religious practices of the Indians.

In dissent Mr. Justice Hutcheon held:[14]

> The issue in this case is whether Anderson Jack and George Louie Charlie were guilty of an offense when they hunted and killed a deer out of season. The hunting and killing was part of a religious ritual of the Coast Salish people of 20,000 years duration. The ritual is not harmful to society, is not opposed to the common good and is not in violation of the rights of any other individual. I have concluded that they were not guilty of an offense and that this appeal should be allowed. There is no suggestion that the loss of one deer for the purpose of the ritual would impair the legislative purpose. I think that the freedom of religion of Jack and Charlie ought not to be taken away by the application of an enactment of general application in the absence of evidence of some compelling justification.... In my opinion, the Wildlife Act ought to be read so as to acknowledge the right of Jack and Charlie on these facts to practise their religion where no compelling interest of society exists.

An argument raised for the first time before the Supreme Court of Canada by the province of British Columbia was that the hunting itself was not a religious practice. The Supreme Court of Canada agreed, holding that there was nothing in the evidence to suggest that the hunting and killing of the deer on Pender Island was part of a religious ritual. The court agreed with the trial judge who said that the Wildlife Act did not interfere with the religion of the people because it was possible to use stored or frozen deer meat for the burning.[15] It is significant that although the judges could envision a proper burning with stored deer meat, the Indians could not.

The court also failed to consider that the preparation for the burning was considered by the Indians as a sacred quest directed by the Shaman's strict instructions. It is evident in the following quote analogizing the obtaining of the meat with the obtaining of sacramental wine:[16]

> No clergyman could raise a defence based on religious freedom, to a charge of obtaining wine illegally while liquor stores were closed, simply because it was intended to use the wine for the sacrament of Holy Communion. Similarly a defence based on "freedom of religion" must fail the Appellants in this case, where the charge is killing a deer in the closed season. Since killing the deer is not, in itself, ceremonial, the *actus reus* of the offence cannot be regarded as a religious observance. If it is not such an observance, then logically, its prohibition by the Wildlife Act raises no question of religious freedom.

The reasoning suggests that if the Indian practice more closely paralleled Judeo-Christian religious practices and if some overt act, such as the saying of a prayer, took place when the deer was shot, that kind of evidence would flag to the courts a religious ceremony worthy of judicial protection. By defining religion as a ceremony and ignoring or refusing to give weight to the evidence of the Indian people which described the religious practice as understood and as practised by them, the Supreme Court of Canada set itself as the judge of Indian religious orthodoxy and then failed to understand the evidence which described the essence of the religious practices and beliefs.

. . . .

CONCLUSION

Since the enactment of the Constitution Act, 1982, which entrenches aboriginal and treaty rights, Indian Nations are increasingly turning to the courts to compel governments to negotiate just land claims. But it is questionable whether the courts can or should settle issues involving aboriginal rights. Relations between Nations is certainly a political matter. However, courts could have a role in building the foundation for meaningful political negotiations between the Indian Nations and the Crown.

Judges hearing cases such as those discussed above must not only be sensitive to their own biases, but they must also hear evidence before them with open minds so that they can understand another world view as it is understood by the Indians. Without such judicial sensitivity, judges will fail to protect the rights Indians say are necessary for their survival. Should the courts fail in this responsibility, future negotiations with governments regarding native rights will be jeopardized.

Endnotes

1. *Constitution Act, 1982*, Pt. II, s. 35 [am. SI/84–102, Sched., s. 2]
2. (1977), 34 C.C.C. (2d) 377 (S.C.C.).
3. *Ibid.* at 380.
4. (1971), 17 F.L.R. 141 (S.C.).
5. *Ibid.* at 265.
6. *Ibid.* at 267.
7. *Ibid.* at 270–73.
8. [1985] 4 C.N.L.R. 88 (S.C.C.).
9. *Ibid.* at 90, 91.
10. *Wildlife Act*, S.B.C. 1966, c. 55 [see now 1982, c. 57], s. 4(1)(c) [now s. 27(1)(c)].
11. *R. v. Jack* (1980), 50 C.C.C. (2d) 337 (B.C. Prov. Ct.).
12. *R. v. Jack*, [1982] 4 C.N.L.R. 99 (B.C. Co. Ct).
13. *R. v. Jack* (1983), 139 D.L.R. (3d) 25 (B.C.C.A.).
14. *Ibid.* at 41.
15. See *supra* note 8 at 100.
16. *Ibid.* at 101.

Further Reading

Richard Delgado, "When a Story is Just a Story: Does Voice Really Matter?" (1990), 76 *Virginia Law Review* 95–116.

Carol Gilligan, *In a Different Voice* (Cambridge: Harvard University Press, 1982).

4   Legal Method and Social Inquiry

A. Sources of Law and Legal Authority

Introduction to Legal Method†
J. Farrar and A. Dugdale

ANY law library contains volumes of reports of case decisions and statutes. These are the two main sources of our law. Judgments in cases are sources of law, for what a court declares the law to be in one case "authority" in the sense that it must be taken into account by other judges (and consequently legal advisers) when they are determining what law should apply to other similar fact situations. If say, you want to know whether a professional man such as an accountant owes a duty of care to someone who has suffered a loss as a result of his actions, you will be able to find the likely answer by consulting previous case decisions in which a court has declared the extent of a professional man's duty. These "authorities" provide the guidelines for both future cases and legal advice generally.

Until the nineteenth century case law was the main source of law, statutes being of relatively minor importance. But today their roles are reversed, indeed some would say that statutes are too dominant, that our system is "choking on statutes" many of which are in need of repeal or amendment if only the legislature had time. The reasons for the growth of statutes as a source are several. Partly it is because the social and economic problems of the twentieth century have demanded more sophisticated legal techniques than can be provided by case law alone. The administrative regulatory or social benefit conferral techniques discussed in Chapter 2 require laws establishing complex procedures, requirements, rights and duties which can only be expressed with sufficient precision in a statute. Again the speed of changes has far outstripped the capacity of case law alone to create new rules. Thus, the regulation of credit cards or data banks cannot

be left to await the development of suitable case law principles. It requires an immediate response which can only be provided by the legislature. Legislation has another important advantage as a source; it attracts widespread publicity. If the aim is to influence behaviour, e.g., persuading car occupants to wear seat belts, it is better achieved by a well publicised statute rather than by a little heard of case law decision.

Although the Legislature passes statutes, it does not apply them. The task of applying the provisions of the statute to a particular fact situation is ultimately one for the courts and in exercising this function judges are called upon to interpret the meaning of the statute. To appreciate the role of Statutes as a source of law, it is then necessary to understand the approaches to interpretation which the courts adopt. Indeed the appellate courts probably spend more of their time on cases involving statutory interpretation than on those involving case law.

· · · ·

One comment should be made about the sources as a whole. They do not provide a neatly ordered legal framework under which one particular fact situation is covered by one particular source of law. Rather the sources frequently overlap and on occasions conflict. Different case law sources may be potentially applicable to the same fact situation. The conflict between the case law authorities of equity and the common law are but an extreme example of this problem. Statutes may also overlap in a particular context. There may occasionally be a conflict between

† Farrar, John, and Dugdale, Anthony, eds., *Introduction to Legal Method*, 2nd ed. (London: Sweet & Maxwell, 1984), 70–72, 182, 187–89, 286–88. Reprinted by permission of Sweet & Maxwell Ltd.

their provisions or the way in which they have been interpreted. Both statutory and case law sources may overlap, it being left to the courts to resolve their competing claims to be applied to the situation in question. By contrast, it might seem that the sources of the civil law systems, namely codes supplemented by doctrine, i.e., learned writings, present a clearer picture. It has been said that, whilst the framework of sources of the civil law systems possess the order of a Louis XIV formal garden, that of our system is more akin to Hampton Court maze.

. . . .

We have seen that the common law is largely the product of the judiciary. On the continent, until the codifications of the nineteenth century, learned writings (which are usually referred to as *doctrine*) were a fundamental source of law. In England learned writers have traditionally played a subordinate role and their writings have never enjoyed the status afforded to continental doctrinal writings before the codifications. The position on the continent since codification seems to be that doctrine still enjoys high prestige but is now really an important *secondary* source in areas governed by the codes and other legislation. This latter role should not be underestimated since, as David and Brierley point out, doctrine creates the legal vocabulary and ideas used by legislators, and influences the methods of statutory interpretation.

THE POSITION OF DOCTRINE IN ENGLISH LAW

The position of learned writings in English law has in fact varied at different periods of legal history. Certain classical authors are recognised as authorities and there has gradually been a relaxation of the strange, necromantic rule allowing only the citation of dead authors.

THE CITATION OF MODERN WRITERS

The old rule of practice was that the works of living authors could not be cited but could be plagiarised by counsel by incorporation into their own submissions to the court. Various reasons have been given for this — the fear that living authors would change their minds and render the law uncertain; the growth of law reporting rendered it unnecessary to cite secondary sources; and the notion that the passage of time would result in the elimination of errors by subsequent editors. Sir Robert Megarry V.-C., who speaks with considerable knowledge and experience in these matters, in his *Miscellany-at-Law* (1955), p. 328, adds the further reason that

there are a number of living authors whose appearance and demeanour do something to sap the confidence in their omniscience which the printed page may have instilled; the dead, on the other hand, so often leave little clue to what manner of men they were save the majestic skill with which they have arrayed the learning of centuries and exposed the failings of the bench.

The old rule has become honoured more in its breach than its observance. There is an interesting exchange between counsel and the Bench in *R. v. Ion* (1852), 2 Den. 475, 488.

Metcalfe (counsel):.... In the 11th edition of a work, formerly edited by one of your Lordships, *Archbold on Criminal Pleading* by Welsby, Mr. Welsby, who may be cited as authority, comments on the words 'utter or publish'...

Pollock C.B.: — Not yet an authority.

Metcalfe: — It is no doubt a rule that a writer on law is not to be considered an authority in his lifetime. The only exception to the rule, perhaps, in the case of Justice Story.

Coleridge J.: — Story is dead.

Cresswell J.: — No doubt the cases are carefully abstracted by Mr. Welsby in the passage you refer to.

Lord Campbell C.J.: — It is scarcely necessary to say that my opinion of Mr. Welsby is one of sincere respect.

The reporter, Denison, appends a footnote to the effect that the rule seemed to be more honoured in the breach than in its observance and he refers to a number of writers who had been cited in their lifetime.

There are numerous conflicting passages in the reports on the application of the rule but certainly the practice has now developed of citing living authors. It may be as Hood Phillips maintains that the judges allow themselves more latitude than they do counsel.

In 1947 Lord Denning wrote in the *Law Quarterly Review* that "the notion that (academic lawyers) works are not of authority except after the author's death, has long been exploded. Indeed the more recent the work, the more persuasive it is." This view has not been universally accepted but there seems to be an increasing tendency to accept academic writings as a convenient secondary source of law or alternatively as a source of suggestions of what the law should be where there is a gap or the law is unclear.

As Lord Denning said such books "are written by men who have studied the law as a science with more detachment than is possible to men engaged in practice."

Sir Robert Megarry, who is both a writer and a judge, expressed the matter a little more cautiously in *Cordell v. Second Clanfield Properties Ltd.*, [1968] 2 Ch. 9, 16 when he said:

> the process of authorship is entirely different from that of judicial decision. The author, no doubt, has the benefit of a broad and comprehensive survey of his chosen subject as a whole, together with a lengthy period of gestation and intermittent opportunities for consideration. But he is exposed to the peril of yielding to preconceptions, and he lacks the advantage of that impact and sharpening of focus which the detailed facts of a particular case bring to the judge. Above all, he has to form his ideas without the aid of the purifying ordeal of skilled argument on the specific facts of a contested case. Argued law is tough law. This is as true today as it was in 1409 when Hankford J. said: 'Homme ne scaveroit de quel metal un campane fuit, si ceo ne fuit bien batu, quasi diceret, le ley per bon disputacion serra bien conus'; [Just as it is said 'A man will not know of what metal a bell is made if it has not been well beaten (rung)' so the law shall be well known by good disputation] and these words are none the less apt for a judge who sits, as I do, within earshot of the bells of St. Clements. I would therefore give credit to the words of any reputable author in a book or article as expressing tenable and arguable ideas, as fertilisers of thought, and as conveniently expressing the fruits of research in print, often in apt and persuasive language. But I would do no more than that; and in particular, I would expose those views to the testing and refining process of argument. Today, as of old, by good disputing shall the law be well known.

Law, Politics and the Judicial Process in Canada[†]
F.L. Morton

ONE of the most distinctive characteristics of the judicial process is its formalized method of reasoning. Because their authority flows from the public perception that they are "merely" applying pre-existing rules to resolve new disputes, judges are not permitted the broad prerogative enjoyed by the legislative and the executive branches. Unlike the latter, courts are not supposed to create new policies to deal with new problems. In their oral or written judgments, judges must explain where and how they derived the "rule" used to settle a case. There are three principal sources for these "rules": a written constitution, legislative statutes (including administrative regulations), and prior judicial decisions, known as precedents. Constitutional interpretation is the subject of the following two chapters. This chapter is concerned with the role of precedent and statutory interpretation in judicial reasoning.

Until the middle of the nineteenth century, most internal or domestic law in English-speaking societies was common law. Common law originated in the judicial recognition and enforcement of traditional usages and customs of the Anglo-Saxon and later Norman peoples in the British Isles. As these judicial decisions were made, they in turn became part of the common law. The common law in contemporary Canadian society consists of all previous judicial decisions by Canadian and British courts, as they are recorded in the case reports of these nations. The common law system is distinguished from the civil law system by its basis in precedent rather than legislative enactment. The civil law system originated in ancient Roman law, developed on the European continent, and was imported into Quebec by the French. It is based on a single, comprehensive code, enacted by the legislature.

The law of precedent, or *stare decisis*, is a self-imposed judicial rule that "like cases be decided alike." As Gordon Post explains, the law of precedent is essentially a formalization of the common sense use of past experience as a guide to present conduct. The value of judicial adherence to *stare decisis* is two-fold. First, continuity and certainty in the law is a prerequisite of civilized human activity. If there is no reasonable guarantee that what is valid law today will still be valid law tomorrow, personal,

† Morton, F.L., *Law, Politics and the Judicial Process in Canada* (Calgary: University of Calgary Press, 1984), 185–89. Reprinted by permission of F.L. Morton, Department of Political Science, University of Calgary.

economic, and political intercourse would grind to a halt. In each of these spheres of human activity, present-day decisions and activities are predicated on expectations about the future. Ensuring a high degree of predictability and continuity between the present and the future is one of the primary purposes of a political regime. As the institutions charged with interpreting and adapting the laws over time, the courts are responsible for maintaining continuity and certainty. As Dicey said, "A law which was not certain would in reality be no law at all." Adherence to the rule of precedent — "deciding like cases alike" — is the mechanism that provides this certainty.

The rule of precedent also contributes to guaranteeing the "rule of law, not of men." One of the ideals of the Western tradition's conception of justice is that the laws be applied equally and impartially to all persons. This ideal precludes any *ad hoc* application of the laws, and demands instead that laws be applied uniformly, or that any deviation from the rule be justified on principle — that is, by another rule. The idiosyncrasies or personal preferences of a judge are not permissible grounds for judicial decisions. This would re-introduce the "rule of men" rather than the "rule of law." By minimizing the discretion or freedom of individual judges, *stare decisis* preserves the "rule of law."

It should be emphasized that *stare decisis* minimizes but does not eliminate the element of judicial discretion or creativity. While legal reasoning presents itself as a deductive process, the reality is a more subtle blend of both inductive and deductive reasoning. Legal reasoning is accurately described as "reasoning by example."[1] The judges are essentially asking, "Whether the present case resembles the plain case 'sufficiently' and in the 'relevant' aspects."[2] In determining what is "sufficient" and what is "relevant," the judge must ultimately make certain choices. Because of this element of choice, a judge is responsible for striking the balance between continuity and innovation. The central thrust of the theory of legal realism has been to emphasize this element of choice and judicial discretion, and the ensuing responsibility of the judge for his choice.

Weiler's analysis of the Supreme Court's responsibility for the development of tort law is based on this legal realist perspective. Weiler argues that judges can no longer claim that precedent "dictates" nonsensical or patently unfair legal conclusions. Judges must be critical in their use of precedent, and go beyond the surface "rule" to discover the animating "principle." The proper function of the common law judge, according to Weiler, is to derive specific rules from more general principles, as the situation demands. Since situations change, rules must change also. While the "cattle trespass" exemption to normal tort law responsibility may have been appropriate to the rural, agricultural society of eighteenth century England, it had become a dangerous anachronism in twentieth century

Canada. Similarly in *Boucher v. The King*, the Court was faced with a conflict between the definition of "seditious libel" developed in nineteenth century, homogeneous, protestant Britain, and the norms of freedom of religion and speech in twentieth century, pluralistic Canada. Appeal court judges have a duty, says Weiler, to adapt the common law to the changing needs and circumstances of contemporary society.

Strict adherence to *stare decisis* is yet another aspect of the "adjudication of disputes" function of courts that poses problems for judicial policy-making. Refusal to disavow or change past decisions plays no constructive role in a policy-making institution, as the examples of legislative and executive practice make clear. While certainty and continuity are legal virtues, adaptability and innovation are more important in the policy-making process. The case for abandoning a strict adherence to precedent is especially strong in constitutional law. Not only is policy-impact more probable, but constitutional law lacks the flexibility of common law and statutes. If the courts make a "mistake" in the latter areas, it can be corrected by remedial legislation. But if the Supreme Court makes a constitutional decision with undesirable policy consequences, the only direct way to correct the damage is through formal constitutional amendment, an extremely cumbersome and difficult process.[3] Predictably, the U.S. Supreme Court was the first court of appeal in a common law nation to abandon *stare decisis* as an absolute requirement. The demotion of *stare decisis* from a binding rule to a guiding principle is another index of a court's evolution toward a greater policy-making role.

The recent advent of judicial realism in Canadian jurisprudence has brought with it a decline in the status of the rule of *stare decisis*. Long after the American Supreme Court had abandoned absolute adherence to precedent, the Canadian Supreme Court continued to perceive itself as bound to adhere not only to its own previous decisions but those of the British House of Lords as well. This latter restriction is attributable to the role of the Judicial Committee of the Privy Council as Canada's final court of appeal until 1949. Ten years after the abolition of that role, the Supreme Court declared its independence from British precedents as well. In 1966 the British House of Lords officially declared that, when appropriate, it would no longer follow its own prior decisions. However, the Supreme Court of Canada continued to profess strict adherence to its prior decision until the 1970's. Under the leadership of Bora Laskin, the Canadian Supreme Court began to move in the same direction. In 1972, before his appointment as chief justice, Laskin had written that *stare decisis* was "no longer an article of faith in the Supreme Court of Canada, but it still remains a cogent principle."[4] Speaking as the new Chief Justice at the Centennial Symposium of the Supreme Court in 1975, Laskin repeated that *stare decisis* was no longer "an inexorable rule," but rather, simply an important element of the judicial process, a necessary consideration which should give pause to any but the most sober conclusion that a previous decision or line of authority is wrong and ought to be changed.[5]

Practising what he preached, Laskin led the Supreme Court to overturn three precedents during the next three years, including an old Privy Council decision dealing with the federal division of powers.[6] The abandoning of strict adherence to *stare decisis* is yet another indicator of the Supreme Court's institutional evolution toward more of a policy-making court.

The second principal source of law is legislative statutes. Beginning in the nineteenth century, legislatures in Great Britain, Canada, and the United States began to codify large portions of the common law. In large part this was a democratic reaction against the perceived elitism of the "judge-made" character of the common law. By reducing the confusing maze of common law precedent to clearly worded, legislative statutes, it was thought that the law would be made easier for "the people" to understand, and that the democratic authority of "government by consent" would be enhanced.

In 1892 the Canadian Parliament abolished all criminal offenses at common law, and replaced them with a comprehensive statute, the *Criminal Code*. In so doing, Parliament hoped to reap the alleged advantages of codification mentioned above, including restricting judicial discretion in the criminal law. Since crimes were now clearly and authoritatively defined, judges would simply apply the law as Parliament had written it. It would no longer be necessary to refer to a vast and confusing system of precedent to apply the criminal law, or so it was hoped.

In fact, precedent and *stare decisis* quickly found their way back into the criminal law. Perhaps, as Parker has suggested, it was (and still is) impossible for judges and lawyers trained in the common law tradition to properly construe a code of law.[7] More likely the common law "habit" simply compounds a more serious problem — the ultimate ambiguity of statutory terminology itself. Try as they might, legislators will never be able to draft statutes that anticipate and encompass all possible future situations. This is due in part to the inherent tension between the generality of words and the specificity of reality, and in part to human ignorance of the future. As new situations inevitably arise, the applicability of the original wording of statutes becomes increasingly questionable.

. . . .

The preceding argument notwithstanding judicial discretion in interpreting statutes, including the *Criminal Code*, is much more circumscribed than in interpreting the common law. As Weiler says, judges can develop new torts, but not new crimes, and there are sound reasons for preferring this arrangement. As issues of tort law are rarely the subject of partisan political controversy, an innovative court cannot be accused of usurping the legislative function. The controversies over capital punishment and abortion show that the same is not true of the criminal law. In the area of tort law, judicial expertise is very high, relative to other policy-making institutions. Finally, judicial initiatives in substantive criminal law would pose the threat of punishing innocent persons. No comparable problem of "due process" arises in tort law.

While codification and statutes clearly circumscribe the limits of judicial law-making, there is still the element of judicial "choice" and its accompanying responsibility. This is especially true of the *Criminal Code*, which authorizes the continued use of common law defenses such as *mens rea*. Once again, Weiler argues that judges should go beyond superficial resemblances of wording of facts and grasp the principles that animate this area of law. The examples used appear to be contradictory decisions concerning the availability of the *mens rea* defense. Weiler suggests that these can be reconciled by reference to the underlying competition between the "crime control" and "due process" principles of criminal law. Different judges could reasonably reach different conclusions in these two cases. The essential point from Weiler's perspective is not so much what a judge decides, but how he decides the case. A final appellate court should explicitly ground its decision in the underlying principles, and explain why the particular circumstances of this case dictated favouring one over the other. Failure to do so is a failure to live up to the standards of judicial craftsmanship that can reasonably be expected from a final appellate court in an age of legal realism.

Endnotes

1. Edward H. Levi, *An Introduction to Legal Reasoning* (Chicago: University of Chicago Press, 1949), 1.

2. H.L.A. Hart, *The Concept of Law* (Oxford: Oxford University Press, 1961), 124.

3. This is not true of judicial decisions based on sections 2 and 7 through 15 of the *Charter of Rights*, which are subject to the section 33 "legislative override" provision.

4. "The Institutional Character of the Judge" (1972), 7 *Israel Law Review* 341. Partially reprinted in *Reading* 12.2.

5. Reprinted in *Reading* 3.1.

6. *R. v. Paquette*, [1977] 2 S.C.R. 189; *McNamara Const. Western Ltd. v. The Queen*, [1977] 2 S.C.R. 654; and *Reference re Agricultural Products Marketing Act*, [1978] 2 S.C.R. 1198.

7. Graham Parker, *An Introduction to Criminal Law*, 2nd ed. (Toronto: Methuen, 1983), 43.

The Problem of Legal Method[†]
C. Smart

By drawing on other disciplines we are now asking if not only the practice of law silences women's aspirations and needs, and conversely privileges those of men, but whether the very construction not only of the legal discourse, but representations of the discourse in the academy (the construction of our understanding and knowledge of law), is the product of patriarchal relations at the root of our society. (Bottomley 1987: 12)

ANNE Bottomley is here raising the question of whether the very core of law — the means by which law is differentiated from other forms of knowledge — is gendered. We are now familiar with other forms of feminist criticism — for example the criticism of law for excluding women (Sachs and Wilson 1978), or criticism of the content of legislation (Atkins and Wilson 1978), or the criticism of the specific practices of law (Adler 1987). It is a fairly recent innovation for feminists to start to criticize the very tools of legal method which have been presumed to be neutral.

As Bottomley suggests, this form of critique is not new in other disciplines. Sociology, for example, has long been reflexive about its methodology and methods and there is a large feminist literature available in this field. As early as 1974 Dorothy Smith, in an article of major importance, argued that it was not sufficient to add women to the subject matter of the social sciences without radically altering the perspective and method of these disciplines. In law this critique has taken longer to materialize. This is undoubtedly linked to the status of law and its claims to Truth. Sociology's claim to truth has always been shaky, not so law's. But in all areas of the academe radical (i.e., at root) dissent from the dominant paradigm of knowledge production causes problems for the dissenter. As Lahey (1985) has argued, to follow radically different ways of thinking can amount to professional suicide.

In the discipline of law there is almost a double suicide involved. Not only does the dissenter challenge academic standards, but also the standards of law as a profession. Inasmuch as law has a direct practical application, the dissenter in law is more subversive than in a discipline like sociology. The former challenges the standing of judges, barristers, and solicitors as well as academic law-

yers. Little wonder then that feminism has such a hard time taking root in law.

Mary Jane Mossman (1986) has suggested that law (at least legal method) is probably impervious to the feminist challenge. It is perhaps worth considering her view in some detail. In her article "Feminism and Legal Method: The Difference It Makes" Mossman identifies three main elements to traditional legal method. These are boundary definition, defining "relevance," and case analysis. The first element, boundary definition, is the process whereby certain matters are identified as outside the realm of law. Hence some issues may be identified as political or moral. It is of course important to recognize that these boundaries may move and that they are little more than a convenience. For example in the UK prostitution is defined as a moral issue, not a matter for law. However, soliciting for the purposes of prostitution which, by definition, causes a nuisance, is a legal matter. The point that Mossman makes however, is that boundary definitions are important not as a consequence of where the boundaries are drawn, but as a consequence of the neutrality that it confers on the law. So when lawyers and judges maintain that it is the job of the legally-trained mind to interpret the law, and not to pass judgement on issues outside the law, they gain credibility. They assert a terrain within which legal method is entirely appropriate, but they also appear to keep out of subjective areas like moral evaluations, or political bias.

The second element of method is the defining of relevance. So, for example, the student of law learns that it is relevant in cases of rape to know the "victim's" sexual history. If she has had a sexual relationship with the accused this must be made known, and even where it is not with the accused it may be deemed relevant. The sexual history of the accused is, of course, never relevant. In learning this the student of law learns how to defend a rape case successfully and he or she also learns another technique of oppressing women. Yet law is impervious to this critique because the formulation of the rules guiding rape cases are shrouded in the mists of time — and by the myths of neutrality. The student who argues that this should not be relevant will never make a "good" lawyer.

The third element is case analysis. This is where the legally-trained mind searches out cases which may constitute the precedent of a judicial decision. Some cases become "good" law, i.e., should be followed, others mysteriously become "bad" law and are ignored. But even among cases that lawyers call "good" law there is a vast

† Smart, Carol, "The Problem of Legal Method" in *Feminism and the Power of Law* (London: Routledge, 1989), pp. 20–25. Reprinted by permission of Routledge, International Thomson Publishing Services Ltd., Hampshire, U.K.

choice. This raises the question of how they know which ones are relevant. Sumner (1979) has argued that judges merely make their decisions and select the cases accordingly. In other words the cases are decided in a *post hoc* fashion; logic does not inexorably lead the judge to the *right* decision. This, of course, is heresy to the legal positivists, yet the observation that cases heard on appeal can overturn previous decisions — several times — should be enough to produce scepticism about the infallibility of the case analysis method.

In all of these areas, Mossman argues that it is possible for law to evade the feminist challenge, indeed to identify it is irrelevant nonsense. Women lawyers are faced with the choice of being good feminists and bad lawyers, or the converse. However, whilst accepting the strength of Mossman and Lahey's argument, it may be that they both take law too seriously. Legal method can be deconstructed, and it is well known that law in law schools is quite different to the practices of lawyers "outside." It is important to recognize the power that accrues to law through its claim to truth, but law is both more and less than this in practice. It is more than this because the focus on legal method is narrowly "judge-oriented" and a lot of law in practice never gets near a judge; it is less than this because although law makes a claim to truth, many lawyers do not, and they too deflate this view of law in their daily practice. The extension of law's domain to which I referred above is not necessarily regarded by everyone as legitimate. It is, for example, fairly common to hear the utterance that more law simply means more money lining the pockets of lawyers. Such utterances indicate that not everyone accepts law's image of itself, nor welcomes the extension of legal terrain; they may even mark the beginnings of a resistance to the power of law.

I would like to return to the point about the focus on legal method being narrowly judge-oriented. In her book *Women's Law* (1987), Stang Dahl describes in detail how the new discipline of Women's Law began in the Law School of the University of Oslo, and what its orientation is. I cannot do justice to her pioneering work here, but I wish to highlight some of the important points she makes about challenging traditional law and legal method (or doctrine as she calls it). Stang Dahl accepts the idea that law should retain its own method, she states,

> Legal doctrine, i.e., the interpretation of law according to prescribed methodology, should remain the core area of legal science because it is there that lawyers have their own tools and distinct craft. (Stang Dahl 1987: 32)

This is surprising given the drift of most feminist work in North America and the UK. However, it becomes clear that Stang Dahl does not include in her idea of doctrine all the elements that Mossman includes. So, for example,

she points out how Women's Law challenges the usual direction of law by encouraging "the use of legal sources 'from below'." By this she means that greater reliance should be placed on custom and public opinion of what law ought to be. This, she argues, allows empirical evidence about women's lives greater influence on the law. So law would become more responsive to the "real" rather than its own internal imperatives. In this way she envisages law and the social sciences coming closer together and a greater role for the women's movement in influencing law.

Stang Dahl's next challenge to traditional law is to emphasize government administration rather than formal law. She argues that legislation (and also the major legal cases of the day) rarely have anything to do with women. In fact she goes so far as to say that even sex discrimination legislation has little to do with women. She argues (rightly in my view),

> That a law which is gender-specific in its formulation need not, however, mean that it is significant for women's position in law or society. The same applies to the directives found in sex discrimination legislation. Even though its express objective gives it an automatic relevance to women's law, and even though the act's enforcement measures are many and comprehensive, this in itself is not tantamount to the law's consequences having special significance for women's lives and rights, either generally or in decisions in individual cases. (Stang Dahl 1987: 29)

In her view the "law" that affects women's lives is more likely to be the administration of welfare benefits, the operation of the private law of maintenance, and the formulation of guidelines and decision-making at the level of bureaucratic operation. Hence she proposes simply to demote the importance of formal law in feminist work. But she does not suggest that this be done by *fiat*; she argues that it is a development which is already occurring within law. High status may still be in the realms of formal law, but the routine and necessary work is elsewhere. This point, in turn, is linked to the point about the narrowness of legal method — and therefore feminist concentration on this method. Stang Dahl argues that legal reasoning which applies abstract norms to the facts of an individual case is only relevant where a judge is the addressee. Hence this method is judge-dominated because, in order to persuade a judge of a particular point, it is necessary to reason in this rigidly legal way. However, such law has little relevance to the lives of women, so women's law in Oslo addresses itself to a different audience. Stang Dahl does not promote this as a way of overcoming law's hegemony, however, I think she says more than she realizes here. Whilst it is true that all law is in some way in the shadow of the judges, it is perhaps important to recognize how little law in practice is ever subjected to legal method. The strategy that seems to come from Stang Dahl's work is therefore not to challenge legal method so much as to ignore it and to focus on law in practice. If Mossman is correct that legal method is impervious to feminist critique then Stang Dahl's option seems more sensible than continuing to push fruitlessly against such an immovable object.

This strategy does not overcome all the problems identified in this chapter of course. Yet it does overcome the problem of colluding with law's overinflated view of itself. Part of the power that law can exercise resides in the authority we accord it. By stressing how powerless feminism is in the face of law and legal method, we simply add to its power. The strategy available to Stang Dahl in Oslo is not, of course, universally available. There are no law schools in the UK that would contemplate such a radical move as to introduce Women's Law as part of a compulsory syllabus. Yet at least this provides a useful model which indicates how the power of formal law can be decentred. But feminism itself as a source of power and resistance even where we do not have the means radically to change law schools and law itself. Weedon has argued that

> even where feminist discourses lack the social power to realize their versions of knowledge in institutional practices, they can offer discursive space for which the individual can resist dominant subject positions. (Weedon 1987: 110–11)

It is therefore important for feminism to sustain its challenge to the power of law to define women in law's terms. Feminism has the power to challenge subjectivity and to alter women's consciousness. It also has the means to expose how law operates in all its most detailed mechanisms. In doing this it can increase the resistance to law and may effect a shift in power. Whilst it is important that feminism should recognize the power that law can exercise, it is axiomatic that feminists do not regard themselves as powerless.

Reading the Law[†]
P. Goodrich

INSTITUTIONAL SOURCES OF LAW

The assumptions that lawyers make as to the inevitability, the validity and the moral benefit of legal regulation are crucial to their practice and to the maintenance of legal rules, to the ideology of law within the industrialized western nations. Such assumptions as to the conceptual unit of law are, however, increasingly infrequently utilized as explicit sources of law, reference to moral, political and economic factors generally being seen as a function of interpretation and argumentation — of implicit or tacit sources of law — rather than of formally designated legal authority. At the same time as stressing the practical importance of the ideational source of law, we would also rapidly point out that the abstract and external, ideational source of law is neither the most obvious nor the most frequently stated meaning of source of law in contemporary legal cultures. The preferred view is currently one which stresses the institutional sources of law rather than directly or consciously elaborating the myth of an origin or essence of law or indeed the dogmatic status of legal science or legal reason as sources of law. The current legal wisdom views law as a tradition and as a process or practice of regulation. Rather than defining law, legal doctrine is now more content to see it as a series of traditionally established tests and similarly established techniques for the interpretation of those texts: 'laws have no necessary unity of content, form or function outside of that derived from the legislative processes and legal apparatuses'. The institutional source of law is here seen to be the established practice of the legal institution and of its officials — law is taken to be what lawyers 'recognize' as law. In complex modern legal orders the material sources of law are various and far from simple; the manner of their recognition is correspondingly a complex 'professional' task, although legal doctrine does not attempt to formulate any explicit rule for verifying valid law. The rule of recognition is rather 'manifest in the general practice on the part of officials...of identifying rules...its existence is *shown* in the way in which particular rules are identified, either by courts or other officials...the rule of recognition of a legal system is like the scoring rule of game'. While this defi-

---

† Goodrich, Peter, *Reading the Law: A Critical Introduction to Legal Method and Techniques* (Oxford: Basil Blackwell, 1986), 13–20. Reprinted by permission of Basil Blackwell Ltd., Oxford, U.K.

nition of the sources of law suffers from numerous defects not the least being that it is a circular or tautological definition which uncritically allows lawyers to define the law, it does carry a useful element of realism with it. Law is defined as the social fact of law, as a long-standing institutional practice subject to the internal discipline and rules of the institution itself. Within the legal institution the material sources of law are to be discovered in a hierarchically organized series of institutional functions or roles; provided that the given rule is not in conflict with some other, hierarchically superior, source of law, it will be deemed valid law.

The concept of recognition refers the student of law or other reader of legal texts to what are somewhat ambiguously termed the 'institutional' or legal sources of law within the specific legal tradition being studied. A classic formulation of this most basic doctrinal meaning of recognition can be taken from the writings of the Austrian jurist Hans Kelsen (1957): 'positive law is an order by which human conduct is regulated in a specific way. The regulation is accomplished by provisions which set forth how men ought to act. Such provisions are called norms and either come from custom, as do the norms of the common law, or are enacted by conscious acts of certain organs aiming to create law, as a legislature acting in its law-making capacity.' Clearly this view of law as defined by its source is too general to be of specific or substantive use: different institutions and different procedures will be found to designate the hierarchy of legal sources of law within different legal orders. The general point made by Kelsen, however, remains valid; it is by examining where the law or rule comes from — its institutional source — that law is recognized as valid within the official community of legal doctrine in a fashion broadly comparable to that whereby the institution of language determines the manner of recognition of utterances as being in a familiar or foreign tongue.

The most basic institutional meaning of source of law refers to the institutional behaviour and practice most generally accepted and adopted by the officials of the legal system examined. Institution is here most generally taken to refer to conventions or to doctrinally agreed roles, as for example in the (unwritten) British constitution and the sources of law within that constitution. The traditional view is one which is expressed by A.V. Dicey in his study of the law of the constitution (Dicey, 1885) in terms of institutionally arranged sources of law. The supreme source of law, then as now, is found in the duly expressed utterances of the institution 'Queen in Parliament', composed of the monarch, House of Lords and the House of Commons acting in agreement. This triumvirate was the supreme source of law within the United Kingdom at the time in which Dicey was writing, supremacy meaning that the enactments of this body could not be overturned by any court of law nor by any other legislative institution within the United Kingdom.

. . . .

The mode of recognition of a valid source of law within the United Kingdom varies according to the hierarchical status of that source: the higher the source in the hierarchy, the more literal and internal the recognition of it is likely to be. Thus in the classic case of *Edinburgh and Dalkeith Railway v. Wauchope*, [1842] 8 Cl & F 710, where it was pronounced by Lord Campbell — in an extremely legalistic vein — that 'all the Court of Justice can do is look to the Parliamentary roll: if from that it should appear that a bill has passed both Houses and received the Royal assent, no court of Justice can inquire into the mode in which it was introduced into Parliament, nor into what was done previous to its introduction, or what passed in Parliament during its progress in its various stages through both Houses.' Consequently the plaintiffs in the case in question, adversely affected by a duly enacted Private Bill, could not resist its adverse effects upon their interests on the grounds that they had received no notification of the Bill. The stated position of the courts in relation to legislation or written law is one of straightforward obedience and application save only in circumstances where there are formal irregularities in the enactment, as in *Stockdale v. Hansard*, [1839] 9 Ad & E 9, a case concerning Parliamentary privilege in which the court conclusively rejected the argument that one branch of the 'Queen in Parliament', the House of Commons alone, could by itself change the law: 'nothing is clearer than that the House does not have that power, and cannot by its own resolutions acquire it.'

As we shall have occasion to observe later, the courts of the common law have traditionally approached legislation and written instruments more generally with something approximating mystical awe. While that attitude has changed somewhat over the past decades and certainly has not often extended to European legislation, it is still useful to distinguish, on formal grounds, the approach to the supreme source of law and that towards secondary or customary sources. The principal institutional distinction to be made is that between legislation (written) and common (unwritten) law. Legislation, both primary and secondary, forms the institutional pinnacle of the hierarchy of sources and, in doctrinal accounts, these are followed by the courts themselves as institutional sources of law predicated upon the concept of a system of precedent. The decision of a higher court (*ratio decidendi*) binds a lower court and, as a general rule, the most recent decision or pronouncement of a court will be binding evidence of a common-law rule for all courts of equal or lower status.

Without at this stage entering too great a degree of detail with respect to the specific institutional sources and methods of legal recognition, we would wish to make certain brief critical observations as to the accuracy of the doctrinal definition of institutional legal source. This concept of an institutional source utilized in legal doctrinal writings is far more a justification for the procedures of law-application than it is an accurate description of legal methods of dispute-settlement or procedures of social control. The very notion of a hierarchy or indeed grammar of legal sources perpetuates, in a secular form, the essentially natural-law conception of the unity and the reason of legal order. It is, in short, an article of faith as much as it is a descriptive account of the workings of the courts. Certainly we may admit that systems of legal control in modern societies tend to adopt very strict criteria or rules governing the formal order of deference within the institution. It is a part of what Foucault (1977, p. 181) terms the 'order of discourse' within disciplinary social formations strictly to organize, enclose and delimit both the topics of speech and who may speak within each given institution of control. An 'analytical space' is organized within which roles and functions are partitioned and in more general terms highly technical rules operate to legitimate and authorize the speakers and discourses of the law. There are, in brief, specifiable times and places and occasions of legal speech, there are ritual affirmations of what is spoken, there are procedures of social and communicational authorization and of sanction with respect to who may speak and what they may say. The legal institution and the rules governing sources of law are best understood not as a unique set of discursive procedures but as one institutional discourse — albeit a formal, highly symbolic and political significance — within a society of diverse institutions and discourses of control. Analytically, it can be pointed out that law is simply one stage in a continuum of disciplinary and normalizing discourses which might very loosely be said to run from educational discourses, the rules of grammar, etiquette and the social, political and moral aspects of collective existence, through to the more explicitly coercive languages of psychiatry, therapy, law and religion. Finally, it should never be forgotten that beyond the discourses of normality and of law are the various arms of State coercion and terror; where law is ineffective or consent to legal order is lacking, then the discourse of order is simply and swiftly replaced by the politics of violence, of confinement, physical subjection and at its most extreme, death at the hands of the military and martial law.

What is peculiar to the legal institution is not that it has rules of office, of ritual procedures, of doctrine and heresy, as well as specific methods of interpretation and application of its rules, but rather that such a tremendous degree of social affirmation is lavished upon those rules and procedures. The primary modes of recognition of valid legal rules have more to do with the symbols of administration and media power that surround the institutional sources of law than they have to do with either the formal procedures or substantive content relating to sources of law (Mathieson, 1981). Certainly there are strong arguments from very diverse theoretical positions which would forcefully claim that

legal administrative power — in both its formal and its substantive aspects — is much less regulated and far more open to manipulation, negotiation and technique generally, interpretation and abuse, than is admitted by legal doctrine. The logic behind this claim can be subdivided along the lines of the distinction already outlined between ideational and institutional sources of law.

With regard to the ideational source of law — with regard, that is, to legal doctrine, the legal profession's belief in the logical and unified character of legal regulation — the argument is a simple one. There is no rational ground for supposing either that legal order is ultimately derivable from a concept of God or that the existent western legal orders in their actual practice come anywhere close to approximating a divine or natural order incarnate. While there are numerous possible arguments for ascribing divine, natural or rational status to legal regulation, these arguments have nothing whatsoever to do with the sources of law in their material functioning or official validity: beliefs as to the metaphysical import of human existence are characteristic ingredients of faith, philosophy and social and political ideologies; they should not be mistaken for substantive sources of law of either an ideational or institutional kind. The reason for this is not in the end so much to do with arguments as to divinity, metaphysics or the distinction between nature and culture as it is to do with the practical operation of legal orders and the methods necessary for accurately describing them.

In terms of institutional sources, we have already loosely indicated that the legal institution is to be seen as part of a continuum of disciplinary institutions within contemporary western social orders. It would be wrong in such circumstances to view the legal system as being a privileged or unique institution: to a large degree it shares its language, methods of self-regulation and techniques of discipline and decision-making with other branches of the State machinery of control. For that reason alone it would seem apposite to direct a number of relatively simple questions at the legal self-description of the rule of law and to take seriously the available evidence on the functioning of legal rules (Henry, 1984, pp. 1–31). Of the more important areas of discussion, areas we shall return to subsequently, the following are among the more interesting and illuminating. First, the pervasive yet little acknowledged role of discretion within decision-making processes throughout the legal order, and not simply within the process of explicit adjudication. The issue is one which we would term the politics of interpretation: the latitude technically available in virtually all areas of legal discourse allowing for judicial choice in the application of legal norms. There is, we shall suggest, an element of politics in virtually all decision-making procedures in both the legal and other arms of the administration, yet it is only in the realm of legal doctrine as to the sources of law that the existence of such discretion is routinely and vigorously denied. To acknowledge the element of discretion in rule-usage of any kind is to take up a position on the margins of legal doctrinal writing, the official view being a restrictive one, expressed, for example, by Viscount Simmonds in the case of *Scruttons Ltd. v. Midland Silicones*, [1962] AC 446:

> to me heterodoxy, or as some might say, heresy, is not the more attractive because it is dignified by the name of reform. Nor will I easily be led by an undiscerning zeal for some abstract kind of justice to ignore our first duty, which is to administer justice according to law, the law which is established for us by Act of Parliament or the binding authority of precedent.... If the principle of '*just quaesitum tertio*' [third party rights] is to be introduced into our law, it must be done by Parliament. (467–8)

Against such a view, a number of theoretical and substantive arguments can be put forward to emphasize the degrees of choice or to pose discretion as a source of law. In summary form, these would include the generality of legal language and the pervasive use of discretionary categories such as those of 'reasonableness', 'fairness', 'consideration of all the circumstances' and like phrases, both in legislative drafting and in the formulation of common-law rules. To issues of the ambiguity of rules, of competition and conflict between rules within a complex and vast system of substantive law, it should be added that in the end the court makes a decision on the specific case before it. Not only does this mean that the law has always to be interpreted and applied to the particular fact-situation before the court, but it allows the court to alter, vary or ignore the legal rule according to what it sees as the merits of the case. In the view of one important American school of potentially radical legal thought, rules are only ever as good as their application: the law is 'what officials do about disputes' (Llewellyn, 1950).

In looking at what officials do about disputes, it is necessary to take into account a vast array of political, economic, social, ethnic and psychological factors relevant to decision-making, and not simply the officially designated or 'recognized' sources of law. It would be extremely naive or ill-intentioned to suppose that only legal factors determine legal outcomes, a point well refuted by sociological studies of courtroom practice (Carlen, 1976; McBarnet, 1981). The contemporary sociological view of legal sources pays greater attention to informal and discretionary factors than it does to officially designated written and unwritten sources of law. An adequate account of legal decision-making processes should thus take into consideration the entire process of social regulation, including also that preponderant number of disputes that never come to court. First, there is the process of selection of cases to be tried, the question of what happens before the trial. The vast majority of disputed social issues, including both private — and public-law conflicts, never come to court. Mechanisms of informal justice (Henry, 1984), of self-regulation and of social dominance — whether politically, economically or sexually based — more generally prevent the majority of conflicts becoming legal conflicts before the courts. Factors such as lack of knowledge and lack of money, as well as the availability of alternative remedies, will frequently resolve private disputes, while bureaucratic and official practices will frequently be directed towards preventing public and penal issues coming before the courts. When such issues do arise in court, the vast majority of defendants in criminal cases plead guilty and overall, where cases are disputed, informal rules concerning courtroom ritual, patterns of acceptable behaviour, modes of dress and modes of speech are likely to be as important to the outcome of the trial as are any formal legal sources. In the courts of first instance the predominant issue is that of establishing credibility with regard to facts, of substantiating a version of what happened, and is seldom a question of disputes as to the meaning or application of formal rules.

In briefly adverting to factors which can be taken to challenge the legal professional account of law and of legal sources, we are concerned to propose a wider definition of law, legal sources and legal texts. Such 'critical' issues will form a central theme in this study and will be analysed in depth in elaborating a theory of reading the law. For the present purpose of analysing the concept of source of law we would simply conclude that any remotely critical account of the legal institution should analyse it both in terms of itself-definition and also in terms of its more general social and political roles. The legal institution forms one branch of the political administration of the modern State. As one element within a complex bureaucracy it would be surprising if it did not have ambitions, goals, values and purposes closely allied to those of government itself. Its ideology is in that sense political and its functions and performances are political and social as well as being distinctively legal. Such a point is not of great originality but it is frequently forgotten or repressed: the law may be defined at its broadest as the characteristic discourse and practice of the legal institution. These discourses and practices should not be read simply in the formal terms of the specifically legal but also as social discourse, as part of a continuing political and administrative dialogue as to the terms and conditions of social life. Legal discourse is in this sense simply one of many competing normative disciplinary discourses, discourses of morality, religion and social custom to which it is closely related and from which it draws many if not all of its justificatory arguments. It is a discourse which should ideally be read in terms of control — of dominance and subordination — and of social power-relations portrayed and addressed to a far more general audience than that of law-breakers and wrong-doers alone (Goodrich, 1986, ch. 7). Finally, it is a discourse that combines both speech and action and consequently changes dramatically over time. It is a discourse which should be read as inherently his-torical and political in that it is a rhetoric aligned to his-torical and social change and it is in that context and at that level of social dialogue that we attempt in this word to read it.

R. v. Chase[†]

APPEAL by the accused from his conviction and sen-tence on a charge of sexual assault contrary to s. 246.1 of the *Criminal Code*.

The judgment of the court was delivered by

ANGERS J.A.: — This is an appeal from a conviction by a judge of the provincial court for an offence of sex-ual assault contrary to s. 246.1(1)(a) of the *Criminal Code* and the sentence of eight months' imprisonment imposed therefor.

The facts are not in dispute. On October 22, 1983, the appellant went to the home of a neighbour. A 15-year-old girl and her 11-year-old brother were downstairs playing pool while their 83-year-old grandfather was upstairs sleeping. The parents were absent. The appellant struggled with the girl and grabbed her by the arms, the shoulders and the breasts. As she fought back, the appellant said: "Come on dear, don't hit me, I know you want it". At one point she said: "he tried to grab for my private, but he didn't succeed because my hands were too fast". Eventu-ally the girl and her brother made a telephone call to a neighbour and the appellant left. The episode lasted a little more than half an hour.

· · · ·

The appellant's third ground of appeal is that there was no evidence to support a conviction for the offence of sexual assault but only of common assault. That argu-ment turns on the meaning of the words "sexual assault" as contained in 246.1(1) which reads:

> **246.1**(1) Every one who commits a sexual assault is guilty of
> (a) an indictable offence and is liable to impris-onment for ten years; or
> (b) an offence punishable on summary conviction.

The words "sexual assault" are not defined in the *Criminal Code*, but the word "assault" is defined in s. 244 as follows:

> **244.**(1) A person commits an assault when
> (a) without the consent of another person, he applies force intentionally to that other per-son, directly or indirectly;

· · · ·

> (2) This section applies to all forms of as-sault, including sexual assault, sexual assault with a weapon, threats to a third party or causing bod-ily harm and aggravated sexual assault.

· · · ·

Webster's New Collegiate Dictionary defines "sex-ual" as:

1. of, relating to, or associated with sex of the sexes and
2. having or involving sex;

The Oxford English Dictionary defines the word:

1. of or pertaining to sex or the attribute of being male or female; existing or predicated with regard to sex;
2. pertaining to sex as concerned in generation or in the processes connected with this;
3. of or pertaining to the organs of sex;
4. characteristic of or peculiar to the one sex or the other, secondary sexual characteristics. Those marks of sex (e.g., the beard in man, the distinctive plumage in birds) which are not immediately connected with the repro-ductive structure.

[†]   *R. v. Chase* (1984), 13 C.C.C. (3d) 187 (edited) (N.B. C.A.).

On the other hand, "sex" is defined in Webster's as:

the sum of the structural, functional, and behavioural characteristics of living beings that subserve reproduction by two interacting parents that distinguish males and females.

The Oxford Dictionary defines the word thus:

the sum of those differences in the structure and function of the reproductive organs on the ground of which beings are distinguished as male and female, and of the other physiological differences consequent on these; the class of phenomena with which these differences are concerned.

Both dictionaries refer to the sexual organs or genitalia as the object of those definitions.

The addition of the word "sexual" to the term assault, in my opinion, suggests that it is now necessary to determine to which part of the body the unlawful force was applied. Based on the meaning of sexual, the concept of a sexual assault as being an intentional and forced contact with the sexual organs or genitalia of another person with that person's consent is rather easily understood. So would, for that matter, the forced and intentional contact of one's sexual organs with any part of another person. The problem in this case is that the contact was not with the sexual organs of the victim but to the mammary gland, a secondary sexual characteristic.

The offensiveness to manners or morals was an appropriate test in indecent assault offences but it cannot be used here without giving a different meaning to the words used by the legislators. On the other hand, to include as sexual an assault to the parts of a person's body considered as having secondary sexual characteristics may lead to absurd results if one considers a man's beard. Nor am I prepared to include those parts of the human body considered erogenous zones lest a person be liable to conviction for stealing a goodnight kiss. In any event, to involve secondary sexual characteristics or erogenous zones or, for that matter, the sexual gratification intent of the accused might well lead the court into the domain of sexology or at least require it to examine the sexual behaviour of the human species. In my view, this was not the intent of the legislation. It seems to me that the word "sexual" as used in the section ought to be given its natural meaning as limited to the sexual organs or genitalia. Section 246.6, which uses such words as "sexual activity" and "sexual contact" reinforces this view.

. . . .

For the reasons that I have stated, I think there was no actual sexual assault in this case but rather a common assault. Therefore, by virtue of s. 613(3) of the *Code*, I would dismiss the appeal against conviction, and substitute a verdict of guilty of common assault.

. . . .

Appeal dismissed; conviction for assault substituted.

R. v. Alderton[†]

APPEAL by accused from his conviction and sentence on charges of break and enter and committing sexual assault and being masked with intent.

The judgment of the court was delivered orally by

MARTIN J.A.: — The appellant was charged...on an indictment containing two counts.

Count 1 charged the appellant with having...broken and entered an apartment and with having committed therein the indictable offence of sexual assault contrary to s. 306(1)(b) of the *Criminal Code*.

Count 2 charged that the appellant on the same date with intent to commit an indictable offence had his face masked with a pair of panty-hose.

The jury returned a verdict of guilty on both counts and following the appellant's conviction, he was sentenced to imprisonment for four years on count 1 and to six months consecutive on count 2. He now appeals against his conviction and, in the alternative, against the sentence imposed.

[†] *R. v. Alderton* (1985), 49 O.R. (2d) 257 (edited) (Ont. C.A.).

The material facts are these. Shortly before 4:00 a.m. on the morning of July 12th, the complainant was asleep alone in her apartment in Owen Sound when she was awakened by the sound of clicking from the door. She heard a footstep and then a man appeared in the doorway to the bedroom. She noticed that he was wearing jeans and a blue T-shirt with darker blue bands at the sleeve and neck. He was wearing a nylon-stocking mask over his head. The man moved towards the bed; the complainant noticed that he was wearing rubber gloves.

The man jumped on the bed, forced the complainant back into the pillows, and held her down with one hand covering her mouth and nose. She heard the sound of tape being pulled from a role and she panicked, struggled, got free and fled from her apartment to that of a neighbour. The police were summoned. The complainant notices that her attacker's breath had a very pronounced odour, rather like a smell of garlic.

. . . .

The second ground of appeal...was that there was no evidence upon which a jury could find that the appellant was guilty of a sexual assault as distinct from an assault. He relied upon the judgment of the New Brunswick Court of Appeal in *R. v. Chase* (1984), 13 C.C.C. (3d) 187, 40 C.R. (3d) 282, 55 N.B.R. (2d) 97; leave to appeal granted

October 1, 1984 (S.C.C.). In that case the New Brunswick Court of Appeal held that seizing the breast of a young girl accompanied by an implicit oral solicitation to have sexual intercourse did not constitute a sexual assault.

Section 246.1(1) of the *Code* provides that every one who commits a sexual assault is guilty of an indictable offence, or an offence punishable on summary conviction.

. . . .

We are, with the greatest deference, unable to accept the views of the court expressed in that case. Without in any way attempting to give a comprehensive definition of a "sexual assault" we are all satisfied that it *includes* an assault with the intention of having sexual intercourse with the victim without her consent, or an assault made upon a victim for the purpose of sexual gratification.

We are all of the view that in the circumstances of the present case, there was ample evidence upon which the jury could find that the appellant committed a sexual assault upon the complainant and, indeed, we think the evidence did not permit of any other conclusion.

. . . .

Accordingly, the appeal for conviction must be dismissed.

R. v. Taylor †

APPEAL by the Crown from the accused's acquittal on charges of assault, sexual assault, use of a weapon in a sexual assault and unlawful confinement.

The judgment of the court was delivered by

LAYCRAFT C.J.A.: — This is a Crown appeal of the acquittal of the respondent on six charges of various offences of assault, sexual assault, use of a weapon in a sexual attack and confinement of a 16-year-old girl. We are required to inquire into the nature of the new offence of sexual assault and to consider whether an act found to be indecent is, nevertheless, not a sexual assault.

. . . .

In November, 1981, the girl involved in these charges was living with her mother in Nova Scotia. The mother found it impossible to control the girl's behaviour and, in particular, to stop her smoking marijuana. In that month she sent her to Edmonton to live with an older daughter of the family who is married to the respondent....

The only other evidence on the purpose of the relocation of the girl is that the mother did it in the hope that "the Taylors could provide some guidance" that the "Mother seemed to have difficulty providing". From this I would infer a delegation to the respondent and his wife of parental authority.

. . . .

† *R. v. Taylor* (1985), 19 C.C.C. (3d) 156 (edited) (Alta. C.A.).

The six charges in this appeal arise from three incidents in January and April, 1983. On January 1, 1983, the respondent discussed with the girl at some length her continued misbehaviour in smoking both drugs and cigarettes. He then took her, dressed in her night-gown, to the basement where she was required to put her hands over her head against a vertical metal support post in the basement. Her hands were bound there by cellulose tape and she was forced to stand in that position for some 15 minutes. The respondent told her, according to her evidence, "that if he ever caught me smoking drugs again he would tie me up to the pole and strip me and beat me".

In April, the respondent heard of further misbehaviour, though this time it was smoking cigarettes rather than marijuana. There then occurred, four days apart, the two further incidents in these charges. On each occasion, the respondent's wife and the other sister living with them were absent from the home. On the first occasion, after the girl had prepared for bed on his orders, he again spoke to her at length about her conduct and then again ordered her to the basement. There he taped her hands to the post as before. This time, however, he pulled her night-gown up to her neck and lowered the panties she was wearing to her ankles so that she stood naked for 5 to 10 minutes. Four days later, apparently for further misconduct, he did the same things again but, in addition, delivered 10 to 12 blows with a wooden paddle to her buttocks. A few red marks were visible on her buttocks the following day when she was examined by a school counsellor.

. . . .

The essential charges are assault, sexual assault and sexual assault with a weapon respectively.

. . . .

The new "sexual assault" offences were part of the *Criminal Law Amendment Act* which came into force on January 4, 1983....

The new provisions do not define "sexual assault". However, "assault" is defined and thus the new offences are an assault with some additional meaning required by the modifier "sexual". In the offences which were replaced this was also true of "indecent assault", a term which gave no difficulty in judicial interpretation. For decades, juries were charged that indecent assault was an assault in circumstances of indecency: *R. v. Louie Chong* (1914), 23 C.C.C. 250, 32 O.L.R. 66; *R. v. Quinton* (1947), 88 C.C.C. 231, [1948] 3 D.L.R. 625, [1947] S.C.R. 234. Though this approach was susceptible to the comment that it was simply an assertion that an assault is indecent if it is indecent, it was nevertheless an approach perfectly understandable by generations of juries, and eminently practicable in the administration of the criminal law.

There are as yet only a few decisions dealing with the new sexual assault offences. The approach used in defining indecent assault has, however, been rejected by the New Brunswick Court of Appeal in *R. v. Chase* (1984), 13 C.C.C. (3d) 187, 40 C.R. (3d) 282, 55 N.B.R. (2d) 97....

In three cases decided since the *Chase* decision, courts have declined to follow it: *Gardynik v. The Queen* (1984), Durham County Court (unreported), a decision of Lovekin Co. Ct. J. [since reported 42 C.R. (3d) 362; *R. v. Lang* (1984), Alberta Court of Queen's Bench (unreported), an oral decision of D.C. McDonald J., and *R. v. Alderton* (January 31, 1985, Ontario Court of Appeal, unreported) [since reported 17 C.C.C. (3d) 204, 49 O.R. (2d) 257, 44 C.R. (3d) 254], an oral decision of Martin J.A. All of these decisions employ a wider meaning of the word "sexual" than did the *Chase* decision. *Gardynik* and *Lang* cite further dictionary definitions and emphasize that the word is used as an adjective.

. . . .

By moving the sexual assault offences out of Part IV of the *Criminal Code* (sexual offences, public morals and disorderly conduct) to Part VI (offences against the person and reputation), Parliament has emphasized that sexual assault is primarily an act of violence and not an act of passion. Nevertheless, Parliament used the word "sexual" as a modifier and prescribed maximum penalties much more severe than those for assault.

Without joining a battle of dictionaries, it is my view that these words were intended to comprehend a wide range of forcible acts within the definition of "assault" to which, in the circumstances disclosed by the evidence, there is a carnal aspect. "sexual assault" is therefore an act of force in circumstances of sexuality as that can be seen in the circumstances.... I would not attempt a comprehensive definition of "Sexual assault". The term includes, however, an act which is intended to degrade or demean another person for sexual gratification. Nothing in the new sections of the *Code*, in my view, restricts the carnal or sexual aspects only to acts of force involving the sexual organs and I respectfully disagree with the restricted meaning expressed in *R. v. Chase, supra*.

By what test is this carnal aspect to be judged? Do we consider the perceptions of the victim or the purpose of the person committing the assault, or is the test for the existence of a sexual aspect of the assault an objective one? In my view, the test must be essentially objective. Viewed in the light of all the circumstances, is the sexual or carnal context of the assault visible to a reasonable observer? Considerations of practicality in the administration of the new law require objectivity and must have been in the contemplation of Parliament. That is not to say that the sexual aspect of a particular assault may not be demonstrated by examining the purpose of the person committing it as that purpose is disclosed in the evidence. The perceptions of the victim may or may not be of assistance. The victim's observations of act, word, expression and gesture which accompany the assault may assist in determining whether it had a sexual aspect. On the other hand, the victim's standards may be unduly sensitive or delicate judged in the light of contemporary standards.

. . . .

In my view, the proper test for the existence of sexual assault was not applied by the trial judge. There must, therefore, be a new trial on the charges of sexual assault and, if the Crown wishes to proceed with them, on the related charges of confinement.

R. v. Chase[†]

APPEAL from a judgment of the New Brunswick Court of Appeal (1984), 13 C.C.C. (3d) 187, 40 C.R. (3d) 282, 55 N.B.R. (2d) 97, 144 A.P.R. 97, dismissing the accused's appeal from his conviction on a charge of sexual assault and substituting a verdict of guilty of common assault. Appeal allowed.

The judgment of the Court was delivered by

McINTYRE J.: — This appeal concerns the meaning of the term 'sexual assault', as it is used in ss. 244 and 246.1 of the *Criminal Code*. For ease of reference, the sections are reproduced hereunder:

   244.(1) A person commits an assault when
   (a) without the consent of another person, he applies force intentionally to that other person, directly or indirectly;
   (b) he attempts or threatens, by an act or gesture, to apply force to another person, if he has, or causes that other person to believe upon reasonable grounds that he has, present ability to effect his purpose; or
   (c) while openly wearing or carrying a weapon or an imitation thereof, he accosts or impedes another person or begs.

   (2) This section applies to all forms of assault, including sexual assault, sexual assault with a weapon, threats to a third party or causing bodily harm and aggravated sexual assault.

   (3) For the purposes of this section, no consent is obtained where the complainant submits or does not resist by reason of

   (a) the application of force to the complainant or to a person other than the complainant;
   (b) threats or fear of the application of force to the complainant or to a person other than the complainant;
   (c) fraud; or
   (d) the exercise of authority.

   (4) Where an accused alleges that he believed that the complainant consented to the conduct that is the subject-matter of the charge, a judge, if satisfied that there is sufficient evidence and that, if believed by the jury, the evidence would constitute a defence, shall instruct the jury, when reviewing all the evidence relating to the determination of the honesty of the accused's belief, to consider the presence or absence of reasonable grounds for that belief.

   246.1(1) Every one who commits a sexual assault is guilty of
   (a) an indictable offence and is liable to imprisonment for ten years; or
   (b) an offence punishable on summary conviction.

   (2) Where an accused is charged with an offence under subsection (1) or section 246.2 or 246.3 in respect of a person under the age of fourteen years, it is not a defence that the complainant consented to the activity that forms the subject-matter of the charge unless the accused is less than three years older than the complainant.

. . . .

---

†   *R. v. Chase*, [1987] 2 S.C.R. 293 (edited) (S.C.C).

The new sexual assault provisions of the *Criminal Code* were enacted in the *Act to amend the Criminal Code in relation to sexual offences and other offences against the person and to amend certain other Acts in relation thereto or in consequence thereof*, S.C. 1980–81–82–83, c. 125. They replace the previous offences of rape, attempted rape, sexual intercourse with the feeble-minded, and indecent assault on a female or male. It is now for the courts to endeavour to develop a realistic and workable approach to the construction of the new sections. The key sections are 244 and 246.1, *supra*. Section 246.1 creates the offence of sexual assault, an expression nowhere defined in the *Criminal Code*. To determine its nature, we must first turn to the assault section, 244(1), where an assault is defined in terms similar, if not identical, to the concept of assault at common law. Section 244(2) provides that the section applies to sexual assaults. It was suggested in argument by the respondent that paras. (a), (b) and (c) of s. 244(1) are to be read disjunctively so that only para. (a) could be applicable to the offence of sexual assault....

Since judgment was given in this case in the New Brunswick Court of Appeal, other appellate courts have dealt with the problem. As far as I am able to determine, none has followed the approach of the Court of Appeal in this case. In *R. v. Alderton* (1985), 49 O.R. (2d) 257, the matter was presented to the Ontario Court of Appeal.

. . . .

In *R. v. Taylor* (1985), 44 C.R. (3d) 263, the matter was considered in the Alberta Court of Appeal.

. . . .

In the British Columbia Court of Appeal, the matter was considered in *R. v. Cook* (1985), 20 C.C.C. (3d) 18. In this case, on facts which clearly revealed conduct which would qualify as sexual assaults, the *Chase* approach was again rejected. Lambert J.A. did not attempt to give a precise definition of sexual assault where Parliament had declined to do so, but he did consider that the characteristic which made a simple assault into a sexual assault was not solely a matter of anatomy. He considered that a real affront to sexual integrity and sexual dignity may be sufficient.

It will be seen from this brief review of the cases that the approach taken by the New Brunswick Court of Appeal in the case at bar has found little, if any, support. All the cases cited have recognized the need for a broader approach and all have recognized the difficulty in formulating one. While I would agree that it is difficult and probably unwise to attempt to develop a precise and all-inclusive definition of the new offence of sexual assault at this stage in its development, it seems to me to be necessary to attempt to settle upon certain considerations which may be of assistance to the courts in developing on a case-to-case basis a workable definition of the offence.

To begin with, I agree, as I have indicated, that the test for the recognition of sexual assault does not depend solely on contact with specific areas of the human anatomy. I am also of the view that sexual assault need not involve an attack by a member of one sex upon a member of the other; it could be perpetrated upon one of the same sex. I agree as well with those who say that the new offence is truly new and does not merely duplicate the offences it replaces. Accordingly, the definition of the term "sexual assault" and the reach of the offence it describes is not necessarily limited to the scope of its predecessors. I would consider as well that the test for its recognition should be objective.

While it is clear that the concept of a sexual assault differs from that of the former indecent assault, it is nevertheless equally clear that the terms overlap in many respects and sexual assault in many cases will involve the same sort of conduct that formerly would have justified a conviction for an indecent assault.... After many years of dealing with the concept of indecent assault, the courts developed the definition, "an assault in circumstances of indecency". This, of course was an imprecise definition but everyone knew what an indecent assault was. The law in that respect was reasonably clear and there was little difficulty with its enforcement. In my view then, a similar approach may be adopted in formulating a definition of sexual assault.

Applying these principles and the authorities cited, I would make the following observations. Sexual assault is an assault within any one of the definitions of that concept in s. 244(1) of the *Criminal Code* which is committed in circumstances of a sexual nature, such that the sexual integrity of the victim is violated. The test to be applied in determining whether the impugned conduct has the requisite sexual nature is an objective one: "Viewed in the light of all the circumstances, is the sexual or carnal context of the assault visible to a reasonable observer" (*Taylor, supra, per* Laycraft C.J.A., at p. 269). The part of the body touched, the nature of the contact, the situation in which it occurred, the words and gestures accompanying the act, and all other circumstances surrounding the conduct, including threats which may or may not be accompanied by force, will be relevant.... The intent or purpose of the person committing the act, to the extent that this may appear from the evidence, may also be a factor in considering whether the conduct is sexual. If the motive of the accused is sexual gratification, to the extent that this may appear from the evidence, it may be a factor in determining whether the conduct is sexual. It must be emphasized, however, that the existence of such a motive is simply one of many factors to be considered, the importance of which will vary depending on the circumstances.

. . . .

Turning to the case at bar I have no difficulty in concluding, on the basis of the principles I have discussed above, that there was ample evidence before the trial judge upon which he could find that sexual assault was committed.

Viewed objectively in the light of all the circumstances, it is clear that the conduct of the respondent in grabbing the complainant's breasts constituted an assault of a sexual nature. I would therefore allow the appeal, set aside the conviction of common assault recorded by the Court of Appeal and restore the conviction of sexual assault made at trial.

Further Reading

M. Galanter, "Notes on the Future of Social Research in Law" in eds. L. Freidman and S. MacAulay, *Law and the Behavioural Sciences* (Indianapolis: Bobbs-Merril, 1977), 18–20.

B. Legal Research: Creating Knowledge About Law

Types of Legal Research[†]

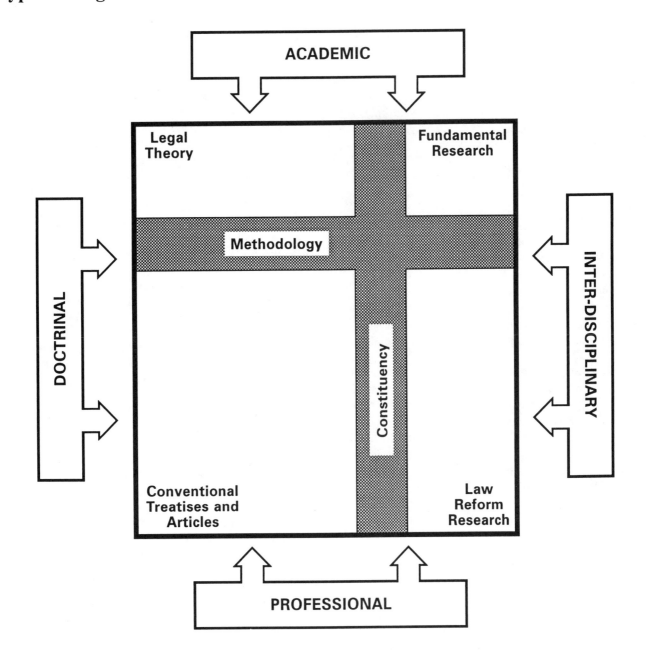

†   Consultative Group on Research and Education in Law, "Types of Legal Research" in *Law and Learning: Report to the Social Sciences and Humanities Research Council of Canada* (Ottawa: SSHRC, Minister of Supply and Services, 1983). Captus Press Inc. thanks the Social Sciences and Humanities Research Council, P.O. Box 1610, Ottawa K1P 6G4, for permission to reproduce a limited edition textbook of *Law and Learning: Report to the Social Sciences and Humanities Research Council of Canada*, originally published by the SSHRC in 1983. Cette publication est disponible en français, au Conseil, sous le titre: *Le droit et le savoir: Rapport au Conseil de recherches en sciences humaines du Canada* par le Groupe consultatif sur la recherche et les études en droit.

Legal Research in a Social Sciences Setting: The Problem of Method†
T.B. Dawson

THE LEGAL STUDIES CONTEXT AND ITS IMPLICATIONS FOR METHOD

In beginning to think about legal studies method, the parameters of legal studies itself must first be sketched in to provide the setting or context for the research to be undertaken. Defining the "field" of inquiry, even in a somewhat preliminary fashion, permits the ambit and focus of appropriate research questions to be established. If nothing else, it answers students who want to know what kind of research they are "supposed to be doing". This discussion of the "research setting" is particularly appropriate insofar as the precise ambit of "legal studies" is a subject of considerable debate.[1] One or other of my colleagues has described aspects of the project in the following terms:[2]

[Legal studies] treats "law" and "legal systems" as its focus of study and commences from the assumption that two of the most crucial questions are: what counts as law...what is the relationship between law and power;

[Legal studies] assumes that law is a social phenomenon which cannot be studied in isolation from its social, economic and political context. However, this does not mean that we should regard law as simply a product, of or reflection of external...forces, values or interests...[but] also ...the law (the legal terrain, juridical field) should be regarded as a site or mechanism through which competing conceptions of social relations and social ordering are articulated, given privileged meanings and contested;

[Legal studies] is firmly rooted in social scientific traditions of enquiry. Legal rules, concepts, structures, institutions and personnel are situated in their social, economic and political contexts. Our legal studies approach goes beyond "law context" or "law as a reflection of social forces". It eschews the professional law school's fascination with doctrine, and on the other hand, empiricism. Rather, a critical approach is taken both internally and externally... Law is examined in its own conceptual terms [and] law is examined in terms of practices;

Legal studies views law as itself a site of knowledge and power, studies the constitution of law in society and permits a range of approaches to the study of law: empirical, deconstructionist, theoretical [etc.];

[Legal studies'] conception of law is of a set of practices and discourses which constitute a "legal" or "juridical field" which is generated by the intersecting activities of agents (judges, lawyers, court officials, legislators, litigants, social activists, etc.), and institutions (courts, legal profession, legislatures, administrations, social movements etc.) To explore this conception of law it is necessary to adopt the concept of a "standpoint" which draws attention to the fact that the legal field, not only appears [to be different], but *is* different when approached from the situation of different participants within the legal field.

Some key ideas in these etchings are that legal studies goes "beyond law in context", eschews a fascination with either doctrine or empiricism, and views law as part of social organization. The focus of study becomes any person, process, or institution which is "endemically legal" in an expanded sense. By moving beyond formal law or state law, legal studies problematizes the very concepts of "law" and "legal practices". It also has a far wiser sweep than "conventional legal scholarship" which tends to be directed to doctrinal analysis of "primary legal sources" (texts) for the purpose of explaining, evaluating, and predicting judicial or legislative decisions or formal law reform.[3] The concept and function of "doctrine" is itself an interesting object of study. In short, the juridical field is itself an object of inquiry, together with interpretive issues related to the standpoints of legal actors and, indeed, of researchers. As my colleague, Alan Hunt has commented:

The [legal studies] project explicitly adopts law as its "object of inquiry" and locates that study *within* the social sciences. The location within social science is contrasted with "interdisciplinary" approaches which make use of the methods of other disciplines but sees these as "tools" or "techniques" to be applied to an *already constituted* object of inquiry.[4]

†   Dawson, T. Brettel, "Legal Research in a Social Sciences Setting: The Problem of Method" (1992), 14 *Dalhousie Law Journal* 445 at 448–50, 451, 453–56, 463–64. Reprinted by permission of Dalhousie Law Journal.

Clearly, methodological implications flow from such ideas. The objective of legal studies research cannot be formulated as being to "find the law" or to apply "found law" to particular situations (doctrinal method). But, at the same time, one cannot simply take a "law" or "the law" and study it "in action in society" in an empirical sense.[5] Because a legal studies perspective disrupts assumptions underlying canons of "data" and "knowledge" about "law" whether "on the books" or "in action", it is not enough, methodologically to simply add together social science knowledge from social data and legal knowledge from law data, and call it "socio-legal" knowledge....

. . . .

...In teaching research methods in legal studies, the aim must be to produce neither (positivist) legal scholars nor (legal) sociologists — and certainly not positivist legal sociologists! Indeed, legal learning as it exists, empirical enquiry as it exists, and the relationship between the two, cannot simply be assumed. Rather, they must be rebuilt in order to construct new, pluralist, and non-positivist ways of looking at the legal system. This, then, is the ongoing challenge.

. . . .

EVOLVING RESEARCH PRINCIPLES

. . . .

The first principle is that one must have a research question. This research question inevitably (and fruitfully) reflects the topic and scope of research and also what the researcher considers to be worthwhile asking and why. From the well-defined research question flow the research trajectory and selection of the appropriate sources and methods. A second principle is that research is an integrated process. Instruction in research method, then, is best directed to developing research strategies and approaches rather than simply instilling isolated technical and bibliographic skills. Researchers must understand what they are doing and why. They must also be efficient and independent. A third principle is that research is about analysis and the creation of new knowledge. The location of sources, no matter how satisfying, in and of itself, to budding library sleuths, is simply preparatory. To complete research, sources must be analyzed within an interpretative framework and be related back to the research question. Accordingly a theory and practice of "reading", is integral to independent and critical thought. The following sections expand on these principles and the tensions from which they sprang.

KNOW YOURSELF (OR, HAVE FUN AND HAVE A RESEARCH QUESTION)

Researching can be a panicked and deadeningly boring exercise for most undergraduate students. They have to write an essay by date X on topic Y for Professor Z. The inevitable tends to be avoided for as long as possible, before being produced as quickly as possible, with as little effort as possible. Research often appears to have been conducted in an *ad hoc* fashion, with sources being regarded as lucky finds. Bad experiences can easily lead to "research aversion", or at the least, to bad habits. Like the Delphic oracle, I suggest that some of the solution to this malaise may lie in the researcher "knowing herself" — in this case experiencing herself in the research process and knowing what she is doing and why she bothers. This breaks down into two components. The first is the need to have the researcher "present" in the research project; the second is the need for focus and direction in the project itself.

From the outset, I wanted to convey to the students that research could be enjoyable and that they could "present" in their research: it could matter to them, they could choose it because it interested them, and they could do what they wanted to do with it. The puzzle was how to convey these ideas in a congruent manner. It was solved in a satisfying manner by Sandra Kirby and Kate McKenna, in their book *Experience, Research Social Change: Methods from the Margins*, which was a course text.[6] They outline two ideas: a self-guided library tour "unlike any you may have been on before", and attention to "conceptual baggage". The library tour is a fascinating innovation, which I have dubbed "library tourism". Students are encouraged to set aside an hour or so to browse in the library however their spirit leads. No expectations, no limits, no end products and no "shoulds". Students can start with a general topic, a specific word, or even just a physical place in the library. The exercise is intentionally open-ended. The tour works on the premise that everyone likes a conversation, and the library is a lively bustle of conversations between authors proposing and debating various ideas, information and opinions. The whole tour is entirely free form.

Students who undertook the adventure were enthusiastic. They were staggered that research could be their own — not just some task set by some professor — and that it could be fun; in fact, that they could *enjoy* following their (research) nose. It also helped students to find out what kind of researcher they were: for example, street of consciousness ("well, I started out with judicial appointments and got interested in judge's wigs and ended up looking at the history of horse racing" or, "I started with the word 'black' and got a reference to black bass, and from their I went to fish parasites, and I found out about one really interesting parasite with an incredibly sexist name, so I began to think about gendered language"), "obsessive/compulsive" ("well, 500 items showed up on the computer in response to my query — so I had to look through them all...yes, every last one of them just in case one might be relevant"), confident or unconfident; associative etc. Many students said it was the first time they had actually *enjoyed* being in the library.

Conceptual baggage is another way in which researchers can come to "know themselves" and work with their strengths and dispositions. By "conceptual baggage", Kirby and McKenna refer to the mix of assumptions, premises, experiences, values and beliefs held by the researcher about the topic/question. The conceptual baggage is often the source of their interest in the topic and the angle taken by the researcher. Awareness of conceptual baggage, which inevitably exists in any researcher, can provide insight about choice of topic and direction. It can alert a researcher to her potential biases. At the same time, conceptual baggage can highlight the strengths and priorities that the researcher is bringing into a project. Instead of pretending it isn't there (objectivity?), acknowledging conceptual baggage ensures that the researcher is there in the research (objectively?). This idea may well be a step in developing scholarship and avoiding advocacy, no matter how well dressed.[7]

Focus in research is a second step in researchers coming to know who they are and what they are doing. The centrepiece of effective research is an effective research question. Research must be animated by a "problem" or "hunch" from which the thesis of the work and its basic questions can be crafted. Easy to say. However, in thinking about how to incorporate this idea into the new course, I ran across two significant "research design issues". The first was the effect that the research question itself might have on research implementation, and the second was how to generate the research problems by which students might be impelled into their own research process.

What I mean by the first design issue, is illustrated by the model of research question generally adopted in texts on legal research. Christopher Wren and Jill Wren,[8] for example, suggest that a legal problem involves analyzing "facts" to isolate "issues" on which "law" can then be located, (with appropriate updating), analyzed (for relevance, weight etc.) and in turn applied, to give a "correct", or at least, arguable opinion as to what a judge might be predicted to do (or should be persuaded to do, from the point of view of an advocate or legal academic). Pretty clearly this view is stimulated by "one right answer" jurisprudence.[9] It also involves an instructional agenda which communicates to students what "thinking like a lawyer" involves and how to define and resolve legal problems. It follows a traditional lawyer/client advice model with a correspondingly limited conceptions of the need and use for legal research. Furthermore, the idea that law in research or practice might be beneficially critiqued, is quite absent from their definition of the task.[10] To Wren and Wren, law tools, then, are ready to use skills are honed

in their use. Of course, as most law tools are, in fact, organized to facilitate this research model, their approach and the assumptions on which it based actually may be quite correct within doctrinal law research.

Of conceptual interest to me was to note how the definition of the research problem effectively sets the trajectory of research implementation: different questions/ assumptions lead to different research directions and resource needs. If we follow the trajectory envisaged by the indexers and cataloguers of traditional documentary law texts, we can easily find ourselves asking only certain kinds of questions and in certain kinds of ways. If we ask different questions, not only may we need different, additional, or alternative tools, but we may have difficulty using existing legal tools: there may be no category or heading for what we are looking for. My students were frustrated in this way more than once. Yet, rather than scampering back to the fold, I think that by asking different kinds of questions, legal studies both defines itself and lays the basis for its method. Thus, the generation of the research problem and its definition are of central importance in thinking about "legal studies research".

My primary objective has been to encourage students to formulate a specific question to which research can be directed, rather than meandering around in a large topic area. Meandering seems to me to be a preliminary part of becoming lost. All topics can generate a host of different questions and angles. The choice of specific approaches is influenced by the particular interest and perspective of the researcher. For example, alternative treatment options for young offenders can raise questions of whether the orders are constitutional (age discrimination etc.), justified (control of juvenile crime by way of adequate punishment and deterrence etc.), or consistent with rights of privacy and consent to treatment. Together with narrowing a topic to a particular question comes the requirement to answer the "so what" aspect by being able to give an account of why the information is worth seeking out and what will be known when the information is gathered together and analyzed. In this way, a context, hunch, and thesis for research can be molded into a helpful research question.

...As any legally trained scholar knows, there is a vast expanse of "formal" law-related material in a number of different categories: judicial and quasi-judicial material; legislation and legislative evaluations; parliamentary material, commission reports, and other government documents; law reform material, — all further bisected by diverse jurisdictions/countries and time periods, historical and current. This terrain is marked by a host of indexes, different categorization schemes and organizational principles, and particularities. Anyone who wants to reliably and intelligently discuss this material must be able to locate it, update it, and know what kind of animal it is. Knowledge of this core of law material cannot be assumed or fudged by legal researchers/students. The effect of a drunk driving law cannot be discussed usefully by a student who can't locate the original legislation and any amendments to it. Equally knowing how to use this material and not be intimated by it seems to be a prerequisite to being able to critique the assumptions and values contained within it, and to be able to take law seriously as an object of inquiry.

However, while law texts may be necessary, they are also not sufficient, to use a current turn of phrase. The research questions which the students generated from use of a legal studies framework, all connected law to social practices. A focus on law texts only, then, gives students only part of what they need to pursue their research. Indeed, if the essence of legal studies is context and standpoint, such "internal" or self-defining law sources are only part of what is required to understand law. Moreover, establishing or accepting, a dichotomy between "law research" and "social research" is not fruitful to the project of "taking law seriously as an objective of inquiry". Law exists in social practices, and modes of ordering or regulation of society are wide ranging.

The social research dimension and interest in the effectiveness of law apparent from the student research questions, pressed me to think about the scope of materials and "sources" relevant to legal studies research. Some sort of empirical material, whether created or located, become necessary. Much of the student interest seemed to reflect the established concern of "law and society" with the "gap problem": a perceived difference between "law on the books" and "law in action". But, while this interest in "gap problem" research indicated that students were anxious to understand law in a broad sense, it gave rise to an additional methodological problem in relation to the use of social research resources. Students must learn how to read, analyze and integrate social research in their law problems in an "authentic" and appropriate way. Too often legal researchers seem to treat social research, especially statistics, in the same way boars might forage for truffles: tasty tidbits to supplement the dinner. Munger and Seron suggest that legal researchers, even critical legal researchers, tend to use social research in a highly selective manner, to support already mapped out arguments.[11] Moreover, the "gap problem" raises issues of what we should, or do, expect law to be like or to achieve. What is, after all, the significance of locating a "gap" between law in practice and law in the books? And, how can a gap, or the "effectiveness" of law be measured?[12]

But, to return to the central issue of process. In this section I have discussed the pitfalls of assuming the body of material and sources for research and I have insisted that technical skills be developed in conjunction with an awareness of the appropriate uses and limitations of the resource tools. A much expanded understanding of legal research materials is necessary to assist informed legal studies research. A strategic approach to research involving the staged introduction of relevant materials and tools reinforces these

ideas. After development of the research question and identification of issues and possible approaches, it was suggested that students follow a pattern of consulting general sources before moving to the most relevant primary or first-hand sources around which the research question hinged. Once identified, the tools by which these sources could be located were introduced. Various approaches to sources were also suggested: topical, key words, statute-based and so forth. As a consequence, not every source was introduced to every student. Ideally, however, those sources and tools that were of concrete relevance were introduced into the research skills of students.

Endnotes

1. See e.g., Galanter, "The Future of Social Research in Law"; Macaulay, "Any 'There' There?" *supra*, note 5; P. Harris, "Approaches to the Teaching of Law through Social Science Perspectives", (Jurisprudence Centre, Carleton University, 1985); J. Hagan, "The New Legal Scholarship: Problems and Prospects" (1986), 1 *Can. J.L. & Society*; Symposium Issue: *Law, Ideology and Social Research* (1986), 9 *Legal Studies Forum*; Special Issue: *Socio-legal Research and Policy Issues* (1988), 10 *Law and Policy*.
2. The discussion of legal studies from which these quotations are taken, was stipulated in part by the development of a Masters Degree in Law in the Department, and in part by a rethinking of our first year Introduction to Law course. A flurry of "thought piece" memos on the topic circulated among faculty working on the first year committee, in the fall of 1989. I have chosen to quote without attribution, but I have the originals on file.
3. See M. Bayles, "The Purposes of Contract Law" (1983), 17 *Valpariso University Law Rev.* 613.
4. A. Hunt, "What is Legal Studies?", at 1.
5. See generally F. Munger, "Law, Charge and Litigation: A Critical Examination of an Empirical Research Tradition" (1988), 22 *Law and Society Review* 57; D. Trubek, "Where the Action is: Critical Legal Studies and Empiricism" (1984), 36 *Stan. L. Rev.* 575.
6. S. Kirby and K. McKenna, *Experience, Research, Social Change: Methods from the Margins* (Toronto: Garamond Press, 1989).
7. See generally R. Cramton, "Demystifying Legal Scholarship" (1986), 75 *Geo. L.J.* 1 at 7–8. Much legal scholarship, he comments, "pretends to an objectively which it does not deliver; it fails to state or examine the premises on which it is based; and it conveys a hubris of truth or righteousness...that is inconsistent with the humility of the true scholar."
8. C. Wren and J. Wren, "The teaching of Legal Research" (1988), 80 *Law Libr. J.* 7.
9. I thank Alan Hunt for this point. Sir Owen Dixon, an eminent former Chief Justice of the High Court of Australia clearly adhered to this view of legal research and judicial decision. See O. Dixon, "Concerning Judicial Method", in *Jesting Pilate* (Australia: Law Book Co., 1965).
10. This omission may be connected to the care taken by Wren and Wren to point out that they are practicing attorneys. This seems to be directed to credentialing their opinions as "relevant" rather than academic — another of the ironies which seem to abound in legal research instruction!
11. Munger and Seron, "Critical Legal Theory", *supra*, note 43.
12. See further Galanter, "The Future", *supra*, note 9; Macaulay, "Any 'There' There?", *supra*, note 5; Cotterrell, "Constitution and Confrontation", *supra*, note 5; David Nelken, "The 'Gap Problem' in the Sociology of Law: A Theoretical Review" (1981), 1 *Windsor Yearbook to Access to Justice* 35.

Research Methods in the Sociology of the Law†
A. Podgorecki

SEVERAL methods can be applied in researching the sociology of law. Before discussing them and presenting examples of their application together with the results and interpretations, it seems useful to define the term 'method' as follows: 'a method is a systematically employed mode of performance.' 'Method' is often used as a synonym for research 'technique.' However, this is not quite a correct usage. A method implies a more general approach to problem-solving in various situations; a technique usually indicates more narrowly defined procedures. Various techniques can be applied within a given method, while a technique rarely offers alternative ways of performance.

A method is a general directive on how a goal-directed process should be arranged; a technique provides a tool or a tested device or know-how most adequate to a given research task. For example, observation can be called a research method including such distinct techniques as studying the court files, overt or secret participation, etc.

THE HISTORICAL-DESCRIPTIVE METHOD

The historical method in sociology assumes the diachronic standpoint in research, reaching back into the past. It makes use of various documents, such as private and official records, memoirs, publications, etc., recorded in any type of writing, cuneiform or hieroglyphics, or in symbols such as seals or coats of arms. The historical method requires expert critical source analysis, indirect or direct. In some cases this method can lack sufficient precision; in others it can yield many interesting results.

THE ETHNOGRAPHIC-COMPARATIVE METHOD

This method is similar to the historical. It consists in studying the functioning of various cultural phenomena in what are called the primitive societies. Contemporary civilized social relations are extremely complex. Primitive societies can sometimes offer opportunities to observe legal behaviors reduced to laboratory simplicity. Since the researches performed by means of the ethnographic-comparative method are usually carried out in cultures which are different from the student's own, the data obtained by it must be very carefully cross-controlled by as many

means as possible. The technique of participant-observer can be very useful here, for after some time it allows the scholar to become more or less identified with the studied cultural environment.

QUESTIONNAIRE AND INTERVIEW METHODS

The interview method consists in a structured or controlled conversation according to a prearranged schedule, and is designed to provide data on facts, opinions or judgments. Such a procedure allows for:

- face-to-face contact of an interviewer with a respondent;
- asking a number of follow-up questions about the same problem;
- asking control questions;
- controlling the situation in which the declarations are made.

Moreover, such a face-to-face conversation permits assessment of the degree to which a respondent is involved in the problems he is asked about. Finally, it allows the perception of new problems which otherwise could have passed unnoticed and the supplementing of the schedule during the research.

A questionnaire is a much less versatile method. It is based essentially on what are called closed questions, offering a list of ready alternative answers. These answers can be quickly and systematically compared.

Methods of opinion polling are sometimes considered as a distinct method because of the importance of the problem, though from a strictly methodological standpoint they can be reduced to either the interview or the questionnaire, or to a combination of the two. These methods can be applied in particular to the study of attitudes toward law and the legal awareness of society. We know that the statutory law is not always known by everyone in detail and that it is by no means accepted by the whole society. We also know that the officially enacted law can sometimes be in actual conflict with the sentiment of the society or of some of its groups. These phenomena have been relatively little investigated and there is now urgent need to fill this gap in our knowledge.

---

† Podgorecki, Adam, "Research Methods in the Sociology of the Law" in *Law and Society* (London: Routledge & Kegan Paul, 1974), 48–51. Reprinted by permission of Routledge, International Thomson Publishing Services Ltd., Hampshire, U.K.

THE MONOGRAPHIC METHOD

This method aims at gaining a thorough knowledge of the functioning of a specified legal institution, and its inherent interactions and tensions, by means of detailed description supplemented by interviewing techniques. The main thrust is a confrontation between actual behavior, and opinions and attitudes about and toward it. Sometimes a participant-observer of the studied unit may be involved, as when a sociologist takes a job in a factory as a worker so as to gain insight into some particular phenomena.

THE EXPERIMENTAL METHOD

In spite of the prevailing belief, the experimental method can be applied to investigations on the functioning of law. Even though intentional experimenting in law-making by passing normative acts so as to obtain some cognitive results is quite exceptional, still unintended experiments do occur quite frequently, especially when law is used as an instrument in administration.

THE STATISTICAL METHOD

Statistical techniques can be very useful in investigations of the functioning of law. Though they are actually applied by lawyers, it must be noted that the use of them is quite narrow: they serve mainly the purposes of description and reporting. They provide quantitative illustrations of the dynamics of certain social processes or serve to arrange the sets of available data in numerical terms. However, they ought always to be called upon for verification of hypotheses concerning the influence of definite factors upon law, or vice versa.

ANALYSIS OF LEGAL MATERIALS

Studies of court and administration files, of statistical data contained in or related to them, of minutes, reports, legislative justifications, motions *de lege ferenda*, are among the materials used in analysis of legal problems. These assist in gaining insights into the functioning of legal precepts — e.g., a deficient functioning of a precept will cause an increase in the number of appeals in cases regulated by it. They also yield data on whether certain precepts are or are not being violated — if they are, the number of relevant cases, appellants, suits, etc., will be magnified. By means of these materials we can also collect data for verification of hypotheses underlying legal precepts or normative enactments.

The above list of the essential sociological methods applied to the sociology of law is by no means mutually exclusive: e.g., the monographic method can involve interviews; the questionnaire and interview methods require the use of statistical processing. However, a presentation of various possible and useful approaches allowing study of the functioning of law seems to be more important than the requirements of any formal classification.

A Guide to Legal Research[†]
J.R. Castel and O. Latchman

ESSENTIAL BACKGROUND

The Relative Weight of Primary Sources of Law

Legislation
The Constitution — The Constitution[1] is the most important statute. All other law, whether enacted by parliament or made by judges, must be consistent with the Constitution. The Constitution governs the division of powers between the federal and provincial governments and bestows fundamental rights and freedoms on individuals and groups.

Statutes — Statutes are laws that are passed by the legislature — federal or provincial. They usually deal with a specific subject. For example, the *Criminal Code*[2] is a comprehensive statute that defines criminal offences, prescribes punishments, and sets out the procedure for administering the *Code*. Assuming that a statute is consistent with the Constitution, it is the law in a given jurisdiction.[3] Statutes are, however, subject to interpretation by the judiciary and administrative tribunals.[4] Such interpretations form part of the law. Accordingly, statutory law can be altered by any of the following: (a) other acts of the legislature (amendments or repeals); (b) judicial or

† Excerpts from Castel, Jacqueline R., and Latchman, Omeela, *The Practical Guide to Canadian Legal Research*, Rev. ed. (Toronto: Carswell, 1994) at 4–8, 39–40. Reprinted by permission of Carswell, a division of Thomson Canada Limited.

administrative tribunal interpretations; and (c) declarations of constitutional invalidity ("striking down").

Regulations — Statutes often empower administrative agencies to make rules ("regulations") which provide detail about how the statute is to be implemented. For example, a statute might say, "It is unlawful to pollute." Regulations might specify what substances constitute pollutants and the registration, licensing, and monitoring requirements for those who handle such pollutants. Regulations, therefore, provide detail that is not found in the statute in the form of: definitions, licensing requirements, registration requirements, insurance requirements, performance specifications, exemptions, forms, etc.

Jurisprudence

Judicial Decisions — Judicial decisions or "case law" are judge-made law. In the absence of a statute on the topic area, case law on the topic will be binding. Note that it cannot be any case law. In order to assess whether a particular decision is binding, you must pay attention to both jurisdiction and level of court. These topics are discussed below. The law in an area that is governed solely by case law, is known as "common law".

Even where statutes exist, judge-made law is necessary to interpret what the words and phrases of the statute mean in relation to specific fact situations. Cases interpret a statute and form part of the law. In fact, if a court has ruled that a section of a statute is to be interpreted in a certain way, even if there are several other rational readings of the section, only the reading endorsed by the court is law.

Decisions of Administrative Tribunals — Administrative tribunals are not courts of law. Traditionally, they have been described as "creatures of statute". This means that their powers to adjudicate are based strictly on the wording of the enabling statute that created the tribunal.

Decisions of administrative tribunals are only meant to be binding on the parties to the particular case. Unlike judicial decisions, they are not "law" — that is, they are not binding precedents. However, in practice, previous decisions of the same tribunal will be very persuasive.

Role of Concurring and Dissenting Opinions — There are situations where the majority of the court agree to decide a case in a certain way and several judges write concurring opinions for the majority. These opinions may differ substantially in their reasoning. Such cases are troublesome to interpret because the exact law is not clearly defined. When dealing with these cases, your analysis must be sensitive to the reasoning employed in all of the concurring judgments.

Dissenting opinions are not binding. However, they can be persuasive depending on the judge.

Importance of Jurisdiction

Only statutes and case law within your jurisdiction are binding. A British Columbia statute, for instance, would never be binding in Nova Scotia. Similarly, a decision from the Saskatchewan Court of Appeal would never be binding in Alberta or any other province outside of Saskatchewan. However, if the same Saskatchewan Court of Appeal decision was appealed to the Supreme Court of Canada, the decision of the Supreme Court of Canada, although dealing with a case that arose in Saskatchewan, would be binding on all of Canada.

Decisions from other jurisdictions, while not binding, may be persuasive, depending on the level of court of the decision, the reputation of the judge or panel of judges who wrote the decision, and the actual jurisdiction. In Canada, the British Columbia and Ontario appellate courts are regarded as very persuasive throughout the country. This is not to say that decisions of these courts will necessarily be followed elsewhere. Yet it is not unusual for courts of other provinces to at least consider decisions from these courts.

Foreign law, while never binding in Canada, may also be persuasive. When an area of Canadian law has not been well developed or is in a state of confusion, courts will often look to the case law of other jurisdictions, particularly Britain and the United States, about a rational approach to the legal problem.

Statutes from other jurisdictions are generally not persuasive. However, there are some exceptions. If another jurisdiction has a similar statute, judicial interpretation of that statute may be relevant persuasive authority. For example, many provinces have similar business corporations legislation. Accordingly, cases decided under one province's statute may be persuasive authority when considering the interpretation of another province's statute. An American example is the Uniform Commercial Code, a comprehensive code dealing with commercial law, that has been passed by many state legislatures. Treatises and articles will identify these similar statutory regimes for you.

Importance of Court Structure

The court structure is hierarchical. The basic rule is that given two decisions from two different levels of court, the decision from the higher court is binding. It is, therefore, essential to know the court structure of the jurisdiction for which you are doing research.

In Canada there are two main court systems — federal and provincial. The highest court in both of these systems is the Supreme Court of Canada. Below is a general overview of the Canadian court structure.[5]

Federal Court System

The federal court system consists of the Federal Court (trial division) and an appellate court called the Federal Court of Appeal. Appeals from the Federal Court of Appeal are heard in the Supreme Court of Canada.

Provincial Court System

The provincial court system comprises a provincial "superior" court of general jurisdiction[6] and an appellate court usually called the Court of Appeal.[7] Appeals from the provincial courts of appeal are heard in the Supreme Court of Canada.

Each province also has "inferior" provincial courts. The judges of these courts are provincially appointed, in contrast to the judges of the above mentioned courts who are all federally appointed. The provincial inferior courts have civil, criminal and, in some provinces, family and youth court divisions. The civil courts are small claims courts, which hear civil cases where the amount claimed or value of property in question does not exceed specified amounts. The criminal courts deal with less serious criminal offences. The pathway of appeals from the inferior provincial courts are determined by the specific statutory provisions regulating the litigation.

How a Case Makes its Way Through the Court Structure

The majority of cases are the result of opposing parties resolving a conflict over:

(a) the constitutionality of a statute;
(b) the legality of an action or activity;
(c) an entitlement to compensation or to a remedial order for an action or activity;
(d) an entitlement to property; or
(e) the rights and obligations between parties.

When the parties litigate, a trial is held and a decision rendered by a judge or a judge and jury. The court in which the trial is held is referred to as the court of first instance. Often this decision will be the final one. However, should one of the parties be dissatisfied with the decision and if that party has a right of appeal, he or she may choose to appeal some or all of the legal and/or factual issues in his or her case to the next level of court. The decision of the appeal court will take precedence over the decision of the trial court.

It may be possible to appeal the decision of an appeal court further. Any subsequent appeal(s), will displace those decisions preceding them in the appeal process, unless the decision is affirmed (i.e., the appeal court decides that the decision of the lower court was correct).

. . . .

LEGAL PERIODICALS

What are Periodicals?

Legal periodicals or journals publish articles, case comments, and book reviews on various areas of law. There are two types of periodicals: (a) general periodicals which publish articles on all areas of law; and (b) topical periodicals which publish articles on specific areas of the law only. Periodicals can be persuasive sources of secondary legal literature depending on the thoroughness and quality of the author's analysis.

When are Periodicals Useful?

Periodicals are particularly useful when you are researching a new field of law or a field which has just undergone changes or developments. Periodicals are published more frequently than treatises, and thus often provide more current information. Periodical articles also tend to be more focused than treatises. A treatise, for instance, may provide an overview of the entire law of contracts; a periodical article, on the other hand, will likely focus on a discrete area of contract law. For this reason, if you are unfamiliar with the area of law, we recommend first looking at a legal encyclopedia or treatise to get an overview and then consulting periodical articles. Case comments of significant decisions are also useful.[8]

Case comments show how a decision has affected the law and, therefore, often contain an overview of the law on the topic. It is useful to look for case comments once you have found the relevant case law on your topic. You will tend to find case comments on decisions that are contentious or have made a significant contribution to the law.

Never assume that an article or case comment has cited all of the relevant law on your topic and always read the case law for yourself to ensure that your interpretation corresponds with the author's. The researcher should be aware that journal articles are often written from a certain political or theoretical perspective.

How are Periodicals Indexed?

Periodical indexes facilitate quick access to journal articles, case comments, and book reviews. There are different volumes for different years. Materials are indexed as follows: articles according to subject; articles according to author; case comments according to case name; case comments according to subject; and book reviews according to author and/or title of the book.

There are seven main periodical indexes:

1. *Current Law Index*;
2. *Index to Legal Periodicals*;
3. *Index to Canadian Legal Periodical Literature*;

4. *Canadian Abridgment: Index to Canadian Legal Literature*;
5. *Legal Journals Index*;
6. *Index to Foreign Legal Periodicals*; and
7. *Index to Periodical Articles Related to Law.*

Current Law Index is the most comprehensive periodical index. It covers over 700 periodicals published in the Commonwealth and the United States. If you are doing in depth research on a topic and require foreign legal analysis, Current Law Index is your best choice. We would recommend using this index in most instances, particularly if you are interested in Canadian and foreign periodical literature.

Index to Legal Periodicals covers over 400 legal journals from Canada, the United States, England, Ireland, Australia, and New Zealand.

Index to Canadian Legal Periodical Literature covers Canadian journals only. Although this is the least comprehensive of the above indexes, if you are looking for Canadian articles and/or case comments only, it is sufficiently thorough.

Canadian Abridgment: Index to Canadian Legal Literature is broader than the *Index to Canadian Legal Periodical Literature* in that it does not restrict itself to indexing periodicals. In addition to periodicals, the following forms of secondary legal literature are indexed: treatises, academic publications (casebooks, theses), essays from edited collections, government publications, law society and bar association publications, continuing legal education materials, and audio-visual materials. If you need to find secondary literature other than periodicals, you should consult the *Canadian Abridgment: Index to Canadian Legal Literature.*[9]

Legal Journals Index covers all legal journals published in the United Kingdom.

Index to Foreign Legal Periodicals covers articles dealing with international and comparative law in addition to the law of common law countries excluding Canada, the United Kingdom, and the United States.

Endnotes

1. *Constitution Act, 1867* (U.K.), 30 & 31 Vict., c. 3 and *Constitution Act, 1982*, being Schedule B to the *Canada Act, 1982* (U.K.), 1982, c. 11.
2. R.S.C. 1985, c. C–46.
3. A statutory provision is binding and assumed to be constitutional unless a court has found it to be unconstitutional or "struck down" the provision.
4. Strictly speaking administrative tribunal decisions are not law. See the section, later in this chapter, on "Decisions of Administrative Tribunals", where the status of such decisions is discussed.
5. For a more specific description of the court structure in your province or territory, consult the chart from the *Canadian Abridgment* reproduced in Appendix I.
6. The names of the provincial superior courts vary from province to province: in Alberta, British Columbia, Manitoba, New Brunswick, and Saskatchewan, they are called the Court of Queen's Bench; in Newfoundland, Northwest Territories, Nova Scotia, Prince Edward Island, and Yukon Territory, they are called the Supreme Court; in Ontario it is called the Ontario Court (General Division); and in Quebec, it is called the Superior Court.
7. In Alberta, British Columbia, Manitoba, New Brunswick, Northwest Territories, Ontario, Saskatchewan, and Yukon Territory, the appellate court is called the Court of Appeal. In Newfoundland, Nova Scotia, and Prince Edward Island, the appellate court is called the Court of Appeal.
8. See Chapter Twenty for a discussion of the mechanics of writing a case comment.
9. For an explanation of how to use the *Canadian Abridgment: Index to Canadian Legal Literature* see Chapter Eleven. The explanation of how to use periodical indexes below does not apply to this index.

A Schema and System for Legal Research[†]
T.B. Dawson

INTRODUCTION

In order to enjoy legal research — the creation of new legal knowledge — it is of critical importance to be focused, systematic and efficient. You need to know what you are looking for, where to find it and how to go about locating, reading and thinking about your data. In the system or schema developed below, there are three stages to effective legal research: planning, execution and action. A central idea is that you should do research that matters to you and that interests you; the rest proposes a method whereby you can actualize your research objectives.

† Dawson, T. Brettel, "A Schema and System for Legal Research", (1990).

STAGE ONE: PLANNING

Before you open a book, plan your general approach: even if you modify it as you discover new information during actual research, you will be much more successful and efficient if you have an idea of the steps you wish to take.

1. Identify a problem which interests you and which you would like to research. Next:
   i. analyze the problem: what do you know about the general subject?
   ii. focus your interest and refine a research question which will help you investigate this problem;
   iii. do some preliminary reading in the general subject area — find a book or an article that is relevant. Note: this is only preliminary — not research!
   iv. consider and note down your 'conceptual baggage': what assumptions are you making? Why are you interested? What do you hope to achieve? What kind of things are you bringing along with you on the research journey?

Even though you will probably be presented with 'essay topics' in your assignments during undergraduate days, it is still necessary to select a topic which interests you and develop a research question and focus that flows out of it. The only difference between being given an 'essay topic' or being asked to directly select your own is that with an essay topic, you are given a point of departure. In whatever research you do, it is also important to consider and take into account the class, gender and race implications of your research and perspective: will your research apply equally to men and women or to aboriginal peoples and non-aboriginal peoples? Are you studying a socially or economically privileged population and what are the research and analysis implications of doing so?

2. Consider the issues which are part of your research problem/research question. This involves three steps:
   i. identification of (relevant issues);
   ii. selection and prioritization of issues for research;
   iii. construction of a 'preoutline' indicating the likely issues and subjects to be considered. This has the advantages of organizing your research into categories, permitting it to cumulate according to subject, assisting you in knowing where you have researched or not, and making your research more easily accessible.

3. Next, consider the type of research which will be required in addressing your research problem and the sources available to you in designing and executing your research project. If you are taking a survey type of approach you will need to design the survey or interview structure carefully, prepare to gather the information, record the data, and reflect upon it. Next you will need to develop an analysis of the data which involves organizing it, describing and linking it, and considering what it means.

4. Generally speaking, at least part of your research will be library based, and you will need to utilize research tools to execute your project.
   i. it is first necessary to prepare a list of search words and phrases to be used in indexes, abstracts, etc. Draw these words from your issues and any fact situation you are dealing with;
   ii. prepare a checklist of sources to be searched (may be added to as you proceed).

STAGE TWO: EXECUTION: THE RESEARCHING STAGE

1. Your objectives in the active research stage are to find, sort, read, evaluate/analyze and update your sources. You should continually evaluate what you are finding in terms of your research question and research issues. Make sure you read the material you are finding too — it is no help to have an enormous pile of references and no idea what they say or where to start on them. Research is not really the mechanics of locating references, essential as this is. Rather, research itself is the step of considering what is contained in the sources themselves: you must also take time to evaluate/analyze this material: what is it saying? How does it advance your research? Do the authors and sources agree with each other? What is the significance of disagreement between them?

2. It is preferable to locate and process primary sources first, followed by secondary sources. Which is which, will depend on the kind of research problem and research question you are working on. The purpose of referring to secondary sources is to help develop arguments and perspectives on the topic. Secondary sources are simply other people's opinions or synthesis of primary sources relevant to their research questions. Your aim should be to come to an

independent conclusion on your own research question.

3. There are various 'finding tools': indexes, digests, abstracts, abridgements, periodical indexes, citators, consolidations, advance sheets, computer and CD-ROM database which you can use to find material relevant to your research question. Refer to the section on 'locating sources of legal knowledge' and to texts such as Margaret Banks, *Using a Law Library*, 4th ed., (Toronto: Carswell, 1985); Douglas MacEllvan, *Legal Research Handbook*, 2nd ed., (Toronto: Butterworths, 1986); Yogis and Christie, *Legal Research and Writing Manual*, 3rd ed., Michael Tosipescu (Toronto: Butterworths, 1988).

Be aware that the organization of legal materials in the library and in the finding tools has been affected by particular views of what is important or 'authoritative' and that the organization reflects existing categorizations. This can affect what it is possible to ask about law and what it is possible to find out about law.

4. It is imperative that you keep complete and accurate notes which record:
  i. source and citation: Generally a complete bibliographic reference should be made and kept separately from your research notes. If you adopt this practice you will be able to abbreviate the source in subject notes and also you will be able to quickly locate bibliographic information;
  ii. topics and search words used;
  iii. content of the source. Here you have a choice of either taking notes on each source separately or organizing content notes according to subjects covered with a note of the source (author, title and page numbers). Separate notes allow you to precis and follow the arguments made; subject notes allow you to cumulate your information on a particular topic or issue and quickly compare the opinions of one author or source and another. When you are taking notes on a case, you should 'brief the case' by taking note of the name, citation, court, legal topics, factual summary, issues, result and reasoning in the decision. Case information can then be put into subject notes where relevant;
  iv. relevant cross references which you want to follow-up. Again, this could be with your content notes or in a separate notebook together with information about the source of the idea or cross-reference;

  v. method of updating employed. It is crucial that your sources are current and accurate. If your source is a statute, you should check to see if it has been amended; if it is a case, you should check to see if it has been appealed or if it has been cited with approval or disapproval in later cases; if it is an article, are there other articles on the topic?

STAGE THREE: ACTION

1. Stop researching and start writing when
  i. you begin to find the same references over and over again and you are no longer finding new sources which are relevant; and
  ii. you have evaluated the materials you have found in terms of the research question.

2. An essay or research paper essay must contain several elements. Be careful, however, not to adopt a formulaic approach to writing research papers. Every topic has different requirements as to content and different ways to be most effectively presented. There are some basics though which must be included:
  i. an introduction which sets out the research topic, the research question and basic issues to be considered in the paper. If these have changed since your preliminary proposal, use the current ideas;
  ii. a main body in which you develop your arguments and discuss your material in a form appropriate to your topic. Be careful to link ideas and develop them logically. Try to have clear opening and closing sentences to each paragraph; and, use paragraphing effectively;
  iii. a conclusion in which you summarize your points and tie them together and relate them to your research question: conclude — what have you established?

The actual writing involves several stages:

4. Be selective. No matter how interesting a point may be, if it does not relate to your research question or establish a relevant point in argumentation it *must* be omitted. Use it in your next paper!

5. Prepare a detailed outline of the content of your paper. Doing so organizes you, directs your writing and prevents you from becoming lost. It also helps you to ensure that everything mentioned in the body of the paper is relevant to the research question being addressed.

6. Prepare a first draft of your paper. Keep in mind what you are trying to achieve in the paper, to whom you are addressing the paper and why you are writing the paper: purpose, audience and occasion. Get to point; try to avoid extended preliminaries and delaying tactics. Pay attention to the 'rules of writing'; ensure that you honestly and correctly attribute your sources in footnotes or end notes; avoid stringing together quotations and calling it an essay — use quotations from the work of others sparingly, and only to support a point you are making. Make sure you comment on the relevance or importance of the point made in any quotation used.

7. Discuss your draft and consider the feedback received.

8. Revise your paper. Yes, the first draft will need to be revised! The objectives of revision are to achieve clarity, an effective and tight structure and brevity. Take several swings through your paper looking for different things each time.
   i.   First, look for 'truth and accuracy' — is your argument and the information on which it is based correct?
   ii. Second, concentrate on structure: is it logical? Do things belong where they are? Is there repetition? Do you develop an argument? Are transitions and linkages smooth and effective?
   iii. Third, look at your paragraphs: do they have topic sentences setting out the basic idea being considered? Is that idea in fact the topic of the paragraph?
   iv. Fourth, review your sentences. Are they sentences? Are they too long? Is the active voice used? Have you used gender-appropriate, non-sexist language?
   v.   Fifth, look at your words. Make sure you are using words which are correct, clear and effective. Keep words and phrases simple; avoid legalese; avoid ambiguity. Be concrete.
   vi. Sixth, and finally, check for spelling, grammar, punctuation. Make sure your citation and foot/end noting is correct. Citation rules are located in manuals such as the *Canadian Guide to Uniform Legal Citation*, 2nd ed. (Toronto: Carswell, 1988). Correct citation is not optional but is essential to a good research product. It may seem a bit tedious to learn correct citation, but once the rules are ingrained in your socio-legal mind, you can use them with ease and elegance. The purposes of citation rules include: permitting the reader to easily locate the sources referred to, correctly representing the original source, acting as a universally understood shorthand to source material, and ensuring conciseness and brevity. Incorrect, incomplete or inaccurate citation is frustrating to a reader and gives the impression that your work is shoddy, careless and inferior.

9. Finalize your paper, proof read it and submit it.

10. If appropriate, do something with your research to make it useful to other people as well as you.

CONCLUSION

Everyone is able to do research — there is nothing mysterious about it. In essence, research is wanting to find something out or to develop a hunch or theory. That said, there are certain skills that need to be developed and refined over time to help a researcher become efficient and at ease with the resources available for research. It is also essential that a researcher be systematic and organized. Researchers need to know where they are going and why, where they have been and what they have discovered. The three stage approach which has been outlined and discussed, focuses on the role of planning, execution and action in research. I hope you will be able to take the ideas advanced and fashion them in your own growth as a researcher.

References

Christopher Wren and Jill Robinson Wren, *The Legal Research Manual: A Game Plan for Legal Research and Analysis*, 2nd ed. (Adams and Ambrose, 1986).

Frank Houdek, ed. *Making 'Wren' Work: A Multidimensional Program for Teaching Legal Research* (Illinois: School of Law, Southern Illinois University, 1989).

Timothy Perrin, *Better Writing for Lawyers* (Toronto: Law Society of Upper Canada, 1990).

Sandra Kirby and Kate McKenna, *Experience, Research and Social Change: Methods from the Margins* (Toronto: Garamond Press, 1989).

Margrit Eichler, *Non-sexist Research Methods* (Boston: Allen and Unwin, 1988).

Non-Sexist Research Methods[†]
M. Eichler

SEXISM IN RESEARCH

Most analyses of sexism in research focus either on one discipline or subject area or else on one type of sexism. Indeed, we do not tend to speak of "types of sexism," but of "sexism," pure and simple. The term "sexism" suggests that we are dealing with *one* problem that may manifest itself in different areas differently, but which nevertheless is a single basic problem — what one might call the "big blob" theory of sexism.

This book takes a different approach. Sexism is here broken down into seven different types. Of these seven types, four are primary and three are derived.

THE SEVEN SEXIST PROBLEMS

Androcentricity

Androcentricity is essentially a view of the world from a male perspective. It manifests itself when ego is constructed as male rather than female, such as when "intergroup warfare" is defined as a "means of gaining women and slaves." In this case, the "group" is defined as consisting only of males, since the women are what is "gained." From an androcentric perspective, women are seen as passive objects rather than subjects in history, as acted upon rather than actors; androcentricity prevents us from understanding that both males and females are always acted upon as well as acting, although often in very different ways. Two extreme forms of androcentricity are *gynopia* (female invisibility) and *misogyny* (hatred of women).

This definition raises a difficulty that must be acknowledged. Theoretically speaking, problems of perspective could come in two versions: one female, one male. The female version would be gynocentricity, or a view of the world from a female perspective. I have labeled this problem androcentricity rather than, for instance, andro-gynocentricity for two reasons. First, the problem is so overwhelmingly biased in the male direction that to accord a female version of the problem equal status would be inappropriate. I have, however, included the few examples of incipient gynocentricity that I found in my search of the literature. Second, it is not really possible to find a form of gynocentricity that is in any way comparable to androcentricity, for the simple reason that we live in an androcentric social, political, and in-

tellectual environment. Thus even when we attempt to take a *consciously* female perspective, this attempt occurs within an overall intellectual environment in which both our vehicle for thought (language) and the content of thought (concepts) are colored by thousands of years of overwhelmingly androcentric thinking. It is therefore both misleading and inaccurate to treat possible gynocentricity as comparable to actual androcentricity. However, it is important to acknowledge that sexism can theoretically come in two forms, and to remind ourselves that neither is acceptable in scholarship.

Overgeneralization/Overspecificity

Overgeneralization occurs when a study deals with only one sex but presents itself as if it were applicable to both sexes. Its flip side is overspecificity, which occurs when a study is reported in such a manner that it is impossible to determine whether or not it applies to one or both sexes. Using a sample of male workers and calling it a study of social class is an instance of overgeneralization; the same problem arises when one uses the term "parents" to refer exclusively to mothers (ignoring fathers). Overspecificity occurs when single-sex terms are used when members of both sexes are involved (e.g., "the doctor...he," or "man is a mammal"). Many (but not all) of the problems involving sexist language belong in this category.

There is considerable overlap between overgeneralization/overspecificity and androcentricity. Nevertheless, one cannot be equated to the other. A study may be androcentric without being over-general, such as when male violence against women is dismissed as trivial or unimportant (thus maintaining male over female interests) although the actors are correctly identified by their sex. A study may also be overgeneral or overspecific without being necessarily androcentric, such as when a study uses all male subjects (e.g., male students) or all female subjects (e.g., mothers) but presents the findings in general terms ("students" respond well to ability grouping, or "parents" tend to teach their children concepts through ostensive definitions).

Gender Insensitivity

Gender insensitivity is a simple problem: it consists of ignoring sex as a socially important variable. It sometimes overlaps with overgeneralization/overspecificity, but the two are not identical: In the case of general insensitivity, sex is ignored to such a degree that the presence

---

† Eichler, Margrit, *Non-Sexist Research Methods* (Cambridge: Unwin Hyman, Inc., 1988), 1–9, 11–15. Reprinted by permission of Routledge, International Thomson Publishing Services Ltd., Hampshire, U.K.

of overgeneralization or androcentricity cannot even be identified. If a study simply fails to report the sex of its respondents, or if a policy study completely ignores the different effects of, let us say, a particular unemployment insurance policy on the two sexes, then we cannot identify whether male or female subjects were included or whether males or females would differentially profit from or be hurt by a particular policy. In a completely gender-insensitive study, it would be impossible to identify other problems because information necessary to do so is missing.

Double Standards

The use of double standards involves evaluating, treating, or measuring identical behaviors, traits, or situations by different means. A double standard is by no means easy to identify, although it may sound easy: it involves recognizing behaviors, traits, or situations as identical when they bear different labels or are described in different terms. For instance, some psychological disorders occur only in one sex. To find out whether or not a given example is an instance of the application of a double standard, one must (1) identify a larger category for the disorder; (2) determine whether there is a complementary disorder for the other sex; (3) identify whether the two are equivalent; and (4) determine whether they are evaluated in different ways. Only when all these preconditions are obtained are we dealing with a double standard. If the disorder appears in only one sex, no double standard is involved.

Identification is not made easier by the fact that a researcher may have used different instruments to measure identical attributes of the sexes. For example, social status is currently derived by using different measures for the sexes (for further discussion of this specific problem, see Chapter 5). However, this different measurement coincides with an actual difference in social standing between the sexes, a difference that we are incapable of measuring adequately because we have no sex-free instrument at our disposal. Identification of a double standard thus involves distancing oneself to some degree from the social context as it is presented — not a simple thing to do, and never perfectly achieved.

A double standard is likely to be inspired by, or lead to, androcentricity, but it need not necessarily do so. Using female-derived categories of social status for women and male-derived categories for men is an instance of a double standard in the use of instruments, but it is neither gender insensitive nor androcentric nor overgeneral/overspecific.

Sex Appropriateness

Sex appropriateness, our first "derived" category, is nothing but a particular instance of a double standard, one that is so accepted within the relevant literature that it is proudly acknowledged with special terms: for example,

"appropriate sex roles," or "appropriate gender identity." The absence of appropriate gender identity is called *dysphoria*, and it is classed as a psychological disorder. Sex appropriateness becomes a problem when *human* traits or attributes are assigned only to one sex or the other and are treated as more important for the sex to which they have been assigned. It is *not* a problem when we are dealing with a truly sex-specific attribute, such as the capacity to ejaculate or to give birth to children. It *is* a problem when it is applied to such human capacities as child rearing (as opposed to child bearing).

This particular example of a double standard has been singled out from the overall discussion of double standards because sex appropriateness is still widely accepted within the social science literature as a legitimate concept.

Familism

Familism is a particular instance of gender insensitivity. It consists of treating the family as the smallest unit of analysis in instances in which it is, in fact, individuals within families (or households) who engage in certain actions, have certain experiences, and so on. It is *not* a problem of sexism when no such attribution occurs. Another manifestation of familism occurs when the family is assumed to be uniformly affected (positively or negatively) in instances in which the same event may have different effects on various family members.

This problem has been singled out from the general discussion of gender insensitivity for the same reason that sex appropriateness has been singled out from the discussion of double standards: It is a very well-accepted practice within the social sciences to engage in familism, and is, at present, still considered to be entirely legitimate.

Sexual Dichotomism

Sexual dichotomism is another subaspect of the use of double standards. It involves the treatment of the sexes as two entirely discrete social, as well as biological, groups, rather than as two groups with overlapping characteristics. It leads to an exaggeration of sex differences of all types at the expense of recognizing *both* the differences *and* the similarities between the sexes. It is particularly important to recognize sexual dichotomism as a form of sexism because it is sometimes used as a "cure" for gender insensitivity. When this occurs, it is simply a case of substituting one form of sexism for another; and it is doubly misleading because it creates the illusion of having achieved a solution.

. . . .

SEXISM AND SCIENTIFIC OBJECTIVITY

One spinoff from the various critiques of sexism in research has been a renewed doubt about the possibility of objectivity in the social sciences. While academicians have traditionally assumed that objectivity is a hallmark of their work, feminist scholars have challenged this assumption. Some feminist researchers even maintain that objectivity is, in principle, impossible to achieve, and that the most we can do is to admit to an unabashed subjectivity, our own as well as everybody else's. However, the logical consequence of such a principled stance is that research, including the implied cumulative knowledge it generates, is impossible.

This seems rather like throwing out the baby with the bathwater. Instead, it is more useful to identify the various components commonly included under the heading of objectivity and look at them separately, in order to eliminate the problematic aspects of objectivity while maintaining the useful ones. One scholar who engages in such a process of separating useful from harmful components of objectivity is Elizabeth Fee. She suggests that the following "aspects of scientific objectivity...should be preserved and defended":

> The concept of creating knowledge through a constant process of practical interaction with nature, the willingness to consider all assumptions and methods as open to question and the expectation that ideas will be subjected to the most unfettered critical evaluation....

Fee also rejects certain aspects of "objectivity" in research. For example, she rejects as not helpful the notion that objectivity requires a distancing of the researcher from the subject matter, and of the production of knowledge from its uses. Likewise, she rejects as unnecessary the divorce between scientific rationality and emotional or social commitment; she also rejects the assumption that knowledge must flow only from the expert to the nonexpert and thus that a dialogue is not possible. She deplores the prevailing split between subject and object, in which the knowing mind is active and the object of knowledge entirely passive. Such a structure of knowledge results in a depersonalized voice of abstract authority that legitimizes domination. Finally, she rejects as impossible the complete freedom of research from its sociopolitical environment.

Though she focuses on the concept of the "scientific process" and not on "objectivity" *per se*, Karen Messing argues that "the ideology and the background on the researcher" can influence the research process at eleven different stages:

- the selection of the scientists,
- their access to facilities for scientific work,
- the choice of research topic,
- the wording of the hypothesis,
- the choice of experimental subjects,
- the choice of appropriate controls,
- the method of observation,
- data analysis,
- interpretation of data,
- the publication of results,
- and the popularization of results.

Jill McCalla Vickers lists as one of her methodological rebellions "the rebellion against objectivity," which she sees as (a) "treating those you study as objects and objectifying their pains in words which hide the identity of their oppressors," or (b) "being detached from that which is studied." She accepts objectivity as "the rules which are designed to facilitate intersubjective transmissibility, testing, replication, etc."

Finally, Evelyn Fox Keller has beautifully demonstrated that objectivity has been largely equated with masculinity. She discusses particularly the misconception that objectivity requires detachment of the knower, both in emotional as well as in intellectual terms. Moreover, she argues that

> the disengagement of our thinking about science from our notions of what is masculine could lead to a freeing of both from some of the rigidities to which they have been bound, with profound ramifications for both. Not only, for example, might science become more accessible to women, but, far more importantly, our very conception of "objective" could be freed from inappropriate constraints. As we begin to understand the ways in which science itself has been influenced by its unconscious mythology, we can begin to perceive the possibilities for a science not bound by such mythology.

It seems, then, that it is possible to be critical of the way in which objectivity has been defined without having to abandon the concept and sink into the morass of complete cultural subjectivism. We need to separate clearly objectivity from detachment and from the myth that research is value-free. Neither of the latter two conditions is, in principle, possible for any researcher (or anybody else). Our values will always intrude in a number of ways into the research process, beginning with the choice of the research question; and we will necessarily always be informed by a particular perspective. Nor is there any need to detach ourselves emotionally from the research process — in fact, this is impossible, and what appears as scholarly detachment is in reality only a matter of careful disguise.

Objectivity remains a useful and important goal for research in the following ways:

1. a commitment to look at contrary evidence;
2. a determination to aim at maximum replicability of any study (which implies accurate reporting of all processes employed and separation between simple reporting and interpretation, to the degree that these are possible);
3. a commitment to "truth-finding" (what Kenneth Boulding has called veracity); and
4. a clarification and classification of values underlying the research: nonsexist research, for instance, is based on the value judgment that the sexes are of equal worth, while androcentric research grows out of the belief that men are of higher worth (and therefore more important) than women.

I find it useful to think of objectivity as an asymptotically approachable but unreachable goal, with the elimination of sexism in research as a station along the way.

SOLVING THE PROBLEM OF SEXISM IN RESEARCH

When we regard a problem as simple, a single solution often seems appropriate. Once we begin to differentiate among different and distinct components of a problem, however, different and distinct solutions become a necessity. When we fail to make the proper distinctions, we may — unwittingly and despite the very best intentions — replace one problem of sexism with another.

The analysis of sexism in language provides a case in point. Early and incisive studies of sexism in language convinced a number or organizations and individuals that sexist language was unacceptable in scholarly research (or elsewhere, for that matter!). Typically, these analyses pointed out the use of so-called generic male terms as sexist, and often they included reference to such demeaning terms as "girls" for "women," or nonparallel terms (Mrs. John Smith but not Mr. Anne Smith, or the use of Mrs. or Miss, which indicate marital status, versus Mr., which does not).

As a consequence of these critiques, guides were published that replaced so-called generic male terms with truly generic terms: policeman became police officer; fireman, fire fighter; postman, mail carrier; workman, worker; chairman, chairperson; mankind, humanity; and so on. In effect, occupational and other terms were "desexed." The generic "he" was replaced with "he or she," or "s/he," or "they," or "one," or "people," and so on. Guides of this type continue to be important and useful, but unless care is taken as to how and when and in what context these gender-neutral terms are used, another form of sexism may inadvertently enter the picture.

The use of male (or sex-specific) terms for generic situations is one form of overgeneralization, one of our sexist problems. However, there is another aspect to the same problem: the use of generic terms for sex-specific situations, which is just as problematic as is the first manifestation. For example, if researchers talk about workers in general while only having studied male workers (constantly and cautiously using "they," "People," "the individual," "the person," and so on, with nary a female in sight), they simply replace one sexist problem with another in the manner in which language is used. Language that employs "nonsexist" generic terms for sex-specific situations creates the same problem in reverse and constitutes at one and the same time an example of both overgeneralization and gender insensitivity. In other words, when the content is sex specific, the language used should also be sex specific.

Sexism takes more than one form, and therefore ways to combat it may also take more than one form. The trick is to develop criteria that help us determine which solution is appropriate when. This is the major purpose of this book.

Good Legal Writing: Of Orwell and Window Panes[†]

P. Samuelson

GEORGE Orwell once wrote that "[g]ood prose is like a window pane."[1] What I take Orwell to have meant by that remark is that when people read good prose, it makes them feel as if they've "seen" something (whatever the author was trying to convey) more clearly.[2] Put another way, if a writer can induce his or her reader to feel that the reader would have come to the same conclusion that the author reached had the reader done his or her own investigation of the subject matter, the writer has achieved a kind of "window pane" effect on the reader.

† Samuelson, Pamela, "Good Legal Writing: Of Orwell and Window Panes" (1984), 46 *University of Pittsburg Law Review* 149 at 149–57. Copyright © 1994 Pamela Samuelson. Reprinted by permission of the author and the publisher.

There are certainly many styles of successful writing. Some charm by exotic imagery, others by suspense, some even by subtle obfuscations. However, the style of writing I have found to be most successful for legal analyses is the sort which Orwell's comment conjures up: flawlessly clear, lucid, and enlightening. As I have worked with law students on supervised writing projects, I have noticed that lucidity does not come naturally to most law students, perhaps because they have been forced in their legal studies to read so much bad writing that they mistake what they've read for the true and proper model. I have also noticed that simply directing someone to be lucid doesn't often help him or her to become so. Over time I have developed a set of ideas about how one can make one's legal prose become like a window pane. In this Essay, I will share those ideas with you.

You will soon notice that this Essay is addressed chiefly to an audience of inexperienced legal writers, most specifically to those law students whom I teach. More experienced writers may find the Essay mildly entertaining, perhaps even picking up a tip or two for improving their own writing technique. I hope that at least some of my readers who are experienced writers, especially those who try, as I do, to teach others to write, find a fellow traveller's exposition helpful to further their own thinking about the mysterious process of learning to write well.

Despite what you may infer from the detailed comments within, I do not believe in a formulaic approach to legal writing.[3] There is no one "right" way to organize, analyze, or write about any legal issue.[4] There are thousands, if not millions, of "right" ways. My aim in reviewing other people's writing is to help them find the analytic approach, organization, and style that will work for the ideas they want to convey. To put it another way, I try to help each of them find his or her "voice" as a writer.[5] No one can learn to write well by aping another person's style. I tell my students: The first thing you must do when you write is be yourself; the second thing you must do is learn to appreciate and enhance your natural strengths as a writer (yes, you have them); and the third thing you must do is understand and work on removing whatever weaknesses are undermining your strengths. I see my role as facilitating this process of self-discovery.

Now for the framework of this Essay: In Section I, [the only section included in this extract (see original article for information contained in other sections) — Eds.], I set forth what are, for me, the six paramount rules of good legal writing. These have general applicability to the whole of one's writing. This is followed in Section II by a set of fourteen additional rules, which pertain, for the most part, to specific aspects of a legal analysis. Sections III and IV briefly advise inexperienced writers on how much research to do for a legal analysis and on strategies for overcoming writer's block. The final section suggests an approach to editing other people's work and communicating with the writers about their work. This approach, in my view, is the one most likely to be successful in yielding the intended result of improving the quality of the writer's next draft. As you'll see, I view an editor's job as well done when he or she has rendered him or herself obsolete. (Now that I have given you this structure, I feel free to be a bit jaunty and jocular, hoping to lead you further into my web.)

THE SIX PARAMOUNT RULES OF GOOD LEGAL WRITING

Have a Point

In order to write a good legal analysis, you've got to have a point (that is, a thesis) you want to make.[6] In reviewing student papers, I have noticed two sorts of problems students have with the seemingly simple point of having a point. One is not to have a point at all. There are two main subcategories of this problem: one is being very descriptive about one's topic,[7] that is, surveying rather than analyzing it; the other is demonstrating the author's ambivalence about the issue.[8] Not having a thesis is unacceptable. So is being ambivalent about what your thesis is. Go ahead. Take a risk. Bite the bullet. Choose your thesis and see where it takes you.[9]

The other sort of problem — one to which enthusiasts, in particular, are prone — is to have twelve or thirteen points. It is very easy, as one begins to get familiar with a subject, to get captivated by the myriad issued which any reasonably interesting subject will raise. One may find it difficult to resist the temptation to put all of the interesting issues in at least the first draft without tying them together in a single thematic structure.

I tell my students: Very few people can write in any depth about more than one major issue at a time, and you probably aren't one of them. From my perspective, the aim of this exercise is to explore one thing (your thesis) in depth. While it may very well be possible to weave some of the more closely related tantalizing issues into the fabric of your paper (or, better, into the footnotes), you must make them work in service of your thesis. However sharp your insight, if it doesn't advance your argument, drop it.

Get to the Point

Quite as important as having a point is getting to it with reasonable dispatch. This means that you should tell your reader what the point is in your first paragraph, if possible, or at the most by the end of the second page.[10] It means that you should start your analysis of the thesis on page two or three, not on page twenty or thirty. It means that you should remind your reader of your thesis as you go along by such means as section title and transitional sentences.[11] Think of your thesis as the spice of your paper. Just as you wouldn't put all the spice for your dinner into your dessert, don't put all of your analysis in the latter third or quarter of your paper.

Adopt a Structure For Your Analysis That Will Allow You to Integrate the Facts, Court Analysis, and Policies Into the Body of Your Argument

The reason many law students seem to take so long to get to the point is that they have adopted what I deem to be an artificial structure, often a structure which could be used for any paper, no matter what its thesis. If this has been your habit, think about breaking it. It's time to try a more unified, more integrated, and more analytical structure. It is time to learn to get to the point on page two. It is time to learn to develop a structure which can be the structure *only* for that paper because it's based on the particular analysis you've developed to support your thesis.

What do I mean when I say law students tend to adopt an "artificial structure?" Here's an example:

I. Introduction
(Often this is an introduction to the general subject matter of the paper. If it mentions the paper's thesis, it often does it in a sentence tucked away at the bottom of page three or five in an inconspicuous place.)

II. Background
(This is often an overview of some of the historical context of the problem and/or of legal concepts which are to be discussed in the analytic section fifteen pages later. It often reads like an encyclopedia or a dispassionate general treatise on the subject.)

III. Facts
(Often this is a recitation of "the facts" of a particular case which will be under the analytic microscope in Section V. It often meanders through the odds and ends of the case, often giving many more facts than is necessary to make the analytic point.)

IV. Court Decision(s)
(This is usually a report on the trial and any appellate court's holdings — usually all of the issues, not just the ones pertinent to the discussion — and sometimes also of arguments rejected or accepted and any titillating dicta, pertinent or not.)

V. Analysis
(Finally. The author now attacks court A for this and court B for that, repeating in the process all the arguments or holdings discussed in the previous section, the facts of the next previous section, and the concepts of the background section, and inadequately developing all of them in terms of their relationships to one another.)

VI. Policy
(If law students mention the policy implications of their thesis at all, the policy issues are trotted out in a page or so near the end, usually held up for display as if they were the recently severed head of John the Baptist. Horrors!)

VII. Conclusion
(This is often a rather mechanical repetition of the kernel of the analysis from Section V. It rarely contains anything new or interesting.)

What's so bad about this structure, you may ask. Lots of things, I will answer. The worst thing about it is that it's the sort of structure that doesn't start getting to the point until page twenty.

A concomitant bad effect is that along the route to your analytic section, your reader is very likely to get distracted by the unfocused discussion of history, concepts, facts, and the like. Your reader isn't your mother who might be willing to read everything you write with fascinated attention.[12] Even if you've told your reader what your thesis is in the first page or so, your reader will have forgotten it by the fifth page of your meandering history. And by the time you get to the analysis itself, your reader will have forgotten the background stuff mentioned in your earlier sections. Unless you repeat in Section V what you said in Section II, a diligent reader may have to turn back to Section II and reread it, which again, is a distraction from the smooth development of your argument.

This brings me to a third bad thing about the kind of structure I've been discussing. It requires a lot of repetition as glue. Repetition is all right if it's necessary, but if you organize an analysis well, there is little or no need to repeat yourself.

A fourth ill effect of this structure is that the potential power of your argument is dissipated by having been so severely chopped up into bits and sprinkled throughout the paper. If the historical context of argument A is discussed on pages four and five, the facts on seven, the courts' holdings briefly on eleven and thirteen, your analysis of them on sixteen, and the policy implications on twenty-two, the forcefulness of the argument will be less than if all are integrated into one section of seven pages. A highly diligent reader will feel forced to do the work for you, but most readers will say, "Ho, hum, I'm glad I got through that mess, but what was it about?"

Remember that the whole point of legal writing is to persuade your reader of your thesis, so you shouldn't structure your paper to impede your ability to persuade. Integrate, and your prose will be like a window pane.

Break Your Analysis Up into its Component Parts and Develop Them Separately, But in an Organized Way

One can only analyze an issue in an organized way. There are a great many ways to organize the analysis of any thesis, but all good ways have this in common: One's analysis must be broken down into component parts, and each element must be examined and developed in an orderly and integrated way. The structure of your paper should reflect the basic components of the argument which has to be made to support your thesis. It's hard to be more specific than this about how to break down the analysis into its component parts because not only does each thesis demand a different set of components, but each writer on the same thesis might use different components or might order his or her components differently.

Do make an outline before you begin to write. It needn't be a formal outline with I, A, 1, a, iii's in it, but it should break the argument up into the basic components and it should reflect the order in which the strongest case for your position can be made. Play around with the ordering of the elements. Ask yourself why what you put first needs to be there.

Try not to have more than three basic elements in your argument. Why, you ask. Simple. Human beings are limited creatures. They get bored or confused if you make six, twelve, or twenty arguments at once. People are pretty good at holding onto two or three basic arguments or components of arguments at the same time. So pander to them; pick what's most important to say in the text and put everything else in footnotes (or in a folder for your next book).

Allow yourself to revise your structure as you go along if, as you write, you find yourself dissatisfied with your initial organization. Reread the paper after you've written it to see if the organization you tried has been successful. If not, try to rework it in outline form before rewriting the whole paper.

Adopt a Measured Tone

The importance of tone is often overlooked by neophyte writers.

To decide what kind of tone your paper should have, think about whom you want to persuade of the point you're making in the paper. When you know to whom the piece is addressed, you will (hopefully) be able to figure out what tone would be most likely to facilitate your goal of convincing that person. If you keep this audience in mind throughout your paper, you will be able to keep the tone constant.

In legal papers, it is generally a good idea to adopt a tone of measured rationality, as if you were saying "let us reason together on this issue." Target the paper as if the audience were a reasonably intelligent and diligent judge who, until now, has had little or no exposure to the issue on which you write but who is about to make an important decision on it.[13] Assume this judge has some serious reservations about the position you take, but has not yet made up his or her mind on the subject. Your job is to anticipate and meet all of his or her objections and other concerns. It is more effective to do this, not in a defensive way but by incorporating those considerations that seem to cut against your position within the framework of your affirmative analysis of the issue.[14]

Too forceful or strident a tone will make the reader feel bludgeoned. This will not only make the reader angry, but it will also distract him or her from perceiving the merit of your argument. Even your supporters, who may look to your piece for intellectual support, may be offended to too harsh a tone.

Too colloquial or journalistic a tone will make the reader think you are not really taking the issue seriously, or are not capable of taking the issue seriously, except perhaps in an emotional way. Too wishy-washy, vague, or ambivalent a tone will cause the reader to doubt whether he or she can gain anything by reading what you have to say about the matter.

The tone of a paper is one of the primary things which will make a reader decide whether to trust or distrust the writer. If the tone is wrong, most readers will stop reading the paper.

Be Concrete and Simplify Whenever Possible

Concreteness is related to tone, but it is worth emphasizing as a separate concern. My advice is this: Whenever there is a choice between saying something in an abstract way or saying it in a concrete way, opt for the concrete expression. Or, if you feel you must speak abstractly, at least give a concrete example to illustrate the abstract point. Abstraction and reification seem to be occupational hazards of the legal profession,[15] but one can fight one's impulses to be abstract. Generally, it is wise to do so.

A friend once told me that Albert Einstein said: "Make things as simple as possible — but no simpler." That is a basic rule of science; it should be a basic rule of writing as well. It should apply to everything about your writing from your theories, to the thread of your argumentation, to your descriptions, and to the language you use to express your ideas.

Almost any subject can be made to seem to be unremittingly complex. The world is, in fact, a complicated place. However, we can understand the world (or one of its facets) only by simplifying it. The more complicated your argument is, the harder it will be for your reader to follow it. That's why if there's a simpler way to develop your argument, use it.[16]

Don't try to impress your reader with fancy words and long, complex sentences structures. (An occasional fancy word is okay.) When you finish writing, go back over your text and prune the sentence structure and wording. We all tend to be a bit prolix (is this a well-placed fancy word?), especially in our early drafts. At least five to ten percent of your text can usually be trimmed without loss of meaning. Often, the excision of that excess five to ten percent will, in fact, enhance the effectiveness of your communication.

Endnotes

1. G. Orwell, "Why I Write", in *A Collection of Essays* 320 (1954).
2. Think of how many of the words we use to describe good writing that are derived from words referring to light or related to light imagery: lucid, enlightening, elucidating, illuminating, dazzling, brilliant, reflective, polished, to name a few.
3. That is, I do not believe every paper should be organized and written in the same way: First, do X, then do Y, then do Z. People get bored by formula-structured work. A writer's aims is to keep his or her reader interested.
4. On occasion I suggest to a writer whose work I'm editing an organization or approach I might use if I were writing on the topic. I do this mostly to help the writer think of alternatives when I see a problem with the existing organization. To the extent I can, I try to work with the writer on the organization and mode of analysis he or she has chosen for the piece.
5. I also find it necessary to tell my students to be aware of my objectivity. There are many ways to analyze an issue and many acceptable outcomes on particular issues. I tell them I will be neither harder nor easier on them if they take the position they think I might espouse. My only concern in reviewing their work is to help them build the best possible argument for whatever position they decide to take. Even harebrained ideas can be made to look respectable.

I also tell my students that for perhaps the last time in a long while, they will be able in their papers to be above the adversarial fray of well-heeled interests. I ask them to disregard what their past, present, or future professors, employers, or clients would think about the issue. Write about the topic, I say, as if it was your responsibility to decide what to do about the problem. Even better, write as if you were explaining to someone who would make the decision why the course of action you recommend or the way of looking at the problem that you have adopted, makes the most sense of all the possible alternatives and is the one most conducive to the best welfare of society. See Section II, Rule 14, regarding consideration of the policy implications of one's thesis.
6. It is often necessary to do some research to refine one's approach to a topic enough to have a thesis about it. I usually require my students to write a summary of the thesis of their paper in the first few weeks of the term in order to prod them to formulate one. I tell them they'll be surprised how much easier it is to do research and organize their thoughts about a topic when they decide what point they want to make.
7. In *A v. B* the court held **X**. In *C v. D* the court held **Y**. The cases are in conflict. Conclusion: too bad, or there is a need for the issue to be resolved, but I don't care to help with it.
8. Now I think **X**; but then there's **Y**; and yet **Z** makes me think something else; so maybe I should go to Hawaii and forget about it.
9. I tell my students it's okay to change their minds about their theses if further research or thought reveals a gaping hole in the roof of the argument.
10. See Section II, Rule 1, regarding my advice on strong first paragraphs.
11. See Section II, Rules 2 & 5, regarding section titles and transitions.
12. For those of you whose mothers don't have this attitude, isn't it true that you'd like her to feel this way?
13. Someone who strongly favors or is adamantly opposed to your position won't need your reasoned analysis to make up his or her mind.
14. See Section II, Rule 7, regarding the advice on respectfully addressing your opponent's arguments.
15. There seems to me to be two main reasons for the typical law student's lust after abstraction. One is that they have spent their first year of law school reading judicial opinions which themselves are replete with abstractions. The second is that in reading the cases for the purpose of extracting abstract principles, law students become intoxicated by the principles and mistake them for the real thing in the cases which are the situations.
16. Scientists will also tell you simpler explanations are also more likely to be true.

One Right Way[†]
H.S. Becker

SCHOLARLY writers have to organize their material, express an argument clearly enough that readers can follow the reasoning and accept the conclusions. They make this job harder than it need be when they think that there is only One Right Way to do it, that each paper they write has a preordained structure they must find. They simplify their work, on the other hand, when they recognize that there are many effective ways to say something and that their job is only to choose one and execute it so that readers will know what they are doing.

† Becker, Howard S., "One Right Way" in *Writing for Social Scientists* (Chicago: University of Chicago Press, 1986) at 43–48. Reprinted by permission of the author and University of Chicago Press.

I have a lot of trouble with students (and not just students) when I go over their papers and suggest revisions. They get tongue-tied and act ashamed and upset when I say that this is a good start, all you have to do is this, that, and the other and it will be in good shape. Why do they think there is something wrong with changing what they have written? Why are they so leery of rewriting?

It might be laziness. You might decide...that it is physically too much trouble to do it again. You just don't feel like retyping a page or cutting-and-pasting any more.

More often, students and scholars balk at rewriting because they are subordinates in a hierarchical organization, usually a school. The master-servant or boss-worker relationship characteristic of schools gives people a lot of reasons for not wanting to rewrite, many of them quite sensible. Teachers and administrators intend their schools' systems of reward to encourage learning. But those systems usually teach undergraduates, instead, to earn grades rather than to be interested in the subjects they study or to do a really good job.... Students try to find out, by interrogating instructors and relying on the experience of other students, exactly what they have to do to get good grades. When they find out, they do what they have learned is necessary, and no more. Few students learn (and here we can rely on our own memories as students and teachers) that they have to rewrite or revise anything. On the contrary, they learn that a really smart student does a paper once, making it as good as possible in one pass. If you really don't care very much about the work you are doing — if it is just a chore to be done for a course, and you have calculated that it is worth only so much effort and no more — then you might reasonably do it once and to hell with it. You have better ways to spend your time.

Schools also teach students to think of writing as a kind of test: the teacher hands you the problem, and you try to answer it, then go on to the next problem. One shot per problem. Going over it is, somehow, "cheating," especially when you have had the benefit of someone else's coaching after your first try. It's somehow no longer a fair test of your own abilities. You can hear your sixth grade teacher saying, "Is this all your own work?" What a student might think of as coaching and cheating, of course, is what more experienced people think of as getting some critical response from informed readers.

Joseph Williams suggested to me that students, being young, simply don't have the experience of life that would let them use their imaginations to get out of their own egocentric worlds. They thus cannot imagine an audience's response or the possibility of a text other than the one they have already produced. That may be true. But the lack of experience may result less from youth than from the way schools infantilize young people. Graduate students certainly appreciate the need for rewriting more

keenly when, contemplating reading their paper at a professional meeting, they envision total strangers assaulting their logic, evidence, and prose.

Such reasons might explain why people don't rewrite, but not the shame and embarrassment they feel at the thought of doing it. These feelings also originate in schools. No one connected with schools, neither teachers nor administrators, tells students how the writing they read — textbooks or their own teachers' research reports, for instance — actually gets done. In fact, as I said earlier...the separation of scholarly work from teaching in almost all schools hides the process from students. (Just as, according to Thomas Kuhn, histories of science hide all the false turns and mistakes in the research programs that produced the successes they celebrate.) Students don't know, never seeing their teacher, let alone textbook authors, at work, that all these people do things more than once, rather than treating their professional work as a quasi-test. Students don't know that journal editors routinely send papers back for revision, that publishers hire editors to improve the prose of books to be published. They don't know that revising and editing happen to everyone, and are not emergency procedures undertaken only in cases of scandalously unprofessional incompetence.

Students think of their teachers, and the textbook authors their teachers stand for, as authorities for another obvious reason: these people stand above them in the school hierarchy. They are the bosses who give the grades and judge whether students' work is good enough. Unless students decide that the educational institutions they attend are frauds (and surprisingly few do, considering the evidence available to them), they will accept the implicit organizational proposition that the people who run schools know what they are doing. Not only, then, do their academic superiors — as far as they can see — never rewrite anything, they also get what they write "right" the first time. So students learn and really believe, at least for a while, that "real writers" (or "professionals" or "smart people") get it right the first time. Only dummies have to do it over and over. This might be another version of the test mentality: the ability to do it right the first time shows superior ability. This, too, is hierarchy, full-blown, at its worst: subordinates taking such evaluations as grades and teachers' comments, which are legitimated by the stratification of schools and scholarship, as ultimate and not-to-be-questioned evaluations of their own personal worth...

All these ideas — about not rewriting, about the school paper as a sign of worth — rest on the fallacious premise that there is a "right answer," a "best way" to do things. Some readers will think I have invented a strawman, that serious students and scholars know there is no One Right Way. But students and scholars do believe in One Right Way, because the institutions they work in embody that idea. The ideas of the right answer and a best way find their natural home in hierarchy. Most people believe that the higher-ups in hierarchical organizations know more and know better than the people lower down. They don't. Studies of organizations show that superiors may know more about some things, but usually know a good deal less about many others. They even know less about the organization's central business, which you might suppose they would know better. But the official theory of the organization, and usually of its environing society, ignores such results, holding that higher-ups really do know better. What they know is, in fact, by definition the "right answer."

No matter that real authorities on any subject know that there is never one right answer, just a lot of provisional answers competing for attention and acceptance. Students, undergraduates particularly, don't like such talk. Why bother learning something that isn't true only to have to learn something else in its place tomorrow? Nor do true-believing scholars like it, whether they have discovered the truth themselves, or are only followers of the discoverers. The leaders of the field must know. What they know is what's in the book. That is real

hierarchy, seen most clearly when a chemistry experiment performed in class fails to produce the "correct" result and the teacher tells students what should have happened and what, therefore, they should write in their notebooks. (Yes, that *does* happen.)

If there is one right answer, and you believe that the authorities who run the institution you work in know it, then you know that your job is to find out the right answer and reproduce it when required, thus showing that you deserve to be rewarded, maybe even to become one of the guardians yourself. That is the undergraduate version. A slightly more sophisticated versions afflicts graduate students and professionals. Since what you are writing is something new, the One Right Way does not exist, but its Platonic ideal exists somewhere and it is up to you to discover it and put it down on paper. I suppose that many of us would like readers to feel that we have found such a preordained right way to say what we say, one that looks as though it could only be that way. But serious writers discover that perfect form (that is, some form that does what they want done, even though not the only possible one), after lengthy exploitation, not the first time.

Style Guide for Law Essays[†]

GENERAL FORM

Each term paper should have (1) a title page, (2) a brief table of contents (only if asked for by your professor), and (3) bibliography (if requested). Plain bond or computer paper should be used with left-hand and top margins, one and one-half inches wide, and right-hand and bottom margins one inch wide. If word-processed (preferable), the text should be double-spaced. The pages should be numbered and the original copy should be handed in.

PRELIMINARY

The importance of taking your original notes carefully cannot be overstated. Be sure to write down a full description of the source, including all the bibliographical information that you will need. Record the number of the page(s) from which each note is taken.

FOOTNOTES

In order to avoid charges of plagiarism, footnotes or endnotes should be used in the following instances:

(a) when quoting directly from another's work
(b) when paraphrasing the statements of others
(c) when discussing opinions and theories of others
(d) when presenting information which is not a matter of general knowledge
(e) when explaining and amplifying statements made in your text.

Each footnote should be listed in the text by an arabic figure, placed on a level with apostrophes, at the end of the passage to which it refers. Footnotes should be numbered consecutively throughout the paper. The footnotes themselves should be placed at the bottom of each page and identified in order by number. Endnotes should be placed at the end of your paper (before the bibliography) and also identified by number.

[†] "Style Guide for Law Essays", Department of Law, Carleton University, 1994.

THE COMPLETE CITATION

The first time a work is cited in a footnote, complete bibliographical information should be given.

Examples for Books

A full citation includes author's name, title (underlined *or* italicized), volume number (if any), place of publication, publisher, date and pinpoint.

One Author:

¹ G. Parker, *An Introduction to Criminal Law* (Toronto: Methuen, 1983) at 73.

Joint Authors:

² R.H. Floyd, C.S. Gray & R.P. Short, *Public-Enterprises in Mixed Economies* (Washington, D.C.: International Monetary Fund, 1984).

More Than Three Authors:
Cite only the first author and use "*et al.*"

³ J.B. Laskin *et al.*, *Debtor and Creditor: Cases, Notes, and Materials*, 2d ed. (Toronto: University of Toronto Press, 1982).

Editor of a Collection as Author:

⁴ W.T. McGrath, ed., *Crime and its Treatment in Canada* (Toronto: Gage Publishing Limited, 1980).

Examples of Journal Articles

A full citation includes author's name, title of article (in quotes), year of publication, volume number, name of journal, page and pinpoint.

One Author:

⁴ M.R. Goode, "*Mens Rea* in *Corpore Reo*: An Exploration of the Rapists' Charter" (1983) 7 *Dalhousie L.J.* 447 at 448.

Joint Authors:

⁵ G.A. Ferguson & D.W. Roberts, "Plea Bargaining: Directions for Canadian Reform" (1974), 52 *Can. Bar Rev.* 497 at 503.

SHORTENED FORM OF CITATION

Use this shortened form only when complete citation has already been used in an earlier footnote or endnote. Include only author's surname, a reference to the earlier footnote or endnote, and the page references. For example:

⁶ Parker, *supra* note 1 at 8. (Note: *supra* is Latin for "above")

If the work being cited is the same as that *immediately* above it, *Ibid*, may be used. For example:

⁶ Parker, *supra* note 1 at 8.
⁷ *Ibid.* at 10.

CASES

Cases decided in different courts in various jurisdictions have been collected and printed in series of case reports. One series of case reports usually deals with cases from one jurisdiction, cases from one level of court, or cases concerning one legal subject. For example, in Ontario, the *Ontario Reports* report cases decided in Ontario. An example of a series of case reports dealing with one particular topic is *Canadian Criminal Cases*, which is a collection of cases from all across Canada that relate to criminal law matters.

When referring to a case reported in a series of case reports, the citation of the case is given so that others can find the full text of the decision if they wish. Cases are always cited as follows: name of the case, date of the decision or the volume of the series in which the case is found, volume number, name of the law reports, series, page number, name of the court giving the decision. If the date is given in square brackets, that means that the date is important in finding the correct volume of the reports; each year the volume numbers start over again (i.e., there are volumes 1, 2, and 3 in each year). Sometimes, only one volume exists for each year and only a date is given in square brackets. If the date is given in round brackets, then it is not required to find the case. You merely have to look at the volume number. For example:

R. v. Stanley (1977), 36 C.C.C. (2d) 216 (B.C.C.A.).

R. v. Landry, [1991] 1 S.C.R. 99 at 110, 62 C.C.C. (3d) 117, Lamer C.J.

Examples of Frequently Used Law Report Series
- C.C.C. Canadian Criminal Cases (criminal law cases — Canada)
- R.F.L. Reports of Family Law (family law cases — Canada)

- O.R.   Ontario Reports (cases from Ontario)
- O.L.R.   Ontario Law Reports (old series — no longer used)
- O.W.N.   Ontario Weekly Notes (old series — no longer used)
- W.W.R.   Western Weekly Reports (cases — Western Canada)
- D.L.R.   Dominion Law Reports (cases from all of Canada)
- S.C.R.   Supreme Court Reports (cases from the Supreme Court of Canada)
- All E.R.   All England Law Reports (cases from England and other parts of the Commonwealth)

Please note that there are often more than one series of any particular law report. For example, there are four series of the *Dominion Law Reports*, three of *Reports of Family Law*, and two of the *Ontario Reports*. The series are indicated as follows:

First series: (1976), 25 R.F.L. 213
Second series: (1981), 18 R.F.L. (2d) 400
Third series: (1987), 6 R.F.L. (3d) 234

LEGISLATION

Citation of legislation should include the title of the statute, statute volume, the jurisdiction, the year, the chapter number and pinpoint. For example:

Canada Evidence Act, R.S.C. 1970, c. E–10, s. 19(a).
City of Moncton Act, 1990, S.N.B. 1990, c. 69.

BIBLIOGRAPHY

At the end of the paper, after footnotes and/or endnotes, list all books, pamphlets, articles, newspapers, documents, legislation, etc., which you used in preparation of the paper. Refer also to interviews conducted. All but the first line of each reference should be indented. In the bibliography, authors are cited by giving the last name first, and alphabetically. You may wish to list cases and legislation separately from other sources used. For example:

Floyd, R.H., C.S. Gray & R.P. Short, *Public Enterprises in Mixed Economies*. Washington, D.C.: International Monetary Fund, 1984.
Goode, M.R., "*Mens Rea* in *Corpore Reo*: An Exploration of the Rapists' Charter" (1983), 7 *Dalhousie Law Journal* 447.
Parker, G., *An Introduction to Criminal Law*. Toronto: Methuen, 1983.

For a more detailed discussion of citation, refer to other style handbooks. Examples of legal handbooks are:

Canadian Guide to Uniform Legal Citation, 3d ed. (Toronto: Carswell, 1992).
MacEllven, D.T., *Legal Research Handbook*, 3d ed. (Toronto: Butterworths, 1993).

A free writing Tutorial Service is available to students of Carleton University. For more information, call 788–6632 or inquire at Paterson Hall, Room 215.

Plagiarism and Acknowledging Sources[†]
J. Johnson

AVOIDING PLAGIARISM

If you take notes carefully and record your sources accurately, you will be able to document your sources when you write your paper. You must give others credit when you use their words or when you paraphrase or summarize their original ideas. Failure to do so is called *plagiarism*, which means literary theft, and may lead to a legal suit if the plagiarized material is published uncredited. In college, plagiarism is also unacceptable. The best way to avoid plagiarism is by converting the ideas of your source into your own words — as summary or paraphrase — as

---

[†]   Excerpts from Johnson, Jean, *The Bedford Guide to the Research Process* (New York: St. Martin's Press, 1987) at 96–98, 151–59. Copyright © 1987. Reprinted by permission of St. Martin's Press, Incorporated.

you take notes or, if you quote directly, by making sure that you use quotation marks. Whenever you write down any information from a source, be sure to note where you found it so that you can cite that source in your paper. If someone else's words are on your note cards without identification, you may end up with the same words in your paper, which is unarguably plagiarism. You may also slip into plagiarism by failing to take notes at all and instead trying to write your paper directly from photocopied material or from books. Without the intermediate stage of putting the information into your own words on cards, it is easy to use the words of the original source without realizing it.

But, you might ask, do I have to document every bit of information I put into my paper? Must I have a footnote for every sentence? Because a good bit of what you write will be yours and some of it will be general knowledge, you will not need to document every sentence in your paper, but you must, as a careful researcher, record your sources on your note cards so that you will know to whom to give credit. Suggestions for documenting your paper will be given [later in the book — Eds.].

The preceding sections [not included in this extract (consult original for more information) — Eds.] on paraphrasing and summarizing show how to take notes that do not plagiarize. You will not get into trouble if you make the information part of your own thinking and then put it down in your own words. Trouble arises when you take notes mechanically, without actually understanding what you are writing. Plagiarism usually takes one of the following three forms:

1. Word-for-word transcription of the entire passage.
2. A paraphrase using the basic sentence structure of the source with a few of the words of phrases of the note taker substituted for those of the source.
3. A paraphrase using the note taker's sentence structure and many of his or her words but with key words of the author used, without quotation marks.

Here are some examples of note taking illustrating the last two of these types of plagiarism. The notes are based on this passage from *The Greek Experience*, by C.M. Bowra.

> The essence of the heroic outlook is the pursuit of honour through action. The great man is he who, being endowed with superior qualities of body and mind, uses them to the utmost and wins the applause of his fellows because he spares no effort and shirks no risk in his desire to make the most of the gifts and to surpass other men in his exercise of them.

In the following paraphrase, the writer keeps the basic structure of the original and merely changes a few of the words. This is plagiarism.

> The main idea in the heroic outlook is striving to achieve honor by being active. The great man, having the highest qualities of body and mind, uses them to the greatest extent and is applauded by his comrades because he will pay any price in his desire to make the best of his gifts and to do better than other men in his use of them.

The following note uses the note taker's sentence structure, but borrows key words and phrases without quotation marks. This also is plagiarism.

> The Greeks believed that the hero had superior qualities of body and mind. In his desire to make the most of his gifts the great man would spare no effort in his desire to use his gifts in surpassing other men.

An acceptable paraphrase would be as follows:

> Heroism to the Greeks meant the demonstration of superiority through great deeds. The Greeks believed that the hero was a man who was superior to other men and who was willing to use his great qualities even if he risked his life doing so. He deserves the praise he gets from his fellowmen.

Or a combination of paraphrase and quotation may be used:

> The Greeks' idea of heroism was "the pursuit of honour through action." The hero has "superior qualities of body and mind" and he will take any risk in order to demonstrate his heroism to his fellowmen.

These paraphrases can now be integrated into a paper with no danger of plagiarism. Of course, the source must be cited; instead of using a footnote, the writer might give the author's name in the text as part of the introduction to the passage. Notice that single words do not have to be put between quotation marks unless they show an original or distinctive use by the source; the word *superior* as used in the first acceptable paraphrase does not indicate a special use of the word and so no quotation marks are necessary. Notice also that quoted material must be given exactly as it is in the original; in the second example the writer uses the British spelling of *honor*.

Exercises

1. Photocopy a short article or part of a long article from an encyclopedia or periodical on a subject related to your topic. On note cards, summarize the material on the photocopy in a short paragraph and paraphrase some of it. Intersperse a few words from the original if you wish (being careful to use quotation marks), but the notes should be primarily in your own words. In class exchange your notes and photocopy with another class member; then write a comment to the person whose paper you have, answering the following questions: (a) Are the summary and paraphrase accurate? (b) Do they avoid plagiarism?

2. Record the following in your search log:
   - The most interesting bit of information you have learned about your subject so far.
   - The most frustrating experience you have had so far in your research.
   - The most enjoyable part of your research process until now.
   - Exchange your observations with your classmates.

3. Write an evaluation of at least three of your sources, including both a book and an article, if possible. Explain in detail how you arrived at your evaluation and the sources that guided you.

4. In your search log, write a summary of the progress you have made in recording and evaluating your sources.

. . . .

ACKNOWLEDGING YOUR SOURCES

When to Acknowledge Your Sources

You must give credit in your paper for ideas or information that belongs to someone else, whether you quote it, summarize it, or paraphrase it. Explaining where you got your material is part of the information about your subject that belongs in your paper. It gives readers a chance to judge its reliability and accuracy and also makes it possible for them to look up more about the subject if they want to. Failure to give the source is literary theft or plagiarism. (For suggestions on avoiding plagiarism, see [p. 120].)

But give citations only when they are necessary. Every footnote or endnote number or parenthetical citation disturbs the flow of your writing to some extent. You do not need to cite your source in the following instances:

1. When your information is common knowledge.

   Mars was the Roman god of war.
   Dwight Eisenhower became president in 1953.

Although it may be difficult sometimes to identify what is common knowledge, in most cases you should not have trouble. Any date, like the one given in the example, that can be verified in an encyclopedia, newspaper, or almanac need not be documented, even though many people might not remember it.

2. When the information is accepted as true by most people.

   Alcoholism impairs the functions of the brain, liver, stomach, and lungs.

This kind of information may be harder to identify. You may be gathering information on a subject you know little about and everything is new to you. In doing research for a paper on drugs, you may read that most former heroin addicts are unable to stay away from heroin permanently. Is this common knowledge among doctors and heroin users? When you aren't sure whether it's common knowledge, and when your readers are people at the same level of knowledge as you who might question the validity of your information or wonder where you got it, you should document it.

3. When the statements or observations are your own.

   No one should be locked into full-time custodial care when alternative means of treatment are available.

You should always cite your source in these instances:

(a) When the information is exclusively the idea or discovery of one person or a group of people. All direct quotations and most paraphrases and summaries of factual information fit this description.

   As crime rates rise, more prisoners stay longer in prisons that are already crammed well past their planned capacity (Jenson 1980).

The statement that "more prisoners stay longer" in crowded prisons needs to be documented by citing the person who has the figures to back up this information.

   In 1981 only 8 percent of architects reported using computers; in 1986, 32 percent of architects are expected to be using computers in their work ("Computers" 20).

You should give the source of any figures unless you compiled them.

(b) When your readers might like to find out more about the subject.

In his "Health Care for All Americans" bill, Senator Kennedy proposed the creation of a comprehensive plan to control health care expenditures (Riegle).

(c) When your readers might question the accuracy or authenticity of the information. Ask yourself whether your readers are likely to ask "Where did you find that?" or "Who said that?"

One species of mammal becomes extinct each year (Ziswiler 17).

(d) When you use a direct quotation of one word or more.

In his later years Lowell called Rousseau "a monstrous liar" (*Letters* 466).

How to Acknowledge Your Sources

The documentation within your text can be placed in footnotes or within parentheses; the documentation at the end of your paper will be a list called Works Cited, References, or Bibliography. Your choice of documentation style depends either on your subject or on the preference of the person or organization you are writing for. Check with your instructor to find out what style is required for your paper. The style commonly used by writers in the humanities (English, foreign languages, history, and philosophy) is known as the author/page style and is recommended by the Modern Language Association in the *MLA Handbook* (1984). This style is frequently used by writers in other disciplines, too, so if you are in doubt as to which style to use or if your instructor does not express a preference, the author/page style will probably be acceptable. [Consult original for] detailed guidelines for using this system as well as two sample papers illustrating its use.

A variant of this style is the use of footnotes at the bottom of the page or endnotes on a separate page at the end of the paper. Until 1983, footnotes or endnotes were advocated in the *MLA Handbook*, and many writers in the humanities still use them. You'll find suggestions for using them also in Chapter 11 [of the original].

The author/date system is favoured by writers in the social sciences, biology, earth sciences, and business and is recommended in the *Publication Manual of the American Psychological Association* (1983). Details for using this system and a sample paper are given in [the original].

A third major documentation style is the number system, preferred by writers in the applied sciences, medical sciences, and engineering and outlined in the *CBE Style Manual*, published by the Council of Biology Editors (1983). The use of this style is explained and a sample paper is provided in [the original].

The three major systems — author/page, author/date, and the number system — recommend that documentation information be given in parentheses within the paper with a list of references placed at the end. The following guidelines give some of the most frequent uses of these systems. You will find details for each system in [the original].

While you are writing your first draft, be sure to give the source in parentheses so that you will know where the material came from when you write your final draft. No matter what citation system you use in your final draft, give at least the author and page number of every summary, paraphrase, or quotation as you write your first draft.

Author/Page System

If you use the author/page system of citation, you need to supply the author's last name and the page number of the work, either in your text or in parentheses. Readers who want to know the name of the work and the publication facts can look those up in the list of works cited at the end of your paper. Place the parenthetical citation as near as possible to the information you are documenting, either where a pause occurs or at the end of the sentence.

When should you put the author's name in your text and when should you put it in the citation? To decide the answer, consider the needs of your readers. If the name of the author is a significant part of the information you are giving, give the name in your text, leaving only the page number for your citation.

According to Van Doren (4), early American fiction writers were often charged with corrupting the public morals.

Here the page number is placed after the name of the author instead of after the information given because a pause occurs there.

When the information you are giving or the point you are making is more important than the author, place the author's name as well as the page number in the parenthetical citation.

The Alliance adopted the free silver plank in its platform of 1887 (Hicks 132).

Note that there is no punctuation between the author and page number and that the period marking the end of the sentence comes after the parenthetical citation.

However, if you have included more than one work by an author in your list of works cited, you will have to include a brief title in your citation.

As early as 1884, both major parties recognized labor in their platforms (Destler, *American Radicalism* 141).

You might refer, in your text, to a whole work; in that case you would not need a parenthetical citation.

In *My Antonia*, Willa Cather allows the narrator to overshadow the heroine.

When you have a long quotation set off from the rest of the text, place the citation in parentheses two spaces after the punctuation mark at the end of the quotation.

In *The Jungle*, Upton Sinclair depicted the horrors of slaughterhouses in passages like this:

> The fertilizer works of Durham's lay away from the rest of the plant. Few visitors ever saw them, and the few who did would come out looking like Dante, of whom the peasants declared that he had been into hell. To this part of the yards came all the "tankage," and the waste products of all sorts; here they dried out the bones — and in suffocating cellars where the daylight never came you might see men and women and children bending over whirling machines and sawing bits of bone into all sorts of shapes, breathing their lungs full of the fine dust. (129)

In the author/page system, as in the other systems, you would not put any documentation in footnotes or endnotes. The only notes you might use are content or explanatory notes to explain a point further or cite other bibliographic sources. If you use these, you would put them at the end of the paper before the Works Cited section. In the text you would place a superscript numeral, like this,[1] to refer your readers to a note at the end of the paper in a section labelled Notes:

[1]   See also Schlesinger (717), who points out that Adams was fascinated with politics throughout his career.

Leave one space between the superscript number and the beginning of the note.

Explanatory or content notes are explained further in [the original]; you will find other examples of their use in the sample papers in [the original].

Author/Date System

For those who use the author/date system (writers in the social sciences, biology, business, economics, linguis-

tics and earth sciences), the date of the information cited, as well as the name of the author, is important and must appear either in your text or in a parenthetical citation. The list of sources appears at the end of the paper arranged in alphabetical order and usually titled References. A few of the most commonly used citations are given here; you'll find others in [the original], along with a sample paper.

As you would want to do with any of these systems, make sure you introduce your source rather than just giving a quotation or paraphrase with a citation at the end.

If you use the author's name as part of your text, place the date in parentheses following the name:

Wellington's study (1982) clearly showed that...

If the date is important enough to be included in the text, you should need no citation:

Wellington's 1982 study showed that...

Perhaps you will want to put both the author and date in the parenthetical citation:

At least one authority (Wellington, 1982) has pointed out that...

Note the comma between the author's name and the date.

Some instructors and some publishers prefer that page numbers be given with each citation. In any case, when you quote directly from someone else's work you *must* give a page number. When the author and the quotation are separated, the date is usually given directly after the name of the author; and the page number follows the quotation.

According to Lowe (1979), prison "should be the last alternative" (p. 14).

With a quotation of more than forty words, indent the whole passage five spaces from the left margin. If there are any paragraphs within the passage, indent the first line of each one five more spaces.

Barlow and Seidner (1983) reported the following results:

> The majority of relationship problems are connected with the phobia. This seemed clearly true in the first client where the relationship was basically very strong.... Nevertheless, relationship issues improved considerably as phobia improved. This girl was referred for further therapy concerning interpersonal relationships and career choices following treatment.

The second client, on the other hand, came from a severely disturbed family with constant conflict. The mother held the family together by trying to accommodate everybody but was hospitalized occasionally for periods of amnesia lasting several days during times of particularly intense family stress. (p. 525)

Note the location and punctuation of the page number for a block quote — two spaces after the final period.

Number System

The number system is used by writers in chemistry, physics, mathematics, medicine, and nursing and by some writers in biology. (A few chemistry journals use the author/date system.) With this system, citations start with "1" and are numbered consecutively throughout the paper. If a reference is repeated, its original number is repeated. Items in the list of references at the end of the paper are given in numerical order. Some writers use a variation of this system: the list of references is in alphabetical order and, consequently, the numbers in the text are not in serial order. For more details on the use of the number system of citation and a sample paper, see [the original].

A citation using the number system appears this way.

Paroxysmal tachycardia occurs more often in young patients with normal hearts (5).

In a variation of the number system, some writers use both the number and the name of the author(s).

Paroxysmal tachycardia occurs more often in young patients with normal hearts (Krupp and Chatton 5).

. . . .

[MORE ON] AVOIDING PLAGIARISM

Plagiarism is using others' words or ideas without attribution (see [above] for suggestions on avoiding plagiarism while taking notes). The use of summaries, paraphrases, and quotations from others without citing the source is plagiarism; using verbatim quotations without enclosing them in quotation marks is also plagiarism.

Plagiarism results from a writer's failure to integrate information from sources into his or her own thinking. Such failure often originates in inadequate paraphrasing and summarizing when you take notes; attempts to shorten the process and write directly from sources can lead to plagiarism. Besides the academic and legal penalties for

plagiarism, one of the most unfortunate results is the writer's loss of the pleasure that comes from discovery of knowledge (plagiarism is evidence of the lack of such discovery) and the subsequent pleasure of telling about it.

Plagiarism is usually recognizable because the borrowed material is written in a different style from that of the author of the paper. Sometimes the borrowed material alternates with the writer's words with resulting distortion and lack of clarity. Often terms that were explained earlier in the original are not explained in the paper. Writers involved with their audiences do not write this way. But the writer who uses others' writing instead of his or her own is not concerned primarily with communicating to the reader, and most readers can sense this. [Below,] is an example of plagiarism in the introduction to a paper. You will find it difficult to understand, even though it is the beginning of the paper, and you will probably lose interest rather quickly. The plagiarized passages are [italicized].

Although the writer cites a source, his citation is given only at the end of the last sentence. Therefore, a reader has to conclude that everything else is his own. Yet it is obvious that to make such sweeping generalizations about large periods of history, the writer would have had to engage in years of research and would need to produce a book-length work to give the details on which they were based. The scope is beyond a student writer at almost any level. Lack of clarity and coherence are the result of stitching together unexplained generalizations from another writer with a few words of the writer's own.

Plagiarism is a rhetorical as well as an ethical problem. It results from interconnected failures in thinking, note taking, and writing. Here are some suggestions for avoiding plagiarism.

1. Make a schedule when you start work on your paper and follow it as closely as possible. When you find yourself rushing to meet a deadline, it is easy to get careless and save time by using someone else's words.

Example of Plagiarism

Original
The long epoch from the Second Awakening to the war with Spain was also a century of great tribulation, an "ordeal of faith" for church-going America....

On the intellectual level the new challenges were of two sorts. First, there was a set of specific problems that had to be faced separately: Darwin unquestionably became the nineteenth century's Newton, and his theory of evolution through natural selection became the century's cardinal idea.... Accompanying these specific problems was a second and more general challenge: the rise of positivistic naturalism, the cumulative result of modern methods for acquiring knowledge. In every discipline from physics to biblical criticism, myth and error were being dispelled, and the result of this activity was a world view which raised problems of the most fundamental sort. (Sydney E. Ahlstrom, *A Religious History of the American People* [New Haven; Yale University Press, 1972], pp. 763–64)

Plagiarized version

The long epoch *from the Second Awakening* of 1785 and *the war with Spain* in 1898 *was a century of tribulation and ordeal* for religious Americans. During this period, but most notably between the years 1865–1900, many intellectual clergymen created a new Liberal Theology built on the tenets of Darwinism and positivistic naturalism, while the unlettered population remained staunchly conservative based on the orthodoxy of the Puritans.

The *intellectuals* dealt with *two challenges*, each of them separately. First, there was *Darwin*, who had *become by (1865) the Newton of the nineteenth century*, whose *theory of natural selection had become the century's cardinal idea.*

The second was a more general challenge: *the rise of positivistic naturalism*, or *the cumulative result of modern methods for acquiring* information. *In every discipline from physics to biblical* exegesis, *myth and error were being dispelled*, and the *result*ing *world view raised fundamental problems* concerning faith and the deterministic principles held by the church (Ahlstrom 763–64).

2. Choose a topic that you want to learn about and will want to tell others about. If you are genuinely interested in your subject you will want to use your own words to explain it.

3. Make sure you understand the materials you are reading; if you don't understand them, don't use them in your paper. If you don't comprehend your information, you will have to use someone else's words to explain it.

4. Take notes only after you have integrated your reading into your own thinking. Use paraphrasing and summarizing as much as possible in order to ensure that the material has become your own.

5. Before you write, review your notes carefully and make sure you understand how and where they will fit into your paper. If you don't see the connection between your information and your over-all purpose, it will be difficult for you to use your own words.

6. Avoid writing directly from your sources. It's difficult not to use the words you see right before you.

If you follow these guidelines, it's unlikely that you will find yourself plagiarizing. Even more important, you will have the pleasure of writing a paper that you yourself will enjoy reading.

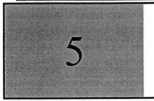

Law and the State: Constitutional Bases of Law

5

Introduction to the Study of the Law of the Constitution[†]
A.V. Dicey

THE RULE OF LAW: ITS NATURE AND GENERAL APPLICATIONS[1]

Two features have at all times since the Norman Conquest characterised the political institutions of England.

The first of these features is the omnipotence or un-disputed supremacy throughout the whole country of the central government. This authority of the state or the nation was during the earlier periods of our history represented by the power of the Crown. The King was the source of law and the maintainer of order. The maxim of the courts, *tout fuit in luy et vient de lui al commencement,*[2] was originally the expression of an actual and undoubted fact. This royal supremacy has now passed into that sovereignty of Parliament which has formed the main subject of the foregoing chapters.[3]

The second of these features, which is closely connected with the first, is the rule or supremacy of law. This peculiarity of our polity is well expressed in the old saw of the courts, "La ley est le plus haute inheritance, que le roy ad; car par la ley il meme et toutes ses sujets sont rules, et si la ley ne fuit, nul roi, et nul inheritance sera."[4]

This supremacy of the law, or the security given under the English constitution to the rights of individuals looked at from various points of view, forms the subject of this part of this treatise.

. . . .

Three Meanings of Rule of Law

When we say that the supremacy or the rule of law is a characteristic of the English constitution, we generally include under one expression at least three distinct though kindred conceptions.

We mean, in the first place, that no man is punishable or can be lawfully made to suffer in body or goods except for a distinct breach of law established in the ordinary legal manner before the ordinary courts of the land. In this sense the rule of law is contrasted with every system of government based on the exercise by persons in authority of wide, arbitrary, or discretionary powers of constraint.

. . . .

Every Man Subject to Ordinary Law Administered by Ordinary Tribunals

We mean in the second place,[5] when we speak of the "rule of law" as a characteristic of our country, not only that with us no man is above the law, but (what is a different thing) that here every man, whatever be his rank or condition, is subject to the ordinary law of the realm and amenable to the jurisdiction of the ordinary tribunals.

. . . .

There remains yet a third and a different sense in which the "rule of law" or the predominance of the legal spirit may be described as a special attribute of English institutions. We may say that the constitution is pervaded

† Dicey, A.V., *Introduction to the Study of the Law of the Constitution*, 10th ed., (New York: St. Martin's Press, 1965), 183–84, 187–88, 193, 195–96, 202–03. Copyright © 1965, Macmillan Press Ltd. Reprinted by permission of Macmillan Press Ltd., Hampshire, U.K.

by the rule of law on the ground that the general principles of the constitution (as for example the right to personal liberty, or the right of public meeting) are with us the result of judicial decisions determining the rights of private persons in particular cases brought before the courts[6] whereas under many foreign constitutions the security (such as it is) given to the rights of individuals results, or appears to result, from the general principles of the constitution.

This is one portion at least of the fact vaguely hinted at in the current but misguiding statement that "the constitution has not been made but has grown." This *dictum*, if taken literally, is absurd.

> Political institutions (however the proposition may be at times ignored) are the work of men, owe their origin and their whole existence to human will. Men did not wake up on a summer morning and find them sprung up. Neither do they resemble trees, which, once planted, are 'aye growing' while men 'are sleeping.' In every stage of their existence they are made what they are by human voluntary agency.[7]

Yet, though this is so, the dogma that the form of a government is a sort of spontaneous growth so closely bound up with the life of a people that we can hardly treat it as a product of human will and energy, does, though in a loose and inaccurate fashion, bring into view the fact that some polities, and among them the English constitution, have not been created at one stroke, and far from being the result of legislation, in the ordinary sense of that term, are the fruit of contests carried on in the courts on behalf of the rights of individuals. Our constitution, in short, is a judge-made constitution, and it bears on its face all the features, good and bad, of judge-made law.

. . . .

Summary of Meanings of Rule of Law

That "rule of law," then, which forms a fundamental principle of the constitution, has three meanings, or may be regarded from three different points of view.

It means, in the first place, the absolute supremacy or predominance of regular law as opposed to the influence of arbitrary power, and excludes the existence of arbitrariness, of prerogative, or even of wide discretionary authority on the part of the government. Englishmen are ruled by the law, and by the law alone; a man may with us be punished for a breach of law, but he can be punished for nothing else.

It means, again, equality before the law, or the equal subjection of all classes to the ordinary law of the land administered by the ordinary law courts and "rule of law" in this sense excludes the idea of any exemption of officials or others from the duty of obedience to the law which governs the citizens or from the jurisdiction of the ordinary tribunals; there can be with us nothing really corresponding to the "administrative law" (*droit administratif*) or the "administrative tribunals" (*tribunaux administratifs*) of France.[8] The notion which lies at the bottom of the "administrative law" known to foreign countries is, that affairs or disputes in which the government or its servants are concerned are beyond the sphere of the civil courts and must be dealt with by special and more or less official bodies. This idea is utterly unknown to the law of England, and indeed is fundamentally inconsistent with our traditions and customs.

The "rule of law," lastly, may be used as a formula for expressing the fact that with us the law of the constitution, the rules which in foreign countries naturally form part of a constitutional code, are not the source but the consequence of the rights of individuals, as defined and enforced by the courts; that, in short, the principles of private law have with us been by the action of the courts and Parliament so extended as to determine the position of the Crown and of its servants; thus the constitution is the result of the ordinary law of the land.

Endnotes

1. Sir Ivor Jennings has been a most formidable critic of Dicey and in particular of this Part. See especially *The Law and the Constitution* (4th ed., 1952), ch. i, ii, vi, and App. ii, and the article, "In Praise of Dicey", in *Public Administration*, vol. xi, No. 2 (April, 1935). — Ed.
2. Year Books, xxiv Edward III, cited Gneist, *Englische Verwaltungsrecht* (1867), vol. i, p. 454.
3. See Part i, *ante*.
4. Year Books, xix. Henry VI, cited Gneist, *op. cit.*, vol. i, p. 455.
5. For first meaning see p. 188, *ante*.
6. *Cf. Calvin's Case* (1608) 7 Co. Rep. 1a; *Campbell v. Hall* (1774), Lofft. 655; K. & L. 487; *Wilkes v. Wood* (1763), 19 St. Tr. 1153; *Mostyn v. Fabrigas* (1774), 1 Cowp. 161. Parliamentary declarations of the law such as the *Petition of Right* and the *Bill of Rights* have a certain affinity to judicial decisions. [When the author refers to the general principles of the constitution in this context, it is clear from his examples that he is dealing with the means of protecting private rights. The origin of the sovereignty of Parliament cannot be traced to a judicial decision and the independence of the judges has rested on statute since the *Act of Settlement*, 1701. — Ed.]
7. Mill, *Considerations on Representative Government* (3rd ed., 1865), p. 4.
8. See ch. xii and *cf.* pp. cxiii *et seq.*, App. 1, *post*, and Jennings, *The Law and the Constitution* (4th ed., 1952), App. ii.

The "Living Tree" Approach to Interpreting the BNA Act[†]

LORD SANKEY: —

. . . .

The *British North America Act* planted in Canada a living tree capable of growth and expansion within its natural limits. The object of the Act was to grant a Constitution to Canada. "Like all written constitutions it has been subject to development through usage and convention."

Their Lordships do not conceive it to be the duty of this Board — it is certainly not their desire — to cut down the provisions of the Act by a narrow and technical construction, but rather to give it a large and liberal interpretation so that the Dominion to a great extent, but within certain fixed limits, may be mistress in her own house, as the Provinces to a great extent, but within certain fixed limits, are mistresses in theirs.

The Origins of Judicial Review in Canada[††]
J. Smith

FOR many years students have been taught that the practice of judicial review in Canada is less important than it is in the United States. This is because it has had less scope, and it has had less scope because, until recently, Canada's written constitution, unlike the American Constitution, included no bill of rights. Whereas in both countries the courts, acting as "umpires" of their respective federal forms of government, have had the power to declare laws beyond the competence of the jurisdiction enacting them, the American courts have had the additional and, to many, fascinating power to enforce against governments the guarantees of the rights of citizens contained in the Bill of Rights. Obviously this line of comparison is outmoded now. After a prolonged and at times bitter debate, the federal government and nine of the ten provincial governments reached agreement last year on a set of amendments to the *British Northern America Act*, among them a Charter of Rights and Freedoms. As a result, the breadth of the courts' power of judicial review more closely approximates that possessed by their American counterparts. Is this development consistent with the nature of Canada's constitutional arrangements? Does the Charter provide the basis of the completion of an initially limited power?....

...One of the most thorough studies available is B.L. Strayer's *Judicial Review of Legislation in Canada*. Strayer argues that the *BNA Act, 1867* and related acts did not vest explicitly in the courts the power of judicial review. Nor can our common law inheritance be held responsible for it. Instead, judicial review is a product of the British colonial system, "implicit in the royal instructions, charters, or Imperial statutes creating the colonial legislatures." Since these legislatures were bodies of limited power, the colonial charters establishing them typically included clauses prohibiting them from passing laws repugnant to Imperial statutes....

...As early as the fifteenth century, it was customary for the King's Privy Council rather than English domestic courts to hear appeals arising out of colonial matters. This practice was regulated by the *Privy Council Acts* of 1833 and 1844, which established the Judicial Committee of the Privy Council, specified its membership and authorized it to hear appeals from colonial courts. Thus the Judicial Committee acted as the highest appellate court for the colonies. As Strayer points out, it showed no inclination to question its authority to review the validity of colonial legislation, undoubtedly because the colonies themselves possessed only limited or subordinate legislative powers. He attributes considerable importance to the precedent it set throughout the Empire for the exercise of a similar power by colonial courts. According to Strayer, we must look to the British colonial system, and especially its doctrine of judicial review of colonial legislation, for the origin of judicial review in Canada: "The constitutional law of the Empire in 1867 apparently embraced the convention that where legislative powers were granted subject

†   Excerpt from *Edwards v. A.G. for Canada*, [1930] A.C. 124.

††   Smith, Jennifer, "The Origins of Judicial Review in Canada" (1983), 16 *Canadian Journal of Political Science* 115 at 115–17. Reprinted by permission of Canadian Political Science Association, Ottawa, Ontario.

to limitations the courts would enforce those limitations. The BNA Act was drafted and enacted in this context."...

...Thus he [Strayer] is faced with the fact that following Confederation, the Canadian courts took up the power of judicial review, and concludes that this was the result of both pre-Confederation practice and the federal character of the new constitution: "There was a continuity of judicial practice because the Imperial structure had not changed basically.... Colonial legislatures, whether Dominion or provincial, were limited legislatures, and courts could enforce the limitations." The inner logic of federalism with its distribution of legislative powers pointed to the need for something like the kind of judicial enforcement that pre-Confederation practice had established.

Strayer's search for an explanation of judicial review arises out of his insistence that it is not "absolute," that is, not fully guaranteed in the *BNA Act*. In his opinion, the relevant clauses of the Act gave Parliament and the local legislatures too much regulatory power over the courts to support such a view, power more in keeping with the principle of parliamentary as opposed to judicial supremacy. Indeed, according to W.R. Lederman, Strayer implies that an "element of judicial usurpation" figures in its establishment, an implication Lederman cannot accept. By contrast, Lederman reads into sections 96 to 100 of the Act an "intention to reproduce superior courts in the image of the English central royal courts." If he can demonstrate that these English courts had acquired a "basic independence" enabling them to withstand even the undoubted supremacy of the British Parliament, then courts deliberately modelled after them in Canada would assume a similar status. In "The Independence of the Judiciary," Lederman undertakes such a demonstration....

...Strayer takes note of this argument and dismisses it by observing that the jurisdiction of Lederman's royal courts was subject to the British Parliament's control and that in any event it never included the power to review the validity of Parliament's acts "in spite of the pretensions of Coke and others." Canadian superior courts can hardly claim by inheritance an inviolable right of judicial review their English forebears never possessed. Lederman's rejoinder is that Canadian courts, both before and after 1867, have never faced legislatures equipped with the full supremacy of the British Parliament. Indeed, until 1931 they dealt with subordinate colonial legislatures, and while the Statute of Westminster substituted equality in the place of subordination, the constitution itself remained a British statute. Thus the power to review acts of subordinate bodies undertaken by Canadian courts before 1931 was well established by "history, custom, precedent and the need of federalism" and after 1931 merely continued as a matter of course.

. . . .

Viewed in the light of the older controversy about the court, the debate culminating in the recent set of amendments contained in the *Constitution Act, 1982*, took a familiar turn. In the earlier contest, both opponents and partisans of judicial review focused attention on its implications for the federalism. While some saw in it a solution to conflicts arising out of competing in favour of Parliament's control of the constitution. Over a century later, the issue of judicial versus parliamentary supremacy surfaced again in connection with the proposed Charter of Rights and Freedoms. Prime Minister Pierre Trudeau, a determined champion of the notion of a charter, often defended his cause without even referring to the risk it necessarily imposes on the courts. Instead, he claimed that it would "confer power on the people of Canada, power to protect themselves from abuses by public authorities." A charter would liberate people by preventing governments from denying specified freedoms. On the other hand, opponents of the idea like the then premier of Saskatchewan, Allan Blakeney, attempted to counter the undeniable appeal of this claim by drawing attention to the role of the courts that is implied. According to Blakeney, including rights in a written constitution means transferring responsibility for them from duly elected legislatures, the democratic seat of governments, to nonelected tribunals. It amounts to requiring the courts to make "social judgments" in the course of interpreting a charter's clauses, judgments which, in his view, properly belong to "the voters and their representatives." In the event, a Charter of Rights and Freedoms now forms part of Canada's newly amended constitution. Are we entitled to conclude, then, that acceptance of the Charter, and the increased scope for judicial review that it entails, signals a resolution of the issue of parliamentary versus judicial supremacy in favour of the latter? The answer is not quite.

It is true, as Peter Russell points out, that section 52 of the *Constitution Act, 1982*, by declaring the Constitution of Canada to be the "supreme law" and any law inconsistent with its provisions to be of "no force or effect," gives the courts' power to invalidate unconstitutional laws an explicit constitutional footing for the first time. Further, under the provisions of the new amending formula, the composition of the Supreme Court is protected from easy change by the stringent requirement of unanimity on the part of the Senate, the House of Commons and provincial legislative assemblies. The court is also listed under section 42(1) as an item that can be amended only in accordance with the general formula set out in section 38(1). Thus the court is constitutionally entrenched. However, neither the federal government's power to appoint Supreme Court justices nor the nonjudicial advisory task required by the reference mechanism is affected. More important still is the fact that the Charter itself, to the disappointment of its partisans, contains a provision enabling the legislative bodies of both levels of government to override some of its guarantees, namely, those dealing with fundamental freedoms, legal rights and equality rights. The provision is qualified to the extent that legislatures choosing to avail themselves of it are required to declare, expressly their intention and reconsider the matter every five years, and there has been speculation about the likely effect of these qualifications on politicians' willingness to resort to the "override." Nevertheless, its very appearance in the context of the Charter strikes an incongruous note and is testimony to the strength of the lingering tradition of parliamentary supremacy. Finally, there is the first clause of the Charter which subjects its guarantees to "such reasonable limits prescribed by law as can be demonstrably justified in a free and democratic society." Ultimately it is up to the Supreme Court to stake out the "reasonable limits." In the meantime, we do know that they are held to exist, that there is thought to be something higher than, or beyond the Charter's guarantees to which appeal can be made in order to justify their denial or restriction. And the initiative in this regard is secured to governments. While the courts' power of judicial review has undoubtedly surmounted the rather narrow, partisan function envisaged for the new Supreme Court in 1875 by Macdonald, the principle of parliamentary supremacy persists.

The Environment of Canada's Judicial System[†]
P.H. Russell

SOCIAL AND ECONOMIC DEVELOPMENT

As an industrialized and urbanized society, Canada has experienced, to a relatively high degree, what the political sociologists refer to as "modernization." This modernization has been accompanied by increased complexity in Canadian law and increased professionalization of Canada's legal institutions. For the judicial system this has meant, among other things, an increased insistence on the possession of professional legal credentials by those adjudicating disputes about the law. Thus in Canada we have witnessed nearly a complete repudiation of the lay person as judge and a tendency to regard juries as technically too incompetent to be reliable fact-finders. Growing professionalism has also been felt although in a much more delayed fashion, in the administration of Canadian courts, where there is increasing recognition of the merit of applying specialized administrative skills and the techniques of the computer age to managing court case flows.

But the effects of the modernization of Canadian society on its judicial system have been more pervasive and profound than a tendency to specialization. As industrialization and urbanization weaken traditional social bonds of family and community, basic social attitudes and relations are altered. We become a society of strangers relying increasingly, each of us, on formal positive law to define our rights and obligations; as a consequence, we turn increasingly to formal adjudication to settle our differences. This transformation of social relations from those based on custom and informal sources of authority to a system depending much more on legally defined rights and duties tends to expand the role of adjudicative agencies. This can be seen in fields as far apart as family law and federalism: as squabbling spouses and government turn to positive law as a guide to good conduct, they resort increasingly to courts to adjudicate conflict. Another facet of the social alienation accompanying modernity is increased reliance on enforcement of the criminal law rather than more informal communal sanctions as a means of maintaining social order. This, too, places increased burdens on Canadian courts, not so much to adjudicate disputes (few criminal charges produce not guilty pleas and formal court adjudication) but to provide a judicial presence in the processing of those selected by the police for criminal prosecution.

Socio-economic development does not affect the business of courts in industrialized societies in a uniform way. The impact is considerably influenced by the litigiousness of a people — that is to say, their general propensity to settle disputes by pressing claims to formal adjudication rather than negotiating settlements more informally. A litigious tendency may be present in a society quite independently of its level of modernization. Among modern industrialized countries, England, New Zealand, and the United States have much higher civil case loads per capita than Italy, Japan, or Spain. The preference of the Japanese of mediation and conciliation over adjudication is reflected in the small size of their legal profession: 1 lawyer for each 10,000 of population compared with a ratio of 1 to 400 in the United States. No systematic research has been done on the litigiousness of Canadians, but the fact that on a per capita basis the Canadian judiciary and legal

---

[†]   Russell, Peter H., "The Environment of Canada's Judicial System" in *The Judiciary in Canada* (Toronto: McGraw-Hill Ryerson Limited, 1987), 31–39. Reprinted by permission of McGraw-Hill Ryerson Limited, Whitby, Ontario.

profession are roughly comparable in size to their American counterparts suggests that Canada is one of the more litigious of the industrialized and urbanized countries, perhaps only slightly less so than the United States. Canadian patterns may have been brought closer to American ones by the rapid expansion of the legal profession and legal aid programs over the past decade or so. These developments, while not necessarily altering the general disposition of Canadians to litigate, have made the option of taking disputes to court more available to people of limited means.

Increases in the number and complexity of laws, in the number of lawyers, and even in the litigiousness of the population, do not necessarily lead to a mushrooming of court business and expansion of the courts. Much depends on the relative attractiveness of judicial institutions as dispute-settling mechanisms and the availability of alternatives. The evidence in Canada suggests that very little of the increased need for adjudicative services generated by social change and industrial development has been taken care of by the general jurisdiction trial courts (i.e., the superior, district, and county courts of the provinces), which at the time of Confederation were regarded as the most important of Canada's judicial institutions. These provincial courts, staffed by federally appointed judges — the original linchpins of Canada's judicial system — have scarcely expanded at all. Whereas the number of judges serving at this level was 2.52 per 100,000 of population in 1867, by 1975 the ratio had actually declined to 2.23 per 100,000. Some of this increased demand for adjudication, especially in the field of criminal justice, has been met by the provincially appointed judges in the so-called lower courts of the provinces, and a little, on the civil side, by the major federally established trial court, the Federal Court of Canada. But probably a great deal more has been taken care of outside the formal court system through private arbitration and administrative tribunals. Improvements in the administration of courts may begin to reverse this trend by reducing some of the delay and inconvenience which in the past drove business away from the courts. Another factor working in the same direction is the Canadian version of what in the United States is referred to as the "public law explosion." On the one hand, the expanded use of the criminal sanction by the state; on the other hand, the expanded range of statutory and even constitutional rights that can be claimed by the individual or corporation against the state generate disputes which in our society must finally be settled by the courts.

POLITICAL BELIEFS AND IDEOLOGY

Here we encounter the second environment influence on the judicial system: political beliefs and ideology. An increase in the degree of independence enjoyed by Canadian courts and their added capacity to serve as vehicles for challenging government has been closely related to a strengthening of support of liberalism in Canada's political culture. This growth in respect for liberal values — for the rights of individuals and the value of preventing excessive and illegal exercises of governmental authority — has not, to be sure, developed to the point of extinguishing strong conservative tendencies in Canada's political culture. Canada was founded by counter-revolutionaries suspicious of the excesses of American democracy. The continued popularity of the national police force, the RCMP (despite the exposure of its infringements of the legal rights of Canadians and its intolerance of political dissent), as well as popular support for the invocation of the *War Measures Act* in the 1970 October crisis, point to the survival of this conservative strain. But liberal critics of these recent manifestations of Canadians' respect for authority and fear of disorder often fail to mark the liberalization of political attitudes that has been occurring in Canada. Manifestations of moral outrage and the favourable treatment it receives in the popular media are, in themselves, an indication of this change.

A growing egalitarianism in Canadian society has fostered the extension of liberal values to all classes in society. This tendency has had important consequences for the functioning of the courts. Legal aid (the provision of publicly funded legal counsel to indigent persons) is, as we have noted, a leading example of this trend. Another is reform of the criminal justice system which has taken place over the last century. The reduction of close ties between the criminal courts and the police, bail reform, and an upgrading of the qualifications of the judges who preside over the country's busiest criminal courts are part of this movement. These reforms are relatively modest; none goes as far as critics of the system might wish. But the direction of change is clearly liberal.

A further illustration of this liberalization of attitudes and its effect on the judicial system is the change which has taken place in the appeal system in criminal cases. Up until 1892 there was no right of appeal in criminal cases. When a right of appeal was included in the *Criminal Code*, it was typical of the mixture of values in Canadian society that not only was the accused given a right to appeal his conviction but the crown was also given a right to appeal the accused's acquittal, even if the verdict was rendered by a jury. The review of trial court decisions in criminal cases has become an increasingly important function of Canada's courts of appeal. We can get some idea of how much Canadian attitudes have changed by noting that in 1975 when the crown successfully appealed a jury's acquittal of Dr. Morgentaler, a Montreal physician who ran an abortion clinic, there was a sufficient public outcry to bring about an amendment of the *Criminal Code* removing the power of appeal courts to substitute a guilty verdict for an acquittal in a case heard by judge and jury.

An egalitarian extension of legal rights has also affected the work of courts in non-criminal areas. New legal rights have been established for classes of persons whose bargaining position was relatively weak: for example, wives in relation to husbands, children in relation to parents, employees in relation to employers, students and professors in relation to university officials. The establishment of these rights means that disputes which might have been settled informally are now often litigated and go to court. Dispute settlement through informal negotiation becomes less acceptable when social and economic "underdogs" believe their interests will be better protected by claiming rights in court rather than counting on the benevolence of those in positions of power.

A similar reduction of trust in those exercising political authority has made Canadians more interested in the liberal notion of building checks and balances into their system of government. Canadians may continue to believe that the purpose of government is as much to provide for peace, order and good government as it is to protect the rights and liberties of the individual, but they have become increasingly apprehensive about the problems of controlling the governmental leviathan. Several generations of experience under big government have generated scepticism about the inherent good sense and self-restraint of those who govern. The nineteenth-century achievement of responsible government has proved to be no panacea for ensuring that government is accountable to the people. The decline of the legislature's significance in law-making and in its capacity for monitoring government operations has been evident for many years. Cabinet government concentrates enormous power in the hands of a very few politicians and officials. There may be some dim recognition that the vitality of the division of powers and competition between federal and provincial governments in Canada by dispersing power enhances political liberty. Still, both provincial and federal governments are recognized as centres of power against whose arbitrary and unlawful activities citizens need further institutional protection.

Increasing this liberal impulse looks to the judiciary for such protection. Where there is fear that government will abuse newly acquired powers, the judiciary is brought in to guard against this danger. A good example is the inclusion of a requirement for judicial warrants in the legislation that legalized electronic eavesdropping by the police. More recently, in the debate over a federal *Access to Information Act*, distrust of the government forced the inclusion of a provision giving the courts, in most instances, the final word in deciding whether government refusals to provide information fall within statutory criteria.

This tendency in the Canadian political system to rely on the judicial process as a means of preventing abuse of power and protecting rights may now be at a turning point. Canada's new constitutional *Charter of Rights and Freedoms* significantly expands expectations about the judici-

ary's capacity and inclination to check government. The apparent popularity of increasing the power of judges at the expense of the power of politicians and officials demonstrates the extent to which Canadians, at this point in their history, regard their judges as less tied to the interests of government; they are seen in a fundamental sense as being less political and more trustworthy than those holding executive and legislative positions. But, again, it is important to point out that this perception of the judiciary as the politically neutered branch of government may well be undermined by the political nature of the judiciary's responsibilities under the new Charter.

CANADA'S LEGAL CULTURE

The third and most direct of the environmental influences on the judicial system is a country's legal culture. The basic character of Canada's legal system, and hence of its judicial system, might be expected to reflect the legal cultures of the two European peoples, the English and the French, who founded Canada. But this expectation is not borne out by the facts. So dominant has the English common law system been that it is misleading to think of Canada's legal culture as fundamentally dualistic. This is especially true of its judicial system, which has been even more thoroughly anglicized than the substantive law. As far as the legal culture of Canada's original inhabitants is concerned, it was totally ignored and for all practical purposes obliterated by the European settlers. Thus, in legal terms, Canada today belongs essentially to the common law world although as with all the common law countries, there are some distinctive wrinkles stemming from the country's particular circumstances.

There is a strong element of legal dualism in Quebec's history. Soon after the British conquest of New France, through the *Quebec Act* of 1774, the laws of the French Canadians were made the basis of the colony's civil law, while its criminal law was to be British. Despite this original dualism, French civil law was subjected to powerful common law influences. The principal vehicle for this process of anglicization was the judicial system. British governors selected the judges and for the most part they chose persons whose legal knowledge, if it existed at all, was based on English experience. Most importantly, the appeal was dominated by English Canadians and British judges. Consequently the judicial method in both civil and criminal law became the common law method, with its emphasis on judicial precedent. These common law techniques were so firmly embedded by the time a *Civil Code* was adopted in Quebec that English-style judicial precedents rather than French civilian doctrine became the dominant force in interpreting the code. The anglicization of Quebec's civil law system is a testament to the quiet way in which power can flow through a judicial system, especially one with a powerful appeals hierarchy.

An essential part of the Confederation settlement in 1867 was that Quebec, as the province in which the French Canadians could maintain a majority, would be able to preserve the distinctive language, religion, and laws of the French-Canadian people. Section 92(13) of the *British North America Act* gave all the provinces jurisdiction over "property and civil rights" — a concept that embraces most of the subjects included in Quebec's *Civil Code* and *Code of Procedure*. Thus Quebec has retained legislative jurisdiction over those matters which are central to the French civil law tradition. On particular points of substantive law and civil procedure Quebec civil law differs from the laws of the common law provinces, although under the impact of secularization and modern commerce these differences have narrowed and may not be more significant than differences that exist in some areas of statutory law among the common law provinces. Since Confederation the highest court of appeal, whose opinions interpreting Quebec's civil law bind Quebec judges, has been, first, an imperial court, the Judicial Committee of the Privy Council, and then the Supreme Court of Canada. Although Quebec judges have always been in a minority position on the latter court, more often than not they have been the dominant influence on the panels hearing civil law cases from Quebec.

For our purposes here the most important point is that the judicial institutions of Quebec, despite any residue of French civil law and procedure that survives, bear the essential features of English common law courts. A lawyer from English-speaking Canada, or for that matter from virtually any other part of the English-speaking world, who wished to practise in Quebec, would not have to adapt to an alien judicial system. It is only in very recent years that Quebec court reformers have begun to look to continental French institutions for inspiration — for instance, to the idea of a career judiciary based on a special legal education for judges. So far, this application of Quebec nationalism to judicial institutions has not borne fruit in any concrete changes.

Some of the features of the common law tradition that have important consequences for the role of the judiciary in Canada (for example, the use of juries and the adversary system) have already been mentioned and will be referred to later in the text. In this introductory discussion of judicial power there are two features of common law systems that deserve special emphasis: the central importance of the judges, and the power of the legal profession.

In any legal system based on the common law tradition, the judge has a preeminent position as compared with other legal functionaries. Common law is indeed judge-made law. On many subjects of contemporary legislative interest, common law rules are dwarfed in importance by statutes enacted by the legislature, by delegated legislation

or regulations enacted by the executive, and in Canada by the written Constitution. Long ago common law judges accepted their subordination to Parliament as a sovereign law maker, and in Canada they must accept the Constitution of Canada as the highest source of law. Even so, judicial decisions applying and interpreting regulations, statutes, and the Constitution, as we have already stressed, can have a tremendous influence on the policies that are actually effected and the rights that are actually established through these other sources of law. It is true that the difference between the legislative role of the judge in the common law system as compared with the civil law system has been exaggerated. Modern scholarship on civil law systems has revealed the important role that judicial interpretation and judicial opinions play in applying civil law codes, despite the civil law system's theoretical denial of their importance. Nevertheless the fact remains that it is the common law system that openly accepts the judicial opinion with all its potential for law development as an integral part of the system.

The pre-eminence of the judge in the common law system extends beyond the judge's law-making role. It is also manifest in the social and political status of the judge. In continental Europe the legal scholar has a high, if not a higher, status than the judge. This is certainly not the case in Canada. The lustre of the judicial position in Canada is reflected in the practice, already commented upon, of assigning judges major extra-judicial responsibilities, notably on royal commissions and commissions of inquiry, on matters of great public interest. A symbolic indication of the high status of the judicial office in Canada is that the chief justice of the country's highest court, the Supreme Court of Canada, in the absence or incapacity of the governor general, represents the head of state. Whether or not there is validity in the generalization that Canadian judges are self-restrained or uncreative in the exercise of their judicial powers, the high status accorded them in the Canadian legal and political systems continues to be a significant political resource for the Canadian judiciary.

The prestige and power of judges in the common law system is closely related to the strength of the legal profession. It might even be said that the pre-eminent position of the bench within common law legal systems largely derives from the pre-eminent position of the bar within common law societies. Going back to the roots of the common law judicial system in England, it was the ability of a small guild of private legal practitioners centred in the Inns of Court in London — first the sergeants, then the barristers — to monopolize appointments to the Royal Courts of Justice that was decisive in ensuring that the common law judiciary would not develop in the continental fashion as a career branch of government service. Instead, judicial positions in the higher courts would be awarded to persons who had distinguished themselves in private legal practice. The bench in Canada, even at its lowest levels, is recruited almost exclusively from the bar. Thus, in studying the forces that shape the Canadian judiciary it is essential to take into account the nature of the Canadian legal profession. Access to that profession, its education system, and the characteristics of private practice will have a great deal to do with determining what kinds of men and women become judges in Canada.

In Canada the bar is considerably less elitist than in England. Instead of the English division between a small group of barristers who plead cases in court and a great mass of solicitors advising clients and transacting legal business out of court, or France's four or five separate legal professions (advocates, avoues, notaries, and judges), Canada has a fused and unified legal profession. There are specializations within this profession, but all Canadian lawyers belong to a single profession. Further, the Canadian bar is not concentrated in a single metropolitan centre but is dispersed across the country; there are centres of professional activity in every Canadian province. Thus the professional pool from which Canadian judges are recruited is much larger and more diverse than the tiny coterie of London-based barristers from which English judges are drawn. As a social interest group, geographical dispersal is more than compensated for by professional unity. The Canadian bar's ability to assert itself as a unified profession has few parallels in other countries.

Some lawyers might object to the suggestion that they belong to a private interest group. Formally, as members of the bar, they are "officers of the court," and in that sense belong to a public institution. Nevertheless, the profession has emphasized the need to maintain its independence of government. It has insisted, successfully, on its own self-government, on controlling the standards of professional education and in most provinces, on keeping private legal practitioners, rather than salaried lawyers, as the mainstay of publicly funded legal aid programs. The rationale for this commitment to the profession's independence has been fundamentally ideological: recognition of the value in a liberal state under the rule of law of ensuring that individuals and groups have access to legal counsel not controlled by the government.

If the press can be referred to as the fourth estate, the legal profession as a private organization providing an essential public service might be thought of as a fifth estate in Canada. The power of this fifth estate is exercised through its professional activities and advocacy, and also through the participation of so many of its members at the highest levels of the political branches of government. The private practice of law provides exceptional opportunities for those who wish to take their chances in electoral competition. No other profession or occupational group has been so well represented in legislatures and cabinets at both the federal and provincial levels. Among other things, the political prominence of the profession means that the views of professional lawyers are paramount in shaping policies with regard to judicial institutions and judicial reform. No major changes in the structure or functioning of Canada's courts can take place without the approval of leaders of the bar.

It would be a mistake, however, to think of the bar as an unchanging monolithic force. The winds of change which affect all other important social institutions are beginning to bring about significant changes in the size and shape of Canada's legal profession. The last decade has seen a major transformation. The ranks of the profession have expanded so that on a per capita basis it approximates the size of the American profession. The dominant position of males and the charter ethnic groups has declined. Most significantly, the political diversity of the profession would appear to have increased with the formation of radical breakaway organizations outside of the professional establishment. In the long run, all of this is likely to have profoundly important effects on the social and political orientation of the Canadian judiciary.

Constitution Act, 1982 (Part I)[†]

WHEREAS Canada is founded upon principles that recognize the supremacy of God and the rule of law:

1. The *Canadian Charter of Rights and Freedoms* guarantees the rights and freedoms set out in it subject only to such reasonable limits prescribed by law as can be demonstrably justified in a free and democratic society.

2. Everyone has the following fundamental freedoms:
(a) freedom of conscience and religion;
(b) freedom of thought, belief, opinion and expression, including freedom of the press and other media of communication;
(c) freedom of peaceful assembly; and
(d) freedom of association.

[†] *Constitution Act, 1982* (Part I), *Canadian Charter of Rights and Freedoms*, selected sections.

3. Every citizen of Canada has the right to vote in an election of members of the House of Commons or of a legislative assembly and to be qualified for membership therein.

. . . .

6.(1) Every citizen of Canada has the right to enter, remain in and leave Canada.

7. Everyone has the right to life, liberty and security of the person and the right not to be deprived thereof except in accordance with the principles of fundamental justice.

8. Everyone has the right to be secure against unreasonable search or seizure.

9. Everyone has the right not to be arbitrarily detained or imprisoned.

10. Everyone has the right on arrest or detention
(a) to be informed promptly of the reasons therefor;
(b) to retain and instruct counsel without delay and to be informed of that right; and
(c) to have the validity of the detention determined by way of *habeas corpus* and to be released if the detention is not lawful.

. . . .

12. Everyone has the right not to be subjected to any cruel and unusual treatment or punishment.

. . . .

15.(1) Every individual is equal before and under the law and has the right to the equal protection and equal benefit of the law without discrimination and, in particular, without discrimination based on race, national or ethnic origin, colour, religion, sex, age or mental or physical disability.

(2) Subsection (1) does not preclude any law, program or activity that has as its object the amelioration of conditions of disadvantaged individuals or groups including those that are disadvantaged because of race, national or ethnic origin, colour, religion, sex, age or mental or physical disability.

. . . .

24.(1) Anyone whose rights or freedoms, as guaranteed by this Charter, have been infringed or denied may apply to a court of competent jurisdiction to obtain such remedy as the court considers appropriate and just in the circumstances.

(2) Where, in proceedings under subsection (1), a court concludes that evidence was obtained in a manner that infringed or denied any rights or freedoms guaranteed by this Charter, the evidence shall be excluded if it is established that, having regard to all the circumstances, the admission of it in the proceedings would bring the administration of justice into disrepute.

. . . .

26. The guarantee in this Charter of certain rights and freedoms shall not be construed as denying the existence of any other rights or freedoms that exist in Canada.

. . . .

28. Notwithstanding anything in this Charter, the rights and freedoms referred to in it are guaranteed equally to male and female persons.

. . . .

31. Nothing in this Charter extends the legislative powers of any body or authority.

. . . .

33.(1) Parliament or the legislature of a province may expressly declare in an Act of Parliament or of the legislature, as the case may be, that the Act or a provision thereof shall operate notwithstanding a provision included in section 2 or sections 7 to 15 of this Charter.

. . . .

(3) A declaration made under subsection (1) shall cease to have effect five years after it comes into force or on such earlier date as may be specified in the declaration.

(4) Parliament or a legislature of a province may re-enact a declaration made under subsection (1).

Popular Rights in (And Out Of) The Constitution[†]
G. Starr

INTRODUCTION

So many fears are calmed. For those who thought the Trudeau *Charter* was opening a future of godless communism, it is declared that we recognise "the supremacy of God and the rule of law".[1] Those who worry about the erosion of their property rights are re-assured by the continuance of the *Canadian Bill of Rights* and such provincial equivalents as there are. And monarchists and others who dread republicanism find, under the heading "Democratic Rights", nothing more threatening than a right to vote and the ancient constitutional provisions respecting the frequency of elections and the sittings of legislative bodies; what had been merely statutory in the *War Measures Act* is made constitutional through provision for abrogation in time of "real or apprehended war, invasion or insurrection".[2] The searcher for evidence of the rights of the people to participate in the political life of Canada will find virtually "no new thing under the sun". The cynic within will easily conclude that the *Charter* is a creature of smoke and mirrors.

This paper proposes, however, that, while there is only one provision in the *Constitution Act, 1982*, which actually enhances the power of the people, there is a possibility of using the *Charter* to broaden the base of popular power. Although the expansion of judicial power by the *Charter* has received considerable attention in the last two years, there are actually important limitations on the judicial power (and on the legislative power) introduced by the *Constitution Act, 1982*. Some of these limitations can be used to broaden and deepen popular power, to add to the weight of public opinion and to sharpen the impact of the popular will. At least in theory.

Sections 2 to 5, although divided under the two headings, "Fundamental Freedoms" and "Democratic Rights", include the *Charter* provisions which deal directly with what I characterise as "popular rights". In these four sections are embodied all the guarantees we have of the right of people to participate in the "free and democratic society" contemplated by section 1.

What the *Charter* denominates "fundamental freedoms" have been called either "political rights" (as by then Minister of Justice Trudeau in his 1968 document *A Canadian Charter of Human Rights*) or "civil liberties" (as by many whose views on the subject are strongly influenced by American individual rights theories). Implicit in both "fundamental freedoms" and "civil liberties" as labels is the individualistic notion, a progeny of the Enlightenment, of creating a sphere of individual autonomy on which the sovereign power might not intrude. Historically, and continuing well beyond the zenith of natural law, private property was at the conceptual core of this notion. Viewed through these lenses, the "freedoms" protected by section 2 might be summed up (more emphatically if property were in their midst) by the revealing Anglo-American phrase "the right to be left alone".

Although they will be invoked (and upheld) in support of individualistic and selfish causes, I will consider these "freedoms" here for their importance to collective action. Indeed, with possible factual exceptions in the areas of conscience, religion, thought, belief and opinion, the freedoms protected by section 2 presuppose co-operation and community of purpose. Were it otherwise, freedom of the press (even as a concept) would indeed be limited to those who own one. To state the obvious, "assembly" requires three or more people and "association" two as a notional minimum.

While I will not shun the expression "fundamental freedoms", I will regard the areas of activity protected by section 2 as "political rights". With the right to stand for election and the right to vote classed by *Charter* headings as "democratic rights", the total of "political rights" and "democratic rights" may be regarded as "popular rights" — rights of "everyone" or "every citizen" to participate, if only in the extra-parliamentary opposition, in the political determination of the path of the state.

POLITICAL RIGHTS

The first observation about section 2 is that it is subject to section 1. By having the standards of permissible limitations enunciated in s. 1 of the *Charter*, we avoid the untenable proposition, as espoused in the American *Bill of Rights*, that the legislature "shall make no law abridging". A function of this express limitation in s. 1 is that we also preclude judges and administrators from making up limitations *ex post facto*. Limitations, to be recognised at all, must be "prescribed by law". Commentators (and most judges who have expressed themselves on the matter) agree that "demonstrably justified" places the onus on the party seeking to uphold the challenged law. While awaiting a stable articulation of judge-made law on this issue, the defence of political rights will require advocacy that prevents judges adopting easy conclusions that "limits prescribed by law" are *prima facie* "reasonable", thereby

† Starr, Gail, "Popular Rights in (And Out Of) The Constitution" (1984), 2 *Socialist Studies* at 8–16. Reprinted by permission of the Society for Socialist Studies, Economics, and Labour Studies, University of Manitoba.

begging the question as to whether they are "demonstrably justified". As our judges, both home-grown and imperial, have displayed a propensity for skipping over an inquiry into "matters coming within classes of subjects" to get to heads of legislative competence, we should, by now, know how to expose such practices.

The second internal *Charter* limitation on section 2 is the legislative override provided by section 33. Parliament or a provincial legislature may by legislative declaration override any provision of section 2 (and of section 7 through 15). Section 33, which Professor David Cruickshank appropriately suggests we should call "the rights-denial clause", seems to provide only for the *negation* of rights granted or affirmed by section 2 and 7 to 15 of the *Charter*. However, ironically in view of the way it is formulated, it may also have important uses in the *protection* of popular rights. Most relevant are those rights declared in section 2.

The legislative override is available only within the sphere of legislative competence possessed by the legislature seeking to override the *Charter*. This refers to the division of powers represented principally by sections 91 and 92 of the *Constitution Act, 1867*. And section 31 of the *Charter* provides, unambiguously, that "(n)othing in this *Charter* extends the legislative powers of any body or authority." To the extent, therefore, that legislative denial of section 2 rights would be aimed at making criminal certain exercises of those rights, only Parliament would be competent to do so. Accordingly, with a clear sense of *deja vu*, provincial legislative attempts to override section 2 protection may be challenged as invasions of the exclusive federal criminal law power. Suggestions for employing this argument will be offered in the context of specific section 2 rights, especially freedom of peaceful assembly.

This argument will in some cases have to draw on the "implied Bill of Rights", a Canadian judicial approach to the relationship between citizen and state which is, with respect to our pre-*Charter* jurisprudence, of doubted vitality. However, to the extent that the implied Bill of Rights survives, it could be a weapon for challenging provincial legislation restricting political rights. Strong *dicta* exist suggesting that the fundamental freedoms implicit in having a constitution "similar in principle to that of the United Kingdom" can never be "local matters". Some *dicta* are available, in the implied Bill of Rights cases, to suggest that neither level of government can limit certain of these rights.[3]

Freedom of Conscience and Religion

Some have suggested that the addition of "conscience" to the freedom as it was expressed in the *Canadian Bill of Rights* will extend the protection to quasi-religious groups and to "non-religious aspects" of religious systems. This remains to be seen; bigamy will not be

excused by the courts merely because it is allowed by the religion of the accused. The balancing required by section 1 will test the boundaries of whatever may be newly permitted by the change in phrasing.

What the change in wording does make possible is the development of a concept of freedom *from* religion. Freedom from religion would include freedom from having elements of one's life dictated by prevailing patterns of religious belief. Prayers and religious study in public schools and Sunday observance legislation come to mind. The Provincial Court of Alberta, in Calgary, has declared section 4 of the *Lord's Day Act* contrary to the provisions of the *Charter* and, therefore, of no force or effect. Sunday observance legislation was recharacterised as having nothing to do with the criminal law power.[4] Further, although not mentioned specifically in the reasons for judgment, the provision of section 27 of the *Charter*, that it should be interpreted "in a manner consistent with the preservation and enhancement of the multi-cultural heritage of Canadians", provides an additional buttress to the reasoning of Judge Stevenson.

While the general prospect held out by section 2(a), especially when read with section 27, is of a secular society, section 29 makes clear that existing Constitutional guarantees relating to separate schools remain undisturbed. Whether the preamble to the *Charter* can be invoked for any particular purpose is an open question.

Freedom of Expression

Subsection (b) of section 2 identifies a number of elements of the freedom of expression. The *Canadian Bill of Rights* protected only speech. Gestures and other forms of symbolic speech will now come under the protection. In a technologically forward-looking expansion, freedom of the press is extended to "other media of communication". This larger collocation of phrases elaborating the identified freedoms suggests that the whole may be greater than the sum of its parts. There are concepts here to work with in building arguments for the right to effective speech, for the right to be heard, for the right to respond to image advertising, for the right of access to outlets of information, etc. More will be said about the protection of thought, belief, and opinion.

Freedom of Peaceful Assembly

The *Canadian Bill of Rights* protected "freedom of assembly and association". The *Charter* divides the two and qualifies assembly by the requirement that it be peaceful. I hope that this change, read with the expansion of "expression" described above, will render the reasoning of Mr. Justice Beetz in *Dupond*[5] obsolete.

Under the *Canadian Bill of Rights*, the protection offered to assembly and association rights was never successfully invoked. We grew used to there being no effective protection of the right to assemble. In Vancouver the city's interest in having its noise by-law enforced was held to be sufficient to prohibit Hare Krishna groups from chanting along the sidewalks. In Calgary the whimsical issuance, or non-issuance, of parade permits was upheld against Chilean exiles seeking to mount a modest demonstration against the excesses of the Pinochet regime. And in Montreal, in the only case of its type to reach the Supreme Court of Canada, the dual fear that either assembly might become effective to mobilise public opinion or that the police budget would be exhausted in preventing it, was sufficient to justify city by-laws prohibiting *any* demonstration for a period of 60 days.[6] Thus, even during the period of our history when the *Canadian Bill of Rights* expressly protected assembly and association, we saw our highest court approve a local measure as repressive as the 1920's Toronto by-laws which forbade meetings at which anyone was to speak in a language other than English.[7]

With the constitutional recognition of the right of assembly now qualified, in terms, only by the requirement that it be ''peaceful'', it may be argued that the only justification for restricting the exercise of the right would be to prevent riot, and that that is covered by the *Criminal Code*. As, historically, almost all limitations on the right of assembly have been placed there by local and provincial authorities, this may be a potent argument. Again, the ''implied Bill of Rights'' argument, to the effect that this right is so fundamental to Canadian society as to be beyond the reach of either level of government, must be pressed.

Freedom of Association

The most continuous struggle for recognition of the freedom of association has been waged by trade unions. Major episodes have also included the occasional banning of the Communist Party of Canada, through the *Criminal Code*, and of the F.L.Q., first under the *War Measures Act* and then under the ''Turner law''.[8] It is not known whether this characteristic of the freedom's history played any part in the drafter's decision to separate assembly from association, but the decision to recognise association as a separate right may help us argue that it be broadened. Because of this history of the concept and its realisation, it may now be easier to argue that it includes the right to form a union, the right to bargain collectively, and the right to strike. In any event, its separate recognition may contribute to pushing back the lines drawn by prohibitions on conspiracy and sedition.[9]

The history of the struggle for recognition of the right will also need to be employed to argue that the constitutional recognition of the positive right does not include recognition of its converse. (It is suggested that the differences in historical development of recognition of the two rights mandate the contrary argument, as set out above, with respect to the

freedom of religion.) Thus, the freedom of *dis*association, contrary to the results obtained under the *European Convention* with respect to the closed shop,[10] must be seen as a right *not* protected by the *Charter*.

Section 2 as an Entity

Subsection (b) expressly contemplates a freedom of ''thought, belief and opinion''. The presence of these words might be dismissed as conferring nothing, recognising nothing. Many would dismiss them as hollow; a few contend that they cannot be invaded anyway. But they can be and are invaded daily. This recognition in the *Charter* may presage a broadening of popular rights.

The experience of the left in Canada demonstrates, even if Orwell had not already shown it to be possible, that the state can know every preference, every value, every deeply held opinion by simply taking note of what an individual does. Through surveillance, through intimidation and through harassment, both subtle and unsubtle pressure is exerted to conform, to be quiet, to cease challenging, to be inactive except in harmless individualistic pursuits.[11]

The seemingly innocuous words of subsection 2(b), taken together with the other rights protected by section 2, constitute a whole larger than the sum of its parts. This may be a kind of right to privacy, but one founded on the dignity and worth of persons as social and political beings, rather than on the licence of the individual in relation to his own property. We will make more headway in using section 2 to broaden collective interests if we regard it as a right *to be with* and consistently oppose its interpretation to vindicate the dubious right to be left alone. In this way it becomes the basis upon which we can, together, demand the recognition of additional political rights.

DEMOCRATIC RIGHTS

''Democratic rights'' in sections 3 through 5 of the *Charter* provide for the merely elementary components of electoral democracy. Only s. 3 contains anything new. Section 4 and 5 enshrine British norms developed well before Confederation and already a part of our constitutional law.

Any Canadian who paid much attention to the ten year build-up which culminated in patriation will have noticed that, whether the bargaining table was situated in Victoria, Ottawa or Quebec, the only people at it were politicians. To be sure, Liberal roadshow after Liberal roadshow toured the country, listening conspicuously to what real people might like to have in their constitution.[12] The only groups to have any effect on the final text were women and native people, the two groups politically astute enough to act on the knowledge that politicians seizing a once-in-a-lifetime opportunity to divide up the pie would be influenced only by those who stayed within a figurative shouting distance of the bargaining table. The historic gains won by these two groups are outside the scope of this paper. But these victories represent the only concessions wrested by the people from the politicians.

The guarantee, provided by s. 3, that "every citizen of Canada" can vote in an election to the House of Commons or to the Legislative Assembly of a province represents an expansion of the right, at least insofar as it has received statutory recognition. Judges, convicted prisoners and mentally incompetent persons are today generally denied the right to vote.[13] Since patriation, challenges to denials of the right to vote have been brought by remand prisoners,[14] convicted prisoners,[15] judges,[16] and probationers.[17] Such statutory restrictions will be subject to judicial "balancing" of the restriction as against the provisions of s. 1.

Section 3 also provides that "every citizen of Canada has the right...to be qualified for membership" in the House of Commons or a Legislative Assembly. Again, age and residency requirements might be challenged through a combination of s. 3 provisions and equality (s. 15) or mobility (s. 6) arguments. But these provisions will not be of crucial significance to many people. As s. 3 is limited, by its own terms, to House of Commons and provincial legislature members, there is no threat to the prohibition against a bankrupt being a Senator.[18] Accordingly, we can expect a continuation of the tradition that Senators will be appointed only from the ranks of the suitably privileged.

Sections 4 and 5, as we suggested above, continue the requirements that, "real or apprehended war, invasion or insurrection" not intervening, there shall be elections at least every five years, and that parliament and provincial legislatures shall sit at least once every twelve months. Little is new, and no significant additional power is conferred upon the people.

LEGISLATIVE OVERRIDE

It was suggested in the introduction that there were important limitations on both legislative and judicial power, provided for in the *Charter*, which might operate to add to the power of people. These possibilities lie within the provisions of s. 33 of the *Charter*, the "legislative override" of the "rights denial" section. Underlying this section is a schizophrenic theory which will be argued and applied in a schizophrenic fashion. A major theme of the *Constitution Act, 1982*, as chiefly expressed in sections 52 and 24, is that the *Constitution* is "the supreme law of Canada" and that courts are the final arbiters as to when it has been violated and what remedy should be provided. Citizens can claim from the judiciary a remedy for wrongs committed by the state through its executive and legislative organs. Yet, over against this lies a (sometimes grudging) recognition that judicial review,

even when undertaken by an independent judiciary, is fundamentally anti-democratic. The conflicting impulses — now to trust an independent judiciary, now to trust elected representatives — produce a "clear" mandate which, with respect to s. 2 or sections 7 to 15, can always be drawn back.

It is the quintessential Canadian solution. What can be said in its favour is this: when, and to the extent that, Canadian electoral democracy can be made to function in objectively democratic ways, the Canadian people (or, as appropriate, the people of a province) *may* have the last word about what the *Charter* should provide. That statement is supportable only by calling attention to the fact that if a government, through the legislature it controls, deliberately and in terms enacts legislation which is to operate notwithstanding *Charter* protections, such an enactment can be an election issue and, if opposition to that enactment is sufficiently popular and effective, the people can "throw the rascals out".

The provinces, from whom most legislative derogations from the *Charter* may be expected in the short run, have not had their legislative powers broadened in any respect by the *Charter*; s. 31 makes that clear. "Distribution of powers" arguments will still be pertinent. With respect to s. 2, therefore, when a provincial legislature seeks to deny one of the protected rights, it will be possible to argue that such legislation cannot be "demonstrably justified" except as an exercise of the criminal law power, which is exclusively federal. And here again, the "implied Bill of Rights" argument may be marshalled. Similar arguments will be telling where provincial legislation seeks to override the protections offered by section 7 through 15. The provincial interest in quasi-criminal offences and penalties is not momentous enough to demonstrably justify overriding these fundamental legal rights.

Insofar as equality rights are concerned, s. 15 can be overridden by either Parliament or a provincial legislature; however, section 28 (with respect to which there is no override) prohibits, to both levels of government, discrimination based on gender. Section 28 also suggests that gender-based discrimination that does not meet the s. 1 requirement can be challenged immediately, notwithstanding the three year suspension of other equality rights provided by s. 32(2).

"DISAPPEARED" RIGHTS

There was, in most drafts of the *Constitution Act, 1982*, save for the one that was enacted, an important provision of a popular right. In the early drafts, part or all of the patriation package would have been the subject of a referendum. When the politicians reached the final bargaining table the referendum provision was quietly abandoned. The first of the Liberal roadshows to begin to focus public attention on constitutional issues aimed at amendment and patriation was the MacGuigan-Molgat Committee, the Special Joint Committee of the Senate and the House of Commons on the Constitution of Canada, which submitted its report in 1972.[19] A number of the individuals appearing before the MacGuigan-Molgat Committee suggested that a referendum mechanism be incorporated into the constitutional amendment process. The report of the committee did not mention the issue.

A few years later another road show was mounted, this one carrying out its consultations with the public at the same time as federal and provincial politicians were working away at the real bargaining tables. A similar pattern of representations was made to the Pepin-Robarts Commission. It did recommend the referendum mechanism.[20]

Meanwhile, at the bargaining table, referendum provisions found their way into some of the tentative agreements reached among politicians, most notably the *Victoria Charter*. Accounts of discussions leading to these various (and ultimately abortive) proposals suggest that only the federal delegation held any brief for the referendum. Only a few of Mr. Trudeau's closest advisors, notably Michael Kirby, actually favoured such a provision.[21]

In the end, or at least as close to the end as 5 November is to 2 December 1981, this provision (as it appeared in the penultimate version) disappeared. There was never an explanation. So far as can be ascertained, politicians actually at the various bargaining tables never made strong public statements against the notion of the referendum. But there was no commitment to it.

What is at least as important as the disappearance of referendum provisions in 1982 is that the politicians assured themselves the same closed forum for the next mandatory review of the *Constitution*. Section 49 of the *Constitution Act, 1982* provides:

> A constitutional conference composed of the Prime Minister of Canada and the first ministers of the provinces shall be convened by the Prime Minister of Canada within 15 years after this Part comes into force to review the provisions of this Part.

The "Part" being referred to is Part V of the *Constitution Act, 1982*, headed *Procedure for amending Constitution of Canada*.

If the political aspirations and values of people other than elected politicians are to be given expression in the development of the Canadian constitution, less than 13 years remain in which to create a climate in which politicians would find it unthinkable to sit down alone for the

further amendment of the constitution. We will need every "popular right" we can argue for.

Endnotes

1. *Canadian Charter of Rights and Freedoms*, being Part I of the *Constitution Act, 1982*, Preamble.
2. *Ibid.*, s. 4(2).
3. For a review of the pertinent elements of the "implied bill of rights" and a careful analysis of subsequent treatment in the Supreme Court of Canada, see Cline and Finley, "Whither the Implied Bill of Rights" (1980–81), 45 *Sask. L. Rev.* 137.
4. *R. v. Big M Drug Mart* (1983), 25 *Alta. L.R.* (2d) 195 (Prov. Ct.) affirmed as to *Charter* reasoning (with the recharacterisation emphatically disapproved), in (1983), 49 A.R. 194 (C.A.). Leave to appeal to the Supreme Court of Canada granted, appeal to be heard in session commencing 24 January 1984.
5. *A.-G. Can. & Dupond v. Montreal* (1978), 2 S.C.R. 770.
6. *Ibid.*
7. See L.R. Betcherman, *The Little Band* (1982).
8. *Public Order (Temporary Measures) Act*, S.C. 1970–71–72, c. 2.
9. For a useful discussion of judicial themes, their development and apparent pre-*Charter* prospects, see MacKinnon, "Conspiracy and Sedition as Canadian Political Crimes" (1977), 23 *McGill L.J.* 622, and by the same author, "Developments in the Law of Criminal Conspiracy" (1981), 59 *Can. Bar. Rev.* 301.
10. *Young, James & Webster v. U.K.* (Closed Shop Case) decision of 25 November 1980, 44 Eur. Court H.R., Series A at I. Also reported in (1981), 3 *H.R.L.J.* 185.
11. No less conservative a body than the Canadian Bar Association has made a similar point in its major published statement on the *Constitution*. See Canadian Bar Association on the Constitution, *Towards A New Canada* (1978) at 16–18.
12. The pattern was established by the Lamontagne-Macguigan Committee (later the Molgat-MacGuigan Committee) in operation from 1970–72, which heard enough from the citizenry to fill about 8,000 pages with a record of what they had said, and which put a bit of that content into its recommendations. See that committee's final report: Can. Special Joint Committee of Senate and H. of C., *Constitution of Canada: Final Report* (1972). A replay occurred in 1977–79 with the Pepin-Robarts Task force on Canadian Unity. As would be expected, considering the title and the mandate of this body, the results were less focused. See its three reports, entitled: *A Time to Speak* (1979); *Coming to Terms* (1979); *A Future Together* (1979). A third road show, the Chretien-Romanow careenings of July and August of 1981, was limited to consultation among politicians. Things were getting serious by then.
13. See, as typical examples, *Canada Elections Act*, R.S.C., 1970, c. 14 (1st Sup.) s. 14(4); and *Elections Act*, R.S.A. 1980, c. E–2, s. 41.
14. *Re Maltby et al. v. A.-G. Sask. et al.* (1982), 20 S.R. 366 (Sask. Q.B.) (Successful).
15. *Jolivet v. The Queen*, unreported, 17 Aug. 1983, B.C.S.C. (Unsuccessful).
16. Apparently successful in Saskatchewan without being tested in court.
17. *Reynolds v. A.-G. B.C.* (1983), 2 W.W.R. 413 (B.C.S.C.) (Successful).
18. *Constitution Act, 1867*, s. 31(3).
19. See note 12.
20. See *A Future Together* (1979) note 12 at 103–104 and Recommendation 65 at 130–131.
21. The most trenchant journalistic account, although somewhat episodic, would appear to be R. Sheppard and M. Valpy, *The National Deal* (1982). An invaluable account by a Constitutional lawyer/historian is McConnell, "Annual Survey of Canadian Law: Constitutional Law" (1982), 14 *Ottawa L. Rev.* 502.

6

Law and Social Ordering

A. Law and Domination: Criminal Law

The Treason Trial of David MacLane [1797]†
R. DeSalaberry

THE Court opened at 7 o'clock a.m. precisely. David Maclane was placed at the bar. The jurors empanelled by the sheriff were called over — eleven were challenged on the part of the Crown, and twenty-four by the prisoner. The following gentlemen were sworn: John Blackwood, John Crawford, John Mure, John Jones, James M. Goddard, Henry Cull, John Painter, David Munro, James Irvine, James Orkney, Robert Morragh, Georges Symes. Then Mr. Lind, Clerk of the Arraigns said: "David Maclane, hold up your hand. Gentlemen of the Jury, the prisoner David Maclane stands indicted (here he read the indictment of which I have presented already the substance). Upon this indictment he hath been arraigned and upon his arraignment hath pleaded not guilty, and for his trial hath put himself upon God and the country, which country you are. Your charge is to enquire whether he be guilty of the felony and high treason whereof he stands indicted or not guilty. If you find him guilty, you are to enquire what goods or chattels, lands or tenements he had at the time of the felony and high treason committed, or at any other time since. If you find him not guilty, you are to enquire whether he fled for it. If you find that he did fly for it, you shall enquire of his goods and chattels as if you had found him guilty. If you find him not guilty and that he did not fly for it, say so, and no more. Hear you evidence."

Then Mr. Caron addressed the jury on behalf of the Crown and was followed by the Attorney-General who gave them the law and the facts on which the charge was based and which were to be brought forth by the witnesses William Barnard, Elmer Cushing, Francis Chandonet, Thomas Butterfield, Charles Frichette, John Black and Herman W. Ryland. Barnard had met the accused for the first time in Vermont at dark in a house near the border line. Maclane confidentially told him under a solemn promise of secrecy that his business was to bring about a revolution in Canada, and that the Canadians would have everything done for them for that purpose. He offered him to take the lead, adding that if Barnard undertook the task his fortune would be made.

A second interview took place at Montreal a few days later and again the matter was pressed upon Barnard, who this time informed Mr. McCord, one of the magistrates at Montreal. Barnard met the accused a third time at Laprairie, a village on the south shore of the St. Lawrence, about 9 miles above Montreal, on the second of November, when the same proposals were renewed and the promise made that an army would invade the province in the spring. He wanted to know where the seminary of Montreal kept their money and wished to be informed who the principal merchants were and in what part of their houses they kept their cash.

Elmer Cushing the second witness kept a tavern called the "American Coffee House" at Montreal, and the accused stopped at his place on the 5th of November. Cushing observed that his clothes were covered with small burrs, and asked him where he had been. He answered that he had been on every part of the mountain, which might be made a place of great command over Montreal in case of war. Maclane then exacting a promise of secrecy, which was given, told the witness that there would be a severe attack upon the province early in the spring; that he was employed by the French Minister at Philadelphia in forwarding the plan; that

---

† DeSalaberry, R., "Treason Trial of David McLane [1797]" originally appeared as "The First State Trial in Lower Canada" (Sept., 1927), VII *Canadian Bar Review* at 472–77. Reprinted by permission of the Canadian Bar Association, Ottawa, Ontario. Captus Press Inc. has employed its best effort to locate the copyright holder in order to reprint this work with permission.

the attack would be made by a fleet from France, which would bring from ten to fifteen thousand land forces. He went to his saddlebags, took out a pair of shoes, one of which had a hole near the toe, and pulled out a paper signed Adet. He assured Cushing he would have any reward he might ask for if he took an active part and that if he ever revealed what he had heard it should fare hard with him; that his life would be taken immediately.

Francis Chandonet, the third witness, was an American subject. He had met the prisoner at Watson's Tavern in the course of the previous summer, a little below "Ile aux Noix" and sometime also in the beginning of the winter. Maclane had come across Lake Champlain, and told the witness that he had come on most important business which he would reveal under promise of secrecy. He then told him he was employed by the French to sound the minds of the people, and that the plan was to secrete a quantity of arms and ammunition on rafts in the spring to be brought into the province by Lake Champlain, and the St. Lawrence, that he thought a quantity might likewise be concealed in the rafts of firewood made in the Cateauguay River, and he pressed very hard upon the witness to take part with him, which the latter refused to do.

Thomas Butterfield, from Swaton, U.S., the next witness, was an accomplice. He had promised to assist Maclane in all his enterprises against Canada and also was under his pay. The prisoner had told him he and a man named Frichette were going to Quebec to lay some plan to take the garrison.

Frichette was then heard. He met the prisoner at St. John's, who asked him if he had horses to sell. Both went into the field where Frichette, being bound by an oath to secrecy, was asked by the accused if the Canadians were disposed to revolt, to which Frichette answered they were not desirous of war, and the prisoner then stated that he had come to take Quebec — that five hundred men with pikes could do it. He asked him to conduct him to Quebec through the land, to which the witness agreed. They passed behind the Fort of St. John's before daylight, and proceeded on the south shore road to St. Nicholas. They left St. Nicholas, and crossed the St. Lawrence to Wolfe's Cove. The prisoner set Frichette from there to Quebec to bring one Mr. Black to him. When Mr. Black arrived he told the prisoner that Frichette had informed him of the intentions of his journey. He advised him to go back without making the attempt, as he thought it could not succeed as the Canadians were not disposed to rise and could not therefore be depended upon.

The prisoner afterwards informed Mr. Black he had a letter for him, and another person. Mr. Black opened and read the letters and advised the prisoner to tear them to pieces, and bury them, which was done. At Mr. Black's request he explained his plan of the taking of Quebec. The troops he said would be so surprised that they would not know which way to turn. Mr. Black told Maclane not to be afraid and to come to Quebec to his house, dressed like a gentleman, and take a walk about the town. The prisoner expressed his dislike to come into town, but Mr. Black insisted and finally Maclane consented to go. Mr. Black did not approve of his coming in company with him, to avoid suspicion. He wanted Frichette to bring Maclane to his house in the evening which accordingly was done. The prisoner desired to be called by the name of Felt, from St. John's, till he went to Mr. Black's.

Mr. Black then gave evidence. He corroborated Frichette and related to the Jury that the prisoner had explained his plan, which was that of humanity. That he was sorry to see a great people labouring under the tyranny of England; that he proposed to push the British from the continent of America. He said he left Mr. Adet on the 7th of April, who was going to France on the 10th, and that both he and the Spanish minister were concerned in the measures. That besides these measures there were fifteen thousand men at the line ready at a nod. He inquired much concerning the property, public and private, that there was at Quebec, and he said the property was intended to be given to those who should take the city. Black advised him to come to town after dark. The prisoner finally consented and was conducted to his house by Frichette. As soon as Black came back to town he gave information to a magistrate, Mr. Young, and the prisoner was apprehended the same evening, about eleven o'clock at his house.

The last witness was Herman Witsius Ryland, Secretary to His Excellency the Governor-General, who made the arrest. This concluded the evidence of the Crown. The defence produced no witnesses. David Maclane made a long speech to the Jury in which he denied the charge, but unfortunately it was not conclusive. His two counsel made a strong appeal to the feelings of the Jury. The Attorney-General replied. Chief Justice Osgood then made a forcible address to the Jury, but very fair and moderate, summing up the evidence in a clear, precise and impartial manner.

Then the Jury withdrew for twenty minutes and returned. The Clerk of Arraigns then said:

"Gentlemen answer to your names."

"Gentlemen, are you all agreed upon your verdict?" — "Yes."

"Who shall speak for you?" — "Our foreman."

"David Maclane hold up your hand. Jurors, look upon the prisoner; how say you — is he guilty of the felony and high treason whereof he stands indicted, or not guilty?"

Foreman: "Guilty."

"What goods or chattels, lands or tenements had he at the time of the felony and high treason by him committed?"

Foreman: "None to our knowledge."

"Gentlemen of the Jury, the Court discharges you and thanks you for your services."

The Attorney-General: "Upon the verdict as recorded, I humbly move for judgment of death against the prisoner."

Clerk of Arraigns: "David Maclane, hold up you hand. You have been indicted of felony and treason, have been arraigned and pleaded not guilty thereto, and for your trial have put yourself on God and country, which country has found you guilty — what have you to say for yourself why the court should not give judgment of death upon you according to law."

Prisoner: "I have nothing more to say."

Proclamation being made, the Chief Justice Pronounced the sentence of death as follows: —

It remains that I should discharge the painful duty of pronouncing the sentence of the law which is: That you, David Maclane, be taken to the place from whence you came, and from thence you are to be drawn to the place of execution, where you must be hanged by the neck, but not until you are dead; for you must be cut down alive and your bowels taken out and burnt before your face; then your head must be severed from your body, which must be divided into four parts, and your head and quarters be at the King's disposal — and may the Lord have mercy on your soul.

The Attorney-General moved that a day should be fixed for the execution, and the Court appointed Friday, the 21st of July.

The trial had commenced at 7 a.m. and was concluded at 9 p.m. the same day.

On Friday, the 21st, the prisoner was taken from the gaol and placed upon a hurdle which moved in slow solemnity towards the place of execution. At about a quarter after ten, the hurdle drew up close to the gallows. As soon as it stopped, Maclane rose up dressed in white linen and wearing a white cap on his head. The Rev. Mr. Mountain and the Rev. Mr. Sparks attended him, and with them he continued in fervent prayer for some minutes. He then informed the executioner that he was ready and was by him directed to ascend the ladder, which he immediately did. But the executioner observing that he was too high, he descended a step or two and then addressed the spectators in the following words:

This place gives me pleasure; I am now going where I have long wished to be and you, who now see me, must all follow me in a short time, some of you perhaps in a few days; let this be a warning to prepare for your own deaths.

Then addressing himself to the military who were drawn up in a hollow square, he added: "You with arms in your hands, you are not secure here even with your arms. I am going where I shall be secure without them." He immediately drew the cap over his face, exclaiming: "Oh! God, receive my soul. I long to be with my Jesus," and dropped his handkerchief as a signal to the executioner, who instantly turned him off. He struggled with death but a short time. The body hung for about twenty-five minutes, and was then cut down. A platform, with a raised block upon it, was brought near the gallows, and a fire was kindled for executing the remainder of the sentence. The head was cut off, and the executioner holding it up to public view proclaimed it "the head of a traitor." An incision was made below the breast and a part of the bowels taken out and burnt. The four quarters were marked with a knife but not divided from the body.

The whole of the execution took about two hours.

Law, State, and Class Struggle[†]
A. Hunt

INTRODUCTION

This chapter sets out to examine the way in which law operates to maintain class domination. The argument that is developed shows that law should not simply be regarded as part of the coercive armoury of the state; but also must be understood as making a major contribution to what will be called "ideological domination." Ideological domination consists of those processes that produce and reaffirm the existing social order and thereby legitimize class domi-

† Hunt, Alan, "Law, State, and Class Struggle" in *Explorations in Law and Society: Towards a Constitutive Theory of Law* (London: Routledge, 1993) at 17–35. Originally from (1976), 20 *Marxism Today* 178–87. Reprinted by permission of Alan Hunt and Statesman Newspaper and Society, U.K.

nation. The processes involved in creating and reproducing ideological domination play a major part in ensuring the continuation of capitalist social relations.

There has been relatively little attention paid by Marxists to law. This absence of discussion has resulted in a tendency for the more obvious repressive characteristics to be stressed; and as a consequence the more pervasive contribution of law to the maintenance of capitalist society has not been sufficiently explored. The analysis of law in this wider context is of considerable political importance. Marxists are increasingly being forced to come to grips with the fact that modern capitalism has exhibited very considerable "staying power." In the period since the Second World War capitalism in Western Europe has shown what may be best described as relative stability; that is to suggest that despite the occurrence of very deep economic, social and political crises the capitalist social order in the major Western European states has survived substantially intact. This chapter examines the extent and the manner in which legal systems contribute to the perpetuation of capitalist systems.

STATE AND LAW

In class societies the economic and social dominance of an exploiting class does not sustain itself automatically. The exploiting class always strives to turn itself into a ruling class by means of an institutional structure, the state, which operates to sustain and to reproduce that position. While the state is a product of class antagonism it takes on the appearance of being an entity which stands above society and which embodies the interests of the community as a whole. This apparently *universal* quality is especially significant with reference of legal systems:

> Right, law, etc. are merely the symptom, the expression of *other* relations upon which State power rests.... These actual relations are in no way created by the State power; on the contrary they are the power creating it. The individuals who rule in these conditions, besides having to constitute their power in the form of the *State*, have to give their will, which is determined by these definite conditions, a universal expression as the will of the state, as law. (Marx/Engels 1968: 366)

The distinctive feature then of legal systems of class societies is the fact that they embody the material interests of the ruling class in a universal form, and thus present law as the embodiment of the interests of the community as a whole:

> In a modern state, law must not only correspond to the general economic condition and be its expression, but must also be an *internally coherent* expression which does not owing to inner contradictions, reduce itself to nought. And in order to achieve this, the faithful reflection of economic conditions suffers increasingly. All the more so the more rarely it happens that a code of law is the blunt, unmitigated, unadulterated expression of domination of a class — this in itself would offend the "conception of right". (Engels 1890: 504)

This striving of "internal coherence," in which law comes to be seen as the embodiment of universal notions of "justice" and "right," needs to be explored. At the hands of bourgeois legal and political theorists it has been used to provide an ideological dogma, important in bourgeois political and legal theory, of the doctrine of the "separation of powers." The essence of this view is that the character of the democratic state is defined as one in which there exists a separation between the major components of the state. Specifically it is argued that not only is there, but also that there ought to be, a separation between the legislature, which makes the laws, and the judiciary, which apply those laws.

The doctrine of the separation of powers has played, and continues to play a central part in bourgeois theory of the law and the state. There has been a tendency of Marxists in seeking to expose the ideological character of this doctrine to react against it by asserting the identity of the state and law. Thus the legal system has been presented simply as the direct and totally subservient agent of the state. Such a position is too simple, but more importantly it obscures the real class character of the legal system as a mechanism whereby the existing form of class domination is perpetuated and reproduced.

We need to start by asking, how does it come about that a separation appears to exist between law and state? Engels provides a useful starting point:

> But once the state has become an independent power *vis-à-vis* society, it produces forthwith a further ideology. It is indeed among professional politicians, theorists of public law and jurists of private law that the connection with economic facts gets lost for fair [*sic*]. Since in each particular case the economic facts must assume the form of juristic motives in order to receive legal sanction; and since, in so doing, consideration of course has to be given to the whole legal system already in operation, the juristic form is, in consequence, made everything and the economic content nothing. (Engels 1958: 396–97)

If these ideological functions are to be fulfilled they cannot operate exclusively as ideological forces, they must find some expression in the actual practice embodied within the legal system. As a consequence the legal system operates in a manner which cannot be explained exclusively by reference to the dictates of the state as a whole.

The doctrine of the separation of powers appeals to the independence of the judiciary. Yet this independence is clearly very restricted. Judicial appointments are made by the highest representatives of the political apparatus of the state.[1]

But what does need to be stressed is that even the relative degree of autonomy sets up stresses and contradictions within the state as a whole. Decisions by courts do not always please the holders of state power. The protracted struggle between the courts and Nixon throughout the "Watergate affair" is perhaps the most important recent example of such a tension in operation, in which the conflict between court and state contributed in no small measure to the downfall of Nixon.

But the tension between courts and state may also have advantages for the holders of state power. The institutional complexity of the English legal system allowed the government to brush the cobwebs off the Official solicitor whose intervention facilitated the release of the "Pentonville 5" in 1972 when faced with the prospect of a General Strike. Frequently it serves as a convenient smoke-screen behind which to hide; Roy Jenkins, as Home Secretary, consistently used the excuse of separation between government and courts to refuse to intervene and secure the release of the Shrewsbury pickets.

This discussion points toward the general conclusion that the relationship between the state and the legal system must always be a matter for concrete examination. While the general dependence of the law on the state as a whole is an important proposition within Marxist theory, this must not be treated as if it suggested a complete identity between law and state.

DOMINATION AND HEGEMONY

Domination is a universal feature of class society. It consists in the subjection of one or more classes to another class (or grouping of classes) in such a way that exploitative relations are perpetuated. But the form that domination takes varies with the form of the exploitative class relations; thus the domination of slave by slaveholder differs from the employer's domination of the factory worker. Domination must be viewed not as a single act but as a process that reproduces the conditions for exploitative social relations.

Domination can only be based for very short periods of time on direct physical coercion. Even the most barbarous and coercive systems do not rely exclusively upon coercive violence. Direct coercion will often play a major part in the establishment of a new system of class power, but, however much it continues to depend on physical repression, it will strive to promote other means of consolidating its domination.

An extremely fruitful approach to the discussion of domination is provided by the early leader of the Italian Communist Party, Antonio Gramsci, who made use of the concept of "hegemony." He used it to identify the processes that create

> the "spontaneous" consent given by the great mass of the population to the general direction imposed on social life by the dominant fundamental group (i.e., the ruling class). (Gramsci 1971: 12)

The vital characteristic of "hegemony" is that it is an active process; it is concerned not only with the *fact* of consent, but focuses on the creation and the mobilization of that consent. One major facet of the class struggle that takes place within capitalist societies is the continual struggle for influence over the ideas, perceptions, and values of members of the different classes. The maintenance of capitalism would be impossible unless the capitalist class was able to decisively influence the ideas, attitudes and consciousness of the working class.

It is important to stress that the ideological struggle is not simply concerned with the conflict between general theories of society. It is concerned with every aspect of the way in which people think about, react to, and interpret their position in class society.

COERCIVE AND IDEOLOGICAL DOMINATION

In examining the part that is played by law in the class struggle it is useful to distinguish between two different aspects. Law plays an important role in sustaining the domination of the ruling class because it operates both as a form of *coercive domination* and of *ideological domination*. It will also be necessary to stress that they are not simple alternatives. I hope to show the way in which these two elements are closely bound together and as such contribute to the special effectiveness of law as a mechanism of social order.

Let us first consider the coercive character of law. The legal system is able to call upon the organized power of the state. This repression operates both through specific institutions, which range from the courts themselves to the prison system, probation service, etc. In addition it also operates more generally through the police system that operates with wide-ranging powers, sanctioned by law, but able to act with a very considerable degree of autonomy.

Legal coercion operates at a number of different levels. Of greatest importance is the application of coercion to protect the *general conditions* of the capitalist order. First and foremost coercion is applied to protect and reinforce the property relations of capitalist society. There exists an increasingly complex body of "offences against property" that are concerned with the defense of private property. First they are important in demarcating the "lawful" from the "unlawful"; they differentiate between the unlawful appropriation of property, the acts of the "criminals," and the lawful forms of appropriation that are the hallmark of the capitalist system. Just how close is the dividing line between lawful and unlawful appropriation has been clearly revealed by recent bribery and corruption cases. But second, it is not only the offender that is coerced, but all members of society because the coercion of the offender reinforces the values, attitudes, and behavior associated with the existence of private property. It is for this reason that it was stressed above that the coercive and ideological functions of law are closely related.

While the criminal law protects the property interests of the capitalist class it operates more generally to protect the "private property" of all members of society. Indeed it is important to recognise that the vast majority of "property offences" are committed, not against the property of the capitalist class, but rather against the property of noncapitalists. Property offences are usually directed against the privately owned consumption goods of working people.

Another way in which legal coercion is applied to defend the *general* conditions of capitalist society is with respect to "offences against the person." Again this area of the criminal law does not merely act against offences against members of the capitalist class. The significance of this type of legal coercion is that some level of general social order is a necessary precondition for the maintenance of its specifically capitalist content.

One of the most important manifestations of legal coercion is the application of law for the direct protection of the state itself. The state has at its disposal a veritable armory of measures that are ready to be invoked to defend the existing political order. These range from a number of traditional offences such as treason, treachery, and sedition (which have been invoked fairly infrequently in the recent past), through such legislation as the *Official Secrets Act* of 1911 and 1920 and the *Incitement to Disaffection Act* 1934, to the wide ranging emergency powers that the ruling class has gradually accumulated. *The Emergency Powers Acts* of 1920 and 1964 give very extensive powers to the civil and military authorities to intervene in the class struggle. These powers have been used on no less than eight occasions since the War; on four of these occasions by the Health government against dockers, power supply workers, and the miners; Labour Governments have not shrunk from invoking them.

In the recent past Northern Ireland has been a fertile source of emergency regulations. *The Northern Ireland (Emergency Provisions) Act* 1973 and the *Prevention of Terrorism (Emergency Powers) Act* 1974 have aided the British government's struggle against the Irish people and their scope has been extended to the mainland.[2]

The ruling class also has at its disposal a wide range of legal devices that can be used against offences against public order. These range through riot, affray, unlawful assembly and breach of the peace. Of particular importance is the *Public Order Act* 1936, supposedly introduced to curb the Fascists, but used systematically against the Left. It is interesting to observe the skill of the police and courts in making use of "appropriate" legal mechanisms. A good example has been the recent resuscitation of the *Conspiracy and Protection of Property Act* 1875.

In protecting the existing political order the law does not only have at its disposal the wide ranging powers contained in the legislation discussed above. The general principles of criminal law offer not only ample scope, but also special advantage. It is often in the interest of the ruling class to seek to depoliticize the class struggle. One of the means that is frequently invoked is to charge the "political offender" with ordinary crimes. This can be achieved by using a charge that is incidental to the main social or political issue involved; the most favored police strategy being to invoke charges involving or implying violence. A very good example of this technique is to be seen in the trial of the Shrewsbury pickets. The use of such charges allows the political issues to be ignored while branding the defendants as "common criminals," a tactic favored by Roy Jenkins and Frank Chapple in their attacks on the Shrewsbury pickets.

A related prosecution strategy is to use blanket charges; much in favor in the recent past has been the use of conspiracy charges. These are not only significant in that they allow the prosecution to evade some of the restrictions with regard to the evidence and procedure that normally apply. But in addition, through the orchestration by the mass media, to create impressions of the existence of an unspecified "threat to law and order."

The legal order has at its disposal this powerful armoury of techniques of legal coercion that enable it to directly intervene in the class struggle to defend the interest of the existing order. This direct intervention in the class struggle stands out most sharply in the case of industrial and trade union laws.[3] The history of trade union law, from the *Combination Act* 1800 to the *Industrial Relations Act* 1971, is testimony to the attempt to provide a legal framework favorable to the interests of capital as opposed to those of labor. Yet it is the testimony of the extent to the resistance that over the period as a whole has not only forced tactical retreats, but has also witnessed significant advances in the legal positions of trade unions.

I will return later to take up this question of law as an arena of class struggle.

What stands out in sharp relief is the extent to which the ruling class utilizes a legal framework for sustaining and buttressing their class interests. But a certain degree of care is needed in drawing conclusions from this common ground. The argument is frequently advanced that in periods of crisis the capitalist class resort to an increasingly repressive strategy and embark on major attacks on civil liberties. This type of analysis is very clearly presented in John Hostettler's article "Trends to Authoritarian Rule in Britain" (*Marxism Today*, Dec. 1973). This line of argument is sometimes presented in such a way that it obscures important contradictory dimensions, which if correctly considered throw much light on the specific role of law within capitalist society.

The lurch of legal authoritarianism is checked by an equally strong need on the part of the ruling class to maintain the legitimacy of their class rule. This contradiction is not an interaction between two equal forces that smoothly balance each other out; hence there are periods in which there are major shifts toward authoritarianism, but equally there are periods of movement toward more liberal and less coercive forms. The particular result at any point in time is a complex result of the level of class struggle itself.

There is a more general, and possibly more fundamental, political point that underlies this discussion that needs to be more fully discussed. Lenin was correct when he argued that

> bourgeois states are most varied in form, but their essence is the same; all these states, whatever their form in the final analysis are inevitably the dictatorship of the bourgeoisie. (CW 25: 413).

Yet there has been a tendency (which is present in Lenin as well as in others) to regard bourgeois democracy as simply a sham or fraud designed to conceal the class character of the rule of the bourgeoisie. Capitalism has been in existence long enough to demonstrate that its most persistent, stable and "successful" form has proved to be the *bourgeois democratic* political form. Thus for the bourgeoisie whatever pressures manifest themselves toward the "authoritarian solution" there is at the same time a profound concern to sustain the legitimacy of the capitalist order.

This analysis does not lead to the conclusion that the resort by the ruling class to fascism or to military coup is impossible. The tragic example of Chile is too urgent to allow such a naive conclusion. But this analysis does insist that the resort to fascism is not the automatic response of a capitalist class in crisis. We should have no illusions about the fact that the capitalist class has been prepared, in the final analysis, to abandon bourgeois democracy. But

we should be equally insistent that the interests of the bourgeoisie have been best served where they have been able to sustain their class rule within the bourgeois democratic form and that the ruling class itself has an interest in the preservation of bourgeois democracy.

The legal order plays a central role within bourgeois democracy. Thus while the coercive role of the legal order has been emphasized in the first half of this article it is now necessary to draw attention to and to examine the contribution made by the legal system to sustaining the legitimacy of the bourgeois democratic order. In other words it is necessary to discuss law as a method of ideological domination.

LAW AS IDEOLOGICAL DOMINATION

Repressive and ideological domination are in no sense alternatives. On the contrary they are interdependent; they interact and reinforce each other. While the coercion of the criminal law is directed against those it punishes, its ideological effects are directed much wider. For example, the jailing of the Shrewsbury pickets was legal violence against the accused which was concerned with more than "deterring" others; it was an ideological offence against the strategy of the "flying picket" developed by the miners and applied so effectively by building workers.

Ideological domination describes those activities and processes whereby the assent to the existing social order is produced and mobilized. The notion of assent embraces both the idea of legitimacy as active assent and also acceptance as the passive form. The means by which assent is produced are ideological in that it involves the production and dissemination of ideas that affect social practice through the determination of the social consciousness of individuals, groups, and classes. This process is one of domination in that it involves two elements; first, a differential ability of groups and classes in society to produce, communicate, and disseminate ideas, and second, these ideas, directly or indirectly, have consequences for the maintenance of the existing social order.

Law is ideological in that it conveys or transmits a complex set of attitudes, values, and theories about aspects of society. Its ideological content forms part of the dominant ideology because these attitudes, values, etc. are ones that reinforce and legitimize the existing social order.

The most pervasive ideological effect of law is to be found in the fact that legal rules and their application give effect to existing social relations. The rules of law affirm the social and economic relations that exist within capitalist society. Thus the law of property is not only based on the inequality of property ownership but it reinforces it by allowing and facilitating the owners of property to make use of that property as capital. The complex of legal rules relating to mortgages, trusts, leases, etc. not only allows but also enables property to be used as capital. The law relating to contracts and commercial activity gives effect to the mechanisms of the market.

Similarly labor law facilitates the capitalist form of the relationship between labor and capital; it gives effect to the economic fact of the dependence of the majority on the sale of their labor power. It embodies the economic power of capital over labor by granting to the employer rights regarding not only the control of labor but also over hiring and firing of labor.

Rules of law impinge on almost every form of social relations. For example, family law, despite the reforms of the past decades, incorporates the fact of the dominant role of the husband over the wife, of the parents over the children. Likewise the law of landlord and tenant underlines the power of landlords over tenants in regard to the supply of housing. It is important to stress that the legal rules do not *create* the social relations that make up capitalist society. But by stating them as principles and by enforcing them the law operates not only to reinforce these relations but also to legitimize them in their existing form. This function is further advanced by the role of law in conferring authority upon officials such as the police, magistrates, etc.

The rules of law not only define social relations but confer rights and powers on certain categories of individuals. Thus, for example, landlord and tenant law not only incorporates the economic fact of the monopolization of housing by private interests, but it also legitimizes that economic power by granting rights to landlords to extract rent, to impose conditions, and to evict tenants. The legal system not only reinforces existing social and economic relations, but in addition it confers authority on dominant social interests.

One important aspect that should not be overlooked is the extent to which law operates to regulate the mutual interests of the bourgeoisie. It provides a mechanism for the resolution of disputes and conflicts that arise *between* capitalist interests:

> The administration of...civil justice is concerned almost exclusively with conflicts over property and hence affects almost exclusively the possessing classes. (Marx 1958: II, 34)

Company law, for example, is concerned in the main with the respective interests of shareholders and directors. Much commercial law is likewise concerned with the interests of merchants, middleman, and dealers.

The law regulating the interests of the propertied classes is detailed and complex, but it has a significant common core. The operation of capitalistic functions is facilitated where the law provides a degree of certainty and predictability. What bourgeois legal theory fails to recognize is that it is only that element of law that regulates the mutual interests of the bourgeoisie, and not the whole of law in a capitalist society that exhibits this quest for certainty.

It is necessary to consider more closely the nature of the correspondence between legal rules and the social relations to which they relate. Legal rules do not simply "reflect" social relations. The rules of law have an added ideological dimension. To explain this it is important to recall that a central feature of capitalist society is that its essential features are obscured or concealed by the very nature of the operation of the capitalist economy. Marx insisted on the need to distinguish between how things appear (the "appearance" or "phenomenal form") and how they really are ("real substratum" or "essence").

The "real" relations that exist find themselves expressed in legal rules in a distorted or truncated form because the law gives effect to only the appearance ("phenomenal form") of social relations. This theoretical point could be taken further by applying the argument developed by Marx in the famous section on "the fetishism of commodities" in *Capital* Vol. I in which he shows how our comprehension of commodities embodies not the real social relations of production which create them, but simply as things; and as a result what are relations between people come to be seen as relations between things.

So legal rules appear abstracted from social relations, and are therefore a "fetishistic" expression of social relations. Legal rules are further divorced from the social relations to which they refer because they (like the state itself) appear separated, independent of society; they seem to have an independent origin and life of their own. Thus as ideological forms of social relations legal rules are doubly removed from the real world.

Legal rules express the appearance of social relations:

> This phenomenal form, which makes the actual relations invisible...forms the basis of all the juridical notions of both labourer and capitalist, of all the mystifications of the capitalist mode of production, of all its illusions as to liberty. (Marx 1961: I, 540)

Marx showed how our initial perception of the capitalist economy focuses on the process of circulation and exchange, and thus ignores the production process itself. It is significant to note that legal rules follow this pattern and reduce social relations to a system of exchanges. The key legal concept of bourgeois law is that of *contract*. All the most important relations within capitalist society are moulded into the form of contractual relations.

By treating social relations as "contracts" bourgeois law strips them of their most important characteristics. Perhaps the most important example is in the labor relationship between employers and workers. At law the labor relation is a contract between individual employer and individual employee; they are therefore presumed to bargain over the terms of the contract. This individualizing of the contract of employment by focusing on it as an individual exchange excludes the social character of the relation between capital and labor. It is incapable of embracing the increasingly collective determination of labor relations through negotiations between trade unions and employers' federations. English law has reduced itself to great confusion in attempting to preserve the "individual contract" while taking some note of the real "collective contract."

It is not only economic relations that are reduced to contractual form. A wide range of other social relations is similarly treated. Thus, for example, the social institution of marriage is enshrined in law as a contract within which the "parties" have obligations that derive from the contract, and the "breach" of which can result in the contract being terminated, i.e., in divorce. Yet by expressing the marriage relationship in contractual form the law inadvertently exposes something of the real economic basis on which the bourgeois marriage is based, founded on the economic dependence of women.

The principles of contract have been so pervasive that they have been developed into a contractual ideology which continues to have wider ranging influences. Contractual ideology leans heavily on the notions of freedom and equality. But the "freedom" and "equality" to which it refers is purely *formal*; that is individuals are regarded as free if there is no legal bar to them entering into a contract, and are therefore deemed to be equal. It is a notion of equality brilliantly captured by Anatole France:

The law in its majestic impartiality forbids rich and poor alike to sleep under bridges, to beg in the streets and steal bread (1927: 91)

These formal notions of freedom and equality fare characteristic of bourgeois legal and political theory. They do violence to social reality because they are incapable of grasping the real inequality and lack of freedom that results from the dependence of all workers on the sale of their labor.

This discussion has focused on the way in which the rules of law, far from being pure or independent creations, are but a distorted expression of the existing social relations which are thereby reinforced and legitimised. This ideological character of legal rules is extended by two further considerations.

One of the difficulties in penetrating the ideological form of bourgeois law stems from the fact that it operates by abstracting the cases that come before the courts from their social and class context. They are thereby reduced to the status of being pure *technical* issues, apparently divorced from any political or ideological overtones. If, for example, a householder inquires why it is that tax relief is granted on mortgage payments but not on rent, the law

replies that it is not a question of relief on mortgage or rent, but on interest repayments. By focusing on a technical distinction the law thereby obscures the social and economic reality.

Second, the law further depoliticizes social issues through the universal form of many legal rules. The fact that rules of criminal law protect the person and property of all members of society not only hides the fundamental class differences, but it also treats the capital of the employer and the personal belongings of the worker as if they were the same. The ideological significance is that it induces the view that all classes in society have a common interest in the protection of private property. Thereby the legal system is aided in fulfilling the ideological function of asserting the unity of interests of all classes. The ideology of the "rule of law" operates to assert and reinforce, and even seeks to celebrate, a social unity and cohesion in the face of the manifest class differentiation of capitalist society.

There is one further facet of the ideological character of law. It is directly ideological in the sense that the legal system propagates a range of views about the nature of the social and political system. This general ideological character of law is contained in what I will call "bourgeois legal ideology."

Bourgeois legal ideology is the fundamental component of the justification of the bourgeois democratic state; many of its elements directly enter into the consciousness of wide sections of the population. The central element of this ideology is the doctrine of "the rule of law." Its classic expression is to be found in Dicey:

When we speak of the "rule of law" as a characteristic of our country we mean, not only that with us no man is above the law, but (what is a different thing) that every man, whatever be his rank or condition, is subject to the ordinary law of the realm.... With us every official, from the Prime Minister down to a constable...is under the same responsibility for every act done without legal justification as any other citizen. (1967: 193)

The fundamental tenet is that both the ruled and the rulers are equally subject to a common system of the law. The "law" itself is thus viewed as something separate from the interests of classes. As such it plays a central role in the legitimation of the bourgeois democratic political order.

One particularly interesting feature of bourgeois legal ideology in the context of English law is the way in which it holds itself out as the protector of the individual against the incursions of the state. This antithesis between individual and state has a lengthy history in bourgeois legal thought. Its roots were in the historical alliance between

147

the common law judges and the bourgeois interests against the absolutism of the Stuarts. It became more fully elaborated during the nineteenth century as the legal reflex of laissez-faire ideology. And in the twentieth century it has been used as the basis of antistate attitudes that characterize one element of the conservative reaction to the growth of the Welfare State.

In addition to explicit constitutional principles bourgeois legal ideology consists of a range of important background or implicit assumptions. The intention is only to roughly sketch some of these assumptions, but at the same time to argue that the more the "law and order" debate moves into the center of the political stage the more important it becomes to develop a systematic critique of bourgeois legal ideology.

Almost all discussion about law is based on the assumption that the existence of law is an inevitable or natural feature of social life. Hence law becomes identified with "civilization"; the absence of law is seen as synonymous with the absence of civilization. The classic expression of this assumption is the equation of the absence of law with anarchy; in its classical form in the political philosophy of Hobbes the absence of law implies a condition of "the war of all against all." The whole of society is presumed to have an interest in the existence of law, and is therefore closely connected with the "universalism" of law discussed above.

A closely associated assumption insists on the inherent rationality of law. The existence of rules of social life brought together or codified as law is presented as socially desirable in that it makes social life more certain and predictable. Social life is viewed as if it were a game or a sport in which it is essential that all the "players" adhere to the same rules; without this common set of rules social life would revert to anarchy. Such an attitude places stress on the desirability of rules *as such*, and hence leaves unquestioned the content of those rules and any questions concerning the social and economic interests that are embodied in the rules.

Flowing directly from the insistence on the naturalness and rationality of law is the insistence that adherence to law is natural, and as a corollary, that nonadherence to law is unnatural or deviant. The very existence of a state is treated as a sufficient condition to make obedience to law obligatory for all citizens. The assumption is made that the offender who violates the law is a deviant whose deviation stems from some pathological condition. While the nature of the pathology appealed to has varied, from the genetic inferiority of the "lower orders" to deficiencies in "socialization," the same assumption of the naturalness of obedience to law persists. It is interesting to note that in the recent past this essentially conservative tradition has come under increasing attack from criminologists, and that radical theories of crime are being developed which draw upon Marxism (Taylor, Walton, and Young 1972).

These interrelated attitudes and assumptions about law are not usually expressed in a coherent form: they are a cluster of ideas, but they add up to an assertion of the "sanctity of law" that forms the heart of the pervasive and powerful "law and order" ideology. This ideology finds expression not only in the moralizing editorials of the *Times*, but also forms an important part of widespread and diffuse social attitudes. The essential substance of these views is that they appeal to the sanctity of law, elevated above social life itself, and thereby ignore the class content of law and its role in legitimising the existing forms of class domination.

There is one final aspect of the ideological character of law that needs to be mentioned. The most formal and systematic expression of legal ideology is provided by jurisprudence or legal theory. The history of jurisprudence consists in successive attempts to provide a justification for obedience to law. The central concern has been to provide a socially persuasive account of the legitimacy of the existing legal order, and through that of the social order itself. However, a very interesting development has occurred within jurisprudence which is worth noting. Increasingly a number of liberal academics have been afflicted with growing self-doubt and disillusionment with the whole edifice of law, and are increasingly aware of a very real decline in the legitimacy of the existing legal order (Rostow 1970; Wolff 1971).

The operation of law is, therefore, not confined to simply giving effect to the direct and immediate interests of the ruling class. It must be understood as having an ideological function of an extensive character. Within capitalist society the legal system not only provides substantial ideological underpinnings to the existing capitalist organization of society. It also provides a consistent and coherent legitimation of a multitude of key institutions and principles that are central to the smooth operation of a system of capitalist social relations.

It is this ability to integrate two critical functions, on the one hand to give practical effect to the interests of the dominant class, and, at the same time, to provide a justification or legitimation for these interests in terms of some higher and apparently universal interest of all classes that demonstrates the real power and influence of law in capitalist society.

LAW AND CLASS STRUGGLE

Our attention has been focused on the part that law plays in the process of reproducing capitalist social order. Yet law is not simply an instrument which can be wielded at will by an omnipotent ruling class. Precisely because it is an active element in the class struggle, it is at the same time affected by and involved in the class struggle. The law and the legal system form part of the context within which the class struggle takes place, and it is itself an arena in which that struggle occurs. To recognize that class struggle occurs *within* the legal system is not to suggest that the legal system is some neutral territory over which the class struggle wrestles for control. As a major component of the state law is necessarily part of the process through which the ruling class seeks to preserve its domination.

To argue that class struggle occurs within law is only the first step in examining the way in which class struggle makes itself evident within law. It has been argued above that law plays a central part in bourgeois democratic society, not only in theory but also in practice. The form taken by the class struggle has its boundaries broadly defined by the existing law. Thus, for example, trade union activity in Britain is pursued by forms of struggle that are recognized as being lawful. Some of the most important stages in the history of British trade unionism have been periods when struggle has occurred around attempts by the ruling class to narrow or restrict this lawful sphere of operations. The struggle against the *Industrial Relations Act* was a classic example of this type of struggle.

While law plays this important part of defining the parameters of class struggle, it also needs to be recognized that it does not necessarily stay confined within this framework. Indeed a change in this boundary or its breach will normally mark a critical phase in the class struggle. For example, a very important stage of the struggle against the *Industrial Relations Act* occurred in the months after it had been put on the statute book. The right-wing inside the Labour Movement argued that despite the objection they had to the Act it was now "law" and had to be accepted. The critical phase was the decisions make in the individual unions and within the TUC (Croydon and Blackpool Congresses 1971) as to whether they would "register" under the Act, and thus come within "the law," or whether to remain unregistered and to conduct trade union activity without the forms of protection that had been established since the beginning of the century.

Not only does law play an important part in defining the parameters of the class struggle, but many important stages in the class struggle take place around demands for legislative reforms. Marx himself gave considerable attention to one very important example of such struggles, the early *Factory Acts* (in particular the *Factories Regulation Act* of 1833). His chapter in *Capital* Volume I, on "The Working-Day" is a classic study of the interrelation and interaction of class forces in a struggle for legislative control of working hours.

> The creation of a normal working-day is, therefore, the product of a protracted civil war, more or less dissembled, between the capitalist class and the working-class. (1961: I, 231–302)

Elsewhere he summarized the significance of the victory underlying the Act in the following terms:

> it was the first time that in broad daylight the political economy of the middle class succumbed to the political economy of the working class. (1958: I, 383)

His analysis makes clear that the factory acts were not simply the direct result of class struggle between the capitalist and working classes. Two particular features of the analysis are worth drawing attention to. The first concerns the relationship between the state and the capitalist class. The advent of machinery and industrial production in the textile industry gives rise to a veritable orgy of exploitation in which the working-day is extended to such lengths that a real threat is posed to the survival of the work force. At this stage the state represents the collective interests of capital, as distinct from the interests of individual capitalists.

Second, he stresses the divisions between the various sections of the capitalist class. Not only is there the division between the landed and industrial capitalists, which led the Tories as representatives of landed capital, to support factory legislation. But more important are the divisions between the more advanced sections of industrial capital and the smaller, more traditional employers. The passage of the factory acts represented a victory not only for the working class, but also for the more advanced sections of capital, who triumphed over their less efficient rivals. The overall analysis therefore brings out with great sharpness the way in which the development of the productive forces, in association with the more or less conscious struggle of various classes, finds its expression in legislation.

In his discussion of factory legislation Marx showed clearly how each legislative victory was only partial; while each was a major practical and idelogical victory, the employers, with the direct complicity of the magistrates and judges, impeded the effective enforcement of the provisions of the statutes.

CONCLUSION

In this chapter I have stressed the importance of law in capitalist society, and as a consequence argued that it is a question that requires a more thorough analysis by Marxists. While this chapter does not complete that task, it has sought to raise a number of questions, and to stress a number of areas for discussion. Some of these have been of a general nature that revolve around an assertion of law as an important agency in the maintenance of capitalist social relations. In particular I have argued the need to understand the significance of law as a system of ideological-coercive domination. It is through this emphasis on this combined process, rather than as two distinct or separate processes, that we can achieve a better understanding of the specific functioning of law within capitalist society, and is also of assistance in achieving a fuller theoretical treatment of the capitalist state.

The legal system within the bourgeois democratic state operates in such a way as to legitimize the class rule of the bourgeoisie. This legitimation involves not only the recognition and reinforcement of the social and economic relations of capitalism. It also encompasses the reification of law (through which law appears to be a power above and outside society) in which the social and political relations of capitalist society are presented as natural and universal. Law then operates to provide ideological reinforcement to those processes that make the reality of class and class power less visible.

The really difficult question is posed by the fact that bourgeois democratic society is not entirely a facade and a fraud. If it were its veils and deceits would have been stripped away long ago. Its strength and persistence result from the fact that in varying degrees it has successfully combined the continued social, political and economic dominance of the capitalist class with, at the same time, a significant level of involvement of the exploited classes sufficient to ensure a relatively high level of acceptance of, and even commitment to, the existing order.

Within the bourgeois democratic state law provides, alongside those aspects that reinforce the domination of the ruling class, an important set of rights, protections, and powers that in varying degrees incorporate certain class

interests of the nonruling classes. The most obvious examples of these are such things as the right to vote, to form trade unions, to take strike action, etc.

It is important to recognize that most of these have been secured as the result of class struggle. But these facts should not lead us to view them simply as concessions wrung from the capitalist. Once granted they become woven into the fabric of bourgeois democracy. It should also be noted that we need to recognize that the range of legal rights that may be used to the advantage of the working class extends beyond the range of the more obvious "political" rights mentioned. The law confers rights and protections on all classes as "citizens" in bourgeois democracy. It is of course important to stress the inequality of their application and the inequality of access to legal redress. Yet this does not negate their political and ideological importance. Their very existence plays a significant part in securing the acceptance of, and allegiance to, the existing capitalist social order.

Endnotes

1. In Britain, judicial appointments are made on the initiative of the Lord Chancellor, himself a member of the Cabinet, and as such, a directly "political" appointment. In the United States, the political character of judicial appointments is even more apparent.
2. For details on the use of law in Northern Ireland, see Boyle et al. (1975).
3. For a concise history of trade union law, see Wedderburn (1965).

Desperate Women and Compassionate Courts: Infanticide in Nineteenth-Century Canada†
C. Backhouse

INFANTICIDE is one of the oldest, most widely known means of population control.[1] In the time of Plato and Aristotle it was generally accepted and even recommended for eugenic reasons.[2] Jean-Louis Flandrin has claimed that even as late as the seventeenth century, infanticide was the principal means of birth control in France: 'Women pregnant out of wedlock would regularly murder their new-born bastards, and married couples had no compunction about smothering or abandoning unwanted children

in hard times.'[3] The general acceptance of infanticide may have related to the ineffectiveness or unavailability of other methods of fertility control; when circumstances made child rearing impossible, infanticide was adopted as a last resort. Furthermore the fragility of infant life in an era of limited medical knowledge must have helped create an environment in which the death of newborn children was a customary feature of daily life. Deliberate child murder may have seemed less reprehensible under these

† Backhouse, Constance, "Desperate Women and Compassionate Courts: Infanticide in Nineteenth-Century Canada" (1984), 34 *University of Toronto Law Journal* at 447–54. Reprinted by permission of University of Toronto Press.

conditions. Given this background, it is not surprising that infanticide was a prevalent feature of nineteenth-century Canadian life. If one can judge reliably from the number of legislative enactments and court trials, infanticide appears to have been frequently resorted to by Canadian women who were determined not to rear an unwanted child.[4] This paper analyses the response of the legal system to their efforts.

It was during the nineteenth century that the law first began to forbid the use of birth control and abortion.[5] The legal system, which was created and operated exclusively by men, was starting to assert pervasive control over the fertility of women. A logical extension of these initiatives would have been to mete out harsh criminal punishment to women committing infanticide. Yet male judges and male jurors exhibited remarkable lenience when faced with women who were accused of infanticide, and in most cases the women were discharged and set free. The courts regularly returned verdicts of not guilty despite overwhelming evidence to the contrary. Their response is one of the strongest indications of the attitude towards infanticide in the nineteenth century — that of compassion, tolerance, and sympathy. From the perspective of the twentieth century, this compassion may seem misplaced, at least with respect to the many unwanted infants who met their untimely end in rather violent ways. However an examination of the conditions that confronted these women and their lack of alternatives leads to the inescapable conclusion that infanticide was often an obvious and necessary last resort.

The legal records indicate that the vast majority of women who were charged with infanticide were unmarried. The disgrace which attached to unwed pregnancy in Victorian times was intense and all-encompassing. Family and friends might cut off all relations, and the poor woman would be forced to leave her home and neighbourhood to seek anonymity. The difficulties of trying to support herself and her child would have been nearly insurmountable because women's wages were not set high enough to support themselves, let alone dependent children.[6] Unless she could find a charitable organization to take her in, prostitution would be her only resort. Many unmarried pregnant women, often extremely young, were desperate to conceal their pregnancy and do away with their child before their lives were disastrously transformed. These women were determined to exert some control over their fate, even through infanticide if necessary. A description of the statutes enacted in nineteenth-century Canada and the many court trials which considered these laws will indicate the extent to which the law failed to sanction their behaviour and will also illustrate that society generally respected these women's decisions.

THE STATUTORY FRAMEWORK

English common law treated child murder just like other forms of murder, as a felony punishable by death.[7] It was extremely difficult to prove a charge of murder in infanticide cases, however, since so many babies died at birth from natural causes or from improper medical treatment. To complicate matters, some women concealed their pregnancies, gave birth in secret, and then tried to hide the child's body in order to escape detection. If she was caught, the terrified mother would claim that the child was stillborn or died right after birth despite her attempts to save it. While in some cases this was no doubt true, in others it was a fabrication. To prevent this, an unusual statute was enacted in a number of Canadian jurisdictions to punish the 'concealment' of the birth of an infant.

The Nova Scotia and Prince Edward Island statutes, passed in 1758 and 1792 respectively, read as follows:

> [I]f any woman be delivered of any issue of her body, male or female, which being born alive, should by the laws of the realm of England be a bastard, and that she endeavour privately, either by drowning or secret burying thereof, or in any other way, either by herself, or the procuring of others, so to conceal the death thereof, as that it may not come to light whether it were born alive or not, but be concealed, the mother so offending shall suffer death as in the case of murder, except such mother can make proof by one witness, that the child whose death was by her so intended to be concealed, was born dead.[8]

These statutes were modelled upon English legislation[9] and were later extended to Quebec and Upper Canada by way of general legislation receiving English criminal law into the colonies.[10] Prosecutors were no longer forced to prove that the mother had actually murdered her newborn child; all that was required was evidence that the mother had given birth, that the child had died, and that the mother had attempted to conceal this fact. At this point there was an automatic presumption of guilt, upon which the mother could be put to death as a murderer. No matter how credible and convincing the mother's testimony might have been, courts were instructed to convict unless she could provide some other person as a witness to her innocence. This witness would have to testify that he or she had seen the mother give birth and that the child had been stillborn. Since the purpose of concealment would have been destroyed by inviting a witness to attend the birth, it must have been clear to the legislators that few women accused of this crime would be able to meet his burden of evidence. They must have known that they were sentencing innocent women to death in the many cases where a woman attempted to conceal her childbirth but the foetus was still-born or died of natural causes.

Several other features of the statute are also of interest. The legislation applied solely to 'bastard' children, and not to the concealment of children born inside wedlock. Presumably the legislators had concluded that mothers would not commit infanticide against legitimate children. While there is no doubt that some married women were committing infanticide, they may have had less reason to conceal their pregnancies, since they would suffer no loss of reputation comparable to that of unwed mothers. The subsequent death of a legitimate child could be brushed aside as a natural event, with no one to claim the contrary. The legislation could conceivably have encompassed married women giving birth inside wedlock, thus forcing them to have witnesses at all births to testify as to the condition of the infant when born. However, this may have been viewed as an unwarranted intrusion upon the privacy of married couples. Furthermore, the legislators may have believed that husbands were the best safeguard to prevent their wives from concealing childbirth or committing infanticide. It is also interesting that the legislature found it necessary to specify that the statute was to apply to female children as well as to male children. In pre-industrial societies female children had most often been chosen for elimination.[11] Knowledge of historical imbalances in the ratio of female to male infanticide victims may have prompted the legislators to leave no room for doubt that female children were to be given equal protection.[12]

There are no reported Canadian cases under these first concealment statutes, which is not surprising in view of the paucity of reported decisions up until the end of the first quarter of the nineteenth century. Two trials, unearthed through the archival research of Robert L. Fraser, have emerged as landmark cases; both of them occurred in the province of Upper Canada.

Angelique Pilotte, a twenty-year-old native Indian woman, was tried for the concealment of her illegitimate child in Niagara on 8 September 1817.[13] While employed as a domestic servant, Angelique had travelled to France, where she met a British officer with whom she had an 'unhappy connection.' Returning to Quebec alone and pregnant, she managed to obtain another domestic position by concealing her pregnancy. Angelique's ability to hide her condition was so great that even the female servant who shared her bed knew nothing about it. Rising from bed on the night of 30 July 1817, Angelique went out to a nearby field and gave birth to a male infant about 2:00 a.m. The child seems to have been born alive, although it was sickly and did not cry at all. After staying there an hour or so, Angelique wrapped the infant's body tightly in a cloth and left him behind a stable until about 2:00 am the next night, when, fearful of her mistress's reaction, she buried him in a shallow grave. When the child's body was discovered, Angelique's mistress suspected her. Confronted by accusations, Angelique, who seemed unaware that concealing the birth of a child was a crime under English law, immediately confessed to having given birth and was held for trial 'in a state of extreme convulsion.'

The wording of the statute made proof of the cause of death irrelevant unless there was evidence to this effect from witnesses other than that mother. However, both trial lawyers seemed anxious to bring out evidence concerning the reasons for the child's death. Henry John Boulton, the prosecutor, introduced evidence from a local surgeon who testified that the infant's body 'was perfect in form, and had every appearance of mature birth.' He also stated that a live chid 'so tightly pinned up [by cloth] must necessarily be smothered.' Under cross-examination by the defence counsel, Bartholomew C. Beardsley, however, he admitted that the child's death might have also been caused by 'the want of proper assistance at the time of delivery.' The surgeon also added that it was usual for babies to cry after birth, and it was therefore surprising that Angelique's child had never uttered a sound. The child might have died, then, from any number of causes — from natural birth defects, from lack of medical attention at the delivery, from lack of food or exposure, from choking under the tightly wrapped cloth, or from being buried in the field. The evidence, however, was clearly sufficient to convict Angelique under the concealment charge, and the jury took little time in concluding that she was guilty. Although the jury 'strongly' urged mercy, William Campbell J. concluded that Angelique had been convicted on 'clear and sufficient evidence' and sentenced her to be hanged on 11 September 1817.

The sentence brought a great outcry from the community, and a surprising number came forward to plead for clemency on Angelique's behalf. Petitions for mercy came from some of the most respected members of the community including a number of military officers stationed in the area and more than a dozen magistrates. Particular attention was focused upon Angelique's Indian heritage. Emphasizing that she had not even 'the slightest instruction in the principles of Christian religion,' a petition from Angelique's lawyer claimed that she knew only the 'customs and maxims of her own nation' and was guilty only of the 'invariable custom of Indian women to retire and birth forth their children alone and in secret.' The absurdity of convicting an Indian woman under an imperial concealment statute was the key argument in the document. Eight months later, Angelique was notified that a royal pardon had commuted her sentence to one year's imprisonment. While all involved were no doubt relieved that Angelique would not be hanged, some must have continued to wonder whether she had really murdered her child, a fact that had never been determined at trial. Her mistress had publicly stated that Angelique was 'so simple and ignorant as not to know right from wrong, nor that she thought it a crime to kill her own child.' This woman may have hit upon the critical issue involved in the case — that Angelique had viewed infanticide as a normal event, something which was practised by many Indian women without fear of criminal sanction. Further research about North American Indian cultures would be necessary before one could know for certain whether Angelique's response to an unwanted pregnancy was a common one in the Indian community at this time.

The second landmark case involved Mary Thompson, a young woman who came from an impoverished, landless family living in the area of York. She was tried on 17 October 1823 at York for the concealment of the birth of her illegitimate child.[14] When Mary had discovered she was pregnant, she confided in her married sister, who promised to assist her during the delivery. However Mary had miscalculated the date of delivery and, taken by surprise, she had given birth alone, without assistance. She killed the child immediately, which she claimed was an act prompted by 'the pains and anguish of childbirth.' The child was found with 'a fracture of the skull, braine, and extravagate [*sic*] blood,' and the twelve jurors who tried the case had little difficult returning a verdict of guilty. In spite of the jury's recommendation for 'merciful consideration,' William Dummer Powell CJ sentenced Mary to be hanged on 20 October 1823.

Mary's father put forth the only major petition urging clemency; nevertheless Powell CJ delayed the execution and gave consideration to seeking royal review. During the trial the judge had permitted the introduction of evidence that the dead child's lungs had floated when immersed in water; this had been accepted as conclusive proof that the child had been born alive. After the trial, Powell CJ learned that this evidence was no longer considered legally reliable in England, and he decided that the case should be given royal consideration. This decision is somewhat perplexing, since under the concealment statute the question of whether the child was born alive was of no consequence unless there was some witness who could attest to this fact. However on 6 August 1824 Mary Thompson was granted a general pardon, and hence a lesser sentence than that served by Angelique Pilotte.

. . . .

Both the cases discussed resulted in convictions, but both courts seemed preoccupied with the technically irrelevant evidence concerning the cause of the child's death. The courts were straining for evidence with which to avoid the harsh death penalty, although in neither case were they able to muster enough material to warrant a finding of not guilty. It is evident that the concealment statute was viewed as overly harsh, both by the community which reacted with concern to the sentence in the case of Angelique Pilotte and by the legal officials who sought for, and were granted the commutation of the death penalty following both trials.

. . . .

Endnotes

1. See Langer, "Infanticide: A historical survey" (1974), 1 *Hist. of Childhood Q.* 353 at 353–5; Shorter, "Infanticide in the past" (1973), 1 *Hist. of Childhood Q.* 178 at 179; Gordon *Woman's Body, Woman's Right* (1974), at 32–5.
2. Gordon, *supra* note 1, at 32, 35.
3. Shorter, *supra* note 1, quotes this material from an unpublished manuscript by Flandrin at 179.
4. See Ward, "Unwed motherhood in nineteenth-century English Canada" in *Historical Papers* (Ottawa: Canadian Historical Assoc., 1981) 34 at 44–5 for an excellent article describing widespread prevalence of infanticide based on arrest records for Toronto between 1860 and 1899.
5. See my "Involuntary motherhood: Abortion, birth control and the law in nineteenth-century Canada" forthcoming in *Windsor Access to Justice Yearbook*.
6. See Ward, *supra* note 4, for a description of the many obstacles facing women pregnant outside wedlock.
7. In earlier times this had not always been the case. It was not until 318 AD that the Christian Emperor Constantine first declared the slaying of a son or daughter by a father to be a crime.
8. *An Act relating to Treasons and Felonies* (1758), 32 Geo. II, c. 13, s. 5 (N.S.); *An Act relating to Treasons and Felonies* (1792), 33 Geo. III, c. 1, s. 5 (P.E.I.).
9. In fact the statutes were exact duplicates of an English statute entitled *An act to prevent the destroying and murdering of bastard children*, (1623), 21 James I, c. 27, s. 2 (Eng.).
10. *An act for the further introduction of the criminal law of England into this province, and for the more effectual punishment of certain offenders* (1800), 40 Geo. III, c. 1, s. 1 (Upper Canada). The Quebec reference is taken from Fred Kaufman J.'s introduction to Burbidge *Digest of the Criminal Law of Canada* (1980, orig. pub. 1890), foreword at 1.
11. See Gordon, *supra* note 1, at 34 and Dellapenna, "The history of abortion: Technology, morality and the law" (1979), 40 *U. Pitts. L.R.* 359 at 396.
12. The nineteenth-century legal materials discussed *infra* reveal no significant differentiation between the number of male and female infants killed.
13. This account of the trial of Angelique Pilotte is drawn from the unpublished manuscript prepared by Robert L. Fraser for the *Dictionary of Canadian Biography*, vol. 5, biography No. T–427c.
14. This account of the trial of Mary Thompson is drawn from an unpublished manuscript prepared by Robert L. Fraser for the *Dictionary of Canadian Biography*, vol. 6, biography No. T–654.

Police Under Fire†

AT 7:45 p.m. on Dec. 8, a .38–calibre bullet smashed through the rear window of a stolen black Nissan Maxima sedan and into the brain of its 17-year-old driver. Fifteen hours later, Michael Wade Lawson died when doctors disconnected his body from a life-support system at Mississauga Hospital, just west of Toronto. The moments of shattering gunfire left a legacy of anger and distrust. The youth happened to be black. The bullet that killed him was one of several fired by two plainclothes policemen. The next day, the Peel Regional Police Force declared that the officers had fired at the high-powered Maxima in self-defence after its driver, ignoring an order to stop, drove directly at them. But Lawson's grieving family and friends accused the police of racist violence. Lawson, said mourner Milton Blake at the Youth's funeral, had been "cut down by the hunter's gun, sealed by the badge of law." Added Dari Meade, a member of Toronto's Black Action Defence Committee: "We want murder charges."

Tragedies

Lawson's death was a sad addendum to a growing list of tragedies that has forced a painful reassessment of relations between Canadian police and the communities they are sworn to serve. Among some Canadians — especially the expanding communities of visible minorities — there is vocal suspicion that police forces are, at best, out of touch with a changing society and, at worst, racist. In squad cars and station houses across the country, meanwhile, policemen and a growing number of policewomen say that it has become more difficult and dangerous to keep the peace and enforce the law. As grievances mount on both sides, so do the number of victims. Spokesmen for police point to the toll of suicide and divorce among serving officers, while the mourning relatives of police shootings point to the dead.

Controversial

Lawson was the second black Toronto-area resident in four months to die after being shot by police, and the most recent in a series of controversial killings. Last Aug. 9, a policeman shot and killed Lester Donaldson, a 44-year-old black man, in a Toronto rooming house. A police spokesman quoted Const. David Deviney as saying that he fired at Donaldson to defend his partner when Donaldson lunged at him with a knife. In Montreal last February, black leaders alleged racism when a jury acquitted Const.

Allen Gosset of a manslaughter charge after he had shot and killed an unarmed black 19-year-old, Anthony Griffin, the previous November. Griffin — wanted for breaking and entering — had heeded an order to surrender after briefly bolting from police custody.

During the month following Gosset's acquittal — which the Crown is now appealing — Manitoba Indian leader John Joseph Harper died from a police bullet fired during a scuffle with Winnipeg constable Robert Cross on a city street. Then, in June, Vancouver police shot and killed a distraught, knife-wielding psychiatric patient, Gregory Coghlan, in what a coroner's jury later determined to be "victim-precipitated homicide...a species of suicide."

After each eruption of fatal police gunfire, investigators groped for explanations. In Quebec and Manitoba, commissions have begun inquiries into police treatment of racial minorities. And one week after Lawson's death, Ontario Solicitor General Joan Smith named a five-member civilian panel to examine relations between the police and minority groups.

Spokesmen for ethnic minorities are the most vocal critics of police conduct across the country. Among the general public, surveys conducted by Gallup Canada Inc. show that 50 per cent of Canadians consider the country's 52,500 police officers to be highly or very highly trustworthy — as many as had expressed the same opinion in 1976. But even among those who express general satisfaction with the police, say observers of community attitudes, personal contacts with police officers are seldom either welcome or relaxed. "We have a love/hate relationship with police," observed John Sewell, a former mayor of Toronto and author of the 1985 study *Police*. "We need them to save us from dangerous situations yet we feel they impinge on our lives."

For their part, police officers across Canada told *Maclean's* that they view their fellow citizens with growing distrust, frustration and a sense of deepening isolation. "A police officer coming on a case is resented by everyone," said Robert Menard, 54, a burly 30-year veteran of the Montreal Urban Community police force, for one. "But how the hell can a civilian understand what we deal with every day? You are God damned right we are frustrated."

Pressures

There are 13,483 Royal Canadian Mounted Police who enforce federal law and provide rural service in eight provinces and the North. Provincial police forces operate

---

† "Police Under Fire" *Maclean's*, January 9, 1989, 30–33. Reprinted by permission of *Maclean's Magazine*, Maclean Hunter Publishing Ltd.

in Ontario and Quebec, while most cities and towns have their own municipal police. Many of them who spoke to *Maclean's* correspondents said that the mounting pressures of their work — and the strident pitch of public criticism — have resulted in low morale and a growing number of stress-related personal problems. According to one survey, as many as 75 per cent of police marriages end in divorce (page 36). In Halifax, Montreal and Calgary, among other cities, the rising number of stress-linked complaints — including alcohol abuse, domestic violence and depression — has prompted the establishment of counselling services for emotionally troubled officers. Social scientists and other observers say that a number of factors have converged to raise the level of stress on Canadian police. In an increasingly urbanized society, economic pressures, the growing use of drugs and an influx of immigrants from cultures with different traditions and attitudes toward the law have contributed to a rising level of violent crime that police must routinely deal with (page 34). At the same time, the 1982 *Charter of Rights and Freedoms*, with its clear definitions of individual rights, and the 1984 *Young Offenders Act* — which some officers say limits their ability to deal with criminals under 18 — have intensified the scrutiny when police fall short of demanding standards of conduct.

Discipline

There is impassioned debate, however, over what must be corrected in order to restore the tarnished honour of the policeman's badge. Sewell blames the military-style discipline that still pervades most police forces. "Look at the conditions of the normal cop on the beat," he said in an interview. "They are treated badly in a 19th-century management structure. And they lash out." On the other hand, the director of the University of Regina's Prairie Justice Research School, James Harding, criticizes the recruitment into uniform of "kids who see police work as a mandate to play rough." In Montreal, newspaper columnist George Springate, a former city policeman who also served for 11 years in the Quebec legislature, says that the public demands too much of police. "We have to stop picking on the police, expecting them to be saviours for everything that goes wrong in society," said Springate. "They aren't miracle workers."

The debate has acquired new urgency with the recent rash of controversial shootings involving police officers. On the Mississauga street of new brick homes where Wade Lawson's life ended, the red spray paint that investigators had used to mark the spot where the stolen Maxima came to rest quickly disappeared under a mid-December dusting of snow. Other details have emerged slowly in brief statements by police and in news reports.

Tip

The events that led to Lawson's death began shortly after midnight on Dec. 8, when the Grade 11 high-school student stepped from a car driven by his cousin, Dale Ewers, and crossed a Mississauga street to the parking lot of a Nissan dealership at about the time that someone stole a black Maxima. Within hours, a tip from a security guard at a nearby motel led constables Darren Longpre and Anthony Melaragni to set up a daylong surveillance near Ewer's home. Shortly after 7:30 p.m., Ad Maxima, bearing stolen New York state licence plates, pulled into a driveway facing the house and a passenger got out. As the car backed onto the street and began to drive away, Longpre and Melaragni got out of their own car to intercept it.

According to the statement issued by the Peel regional police, Longpre and Melaragni approached the stolen Maxima and identified themselves to two occupants with the intention of placing them under arrest. But when the car "accelerated directly at" the two officers, the statement continued, they opened fire "in defence of their lives," unleashing at least half a dozen bullets. Indeed, the Toronto *Globe and Mail* later reported that officers close to the investigation had said that the Maxima knocked one of the policemen to the ground as it sped away, prompting both officers to fire at the fleeing automobile. That report added that one of the bullets fired had penetrated the car's rear window, ricocheted inside the vehicle and struck Lawson in the back of the head.

'Nigger'

However, another youth who was in the car at the time of the shooting, but who escaped uninjured, told a Lawson family lawyer that he had heard nothing before the police opened fire. And the 17-year-old youth, who has been charged with possession of stolen property and cannot be named under the *Young Offenders Act*, added that after the officers pulled him from the Maxima, one policeman kicked him and called him a "nigger."

The day after the shooting, Peel Police Chief William Teggart requested an Ontario Provincial Police investigation of the affair. The OPP report, which could recommend criminal charges against the Peel police officers, is expected to be completed late this month. Still, even while the investigation continued, one local black activist, Al Peabody, predicted that its findings would be "a whitewash." Added the youth's father, Winston Lawson, who owns a gravel business: "They are police investigating other police. Naturally, they have sympathy for each other." The charge was dismissed by OPP spokesman Insp. Robert Guay. Declared Guay: "The OPP is a credible force. The family can be assured of a thorough, unbiased investigation." By late last week, however, the OPP had not laid charges against either Longore or Melaragni.

Risk

Many police officers express a growing sense of injury. Complaints of police brutality are far outnumbered by police accounts of violence suffered at the hands of the public. A badge and uniform are no protection against daily dangers that range from a drunk's wildly thrown punch to the fear of AIDS infection through contact with an accident victim's blood. In addition, there is the ever-present risk of death from criminal gunfire. Between 1978 and 1987, 35 on-duty police officers have been killed in Canada.

Beyond the fear for their own safety, police officers interviewed by *Maclean's* expressed a deepening sense of grievance. They complained about high demands and low salaries. First-class constables typically earn between $42,000 and $47,000 a year across the country. As well, work loads have become heavier, as Canada's crime rate recorded a 27 per cent increase between 1978 and 1986 — with violent crimes jumping by 45 per cent — while police forces grew by only six per cent over the same period. At the same time, the very nature of police work forces officers into close daily contact with society's least successful members. "We deal with the dregs of society," said Montreal's Menard, who was shot in the left lung and right leg while trying to prevent a bank robbery in 1985. "We deal with violence, with abuse. We deal with what you as a civilian don't want to have anything to do with."

Often there is little time to weigh choices before reacting. Noted Menard: "We make a judgment call in very tense and explosive situations in an instant, and we must be right the first and only time." In such conditions, said John Sawatsky, a Toronto-based psychologist who counsels OPP members, it is not surprising that an officer sometimes makes a wrong decision. "People who are stressed as much as police officers," said Sawatsky, "sometimes lose their judgment." The consequences for a reaction that appears in retrospect to have been wrong can be a fine, dismissal from the force or criminal charges. "At the back of a policeman's mind," said Jacques Duchesneau, the head of Montreal's organized crime squad, "is always the thought that one quick reaction could live with you for a long time."

Duchesneau, like many police officers, says that the decisions have become more complex in the 1980s. Growing Caribbean, Chinese and Vietnamese communities have become targets for ethnic criminal organizations that are difficult for Canadian police — still overwhelmingly white — to penetrate. Calgary Police Chief Ernest Reimer, who will retire this month at 55, says that "there is a heavy degree of mistrust [of the police] in these new ethnic communities." In many cities, the mistrust is reinforced by an imbalance between the ethnic makeup of police and that of the city they serve. In Toronto, although visible minorities account for 20 per cent of the city's 2.2 million people, according to Sher Singh, chairman of the Toronto Council on Race Relations and Policing, they number only five per cent of its 5,400 police — and hold no ranks above staff inspector.

Work Load

Beyond the charged emotions that radiate from each controversial shooting, however, statistics suggest that Canadian policemen fare well when breakdowns in discipline are weighed against their work load. Among the few forces that release such figures, the RCMP recorded 2,500 complaints about its officers in 1987 — fewer than 0.09 per cent of its three million contacts with the public. The figure for Toronto's force was even lower: fewer than 0.08 per cent of the 1,045,000 calls Toronto police answered last year led to complaints against the force. Fatal shootings by Canadian police — an average of eight each year between 1961 and 1981 — are few by comparison with those in the United States, where police kill at least one person every day.

Still, many Canadian police officers acknowledge that they must do more to regain public confidence. Some steps have already been taken. Educational standards for police recruits have risen. As well, police training programs have been redesigned to emphasize psychology and communication skills and to discourage cadets from viewing themselves as gun-toting enforcers. In answer to allegations that they fail to reflect their community's ethnic mix, urban forces in Toronto and Vancouver have launched active recruiting drives in the two cities' burgeoning immigrant communities.

At the same time, governments increasingly are moving toward the establishment of civilian review boards to investigate complaints against the police. Complaints against RCMP members have been handled by a civilian review panel since last September. And legislation introduced in the Quebec national assembly in November will give civilian panels the right to hold public inquiries into allegations of police misconduct in that province. Similar boards already exist in Nova Scotia and in the cities of Calgary and Toronto. But the spread of civilian panels has been slowed by police resistance.

Tension

Meanwhile, the commissions appointed after the Lawson, Griffin and Harper shootings continue to search for new measures to restore the corroded relationship between police and the public. Their tasks are complicated by deep emotions on both sides of a complex issue. "Police feel abandoned," said Springate. "And as they come under public criticism, they tend to withdraw more into themselves." In Mississauga, meanwhile, Milton Blake told Wade Lawson's mourners last month that "we must rise up to become the protectors of our own interests." But such sentiments seemed unlikely to help reduce the tension in any future confrontation between armed police and the citizens they are sworn to protect.

Nova Scotia Royal Commission on the Donald Marshall Jr. Prosecution[†]

INTRODUCTION

We find:

- That the criminal justice system failed Donald Marshall, Jr. at virtually every turn from his arrest and conviction in 1971 up to — and even beyond — his acquittal by the Supreme Court of Nova Scotia (Appeal Division) in 1983.
- That this miscarriage of justice could have and should have been prevented if persons involved in the criminal justice system had carried out their duties in a professional and/or competent manner.
- That Marshall was not the author of his own misfortune.
- That the miscarriage of justice was real and not simply apparent.
- That the fact that Marshall was a Native was a factor in his wrongful conviction and imprisonment.

On May 28, 1971, four people came together in a brief, unplanned nighttime encounter in Wentworth Park in Sydney, Nova Scotia. One of them, a 17-year-old black youth named Sandford (Sandy) William Seale, was killed. Another, a 17-year-old Micmac Indian named Donald Marshal, Jr., was wrongfully convicted of his murder, and was sentenced to life imprisonment in November 1971. Eleven years later, after Marshall's lawyer, Stephen Aronson, brought forward information suggesting Marshall did not commit the murder, the RCMP reinvestigated the case for a second time. After that investigation confirmed that Marshall did not kill Seale, he was released on parole and subsequently acquitted by the Supreme Court of Nova Scotia (Appeal Division) in May 1983. A third man, Roy Newman Ebsary, who was one of the four people who had come together in Wentworth Park that night, was charged with killing Seale and was convicted of manslaughter following three trials. He was sentenced to three years in prison. In 1986, the Court of Appeal reduced his sentence to one year. He died in 1988.

The events that took place in Wentworth Park in those few moments on that spring night in 1971 have spawned numerous official inquiries and proceedings, including three formal police investigations, two preliminary inquiries, four trials, three appeals to the Supreme Court of Nova Scotia (Appeal Division), a Reference to the Court of Appeal and two Royal Commissions, including this one.

The cost in dollars has been tremendous. The toll in human anguish has been incalculable.

The principal task of this Royal Commission has been to determine why Donald Marshall, Jr. was wrongfully convicted and to make recommendations to ensure that such a miscarriage of justice does not happen again.

First, what did go wrong? Although we will examine in detail each of the relevant events of the Marshall case from its beginning on May 28, 1971, to our appointment on October 28, 1986, we can begin with the following general conclusions that flow from our consideration of all of the evidence.

The criminal justice system failed Donald Marshall, Jr. at virtually every turn, from his arrest and wrongful conviction in 1971 up to — and even beyond — his acquittal by the Court of Appeal in 1983. The tragedy of this failure is compounded by the evidence that this miscarriage of justice could have — and should have — been prevented, or at least corrected quickly, if those involved in the system had carried out their duties in a professional and/or competent manner.

If, for example, the Sergeant of Detectives of the Sydney City Police Department had not prematurely concluded — on the basis of no supporting evidence and in the face of compelling contradictory evidence — that Donald Marshall, Jr. was responsible for the death of Sandy Seale, Marshall would almost certainly never have been charged with the crime. If the Crown prosecutor had provided full disclosure to Marshall's lawyers of the conflicting statements provided by alleged eyewitnesses; if Marshall's lawyers had conducted a more thorough defence, including pressing for such disclosure and conducting their own investigations into the killing; if the judge in the case had not made critical errors in law; Marshall would almost certainly not have been convicted.

Even after he was convicted and sent to prison, however, there were numerous other occasions when this miscarriage of justice should have been discovered and rectified, but was not.

For example, when the Crown received evidence shortly after Marshall's conviction suggesting Roy Ebsary might have been involved in the killing, it did not disclose this information to Marshall's counsel. When the RCMP reinvestigated the murder as a result of that new evidence, it did so in such an entirely inadequate and unprofessional manner that it prevented his wrongful conviction from being discovered. During Marshall's appeal of his convic-

---

[†]   *Nova Scotia Royal Commission on the Donald Marshall Jr. Prosecution*, Volume I, 1989, pp. 15–18, Province of Nova Scotia.

tion, his lawyers failed to identify and argue critical errors of law which occurred during the trial. Similarly, the Court of Appeal failed to identify these errors.

When Marshall's wrongful conviction was finally discovered in the early 1980s, the Court of Appeal compounded the miscarriage of justice by describing Marshall as having contributed in large measure to his own conviction and by stating that any miscarriage of justice in the case was more apparent than real.

This Commission has concluded that Donald Marshall, Jr. was not to blame for his own conviction and that the miscarriage of justice against him was real.

That is the inescapable, and inescapably distressing, conclusion we have reached after listening to 113 witnesses during 93 days of public hearings in Halifax and Sydney in 1987 and 1988 and after sifting through 176 exhibits submitted in evidence during those hearings.

But concluding that Donald Marshall, Jr. was the victim of a miscarriage of justice does not answer the complex question of why Marshall came to be wrongfully convicted and imprisoned in the first place. Was it because he was a Native? Was it because he was poor?

To answer those admittedly difficult questions, this Commission has looked not only at how the criminal justice system in Nova Scotia operated in the Marshall case, but it has also compared the handling of the Marshall case with the way in which the system dealt with cases involving powerful and prominent public officials. At the same time, we commissioned independent research studies to find out how Natives and Blacks are treated in the criminal justice system.

From all of that, the evidence is once again persuasive and the conclusion inescapable that Donald Marshall, Jr. was convicted and sent to prison, in part at least, because he was a Native person. We will look at these issues in more detail in our section on visible minorities in the justice system later in this volume.

Having reached these conclusions, we take the next logical step in fulfilling our mandate and ask what can and should be done to make sure that the criminal justice system lives up to this promise of equal justice for all? That too is a question we will deal with later in this volume of our Report.

There are certain issues, however, that we will not be addressing in our Report. For example, this Royal Commission is not recommending that criminal charges be laid against any specific individuals arising out of the findings of fact we will make. Although some counsel urged us to do so during their final arguments to the Royal Commission, it is our opinion that a decision on whether or not any charges should be laid is one that should be taken by the appropriate authorities after due consideration of all

relevant factors. We agree with the sentiments expressed by the Attorney General of Ontario when establishing the Grange Commission, sentiments which were concurred in by the Ontario Court of Appeal in *Re Nelles et al. and Grange et al.* (1984), 9 D.L.R. (4th) 79 at p. 84:

> The purpose of a public inquiry is not to attach criminal culpability. It is not a forum to put individuals on trial. The just and proper place to make and defend allegations of crime or civil liability is in a court of law.
>
> In this context, I am reminded of the remarks of an eminent Ontario jurist, Mr. Justice Riddell of the Ontario Court of Appeal, whose observations almost 50 years ago are equally applicable today.
>
> A Royal Commission is not for the purpose of trying a case or a charge against anyone, any person or any institution — but for the purpose of informing the people concerning the facts of the matter to be enquired into. The object of a Royal Commission is to determine facts, not try individuals or institutions, and this consideration is sufficient to guide the Commissioner in the performance of his duty.

The Court went on to say:

> A public inquiry is not the means by which investigations are carried out with respect to the commission of particular crimes.... Such an inquiry is a coercive procedure and is quite incompatible with our notion of justice in the investigation of a particular crime and the determination of actual or probable criminal or civil responsibility.

We share this view.

Further, we are not — as some have also urged us to do — specifically recommending that Donald Marshall, Jr. receive additional compensation. The Commission accepted that a settlement had been negotiated, and accordingly, heard no evidence on the amount of compensation that may have otherwise been appropriate. However, the Commission did examine the process by which compensation was ultimately negotiated and paid. We have concluded that the negotiations were strongly influenced by factors which, in our view, were either wrong or inappropriate, and that as a result the compensation process was so seriously flawed that the amount paid should be reevaluated.

Is There a Place for the Victim in the Prosecution Process?[†]

P. Clarke

VICTIMS of crime once were the central actors in bringing offenders to justice. Today they are neglected outsiders in a system which could not function without them, yet is not accountable to them, provides no role for them and does not necessarily serve them, for ours is "an adversary system in which the victim is not one of the adversaries" (Federal-Provincial Task Force, 1983:5).

Victims are organizing, in one of the significant developments in the justice system, to complain of their expulsion and to demand more participation. Sometimes they bypass the system entirely, either by systems of private justice or in extreme cases by becoming their own prosecutor, judge and executioner.

A number of jurisdictions have tried a number of ways over the past twenty years to answer the demands of victims, and in Canada a Federal-Provincial Task Force on Justice for Victims has made recommendations some of which have been embodied in proposed legislation. The question is no longer, the Task Force says, "whether the victim should participate in the (criminal justice) process or not. The question is rather the extent of that participation" (1983:7).

This paper will look at the current status of the victim in the prosecution process, the reasons for that status in the historic development of the process, and some reasons for the growth of the victims' rights movement. It will review proposals to change the victim's status but will argue that, as far as genuine participation is concerned, the proposed changes will be more cosmetic than real. That is because of the nature of the process, the nature of bureaucratic systems to resist change, and the aims and purposes of the criminal justice system. The exclusion of victims is not an accident or oversight which can be remedied by minor tinkering with a process whose purpose is to provide justice for victims. It is a necessary and inevitable fact of a process with a totally different purpose. If victims dare to find remedies for their victimization, they must find them outside the prosecution process.

EVOLUTION OF THE PROSECUTION PROCESS

Before there was a formal legal system, all wrongs were private wrongs. Victims and their families exacted the penalties. To temper and regulate such private justice, in Anglo-Saxon law there gradually grew a system of restitution with fixed payments for various wrongs. At the same time there grew the notion that while some incidents were private disputes, which in the development of law became torts to be dealt with in civil courts, other acts threatened the fabric of society and destroyed "the King's peace". For such acts the offender made payment not only to the victim but also to the lord or the king. Holdsworth (1909:38) claims this was "the germ of the idea that wrong is not simply the affair of the injured individual — an idea which is the condition precedent to the growth of a criminal law".

Gradually as this idea developed, the victim lost control of the conflict and it became the property of the state. The focus shifted from a dispute between the offender and the victim, in which the offender was bound to make reparation to the person he had injured, to the relationship between the offender and society, in which the offender had injured society and must be punished by society. Common law developed to prevent victims from receiving reparations until they did all they could to bring the offender to justice and forbid victims to agree not to prosecute in order to get back their property. Individuals could not condone a crime against the state (Hudson and Galway, 1975:24).

The key to a criminal proceeding thus became, in essence, the exclusion of the victim as one of the parties. Full participation by the victim, Christie says (1977:3), presupposes elements of civil law.

Just as the state came to replace the victim as the injured party, so it gradually replaced the victim as the prosecuting party. Until the late 18th century, trials normally were conducted by the victim-prosecutor and the defendant (Beattie, 1986:13). By the 19th century Blackstone was able to state categorically that the sovereign "is therefore the proper person to prosecute for all public offences and breaches of the peace, being the person injured in the eye of the law" (Hagan, 1983:268).

In the evolution of the prosecution process, then, two important things have happened, according to Christie (1977:3), one, that both parties are being represented; and second, that the one represented by the state, the victim, "is so thoroughly represented that for the most part he has been pushed completely out of the arena". The victim is a double loser: his property may have been stolen by the offender, but "his conflict has been stolen by the state" (Christie, 1982:93). When the private conflicts become state property, they are made to serve "the ideological interests of state-subject authority relations and the organizational interests of the individual citizens" (Ericson and Baranek, 1982:4).

† Clarke, Patricia, "Is There a Place for the Victim in the Prosecution Process?" (1987), 8 *Canadian Criminology Forum* 227. Reprinted by permission of the Canadian Criminology Forum, Toronto, Canada.

ROLE OF THE VICTIM IN THE PROSECUTION PROCESS

This transfer of the dispute between two persons into a dispute between one of them and the Crown means, according to Shearing and Stenning (1983:9), that victim neglect is not a "minor deficiency" in the justice system but arises from a "fundamental feature". The state owns the conflict and the roles left to victims are; (1) to supply the system with raw material; (2) to give the evidence the system requires; and (3) to serve as a "ceremonial" or "symbolic" presence (Hagan, 1983:7) which legitimizes the mobilization of the law against the accused.

The fundamental policy objectives of the criminal justice system are based on a classical concept of society as a contract between a neutral arbitrating state and rational individuals. The state provides society and its members with a reasonable degree of security, and ensures just treatment for the accused (Griffiths et al., 1980:6). Punishments must be established if the sovereign is to "defend the public liberty, entrusted to his care, from the usurpation of individuals" (VOLD, 1979:24), and they must be fixed, known and in relation to the crime. These policy objectives ignore the victim as such, other than as a member of society. The second objective implies, far from participation by the victim, a moderation and rationality in the punishment the accused might otherwise receive from those who believe themselves wronged. The resulting court process may be seen as a sort of morality play where certain values are publicly affirmed, certain conduct publicly denounced, and certain persons identified, blamed and rejected as "criminals". "The process uses accused persons to help define the relationship between the individual and the state" (Ericson and Baranek, 1982:215). Victims and their needs simply are not part of the script.

As the process has evolved, the chief power left to victims is the power not to surrender their conflict to the state — not to report the victimization. More than half of victims appear to exercise this right (Task Force, 1983:14). Once the state takes over, they lose virtually all other power. They have no right to testify, although they may do so if they are called by the Crown and if theirs is the uncommon case which goes to trial. Approximately up to 70% of cases are settled by a guilty plea. They have no right to express their views on bail or sentencing, though a judge or prosecutor is free to ask for them. They have no right to receive restitution, although they may in certain circumstances have a right to apply for it.

In the prosecution, the Crown represents the interests of the community, which may or may not coincide with the interests of the victims. The Crown must consider, for example, priorities on police time and court time for investigating and prosecuting, availability of evidence, chances of a conviction, public attitudes toward the offence, desirability of plea negotiations, the protection of the community and the rehabilitation of the offender. The victim has no way to challenge these Crown decisions.

Not only does the Crown have to consider wider concerns than those of the victim, but it can be argued that to seem to represent the victim, or to press the victim's claim, might prejudice the Crown's function as an impartial presenter of all the evidence. Indeed, for the Crown to give any assistance or status to the alleged victim, which would not be given to any witness, might compromise the rights of the accused. Even to equate the complainant with a victim could prejudge facts to be proved, for instance in a sexual assault case where consent is an issue.

THE VICTIM MOVEMENT

Having been detached over the centuries from the prosecution process, some victims have organized to attempt to get back in. In the last few years such groups have mushroomed across North America. In Canada 28 groups claim 150 chapters in every province and 250,000 to 400,000 members (Toronto Star, 1984:1). Their numbers comprise an effective lobby, but are only a fraction of those eligible. Individual victims in Canada number at least 1.6 million a year. Organizational victims may be even more numerous: in a study by Hagan (1983:35) they made up two-thirds of a random sample.

A number of factors appear to be involved in the birth and growth of victim groups. First, is "a widespread and apparently increasing fear of crime" of which Taylor (1983:93) says "countless research studies" have provided evidence. The fear, partly justified and partly promoted by the media, is expressed in purchases of burglar alarms and double-locks, in self-defence classes, in private security patrols and programmes such as Neighbourhood Watch, and in victim groups.

Second, is the law and order movement, which argues that the criminal justice system is "soft on criminals", thereby turning them loose to create more victims. It supports more "rights" for victims to balance what it claims are too many rights for "criminals".

Third, is the women's movement, which began with advocacy and assistance for rape victims and in some jurisdictions achieved changes in statutes and rules of evidence which provided more rights for victim-witnesses.

Fourth, is the self-help movement, growing out of the protest movements of the 1960's, which leads people who don't trust big government or bureaucracy to form their own groups to represent themselves.

Fifth, is the general humanitarian impulse to help people in trouble (and earn political points) which in other fields has led to worker compensation programmes or the motorists' unsatisfied judgement fund.

Victim advocacy groups differ in their concerns and their goals. Some complain most about neglect, carelessness and insensitivity from police and the courts. They can't find out what is happening in their case, they can't understand what goes on in court and they are not notified when their case is coming up or when it is settled. These groups want more information, more support services, more "sensitivity".

Others complain that victims cannot get restitution for their losses, or even get back their stolen property promptly. According to a 1976 survey in Alameda County, California (Karmen, 1984:148), 30% of victims never got back the stolen property used as evidence, 42% never learned the outcome of their case, and 61% of those eligible for the state's crime compensation fund were not informed of its existence. These victims want more effective compensation schemes and help in applying to them.

Still others such as Mothers Against Drunk Driving want stiffer laws for specific offences. And some want an active role in the prosecution process. They ask to be acknowledged as a party to the proceedings, to be given access to the Crown case, to be supplied with reasons for every decision, even given a veto on plea negotiations and sentence submissions. Donald Sullivan, spokesman for a Canadian conference of victims' groups, says they want laws to give victims "a place in the courtroom" and rights in court "equal to those of the offender" (Toronto Star, 1985:2).

SOURCE OF RIGHTS FOR VICTIMS

A right has three key features (Task Force 1983:130). It is a legal recognition of interest, in this case the victim's interest in this court proceeding. A right for one party implies a responsibility or duty on another party. And it must be legally enforceable, so that one can secure either the right or damages.

At present the justice system is a balance (equal or not) of rights between prosecution and accused. If victims are to have more rights in the prosecution process, are they to come at the expense of the rights of police or the Crown or court officials? These have the greatest interest in encouraging the co-operation of victims, for as much as 87% of police workload — and consequently much of the court workload — comes from incidents reported by citizens (Griffiths et al., 1980:33). Clearly it is in the bureaucratic interests of the system to encourage a steady and increasing clientele. The more incidents that are reported, the higher the crime rate; and high crime rates are an effective argument for bigger budgets. Yet as we have seen, more than half of victimizations are not reported, and many victims "appear to feel that the system would only fail them or ignore them if they involved it" (Task Force, 1983:3).

Victims are essential not only to bringing in the cases but, as witnesses, to prosecuting them successfully. Treat-

ing victims in a "sensitive manner" will encourage their "constructive assistance", says a paper prepared for the Federal Department of Justice (Weiler and Desgagne, 1984:27). Or as Weigend (1983:93) puts it, "Happy victims make better witnesses" — a claim he says is unsubstantiated by any evidence except the "feelings" of the staff of victim/witness assistance programmes.

Sensitivity however does not confer power. It is not a right enforceable by law (Task Force 1983:131). It does not conflict with any of the prerogatives of the prosecution. None of the proposals of the Task Force on Justice for Victims involves any mandatory transfer of power from police or court to victims. They contain phrases such as "to be considered" or "where appropriate". Indeed, the Task Force says the key words in its proposals for victims are "concern, consideration and communication" and that these words sum up how the system can respond to the concerns of victims "without compromising its basic aims". (1983:152)

But the "basic aims", as we have seen, have no necessary connection with justice for victims. There is no transfer of power to victims in proposals which allow them to participate in their cases only at the discretion of judge or Crown. There is no transfer of power, either in the guidelines for fair treatment of victims set out by the Victim Committee of the American Bar Association and quoted with approval by the Task Force. (1983:152) They deal mainly with ways to improve communication between victims and decision-makers in the criminal justice system. Similarly, a case management programme in British Columbia "improved convenience" for victims with no change in the "aims and purposes" of the system (Task Force, 1983:96).

If rights for victims are not to come from the prosecution, then they must come from the accused. If the victim of sexual assault, for instance, wins the right not to have evidence of sexual reputation considered, the accused loses the right to present that evidence. The transfer of rights is particularly evident in the California *Victims' Bill of Rights* of 1982 (Karmen, 1984:232–3), which limits the accused's opportunities for bail, restricts plea bargaining, restricts insanity defence, broadens standards for admissibility of evidence, and permits victims to press for greater penalties in sentencing, to appeal sentences they view as lenient and to argue against parole.

That is further than Canadians appear willing to go. The rhetoric is that the rights of the accused are inviolate, and the Task Force cautions that in focussing on the plight of the victim "we must not lose sight of the need to safeguard the accused" (1983:5). Perhaps it would be more realistic to say, with Ericson and Baranek (1982:233), that both accused and victim are dependents in the prosecution process and that neither has more "rights" than is expedient to allow and not "upset the operation of criminal control in the interests of the state".

PROPOSALS FOR CHANGE

It appears then that victims have almost no enforceable rights in the prosecution process. It also appears that they are excluded from any real rights in the process by its very nature as a conflict between the state and the accused. Within those limits, several ways have been suggested to recognize and recompense the victim.

One is financial reparation. Three of the 79 recommendations of the Task Force deal with this. A second is a "victim impact" statement, to be requested before sentencing, the subject of another Task Force recommendation. A third is a "victims' advocate" who attempts to influence the prosecution process. Two such experiments have been tried in the United States (McDonald, 1976:153). In one a lawyer was employed as a "victim advocate" to attempt to influence the process through out-of-court negotiations. In the other, a volunteer group of victim advocates attended court hearings en masse for a time, until they tired of it, and claimed fewer charges were dismissed or remanded when they were present. The second programme raises questions about fairness to the accused. As Griffiths says (1980:32), "The prototype of community involvement...is the lynch mob." The first raises questions about who pays the advocate. If the victims pay, they may feel twice victimized. If the state pays, that may compromise its stance that the community, not the victim, is the injured party. In any case, such advocates have no standing in court since the victim is not one of the adversaries.

RESTITUTION AND COMPENSATION

The Task Force proposals on reparation would; (1) amend s. 653 of the *Criminal Code* to require judges to consider restitution "in all appropriate cases" and to provide an opportunity for victims to make representations about their ascertainable losses; (2) empower the court to impose a jail term for wilful default on a restitution order; (3) amend s. 388 to raise its present limit on restitution for property damage from $50 to $500. Restitution as part of a probation order under s. 663 would continue unchanged.

"Whenever possible," the Task Force explains, "victims should be restored to the position they enjoyed prior to the victimization" (Task Force, 1983:35). The Law Reform Commission of Canada in its paper on Restitution and Compensation describes restitution as a "natural and just response" to the victim's plight which should be a "central consideration" in sentencing (Working Paper 5, 1974:6,8).

Yet such remedies for the victim already exist. Several sections of the *Criminal Code* make it possible for the court to order restitution. These remedies appear to be seldom used. While Canadian data are lacking (Burns, 1980:29), the Task Force thinks judges are "reluctant" to use them (Task Force, 1983:54). It does not explain why judges would be less reluctant to use its new proposals.

Outside the criminal process, victims may apply to provincial crime injury compensation boards in all provinces except Prince Edward Island, or collect for property losses from private insurance, or file a civil suit both for property loss and for suffering and get judgement not only against the offender but, where negligence can be proved, against third parties.

Restitution provisions in other jurisdictions appear to be an ineffective remedy for victims. In Britain, after passage of new restitution legislation in 1972, of those sent to custody and also given restitution orders only 12% paid the whole sum (Burns, 1980:15). In practice, said the British Advisory Council on the Penal System, a victim's prospects for restitution through a criminal court order "are remote" (Burns, 1980:15). After a study of United States restitution schemes, Burns found them of relatively little use to victims and concluded that their popularity reflected a conception of them as "potentially useful tools for rehabilitating the offender rather than as devices for restoring the victim" (Burns, 1980:12).

The compensation schemes outside the criminal process are not well used either. They are usually limited to victims of violent crime but are available regardless of whether an offender has been identified or convicted. In Ontario, one in 55 eligible victims actually seeks compensation (*Globe & Mail*, 1984:2). A study of the New York and New Jersey schemes showed that fewer than 1% of all victims of violent crime even applied to the boards, and only 35% of those who applied were compensated (Elias, 1983:219).

As for the possibility of civil suit, Allen Linden reported that 1.5% of victims surveyed collected anything by suit, although 74.2% of those studied suffered some economic loss (Linden, 1968:29).

Whether or not restitution is a "natural response", there appear to be a number of reasons why judges are reluctant to use the existing provisions and legislators are reluctant to impose more effective ones — reasons involving the nature of the criminal process, the objectives of sentencing, constitutional division of powers, and sometimes no doubt a combination of ignorance and inertia. Judge Cartwright of York County, in *Regina v. Kalloo* (Unreported; quoted in Moskoff, 1983:11), commented:

> those few Crown counsel who are even aware of the existence of this section (653) which allows the victim of an indictable offence to apply for an order to satisfy loss or damage to property caused in the commission of a crime are equally indifferent to its application.

He went on to suggest that if the Attorney General were paid by commission on completed restitution orders, "blood would be flowing from stones" all over Ontario (Moskoff, 1983:11).

The difficulty of getting blood from stones, however, is one reason restitution orders are seldom made, and civil suit is often useless as well. In making restitution a condition of probation under s. 663(2)(e), a judge is bound to consider an offender's ability to pay. (He is not so bound under 2.653.) Observation of the courts indicates that many offenders, particularly against property, have neither jobs nor assets.

A further reason for caution is the Supreme Court of Canada ruling in *R. v. Zelensky* ((1978), 2 C.R. (3d) 107 (S.C.C.)) that proceedings for restitution under s. 653 must not take on any character of a civil suit, and therefore the criminal court must not determine issues regarding the amount to be awarded. Restitution can be imposed, then, only when the amount is not in dispute, which Moskoff comments makes the section a "toothless tiger" (Moskoff, 1983:11). Burns comments that judges hesitate to order restitution under s. 663 as well, first because they fear using criminal law to enforce civil obligations, and second because they see it as suitable only for simple cases in which there is no dispute either over the amount involved or over the offender's ability to pay (Burns, 1980:25).

In addition, a restitution order once made is hard to enforce. Those made under s. 653 must be enforced by the victim as a civil judgement, if the offender has assets and can be located. Those made under s. 663(2)(e) are intended to be monitored by probation officers. If the probation officers notice that payments have not been made, and if they decide to charge the offender with failure to comply with probation, and if the offender can be located, they must prove the offender "wilfully" defaulted. If they succeed, the maximum penalty is a $500 fine and/or six months in jail. Note that the victim is not the complainant in the enforcement procedure.

The most serious problem with restitution involves the nature of the criminal process. Civil wrongs have grown in law to be those for which injured persons seek their own monetary compensation. Criminal wrongs have become a public relationship between offenders and the state with a public response applied through penal sanctions. The historical tie between the two remains in the *Criminal Code* provisions for restitution (s. 653 and s. 663) which the Law Reform Commission describes as carry-overs "grudgingly grafted onto penal law to save the victim the expense of a civil suit" (Working Paper 5, 1974:9). They enable the victim to circumvent civil procedure by obtaining a criminal judgement, enforceable as if it were civil, by a more expeditious and less expensive process. An example of the civil nature of s. 653 is that it comes into operation "on application" of the victim, not on the initiative of the court.

The *British North America Act* gives jurisdiction over criminal law and procedure to the federal parliament (1867: sect. 91(27)) but authority over property and civil rights to the provinces. This division, says Burns, means "an almost insurmountable obstacle to the establishment of efficient restitution systems in Canada" (1980:29).

Further, criminal courts are constituted to determine a person's criminal responsibility, not his/her civil liability. The two have different standards of proof and different rules of evidence. For example, examination for discovery is a civil procedure not available in the criminal court. An accused person would not have the same safeguards around challenging a victim's claim for damages in criminal court than would be available in civil court. For the criminal court to try to make such a determination raises the danger of infringing on the powers reserved to the civil court. Widespread use of restitution orders might encourage use of the criminal courts as a collection agency, and lead to threatening prosecution to collect a debt.

A further set of problems arises because the focus in sentencing is not on what is pleasing to the victim but on what is good for the offender and for society. Though the Law Reform Commission say restitution is a "rational sanction" and the Zelensky decision accepted its "valid character" as part of the sentencing process, restitution cannot be argued in the criminal court on the basis that it would return the victim to wholeness or compensate for suffering. The only constitutional way to make the civil liability to the victim a valid part of the criminal sentence is to actively locate it within criminal law. The purpose which has been alleged is that it will deprive the offender of the fruits of crime, deter those who might hope to profit illegally, and facilitate the rehabilitation of the accused.

The Law Reform Commission argues that restitution, "involves acceptance of the offender as a responsible person with the capacity to undertake constructive and socially approved acts.... To the extent that restitution works toward self-correction and prevents or at least discourages the offender's commitment to a life of crime, the community enjoys a measure of protection.... The offender too benefits.... He is treated as a responsible human being" (1974:7–8).

These desirable effects, Burns comments, are "entirely speculative" (1980:8). The momentum toward restitution as a sentence seems to him to depend on little more than "an intuitive sense of its rationality" (1980:7).

The Task Force, although it supports expanded restitution proposals, admits "there is little of the kind of 'hard' evidence which might allow us to decide conclusively whether the benefits of restitution outweigh its costs" (1983:92). To be fair, there is little hard evidence on whether any other sentencing dispositions work any better (Griffiths et al., 1980:233–34). The "safest conclusion", says Klein, is that restitution "as a correctional measure simply will not make any difference" (1978:400).

And finally, there are difficulties in implementing effective and just restitution schemes.

Crown attorneys will have discretion whether to recommend restitution, and judges will have discretion whether to order it. Can justice then be equal for offenders, or victims? The victims cannot "shop" for a judge who is known to make restitution orders.

Would the law fall unevenly on the person who steals $10 million and cannot possibly make restitution, and the person who steals $100 and can? If restitution is a correctional measure, imposed for the good of the offender, should it not then be imposed regardless of whether the victim has been paid for the loss by insurance?

Defence counsel often tell the court, in a bid for a more lenient sentence, that full or partial restitution has been made. If this does in fact result in leniency, does that mean that if a rich man and a poor man both break a window, and the rich man can afford to replace it, then he receives a less severe sentence than the poor man for the same offence?

What happens if there are several offenders? If one has no ability to pay, or reneges on payment, do the others pay more to make up the victim's total loss? Suppose there are multiple victims, and as part of plea negotiations some charges are dropped. Which victims are then to receive restitution?

Finally, if victims of crime are entitled to be restored to their original status, why not every victim? Why limit the recompense to those cases of property loss in which an offender can not only be identified, charged, convicted, and sentenced to make restitution but can actually pay damages?

Yet with all their flaws, restitution programmes (inside the criminal process) and compensation schemes (outside of it) have been legislated in many jurisdictions in the last 20 years. Though often underfunded, unadvertised and underused, obviously they have merits for lawmakers. For one, they enable governments faced with rising crime rates and rising public concern over crime to say, "Look what we're doing for the victims." Roger Meiners points out that large numbers of compensation programmes were established at least in part as a palliative for increasing crime and relatively inefficient restitution (Meiners, 1978:9–44). Voters are told that something will be done for them when and if they are victimized and few will find out otherwise. Elias claims compensation has:

> justified strengthened police forces, provided political advantages to its supporters, facilitated social control of the population and yet substantially failed in providing most victims with assistance (1983:213).

A second purpose is to keep the victim from demanding a real role in the prosecution process. As Hagan says, such programmes open the possibility of bringing the victim back into the system without actually doing it, symbolically conveying a sense of concern while doing little to alter the actual origin of the concern (1983:60).

VICTIM IMPACT STATEMENTS

The other proposal of the Task Force, aside from restitution, to bring the victim back into the prosecution process was to amend the *Criminal Code* to "permit" the introduction of a victim impact statement "to be considered" at the time of sentencing (Task Force, 1983:157). Such a statement would presumably enable victims to tell the judge of their suffering and of any monetary loss as a result of the crime. Presumably they would then feel that somebody was paying attention to what happened to them.

At present nothing, except pressure of time, prevents a judge from asking to hear from a victim, or when ordering a pre-sentence report from asking that the victim be consulted. The intent of the Task Force proposal is to require the judge to request such a statement.

That proposal raises serious questions. To the degree that the statement dealt with monetary loss, it could be considered in assessing restitution as part of a sentence, subject to concerns already discussed about the purposes of sentencing and conflict with civil courts, particularly if the amount of the loss were in dispute. Questions arise whether the determination of loss would have to be based on receipts of appraisals, which might be difficult for some victims to produce; whether the statement would have to be sworn; whether it would be subject to contest by the accused, and if contested, whether the whole question would not then have to be referred to a civil court for adjudication.

To the degree that the statement dealt with pain or suffering, its usefulness would be questionable as long as the focus in sentencing is on the protection of society and the rehabilitation of the accused. A shut-in widow whose television set is stolen may suffer more from its loss than the wealthy bachelor who is seldom home, but that should weigh less with the judge than the characteristics of the offence, the previous record of the offender and the perceived need to deter such behaviour in the community. If the purpose of the sentence is to rehabilitate the offender, then its nature should be determined by presumed experts. If its purpose is deterrence, then it should be certain and predictable, not subject to modification by the victim. If the purpose is retribution, then the punishment must fit the crime rather than the victim (Karmen, 1984:155).

Then there is the problem of how the statement will be submitted. Ninety-eight percent of cases are concluded in the provincial courts (Griffiths et al., 1980:146) and about 70% of these without a trial (Griffiths et al., 1980:147). Dockets are crowded, hearings are rushed and pre-sentence reports are rare. If the victim is not present when the accused pleads guilty, how often will judges be willing to delay sentence to hear from the victim?

Perhaps too, it is only an assumption that many victims really want this input, or any input, into their cases. A Philadelphia judge, Lois Porer, who routinely offers victims a chance to speak on sentence, says they seldom do (Karmen, 1984:230). Since victim impact statements were legislated in Connecticut in 1981, only 3% of victims appear at sentence hearings (Karmen, 1984:231). When as an experiment victims were invited to take part in plea-bargaining sessions on their cases in Dade County, Florida, only a third attended. Those who were present generally spoke only in answer to questions, approved what the professionals suggested and were "passive and docile" (Heinz and Kerstetter, 1980:172).

RESISTANCE TO CHANGE

Having looked at the "rights" of the victim in the prosecution process and at proposals to give victims a larger role, it remains to ask: would these proposals, or any proposals, make any real difference in the conduct of the courts?

As we have seen, restitution is seldom ordered. Compensation schemes are seldom used. The majority of victims do not accept the limited opportunities to participate which are offered to them. It is not clear whether the last is because they don't care, or because they don't think it will make any difference, or because as the Dade County study suggests the system is not diligent in notifying them of opportunities (Heinz and Kerstetter, 1980:173).

One of the reasons advanced for helping victims is to encourage them to cooperate with the system in reporting more victimizations. In the United States, the percentage of incidents of violence which were reported to police went from 46% in 1973 to 47% in 1981, and of household burglaries from 47% in 1973 to 51% in 1981, despite the launching of numerous victim-assistance programmes during that period (Karmen, 1984:168).

After reviewing a decade of action and advocacy on behalf of victims in the United States, Weigend concluded it had generated "much rhetoric, more knowledge...but little change" (1983:91).

Criminal justice systems are like any bureaucracy. They operate in their own interests. They are subject to what Karmen calls "goal displacement" (1984:169), which means that they substitute for the official goals of doing justice and serving the public, the unofficial goals of getting through the workload expeditiously, covering up mistakes and making themselves look as essential as possible so funding won't be cut. As King points out:

> Imagine for example the approach of the victim of a serious crime. He wishes to see the offender punished and deterred from further offences. Now compare that approach with that of a court administrator, whose major concern is the efficient running of the system, clearing the workload for the day and avoiding any unnecessary

delays.... The one looks to the magistrate to revenge his loss...and to compensate him, the victim, while another looks at his watch and wonders how long the case is going to last and whether the morning list will be completed by one o'clock (1981:13–14).

A place for victims in the prosecution process is limited to one that does not interfere with the smooth working of the system or the privileges and convenience of its principles.

Most reforms, as we have seen, seem to be intended to inform or assist or conciliate the victim, and these are worthy goals, but they involve no real rights or participation. Where the victim has been granted a role in the process, it appears to be subject to foot-dragging (the Dade County experiment), discretion (to be "considered" or to be applied "where appropriate") or co-opting.

The fate of reforms in the role of the victim is not surprising. Ericson and Baranek state:

> It is a common feature of bureaucratic organizations that rules intended to influence the action of agents are routinely absorbed by the agents to conform with their existing practices (1982:224).

Exciting reforms are "translated into mechanisms of convenience by control agents and relegated to their pragmatically appropriate place" (Ericson and Baranek, 1982:231).

CONCLUSION

If the public criminal justice process is impervious to change which would allow the victim any real participation, what then?

Organizational victims already bypass the public prosecution and set up their own system to deal with incidents which are classified not as "crime" (which by definition involves the public interest) but as "loss" (Shearing and Stenning, 1983:7). In these victim-oriented systems, run by and for victims, the priority is on restitution or compensation for the loss and prevention of future losses.

Then there are proposals, for example Christie's (1977, 1982), for similar decriminalization of offences against individuals. Christie argues that we "create crime by creating systems that ask for the word" (1982:74). He proposes to remove conflicts from the professionals and return them to the accused and the victims, and to set up quasi-civil procedures to assess compensation and penalties. Pointing out that "several less-industrialized countries" apply civil law where Europe applies criminal law (1982:92), he asks, "Could we imagine social systems where the parties by and large relied on civil solutions?" (1982:96).

Ericson and Baranek, discussing such proposals, are skeptical. Decriminalization may simply imply some other form of social control. Diversion programmes may lead to more cumbersome procedures and increase the number of persons subject to control (1982:228). They add, "All reform alternatives include an added role for some group of professionals" (1982:233).

It is also important to note that there is the vigilante, who tries his own case and administers his own justice, celebrated in the movies *Death Wish* and *Deadly Force* ("When the cops won't and the courts can't...he will give you justice!" (Karmen, 1984:247)) and emulated by Bernhard Goetz of New York.

In Canada, at least, rates of reported crime are not escalating in a way that justifies the vigilante. But one of the arguments for compensating victims of crime rests on the assumption that they do not carry out their own justice. In Taylor's analysis (1983), a crucial function of the capitalist state is to maintain conditions under which production can flourish. One of these conditions is a "justice" system. There must be an overall sense in society of a free contract whereby the state protects the person and the property of its citizens, in exchange for those citizens subjugating themselves to the state. The loss of liberty thereby involved is offset and made legitimate by the overall protection of the freedom of the citizen which is provided by a police force and a legal and penal system (1983:135). In other words, citizens give up the right to protect themselves and to pursue their own vengeance, and the state contracts to protect them and collects taxes from them to do so. Therefore, it can be argued that if the state fails in its side of the contract, it should compensate the victims.

Similar arguments for compensating crime victims can be raised on the basis of sociologist Emile Durkheim's theories that crime is normal, even necessary to a healthy society (Vold, 1979:204–208). Durkheim argued that society makes certain demands on its members, and fulfilling theme demands is an important source of social solidarity. But the demands are constructed so that inevitably a certain identifiable group will not be able to fulfill them. This enables the rest to feel a sense of moral superiority which he says is the primary source of the social solidarity.

Durkheim informed us that it is not only inevitable that some will oppose the collective conscience, it is also healthy. Progressive social change comes about because some people dare to differ. Thus crime is the price society pays for the possibility of progress — all the more reason why society should compensate those few who are martyrs to its health.

What would we do if we were really serious about helping victims of crime? We would fund adequately and advertise widely a government-supported compensation fund. It would not be funded, as is often suggested, by convicted offenders, for that would imply that offenders are a distinct group and would hold all in that group, who happened to be caught, liable for the damage inflicted by some. Rather it might be funded like medical insurance (one might contribute to OHIP and to VICE — Victims Insurance (against) Criminal Enterprises), recognizing first, that there are more offenders than ever that are caught; second, that the definition of which acts are crimes and therefore which persons are offenders is made by society and changes from time to time; and third, that society has an obligation to those who suffer from one of its inevitable features. We would allow compensation both for material loss and for pain and suffering, and whether or not an offender has been identified. Yes, there would be cheating, just as people cheat now on claims for private insurance. But if private insurers live with that risk, surely a public scheme can.

Victim Power: Too Much For Anyone's Good?[†]
K. Makin

Now, no one can say no to people once shunted aside.

RARELY has a grassroots movement acquired power and influence as swiftly as have victims of violence, the self-described "forgotten people of the justice system," in the past decade.

Few could deny that victim issues have long needed attention, or that many of the movement's recent victories have been well-deserved.

---

† Makin, Kirk, "Victim Power: Too Much For Anyone's Good?" *Globe and Mail*, August 26, 1989, D2. Reprinted by permission of The Globe and Mail.

But a significant part of the victim lobby lacks sophistical and balance, and many in the justice system feel that some of its strongest voices border on the hysterical, or that the movement's leaders tend to be either weak and politically naive or brash and pushy.

"It is the golden age of victims," commented Robert Wakefield, former president of the Defence Counsel Association of Ottawa. "They are a very powerful lobby with undeniable appeal. No one can say no to them."

Politicians meet victim advocates on short notice and echo their demands in speeches. The media love their availability and hunger for their strident views, rewarding them with massive, unquestioning publicity.

Among the triumphs of the victims lobby in the past few years:

- Much harsher penalties for impaired drivers and spouse-beaters;
- A fee charged to convicted criminals to help pay for victim services;
- The use in many provinces of victim impact statements during sentencing;
- Education programs in schools;
- Training programs for Crown attorneys to teach them to deal delicately with victims and to keep them informed of legal developments;
- The non-disclosure in legal proceedings of the names of victims of sexual assault;
- Increases in compensation funds for crime victims;
- Victim and witness services in courthouses and government ministries across the country.

As well, all levels of government funnel money into victim conferences, task force studies, surveys, films, pamphlets and pilot programs.

"I don't think you can have a conference these days without looking at victim issues," one federal official said.

Some authorities on victimization say that for every group that starts up, two disappear.

"It is an unregulated area," said Susan Lee, a victim specialist with Ontario's Ministry of the Attorney-General. "Anyone can set up shop, contact victims for support and publicly push their own agenda."

Ms. Lee supports such groups, but many players in the justice system fear their power and resent their simplistic view of the world. They fear that this new-found lobbying power could upset a delicate balance of legal rights that has taken generations to establish.

Mr. Wakefield asserted that most victim activists, for example, brush aside concepts such as the presumption of innocence or the rehabilitation of criminals.

"They just want more charges laid, no plea bargaining, no acquittals, whopping sentences, and compensation for themselves," he said. "Victims are attempting to exploit our genuine sympathy for them and use it to alter the outcome of trials.

"It is changing the sentencing procedures. Where does genuine concern of the courts for public perception stop, and mob rule begin? Should the courts pander to popular sentiment?

"There is more to the criminal justice system than public popularity. I think the system is very strong, but we are slowly losing it. It is being twisted to appease interest groups."

Most disturbing, Mr. Wakefield said, is that judges, who must hover above the fray and apply established case law, are more and more frequently citing public discontent as one reason for harsh sentences.

Many activists bolster their arguments by distorting the facts of individual crimes, Mr. Wakefield said. "Whenever it comes to a hard, logical issue they retreat to their emotional trauma, and how we should feel sorry for them."

Irwin Waller, a University of Ottawa criminologist who specializes in victim issues, divides victim groups into three categories relating to drunk driving, violence, and specialties such as sexual assault or spouse battering.

Although rape crisis centres were probably the forerunners of the victim movement, Ms. Lee dates the real surge to 1981, when a federal-provincial conference gave the victim issue a high profile.

The questions raised at the time were simple: Why were victims kept in the dark about their cases? Why were witnesses kept waiting for hours in courtroom hallways? Why did no one in authority talk to victims about the trauma they had experienced?

After a serious crime, Ms. Lee said, victims typically go through several identifiable stages.

First there is disorientation and fear. Then comes a "recoiling," during which a victim may be nervous and sleepless and may even change his or her residence. At this stage, Ms. Lee said, the individual needs someone sympathetic to talk to, something at which some victim groups excel.

The final stage, Ms. Lee said, involves "reorganization," in which the victim may use counselling to overcome psychological effects

Many never reach this stage, becoming mired in guilt or sadness. Some try to work out their emotions through endless battles with the justice system.

"It is easy to get involved in the justice system and diffuse the pain," said Julie Cullen, director of Victim Witness Services at the British Columbia Attorney-General's ministry. "You focus on the system and lash out at it. But years later, you have to go back and deal with it."

Some victim advocates jeopardize their influence with hysteria, said Richard Fischer, director of the California Centre on Victimology.

167

"Some people are not emotionally stable even before they are victimized, and the victimization can make them worse," he said. "There are a lot of fanatical people who just cannot be helped.

"It is really sad to see someone whose daughter was killed 10 years ago and who was never strong enough emotionally to move on in their life."

That is why the time has passed when crime victims should counsel other victims or lead groups lobbying for change, Mr. Fischer said. In the United States these people have been shunted aside in favor of trained, professional victim counsellors and lobbyists.

"I think it is important to have a real, comprehensive therapeutic approach," he said. "There is an enormous need for specialist."

Most established U.S. groups are careful and pragmatic in selecting legislation they want to promote or quash, Mr. Fischer said, "I think we are probably one of the most powerful groups in the country in influencing legislation."

Prof. Waller argues that there is a place for both types of victim groups. "If you look at groups like NOVA (a giant U.S. victim group), what they are arguing for is much more thought-out and objective and reasonable and better argued. However, it does take people who have the amount of emotion of (Canadian victim advocates) Don Sullivan or Gary Rosenfeldt to get the media and politicians interested."

As a former director of an umbrella organization of victims' groups, Ms. Cullen has seen things from both sides. Although many groups fill an important need, she said, some are dangerously untrained.

"You wonder how effective they are in helping grieving parents when they are grieving themselves. It seems to me they may do more harm than good."

Another concern is the potential harm that aggressive recruiting by a group can cause recent victims of crime.

"Some are like a boiler-room operation as far as I am concerned," Ms. Cullen said. "You've got people who are at their most vulnerable point."

By counselling and recruiting others, she said, they may simply perpetuate the problem of unresolved feelings.

Further Reading

H. Rubel, "Victim Participation in Sentencing Proceedings" 28 *Criminal Law Quarterly* 226–50.

R. Abel, "Pounds of Cure, Ounces of Prevention" (1985), 73 *California Law Review* 1003–23.

B. Law and Private Ordering: Legal Relations and Social Relations

Non-Contractual Relationships in Business: A Preliminary Study[†]
S. Macaulay

The Adjustment of Exchange Relationships and the Settling of Disputes

While a significant amount of creating business exchanges is done on a fairly noncontractual basis, the creation of exchanges usually is far more contractual than the adjustment of such relationships and the settlement of disputes. Exchanges are adjusted when the obligations of one or both parties are modified by agreement during the life of the relationship. For example, the buyer may be allowed to cancel all or part of the goods he has ordered because he no longer needs them; the seller may be paid more than the usual contract price by the buyer because of unusual changed circumstances. Dispute settlement involves determining whether or not a party has performed as agreed and, if he has not, doing something about it. For example, a court may have to interpret the meaning of a contract, determine what the alleged defaulting party has done and determine what, if any, remedy the aggrieved party is entitled to. Or one party may assert that the other is in default, refuse to proceed with performing the contract and refuse to deal ever again with the alleged defaulter. If the alleged defaulter, who in fact may not be in default, takes no action, the dispute is then "settled."

Business exchanges in non-speculative areas are usually adjusted without dispute. Under the law of contracts, if B orders 1,000 widgets from S at $1.00 each, B must take all 1,000 widgets or be in breach of contract and liable to pay S his expenses up to the time of the breach plus his lost anticipated profit. Yet all ten of the purchasing agents asked about cancellation of orders once placed indicated that they expected to be able to cancel orders freely subject to only an obligation to pay for the seller's major expenses such as scrapped steel. All 17 sales personnel asked reported that they often had to accept cancellation. One said, "You can't ask a man to eat paper [the firm's product] when he has no use for it." A lawyer with many large industrial clients said,

> Often businessmen do not feel they have "a contract" — rather they have "an order." They speak of "cancelling the order" rather than "breaching our contract." When I began practice I referred to order cancellations as breaches of contract, but my clients objected since they do not think of cancellation as wrong. Most clients, in heavy industry at least, believe that there is a right to cancel as part of the buyer-seller relationship. There is a widespread attitude that one can back out of any deal within some very vague limits. Lawyers are often surprised by this attitude.

Disputes are frequently settled without reference to the contract or potential or actual legal sanctions. There is a hesitancy to speak of legal rights or to threaten to sue in these negotiations. Even where the parties have a detailed and carefully planned agreement which indicates what is to happen if, say, the seller fails to deliver on time, often they will never refer to the agreement but will negotiate a solution when the problem arises apparently as if there had never been any original contract. One purchasing agent expressed a common business attitude when he said,

> if something comes up, you get the other man on the telephone and deal with the problem. You don't read legalistic contract clauses at each other if you ever want to do business again. One doesn't run to lawyers if he wants to stay in business because one must behave decently.

Or as one businessman put it, "You can settle any dispute if you keep the lawyers and accountants out of it. They just do not understand the give-and-take needed in business." All of the house counsel interviewed indicated that they are called into the dispute settlement process only after the businessmen have failed to settle matters in their own way. Two indicated that after being called in house counsel at first will only advise the purchasing agent, sales manager or other official involved; not even the house counsel's letterhead is used on communications with the other side until all hope for a peaceful resolution is gone.

Law suits for breach of contract appear to be rare. Only five of the 12 purchasing agents had ever been involved in even a negotiation concerning a contract dispute where both sides were represented by lawyers; only two

---

† Macaulay, Stewart, "Non-Contractual Relationships in Business: A Preliminary Study" (1963), 28 *American Sociological Rev.* 55 at 60–67.

of ten sales managers had ever gone this far. None had been involved in a case that went through trial. A law firm with more than 40 lawyers and a large commercial practice handles in a year only about six trials concerned with contract problems. Less than 10 per cent of the time of this office is devoted to any type of work related to contracts disputes. Corporations big enough to do business in more than one state tend to sue and be sued in the federal courts. Yet only 2,779 out of 58,293 civil actions filed in the United States District Courts in fiscal year 1961 involved private contracts. During the same period only 3,447 of the 61,138 civil cases filed in the principal trial courts of New York State involved private contracts. The same picture emerges from a review of appellate cases. Mentschikoff has suggested that commercial cases are not brought to the courts either in periods of business prosperity (because buyers unjustifiably reject goods only when prices drop and they can get similar goods elsewhere at less than the contract price) or in periods of deep depression (because people are unable to come to court or have insufficient assets to satisfy any judgment that might be obtained). Apparently, she adds, it is necessary to have "a kind of middle-sized depression" to bring large numbers of commercial cases to the courts. However, there is little evidence that in even "a kind of middle-sized depression" today's businessmen would use the courts to settle disputes.

At times relatively contractual methods are used to make adjustments in ongoing transactions and to settle disputes. Demands of one side which are deemed unreasonable by the other occasionally are blocked by reference to the terms of the agreement between the parties. The legal position of the parties can influence negotiations even though legal rights or litigation are never mentioned in their discussions; it makes a difference if one is demanding what both concede to be a right or begging for a favour. Now and then a firm may threaten to turn matters over to its attorneys, threaten to sue, commence a suit or even litigate and carry an appeal to the highest court which will hear the matter. Thus, legal sanctions, while not an everyday affair, are not unknown in business.

One can conclude that while detailed planning and legal sanctions play a significant role in some exchanges between businesses, in many business exchanges their role is small.

TENTATIVE EXPLANATIONS

Two questions need to be answered: (A) How can business successfully operate exchange relationships with relatively so little attention to detailed planning or to legal sanctions, and (B) Why does business ever use contract in light of its success without it?

Why are Relatively Non-Contractual Practices so Common?

In most situations contract is not needed. Often its functions are served by other devices. Most problems are avoided without resort to detailed planning or legal sanctions because usually there is little room for honest misunderstandings or good faith differences of opinion about the nature and quality of a seller's performance. Although the parties fail to cover all foreseeable contingencies, they will exercise care to see that both understand the primary obligation on each side. Either products are standardized with an accepted description or specifications are written calling for production to certain tolerances or results. Those who write and read specifications are experienced professionals who will know the customs of their industry and those of the industries with which they deal. Consequently, these customs can fill gaps in the express agreements of the parties. Finally, most products can be tested to see if they are what was ordered; typically in the manufacturing industry we are not dealing with questions of taste or judgment where people can differ in good faith.

When defaults occur they are not likely to be disastrous because of techniques of risk avoidance or risk spreading. One can deal with firms of good reputation or he may be able to get some form of security to guarantee performance. One can insure against many breaches of contract where the risks justify the costs. Sellers set up reserves for bad debts on their books and can sell some of their accounts receivable. Buyers can place orders with two or more suppliers of the same item so that a default by one will not stop the buyer's assembly lines.

Moreover, contract and contract law are often thought unnecessary because there are many effective non-legal sanctions. Two norms are widely accepted. (1) Commitments are to be honored in almost all situations; one does not welsh on a deal. (2) One ought to produce a good product and stand behind it. Then, too, business units are organized to perform commitments, and internal sanctions will induce performance. For example, sales personnel must face angry customers when there has been a late or defective performance. The salesmen do not enjoy this and will put pressure on the production personnel responsible for the default. If the production personnel default too often, they will be fired. At all levels of the two business units personal relationships across the boundaries of the two organizations exert pressures for conformity to expectations. Salesmen often know purchasing agents well. The same two individuals occupying these roles may have dealt with each other from five to 25 years. Each has something to give the other. Salesmen have gossip about competitors, shortages and price increases to give purchasing agents who treat them well. Salesmen take purchasing agents to dinner, and they give purchasing agents Christmas gifts hoping to improve the chances of making a sale. The buyer's engineering staff may work with the seller's engineering staff to solve problems jointly. The seller's engineers may render great assistance, and the buyer's engineers may desire to return the favour by drafting specifications which only the seller can meet. The top executives of the two firms may know each other. They may sit together on government or trade committees. They may know each other socially and even belong to the same country club. The inter-relationships may be more formal. Sellers may hold stock in corporations which are important customers; buyers may hold stock in important suppliers. Both buyer and seller may share common directors on their boards. They may share a common financial institution which has financed both units.

The final type of non-legal sanction is the most obvious. Both business units involved in the exchange desire to continue successfully in business and will avoid conduct which might interfere with attaining this goal. One is concerned with both the reaction of the other party in the particular exchange and with his own general business reputation. Obviously, the buyer gains sanctions insofar as the seller wants the particular exchange to be completed. Buyers can withhold part of all of their payments until sellers have performed to their satisfaction. If a seller has a great deal of money tied up in his performance which he must recover quickly, he will go a long way to please the buyer in order to be paid. Moreover, buyers who are dissatisfied may cancel and cause sellers to lose the cost of what they have done up to cancellation. Furthermore, sellers hope for repeats for orders, and one gets few of these from unhappy customers. Some industrial buyers go so far as to formalize this sanction by issuing "report cards" rating the performance of each supplier. The supplier rating goes to the top management of the seller organization, and these men can apply internal sanctions to salesmen, production supervisors or product designers if there are too many "D's" or "F's" on the report card.

While it is generally assumed that the customer is always right, the seller may have some counterbalancing sanctions against the buyer. The seller may have obtained a large downpayment from the buyer which he will want to protect. The seller may have an exclusive process which the buyer needs. The seller may be one of the few firms which has the skill to make the item to the tolerances set by the buyer's engineers and within the time available. There are costs and delays involved in turning from a supplier one has dealt with in the past to a new supplier. Then, too, market conditions can change so that a buyer is faced with shortages of critical items. The most extreme example is the post World War II gray market conditions when sellers were rationing goods rather than selling them. Buyers must build up some reserve of good will with suppliers if they face the risk of such shortage and desire good treatment when they occur. Finally, there is reciprocity in buying and selling. A buyer cannot push a supplier too far if that supplier also buys significant quantities of the product made by the buyer.

Not only do the particular business units in a given exchange want to deal with each other again, they also want to deal with other business units in the future. And the way one behaves in a particular transaction, or a series of transactions, will colour his general business reputation. Blacklisting can be formal or informal. Buyers who fail to pay their bills on time risk a bad report in credit rating services such as Dun and Bradstreet. Sellers who do not satisfy their customers become the subject of discussion in the gossip exchanged by purchasing agents and salesmen, at meetings of purchasing agents' associations and trade associations, or even at country clubs or social gatherings where members of top management meet. The American male's habit of debating the merits of new cars carries over to industrial items. Obviously, a poor reputation does not help a firm make sales and may force it to offer great price discounts or added services to remain in business. Furthermore, the habits of unusually demanding buyers become known, and they tend to get no more than they can coerce out of suppliers who choose to deal with them. Thus, often contract is not needed as there are alternatives.

Not only are contract and contract law not needed in many situations, their use may have, or may be thought to have, undesirable consequences. Detailed negotiated contracts can get in the way of creating good exchange relationships between business units. If one side insists on a detailed plan, there will be delay while letters are exchanged as the parties try to agree on what should happen if a remote and unlikely contingency occurs. In some cases they may not be able to agree at all on such matters and as a result a sale may be lost to the seller and the buyer may have to search elsewhere for an acceptable supplier. Many businessmen would react by thinking that, had no one raised the series of remote and unlikely contingencies, all this wasted effort could have been avoided.

Even where agreement can be reached at the negotiation stage, carefully planned arrangements may create undesirable exchange relationships between business units. Some businessmen object that in such a carefully worked out relationship one gets performance only to the letter of the contract. Such planning indicates a lack of trust and blunts the demands of friendship, turning a cooperative venture into an antagonistic horse trade. Yet the greater danger perceived by some businessmen is that one would have to perform his side of the bargain to its letter and thus lose what is called "flexibility." Businessmen may welcome a measure of vagueness in the obligations they assume so that they may negotiate matters in light of the actual circumstances.

Adjustment of exchange relationships and dispute settlement by litigation or the threat of it also has many costs. The gain anticipated from using this form of coercion often fails to outweigh these costs, which are both monetary and non-monetary. Threatening to turn matters over to an attorney may cost no more money than postage or a telephone call; yet few are so skilled in making such a threat that it will not cost some deterioration of the relationship between the firms. One businessman said that customers had better not rely on legal rights or threaten to bring a breach of contract law suit against him since he "would not be treated like a criminal" and would fight back with every means available. Clearly actual litigation is even more costly than making threats. Lawyers demand substantial fees from larger business units. A firm's executives often will have to be transported and maintained in another city during the proceedings if, as often is the case, the trial must be held away from the home office. Top management does not travel by Greyhound and stay at the Y.M.C.A. Moreover, there will be the cost of diverting top management, engineers, and others in the organization from their normal activities. The firm may lose many days work from several key people. The non-monetary costs may be large too. A breach of contract law suit may settle a particular dispute, but such an action often results in a "divorce" ending the "marriage" between the two businesses, since a contract action is likely to carry charges with at least overtones of bad faith. Many executives, moreover, dislike the prospect of being cross-examined in public. Some executives may dislike losing control of a situation by turning the decision-making power over to lawyers. Finally, the law of contract damages may not provide an adequate remedy even if the firm wins the suit; one may get vindication but not much money.

Why do Relatively Contractual Practices ever Exist?

Although contract is not needed and actually may have negative consequences, businessmen do make some carefully planned contracts, negotiate settlements influenced by their legal rights and commence and defend some breach of contract law suits or arbitration proceedings. In view of the findings and explanation presented to this point, one may ask why. Exchanges are carefully planned when it is thought that planning and a potential legal sanction will have more advantages than disadvantages. Such a judgment may be reached when contract planning serves the internal needs of an organization involved in a business exchange. For example, a fairly detailed contract can serve as a communication device within a large corporation. While the corporation's sales manager and house counsel may work out all the provisions with the customer, its production manager will have to make the product. He must be told what to do and how to handle at least the most obvious contingencies. Moreover, the sales manager may want to remove certain issues from future negotiation by his subordinates. If he puts the matter in the written contract, he may be able to keep his salesmen from making concessions to the customer without first consulting the sales manager. Then the sales manager may be aided in his battles with his firm's financial or engineering departments if the contract calls for certain practices which the sales manager advocates but which the other departments resist. Now the corporation is obligated to a customer to do what the sales manager wants to do; how can the financial or engineering departments insist on anything else?

Also one tends to find a judgment that the gains of contract outweigh the costs where there is a likelihood that significant problems will arise. One factor leading to this conclusion is complexity of the agreed performance over a long period. Another factor is whether or not the degree of injury in case of default is thought to be potentially great. This factor cuts two ways. First, a buyer may want to commit a seller to a detailed and legally binding contract, where the consequence of a default by the seller would seriously injure the buyer. For example, the airlines are subject to law suits from the survivors of passengers and to great adverse publicity as a result of crashes. One would expect the airlines to bargain for carefully defined and legally enforceable obligations on the part of the airframe manufacturers when they purchase aircraft. Second, a seller may want to limit his liability for a buyer's damages by a provision in their contract. For example, a manufacturer of air conditioning may deal with motels in the South and Southwest. If this equipment fails in the hot summer months, a motel may lose a great deal of business. The manufacturer may wish to avoid any liability for this type of injury to his customers and may want a contract with a clear disclaimer clause.

Similarly, one uses or threatens to use legal sanctions to settle disputes when other devices will not work and when the gains are thought to outweigh the costs. For example, perhaps the most common type of business contracts case fought all the way through the appellate courts today is an action for an alleged wrongful termination of a dealer's franchise by a manufacturer. Since the franchise has been terminated, factors such as personal relationships and the desire for future business will have little effect; the cancellation of the franchise indicates they have already failed to maintain the relationship. Nor will a complaining dealer worry about creating a hostile relationship between himself and the manufacturer. Often the dealer has suffered a great financial loss both as to his investment in building and equipment and as to his anticipated future profits. A cancelled automobile dealer's lease on his showroom and shop will continue to run, and his tools for servicing, say, Plymouths cannot be used to service other makes of cars. Moreover, he will have no more new Plymouths to sell. Today there is some chance of winning a law suit for terminating a franchise in bad faith in many states and in the federal courts. Thus, often the dealer chooses to risk the cost of a lawyer's fee because of the chance that he may recover some compensation for his losses.

An "irrational" factor may exert some influence on the decision to use legal sanctions. The man who controls a firm may feel that he or his organization has been made to appear foolish or has been the victim of fraud or bad faith. The law suit may be seen as a vehicle "to get even" although the potential gains, as viewed by an objective observer, are outweighed by the potential costs.

The decision whether or not to use contract — whether the gain exceeds the costs — will be made by the person within the business unit with the power to make it, and it tends to make a difference who he is. People in a sales department oppose contract. Contractual negotiations are just one more hurdle in the way of a sale. Holding a customer to the letter of a contract is bad for "customer relations." Suing a customer who is not bankrupt and might order again is poor strategy. Purchasing agents and their buyers are less hostile to contracts but regard attention devoted to such matters as a waste of time. In contrast, the financial control department — the treasurer, controller or auditor — leans toward more contractual dealings. Contract is viewed by these people as an organizing tool to control operations in a large organization. It tends to define precisely and to minimize the risks to which the firm is exposed. Outside lawyers — those with many clients — may share this enthusiasm for a more contractual method of dealing. These lawyers are concerned with preventive law — avoiding any possible legal difficulty. They see many unstable and unsuccessful exchange transactions, and so they are aware of, and perhaps overly concerned with, all of the things which can go wrong. Moreover, their job of settling disputes with legal sanctions is much easier if their client has not been overly casual about transaction planning. The inside lawyer, or house counsel, is harder to classify. He is likely to have some sympathy with a more contractual method of dealing. He shares the outside lawyer's "craft urge" to see exchange transactions neat and tidy from a legal standpoint. Since he is more concerned with avoiding and settling disputes than selling goods, he is likely to be less willing to rely on a man's word as the sole sanction than is a salesman. Yet the house counsel is more a part of the organization and more aware of its goals and subject to its internal sanctions. If the potential risks are not too great, he may hesitate to suggest a more contractual procedure to the sales department. He must sell his services to the operating departments, and he must hoard what power he has, expending it on only what he sees as significant issues.

The power to decide that a more contractual method of creating relationships and settling disputes shall be used will be held by different people at different times in different organizations. In most firms the sales department and the purchasing department have a great deal of power to resist contractual procedures or to ignore them if they are formally adopted and to handle disputes their own way. Yet in larger organizations the treasurer and the controller have increasing power to demand both systems and compliance. Occasionally, the house counsel must arbitrate the conflicting positions of these departments; in giving "legal advice" he may make the business judgment necessary regarding the use of contract. At times he may ask for an opinion from an outside law firm to reinforce his own position with the outside firm's prestige.

Obviously, there are other significant variables which influence the degree that contract is used. One is the relative bargaining power or skill of the two business units. Even if the controller of a small supplier succeeds within the firm and creates a contractual system of dealing, there will be no contract if the firm's large customer prefers not to be bound to anything. Firms that supply General Motors deal as General Motors wants to do business, for the most part. Yet bargaining power is not size or share of the market alone. Even a General Motors may need a particular supplier, at least temporarily. Furthermore, bargaining power may shift as an exchange relationship is first created and then continues. Even a giant firm can find itself bound to a small supplier once production of an essential item begins for there may not be time to turn to another supplier. Also, all of the factors discussed in this paper can be viewed as *components* of bargaining power — for example, the personal relationship between the presidents of the buyer and the seller firms may give a sales manager great power over a purchasing agent who has been instructed to give the seller "every consideration." Another variable relevant to the use of contract is the influence of third parties. The federal government, or a lender of money, may insist that a contract be made in a particular transaction or may influence the decision to assert one's legal rights under a contract.

Contract, then, often plays an important role in business, but other factors are significant. To understand the functions of contract the whole system of conducting exchanges must be explored fully. More types of business communities must be studied, contract litigation must be analyzed to see why the non-legal sanctions fail to prevent the use of legal sanctions and all of the variables suggested in this paper must be classified more systematically.

Questions

1. What are the implications of Macaulay's study for our understanding of the role of law in society?
2. Is there a useful distinction to be made between looking at the role of contract law in providing a legal framework for business relations, and the role of the legal profession and the courts in resolving disputes arising out of business relations?
3. How does the situation described by Macaulay differ from the legal framework governing collective bargaining and labour relations, in which arbitration is used to resolve disputes, rather than formal adjudication through the courts? See M. MacNeil, "Rights Arbitration: Current Practices, Problems and Innovative Suggestions", in A. Sethi, ed. *Collective Bargaining in Canada* (Nelson Canada, 1989).

The Use of 'Contracts' as a Social Work Technique[†]
D. Nelken

Introduction: What are Social Work Contracts?[1]

The use of contracts as a tool of social work intervention is now widespread.[2] The various factors that help to account for the spread of this way of working look likely to lead to greater use of this technique. Yet there has still hardly been any research into the reasons for the use of this method, the kinds of contracts used in different situations and the success which has attended their use. Indeed, the problem of deciding what "success" would mean in any project set up to evaluate contracts has hardly been confronted. The promise of effective use of contracts for the benefit of clients, field social workers, social work management and policy makers is so great that the topic is one which cries out for careful investigation and appraisal. But beyond these policy issues the use of social work contracts provides an ideal setting for observing the difficulties of securing "agreement" in a structured situation of unequal power and, by the same token, a rare insight into the modalities of a new form of social control.[3]

There is also an important, if sometimes elusive, legal side to these developments. Because the use of social work contracts involves the fusion of "juridical" and "disciplinary" forms of power,[4] probably the least helpful question to ask is — are these really "legal" contracts? Social work contracts are unlikely to be legally binding because there is no "intention to create legal relations" in addition to other legal defects; in any case they normally only reinforce already existing legal obligations. Nevertheless some discussions in the social work literature do look to the rules of contract law to provide principled guidance to social workers in relation to problems of inequality, duress or undue influence. They seek to establish if "consideration" is required and whether the inclusion of standard non-negotiable terms is acceptable.[5] Rather than these questionable analogies, however, it may be that social workers have more to learn from sociological studies of the way legal contracts *are actually used*, especially as these investigations demonstrate the extent to which the success of contractual agreements depends on the existence of further reasons for the parties to wish to continue their relationship.[6] Other valuable enquiries would include the public law status of these ostensibly private legal forms, as well as the question of how far the social work profession may have adopted and adapted the language of contract as a form of *self-protection* against legal review. However, as this is an introductory paper, these matters will not be enforced here. I propose instead to try to show some of the interest and perhaps also the significance of the topic of social work contracts by describing the background and context of their use and reporting on a pilot study which I carried out into the attitudes of social workers and others to the use of this technique.

What are social work contracts? As will be seen, the term covers a promiscuous variety of techniques for achieving agreement, setting conditions, co-ordinating arrangements, identifying tasks and so on. Moreover, contracts range from complex written forms to mere oral agreements. The only common denominator — if there is one — is that social work contracts identify an agreement (on its face voluntary) between social workers and others concerning the content of social work. Even this definition fits some types of social work contracts better than others. One of the first necessities of research in this area is the formulation of a satisfactory typology of social work contracts.

Contracts similar to those used in social work are increasingly becoming the stock-in-trade of others involved in welfare and educational interventions. Thus marriage counsellors arrange for unhappy spouses to enter into contracts to encourage mutual satisfaction, divorce mediators use contracts to establish the outcome of their conciliation work and children excluded from school are issued with contract forms which they must use to write acknowledgement of past misdeeds and warrants of future good behaviour before they gain re-entry to school. Contracts are also utilized as part of the increasing vogue for mediation and conciliation, as well as by professions drawing on psychology and psychiatry. Welfare contracts are therefore not unique to social work. Nor are they necessarily borrowed directly from the lawyer's use of contract. Putting the responsibility on people to comply with their own volunteered agreements is a widespread feature of institutional, business and, of course, family life. Nonetheless there seems to be enough in common in this special area of the use of contrasts for a study of social work contracts in their own right.

Endnotes

1. Although I have used the term contracts without quotation marks throughout this paper, it will be clear from the argument that this is not because I subscribe to the view that they are binding legal contracts.

---

† Nelken, David, "The Use of 'Contracts' as a Social Work Technique" (1987), 40 *Current Legal Problems* at 207–08. Reprinted by permission of Oxford University Press.

2.   Although I have not yet been able to carry out systematic comparative research I have information that social work contracts are used extensively throughout Britain as well as in the United States, Scandinavia and France.
3.   See D. Nelken, "Social Work Contracts and Social Control" in R. Mathews, ed., *Reconstructing Criminal Justice* (Forthcoming).
4.   M. Foucault, *Discipline and Punish* (1977); J. Donzelot, *The Policing of Families* (1979).

5.   J. Corden, "Contracts in Social Work Places" (1980), 10 *British Journal of Social Work* 143–61.
6.   S. MacAulay, "Non-Contractual Relations in Business: A Preliminary Study" (1963), 28 *Am. Soc. Rev.* 55–67; H. Beale and T. Dugdale, "Contracts between Businessmen: Planning and the use of Contractual Remedies" (1975), 2 *Brit. J. Law and Soc.* 45–60.

Bargaining in the Shadow of the Law: The Case of Divorce[†]

R.H. Mnookin

I wish to suggest a new way of thinking about the role of law at the time of divorce. It is concerned primarily with the impact of the legal system on negotiations and bargaining that occurs *outside* of court. Rather than regard order as imposed from above, I see the primary function of contemporary divorce law as providing a framework for divorcing couples themselves to determine their respective rights and responsibilities after dissolution. This process, by which parties to a marriage are empowered to create their own legally enforceable commitments, I shall call "*private ordering.*"[1]

Available evidence concerning how divorce proceedings actually work suggests that a re-examination from the perspective of private ordering is long overdue. "Typically the parties do not go to court at all until they have worked matters out and are ready for the rubber stamp."[2] Both in the United States and England the overwhelming majority of divorcing couples resolve or settle the distributional questions concerning marital property, alimony, child support, and custody without bringing any contested issue to the court for adjudication.[3]

This new perspective and the use of the term "private ordering" is not meant to suggest an absence of important social interests in how this process works, or in the fairness of the outcomes. The implicit policy questions are ones of emphasis and degree: to what extent should law permit and encourage divorcing couples to work out their own arrangements? Within what limits should parties be empowered to make their own law that they bring into existence by their agreement? What procedural or substantive safeguards are necessary because of various social interests? Nor is this new perspective meant to imply that the law and the legal system are unimportant. For divorcing spouses and their children, family law is inescapably relevant. The legal system affects *when* a divorce may occur; *how* a divorce must be procured; and *what happens* as a

consequence of divorce. The primary purpose of this paper is to develop a framework for thinking about how the legal rules and procedures used in court for adjudicating disputes affect the bargaining process that occurs between divorcing couples *outside* the courtroom.

Before setting out together, let me provide you with a road map of where we are going. Our first stop involves an examination of the degree to which the law today authorises private ordering at the time of divorce. In other words, to what extent can a divorcing couple create their own legally enforceable commitments? In this context, I will also explain why I think the legal system should provide divorcing couples broad power through agreement to resolve the various questions that arise.

Secondly, against this background, I present a simple bargaining model to suggest how the legal system affects negotiations between spouses and their representatives at the time of divorce.

Finally, I will apply this framework to several issues that have dominated much of the academic discussion concerning family law during recent years:

1.   The advantages and disadvantages of discretion conferring legal standards for child custody;
2.   Goldstein, Freud and Solnit's proposed standard for visitation;
3.   The role of lawyers in the divorce process; and
4.   The role of courts in "undisputed" divorces.

Let us now turn to the question of the extent to which the law today sanctions private ordering. At the outset it is important to recall that a legal system might allow varying degrees of private ordering upon the dissolution of marriage. Until the no-fault revolution, the law concerning divorce did reflect a highly regulatory model that attempted to restrict private ordering. Couples had no for-

†   Mnookin, Robert H., "Bargaining in the Shadow of the Law: The Case of Divorce" (1979), 32 *Current Legal Problems* at 65–70, 93–95, 96–102. Reprinted by permission of Oxford University Press.

mal power to end their marriage by mutual agreement. Divorce was granted only after an official inquiry by a judge, who had to determine whether there were "appropriate grounds," which were themselves very narrowly defined in terms of marital offences. If a divorce were granted, the State asserted broad power to impose distributional consequences, and to have continuing regulatory jurisdiction over the children and their relationship to their parents. Doctrines such as collusion, connivance and condonation were meant to curtail the degree to which parties themselves could through agreement bring about a divorce; and the procedural requirements reflected the view, in R.M. Jackson's words, that both the petitioner and the respondent were "suspicious characters."[4] Obviously, the marital offence regime — even at its most restrictive — could not entirely eliminate collusion. Some divorcing spouses worked things out for themselves and then (with the help of their lawyers) staged a carefully rehearsed and jointly produced play for the court.[5] Nonetheless, the legal system was structured to minimise private ordering.

Dramatic changes in divorce law during the past decade now permit a substantial degree of private ordering. The "no fault revolution" has made the fundamental decision of whether there shall be divorce largely a matter of private concern. Parties to a marriage can now explicitly create circumstances that will allow divorce. Indeed, the reality is that agreement between spouses is not even necessary — either spouse can unilaterally create the grounds for dissolution simply by separation for a sufficient period of time.[6]

What about the parties' power to decide for themselves the consequences of divorce? Here the presence of children makes an important difference. Where the divorcing couple has no children, the law both in England and the United States largely recognises the power of the parties upon separation or divorce to make their own arrangements concerning marital property and alimony.[7] A spousal agreement may be subject to some sort of judicial proceeding — or submission to a Registrar — but on both sides of the Atlantic the official review appears to be largely perfunctory.[8] In some American states, a couple may if they choose make their agreement binding and final — i.e., not subject to later modification by a court after the divorce.[9] In England, strictly speaking, this probably is not possible.[10] Nonetheless, English courts are very slow after a divorce is granted to modify an agreement intended to be binding or an order issued with the consent of the parties.[11]

Where there are minor children, existing law imposes substantial doctrinal constraints. For those allocational decisions that directly affect children — that is, child support, custody and visitation — parents lack the formal power "to make their own law." The court, exercising the state's *parens patrine* power, is said to have responsibility to determine who should have custody and on what con-

ditions. Private agreements concerning these matters are possible, and common, but these agreements cannot bind the court which is said to have an independent responsibility for determining what arrangements best serve the child's welfare.[12] Thus, the court has the power to reject a parental agreement, and order some other level of child support or some other custodial arrangement, if that is thought more desirable.[13] Moreover, even if the parties' initial agreement is accepted by the court, the parties entirely lack the power to provide for finality. A court may at any time during the child's minority reopen and modify the initial decree in light of any subsequent change in circumstances.[14] The parties entirely lack the power to deprive the court of this jurisdiction.

These limitations on parental power reflect a variety of policy concerns. They may acknowledge the fact that the child, although profoundly affected by the bargain, is not normally a meaningful participant in the negotiating process. A parental agreement concerning custody, visitation or support may not reflect the child's interests but instead the interests of the parents. A parent eager to escape an unhappy marriage may agree to custodial arrangements and levels of support that are less advantageous to the child than some feasible alternative. Judicial scrutiny and continual supervision of the elements of the separation agreement concerning the child might therefore be seen as a safeguard of the child's interests.

Available evidence concerning how the legal system in fact processes undisputed divorce cases involving minor children suggests that in fact parents have very broad powers to make their own deals. Typically separation agreements are rubber stamped even in cases involving children. A study of custody here in England suggests, for example, that courts rarely set aside an arrangement acceptable to the parents.[15] Anecdotal evidence in America suggests that the same is true in the U.S.

That the legal system in fact gives parents broad discretion is less than surprising when one considers a number of factors. First, getting information is difficult when there is no dispute. There are usually very limited resources for a thorough or an independent investigation of the family's circumstances. Secondly, the applicable legal standards are extremely vague and give registrars or judges very little guidance as to what circumstances justify overriding a parental decision.[16] Finally, there are obvious limitations on a court's practical power to control parental behaviour once they leave the courtroom. For all these reasons, it is not surprising that most courts behave as if their function in the divorce process is dispute settlement. Where there is no dispute, busy judges or registrars are typically quite willing to rubber stamp a private agreement, thus conserving resources for disputed cases.

Before proceeding, I should make clear the reasons I think law should give divorcing spouses broad powers to make their own agreement. When a couple can resolve distributional consequences of divorce without resort to court for adjudication, there are obvious and substantial savings. The cost of litigation, both private and public, is minimised. The pain of an adversarial proceeding is avoided. Recent findings from psychological studies suggest the desirability from a child's perspective in having parents agree on custodial arrangements. Moreover, through a negotiated agreement the parties can often avoid the risks and uncertainties of litigation which sometimes involve all or nothing consequences. Given the substantial delays that often characterise contested judicial proceedings, an agreement can often provide significant time-savings for the parties, thus allowing the spouses to proceed with their lives. Finally, a solution agreed to by the parties seems more likely to be consistent with their own preferences and accepted by them over time than a result that is simply imposed by a court.

For divorces where there are no minor children, divorcing couples should have very broad powers to make their own arrangements; significant limitations are inconsistent with the premises of no fault divorce. After all, who can better evaluate the comparative advantages of alternative arrangements than the parties themselves? In John Stuart Mill's words, each spouse "is the person most interested in his own well-being...with respect to his own feelings and circumstances, the most ordinary man or woman has means of knowledge immeasurably surpassing those that can be possessed by anyone else."[17] Courts should not, of course, enforce agreements that reflect fraud or overreaching. Nor do I wish to minimise the importance of appropriate standards for alimony and marital property for, in ways that I will describe shortly, these standards very much affect negotiated outcomes. Nonetheless, against a backdrop of fair standards, parties should be encouraged to settle for themselves these economic issues. The state should provide an efficient and fair mechanism for enforcing such agreements, and for settling disputes when the parties are unable to agree.

Where there are minor children, the state obviously has broader interests than simply dispute settlement. The state also has a responsibility for *child protection*. To acknowledge this responsibility, however, is not to define its limits. Indeed the critical questions concern the proper scope of the child protection function at the time of divorce, and the mechanisms that best achieve this goal.

For reasons I have spelled out at length elsewhere,[18] the actual determination of what is in fact in a child's best interest is ordinarily quite indeterminate: it requires predictions beyond the capacity of the behavioural sciences. It also involves the imposition of values about which there appears to be little consensus in our societies today. Thus the fundamental question is: who decides on behalf of the child? To what extent should the child's parents be given the freedom to decide between themselves how responsibility for their children is to be allocated following di-

vorce? I believe divorcing parents should be given considerable freedom to decide custody matters — subject only to the same minimum standards for child protection that the State imposes on *all* families with respect to neglect and abuse. A negotiated resolution is desirable from the child's perspective for several reasons. Since a child's social and psychological relationships with *both* parents ordinarily continue after the divorce, a process that leads to agreement between the parents is preferable to one that necessarily has a winner and a loser. A child's future relationship with each of his parents may be better maintained and his existing relationship less damaged by a negotiated settlement than by one imposed by a court after an adversarial proceeding. Moreover, the parents will know more about the child than the judge, since they have better access to information about the child's circumstances and desires. Indeed, given the basic indeterminacy of anyone knowing what is best for the child, having a privately negotiated solution by those who will be responsible for care after the divorce seems much more likely to match the parents' capacities and desires with the child's needs. These advantages suggest that courts should not second-guess parental agreements unless judicial intervention is required by the strict child-protection standard implicit in neglect laws.

If parents have the authority to decide, there can be no doubt that some parents will make mistakes. But so do judges. Parents (not the state) are primarily responsible for their children after divorce. Part of this responsibility involves attempting, themselves, to agree upon some allocation of responsibilities in the future. This is not to suggest that the State does not have an important responsibility to inform parents concerning the child's needs during and after divorce; nor does it mean that the State does not have an important interest in facilitating parental agreement. Nevertheless, the law in action (which acknowledges substantial parental power) strikes me as preferable to existing doctrine (which imposes substantial restrictions on parental power to decide for themselves).

Everyone may not share these premises concerning the desirability of private ordering. But no matter what one's thinking on these questions, the fact that most divorcing couples do not bring disputes to court for adjudication suggests the appropriateness of analysing how the legal system affects the bargaining behaviour of divorcing couples.

．．．．

An Evaluation of the Lawyer's Role

If one accepts the proposition that the primary function of the legal system should be to facilitate private ordering and dispute resolution, then several important questions come into sharp focus. To what extent does the participation of lawyers facilitate dispute resolution? Are there alternative procedures (in which lawyers play a lesser role) that are less costly and more fair? Many observers are very critical of the way some lawyers behave in divorce negotiations. Lawyers may "heat up" the process, make negotiations more adversarial and painful than they would otherwise be, and make it more difficult and costly for the spouses to reach agreement. Indeed, it may well be that lawyers more than lay people are prepared to adopt negotiating strategies involving threats, and the strategic misrepresentation of their client's true preferences in order to reach a more favourable settlement for the client. Ivan Illich has recently suggested that a broad range of illnesses are in fact "iatrogenic,"[19] i.e., induced and created by medical treatment and the health industry. The same charge might be laid on the legal profession. The participation of lawyers in the divorce process may on balance lead to more disputes and higher costs without improving the fairness of the outcomes.

There are also arguments that lawyers facilitate dispute settlement. The participation of lawyers may make negotiations more rational, may minimise the number of disputes, may increase the opportunities for resolution out of court, and may insure that the outcomes reflect the applicable legal norms. Professor Eisenberg has suggested how a pair of lawyers — each acting for his client — may make the process of negotiation in dispute settlement very much like adjudication, i.e., a process where "rules, precedents, and reasoned elaboration — may be expanded to determine outcome..."[20] Where each spouse has a lawyer, the lawyers

> are likely to find themselves allied with each other as well as with the disputants, because of their relative emotional detachment, their interest in resolving the dispute, and, in some cases, their shared professional values. Each therefore tends to take on a Janus-like role, facing the other as an advocate of that which is reasonable in the other's position.... Because a lawyer is both a personal advisor and a technical expert, each actor-disputant is likely to accept a settlement his lawyer recommends. Because of their training and the fact that typically they become involved only when formal litigation is contemplated, lawyers are likely to negotiate on the basis of *legal* principles, rules, and precedents. When these two elements are combined, the result is that paired legal affiliates typically function as a coupled unit which is strikingly similar to a formal adjudicative unit in terms of both input and output. Indeed, in terms of sheer number of dispute-settlements effected, the most significant legal dispute-settlement institution is typically not the bench, but the bar.[21]

The perspective of private ordering exposes these various roles and raises the obvious question: what in fact do lawyers do in the process? Lawyers may serve various functions, and yet we know very little about how in fact lawyers behave. Obviously, lawyers are not of all one piece. Their styles differ. Some lawyers may prefer (and be more effective at) certain roles. Some lawyers are known within the profession as negotiators who strive to find middle ground acceptable to both sides; others are fighters, who love the courtroom battle. Research could usefully explore how much specialisation there is, and the extent to which clients (when they are choosing a lawyer at the time of divorce) have any notion at all of their lawyers' skills or tastes for these various roles. More generally, systematic empirical research might illustrate how often (and in what circumstances) lawyers facilitate dispute settlement at the time of divorce, and how often (and in what circumstances) they hurt.

This framework also suggests how timely it is to re-examine the question of why the legal profession should have a monopoly with respect to these roles, and the extent to which it does in fact have such a monopoly. How well are lawyers trained to perform these various roles? Other professionals or para-professionals might serve some of these functions as well as lawyers at a substantially lower cost. This is most obviously the case where there is no dispute, and the attorney's role is essentially that of "clerk." A recent study in Connecticut suggests that in most uncontested divorces, clients believe their lawyer did no more than fill out the necessary forms (a complaint, a claim for a hearing, and a decree) and made an appearance at a *pro forma* hearing. Moreover, the same study suggests that because the forms and procedures are complicated, do-it-yourself "divorce dissolution kits" (without additional lay assistance) pose rather little threat to the monopoly of the organised bar.[22] Most people lack the time, confidence, or ability to navigate through the legal shoals themselves — even where they have no dispute with their spouse. This suggests that procedural reform aimed at simplifying the procedure for uncontested divorce could substantially reduce transaction costs in many cases.

· · · ·

THE ROLE OF COURTS

Let us consider the role of courts in the divorce process from the perspective of private ordering. Obviously, the judicial system provides a mechanism for dispute settlement through adjudication where the parties have not been able to agree. But courts also play a role in a much larger number of cases than those where the dispute is adjudicated. Because each party knows the other can invoke the court's power to settle their differences, the presence of the judiciary exerts considerable pressure towards settlement. Indeed, anecdotal evidence suggests that courts often put pressure on the parties in disputed cases "to settle their own differences" through private negotiations, thus avoiding the need for adjudication.

One striking feature of the present day system, however, is the requirement that undisputed cases pass through court. With a narrow exception recently enacted in California, every American state requires a judicial proceeding to secure a divorce in all cases. From a historical perspective, this requirement is not surprising: it represented a regulatory mechanism to ensure that divorces were only granted in narrowly defined circumstances. Before the no-fault revolution, dispute settlement was not the primary function of divorce proceedings.

The no-fault revolution has now empowered either spouse unilaterally to create the circumstances for divorce. The state no longer purports to have an interest preventing re-marriage where either spouse wants to dissolve an earlier marriage. Ironically, however, the shell of the same administrative and regulatory mechanisms has been preserved. Indeed, this analysis suggests a policy question of substantial importance: where there is no dispute between the divorcing spouses concerning the allocation implications of their divorce, why should a judicial proceeding be required? Absent a dispute, why should a court have any role? Why require a costly legal transaction in court when the questions can be resolved by negotiations?

It would not be difficult to imagine the elimination of a judicial proceeding in undisputed divorce cases. Getting married obviously does not require judicial proceedings. Why should getting a divorce?[23] The requirement of a judicial proceeding probably imposes significant transaction costs, both public and private. Because even uncontested divorces must go through court, parties may end up hiring a lawyer, even where the lawyer's function is basically that of a clerk. An appearance by a lawyer in court takes time — time for which the parties are charged. Moreover a judicial proceeding requires the use of judicial resources as well as the time of the parties themselves. Some countries have largely eliminated the requirement that undisputed divorces go through court; it certainly seems timely to examine the justifications for the requirement, and to ask whether there might not be alternatives that are preferable which cost less.

While the analysis that follows is necessarily preliminary, it is useful to identify and examine four arguments in defence of a judicial proceeding, in uncontested divorce cases.

Ceremonial Function

A judicial proceeding might be thought to serve a ceremonial function that re-confirms, both for the divorcing parties and the general public, the seriousness with which the state takes marriage and divorce. Rituals are important, and the court proceeding can be seen as a socially imposed divorce ritual. But as a ritual, the court proceeding for uncontested divorces, seems peculiar. The marriage ceremony itself is, after all, extremely simple, and does not require lawyers and a judge. Moreover, in most states, the parties themselves are not usually required to appear in court in order to procure a divorce. Their lawyers, instead, can appear for them. If the ritual were for the benefit of the parties, presumably their presence would be required. In all events, one can ask how well the existing requirement serves the ceremonial function? Is the purpose of the requirement ceremonial? Or is it more like a civil fine, imposed on a divorcing couple; a fine payable not to the treasury but to the divorce bar?

Review Ensures Fair Outcomes:
Fairness Between the Spouses

The requirement of judicial approval of post-marital agreements might be justified on the ground that the state has an interest in ensuring that the results of the bargaining process are fair, as between the spouses. A judicial proceeding might protect people from their own ignorance, and might also be thought to prevent unfair results arising from unequal bargaining capacity between the spouses. These arguments have a plausible air, but the reality of the present day system might suggest that they mean very little in practice. Courts typically rubber stamp an agreement reached between the parties. Moreover, there are reasons to doubt that the requirement of judicial review is very often necessary for these purposes. there may well be cases where one spouse (presumably the husband) is highly sophisticated in business matters, while the other spouse (the wife) is an innocent lamb being led to the slaughter. But typically married couples generally have similar educational and cultural backgrounds. Moreover, most individuals perceive very well their own financial interests and needs at the time of divorce.

If there are systematic biases in the process, a more appropriate safeguard would be to change the *substantive standards* concerning who gets what. For example, if it is thought that husbands systematically provide their wives with an insufficient share of the family's assets, or with inadequate alimony, after marriages of long duration where the wife has not worked, the *legal standards* can be changed to provide greater claims for the wife. Moreover, procedural mechanisms can then be developed that require review and a hearing only in those cases where the spousal agreement falls outside the norm (e.g., where marital property was divided very unequally, or where alimony claims were being waived). In practice today, I suspect judges or registrars attempt to identify such cases for intensive examination. At the present time, however, cases falling within the normal range must also pass through a judicial proceeding, with its attendant costs. A system where the state defines reasonable norms, and then permits couples to reach agreement outside the norms provided there were additional procedural safeguards, would seem both more effective and less costly.

Effect on Out-of-Court Settlements

It might be though that the requirement that undisputed cases go to court, improves the private settlement process outside of court. Knowing that they will have to display their agreement to a judge, the parties (and their attorneys) may deal with each other in a fairer way and be more likely to reach an agreement reflecting the appropriate social norms. Behavioural scientists have suggested that the presence of an "audience" can affect bargaining.[24] With respect to out-of-court negotiations, the judge represents both an "actual" audience and "abstract" audience. He is an actual audience in that parties know that eventually they may have to explain their agreement to a judge. This may mitigate extreme claims. The judge also represents an abstract audience as well, which symbolically represents the social interests in the child and various notions of honour, reputation, and history.

It is extremely difficult to evaluate this argument, and to know how the requirement of judicial proceedings in undisputed cases affects negotiations in such cases. A requirement that disputed cases alone would go before a court might be sufficient to bring the "audience" benefits to the process of negotiation. Moreover, it is possible that the requirement of judicial approval makes dispute settlement more not less difficult. For one thing, the requirement probably means that lawyers are more often involved in the process than would otherwise be the case. As earlier noted, it at least seems an open question whether having lawyers in the process facilitates dispute resolution in those case where the parties might otherwise reach agreement anyway. Moreover, there is always the possibility that in the occasional case where the judge does upset the agreement reached by the parties, the eventual outcome may on balance be no more desirable (or even less desirable) than would otherwise be the case.

Child Protection

Where a divorcing couple has minor children, the state has an important interest in child protection. The requirement of court review of private agreements relating to custody or child support might be justified on this ground. For one thing, from the child's perspective, the quality of negotiated agreements may be improved. Some parents might otherwise engage in divorce bargaining on the basis of preferences that reflected narrowly selfish interests, rather than concern for the child. The review requirement might serve as an important reminder to the parents of the social concern for their children, and may somehow con-

strain otherwise selfish behaviour. Even a selfish spouse may be more concerned about his reputation as a parent if there is some sort of public process. Especially in cases where there are children, the judge may represent an important "audience" whose unseen presence affects bargaining behaviour. Finally, although most parental agreements are approved after only superficial examination by the judge, some agreements are in fact disapproved: to the extent courts succeed in identifying arrangements that are disadvantageous to a child in a particular case and in imposing some better alternative, the child's welfare is obviously improved.

A variety of arguments can be made on the other side, however. For one thing, what evidence we have suggests that in operation courts rarely overturn parental agreements. Given the resources that are devoted to this task there is little reason to believe that the process today in fact operates as much of a safeguard where there is no parental dispute. Moreover, the process itself probably imposes not insubstantial transaction costs — both public (in terms of traditional resources expended) and private (in terms of the cost to the parties, the legal fees and time). These extra transaction costs might otherwise enure (at least in part) to the benefit of the children.

There are also reasons to think that, in the vast majority of cases, this review may well be unnecessary. For one thing, the custodial spouse will typically perceive very clearly the economic consequences for the child of any support arrangement that he or she agrees to. There is after all, considerable joint consumption between the custodial parent and the child. Moreover, child support payments (like alimony and the earnings of the custodial spouse) typically go into a single economic pot that supports both the custodial parent and the child. In other words, the economic interests of the child and the economic interests of the custodial parent substantially coincide.

A second safeguard — banal as it sounds — is that most parents care deeply for their children. No court proceeding can of course require parents to love their children, and prevent selfish calculation by a divorcing parent. Nevertheless, to the extent that divorcing parents do love their children there is every reason to think that they will in fact themselves be very concerned with making arrangements that are beneficial to the child. Perhaps there are good reasons not to trust parents with child-rearing responsibilities on or after divorce. That was certainly the implicit attitude during the heyday of the marital offence regime. But is it really appropriate today? Indeed, it is interesting to compare the review requirements imposed by law if the child's family is disrupted by divorce with the review requirements imposed if the family is disrupted by the death of one of the parents. American law permits a parent to disinherit his minor children. A decedent cannot, however, disinherit his spouse and in effect present day law trusts the surviving parent with child-rearing responsibility in the light of existing economic resources. With respect to any inheritance of any surviving spouse, there is no supervision imposed by operation of law on how he or she spends the inheritance, and there is no examination of what portion is spent on the child. Instead, the surviving parent is trusted to look after the child, subject of course to the minimum limitations imposed by the child neglect laws which apply to all parents.

The review requirement may, ironically, send an inappropriate set of signals to parents at the time of divorce: it may suggest to them that because of the divorce they are no longer trusted to be adequate parents, and that the state will now assume special responsibility for their children. Indeed, court review might conceivably induce more selfish behaviour on the part of parents who take the attitude that it is the court's job, not their own responsibility, to be concerned with the interests of their children. In fact, the state does not and cannot assume a broad role for child-rearing responsibility after divorce.

CONCLUSION

Viewing the process of dissolution from the perspective of private ordering does not make previously intractable family law problems disappear. If anything, the world seems even more complex, for analysis involves the examination of the effects of alternative rules and procedures on informal and formal bargaining outside of court about which we have little understanding. There is little existing theory to inform the enquiry. There now exists no bargaining theory that can yield accurate predictions of the expected outcomes, assuming different legal rules where rational self-interested parties are negotiating over money issues. Where there are minor children involved, the parents are not simply bargaining over money; they also must be necessarily concerned with allocating child-rearing responsibilities in the future. We have tried to suggest how the variability of parental preferences with respect to custody makes the task of analysing bargaining especially difficult. Furthermore, rational bargaining may be in short supply when a family is in the process of breaking up. Some divorcing spouses seem motivated by spite or envy, more than a careful assessment of self-interest in the light of available alternatives. Where bargaining is motivated by emotional drives, the assessment of the effects of alternative legal rules seems even more speculative. Finally, it must sadly be reported that there has been little empirical work which has involved the systematic observation of how the process of private ordering in fact works today.

Given the absence of powerful theory or systematic data, this essay makes no claims at being definitive. It instead has suggested a theoretical perspective that permits a broader analysis of the probable consequences of family law rules and procedures. It also more sharply exposes a set of questions of enormous social importance. If one accepts the proposition that disputes settlement should be the primary goal of the legal system, the analysis does not imply that the state should simply withdraw all resources from the process, and leave it to the divorcing spouses to work things out on their own, unassisted by any professional help. Instead, this inquiry should underline the desirability of learning more about how alternative procedural mechanisms might facilitate dispute resolution during a typically difficult and painful time in the lives of parents and children alike.

The perspective certainly has implications far broader than family law. In a wide variety of contexts, individuals bargain in the shadow of the law. Few automobile accident claims are ever tried; most are settled out of court. Criminal prosecutions are typically resolved by a plea bargain, not an adjudication of guilt. Most administrative proceedings result in consent agreements not trials. In each of these contexts, the preferences of the parties, the entitlements created by law, transaction costs, and attitudes towards risk, will presumably substantially affect the negotiated outcomes. Indeed, I hope this essay will stimulate and encourage further work by others in a variety of contexts. Theoretical and empirical research concerning how people bargain in the shadow of law should provide us with a richer understanding of how the legal system affects behaviour, and allow a better appraisal of the consequences of reform proposals.

Endnotes

1. According to Professor Lon Fuller "A central purpose of law is to furnish base lines for human interaction." See L. Fuller, "Human Interaction and the Law" (1970), *The American Journal of Jurisprudence* 1 at 24.
2. Friedman and Percival, "A Tale of Two courts: Litigation in Alameda and San Benito Counties" (1970), 10 *Law and Society Review* at 267, 270.
3. There are no data that permit precise estimates on a national basis. Nonetheless, available evidence suggests that only a very small percentage of cases are contested in court. See Friedman and Percival, *supra* note 3. John Eekelaar found that of divorces when there were minor children, only 6.9 per cent, were contested (J. Eekelaar and E. Clive, *Custody After Divorce: The Disposition of Custody in Divorce Cases in Great Britain*, Family Law Studies No. 1, Centre for Socio-Legal Studies, Wolfson College, Oxford; Baker, Eekelaar, Gibson and Raikes, *The Matrimonial Jurisdiction of Registrars*, Family Law Studies No. 2, Centre for Socio-Legal Studies, Wolfson College, Oxford). It has been estimated that, in 1974, under one-third of divorces in England involved a request for an order for financial provision. Many of these were not disputed. See J. Eekelaar, *Family Law and Social Policy* (1977), p. 303, n. 95.
4. R.M. Jackson, *The Machinery of Justice*, 7th ed. (1974), 54.
5. See O.R. McGregor, *Divorce in England: A Centenary Study* (1957), 134–36; H. O'Gorman, *Lawyers and Matrimonial Cases: A Study of Informal Pressures in Private Professional Practice* (1963).
6. See *Matrimonial Causes Act* 1973, s. 1(1). For a summary of the law in American states, see Freed, "Grounds for Divorce in the American Jurisdiction" (1973), 8 *Fam. L.Q.* 401. It now appears that only three states in America, Illinois, Pennsylvania, and South Dakota retain ex-

clusively fault grounds for divorce. Project, "The Unauthorised Practice of Law and *Pro Se* Divorce: An Empirical Analysis" (1976), 86 *Yale L.J.* 104, 105, n. 1.

7. See J.G. Miller, *Family Property and Financial Provision* (1974), 144–57; *Uniform Marriage and Divorce Act*, 306.

8. See Foote, Levy and Sander, *Cases and materials on Family Law* (1976), 904: ("Only rarely do courts interfere with the agreement worked out by the parties."). W. Baker, J. Eekelaar and C. Gilson, *The Matrimonial Jurisdiction of Registrars, op. cit., supra,* at 58, 59, suggesting that commonly "it is the practice in consent applications not to require any information in addition to that presented to the court, even if the file contains no information at all." The report goes on to say that commonly registrars "would investigate only if something was obviously wrong," at least if there were no children. For a discussion of a power of English courts to modify or alter a spousal agreement, see *Rayden on Divorce,* 12th ed., vol. 1, (1974), Chap. 22b, 846–56.

9. See e.g., *California Civil Code* 4811 (b) (West Supp. 1978).

10. See *Matrimonial Causes Act,* 1973, s. 34, s. 35.

11. In England, divorcing spouses lack the power by agreement to oust the court's jurisdiction in maintenance matters; the court always has jurisdiction to modify an agreement in light of changed circumstances. *Matrimonial Causes Act,* 1973, ss. 34, 35. In practice, however, after the divorce has been granted, courts are slow to vary the parties' prior agreement, especially ones originally entered into with legal advice. *Wright v. Wright,* [1970] 1 W.L.R. 1219; [1970] 3 All E.R. 209. When issuing its own orders concerning maintenance, a court has discretion to depart from any agreement the parties may have come to before the proceedings. *Matrimonial Causes Act,* 1973, ss. 23–25. But a recent decision emphasises the deference owed by the court to arms length agreements negotiated with legal advice. In *Dean v. Dean,* [1978] 3 All E.R. 758, 767, the court said that in exercising its duties under the *Matrimonial Causes Act,* a court "at the same time...owes a duty to uphold agreements validly arrived at and which are not on the fact of them, or in fact, against public policy. In general terms also, it is wrong for the court to stir up problems with parties who have come to an agreement." After a court issues an order, even one made by consent of the parties (*Matrimonial Causes Act* of 1973, s. 31), the court is free later to modify the original order. But consent orders are not readily modified later by courts, "since to do so might seriously undermine the value of such orders and so discourage parties from agreeing to them." *B. (G.C.) v. B. (B.A.),* [1970] 1 All E.R. 913, 917 (Ormrod J.). Finally, the House of Lords recently made clear that a court may by order "achieve finality" at the time of divorce if the court thought it appropriate, practical and just.

Minton v. Minton, The Times, November 23, 1978 (H.L.). Lord Scar-

man interpreted s. 23(1) of the *Matrimonial Causes Act,* 1973 as reflecting the principle of "the clean break." An object of the modern law was to encourage each [spouse] to put the past behind them and begin a new life which was not overshadowed by the relationship which had broken down. It would be inconsistent with that principle if the court could not make, as between the spouses, a genuinely final order unless it was prepared to dismiss the application.

12. See *Matrimonial Causes Act,* 1973, s. 41(1) which requires a court to review the arrangements for the children before entering decree. See also ss. 23, 25(1), 25(2), 42(1); *Guardianship of Minors Act,* 1971, s. 1; *Uniform Marriage and Divorce Act,* s. 306(f).

13. See e.g., *California Civil Code* 4811(a) (West Supp. 1978); *Daily v. Daily,* 175 Ark. 161, 164, 298 S.W. 1012, 1013 (1927).

14. *Matrimonial Causes Act,* 1973, ss. 31, 35(2)(b); *Guardianship of Minors Act,* s. 9(4). See *Re F. (W.) (an Infant),* [1969] 2 Ch. 269; [1969] 3 All E.R. 595. See *Uniform Marriage and Divorce Act,* s. 306(f).

15. With respect to child custody matters John Eekelaar found that in uncontested cases, the court adjourned for further information or negotiation in less than 10 per cent of cases; a welfare report was available in only 8.2 per cent of uncontested cases; and that the courts changed the child's residential status quo in only 0.6 per cent of the uncontested cases. Eekelaar and Clive, *supra* at 66, 67.

16. For a general discussion of the indeterminacy of the dominant standards in custody cases, see Mnookin, "Child Custody Adjudication: Judicial Functions in the Face of Indeterminacy" in *Law and Contemporary Problems,* vol. 29(2), 226.

17. *On Liberty,* 133 (Everyman edition).

18. See Mnookin, *supra,* n. 17.

19. See I. Illich, *Medical Nemesis* (1976).

20. Eisenberg, "Private Ordering Through Negotiation: Dispute Settlement and Rule-Making" (1976), 87 *Harv. L.R.* 637, 638.

21. *Ibid.* at 664–65.

22. Project, "The Unauthorised Practice of Law and *Pro Se* Divorce: An Empirical Analysis" (1976), 86 *Yale L.J.* 104.

23. The parties might simply be permitted to file with an appropriate state agency a document that automatically leads to a divorce, perhaps after an appropriate waiting period? Any agreement the couple had concerning their respective property rights, or custody issues might be appended. Where there is no dispute over these issues, this agreement would bind the parties, perhaps following review if it involved an arrangement that was very unusual.

24. See J. Rubin and B. Brown, *The Social Psychology of Bargaining and Negotiations* (1975), 43–54.

Notes

1.   In what respects is the trend towards legalization of marriage dissolution described and advocated by Mnookin similar to and/or distinct from the informal contractual use of wife sale described by Hardy and O'Donovan?

2.   Perhaps the most crucial distinction is that in The Mayor of Casterbridge the wife, although consenting, is the object of the transaction, rather than a contracting party in her own right. To what extent does this significant change in the legal status of the wife as a party to the contract alter the appropriateness of contract as a mode of allocating rights and responsibilities on the breakdown of a marriage?

3.   Note: See also Katherine O'Donovan "Wife Sale and Desertion as Alternatives to Judicial Marriage Dissolution" in John Eckelaar and Sanford Katz, eds., *The Resolution of Family Conflict: Comparative Legal Perspectives* (Toronto: Butterworths, 1984).

C. Understanding Legal Repression and Legal Regulation

Democracy and Capitalism[†]
S. Bowles and H. Gintis

POWER may be wielded in numerous ways. Historically, armed force has been a central pillar of power, as liberal theory rightly stresses. But the arsenal of domination goes beyond the gun. Control of the tools with which we produce our livelihood and the words that give our lives and loyalties their meanings have been no less central to the exercise of power.

Debates among Marxian and liberal theorists concerning the roots of domination have tended to adopt an impoverished conception of power. The liberal concern with the despotic state is matched in its narrowness by the Marxian concern with class domination. Each ignores the undeniable insights of the other; both give scant theoretical attention to forms of power that cannot be reduced to either state despotism and class. The most ubiquitous of these excluded forms of power is the domination of women by men.

Equally important, the grand debates between the liberal and Marxian political traditions skirt a central concern of democratic theory, the relationship between power and freedom. Democracy promises the collective accountability of power, but it promises another, more constructive concept as well; namely, the ability of people to effectively carry out their individual and common projects unencumbered by arbitrary constraint. For the liberal, this positive side of power — agency — is rendered minimally, as political liberty and the freedom to contract with whomever one pleases. Both of these liberal forms of freedom represent the absence of constraint rather than personal or collective empowerment. They are, in Isiah Berlin's apt terminology, "negative freedoms." For the classical Marxist, agency is the ability of an emerging class to carry out a historic project dictated by the onward march of the productive forces of society. Neither the liberal nor the Marxian definition encompasses the vision of people and of a people free to be the architects of their own personal and social histories.

We will address the problems raised for democratic theory by these partial conceptions of power in this chapter and in chapter 5, which considers the question of the individual and agency. Here we will develop a conception of power, the structures of social domination, and the resistance to domination capable of understanding the historical dynamics of diverse forms of power — patriarchal, state, class, or other. We will analyze the reproduction of patriarchal domination both as a central issue of democracy in its own right and as an illustration of our approach.

. . . .

The underlying logic of our argument contrasts in two important ways with dominant conceptions in social theory. First, though we affirm that historical change is structured, systematic, and hence understandable in more than simply empirical terms, we reject the notion that either stability or change obeys a single logic, whether of enlightenment, modernization, or the advance of productive capacities. Underlying this denial is our second fundamental commitment, a rejection of the concept of power as unitary; it is the notion that power emanates from a single source in society that provides the bedrock of what might be called the unitary conception of history.

We believe that an alternative conception of power, social structure, and history can make better sense of the historical clash of rights in liberal democratic capitalism and the political nature of the economy. The next two sections develop such a conception of power, in terms of the following five propositions.

First, power is heterogeneous, wielding a variety of weapons, yielding to a host of counterpressures, and obeying no single logic. Here we focus on the distinct forms of domination and solidarity based on class, state, and gender.

Second, power is not an amorphous constraint on action but rather a structure of rules empowering and restraining actors in varying degrees. These distinct sets of rules may be embodied in concrete institutions (for example, the World Bank), in linguistic convention (as in the generic term *man*), in unwritten custom (for example, primogeniture), in legal practice (as in the formal recognition of collective bargaining for wages), and, as we have

---

seen, in more general conceptions of property and personal rights.

Third, the perpetuation of any power structure is generally problematic. Further, a structure of power is secured or toppled not only by history-making collective struggles, but more prosaically by a complex society-wide web of everyday individual action and compliance.

Fourth, distinct structures of power — be they the liberal democratic state, the patriarchal family, the capitalist economy, or other — are not merely juxtaposed, they are bound together in a common process of social reproduction. Each one may contribute to the survival of another; or they may foster mutually corrosive and subversive impulses.

And fifth, because people's lives are generally governed by more than one distinct power structure — for example one may be a worker, a wife, and a citizen — we experience power as heterogeneous, and are often able to bring the experiences within one system of power to bear in the pursuit of our projects within another. The clash of rights, based on impressive ability of elites and democratic movements alike to extend rights from one sphere of society to others, is the most important historical example of this transportation of practices from one social realm to another.

We refer to our approach as a historical-structural model of power. As we deny the usefulness of a general theory of power and its reproduction, we will seek to develop these five propositions in a particular historical setting; that is, the liberal capitalist nations of Europe and North America over the past two centuries.

A POLITICAL CONCEPTION OF FAMILY, STATE, AND ECONOMY

It has become fashionable, in reacting against the traditional unitary conception of power, to profess a richly textured alternative notion — an idea of power as likely to be illuminated by the study of words and symbols as of armaments and property. Michel Foucault, for instance, writes:

> The analysis made in terms of power, must not assume that the sovereignty of the state, the form of the law or the overall unity of a domination are given at the outset.... Power is everywhere....

This acute and welcome sensitivity to the ubiquity of power, however, can easily slip into treating power *per se* as domination, and replacing a critique of domination with a diffuse critique of authority of no particular use to democratic social movements. Thus Thomas Wartenberg notes, in a perceptive analysis of Foucault's attempt at deconstructing power, that

at the political level, this problem asserts itself in Foucault's failure to distinguish different types of repressive societies.... Though all social systems do exist by means of a structuring of human beings to meet the needs of that system, we need to have a way to talk about how much pain such structuring inflicts upon the creatures for whom it exists.

We also need, we might add, a way to talk about the *structure* of power in order to assess its *accountability*.

Our conception of power is at once a theory of domination and a theory of structural change flowing from collective resistance to domination. It is at the same time a structural theory and a theory of social action. Marx, in criticizing Ludwig Feuerbach, lamented the fact that materialist thought tended to denigrate action in favor of structure: "Hence it happened that the active side, in contradistinction to materialism, was developed by the idealism." Analogously, structural theories of power often support a conception either of unquestioned, monolithic, uncontested domination or of the mechanistic inevitability of the collapse of domination.[1] The commonplace observation that structures do not reproduce or destroy themselves but are perpetuated or overturned by *what people do* finds no place in most structural theories. The active side of power is more fully developed by theories of choice.

Theories of choice, however — for reasons we will address in the next chapter — generally fail to provide an adequate account of the forms of collective action central to an active and historical conception of power. By developing the relationship between domination and solidarity, we seek to avoid both the individualism of choice theories and the presumption of a pregiven logic of either stability or crisis in structural theories. More positively, we will embrace the fundamental tenet of structural theories — that individual action is highly regulated — in a framework that insists that the historical dynamics of the structures regulating choice are themselves the result, however indirect and unintended, of individual action.

Vertical relationships of superior to subordinate, of employer to worker, of man to woman, of despot to subject, of white to black, provide the raw materials with which people construct the corresponding horizontal structures of social bonding — class consciousness, democratic nationalism, racial unity, and the like. (This rudimentary statement of the conditions of collective action simply generalizes Marx's insight that the structure of exploitation might provide the conditions for the unification of the exploited. We will turn to this issue in some detail in chapter 6.) These structures of social bonding allow people to forge from their individual experiences of oppression (and those of other people) an ensemble of cultural and organizational tools upon which collective action may be based.

The active side of power surely includes the exercise of domination by the powerful and the complicity of the oppressed in their oppression. But it also includes revolutionary collective action: forging communicative and organizational tools of bonding from the cacophony of discourses to which the mosaic of domination gives rise, and putting these tools to use in transforming structures of power. The clash of rights in liberal democratic capitalism, in particular, has seen both the collective action of the dispossessed in pitting personal rights against the privileges of wealth, race, and gender as well as the counterstrategies of the privileged in shoring up patriarchal rights, property rights, and "skin privilege."

Recognition of the heterogeneity of power invites a more searching analysis of the way in which distinct spheres of social life regulate social action in such a manner as to produce systems of domination *and* the possibility of their elimination.

Power is the capacity to render social action effective. It is coextensive with neither the state, nor with physical force, nor with face-to-face command. Power may be exercised through the ability to overcome the resistance of others — as in Max Weber's conception — but it may equally be exercised through the ability to avoid resistance, either through control over which issues become contestable or through influence over others' wants, sentiments, desires, or, more generally, objectives.

. . . .

We focus on three general forms of the asymmetrical exercise of power: domination through the monopoly of the means of coercion, through the exercise of property rights, and through the operation of gender-based privilege. These are certainly not the only forms of domination observed in modern society. Race, ethnicity, religion, language, and region, among others, have served as major bases of social oppression and *loci* of bitter conflict. We focus on these three forms of domination not because other forms are less general, affecting particular liberal democratic capitalist societies in widely differing degrees and in quite distinct manners.[2]

Each of these three forms of domination may be considered to be a means of regulating social action. Thus, in three distinct ways, action is structured by a specific set of rules of the game: (a) the forms and rewards of participation of individuals in a practice are socially regulated; (b) the range of feasible alternative forms of practice are socially delimited; and (c) the potential effectiveness of distinct types of practice are socially mediated.

Endnotes

1. Many who have stressed the centrality of power (Marxists, anarchists, humanists, and others) have courted the danger of ultimately reducing history to the mechanical unfolding of a system of power's pregiven logic. As a result, the prospect of emancipation has often been sought either in the indomitable and freedom-loving human spirit, or in the structurally given inevitability of systemic collapse. However, we see no need to pin our democratic hopes either on human nature or on the accident-prone character of the structures that dominate our lives. The ubiquity of unaccountable power does not imply its invincibility.

2. Our analysis of domination in liberal democratic capitalist societies is situated on a level of abstraction between "capitalist society in general" or "patriarchal society in general" and particular concrete societies such as the United States in the post-World War II era. A more concrete study would require attention to other axes of domination, in the case of the United States, race and imperialism in particular.

The Hegemonic Function of the Law[†]
E.D. Genovese

WHEN Mao Tse-tung told his revolutionary army, "Political power grows out of the barrel of a gun," he stated the obvious, for as Max Weber long before had observed as a matter of scientific detachment, "The decisive means for politics is violence." This viewpoint does not deny an ethical dimension to state power; it asserts that state power, the conquest of which constitutes the object of all serious political struggle, represents an attempt to monopolize and therefore both discipline and legitimize the weapons of violence.

One of the primary functions of the law concerns the means by which command of the gun becomes ethically sanctioned. But if we left it at that, we could never account for the dignity and elan of a legal profession in, say,

† Genovese, Eugene D., "The Hegemonic Function of the Law" in *Roll, Jordon, Roll: The World The Slaves Made* (New York: Pantheon Books, 1974), 25–49. Copyright © 1972, 1974 by Eugene D. Genovese. Reprinted by permission of Pantheon Books, a division of Random House, Inc.

England, that has itself become a social force; much less could we account for the undeniable influence of the law in shaping the class relations of which it is an instrument of domination. Thus, the fashionable relegation of law to the rank of a superstructural and derivative phenomenon obscures the degree of autonomy it creates for itself. In modern societies, at least, the theoretical and moral foundations of the legal order and the actual, specific history of its ideas and institutions influence, step by step, the wider social order and system of class rule, for no class in the modern Western world could rule for long without some ability to present itself as the guardian of the interests and sentiments of those being ruled.

The idea of "hegemony," which since Gramsci has become central to Western Marxism, implies class antagonisms; but it also implies, for a given historical epoch, the ability of a particular class to contain those antagonisms on a terrain in which its legitimacy is not dangerously questioned. As regards the law specifically, note should be taken of the unhappy fate of natural-law doctrines and assorted other excursions into "revolutionary" legal theory. The evolutionary bourgeoisie, during its rise to power in Europe, counterposed natural-law doctrines to feudal theory but once in power rushed to embrace a positive theory of law, even while assimilating natural-law doctrines to a new defense of property. Nor did the experience of the Communist movement in Russia differ after its conquest of power. However much sentimentalists and utopians may rail at the monotonous recurrence of a positive theory of law whenever revolutionaries settle down to rebuild the world they have shattered, any other course would be doomed to failure. Ruling classes differ, and each must rule differently. But all modern ruling classes have much in common in their attitude toward the law, for each must confront the problem of coercion in such a way as to minimize the necessity for its use, and each must disguise the extent to which state power does not so much rest on force as represent its actuality. Even Marxian theory, therefore, must end with the assertion of a positive theory of law and judge natural-law and "higher-law" doctrines to be tactical devices in the extralegal struggle.

In southern slave society, as in other societies, the law, even narrowly defined as a system of institutionalized jurisprudence, constituted a principal vehicle for the hegemony of the ruling class. Since the slaveholders, like other ruling classes, arose and grew in dialectical response to the other classes of society — since they were moulded by white yeomen and black slaves as much as they moulded them — the law cannot be viewed as something passive and reflective, but must be viewed as an active, partially autonomous force, which mediated among the several classes and compelled the rulers to bend to the demands of the ruled. The slaveholders faced an unusually complex problem since their regional power was embedded in a national system in which they had to share power with an antagonistic northern bourgeoisie. A full evaluation of the significance of the law of slavery will have to await an adequate history of the southern legal system in relation to the national; until then a preliminary analysis that risks too much abstraction must serve.

The slaveholders as a socio-economic class shaped the legal system to their interests. But within that socio-economic class — the class as a whole — there were elements competing for power. Within it, a political center arose, consolidated itself, and assumed a commanding position during the 1850s. The most advanced fraction of the slaveholders — those who most clearly perceived the interests and needs of the class as a whole — steadily worked to make their class more conscious of its nature, spirit, and destiny. In the process it created a world-view appropriate to a slaveholders' regime.

For any such political center, the class as a whole must be brought to a higher understanding of itself — transformed from a class-in-itself, reacting to pressures on its objective position, into a class-for-itself, consciously striving to shape the world in its own image. Only possession of public power can discipline a class as a whole, and through it, the other classes of society. The juridical system may become, then, not merely an expression of class interests, nor even merely an expression of the willingness of the rulers to mediate with the ruled; it may become an instrument by which the advanced section of the ruling class imposes its viewpoint upon the class as a whole and the wider society. The law must discipline the ruling class and guide and educate the masses. To accomplish these tasks it must manifest a degree of evenhandedness sufficient to compel social conformity; it must, that is, validate itself ethically in the eyes of the several classes, not just the ruling class. Both criminal and civil law set standards of behavior and sanction norms that extend well beyond strictly legal matters. The death penalty for murder, for example, need not arise from a pragmatic concern with deterrence, and its defenders could justifiably resist psychological arguments. It may arise from the demand for implementation of a certain idea of justice and from the educational requirement to set a firm standard of right and wrong. "The Law," as Gramsci says, "is the repressive and negative aspect of the entire positive civilising activity undertaken by the State."

The law acts hegemonically to assure people that their particular consciences can be subordinated — indeed, morally must be subordinated — to the collective judgment of society. It may compel conformity by granting each individual his right of private judgment, but it must deny him the right to take action based on that judgment when in conflict with the general will. Those who would act on their own judgment as against the collective judgment embodied in the law find themselves pressed from the moral question implicit in any particular law to the moral question of obedience to constituted authority. It appears mere egotism and antisocial behavior to attempt to go outside the law unless one is prepared to attack the entire legal system and therefore the consensual framework of the body politic.

The white South shaped its attitude toward its slaves in this context. With high, malicious humor, William Styron has his fictional T.R. Gray explain to Nat Turner how he, a mere chattel, can be tried for the very human acts of murder and insurrection:

> ...The point is that *you* are *animate* chattel and animate chattel is capable of craft and connivery and wily stealth. You ain't a wagon, Reverend, but chattel that possesses moral choice and spiritual volition. Remember that well. Because that's how come the law provides that animate chattel like you can be tried for a felony, and that's how come you're goin' to be tried next Sattidy.
>
> He paused, then said softly without emotion: "And hung by the neck until dead."

Styron may well have meant to satirize Judge Green of the Tennessee Supreme Court, who declared in 1846, "A slave is not in the condition of a horse." The slave, Judge Green continued, is made in the image of the Creator: "He has mental capacities, and an immortal principle in his nature that constitute him equal to his owner, but for the accidental position in which fortune has placed him.... The laws...cannot extinguish his high born nature, nor deprive him of many rights which are inherent in man." The idea that chattels, as the states usually defined slaves, could have a highborn nature, complete with rights inherent in man, went down hard with those who thought that even the law should obey the rules of logic.

Four years before Judge Green's humane observations, Judge Turley of the same court unwittingly presented the dilemma. "The right to obedience..." he declared in *Jacob (a Slave) v. State*, "in all lawful things...is perfect in the master; and the power to inflict any punishment, not affecting life or limb...is secured to him by law." The slave, being neither a wagon nor a horse, had to be dealt with as a man, but the law dared not address itself direct to the point. Had the law declared the slave a person in a specific class relationship to another person, two unpleasant consequences would have followed. First, the demand that such elementary rights as those of the family be respected would have become irresistible in a commercialized society that required the opposite in order to guarantee an adequate mobility of capital and labor. Second, the slaveholders would have had to surrender in principle, much as they often had to do in practice, their insistence that a slave was morally obligated to function as an extension of his master's will. However much the law generally seeks to adjust conflicting principles in society, in this case it risked undermining the one principle the slaveholders viewed as a *sine qua non*.

Yet, as Styron correctly emphasizes in the words he gives to T.R. Gray, the courts had to recognize the humanity — and therefore the free will — of the slave or be unable to hold him accountable for antisocial acts. Judge Bunning of Georgia plainly said, "It is not true that slaves are only chattels...and therefore, it is not true that it is not possible for them to be prisoners...." He did not tell us how a chattel (a thing) could also be nonchattel in any sense other than an agreed-upon fiction, nor did he wish to explore the question why a fiction should have become necessary. Since much of the law concerns agreed-upon fictions, the judges, as judges, did not have to become nervous about their diverse legal opinions, but as slaveholders, they could not avoid the prospect of disarray being introduced into their social philosophy. Repeatedly, the courts struggled with and tripped over the slave's humanity. Judge Hall of North Carolina, contrary to reason, nature, and the opinion of his fellow judges, could blurt out, *en passant*, "Being slaves, they had no will of their own...." If so, then what of the opinion expressed by the State Supreme Court of Missouri: "The power of the master being limited, his responsibility is proportioned accordingly"?

The high court of South Carolina wrestled with the conflicting principles of slave society and came up with an assortment of mutually exclusive answers. Judge Waites, in *State v. Cynthia Simmons and Lawrence Kitchen* (1794): "Negroes are under the protection of the laws, and have personal rights, and cannot be considered on a footing only with domestic animals. They have wills of their own — capacities to commit crimes; and are responsible for offences against society." The court in *Fairchild v. Bell* (1807): "The slave lives for his master's service. His time, his labor, his comforts, are all at the master's disposal." Judge John Belton O'Neall in *Tennent v. Dendy* (1837): "Slaves are our most valuable property.... Too many guards cannot be interposed between it and violent unprincipled men.... The slave ought to be fully aware that his master is to him...a perfect security from injury. When this is the case, the relation of master and servant becomes little short of that of parent and child." But in Kentucky, the high court had pronounced in 1828: "However deeply it may be regretted, and whether it be politic or impolitic, a slave by our code is not treated as a person, but (*negotium*) a thing, as he stood in the civil code of the Roman Empire." But one year later we hear: "A slave has volition, and has feelings which cannot be entirely disregarded." And again in 1836: "But, although the law of this state considers slaves as property, yet it recognizes their personal existence, and, to a qualified extent, their natural rights."

The South had discovered, as had every previous slave society, that it could not deny the slave's humanity, however many preposterous legal fictions it invented. That discovery ought to have told the slaveholders much more. Had they reflected on the implications of a wagon's inability to raise an insurrection, they might have understood that the slaves as well as the masters were creating the law. The slaves' action proceeded within narrow limits, but it realized one vital objective: it exposed the deception on which the slave society rested — the notion that in fact, not merely in one's fantasy life, some human beings could become mere extensions of the will of another. The slaves grasped the significance of their victory with deeper insight than they have usually been given credit for. They say that they had few rights at law and that those could easily be violated by the whites. But even one right, imperfectly defended, was enough to tell them that the pretensions of the master class could be resisted. Before long, law or no law, they were adding a great many "customary rights" of their own and learning how to get them respected.

The slaves understood that the law offered them little or no protection, and in self-defense they turned to two alternatives: to their master, if he was decent, or his neighbors, if he was not; and to their own resources. Their commitment to a paternalistic system deepened accordingly, but in such a way as to allow them to define rights for themselves. For reasons of their own the slaveholders relied heavily on local custom and tradition; so did the slaves, who turned this reliance into a weapon. If the law said they had no right to property, for example, but local custom accorded them private garden plots, then woe to the master or overseer who summarily withdrew the "privilege." To those slaves the privilege had become a right, and the withdrawal an act of aggression not to be borne. The slaveholders, understanding this attitude, rationalized their willingness to compromise. The slaves forced themselves upon the law, for the courts repeatedly sustained such ostensibly extralegal arrangements as having the force of law because sanctioned by time-honored practice. It was a small victory so far as everyday protection was concerned, but not so small psychologically; it gave the slaves some sense of having rights of their own and also made them more aware of those rights withheld. W.W. Hazard of Georgia ran the risk of telling his slaves about their legal rights and of stressing the legal limits of his own power over them. He made it clear that he had an obligation to take care of them in their old age, whereas free white workers had no such protection, and argued deftly that their being whipped for insubordination represented a humane alternative to the practice of shooting soldiers and sailors for insubordination. His was an unusual act, but perhaps not so risky after all. He may have scored a few points while not revealing much they did not already know.

The legal status of the slave during the seventeenth century, particularly in Virginia, still occasions dispute. We cannot be sure that the position of the earliest Africans differed markedly from that of the white indentured servants. The debate has considerable significance for the interpretation of race relations in American history. It remains possible that for a brief period a less oppressive pattern of race relations had had a chance to develop in the Upper South; it is doubtful that any such alternative ever existed in South Carolina, which as a slave society virtually derived from Barbados. In any case, before the turn of the century the issue had been resolved and blacks condemned to the status of slaves for life.

The laws of Virginia and Maryland, as well as those of the colonies to the south, increasingly gave masters the widest possible power over the slaves and also, through prohibition of interracial marriage and the general restriction of slave status to nonwhites, codified and simultaneously preached white supremacy. Kenneth Stampp writes: "Thus the master class, for its own purposes, wrote chattel slavery, the caste system, and color prejudice into American custom and law." These earliest, Draconian slave codes served as a model for those adopted by new slave states during the nineteenth century. Over time they became harsher with respect to manumission, education, and the status of the free Negro and milder with respect to protection for slave life; but most of the amelioration that occurred came through the courts and the force of public opinion rather than from the codes themselves. At the end of the antebellum period the laws remained Draconian and the enormous power of the masters had received only modest qualification. The best that might be said is that the list of capital crimes had shrunk considerably, in accordance with the movement toward general sensibility, and that the ruthless enforcement of the eighteenth century had given way to greater flexibility during the nineteenth. The laws, at least as amended during the early nineteenth century, tried to protect the lives of the slaves and provided for murder indictments against masters and other whites. They also demanded that masters, under penalty of fine or imprisonment, give adequate food, clothing, shelter, and support to the elderly. But these qualifications added confirmation to the power of the master over the slaves' bodies as well as labor time. Nowhere did slave marriages win legal sanction, and therefore families could be separated with impunity. Only Louisiana effectively limited this outrage by forbidding the sale away from their mothers of children under the age of ten. Most significantly, blacks could not testify against whites in court, so that enforcement of the laws against cruel or even murderous masters became extremely difficult.

If harsh laws did not mean equally harsh practice, neither did mild laws mean equally mild practice. Kentucky had one of the mildest of slave codes, including the notable absence of an antiliteracy provision, but it probably suffered more personal violence and lynching than most other states, although much more often directed against allegedly negrophile whites than against blacks. The South had become the region of lynching *par excellence* during antebellum times, but of the three hundred or so victims recorded between 1840 and 1860, probably less than 10 percent were blacks. Occasionally, the lynch fever struck hard, as in the wake of an insurrection scare. In these cases the most respectable planters might find themselves side by side with the poor whites in meting out fearful summary punishments; but for the blacks the danger of lynching remained minimal until after emancipation. The direct power of the masters over their slaves and in society as a whole, where they had little need for extralegal measures against blacks, provided the slaves with extensive protection against mob violence. So strong a hold did this sense of justice take on the master class that even during the war prominent voices could be heard in opposition to panicky summary actions against defecting slaves. Charles C. Jones, Jr., then a lieutenant in the Confederate army, wrote his father: "A trial by jury is accorded to everyone, whether white or black, where life is at stake.... Any other procedure, although possibly to a certain extent justified by the aggravated character of the offense and upon the grounds of public good, would in a strictly legal sense certainly be *coram non judice*, and would savor of mob law." As Lieutenant Jones undoubtedly understood, an easy attitude toward indiscriminate mob violence against blacks would do more than threaten slave property; it would also threaten the position of the master class in society and open the way to initiatives by the white lower classes that might not remain within racial bounds. The masters felt that their own direct action, buttressed a legal system of their own construction, needed little or no support from poor white trash. Order meant order.

The extent to which the law, rather than mobs, dealt with slave criminals appeared nowhere so starkly as in the response to rape cases. Rape meant, by definition, rape of white women, for no such crime as rape of a black woman existed at law. Even when a black man sexually attacked a black woman he could only be punished by his master; no way existed to bring him to trial or to convict him if so brought. In one case an appellate court reversed the conviction of a black man for attempted rape, probably of a white woman, because the indictment had failed to specify the race of the victim.

Rape and attempted rape of white women by black men did not occur frequently. Ulrich Bonnell Phillips found 105 cases in Virginia for 1780 to 1864, with a few years unaccounted for. Other states kept poor records on slave crime, although enough cases reached the appellate courts to make it clear that every slaveholding area had to face the issue once in a while. But even these infrequent cases provide a body of evidence of contemporary white southern attitudes.

On the whole, the racist fantasy so familiar after emancipation did not grip the South in slavery times. Slaves accused of rape occasionally suffered lynching, but the overwhelming majority, so far as existing evidence

may be trusted, received trials as fair and careful as the fundamental injustice of the legal system made possible. Sometimes slaves did run into injustices even at law. A slave accused of raping a widow in Louisiana in 1859 went to the gallows on evidence that a local planter thought woefully insufficient. No positive identification had been made, he charged, and the evidence as a whole was slender. "I consider him," he wrote in his diary, "to be a victim of what is deemed a necessary example."

The astonishing facts — astonishing in view of post emancipation outrages — are that public opinion usually remained calm enough to leave the matter in the hands of the courts and that the courts usually performed their duty scrupulously. The appellate courts in every southern state threw out convictions for rape and attempted rape on every possible ground, including the purely technical. They overturned convictions because the indictments had not been drawn up properly; because the lower courts had based their convictions on possibly coerced confessions; or because the reputation of the white victim had not been admitted as evidence. The calmness of the public and the judicial system, relative to that of postbellum years, appeared most pointedly in reversals based on the failure to prove that black men who approached white women actually intended to use force. The Supreme Court of Alabama declared in one such instance: "An indecent advance, or importunity, however revolting, would not constitute the offence...." The punishment for rape remained death; punishment by castration receded, although in Missouri it survived into the late antebellum period.

The scrupulousness of the high courts extended to cases of slaves' murdering or attempting to murder whites. In Mississippi during 1834–1861, five of thirteen convictions were reversed or remanded; in Alabama during 1825–1864, nine of fourteen; in Louisiana during 1844–1859, two of five. The same pattern appeared in other states.

A slave could kill a white man in self-defense and escape conviction, provided that his own life stood in clear and imminent danger. In a celebrated case in Virginia in 1791, Moses, a slave, killed his overseer and escaped conviction despite much controversy in the white community. The court accepted testimony that Moses had served honestly and faithfully and that he had killed only when the overseer tried to kill him. During the nineteenth century the southern courts said plainly that a slave had the right to resist an assault that threatened his life, even to the point of killing his attacker. In practice, these rulings meant that a white man who attacked a slave with a deadly weapon risked the consequences; they did not mean that a slave had the right to make a judgment on the potential effects of, say, a prolonged whipping.

A brace of famous cases in North Carolina brought the theoretical questions to the surface and exposed the ultimate absurdity of defining a slave as chattel. In 1829,

Judge Thomas Ruffin, one of the South's most respected jurists, handed down a decision he freely admitted to have ghastly implications. A lower court had held that, as a matter of law, a master could be charged with committing battery upon a slave, much as a parent could be charged with unduly harsh physical punishment of a child. Judge Ruffin explained the Supreme Court's reversal in words that reveal as much about new attitudes toward the rights of children and the limits of parental authority as about anything else:

> There is no likeness between the cases. They are in opposition to each other and there is an impassable gulf between them — the difference is that which exists between freedom and slavery — and a greater cannot be imagined. In the one the end in view is the happiness of the youth born to equal rights with that governor on whom the duty devolves of training the young to usefulness in a status which he is afterwards to assume among free men.
>
> With slavery it is far otherwise. The end is the profit of the master, his security and public safety; the subject, one doomed in his own person, and his posterity, to live without knowledge, and without the capacity to make anything his own, and to toil that another may reap the fruits. What moral considerations, such as a father might give to a son, shall be addressed to such a being, to convince him what, it is impossible but that the most stupid must feel and know can never be true — that he is thus to labour upon a principle of natural duty, or for the sake of his own personal happiness, such services can only be expected from one who has no will of his own; who surrenders his will in implicit obedience to that of another. Such obedience is the consequence only of uncontrolled authority over the body. There is nothing else which can operate to produce the effect. The power of the master must be absolute to render the submission of the slave perfect. I must freely confess my sense of the harshness of this proposition, I feel it as deeply as any man can. And as a principle of moral right, every person in his retirement must repudiate it. But in the actual condition of things, it must be so. There is no remedy. This discipline belongs to the state of slavery.

Never has the logic of slavery been followed so faithfully by a humane and responsible man. As Ruffin knew, no civilized community could live with such a view. Perhaps he had hoped that the legislature would find a way to remove the high court's dilemma. It did not. The court had to reconsider its attitude.

In 1834, in *State v. Will*, the liberal Judge Gaston, speaking for the same court, handed down a radically different doctrine at once infinitely more humane and considerably less logical. Judge Gaston considered some things more important than logical consistency. Will, a slave, had tried to run away from an overseer who was attempting to whip him. The overseer thereupon got a gun and tried to shoot him. Will killed the overseer; accordingly, he entered a plea of innocent by reason of self-defense. The Supreme Court, under Judge Gaston's leadership, overturned Will's conviction and sustained the plea. Judge Ruffin must have been relieved; he remained silent and did not dissent from a ruling that so clearly contradicted the philosophy inherent in his own previous judgment. The aftermath of the case also reveals something about the southern legal system. On the assumption that Will's life would be unsafe from extralegal white retaliation, his master sold him and his wife to Mississippi. A few years later she arranged to be sold back to her old place. Her fellow slaves greeted her with surprise, for they had not expected her to leave her husband. She had not. Will had killed another slave in Mississippi and had been convicted of murder and executed. As the poor woman recalled, "Will sho'ly had hard luck. He killed a white man in North Carolina and got off, and then was hung for killing a nigger in Mississippi."

The courts could never have sustained the right of a slave to self-defense if public opinion had been hostile. For the most part, it was not. Especially in cases in which the victim was an overseer or a poor man, the white attitude was that he got what he deserved. Armstead Barrett, an ex-slave of Texas, recalled that when a brutal overseer finally went too far, two slaves picked up their hoes one day and hacked his head off. The master calmly sold them. In so doing, he protected his investment, for compensation never equalled market value; but we can hardly believe that in such cases of violence against whites monetary considerations easily overpowered the others. In South Carolina a master abused his slaves and was believed responsible for the death of one or more. A committee of local citizens waited on the master to suggest, no doubt with grave courtesy and respect, that he leave the area immediately. He did. In Georgia slaves killed a cruel master without evoking the ire of local whites, who considered that he had deserved his fate. In Missouri, an ex-slave recalled that at the age of ten she had blinded her old mistress by hitting her with a rock in retaliation for the wanton and unpunished murder of her baby sister, who had made a nuisance of herself by excessive crying. The slave girl was owned by the mistress's daughter, who refused to have her punished and said, "Well, I guess mamma has larnt her lesson at last."

In seventeenth-century Virginia a master could not murder a slave. He might cause his death, but he could not, legally, murder him. Would a man willingly destroy his own property? Certainly not. Therefore, no such crime as the murder of one's own slave could present itself to a court of reasonable men. In time, Virginia and the other slaves states thought better of the matter. In 1821, South Carolina became the last of the slave states to declare itself clearly in protection of slave life. During the nineteenth century, despite state-by-state variations, slaveholders theoretically faced murder charges for wantonly killing a slave or for causing his death by excessive punishment. The Virginia Supreme Court in 1851 upheld the conviction of a master for causing the death of a slave by "cruel and excessive whipping and torture": "But in so inflicting punishment for the sake of punishment, the owner of the slave acts at his peril; and if death ensues in consequence of such punishment, the relation of master and slave affords no ground or excuse or palliation." The court unanimously ruled that a murder had been committed.

South Carolina responded more slowly to the demands for liberalization than did other states, although Chancellor Harper may have been right in declaring: "It is a somewhat singular fact that when there existed in our State no law for punishing the murder of a slave other than a pecuniary fine, there were, I will venture to say, at least ten murders of freedom for one murder of a slave." White folks in South Carolina, gentlemen all, always had played rough with each other and everyone else. When whites were convicted of killing slaves, they usually got off lightly, although less so as time went on. By 1791 the prosecution insisted that a white man deserved the death penalty in a clear case of murder, especially since such crimes against slaves were increasing and had to be deterred. The murderer received a fine of £700, which he was unable to pay; accordingly, he went to prison for seven years at hard labor. The same year a white man convicted of manslaughter of a slave paid £50. After a tougher law was passed in 1821 in South Carolina a man killed a slave, not with premeditation but "in heat of passion," and received a fine of $350.

The law of 1821 established three categories: murder, killing in heat of passion, and killing by undue correction — generally, excessive whipping. The change aimed at increasing the penalty for murder. Judge O'Neall commented: "The act of 1821 changed the murder of a slave from a mere misdemeanor, which it was under the act of 1740, to a felony.... It, in a criminal point of view, elevated slaves from chattels personal to human beings in the place of the State." The authorities enforced the law as best they could, but its strength may be measured by the sentence meted out to a woman convicted of killing a slave by undue correction in 1840 — a fine of $214.28.

The courts moved to eliminate the excuses for killing blacks. In Louisiana, for example, a white man was found guilty of killing a free man of colour who had insulted him. The court observed that whites did not have to suffer insults from Negroes, slave or free, and had adequate recourse at law; therefore, the provocation could not excuse the defendant's extralegal action. In Texas a white man killed another man's slave, who had raised a hand to him. He was found guilty of manslaughter and appealed, but the high court sustained the verdict, citing precedent in Tennessee, and added, "The only matter of surprise is that it should ever have been doubted."

When whites did find themselves before the bar of justice, especially during the late antebellum period, they could expect greater severity than might be imagined. The penalties seldom reached the extreme or the level they would have if the victim had been white; but neither did they usually qualify as a slap on the wrist. If one murderer in North Carolina got off with only eleven months in prison in 1825, most fared a good deal worse. Ten-year sentences were common, and occasionally the death penalty was invoked.

The greatest difficulty in securing enforcement of the laws against murdering or mistreating slaves did not stem from the laxness of the authorities or from the unwillingness of juries to convict, or from any softness in the appellate courts. Public opinion might remain silent in the face of harsh treatment by masters; it did not readily suffer known sadists and killers. But neither did it suffer blacks to testify against whites, and therein lay the fatal weakness of the law. Moreover, the authorities and public opinion more readily come down hard upon overseers or small slaveholders than upon gentlemen of standing.

Despite the efforts of the authorities and the courts, masters and overseers undoubtedly murdered more slaves than we shall ever know. If the number did not reach heights worthy of classification as "statistically significant," it probably did loom large enough to strike terror into the quarters. It could happen. It sometimes did. And the arrests, convictions, and punishment never remotely kept pace with the number of victims.

Despite so weak a legal structure, the slaves in the United States probably suffered the ultimate crime of violence less frequently than did those in other American slave societies, and white killers probably faced justice more often in the Old South than elsewhere. The murder of a slave in Barbados drew little attention or likelihood of punishment. Effective protection was out of the question in Saint-Dominique. The Catholic slaveholding countries of Spanish and Portuguese America abounded in unenforceable and unenforced protective codes. Wherever the blacks heavily outnumbered the whites, as they did in so much of the Caribbean, fear of insurrection and insubordination strangled pleas for humanity. The bleak record of the southern slave states actually glows in comparison. These observations reveal something about the sociology of law and power. But they would not likely have provided much comfort to the slaves of South Carolina or Mississippi.

Frederick Law Olmsted pointed out the consequences of the South's position, especially for those regions in which white testimony could not be expected:

> The precariousness of the much-vaunted happiness of the slaves can need but one further reflection to be appreciated. No white man can be condemned for any cruelty or neglect, no matter how fiendish, on slave testimony. The rice plantations are in a region very sparsely occupied by whites: the plantations are nearly all very large — often miles across: many a one of them occupying the whole of an island — and rarely is there more than one white man upon a plantation at a time, during the summer. Upon this one man each slave is dependent, even for the necessities of life.

South Carolina tried to protect its slaves in cases of wanton cruelty or murder by providing that the master had responsibility for their condition, so that physical evidence on a body or the condition of a corpse could constitute circumstantial evidence adequate for conviction. What the law gave, the law took away, for it also provided that a master's oath of innocence had to be respected. Apart from the general absurdity of such a provision, the State Supreme Court's outstanding jurist, John Belton O'Neall, fumed, "This is the greatest temptation ever present to perjury, and the Legislature ought speedily to remove it."

The tenacious opposition to black testimony against whites proved a disadvantage to the planters themselves. If, for example, a white man robbed a plantation, the testimony of the owner's slaves had to be ignored. If a white man killed another's slave and thereby also robbed him of hundreds or thousands of dollars, the slaveholder had to settle accounts by personal violence or not at all unless some other white man had witnessed the crime. In Louisiana in 1840 the ultimate irony occurred, when a white man who had incited slaves to insurrection had to be acquitted because their confessions could not be used against him. In this as in so many other ways, the racism of the whites worked against them; but they regarded these expensive inconveniences as necessary evils and bore them doggedly.

"It is remarkable at first view," wrote George Fitzhugh, the proslavery ideologue of Virginia, "that in Cuba, where the law attempts to secure mild treatment to the slave, he is unhumanely treated; and in Virginia, where there is scarce any law to protect him, he is very humanely governed and provided for." This self-serving sermon, with its exaggeration and its kernel of truth, became standard fare for the apologists for slavery and has won some support from subsequent historians. The slaveholders did not intend to enforce their severe legislation strictly and considered it a device to be reserved for periods of disquiet and especially for periods of rumored insurrectionary plots. In practice this easy attitude confirmed the direct power of the master. For example, although state or local laws might forbid large meetings of slaves from several plantations, the planters normally permitted religious services or balls and barbecues unless they had some reason to fear trouble. The local authorities, generally subservient to the planters, usually looked the other way. Thus in Ascension Parish, Louisiana, the local ordinance declared: "Every person is prohibited from permitting in his negro quarters any other assemblies but those of his slaves and from allowing his slaves to dance during the night." Enforcement of such an edict would have required that masters constantly punish their slaves, who were not to be denied, and thereby ruin the morale of their labor force. Planters who agreed to such an edict had either let themselves be swept away by some momentary passion or intended it for emergency enforcement. The laws of most states also forbade teaching slaves to read and write. Most slaveholders obeyed these laws because they thought them wise not because they expected punishment of violators. In many of the great planter families various individuals, especially the white children, taught slaves to read. Some slaveholders violated the laws against giving slaves guns to hunt with, although they no doubt screened the beneficiaries with care. The law existed as a resource to provide means for meeting any emergency and to curb permissive masters. But the heart of the slave law lay with the master's prerogatives and depended upon his discretion. In this sense alone did practice generally veer from statute.

A slaveholding community did not intervene against a brutal master because of moral outrage alone; it intervened to protect its interests. Or rather, its strong sense of interest informed its moral sensibilities. "Harmony among neighbors is very important in the successful management of slaves," wrote a planter in an article directed to his own class. A good manager among bad ones, he explained, faces a hopeless task, for the slaves easily perceive differences and become dissatisfied. It does no good, wrote another, to enforce discipline on your plantation if the next planter does not. These arguments cut in both directions. They called for strict discipline from those who tended to be lax and for restraint from those who tended to be harsh.

What the law could not accomplish, public opinion might. A brutal overseer threatened by arrest could be made to understand that, however his trial might turn out, the community would welcome his departure. J.H. Bills reported from one of his plantations in Mississippi: "A jury of inquest was held yesterday over the body of a negro fellow, the property of the John Fowler estate, whose verdict was, I understand, that he came to his death by a blow given him on the head by Mahlon Hix a few days before. Hix left a country this morning."

A more difficult question concerned atrocities by respected masters. When in Richmond, Virginia, Fredrika Bremer heard some slaveholders talking about a rich neighbor who treated his slaves savagely. They condemned him, but had nevertheless accepted an invitation to his party. When questioned, they explained that they did not wish to offend his wife and daughters. Miss Bremer thought that his money and power had played a part in their decision. She noted a five-year sentence handed down on a master for barbarously killing a favorite house slave. When the entire community expressed outrage at the crime and approved the prison term, she concluded that that was about what it took to provoke a meaningful reaction.

Ex-slaves from various parts of the South recalled community interventions and moral pressure on cruel masters. Haga Lewis of Texas said that her master filed charges against some neighbors for underfeeding and excessive whipping. A.M. Moore, an educated preacher from Harrison County, Texas, added, "I've known courts in this county to fine slaveowners for not feeding and clothing their slaves right." George Teamoh of Virginia recalled that his mistress gave runaways from cruelty refuge on her place. Lou Smith of South Carolina recalled a slave's slipping off to tell white neighbors that his master had savagely whipped a slave and left him bleeding. The neighbors forced the master to have the slave attended by a doctor. And others testified that brutal masters had constant trouble from irate fellow slaveholders, none of whom, however, seemed willing to take direct action unless something atrocious had occurred.

Cruel and negligent masters did not often face trial. Some did, primarily because of the efforts of other slaveholders. A slaveholder in certain states could be convicted on circumstantial evidence alone, if the decision in *State of Louisiana v. Morris* (1849) may be taken as a guide. Even then, no conviction was likely without an aroused public opinion. These convictions, inadequate as they were, reminded the community of what was expected of individual behaviour.

Fortunately for the slaves, in many communities one or two souls among the slaveholders ran the risks of personal retaliation to keep an eye on everyone else's plantations. Captain J.G. Richardson of New Iberia, Louisiana, made no few enemies by compelling prosecution of delinquent fellow slaveholders, and others like him cropped up here and there. The private papers of the slaveholders, as well as their public efforts, suggest that they could become enraged at local sadists and would take action in the extreme cases.

Moral suasion and active intervention had limits. Much cruelty occurred because average masters lost their tempers — something any other master had to excuse unless he saw himself as a saint who could never be riled — and little could be done about someone who stopped short of atrocities as defined by other slaveholders and who did not much care about his neighbors' criticism. Yet moral pressure, if it could not prevent savages from acting sav-

agely, did set a standard of behavior to which men who cared about their reputations tried to adhere.

Although we do not have a thorough study of the place of the slave law in the southern legal system and of the relationship of the southern legal system as a whole to that of the United States and Western Europe, tentative appraisals must be risked if much sense is to be made out of the broader aspects of the master-slave relationship. Two questions in particular present themselves: the general character of the southern legal system; and the relationship between the legal status of the slave and his position in what appears to many to have been extralegal practice.

The two questions merge. The dichotomy, made current by Ulrich Bonnell Phillips, of a decisive distinction between law and practice or custom, requires critical examination. W.E.B. Du Bois's comment on the proslavery apologetics to which such a distinction has sometimes been applied says enough on the level on which he chose to leave the matter:

> It may be said with truth that the law was often harsher than the practice. Nevertheless, these laws and decisions represent the legally permissible possibilities, and the only curb upon the power of the master was his sense of humanity and decency, on the one hand, and the conserving of his investment on the other. Of the humanity of large numbers of Southern masters there can be no doubt.

The frontier quality of much of the Old South inhibited the growth of strong law-enforcement agencies, but this quality itself cannot be separated from the geographic advance of slave society. The plantation system produced an extensive pattern of settlement, relative to that of the Northwest, and resulted in the establishment of a multitude of separate centers of power in the plantations themselves. At the same time, the nonplantation areas found themselves developing as enclaves more or less detached from the mainstream of southern society. Thus, whereas the frontier steadily passed in the free states and even the formative stages of civilization rested on a certain civic consciousness, it not only passed less rapidly in the slave states but actually entrenched itself within the civilization being built. This process imparted a higher degree of apparent lawlessness — of the extralegal settlement of personal disputes — to southern life. Its spirit might be illustrated by the advice given to Andrew Jackson by his mother: "Never tell a lie, nor take what is not your own, nor sue anybody for slander or assault and battery. *Always settle them cases yourself!*"

This "violent tenor of life," to use an expression Johan Huizinga applied to late medieval Europe, provided one side of the story; the intrinsic difficulty of developing a modern legal system in a slave society provided another.

Southerners considered themselves law-abiding and considered northerners lawless. After all, southerners did not assert higher-law doctrines and broad interpretations of the Constitution. Rather, as Charles S. Sydnor has argued, they understood the law in a much different way and professed to see no contradiction between their code of honor, with its appeal to extralegal personal force, and a respect for the law itself. Notwithstanding some hypocrisy, their view represented a clumsy but authentic adjustment to the necessity for a dualistic, even self-contradictory, concept of law prefigured in the rise of a rational system of law in European civilization.

At first glance, the legal history of Western Europe represents an anomaly. The law arose in early modern times on rational rather than traditional, patrimonial, or charismatic foundations, however, many elements of these remained. As such, it assumed an equality of persons before the law that could only have arisen from the social relationships introduced by the expansion of capitalism and the spread of bourgeois, marketplace values, although to a considerable extent it derived from Roman tradition. Max Weber's distinction between "capitalism in general" and "modern capitalism," however suggestive, cannot resolve the apparent contradiction.

As Weber clearly understood, the ruling class of Roman society, and therefore the society itself, rested on slave-labor foundations. We do not have to follow Rostovtzeff, Salvioli, and others in projecting an ancient capitalism or a cycle of capitalisms in order to establish a firm link between ancient and modern civilization in Western Europe, as manifested in the continuity of legal tradition. Slavery as a mode of production creates a market for labor, much as capitalism creates a market for labor-power. Both encourage commercial development, which is by no means to be equated with capitalist development (understood as a system of social relations within which labor-power has become a commodity). Ancient slave society could not, however, remove the limits to commercial expansion — could not raise the marketplace to the center of the society as well as the economy — for its very capitalization of labor established the firmest of those limits. The modern bourgeoisie, on the other hand, arose and throve on its ability to transform labor power into a commodity and thereby revolutionize every feature of thought and feeling in accordance with the fundamental change in social relations. It thereby created the appearance of human equality, for the laborer faced the capitalist in relation of seller and buyer of labor-power — an ostensibly disembodied commodity. The relationship of each to the other took on the fetishistic aspect of a relationship of both to a commodity — a thing — and cloaked the reality of the domination of one man by another. Although ancient slavery did not create a market for labor-power, it did, by creating a market for human beings and their economic products, induce a high level of commercialization that,

together with the successful consolidation of a centralized state, combined to bequeath a system of law upon which modern bourgeois society could build. The rise of capitalism out of a seigneurial society in the West owed much to cultural roots that that particular kind of seigneurialism had in a long slaveholding past.

The slave South inherited English common law as well as elements and influences from continental Roman and Germanic communal and feudal law. But by the time the slave regime underwent consolidation, the legal system of the Western world had succumbed to a bourgeois idea of private property. The southern slaveholders had been nurtured on that idea but also had to draw upon earlier traditions in order to justify their assimilation of human beings to property. In so doing, they contradicted, however discreetly, that idea of property which had provided the foundation for their class claims.

The slaveholders could not simply tack the idea of property in man onto their inherited ideas of property in general, for those inherited ideas, as manifested in the bourgeois transformation of Roman law and common law, rested precisely upon a doctrine of marketplace equality within which — however various the actual practice for a protracted period of time — slavery contradicted first principles. The southern legal system increasingly came to accept an implicity duality: a recognition of the rights of the state over individuals, slave or free, and a recognition of the rights of the slaveholders over their slaves. Since the slaveholders' property in man had to be respected, the state's rights over the slaveholders as well as the slaves had to be circumscribed. At first glance, this arrangement appears simple enough: considered abstractly, a system in which the state, representing above all the collective will of the slaveholding class, could lay down rules for the individual slaveholders, who would, however, have full power over their chattels. But the slaves, simply by asserting their humanity, quickly demolished this nice arrangement. The moral, not to mention political, needs of the ruling class as a whole required that it interpose itself, by the instrument of state power, between individual masters and their slaves. It is less important that it did so within narrow bounds than that it did so at all. The resultant ambiguity, however functional in quiet times, ill prepared the South to meet the test of modern war.

Even in peacetime the slaveholders had to pay dearly for their compromises. Among other things, as Charles S. Sydnor saw and as Robert Fogel and Stanley Engerman have reflected on further, the reintroduction of precapitalist elements into the legal system weakened the economic organization and business capacity of the planters. These questions await a full exploration at other hands.

The immediate concern is with the effect of the imposed duality created by the reintroduction as well as the continuation of precapitalist ideas of power and property into an inherited system of bourgeois-shaped rational jurisprudence. This momentous reintroduction was effected with some ease because the idea of the state's having a monopoly of the legal means of coercion by violence had had only a brief history — roughly, from the conquest of state power by the bourgeoisies of England and Holland during the seventeenth century and of France at the end of the eighteenth. Nor had traditional ideas simply disappeared. Not only from the Left, but more powerfully from the Right, they continued to do battle within even the most advanced capitalist countries.

The slaveholders fell back on a kind of dual power: that which they collectively exercised as a class, even against their own individual impulses, through their effective control of state power; and that which they reserved to themselves as individuals who commanded other human beings in bondage. In general, this duality appears in all systems of class rule, for the collective judgment of the ruling class, coherently organized in the common interest, cannot be expected to coincide with the sum total of the individual interests and judgments of its members; first, because the law tends to reflect the will of the most politically coherent and determined fraction, and second, because the sum total of the individual interests and judgments of the members of the ruling class generally, rather than occasionally, pulls against the collective needs of a class that must appeal to other classes for support at critical junctures. But the slaveholders' problem ran much deeper, for the idea of slavery cannot easily be divorced from the idea of total power — of the reduction of one human being to the status of an extension of another's will — which is phenomenologically impossible, and more to the point, as Judge Ruffin had to face, politically impossible as well. Repeatedly, the slaveholders' own legal apparatus had to intervene, not primarily to protect the slaves from their masters, but to mediate certain questions among contending manifestations of human action. In so doing, it discredited the essential philosophical idea on which slavery rested and, simultaneously, bore witness to the slaves' ability to register the claims of their humanity.

Confronted with these painful and contradictory necessities, the slaveholders chose to keep their options open. They erected a legal system the implications of which should have embarrassed them and sometimes did; and then they tried to hold it as a reserve. They repeatedly had to violate their own laws without feeling themselves lawbreakers. The slave laws existed as a moral guide and an instrument for emergency use, although the legal profession and especially the judges struggled to enforce them as a matter of positive law; wherever possible, the authority of the master class, considered as a perfectly proper system of complementary plantation law, remained in effect. But since no reasonable formula could be devised to mediate between counterclaims arising from the two sides of this dual system, much had to be left outside the law altogether.

Several of the many ramifications of this interpretation bear on the position and condition of the slaves. We have already found reason to qualify the oft-repeated charge that the legal system of the South did not offer the slaves the protection offered by the slave codes of the Catholic countries. Further observations are now in order. The ethos informing the Catholic slave codes did play a significant role in shaping the slave societies of Portuguese and Spanish America, but the role of the law itself cannot readily be deduced either from that ethos or from the codes themselves. The system of enforcement in the United States, conditioned by Anglo-American standards of efficiency and civil discipline, generally exceeded that in, say, Brazil, where effective power law with the *senbores de engenbo* — *the great sugar planters. And the Spanish slogan, ¡Obedezco pero no cumplo!* (I obey, but I do not comply) says enough. More to the point, the slave codes of Brazil, the various Caribbean colonies, and Spanish South America had been drafted by nonslaveholders in the several metropolitan capitals and had had to be imposed upon resistant planters with enormous power of their own. The British, for their part, showed great reluctance to impose a slave code on the Caribbean planters. The slave codes of the southern United States came from the slaveholders themselves and represented their collective estimate of right and wrong and of the limits that should hedge in their own individual power. Their positive value lay not in the probability of scrupulous enforcement but in the standards of decency they laid down in a world inhabited, like most worlds, by men who strove to be considered decent. These standards could be violated with impunity and often were, but their educational and moral effect remained to offer the slaves the little protection they had.

For the slaves, two major consequences flowed from the ambiguities of the system. First, they constantly had before them evidence of what they could only see as white hypocrisy. An ex-slave commented on the antimiscegenation laws and their fate at the hands of the white man: "He made that law himself and he is the first to violation." No respect for the law could easily rise on such a foundation. Since the slaves knew that the law protected them little and could not readily be enforced even in that little, the second consequence followed. For protection against every possible assault on their being they had to turn to a human protector — in effect, a lord. They had to look to their masters for protection against patrollers, against lynching, against the strict enforcement of the law itself, as well as against hunger and physical deprivation. And they had to look to some other white man to shield them against a harsh or sadistic master. Thus, the implicit hegemonic function of the dual system of law conquered the quarters. But not wholly and not without encouraging a dangerous misunderstanding.

As the masters saw, the working out of the legal system drove the slaves deeper into an acceptance of paternalism. As the masters did not see, it did not drive them into an acceptance of slavery as such. On the contrary, the contradictions in the dual system and in the slave law *per se*, which had developed in the first place because of the slaves' assertion of their humanity, constantly reminded the slaves of the fundamental injustice to which they were being subjected. Paternalism and slavery merged into a single idea to the masters. But the slaves proved much more astute in separating the two; they acted consciously and unconsciously to transform paternalism into a doctrine of protection of their own rights — a doctrine that represented the negation of the idea of slavery itself.

The Power of Law[†]
C. Smart

INTRODUCTION

This book is an exploration of how law exercises power and the extent to which it resists and disqualifies alternative accounts of social reality. Initially, it is important to clarify what is meant by the term 'law', since using this concept in the singular tends to imply that law is a body of knowledge/rules which is unified in intent, theory, and practice. In fact I reject this notion of the unity of law because law operates with conflicting principles and contradictory effects at every level from High Court judgements to administrative law. As Hirst (1986) has pointed out, there is now considerable dispute over what law is. Notwithstanding this, the collectivity to which the label law is applied presents us with the appearance of unity and singularity. Hence law constitutes a plurality of principles, knowledges, and events, yet it claims a unity through the common usage of the term 'law'. I shall argue that it is in fact empowered by its 'singular' image. It is important to acknowledge that the usage of the term 'law' operates as a claim to power in that it embodies a claim to a superior and unified field of knowledge which concedes little to other competing discourses which by comparison fail to promote such a unified appearance. I shall therefore retain the term 'law' because this power to define (itself and other discourses) is part of the power of law that I wish to explore. In addition it is law's ability to impose its definition of events on everyday life that interests me. For example I shall examine how law's definition of rape takes precedence over women's definitions and how law manages to retain the ability to arrogate to itself the right to define the truth of things in spite of the growing challenge of other discourses like feminism.

In the following chapters I shall attempt to push forward feminist theorizing in relation to law and to establish a new basis for its challenge to legal discourse. At present it seems as if feminist 'legal theory' is immobilized in the face of the failure of feminism to affect law and the failure of law to transform the quality of women's lives. Feminist scholarship has become trapped into debates about the 'usefulness' of law to the emancipation of women, or the relative merits of 'equality' versus 'difference' as strategies, or the extent to which law reflects the interest of patriarchy, or simply men. These are necessary debates but they have the overwhelming disadvantage of ceding to law the very power that law may then deploy against women's claims. It is a dilemma that all radical political movements face, namely the problem of challenging a form of power without accepting its own terms of reference and hence losing the battle before it has begun. Put simply, in accepting law's terms in order to challenge law, feminism always concedes too much. I shall therefore explore some ways of avoiding this process and shall indicate the importance of attempting to 'de-centre' law wherever this is feasible. By this I mean that it is important to think of non-legal strategies and to discourage a resort to law as if it holds the key to unlock women's oppression. I include in this 'resort to law' not only matters of direct policy proposals but also matters of scholarship. For example I raise fundamental doubts about striving to achieve a feminist jurisprudence if such an enterprise merely challenges the form of law but leaves untouched the idea that law should occupy a special place in ordering everyday life. I am not suggesting we can simply abolish law, but we can resist the move towards more law and the creeping hegemony of the legal order.

To some extent this requires a reconceptualization of familiar issues as well as an attempt to think in a different mode. So I make no apologies for going over familiar terrain such as rape — but I propose to do so in a new

---

† Smart, Carol, "The Power of Law" in *Feminism and the Power of Law* (London: Routledge, 1989), 4–13. Reprinted by permission of Routledge, International Thomson Publishing Services Ltd., Hampshire, U.K.

way. This also means that I do not make policy proposals on, for example, how the law of rape should be reformed. Rather I concentrate on how to sustain feminist discourse in the face of renewed challenges to its legitimacy and on the task of deconstructing the discursive power of law. It is not solely important to promote feminist policies — indeed we are increasingly aware of their limitations. Rather it is my argument that law must also be tackled at the conceptual level if feminist discourses are to take a firmer root.

THE INFLUENCE OF FOUCAULT

Concepts like truth, power, and knowledge are central to this enterprise and it is therefore important to acknowledge their source in the work of Foucault. (For a full exposition of his work it is necessary to look to detailed works like Gordon 1980; Smart 1983, 1985; Cousins and Hussain 1984; Couzens Hoy 1986.) I shall therefore, in the following section, give some consideration to the value of these concepts in relation to a feminist analysis of law. In particular I shall challenge the theme which is fairly explicit in Foucault's work, namely that it is more fruitful to study the processes of power outside legal institutions because the power of legal discourse is diminishing. I do not reject the idea that non-juridical modes of regulation are increasingly important, but I shall put forward the idea that juridical power remains a formidable obstacle to feminism and that, whilst other mechanisms of discipline develop, law itself can deploy these mechanisms to enhance its own power. I therefore propose that the concentration on disciplinary mechanisms (for example of psychiatry and psychology) should not induce a belief that law is a less significant site of power relations. Finally I shall consider the problem of legal method (i.e., the process by which law arrives at its version of Truth) and how in the process it disqualifies other knowledges which may be rooted in feminism.

POWER, TRUTH, KNOWLEDGE

Power

...in the case of the classic, juridical theory, power is taken to be a right, which one is able to possess like a commodity, and which can in consequence transfer or alienate, either wholly or partially, through a legal act or through some act that establishes a right, such as takes place through cession or contract. Power is that concrete power which every individual holds, and whose partial or total cession enables political power or sovereignty to be established. (Gordon 1980: 88)

It is this formulation of the concept of power that Foucault rejects. He attempts to construct a non-economic analysis of power which better reflects the mechanisms of power in the twentieth century. The idea of power as a commodity which some people, or a class of people, may 'own' (usually because they command wealth or economic resources) is inadequate to an understanding of contemporary society. His argument is that society has become transformed such that, whilst in the past the linkage of power and judicial rights may have been valid, this is no longer the case. The transformation that Foucault identifies is the development of the disciplinary society. By this he means the growth of new knowledges (e.g., medicine, criminology, pedagogics, epidemiology, etc.) which came to constitute the 'modern episteme'. These knowledges create new fields of exploration and bring with them new modes of surveillance and regulation of the population. Hence the criminal is no longer someone who breaks the law and who must be punished. He is pathologized, he needs to be subjected to close surveillance and ultimately to cure or normalization. This process, which Foucault has explored in depth in *Discipline and Punish* (1979b), *The Birth of the Clinic* (1975), *Madness and Civilisation* (1971), *The History of Sexuality* (1979a), is one which applies to all areas of social life. Foucault has identified a new mode of regulation, the mechanism of discipline — 'a closely linked grid of disciplinary coercions whose purpose is in fact to assure the coercion of this same social body' (Gordon 1980: 106).

Foucault's concentration on the growth of the disciplinary society reflects his greater interest in the mechanisms of power than the 'old' questions of who has power. He also rejects the tendency which is apparent in the traditional formulation of power, of treating power as if it were negative, repressive and juridical. He maintains that power is creative and technical. By this it is meant that the mechanisms of power create resistances and local struggles which operate to bring about new forms of knowledge and resistance. Hence power is productive, not simply a negative sanction which stops or restricts oppositional developments. However, it is clear that although Foucault's reconceptualization of power opens new ways of understanding, it is very hard to abandon the old concept of power. Hence we not only continue to talk about power as a commodity, we also act as if it were. As Taylor (1986) has argued,

Foucault's thesis is that, while we have not ceased talking and thinking in terms of this model (i.e., power as a system of commands and obedience), we actually live in relations of power which are quite different, and which cannot be properly described in its terms. What is wielded through the modern technologies of control is something quite different, in that it is not concerned with law but with normalization. (Taylor 1986: 75)

The question that this raises is 'why do we still look to the old forms of power if they are no longer appropriate?' Interestingly, Foucault does not dismiss law and the old forms of power altogether as Taylor implies. It is, however, hard to be clear on what he has to say in this area since, by his own admission, Foucault was more interested in the mechanisms of power at its extremities (i.e., where it is least law-like) than power at its core (i.e., law itself and legal institutions). He does not appear to be saying that law, and the old contrivances of power, are no longer relevant — although he seems to argue that they will become so. Hence, we should talk of two parallel mechanisms of power which operate symbiotically, but where the old mechanism will be eventually colonized by the new.

> And I believe that in our times power is exercised simultaneously through this right and these techniques and that these techniques and these discourses, to which the disciplines give rise, invade the area of right so that the procedures of normalisation come to be ever more constantly engaged in the colonisation of those of law. (Gordon 1980: 107)

So Foucault sees the old power (and hence the significance of law) diminishing. I am less certain that this is happening. Rather it is possible to posit a move in the opposite direction, for example the growing legalization of everyday life from the moment of conception (i.e., increasing foetal rights) through to the legal definition of death (i.e., brain death or 'body' death). It may be that law is being colonized in some instances, but in others law may be extending its influence as I shall argue below.

We need therefore to think in terms of two parallel mechanisms of power, each with its own discourse, the discourse of rights and the discourse of normalization. Foucault tells us far more about the latter than the former, yet the former is by no means redundant (even if it is doomed to become so). This raises a number of issues. For example, what is the relationship between the two mechanisms in specific areas as opposed to broad generalities? Might we see an uneven development of this colonization of law? What does this mean for political strategy, if anything? Foucault suggests, for example, that there is little point in turning to law (the discourse of rights) as a strategy to deal with the encroachment of surveillance, since they are now symbiotically linked. I shall not answer all these questions in this chapter, but I shall explore the interface between the two mechanisms to try to give some substance to this, so far, abstract discussion. Before this I must give brief consideration to the notions of truth and knowledge.

Truth/Knowledge

In using the concept of truth Foucault does not mean 'the ensemble of truths which are to be discovered and accepted'. On the contrary Foucault uses it to refer to 'the ensemble of rules according to which the true and the false are separated and specific effects of power attached to the true' (Gordon 1980: 132). He is not concerned with what is considered to be the usual quest of science, namely to uncover the truth, rather he is interested in discovering how certain discourses claim to speak the truth and thus can exercise power in a society that values this notion of truth. He argues that making the claim to be a science is in fact an exercise of power because, in claiming scientificity, other knowledges are accorded less status, less value. Those knowledges which are called faith, experience, biography, and so on, are ranked as lesser knowledges. They can exercise less influence, they are disqualified. Defining a field of knowledge as science is to claim that it speaks a truth which can be favourably compared to partial truths and untruths which epitomize non-scientific discourse.

Foucault does not compare the scientist's claim to truth, and hence exercise of power, with the lawyer's claim. Law does not fit into his discussion of science, knowledge, and truth because, as I have pointed out, he identifies it in relation to the regime of power that predates the growth of the modern episteme. Yet I wish to argue that there are very close parallels in terms of this 'claim to truth' and the effect of power that the claim concedes. I am not saying that law attempts to call itself a science, but then it does not have to. Law has its own method, its own testing ground, its own specialized language and systems of results. It may be a field of knowledge that has a lower status than those regarded as 'real' sciences, none the less it sets itself apart from other discourses in the same way that science does.

It might be useful to provide an example here. In the area of family law there has been a steady encroachment of what has become known as the welfare principle. Hence decisions about children tend to be based on the concept of welfare rather than more traditional legal concepts like rights. As a consequence it has become necessary for law to differentiate itself from social work. Those with legal training distinguish their own knowledge base, and give higher value to their own skills than those of lay people who are inside the legal system (e.g., magistrates and social workers). The following statements from interviews carried out with solicitors in Sheffield in 1980 reveal clearly the hierarchy of knowledge that is presumed in law. (A full exposition of these interviews can be found in Smart 1984.)

1. At times I wish [the judge] would just take notice of the parties themselves and *do a lawyer's appraisal* of individuals, rather than at times, [taking notice of] in my book, inex-

perienced, undertrained operatives...[i.e., social workers].

2. [Referring to the influence of welfare reports] I think that it depends a lot on the judge in the County Court. I think the magistrates' courts are more influenced. I think that judges are used to making up their minds on the *basis of the evidence* and what they think about the parties before them, whereas the magistrates tend to be less self-confident...

3. [Referring to magistrates in general] ...you have to be a very expert practitioner before you can accurately predict which way [magistrates] are going to jump...they're pretty fickle anyway, and they make decisions which don't appear to be based on anything *normal*.

So law sets itself about knowledges like psychology, sociology, or common sense. It claims to have the method to establish the truth of events. The main vehicle for this claim is the legal method which is taught in law schools and which I shall discuss in more detail below. A more 'public' version of this claim, however, is the criminal trial which, through the adversarial system, is thought to be a secure basis for findings of guilt and innocence. Judges and juries can come to correct legal decisions; the fact that other judges in higher courts may overrule some decisions only goes to prove that the system ultimately divines the correct view.

Law's claim to truth is not manifested so much in its practice, however, but rather in the ideal of law. In this sense it does not matter that practitioners may fall short of the ideal. If we take the analogy of science, the claim to scientificity is a claim to exercise power, it does not matter that experiments do not work or that medicine cannot find a cure for all ills. The point is that we accord so much status to scientific work that its truth outweighs other truths, indeed it denies the possibility of others. We do not give quite such a status to law, although we operate as if the legal system does dispense justice (i.e., correct decisions), and we certainly give greater weight to a judge's pronouncement of guilt than a defendant's proclamation of innocence. Indeed there are those who would say that 'law is what the judges say it is'. The judge is held to be a man of wisdom, a man of knowledge, not a mere technician who can ply his trade.

If we accept that law, like science, makes a claim to truth and that this is indivisible from the exercise of power, we can see that law exercises power not simply in its material effects (judgements) but also in its ability to disqualify other knowledges and experiences. Non-legal knowledge is therefore suspect and/or secondary. Everyday experiences are of little interest in terms of their

meaning for individuals. Rather these experiences must be translated into another form in order to become 'legal' issues and before they can be processed through the legal system (Cain 1979). For the system to run smoothly, whether it is criminal or civil, the ideal is that all parties are legally represented and that the parties say as little as possible (i.e., they are mute). The problem for the lawyer is that the litigant may bring in issues which are not, in legal terms, pertinent to the case, or s/he might inadvertently say something that has a legal significance unknown to her/him. So the legal process translates everyday experience into legal relevances, it excludes a great deal that might be relevant to the parties, and it makes its judgement on the scripted or tailored account. Of course parties are not always silenced, but I hope to show in Chapter Two that how they are allowed to speak, and how their experience is turned into something that law can digest and process, is a demonstration of the power of law to disqualify alternative accounts.

Law sets itself outside the social order, as if through the application of legal method and rigour, it becomes a thing apart which can in turn reflect upon the world from which it is divorced. Consider the following quotation from Lord Denning, written when he was Master of the Rolls (i.e., head of the Court of Appeal).

By a series of Acts of Parliament, however, starting in 1870, all the disabilities of wives in regard to property have been swept away. A married woman is now entitled to her own property and earnings, just as her husband is entitled to his. Her stocks and shares remain hers. Her wedding presents are hers. Her earnings are hers. She can deal with all property as fully as any man.... No longer is she dependent on her husband. She can, and does, go out to work and earn her own living. Her equality is complete. (Denning 1980: 200)

In this conceptualization it is law that has given women equality (accepting for the moment that they do have formal equality). In this way law is taken to be outside the social body, it transcends it and acts upon it. Indeed the more it is seen as a unified discipline that responds only to its own coherent, internal logic, the more powerful it becomes. It is not simply that in this passage Denning omits to point out how many women chained themselves to railings, demonstrated and lobbied in Parliament to change the law, nor that he ignores the dramatic changes to women's economic position which occurred quite independently of law, it is rather that he constructs law as a kind of sovereign with the power to give or withhold rights. (Here we are back to Foucault's notion of the 'old' power of law.) Linked to this idea, law is constructed as a force of linear progress, a beacon to lead us out of darkness. The significance of this is not that one judge, no matter how eminent, should state this, but that this has become a commonsense approach. The idea that law has the power to right wrongs is pervasive. Just as medicine is seen as curative rather than *iatrogenic*, so law is seen as extending rights rather than creating wrongs. It is perhaps useful to coin the term *juridogenic* to apply to law as a way of conceptualizing the harm that law may generate as a consequence of its operations. (Examples of the juridogenic potential of law are explored in later chapters.) But there are two issues here. One is the idea of law as a force for good (or bad); the other is the idea of law as a force at all — both have to be subject to scrutiny. If we stop at the point of considering whether law is a force for good or bad we concede that law is a force — indeed it implies that we simply wish to redirect its purpose. If we go one step further we can begin to problematize, to challenge, and even to redefine law's supposedly legitimate place in the order of things. Ultimately this is the most necessary project.

Lastly in this section on truth and knowledge, I want to consider how law extends itself beyond uttering the truth of law, to making such claims about other areas of social life. What is important about this tendency is that the framework for such utterances remains legal — and hence retains the mantle of legal power. To put it figuratively, the judge does not remove his wig when he passes comment on, for example, issues of sexual morality in rape cases. He retains the authority drawn from legal scholarship and the 'truth' of law, but he applies it to non-legal

issues. This is a form of legal imperialism in which the legitimacy law claims in the field of law extends to every issue in social life. Hence Lord Denning states,

> No matter how you may dispute and argue, you cannot alter the fact that women are quite different from men. The principal task in the life of women is to bear and rear children:... He is physically the stronger and she the weaker. He is temperamentally the more aggressive and she the more submissive. It is he who takes the initiative and she who responds. These diversities of function and temperament lead to differences of outlook which cannot be ignored. But they are, none of them, any reason for putting women under the subjection of men. (Denning 1980: 194)

Here Denning is articulating a Truth about the natural differences between women and men. He combines the Truth claimed by sociobiology (i.e., a 'scientific' truth) with the Truth claimed by law. He makes it clear that there is no point in argument; anyone who disagrees is, by definition, a fool. Hence the feminist position is constructed as a form of 'disqualified knowledge', whilst the naturalistic stance on innate gender differences acquires the status of a legal Truth. In this passage both law and biological determinism are affirmed, whilst law accredits itself with doing good.

The Cultural Effects of Judicial Bias[†]
J. Ryan and B. Ominayak

INTRODUCTION

There are approximately 850,000 native people in Canada, comprised of three groups — Indians, Métis and Inuit — making up about 3 per cent of the Canadian population. Approximately one half of the native people are registered. They are referred to as "status" Indians: that is, they have a legal definition under the *Indian Act*.[1] This Indian population and the Inuit are the sole responsibility of the federal government and are administered by the Department of Indian Affairs and Northern Development ("DIAND"). The remaining population of native descent is not "regis-

tered" and they are generally referred to as "non-status" Indians and Metis; they are the responsibility of provincial governments.

Another statute and one on which aboriginal land claims rest is the *Royal Proclamation of 1763*[2] which makes reference to the rights of aboriginal populations to maintain their territories for hunting, fishing and trapping. However, the arbitrary constraints placed on Indians by a colonial administration in Canada continue to reflect the prevailing political values of the seventeenth century. Policies emanating from political decisions maximize access to power, wealth, and land in the interests of white Canadians rather

† Ryan, Joan, and Ominayak, Bernard, "The Cultural Effects of Judicial Bias" in eds. S. Martin and K. Mahoney, *Equality and Judicial Neutrality* (Calgary: Thomson Professional Publishing Canada, 1987), 346–57. Reprinted by permission of Carswell, a division of Thomson Canada Limited, and by Sheilah Martin and Kathleen Mahoney.

than those of aboriginal populations despite the legislative quasi-protection of aboriginal territories.[3]

Canadian Confederation took place in 1867 under British rule. As Canada emerged out of New France (in the political sense) and as more and more settlers arrived from Europe, it became clear that Indian populations would have to cede their lands to the newcomers and become less visible. The *Indian Act* and the treaties accomplished both these ends. The *Indian Act* was a mandate for government administrators to control the lives of Indians on reserves. It defined who was Indian legally and, therefore, who was entitled to government benefits under the Act.

On behalf of the British government, settlements regarding land were made with most Indian groups across Canada in the late 1800s.[4] The treaties completed the surrender of traditional Indian lands from the borders of Ontario to the borders of British Columbia — millions of acres. In essence, they were peace treaties. As well, the agreement was that the government would provide reserve lands, held in trust and that Indians would occupy those lands but retain hunting, fishing, and trapping rights in unoccupied Crown lands. Disputes today between government and Indian bands focus on the failure of government to maintain its part of the treaties.

The relationships between Indians and non-Indians, as pointed out previously, have changed over time. These relationships have reflected varying historical conditions as the two groups progressed. However, it is clear that *at all times*, the relationships reflect an attempt by the dominant group to control Indians and that the dominant group has, *at all times*, retained power (and thus control) over native people.

In order to fully appreciate the thrust of historical relationships and policies in the failure of native peoples to achieve self-determination, it is important to define the latter. My definition essentially argues that self-determination is the maximum utilization of both human and environmental resources under local control. The *under-development* of native groups applies to those situations in which resources are not used maximally and where they are not under local control. Finally, where no resources exist for political and economic development under local control, we can talk about *non-developed* areas, rather than under-developed ones. Another process is one which I call *de-development*, this is the case in several Indian situations in which local control and maximum use of total resources has peaked and then diminished due to external factors or, more likely, a combination of these. I suggest that de-development is the process which has occurred in the past in which subsistence economies have been altered to adapt to a cash economy, and in which the control of environmental resources has passed to externally controlling agencies such as governments, oil companies, and the like. Along with such economic shifts come the preponderance

of shifts in local political, ritual, social and environmental systems with the result that the locus of control becomes totally external, thus creating dependency and powerlessness. This is reflected in the ever-increasing statistics on suicide, homicide, abuse of alcohol, criminal charges, incarceration, as well as in the use of militancy and confrontation as adaptive measures of Indian reserves. Such adaptations are dysfunctional at both the corporate and individual levels. The mythology of quasi-political and economic gains potentially available through the assimilative model is a most dangerous one. The process of de-development brings us to a discussion of the issues of tribal diversity and ideology which are inextricably linked to identity and autonomy.

THE NATURE OF SUBSISTENCE SOCIETIES

The persistence of tribal societies in Canada is dependent on the maintenance of the linkage with their land and family, since these are the critical factors which provide a past and promise a future. If the women of the Six Nations cease to be clan mothers, or if the Haida clan matriarchs all die in jail, those societies will cease to exist because the very roots of their civilization will have been fractured beyond repair. If the Northwest Coast carvers stop carving their history in the round in three dimensions, they will have no future either because without a past, there can be no future. If the Cree give up their land to oil companies, they too will be destroyed because in their land rests collaborative survival, kinship, and a political and economic past and future. People, land, spirits, economies, the past, the present and future of tribal societies will remain viable only as long as they remain on the same plane; expandable, evolving, interactive, adaptive and interrelated. If the circle breaks, or is broken externally, then the society itself breaks, too, and those who survive become other than who they are now.

The Lubicon Lake Cree people always lived off the land until 1984 when hunting and trapping became impossible. Prior to that, the small community had a life-style that integrated all aspects of the culture. Senior men — the elders — drew their status from their expertise as hunters and trappers. They were also the community leaders. Women drew their status from their ability to use the food and hides from the hunt, to prepare hides, to tan furs, to preserve food by drying and freezing, and so on. It was an egalitarian society, one in which each person had a rightful and acknowledged place, one in which roles were taught and learned effectively and in which expectations were clear. It was an integrated society in which the socialization of the youngest generation was done by alternate ones and included all aspects of ritual, social, economic and political realities. There was a pattern to the life-style which flowed through time. There was a seasonality which allowed for fun and leisure as well as the hardships of the hunt and the trapline. It was a healthy existence; it was balanced and it worked.

It worked until it was fractured by the ingress of the multinational oil and gas companies whose activities moved the animals farther away and eventually out of reach. Berger states,[5]

> Subsistence activities link the generations and the extended family into a complex network of associations, rights and obligations. This network both reflects and recreates the social order and gives meaning to each person's contributions and rewards.
>
> ...Order in a village is based on subsistence activities and depends upon earned respect and consensus, not on authority and coercion.
>
> ...Subsistence enables the native peoples to feel at one with their ancestors, at home in the present, confident of the future.

It is those linkages which the courts and many others fail to understand. It is the economic argument that baffles them; they fail to understand that subsistence economies are labour intensive and non-accumulative but that the quality of life is high even though its materialistic base is not extensive. In many cases, a hunter or trapper can only own what he can carry and thus possessions are modest but totally adequate to the task. At Lubicon Lake, it was possible to use horses in the bush and in winter to use dogs; this meant that trappers could take their families with them and as a result many cabins were built out on the lines. Graves were also to be found along the lines because people buried their dead within their own trapping territories.

The conflict between the companies and the Indians over the use of land brings forward the issue of who controls whom, for the industrialists seek to control traditional lands that have been in the stewardship of Indians for many centuries. As Berger notes,[6]

> The industrial system that has created the great cities is not only a creator of wealth but also a shatterer of traditional societies and a powerful instrument of control in the new social systems to which it gives rise...we have neglected to consider seriously the possibility of restructuring our own relations with traditional societies to ensure that their subsistence economies may not only be preserved but enabled to thrive.

Again, Berger re-emphasizes this point when he states,[7]

> Their determination to retain their own cultures does not mean that they wish to return to the past,

it means they refuse to let their future be dictated by others...the right of native peoples to their own distinct place in the contemporary life of the larger nation must be affirmed.

In a short four years, the homelands of the Lubicons have been scarred with seismic roads, burned by unfought fires, and trampled by bulldozers. The silence has been broken with the sounds of trucks and pumps. All of this activity has been undertaken unilaterally by the multinational oil and gas companies with the agreement of the province of Alberta. No one asked the Cree if they had concerns about the way development should proceed, or if it should proceed, on the lands. The outcome has been the loss of a viable economy. As the land base was disrupted human lives were shattered because the relationship with the land was broken. This mean a loss of linkage to the past, to the spirit world, to ancestors, to identity and to affirmation of self. It created a vacuum which was overwhelming because all roles were negated and no others could replace them fast enough to make them workable. The rhythm of life was broken and we began to see the predictable results: people became depressed, they drank, they abandoned themselves, they had no context, they could not find new meanings in old lands, they had no money, no access to work, they lost status, dignity, identity, responsibility. They became angry and turned it inward; they became dependent and isolated. The isolation was damaging to individuals and to the collective; people who are very competent to make decisions when seeking consensus and relying upon the wisdom of elders, do not necessarily know how to make individual decisions. Where there is no work, no activity, no vision of a future and the links with the past are shattered, there is no present and everything becomes meaningless. So, marriages break down and children are ignored because no one has anything to offer them. Erikson notes,[8]

> ...the cultural bonds that connect people to one another and to places in which they live are a kind of tissue that can be damaged and even destroyed by too sharp and too sustained an assault.... Collective trauma...works its way slowly into the awareness of those who come to suffer from it...it is a form of shock...that the community no longer exists as an effective source of support and that an important part of their world had disappeared without so much as a sound.

THE LUBICON LAKE CREE: ABORIGINAL ISSUES

The Lubicon Lake people live in the northeast area of the Peace River district of Alberta. They number 387 persons and they have always been a hunting and trapping society.

Their traditional homelands spread over 8,500 square miles between the Peace and the Loon/Wabasca Rivers. Currently, they live in the community of Little Buffalo on Lubicon Lake.

The Lubicons are in dispute over their traditional lands to which they claim Indian title. Their aboriginal rights, guaranteed under the *Royal Proclamation of 1763*, were never extinguished by Treaty 8 because the treaty party never met with the Lubicon Lake Cree people in the 1800s. The Lubicons have continued their hunting and trapping life-style until recently when oil and gas developments in their aboriginal lands made it impossible for them to continue their subsistence activities.

In the 1940s, some settlers arrived to farm in the area, and the Lubicons became aware that other bands had been allocated reserves and were at the west end of Lubicon Lake which is the core of their 8,500 square mile traditional territories. Based on the Treaty 8 formula for current population, the Band was allocated 25 square miles as a reserve area. The area was held by Alberta in trust pending the federal survey and assignment. However, Canada never acted on the survey and eventually Alberta unilaterally removed the land from the Alberta Land Registry. Currently, the Cree are considered to be squatters on their own homelands. In 1984, Alberta unilaterally decreed the town site at Little Buffalo to be a hamlet. The province then set about to convince people to drop their aboriginal claim and to accept two-acre plots of land as part of an organized settlement of the area. The Cree declined and pursued their land claim in the federal courts; they sought an interim injunction in the Alberta Court of Queen's Bench to stop further oil and gas explorations and extractions in their hunting and trapping territories.

Oil and gas developments had started in the hunting and trapping territories in the 1950s, but these activities initially were spread over a large territory, involving low-key operations with little heavy duty equipment. They were mostly unsuccessful and resulted in the abandonment of most wells. In the 1950s, 11 wells were drilled and abandoned; in the 1960s, 24 wells were drilled and abandoned; by the 1970s, however, 34 wells were drilled and most remained operative. It was at this point that the Cree became aware of the major increase in oil and gas activity, noticed the decrease of game in the area, and recognized problems with having strangers in their homelands who were acting unilaterally.

This concern turned to alarm when a high grid road was constructed from Peace River into the Lubicon Lake area in 1978.[9] This road allowed the oil companies to roll their heavy duty trucks and equipment into the homelands of the Lubicons. It also opened up the area for more non-native settlement, hunting, logging, and fishing, with their subsequent consequences on the land base. To allow access to the 135 wells put in place between 1980 and 1984 and for further exploration, 4,053 miles of seismic

roads were cut in the hunting and trapping territories; the Shell Oil Company drained a lake to cool their *in situ* plant; further, a Union Oil Company pipeline to deliver the gas went in on the border of the 25-square mile reserve. In 1983, Alberta failed to fight a fire in the prime beaver breeding and moose habitat, with the result that 27,000 acres burned, Alberta further leased every square inch of the hunting and trapping territories to multinational companies for oil and gas exploration. Renewal leases were advertised during the interim injunction hearings.

Needless to say, the outcome of all the extractive industrial activities was devastating for the Lubicon Lake people and for their lands. Traplines were destroyed, game moved out of the area, and harassment of trappers by field oil company personnel was intense. Harassment by the province was also considerable and took the form of pressuring fur buyers not to buy from the Lubicons, pressuring individuals to opt out of the aboriginal claim and to accept municipal lots. Indian cars were run off the road by oil company employees. Tax notices were sent to residents by Alberta which also forced people to take their horse fences down because it was municipal land.

In 1980, the Lubicons filed an action in the federal courts[10] against the federal government and Alberta and against the oil companies in the area. The application was dismissed for lack of jurisdiction of that forum.

In 1982, the Lubicons filed for an interim injunction against 11 multinational oil companies and Petro-Canada in the Court of Queen's Bench, Alberta.[11] They sought a declaration of aboriginal rights or, alternatively, treaty rights. They sought a halt to all oil and gas activities in a 15-square mile radius of Lubicon Lake (their summer harvesting area) and they sought a limited injunction in the remaining hunting and trapping territories.

The intent of the Cree was to protect their lands from further destruction pending the outcome of their application for recognition of their aboriginal status and their aboriginal land claim. The courts were not sympathetic, and despite the fact that everyone recognized that another drilling season would enhance the income of the oil companies and further diminish the hunting and trapping incomes of the lubicons, the court allowed the defendant lawyers to delay proceedings with the result that the injunction hearings took one year and three days.[12] Finally, after 20 days of argument, the judge dismissed the Cree application and assigned unprecedented court costs to the Cree for approximately $200,000.

The Cree then turned to the Alberta Court of Appeal. They also publicized their dilemma and sought political and financial support from various sources. A legal defence fund was established, a major search for political support across the world was initiated. The Alberta Court of Appeal denied the appeal after waiting six months to hear it. The Supreme Court of Canada denied leave to appeal at the level. The oil and gas developments in the

Lubicon Lake area and the failure of the courts to grant an interim injunction have had dire consequences on the life-style of the Cree, and these cumulative negative results are reflected in increased rates of welfare, social pathology, decrease in income, the destruction of a way of life and of the quality of life for individuals. The impacts were labelled "genocidal consequences" by the World Council of Churches delegation which visited the area in 1984.[13]

GENOCIDAL CONSEQUENCES

The history of colonialism and de-development outlined in the preceding sections took its toll on Indian populations in Canada in uneven ways. The Lubicon people were relatively isolated from its effect until the 1940s because they were living in the bush and were able to sustain their cultural life-style until the land base came under attack. It was entirely predictable that once the land base was threatened, lives would be too. However, Canada and Alberta and the general Canadian public could not accept that a hunting and trapping society was viable, that the Cree wished to pursue their traditional life-style, and that they would fight to do so. Not surprisingly, the courts reflected the prevailing sentiments of the majority society in their decisions and in so doing failed to comprehend the magnitude of their decisions. The outcome of those judicial decisions has led to the systematic destruction of a way of life and of the basis of that life: the land. Unfortunately, the judges who denied the interim injunctive relief to the Lubicon people are not accountable for the outcomes of their decisions. Those outcomes have clear genocidal consequences. We should be clear on the terms we are using. The term "genocide" is not used lightly here and it predictably evokes strong aversive reactions on the part of the reader. However, it is important to use the term because it is accurate and the reactions to it are important to deal with. The term is most familiar when attached to the accounts of the holocaust and there is no ambivalence about the annihilation of millions of Jewish people. Webster defines the term as "the systematic destruction of a way of life, of a culture, of a people"[14] and it is in that sense that we use it. No one is suggesting that people at Lubicon Lake are being gassed to death, or shot as were the Beothuks of Newfoundland. However, there are many ways to be systematically destroyed and death at many levels is the result. We have already seen some of those results in the last few years at Lubicon, results the courts said could not be considered because they were "fears of the future" and therefore not factual.[15] However, in the court proceeding evidence was presented by indicating the beginning of the destruction. The judges chose not to believe it.

The second term that is used consistently in this paper is "institutionalized racism". This I use in the sense of entrenched attitudes, carefully taught and assumed, usually unconscious and which are exhibited in often subtle but hostile racist behaviour towards people of another class and colour. Such behaviour is a normative part of bureaucratic behaviour within both the federal and provincial Indian affairs administration. The term harkens back to the concepts of the noble savage, the wardship mentality, the moral majority position. Racism is endemic in our society and is expressed most often in ethnocentric, moralistic ways. Its effect is the denigration of the value of other cultures, and it is a constant challenge to the dignity and acceptability of native peoples. Frideres states,[16]

> According to racist theory, no amount of efforts by natives or assistance from whites could compensate for the natives' natural inferiority. This conviction is evident in the government's decision to establish native reservations. The reserves were to act as holding pens for worthless people, inferior children, wards of the nation.

Further, Frideres holds that the current myth of equality, that is, that all humans are equal no matter how different they are, is equally discriminatory because the mythology acts as a rationale to deny special privileges, programs and affirmative action.

JUDGMENTS

Over 8,000 pages of evidence, affidavits, testimony, and legal arguments were produced during the application by the Lubicon Lake people for an interim injunction. Basically, their argument was that they held Indian title to their homelands, that those lands were being destroyed by the oil and gas companies operating in the area and that they feared for their lives and livelihood. Evidence was argued on many details of the application by the affidavits, including my own, testifying that the continuance of such activities would destroy the integrity of the cultural group and therefore destroy the society, as well as individuals, was never challenged until the judgments. These judgments were based on assumptions which I think are irrelevant in the consideration of cross-cultural situations. For example, if the premise is used that the greater good of the greater number is the key component of balance of convenience arguments, then minority groups will never be able to receive justice in the courts. In this case, the arguments were advanced and upheld by the court decisions that the companies would suffer the greater injustice if they were enjoined because they would lose their competitive edge in the industry; that the appellants could not provide compensation for the loss of income for the companies if they lost the trial action; and that the coffers of the Alberta Heritage fund (and therefore the people of Alberta) would suffer if the Cree were to receive injunctive relief.

Let us look at that for a moment. First, the companies estimated a loss of $90 million if they were enjoined for six months. That calculation did not include the loss of jobs and the loss of competitive edge in the industry. By comparison, the Cree would lose *only* $80,000 (20 trappers times an average income of $4,000). Therefore, it was acceptable to the courts for the Cree to lose less than for the companies to lose more. Further, such capitalistic arguments failed to comprehend that cash income was not all that was at stake for the Cree. The oil would have remained in the ground and would not have rotted during the injunctive period; the assets of the company would still have been there; they would have lost time but, in the long run, they would not have lost money. For the Cree, however, the loss of their land resulted not only in a loss of income but also in a loss of a way of life. The courts did not understand, or accept that the destruction of the land was not compensatory because one cannot pay for something that is irreplaceable, as is a way of life. In the Court of Queen's Bench, Justice Forsyth was quite clear about his disregard of the importance of life-style to the Cree when he said[17]

> The evidence simply does not establish a way of life by the applicants which is being destroyed by the respondents...
> ...the evidence of lifestyle being affected is limited to a few individuals who hunt and trap in the area...

Further, Forsyth J. in his judgment states:[18]

> This is not a case of an isolated community in the remote north where access is only available by air on rare occasions and whose way of life is dependent to great extent on living off the land itself. The twentieth century, for better or for worse, has been part of the applicants' lives for a considerable period of time. The influence of the outside world comes from various sources, in many cases not connected with any of the activities of any of the respondents.

The honourable judge was wrong in his assessment of the dependency of the Lubicon people on the land, and seemingly chose not to credit their own submissions and affidavits which clearly outlined the extent of their activities on the land, the integrity of their hunting and trapping culture and its economic, social, ritual and political complexity. Further, in stating that the Lubicon people are part of the twentieth century, the judge denies them the options

of being hunters and trappers at the same time as they utilize aspects of the majority culture to enhance their own life-styles. It becomes an either/or proposition far removed from the reality of the very viable and stable land-based Cree society. The statement also raises questions about how Indians are viewed in the eyes of the court, or at least in this instance. Staroszik comments,[19]

> We can only assume from the Court's decision that Indians in general do not have a culture or a way of life which qualifies for the protection of the law unless they fulfill the Victorian image of the "noble savage" living in a pristine and unadulterated wilderness environment having no contact with technology or other phenomenon of so called "civilization".

Bankes comments in a similar vein on Forsyth J.'s decision when he says,[20]

> Forsyth was of the view that the plaintiffs could hardly establish a threat to a traditional way of life when they had already gone a long way towards joining the mainstream of 20th century society. In other words, the Lubicon Band had nothing left worth protecting. That, with respect, seems to be a very harsh conclusion, and more to the point, an inappropriate one to be made at the interim injunction stage. It also indicates a judicial view that the aboriginal peoples of Canada have rights so long as they remain in a fossilized or primitive state but their rights are progressively diminished to the extent that they avail themselves of the benefits and the burdens of the 20th century.

If one looks carefully at the assumptions that the native life-styles are not commensurate with valued types of twentieth century living, then the double-edged dilemma is clear: whatever one is as a native, it is not good enough, or defensible, or acceptable. It is clear to me that the court failed to accept the statements of the Cree as believable because the Cree did not fit into the suitable categories of mythological Indians, that is, they had a viable way of life which was under assault, but because they used the technological trappings of our society, they ought not to be hunters and trappers. In other words, the court reflected the institutionalized, racist view of Canadian society while also applying criteria which were irrelevant to minority group arguments.

A further example of this bind arises in the issue of the ability to pay. It was conceded that if the companies lost the case, they had the ability to pay but if the Lubicons lost, they could not compensate the companies for their losses. Forsyth J. addressed this issue in his judgment[21]

...I am more than satisfied that the respondents would suffer large and significant damages if injunctive relief in any of the forms sought by the applicants were granted. Furthermore, the respondents would suffer a loss of competitive position in the industry *vis-à-vis* the position of other companies not parties to this action. That loss coupled with the admitted inability of the applicants to give a meaningful undertaking to the court as to damages...reinforces my decision that injunctive relief in this case is not appropriate.

And Kerans J.A. writing for the Alberta Court of Appeal supports the lower court judgment when he says,[22]

In any event, we agree with him that, on the balance of convenience, the harm done to the respondents would far outweigh any harm done to the applicants during the interval before trial.

The "interim before trial" was known to be at least a year. The Kerans J.A. judgment was written in January 1985 and trial was to be some time in 1986: in fact, a specific date for 1988 has yet to be set. Bankes,[23] discussing the *Meares Island* case along with the *Lubicon and Bears Island* cases, summarizes his impressions of the court decisions in the following way,

I would suggest that the judgments show a tremendous skepticism of the claims made by the bands and an unwillingness to take them seriously...the skepticism as to the nature of Indian rights also extends to skepticism as to the need to protect a unique Indian way of life.

In essence, we have evidence here of judicial bias against those whose lives are not only different and therefore somehow suspect, but also who are too poor to provide an undertaking thus making them doubly suspicious. We are left then with the conclusion that the poor cannot look to the courts for injunctive relief against the rich and so we have a class bias as well as a racial one. Staroszik supports this analysis when he states:[24]

...the court has, in effect, determined that it is the greater public interest that the substantial economic activity proceed and that the loss of the plaintiff's culture and society, even if irreparable, on balance is not significant compared to the gains of industry and the government.

CONCLUSION

There were many other issues which arose in court which could be addressed here and which reflected the institutionalized bias of the courts against minority people. I believe that the courts failed to understand the nature of hunting and trapping societies and lacked the will to accept the evidence put forth by the Cree. For the judges, and the defendant lawyers, it was the first time they had had direct contact with native people. The language barriers were considerable since not only was English used entirely but it was used in a legalistic way. The Cree elders spoke no English and it fell to the chief to interpret not only what was said but what it meant. The differential views of justice, of truth, of morality were painfully clear in this cross-cultural situation. While the Cree sat with their pictures of bulldozed traplines, the companies argued that they had no policy to bulldoze lines and were not responsible for such damages. They argued that they were good corporate citizens, operating legally and monitored by Alberta. It was hard to find the real truths in the midst of the posturing and it became clear early in the proceedings that even "facts" are disputable.

The differential perceptions of events also gave rise to some anguish and anger. The companies argued that they had adhered to the law by sending advance notice to the Band of their activities in the area so the trappers could pull their lines. Indeed some did, but the mail went to Peace River or to the Band office while the trappers were out on their lines and no mail could reach them there. The companies did not feel they needed to provide such information through their field personnel who might talk to the trappers. This lack of goodwill and the belief that all of this was just a nuisance anyway failed to address the real issues, that is, the loss of food and income from traplines, and in some cases, the loss of the trapline itself. The ramifications of those losses were not recognized or accepted by the companies or the courts. This type of attitude and behaviour I have to label as racism because it fails to acknowledge and respect the way of life of a racial minority as valid.

Finally, the courts, in refusing to accept arguments that predicted the destruction of the community should the land base continue to be destroyed on the grounds that these were not facts of the present and were based on "fear of the future", gave authority to the companies to pursue that destruction. In so doing, the courts condemned the Lubicon Lake people to misery, poverty, suicide, despair and all the genocidal consequences which were accurately predicted during the hearings.

Endnotes

1. R.S.C. 1970, c. I–6.
2. *Royal Proclamation*, R.S.C. 1970, App. I.
3. Canada, Department of Indian Affairs and Northern Resources, *The Historical Development of the Indian Act* (1978).
4. Canada, *Indian Treaties and Surrenders* (1905).
5. Berger, *Village Journey* (1985) at 52 ff.
6. *Ibid.*
7. *Ibid.*
8. Erikson in Shilnyk, *A Poison Greater than Love* (1985) at xiii–xviii.
9. This road construction was opposed by the Cree who filed a *caveat* against Alberta in 1975 to stop the road from being built. Alberta responded by passing Bill 29 which prohibited people from filing caveats against the province. Alberta applied the Bill retroactively and the road went through.
10. *Lubicon Lake Band v. R.* (1980), 117 D.L.R. (3d) 247 (Fed. T.D.).
11. *Ominayak v. Norcen Energy Resources Ltd.* (1982), 23 *Alta. L.R.* (2d) 284, additional reasons at 24 *Alta. L.R.* (2d) 151 (*sub nom. Lubicon Lake Indian Band v. Norcen Energy Resources Ltd.*) (Q.B.).

12. Staroszik, "*Ominayak v. Norcen* Case Notes" (1985), *Environmental Law Centre Newsletter* at 2.
13. World Council of Churches, *Brief to the Prime Minister of Canada* (1985).
14. *Webster's New Collegiate Dictionary* (1956).
15. Judgment of Forsyth J., *supra*, note 11.
16. Frideres, *Native People in Canada: Contemporary Conflicts* (1984) at 304.
17. (1983), 29 *Alta. L.R.* (2d) 151 at 157 (Q.B.).
18. *Ibid.* at 157–58.
19. Staroszik, "*Ominayak v. Norcen et al.* Case Notes" (1985), *Environmental Law Centre Newsletter* at 7.
20. Bankes, "Judicial Attitudes to Aboriginal Resource Rights and Title" (1985), 13 *Resources* 3.
21. Judgment of Forsyth J. (1983), 29 *Alta. L.R.* (2d) 151 at 158 (Q.B.).
22. Judgment of Kerans J.A. (1984), 36 *Alta. L.R.* (2d) 137 (C.A.).
23. See *supra*, note 22 at 4.
24. Staroszik, "*Ominayak v. Norcen et al.* Case Notes" (1985), *Environmental Law Centre Newsletter* at 8.

7

Dispute Resolution

A. Types of Disputes and Processes for Resolution

The Mediator and the Judge[†]
T. Eckhoff

MEDIATION consists of influencing the parties to come to agreement by appealing to their own interest. The mediator may make use of various means to attain this goal. He may work on the parties' ideas of what serves them best, for instance, in such a way that he gets them to consider their common interests as more essential that they did previously, or their competing interests as less essential. He may also look for possibilities of resolution which the parties themselves have not discovered and try to convince them that both will be well served with his suggestion. The very fact that a suggestion is proposed by an impartial third party may also, in certain cases, be sufficient for the parties to accept it (*cf.* Schelling, 1960, pp. 62, 63, 71 and 143 ff.). The mediator also has the possibility of using promises or threats. He may, for instance, promise the parties help or support in the future if they become reconciled or he may threaten to ally himself with one of them if the other does not give in. A mediator does not necessarily have to go in for compromise solutions, but for many reasons he will, as a rule, do so. The compromise is often the way of least resistance for one who shall get the parties to agree to an arrangement. As pointed out by Aubert (1963, p. 39) it may also contribute to the mediator's own prestige that he promotes intermediate solutions. Therewith he appears as the moderate and reasonable person with ability to see the problem from different angles — in contrast to the parties who will easily be suspected of having been onesided and quarrelsome since they have not managed to resolve the conflict on their own.

In order that both parties should have confidence in the mediator and be willing to co-operate with him and listen to his advice, it is important that they consider him impartial. This gives him an extra reason to follow the line of compromise (Aubert, 1963, p. 39, and Eckhoff, 1965, pp. 13–14). For, by giving both parties some support, he shows that the interests of one lie as close to his heart as those of the other. Regard for impartiality carries with it the consequence that the mediator sometimes must display caution in pressing the parties too hard. That the mediator, for instance, makes a threat to one of the parties to ally himself with the opponent unless compliance is forthcoming, may be an effective means of exerting pressure, but will easily endanger confidence in his impartiality. This can reduce his possibilities for getting the conflict resolved if threats do not work and it can weaken his future prestige as a mediator.

The conditions for a mediator are best in cases where both parties are interested in having the conflict resolved. The stronger this common interest is, the greater reason they have for bringing the conflict before a third party, and the more motivated they will be for co-operating actively with him in finding a solution, and for adjusting their demands in such a way that solution can be reached.

If the parties, or one of them, is, to begin with, not motivated for having the conflict resolved, or in any case not motivated to agree to any compromise, such motives must be *created* in him, for instance with the help of threats or sanctions. Cases may occur where the parties (or the unwilling one of them), may have a mediator forced upon them, and under pressure of persuasion from him or from the environment agree to an arrangement. But mediation under such circumstances presents difficulties, among other reasons, because it demands a balancing be-

---

†   Eckhoff, Torstein, "The Mediator and the Judge" in ed. Vilhelm Aubert, *Sociology of Law* (Penguin Books, 1969), 171–81. Reprinted from "The Mediator and the Judge" (1966), 10 *Acta Sociologica* 158–66, by permission of the Scandinavian University Press.

tween the regard for impartiality and the regard for exertion of sufficient pressure. If the conditions for resolving the conflict by a judgement or administrative decision exist these will, as a rule, be more effective procedures than mediation in the cases described here.

That normative factors are considered relevant for the solution, can in certain cases be helpful during mediation. By referring to a norm (e.g., concerning what is right and wrong) the mediator may get the parties to renounce unreasonable demands so that their points of view approach each other. Even if the parties do not feel bound by the norms, it is conceivable that others consider it important that they be followed and that the mediator can therefore argue that a party will be exposed to disapproval if he does not accommodate.

The norms will be of special support for the mediator if the parties are generally in agreement on their content and are willing to submit to them, so that the reason that there is a conflict at all can be traced back to the fact that the norms do not cover all aspects of the difference. The remainder which is not covered will then have the features of a fairly pure conflict of interests where the norms have brought the points of departure nearer one another than they would otherwise have been.

If, however, the parties consider the norms as giving answers to the questions being disputed, but disagree on what the answers are, the possibilities for mediation will, as a rule, be weakened. In the first place, the probability that the conflict will at all be made the object of mediation is reduced, among other reasons, because bringing it before a judge will often be possible and more likely in these cases. Secondly, mediation which has been begun may be made difficult because of the parties' disagreement concerning the norms or the relevant facts. This is the more true the more inflexibly the opinions are opposed to each other and the more value-laden they are. The parties' resistance to compromising on questions of rights or truth makes itself felt also when the mediator appears in the arena. Perhaps the presence of a third party will make the parties even more set on asserting their rights than they otherwise would have been. The mediator can try to 'de-ideologize' the dispute by arguing that it is not always wise to 'stand on one's right' and that one should not 'push things to extremes', but go the 'golden middle road'.[1] Sometimes he succeeds in this and manages to concentrate attention on the interest-aspects, so that the usual mediation arguments will have an effect. But it may also go the other way. The mediator lets himself be influenced by the parties to see the normative aspects as the most important, and ends up by judging instead of mediating. And even if he does not go so far, his opinions concerning norms and facts may inhibit his eagerness to mediate. In any case, it may be distasteful for him to work for a compromise if he has made up his mind that one of the parties is completely right and the other wrong.

Hoebel's survey (1954) of conflict-resolution in various primitive cultures confirms the impression that conditions are, generally speaking, less favourable for mediation than for other forms of conflict-resolution when the conflicts are characterized by disagreements about normative factors. Most of the third party institutions he describes have more in common with what I in this article call judgemental and administrative activity than with mediation. The only example in Hoebel's book of the development of a pure mediation institution for the resolution of disputes which have a strongly normative element, is found among the Ifugao-people in the northern part of Luzon in the Philippines. This is an agricultural people without any kind of state-form but with well developed rules governing property rights, sale, mortgage, social status (which is conditional on how much one owns), family relations, violation of rights, etc. Conflicts concerning these relations occur often. If the parties do not manage to solve them on their own they are regularly left to a mediator, who is called a *mokalun*. This is not a permanent office that belongs to certain persons but a task to which the person is appointed for the particular case. In practice the *mokalun* is always a person high rank and generally someone who has won esteem as a headhunter. He is chosen by the plaintiff, but is regarded as an impartial intermediary, not as a representative for a party. The parties are obligated to keep peace so long as mediation is in progress and they may not have any direct contact with each other during this period. The *mokalun* visits them alternately. He brings offers of conciliation and replies to these offers, and he tries, with the help of persuasion, and also generally with threats, to push through a conciliation. If he attains this he will receive good pay and increased prestige. If the mediation is not successful the conflict will remain unresolved and will perhaps result in homicide and blood feuds, for the *mokalun* has no authority to make decisions which are binding on the parties.

It is easy to point to features in the Ifugao culture which can have favoured the growth of such a method of conflict-resolution. On the one hand, there has obviously been a strong need to avoid open struggle within the local society, among other reasons, because the people were resident farmers who had put generations of work into terraces and irrigation works. On the other hand, there was no political leadership and no organized restraining power, and the conditions were therefore not favourable for conflict-resolution by judgement or coercive power. Nevertheless, it is noteworthy that the mediation arrangement functioned so well as it did, considering that it was applied to conflicts where divergent opinions of right and wrong were pitted against each other. It is natural to make a comparison with our present international conflicts, where the conditions are parallel to the extent that the danger for combat actions and the absence of other kinds of third party institutions create a strong need for mediation, but where the mediation institutions so far developed have been far less effective.

The *judge* is distinguished from the mediator in that his activity is related to the level of norms rather than to the level of interests. His task is not to try to reconcile the parties but to reach a decision about which of them is right. This leads to several important differences between the two methods of conflict-resolution. The mediator should preferably look forward, toward the consequences which may follow from the various alternative solutions, and he must work on the parties to get them to accept a solution. The judge, on the other hand, looks back to the events which have taken place (e.g., agreements which the parties have entered into, violations which one has inflicted on the other, etc.) and to the norms concerning acquisition of rights, responsibilities, etc. which are connected with these events. When he has taken his standpoint on this basis, his task is finished. The judge, therefore, does not have to be an adaptable negotiator with ability to convince and to find constructive solutions, as the mediator preferably should be. But he must be able to speak with authority on the existing questions of norms and facts in order to be an effective resolver of conflicts.

The possibility for judging in a dispute presupposes that the norms are considered relevant to the solution. The norms may be more or less structures. They may consist in a formal set of rules (e.g., a judicial system, the by-laws of an organization of the rules of a game), in customs or only in vague notions of what is right and just. The normative frame of reference in which a decision is placed does not have to be the same — and does not even have to exist — for all those who have something to do with the conflict. What one person perceives as a judgement another may perceive as an arbitrary command. If, however, *none* of those involved (the parties, the third party, the environment) applies normative considerations to the relationship because all consider it a pure conflict of interests, decision by judgement is excluded.

A decision may be a 'judgement' (in the sense in which the term is used here) even if the parties do not comply with it. But the greater the possibility that a judgement will be lived up to, the more suitable judgement will be as a method for conflict-resolution, and the better reason will the person who desires a solution have for preferring that procedure. It is therefore of significance to map out the factors which promote and hinder compliance to judgements.

The parties' interests in the outcome play an important role in this connexion. If the main thing for them is to have the dispute settled, and it is of secondary importance what the content of the solution is, it will require very little for them to comply with the judgement. If, on the other hand, there are strong and competing interests connected with the outcome, so that submission to the judgement

implies a great sacrifice for one or both of the parties, the question of compliance is more precarious.

That one party (voluntarily or by force) submits to a judgement in spite of the sacrifice it means for him, may be due in part to norms and in part to the authority of the judge. There may be many reasons for the parties' respect for those *norms* on which the judge bases his decision; for instance, they may be internalized, or one fears gods' or people's punishment if one violates them, or one finds it profitable in the long run to follow them (e.g., because it creates confidence in one's business activities if one gains a reputation for law-abidance or because it makes the game more fun if the rules are followed). If the parties are sufficiently motivated to comply with the norms and give exhaustive answers to the question under dispute, then relatively modest demands are made on the judge's authority. If he is regarded as having knowledge of the norms and as having ability to find the facts, this will be sufficient to assure that his judgements are respected. Sometimes this is a simple assignment which many can fulfill. We may, for instance, take the case of two chess players who have not yet completely learned the rules of the game and who disagree as to whether it is permissible to castle in the present position. They ask a more experienced player who is present and comply without question to his decision because they consider it obvious that the rules should be followed and know that he is acquainted with them. But there are also cases where insight into norms, and perhaps also ability to clarify the factual relations in the matter, presuppose special expertise which only a few have. The kind of expertise required varies with the nature of the normative ideas. It may be, for instance, that contact with supernatural powers is considered to provide special prerequisites for finding out what is true and right, or it may be life-experience or professional studies. Monopolizing of insight may be a natural consequence of the fact that a norm system is large and cannot be taken in at a glance, but there are also many examples of systematic endeavours on the part of experts to prevent intruders from acquiring their knowledge.

If the parties are not sufficiently strongly motivated to comply with the norms which regulate their mutual rights and duties, or if they do not regard these as giving exhaustive answers to the matter of dispute, the judgement must appear as something more than a conveyance of information in order to command respect. The parties must, in one way or another, be bound or forced to adhere to it. One condition which may contribute to this is that, in addition to the primary norms which define the parties' mutual rights and obligations, there is also a set of secondary norms of adjudication which single out the judge as the proper person to settle the dispute and which possibly also impose upon the parties the duty to abide by his decision. That the judge is in this way equipped with *authority* is in many cases sufficient reason for the parties to consider themselves bound to live up to his decisions. But the establishment of authority often presupposes power, and even if the authority-relationship is established, it may sometimes be necessary to press through a decision by force. The power can reside with the judge, with someone he represents (e.g., the state) or with others who are interested in the decision being respected (e.g., the winning party or his relatives or friends). And it can have various bases: physical or military strength, control of resources on which the parties are dependent, powers of sorcery, etc. How *much* power is necessary depends partly on what other factors promote and hinder compliance, and partly upon the relative strength of the enforcing authority and the disobedient party.

That the parties and others have confidence in the judge's impartiality promotes compliance to judgements. It strengthens the belief that the decisions he makes are right and it facilitates enforcement by making the application of force more legitimate. As mentioned before, it is also important for the mediator to appear impartial, but the manner of showing impartiality is different for the two kinds of third parties.[2] To a certain extent the judge can display that he gives equal consideration to both parties, for instance, by giving both the same possibilities for arguing and for presenting evidence. But he cannot, like the mediator, systematically endeavour to reach compromises, because the norms sometimes demand decision in favour of one of the parties. If he finds that one party is completely right he must judge in his favour, and the outcome of the case will not in itself be a testimony to his giving equal consideration to both.

But the judge has other possibilities for appearing impartial. Sometimes his person gives sufficient guarantee. He is, for instance, because of his high rank, his contact with supernatural powers or his recognized wisdom and strength of character regarded as infallible, or at least freed from suspicion of partisanship. The privilege of the judge to assume a retired position during the proceedings and not to engage in argumentation with the parties makes it easier to ascribe such qualities to him than to the mediator. Another significant factor is that there are, as a rule, small possibilities for checking the rightness of a judgement because this presupposes knowledge of both the system of norms and the facts of the particular case. To maintain a belief that certain persons are infallible can, nevertheless, present difficulties, especially in cultures characterized by democratization and secularization. To reduce or conceal the human factor in decision-making will therefore often be better suited to strengthening confidence in the decisions. Letting the judge appear as a 'mouthpiece of the law', who cannot himself exert any influence worth mentioning on the outcome of the cases, tends to remove the fear that his own interests, prejudices, sympathies and antipathies may have impact on his rulings.

Tendencies to overestimate the influence of the norms and underestimate the influence of the judge may also have other functions than strengthening confidence in the judge's impartiality. Firstly, these tendencies contribute to the transmission of authority from the norm system to the individual decisions. Secondly, the conditions are favourable for a gradual and often almost unnoticeable development of a norm system through court practice, so that the resistance to change is reduced. An thirdly, the judge will be less exposed to criticism and self reproach when he (both in his own and others' eyes) avoids appearing as personally responsible for his decisions. This is important because it might otherwise involve great strain to make decisions in disputes where the parties' contentions are strongly opposed to each other, where there are perhaps great interests at stake for both, and where it may be extremely doubtful who is right (*cf.* Eckhoff and Jacobsen, 1960, especially pp. 37 ff.). It is therefore not surprising that many techniques have been used in the various judicial systems for the purpose of eliminating, limiting or concealing the influence of the judge. The use of ordeals and drawing of lots in the administration of justice (*cf.* Eckhoff, 1965, pp. 16–17; and Wedberg, 1935) may be mentioned as examples of this, and the same is true for the technique of judicial argumentation which gives the decisions the appearance of being the products of knowledge and logic, and not of evaluation and choice.

Judicial activity and formation of norms serve to support each other mutually. On the one hand, the judge is dependent on normative premises on which he can base his decisions. The greater the relevance attributed to them, and the stronger the ideological anchoring of the norm system, the more favourable are the conditions for conflict-resolution by judgement. On the other hand, the activity of judges can contribute to the spreading of knowledge about norms, to their increased recognition and authority, and to a gradual extension of the norm system to cover new types of conflict situations.

The activity of judging is in these respects quite different from the activity of mediating. As mentioned before, the task of the mediator becomes more difficult the more emphasis the parties place on the normative aspects of the conflict (presupposing that there is disagreement about these, as there usually will be in conflict situations). The mediator, therefore, must try to 'de-ideologize' the conflict, for instance, by stressing that interests are more important than the question of who is right and who is wrong, or by arguing that one ought to be reasonable and willing to compromise. The use of mediation in certain types of disputes may tend to create or reinforce the norm that willingness to compromise is the proper behaviour in conflict situations, and thereby to reduce the significance of such norms as judges base their decisions on.

The contrasts between the two types of third-party intervention make it difficult to combine the role of the judge and the role of the mediator in a satisfactory way. Indeed it does happen that a third party first tries to mediate between the parties and if that does not succeed, passes judgement.[3] Also the reverse is conceivable: that a third party first passes judgement and then proceeds to mediate when he sees that the judgement will not be respected. But in both cases attempts to use one method may place hindrances in the way of the other. By mediating one may weaken the normative basis for a later judgement and perhaps also undermine confidence in one's impartiality as a judge; and by judging first one will easily reduce the willingness to compromise of the party who was supported in the judgement, and will be met with suspicion of partiality by the other.

When the establishment of new third-party institutions is sought, for instance, by a legislator who is looking for new ways of settling labour conflicts, or by those who are working for the peaceful adjustment of international conflicts, there may be a dilemma about which way to go. Should one go in for building up the norm system, and for strengthening the normative engagement with the aim of having as many conflicts as possible decided by judgement? Or ought one rather rely on 'de-ideologization' and mediation? In considering such questions it is important not to let oneself be led by superficial analogies but to take account of all the relevant factors. Regarding international conflicts, for instance, one must consider that there is no superior instance which is powerful enough to force a powerful state

to obedience. This has the consequence that courts can hardly be effective organs for the resolution of conflicts where substantial interests are at stake. Mediation also presents difficulties, among other reasons because the parties often place great emphasis on the moral and legal aspects of the conflict, and have strongly divergent opinions concerning both norms and (perhaps especially) the relevant facts. But there is good reason to believe that the difficulties in mediation are, after all, easier to overcome and that endeavours should therefore go in the direction of reducing the normative engagement.

Endnotes

1. Confucius considered this as one of the conflict-resolver's most important tasks. His teaching that the parties tending to assert their rights must be dampened, so that one could get them to compromise, has left deep marks in the East-Asiatic ideology of conflict-resolution. This is probably one of the reasons that the idea of the Rule of Law has had such difficulty in winning support in the East. *Cf., The Dynamic Aspects of the Rule of Law in the Modern Age*, issued by the International Commission of Jurists, 1965, pp. 31–2.
2. *Cf.* Eckhoff (1965, pp. 12 ff.), where there is a survey of various ways in which conflict-resolvers can show their impartiality.
3. The *Norwegian Civil Procedure Act* (of 13 August 1915, p. 99) provides that the judge may, at any stage of the case, attempt to mediate between the parties.

Further Reading

Alan Milner, "Settling Disputes: The Changing Face of English Law" (1974), 20 *McGill Law Journal* 521–33.

V. Aubert, "Law and Conflicts", in *In Search of Law* (Oxford: Basil Blackwell, 1983), 58–75.

R. Abel, "Delegalization: A Critical Review of its Ideology Manifestations and Social Consequences" (1980), 6 *Jahrbuch Fur Rechts-Soziologie und Rechtstheorie* 27–43.

J. Inverarity et al., "Legal Procedure and Social Structure: The Contribution of Max Weber" in *Law and Society, Sociological Perspectives on Criminal Law* (Toronto: Little Brown & Co., 1983), Chapter 3.

B. Adjudication

The Judge and the Adversary System[†]
N. Brooks

THE ROLE OF THE JUDGE
IN THE ADVERSARY SYSTEM

A thorough discussion of this subject would require an examination of the judge's role at each stage of the litigation process: at the pre-trial investigative stage; at the pre-trial procedural stages; at the trial; at the sentencing hearing; and at the hearing to determine law and policy. While the same principles may be applicable to each stage, the discussion in this paper will focus on the role of the trial judge in the conduct of the trial. The trial has a first claim on our attention since it is at this stage of the litigation process that all aspects of the adversary system bear most directly on the judge's role. Moreover, restricting the discussion in this way will permit, in the time available, a more detailed development of the central theoretical themes of the subject.

In determining the precise role that he will assume in discharging his responsibilities at trial, a judge will undoubtedly consider a wide range of factors: the peculiarities of his own temperament and abilities, the significance of the particular case to the parties and to the public, the complexity of the factual and legal issues raised by the case, and the effectiveness of the parties or their counsel in presenting the case. However, whatever other factors a judge might consider in defining the precise nature of the role he will play, the fact that he is an arbiter in an adjudicative proceeding that is adversarial in nature necessarily prescribes for him the parameters of his involvement in the proceeding. In this paper I will develop this theme by speculating about the justifications which have been or might be advanced supporting the adversary system, and then exploring the limitations that these justifications impose on the judge's role in conducting a judicial trial.

Although even a careful analysis of the underlying premises of the adversary system may not result in a statement of principles that would lead each of us to resolve particular problems as to the judge's intervention in the trial in the same way, it should provide us with some general sense of his role. Obviously, if we do not stand upon common ground in our understanding of the adversary system, or in our understanding of its premises, any discussion of the judge's role will be mere rhetoric or sophistry. While at the end of the day, an attempt to refine the judge's role in the trial may appear to be trivial because of the obvious constraints that the adversary system, by any understanding, places on the judge's intervention in the trial, the issue is too important for any refinement to be trivial. Judge Breitel, a Justice of the Appellate Division, Supreme Court of New York, addressing a conference on judicial ethics noted, "Consciously or unconsciously the most important decision that the judge makes for himself is whether he will play an affirmative or quiescent role in the performance of his function." Also, because the issue is so central to our whole concept of the judicial trial, the importance of a clear understanding of the judge's role transcends the few instances where it becomes a matter of practical concern in any particular trial.

Definition of "Adversary System"

The greatest impediment to clear thinking about the judge's role in the adversary system is the variety of meanings that are often assigned to the concept of the adversary system. Therefore, before examining the premises underlying the adversary system let me make clear the sense in which that concept is used in this paper by distinguishing it from various senses in which it is often misleadingly used.

The term is being used in this paper to refer generally to a procedural system in which the parties and not the judge have the primary responsibility for defining the issues in dispute and for carrying the dispute forward through the system. Thus, it should not be confused with what might more accurately be referred to as the adjudicative process. Adjudication is a method of settling disputes that is commonly contrasted with other methods of dispute resolution such as mediation, negotiation and conciliation. Used in this context, it refers characteristically to a means of resolving disputes in which some general principle or rule of law is applied to the facts that gave rise to the dispute and in which the parties involved are able to participate by presenting proofs and reasoned argument.

Professor Lon Fuller, who in a series of essays clarified the tasks for which adjudication because of its institutional framework was well-suited as a means of social

---

†   Brooks, Neil, "The Judge and the Adversary System" in ed. Allen Linden, *The Canadian Judiciary*, (Toronto: Osgoode Hall Law School, 1976), at 89–118. Reprinted by permission of Professor Neil Brooks.

ordering, argued that an adversary presentation is essential to adjudication. He postulated that the fundamental characteristic of adjudication is the opportunity it provides for the affected parties to participate in the decision-making by presenting proofs and arguments. He concluded that only the adversary system is capable of affording this requisite degree of participation. Whether or not these two concepts need to be so closely wed, it remains useful in analysing the judge's role to distinguish between them.

While I do not intend to get diverted from my central task by embarking on a critical analysis of the adversary system, it will assist in clarifying the judge's role in the adversary system to mention two criticisms which are sometimes directed at it, but which are more appropriately seen to be criticisms of adjudication as a form of dispute resolution. An understanding of the criticisms will illustrate the point that adjudication is a means of resolving disputes; the adversary system is a procedural system in which the parties and not the judge assume the primary role in defining the dispute and in presenting proof. Firstly, it is sometimes suggested that the adversary system is an inappropriate method of dealing with polycentric problems. In defining a polycentric problem, Professor Lon Fuller, who coined the phrase in this context, analogized it to a spider web, "[a] pull on one strand will distribute tensions after a complicated pattern throughout the web as a whole...each crossing of strands is a distinct centre for distributing tensions." One difficulty of resolving a polycentric problem, then, is that a principle of sufficient generality cannot be formulated to account for the diverse effects of shifting one interest in such a problem. However, this is a problem which presents itself when an attempt is made to resolve such a problem of adjudication. Thus it is not properly seen as a criticism of the adversary system.

Secondly, it is sometimes argued that the adversary system is deficient because it presents an all-or-nothing proposition — there are always winners and losers — and, as a consequence, the total satisfaction of the parties is often reduced. This is particularly the case in areas such as family law, labour law, or criminal law where the parties are part of a close social or economic relationship. Again the adversary system is here a victim because of its close association with adjudication. The attempt at the outset to adjudicate this kind of claim is more properly criticized.

The term adversary system is also frequently used to contrast contemporary Anglo-American criminal procedure with the proceedings before the Court of Star Chamber or other so-called inquisitorial systems of medieval Europe. Used in this sense, the adversary system is taken to describe a proceeding which is conducted in public, in which the accused has been charged with a specific crime, in which the accused has the right to remain silent and a right to counsel, and in which the prosecution must prove the accused's guilt beyond a reasonable doubt. Basically,

it is taken to characterize a procedural system which shows concern for the protection of the innocent, and the protection of social values other than the conviction of the guilty, such as the dignity of the individual. While the terms are often used interchangeably, it assists clarity of thought if the term accusatorial is used to refer to such a system and the term adversarial used to refer, again, simply to a method of proof-taking in which the parties play the leading role. While Anglo-Americans might like to think that the two concepts — adversarial and accusatorial — march together, that is not necessarily the case. In the sense that the terms are used here the inquisitorial systems which are prevalent in many European countries could be as accusatorial as the Anglo-American adversary system. Indeed, in practice, such systems might afford more protection to the innocent accused and to the dignity and freedom of the individual. The confusion in usage is compounded because the term inquisitorial is used to describe both the procedure before, for instance, the Court of Star Chamber or the Spanish Inquisition and the procedures of modern continental European countries.

Which leads me to a third sense in which the term adversary system is sometimes used — that is, as a term which refers to Anglo-American judicial procedure to distinguish it from judicial procedures in continental Europe. When the phrase is used in this sense it is deprived of meaningful content. There are undoubtedly many obvious differences between common law and civilian systems; there are also many points of similarity — to compare them generally tells us little about either system. If the evolution of the two systems is considered, including the evolution that is presently going on, the distinction becomes even more blurred. Furthermore, legal procedures in the countries on the European continent vary greatly, the difference between any two such countries might be more substantial than the difference between any one of them and Anglo-American procedure. In fairness to those who make the comparison, they may be referring generally to the role of the judge. Used narrowly in this way the terms, as antonyms, have some meaning. The judge assumes a much larger role in the litigation process in most European systems than he does in the Anglo-American system.

The adversary system, as that term is used by many proceduralists and as it will be used in this paper, embodies two distinct principles. The issues resolved by these two principles raise the two most basic questions that confront any adjudicative procedural system. The first issue is what should the respective functions of the parties and the judge be with reference to the initiation and content of the adjudication. The adversary system rests on the principle of party-autonomy. That is to say, that the parties have the right to pursue or dispose of their legal rights and remedies as they wish. The second issue is what should the respective functions of the parties and the judge be with reference to the progress of a dispute through the procedural system once initiated and defined. The adversary system rests on the principle of party-prosecution. This principle holds that the parties have the primary responsibility to choose without interference from the judge the manner in which they will go forward with their case and the proofs they will present for the judge's consideration in adjudicating the dispute.

Party-Autonomy

In defining the judge's role in the conduct of the trial it is, of course, the principle of party-prosecution that requires careful analysis. However, to place that examination in perspective, the principle of party-autonomy must be briefly examined. The principle of party-autonomy has two aspects. First, it limits the judge's function to disputes which have been presented to him. A judge plays a role only when a conflict has arisen between two or more parties, and at least one of them seeks the assistance of the judge in resolving the dispute. John Chipman Gray, in defining a judge, summarized this principle: "A judge of an organized body is a man appointed by that body to determine duties and the corresponding rights upon the application of persons claiming those rights." The authors of a casebook on civil procedure described the principle more prosaically: "Courts ought not to function as self-propelled vehicles of justice and right like King Arthur's knights in Good Humor trucks." Lon Fuller quotes a socialist critic of bourgeois law who caricatured this premise of the adversary system by asserting that courts in such a system "are like defective clocks; they have to be shaken to set them going". Fuller noted that, "[h]e of course added the point that the shaking costs money".

The second aspect of party-autonomy is that the parties have the sole responsibility for defining the dispute that they would like adjudicated. Thus, if the parties want the judge to decide one dispute, he will not insist on resolving another even though he perceives the other issue to be the real cause of the conflict between the parties.

Both aspects of party-autonomy are subject to qualifications. While the judge cannot initiate proceedings, he can prevent the parties from initiating certain proceedings. The courts have an important social function to perform by resolving disputes. Thus the judge can prevent parties from using the litigation process to resolve hypothetical or moot problems. He can judicially notice all facts that he considers beyond reasonable dispute and thus prevent the parties from consuming the time of the court by presenting evidence on clear factual issues. He can also prevent misuses of the process by a judicial screening of cases, he can give judgment on the pleadings or give a summary judgment. Indeed he is assisted in controlling the use of the court's process by counsel for the parties. Lawyers have a professional responsibility to ensure the

claims and defences they put forward have merit and are related to a real conflict.

In criminal cases, the judge's role in controlling the issues disputed is even greater than his responsibility in civil cases. While the judge cannot control the criminal cases to reach his docket, nor find the accused guilty of a crime he is not charged with, nor insist that the Crown amend the indictment to add charges, he does not permit the accused or the Crown complete autonomy in defining the issues contested. For instance, he can prevent the Crown from initiating the case if he concludes that the Crown is abusing the process. There is also an increasing recognition of the judge's responsibility to examine the factual basis of a plea of guilty. In the United States a Presidential Commission has recently recommended that the guilty plea be abolished entirely because, among other things, it leaves too much of the public interest to the parties.

The limits of the principle of party-autonomy can, of course, only be defined by reference to the reasons why it is regarded as being an essential principle of the Anglo-American procedural system. Two justifications sometimes put forward fail to appreciate that party-autonomy is only a principle which defines the respective roles of the parties and the judge. In civil cases, it has been said that the principle of party-autonomy — that the judge only operates when the parties present him with a dispute to resolve — rests on the judgment that "the social interest in securing general observance of the rules of private law is sufficiently served by leaving their enforcement to the self-interest of the parties more or less directly affected." However, while this reason might explain why the state need not become involved in the enforcement of the civil law, it does not go directly to the issue of the roles of the parties and the judge in initiating actions. In many areas where there is an important public interest in the enforcement of the civil law, as in the enforcement of the criminal law, the state, through an administrative agency, might initiate actions enforcing the law. And yet, since it is not the judge who initiates such actions, the principle of party-autonomy would be satisfied.

Others have suggested that the principle of party-autonomy reflects a political ideology. Thurman Arnold asserted, "...the civil trial dramatizes the moral beauty of the noninterference of government in private affairs.... The whole ideology, and procedural organization of the civil trial is designed to insulate the court and the government from taking the initiative in enforcing or even protecting the civil rights of individuals". Thurman Arnold was at the time decrying the resistance to the New Deal and exploring its causes. He went on, "[t]his role of the civil trial as a symbol of individual freedom from active interference by the government makes it a most important factor in preserving conservative traditions in the face of new legislation". While party-autonomy may reflect a *laissez-faire* philosophy, Arnold's point goes to the role of the government generally in the enforcement of the civil law.

Both of the above reasons given for the principle of party-autonomy stem from the misconception of what the principle demands. The principle does not require that the state refrain from initiating civil actions. It merely requires that the judge not initiate them. Fleming James more correctly stated the rationale when he noted, "...the adversary system and party-(autonomy) may well exist in areas extensively regulated by government in what is deemed to be the public interest. Their existence stems not from *laissez-faire* or a philosophy of individualism but rather from a notion of the proper allocation of function between the parties to a dispute (one of whom may be the government) and the tribunal which is to decide it, under any economic or social order, at least in a free society". Professor Lon Fuller also argued that the principle that an arbiter should not act on his own motion in initiating a case rests not on a political philosophy, but on a judgement that it increased the effectiveness of adjudication: "...it is generally impossible to keep even the bare initiation of proceedings untainted by preconceptions about what happened and what its consequences should be. In this sense, initiation of the proceedings by the arbiter impairs the integrity of adjudication by reducing the effectiveness of the litigant's participation through proofs and arguments."

Party-Prosecution

The second major premise of the adversary system, as that term is used by most proceduralists, is the principle of party-prosecution. This principle holds that the parties have the right and the responsibility to choose the manner in which they will go forward with their case and the proof they will present to support it. The judge's role is to passively evaluate the merits of the case as and when it is presented to him.

In the remainder of this paper I will explore the reasons why the principle of party-prosecution is adhered to at trial, and offer some general comments on the parameters that these reasons place upon the judge's intervention in the conduct of the case. The conclusion that I reach is that viewed in this way the adversary system does not impose as severe restraints on the judge's intervention as is often assumed, and that in appropriate cases the judge should, if he deems it necessary, play a much larger role in the conduct of the case. My argument will be a plea for more judicial activism in controlling the conduct of the trial.

The principle of party-prosecution at trial rests, in the main, upon two broad empirical assumptions. Firstly, that the legitimacy of adjudication as a means of social ordering is enhanced if it is conducted according to an adversarial presentation. Secondly, that more accurate fact-finding is likely to result if parties motivated by self-interest are given the responsibilities of investigating facts and presenting arguments, and if the decision-maker remains passive.

The Adversary System increases the Acceptability of Adjudication

Every means of social ordering used by the state must be acceptable not only to those immediately affected by its particular sanctions but also to all those governed by the state. This need for legitimacy is particularly paramount in a free society with respect to adjudication since a judge's decision might be perceived, in some sense at least, to be undemocratic.

Legitimacy or acceptability is a derivative value. That is to say, a decision-making process will be acceptable to the extent that it meets all the criteria that people expect of that decision-making process. With respect to adjudication these expectations undoubtedly include such considerations as expediency, finality, inexpensiveness, and the protection of privacy and other social values. To the extent that the adversary system furthers these values it will render the adjudicative process more acceptable than would some other procedural device for finding the facts. But aside from these considerations, which are necessary attributes of any acceptable adjudicative proceeding, it is often argued that the adversary system has unique characteristics which render it in judicial trials a more acceptable procedure in our society than other methods of fact-finding. The reasons for the acceptability of the adversary system, if indeed it is more acceptable than other methods of fact-finding, must rest ultimately upon complex questions of political theory and psychology. I can only be suggestive here, in part repeating what others have speculated. Four reasons might be given as to why the adversary system is a more acceptable method of fact-finding in judicial trials than any other method.

Relationship to the Prevalent Political and Economic Theory

The adversary system yields greater satisfaction to the litigants and others because it is a procedure that is consistent with the prevalent social and political ideology of western society. An assertion made in the editorial page of a bar association journal illustrates this argument: "If you believe in the Anglo-Saxon common law tradition, that the individual is the important unit of our society, and the state exists to serve him, then it seems that the adversary system is preferable. If you hold a corporate view of society, that is to say, that the community is the important unit, and that the citizen must be primarily considered as a part of the corporate unit, then it seems you should champion the inquisitorial system..."

Jerome Frank is well known for linking the adversary system with economic theory. In his writings he repeatedly associated it with classic, *laissez-faire*, economic theory and unbridled individualism. Surprisingly, however, only recently has scholarship emerged in the English language which attempts to seriously study the influence of political and economic theory on judicial procedure. Naively, perhaps, the assumption has been made that procedure is value-free. Scholars who have turned their attention to this question in recent years seem to agree that at least at a very general and theoretical level there are connections between ideology and procedural choices. The connection may not be direct, nor empirically demonstrable. However, at least arguably, the adversary system can be seen as reflecting the political and economic ideology of classic English liberalism in three ways: by its emphasis upon self-interest and individual initiative; by its apparent distrust of the state; and, by the significance it attaches to the participation of the parties.

The adversary system legitimizes, indeed necessitates, a self-interested role for the parties. Thus one of its premises would appear to be consistent with the premise of the capitalist system of economic organization that if each individual strives to promote his self-interest an optimum allocation of resources will result. As Professors Neef and Nagel note, "...at the base of the adversary proceeding we encounter the old *laissez-faire* notion that each party will (or indeed can) bring out all the evidence favorable to his own side, and that if the accused is innocent (if his is the best case) he can act to 'out-produce' the presentation made by his competitors". With this competitive individualism at its base, if the party with the better case — that is the case that is correct on the facts — were to lose, that result would be satisfactory in an adversary system because he, not the system, would be the author of his defeat. Initiative is rightly rewarded, laziness or ignorance penalized. This justification for the adversary system is illustrated in a statement made in a commentary on the Japan *Code of Civil Procedure* that was enacted after World War II when Japan adopted the adversary system.

> [S]ince civil litigation is essentially a dispute concerning private rights, as a matter of course, the responsibility and duty to present proof rests with the parties; it is neither the responsibility nor the duty of the court.... When the necessary facts to maintain the allegation of a party cannot be proven, the disadvantage should be borne by such party, and it is sufficient grounds for the court to issue him an unfavorable determination. The disadvantage is a consequence invited by the party himself, over and beyond which the court should neither assist a party on one side nor interfere.

If this is one of the justifications for the adversary system then not many people today would likely perceive of it as placing very serious constraints on the judge's

intervention in the trial. *Laissez-faire* theory is no longer taken as being determinative in the economic and social fields. It would be incongruous if its basic postulate was still the premise used to define the respective roles of the parties and the judge in a judicial trial.

A basic socialist value is a strong emphasis on collectivism. The interests of the state and the individual are assumed to coincide, state power is not distrusted. On the other hand, liberal political philosophy is premised on a distrust of the state and public officials. The adversary system can thus be viewed in a liberal state as a means of decentralizing power, and as an attempt to prevent abuses of political power. This view finds some support in the fact that the genesis of at least some rules of procedure and evidence can also be explained on the basis of a felt concern to decentralize power. Professor Friedman in his recent text, a *History of American Law*, notes that the law of evidence "...was founded in a world of mistrust and suspicion of institutions; it liked nothing better than constant checks and balances..." This concern in an adversary system to decentralize power was illustrated during the period of Jacksonian democracy in the United States when a serious effort was initiated to take many rights from the judge including not only the right to comment upon the evidence but also the right to summarize the evidence to the jury.

Again, assuming this to be a premise of the adversary system, it would not appear to require that the judge be totally passive in the conduct of the trial. Indeed since in most cases he has the responsibility for the ultimate disposition of the case it would be incongruous to attempt to prohibit him from intervening in the proof-taking under the belief that his power was being constrained. This premise of the adversary system might have more relevance in defining the limits of party-autonomy.

Finally, the adversary system can be seen as being consistent with our prevalent political philosophy because it affords the parties the opportunity to participate in the making of decisions that affect their interests. Both psychological and theoretical literature in political philosophy support the view that the most acceptable type of decision in a democracy is personal choice. However, since it is clearly impossible to realize personal choice in many situations the best alternative is a system that assures to those affected by the decision some participation in the decisional process. A procedural system in which the judge assumes the primary responsibility for eliciting the proof, but permits the parties to assist in the proof-taking, would provide the parties a measure of participation in the decision-making process. However, Fuller argues that the adversary system "heightens the significance of...participation" and thus "lifts adjudication toward its optimum expression". For this reason, he concludes that the adversary system is an essential characteristic of the adjudicative process.

The extent to which the judge's intervention in the trial, either in clarifying evidence or in calling for new evidence, impairs the parties' sense of participation is obviously an extremely complex question that cannot be explored in any detail here. In some instances, however, it might clearly be a consideration that leads the judge to the conclusion that he should not intervene. But in other situations his intervention in the form of asking questions might actually increase the meaningfulness of the parties' participation. Everyone has different cognitive needs and if the judge makes these needs known to the parties then it will make their participation more meaningful — obviously their participation will be meaningless unless the judge's understanding of the case is the meaning that they are attempting to convey to him. Also, even if the judge were to call additional proof, so long as he gives the parties the opportunity to test such proof and call rebutting proof their participation in the decision-making process would appear to remain meaningful.

Cathartic Effect

Particularly in civil suits the adversary system might be a more acceptable procedure for fact-finding than the inquisitorial system because it satisfies the psychology of the litigants by legitimizing a courtroom duel which is a sublimation of more direct forms of hostile aggression. It has been suggested that there are psychological benefits in the "battle atmosphere" of adversary litigation. Charles Curtis in his book *It's Your Law* summarized this argument. He said:

> The law takes the position that we ought to be satisfied if the parties are; and it believes that the best way to get this done is to encourage them to fight it out, and dissolve their differences in dissention. We are still a combative people not yet so civilized and sophisticated as to forget that combat is one way to justice.

The use of the adversary system to satisfy the primeval competitive urges of the litigants might be suggested by its genealogy. The ancestry of the trial is of course the blood feud, trial by battle and individual or class acts of revenge. The justification for the adversary system is also apparent in the frequent analogy of the judicial trial to a sporting event. It leads lawyers to talk of tactics and strategy and to refer to the judge as an umpire. This view of the adversary process is most clearly perceived if the trial is regarded as a "game", using that word in the sense that it is used by game theorists. The "sporting theory of justice" describes the rules of the game. There has been a social disturbance and the game is played only to gain some relief or satisfaction.

The adversary system viewed as part of a game perhaps explains the system's acceptance of the result when a party loses on a technicality, even if his loss was due to a violation of one of the technical rules of evidence of procedure which regulate the game. If Justice is equated to the satisfaction of the litigants then the adversary system, which is directly responsible for this satisfaction, becomes an end in itself. The true facts of the case are less important than how well the parties play the game. Reasoning from this premise, Charles Curtis concluded:

> Justice is something larger and more intimate than truth. Truth is only one of the ingredients of justice. Its whole is the satisfaction of those concerned.... The administration of Justice is no more designed to elicit truth than the scientific approach is designed to extract justice from the atom.

If this justification for the adversary system is correct then the judge's role in the trial would be a limited one. However, the basic premise of the argument is disputable. As one author posed the question: "Is the battle atmosphere of trial proceedings truly cathartic, in the sense of relieving tensions and aggressions that would otherwise find more destructive outlets, or does it instill an aggressive approach to problems that is incompatible with the need to compromise and co-operate in the vast majority of interpersonal contacts?" Unfortunately, no serious effort has been made to resolve this question by asking the ultimate consumers of the system — the litigants. Basing a judgement on common experience, however, most people would probably agree with Professor Garlan who wrote at the height of the legal realist movement, referring to the jurisprudential theory of what he called "sporting fairness":

> The game has become too brutal, too destructive of human life, too exhaustive to those who win, and too fatal for those who lose. Living begins to look more like a struggle, than a game. The participant's sense of humor and sense of balance are worn, and the sporting morale is breaking up into a fighting morale. The sides are too unequal for successful competition, and, in the eyes of the defeated, the game looks more like exploitation than competition.

While we know very little about the psychology of litigants, I suspect that most of them do not view social conflicts as social events. They come to court expecting justice, and unless the rules of substantive law are perverse, that means they expect their dispute to be resolved according to the law. A theory about the judge's role that begins by assuming that rules of evidence and procedure are simply rules of competition is therefore deficient.

219

Role of Counsel

A third aspect of the adversary system that might render it more acceptable than the inquisitorial system is the role played by counsel. It has been hypothesized that "[i]f parties perceive their adversary attorneys as having interests convergent with their own, they may begin to experience the comforting strength of belonging to a coalition the total purpose of which is to gain a favorable verdict at the expense of the opposing party". Also the lawyer will be a person who, in some sense, shares in the litigant's defeat. Certain institutional characteristics of the adversary system might encourage this coalition and the apparent identity of interest between the adversary lawyer and his client. However, assuming this to be true, intervention in the trial proceedings by the trial judge is unlikely to destroy in any way this coalition or this sense of shared purpose.

Appearance of Impartiality

Finally, the adversary system might be more acceptable than an inquisitorial system because it gives the tribunal the appearance of impartiality. Proponents of the Anglo-American procedural system attach great importance to the appearance of impartiality. While its importance cannot be denied, the intelligent control of the conduct of the trial need not leave a judge open to the charge of partiality. The possible appearance of impartiality is a matter a judge should consider when intervening, and to that extent it limits his intervention. For instance, if a judge calls a witness he must ensure that the parties have an opportunity to test the testimony of the witness and to call rebutting evidence or he might be open to the charge that he is shaping the record. If a witness is evasive in answering questions the judge must ensure that he does not appear hostile towards the witness. However, if the judge intervenes in a fair and dispassionate manner this consideration should not seriously impair his ability to intervene when he thinks it is necessary.

The Adversary System Increases the Accuracy of Fact-Finding

A second justification given for the adversary system is that it is a better fact-finding mechanism than the inquisitorial system. That is to say, given all the interests that must be balanced in a procedural system more accurate factual judgments about past events are likely to be achieved using the adversary system than using some other system. This justification rests, in turn, upon two premises. The first premise is that the adversary system will result in a more thorough investigation of the facts than the inquisitorial system. The second premise is that under the adversarial system the trier of fact is more likely to reach the correct decision because during the proceedings he will not acquire a bias towards one conclusion or the other. He will be able to remain completely disinterested in the outcome until all

the proof has been elicited and the arguments made. In order to define the role of the judge in the adversary system these two premises must be explored in detail.

Parties Motivated by Self-Interest are Likely to be Most Diligent in Presenting and Critically Evaluating all the Evidence

The first premise of this justification for the adversary system is that in an adversary proceeding the judge will, when he makes his decision, be more informed as to the facts than a similarly situated judge in an inquisitorial system. This is so, it is argued, because parties who are given a free hand in pursuing their perceived self-interest are more likely than an official motivated only by official duty to transmit to the judge all evidence favorable to their case and to critically test all unfavourable evidence presented to him. Empirical studies have attempted to test whether this premise is correct. However, for purposes of defining the judge's role in the adversary system the premise must be accepted as true.

The parties do not have complete control over the presentation and testing of proof and this premise of the adversary system does not require them to have such control. Control is given to the parties to promote accurate fact-finding and to further achieve this end the parties are constrained in the conduct of their case by rules of procedure and evidence. The need for these rules arises because if this premise of the adversary system is to achieve its objective a number of factors must be present in the litigation of particular disputes. The rules are intended, in part, to ensure that these factors are present. If these factors are not present in a particular case the adversary system will not achieve its goal of accurate fact-finding; or if it is to achieve this end in their absence the judge may have to regulate his conduct accordingly. Thus the judge, in defining his role must be sensitive to the presence or absence of these factors. For purposes of clarity I will discuss these factors as assumptions of the premise that the adversary system is an accurate fact-finding mechanism because parties motivated by self-interest will present and critically test all relevant evidence.

ASSUMPTION 1: The Parties are Initially Motivated

The first assumption that this premise of the adversary system makes is that the parties are initially motivated to seek out all the evidence favorable to their case. This obviously depends upon both parties being equally interested in the outcome of the case, that is, equally interested in pursuing their respective rights and remedies and in opposing the rights of the other party. If this is not the case, if one of the parties is not motivated to oppose the other party's case, the requisite factual investigation and presentation of proof will not take place. By way of illustration, one area where the parties may not be sufficiently interested in defending their legal rights, and in which, therefore, the adversary system breaks down, is in the area of divorce. A divorce cannot be granted under the *Divorce Act* unless the judge is satisfied that there has been no condonation or connivance on the part of the petitioner. But since both parties in a particular case may want to be divorced, neither will be motivated to bring such evidence forward. In England, in recognition of the lack of motivation on the part of the parties in a divorce case, and of the state's interest in ensuring that divorces are only granted where the law authorizes them, an officer called the Queen's Proctor has been appointed. His duty is to intervene in divorce cases and ferret out facts that might suggest a collusive divorce. In Canada, while a Queen's Proctor has been officially appointed in some provinces, he is seldom called upon to discharge his duties. However, section 9 of the *Divorce Act* would appear on a literal reading to require the judge to embark on his own investigation of the possibility of condonation or connivance in the undefended divorce cases.

ASSUMPTION 2: *The Parties Will Sustain their Motivation*

A second assumption of this premise of the adversary system is that throughout the proceedings both parties will sustain their motivation to present all the evidence. A number of rules of evidence have been developed to encourage parties to diligently pursue all the evidence favorable to their side; at least these rules can, in part, be understood by reference to this need. The privilege against self-incrimination, for instance, is sometimes justified on this basis. By denying the police the right to compel the accused to incriminate himself the rule forces them to seek more reliable evidence. In the same way rules requiring the corroboration of certain witnesses who are generally assumed to be unreliable might be justified on the basis that they compel the Crown to search for additional independent evidence. It is interesting to note that these rules apply in the main against the prosecution in criminal cases — they encourage the police to seek additional evidence. Perhaps this is so because there is a fear that, at least in some cases, the prosecution motivated only by official duty, may not otherwise display the diligence in pursuing evidence that the adversary system demands.

A further rule of evidence that has the effect of encouraging the parties to independently investigate all evidence in their favour is the solicitor-client privilege — at least that part of it that the Americans call the work product rule. This rule, in general, prevents one lawyer or litigant from demanding disclosure, particularly before trial, of the other litigant's trial briefs, witness statements and related materials prepared or collected for use in the litigation. If a litigant could compel such disclosure there would be a great temptation for each litigant to rely on the other to do the investigations and to gather the necessary information. Eventually, litigants would become more and more reluctant to make an independent effort to collect information and to prepare arguments for trial. Thus, the rule contributes to the efficiency of the adversary scheme of litigation. Professor Maguire observed, "so long as we depend upon thorough advanced preparation by opposing trial counsel to accumulate the necessary information about law, fact and evidence, we must not let the drones sponge upon the busy bees. Otherwise it would not be long before all lawyers become drones".

As well as forming the basis of a number of rules of evidence and procedure this assumption of party-prosecution has a more direct implication in defining the judge's role. In a system that relies on party prosecution the judge cannot intervene to such an extent in the trial that the parties begin to rely upon him to search out the facts favourable to their case and thus become less diligent themselves in seeking out the facts. There is some evidence that this attitude on the part of litigants results when the court assumes a large responsibility for proof-taking. At least it is a concern that has been expressed in countries in which the judge assumes such a role. For example, in Japan, when the adversarial system was adopted in 1948 the commentators on the new *Code of Civil Procedure* noted that, "[e]xcessive interference by the Court dampens the zeal of the parties and instead — it being entirely impossible under the present trial system for the court completely to gather all evidence *ex officio* — produces a result which is accidental in nature. This is the reason why we thoroughly follow the doctrine of party presentation under the new constitution, in which the freedom and responsibility of the individual is made a fundamental principle."

In some cases a judge might justifiably be unwilling to intervene to correct an oversight or to call further proof in order to discipline a prosecutor in a criminal case for the inefficient presentation of a case. However, within the framework of the present Anglo-American trial increased intervention by the judge would likely have little impact on the parties' presentation of their case. The stakes in most cases are too high to risk leaving important proof-taking to the judge's initiative. Even if increased judicial intervention did not have the effect in some cases of weakening the parties' presentation of proof, there is the further question of "whether in the long run this is outweighed by benefits, such as helping the party represented by an ineffective lawyer".

ASSUMPTION 3: *The Parties Have Equal Capacity, Skill and Resources*

Party-prosecution, as a principle of the adversary system, rests on a third assumption: that each party has the ability, skill, and resources to search out the evidence favorable to his case and to present it to the court. Do the parties always have the capacity or ability to obtain access to all facts favourable to their case? The adversary system encourages parties to assume a self-interested role. While casting the parties into this role it ensures that they will be diligent in presenting evidence favorable to their cause, it also legitimizes or at least would appear to sanction their suppressing evidence that is unfavorable to their case. This temptation laid before the parties is regarded by many as the greatest obstacle to accurate fact-finding in the adversary system. Professor Brett argued that because "...neither of the rival theorists...[is] bound to put forward all the data in his possession — indeed...each...regard it as proper to suppress any 'inconvenient' or inconsistent observations of whose existence he...[knows,] 'the adversary system' must be regarded as basically unscientific in approach, and unsound". He further asserted that Macaulay's justification of the adversary system that "we obtain the fairest decision when two men argue, as unfairly as possible, on opposite sides, for then it is certain that no important consideration will altogether escape notice", confuses an incentive to obtain contradictory evidence with the capacity or ability to obtain it. Jerome Frank also noted, in supporting his contention that the "fight" theory of litigation does not coincide with the "truth" theory, that "frequently the partisanship of the opposing lawyers blocks the uncovering of vital evidence or leads to a presentation of vital testimony in a way that distorts it". There is little a judge in any system can do to prevent the parties from suppressing or falsifying evidence. A number of rules of evidence and procedure, however, attempt to provide both parties with access to as much evidence as possible. While these rules do not bear directly on the judge's role they are important in increasing our understanding of the adversary system and thus at least indirectly the judge's role in it.

First, rules of pre-trial discovery assist the parties in obtaining evidence. In civil cases, these rules generally permit a party to question the other prior to the trial about his knowledge of the facts in the case. It has been argued that pre-trial discovery is inconsistent with the adversary system. However, this argument confuses means with ends. If one begins the analysis by looking at the reasons for the adversary system, the better view would appear to be that of Professor Goldstein who concluded the discovery "has as its object the harnessing of the full creative potential of the adversary process, bringing each party to trial as aware of what he must meet as his finances and his lawyer's energy and intelligence permit".

Another device used both by the common law and by the legislatures to overcome the danger that the parties will suppress evidence and thus render the adversary system self-defeating is the presumption. While presumptions are sometimes created for reasons of social policy, or in order to expedite proof-taking, many presumptions oper-

ate against the party who has the superior access to the proof with respect to a particular fact. Thus it forces him to come forward with evidence that his opponent would have difficulty obtaining. A simple illustration is the presumption that arises if a bailor proves that he delivered property to a bailee in good condition and that the property was returned to him in a damaged condition. Because the bailor is not likely to have access to evidence relating to the bailee's negligence the damage will be presumed, at common law, to have been caused by the negligence of the bailee. Thus the bailee will have to come forward with sufficient evidence to prove that the damage was not caused by his negligence. In another situation a higher than normal standard of proof is placed on a party because he has control over the proof. The prosecutor must prove beyond a reasonable doubt that a confession is voluntary before the confession is admissible in evidence. At least one justification for imposing this high standard of proof is that the accused's adversary, the prosecution, has the ability, to some extent, to control the proof that relates to the voluntariness of a confession. The police can usually take statements under circumstances in which there can be no doubt as to their voluntariness. The accused, if the burden were placed on him to prove involuntariness, would likely be able to produce only his own testimony as proof. If the burden on the Crown were to prove voluntariness only on the balance of probability, the confession would usually be admitted since the issue would resolve itself into the question of who is likely to be more credible, the police or the accused.

To assist a party in gaining access to all the evidence favorable to his case an adverse inference is drawn against a party who fails to disclose to the court evidence which is within his power to produce. This inference rests on the assumption that an "honest and fearless claimant" will produce all the evidence favorable to his case and over which he has control. Therefore if he fails to produce evidence over which he has control, it can be inferred that the evidence is unfavourable to his cause. As well as drawing an adverse inference against a party who fails to produce evidence over which he has control, conduct by a party which renders it difficult or impossible for the other party to produce certain evidence will be regarded by the court as an admission of guilt or liability against that party. "Spoliation" admissions might include such things as the destruction or concealment of relevant documents or objects, intimidation, or the fabrication of evidence.

Finally, to ensure that the party's strong sense of self-interest and stake in the trial does not result in the degeneration of the trial into fraud and deceit, interposed between the litigant and the process is a lawyer; a person who will, to a large extent, conduct the proceedings and who has a responsibility not only to the litigant, his client, but also to the process. While the exact nature of the lawyer's responsibility to the process is the subject of dispute, there is agreement that he has a responsibility in most cases to protect the process from evidence he knows to be falsified.

For this assumption of the adversary system to be operative both parties must also have equal resources to investigate and collect facts favorable to their case, and both must be of equal skill in presenting these facts and in testing the facts presented that are unfavorable to their case. If the adversaries do not have equal representation — if for instance the accused in a criminal trial is unable to avail himself of effective counsel — this premise, upon which the adversary system rests, will be impaired. But even when both parties are represented by counsel, the quality of the representation will obviously seldom be equal. What is the role of the judge if one party is not represented or if his representation is inadequate? In such a situation the adversary system will fail to achieve its objective. The judge should not hesitate to intervene. Whatever dangers arise when a judge intervenes in such a situation, they are outweighed by the serious danger that is present if he does not intervene. Professor Fleming James noted that "[a]nything that the law of procedure or the judge's role can do to equalize opportunity and to put a faulty presentation on the right track so that disputes are more likely to be settled on their merits, will in the long run bolster up rather than destroy the adversary system, and will increase the moral force of the decisions." Judge Breitel, in an article on judicial ethics, describes how, when he first went to the bench, he tried to be detached and disciplined in his conduct of the case — which he believed to reflect the ideal role of a judge in the adversary process. After several months, however, and after seeing numerous cases where the lawyers were not equal or were unequal to their task, he began, he says, "to feel revulsion and pangs of conscience". He concluded, "[p]assivity and silence in such a situation ceased to be an acceptable role. Indeed, it made the function and responsibility of being an umpire judge a distortion, an intolerable distortion of the whole process of the administration of justice". Canadian case authorities would appear to support the proposition that when the parties' representation is unequal, the judge has a responsibility to intervene to a greater extent than he otherwise would.

In many inquisitorial systems one of the principal justifications given for increasing the authority of the judge is the need to equalize the parties. The major innovation of the Austrian *Code of Civil Procedure* of 1895, which has had a great influence upon the legislation of many other European countries, was "...its emphasis on a more active role for the judge in both expediting the proceedings and of promoting the social aim of effective quality of the parties". Socialist scholars have contended that there is a reluctance in bourgeois jurisprudence to give the judge a stronger role precisely so that the weaker party can be manoeuvred by the system into a disadvantaged position.

A final aspect of this assumption of the adversary system is the necessity that both parties have the resources to carry out a thorough investigation of the facts. This, of course, is seldom the case. Jerome Frank suggested that in all cases there should be some kind of government intervention to help an impecunious litigant obtain evidence. In criminal cases the state's facilities for investigation are obviously far superior to those of the ordinary defendant. It might be possible to reduce this disparity by providing legal aid programs with the resources necessary to locate and investigate evidence favorable to the accused. A more efficient remedy, since it does not involve the costly duplication of investigative efforts, would be to place the results of government investigations in the hands of the defence. In the United States a rule of procedure that will have this result is emerging. Clearly if we do not wish to be accused of continuing to tolerate a system whose operations negate the reason for having it we will have to continue to move in this direction.

In some areas the adversary system might have to be completely abandoned because the potential parties are not likely to have sufficient resources to pursue their remedies. Where one spouse has been deserted, for instance, we assume that he or she will bring an action for maintenance. But because of the lack of resources this remedy is seldom pursued. The adversary system is simply not an adequate means of protecting civil rights in this area. Judicial intervention obviously cannot overcome this problem, and resort may be needed to administrative investigative bodies.

ASSUMPTION 4: *The Parties will be Given the Opportunity to Test Adverse Evidence*

Party-prosecution assumes that each party will have the opportunity and the ability to thoroughly test the evidence unfavorable to his case. It assumes, also, that this testing of adverse evidence must be done by an adversary cross-examination as opposed to a dispassionate inquisitorial examination. Opinions on the utility of cross-examination are sharply divided. However, a judge presiding over an adversary proceeding must, to some extent at least, assume its efficacy. Numerous rules of evidence, the hearsay rule, the best evidence rule, and the opinion evidence rule, attempt to ensure that the parties will be given the opportunity to confront and cross-examine as effectively as possible the evidence that is introduced against them. But whatever the value of cross-examination in revealing and in testing evidence, it can present grave dangers to the process. In some cases it will have the effect of misleading the trier of fact. Cross-examination, even with the best of intentions on the part of the cross-examiner, may make reliable testimony look debatable, and clear information look confused. Witnesses on the witness stand, in a strange setting, compelled to give their testimony in an unnatural manner, and under the threat of a rigorous cross-examination, can very easily be led to say things that do not accurately represent their recollections. But more seriously, counsel might well use techniques in questioning a witness by which he deliberately attempts to force the witness to narrate his testimony in a way that gives a misleading impression as to his honest recollections.

Cross-examination has other costs of equal or greater significance, costs in terms of human dignity. Cross-examination sometimes results in the total humiliation and destruction of a witness without any corresponding benefits. But I have introduced here a value extrinsic to the adversary system, and I wish to discuss the judge's role only in terms of the assumptions of that system. The point is that if cross-examination is to achieve its purpose in the adversary system, the judge must ensure that it is not used as an instrument to distort and obscure testimony. That is not abandoning his role in the adversary system, it is assuming the responsibility of his role. Eliciting the testimony of children is an area, for instance, where there might be a need for strong intervention by the judge, perhaps to the point where all the questions directed to the child are asked through the judge. Harsh and critical cross-examination techniques can confuse the child to the point where he is unable to give intelligible answers.

The judge is also in a dilemma when cross-examination has proved to be ineffective, or when counsel declines to cross-examine a witness about whose perception of the event described, for instance, the judge is in serious doubt. Should he ask questions, the answer to which he feels might assist him in evaluating the witness's perception? The answer would appear obvious. While certain dangers arise when the judge asks questions, these dangers are overridden by the fact that if the questions are not asked, the adversary system will have failed to achieve its objective.

ASSUMPTION 5: All Interests Affected are Represented

Finally, the principle of party-prosecution assumes that all interests affected by the adjudication are represented by the parties. The adversary system depends upon the parties to bring forward the information upon which the judge will rely in reaching his decision. In reaching a decision the judge must reconcile all the competing interests affected by his decision. If he does not receive information about some of these interests because they are interests of no immediate concern to the parties before him the adversary system will be a defective method of fact-finding for that decision. The importance of this assumption can be illustrated by reference to two areas. In a custody proceeding the adversaries are commonly seen to be the parents of the child, both of whom will supply the court with information as to why they should take custody

of the child. Both will obviously be arguing in their own perceived best interest. However, the real issue in the case is the best interest of the child. In such a situation it is possible that facts relevant to the real issue in the case will not be presented to the judge by the parties and if he is to reach a decision based on all relevant information, he will have to intervene in the fact-finding.

Another area in which the adversaries will not represent all the interests might be described broadly, if not with some circularity, as being the area of public interest law, such as environmental, consumer protection law. Again, in these areas, the wise judge might well call upon the intervention of third parties to represent those interests not represented by the immediate parties to the particular dispute. At the appellant level this is commonly done by means of asking for or inviting *amicus curiae* factums. Justice Thurgood Marshall of the United States Supreme Court recently called upon the organized bar to finance public interest law on the grounds that the practice of public interest law is a vital function of the adversary system since that system presupposes representation of all interests affected.

The Adversary System Counteracts Bias in Decision-Making

The second reason often given as to why the adversary system leads to more accurate fact-finding than an inquisitorial system is that the adversary system permits the judge to remain unbiased as between the parties throughout the proceedings. Bias is a word used in a wide variety of senses, many of which shade into each other. In this context, where important consequences are being drawn from the concept, it is particularly important to be clear about its meaning.

Bias in this context does not mean, as it commonly means in other contexts, a preconceived point of view about issues of law or policy, a personal prejudice against certain types of parties, or bias in the sense of being personally interested in the outcome of the case. No fact-finding mechanism can remove these types of biases. It refers to a bias or prejudgment that is acquired by a decision-maker because of the mechanism of fact-finding used. If the judge takes an active part in proof-taking, it could be argued that he might acquire a bias towards one party or the other for one of the following reasons:

1. If the judge questions a witness and the witness is evasive, disrespectful, hostile, or in some way does not live up to the expectations of the judge, the judge may become antagonistic towards the witness and therefore tend to discredit his testimony.
2. If the judge in proof-taking is responsible for having some important evidence revealed, he may tend to give too much weight to that evidence, either because

he is overly impressed with the skilful manner in which the evidence was presented, or because it is important to him that his intervention is seen to have served a useful purpose.

3. The judge may, in his investigation, become so concerned about a detail of the case that the balance of the evidence will escape his careful attention. This is perhaps the kind of consideration that judges are concerned about when they assert that their ability to evaluate the credibility of a witness is impaired if they themselves become too involved in examining a witness. That is to say, as an investigator preoccupied with his own line of thought, the judge may unconsciously fail to explore important points, may amass so much detail that obvious truths are obscured, or may not carefully observe all of the diverse matters, such as demeanor evidence, that he should take into consideration in evaluating the probative value of testimonial proof.

4. A fourth source of bias that is not present in the adversary system, but which one might argue is present in the inquisitorial system, is the bias that is acquired when the judge is presented with a file of the evidence before the case is heard by him. In an inquisitorial system the judge will of course have had to study the documents contained in the file with some care if he is to be effective in carrying out the proof-taking at trial. There is an obvious danger that the information supplied in the file will bias the judge towards one side or the other. As Glanville Williams noted, "Our reaction to the French system is that it creates a danger that the point of view of the prosecution will communicate itself to the judge before the case has been heard."

5. Finally, it has been contended that the adversary system is an unbiasing fact-finding technique because it counteracts what psychologists call decision-maker bias. Decision-maker bias is acquired when a decision-maker himself investigates the facts upon which he is to rest his judgement. It arises because of the need when one begins to investigate facts to form certain tentative hypotheses about the reality that one is called upon to reconstruct. More or less imperceptively, these preconceptions influence the course of the investigation. As well, facts which confirm the original hypothesis will make a strong imprint upon the mind, while facts that run counter to it are received with diverted attention. This bias, which arises from the process of fact-finding, is avoided in the adversary system, it is argued. It is avoided because, in the adversary system, the judge, since he is not responsible for the investigation, is able to avoid any judgment of the case until he has heard all the evidence.

While all of these kinds of bias may be present in an adversary proceeding, none of them should limit to any great extent, within the framework of our present trial, the judge's intelligent intervention in the case. A recognition of their presence should permit the judge to conduct the proceedings in a fashion that minimizes the dangers that might arise.

Conclusion

I suggested at the outset of this paper that the role of the judge, at least the limits of his intervention in the conduct of the trial, must be established by a careful reference to the premises of the adversary system. However, in some sense, that is only a starting point in defining his role. The adversary system is not a moral axiom. We do maintain it for its own sake, and the values that we seek by use of the adversary system — the acceptability of the process, and accuracy in fact-finding — are only two of the process values that must be pursued in any system of adjudication. As well as these values, any procedural system designed to resolve disputes must strike a balance among many other process values such as finality, expedition, administrative efficiency, and the protection of the dignity of the participants. Interests extrinsic to the process must also be considered, for instance, the protection of important relationships, the control of governmental power, and the protection of the innocent in criminal cases. This is not the place to expand on these interests and their implications, I merely mention them, and the fact that they must be considered by the judge in defining his role in particular situations, in order to place the discussion in this paper in its larger context.

I do not intend to explore the specific instances where a judge might be called upon to intervene in a trial. However, I will make reference to one such instance to illustrate how the premises of the adversary system could form the guidelines upon which the judge relies in defining the extent of his intervention. If a judge decided that a person, whom neither party had called, could perhaps give relevant testimony, the following dangers, in terms of the adversary system, might arise if he called that person as a witness himself: it could weaken the motivating force of the parties in calling all evidence favorable to their case, they might become careless about calling evidence knowing that if they do not call the evidence the judge will, or they might not call a witness hoping that the judge will and thus give a witness favorable to them the appearance of objectivity; it might bias the trier of fact in favour of that witness's testimony, the judge might acquire a commitment to the witness's credibility because of his interest in making his efforts appear worthwhile, the jury might give a witness called by the judge undue weight because of the witness's apparent objectivity; it could give the judge the appearance of partiality, if the witness gives testimony adverse to the accused, for instance, the judge, who called the witness, might appear to be biased against the accused; it could render the judge's ultimate decision less acceptable to the parties, if they view his intervention as an unjustified intrusion in their private fight; or, it could lead to inaccurate fact-finding if the judge called the witness at a time which made it difficult for one of the parties to lead evidence rebutting the testimony, or at a time when it had the effect of weakening the persuasive force of one of the parties' case. As well as these considerations, when the judge calls a witness a number of purely pragmatic procedural considerations arise: who can examine, cross-examine and impeach the witness; if the judge questions the witness, how do the parties effectively object to any improper questions or other procedural errors; and, how does the judge, who does not likely have any detailed or even perhaps general knowledge about the proof in the case until it unfolds before him, know that his intervention is not going to simply waste time.

While I do not have time to explore each of these dangers, and others that might rise in specific contexts, in detail, it should be clear that they provide the judge a wide latitude in which to call witnesses in appropriate cases. A similar analysis could be done for each specific instance

where a judge might intervene in a trial. Giving due considerations to the dangers that might be present in specific instances, if the judge thinks in a particular case it would be helpful, I see no reason why he should hesitate, for instance, to call his own witnesses, to question witnesses both to clarify and to develop additional evidence, to invite witnesses to give a narrative account of their testimony, to invite perhaps three or four witnesses to be sworn and take their evidence in a conference-room style, to intervene to protect witnesses from harassment and confusing questions, or to advise the parties in the presentation of their case so that they do not commit procedural errors.

In conclusion, there is undoubtedly considerable experience and knowledge of human nature captured in the adversary system. What I have attempted to do is re-examine the assumptions of the adversary system and review the judge's role in light of these assumptions. My conclusion is that the adversary system imposes on the judge as well as the parties an important and active role in the conduct of the trial. The adversary system is not an end in itself; it is a procedural device which we have adopted in the pursuit of more ultimate process values. The judge has responsibility not only to arrive at a decision but also to ensure that these process values are attained.

'Fight' Theory vs. 'Truth' Theory[†]
Judge J. Frank

THERE is one most serious handicap in litigation that has received little attention: With the ablest lawyer in the world, a man may lose a suit he ought to win, if he has not the funds to pay for an investigation, before trial, of evidence necessary to sustain his case. I refer to evidence not in the files of the other party and therefore not obtainable by "discovery" procedure. What I mean is this: In order to prove his claim, or to defend against one, a man may need to hire detectives to scour the country — even sometimes foreign countries — in order to locate witnesses who alone may know of events that occurred years ago, or to unearth letters or other papers which may be in distant places. Or, again, he may need the services of an engineer, or a chemist, or an expert accountant, to make an extensive — and therefore expensive — investigation. Without the evidence which such an investigation would reveal, a man is often bound to be defeated. His winning or losing may therefore depend on his pocket-

book. He is out of luck if his pocketbook is not well-lined with money. For neither his lawyer nor any legal-aid institution will supply the needed sums. For want of money, expendable for such purposes, many a suit has been lost, many a meritorious claim or defense has never even been asserted.

Let me illustrate. Fisher, in his recent excellent book, *The Art of Investigation*, writes: "The percentage of witnesses who cannot be found if enough effort is exerted is infinitesimal. A famous investigator once said that the man who could not be found is the man at the bottom of the sea, and even then he must be at the bottom at its points of greatest depth. Anyone alive can be found if enough effort is put forth." That statement may be exaggerated. But you get the point: Suppose there is one man, John Brown, who alone could testify to a crucial event — such as that Sam Jones was in New York City on June 12, 1948. Brown is missing. He may be in China, India or Peru. If

---

† Frank, Jerome, "'Fight' Theory vs. 'Truth' Theory" in *Courts on Trial: Myth and Reality in American Justice* (Ewing, NJ: Princeton University Press, 1949), 94–99. Copyright © 1949 by Princeton University Press (renewed 1976). Reprinted by permission of Princeton University Press.

he can be found, and if he testifies, the plaintiff will win his suit; otherwise he will lose it. If the plaintiff can afford to pay enough to investigators to scour the world for the missing witness, he may be located. If the plaintiff is a man of means, he will hire such investigators. But if he has little money, he can't do so — and will lose his case which may involve all his worldly goods.

That is not true justice, democratic justice. This defect in our judicial system makes a mockery of "equality before the law," which should be one of the first principles of a democracy. That equality, in such instances, depends on a person's financial condition. The tragedy of such a situation is etched in irony when a man's impoverished condition has resulted from a wrong done him by another whom he cannot successfully sue to redress the wrong. Many of our state constitutions contain a provision that "every person ought to obtain justice freely and without being obliged to purchase it." But, as things stand, this is too often a provision in words only. For the advantage in litigation is necessarily on the side of the party that can "purchase justice" by hiring private assistance in obtaining evidence when his adversary cannot. Unless we contrive some method to solve the problem I have posed, we must acknowledge that, in a very real sense, frequently we are "selling justice," denying it to many under-income persons. It should shock us that judicial justice is thus often an upper-bracket privilege. Here we have legal *laissez-faire* at its worst.

That brings me to a point which the fighting theory obscures. A court's decision is not a mere private affair. It culminates in a court order which is one of the most solemn of governmental acts. Not only is a court an agency of government, but remember that its order, if not voluntarily obeyed, will bring into action the police, the sheriff, even the army. What a court orders, then, is no light matter. The court represents the government, organized society, in action.

Such an order a court is not supposed to make unless there exist some facts which bring into operation a legal rule. Now any government officer, other than a judge, if authorized to do an act for the government only if certain facts exist, will be considered irresponsible if he so acts without a governmental investigation. For instance, if an official is empowered to pay money to a veteran suffering from some specified ailment, the official, if he does his duty, will not rely solely on the applicant's statement that he has such an ailment. The government officer insists on a governmental check-up of the evidence. Do courts so conduct themselves?

In criminal cases they seem to, after a fashion. In such cases, there is some recognition that so important a governmental act as a court decision against a defendant should not occur without someone, on behalf of the government itself, seeing to it that the decision is justified by the actual facts so far as they can be discovered with reasonable diligence. For, in theory at least, usually before a criminal action is begun, an official investigation has been conducted which reveals data sufficient to warrant bringing the defendant to trial. In some jurisdictions, indigent defendants *charged* with crime are represented by a publicly-paid official, a Public Defender — a highly important reform which should everywhere be adopted. And the responsibility of government for mistakes of fact in criminal cases, resulting in erroneous court judgments, is recognized in those jurisdictions in which the government compensates an innocent convicted person if it is subsequently shown that he was convicted through such a mistake.

In civil cases (non-criminal cases), on the whole a strikingly different attitude prevails. Although, no less than in a criminal suit, a court's order is a grave governmental act, yet, in civil cases, the government usually accepts no similar responsibilities, even in theory. Such a suit is still in the ancient tradition of "self help." The court usually relies almost entirely on such evidence as one or the other of the private parties to the suit is (a) able to, and (b) chooses to, offer. Lack of skill or diligence of the lawyer for one of those parties, or that party's want of enough funds to finance a pre-trial investigation necessary to obtain evidence, may have the result, as I explained, that crucial available evidence is not offered in court. No government official has the duty to discover, and bring to court, evidence, no matter how important, not offered by the parties.

In short, the theory is that, in most civil suits, the government, through its courts, should make orders which the government will enforce, although those court-orders may not be justified by the actual facts, and although, by reasonable diligence, the government, had it investigated, might have discovered evidence — at variance with the evidence presented — coming closer to the actual facts.

Yet the consequence of a court decision in a civil suit, based upon the court's mistaken view of the actual facts, may be as grave as a criminal judgment which convicts an innocent person. If, because of such an erroneous decision, a man loses his job or his savings and becomes utterly impoverished, he may be in almost as serious a plight as if he had been jailed. His poverty may make him a public charge. It may lead to the delinquency of his children, who may thus become criminals and go to jail. Yet in no jurisdiction is a man compensated by the government for serious injury to him caused by a judgment against him in a non-criminal case, even if later it is shown that the judgment was founded upon perjured or mistaken testimony.

I suggest that there is something fundamentally wrong in our legal system in this respect. If a man's pocket is picked, the government brings a criminal suit, and accepts responsibility for its prosecution. If a man loses his life's savings through a breach of a contract, the government accepts no such responsibility. Shouldn't the government perhaps assume some of the burden of enforcing what we call "private rights"?

Some few moves have been made in the right direction. In an English divorce court, an official, the King's Proctor, brings forward evidence, bearing on possible collusion, not offered by either contestant; some American states provide that the public prosecutor shall do likewise in divorce actions. In our own Domestic Relations Courts, government officers procure and present most of the evidence. Lawyers for any of the parties may cross-examine any witness, may offer additional evidence, and may argue about the applicable legal rules. The advantages of the adversary method are fully preserved, but the fighting spirit is much diminished. Under the *Chandler Act*, enacted in 1938, in certain types of cases relating to corporate reorganization, the SEC, at large public expense, uses its expert staff to obtain and present to the court evidence which usually no private party could afford to procure; the judge and the private parties may treat this evidence like any other evidence, and the parties may introduce further supplementary or conflicting evidence.

Many of our administrative agencies have large and efficient staffs to conduct investigations in order to ferret out evidence put before those agencies in their own administrative proceedings. I know, from personal experience, that not much evidence escapes an agency like the SEC. Mr. Justice Jackson has said: "Such a tribunal is not as dependent as the ordinary court upon the arguments of skilled counsel to get at the truth. Skilled advocacy is neither so necessary to keep such a body informed nor is stupid or clever advocacy so apt to blur the merits of a controversy."

I do not suggest that courts, like such administrative bodies, conduct their own investigations through their own employees. I do suggest that we should consider whether it is not feasible to provide impartial government officials — who are not court employees, and who act on their own initiative — to dig up, and present to the courts, significant evidence which one or the other of the parties may overlook or be unable to procure. No court would be bound to accept that evidence as true. Nor would any of the parties be precluded from trying to show the unreliability of such evidence (by cross-examination or otherwise) or from introducing additional evidence. Trials would still remain adversary. As I concede that to use that device in all civil cases would lead to many complications, I do not urge that it be at once generally adopted. But I think experiments along those lines should now be made.

This proposal resembles somewhat the procedures long used in criminal cases on the European continent. Critics may oppose it on that ground, saying that we should not take over ideas from countries which have been less democratic than ours. To any such argument, Woodrow

Wilson gave the answer: "But why should we not use such parts of foreign contrivances as we want if they may be in any way serviceable? We are in no danger of using them in a foreign way. We borrowed rice, but we do not eat it with chopsticks."

It will also be said that any such proposal is absurdly radical. Yet something of the sort was endorsed by President Taft, by no means a radical. More than thirty years ago he said: "Of all the questions...before the American people I regard no one as more important than this, the improvement of the administration of justice. We must make it so that the poor man will have as nearly as possible an opportunity in litigating as the rich man, and under present conditions, ashamed as we may be of it, this is not the fact." Moreover, we now have public-utility commissions which, on behalf of private persons, bring rate-suits against utility companies. With that in mind, Willoughby wrote a book, published in 1927 by the conservative Brookings Institution, in which he proposed the appointment of a "public prosecutor of civil actions." If a complaint were made to the prosecutor, he would first try to settle the matter or to have the parties agree to submit the dispute to arbitration. Only if these efforts failed would he bring suit. No one would be obliged to retain prosecutor; his employment would be optional; and, if any action were brought on a person's behalf by the prosecutor, that person would be at liberty to retain a private lawyer to assist in the preparation for, and conduct of, the trial. That idea, I think, merits public discussion and consideration. Were it adopted, it should perhaps be supplemented to include a practice now adopted, in some states, by the Public Defender in criminal actions: That official is authorized to expend public funds to seek out and procure what he regards as essential evidence.

Statutes in some jurisdictions authorize the trial judge to call as a witness an expert selected by the judge. Judges might sometimes avail themselves of that power to help indigent or under-income litigants. But I believe that none of those statutes, as they now read, provides for payment by the government to judge-called experts in non-criminal suits. Moreover, those statutes will not meet the difficulties of a prospective litigant when making up his mind whether to bring or defend a suit. Nor do they permit expenditures for detectives and other investigators not regarded as "experts." Nevertheless, this expedient might be expanded so as partially to solve the problem I have presented.

None of these proposals, if adopted, would usher in the millennium. Official evidence gatherers, or public prosecutors of civil actions, will make mistakes, or become excessively partisan. The trial process is, and always will be, human, therefore fallible. It can never be a completely scientific investigation for the discovery of the true facts.

Further Reading

Peter H. Russell, *The Judiciary in Canada: The Third Branch of Government* (Toronto: McGraw-Hill Ryerson, 1987), Chapter 1.

Anne Strick, "Trial by Battle", *The Centre Magazine*, May/June 1978.

Paul Weiler, "Two Models of Judicial Decision-Making" (1968), 46 *Canadian Bar Review* 406.

L. Fuller, "The Forms and Limits of Adjudication", 92 *Harvard Law Review* 353.

C. Alternatives to Adjudication: Settlement-Oriented Dispute Resolution Mechanisms

Against Settlement[†]
O.M. Fiss

IN a recent report to the Harvard Overseers, Derek Bok called for a new direction in legal education.[1] He decried "the familiar tilt in the law curriculum toward preparing students for legal combat," and asked instead that law schools train their students "for the gentler arts of reconciliation and accommodation."[2] He sought to turn our attention from the courts to "new voluntary mechanisms"[3] for resolving disputes. In doing so, Bok echoed themes that have long been associated with the Chief Justice,[4] and that have become a rallying point for the organized bar and the source of a new movement in the law. This movement is the subject of a new professional journal,[5] a newly formed section of the American Association of Law Schools, and several well-funded institutes. It has even received its own acronym — ADR (Alternative Dispute Resolution).

The movement promises to reduce the amount of litigation initiated, and accordingly the bulk of its proposals are devoted to negotiation and mediation prior to suit. But the interest in the so-called "gentler arts" has not been so confined. It extends to ongoing litigation as well, and the advocates of ADR have sought new ways to facilitate and perhaps even pressure parties into settling pending cases. Just last year, Rule 16 of the *Federal Rules of Civil Procedure* was amended to strengthen the hand of the trial judge in brokering settlements: The "facilitation of settlement" became an explicit purpose of pre-trial conferences, and participants were officially invited, if that is the proper word, to consider "the possibility of settlement or the use of extrajudicial procedures to resolve the dispute."[6] Now the Advisory Committee on Civil Rules is proposing to amend Rule 68 to sharpen the incentives for settlement: Under this amendment, a party who rejects a settlement offer and then receives a judgment less favorable than that offer must pay the attorney's fees of the other party.[7] This amendment would effect a major change in the traditional American rule, under which each party pays his or her own attorney's fees.[8] It would also be at odds with a number of statutes that seek to facilitate certain types of civil litigation by providing attorney's fees to plaintiffs if they

win, without imposing liability for the attorney's fees of their adversaries if they lose.[9]

The advocates of ADR are led to support such measures and to exalt the idea of settlement more generally because they view adjudication as a process to resolve disputes. They act as though courts arose to resolve quarrels between neighbors who had reached an impasse and turned to a stranger for help.[10] Courts are seen as an institutionalization of the stranger and adjudication is viewed as the process by which the stranger exercises power. The very fact that the neighbors have turned to someone else to resolve their dispute signifies a breakdown in their social relations; the advocates of ADR acknowledge this, but nonetheless hope that the neighbors will be able to reach agreement before the stranger renders judgment. Settlement is that agreement. It is a truce more than a true reconciliation, but it seems preferable to judgment because it rests on the consent of both parties and avoids the cost of a lengthy trial.

In my view, however, this account of adjudication and the case for settlement rest on questionable premises. I do not believe that settlement as a generic practice is preferable to judgment or should be institutionalized on a wholesale and indiscriminate basis. It should be treated instead as a highly problematic technique for streamlining dockets. Settlement is for me the civil analogue of plea bargaining: Consent is often coerced; the bargain may be struck by someone without authority; the absence of a trial and judgment renders subsequent judicial involvement troublesome; and although dockets are trimmed, justice may not be done. Like plea bargaining, settlement is a capitulation to the conditions of mass society and should be neither encouraged nor praised.

THE IMBALANCE OF POWER

By viewing the lawsuit as a quarrel between two neighbors, the dispute-resolution story that underlies ADR implicitly asks us to assume a rough equality between the contending parties. It treats settlement as the anticipation

†   Fiss, Owen M., "Against Settlement" (1984), 93 *Yale Law Journal* at 1073–90. Reprinted by permission of The Yale Law Journal Company, Fred B. Rothman & Company, and the author.

of the outcome of trial and assumes that the terms of settlement are simply a product of the parties' predictions of that outcome.[11] In truth, however, settlement is also a function of the resources available to each party to finance the litigation, and those resources are frequently distributed unequally. Many lawsuits do not involve a property dispute between two neighbors, or between AT&T and the government (to update the story), but rather concern a struggle between a member of a racial minority and a municipal police department over alleged brutality, or a claim by a worker against a large corporation over work-related injuries. In these cases, the distribution of financial resources, or the ability of one party to pass along its costs, will invariably infect the bargaining process and the settlement will be at odds with a conception of justice that seeks to make the wealth of the parties irrelevant.

The disparities in resources between the parties can influence the settlement in three ways. First, the poorer party may be less able to amass and analyze the information needed to predict the outcome of the litigation, and thus be disadvantaged in the bargaining process. Second, he may need the damages he seeks immediately and thus be induced to settle as a way of accelerating payment, even though he realizes he would get less now than he might if he awaited judgment. All plaintiffs want their damages immediately, but an indigent plaintiff may be exploited by a rich defendant because his need is so great that the defendant can force him to accept a sum that is less than the ordinary present value of the judgment. Third, the poorer party might be forced to settle because he does not have the resources to finance the litigation, to cover either his own projected expenses, such as his lawyer's time, or the expenses his opponent can impose through the manipulation of procedural mechanisms such as discovery. It might seem that settlement benefits the plaintiff by allowing him to avoid the costs of litigation, but this is not so. The defendant can anticipate the plaintiff's costs if the case were to be tried fully and decrease his offer by that amount. The indigent plaintiff is a victim of the costs of litigation even if he settles.[12]

There are exceptions. Seemingly rich defendants may sometimes be subject to financial pressures that make them as anxious to settle as indigent plaintiffs. But I doubt that these circumstances occur with any great frequency. I also doubt that institutional arrangements such as contingent fees or the provision of legal services to the poor will in fact equalize resources between contending parties: The contingent fee does not equalize resources; it only makes an indigent plaintiff vulnerable to the willingness of the private bar to invest in his case. In effect, the ability to exploit the plaintiff's lack of resources has been transferred from rich defendants to lawyer who insist upon a hefty slice of the plaintiff's recovery as their fee. These lawyers, moreover, will only work for contingent fees in certain kinds of cases, such as personal-injury suits. And

the contingent fee is of no avail when the defendant is the disadvantaged party. Governmental subsidies for legal services have a broader potential, but in the civil domain the battle for these subsidies was hard-fought, and they are in fact extremely limited, especially when it comes to cases that seek systemic reform of government practices.[13]

Of course, imbalances of power can distort judgment as well: Resources influence the quality of presentation, which in turn has an important bearing on who wins and the terms of victory. We count, however, on the guiding presence of the judge, who can employ a number of measures to lessen the impact of distributional inequalities. He can, for example, supplement the parties' presentations by asking questions, calling his own witnesses, and inviting other persons and institutions to participate as *amici*.[14] These measures are likely to make only a small contribution toward moderating the influence of distributional inequalities, but should not be ignored for that reason. Not even these small steps are possible with settlement. There is, moreover, a critical difference between a process like settlement, which is based on bargaining and accepts inequalities of wealth as an integral and legitimate component of the process, and a process like judgment, which knowingly struggles against those inequalities. Judgment aspires to an autonomy from distributional inequalities, and it gathers much of its appeal from this aspiration.

. . . .

THE LACK OF A FOUNDATION FOR CONTINUING JUDICIAL INVOLVEMENT

The dispute-resolution story trivializes the remedial dimensions of law-suits and mistakenly assumes judgment to be the end of the process. It supposes that the judge's duty is to declare which neighbor is right and which wrong, and that this declaration will end the judge's involvement (save in that most exceptional situation where it is also necessary for him to issue a writ directing the sheriff to execute the declaration). Under these assumptions, settlement appears as an almost perfect substitute for judgment, for it too can declare the parties' rights. Often, however, judgment is not the end of a lawsuit but only the beginning. The involvement of the court may continue almost indefinitely. In these cases, settlement cannot provide an adequate basis for that necessary continuing involvement, and thus is no substitute for judgment.

The parties may sometimes be locked in combat with one another and view the lawsuit as only one phase in a long continuing struggle. The entry of judgment will then not end the struggle, but rather change its terms and the balance of power. One of the parties will invariably return to the court and again ask for its assistance, not so much because conditions have changed, but because the conditions that preceded the lawsuit have unfortunately not changed. This often occurs in domestic-relations cases, where the divorce decree represents only the opening salvo in an endless series of skirmishes over custody and support.[15]

The structural reform cases that play such a prominent role on the federal docket provide another occasion for continuing judicial involvement. In these cases, courts seek to safeguard public values by restructuring large-scale bureaucratic organizations.[16] The task is enormous, and our knowledge of how to restructure on-going bureaucratic organizations is limited. As a consequence, courts must oversee and manage the remedial process for a long time — maybe forever. This, I fear, is true of most school desegregation cases, some of which have been pending for twenty or thirty years.[17] It is also true of antitrust cases that seek divestiture or reorganization of an industry.[18]

The drive for settlement knows no bounds and can result in a consent decree even in the kinds of cases I have just mentioned, that is, even when a court finds itself embroiled in a continuing struggle between the parties or must reform a bureaucratic organization. The parties may be ignorant of the difficulties ahead or optimistic about the future, or they may simply believe that they can get more favorable terms through a bargained-for agreement. Soon, however, the inevitable happens: One party returns to court and asks the judge to modify the decree, either to make it more effective or less stringent. But the judge is at a loss: He has no basis for assessing the request. He cannot, to use Cardozo's somewhat melodramatic formula, easily decide whether the "dangers, once substantial, have become attenuated to a shadow,"[19] because, by definition, he never knew the dangers.

The allure of settlement in large part derives from the fact that it avoids the need for a trial. Settlement must thus occur before the trial is complete and the judge has entered findings of fact and conclusions of law. As a consequence, the judge confronted with a request for modification of a consent decree must retrospectively reconstruct the situation as it existed at the time the decree was entered, and decide whether conditions today have sufficiently changed to warrant a modification in that decree. In the *Meat Packers* litigation, for example, where a consent decree governed the industry for almost half a century, the judge confronted with a request for modification in 1960 had to reconstruct the "danger" that had existed at the time of the entry of the decree in 1920 in order to determine whether the danger had in fact become a "shadow."[20] Such an inquiry borders on the absurd, and is likely to dissipate whatever savings in judicial resources the initial settlement may have produced.

Settlement also impedes vigorous enforcement, which sometimes requires use of the contempt power. As a formal matter, contempt is available to punish violations of a consent decree.[21] But courts hesitate to use that power to enforce decrees that rest solely on consent, espe-

cially when enforcement is aimed at high public officials, as became evident in the *Willowbrook deinstitutionalization case*[22] and the recent *Chicago desegregation case*.[23] Courts do not see a mere bargain between the parties as a sufficient foundation for the exercise of their coercive powers.

Sometimes the agreement between the parties extends beyond the terms of the decree and includes stipulated "findings of fact" and "conclusions of law," but even then an adequate foundation for a strong use of the judicial power is lacking. Given the underlying purpose of settlement — to avoid trial — the so-called "findings" and "conclusions" are necessarily the products of a bargain between the parties rather than of a trial and an independent judicial judgment. Of course, a plaintiff is free to drop a lawsuit altogether (provided that the interests of certain other persons are not compromised), and a defendant can offer something in return, but that bargained-for arrangement more closely resembles a contract than an injunction. It raises a question which has already been answered whenever an injunction is issued, namely, whether the judicial power should be used to enforce it. Even assuming that the consent is freely given and authoritative, the bargain is at best contractual and does not contain the kind of enforcement commitment already embodied in a decree that is the product of a trial and the judgment of a court.

JUSTICE RATHER THAN PEACE

The dispute-resolution story makes settlement appear as a perfect substitute for judgment, as we just saw, by trivializing the remedial dimensions of a lawsuit, and also by reducing the social function of the lawsuit to one of resolving private disputes: In that story, settlement appears to achieve exactly the same purpose as judgment — peace between the parties — but at considerably less expense to society. The two quarrelling neighbors turn to a court in order to resolve their dispute, and society makes courts available because it wants to aid in the achievement of their private ends or to secure the peace.

In my view, however, the purpose of adjudication should be understood in broader terms. Adjudication uses public resources, and employs not strangers chosen by the parties but public officials chosen by a process in which the public participates. These officials, like members of the legislative and executive branches, possess a power that has been defined and conferred by public law, not by private agreement. Their job is not to maximize the ends of private parties, nor simply to secure the peace, but to explicate and give force to the values embodied in authoritative texts such as the Constitution and statutes: to interpret those values and to bring reality into accord with them. This duty is not discharged when the parties settle.

In our political system, courts are reactive institutions. They do not search out interpretive occasions, but instead wait for others to bring matters to their attention. They also rely for the most part on others to investigate and present the law and facts. A settlement will thereby deprive a court of the occasion, and perhaps even the ability, to render an interpretation. A court cannot proceed (or not proceed very far) in the face of a settlement. To be against settlement is not to urge that parties be "forced" to litigate, since that would interfere with their autonomy and distort the adjudicative process; the parties will be inclined to make the court believe that their bargain is justice. To be against settlement is only to suggest that when the parties settle, society gets less than what appears, and for a price it does not know it is paying. Parties might settle while leaving justice undone. The settlement of a school suit might secure the peace, but not racial equality. Although the parties are prepared to live under the terms they bargained for, and although such peaceful coexistence may be a necessary precondition of justice,[24] and itself a state of affairs to be valued, it is not justice itself. To settle for something means to accept less than some ideal.

I recognize that judges often announce settlements not with a sense of frustration or disappointment, as my account of adjudication might suggest, but with a sigh of relief. But this sigh should be seen for precisely what it is: It is not a recognition that a job is done, nor an acknowledgment that a job need not be done because justice has been secured. It is instead based on another sentiment altogether, namely, that another case has been "moved along," which is true whether or not justice has been done or even needs to be done. Or the sigh might be based on the fact that the agony of judgment has been avoided.

There is, of course, sometimes a value to avoidance, not just to the judge, who is thereby relieved of the need to make or enforce a hard decision, but also to society, which sometimes thrives by masking its basic contradictions. But will settlement result in avoidance when it is most appropriate? Other familiar avoidance devices, such as *certiorari*,[25] at least promise a devotion to public ends, but settlement is controlled by the litigants, and is subject to their private motivations and all the vagaries of the bargaining process. There are also dangers to avoidance, and these may well outweigh any imagined benefits. Partisans of ADR — Chief Justice Berger, or even President Bok — may begin with a certain satisfaction with the *status quo*. But when one sees injustices that cry out for correction — as Congress did when it endorsed the concept of the private attorney general[26] and as the Court of another era did when it sought to enhance access to the courts[27] — the value of avoidance diminishes and the agony of judgment becomes a necessity. Someone has to confront the betrayal of our deepest ideals and be prepared to turn the world upside down to bring those ideals to fruition.

THE REAL DIVIDE

To all this, one can readily imagine a simple response by way of confession and avoidance: We are not talking about *those* lawsuits. Advocates of ADR might insist that my account of adjudication, in contrast to the one implied by the dispute-resolution story, focuses on a rather narrow category of lawsuits. They could argue that while settlement may have only the most limited appeal with respect to those cases, I have not spoken to the "typical" cases. My response is twofold.

First, even as a purely quantitative matter, I doubt that the number of cases I am referring to is trivial. My universe includes those cases in which there are significant distributional inequalities; those in which it is difficult to generate authoritative consent because organizations or social groups are parties or because the power to settle is vested in autonomous agents; those in which the court must continue to supervise the parties after judgment; and those in which justice needs to be done, or to put it more modestly, where there is a genuine social need for an authoritative interpretation of law. I imagine that the number of cases that satisfy one of these four criteria is considerable; in contrast to the kind of case portrayed in the dispute-resolution story, they probably dominate the docket of a modern court system.

Second, it demands a certain kind of myopia to be concerned only with the number of cases, as though all cases are equal simply because the clerk of the court assigns each a single docket number. All cases are not equal. The *Los Angeles desegregation case*,[28] to take one example, is not equal to the allegedly more typical suit involving a property dispute or an automobile accident. The desegregation suit consumes more resources, affects more people, and provokes far greater challenges to the judicial power. The settlement movement must introduce a qualitative perspective; it must speak to these more "significant" cases, and demonstrate the propriety of settling them. Otherwise it will soon be seen as an irrelevance, dealing with trivia rather than responding to the very conditions that give the movement its greatest sway and saliency.

Nor would sorting cases into "two tracks," one for settlement, and another for judgment, avoid my objections. Settling automobile cases and leaving discrimination or antitrust cases for judgment might remove a large number of cases from the dockets, but the dockets will nevertheless remain burdened with the cases that consume the most judicial resources and represent the most controversial exercises of the judicial power. A "two track" strategy would drain the argument for settlement of much of its appeal. I also doubt whether the "two track" strategy can be sensibly implemented. It is impossible to formulate adequate criteria for prospectively sorting cases. The problems of settlement are not tied to the subject matter of the suit, but instead stem from factors that are harder to identify, such as the wealth of the parties, the likely post-judgment history of the suit, or the need for an authoritative interpretation of law. The authors of the amendment to Rule 68 make a gesture toward a "two track" strategy by exempting class actions and shareholder derivative suits, and by allowing the judge to refrain from awarding attorney's fees when it is "unjustified under all of the circumstances."[29] But these gestures are cramped and ill-conceived, and are likely to increase the workload of the courts by giving rise to yet another set of issues to litigate.[30] It is, moreover, hard to see how these problems can be avoided. Many of the factors that lead a society to bring social relationships that otherwise seem wholly private (e.g., marriage) within the jurisdiction of a court, such as imbalances of power or the interests of third parties, are also likely to make settlement problematic. Settlement is a poor substitute for judgement; it is an even poorer substitute for the withdrawal of jurisdiction.

For these reasons, I remain highly skeptical of a "two track" strategy, and would resist it. But the more important point to note is that the draftsmen of Rule 68 are the exception. There is no hint of a "two track" strategy in Rule 16. In fact, most ADR advocates make no effort to distinguish between different types of cases or to suggest that "the gentler arts of reconciliation and accommodation" might be particularly appropriate for one type of case but not for another. They lump all cases together. This suggests that what divides me from the partisans of ADR is not that we are concerned with different universes of cases, that Derek Bok, for example, focuses on boundary quarrels while I see only desegregation suits. I suspect instead that what divides us is much deeper and stems from our understanding of the purpose of the civil law suit and its place in society. It is a difference in outlook.

Someone like Bok sees adjudication in essentially private terms: The purpose of lawsuits and the civil courts is to resolve disputes, and the amount of litigation we encounter is evidence of the needlessly combative and quarrelsome character of Americans. Or as Bok put it, using a more diplomatic idiom: "At bottom, ours is a society built on individualism, competition, and success."[31] I, on the other hand, see adjudication in more public terms: Civil litigation is an institutional arrangement for using state power to bring a recalcitrant reality closer to our chosen ideas. We turn to the courts because we need to, not because of some quirk in our personalities. We train our students in the tougher arts so that they may help secure all that the law promises, not because we want them to become gladiators or because we take a special pleasure in combat.

To conceive of the civil lawsuit in public terms as America does might be unique. I am willing to assume that no other country — including Japan, Bok's new paragon[32] — has a case like *Brown v. Board of Education*[33] in which the judicial power is used to eradicate the caste structure. I am willing to assume that no other country conceives of law and uses law in quite the way we do. But this should be a source of pride rather than shame. What is unique is not the problem, that we live short of our ideals, but that we alone among the nations of the world seem willing to do something about it. Adjudication American-style is not a reflection of our combativeness but rather a tribute to our inventiveness and perhaps even more to our commitment.

Endnotes

1. Bok, "A Flawed System", *Harv. Mag.*, May–June 1983, at 38; reprinted in *N.Y. St. B.J.*, Oct. 1983, at 8, *N.Y. St. B.J.*, Nov. 1983, at 31; excerpted in (1983), 33 *J. Legal Educ.* 570.
2. Bok, *supra* note 1, at 45.
3. *Id.*
4. See e.g., Burger, "Isn't There a Better Way?" (1982), 68 *A.B.A.J.* 274; Burger, "Agenda for 2000 A.D. — A Need for Systematic Anticipation" (1976), 70 *F.R.D.* 83, 93–96.
5. The *Journal of Dispute Resolution*, published by the University of Missouri-Columbia School of Law, is scheduled to begin publication in June, 1984.
6. Fed. R. Civ. P. 16. In a similar spirit, the Second Circuit has instituted a Civil Appeals Management Plan (CAMP), which empowers a court officer to direct the parties to a civil appeal to appear at a pre-argument conference "to consider the possibility of settlement," before their case is scheduled for argument. CAMP 4–5, reprinted in 2d Cir. R. 54. Conferences are held in approximately 90% of the cases assigned to CAMP; staff counsel grant requests by the parties not to hold pre-argument conferences because of "unsettleable issues" in fewer than one in ten cases. Letter from Vincent Flanigan, Management Analyst, Second Circuit Judicial Conference, to Owen M. Fiss (Apr. 12, 1984). For a review of the debate over CAMP's success, see Hoffman, "The Bureaucratic Spectre Newest Challenge to the Courts" (1982), 66 *Judicature* 60, 70 & nn. 42–44. For a discussion of the problems which arise when judges become deeply involved in pre-trial attempts to facilitate settlement, see Resnik, "Managerial Judges" (1982), 96 *Harv. L. Rev.* 374.
7. In pertinent part, Rule 68 currently provides:
> At any time more than 10 days before the trial begins, a party defending a claim may serve upon the adverse party an offer to allow judgment to be taken against him for the money or property or to the effect specified in his offer, with costs then accrued.... If [the offer is rejected and] the judgment finally obtained by the offeree is not more favorable than the offer, the offeree must pay the costs incurred after the making of the offer.

Fed R. Civ. P. 68. The term "costs" has been interpreted not to include attorneys' fees. *Roadway Express v. Piper*, 447 U.S. 752, 759–63 (1980); *Chesny v. Marek*, 720 F. 2d 474, 480 (7th Cir. 1983), *cert. granted*, 52 U.S.L.W. 3770 (U.S. Apr. 23, 1984) (No. 83–1437).
> The proposed amended rule would provide, in pertinent part:
> At any time more than 30 days before the trial begins, any party may serve upon an adverse party an offer, denominated as an offer under this rule, to settle a claim for the money or property or to the effect specified in his offer and to enter into a stipulation dismissing the claim or to allow judgment to be entered accordingly....
> If the judgment finally entered is not more favorable to the offeree than an unaccepted offer,...the offeree must pay the costs and expenses, including reasonable attorneys' fees, incurred by the offeror after the making of the offer.... The

amount of the expenses and interest may be reduced to the extent expressly found by the court, with a statement of reasons, to be excessive or unjustified under all of the circumstances. In determining whether a final judgment is more or less favorable to the offeree than the offer, the costs and expenses of the parties shall be excluded from consideration. Costs, expenses, and interest shall not be awarded to an offeror found by the court to have made an offer in bad faith.

...This rule shall not apply to class or derivative actions under Rules 23, 23.1, and 23.2

Committee on Rules of Prac. & Proc. of the Judicial Conference of the United States, "Preliminary Draft of Proposed Amendments to the Federal Rules of Civil Procedure" (1983), 98 *F.R.D.* 339, 361–63.

8. See *Aleyska Pipeline Serv. Co. v. Wilderness Soc'y*, 421 U.S. 240, 247 (1975).

9. The *Civil Rights Attorney's Fees Awards Act* of 1976 provides that, in a variety of civil rights actions, a "court, in its discretion, may allow the prevailing party...a reasonable attorney's fee as part of the costs." 42 U.S.C. 1988 (1976 & Supp. V 1981). The Supreme Court has read the Act to mean that prevailing plaintiffs should normally recover their attorneys' fees, while prevailing defendants are not normally entitled to such awards. See *Christiansburg Garment Co. v. EEOC*, 434 U.S. 412, 416–18 (1978).

In *Delta Air Lines v. August*, 450 U.S. 346 (1981), the Court held that Rule 68 does not allow a prevailing defendant to recover any costs (including attorney's fees) from a Title VII plaintiff even though the defendant had proposed a settlement prior to trial. The Court found that such an application of Rule 68 would be contrary to the concept of the private attorney general underlying Title VII. *Id.* at 360 n.27. Given the Court's insistence in *Alyeska Pipeline* that any expansion of the concept of the private attorney general would require specific statutory authorization, 421 U.S. at 263–64, and given Congress' response — the 1976 Act — it would be ironic for the Supreme Court to use its rulemaking power to constrict the use of private attorneys general by amending Rule 68. In *Chesny v. Marek*, 720 F. 2d 474, 479 (7th Cir. 1983), *cert. granted*, 52 U.S.L.W. 3770 (U.S. Apr. 23, 1984) (No. 83–1437). Judge Posner interpreted the "costs" provision of current Rule 68 to exclude attorney's fees. He found that including them would deter private attorneys general, would thus involve "substantive" not "procedural" effects, and would therefore exceed the bounds of the *Rules Enabling Act*, 28 U.S.C. 2072 (1976). Judge Posner also noted that by the mid-1970's, Congress had enacted between 75 and 90 separate fee-shifting statutes. *Id.* at 477.

For statutes in other fields of law that award attorney's fees to prevailing plaintiffs but not to prevailing defendants, see e.g., 5 U.S.C. 552a(g)(B) (1982) (Privacy Act); 15 U.S.C. 15 (1982) (antitrust).

10. Martin Shapiro provides one formulation of the dispute-resolution story. See M. Shapiro, *Courts: A Comparative and Political Analysis* (1981), 1–2.

11. See Posner, "An Economic Approach to Legal Procedure and Judicial Administration" (1973), 2 *J. Legal. Stud.* 399; Priest, "Regulating the Content and Volume of Litigation: An Economic Analysis" (1982), 1 *Sup. Ct. Econ. Rev.* 163; Shavell, "Suit, Settlement, and Trial: A Theoretical Analysis Under Alternative Methods for the Allocation of Legal Costs" (19??), 11 *J. Legal. Stud.* 55.

12. The offer-of-settlement rule of the proposed Rule 68 would only aggravate the influence of distributional inequalities. It would make the poorer party liable for the attorney's fees of his adversary, which are likely to be greater than the plaintiff's own legal fees when the defendant retains higher-priced counsel. Thus, fee shifting presents a greater risk to plaintiffs than to defendants. In cases where the prevailing plaintiff is entitled to attorney's fees pursuant to a specific statute, the defendant already has an incentive to settle, namely, to avoid becoming responsible for the plaintiff's legal expenses at trial. (He would still be liable for the plaintiff's pre-trial expenses if the court found that the settlement was sufficiently favorable to make the plaintiff a prevailing party, see *Maher v. Gagne*, 448 U.S. 122, 129–30 (1980), but these expenses are presumably significantly lower than the expenses of actually completing pre-trial preparation and proceeding to trial.) Rule 68 thus does not make the defendant more amenable to settlement. It does, however, place ad-

ditional burdens on plaintiffs, because under Rule 68 they would risk incurring the attorney's fees of the defendant. See *Bitsouni v. Sheraton Hartford Corp.*, 33 Fair Empl. Prac. Cas. (BNA) 898, 901–02 (D. Conn. 1983).

13. See 42 U.S.C. 2996f(b)(3), (6), (8), (9) (Supp. V 1981) (restricting use of Legal Services Corporation funds for, *inter alia*, political, abortion-rights, and desegregation litigation).

14. In a case challenging conditions in Texas' state prison system, for example, Judge Justice ordered the United States to appear as an *amicus curiae* "(i)n order to investigate the facts alleged in the prisoners' complaints, to participate in such civil action with the full rights of a party thereto, and to advise this Court at all stages of the proceedings as to any action deemed appropriate by it." *In re Estelle*, 516 F. 23 480, 482 (5th Cir. 1975) (quoting unpublished district court order), *cert. denied*, 426 U.S. 925 (1976). The decree which was eventually entered found systemic constitutional violations and ordered sweeping changes in the state's prisons. See *Ruiz v. Estell*, 503 F. Supp. 1265 (S.D. Tex. 1980), *motion to stay order granted in part and denied in part*, 650 F. 2d 555 (5th Cir. 1981), *add'l motion to stay order granted in part and denied in part*, 666 F. 2d 854 (5th Cir. 1982).

15. Domestic relations cases form the largest subject-matter category of cases on state court dockets. See Nat'l. Center for State Courts, *State Court Caseload Statistics: The State of the Art* (1978), 53. Much of this litigation occurs after the entry of initial decrees. See Oldham, "Book Review" (1983), 54 *U. Colo L. Rev.* 469, 478–80 (reviewing L. Weitzman, *The Marriage Contract* (1981)).

16. I define the relationship between structural reform and the dispute-resolution story more fully elsewhere. See Fiss, "The Social and Political Foundations of Adjudication" (1982), 6 *L. & Hum. Behav.* 121.

17. See e.g., *Clark v. Board of Educ.* 705 F. 2d 265 (8th Cir. 1983) (continuation of Little Rock desegregation case); *Brown v. Board of Educ.*, 84 F.R.D. 383 (D. Kan, 1979) (seeking intervention in original Topeka desegregation case on behalf of class represented by Linda Brown's daughter).

18. In *United States v. United Shoe Mach. Corp.*, 391 U.S. 244 (1968), for example, the government successfully reopened a decade-old decree because competition in the shoe machinery market had not yet been attained.

19. *United States v. Swift & Co.*, 286 U.S. 106, 119 (1932).

20. See *United States v. Swift & Co.*, 189 F. Supp. 885, 904, 910–12 (N.D. III. 1960), *aff'd* 367 U.S. 909 (1961). For a history of the Meat Packers' consent decree over a fifty-year period, see O. Fiss, *Injunctions* (1972), 325–99.

21. See D. Dobbs, *Handbook on the Law of Remedies*, § 2.9, at 93–94, 99 n. 25 (1973).

22. *New York State Ass'n for Retarded Children v. Carey*, 631 F. 2d 162, 163–64 (2d Cir. 1980) (court unwilling to hold governor in contempt of consent decree when legislature refused to provide funding for committee established by court to oversee implementation of decree). The First Circuit explicitly acknowledged limitations on the power of courts to enforce consent decrees in *Brewster v. Dukakis*, 687 F. 2d 495, 501 (1st Cir. 1982), and *Massachusetts Ass'n for Retarded Citizens v. King* 668 F. 2d 602, 610 (1st Cir. 1981).

23. In *United States v. Board of Educ.* 717 F. 2d 378, 384–85 (7th Cir. 1983), the Court of Appeals found that the district court had acted too hastily in ordering the United States to provide additional financial support for Chicago's voluntary desegregation program pursuant to the consent decree which the federal government and the school board had entered into with the plaintiffs. The Seventh Circuit instead instructed the district court to give the federal government time to comply voluntarily with its obligations.

24. Some observers have argued that compliance is more likely to result from a consent decree than from an adjudicated decree. See O. Fiss and D. Rendleman, *Injunctions*, 2nd ed. (1984) 1004. But increased compliance may well be due to the fact that a consent decree asks less for the defendant rather than from its creating a more amicable relationship between the parties. See McEwen and Maiman, "Mediation in Small Claims Court: Achieving Compliance Through Consent" (1984), 18 *Law & Soc'y Rev.* 11.

25. See generally A. Bickel, *The Least Dangerous Branch* (1962), 111–99 (discussing "the passive virtues"). For an analysis of the doctrines of vagueness and overbreadth as techniques for avoidance, see Note, "The Void-for-Vagueness Doctrine in the Supreme Court" (1960), 109 *U. Pa. L. Rev.* 67.

26. For a discussion of the role of the private attorney general, see *supra* notes 9 and 22. The *Federal Question Jurisdictional Amendments Act* of 1980, Pub. I. No. 96–486, 94 Stat. 2369 (codified at 28 U.S.C. 1331 (Supp. V 1981)), which eliminated the jurisdictional amount in federal question cases, reflects a similar sentiment: A claim's significance cannot be measured simply by the amount of money involved. See H.R. Rep. No. 1461, 94th Cong., 2d Sess. 2, reprinted in 1980 U.S. Cong. Code & Ad. News 5063, 5063–64.

27. For a discussion of the Supreme Court's decisions during the 1960's and early 1970's suggesting that access to the courts and the opportunity to litigate are essential due process rights, see Michelman, "The Supreme Court and Litigation Access Fees" (pts. 1 & 2) (1973), *Duke L.J.* 1153; (1974), *Duke L.J.* 527.

28. See *Crawford v. Board of Educ.*, 46 Cal. App. 3d 872, 120 Cal. Rptr. 334 (Ct. App. 1975), *aff'd*, 17 Cal. 3d, 551 P. 2d 28, 130 Cal. Rptr. 724 (1976). For a recent recounting of the history of the 20 years of litigation, see *Crawford v. Board of Educ.*, 103 S. Ct. 3211, 3214–15 (1982).

29. 98 *F.R.D.* at 362.

30. It is far from clear that either the current offer-of-judgment rule or the proposed amendments are likely to reduce the overall volume of litigation. Although such a rule increases the potential costs a plaintiff faces should he lose, and thus means a plaintiff will be willing to settle for a smaller amount than he would demand if there were no potential liability for the defendant's expenses, it also increases the potential benefits a defendant will receive should his offer exceed the amount the plaintiff recovers at trial (since the defendant will both retain the difference between the offer and the amount actually recovered and will recover his expenses), and thus means a defendant will offer less in a settlement. There is no reason to assume that the gap between the plaintiff's demand and the defendant's offer will be relatively smaller because of the offer-of-judgment rule. See Priest, *supra* note 11, at 171.

Moreover, Rule 68 makes no exception for cases seeking non-monetary relief, such as injunctions. It thus requires the court to decide whether the injunction actually obtained was in fact "better" or "more favorable" than the decree the defendant was willing to enter prior to trial.

The "reasonability" language of the proposed rule, *supra* note 7, creates potential attorney-client conflicts that may also spark litigation. By implication, a court which grants an offeror all of his expenses has decided that the offeree was unreasonable in his refusal. If the offeree based that refusal on the advice of counsel, then that advice was unreasonable, and a malpractice suit can be expected to recover fees assessed against the client in the original case.

The proposed rule's exclusion of costs and attorney's fees from the assessment of whether an offer is more or less favorable than an eventual judgment, 98 *F.R.D.* at 362, may cause additional conflicts between plaintiffs and their attorneys. Suppose that a defendant offers a plaintiff $100,000 as full relief including attorney's fees and costs. If the plaintiff accepts this offer, then his attorney forfeits the right to attorney's fees under a statutory fee-shifting scheme. If, however, the plaintiff refuses the offer, then the plaintiff may be liable to the defendant for the defendant's attorney's fees and costs, even though the plaintiff's total "recovery" at trial — for example, $80,000 on the merits and $30,000 in attorneys' fees — exceeds the defendant's offer because the plaintiff recovered less on the merits. In these circumstances, the lawyer may press his client to litigate because this will assure the lawyer his fee, even though the client will thereby be exposed to possible liability for the defendant's costs and expenses.

31. Bok, *supra* note 1, at 42.

32. *Id.* at 41. As to the validity of the comparisons and a more subtle explanation of the determinants of litigiousness, see Haley, "The Myth of the Reluctant Litigant" (1978), 4 *J. Japanese Stud.* 359, 389 ("Few misconceptions about Japan have been more widespread or as pernicious as the myth of the special reluctance of the Japanese to litigate."); see also Galanter, "Reading the Landscape of Disputes: What We Know and Don't Know (And Think We Know) About Our Allegedly Contentious and Litigious Society" (1983), 31 *UCLA L. Rev.* 4, 57–59 (paucity of lawyers in Japan due to restrictions on number of attorneys admitted to practice rather than to non-litigiousness).

33. 347 U.S. 483 (1954); 349 U.S. 294 (1955).

For Reconciliation†

A.W. McThenia and T.L. Shaffer

PROFESSOR Owen Fiss, in his recent comment, *Against Settlement*,[1] weighs in against the Alternative Dispute Resolution (ADR) movement. He brings to the discussion his often stated preference for adjudicative, which he views as "a tribute to our inventiveness,"[2] to be encouraged because it is a forum for the articulation of important public values. Fiss argues that the entire movement for alternatives to litigation is misplaced. He understands that the movement's claim to legitimacy turns on the inefficiency of the legal system and on popular dissatisfaction with law as a means for maintaining order,[3] and he challenges this claim.

Fiss attacks a straw man. In our view, the models he has created for argument in other circumstances[4] have become mechanisms of self-deception not only for him but for most of those who write about alternatives to litigation. His understanding that the plea of ADR advocates is based on efficiency reduces the entire question to one of procedures. Fiss's argument rests on the faith that justice — and he uses the word — is usually something people get from the government. He comes close to arguing that the branch of government that resolves disputes, the courts, is the principal source of justice in fragmented modern American society.[5]

† McThenia, Andrew Wolfe, and Shaffer, Thomas L., "For Reconciliation" (1985), 94 *Yale Law Journal* at 1660–68. Reprinted by permission of The Yale Law Journal Company, Fred B. Rothman & Company, Professor McThenia and Professor Shaffer.

Fiss's view that the claims of ADR advocates arise from a popular dissatisfaction with law reduces the issue to one of order.[6] As his first stated understanding reduces justice to statism, this understanding reduces justice (or, if you like, peace) to a tolerably minimum level of violence in the community. In our view, an appropriate engagement of the Fiss attack on ADR must go all the way back to these two characterizations in his argument against ADR and in favor of court-dominated dispute resolution. We are not willing to let him frame the issue.

Certain themes recur in the ADR literature. Many advocates of ADR make efficiency-based claims. And a plea for ending the so-called litigation explosion, and for returning to law and order, runs through the rules-of-procedure branch of the ADR literature.[7] But the movement, if it is even appropriate to call it a single movement, is too varied for Fiss's description. Rather than focusing on the substance of claims made for ADR, Fiss has created a view of the function of courts that he can comfortably oppose.

In an earlier and provocative article, Fiss called for both a recognition and an affirmation of the expanded role of courts in modern America.[8] He urged an explicit recognition that "[a]djudication is the social process by which judges give meaning to our public values."[9] Further, he argued that a new form of adjudication, "structural reform," be celebrated as "a central — maybe the central — mode of constitutional adjudication."[10] To develop his thesis and to meet Professor Lon Fuller's arguments on the limits of adjudication,[11] Fiss resorted to modelling. He contrasted his preferred view of adjudication, "structural reform," with what he described as a "traditional" model of adjudication. Although it is not clear whether he understood the *substance* of the two types of adjudication to be fundamentally different,[12] he clearly viewed the *form* of structural reform litigation as "breathtakingly different"[13] from the "dispute resolution" or "traditional" model of adjudication.

While Fiss was initially content to construct contrasting models of adjudication simply in order to accentuate his position and argue against Fuller's, he has in more recent writings asserted that one of these models, that of traditional dispute resolution, has a life of its own, a life that has "long dominated the literature and our thinking."[14] In fact, Fiss's later positive description of structural reform continues to flower, while his negative description of traditional adjudication has become abstract and lifeless. Fiss's response to the imperfections of life that lay bare the difficulties with his model of structural reform has been, it seems to us, to provide a shrill description of traditional judicial dispute resolution.[15]

Fiss's description of traditional dispute resolution is a story of two neighbors "in a state of nature" who each claim a single piece of property and who, when they cannot agree, turn to "a stranger" to resolve their dispute.[16] He asserts that traditional dispute resolution depicts a sociologically impoverished universe,[17] operates in a state of nature where there are no public values of goals[18] except a supposed "natural harmony" of the *status quo*,[19] and calls on the exercise of power by a stranger.[20] That was never Fuller's position. Nor do we find much support in the literature or in reality for such a view of traditional adjudication. If there ever was such a world we expect it was "nasty, brutish and short." However, we don't really believe that traditional adjudication ever bore much resemblance to that story. Yet this is the view of the world that Fiss attributes to the advocates of ADR; his attack on ADR is premised on that notion.[21]

Models are, of course, human creations. The good ones contain elements of the creator's perception of the world and of the reality he seeks to perceive.[22] They are designed to invite conversation and to appeal to the reader in a search for understanding. They are abstractions; but to be effective, they must have some connection either with the creator's view of reality or with what he wants the world to be like. Fiss's model of structural reform is, in this way, an effective model.[23] While it may not depict the world that many of us observe, it does reflect his view of the world he wishes he could find. It reflects, we suspect, more his hope than his actual belief. We honor that. The model is rich. It leads to conversation and debate.

But Fiss's model of traditional dispute resolution is flat; it is only an abstraction, and is therefore also a caricature. It has no relation to the world as it is; it does not appeal to the reader as a convincing way to understand adjudication or its alternatives. It does not permit one to express hope in alternatives to adjudication.

In any event, after setting up his "state of nature" model of dispute resolution, Fiss attributes that view of the world to the advocates of ADR. He understands pleas to consider alternatives to current means of resolving disputes as turning on the inefficiency of traditional adjudication (his negative model), and popular dissatisfaction with it. He equates the ADR movement with those who urge settlement more than judgment and who seek a "truce more than a true reconciliation."[24] He argues that settlement is "a capitulation to the conditions of mass society," a capitulation that "should be neither encouraged nor praised."[25] He assumes that the ADR movement is one that wants peace at any price and treats settlement as "the anticipation of the outcome of trial,"[26] that is, trial in his stranger-judge, negative model of adjudication.

Fiss is against settlement because he views the matters that come before courts in America, and that are inappropriate for ADR, as including cases in which: (1) there are distributional inequities; (2) securing authoritative consent or settlement is difficult; (3) continued supervision following judgment is necessary; and (4) there is a genuine need for an authoritative interpretation of law.[27] Fiss characterizes disputes in this limited way — as arguments between two neighbors, one of whom has vastly superior bargaining power over the other. It is then easy for him to prefer litigation to settlement, because litigation is a way to equalize bargaining power.

The soundest and deepest part of the ADR movement does not rest on Fiss's two-neighbors model. It rests on values — of religion, community, and work place — that are more vigorous than Fiss thinks. In many, in fact most, of the cultural traditions that argue for ADR, settlement is neither an avoidance mechanism nor a truce. Settlement is a process of reconciliation in which the anger of broken relationships is to be confronted rather than avoided, and in which healing demands not a truce but confrontation. Instead of "trivializing the remedial process,"[28] settlement exalts that process. Instead of "reducing the social function...to one of resolving private disputes,"[29] settlement calls on substantive community values. Settlement is sometimes a beginning, and is sometimes a postscript, but it is not the essence of the enterprise of dispute resolution. The essence of the enterprise is more like the structural injunction, about which Fiss has written so eloquently, than like an alternative to the resolution-by-stranger described by his negative model.[30]

The "real divide"[31] between us and Fiss may not be our differing views of the sorts of cases that now wind their way into American courts, but, more fundamentally, it may be our different views of justice. Fiss comes close to equating justice with law. He includes among the cases unsuited for settlement "those in which justice needs to be done, or to put it more modestly, where there is a genuine social need for an authoritative interpretation of law."[32] We do not believe that law and justice are synonymous. We see the deepest and soundest of ADR arguments as in agreement with us: Justice is not usually something people get from the government. And courts (which are not, in any case, strangers) are not the only or even the most important places that dispense justice.[33]

Many advocates of ADR can well be taken to have asked about the law's response to disputes, and alternatives to that response, not in order to reform the law but in order to locate alternative views of what a dispute is. Such alternatives would likely advance or assume understandings of justice (or, if you like, peace) that are also radically different from justice as something lawyers *administer*, or peace as the absence of violence. They assume not that justice is something people get from the government but that it is something people give to one another. These advocates seek an understanding of justice in the way Socrates and Thrasymachus did in the *Republic*: Justice is not the will of the stronger; it is not efficiency in government; it is not the reduction of violence; Justice is what we discover — you and I, Socrates said — when we walk together, listen together, and even love one another, in our curiosity about what justice is and where justice comes from.

Most of us who have gone to college know something about Socrates. Many more of us who grew up in the United States know something about Moses and Jesus. It is from Torah and Gospel, more than from Plato, that we are most likely to be able to sketch out radical alternatives to the law's response to disputes. As a matter of fact, our religious culture contains both a theoretical basis for these alternatives and a way to apply theory to disputes.

In the Hebraic tradition (as in the Islamic), scripture is normative. Judaism, for example, does not merely seek to follow Torah; it loves Torah, it finds life in Torah, it celebrates Torah as one might celebrate the presence of a lover, or of a loving parent, or of a community that nourishes peace — commitment to common well being, and even a feeling of being well. (Salvation is not too strong a word for it.) Justice is the way one defines a righteous life; justice does involve according other persons their due but, more radically, in the Hebraic view, it involves loving them. Such a justice is the product of piety, to be sure, but not piety alone; it is the product of study, of reason, and of attending to the wise and learning from them how to be virtuous.[34] *Quare fidem intellectum.*[35]

The Christian side of the Hebraic tradition has, or should have, all of this. It also has a unique procedure established in St. Matthew's Gospel — a *system* backed up by stern condemnation of Christians who turn from the Gospel and seek instead the law's response to disputes. In this system — as well as Judaism[36] — the religious community claims authority to resolve disputes and even to coerce obedience. The procedure involves, first, conversation; if that fails, it involves mediation; if mediation fails, it involves airing the dispute before representatives of the community. If the dispute goes so far as judgment, the system — as is also the case in Judaism — permits pressure: "[I]f he refuses to listen to the community, treat him like a pagan or a tax collector. I tell you solemnly, whatever you bind on earth shall be considered bound in heaven; whatever you loose on earth shall be considered loosed in heaven."[37]

Thus, the procedure gives priority to restoring the relationship. Hebraic theology puts primary emphasis on relationships, a priority that is political and even ontological, as well as ethical, and therefore legal.[38] And so, most radically, the religious tradition seeks not *resolution* (which connotes the sort of doctrinal integrity in the law that seems to us to be Fiss's highest priority) but *reconciliation* of brother to brother, sister to sister, sister to brother, child to parent, neighbor to neighbor, buyer to seller, defendant to plaintiff, *and judge to both*. (The Judge is also an I and a Thou.) This view of what a dispute is, and of what third parties seek when they intervene in disputes between others, provides an existing, traditional, common alternative to the law's response. The fact seems to be that this alternative has both a vigorous modern history and a studiable contemporary vitality (Jerrold Auerbach[39] to the contrary notwithstanding).

Contemporary manifestations of the Hebraic tradition claim adherence to a moral authority that is more important than the government.[40] The Torah is the wisdom of God, the Gospel is the good news that promises a peace the world cannot give. From one perspective, theology makes such religious views of dispute and resolution seem peripheral. That impression is deceptive, though: In the aggregate these views of what a dispute is are consistent with one another and, as such, consistent with the moral commitments of most people in America. The numbers of people in this country who might find them so is not declining; it is increasing. "In the aggregate" is an appropriate consideration, as one assays radical alternatives to the law's response to disputes, because there is substantial commonality among the practitioners of this radical Hebraic alternative. Religious systems of reconciliation rest on a substantively common theology and on a substantively common argument that, contrary to the implications of Fiss's view of justice, the government is not as important as it thinks it is.

Professor David Trubek ends a recent and pessimistic essay on alternative dispute resolution[41] with a paradox: "[N]o one," he says, "really seems to believe in law any more."[42] The "elites" who complain of a litigation explosion — Chief Justice Warren Burger and others "who champion alternatives"[43] — "question the law's efficacy."[44] But so do those who criticize the law as political and oppressive, most notably scholars in the Critical Legal Studies movement. The elites exalt an informalism they don't believe in, Trubek says; and the radicals exalt a formalist they distrust. Apparently the new legal-process school — or at least one of its eloquent spokesmen, Owen Fiss — still believes in law. Fiss's writing on structural reform is powerful. It may not reflect the way the world actually is, but it is a statement of hope. And that is important in an age of nihilism. But we suspect those who believe in law and in nothing else; we hope Fiss is not among them. Informalism of the Chief Justice's formulation[45] may deserve distrust. But informalism has some contemporary manifestations — many of them resting on the most ancient and deepest of our traditions — that deserve trust and even celebration. These manifestations too are statements of hope. Suggestions for alternatives to litigation need to be critically examined — no doubt many of them are hollow. What they do not need, and what the legal community does not need, is an argument that reduces these alternatives to a caricature.

Endnotes

1. Fiss, "Against Settlement" (1983), 93 *Yale L.J.* 1073 [hereinafter cited as *Against Settlement*].
2. *Id.* at 1090.
3. Professor Fiss equates settlement with ADR and says that settlement should be treated as a "highly problematic technique for streamlining

dockets." *Id.* at 1075. His citations to the underlying story of ADR are to the law and economics literature. *Id.* at 1076 n. 11. He attributes to President Bok the view that litigation "is evidence of the needlessly combative and quarrelsome character of Americans." *Id.* at 1089.
4. See O. Fiss, *The Civil Rights Injunction* (1978); Fiss, "The Supreme Court, 1974 Term — Foreword: The Forms of Justice" (1979), 93 *Harv. L. Rev.* 1 [hereinafter cited as *Forms of Justice*]; Fiss, "The Social and Political Foundations of Adjudication" (1982), 6 *Law & Hum. Behav.* 121 [hereinafter cited as *Foundations of Adjudication.*]
5. In describing those cases unsuitable for ADR Fiss includes "those in which justice needs to be done, or to put it more modestly, where there is a genuine social need for an authoritative interpretation of law." Fiss, *Against Settlement, supra* note 1, at 1087.
6. *Id.* at 1075.
Consent is often coerced; the bargain may be struck by someone without authority; the absence of a trial and judgment renders subsequent judicial involvement troublesome; and although dockets are trimmed, justice may not be done. Like plea bargaining, settlement is a capitulation to the conditions of mass society and should be neither encouraged nor praised.
7. See e.g., J. Auerbach, *Justice Without Law?* (1983); 1 R. Abel, ed., *The Politics of Informal Justice: The American Experience* (1982); 2 R. Abel, ed., *The Politics of Informal Justice: Comparative Studies* (1982); Burter, "Isn't There a Better Way?" (1982), 68 *A.B.A.J.* 274; Posner, "An Economic Approach to Legal Procedure and Judicial Administration" (1973), 2 *J. Legal Stud.* 399. For a statement raising questions about the existence of a legal explosion, see Galanter, "Reading the Landscape of Disputes: What We Know and Don't Know (And Think We Know) About Our Allegedly Contentious and Litigious Society" (1983), 31 *UCLA L. Rev.* 4, 7.
8. Fiss, *Forms of Justice, supra* note 4.
9. *Id.* at 2.
10. *Id.*
11. Professor Fuller's essay, "The Forms and Limits of Adjudication", was published posthumously at (1978), 92 *Harv. L. Rev.* 353. Typed versions of it were circulated some years prior to that time. See also Fuller, "Adjudication and the Rule of Law" (1969), 54 *Proc. Am. Soc'y Int'l L.* 1; Fuller, "Collective Bargaining and the Arbitrator" (1963), *Wis L. Rev.* 3.
12. See Fiss, *Forms of Justice, supra* note 4. At one point Fiss asserts that the function of adjudication throughout the 19th and 20th centuries was not to resolve disputes, *Id.* at 36, but at other places he acknowledges that the historical work of courts may have been akin to dispute resolution. *Id.* at 35–36. In his later writings, perhaps in response to criticism that he had failed "to place institutional litigation in perspective as part of a more complex legal and political tradition," Eisenberg and Yeazell, "The Ordinary and the Extraordinary in Institutional Litigation" (1980), 93 *Harv. L. Rev.* 465, 516. Fiss asserts that it has always been the role of adjudication to give meaning to our public values "continuous with the role of courts under the common law." But he claims that "a *new form* of constitutional adjudication has emerged." Fiss, *Foundations of Adjudication, supra* note 4 at 121.
13. Fiss, *Forms of Justice, supra* note 4, at 17.
14. Fiss, *Foundations of Adjudication, supra* note 4, at 122.
15. Professor Fiss has more recently come to hear the criticism of his model for structural reform. "One obvious threat to the integrity of the judicial process, which has been minimized in my earlier work but which is becoming of increasing concern to me, is the bureaucratization of the judiciary." Fiss, *Foundations of Adjudication, supra* note 4, at 126. Many of his arguments in favor of structural reform were initially challenged by Professor Eisenberg and Yeazell. See Eisenberg and Yeazell *supra* note 12. See also Horowitz, "The Judiciary: Umpire or Empire?" (1982), 6 *Law & Hum. Behav.* 124; Resnick, "Managerial Judges" (1982), 96 *Harv. L. Rev.* 374. In *Foundations of Adjudication*, Fiss discusses the internal strains on his model of structural reform: "These dynamics place strains upon the idea of structural reform, and yet, I would insist, they do not render that mode of adjudication either incoherent or beyond the reach of the judicial power." Fiss, *Foundations of Adjudication, supra* note 4, at 127.

16. Fiss, *Foundations of Adjudication, supra* note 4, at 127, Fiss, *Against Settlement, supra* note 1, at 1075.

17. Fiss, *Foundations of Adjudication, supra* note 4, at 122–23.

18. *Id.* at 123.

19. *Id.* at 124.

20. *Id.*

21. "They [advocates of ADR] act as though courts arose to resolve quarrels between neighbors who had reached an impasse and turned to a stranger for help" Fiss, *Against Settlement, supra* note 1, at 1075.

22. See Frug, "The Ideology of Bureaucracy in American Law" (1984), 97 *Harv. L. Rev.* 1276, 1282.

23. While one might disagree with Professor Fiss's description of structural reform, one must acknowledge the eloquence of his language. Criticism of his scholarship rests more on logic than formulation. One of the major criticisms of his 1979 work, *Forms of Justice, supra* note 4, was that by setting up his either/or worlds, Fiss had exaggerated the discontinuity between past and present, see *supra* note 12. In effect, he had cut the model of structural reform free from history. To suggest that something radically different was under way in adjudication made structural reform suspect and vulnerable to attack. Eisenberg and Yeazell also criticized Fiss for exaggerating the difference in form between traditional litigation practices and remedies, and the model of structural reform. See Eisenberg and Yeazell, *supra* note 12, at 516.

24. Fiss, *Against Settlement, supra* note 1, at 1075.

25. *Id.*

26. *Id.* at 1076.

27. *Id.* at 1087.

28. "The dispute-resolution story trivializes the remedial dimensions of lawsuits and mistakenly assumes judgment to be the end of the process." *Id.* at 1082.

29. *Id.* at 1085.

30. See Riskin, "Mediation and Lawyers" (1982), 43 *Ohio St. L.J.* 29.

31. This is Professor Fiss's phase. See Fiss, *Against Settlement, supra* note 1, at 1087.

32. *Id.*

33. See T. Shaffer, *On Being a Christian and a Lawyer* (1981), 135–36; Shaffer, "The Legal Ethics of the Two Kingdoms" (1983), 17 *Val. U.L. Rev.* 1.

Professor Milner S. Ball, who discussed this comment with us, suggested that Fiss is not arguing so much against religious or community-based ADR as against DR (deregulation). Fiss may, Ball suggests, be asking us to consider whether an overly enthusiastic support of settlement is not another form of the deregulation movement, one that permits private actors with powerful economic interests to pursue self-interest free of community norms. We may, Ball suggests, be reacting to Fiss's overly inductive statements about ADR; he may have over-stated, and

we may have over-reacted. Thus, we may have more common ground than we think. Ball's suggestion is one we will enjoy pursuing. When we do, we will want to tell Ball that the powerful economic interests are as much members of the fragmented but also reconciling community as the oppressed are. And we will want to tell Fiss that it may make a general and important difference that, in almost any kind of ADR, (a) the parties talk to one another, rather than to the government; and that (b) the third party, if there is one present, comes not as a resolver of disputes but as a neighbor.

34. See Passamaneck and Brown, "The Rabbis — Preventive Law Lawyers" (1973), 8 *Israel L. Rev.* 538. We use "Hebraic" here, as Will Herberg does, to mean the ethical tradition common to Christians and Jews. See W. Herberg, *Judaism and Modern Man: An Interpretation of Jewish Religion* (1980), 139.

35. "Faith seeking understanding."

36. See e.g., W. Jacob, ed., *American Reform Responsa: Collected Responsa of the Central Conference of American Rabbis, 1889–1983* (1983); I. Goldstein, *Jewish Justice and Conciliation: History of the Jewish Conciliation Board of America, 1930–1968 and a Review of Jewish Judicial Autonomy* (1981); I. Singer, *In My Father's Court* (1966); J. Yaffe, *So Sue Me! The Story of a Community Court* (1972); Baron, "The Treatment of Jewish Law in American Decisions" (1974), 9 *Israel L. Rev.* 85; Meislin, "Jewish Law in American Tribunals" (1972), 7 *Israel L. Rev.* 349.

37. *Matthew* 18: 17–18.

38. See M. Buber, *I and Thou*, W. Kaufmann, trans. (1970); M. Buber in N. Glatzer, ed. *On Judaism* (1967).

39. J. Auerbach, *supra* note 7.

40. See *supra* note 36. For sources on systems of reconciliation, see (1) Jewish: A. Goren, *New York Jews and the Quest for Community: The Kehillah Experiment, 1908–22* (1970); (2) Canon Law: Coing, "English Equity and the Denunciatio Evangelica of the Canon Law" (1955), 71 *Law Q. Rev.* 223. Our seminar, see *supra* note [not included in this work — publisher's note.], also considered German and French treatises on what is usually called arbitration in common law, the former in preliminary translations done for us by Mrs. Maria Colvin; (3) Peace church (Anabaptist): L. Buzzard and R. Kraybill, *Mediation: A Reader* (1980); R. Kraybill, *Repairing the Breach: Ministering in Community Conflict* (1980); (4) Evangelical Christian: L. Buzzard and L. Eck, *Tell It to the Church* (1982); C. Cassity, *Resolution of Disputes Between Christians*, Rev. ed. (1981). The Buzzard and Eck book contains a useful bibliography.

41. Trubek, "Turning Away From Law?" (1984), 82 *Mich. L. Rev.* 824.

42. *Id.* at 835.

43. *Id.*

44. *Id.*

45. Burger, *supra* note 7.

Ontario Backs New Study to Resolve Disputes Faster[†]
D. Downey

A fund to finance a study of a faster way of resolving civil disputes was announced yesterday by Ontario Attorney-General Ian Scott.

"This fund will allow the citizens of Ontario to evaluate whether alternative dispute resolution can reduce the delays and expenses of the litigation system," Mr. Scott said at a news conference.

But he said that the alternative system, if it were implemented, would not provide a solution to what he referred to as "court problems." In recent months, a back-

---

[†] Downey, Donn, "Ontario Backs New Study to Resolve Disputes Faster", *Globe and Mail*, March 28, 1990, A8. Reprinted by permission of The Globe and Mail.

log of cases has meant that several accused people have been freed without trial because the delays have infringed their rights under the Charter of Rights and Freedoms.

Natalie Rockhill, chairman of the conflict-resolution service at Toronto's St. Stephen's Community House, said the system is an alternative for people who have called police or tried to go to the courts, when they really should have sat down and discussed the problem. It is ideally suited for disputes between neighbors over barking dogs, noisy stereos, fences, parking infringements or leaking drainpipes, she said.

St. Stephen's, which began offering its conflict service in 1985, claims an 85 per cent success rate in cases where an agreement was reached. It is one of a handful of such centres in Ontario.

Parties in the dispute-settling process participate voluntarily. It either complements or is an alternative to the court system, Mr. Scott said.

The province and two private donors have contributed more than $1.2-million to the four-year study. The Donner Canadian Foundation has contributed $320,000, the Law Foundation of Ontario has contributed $300,000 and the province has contributed $500,000.

The project is the first of its kind in Canada, Mr. Scott said. It will include pilot projects, but these have yet to be determined.

B.C. Chief Justice Puts Boots to Alternative Dispute Resolution[†]
B. Daisley

B.C.'s chief justice, Allan McEachern, has delivered a hard-hitting attack on the modern trend towards alternate dispute resolution (ADR).

Speaking at a University of British Columbia law student-sponsored conference on ADR in personal injury litigation earlier this month, the chief justice described the evils of non-judicial settlement which, he says, "tends to favour the unreasonable and the stubborn and the dishonest at the expense of the decent people."

Describing ADR as nothing more than a trend of the 1980s — replacing the '60s and '70s love for law reform — he said arbitration "sometimes becomes just another layer of expense in an already too-expensive procedure."

Putting on his "black hat" to talk about the undiscussed disadvantages of conciliation and mediation, the chief justice warned the assembled students, lawyers and professors that ADR is often supported by "earnest, well-intentioned people who, for a variety of reasons, are anxious to re-organize society and procedures of courts with naive, theoretical concepts of humanity and efficiency."

Social workers think they can resolve social problems best, while engineers feel they are best equipped to handle construction disputes, he noted.

"The problem with all these theories," the judge said, "is that they never recognize the human element. They assume that all people in disputes are honest, decent, rational, understanding people" who are anxious to compromise.

As Chief Justice McEachern sees it, this overlooks the reality "that litigants as a class of people are often not very nice people, or if they're nice people then once infected with the litigation virus, they become, if not dishonest, at least badly distorted."

According to the judge, ADR ignores the fact that not all disputants are interested in settlement or honesty and that some do not even have valid claims.

He also noted ADR emphasizes compromise while there are some cases that should not be compromised. "We will have a very soft and compliant society if no one is allowed to say No,'" he said.

Non-consensual litigation, on the other hand, puts each side on an equal footing and the parties do not have to put up with posturing and bluffing. Another factor the chief justice noted was that cross-examination often brings out the truth. "I don't think ADR is a successful device for discovering or uncovering the truth. I think it starts with a bias towards compromise."

Good counsel, he said, can do just as good a job as a social worker or an engineer in dispute resolution.

While not exposed to any means of resolving a case, the chief justice told the crowd society's decent people need the non-nonsense, straightforward procedures of courtroom litigation to fight unreasonable claims and not the "soft" procedures ADR offers.

Turning to another point, he noted ADR's proponents often ignore conventional litigation's tremendous settlement rate: "Lawyers doing what they do best and for

---

†   Daisley, Brad, "B.C. Chief Justice Puts Boots to Alternative Dispute Resolution", *The Lawyers Weekly*, February 4, 1989, 2. This article originally appeared in the Feb. 4, 1989 issue of *The Lawyers Weekly*. Reprinted by permission.

which they seldom get much credit are able to resolve huge volumes of litigation using the court process but without requiring trials.''

He pointed out that B.C.'s commercial arbitration centre has heard approximately 170 disputes, while a great many individual Vancouver lawyers settle more cases in a year.

Dispute Settlement in Commercial Law Matters[†]
P. Davidson

MEDIATION AND CONCILIATION

Mediation and conciliation are the least formal of the alternate methods of dispute settlement and are sometimes used as a first attempt to resolve the conflict. Both of these methods are extensions of the bilateral negotiations between the parties and are in fact negotiations with a third party helper or interviewer.

Mediation is a process in which the mediator acts as a "go-between" in an attempt to bring the parties together in arriving at a solution to their problems. The mediator does not decide the dispute. On the contrary, the final resolution is a decision solely of the parties and the mediator's only function is to act as an intermediary to bring the parties together to resolve the dispute themselves.

In conciliation proceedings, the conciliator takes a more active role in helping to resolve the dispute. Conciliation is a process whereby the dispute is referred to a conciliator who investigates the subject-matter of the dispute and attempts to reconcile opposing contentions. The conciliator then formulates proposals for settlement, which the parties are free to accept or reject. Again, as with mediation the conciliator does not finally decide the dispute. The final decision is that of the parties, except that with conciliation the parties now have had the advantage of having an independent third party recommend a decision after investigation of the facts.

Both mediation and conciliation may be provided for in the initial contract between the parties, or may be the subject-matter of an agreement to mediate or conciliate after the dispute has arisen. Provision should be made for how the mediator or the conciliator is to be chosen and for how the proceedings are to be initiated and conducted. As mentioned, in both mediation and conciliation the final resolution is up to the parties and the effectiveness of these methods depends to a large degree on the good will of the parties. Once a final resolution has been arrived at, however, it should then be reduced to contract form so that if one party later changes its mind, the other may sue on the agreed resolution and not have to reopen the whole dispute.

ARBITRATION

Arbitration is a more formalized method of dispute settlement than mediation or conciliation. In essence, arbitration is the process of submitting a disagreement to one or more impartial arbitrators, outside the court system and sometimes without the participation of lawyers, with the understanding that both parties will abide by whatever decision is reached. Arbitration differs from conciliation in that the decision given by the arbitrator — the award — is binding on the parties and may be enforced against a recalcitrant party.

Arbitration has a long history in commercial matters and has been followed in nearly every society from the earliest times. As early as 580 A.D., King Recaredo of Spain, in the *Codex Visigothorum*, ordered that "when the merchants from abroad litigate among themselves, let none of our judges undertake to settle their business; rather that they seek among themselves one of the group to rule on the controversy". In 1601, the first statute relating to insurance in England provided for arbitration of disputes and in 1609, Lord Coke enforced a bond under which the obligor promised to pay a sum of money if he did not submit to arbitration. Arbitration was brought into Canadian law by the common law system of England and the civil law system of France. Every province and territory now has an Arbitration Act.

The reasons for preferring arbitration to litigation are many. Once of the main reasons is that arbitration is held in private and avoids publicity. Publicity of commercial disputes is adverse to the interests of both parties in that a resolution may require the disclosure of trade secrets, business procedures, and other matters which could damage the interests of both parties and which they would

---

†   Davidson, Paul, "Dispute Settlement in Commercial Law Matters" (1982–3), 7 *Canadian Business Law Journal* at 197–201. Reprinted by permission of Professor Davidson and Canadian Business Law Journal.

rather keep confidential. Further more, the private atmosphere and informality of the proceedings create a climate more conducive to the friendly resolution of the dispute than does the adversarial court procedure. Business men who wish to maintain friendly commercial relations notwithstanding a dispute over a particular transaction do not wish to publicize such differences or have the "win or lose", "all or nothing" situation of a court decision. The latter can often be avoided in arbitration, particularly where the parties to the arbitration authorize the arbitrator to decide in equity and free him from the strict application of rules of law.

Another advantage of arbitration is that the parties may choose as arbitrators specialists in the field in question, who are experienced in the trade and knowledgeable as to the customs and usages of the branch of trade involved. Further, a well organized arbitration is generally much speedier than a court procedure where delays can extend over many years. Also, costs may be less in arbitration proceedings than in court proceedings, although this depends on the nature of the dispute and the complexity of the case.

Arbitration can also help reduce "litigation neurosis". Many individuals have a fear of legal proceedings and particularly of involvement in a court proceeding. Consequently, instead of pursuing their remedies in a court, many would rather simply leave the matter lie even though they feel unjustly treated. A provision for arbitration, with its less formal proceedings, may dispel some of those feelings and allow these individuals more equal access to justice.

Unpacking the 'Rational Alternative': A Critical Review of Family Mediation Movement Claims[†]

M.J. Bailey

INTRODUCTION

The family mediation movement marches ahead, making its way with claims that are problematic on both theoretical and methodological grounds. These claims include the following:

1. family law cases are inherently unsuited to adjudication and are inherently suited to mediation;
2. mediation reduces the hostilities of divorce;
3. joint custody and mediation as a means of achieving that custody results are in the best interests of children;
4. mediation costs less than litigation;
5. higher levels of support result from mediation;
6. parties are more likely to comply with a mediated agreement; and
7. mediation empowers the parties by allowing them to fashion their own arrangements.

Family mediation proponents are not, of course, unanimous on these issues, but the majority of those in the movement adopt all or most of these positions. This paper critically examines these claims with reference to representative examples of the mediation literature.

. . . .

MEDIATION REDUCES HOSTILITIES

Divorce is an Emotional Not a Legal Issue

Mediation proponents have created a discourse in which divorce is an emotional problem which should be within the exclusive jurisdiction of the helping professions:

> [A]ll the available evidence suggests that the adversarial system is poorly suited to the resolution of disputes between divorcing spouses. The judicial emphasis on discovery of facts using proper legal procedure, and the reliance by lawyers on tactics designed to win, fits poorly with the emotional processes which underpin conflict over substantive issues, it is neither willing nor able to grapple with key emotional issues and, for this reason, is fundamentally unsuited to the resolution of divorce cases.[1]

Of course many disputes other than family law cases involve emotionally charged conflicts — intentional torts

†   Bailey, Martha J., "Unpacking the 'Rational Alternative': A Critical Review of Family Mediation Movement Claims" (1989), 8 *Canadian Journal of Family Law* at 61–62, 70–76, 86–94. Reprinted by permission of Professor Bailey and the Canadian Journal of Family Law.

are only one obvious example. Yet we are not concerned about the court's failure to "grapple with" the emotional aspects of such cases. The court is not expected to — the plaintiff seeks legal redress from the court and obtains help with emotional problems, if required, elsewhere.

Proponents assume that emotional conflicts in family law cases are particularly acute and that the legal issues will not be satisfactorily resolved unless hostilities are resolved in mediation. This claim is not supported by the research (discussed below), and is closely related to the assumption that couples continue to have close and informal contact after separation, and that their relationships must therefore be healthy. Having successfully transformed divorce into a restructuring rather than a termination of family ties, the helping professions now stress the importance of resolving emotional issues to ensure the success of the post-divorce relationships.

Mediators have an interest in promoting the ideology of family system preservation because of the expanded employment opportunities this ideology ensures. When divorce was considered a pathology, those in the "helping professions" were employed to counsel reconciliation. Under the current no-fault divorce regime, social workers have moved away from the goal of formal reconciliation and have moved toward "reconciling" couples to a continuing post-divorce relationship involving joint custody.[2] Robert J. Levy notes that the mediation

> 'movement' has been swelled by those who were previously employed by the custody investigation 'movement', the conciliation court 'movement', the compulsory marriage counseling at divorce 'movement' — in short, by persons who may have professional careers riding on widespread acceptance of the 'mediation alternative'.[3]

While stressing the emotionally charged nature of divorce and criticizing the legal system for its failure to deal with those issues, many mediators fail to provide adequate legal safeguards for the parties. For example, Irving and Benjamin, who score "[t]he judicial emphasis on the discovery of facts using proper legal procedure",[4] state that "unlike the adversary system which assumes that people will lie and builds in a series of procedures to detect it, mediation has no such procedures".[5] Financial disclosure should not be required but "encouraged", say the authors, by overcoming the "trust vacuum" in which most separating couples operate.[6] "Feeling states" and "goals" must also be disclosed, they argue, and this aspect is presented as having as much importance as financial disclosure.

The approach advocated by Irving and Benjamin benefits those who wish to hide assets and disadvantages their partners. Eschewing legal safeguards and making trust the issue run counter to accepted negotiation practice.

For example, Roger Fisher and William Ury, in a standard text on negotiation, suggest "making the negotiation proceed independent of trust. Do not let someone treat your doubts as a personal attack.... A practice of verifying factual assertions reduces the incentive for deception, and your risk of being cheated".[7] Women, who are almost always the claimants in family law cases, are put at particular risk if trust is betrayed in the mediation process. Irving and Benjamin have no answer to this problem other than to say that the courts are available as a "backup"[8] and that failure to make full disclosure "is likely an issue which an evolving mediation profession will need to address".[9] The ability of the mediation profession to address the issue of disclosure is impaired by its characterization of separation as an emotional issue and its rejection of procedural safeguards because of their legalizing effect.[10]

Reducing Hostilities

Many mediators claim that litigation exacerbates hostilities and that mediation reduces the emotional tensions between parties, often expressing particular concern about the detrimental impact of litigation on children. These advocates often fail to distinguish between the causes and effects of family dissolution and litigation in their effects on children. For example, Bennett Wolff advocates mediation with the argument that, "The harmful effects of the adversary process most seriously impact the children, especially the younger ones. They may not possess an adequate psychic capacity to intellectually understand divorce and to appropriately tolerate their intense feelings generated by the family breakup".[11] Of course the effects on children of divorce do not in themselves support either mediation or litigation as a preferred procedure.

Mediation advocates also fail to note that, even if litigation in itself were shown to be emotionally harmful, in some cases it may well be less detrimental to the child than any available alternative. For example, the side effects of litigation are probably less damaging to a child than being delivered into the custody of an abusive parent who will not give up the claim for custody. Perhaps the alleged trauma of litigation is less detrimental to children than the reality of living in poverty pursuant to an inadequate settlement which many children are currently experiencing. This is not to say that litigation assures adequate child support, only that it may be the only possibility of getting some financial assistance when dealing with a recalcitrant spouse.

Mediators' criticisms of the adversary system, described in Department of Justice research as "highly polemical and simplistic",[12] often involve the assertion of "the advantages of mediation by juxtaposing it with litigation or a court battle".[13] They suggest that "litigation" inevitably involves the hotly contested trials and fail to acknowledge that litigation usually involves a settlement which is processed through the courts. When mediation advocates do compare mediation with negotiations between lawyers, a more common method of resolving family law cases than either mediation or trials, the polemic against the adversary system is continued by mediators against lawyers. For example Irving and Benjamin claim:

> The win-lose mentality of adversarial proceedings promote and support the use of pressure tactics, manipulation, the concealment or distortion of facts as well as competitive strategies as necessary and justifiable means of winning. The tendency for lawyers to promote increased conflict between spouses and to prohibit them from seeking nonadversarial solutions is well known.[14]

Research in both Canada and the United States has found that this adversarial portrait of lawyers is inaccurate, that the attitudes of mediators and lawyers toward settlement are similar, and that the outcomes of mediation are probably very similar to those achieved by lawyers in negotiation.[15]

Often mediation advocates do not consider nonmediated negotiated settlements at all, but implicitly impute the disadvantages of full-scale litigation to the "adversary system" in general, and suggest that mediation is the only "rational alternative".[16] Mediation research, which tends to be conducted by mediation proponents, often underrepresents or excludes uncontested cases from the sample groups, and this research is used to support claims about family law cases in general and in favour of mandatory mediation. Yet the vast majority of cases are settled, and in most divorces the respondent does not even file an answer.[17] The research used by proponents to support the claim that the adversary system increases hostility between parents and that mediation alleviates hostility suffers this deficiency.

For example, Irving and Benjamin conducted a study at the Provincial Court (Family Division) in Toronto over a ten month period in 1978–79.[18] They studied only couples who agreed to participate in court-connected counselling or other parties who used the court system. Of their original study sample of 193 couples, only ninety remained to completion. Half of the sixty-one couples who had reached agreement were contacted for one year follow-up interviews — the couples who had not reached agreement were not contacted. Of those contacted, sixteen couples and nine individuals, a total of forty-one persons, gave follow-up interviews. Of these forty-one persons, twenty-one reported that their overall family situation had "improved in the year following counselling".[19] Irving and Benjamin also report that the majority felt that marital conflict existing when the couple first went to court was reduced and had "positive feelings" about counseling. On the basis of this data, the authors claim, *inter alia*, to have

"highlight[ed] the qualitative aspects of divorce litigation, namely, the intense and prolonged emotional turmoil typically associated with it. To the extent that such turmoil clouds judgment and intensifies hostility, it can often prolong conflict and worsen an already traumatic situation".[20] One wonders how they can make this claim in view of their small sample size, equivocal results and, most importantly, the lack of any court control group.

Kathryn Dunlop did include a court control group in her study, which looked at forty-nine persons who had reached agreement in mediation at the Frontenac Family Referral Service in Kingston, and nineteen persons who used the court process.[21] Her findings that a higher percentage of mediation clients perceived an improvement in their problems, an increased ability to discuss problems with their partners, and an improved relationship with their children are of limited value as far as proving a causal link to mediation because of her selection of only couples who had reached agreement in mediation.

Pearson and Thoennes included couples who did not reach agreement in mediation in their Denver comparison of mediating couples who reached agreement, mediating couples who did not reach agreement, those who rejected mediation and a control group using court process.[22] They found that a lower percentage of those who unsuccessfully mediated showed an improvement in their relationship with their spouse than of those who rejected mediation or the control group. Those who mediated successfully, that is, reached an agreement, showed the most improvement. Because they excluded uncontested cases from their study, however, their study gives an exaggerated picture of the contentiousness of custody cases and cannot support claims regarding the general population of family law cases.

The research project completed by the Department of Justice, which was more comprehensive than any other study of mediation[23] and notable for having *not* been conducted by persons in the mediation business, also includes an overrepresentation of both mediated and contested cases, but at least notes that such cases "comprise a minority of all cases dealt with in family courts".[24] The study also addresses the effects of such overrepresentation on research results and does include some uncontested cases in its sample. This study refutes the claim that litigation (in the sense of court processing of contested and uncontested cases) exacerbates hostilities and harms children and found, not only a low level of conflict between divorcing couples, but also a correlation between higher levels of conflict and the use of mediation:

> About 43 percent of the men and 52 percent of the women described their present relationship as friendly, cordial or at least business-like, with respect to the children. In contrast, about 21 percent of the men and 16 percent of the women said

that the present relationship was tense or hostile. Nor does mediation seem to have an impact in the anticipated direction. In all, about 47 percent of the men and women who did not use mediation described their relationship as friendly, cordial or business-like, compared with about 37 percent of those who attended mediation. It must be kept in mind, however, that those who chose to mediate their case were sometimes those who started out with the most conflict and were attempting to work out a shared parenting arrangement.[25]

This study also found that few ex-spouses experienced post-divorce parenting problems — 13.4 percent of the men and 19.7 percent of the women. Those who had attended mediation were slightly more likely to be experiencing post-divorce parenting problems than those who had not.[26] Although this study did not include assessments of children, these results do provide some evidence in rebuttal of mediators' unsubstantiated claims about the hostility generated by litigation and its negative effects on children.

· · · ·

COSTS

Irving and Benjamin make a typical argument of mediation advocates: "On average mediation clients, both public and private, pay hundreds of dollars less for service than those who have their divorce processed through the courts".[27] They base this claim, however, at least in part on the Denver study of court-connected custody mediation conducted by Pearson and Thoennes which excluded uncontested cases.[28] The relatively low costs of having uncontested divorces, which form the large majority of cases "processed through the courts", were not included in their calculations.

Even the cost savings Pearson and Thoennes did find are equivocal. Those who reached agreement in mediation paid an average of $1,630 in legal fees, but those who mediated without reaching agreement paid an average of $2,000 as compared with $1,800 for those who rejected mediation,[29] information not mentioned by Irving and Benjamin. The nonmediation control group's average legal fees were $2,360, but it should again be noted that uncontested cases were excluded from the study.

The Canadian Department of Justice study found that mediation does not reduce legal costs, but results in higher legal fees. Women who mediated paid an average of $1,599 in legal fees compared with $1,214 for those who did not, a difference of $385, and men who mediated paid an average of $2,019 in legal fees compared with $1,511, a difference of $508.[30] The argument that those who went to mediation

would have had even higher legal costs if they had not mediated because of the more contentious nature of their cases was also contradicted by the study:

> [I]n general, where clients said that no matters were ever in dispute, the average legal fees were estimated at $658, compared with an average of $1,758 when one or matters [*sic*] were, at least initially, in dispute. Those with nothing to dispute and who, nevertheless, attended mediation estimated their legal fees at $937, compared with $627 for those who did not attend mediation. Where matters were initially in dispute, the mediation group estimated legal fees at $2,071, compared with $1,582 for non-mediation clients, a difference of $489. When legal fees are broken down by clients' assessments of whether the case was contested or uncontested, they are still higher for those in the mediation group.[31]

The Ontario Association for Family Mediation (OAFM) lobbies for mandatory court-connected mediation, arguing that "litigation is often prohibitively expensive for most families".[32] Family Mediation Canada continues to assert that "Research has found that mediation is typically less costly from both a financial and emotional aspect than litigation."[33] Yet the evidence shows that mediation is not less expensive for the parties.

Mediation may reduce government costs of processing family law cases. Mediation services cost less per hour than court time, and some studies show that mediated cases require less court time and therefore result in a savings for government.[34] Some mediation advocates assume cost savings to government on the basis of high settlement rates in mediation, without examining settlement rates of nonmediated cases or undertaking any other cost analysis.[35] The Department of Justice study did not reveal a significant saving in court time resulting from mediation. In the Winnipeg portion of the study, the judges and lawyers interviewed on this question were divided as to whether mediation led to a saving in court time.[36] The study of Saskatoon, St. John's, and Montreal found that mediation clients were somewhat more likely to spend less than an hour in court — 77 percent versus 56 percent of nonmediated cases. A slightly higher percentage of mediated cases, however, returned to court at least once — 36 percent versus 31 percent of nonmediated cases.

At this point the evidence as to whether mediation reduces the use of court time is equivocal, and existing data will have to be examined in light of the developing role of courts in the mediation process. Mr. Justice Zuber, in his report on court reform in Ontario, has recommended that judges be trained in mediation,[37] and specifically suggests that judges in family law cases may take on the role of mediator.[38] If judges become further involved in the process, the costs of mediation will change because of the different salary levels of judges and those currently providing mediation services. Of course, other changes to the current structure of mediation services may also affect costs.

SUPPORT OUTCOMES

There is some evidence that mediation results in higher support awards. The Department of Justice study found that support awards in mediated cases are about 22 percent higher than in nonmediated cases.[39] When this figure is adjusted for income, because of the relative affluence of those who use mediation, there is a somewhat smaller but still very significant difference. There are, however, two *caveats* relating to this evidence on mediation. First, the three sites from which the Department of Justice figures are drawn show very disparate results. In Montreal, the only research site offering comprehensive mediation, support in the mediated cases was 28 percent higher than in nonmediated cases; in Saskatoon the difference was 11 percent; and in St. John's support levels in mediated cases were 4.5 percent *below* those in nonmediated cases.[40] Support levels may be affected by, *inter alia*, the method of mediation. The Department of Justice study notes connection between higher support levels in Montreal and the comprehensive mediation offered at the site. Other variables may also affect support results.

The second point is that the higher levels of support resulting from mediation, "though no doubt important to the well-being of these families, are not large enough to offset the wider inequalities which result in an impoverished situation for many women and their children following divorce and separation".[41] Women may achieve somewhat higher support but in most cases not enough to lift them and their children out of poverty. However, because in mediation "the ultimate authority belongs to the disputants",[42] responsibility is shifted to the women who "agree" to continuing but slightly reduced poverty.

With regard to this last point, it is useful to look at the context in which family mediation has developed — a society with a growing belief in the inefficiency of government, and the efficiency of the marketplace in allocating resources. The current reaffirmation of the efficiency of the private marketplace has been paralleled by a growing belief in the efficiency of private ordering of family disputes.[43] Michael Ignatieff's analysis of the reemphasis on the free market may also be applied to the current trend toward private family ordering:

> Market signals are more accurate and more responsible predictors than government-backed planning based on social science indicators...[but] there was a further specifically political attraction in the market model besides its predictive

plausibility. One of the crucial functions of the market solution — denationalization, privatization — has been to take distributional conflicts out of the political arena.[44]

Similarly, private ordering appears to remove distributional conflicts between separating couples from the government's area of responsibility. To draw on Ignatieff's point, the efficiency arguments on behalf of mediation may simply mask the evasion of responsibility for distributional outcomes.

COMPLIANCE

Mediation is supposed to increase compliance in making support payments by giving the parties a sense of participation and a strong commitment to the mediated agreement[45] and by reducing the "anger, feelings of loss, sense of injustice and separation from their children that many divorcing fathers experience".[46] The OAFM lobbies for mandatory mediation with the claim that 85 percent of support orders are not complied with,[47] but has not shown that mediation improves compliance rates.

In their Denver mediation study, Pearson and Thoennes found that, at two to three month and six month follow-ups after the court order, the compliance rate was highest for those who reached agreement in mediation.[48] The lowest compliance rate, however, was among those who had mediated but did not reach agreement — compliance rates were higher for those who rejected mediation and for the control group. Compliance rates for uncontested cases were not included in their study.

The Department of Justice study found that, overall, mediation did not have a positive impact on compliance with support orders.[49] In Montreal the compliance rate was much higher among those who mediated (97% versus 66%), but in Saskatoon and St. John's there was no significant difference between mediated and nonmediated cases, and in Winnipeg, where custody mediation is mandatory, there is a greater likelihood of default among those who reached full or partial agreement in mediation than among those who did not.

The research on this issue is ambiguous. It appears that some forms of mediation may positively affect compliance while others do not, but the relevant variables are not clear. There is not sufficient evidence at this point to make the general claim that mediation leads to greater compliance.

EMPOWERMENT

John Stuart Mill made the argument that men and women should be allowed to govern themselves as far as possible because they are in the best position to determine their own cases:

[W]ith respect to his own feelings and circumstances the most ordinary man or woman has means of knowledge immeasurably surpassing those that can be possessed by anyone else. The interference of society to overrule his judgement and purposes in what only regards himself must be grounded on general presumptions which may be altogether wrong and, even if right, are as likely as not to be misapplied to individual cases, by persons no better acquainted with the circumstances of such cases than those are who look at them merely from without.[50]

Mill acknowledged, however, that, "In the conduct of human beings towards one another it is necessary that general rules should for the most part be observed in order that people may know what they have to expect".[51] He also said "As soon as any part of a person's conduct affects prejudicially the interests of others, society has jurisdiction over it, and the question whether the general welfare will or will not be promoted by interfering with it becomes open to question."[52]

The increasing tension is between the efficiency of self-rule and the duty of not injuring others is expressed in Post-Mill liberalism's seemingly schizophrenic support for growing government intervention accompanied by expressions of renewed allegiance to the principle of liberty.[53] Modern family law seems to be a quintessential expression of this schizophrenia because it seeks to create a near-comprehensive scheme for marriage dissolution, yet simultaneously gives the parties freedom to disregard it and fashion their own scheme. On the one hand we have rules governing marriage dissolutions "in order that people may know what they have to expect", and on the other hand we encourage the parties to exercise their freedom to dissolve their marriage in a way that suits them. One interpretation of this schizophrenia is that family law acknowledges the potentially prejudicial effect of marriage dissolution on one or both parties and society's jurisdiction over it by the enunciation of rules, but, by permitting parties to ignore these rules, family law stops short of claiming complete jurisdiction on the grounds of general welfare.

Mediation proponents have taken up Mill's argument concerning the benefits of individual autonomy:

The ultimate authority in mediation belongs to the participants themselves, and they may fashion a unique solution that will work for them without being strictly governed by precedent of being unduly concerned with the precedent they may set for others. They may, with the help of their mediator, consider a comprehensive mix of their needs, interests, and whatever else they deem relevant regardless of rules of evidence or strict

adherence to substantive law. Unlike the adjudicatory process, the emphasis is not on who is right or wrong or who wins and who loses, but rather upon establishing a workable solution that meets the participant's [*sic*] unique needs. Mediation is a win/win process.[54]

The typographical error in this quoted passage is ironic because, for the most part, mediation proponents have failed to address the distinction between self-rule and what one might call "couple-rule". The parties may have incompatible interests and wishes. One party's judgment may be overruled, to use Mill's terms, not directly by society, but by the other party. Granting the parties control over the outcome will not necessarily result in a solution that is best for each of the parties, but "may enable one party to enforce a solution which would not have been tolerated by an even-handed outsider."[55] Mediation is touted as allowing the couple the freedom to make their own standards of fairness.[56] To the extent that the weaker party's standards are overruled by the other's, this freedom claim is untenable.

Clients are said to be empowered by their freedom to determine their own cases in accordance with their personal standards of fairness. The relationship between this freedom or autonomy and the existing legal framework, however, has not been fully explained. Robert H. Mnookin and Lewis Kornhauser make the point that divorce settlements take place "in the shadow of the law", that is, are affected by and reflect to some degree existing procedural and substantive laws.[57] According to Mnookin and Kornhauser, private ordering does not delegalize settlements, but only dejudicializes them. The extent to which the law does or should affect settlements, however, is not clear.

Mediators themselves have not come to terms with the problem of the extent to which legal norms should limit the "autonomy" of the parties. Not all mediators have been legally trained, and some may be unaware of likely legal outcomes. The OAFM's *Code of Conduct* requires the mediator to advise participants if the mediator believes that the agreement being reached is unreasonable,[58] but does not correlate reason with legal norms. Perhaps because of their claim that parties may set their own standards of fairness, mediators express confusion about the meaning of substantive fairness and their role, if any, in ensuring same.[59]

Mediation purportedly allows couples to decide their own standard of fairness in financial matters, but deviation from legal standards may result in injury to one of the parties. Mnookin and Kornhauser, while suggesting that judicial review of divorce settlements is usually unnecessary, have said that cases of unequal bargaining power could be addressed by judicial review of settlements falling outside a broad range of norms.[60] Setting a high threshold for intervention, however, is problematic because gender inequality will reduce the *de facto* legal entitlements of women to that which a court will not overturn.

Other mediation proponents take a more cavalier attitude toward the place of law in mediation. Leonard Marlow argues that divorce mediation "rejects the idea that...legal rules and principles embody any necessary wisdom or logic. In fact, it views them as being arbitrary principles, having little to do with the realities of a couple's life and not superior to the judgments that the couple could make on their own".[61] Marlow suggests that mediators not feel bound by legal rules which are "limiting factors",[62] and yet at times useful to the mediator "as an intervention of strategy to achieve a desired result".[63] The desired result is "a fairer agreement than the law would provide".[64] It is apparently the mediator who decides what is fair, and "from his [the mediator's] standpoint, the problem is that the expectations created by these rules and principles will produce an agreement between the parties that is not fair".[65] Marlow does not explain why the values of a mediator should be preferable to those of a judge or legislator, or why the parties should give away their legal bargaining counters and put their trust in individual mediators' notions of fairness.

Neither the high threshold for intervention recommended by Mnookin and Kornhauser, nor the substitution of the mediator's notions of fairness for law suggested by Marlow are satisfactory to women who, as the less advantaged parties, rely on legal entitlements. The ideal of the parties achieving their own standard of fairness is unlikely to be reached in a situation of inequality.

Mediators also claim to correct power imbalances between the parties. They have failed, however, to recognize and address a basic issue of mediation — systemic power imbalances. Family mediation generally deals with a dispute between a man and a woman, so the issue of gender inequality must be addressed. Some mediators acknowledge that women are usually the "weaker" party, even that this "weakness" is caused by conformity to current social norms; but, consistent with the liberal discourse in which mediation is situated, addressing this problem is seen as being in conflict with the ideal of neutrality.[66] Their insight that women happen to be the weaker party leads them, at best, to a case-by-case approach of "helping" women on an individualized basis rather than to a political analysis that would call into question the initial premises of mediation. Other mediators discuss inequality of bargaining power in a gender neutral way, suggesting that disparities in power are solely the result of personal characteristics of individuals and unrelated to gender.[67] Still others accept the argument of fathers' rights groups that women have more power than men, at least with regard to custody.[68] Regardless of the model or individual mediator's approach, the rule is to treat psychological, economic, and emotional imbalances as personal matters to be addressed on an individualized basis rather than as existing within a framework of systemic imbalance.[69]

CONCLUSION

The growth of the family mediation movement has been sustained by claims which are open to question. Supporters of mediation — mediators, fathers' rights groups, the three branches of government — should address the problems with the research if they hope to establish the legitimacy of the movement and avoid charges of self-interest. Mediation is a method of dispute resolution we may want to use, but only with a clearer understanding of its problems and possibilities.

Endnotes

1. Howard H. Irving and Michael Benjamin, *Family Mediation* (Toronto: Carswell, 1987) at 40.
2. Fineman, *supra* note 17 at 744.
3. Robert J. Levy, "Comment on the Pearson-Thoennes Study and on Mediation" (1984), 17 *Fam. L.Q.* 425 at 432–33 [footnotes omitted].
4. Irving and Benjamin, *supra*, note 1 at 40.
5. *Ibid.* at 54.
6. *Ibid.* at 83.
7. Roger Fisher and William Ury, *Getting to Yes* (New York: Penguin Books, 1983) 138.
8. Although a court may set aside a domestic contract for failure to make financial disclosure pursuant to the *Family Law Act, supra*, note 19, s. 56(4)(a), this remedy is discretionary and depends, inter alia, on whether a particular judge considers the undisclosed assets "significant", a highly elastic term: *Demchuk v. Demchuk* (1986) 1 R.F.L. (3d) 176 (Ont. H.C.).
9. Irving and Benjamin, *supra*, note 1 at 54.
10. Wolff, *supra* note 35 at 76 writes: "One of the advantages of mediation is its nonlegal and flexible nature. The process is less restricted by the rules of procedure and evidence than the adversary system."
11. *Ibid.* at 75.
12. Richardson, *supra*, note 15 at 19.
13. Harriet Sachs, "The Dejudicialization of Family Law: Mediation and Assessments" in Elizabeth Sloss, ed., *Family Law in Canada: New Directions* (Ottawa: Canadian Advisory Council on the Status of Women, 1985) 85 at 88.
14. Irving and Benjamin, *supra*, note 1 at 39 [references omitted]. For an example of an American commentator making similar claims see Winks, *supra*, note 27 at 622–23.
15. Richardson, *supra*, note 15 at 19–20; Kenneth Kressel, *The Divorce Process* (New York: Basic Books, 1985) at 178.
16. A number of mediation advocates use this phrase. See for example H. Jay Folberg, "Divorce Mediation — The Emerging American Model" in Eekelaar and Katz, *supra*, note 28, 193 at 210.
17. D.C. McKie, B. Prentice and P. Reed (Statistics Canada), *Divorce: Law and the Family in Canada* (Ottawa: Supply and Services Canada, 1983) 151.
18. Howard H. Irving and Michael Benjamin, "A Study of Conciliation Counselling in the Family Court of Toronto: Implications for Socio-Legal Practice" in Eekelaar and Katz, *supra*, note 28 at 268.
19. *Ibid.* at 282.
20. *Ibid.* at 285.
21. *Couples in Crisis, supra*, note 41 at 70ff.
22. Jessica Pearson and Nancy Thoennes, "Mediating and Litigating Child Custody Disputes: A Longitudinal Evaluation" (1984), 17 *Fam. L.Q.* 497.
23. The Department of Justice study, which looked at court-connected mediation in Winnipeg, Saskatoon, Montreal, and St. John's, has two

parts. The first part, which looked exclusively at Winnipeg, where there is mandatory mediation of contested custody cases, included 282 questionnaires to persons entering mediation and 138 telephone interviews with clients 3–4 months after mediation terminated, as well as a review of the court-record and archival data and interviews with lawyers, mediators and judges. The second part, called the Divorce and Family Mediation Study, looked at the remaining three cities and included interviews with 905 divorced or separated persons including 324 who had used mediation, examination of court files and interviews and surveys of lawyers and mediators: Richardson, *supra*, note 15 at 12–14.

24. *Ibid.* at 13.

25. *Ibid.* at 59.

26. *Ibid.* at 39.

27. Irving and Benjamin, *supra*, note 1 at 241. See also Gifford, *supra*, note 39 at 409, where the author assumes cost savings for clients simply on the basis of the high settlement rate in nonmediated cases or conducting any research or analysis of client costs. Many advocates assume the cost benefits of mediation to clients without any reference to supporting research or analysis. See for example Winks, *supra*, note 29 at 648.

28. Pearson and Thoennes, "Mediating and Litigating Child Custody Disputes", *supra*, note 64.

29. *Ibid.* at 507–08.

30. Richardson, *supra*, note 15 at 40.

31. *Ibid.*

32. Letter from President and Board Members of the OAFM to Attorney General Ian Scott and Patrick Monohan, Senior Policy Advisor (16 March 1987), reprinted in (1987), 4:2 *OAFM Newsletter* 1 [hereinafter *OAFM Letter*].

33. "Family Mediation", a brochure delivered by Family Mediation Canada to the writer on 10 April 1989.

34. See for examples the 1981 study conducted by Dr. D. Gardner comparing mediation and court outcomes at four Family Courts in Ontario for cost effectiveness, reported in *Couples in Crisis*, *supra*, note 41 at 43ff.

35. See for example Gifford, *supra*, note 15 at 41.

36. Richardson, *supra*, note 15 at 41.

37. Honourable T.G. Zuber (Ontario Ministry of the Attorney General), *Report of the Ontario Courts Inquiry* (Toronto: Queen's Printer for Ontario) at 202.

38. *Ibid.* at 211.

39. Richardson, *supra*, note 15 at 32.

40. *Ibid.* In her B.C. study, Gifford too found slightly higher levels of child support resulting from court orders than from mediated agreements: *supra*, note 48 at 405–06.

41. *Ibid.*

42. Ryan, "The Lawyer as Mediator", *supra*, note 30 at 108.

43. Frances E. Olsen, "The Family and the Market: A Study of Ideology and Legal Reform" (1983), 96 *Harv. L. Rev.* 1497 at 1502.

44. Michael Ignatieff, "The Myth of Citizenship" (1987), 94:4 *Queen's Q.* 966 at 981.

45. Sander, "Towards a Functional Analysis", *supra*, note 28 at xiii.

46. Jessica Pearson and Nancy Thoennes, "Custody Mediation in Denver: Shorter and Longer Term Effects" in Eekelaar and Katz, *supra*, note 28, 248 at 250.

47. *OAFM Letter*, *supra*, note 131.

48. Pearson and Thoennes, "Custody Mediation in Denver", *supra*, note 145 at 256.

49. Richardson, *supra*, note 15 at 33.

50. John Stuart Mill, *On Liberty* (Harmondsworth: Penguin Books, 1974) at 143 [first published in 1859].

51. *Ibid.*

52. *Ibid.* at 141.

53. Gertrude Himmelfarb, "Introduction" in J.S. Mill, *On Liberty, ibid.* 7 at 47.

54. Jay Folberg and Alison Taylor, *A Comprehensive Guide to Resolving Conflict Without Litigation* (San Francisco: Jossey-Bass, 1984) at 10.

55. Simon Roberts, "Mediation in Family Disputes" (1983), 47 *Modern L. Rev.* 537 at 540.

56. Mary-Lynne Fisher and Linda L. McFadden, "Premarital and Remarital Mediation: Complementary Roles for Lawyers and Therapists" (1984–85), 24 *J. of Fam. L.* 451 at 455.

57. Robert H. Mnookin and Lewis Kornhauser, "Bargaining in the Shadow of the Law: The Case of Divorce" (1979), 99 *Yale L. Rev.* 950.

58. OAFM *Code of Conduct*, s. 10(d), reprinted in Alistair Bissett-Johnson, "Mediation of Property and Support Disputes" in James G. McLeod, ed., *Family Dispute Resolution* (Toronto: Carswell, 1987) 99 at 109ff.

59. Irving and Benjamin, *supra*, note 43 at 55 and 85.

60. Mnookin and Kornhauser, *supra*, note 156 at 993.

61. Leonard Marlow, "The Rule of Law in Divorce Mediation" (1985), 9 *Mediation Q.* 5 at 10.

62. *Ibid.* at 10.

63. *Ibid.* at 12.

64. *Ibid.* at 11.

65. *Ibid.* at 11.

66. See for example Irving and Benjamin, *supra*, note 52 at 54 and 82.

67. See for example Robert H. Mnookin, "Divorce Bargaining: The Limits on Private Ordering" in Eekelaar and Katz, *supra*, note 1 at 364; Barbara Landau, Mario Bartoletti and Rith Mesbur, *Family Mediation Handbook* (Toronto: Butterworths, 1987) at 88–89; Kelly, "Mediation and Psychotherapy", *supra*, note 23 at 39.

68. For an example of a mediator making this arrangement see Vivian Kerenyi, "Women and Mediation" (1987), 3:2 *Resolve* 4. An example of the claim being made on behalf of a fathers' rights group is P. Nagy, "Children and the New Divorce Act" (1986), 2:2 *Resolve* 15 (Resolve is the newsletter of Family Mediation Canada).

69. See for example Kelly, "Mediation and Psychotherapy", *supra*, note 23 at 39; Weissman and Leick, *supra*, note 152 at 283; Irving and Benjamin, *supra*, note 52 at 82. Martha Shaffer also makes this point at *supra*, note 21 at 179–80.

A Way of Thinking about Collective Bargaining: Circumstance, Policy, Law and Actuality[†]

A.W.R. Carrothers

POLICY

Collective bargaining, as a private sector phenomenon, is a mechanism for the redistribution of wealth generated by an enterprise, among the competing factors of production, through the price of "materials", the cost of "capital", the wages of "labour", and the profits of "enterprise". It is a stratagem by which the worker can, in some measure, participate in the determination of his economic destiny. It redistributes power and authority within the community of the work place. It provides a form of government with which priorities of interests may be reconciled. It is thus an instrument of industrial democracy. The argument is made that in a political democracy with a mixed enterprise system, where the stratagem of collective bargaining not at hand, the benefits deriving from it would be demanded of the state to the detriment of the enterprise system. Thus, collective bargaining may be viewed as a natural concomitant of private enterprise, of public enterprise and even of public service.

Collective bargaining is something more than an inevitable historical event in the economic development of a political democracy, to be managed accordingly. It claims the higher ground of conscious policy, to be understood, crafted with care, put in place, maintained, appraised and overhauled.

What are the components of collective bargaining as policy?

In order to have an effective process of collective bargaining, a legal system must protect employees in three principal areas of activity: first, in forming themselves into a functional collectivity, conventionally called a trade union; second, in securing from the employer, a relationship of effective negotiation with a view to reaching agreement over terms and conditions of employment (in effect a mutual duty, and hence a reciprocal mutual right, to bargain in good faith); a third, in the event that negotiations fail, in invoking meaningful economic sanctions against the employer with a view to inducing agreement. Conventionally such sanctions consist of striking, that is, a collective withdrawal of services, and peaceful picketing, that is, the physical presence of persons at the work place advertising their position that the observer not do business with the employer (the boycott). Engaging in political activity to gain the same or similar objectives should not

be overlooked, as students of the French and Italian scenes will confirm.

The first of these freedoms, the right to organize, can be defeated if the employer should engage in threats of harm or promises of reward to the individual employee to induce him to avoid union membership or to work against union organization. In North America, after World War One, employers created or supported company or plant unions as a plausible alternative to independent unions. But independence from the employer is a quality essential to a bargaining agent.

The establishment of the freedom of union organization presents an example of a series of policy choices. First is the selection of collective bargaining as national economic and social policy. Second is the recognition of the policy of independent unionism. Third is the policy of choice of whether independent unions should develop extra-legally, as they did in the United Kingdom, or under the protection of the law, as they did in North America. That decision will in turn inform the substantive law.

It is an enormously important policy question whether and to what extent the collective bargaining system should be extra-legal; where it is intra-legal, whether and to what extent it should be self-operative or be managed by a public authority; and where there is to be a public agency, how that agency should be composed, what should be its jurisdiction, and how its function should relate to the courts and to the exercise of executive discretion. The theme of the selection of interdependent policies is inherent in the whole of this paper.

The second freedom is the right to collective bargaining proper. The vast bulk, and the best, of human relationships have at their core the element of consensus, of mutuality, of agreement, of common intent. Legal systems cannot compel people to agree. Nor have legal systems been prone to require people to bargain with a view to reaching an agreement. Trial judges have been known, on occasion, to persuade counsel to settle an awkward case, and labour arbitrators recognize a role of mediation as an adjunct of their quasi-judicial function. But the duty to bargain in good faith is not easy to define, bad faith bargaining is not easy to identify, and the role of legal sanctions is not easy to appraise.

Once the policy choice is taken that an employer has a duty to bargain in good faith, a series of derivative policy question arises. With what union does the duty arise? What

---

† Carrothers, A.W.R., "A Way of Thinking about Collective Bargaining: Circumstance, Policy, Law and Actuality" (1985), 40 *Relations Industrielles* 351 at 355–63. Reprinted by permission of the author and the publisher.

evidence should be required that the union has the support of the employees? If membership in the union is to be the test, should the union be free to define and determine membership or should the right to membership be prescribed by the law?

Let us assume that there has been established a bargaining nexus between a union and an employer, that they have bargained in good faith, and that they have reached an impasse. (Where the parties reach agreement the derivative policy question arises as to whether and how the resulting collective agreement is to be enforced and administered: what kind of standing, if any, the collective agreement is to have at law.)

The third freedom, the right to invoke meaningful economic sanctions, is easy to state and enormously complicated in its execution. It should be recognized that, except where both the supply of and demand for labour is inelastic, freedom of speech in the form of a capacity to persuade becomes a significant component in the effectiveness of economic sanctions. The right to strike involves matters of definition and declaration of right. If the right to strike does not preclude the employer from continuing its operations, the union will seek to close down the operations by persuading others not to take employment and not to do business with the employer or deal in the employer's product. The conventional means of persuasion has become the picket line, backed by the ethic that picket lines are not to be crossed. The object is the boycott. Assuming an absence of wrongful behaviour in the picketing activity, to whom should the union be free to address its message, against whom should it be free to address it, and where?

1. to its members who have been called on strike?
2. to other employees who are not members of the union?
3. to employees who are members of another union?
4. to persons wishing to do business with the employer?
5. to persons who have been doing business with the employer and wish to continue?
6. to suppliers of the employer?
7. to purchasers of the employer's product?
8. at the place of business of the supplier or the purchaser?
9. at other plants of the employer?
10. at plants of other employers in the industry who may or may not be servicing the needs of the employer's customers?
11. at the operations of corporate subsidiaries of the employer?
12. at private homes?

Should the response to the questions depend on:

1. the merits of the dispute?
2. the relative economic strength of the parties (a) at the time of the impasse or (b) in the course of the dispute?

3. the impact of the dispute, of its settlement, and of the terms of settlement on government policies at large?
4. whether the public, as a collectivity of innocent and impotent bystanders (the question may be asked whether the public is ever entirely innocent or impotent), is directly prejudiced by the dispute?
5. in what way, and in what degree, the public is prejudiced?

What as a matter of policy, should be the legitimacy of the general strike?

Some of these questions may support a policy response simply as a matter of reflection. They have been arranged in a descending order of a probable affirmative answer. Others of these questions will support a policy response (what *should* be the extent of permissible conduct?) only following an appraisal of specific actualities in all their complexities.

In the United States, and more so in Canada, these questions have been the subject of a kind of codification, with a heavy gloss of case law, administrative decision and regulation, and ad hoc or discretionary legislation and executive action. The general area has been addressed recently by United Kingdom Parliament, but the employer has been reluctant to take up the legal sword, such is the antipathy in that country to legalism in industrial relations.

Can there be collective bargaining without the right to strike? It is argued that if strikes are made illegal all that that will produce is illegal strikes. It is argued further that where the public interest in the delivery of goods and services overrides the public interest in collective bargaining, those who are charged with imposing a solution, must have access to relevant information derived from a relatively free market of which free collective bargaining is a component. In the United States the right to strike is, with few exceptions, denied to the public service. In the United Kingdom there is a quasi-judicial system that keeps terms of public service employment relatively sweet. In Canada there is a right to strike in the federal public service with substantial constraints to protect the performance of essential services. Ad hoc legislation to terminate lawful strikes in the public interest is prevalent in Canada. It is virtually unknown in the United Kingdom and the United States.

If the right to strike is to be denied, what is to take its place to resolve an impasse? The procedure most often used is the quasi-judicial process of arbitration, but a settlement imposed by executive action is not out of the question. It is a policy choice.

The three basic freedoms of collective bargaining involve an obligation in others not to interfere with those freedoms. Yet others have claims of their own which compete with those freedoms and mark their limits. The patrolling of the shifting interface of competing rights and freedoms is the hard and continuing task of the politico-legal system, for freedoms are not absolute. They cannot be and coexist.

There are two freedoms which compete with the collective bargaining trilogy of employee collectivities which demand special attention. The first is the right of the individual employee to work. The second is the right of the employer to manage.

In any organization the interests of the individual must be subservient to the interest of the collectivity to the extent necessary for the pursuit of its objectives. The individual surrenders his freedom in one direction in order to gain benefits in another.

Where the individual has a choice and opts out, he cannot be heard to complain. Where he opts in, he has acquired something of value which the law might be concerned to protect. Where the individual has no choice but to join an organization, the law ought to be concerned to protect his access and his continuing membership.

A trade union is such a collectivity. A union is bound to seek security of employment for its members. It will bargain for it. It will seek to protect its present members who are employees and its members who are unemployed or may become unemployed. It will seek to make membership in the union a condition prior to taking employment, and as a condition of continuing in employment. Obviously access to membership and continuation in membership is of overwhelming interest to the employee. The individual will therefore assert from the law the right of access to membership and to participation according to the rules of the union, and the right to fair rules.

In 1851 Sir Henry Maine, in his book *Ancient Law*, observed that the development of the individual in a progressive legal system marked a growth from status to contract. The position of the individual worker in a modern industrial society has taken on fundamental characteristics of status. He can make no separate agreement with his employer. He has no personal right to be present at the bargaining table. If he enters into employment after the bargaining is over, he has no vote on the terms of the collective agreement. He has no right of access to the administration of the collective agreement. If he has a personal grievance against his employer he is dependent on the decision of the trade union whether to process his case. His contract of employment is thus largely nominal, and is controlled by externalities. If I am right in an earlier statement that the bulk and the best of human relationships are at their core consensual, the contract of union membership can be the lifeline of the individual to the best of human relationships as they relate to the work place, to his sense of worth and to his sense of personality.

The protection of the right to work as against the union involves such policy questions as to whether the law should regulate union security clauses so as to protect the individual where he has been denied union membership; whether the law should prescribe minimum protective provisions in union constitutions, as it does for "members" in the constitutions of public business corporations; and whether the law should impose fair processes on a union's internal affairs, not as a matter of agreement (on the theory that such processes are implicit in the contract of membership), but as a matter of policy and therefore of law.

I come now to the fifth on my list of the freedoms to be accommodated in a collective bargaining system, the freedom of the employer to manage.

Just as employees may need protection from an employer's efforts to impede free trade unionism, so may an employer need protection from a union's importunities against it. If the law embarks upon a recitation of a code of employer improper behaviour, it will be hard pressed not to recite prohibited behaviour by unions and employees. The employer's best protection is his own freedom of speech, and his freedom of assembly into employers' associations.

The list of competing rights, freedoms and interests does not stop there. The public, in the sense of collectivity of private citizens, has a claim to access to goods and services. The public, as the totality of its citizens, has an overriding claim that the government must govern. Collective bargaining is not an "extra-parliamentary process".

People in the Legal Process: Access to "Justice"

A. Who Uses the Law and Why?

Why the 'Haves' Come Out Ahead: Speculation on the Limits of Legal Change[†]
M. Galanter

THIS essay attempts to discern some often general features of a legal system like the American by drawing on (and rearranging) commonplaces and less than systematic gleanings from the literature. The speculative and tentative nature of the assertions here will be apparent and is acknowledged here wholesale to spare myself and the reader repeated disclaimers.

I would like to try to put forward some conjectures about the way in which the basic architecture of the legal system creates and limits the possibilities of using the system as a means of redistributive (that is, systematically equalizing) change. Our question, specifically, is, under what conditions can litigation be redistributive, taking litigation in the broadest sense of the presentation of claims to be decided by courts (or court-like agencies) and the whole penumbra of threats, feints, and so forth, surrounding such presentation.

For the purposes of this analysis, let us think of the legal system as comprised of these elements:

(a) A body of authoritative normative learning, for short, RULES
(b) A set of institutional facilities within which the normative learning is applied to specific cases, for short, COURTS
(c) A body of persons with specialized skill in the above, for short, LAWYERS
(d) Persons or groups with claims they might make to the courts in reference to the rules, etc., for short, PARTIES

Let us also make the following assumptions about the society and the legal system:

(a) It is a society in which actors with different amounts of wealth and power are constantly in competitive or partially cooperative relationships in which they have opposing interests.
(b) This society has a legal system in which a wide range of disputes and conflicts are settled by court-like agencies which purport to apply pre-existing general norms impartially (that is, unaffected by the identity of the parties).
(c) The rules and the procedures of these institutions are complex; wherever possible disputing units employ specialized intermediaries in dealing with them.
(d) The rules applied by the courts are in part worked out in the process of adjudication (courts devise interstitial rules, combine diverse rules, and apply old rules to new situations). There is a living tradition of such rule-work and a system of communication such that the outcomes in some of the adjudicated cases affect the outcome in classes of future adjudicated cases.
(e) Resources on the institutional side are insufficient for timely full-dress adjudication in every case, so that parties are permitted or even encouraged to forego bringing cases and to "settle" cases, that is, bargain to a mutually acceptable outcome.

† Galanter, Marc, "Why the 'Haves' Come Out Ahead: Speculation on the Limits of Legal Change" (1975), 9 *Law and Society Review* at 95–151. Reprinted by permission of the Law and Society Association.

(f) There are several levels of agencies, with "higher" agencies announcing (making, interpreting) rules and other "lower" agencies assigned the responsibility of enforcing (implementing, applying) these rules. (Although there is some overlap of function in both theory and practice, I shall treat them as distinct and refer to them as "peak" and "field level" agencies.)

(g) Not all the rules propounded by "peak" agencies are effective at the "field level," due to imperfections in communication, shortages of resources, skill, understanding, commitment and so forth. (Effectiveness at the field level will be referred to as "penetration.")

A TYPOLOGY OF PARTIES

Most analyses of the legal system start at the rules end and work down through institutional facilities to see what effect the rules have on the parties. I would like to reverse that procedure and look through the other end of the telescope. Let's think about the different kinds of parties and the effect these differences might have on the way the system works.

Because of differences in their size, differences in the state of the law, and differences in their resources, some of the actors in the society have many occasions to utilize the courts (in the broad sense) to make (or defend) claims; others do so only rarely. We might divide our actors into those claimants who have only occasional recourse to the courts (one-shotters or OS) and repeat players (RP) who are engaged in many similar litigations over time. The spouse in a divorce case, the auto-injury claimant, the criminal accused are OSs; the insurance company, the prosecutor, the finance company are RPs. Obviously this is an oversimplification; there are intermediate cases such as the professional criminal. So as we ought to think of OS–RP as a continuum rather than as a dichotomous pair. Typically, the RP is a larger unit and the stakes in any given case are smaller (relative to total worth). OSs are usually smaller units and the stakes represented by the tangible outcome of the case may be high relative to total worth, as in the case of injury victim or the criminal accused. Or, the OS may suffer from the opposite problem: his claim may be so small and unmanageable (the short-weighted consumer or the holder of performing rights) that the cost of enforcing them outruns any promise of benefit. See Finklestein (1954: 284–86).

Let us refine our notion of the RP into an "ideal type", if you will a unit which has had and anticipates repeated litigation, which has low stakes in the outcome of any one case, and which has the resources to pursue its long-run interests. (This does not include every real-world repeat player; that most common repeat player, the alcoholic

derelict, enjoys few of the advantages that may accrue to the RP [see below]. His resources are too few to bargain in the short run or take heed of the long run.) An OS, on the other hand, is a small unit whose claims are too large (relative to size) or too small (relative to the cost of remedies) to be managed routinely and rationally.

We would expect an RP to play the litigation game differently from an OS. Let us consider some of his advantages:

1. RPs, having done it before, have some advance intelligence; they are able to structure the next transaction and build a record. It is the RP who writes the form contract, requires the security deposit, and the like.

2. RPs develop expertise and have ready access to specialists. They enjoy economies of scale and have low start-up costs for any case.

3. RPs have opportunities to develop facilitative informal relations with institutional incumbents.

4. The RP must establish and maintain credibility as a combatant. His interest in his "bargaining reputation" serves as a resource to establish "commitment" to his bargaining positions. With no bargaining reputation to maintain the OS has more difficulty in convincingly committing himself in bargaining.

5. RPs can play the odds. The larger the matter at issue looms for OS, the more likely he is to adopt a minimax strategy (minimize the probability of maximum loss). Assuming that the stakes are relatively smaller for RPs, they can adopt strategies calculated to maximize gain over a long series of cases, even where this involves the risk of maximum loss in some cases.

6. RPs can play for rules as well as immediate gains. First, it pays an RP to expend resources in influencing the making of the relevant rules by such methods as lobbying. (And his accumulated expertise enables him to do this persuasively.)

7. RPs can also play for rules in litigation itself, whereas an OS is unlikely to. That is, there is a difference in what they regard as a favorable outcome. Because his stakes in the immediate outcome are high and because by definition OS is unconcerned with the outcome of similar litigation in the future, OS will have little interest in that element of the outcome which might influence the disposition of the decision-maker next time around. For the RP, on the other hand, anything that will favorably influence the outcomes of future cases is a worthwhile result. The larger the stake for any player and the lower the probability of repeat play, the less likely that he will be concerned with the rules which govern future cases of the same kind. Consider two parents contesting the custody of their only child, the prizefighter vs. the IRS for tax arrears, the convict facing the death penalty. On the other hand, the player with small stakes in the present case and the prospect

of a series of similar cases (the IRS, the adoption agency, the prosecutor) may be more interested in the state of the law.

Thus, if we analyze the outcomes of a case into a tangible component and a rule component, we may expect that in case 1, OS will attempt to maximize his tangible gain. But if RP is interested in maximizing his tangible gain in a series of cases 1...n, he may be willing to trade off tangible gain in any one case for rule gain (or to minimize rule loss). We assumed that the institutional facilities for litigation were overloaded and settlements were prevalent. We would then expect RPs to "settle" cases where they expected unfavorable rule outcomes. Since they expect to litigate again, RPs can select to adjudicate (or appeal) those cases which they regard as most likely to produce favorable rules. On the other hand, OSs should be willing to trade off the possibility of making "good law" for tangible gain. Thus, we would expect the body of "precedent" cases that is, cases capable of influencing the outcome of future cases to be relatively skewed toward those favorable to RP. Of course it is not suggested that the strategic configuration of the parties is the sole or major determinant of rule-development. Rule-development is shaped by a relatively autonomous learned tradition, by the impingement of intellectual currents from outside, by the preferences and prudences of the decision-makers. But courts are passive and these factors operate only when the process is triggered by parties. The point here is merely to note the superior opportunities of the RP to trigger promising cases and prevent the triggering of unpromising ones. It is not incompatible with a course of rule-development favoring OSs (or, as indicated below, with OSs failing to get the benefit of those favorable new rules).

In stipulating that RPs can play for rules, I do not mean to imply that RPs pursue rule-gain as such. If we recall that not all rules penetrate (i.e., become effectively applied at the field level) we come to some additional advantages of the RPs.

8. RPs, by virtue of experience and expertise, are more likely to be able to discern which rules are likely to "penetrate" and which are likely to remain merely symbolic commitments. RPs may be able to concentrate their resources on rule-changes that are likely to make a tangible difference. They can trade off symbolic defeats for tangible gains.

9. Since penetration depends in part on the resources of the parties (knowledge, attentiveness, expert services, money), RPs are more likely to be able to invest the matching resources necessary to secure the penetration of rules favorable to them.

It is not suggested that RPs are to be equated with "haves" (in terms of power, wealth and status) or OSs with "have-nots." In the American setting most RPs are larger, richer and more powerful than are most OSs, so these categories overlap, but there are obvious exceptions. RPs may be "have-nots" (alcoholic derelicts) or may act as champions of "have-nots" (as government does from time to time); OSs such as criminal defendants may be wealthy. What this analysis does is to define a position of advantage in the configuration of contending parties and indicate how those with other advantages tend to occupy this position of advantage and to have their other advantages reinforced and augmented thereby. This position of advantage is one of the ways in which a legal system formally neutral as between "haves" and "have-nots" may perpetuate and augment the advantages of the former.

Digression on Litigation-Mindedness

We have postulated that OSs will be relatively indifferent to the rule-outcomes of particular cases. But one might expect the absolute level of interest in rule-outcomes to vary in different populations: in some there may be widespread and intense concern with securing vindication according to official rules that overshadows interest in the tangible outcomes of disputes; in others rule outcomes may be a matter of relative indifference when compared to tangible outcomes. The level and distribution of such "rule mindedness" may affect the relative strategic position of OSs and RPs. For example, the more rule minded a population, the less we would expect an RP advantage in managing settlement policy.

But such rule mindedness or appetite for official vindication should be distinguished from both (1) readiness to resort to official remedy systems in the first place and (2) high valuation of official rules as symbolic objects. Quite apart from relative concern with rule-outcomes, we might expect populations to differ in their estimates of the propriety and gratification of litigating in the first place. Such attitudes may affect the strategic situation of the parties. For example, the greater the distaste for litigation in a population, the greater the barriers to OSs pressing or defending claims, and the greater the RP advantages, assuming that such sentiments would affect OSs, who are likely to be individuals, more than RPs, who are likely to be organizations.

It cannot be assumed that the observed variations in readiness to official tribunals is directly reflective of a "rights consciousness" or appetite for vindication in terms of authoritative norms. Consider the assertion that the low rate of litigation in Japan flows from an undeveloped "sense of justiciable rights" with the implication that the higher rate in the United States flows from such rights-consciousness. But the high rate of settlements and the low rate of appeals in the United States suggest it should not be regarded as having a population with great interest in securing moral victories through official vindication. Mayhew (1973:14, Table I) reports a survey in which a sample of Detroit area residents were asked how they had wanted to see their "most serious problem" settled. Only a tiny minority (0% of landlord-tenant problems; 2% of neighborhood problems; 4% of expensive purchase problems; 9% of public organization problems; 31% of discrimination problems) reported that they sought "justice" or vindication of their legal rights: "most answered that they sought resolution of their problems in some more or less expedient way."

Paradoxically, low valuation of rule-outcomes in particular cases may co-exist with high valuation of rules as symbolic objects. Edelman (1967: chap. 2) distinguishes between remote, diffuse, unorganized publics, for whom rules are a source of symbolic gratification and organized, attentive publics directly concerned with the tangible results of their application. Public appetite for symbolic gratification by the promulgation of rules does not imply a corresponding private appetite for official vindication in terms of rules in particular cases. Attentive RPs on the other hand may be more inclined to regard rules instrumentally as assets rather than as sources of symbolic gratification.

We may think of litigation as typically involving various combinations of OSs and RPs. We can then construct a matrix such as Figure 1 and fill in the boxes with some well-known if only approximate American examples. (We ignore for the moment that the terms OS and RP represent ends of a continuum, rather than a dichotomous pair.)

On the basis of our incomplete and unsystematic examples, let us conjecture a bit about the content of these boxes:

BOX I: OS vs. OS

The most numerous occupants of this box are divorces and insanity hearings. Most (over 90 percent of divorces, for example) are uncontested. A large portion of these are really pseudo-litigation, that is, a settlement is worked out between the parties and ratified in the guise of adjudication. When we get real litigation in Box I, it is often between parties who have some intimate tie with one another, fighting over some unsharable good, often with

Initiator, Claimant

	One-shotter	Repeat Player
One-shotter	• Parent v. Parent (Custody) • Spouse v. Spouse (Divorce) • Family v. Family Member (Insanity Commitment) • Family v. Family (Inheritance) • Neighbor v. Neighbor • Partner v. Partner **I — OS vs OS**	• Prosecutor v. Accused • Finance Co. v. Debtor • Landlord v. Tenant • I.R.S. v. Taxpayer • Condemnor v. Property Owner **II — RP vs OS**
Repeat Player	• Welfare client v. Agency • Auto dealer v. Manufacturer • Tenant v. Landlord • Injury Victim v. Insurance Company • Bankrupt Consumer v. Creditors • Defamed v. Publisher **III — OS vs RP**	• Union v. Company • Movie Distributor v. Censorship Board • Developer v. Suburban Municipality • Purchaser v. Supplier • Regulatory Agency v. Firms of Regulated Industry **IV — RP vs RP**

(Left label spanning rows: **Defendant**)

FIGURE 1
A Taxonomy of Litigation by Strategic Configuration of Parties

overtones of "spite" and "irrationality." Courts are resorted to where an ongoing relationship is ruptured: they have little to do with the routine patterning of activity. The law is invoked *ad hoc* and instrumentally by the parties. There may be a strong interest in vindication, but neither party is likely to have much interest in the long term state of the law (of, for instance, custody or nuisance). There are few appeals, few test cases, little expenditure of resources on rule-development. Legal doctrine is likely to remain remote from everyday practice and from popular attitudes.

BOX II: RP vs. OS

The great bulk of litigation is found in this box; indeed every really numerous kind except personal injury cases, insanity hearings, and divorces. The law is used for routine processing of claims by parties for whom the making of such claims is a regular business activity. Often the cases here take the form of stereotyped mass processing with little of the individuated attention of full-dress adjudication. Even greater numbers of cases are settled "informally" with settlement keyed to possible litigation outcome (discounted by risk, cost, delay).

The state of the law is of interest to the RP, though not to the OS defendants. Insofar as the law is favorable to the RP it is "followed" closely in practice (subject to discount for RP's transaction costs). Transactions are built to fit the rules by creditors, police, draft boards and other RPs. Rules favouring OSs may be less readily applicable, since OSs do not ordinarily plan the underlying transaction, or less meticulously observed in practice, since OSs are unlikely to be as ready or able as RPs to invest in insuring their penetration to the field level.

BOX III: OS vs. RP

All of these are rather infrequent types except for personal injury cases which are distinctive in that free entry to the arena is provided by the contingent fee. In auto injury claims, litigation is routinized and settlement is closely geared to possible litigation outcome. Outside the personal injury area, litigation in Box III is not routine. It usually represents the attempt of some OS to invoke outside help to create leverage on an organization with which he has been having dealings but is now at the point of divorce (for example, the discharged employee or the cancelled franchisee). The OS claimant generally has little interest in the state of the law; the RP defendant, however, is greatly interested.

BOX IV: RP vs. RP

Let us consider the general case first and then several special cases. We might expect that there would be little litigation in Box IV, because, to the extent that two RPs play with each other repeatedly, the expectation of continued mutually beneficial interaction would give rise to informal bilateral controls. This seems borne out by studies of dealings among businessmen and in labour relations. Official agencies are invoked by unions trying to get established and by management trying to prevent them from getting established, more rarely in dealings between bargaining partners. Units with mutually beneficial relations do not adjust their differences in courts. Where they rely on third parties in dispute-resolution, it is likely to take a form (such as arbitration or a domestic tribunal) detached from official sanctions and applying domestic rather than official rules.

However, there are several special cases. First, there are those RPs who seek, not furtherance of tangible interests, but vindication of fundamental cultural commitments. An example would be the organizations which sponsor much church-state litigation. Where RPs are contending about value differences (who is right) rather than interest conflicts (who gets what) there is less tendency to settle and less basis for developing a private system of dispute settlement.

Second, government is a special kind of RP. Informal controls depend upon the ultimate sanction of withdrawal and refusal to continue beneficial relations. To the extent that withdrawal of future association is not possible in dealing with government, the scope of informal controls is correspondingly limited. The development of informal relations between regulatory agencies and regulated firms is well known. And the regulated may have sanctions other than withdrawal which they can apply; for instance, they may threaten political opposition. But the more inclusive the unit of government, the less effective the withdrawal sanction and the greater the likelihood that a party will attempt to invoke outside allies by litigation even while sustaining the ongoing relationship. This applies also to monopolies, units which share the government's relative immunity to withdrawal sanctions. RPs in monopolistic relationships will occasionally invoke formal controls to show prowess, to give credibility to threats, and to provide satisfactions for other audiences. Thus we would expect litigation by and against government to be more frequent than in other RP vs. RP situations. There is a second reason for expecting more litigation when government is a party. That is, that the notion of "gain" (policy as well as monetary) is often more contingent and problematic for governmental units than for other parties, such as businesses or organized interest groups. In some cases courts may, by proffering authoritative interpretations of public policy, redefine an agency's notion of gain. Hence government parties may be more willing to externalize decisions to the courts. And opponents may have more incentive to litigate against government in the hope of securing a shift in its goals.

A somewhat different kind of special case is present where plaintiff and defendant are both RPs but do not deal with each other repeatedly (two insurance companies, for example.) In the government/monopoly case, the parties were so inextricably bound together that the force of informal controls was limited; here they are not sufficiently bound to each other to give informal controls their bite; there is nothing to withdraw from! The large one-time deal that falls through, the marginal enterprise — these are staple sources of litigation.

Where there is litigation in the RP vs. RP situation, we might expect that there would be heavy expenditure on rule-development, many appeals, and rapid and elaborate development of the doctrinal law. Since the parties can invest to secure implementation of favorable rules, we would expect practice to be closely articulated to the resulting rules.

On the basis of these preliminary guesses, we can sketch a general profile of litigation and the factors associated with it. The great bulk of litigation is found in Box II; much less in Box III. Most of the litigation in these Boxes is mass routine processing of disputes between parties who are strangers (not in mutually beneficial continuing relations) or divorced and between whom there is a disparity in size. One party is a bureaucratically organized "professional" (in the sense of doing it for a living) who enjoys strategic advantages. Informal controls between the parties are tenuous or ineffective; their relationship is likely to be established and defined by official rules; in litigation, these rules are discounted by transaction costs and manipulated selectively to the advantage of the parties. On the other hand, in Boxes I and IV, we have more infrequent but more individualized litigation between parties of the same general magnitude, among whom there are or were continuing multi-stranded relationships with attendant informal controls. Litigation appears when the relationship loses its future value; when its "monopolistic" character deprives informal controls of sufficient leverage and the parties invoke outside allies to modify it; and when the parties seek to vindicate conflicting values.

LAWYERS

What happens when we introduce lawyers? Parties who have lawyers do better. Lawyers are themselves RPs. Does their presence equalize the parties, dispelling the advantage of the RP client? Or does the existence of lawyers amplify the advantage of the RP client? We might assume that RPs (tending to be larger units) who can buy legal

services more steadily, in larger quantities, in bulk (by retainer) and at higher rates, would get services of better quality. They would have better information (especially where restrictions on information about legal services are present). Not only would the RP get more talent to begin with, but he would on the whole get greater continuity, better record-keeping, more anticipatory or preventive work, more experience and specialized skill in pertinent areas, and more control over counsel.

One might expect that just how much the legal services factor would accentuate the RP advantage would be related to the way in which the profession was organized. The more members of the profession were identified with their clients (i.e., the less they were held aloof from clients by their loyalty to courts or an autonomous guild) the more the imbalance would be accentuated. The more close and enduring the lawyer-client relationship, the more the primary loyalty of lawyers to the clients rather than to courts or guild, the more telling the advantages of accumulated expertise and guidance in overall strategy.

What about the specialization of the bar? Might we not expect the existence of specialization to offset RP advantages by providing OS with a specialist who in pursuit of his own career goals would be interested in outcomes that would be advantageous to a whole class of OSs? Does the specialist become the functional equivalent of the RP? We may divide specialists into (1) those specialized by field of law (patent, divorce, etc.), (2) those specialized by the kind of party represented (for example, house counsel). and (3) those specialized by both field of law and "side" or party (personal injury plaintiff, criminal defense, labour). Divorce lawyers do not specialize in husbands or wives, nor real estate lawyers in buyers or seller. But labour lawyers and tax lawyers and stockholders-derivative-suit lawyers do specialize not only in the field of law but in representing one side. Such specialists may represent RPs or OSs. Figure 2 provides some well-known examples of different kinds of specialists:

Most specializations cater to the needs of particular kinds of RPs. Those specialists who service OSs have some distinctive features:

First, they tend to make up the "lower echelons" of the legal profession. Compared to the lawyers who provide services to RPs, lawyers in these specialties tend to be drawn from lower socio-economic origins, to have attended local, proprietary or part-time law schools, to practise alone rather than in large firms, and to possess low prestige within the profession. (Of course the correlation is far from perfect; some lawyers who represent OSs do not have these characteristics and some representing RPs do. However, on the whole the differences in professional standing is massive).

Second, specialists who service OSs tend to have problems of mobilizing a clientele (because of the low state of information among OSs) and encounter "ethical" barriers

Lawyer

		Specialized by Party	Specialized by Field and Party	Specialized by Field
Client	**RP**	• "House Counsel" or General Counsel for Bank, Insurance Co. etc. • Corporation Counsel for Government Unit	• Prosecutor • Personal Injury Defendant • Staff Counsel for NAACP • Tax • Labour/Management • Collections	• Patent
	OS	• "Poverty Lawyers" • Legal Aid	• Criminal Defense • Personal Injury Plaintiff	• Bankruptcy • Divorce

FIGURE 2
A Typology of Legal Specialists

imposed by the profession which forbid solicitation, advertising, referral fees, advances to clients, and so forth.

Third, the episodic and isolated nature of the relationship with particular OS clients tends to elicit a stereotyped and uncreative brand of legal services. Carlin and Howard (1965:385) observe that:

> The quality of service rendered poorer clients is...affected by the non-repeating character of the matters they typically bring to lawyers (such as divorce, criminal, personal injury): this combined with the small fees encourages a mass processing of cases. As a result, only a limited amount of time and interest is usually expended on any one case since there is little or no incentive to treat it except as an isolated piece of legal business. Moreover, there is ordinarily no desire to go much beyond the case as the client presents it, and such cases are only accepted when there is a clear-cut cause of action; i.e., when they fit into convenient legal categories and promise a fairly certain return.

Fourth, while they are themselves RPs, these specialists have problems in developing optimizing strategies. What might be good strategy for an insurance company lawyer or prosecutor, trading off some cases for gains on others is branded as unethical when done by a criminal defense or personal injury plaintiff lawyer. It is not per-

missible for him to play his series of OSs as if they constituted a single RP.

Conversely, the demand of routine and orderly handling of a whole series of OSs may constrain the lawyer from maximizing advantage for any individual OS. Rosenthal (1970:172) shows that "for all but the largest [personal injury] claims an attorney loses money by thoroughly preparing a case and not settling it early."

For the lawyer who services OSs, with his transient clientele, his permanent "client" is the forum, the opposite party, or the intermediary who supplies clients. Consider, for example, the dependence of the criminal defense lawyer on maintaining cooperative relations with the various members of the "criminal court community." Similarly, Carlin notes that among metropolitan individual practitioners whose clientele consists of OSs, there is a deformation of loyalty toward the intermediary.

> In the case of those lawyers specializing in personal injury, local tax, collections, criminal, and to some extent divorce work, the relationship with the client...is generally mediated by a broker or business supplier who may be either another lawyer or a layman. In these fields of practice the lawyer is principally concerned with pleasing the broker or winning his approval, more so than he is with satisfying the individual client. The source of business generally counts for more than the client, especially where the client is unlikely to return or to send in other clients. The client

261

is then expendable: he can be exploited to the full. Under these conditions, when a lawyer receives a client...he has not so much gained a client as a piece of business, and his attitude is often that of handling a particular piece of merchandise or of developing a volume of a certain kind of merchandise.

The existence of a specialized bar on the OS side should overcome the gap in expertise, allow some economies of scale, provide for bargaining commitment and personal familiarity. But this is short of overcoming the fundamental strategic advantages of RPs their capacity to structure the transaction, play the odds, and influence rule-development and enforcement policy.

Specialized lawyers may, by virtue of their identification with parties, become lobbyists, moral entrepreneurs, proponents of reforms on the parties' behalf. But lawyers have a cross-cutting interest in preserving complexity and mystique so that client contact with this area of law is rendered problematic. Lawyers should not be expected to be proponents of reforms which are optimum from the point of view of the clients taken alone. Rather, we would expect them to seek to optimize the clients' position without diminishing that of lawyers. Therefore, specialized lawyers have an interest in a framework which keeps recovery (or whatever) problematic at the same time that they favour changes which improve their clients' position within this framework. (Consider the lobbying efforts of personal injury plaintiffs and defense lawyers.) Considerations of interest are likely to be fused with ideological commitments: the lawyers' preference for complex and finely-tuned bodies of rules, for adversary proceedings for individualized case-by-case decision-making. Just as the culture of the client population affects strategic position, so does the professional culture of the lawyers.

INSTITUTIONAL FACILITIES

We see then that the strategic advantages of the RP may be augmented by the advantages in the distribution of legal services. Both are related to the advantages conferred by the basic features of the institutional facilities for the handling of claims: passivity and overload.

These institutions are passive, first, in the sense that Black refers to as "reactive" they must be mobilized by the claimant giving advantage to the claimant with information, ability to surmount cost barriers, and skill to navigate restrictive procedural requirements. They are passive in a further sense that once in the door the burden is on each party to proceed with his case. The presiding official acts as umpire, while the development of the case, collection of evidence and presentation of proof are left to the initiative and resources of the parties. Parties are treated

as if they were equally endowed with economic resources, investigative opportunities and legal skills (*Cf.* Homberger [1971:641]). Where, as is usually the case, they are not, the broader the delegation to the parties, the greater the advantage conferred on the wealthier, more experienced and better organized party.

The advantages conferred by institutional passivity are accentuated by the chronic overload which typically characterizes these institutions. Typically there are far more claims than there are institutional resources for full dress adjudication of each. In several ways overload creates pressures on claimant to settle rather than to adjudicate:

(a) by causing delay (thereby discounting the value of recovery);
(b) by raising costs (of keeping the case alive);
(c) by inducing institutional incumbents to place a high value on clearing dockets, discouraging full-dress adjudication in favour of bargaining, stereotyping and routine processing;
(d) by inducing the forum to adopt restrictive rules to discourage litigation.

Thus, overload increases the cost and risk of adjudicating and shields existing rules from challenge, diminishing opportunities for rule-change. This tends to favour the beneficiaries of existing rules.

Second, by increasing the difficulty of challenging going practice, overload also benefits those who reap advantage from the neglect (or systematic violation) of rules which favour their adversaries.

Third, overload tends to protect the possessor, the party who has the money or goods, against the claimant. For the most part, this amounts to favoring RPs over OSs, since RPs typically can structure transactions to put themselves in the possessor position.

Finally, the overload situation means that there are more commitments in the formal system than there are resources to honour them, more rights and rules "on the books" than can be vindicated or enforced. There are, then, questions of priorities in the allocation of resources. We would expect judges, police, administrators and other managers of limited institutional facilities to be responsive to the more organized, attentive and influential of their constituents. Again, these tend to be RPs.

Thus, overloaded and passive institutional facilities provide the setting in which the RP advantages in strategic position and legal services can have full play.

RULES

We assume here that rules tend to favour older, culturally dominant interest. This is not meant to imply that the rules are explicitly designed to favour these interests, but rather that those groups which have become dominant have successfully articulated their operations to pre-existing rules. To the extent that rules are evenhanded or favour the "have-nots," the limited resources for their implementation will be allocated, I have argued, so as to give greater effect to those rules which protect and promote the tangible interest of organized and influential groups. Furthermore, the requirements of due process, with their barriers or protections against precipitate action, naturally tend to protect the possessor or holder against the claimant. Finally, the rules are sufficiently complex and problematic (or capable of being problematic if sufficient resources are expended to make them so) that differences in the quantity and quality of legal services will affect capacity to derive advantages from the rules.

Thus, we arrive at Figure 3 which summarizes why the "haves" tend to come out ahead. It points to layers of advantages enjoyed by different (but largely overlapping) classes of "haves", advantages which interlock, reinforcing and shielding one another.

ALTERNATIVES TO THE OFFICIAL SYSTEM

We have been discussing resort to the official system to put forward (or defend against) claims. Actually, resort to this system by claimants (or initiators) is one of several alternatives. Our analysis should consider the relationship of the characteristics of the total official litigation system to this use *vis-à-vis* the alternatives. These include at least the following:

1. Inaction "lumping it," not making a claim or complaint. This is done all the time by "claimants" who lack information or access or who knowingly decide gain is too low, cost too high (including psychic cost of litigating where such activity is repugnant). Costs are raised by lack of information or skill, and also include risk. Inaction is also familiar on the part of official complainers (police, agencies, prosecutors) who have incomplete information about violations,

Element	Advantages	Enjoyed by
PARTIES	• ability to structure transaction • specialized expertise, economies of scale • long-term strategy • ability to play for rules • bargaining credibility • ability to invest in penetration	• repeat players large, professional*
LEGAL SERVICES	• skill, specialization, continuity	• organized, professional,* wealthy
INSTITUTIONAL FACILITIES	• passivity • cost and delay barriers • favorable priorities	• wealthy, experienced, organized • holders, possessors • beneficiaries of existing rules • organized, attentive
RULES	• favorable rules • due process barriers	• older, culturally dominant • holders, possessors

* in the simple sense of "doing it for a living"

FIGURE 3
Why the 'Haves' Tend to Come Out Ahead

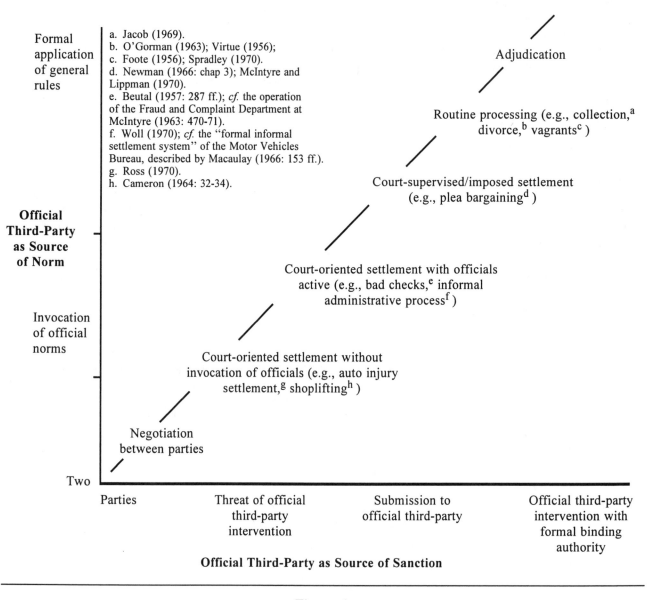

a. Jacob (1969).
b. O'Gorman (1963); Virtue (1956);
c. Foote (1956); Spradley (1970).
d. Newman (1966: chap 3); McIntyre and Lippman (1970).
e. Beutal (1957: 287 ff.); *cf.* the operation of the Fraud and Complaint Department at McIntyre (1963: 470-71).
f. Woll (1970); *cf.* the "formal informal settlement system" of the Motor Vehicles Bureau, described by Macaulay (1966: 153 ff.).
g. Ross (1970).
h. Cameron (1964: 32-34).

Figure 4
'Appended' Dispute-Settlement Systems

limited resources, policies about *de minimus*, schedules of priorities, and so forth.

2. "Exit" withdrawal from a situation or relationship by moving, resigning, severing relations, finding new partners, etc. This is of course a very common expedient in many kinds of trouble. Like "lumping it," it is an alternative to invocation of any kind of remedy system although its presence as a sanction may be important to the working of other remedies. The use of "exit" options depends on the availability of alternative opportunities or partners (and information about them), the costs of withdrawal, transfer, relocation, development of new relationships, the pull of loyalty to previous arrangements and on the availability and cost of other remedies.

3. Resort to some unofficial control system — we are familiar with many instances in which disputes are handled outside the official litigation system. Here we should distinguish (a) those dispute-settlement systems which are normatively and institutionally appended to the official system (such as settlement of auto-injuries, handling of bad checks) from (b) those settlement systems which are relatively independent in norms and sanctions (such as businessmen settling disputes *inter se*, religious groups, gangs).

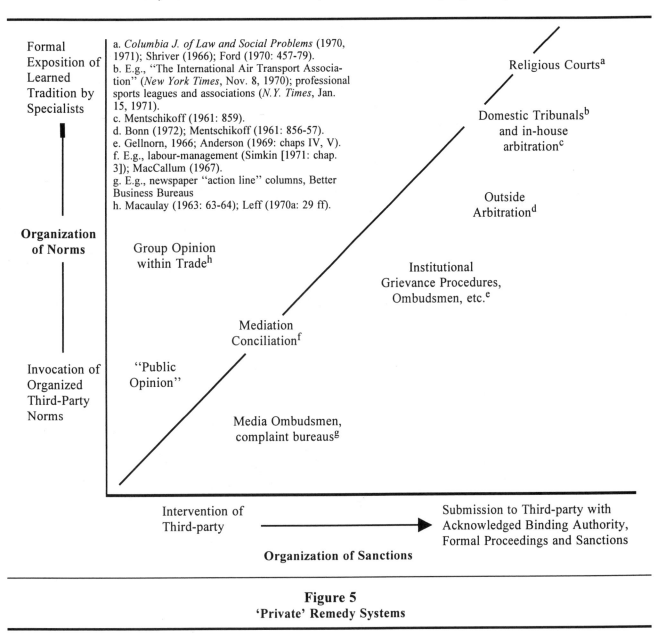

Formal
Exposition of
Learned
Tradition by
Specialists

a. *Columbia J. of Law and Social Problems* (1970, 1971); Shriver (1966); Ford (1970: 457-79).
b. E.g., "The International Air Transport Association" (*New York Times*, Nov. 8, 1970); professional sports leagues and associations (*N.Y. Times*, Jan. 15, 1971).
c. Mentschikoff (1961: 859).
d. Bonn (1972); Mentschikoff (1961: 856-57).
e. Gellnorn, 1966; Anderson (1969: chaps IV, V).
f. E.g., labour-management (Simkin [1971: chap. 3]); MacCallum (1967).
g. E.g., newspaper "action line" columns, Better Business Bureaus
h. Macaulay (1963: 63-64); Leff (1970a: 29 ff).

Religious Courts[a]

Domestic Tribunals[b]
and in-house
arbitration[c]

**Organization
of Norms**

Outside
Arbitration[d]

Group Opinion
within Trade[h]

Institutional
Grievance Procedures,
Ombudsmen, etc.[e]

Mediation
Conciliation[f]

Invocation of
Organized
Third-Party
Norms

"Public
Opinion"

Media Ombudsmen,
complaint bureaus[g]

Intervention of
Third-party

Submission to Third-party with
Acknowledged Binding Authority,
Formal Proceedings and Sanctions

Organization of Sanctions

Figure 5
'Private' Remedy Systems

What we might call the "appended" settlement systems merge imperceptibly into the official litigation system [Figure 4]. We might sort them out by the extent to which the official intervention approaches the adjudicatory mode. We find a continuum from situations where parties settle among themselves with an eye to the official rules and sanctions, through situations where official intervention is invoked, to those in which settlement is supervised and/or imposed by officials, to full dress adjudication. All along this line the sanction is supplied by the official system (though not always in the manner prescribed in the "higher law") and the norm or rules applied are a version of the official rules, although discounted for transaction costs and distorted by their selective use for the purpose of the parties.

From those "appended" systems of discounted and privatized official justice we should distinguish those informal systems of "private justice" which invoke other norms and other sanctions. Such systems of dispute-settlement are typical among people in continuing interaction such as an organized group, a trade, or a university. In sorting out the various types according to the extent and the mode of intervention of third parties, we can distinguish two dimensions: the first is the degree to which the applicable norms are formally articulated, elaborated, and exposited, that is the increasingly organized character of the norms. The second represents the degree to which initiative and binding authority are accorded to the third party, that is, the increasingly organized character of the sanction. Some conjectures about the character of some of

Remedy Systems

OFFICIAL		APPENDED		PRIVATE			
Adjudication	Routine processing	Structurally Interstitial (Officials Participating)	Oriented to Official	Articulated to Official	Independent		Oppositional
	Collections	Plea bargaining, bad check recovery	Auto injury settlement	Businessmen	Churches, Chinese community	Gangs	Mafia Revolutionaries
	Divorce						

Examples

Figure 6
A Scale of Remedy Systems from Official to Private

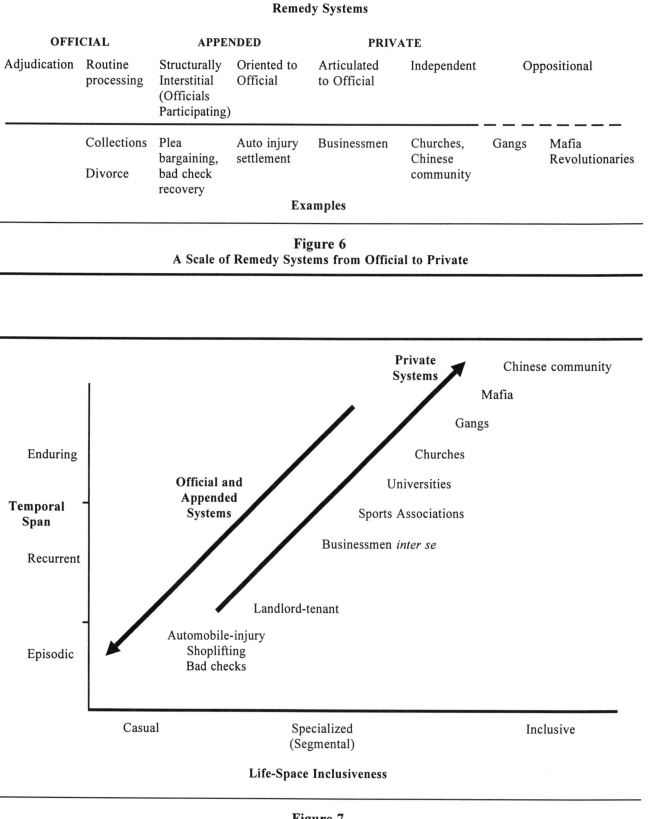

Figure 7
Relationship Between Density of Social Relationships and Type of Remedy System

the common types of private systems are presented in Figure 5.

Our distinction between "appended" and "private" remedy systems should not be taken as a sharp dichotomy but as pointing to a continuum along which we might range the various remedy systems. There is a clear distinction between appended systems like automobile injury or bad check settlements and private systems like the internal regulation of the mafia (Cressey, 1969: Chaps. VIII, IX; Ianni, 1972), or the Chinese community. The internal regulatory aspects of universities, churches, and groups of businessmen lie somewhere in between. It is as if we could visualize a scale stretching from the official remedy system through ones oriented to it through relatively independent systems based on similar values to independent systems based on disparate values.

Presumably it is not accidental that some human encounters are regulated frequently and influentially by the official and its appended systems while others seem to generate controls that make resort to the official and its appended systems rare. Which human encounters are we likely to find regulated at the "official" end of our scale and which at the "private" end? It is submitted that location on our scale [Figure 6] varies with factors that we might sum up by calling them the density of the relationship. That is, the more inclusive in life-space and temporal span a relationship between parties, the less likely it is that those parties will resort to the official system and the more likely that the relationship will be regulated by some independent "private" system. This seems plausible because we would expect inclusive and enduring relationships to create the possibility of effective sanctions; and we would expect participants in such relationships to share a value consensus which provided standards for conduct and legitimized such sanctions in each case of deviance.

The prevalence of private systems does not necessarily imply that they embody values or norms which are competing or opposed to those of the official system. Our analysis does not impute the plurality of remedy systems to cultural differences as such. It implies that the official system is utilized when there is a disparity between social structure and cultural norm. It is used, that is, where interaction and vulnerability create encounters and relationships which do not generate shared norms (they may be insufficiently shared or insufficiently specific) and/or do not give rise to group structures which permit sanctioning these norms.

Figure 7 sketches out such relationships of varying density and suggests the location of various official and private remedy systems. It restates our surmise of a close association between the density of relationships and remoteness from the official system. We may surmise further that on the whole the official and appended systems flourish in connection with the disputes between parties of disparate size which give rise to the litigation in Boxes

II and III of Figure 1. Private remedy systems, on the other hand, are more likely to handle disputes between parties of comparable size. The litigation in Boxes I and IV of Figure 1, then seems to represent in large measure the breakdown (or inhibited development) of private remedy systems. Indeed, the distribution of litigation generally forms a mirror image of the presence of private remedy systems. But the mirror is, for the various reasons discussed here, a distorting one.

From the vantage point of the "higher law" what we have called the official system may be visualized as the "upper" layers of a massive "legal" iceberg, something like this:

Adjudication
Litigation
Appended Settlement Systems
Private Settlement Systems
Exit Remedies/Self Help
Inaction ("lumping it")

The uneven and irregular layers are distinct although they merge imperceptibly into one another. As we proceed to discuss possible reforms of the official system, we will want to consider the kind of impact they will have on the whole iceberg.

We will look at some of the connections and flows between layers mainly from the point of view of the construction of the iceberg itself, but aware that flows and connections are also influenced by atmospheric (cultural) factors such as appetite for vindication, psychic cost of litigation, lawyers' culture and the like.

STRATEGIES FOR REFORM

Our categorization of four layers of advantage (Figure 3) suggests a typology of strategies for "reform" (taken here to mean equalization conferring relative advantage on those who did not enjoy it before.) We then come to four types of equalizing reform:

1. rule-change
2. improvement in institutional facilities
3. improvement of legal services in quantity and quality
4. improvement of strategic position of have-not parties

I shall attempt to sketch some of the possible ramifications of change on each of these levels for other parts of the litigation system and then discuss the relationship between changes in the litigation system and the rest of our legal iceberg. Of course such reforms need not be enacted singly, but may occur in various combinations. However, for our purposes we shall only discuss, first, each type taken in isolation and then, all taken together.

Rule-Change

Obtaining favorable rule changes is an expensive process. The various kinds of "have-nots" (Figure 3) have fewer resources to accomplish changes through legislation or administrative policy making. The advantages of the organized, professional, wealthy and attentive in these forums are well-known. Litigation, on the other hand, has a flavour of equality. The parties are "equal before the law" and the rules of the game do not permit them to deploy all of their resources in the conflict, but require that they proceed within the limiting forms of the trial. Thus, litigation is a particularly tempting arena to "have-nots," including those seeking rule change. Those who seek change through the courts tend to represent relatively isolated interests, unable to carry the day in more political forums.

Litigation may not, however, be a ready source of rule-change for "have-nots." Complexity, the need for high inputs of legal services and cost barriers (heightened by overloaded institutional facilities) make challenge of rules expensive. OS claimants, with high stakes in the tangible outcome, are unlikely to try to obtain rule changes. By definition, a test case litigation deliberately designed to procure rule-change is an unthinkable undertaking for an OS. There are some departures from our ideal type: OSs who place a high value on vindication by official rules or whose peculiar strategic situation makes it in their interest to pursue rule victories. But generally the test-case involves some organization which approximates an RP.

The architecture of courts severely limits the scale and scope of changes they can introduce in the rules. Tradition and ideology limit the kinds of matters that come before them: not patterns of practice but individual instances, not "problems" but cases framed by the parties and strained through requirements of standing, case or controversy, jurisdiction, and so forth. Tradition and ideology also limit the kind of decision they can give. Thus, common law courts for example, give an all-or-none, once-and-for-all decision which must be justified in terms of a limited (though flexible) corpus of rules and techniques. By tradition, courts cannot address problems by devising new regulatory or administrative machinery (and have no taxing and spending powers to support it); courts are limited to solutions compatible with the existing institutional framework. Thus, even the most favorably inclined court may not be able to make those rule-changes most useful to a class of "have-nots."

Rule-change may make use of the courts more attractive to "have-nots." Apart from increasing the possibility of favorable outcomes, it may stimulate organization, rally and encourage litigants. It may directly redistribute symbolic rewards to "have-nots" (or their champions). But tangible rewards do not always follow symbolic ones. Indeed, provision of symbolic rewards to "have-nots" (or

crucial groups of their supporters) may decrease capacity and drive to secure redistribution of tangible benefits.

Rule-changes secured from courts or other peak agencies do not penetrate automatically and costlessly to other levels of the system, as attested by the growing literature on impact. This may be especially true of rule-change secured by adjudication, for several reasons:

1. Courts are not equipped to assess systematically the impact or penetration problem. Courts typically have no facilities for surveillance, monitoring, or securing systematic enforcement of their decrees. The task of monitoring is left to the parties.
2. The built-in limits on applicability due to the piecemeal character of adjudication. Thus a Mobilization for Youth lawyer reflects:

> ...What is the ultimate value of winning a test case? In many ways a result cannot be clear-cut...if the present welfare-residency laws are invalidated, it is quite possible that some other kind of welfare-residency law will spring up in their place. It is not very difficult to come up with a policy that is a little different, stated in different words, but which seeks to achieve the same basic objective. The results of test cases are not generally self-executing.... It is not enough to have a law invalidated or a policy declared void if the agency in question can come up with some variant of that policy, not very different in substance but sufficiently different to remove it from the effects of the court order.

3. The artificial equalizing of parties in adjudication by insulation from the full play of political pressures, the "equality" of the parties, the exclusion of "irrelevant" material, the "independence" of judges, means that judicial outcomes are more likely to be at variance with the existing constellation of political forces than decisions arrived at in forums lacking such insulation. But resources that cannot be employed in the judicial process can reassert themselves at the implementation stage, especially where institutional overload requires another round of decision making (what resources will be deployed to implement which rules) and/or private expenditures to secure implementation. Even where "have-nots" secure favorable changes at the rule level, they may not have the resources to secure the penetration of these rules. The impotence of rule-change, whatever its source, is particularly pronounced when there is reliance on unsophisticated OSs to utilize favorable new rules.

Where rule-change promulgated at the peak ot the system does have an impact on other levels, we should not assume any isomorphorism. The effect on institutional facilities and the strategic position of the parties may be far different then we would predict from the rule-change. Thus, Randall's study of movie censorship shows that liberalization of the rules did not make censorship boards more circumspect; instead, many closed down and the old game between censorship boards and distributors was replaced by a new, rougher game between exhibitors and local government-private group coalitions.

Increase in Institutional Facilities

Imagine an increase in institutional facilities for processing claims such that there is timely full-dress adjudication of every claim put forward; no queue, no delay, no stereotyping. Decrease in delay would lower costs for claimants, taking away this advantage of possessor-defendants. Those relieved of the necessity of discounting recovery for delay would have more to spend on legal services. To the extent that settlement had been induced by delay (rather than insuring against the risk of unacceptable loss), claimants would be inclined to litigate more and settle less. More litigants without stereotyping would mean more contests, including more contesting of rules and more rule change. As discounts diminished, neither side could use settlement policy to prevent rule-loss. Such reforms would for the most part benefit OS claimants, but they would also improve the position of those RP claimants not already in the possessor position, such as the prosecutor where the accused is free on bail.

This assumes no change in the *kind* of institutional facilities. We have merely assumed a greater quantitative availability of courts of the relatively passive variety typical of (at least) "common law" systems in which the case is "tried by the parties before the court..." (Homberger, 1970: 31). One may imagine institutions with augmented authority to solicit and supervise litigation, conduct investigations, secure, assemble and present proof; which enjoyed greater flexibility in devising outcomes (such as compromise or mediation); and finally which had available staff for monitoring compliance with their decrees. Greater institutional "activism" might be expected to reduce advantages of party expertise and of differences in the quality and quantity of legal services. Enhanced capacity for securing compliance might be expected to reduce advantages flowing from differences in ability to invest in enforcement. It is hardly necessary to point out that such reforms could be expected in encounter not only resistance from the beneficiaries of the present passive institutional style, but also massive ideological opposition from legal professionals whose fundamental sense of legal propriety would be violated.

Increase in Legal Services

The reform envisaged here is an increase in quantity and quality of legal services to "have-not" (including greater availability of information about these services). Presumably this would lower costs, remove the expertise advantage, produce more litigation with more favorable outcomes for "have-nots," perhaps with more appeals and more rule challenges, more new rules in their favour. (Public defender, legal aid, judicare, and prepayment plans approximate this in various fashions.) To the extent that OSs would still have to discount for delay and risk, their gains would be limited (and increase in litigation might mean even more delay). Under certain conditions, increased legal services might use institutional overload as leverage on behalf of "have-nots." Our Mobilization for Youth attorney observes:

> ...if the Welfare Department buys out an individual case, we are precluded from getting a principle of law changed, but if we give them one thousand cases to buy out, that law has been effectively changed whether or not the law as written is changed. The practice is changed; the administration is changed; the attitude to the client is changed. The value of a heavy case load is that it allows you to populate the legal process. It allows you to apply remitting pressure on the agency you are dealing with. It creates a force that has to be dealt with, that has to be considered in terms of the decisions that are going to be made prospectively. It means that you are not somebody who will be gone tomorrow, not an isolated case, but a force in the community that will remain once this particular case has been decided.
>
> As a result...we have been able, for the first time to participate along with welfare recipients...in a rule-making process itself... (Rothwax, 1969: 140–41).

The increase in quantity of legal services was accompanied here by increased coordination and organization on the "have-not" side, which brings us to our fourth level of reform.

Reorganization of Parties

The reform envisaged here is the organization of "have-not" parties (whose position approximates OS) into coherent groups that have the ability to act in a coordinated fashion, play long-run strategies, benefit from high-grade legal services, and so forth.

One can imagine various ways in which OSs might be aggregated into RPs. They include (1) the membership association — bargaining agent (trade unions, tenant unions); (2) the assignee — manager of fragmentary rights (performing rights associations like ASCAP); (3) the interest group

— sponsor (NAACP, ACLU, environmental action groups). All of these forms involve upgrading capacities for managing claims by gathering and utilizing information, achieving continuity and persistence, employing expertise, exercising bargaining skill and so forth. These advantages are combined with enhancement of the OS part's strategic position either by aggregating claims that are too small relative to the cost of remedies (consumers, breathers of polluted air, owners of performing rights); or by reducing claims to manageable size by collective action to dispel or share unacceptable risks (tenants, migrant workers). A weaker form of organization would be (4) a clearing-house which established a communication network among OSs. This would lower the costs of information and give RPs a stake in the effect OSs could have on their reputation. A minimal instance of this is represented by the "media ombudsman", the "action line" type of newspaper column. Finally, there is governmentalization utilizing the criminal law or the administrative process to make it the responsibility of a public officer to press claims that would be unmanageable in the hands of a private grievant.

An organized group is not only better able to secure favorable rule changes, in courts and elsewhere, but is better able to see that good rules are implemented. It can expend resources on surveillance, monitoring, threats, or litigation that would be uneconomic for an OS. Such new units would in effect be RPs. Their encounters with opposing RPs would move into Box IV of Figure 1. Neither would enjoy the strategic advantages of RPs over OSs. One possible result, as we have noted in our discussion of the RP v. RP situation, is delegalization, that is, a movement away from the official system to a private system of dispute-settlement; another would be more intense use of the official system.

Many aspects of "public interest law" can be seen as approximations of this reform. (1) The class action is a device to raise the stakes for an RP, reducing his strategic position to that of an OS by making the stakes more than he can afford to play odds on, while moving the claimants into a position in which they enjoy the RP advantages without having to undergo the outlay for organizing. (2) Similarly, the "community organizing" aspect of public interest law can be seen as an effort to create a unit (tenants, consumers) which can play the RP game. (3) Such a change in strategic position creates the possibility of a test-case strategy for getting rule-change. Thus, "public interest law" can be thought of as a combination of community organizing, class action and test-case strategies, along with increase in legal services.

REFORM AND THE REST OF THE ICEBERG

The reforms of the official litigation system that we have imagined would, taken together, provide rules more favorable to the "have-nots." Redress according to the official rules, undiscounted by delay, strategic disability, disparities of legal services and so forth could be obtained whenever either party found it to his advantage. How might we expect such a utopian upgrading of the official machinery to affect the rest of our legal iceberg?

We would expect more use of the official system. Those who opted for inaction because of information or cost barriers and those who "settled" at discount rates in one of the "appended" systems would in many instances find it to their advantage to use the official system. The appended systems, insofar as they are built on the costs of resort to the official system, would either be abandoned or the outcomes produced would move to approximate closely those produced by adjudication.

On the other hand, our reforms would, by organizing OSs, create many situations in which *both* parties were organized to pursue their long-run interest in the litigation arena. In effect, many of the situations which occupied Boxes II and III of Figure 1 (RP v. OS, OS v. RP) the great staple sources of litigation would now be moved to Box IV (RP v. RP). We observed earlier that RPs who anticipate continued dealings with one another tend to rely on informal bilateral controls. We might expect then that the official system would be abandoned in favour of private systems of dispute-settlement.

Thus we would expect our reforms to produce a dual movement: the official and its appended systems would be "legalized" while the proliferation of private systems would "delegalize" many relationships. Which relationships would we expect to move which way? As a first approximation, we might expect that the less "inclusive" relationships currently handled by litigation or in the appended systems would undergo legalization, while relationships at the more inclusive end of the scale (Figure 7) would be privatized. Relationships among strangers (causal, episodic, non-recurrent) would be legalized; more dense (recurrent, inclusive) relationships between parties would be candidates for the development of private systems.

Our earlier analysis suggests that the pattern might be more complex. First, for various reasons a class of OSs may be relatively incapable of being organized. Its size, relative to the size and distribution of potential benefits, may require disproportionately large inputs of coordination and organization. Its shared interest may be insufficiently respectable to be publicly acknowledged (for instance, shoplifters, homosexuals until very recently). Or recurrent OS roles may be staffed by shifting population for whom the sides of the transaction are interchangeable. (For instance, home buyers and sellers, negligent motorists and accident victims.) Even where OSs are organizable, we recall that not all RP v. RP encounters lead to the development of private remedy systems. There are RPs engaged in value conflict; there are those relationships with a governmental or other monopoly aspect in which informal controls may falter; and finally there are those

RPs whose encounters with one another are non-recurring. In all of these we might expect legalization rather than privatization.

Whichever way to movement in any given instance, our reforms would entail changes in the distribution of power. RPs would no longer be able to wield their strategic advantages to invoke selectively the enforcement of favorable rules while securing large discounts (or complete shielding by cost and overload) where the rules favored their OS opponents.

Delegalization (by the proliferation of private remedy and bargaining systems) would permit many relationships to be regulated by norms and understandings that departed from the official rules. Such parochial remedy systems would be insulated from the impingement of the official rules by the commitment of the parties to their continuing relationship. Thus, delegalization would entail a kind of pluralism and decentralization. On the other hand, the "legalization" of the official and appended systems would amount to the collapse of species of pluralism and decentralization that are endemic in the kind of (unreformed) legal system we have postulated. The current prevalence of appended and private remedy systems reflects the inefficiency, cumbersomeness and costliness of using the official system. This inefficient, cumbersome and costly character is a source and shield of a kind of decentralization and pluralism. It permits a selective application of the "higher law" in a way that gives effect at the operative level to parochial norms and concerns which are not fully recognized in the "higher law" (such as the right to exclude low status neighbors, or police dominance in encounters with citizens). If the insulation afforded by the costs of getting the "higher law" to prevail were eroded, many relationships would suddenly be exposed to the "higher law" rather than its parochial counterparts. We might expect this to generate new pressures for explicit recognition of these "subterranean" values or for explicit decentralization.

These conjectures about the shape that a "reformed" legal system might suggest that we take another look at our unreformed system, with its pervasive disparity between authoritative norms and everyday operations. A modern legal system of the type we postulated is characterized structurally by institutional unity and culturally by normative universalism. The power to make, apply and change law is reserved to organs of the public, arranged in unified hierarchic relations, committed to uniform application of universalistic norms.

There is, for example, in American law (that is, in the higher reaches of the system where the learned tradition is propounded) an unrelenting stress on the virtues of uniformity and universality and a pervasive distaste for particularism, compromise and discretion. Yet the cultural attachment to universalism is wedded to and perhaps even

intensifies diversity and particularism at the operative level.

The unreformed features of the legal system then appear as a device for maintaining the partial dissociation of everyday practice from these authoritative institutional and normative commitments. Structurally, (by cost and institutional overload) and culturally (by ambiguity and normative overload) the unreformed system effects a massive covert delegation from the most authoritative rule-makers to field level official (and their constituencies) responsive to other norms and priorities than are contained in the "higher law." By their selective application these field level communities produce regulatory outcomes which could not be predicted by examination of the authoritative "higher law."

Thus its unreformed character articulates the legal system to the discontinuities of culture and social structure: it provides a way of accommodating cultural heterogeneity and social diversity while propounding universalism and unity; of accommodating vast concentrations of private power while upholding the supremacy of public authority; of accommodating inequality in fact while establishing equality at law; of facilitating action by great collective combines while celebrating individualism. Thus "unreform", that is, ambiguity and overload of rules, overloaded and inefficient institutional facilities, disparities in the supply of legal services, and disparities in the strategic position of parties is the foundation of the "dualism" of the legal system. It permits unification and universalism at the symbolic level and diversity and particularism at the operating level.

IMPLICATIONS FOR REFORM

We have discussed the way in which the architecture of the legal system tends to confer interlocking advantages on overlapping groups whom we have called the "haves." To what extent might reforms of the legal system dispel these advantages? Reforms will always be less total than the utopian ones envisioned above. Reformers will have limited resources to deploy and they will always be faced with the necessity of choosing which uses of those resources are most productive of equalizing change. What does our analysis suggest about strategies and priorities?

Our analysis suggests that change at the level of substantive rules is not likely in itself to be determinative of redistributive outcomes. Rule change is in itself likely to have little effect because the system is so constructed that changes in the rules can be filtered out unless accompanied by changes at other levels. In a setting of overloaded institutional facilities, inadequate costly legal services and unorganized parties, beneficiaries may lack the resources to secure implementation; or an RP may restructure the transaction to escape the thrust of the new rule. (Leff,

1970b; Rothwax, 1969: 143; *Cf.* Grossman, 1970). Favorable rules are not necessarily (and possibly not typically) in short supply to "have-nots;" certainly less so than any of the other resources needed to play the litigation game. Programs of equalizing reform which focus on rule-change can be readily absorbed without any change in power relations. The system has the capacity to change a great deal at the level of rules without corresponding changes in everyday patterns of practice or distribution of tangible advantages. (See, for example, Lipsky, 1970: chap. 4, 5). Indeed, rule-change may become a symbolic substitute for redistribution of advantages. (See Edelman, 1967: 40).

The low potency of substantive rule-change is especially the case with rule-changes procured from courts. That courts can sometimes be induced to propound rule-changes that legislatures would not make points to the limitation as well as the possibilities of court-produced change. With their relative insulation from retaliation by antagonistic interests, courts may more easily propound new rules which depart from prevailing power relations. But such rules require even greater inputs of other resources to secure effective implementation. And courts have less capacity than other rule-makers to create institutional facilities and re-allocate resources to secure implementation of new rules. Litigation then is unlikely to shape decisively the distribution of power in society. It may serve to secure or solidify symbolic commitments. It is vital tactically in securing temporary advantage or protection, providing leverage for organization and articulation of interests and conferring (or withholding) the mantle of legitimacy. The more divided the other holders of power, the greater the redistributive potential of this symbolic/tactical role. (Dahl, 1958: 294).

Our analysis suggests that breaking the interlocked advantages of the "haves" requires attention not only to the level of rules, but also to institutional facilities, legal services and organization of parties. It suggests that litigating and lobbying have to be complemented by interest organizing, provisions of services and invention of new forms of institutional facilities.

The thrust of our analysis is that changes at the level of parties are most likely to generate changes at other levels. If rules are the most abundant resource for reformers, parties capable of pursuing long-range strategies are the rarest. The presence of such parties can generate effective demand for high grade legal services, continuous, expert, and oriented to the long-run and pressure for institutional reforms and favorable rules. This suggests that we can roughly surmise the relative strategic priority of various rule-changes. Rule-changes which relate directly to the strategic position of the parties by facilitating organization, increasing the supply of legal services (where these in turn provide a focus for articulating and organizing common interests) and increasing the costs of opponents for instance, authorization of class action suits, award of attorneys fees and costs, award of provisional remedies — these are the most powerful fulcrum for change. The intensity of the opposition to class action legislation and autonomous reform-oriented legal services such as California Rural Legal Assistance indicates the "have" own estimation of the relative strategic impact of the several levels.

The contribution of the lawyer to redistributive social change, then, depends upon the organization and culture of the legal profession. We have surmised that court-produced substantive rule-change is unlikely in itself to be a determinative element in producing tangible redistribution of benefits. The leverage provided by litigation depends on its strategic combination with inputs at other levels. The question then is whether the organization of the profession permits lawyers to develop and employ skills at these other levels. The more that lawyers view themselves exclusively as courtroom advocates, the less their willingness to undertake new tasks and form enduring alliances with clients and operate in forums other than courts, the less likely they are to serve as agents of redistributive change. Paradoxically, those legal professions most open to accentuating the advantages of the "haves" (by allowing themselves to be "captured" by recurrent clients) may be most able to become (or have room for, more likely) agents of change, precisely because they provide more licence for identification with clients and their "causes" and have a less strict definition of what are properly professional activities.

Controlling the Abuse of Small Claims Courts[†]

C.S. Axworthy

INTRODUCTION

One of the greatest problems faced in the operation of small claims courts is the overwhelming predominance of corporate plaintiffs who are attracted to the courts by the cheap, fast, and simple adjudication of their claims. This is to the almost total exclusion of individual claimants. If small claims courts are to prove effective, this problem must be solved.

THE REASONS FOR THE EXISTENCE OF SMALL CLAIMS COURTS

The need for the modern small claims court was recognized in 1913 by Dean Roscoe Pound:

> For ordinary causes our contentious system has great merit as a means of getting at the truth. But it is a denial of justice in small causes to drive litigants to employ lawyers, and it is a shame to drive them to legal aid societies to get as a charity what the state should give as a right.

The legal system exists, then, as an avenue through which every person in society who has a valid claim against another should be able to move to attain satisfaction of that claim. Conversely, it should be a protection to persons against invalid claims from other members of society. The fact that a claim is small or held by a person without the knowledge or capabilities to enforce it should be of no importance whatsoever. If the claim is a valid one it should be capable of enforcement. When a claim cannot be enforced because the relative cost is prohibitive, there is, as Pound has said, a "denial of justice". The administrative cost, complications, and other difficulties are no excuse for these denials of justice. As such, something must be done to enable these claims to be effectively enforced: a very cheap and efficient adjudication process. Prujiner calls this process the "democratisation de la justice". It has been the rationale behind small claims courts.

It is necessary to ask two important questions when formulating proposals for an improved small claims courts. Firstly, what groups of people should the small claims court serve, and the corollary, what groups, if any should be excluded? And secondly, what sort of claims should be included within the court's jurisdiction?

The question involving the type of claim is not really so difficult. There would appear to be a reasonable amount of agreement in Canada that any actions relating to a person's reputation (for example, defamation, malicious prosecution and breach of promise to marry), actions relating to land, or the validity of bequests and wills are not appropriate for a small claims court. It is the more difficult problem, of who can sue in the court, which will be the subject of this discussion.

THE OBJECTIVES OF SMALL CLAIMS COURTS

The courts can attempt to deal with all types of small claims, whether held by business interests or individuals, in response to the general criticism that the judicial process is too expensive for the adjudication of small claims. Or, there can be an effort to provide a "people's court" designed as an instrument through which social justice and equity might be achieved in a forum for those unable to pursue their valid claims through the normal channels.

When the small Claims Court and Conciliation Branch of the Municipal court of the District of Columbia was established, the Committee of the United States Senate responsible for the District stated that the purpose of the court was

> ...to improve the administration of justice in small civil cases and make the service of the municipal court more easily available to all of the people whether of large or small means; to simplify practice and procedure in the commencement, handling, and trial of such cases; to eliminate delay and reduce costs; to provide for installment payment of judgments; and generally to promote the confidence of the public in the courts through the provision of a friendly forum for disputes small in amount but important to the parties.

These have been the objectives behind the formation of most small claims courts. Incidentally, the provision of a forum devoted exclusively to legitimate claims of small value relieves the mounting pressure on the superior courts. However, the extensive use of the courts by business interests has to all intents and purposes defeated most of these objectives and has relegated most small claims courts to the status of debt collection agencies.

[†] Axworthy, Christopher S., "Controlling the Abuse of Small Claims Courts" (1976), 22 *McGill Law Journal* at 480–95. Reprinted by permission of the author.

This is not thought to be a problem by every commentator. One obvious argument, and one which is difficult to refute, is that if a business plaintiff is able to recover his legitimate claims in the cheapest possible way, then those defendants who are ordered to pay their bills are subjected to minimal costs:

It is a quick and easy method of clearing up overdue accounts. A small business can collect these sums without...risking much money in the collection process. The defendant too has advantages. He is given his day in court, and his costs of defending the action are small. He does not have to hire a lawyer and, if he loses, the payments are scaled low to give him every chance to meet them.

Coats, Gantz, and Heathcote view the practice of excluding businesses as inequitable. They say, "[it] does not seem to be substantially fair to exclude an entire class of citizens from a useful adjudicative process for the abuse of a few". It should also be remembered that where debts are owed (either to business or individuals) there should be no obstacle to their recovery.

But the fact of the matter is that since small claims courts are inundated with business claims the real beneficiaries are business interests — not individuals. Where studies have been conducted into the social class of individuals using the court, it has been shown that they are almost all "middle class" and well educated. Moulton concludes that small claims courts are courts of the poor "only in the sense that many poor people are brought in to them by compulsory process".

The now-disbanded United Kingdom Consumer Council suggested a system of small claims courts for England and Wales, which, if set up, would be "genuine people's courts" and therefore that "companies, partnerships, associations, and assignees of debts should not be allowed to sue". The report continued:

The purpose would be to prevent the court's becoming widely used by firms for debt collecting and its approach thus becoming more geared to businesses than to individuals.

This is a real danger, as some American small claims courts have shown. Business representatives are usually easier for the court officers and judges to deal with than are individual litigants: they speak the same language, and are generally more articulate and less emotionally involved in the dispute. If company representatives — particularly representatives of the same companies — became a familiar part of the scene, there would be a danger that individuals would become the "odd" parties, the ones to be dealt with on

sufferance, with the implication that they were wasting the court's time.

The grouping of claims is another illustration of the misuse of the court; it further decreases the cost of recovery and illustrates the "collection agency" characteristic of the small claims court. It has been said that mass

...filing of claims seems to clearly cut against the equality values which the small claims court was designed to effectuate. A drastic procedural change directly affecting debt collection efforts in small claims court by corporations and other business concerns may be called for. Those organizations which are able to afford the services of a collection agency or more expensive court authorized debt collection should be compelled to employ them.

Limiting the number of times any one person (legal or individual) could sue would deal with this problem to a large extent, but, if the court is not to be a collection agency, mass claims must be removed in some way. If commercial interests were prohibited from suing in small claims court, the court could not be used as a commercial debt collection agency. Unfortunately, a consequence of such a decision would be to increase the incidence of such claims in the higher courts. The commercial interests being barred from the small claims court would have no choice, if they wished to enlist the aid of the judicial system, but to bring their actions in these higher courts.

As the small claims adjudication process is so attractive, many actions are instigated which would not be worth-while in its absence. The individual with a claim, especially an individual of limited means, is not normally aware that a small claims court exists to help him pursue his claim. Neither is an individual likely to feel competent to take on a large corporation or even a local businessman. For many people,

...especially the poor, small claims...courts *are* the legal system; it is their experience in these inferior tribunals that shapes the attitudes of low-income litigants toward the law and society it reflects. Thus an appraisal of small claims courts necessarily poses the question of whether we feel it is important to reduce the alienation of the poor and to increase their sense of participation — and their actual participation — in the legal process. It is not enough to look at the surface efficiency of small claims courts and their apparent saving of judicial resources that results without asking how this efficiency and economy is obtained, and at whose expense.

Traditionally, matters which are worth adjudicating have been those which it is economically efficient to adjudicate, i.e., those claims of such an amount that once the legal and other fees have been deducted, a valuable and worth-while amount remains to the successful party. With small claims this cannot possibly be the justification for going to court; the costs involved in normal court action are staggering. By reducing costs small claims courts attempt to reduce the importance of this criterion.

Small claims *are* important, collectively if not individually. There are many more small claims than large ones. And although the amounts may be small in absolute terms, to the claimant they may form enormous sums in relation to his income. As well, more small claims involve disputes between persons of different social and economic status than do large ones. As Ison says,

> ...it is in the handling of small claims, rather than large ones, that the integrity of justice is tested in the processes of interclass reaction. So to the majority of the population, the handling of small claims is far more significant than the handling of larger ones in contributing to the level of their confidence in the administration of justice.

Small claims courts have been set up primarily in order to make civil justice accessible to the poor. They provide an inexpensive and efficient means of dispute settlement for a potentially large number of claimants, but whether they actually perform this function for the poor is debatable, as already pointed out. Small claims courts have failed to provide "a kind of participatory justice where every citizen would have his say, no matter how small his claim".

SOLUTIONS TO THE ABUSE
OF SMALL CLAIMS COURTS

Small claims courts are abused by business claimants who have turned them into debt-collection agencies. They have not responded to the needs of the individual with a small claim. Quebec has sought to rectify this imbalance by excluding from small claims court all those pursuing a commercial claim. This restriction on the use of the court by commercial interests in not as effective as it may seem at first sight. Restricting the availability of default judgments, it is submitted, might provide a more satisfactory alternative. It at least avoids the argument, raised by business interests, that the exclusion from small claims court of commercial matters discriminates against certain legitimate small claims.

One thing is abundantly clear: unless businesses are prevented from commencing actions in the small claims court, they will continue to predominate. Statistics show that few cases are being brought by individuals. Even with

the statutory requirement to prove claims which exists in Alberta, corporate plaintiffs predominate.

Discussions of the use and abuse of small claims courts have centered primarily around the issue of who may be plaintiff. There have been a variety of suggestions:

(a) Do not place any restriction on who can sue in small claims courts;

(b) permit anyone to sue, but split the court into two sections — one for business claims and one for individual claims;

(c) Limit the number of times in any particular time-period that any person (legal or otherwise) can sue in the court;

(d) Permit only businesses with "clean hands" to sue, but do not restrict individual rights in any way;

(e) Bar business plaintiffs from suing in the court altogether;

(f) Permit anyone to sue but require proof of the claim before giving judgment; in other words, exclude default judgments.

No Restriction

Small claims courts are being monopolized by business interests and are not fulfilling the function for which they were specifically designed. In the absence of some other effective measure to control this misuse, there must be some restriction on who may sue in the court.

One Small Claims Court, Two Divisions

Robinson was the first to put forward the proposal that a small claims court might have two divisions, one for commercial claims and one for individual claims:

> Most statutes deal with this problem in a negative way by barring the corporation, partnership, association, and assignee, or one or more of them, from proceeding in the small claims court. However, the proposed procedure to a large extent is applicable to both classes of cases noted. There is no reason why all cases which may appropriately proceed under the simplified practices suggested should not do so. There is then no question of the so-called collection cases being excluded from the positive aspects of this procedure, but because of the special needs of the individual claimant with a small claim, these claims should be heard separately. The purpose of segregating these cases is to provide an atmosphere where the clerks and judge are oriented to the particular problems of the litigant filing and proceeding with his own claim. As we have seen, the bulk of cases, where there is not such a segregation, will be collection cases. This is bound to influence and perhaps determine the flavor of the court. Clerks

and judges cannot be expected to pay the same attention to individual litigants as to the claimant who is before the Court day after day with court business. Busy men must be hurried out while the occasional litigant can afford to wait — so will go the thinking.

Basic to any conception of small claims courts is the recognition that there are different types of claimants requiring different treatment. Separating the business claimants from the individual claimants, either by hearing the cases on different days or by different branches of the court, may correct some of the inegalities created by herding the sheep with the goats. Business plaintiffs who now sue in the small claims court would, under a dual system, use the business section, and those individuals with claims would use another section. This would be an improvement only if, as suggested by Robinson, the segregation of the cases produced clerks and judges more aware of and receptive to the problems of these individuals. Otherwise there would be little advantage gained by a dual system of small claims courts.

Limiting the Number of Suits

Another possible solution is placing a limit on the number of suits that could be brought in any given period. This has been done in a number of American jurisdictions, the argument being that it opens the court to everyone but prevents its abuse. Indeed, Moulton considers that such a move "effectively eliminate[s] the most troublesome suits."

In effect, this is merely another, more subtle, means of removing the corporation from the court, although it can be argued that, as the limitation would affect everyone, prospective business plaintiffs and individuals alike, it is not discriminatory. Still, the arguments tendered against the total exclusion of business plaintiffs from small claims courts can, with equal validity, be used against this tactic. However, discriminatory or not, a limitation on the number of times an action may be brought within a given time period, would serve to curb the abuse by business of the small claims court.

"Clean Hands" Claimants Only

The proponent of the suggestion that only businesses with "clean hands" should be permitted to sue in the court submits that the small claims court judge should have the discretion to decide whether or not a prospective business plaintiff has "clean hands". Those businesses with "honourable claims" would be permitted to sue, while those with "less honourable claims" would have to discount them to collection agencies or enforce them through the normal court structure.

A procedure involving a differentiation between honourable and less honourable claims is rife with uncertainty, although it is conceivable that legislation could lay down *prima facie* instances of "honourable" and "less honourable" claims. And while "[t]wo practices should be discouraged — overextension of credit, and sales which involve shoddy merchandise, overpricing, and misleading representation", without any guidelines, it would be the judge who would decide which business practices tainted the claim to such an extent as to make it "less honourable".

Apart from the problem of uncertainty, this is an attractive proposition. It would permit the inclusion of businesses as plaintiffs in the small claims court, while preventing claims which resulted from oppressive or shabby business practices. Any reticence on the part of judges in holding that shady practices gave rise to less honourable claims, however, would leave the court in the same position which it now occupies — a cheap, fast, efficient, and simple debt-collection procedure with little or no scrutiny of claims before it.

A recent study by the National Institute for Consumer Justice proposed a variation on this theme: a judge should have the power to bar any litigant from appearing for a period of a year if he has "abused or misused" the court. A claimant who had obtained several default judgments based on fraudulent or unfair trade practices or who had filed under a fictitious name to avoid the prohibition on mass filing or who had filed suit without making any effort to resolve the matter with the defendant, would be deemed to have abused or misused the court.

Total Exclusion of Business Claimants

The most sweeping proposal is to exclude businesses from the small claims court, as has been done in Quebec. Article 953(d) of the *Code of Civil Procedure* includes in its requirement that it be "exigible by any physical person in his own name and on his personal behalf, except for a purchaser of accounts, or by a tutor or curator in his official capacity".

If the small claims court were closed to business interests, much of what Prujiner calls commercial "agressivité juridique" would be "defused". It would, perhaps more correctly, be diverted to other courts or collection methods. Exclusion would merely allow the default judgement to be obtained in a higher court, with the subsequent higher costs being paid by the defendant.

This problem can be solved in two ways. A statutory provision could provide that a judgement could not, under any circumstances, in any court, be awarded in the absence of the defendant without proof being shown by the plaintiff. On such a wide scale, this is impractical. The Province of Quebec has chosen the second alternative and has stipulated that an action brought in a higher court by a business, because of the exclusion of businesses from the small

276

claims court, may, at the option of the defendant, be heard in small claims court. In effect, it means that the small claims court is faced with a claim being pursued by a business. If the small claims procedure is as good as is anticipated, if the individual defendant is informed of his choice, and if the advantages of opting for the small claims court are explained to him, surely in almost every case in which option is available it will be exercised. Therefore, the situation will be the same as it was prior to the exclusion of business claimants from the court. It is difficult to see the value to the individual in excluding business claimants from instituting an action in the small claims court and providing for this optional transfer of the hearing.

If the option is not exercised by a defendant where this is available, and the plaintiff is successful in his claim, the costs payable by the defendant will be greater than if the case had been transferred to the small claims court. Default judgments being available in the higher courts is an added problem to defendants, especially if they find it impossible to take time off work to defend the claim against them. The chances of successful defense are no higher and, because of the nature of the court, might even be considered to be lower, than in the small claims court.

Perhaps the only benefit is psychological: the consumer will have chosen to come to the small claims court. It has been suggested that this maintains the integrity and efficacy of the small claims court as the people's court. If the defendant loses, however, he or she will not be any more understanding of the judicial system merely because the defeat took place in a forum chosen, not by the commercial claimant, but by the defendant.

Business or commercial claimants should not be excluded altogether from small claims courts, but if the transfer-option safeguard is used as in Quebec, the danger remains that the court will be sued as a collection agency. In order to prevent this abuse, the procedure must be such as to require more scrutiny before judgment is awarded to recover a debt. This would appear to be most satisfactorily dealt with by restricting or curtailing the availability of default judgments which account for the vast majority of decisions rendered in small claims courts.

Exclusion of Default Judgments

The harmful effects of default judgments cannot be remedied by measures aimed at the litigants. The small claims procedure of the province of Quebec does little to alter the effect of default judgments. Article 965 of the *Civil Code of Procedure*, however, does provide for the judge to scrutinize the evidence more closely than in a traditional type of case; he may render judgment when the defendant does not appear after "examining the exhibits in the record, or, if he considers it necessary, after hearing the proof of the [plaintiff]". It is at the discretion of the

judge whether he actually requires the plaintiff to prove his case.

Alberta is one jurisdiction which has actually tried to come to terms with the difficult problem of default judgments. Section 26 of *The Small Claims Act* provides, in situations where the defendant does not appear, for a judgment to be awarded in his absence. The section, however, stipulates that the magistrate "may in his discretion allow the plaintiff to prove his claim" by oral evidence given under oath by the plaintiff and/or his witnesses or by means of affidavit evidence where the magistrate is satisfied that oral evidence cannot for some good reason be presented to the court. The magistrate, then, has the discretion to require the plaintiff to prove his claim whether or not the defendant appears. The exercise of the discretion would, of course, mean that the plaintiff would receive no benefit from the non-appearance of the defendant: his path to a judgment is no easier. Section 26 gives the magistrate a choice; he may allow the claimant to prove his case, adjourn the trial to a later date or award judgment by default on production of such evidence as he considers sufficient. Thus, the magistrate in Alberta has the discretion to preclude default judgments, in the normal sense, from his court.

There emerge four possible ways of dealing with default judgments.

The *status quo*, as it exists in most provinces, can be maintained: no proof is required for liquidated debts. Or, as in Alberta, discretion may be given to the judge either to award a default judgment or require the claimant to prove his claim. More radical yet, would be a statutory provision *requiring* the claimant to prove his claim, whether or not the defendant makes an appearance. To preclude default judgments being awarded where the defendant does not appear is clearly unacceptable; no defendant would ever appear under such circumstances.

The present system in most provinces would seem equally unacceptable; claimants recover their debts, legitimate or not, very cheaply and efficiently. The vast majority of cases go by default with virtually no assessment of their merits. Neither is judicial discretion in the awarding of default judgments an ideal solution. It is likely to effect very little change in the existing system.

It is, therefore, recommended that legislation provide that, whether the defendant appear or not, the claimant must prove his claim. This would make the award of a judgment to a claimant dependent upon whether he could prove his claim, and would have the result of safeguarding the individual from the commercial plaintiff who at present uses the small claims procedure partly because his claims receive little scrutiny by the judge.

With the requirement that proof be shown, groundless claims or those of doubtful value would either not be brought or would quickly be dispensed with by the judge. Few doubtful claims would result in judgments being awarded against individual defendants. Genuine claims would suffer little or no hindrance; their holders would merely have to prove them. Needless to say, the small claims jurisdiction would have to be exclusive in order for this to be of value. If it were still possible to sue in higher courts the more doubtful claims could be pursued there and so undermine the protection of the individual envisaged by the small claims court.

The use of the adjournment in order to allow the defendant another chance to appear should be more current. The judge should attempt to ascertain why the defendant did not appear and to encourage him to appear at the next hearing. Where an adjournment is decided upon, costs should be awarded to the claimant to compensate him for the results of the defendant's non-appearance and consequent adjournment. The requirements of proof should not be overly rigorous; the judge should require only sufficient proof as to satisfy him as to his decision.

EVIDENCE REQUIRED TO SUBSTANTIATE A CLAIM

For the prohibitive of default judgments to be successful, satisfactory rules of evidence must be applied. Two considerations especially must be borne in mind: adequate evidence must be presented and it must not vastly increase the adjudication costs.

Those provinces precluding default judgments require evidence to be presented in the form of either oral evidence under oath or by affidavit where the presentation of oral evidence is not possible for some reason. The judge, however, can also grant a judgment when the defendant is not present on the "production of such evidence as [he] considers sufficient".

This would appear to be the most suitable solution to the problem, the only difficulty being to ensure that evidence is presented upon which the decision is based. For instance, nothing would be achieved if bogus or doubtful claims could be pursued to judgment in the same manner as they can be processed at present, in spite of the proof requirement.

As the evidence of provision must not increase the cost, small claims adjudication unduly requiring witnesses to appear at the hearing would not be advisable. There may well be instances, however, where the judge wants to see a particular witness, in which case he should be summoned. In most instances evidence by affidavit would appear to be sufficient, although there is the danger of perjury.

Any system of small claims adjudication, in order to be successful, must be flexible and allow the judge discre-

tion. The judge must come to a conclusion based upon the facts presented to him; he must ascertain whether or not the witnesses and parties are reliable; he must make an assessment as to the truth; and he must decide accordingly. Even if this is not considered to be a radical departure from the present system of awarding default judgments, it is much preferable. At least the judge will not be deciding a case on the basis of a book entry and non-appearance of the defendant. This should ensure claims which would otherwise not be scrutinized, and which would be enforced without scrutiny, will be examined and only enforced where they can be proven to the satisfaction of the judge. As long as the practice of standard form affidavits attested to without concern for the truth does not grow up, this provision will be a successful one. The discretion in the judge should prove the means whereby this practice does not arise.

CONCLUSION

There have been two legislative approaches to the problem of the abuse of small claims court. Quebec has precluded business plaintiffs from its small claims courts and has left the rules relating to default judgments unchanged. British Columbia, Alberta, Manitoba, and Saskatchewan have not prevented businesses from suing, but have given the judge the discretion to require claims to be proven, even if they relate to liquidated debts, and the defendant does not appear at the hearing. The remainder of the provinces with small claims courts have not responded to the problem.

It is felt that nothing constructive can be achieved by precluding business claimants from using small claims courts as it merely encourages those claimants to pursue their claims in higher courts, with the attendant higher costs being payable by the losing defendants. Shifting the adjudication to a higher court may well maintain the integrity of the small claims court as a court for individuals, but it does not solve the problem of the indiscriminate enforcement of small claims against individuals, with little concern for their validity. The requirement that all claims be proven to the satisfaction of the court, whether liquidated debts or not, is designed to prevent small claims adjudication from being abused. In order to prevent business claimants from avoiding the proof requirement by bringing their action in higher courts than the small claims court, the jurisdiction of the court should be exclusive; and so every claim falling within the jurisdictional limits, both monetary and subject, should be required to be pursued in the small claims court. Perhaps, in this way, small claims courts will begin to live up to their early expectation and become a genuine "people's court".

Legal Victory Still Leaves Rosa Becker Out In Cold[†]

W. Marsden

MONEY was the operative word, but revenge was what Rosa Becker really wanted.

Revenge for being tossed out on her fanny by her common-law husband Lothar Pettkus, who showed his appreciation for their 18 years by throwing $3,000 on the floor and suggesting she "get lost."

Rosa thought: That's no way to say goodbye. Not after 18 years (during which she literally cleaned and tied his shoes and ran their business).

So, in 1974, she sued for half of all Pettkus's property, and her revenge turned into one of the most celebrated palimony cases in Canadian history.

In 1980, all nine judges of the Supreme Court of Canada awarded her half of a bee farm the couple built up and half-interest in three properties — setting a legal precedent that the late Chief Bora Laskin believed would settle the matrimonial-property issue.

Her victory was front-page news. Editorials applauded. Her lawyer, Gerald Langlois, predicted a $150,000 settlement for the beekeeping business and other properties. Then the excitement died — and now only law books remember Rosa Becker.

She still has not got her revenge.

Eleven years after she launched her suit and five years after the Supreme Court ruled, she has not received one cent from Lothar Pettkus.

Alone in a 9-room farmhouse in Franklin Centre near Ormstown, where she is paid $3,000 a year plus room and board to clean and cook for a dairy farmer and his farmhand, Becker, 58, reflects on Canadian justice:

"It's weird. I don't understand it."

Lothar Pettkus is 52, 5-foot-11, 200 lbs., strong. He likes hunting moose, is an excellent shot, keeps German shepherds, has thin blond hair, blue eyes.

By his calculation, Rosa Becker has lied 460 times to the Supreme Court of Canada in 1980 and 68 times to the Supreme Court of Ontario during a 1982 trial to divide up the property. He's trying to persuade the Ontario ombudsman to investigate his allegations.

"She was lying so badly that she had the (Supreme Court of Canada) judges convinced that this is the truth and it's definitely not the truth," Pettkus says.

(Judge K.A. Flannigan of the Ontario Supreme Court told Lothar Pettkus at a hearing in 1982: "It's the truth because the court found it to be true." But that hasn't stopped Lothar Pettkus.)

Convinced that the courts have been tricked by Rosa and her lawyer and their "lies," he decided that he cannot become a party to the Supreme Court ruling.

"A person who is perjuring herself with her lawyer — I should be party to a criminal act?" he asks rhetorically.

"I am just an innocent citizen sitting back and watching what the law is doing to people like me."

He might prove that, while you can't fight city hall, you sure can fight the Supreme Court of Canada.

Every move Rosa Becker makes, he thwarts, Becker's lawyer Langlois said.

He has exhausted seven lawyers and wielded every available weapon in the justice system to counter the Supreme Court ruling, he said.

Since the Supreme Court judgment, there have been 21 motions, judgments, affidavits, appeals and court orders issued concerning this case and the division of property — and still no money for Rosa Becker.

Court appearances are catfights, with Pettkus at times attempting to retry the case.

At a 1982 hearing into the division of property, Pettkus, between lawyers, represented himself and was questioning Becker about rent received from a West Hawkesbury, Ont., property they owned:

Rosa Becker: In the beginning it was $80 and then it gone up to $100.

Lothar Pettkus: Your honour, that's not true. At the beginning it was $40 and she says April the 14th, this year, that she paid $80. What was the truth now? Tell your honour the truth.

Becker: It was never $40. It was always $80 and then $100 but never $40.

Pettkus: You don't know if it's $80, you don't know if it was $40 and you don't know if it's $100, because you're so confused you can't answer the question proper.

Becker: Can you blame me for being confused after eight years with you in court?

Q: You took me to court.

A: No. I had no choice.

Q: Establish what was paid for in 1980. When you left...

A: I don't care anymore. You want it, shove it, shove it. I'm sick and tired. (Witness leaves courtroom.)

---

† Marsden, William, "Legal Victory Still Leaves Rosa Becker Out In Cold", *Montreal Gazette*, February 16, 1985, B5. Reprinted by permission of The Gazette, Montreal.

Rosa Becker, small, missing some front teeth, remembers when she first met Lothar Pettkus 30 years ago in the spring of 1955.

It was at a German Club dancehall near the Windsor Hotel. She was 28. He was 22. She earned $28 a week in a lace factory. He earned $75 a week as a garage mechanic.

She thought his tall brushcut made his face "look a mile long." They moved in together. He saved his money. They spent hers.

"Things happen in life that you can't explain and that's one of those things," she said without malice.

In 1960, they bought a 125-acre farm for $5,000, which he paid for out of his savings.

In 1971 and 1973, they purchased properties in East and West Hawkesbury in Ontario, where they moved their beekeeping business.

By that time, they were making as much as $30,000 profit a year. She played a major part in every aspect of the business. Everything was in his name.

But Judge Omer H. Chartrand of the Ontario District Court ruled that Rosa Becker's contribution was in the form of "risk capital invested in the hope of seducing a younger defendant into marriage."

He awarded her 40 empty beehives (which without bees are worthless) and $1,200.

The Court of Appeals ruled in 1978 that Chartrand had undervalued Becker's contributions. It gave her half the assets, valued as of 1974 when the two broke up. The Supreme Court agreed and implied that Chartrand's reference to risk capital "lacked gallantry."

The task then was to evaluate the assets as of 1974, apply interest and give Becker her share.

That process, which normally might take a year, is still not over.

Court judgments so far would put Becker's total claim on Pettkus at about $95,000.

In November 1983, Pettkus offered Becker a deal. He would pay her $46,408.90 if she would allow the Hawkesbury properties to be transferred to Pettkus's wife Monique.

Becker refused because she realized this would leave Pettkus without assets and make it impossible for her to receive the balance owing.

Eric Williams, Pettkus's latest lawyer, points to this offer as an example of Pettkus's willingness to settle. "I'll bet you 99 to one she doesn't get better than that offer," he said, adding that Pettkus has always been willing to settle the matter fairly.

Langlois said he attempted to freeze Lothar Pettkus's bank accounts but found only $12. Pettkus said his wife owns everything now.

Indeed, Monique Pettkus is claiming half her husband's interest in the beekeeping business and the East Hawkesbury property where she and Pettkus live with about 550 beehives. This claim will be fought out in court Feb. 21.

When Langlois tried last fall to seize the beehives, Pettkus's wife went to court and appealed the seizure, claiming that the hives are hers. That trial will be heard in March.

When the bees were seized by the court in November, Pettkus refused to feed them. By the time a court order could be obtained demanding that he feed and maintain the hives (valued at $50 each), most of the bees were dead, Monique told *The Gazette*. Without the bees, the business is worthless.

The only cash available is the $69,000 received from the sale last fall of the two Hawkesbury properties. The money is being held by the court.

By this June, Becker's half with interest will total $32,785.10. But all of that will go to pay her legal fees, which Langlois estimates total about $35,000. She also has to pay half the sheriff, appraisal and real-estate broker fees of about $10,000.

There's a good chance she will get all the $69,000, said Langlois. But it will take a fight, perhaps another year.

"That's the tragedy of this whole thing," Langlois said. "He (Pettkus) is ready to pay whatever amount to whatever lawyers it takes and it's clear that he doesn't intend to pay anything to Rosa Becker.

"She has been given the benefit of these judgments but the law has afforded protection to Pettkus on the realization of the funds."

Williams argues that Becker is trying to get blood out of a stone. "No matter how you cut it, the man is not rich."

. . . .

Rosa Becker has visions. Ghosts tell her things.

They tell her her lawyer is conspiring with Lothar Pettkus.

"They (the visions) are always true and I know that makes Gerry Langlois uneasy about me," she said.

In 1983, she asked the Law Society of Upper Canada to investigate Langlois. They did and found "absolutely no evidence of professional misconduct."

She has also asked Chief Justice Brian Dickson of the Supreme Court of Canada to intervene on her behalf. He has refused.

"I can understand Rosa's frustration," Langlois said. He knows about her visions.

In December, he sent Rosa Becker a letter suggesting that he withdraw from the file since she has lost confidence in him.

Meanwhile, he is preparing her next court appearance and his bill.

And she's thinking she might take her case to the World Court. Still seeking revenge.

Last month, the Supreme Court of Canada decided that the entire question of division of matrimonial property needed another look. It decided to hear an appeal from Mary Sorochan, 69, of Two Hills, Alberta.

"After 40 years of common-law marriage, she received nothing from her estranged husband, who argued that he owned their 190-hectare farm before she came on the scene.

She wants recognition for her help in maintaining the farm.

Further Reading

Ontario Law Reform Commission, *Report on Class Actions*, 1982, Volume III, Chapter 17.

David M. Trubek et al., "The Costs of Ordinary Litigation" (1983), 72 *University of California Law Review*, 72–127.

J. Phillips and K. Hawkins, "Some Economic Aspects of the Settlement Process: A Study of Personal Inquiry Claims" (1976), 39 *Modern Law Review* 497.

B. Access to Justice for the Poor

Legal Services and the Poor[†]
R.J. Gathercole

Justice is open to all — like the Ritz Hotel.

MAKING legal services accessible to the poor is an issue that has long confronted the legal profession, although significant developments in legal aid have taken place only in the last two decades. There had been relatively little discussion of whether the poor really are in dire need of lawyers' services; rather lawyers assume that the poor, like the rest of society, need these services almost as much as food, clothing, shelter and medical attention.

Nor have lawyers been modes about what legal services — as provided by lawyers — can accomplish for the poor. Reginald Heber Smith in his classic work, *Justice and the Poor*, published in 1919 and generally regarded as the motivating force of all American legal aid movement, wrote "In vast tracts of the civil law and in all of the criminal law related to the more severe crimes, equality in the administration of justice can be had only by supplying attorneys to the poor." If more legal aid offices were opened and existing staff increased, "that part of the denial of justice which is traceable solely to the inability of the poor to employ counsel will be completely overcome."

Forty-six years later, E. Clinton Bamberger Jr., a young Baltimore attorney who attended an A.B.A. conference to learn about the new neighbourhood legal offices being established in the United States and found himself recruited as the first Director of Legal Services in the Office of Economic Opportunity (O.E.O.) — the central office of the "War on Poverty" — went even further than Smith.

> We cannot be content with the creation of systems rendering free legal assistance to all the people who need it but cannot afford a lawyer's advice. Our responsibility is to marshal the forces of law and the strength of lawyers to combat the causes and effects of poverty. Lawyers must uncover the legal causes of poverty, remodel the systems which generate the cycle of poverty, and design new social, legal and political tools and vehicles to move poor people from deprivation, depression and despair to opportunity, hope and ambition.

These high expectations of what lawyers could accomplish for the poor were not restricted to the United States. In a 1971 study prepared for the National Council of Welfare, a leading Canadian legal aid activist wrote:

> At the lowest level of abstraction, a legal services programme can at least assist in mitigating the surface attributes of poverty. As a service provided to the poor at no cost, it has a redistributive effect. The nature of the day-to-day legal care provided would lessen at least the effect of poverty. Illegal evictions, consumer fraud, and abuses of official discretion, all wrongs to which the poor are particularly vulnerable, could be vigilantly monitored and often remedied. As well, efforts directed at law reform might succeed in gaining even more widespread relief.

. . . .

> The lawyer's business is to assist his client in analysing alternatives. He is expected to be partial, to act as the advocate of those with interests to pursue. This work, carried on in a way which encouraged the participation of the individual and the group in the work involved in the pursuit of grievances could offer the poor an opportunity to come to grips, perhaps for the first time, with problems heretofore beyond reach.

. . . .

> At first, through their lawyers, but later with progressively less and less assistance, the poor could make articulate and knowledgeable inputs into decision-making processes which affect their lives. This new access to the levers of policymaking might be an important first step in the efforts of the poor to gain some control of their own lives. The degree to which this control can be achieved is the degree to which a legal services programme can contribute to the alteration of the structure of poverty in this country.

---

†   Gathercole, R.J., "Legal Services and the Poor" in eds. R.G. Evans and M.J. Trebilcock, *Lawyers and the Consumer Interest* (Toronto: Butterworth & Co. (Canada) Ltd., 1982), 407–19, 423, 425–29. Reprinted by permission of Professors Robert G. Evans and Michael J. Trebilcock.

It is almost 15 years since these goals of the legal aid movement were articulated. During that time virtually every Canadian province that did not already have one, has developed a legal aid program to provide at least the services envisioned by Smith. A Legal Services Corporation has been established in the United States as an outgrowth of the legal services work started in the O.E.O. and the United Kingdom has made some significant, if somewhat overdue improvements in its legal aid services. Nevertheless, the poor in each of these countries are at best only marginally better off for all of these efforts and even the relatively limited goals articulated by Reginald Heber Smith 60 years ago have not been achieved. It is doubtful that they will be in the foreseeable future.

What went wrong? Although the leaders of the legal aid movement in Canada, and elsewhere, were motivated by the best intentions and a genuine desire to help alleviate the problems of the poor, they did not and perhaps could not fully understand their problems. Contrary to their expectations, the fundamental problems of the poor are not susceptible to traditional legal solutions. They are not the traditional middle class legal problems that lawyers are familiar with. As Bernard Veney, Executive Director of the National Clients' Council in the United States put it:

The problems of low-income people are different from the problems of other people; and their cases must be handled differently. Most attorneys in private practice do not have, as a matter of routine, the skills necessary to practice law for poor people...low-income people have lives of constant crisis. What may be a casual matter for someone who has options is a life and death matter for a low-income person because one of the characteristics of poverty is the *absolute lack of options*. That lack of options may mean that to meet one crisis, people do something that is going to cause another crisis further down the line.

So it is not enough just to handle the legal matter that is there on the surface. Unless you are skilled at recognizing this problem, and skilled at recognizing what the possible remedies are, skilled enough to resolve the initial crisis but also take care of the longer-range crisis, you haven't done anything for low-income people.

Most legal aid programs, even if not so designed originally, have tended to develop according to the interests and priorities of lawyers providing the services rather than those of their clients. Legal services are traditionally provided on a one-to-one, private enterprise basis. The legal profession is generally identified with, and identifies itself with the *status quo*. Lawyers cannot accept the fact that the problems of the poor can only be solved through a fundamental restructuring of traditional institutions, not

by suing someone in a court of law. While the motivations ascribed by one observer to the early development of legal aid in the United Kingdom (that "[it] was produced to justify ideologically the operations of the legal system, which was primarily concerned with property interests, by giving the appearance of making equal access to the legal system available to the lower classes") may not be applicable to recent developments in legal aid, the fact remains that the legal profession remains identified in the minds of the poor with the source of their problems rather than with the solution. An equally important consideration is that governments have consistently underfunded legal services, partly because the poor are not a powerful political constituency but also because government departments and agencies are prime targets of legal aid lawyers. Both of these factors will be discussed more fully later. First, a brief history of the development of legal aid is necessary.

JUDICARE VERSUS LEGAL SERVICES

Civil legal aid has generally followed one of the two models — Judicare or legal services. The Judicare model utilizes members of the private bar as the prime deliverers of legal services. They are paid on a fee-for-service basis, usually in accordance with a specified tariff. The administrative responsibility for most Judicare plans is assigned to the legal profession. The underlying philosophy of Judicare is to provide the poor with access to the same services as are available to the rest of society. Judicare plans tend to concentrate on providing legal assistance for serious criminal offences and for civil actions in superior courts. For example, 41% of the Ontario legal aid budget in 1978 was spent on criminal offences and 27% on divorce and other civil matters. There were only 184 small claims and 578 review board cases out of a total of more than 24,000 civil cases. There were insufficient welfare, landlord-tenant, or unemployment insurance cases to justify a separate heading in the annual report. Judicare's emphasis on litigation stresses a "problem solving" rather than "problem preventing" approach. The emphasis is on ensuring that the poor are accorded their "day in court" rather than on substantive reform of existing laws and institutions.

The legal services model did not become a significant alternative to Judicare until the 1960s and early 1970s. This model stresses the use of full-time salaried lawyers and non-legal personnel operating from offices located in low-income communities, generally of the "storefront" variety. Emphasis is placed on providing legal services in areas of prime concern to the poor — welfare, housing, unemployment insurance, workers' compensation, small claims, domestic disputes — providing assistance to groups and organizations in the community, education programs and law reform activities such as lobbying and test case litigation.

The state philosophy of the legal services movement is that the goal of legal aid should be nothing less than the eradication of poverty. Poverty is a question of power — or, more particularly, lack of it — and the role of the lawyer is to assist the poor person to gain the power to change the institutions, both private and public, which contribute to his poverty and control his life. Case-by-case legal services must be provided but only within this overall framework. In jurisdictions that have adopted the legal services model, administration of legal aid is generally the responsibility of an independent board or commission rather than the legal profession.

For years proponents of the two models carried on a sometimes heated debate over their respective merits. Questions of cost-effectiveness, the efficacy of professional control and whether lawyers had any role to play in social change were argued at great length. Generally, the traditional bar and most politicians tended to support the development of Judicare, professional administrative control and limitations on law reform and lobbying activities by legal aid lawyers. Legal services lawyers criticized Judicare for its adherence to traditional legal solutions and its failure to deal with the "real" problems of the poor.

However, it became apparent that neither approach had all the answers and both had important strengths and weaknesses. As a result, most jurisdictions have developed mixed civil legal aid systems, albeit with the emphasis on one of the two models.

. . . .

Canada, as it often does, has borrowed extensively from both the United States and the United Kingdom. Legal aid in Canada falls within provincial constitutional jurisdiction as part of the administration of justice, although the federal government does provide financial assistance to the provinces for legal aid in criminal matters based on a negotiated formula which can vary from province to province. All provinces, with the exception of Prince Edward Island and New Brunswick, have well-developed legal aid programs. Most have a mixed Judicare and legal services system. Quebec, Saskatchewan and Nova Scotia have adopted legal services as the basic model with a limited Judicare component. The other provinces have adopted the Judicare model.

Both the Manitoba and British Columbia plans have a legal services component. Ontario has a fairly extensive network of legal services offices (approximately 40 throughout the province as of September 1980). They initially developed outside the Ontario Legal Aid Plan, are not referred to in the *Legal Aid Act* and have, at best, only the grudging support of the Law Society of Upper Canada. Funding of these offices is now provided for by regulation, amounting to $4.75 million for the 1980–81 fiscal year, and they now are part of the Ontario Legal Aid Plan under the general supervision of the Clinical Funding Committee which allocates their funding and closely monitors their operations. For example, it is empowered by regulation to require a clinic to employ a solicitor and to train personnel to an approved standard.

The Ontario Legal Aid Plan arose from the report of a joint committee of the Law Society and the government of Ontario released in March 1965. This report drew heavily on the English experience in recommending a Judicare plan to be operated by the Law Society and made no reference at all to the American experience. On the other hand, the Quebec Plan, established in 1972 and the Saskatchewan Plan, established in 1974 adopted the American legal services model which by then was well established. Service under both plans is provided primarily by full-time salaried lawyers. However, the Quebec plan has a more significant Judicare component, and is less community based than the Saskatchewan plan. The boards of directors of the Quebec offices (or "bureaux") are appointed by the Commission de Services Juridiques which administers the plan while boards of the Saskatchewan clinics are elected by the communities for which they operate. The Saskatchewan Plan also has a specific mandate to undertaken law reform and related activities. Other provinces have drawn from the Ontario, Quebec and Saskatchewan plans for inspiration depending upon the political views of each provincial government and its susceptibility to the pressures of the provincial bar.

The legal services offices established in Ontario, British Columbia and Manitoba, also imitated the American experience. The first such office in Ontario, Parkdale Community Legal Services, located in a low income area of Toronto, was one of four such offices funded by the federal Department of Health and Welfare on the basis of a study which strongly supported the American approach. Parkdale also received funding from the Council for Legal Education in Professional Responsibility, a branch of the Ford Foundation, which also funded a number of legal services offices in the United States affiliated with law schools as Parkdale was with Osgoode Hall Law School of York University.

The early development of legal aid in Canada produced some tension between the proponents of Judicare and the supporters of the legal services movement. This was particularly true in Ontario, where Judicare was well established and the Law Society was particularly powerful. After a decade or more of relatively peaceful co-existence, however, the clear consensus is that both models are needed. The traditional bar has overcome its initial paranoia about legal services offices, in part because the fundamental social changes that they feared and legal services lawyers hoped for have not materialized, and in part because legal services offices have created work for private lawyers, both through direct referral and through bringing legal action against their clients. Legal services lawyers, on the other hand, have come to accept that the private bar has a role to play in legal aid, both because of its special expertise and its ability to take cases where legal services lawyers might have conflicts of interest.

THE INADEQUACIES OF LEGAL AID

"Comprehensive" legal aid plans have existed for a decade or more, but the fact remains that the poor still have, at best, only limited access to legal services. One main reason is that legal aid is funded from public monies and governments have failed to provide more than minimal funding. This is partly because the poor do not constitute an effective political constituency, but also because the most effective legal aid programs are continually engaged in fighting government agencies. Accordingly, politicians react with, at best, grudging support and, at worst, outright hostility.

. . . .

A recent Canadian example is the decision of the Saskatchewan government in June 1978 to require the legal services offices in that province to cease their practice of referring criminal cases to private lawyers under the Judicare component of the Saskatchewan plan, while concentrating themselves on the provision of the civil legal aid. The legal services lawyers felt that the demands for services could best be met by utilizing the experience of the private bar in criminal matters and developing their own expertise in civil matters, such as housing and welfare. The government, however, stated that budgetary restraints were necessary and money could be saved if the offices did the criminal work themselves because using private lawyers cost more. This, of course, meant that legal services lawyers would be spending most of their time on criminal matters and would have to neglect what they considered to be the more important civil cases. It was not clear whether the government was motivated solely by financial concerns or whether it wanted to limit the effectiveness of legal services offices. After the Saskatoon Legal Assistance Clinic threatened to close rather than comply with the government's directive, the government backed down and agreed to conduct a review of the province's legal aid system. However, the government appears to have succeeded in the end. The 1979–80 *Annual Report* of the Saskatchewan Community Legal Services Commission showed that the number of criminal cases completed by the private bar in the fiscal year dropped to 505 from 2,562 the previous fiscal year. Private bar civil cases also were reduced from 281 to 120.

Governments continue to refuse to fund legal aid adequately. In 1977 Clinton Bamberger claimed that it would cost $500 million to provide basic minimum legal services to the poor in the United States. This represented 5 lawyers for every 10,000 poor people, compared to the ratio in the general population of 14 lawyers for every 10,000 persons. This year, after years of inflation the Legal Services Corporation budget is still under $300 million, with no chance of any increase in the next few years.

In Canada the situation is no better. In Ontario, legal aid is funded through the Ministry of the Attorney General. The Ministry's entire budget represents less that 1% of the provincial budget ($165.5 million out of $17.1 billion in 1980–81). The legal aid component is $43.3 million or about 26% of that total, but a portion of that amount (about $8 million) is received from the federal government as a contribution towards the provision of criminal legal aid. In other words 1/4 of 1% of the provincial budget is allocated to legal aid. The legal aid expenditure in Quebec ($32 million in the 1978–79 fiscal year) has not increased significantly in the past few years. New Brunswick continues to refuse to establish a civil legal aid program mainly for financial reasons. Similar situations exist in other provinces.

Even with adequate funding however, there are inherent weaknesses in existing legal aid programs which result in seriously inadequate access of the poor to legal services. The main weakness is the emphasis on individual case service. This results in a curative rather than a preventive approach to legal problems. It also means that available legal aid resources cannot begin to cope with the potential caseload let alone undertake effective law reform, lobbying or other group-oriented activities.

The emphasis on case-by-case service of both Judicare and legal services plans results from different factors. The Judicare approach is predicated on this type of service delivery. The legal profession is organized on a free enterprise, single lawyer, single client basis and Judicare seeks to apply this approach in delivering legal services to the poor. Legal services offices, however, have to some extent been forced to emphasize individual cases by funding agencies. While lawyers' training and interests and client demand are also important factors, the requirements of funding agencies that individual services be stressed is the predominant reason for the "caseload crisis" faced by most legal services offices. The evaluation of a legal services office is based on its caseload. This is easier to measure than more nebulous factors such as acceptance in the community, long-term interests of clients and law reform. It is also easier to persuade politicians that public money is being properly used if something concrete, e.g., a thousand cases handled, has resulted from the expenditure.

There are other inadequacies in both legal aid models which have to be considered. Judicare suffers from the underlying assumption that all the poor need is access to the same services that lawyers traditionally provide. Not only does this ignore the specific legal problems of the poor, most of which are substantively different than those of the middle class, but reliance on the private bar also creates particular problems. Most law offices are physically and psychologically inaccessible to the poor. They are located some distance from most poor communities and are designed to appeal to traditional clients. Most poor people find this a completely foreign environment, adding to the pressures of dealing with lawyers. The poor person also identifies the private bar with the "other side" — landlords, finance companies, government agencies — that represent the source of his problem.

The private lawyer lacks expertise in the legal problems of the poor. The intricacies of social welfare legislation, for example, are not easily grasped by handling one or two such cases a year. Conflicts of interest can and do arise between the poor and other existing or potential clients of the lawyer (for example in landlord-tenant and debtor-creditor cases). There is an inability to identify patterns and to organize strategies to deal with underlying problems. Most Judicare plans lack effective research components resulting in a great deal of duplication of effort, as individual lawyers continue to re-invent the wheel. The Ontario Legal Aid plan, in existence for some 13 years, has only recently created a research facility and then only because it was one of the conditions imposed by the provincial Attorney General for his support of a tariff increase.

The method of payment — fee for service, usually in accordance with an established tariff — also limits the coverage which can be provided by Judicare. It is not acceptable politically or economically to expend $500 of public funds in an attempt to recover $50 in unpaid welfare benefits, to sue for $200 in Small Claims Court or to force a landlord to effect small but necessary repairs or to cease harassing tenants. Legal aid assistance is therefore given only in very special cases. In Ontario, for example, clients are entitled to legal aid services for indictable criminal matters and for civil cases brought in the "higher" courts. In other civil cases the test is whether a person of modest means would retain a lawyer in the circumstances. Given the present level of legal fees, the answer is usually negative. The result is that Judicare plans tend to concentrate on providing services for serious criminal cases, traditional civil lawsuits (e.g., motor vehicle accidents, collections) and divorce and other family matters. The Ontario Legal Aid Plan, a representative Judicare plan, shows a very high proportion of certificates granted for these types of cases. In his oft-quoted article "Practicing law for Poor People," Stephen Wexler pointed out that "poor people are not just like rich people without money. Poor people do not have legal problems like those of private plaintiffs and defendants in law school casebooks." Judicare plans are premised on the opposite assumption and limit themselves to providing services for those "casebook" problems.

Outside of the United States, most legal services programs came into being because of the deficiencies of Judicare and were specifically tailored to deal with the particular problems of the poor. The salaried lawyers employed in these offices were expected to — and did — develop an expertise in these areas. In jurisdictions where legal services were the basic delivery model, such as the United States and Quebec, provision was made for a substantial research component to assist lawyers in the field and to identify particular problem areas which might require collective action. Emphasis was also supposed to be placed on law reform activities, both judicial and legislative.

However, as noted above, the emphasis in legal services programs as in their Judicare counterparts has been on the provision of individual case services. Although the type of case emphasized has been somewhat different than in Judicare programs, the fact remains that the essential service provided is the same — problem-solving on a one-to-one basis rather than preventive services on a collective basis as was the hope of many of the early proponents of the legal services movement.

There are a number of reasons for this. First and foremost is the inadequate supply of lawyers and other trained personnel to meet the demand. All legal services offices are inundated with requests for service for people who heretofore had no place to turn. The "caseload crisis" has resulted in services becoming increasingly routine, often to the detriment of the client, a high turnover of personnel and a search for some way of limiting demand or choosing only the most significant or deserving cases (by, for example, limiting office hours, requiring appointments, accepting only certain types of cases — all attributes of traditional legal offices). The caseload crisis also creates increasing concern with ethical questions raised by the established codes of professional conduct. These codes, which were drafted with traditional legal practice in mind, are not always helpful in addressing the issues raised in legal services offices. Is the lawyer's obligation to provide services to as many people as possible or to provide a high standard of service to a limited number? The codes of professional conduct appear to demand both. The present situation in legal services is summed up by Gary Bellow:

> [The] realities [of demands for and supply of legal services to the poor] create enormous pressures for routinized, mass processing of cases. It is posited that, given the need, most recipients would rather receive a little help than none at all. The legal aid bar, which is subsidized, after all, to serve the community, feels it must respond to this need by taking many, many more cases than can be carefully, aggressively handled. The patterns of practice that emerge are the 'best that can be done' under these circumstances.

The problem with this notion (which is widely articulated within programs) is that it functions far more as justification than explanation. Obviously, the service being offered does not simply reflect what clients 'really want'. Clients are not told they are receiving only minimal assistance, or that there may be approaches to some of their problems which are not being explored with them. They are also not afforded a choice between efforts which might more generally affect the conditions in the neighbourhood or community in which they live, and some lesser attention to their immediate concerns. What people 'want' is inevitably indeterminate, depending on their knowledge and what they consider possible and desirable. It's an unusual client who would know without being so advised, that a lawyer less committed to routine service might stimulate litigation and concerted action to control exclusions of their children from school, or might offer a way of doing something about the garbage on the street, or the rats in the walls.

It may be argued that more money and more lawyers can overcome these problems. Even if it were realistic (and it is not) to expect that sufficient public money would be made available, this is at best a simplistic solution. We are only scratching the surface of the potential "legal" problems of the poor. All of the lawyers presently practising in Canada would not be sufficient to deal even with the articulated legal problems of the poor. New approaches and solutions have to be found. The traditional method of solving disputes through the courts and quasi-judicial bodies is not only expensive and time-consuming, but in many cases it is totally ineffective. Enforcement of judgments is not undertaken by the state but is left to the individual litigant. Most people lack both the resources and the ability to deal with the time-consuming and somewhat archaic enforcement process with its judgement debtor examinations, writs of execution and garnishment proceedings.

. . . .

If the legal profession as presently structured, even if supplemented by trained non-legal personnel, cannot adequately deal with the problems of the poor, what is the answer? The assumption is that increased access to lawyers and traditional legal services will benefit the poor. In fact that is not the case. The poor need services which will assist them in dealing effectively with their problems; this cannot be done on a case-by-case basis. While there is, and will continue to be, a huge demand for individual case service, the resources do not presently exist to fill that demand and alternative approaches must be considered.

. . . .

The first priority is to determine what services are, in fact, required. Instead of assuming that the poor need more "legal" services, funding agencies should ascertain the views of the poor on this and other issues on this and other issues affecting them. For example, what problems do the poor perceive as most important and what type of solution are they looking for? Do they seek legal assistance because they perceive their problems as legal ones and desire a legal solution or merely because the legal office is the only available alternative? The services should then be designed to meet the needs of the recipients; not, as is the case with present legal systems, the service deliverers.

Without adequate information it is difficult to predict what the future development of legal aid might or should be, but even a casual observation suggests that a fundamental restructuring of the provision of legal services to the poor is required, that greater emphasis should be placed on long term law reform and political organizing and that legislatures rather than courts should be the focus of these efforts.

. . . .

Community organization must also be a priority. An effective tenants' organization prepared to utilize techniques such as rent strikes is more effective in enforcing a landlord's repair obligations than any number of individual court cases, particularly given the problems of enforcement. The welfare bureaucracy is more likely to respond to the immediate pressure of an organized welfare group than to the strictures of a court. When a welfare cheque is not forthcoming on time, this type of pressure, unlike a time-consuming application to a court, can bring quick results. In 1972 Stephen Wexler argued that only effective community organizing could give the poor power to effect change. The passage of time has only proven the validity of this argument.

New methods of dispute resolution are also required. Traditional methods are slow, costly and ineffective. Too much emphasis is placed on due process rather than on effective decision-making. Procedures need to be streamlined and simplified so that individuals can effectively represent themselves. More emphasis should be placed on providing official assistance to persons appearing before tribunals. This would reduce the need for lawyers and allow more effective participation by the individuals concerned.

These changes would have serious ramifications for the legal profession. Lawyers are not necessarily the most effective lobbyists and they are certainly not trained to be organizers. They are trained to provide specific services to individual clients. This means that the lawyer's role in providing services to the poor is limited. Most bar associations and professional governing bodies have opposed any developments along these lines, suggesting that the

287

profession could not operate effectively in the type of service system.

The provision of legal services to the poor should be the responsibility of persons, both lawyers and non-lawyers, specifically trained for that purpose. How should they be trained? There is no scope in this chapter for a discussion of the problems in legal education but there is no doubt that law schools have a dismal record of training lawyers to serve the poor. Law school curricula emphasize traditional legal subjects, with the special legal problems of the poor being dealt with in one or two courses with such titles as "Poverty Law" and "Law and the Poor", a phenomenon that caused Wexler to remark that "[these courses] serve a useful function by making it crystal clear that the remainder of the curriculum deals with law and the rich; they do little, however, to change the law schools' treatment of legal problems, or their perception of the proper roles and concerns of a lawyer." The calendar of the People's Law School of Los Angeles, California, a law school whose aim is "the development and training of lawyers dedicated to the struggle for social change in the communities of oppressed peoples", puts it more graphically:

> In the past, traditional legal institutions have mass-produced lawyers whose concept of lawyering consisted of joining an elite organization dedicated to maintaining the national socio-economic *status quo*, as well as the lawyer's superior position in it, by serving the rich or acting as legal functionaries of the state.... Existing law schools, at their worst, destroy the development of socially-conscious students, and at their best allow only a limited development of skills by a highly motivated and often select group. Traditional legal education almost uniformly teaches the skills which are required to serve the establishment; the non-establishment student, if not an outcast, is nevertheless segregated with a small group concerned with what are institutionally considered the marginal interests of society: the areas of poverty, civil rights, labour and criminal law.

Specially trained people are needed to serve the interests of the poor. If the law schools are not prepared to meet this challenge, other institutions will, and the law schools will be limited to providing training to a limited portion of the legal services community.

In any legal aid system it is crucial that the poor have some control over the nature of the services to be provided. Most legal services plans recognize this and provide for representation of the client community on the board of directors of each legal services clinic. Invariably, however, client representation is limited to one-half or less. Sometimes express provision is made for lawyers and legal staff to form a majority of the board of directors; some-

times the client representation is specifically restricted, but, in either case, the poor are allowed only to participate in, but not control, the decision-making process. Given lawyers' ability and propensity to control meetings, it is unlikely that lawyers' influence would be seriously diminished even if non-lawyers had a majority on any board.

This is another example of the tension that exists between lawyers and the poor. Lawyers are not prepared to trust poor people to make the fundamental decisions about the nature, organization and priority of legal services that should be provided. At the 1978 National Legal Aid and Defender Association annual meeting in Washington, D.C., I saw this tension at work. The National Clients' Council was holding its annual meeting in association with NLADA, and a joint session was held to discuss the issue of client control. The clients were concerned that the tests laid down by the United States Congress concerning membership on the boards of clinics funded by the Legal Services Corporation were too restrictive, and they were specifically opposed to the legislative requirement that lawyers form a majority of the board. They were critical of the legal services lawyers whom they felt had not effectively fought this provision. The lawyers argued that it was Congress and not the profession that had established the guidelines. However, they did not seem uncomfortable with being given this control over legal services boards, and, in fact, tended to depend on it. Arguments ensued over how to provide effective client representation on boards. Most lawyers claimed that clients were not prepared to participate actively. Clients contended that the lawyers did not try hard enough to recruit good people. Despite the fact that the lawyers in the room were dedicated to helping the poor, and the clients were aware that they were not dealing with traditional lawyers, the gulf between the two groups was obvious and deep. The issue, simply put, was control — the lawyers had it and wanted to keep it; the clients wanted at the very least an equal share.

The issue is exacerbated by the fact that, like lawyers, governments are not prepared to give the poor effective control of legal aid programs. Governments, albeit influenced by the profession, established the requirement of lawyer control over legal aid, whether through administration of Judicare plans by the profession or through majority representation on the controlling bodies of legal services programs. This is not, of course, unique to legal aid. Governments always seem to feel safer with professionals in control of social programs.

Codes of Professional Conduct also support lawyer control. A lawyer is responsible for the conduct of any case he undertakes; he must take instructions from his individual client. Any attempt by outsiders, such as boards of directors, to interfere in a case must be resisted. Additionally, a lawyer is under a duty of confidentiality. He cannot disclose details of any case to outsiders without the express consent of the client or in other very limited circumstances. Therefore any attempt by a client-controlled board of directors to determine what cases should or should not be undertaken by lawyers in its employ, or how a particular case should be handled (e.g., whether it should be settled in the interest of the individual client or carried through to litigation in the hope of obtaining a favourable decision which might benefit a broader community) must, under the present Codes, be resisted by a lawyer. meaningful client input into the determination of the services to be provided and the manner of their provision seems possible by non-legal personnel not subject to the same professional constraints. This is not to say that these constraints are necessarily wrong in every case; only that they do militate against effective client control of legal services.

In the final analysis, whether the poor are to receive effective services from the legal profession either through the provision of traditional services by the established bar

or through a more sophisticated and responsive model, depends on whether governments and the people they represent are prepared to make that commitment. Even if the legal profession were to change fundamentally its outlook on legal aid and itself make a profound commitment to providing adequate services to the poor (an admittedly unlikely development) this would not be enough. To date, few, if any, governments or societies have shown any such inclination. There are too many vested interests to overcome. Governments, the economically and politically powerful, and the legal profession, have no immediate interest in alleviating the plight of the poor. Until we are prepared to accept that fundamental changes are required, we will continue to provide, always grudgingly, inadequate legal assistance. The underlying problems will continue to be ignored. The poor, it seems, will always be with us and justice will continue to identified with the Ritz Hotel.

Community Legal Clinics in Ontario[†]
M.J. Mossman

INTRODUCTION

"I would like to add significantly to the resources available to clinics...the clinics are in a position to take the law to those who need it most. It is almost trite to point out that a great many poor people have never been made aware of the right they enjoy under our laws.... The clinics, located in, and run by, local communities, can reach out to advise people of their rights. They take the law to the people...in doing all this, the clinics help convince the poor that they have a stake in this society."[1]

This 1982 statement by Ontario's Attorney-General is one of the positive statements that has been made about legal aid in Canada recently. While it is by no means Mr. McMurtry's first statement of support for the work of community clinics in Ontario, it is of special significance for two reasons. In the first place, it is a public statement of support for clinics in Ontario at a time when general policies of governmental restraint across Canada have resulted in significant, even fatal, cutbacks in legal aid programs.[2] Secondly, the statement demonstrates support for

increased resources for Ontario clinics at the very time when the Minister was deciding to offer only modest tariff increases to Ontario lawyers providing legal aid services under the complementary judicare program.[3] The possibility that resources for community clinics would actually be *increased* in the face of governmental restraint, and the inevitable pressure to restrict expenditures, thus suggests a very high level of support by the Attorney-General for community clinics.

The value of the Minister's personal support for community clinics is substantial; indeed, on some occasions in the past, his personal support appears to have been critical to their survival.[4] Clearly, the fact that the Ministry of the Attorney-General provides substantial funding for legal aid in Ontario, as well as his role under the Regulation in "designating" the funds for clinics out of the overall legal aid budget,[5] place the Minister in an enviable position to nurture community clinics in accordance with his personal support for them. That the Minister's support is desirable seems self-evident; the real issue is whether it is, by itself, the explanation for the survival of Ontario clinics in the face of widespread restraint and cutbacks.

It has become clear in the early 1980's that many legal aid programs, established with idealism and great

---

† Mossman, Mary Jane, "Community Legal Clinics in Ontario" (1983), 3 *Windsor Yearbook of Access to Justice* at 375–89, 394–402. Reprinted by permission of the author.

expectations in the 1960's and 1970's, have been all too easily eroded or destroyed as governmental restraint has become necessary in the face of an economic recession. For all practical purposes, legal aid has been regarded as just one more government program that is too expensive; there has been little or no recognition that legal services for the poor are any different from other social welfare programs. In this context, it is tempting to conclude that the reason that Ontario community clinics survive, even thrive, is the Minister's personal support for them. Such a conclusion, however, denies that the clinic movement has any inherent validity, for it assumes that their continued survival depends solely on his continued goodwill. More importantly, such a conclusion threatens the integrity of independent legal services; to say that legal services can be provided to the poor in Ontario only because, and so long as, the Minister supports the effort to do so by clinics, is to deny to clinics any capacity for independent legal representation of the poor. Even more significantly, it may also deny clinics capacity for any representation of the poor against, most frequently, the government whom the Attorney-General represents in law enforcement matters. The real issue is, therefore, whether Ontario clinics would have the capacity to provide independent legal services to the poor *in the absence of* Mr. McMurtry's personal support.

This paper is an exploration of the special nature of community clinics in Ontario. It asserts that Ontario clinics are unique in terms of their history, their structure, and their focus, and that no other system of clinics has such an inherent capacity to thrive independently of the Minister's personal support. Because of these special attributes, it also follows that no other clinic system has a greater opportunity to use its resources effectively to achieve the goal of equal justice for the poor. The challenge for Ontario clinics is to use their unique opportunity creatively and effectively toward achieving equal justice.[6]

IN THE BEGINNING: A BRIEF HISTORY

The history of community clinics in Ontario is not neat; like the clinic system itself, it is an amalgam of special circumstances relating to particular times in particular communities. The history is also organic and still evolving, and underlies both the structure which has developed and the focus of clinic work. The history of the clinics is also part of the overall history of legal aid in Ontario; an understanding of clinics within the overall legal aid system in Ontario is fundamental to appreciating their significance, both past and present.

"Modern" legal aid programs in Canada developed only recently. The first such program was established in Ontario by the *Legal Aid Act* in 1966.[7] Based on a report (the Joint Committee Report[8]) recommending the estab-

lishment of a publicly-funded legal aid program to replace the services previously provided by lawyers on a charitable basis, the new legal aid plan demonstrated that; "...legal aid should form part of the administration of justice in its broadest sense. It is no longer a charity but a right."[9] Recognition of this principle resulted in the implementation of legal aid programs in most of the Canadian provinces over the next few years.[10]

The establishment of publicly-funded legal aid programs in Canada was a very significant development, and their impact on courts, lawyers, and clients cannot be over-estimated.[11] More importantly, in a society committed to equality, the need for legal aid services is unquestioned.[12] In the context of the Ontario Legal Aid Plan, the objective of equality in the administration of justice was clearly stated; it was intended that the same legal aid services be made available to the poor as were already being provided to fee-paying clients.[13] With the benefit of hindsight, it is easy to appreciate that such a concept of "equal justice" was too narrow, and that the legal services which poor people most needed were those that responded to their problems, not to the problems of fee-paying clients. Gradually, it was recognized that the poor had legal problems quite different from those of the non-poor, and that Ontario's legal aid system, based on the norm of the fee-paying client, often did not provide appropriate assistance.[14] In addition, the Plan's services were criticized because they were provided by the same private practice lawyers who worked on behalf of fee-paying clients. Of course, the use of the same lawyers to provide services to rich and poor alike arguably represented the epitome of equal opportunity — if, but only if, both groups of clients required the same services. As it became clear that lawyers acting for the poor needed to be familiar with poverty law, it also became clear that specialization was desirable and that salaried lawyers were needed because they could devote their energies solely to the legal needs of the poor.

At the same time that such issues were being discussed about the scope of the Plan's legal aid services and the appropriate means of providing them, concerns were also expressed about the legal profession's continued monopoly on decision making in the context of a publicly-funded program. While it might have been appropriate for the Law Society of Upper Canada to administer the earlier charitable legal aid program, it was suggested that the public who paid for the program, and the poor to whom it was directed, deserved some opportunity for input in decisions about legal aid services.[15] These concerns must be understood in the context of scepticism whether lawyers could be trusted to act effectively in the public interest, and increasing concern about their monopoly on legal services. In several provinces which established legal aid programs after 1966, such arguments bolstered the desire for an independent corporation with a Board composed of some non-lawyer members.[16] In Ontario, by contrast, the *Legal Aid Act* granted responsibility for the administration of legal aid to the Law Society of Upper Canada, the governing body of the Ontario legal profession.[17]

The alleged deficiencies of the Ontario Plan were frequently debated in the late 1960's and early 1970's against the backdrop of the American legal services programs and President Johnson's War on Poverty, as well as the Canadian concept of "the just society". In a general way, the ideas about equality of opportunity were fuelled by a growing mistrust of professionals and their monopoly on information and skills to generate a desire for increased community or public participation in decision making and collective action. Notwithstanding that the Ontario Legal Aid Plan had signified a major societal change in attitude as recently as 1966, the currency of such ideas inevitably led to dissatisfaction with both the goals and the methods of the Plan.

Essentially, it was the critics of the Plan who initiated and established alternative legal aid services in response to "unmet needs"; and it is these services which formed the nucleus of the community clinic system now in place. For example, the need to provide assistance for specialized poverty law problems motivated (at least partly) the organization of Injured Workers' Consultants, a program in which injured workers themselves assisted others with compensation claims. The scarcity of lawyers who were familiar with compensation claims as well as the group's desire to engage in self-help, contributed to the creation of a "clinic" with no lawyer involvement at all, a model decidedly different from the Plan's legal aid services.[18] Similarly, the need for help in a developing legal field contributed to the establishment of the Canadian Environmental Law Association; the "clinic" undertook litigation "in the public interest" and acted for client groups, activities which were not then recognized by the Plan as being needed legal services.[19] At the same time, Parkdale Community Legal Services was established, using law students to provide legal services to the poor.[20] Early on, Parkdale decided to confine its services to a defined geographical community and to limit its services to matters for which the Plan would not provide a certificate; a little later, Parkdale also began to set up structures for community input in decisions about the services it offered, thereby demonstrating a need for services other than those offered by the Plan.

All of these early clinics were established in response to "unmet legal needs", and to fill the "gaps" in the services available from the Plan. As is evident from the brief description above, however, early clinics were designed to meet a number of different objectives, using a variety of means. They did not follow any coherent plan or overall set of priorities for alternative legal services. Yet the ideas originally generated by the establishment of these and similar clinics have evolved as the articulated principles of existing community clinics in Ontario. In particular, the experiences of the early clinics identified two principles. One principle is the need to focus clinic services on the legal needs of the poor; in particular, the need to respond to the real needs of poor people, utilizing specialized personnel that includes both lawyers and community workers. The second principle is the need for community involvement in decision making, especially the need to involve the poor community and legal aid clinic clients in decisions about their legal aid services.

The early clinics must also receive credit for the development of a third principle, that of clinic independence. As is apparent, all of the early legal aid clinics were established as alternatives to the government-funded legal aid Plan. On this basis, of course, they could be described as independent of the Plan in every respect. It is unclear to what extent they were also independent of their initial funding sources: the federal Department of Justice, LIP (Local Initiatives Program) grants, university funding and private foundation grants. Parkdale was even funded initially by the American Ford Foundation.[21] However, while it may be that the early clinics were not independent of their initial funding sources, it is nonetheless clear that they operated independently of the Plan in their formative years. The Plan did not direct their activities and accepted no responsibility for them financially. Thus, the third principle which emerges from an assessment of the early experience of Ontario clinics is the independence of clinics from the Ontario Legal Aid Plan. The clinics received no direction nor any financial support from the Plan. They were therefore fully autonomous alternate legal aid clinics, at least *vis-à-vis* the Plan.

Clinic independence from the Plan contributed to the intensity of the debate about legal aid services in Ontario in the early 1970's. As experience with the Plan increased, there were demands for new services, extended office hours and decentralized office locations (particularly in Metro Toronto).[22] There were also demands for public participation and more appropriate delivery models. Eventually, a Task Force was established in January 1974 to examine and evaluate legal aid in Ontario.[23] The Task Force's Report (the Osler Report) later that year recommended a mixture of delivery systems (complementary models) for legal aid services, including in appropriate circumstances the staffed neighbourhood legal aid clinic.[24] The Task Force also recommended the creation of an independent non-profit corporation, Legal Aid Ontario.[25]

The conclusions of the Osler Task Force were regarded as official recognition of the validity of the early clinics' objections to the Plan. In a brief to the Ontario Government,[26] the early clinics supported the Report's recommendations and urged the creation of a new legal aid corporation in which neither the Law Society nor government representatives should have any special status.

However, the brief is also important for identifying the fiscal dilemma then faced by the early clinics:

> There are a number of community based groups that have been providing legal services on an experimental basis to people not normally reached by the private bar. The existence of these groups was a major impetus for setting up the Task Force, they served as the models for many of the Task Force recommendations, and the Report recommends that they be given support by Legal Aid. These groups are in urgent need of funds. Without further monies almost all of them will fold by the end of the year [1976]. We urge the government and other funding sources to respond quickly, before it is too late. These groups form a solid foundation on which to build and develop community legal services. They must not be allowed to die.[27]

The response was a decision that the Ontario Legal Aid plan would fund community legal services projects[28] and the proclamation of a new Regulation under the *Legal Aid Act* in January 1976, the clinical funding Regulation.[29] This decision marked the end of one era and the beginning of another for community clinics. The Regulation authorized the Plan to provide funding to "independent community-based clinical delivery systems",[30] but only "clinical delivery system" was defined in the Regulation.[31] The reference to "independent" clinics, was, moreover, puzzling; it is difficult to understand how the clinics were to remain "independent" of the Plan once the Plan assumed funding responsibilities — and the ambiguity of this reference has produced both immediate and lasting tensions within the clinic system.

The immediate concerns for clinic autonomy were evidenced in ongoing difficulties about the Plan's funding arrangements for them, and by different perceptions of such matters as the confidentiality of client files.[32] In June 1978, the Attorney-General appointed Mr. Justice Grange[33] to review the operation of the clinical funding Regulation and

> to have regard...to the need for independence of clinical delivery systems, funded under the Regulation, the need for accountability for the expenditure of public funds, the need to maintain good standards of service to the public, the need to deliver service at a reasonable cost to the taxpayer, and the need for orderly growth and development of the clinical portion of the Ontario Legal Aid Plan.[34]

The Report of the Commission on Clinical Funding (the *Grange Report*) concluded that clinics funded by the Plan should have autonomy with respect to both policy

and administration, "subject only to accountability for the public funds advanced and for the legal competence of the services rendered."[35] In the words of the Report, the Plan may interfere with the operation of clinics "only if [the Plan] can bring the interference within one or other of the public's legitimate spheres of interest."[36]

In accordance with the *Grange Report's* recommendations, a new clinic funding Regulation was proclaimed in June 1979,[37] repealing and replacing the earlier one. The new Regulation again provided authority for the Plan to fund "independent" community organizations;[38] once again, "independent" was not defined. The new Regulation also established a new structure for funding (and defunding) clinics,[39] along with a new five-person Committee reporting directly to Convocation of the Law Society of Upper Canada and responsible for the administration of Ontario clinics.[40]

In the year since 1979, the clinic system in Ontario has continued to grow and prosper. With the funding of a new clinic in Sioux Lookout in February 1983, the total number of clinics had reached 41, and the 1982–83 annual budget had grown to almost seven million dollars.[41] More significantly, however, the uniqueness of their pattern of development has more clearly emerged; the combination of the focus of clinic work, the structures for decision making in the clinic system and the nature of community involvement in clinic legal services makes Ontario clinics uniquely capable of effective progress toward equal justice for the poor. To a great extent, the history of Ontario clinics as alternative legal aid services and the less receptive environment in Ontario (at least compared to some other Canadian provinces) has resulted in a community clinic system which has more inherent capacity to carry out its mandate than any others. Ironically, the apparent intransigence of the Law Society and the difficulties between clinics and the Plan seem to have produced a system of community clinics which is more effective than anywhere else. What follows is an analysis of why this is so, focusing on the three principles which have been identified: scope of clinic services, structures for decision making in the clinic system and community involvement in clinic legal service.

ONTARIO CLINIC: THEIR UNIQUE CHARACTERISTICS

Scope of Clinic Services

The scope of services provided by Ontario clinics is the product of the history of legal aid in Ontario. The Ontario Legal Aid Plan adopted the judicare delivery system, using private practice lawyers to provide legal aid services modelled on the services usually provided to fee-paying clients. Use of this model naturally resulted in the extension of legal aid services to those problems for which a fee-paying client would retain a lawyer: proceedings before the Supreme Court, or a county or district court or where a client was charged with an indictable offence.[42] In other proceedings, the legal aid client could have representation only subject to the discretion of the area director of the Plan: proceedings in provincial court (family division), small claims court, boards and tribunals; where the client was charged with an offence which would be tried in a summary conviction proceeding (including a violation of a municipal bylaw); or in drawing documents, negotiating settlements, or giving advice "wherever the subject matter or nature thereof is properly or customarily within the scope of the professional duties of a barrister and solicitor."[43]

Perhaps because the latter activities were regarded as less important to fee-paying clients, the legislation denied these services "as of right" to legal aid clients in Ontario and made them subject to the area directors' discretion. Regardless of the reason for the legislative choice, it affected the scope of services initially provided by the alternative legal aid clinics; essentially clinics focussed on the "gaps" in the Plan's legal aid services, and provided "poverty law" services. In doing so, clinics transformed the concept of legal aid in Ontario; by focusing on the legal needs of the poor rather than on the existing needs of fee-paying clinics, clinics extended the full range of services *needed by the poor* in the justice system. From the early clinics' perspective, if it was important to a welfare mother to pursue a claim before the Social Assistance Review Board, then legal aid representation should be available even if such services were not generally required by fee-paying clients. Furthermore, if a group of mothers on welfare wanted to submit a brief on retraining allowances to the Minister, legal aid representation should be available, just as fee-paying clients would obtain legal assistance in making briefs to government on matters of concern to them.

By 1978, the Grange Commission fully endorsed such clinic activities on behalf of the poor[44] and the need for such activities has also been widely accepted in other jurisdictions, both in Canada and elsewhere.[45] Yet the Ontario experience has special significance because it appears to be the only jurisdiction in which there are two completely separate specialized systems in place of delivering legal aid services. That is, while the judicare system operates to provide representation in court proceedings pursuant to the *Legal Aid Act*, the clinics provide legal advice and representation in matters for which certificates may not be granted. Even more significantly, community clinics have gradually directed attention to those legal problems for which certificates are almost never, or only infrequently, granted: welfare, rent review, workers' compensation, unemployment insurance, some immigration and debtor problems, tenancy agreements, etc. On this basis, the clinics have become "specialists in poverty law" problems while the judicare program has continued to extend legal aid services

to the poor on the same terms as it is available to fee-paying clients.[46] The clinics are staffed by lawyers and community legal workers whose interest, skills and training reflect the clinics' service priorities; the private bar, with interests, skills and training in traditional legal advocacy, provides legal representation in criminal, family and some civil matters to both legal aid and fee-paying clients.

The special significance of this functional division of roles in Ontario must be understood by contrast to clinic arrangements in other Canadian provinces in which the clinics conduct "intake" functions for the whole legal aid system, offer substantial legal aid advocacy before criminal and family courts and also make referrals to the private bar in the fee-for-service arrangement.[47] In such cases, both clinic objectives and the functions of personnel are broad and complex. Moreover, it may be difficult to balance competing needs so as to find the necessary time and creativity to prepare a brief on behalf of welfare mothers, for example, and at the same time prepare for a criminal trial. By contrast, the Ontario clinics have an inherent capacity to focus on the specialized legal problems of the poor and to advocate purposefully on their behalf; the Ontario clinic system is an affirmative action program directed to achieving equal justice and capable of performing as a driving force on behalf of the poor. And Ontario clinics feel freer to specialize in the legal problems of the poor, knowing that other legal problems, for which traditional advocacy solutions are more appropriate, can be provided by the judicare program and by personnel who are appropriately trained to do so.[48]

The division of functions between the clinic system and the judicare program in Ontario thus has immense potential for the objectives of clinics. In contrast to jurisdictions in which clinics have become the primary model for delivering legal aid services, the Ontario system permits a specialization of functions for clinics and private practice lawyers which is arguably more efficient. For clinics, however, the real significance is that specialization permits them to really take on the legal problems of the poor and become their effective advocates in the justice system. Ontario clinics need not be merely band-aids because the overall legal aid system permits, and even directs, them to focus their energies on systemic poverty law problems, leaving the representation of accused persons to the private bar.

The clearest evidence of the scope of services which clinics are intended to provide is found in the clinic funding Regulation under the *Legal Aid Act*, which provides that funding for clinics is based on the delivery of:

...legal and paralegal services or both, including activities reasonably designed to encourage access to such services or to further such services and services designed solely to promote the legal welfare of a community.[49]

Quite clearly, the Regulation endorses activities by clinics beyond traditional advocacy and authorizes clinics to engage in action on behalf of the clients to promote the legal welfare of the poor. Since 1979, the clinic contract or certificate, which authorizes funding for each clinic, has also defined the scope of services in the same wording.[50] Thus, both the clinic funding Regulation and the clinic certificate authorize clinics to undertake effective action on behalf of poor clients.

The specialized function of Ontario clinics and their clear mandate to advocate for equal justice for the poor make them unique as legal aid clinics. They are also somewhat unique because the scope of services they offer was not actively designed, but rather grew out of the desire to respond to unmet needs of the judicare system. To say that legal aid services now provided by clinics and the judicare program are complementary is not, however, to suggest that they are without tension. Particularly because of increasing needs and decreasing resources, the judicare program in Ontario may now be in some jeopardy.[51] For this reason (among others), there have been suggestions that some of the services now provided by the judicare program might better be transferred to clinics and that the intake work of area legal aid offices could also be done by clinics. While such proposals may appear superficially attractive, they present a real threat — to the poor — of a loss of legal aid services specializing in poverty law and advocating, in the broadest sense of the word, on behalf of the poor community. The danger for Ontario clinics is that by acquiring the workload of the judicare program, they will inevitably fall prey to the problems of multi-purpose clinics for which there is ample evidence in other jurisdictions. This conclusion does not mean that a clinic system might not be an appropriate means of providing some services now delivered by the judicare program in Ontario, but it does mean that there are serious, even tragic, disadvantages to utilizing the existing community clinic system to deliver judicare services. To do so would mean that the poor would lose their advocates for systemic change in Ontario's justice system.

. . . .

ONTARIO CLINICS IN THE 1980s — AN ASSESSMENT[52]

The preceding analysis of the history of clinics in Ontario, and of the characteristics which make them uniquely capable of surviving in the face of economic recession, is intended as an assessment of the inherent strength of the clinic system in Ontario. In my view, there are significant differences between the Ontario clinic system and clinics which have developed in other jurisdictions. Although this analysis has shown the inherent strength of Ontario clinics and their unique capacity for survival, it would be wrong

to conclude that they are invulnerable. Indeed, by demonstrating the careful balance which has been achieved in the Ontario clinic system, this analysis also points to the delicacy of the balance which must be maintained. In my opinion, community clinics in Ontario have the capacity to meet the legal services crises of the 1980's, just as they have done in the preceding decades, but the emerging issues require an appreciation of community clinics and their potential on the part of government, the legal profession and clinics.

Renewing the Service Mandate: Clinics and the Legal Profession

In this analysis, I have tried to show that the history of Ontario clinics has resulted in a Regulation which defines a broad scope of services; indeed, I have suggested that the Regulation provides a mandate for Ontario clinics to take on the systemic legal problems of the poor rather than to be limited to merely *ad hoc* remedies. A service mandate direct to promoting "the legal welfare of a community" presents both an opportunity and a challenge to eliminate inequality in the justice system.

In relation to the service mandate, there are important choices presently facing Ontario clinics. In the first place, individual clinics must define more systematically the scope of services they want to provide. Too frequently, clinics in Ontario have simply responded to the service needs which have "walked in the front door"; such a passive response approach inevitably means that other legal needs, perhaps more compelling because less often recognized, are not met at all. Moreover, the case-by-case approach, by itself, may frequently do little or nothing to promote the legal welfare of the poor. Thus, while there is a basic clinic responsibility to get involved in the day-to-day legal problems faced by the poor, clinic boards must also systematically assess the nature of the services they provide in terms of the real problems of their low-income community. In addition, both clinic boards and staff must continually reassess the strategies they use to most effectively promote the legal welfare of the community. Moreover, in the context of a clinic system with inherent capacity to achieve so much effective equality for the poor, and taking account of the scarce resources available, clinics as a group may need to begin defining the limits of community control when a board is unwilling to define a service mandate for its community which goes beyond the band-aid *ad hoc* approach.

The second issue facing clinics is the need to define the limits of the service mandate set out in the Regulation, particularly when clinics are actively providing legal services in addition to case-by-case services for clients. In his letter of December 16, 1982,[53] the newly-appointed chairperson of the Clinic Funding Committee endorsed the enthusiasm of the *Grange Report* for a full range of clinic legal services on behalf of the poor. He also expressed the CFC's concern about the consequences of "political activities by clinics". The issues raised by the Chairman's letter are critical for the future of Ontario clinics because they may affect their ability to "promote the legal welfare" of the low-income community. It is essential, first of all, to understand that the service mandate of clinics (promoting the legal welfare of the community) both permits, and indeed requires, clinics to advocate on behalf of the poor in a partisan, and not a neutral, manner. To the extent, therefore, that the chairperson has suggested that clinics "must always be non-partisan", his statement is not consistent with the service mandate of the Regulation. On the other hand, to the extent that his letter suggests a lack of authority in the Regulation for "the possible promotion of any political party when clinic employees are speaking to tenants about rent review", the Chairman's analysis may be more accurate. There is a difference between partisan advocacy on behalf of the poor and partisan political activities; the former is clearly part of the service mandate of Ontario clinics while the latter probably are not. The crucial point is that clinics must themselves define the limit, perhaps in consultation with the CFC, in order to ensure that the limits of the service mandate are not exceeded, but, more importantly, that they are fulfilled. In the context of any such discussion, it will also be of critical importance to understand the boundary between clinic advocacy on behalf of the poor (pursuant to the Regulation) and the strategies which may be necessary to obtain ongoing funding for clinics. To the extent that the chairperson's letter may appear to suggest that ongoing funding for clinics depends on some restraint in their wholehearted promotion of the legal welfare of the poor community, his assertions cannot be accepted.

Finally, the service mandate of clinics requires an appreciation of their role in the context of the Plan's judicare program. To the extent that the judicare program presently faces some jeopardy[54] (for a variety of reasons), the service mandate of clinics may also be affected; notwithstanding their separate structures for delivering legal aid services, clinics and the judicare program are mutually dependent. And although it may be appropriate to consider the efficacy of delivering judicare services by salaried staff, it is critical to understand that the service mandate of community clinics cannot be adapted to the provision of simultaneous judicare services without losing the essence of their present service mandate. The issue is not the appropriate delivery system but the scope of services to be offered. In this respect, both clinics and judicare lawyers have a mutual interest in an acceptable resolution of the judicare dilemma. In addition, both clinics, and other members of the legal profession have a mutual interest in ensuring the equal justice for the poor which community clinics have a mandate to achieve.

Maintaining Independent Legal Service: Clinics and the Government

In this analysis, I have also tried to demonstrate the critical importance of independent legal services provided by clinics and the delicate nature of the structure developed to achieve this objective. I have also noted the additional advantages accruing to clinics through the Minister's personal support for their activities. Ironically, it is the Minister's unqualified support for clinics which has, in recent months, resulted in a weakening of the structures designed to protect clinic independence. Notwithstanding his good intentions, the Minister's actions require careful scrutiny in the interest of the continued capacity for independent clinics to promote the legal welfare of the poor.

As has been demonstrated, the independence of clinics depends substantially on the existence of a CFC which is free from any controlling influence in its decision making. The Minister's decision in early 1982[55] to appoint two of his senior officials to vacant positions on the CFC signified both his personal support for clinics and his concern to ensure that clinic interests received due attention in his Ministry. Unfortunately, his choice also undermined the delicate balance earlier achieved by the CFC, thereby creating a possibility of more overt governmental intervention in the activities of clinics and their advocacy on behalf of the poor. That the Minister's appointees were persons with some experience in legal aid matters and a sincere commitment to clinics is beside the point; their positions placed them, inevitably, in a conflict of interest on any issue where independent legal representation of the poor was inconsistent with governmental (and Ministerial) policies. Moreover, since this potential conflict of interest problem could be identified in advance, it seems that the Minister's choice must have been made only because he was unable to find any equally suitable appointees who were not employees of his Ministry; particularly with respect to the appointee "with previous clinic association", it is unfortunate that the Minister's choice creates an inevitable conflict between the need to protect independence of clinic legal services and the obligation to defend Ministry policy about legal aid services. And it is essential to recognize that these concerns are live issues, particularly taking into account the need to resolve existing problems with the judicare services. The possibility that community clinics might be expected to undertake the delivery of judicare services clearly demonstrates that conflict between the clinics' interest in continued specialization in poverty law problems to promote the legal welfare of the poor and the Ministry's interest in cost-effective delivery of high volume legal aid services. Because two members of the CFC could not vote independently on any such proposal, there must be serious concern about the integrity of CFC decision making, and its continued role in preserving independent legal services for the poor. In this context, the Minister's personal support for clinics and his expressed desire to increase their resources requires very careful assessment.

Achieving Equal Justice: Clinics and their Communities

The requirement in the 1979 Regulation for a clinic to be a community organization reflects the significance of the concept of community in Ontario clinics. As I have suggested, the recognition of the community's importance to successful clinic action on behalf of the poor has steadily increased, particularly since 1979. Moreover, as has been shown, it is the community which offers the final link in the structures for achieving independent legal representation in the face of substantial public funding for legal aid services.

In this context, Ontario clinics must also be confident that their community organizations are scrupulously independent of other community groups, particularly in relation to decision making procedures and financial arrangements. It is critical to the credibility of successful advocacy on behalf of the poor that a community clinic be, and be seen to be, independent. In this way, independence from government is complemented by independence from other community groups. Notwithstanding that many clinics have evolved out of other community groups, the success of a clinic's advocacy, as well as its credibility as an independent legal service, depend on its scrupulous independence from other community groups. In recent months, the recognition of MTLS's (Metropolitan Tenants Association) need to make decisions about priorities for its legal service,[56] independently of the Federation of Metro Tenants, has signalled a recognition of the importance of this principle and of the coming of age of community clinics in Ontario.

The concept of the community is a vital part of Ontario clinics: the community includes the many people over many years who have made their contribution to the growth and success of clinics, as well as the people to whom clinics, in many different ways, have provided assistance. As I have suggested, the Ontario clinics have a unique opportunity to fulfill the promise of legal aid services. The challenge for Ontario's community clinics is the responsibility of achieving equal justice by and for their community: the poor.

Endnotes

1.   The Honourable R. Roy McMurtry, Q.C., Attorney-General for Ontario, "Notes for a Statement to the Ontario Legislature Standing Committee on the Administration of Justice," December 1, 1982, 30–31.

2.   For example, Nova Scotia's legal aid budget was reduced by 25% for 1982–83; British Columbia was required to cut back by $1.3 million from a budget of $17.3 million and decided to institute a user fee and reduce the services provided; in Saskatchewan, certificates to the private bar were withheld for three months in 1982 to save costs; in Manitoba, by contrast, there was a small increase in the 1982–83 budget, but this followed several years of restraint, *Survey Information*, National Legal Aid Research Centre, Ottawa, November 1982; *B.C. Legal Services Society Newsletter*, October 1982.

3.   In response to the Law Society's requested tariff increase of 30%, the Minister announced on January 15, 1983 a 5% increase retroactive to July 1982, with a further 5% increase effective July 1983. There had been no increase since 1979, *Globe and Mail*, January 15, 1982.

4.   S.R. Ellis, Q.C., "A View of the Profession of Law" (1982), *Bar Admission Course Materials*, 19.

5.   R.R.O. 1980, *Reg.* 578, s. 159.

6.   The phrase "equal justice" is taken from Cappelletti, Gordley and Johnson, Jr., *Toward Equal Justice: A Comparative Study of Legal Aid in Modern Societies* (Dobbs Ferry, 1975).

7.   S.O. 1966, c. 80.

8.   *Report of the Joint Committee on Legal Aid*, William B. Common, Q.C., Chairman (March 1965). Mr. Common was then Deputy Attorney-General for the Province of Ontario, and the Committee was composed of members of the Law Society of Upper Canada, appointed by the Treasurer, and members of the civil service of Ontario, appointed by the Attorney-General. See *Joint Committee Report*, 5.

9.   *Id.*, 97.

10.

Newfoundland	*The Legal Aid Act* (1976)
Nova Scotia	*Legal Aid Planning Act* (1970)
	The Legal Act (1977)
New Brunswick	*The Legal Aid Act* (1972)
Quebec	*Loi de l'aide juridique* (1972)
Manitoba	*Legal Aid Services Society of Manitoba Act* (1972)
Saskatchewan	*Act to Amend the Legal Profession Act* (1967)
	The Community Legal Services (Saskatchewan) Act (1974)
British Columbia	*Court Rules of Practice Act* (1968)
	The Legal Services Commission Act (1975)
	The Legal Services Society Act (1979)
Yukon	*Legal Aid Ordinance* (1975)
N.W.T.	*Legal Services Ordinance* (1979)

An Act passed for Prince Edward Island has not been proclaimed; in Alberta, the Legal Aid Society has been incorporated under the Societies Act and the plan functions as an agreement between the province and the Law Society. See Statistics Canada, *Legal Aid 1981* (Ottawa: Minister of Supply and Services Canada, 1981), 10–12.

11.   See, for example, Ontario Law Reform Commission, *Report on Administration of Ontario Courts* (Toronto: Ministry of the Attorney-General, 1973), III, 126–27. See also chapter 7 generally.

12.   In the first Annual Report of the OLAP, this principle was recognized; the Report stated: "There has always existed, even within the most enlightened society, a disparity between the availability of a lawyer to the well-to-do and to the indigent.... Ontario has now taken a giant stride to ensure that no one shall be denied the services or advice of a lawyer because of lack of money...." Ontario Legal Aid Plan, The Law Society of Upper Canada, *Annual Report 1968*, 6.

13.   *Id.*

14.   See, for example, Taman, *The Legal Services Controversy: An Examination of the Evidence* (Ottawa: National Council of Welfare, 1971).

15.   Significantly, the Joint Committee noted in 1965: "The almost unanimous view expressed to the Committee was that the administration should be the exclusive responsibility of the Law Society of Upper Canada. This partnership between the Provincial Government and the Law Society has existed for 14 years and there is no reason in the opinion of the Committee, for any change." See *Joint Committee Report*, 99.

16. For example, Saskatchewan, Manitoba and Quebec. See especially Larsen, "Seven Years with Legal Aid (1972–79): A Personal View of Some Events and Background Literature" (1981), 11 *Man. L.J.* 237.

17. *Act*, s. 2. The Law Society's power is "subject to the approval of the Attorney-General".

18. The early group apparently was funded by a Local Initiatives Program grant.

19. The original group also included a major research focus, the Canadian Environmental Law Research Foundation (CELA).

20. Parkdale opened in September 1971; it seems that both Injured Workers' Consultants (IWC) and CELA commenced at approximately the same time, or a little earlier. Further research on the early beginning of clinics is needed to be any more specific.

21. The Ford Foundation supported clinical legal education programs through Legal Education for Professional Responsibility (CLEPR.).

22. The Plan responded to some of these demands, following the recommendation of the *Community Legal Services Report* (Toronto: Law Society of Upper Canada, 1972).

23. *Report of the Task Force on Legal Aid*, Mr. Justice Osler, Chairman (Ministry of the Attorney-General, 1974).

24. *Id.*, 25.

25. *Id.*, 22–25.

26. Action on Legal Aid, *Delivery of Legal Services: A Brief to the Ontario Government in Response to the Report of the Osler Task Force on Legal Aid Presented February 1976* (June 1977).

27. *Id.* 10 (Recommendation 2).

28. Noticeably, the decision to fund clinics was not accompanied by any recommendation to establish an independent legal services corporation in Ontario.

29. *O. Reg.* 160/76.

30. *Id.*, s. 147.

31. *Id.*, s. 148: " 'Clinical delivery system' means any method for the delivery of legal or para-legal services to the public other than by way of fee for service, and includes preventive law programmes and educational and training programmes calculated to reduce the cost of delivering legal services."

32. A wide range of concerns was discussed at a meeting between members of the Clinical Funding Committee and clinic representatives in January 1978.

33. *Report of the Commission on Clinical Funding*, Mr. Justice Grange, Commissioner (October, 1978).

34. Letter of appointment to Mr. Justice Grange from the Honourable R. Roy McMurtry, Attorney-General (June 27, 1978), para. 4.

35. *Grange Report*, *supra* note 33, 22.

36. *Id.*

37. See new R.R.O. 1980, *Reg.* 578.

38. *Id.*, s. 148(1)(a) and (2).

39. See *Reg.*, ss. 151 and 152 (funding) and s. 155 (defunding).

40. See *Reg.*, ss. 1549 and 150.

41. For 1981–82, clinic expenditures were $5,469,935 out of a total of OLAP expenditures of $56,241,045. Ontario Legal Aid Plan, *Annual Report 1982*, 32.

42. *Legal Aid Act*, R.S.O. c. 234, s. 12.

43. *Id.*, s. 13.

44. See *Grange Report*, *supra* note 33, 1–3 for a list of the "gaps" in the Plan's services to which community clinics responded; in the words of the Report: "It was to plug these gaps that the clinical movement was born".

45. The legislation establishing other legal aid programs in Canada has recognized the need to respond to the specialized problems of the poor.

For two examples, see the Quebec legislation *supra* note 10, s. 4, defining a right to legal aid of "an economically underprivileged person", and the Manitoba experience referred to by Larsen, *supra* note 16.

46. The specialization "away from" routine representation by clinics in family law and criminal law matters has been noticeable in recent years (Clinic Funding Statistics: unpublished). However, university-based clinics, with a larger personnel than other community clinics, have continued to provide such representation. See Mossman, *Report to the Legal Aid Committee and the Clinic Funding Committee on University Clinics* (December 1981).

47. These arrangements exist, for example, in Nova Scotia, Quebec, Manitoba, Saskatchewan, and British Columbia. There are a few "specialized" clinics in other provinces as well — two in Quebec, which are integrated with the provincial plan, fifteen in British Columbia which handle public information, referrals and tribunal matters and one in the N.W.T. None of these programs seems to operate with the same scope as is evident in Ontario. See *Legal Aid 1981, supra* note 10, 33–34 for information on "specialized" clinics, and 42 and 29 for patterns of legal clinics' activities with respect to representation and referrals to the private bar. These patterns are generally confirmed by the *Annual Reports* of provincial legal aid schemes.

48. This assertion is tempered by the problem of increasing needs and decreasing resources of the judicare program, particularly at present: "In Ontario, the demand for legal aid rose 21 per cent [a three-month period]", A.M. Lawson, Director of the OLAP: "There are more and more demands for aid from more and more people who can't afford anything else", James B. Chadwick, Chairman, Legal Aid Committee. See OLAP, *News Update #10* (October 1982).

49. *Reg.*, s. 148(s).

50. Clinic certificate 1982–83, clause I; This clause is not included in the certificates of three university-based clinics which have no community board.

51. Concerns have been expressed by the Director of OLAP and the chairperson of the Legal Aid Committee, *supra*, note 48. In addition, Ontario lawyers who participate in judicare services scheduled protest "study days" in early 1983. The Ontario judicare situation is not unlike that in other provinces, see *supra*, note 2.

52. From May 1979 to September 1983, I was Clinic Funding Manager of the Ontario Legal Aid Plan and on leave from Osgoode Hall Law School.

53. Letter from Roger D. Yachetti, Q.C., chairperson of the Clinic Funding Committee to the Chairpersons of Boards of Directors and Deans of Law Faculties, December 16, 1982.

54. *News Update, supra*, note 48.

55. The Minister had been requested to make an appointment to replace Brian Bellmore, who had earlier resigned; in February 1982, he announced the appointment of J. Douglas Ewart, Director, Policy Development Department, to replace Mr. Bellmore. At the same time, the Minister announced the appointment of Glenn Carter, General Manager (Programs and Administration Division) to replace an existing member of the CFC, Michael Fitzpatrick (Director of Courts Administration). The Minister confirmed that Mr. Ewart, who had worked as a student at Parkdale Community Legal Services in 1971, was a person with "previous clinic association".

56. See *Report: Independent Community Clinics and Other Community Organizations — A Report to the CFC on MTLS and the FMTA* (August 1982); the Report was substantially accepted by MTLS and recently approved by the CFC.

Access to the Courts[†]
G. Brodsky and S. Day

THIS chapter discusses standing to sue, intervenor status, and funding for litigation. The first two are legal issues. When a court deals with standing and intervenor status, it determines who will be recognized as a proper participant in a case. Despite uncertainty about the courts' approach and some important unresolved issues, recent decisions hold out hope that women and other disadvantaged groups may not be barred from participation by narrow rulings. However, even if disadvantaged groups are assisted by a generous approach to standing, their access will be severely restricted if adequate money and resources are not available to support Charter equality rights litigation.

Questions of access are crucial because they determine who can make their voices heard in the courts and who can participate in shaping the interpretations of the new equality guarantees.

RELAXED RULES OF STANDING

There has been a recent relaxation of the rules governing standing, or who the courts will recognize as a party. Traditionally, no person, except an Attorney General, could bring a constitutional challenge unless they were directly affected by the impugned law in a more significant way than were other citizens. But in the past decade, courts have shown increasing flexibility about that requirement. The decision of the Supreme Court of Canada in the case of *Borowski* radically altered the law of standing.

Joseph Borowski was granted standing to challenge section 251 of the *Criminal Code*, a law that was totally inapplicable to him, on the basis of alleged violations of fetal rights under the *Canadian Bill of Rights*. The effect of the standing decision in *Borowski* is that a court challenge may be brought by a citizen who is not affected directed by legislation where there is "no other reasonable and effective manner in which the issue may be brought before the court."

Another example of the relative ease with which constitutional challenges may be initiated arises in the context of criminal prosecutions. Anyone charged with a criminal offence is permitted to challenge the constitutional validity of the law under which she/he has been charged, even if the alleged infringement is not directly applicable to the accused. An implication for women of this broad rule of standing becomes apparent in the context of a sexual assault trial such as that of *R. v. W.D.C.G.* in which a male accused was permitted to argue that section 149(1) of the *Criminal Code* should be struck down because only a "female person" could be a victim of the crime. The accused was not himself suffering from any lack of legislative protection, nor was he being penalized because of his sex. Section 149(1) said:

> Everyone who indecently assaults a female person is guilty of an indictable offence and is liable to imprisonment for five years.

Although the New Brunswick Court of Appeal upheld the law on the basis that it did not penalize men but rather singled out a particular group for protection, the Court did not question the standing of the accused to raise the sex equality challenge, which had the potential to affect all women in Canada.

Further, the principle that a person may challenge legislation on behalf of other persons as part of his or her defence against a lawsuit is apparently not restricted to criminal prosecutions. For example, in *Shewchuk v. Ricard* where the issue was liability of a putative father for child maintenance under a provincial statute, Jerry Ricard, the putative father, was permitted to challenge the legislation on the grounds of underinclusiveness, even though he was not a member of the excluded class. Ricard argued that sections of the *Child Paternity and Support Act* should be struck down because a father who is left with an "abandoned" child in his arms (which Ricard was not) does not have the same remedies open to him to obtain support from the child's mother, as the mother does to obtain support from the child's father.

Third parties have been permitted to make fair trial challenges pursuant to section 11(d) of the Charter, in trials that are not even their own. For example, in the Ontario Court of Appeal, as a result of a sexual assault trial, Canadian Newspapers Co. (a publishing conglomerate) was able to invoke the Charter's fair trial guarantee to challenge a provision of the *Criminal Code* protecting persons who are sexually assaulted from having their names publicized against their will. Canadian Newspapers Co. was not a party in the sexual assault proceeding, and at no point was it suggested that the fair trial rights of the accused had been violated. Despite this, the Ontario Court of Appeal permitted Canadian Newspapers Co. to argue that fair trial rights had been violated.

---

† Brodsky, G., and Day, Shelagh, "Access to the Courts" in *Canadian Charter Equality Rights for Women: One Step Forward or Two Steps Back?* (Ottawa: Canadian Advisory Council on the Status of Women, 1989), 131–40. Reprinted by permission of Canadian Advisory Council on the Status of Women (CACSW), Ottawa, Ontario.

As these cases indicate, relaxing the rules of standing has made challenging women's protections easier; it is not yet clear, however, whether it will also make it easier to represent women who are not in a position to initiate challenges on their own.

In some cases, parties directly affected by inequality are too isolated and too threatened to act on their own behalf. This may be the case, for example, with domestic workers, the majority of whom are women of colour, in Canada on temporary permits. Many of them are reluctant to challenge their poor working conditions and their lack of protection in Canadian labour law. Legitimately, they fear reprisals and deportation. Standing rules should be broad enough to allow another party, such as an advocacy organization, to initiate a challenge in circumstances like these.

Despite the recent relaxation of the rules of standing, however, it is still not clear that non-profit societies will be able to initiate section 15 challenges on women's behalf when there is no directly harmed woman willing or able to be the named plaintiff. Depending on the courts' approach to this issue, groups like INTERCEDE, or the Women's Legal Education and Action Fund (LEAF) may not be able to obtain standing, because section 15 says "every individual has the right to equality", and the courts seem to agree that "individual" does not include corporations.

Corporations do not have equality rights according to most of the courts that have ruled on this issue so far. We believe this is the correct position for the courts to take, because constitutional equality guarantees are not needed to secure the rights of corporations. However, it will be important for the future of equality rights litigation that, when courts make decisions about standing under section 15, they distinguish between not-for-profit societies seeking to bring forward public interest issues on behalf of members of disadvantaged groups and for-profit corporations litigating in their own interests.

Given that many cases affecting but not involving women can be initiated, women's ability to get before the courts themselves is crucial.

A GENEROUS APPROACH TO PUBLIC INTEREST INTERVENORS

Because there has been a general relaxation of the rules governing who can initiate a constitutional case, it is important to establish a similar relaxation of the rules governing who can intervene as well as a generous approach to public interest intervenors.

Inherent Jurisdiction

The power of the courts to hear representations from intervenors is based on their inherent jurisdiction to accept assistance from an *amicus curiae*, that is, a friend of the court. In addition to the powers vested in the courts by virtue of their inherent jurisdiction to allow interventions, most jurisdictions have statutory rules giving the courts wide discretion to grant or deny leave to prospective intervenors.

Automatic Rights of Attorneys General

In contrast to the general principle that decisions concerning intervenor status are discretionary, rules governing many courts give provincial and federal Attorneys General automatic rights of notice and participation in constitutional cases. The imbalance between citizen and state representation permitted by the special rules for Attorneys General has not gone unnoticed. One academic commentator has said:

> There is a certain irony to this in the context of Charter litigation, since the participation of Attorneys General, who will normally (though not always) be united in seeking to uphold the constitutional validity of the challenged legislation, tends to "stack the deck" in favour of government. If the primary purpose of the Charter is to give Canadians a vehicle for asserting rights *against* government, it seems strange that governments that were not initially parties to the litigation should be provided with an automatic vehicle for conveying their message to the courts, while those interested in presenting a non-governmental perspective must depend on the willingness of the courts to let their voices be heard. (Emphasis in original.)

The fact that Attorneys General have automatic rights of intervention is one consideration in favour of a generous approach to interventions by public interest intervenors in constitutional cases.

Public Participation in Charter Litigation

There may be some private law disputes, involving the routine application of established legal principles, that do not have much impact on anyone other than the parties to the dispute. However, this is never the case with Charter litigation. The superordinate status of the Charter means that every time a Charter challenge is brought, laws may be changed. In addition, the Charter is so new that the meaning of its provisions is being tested constantly. It has been argued by the Canadian Civil Liberties Association and others that it is contrary to democratic principles for courts to interpret and apply the Charter, which will affect the lives of all Canadians, without the benefit of representations from a variety of perspectives. These are additional reasons for the courts to take a liberal approach to public interest interventions in Charter cases.

299

The idea that public interest intervenors have a role to play in Charter cases involving important questions of interpretation was accepted by Justice Lamer in the case of *Mark Andrews* at the Supreme Court of Canada. As previously indicated, this case is the first equality rights case to be heard by the Supreme Court of Canada. Though Andrews, being white, British, and a male law graduate, is certainly not disadvantaged, his case has been identified as critical for those who are. Justice Lamer granted intervenor status to LEAF, the Coalition of Provincial Organizations of the Handicapped (COPOH), and the Canadian Association of University Teachers (CAUT), saying in his order:

> ...it is apparent that the Judgement of the Court of Appeal of British Columbia as it now stands is determinative of more issues than that of whether the restrictive bylaw of access to the legal profession to Canadian citizens only is in violation of Section 15 of the Charter. I am accordingly granting these motions to intervene...

The Rights of Intervenors

The rights of a public interest intervenor are usually thought to be less than that of a party. For example, an intervenor will not ordinarily be permitted to add to the evidence or expand the grounds of an appeal. Such restrictions may be appropriate for public interest intervenors in a case such as *Mark Andrews*, where the concern of the intervenors was not with the resolution of the dispute but with the manner in which the Charter is interpreted. However, in a case such as *Schachter* — where the intervenor, LEAF, was advocating a particular resolution of the issues before the court and where women would be directly affected by the outcome of the case, possibly even to a greater extent than the parties themselves — it was appropriate that the intervenor be accorded party rights. In *Schachter*, LEAF was granted intervenor status with all the rights of a party.

Interventions by Feminist Organizations are Needed

There is a further argument that gives a feminist organization with expertise in the area of equality a particularly strong claim to intervenor status in Charter cases. In view of the overwhelming number of male-initiated sex equality cases and the nature of the arguments being made both by their advocates and by counsel for the Attorneys General, it seems doubtful that many Canadian judges will ever be exposed to models of equality that could actually do something positive for women if women are not permitted to intervene in equality cases initiated by men.

The extent of the courts' willingness to hear from disadvantaged groups when they are not parties may well determine the direction of equality rights jurisprudence. There is no way to ensure that the courts will breathe real life into the Charter's equality guarantees. But if only those interpretations espoused by Attorneys General, defence lawyers, and professional groups are before them, the courts' view will be very limited. The equality guarantees cannot be given the full meaning and impact required by a purposive approach unless the courts listen to the voices of those who are disadvantaged.

Trends Concerning the Granting of Intervenor Status

Traditionally, a prospective intervenor had to demonstrate a direct legal interest, such as a proprietary interest, in the subject matter of the dispute. Even in the mid-1980s, it was apparently quite difficult to obtain intervenor status in the Supreme Court of Canada. But the recent trend in Canada seems to be away from a restrictive approach. It is evident from at least one case that the Charter itself has encouraged courts to re-evaluate their traditional view of intervenors. Justice Addy of the Federal Court of Appeal said:

> The narrow view found in common law jurisprudence to the effect that only parties with a triable interest in the actual issues raised in the pleadings have a right to be heard, was developed and established long before administrative law as we know it today really came into being and thus became subject to judicial control and intervention to any extent. A completely different situation now exists especially in Canada where the supervisory role granted to our Courts has been largely extended by reason of the Charter of Rights, as well as by the proliferation of boards and commissions.

In 1987, LEAF was granted intervenor status by the Supreme Court of Canada, courts of appeal, and the Federal Court.

However, women have not been successful in obtaining intervenor status in all jurisdictions and at all court levels. On November 10, 1986, LEAF's application for intervenor status in the case of *Klachefsky v. Brown* was rejected by Justice Huband of the Manitoba Court of Appeal, with costs against LEAF.

The background of the case argued strongly for court assistance from a feminist intervenor. In the court below, a child custody order had been varied in favour of a father because he had a new wife who would be available to the children 24 hours a day whereas their mother, who was starting a new job, would have to rely on child-care services. LEAF sought leave to intervene, with the consent of the children's mother, to argue that if women's equality is to be obtained, child-care services cannot be considered inferior to care at home in the absence of specific evidence that it is so. Concerning the intervenor application in the Court of Appeal, Justice Huband said:

Counsel for the wife is entirely capable of raising and ventilating any issue relative to the *Charter of Rights and Freedoms* should counsel consider that such an argument would advance the cause of her client.

There is a problem with Justice Huband's reasoning. It does not necessarily follow that arguments relevant to women as a group will be raised by an individual woman's lawyer, no matter how capable she/he might be. In particular, if a lawyer suspects that a court will be impatient or uncomfortable about hearing equality rights arguments, her/his sense of duty to her/his client will likely cause her/him to refrain from making such arguments because they would *not* "advance the cause of the client". Indeed, counsel for Ms. Brown did not make equality rights arguments before the Manitoba Court of Appeal, even though she had been agreeable to the arguments being added by an intervenor. Ultimately, the Manitoba Court of Appeal ruled in favour of Ms. Brown, saying that the trial judge had committed a palpable error by placing undue emphasis on the fact that Ms. Brown was going to require paid child-care services.

Roininen is another case in which an intervenor application by a feminist organization was refused. The central question in that case was whether the child apprehension powers of the Superintendent of Child Welfare permitted the apprehension of a fetus *in utero*. The British Columbia Superintendent of Child Welfare had used these powers while Sandy Roininen was in labour in order to force her to undergo a caesarian section. The authorities had set out to test the scope of their legislative power when they apprehended her fetus *in utero*. With the consent of Sandy Roininen, LEAF sought leave to intervene in the subsequent legal proceedings to present relevant Charter issues to the Court. The application of the prospective intervenor before Judge Davis of the British Columbia Provincial Court was denied, on the basis that a provincial court lacks jurisdiction to permit an intervention and, further, that LEAF did not fall within a class of "other persons the court considers appropriate" to participate in a child apprehension hearing.

Judge Davis then proceeded to uphold the initial apprehension order without any discussion about women's rights to refuse medical treatment, arguing that it was simply a case of what was best for the safety and well-being of a child, not a case of women's rights. Need we say more about why the Court required the assistance of an intervenor? The judge's inability to see that state-ordered cutting into women's bodies raises issues of women's rights calls to mind words of Justice Wilson concerning men's perspective on abortion:

It is probably impossible for a man to respond, even imaginatively, to such a dilemma not just because it is outside the realm of his personal experience (although this is, of course, the case) but because he can relate to it only by objectifying it, thereby eliminating the subjective elements of the female psyche which are at the heart of the dilemma.

Having said that the courts should take a generous approach to would-be intervenors, it must be acknowledged that the courts' discretion to permit non-party participation in court cases is open to manipulation by those with nothing different to present to the court but who merely wish to reinforce the position of one of the parties. If such an agenda is made apparent to the court, intervenor status will be denied. In *Borowski*, Justice Matheson of the Saskatchewan Court of Queen's Bench denied Campaign Life Canada (CLC) permission to intervene because

...it was quite apparent that CLC intended, if granted permission to intervene, to substantially support the position advocated by the plaintiff.

If the agenda of a prospective intervenor is disguised, however, it may be possible to obtain intervenor status, notwithstanding a duplicative position. Five years after Campaign Life's application for intervenor status in *Borowski* was refused in the Saskatchewan Court of Queen's Bench, R.E.A.L. Women of Canada (an anti-feminist organization) obtained intervenor status in the *Borowski* appeal at the Supreme Court of Canada. The public position of R.E.A.L. Women on abortion does not differ in any appreciable way from that espoused by Borowski in the case. The group's position is that the "human rights of the unborn" take precedence over women's freedom of choice. This is also Borowksi's position. Of course the final test of R.E.A.L. Women's legitimacy as an intervenor in the *Borowski* case will be whether the group adds anything that is useful to the Court.

Ironically, in documents supporting its application for intervenor status in this case, R.E.A.L. Women espoused equality for women, even though the organization opposes the introduction of many of the laws and programs requisite to that equality. This should not be surprising. Equality is a term of our Constitution. This means that fighting it openly is difficult, whereas manipulating its meaning may be possible. As the equality rights movement in Canada gains momentum, instances of its detractors using the language of equality rights to justify the continued oppression of disadvantaged groups will no doubt become increasingly common. Already affirmative action programs are criticized as being a kind of reverse discrimination, and those opposed to legal protections for lesbians and gay men complain that human rights laws interfere with their liberty and their freedom of religion. It is to be hoped the courts will look with a critical eye upon the submissions of any intervenor, or indeed of any party, who uses the language of equality to advocate limits on women's freedoms and access to resources.

ACCESS: THE PRACTICAL QUESTIONS

Can women and other disadvantaged groups really use the equality rights guaranteed in the Charter, or do they, in practice, remain beyond their reach?

The figures given in Chapters Three and Five, documenting women's participation in equality rights litigation in the first three years, demonstrate dramatically the seriousness of the access problem. Women simply do not have the money, resources, and power necessary to use the law that is there to protect and support them.

Developing the cases to challenge the many inequalities experienced by women and others is a major task. The cases are difficult and complex. It is rarely simple discrimination on the face of legislation that women need to challenge, but rather laws and policies that have an adverse impact, despite their apparent neutrality. Interventions are equally complex because they often concern difficult and important interpretive issues. Because the Charter guarantees are so new, every equality case is a crucial one, and it is important to describe the scope and nature of each sex equality issue as fully as possible for the courts. As we have said earlier, Canadian courts are not familiar with equality issues. This means that every equality-seeker who litigates now must also be an educator. To do this work well requires extensive research, knowledgeable counsel, access to experts, and informed litigants.

This case development is expensive and time-consuming, requiring a special expertise that few activists or lawyers in Canada have acquired thus far. Few women in Canada who act alone have the money or the resources to engage in Charter litigation.

The irony of this situation is that those with the greatest need for the equality guarantees have the least access to them. As described in earlier chapters, corporations and men have better access to the use of equality guarantees than women and other disadvantaged groups.

Public funding is essential if women are to have any meaningful access to the exercise of their Charter rights. A constitutional guarantee of equality is a hollow promise if only the wealthy and advantaged can use it.

The federal government has taken one step to increase access for equality-seekers. In 1985, it established the Court Challenges Program, which is administered by the Canadian Council on Social Development. Litigants with equality cases challenging a federal law or program can apply to the Court Challenges Program for financial support. The program can supply up to $35,000 per court level for lawyers' fees, case research, and disbursements.

Unfortunately, this public funding scheme has some severe shortcomings:

- Funding is available only for challenges to federal laws and policies.

No money is available to support challenges to provincial laws or politics through this program, and no provincial governments have made similar funds available, with one limited exception. Health, education, the terms and conditions of employment, and social services are provincial matters because of the constitutional division of powers between the federal and provincial governments. These are crucial issues for women, but no funding is available to support challenges in these areas.

- $35,000 per court level for all expenses is not enough to cover the development of complex cases.

Lawyers' fees are high, and extensive work is required to develop cases properly. Sophisticated statistical and demographic evidence is needed in some cases. Historical, sociological, and economic studies are needed in others.

In addition, cases for women and other disadvantaged groups cannot be seen as simply individual. Every case will affect other women and perhaps other groups. This means that the preparation of any equality case has an importance beyond its particular factors and beyond the situation of the particular litigant. In these circumstances, the capacity to do thorough and wide-ranging research and to involve those with specialized knowledge and first-hand experience about particular equality issues is essential. The $35,000 ceiling in an improper limit for disadvantaged litigants.

- Funding is available only for lawyers' fees and case-related research.

If the Charter's equality rights are to be used by disadvantaged groups in anything more than a purely haphazard fashion, resources and money are required to allow the development of expertise and litigation capacity. As already stated, equality cases are, by their very nature, not individual in scope. Well-developed cases require knowledge of the patterns of inequality for the whole group, where a particular case fits into this pattern, and what agreements will best serve the equality interest of the group as a whole.

While knowledge of the key issues for each group and the patterns of inequality from which it suffers exists in advocacy organizations for disadvantaged groups, the expertise to turn that information into legal arguments and developed cases does not.

After studying the experience of women in the United States, women in Canada decided that meaningful access to the use of the new equality guarantees would require founding an organization dedicated specifically to the task of developing strategic equality rights litigation for women. In April 1985, women founded the Women's

Legal Education and Action Fund (LEAF), an organization designed to assist women to exercise their new equality rights. As references throughout this report indicate, LEAF has been significantly involved in the Charter sex equality litigation to date.

Recently, organizations representing disabled persons have taken the same decision and founded the Canadian Disability Rights Council. EGALE (Equality for Gays and Lesbians Everywhere) is also developing a litigation capacity, and groups representing racial and ethnic minorities, prisoners, and people with low incomes are considering how they can support effective litigation on behalf of their members.

For groups that have experienced longstanding disadvantage and powerlessness, meaningful access to the use of the equality guarantees requires more than money for lawyers' fees. It requires money to develop awareness, information, and expertise in their communities and to arrange consultation between groups. Without this vital education, research, and consultation, there is likely to be little equality rights litigation that truly represents the interests of women and other disadvantaged groups. As long as governments do not recognize this, any funding schemes they design will continue to perpetuate the inequity between the advantaged and the disadvantaged in terms of their access to the courts.

- The Court Challenges Program is a five-year program; its mandate runs out in March 1990.

Those who apply for funds to the Court Challenges Program are being informed now that the program cannot pay for any litigation expenses after March 1990. Because litigation is often lengthy, litigants cannot be certain that actions they begin now will be completed by that time. In effect, women and other disadvantaged groups are being advised that they cannot rely any longer on the Court Challenges Program, even for support for cases within its mandate.

CONCLUSION

Thus, with all these difficulties, women and other disadvantaged groups struggle to gain access to the law, while institutions, including governments, universities, and hospitals, spend public dollars without restriction to oppose them.

The issue of access is the most basic one, and the state of access is, at present, shocking. There is only one source of funds to support equality rights litigation, and its mandate is too narrow, its funding levels too restricted, its design too unimaginative, and its future too uncertain to provide real access to the exercise of equality rights in Canada. It is to women's credit and to the credit of other disadvantaged Canadians that with so few resources and from such an unequal position, they are still struggling to make their voices heard in the courts.

The following chapter discusses the inadequacy of the theory of formal equality as an interpretive foundation for the Charter's equality guarantees. But the practical issue of access to the courts makes evident the failure of what formal equality offers. Currently, the law allows the advantaged and the disadvantaged alike to pursue their equality claims in court. Nothing in the law bars the disadvantaged: formal equality exists. However, the practical barriers are all too real. Women's disadvantage, their lack of money, resources, and power mean that they do not have equal access to the use of the very guarantees that are designed to advance their equality.

Further Reading

Ontario Law Reform Commission, *Report on Class Actions*, Volume I, 1982, Chapter 4.

Herbert Kritzer, "Fee Arrangements and Fee Shifting: Lessons from the Experience In Ontario" (1984), 47 *Law and Contemporary Problems* 125–38.

C. Marketing Legal Services

The Development of Prepaid Legal Services in Canada[†]
C.J. Wydrzynski

THE ISSUES: COST AND ACCESS

Recently, increased examination of the cost of legal services and the quality of access to legal service providers has spawned a host of suggested reforms to the current system for delivery of legal services. These reforms fall generally within a number of categories. Some reforms which may lower cost and improve access include more economic law office management,[1] changes in substantive and procedural law to allow for more systematic resolution of legal problems,[2] increased efficiency of judicial and administrative decision-making processes,[3] liberalization of the ethical norms which regulate and authorize law practice[4] and even increased or improved government regulation to improve competition in the interest of the consumer.[5] All of these methods offer logical alternatives which should be carefully analyzed. Others, such as government-sponsored comprehensive judicare, suggest fundamental alterations of our present educational and occupational foundations, by amplifying the government's role and seeking to transfer the cost of legal services to the general public through taxes.[6] In a similar manner, improvements to the legal aid structure are more appropriately identified as social concerns or governmental welfare assistance.[7] Generally, all suggested reforms seek to eliminate existing impediments to optimal use of legally trained personnel: to reduce the cost of legal services to the consumer and improve access to those who dispense legal services.

The problems of cost and access can be affected by many of these methods, but many improvements offer a piecemeal, although important, approach to the basic concerns. None of the methods is comprehensive in its approach to the overall improvement of client-access and client-cost issues. Each option offers improvements over the existing mechanisms, but few seek to provide a total relief package for a broad group within the community.

The concept of prepaid legal services[8] is designed to provide an alternative, comprehensive mechanism which addresses the issues of cost and access directly. Its scope is extensive and directed toward a large segment of the currently underserviced population. Prepaid legal service plans incorporate many of the schemes suggested above and such plans probably will encourage other reforms. Such plans offer one alternative, although a highly useful one, for certain groups in society to organize an economically sound method to apportion costs and help to reduce the random and irregular nature of access to capable lawyers.

Essentially, the concept of prepaid legal services can be seen as a self-help mechanism for the consumer. It allows consumers to design an appropriate cost model to fit their needs and to structure an access model which will provide the desired degree of availability of lawyers to the group, given the circumstances and the context in which a group must operate. It is by virtue of such an arrangement that actual consumer needs can be determined. Other forms of analysis engage in speculation about these questions. They tend to exclude the consumer from their perspective, or decide for them what they want in the "public interest". Prepaid legal service plans, within limits, tend to leave this choice where it ought to be left: with those who have the greatest interests at stake.[9]

Prepaid legal service plans are designed largely for a specific economic group within society: the middle-income earner.[10] While there are many statistics to show that middle-income wage earners are a prime group experiencing both cost and access problems, economic common sense dictates that cost and access should be a greater problem for this group than the most affluent in society.[11] As well, the development of provincial legal aid schemes has placed the indigent client in a relatively better cost-access position than the middle-income earner. Historically, the middle-income individual has been provided with the fee-for-service access model. The many inherent problems of this model have been recognized and reforms such as specialization and advertising have been suggested as providing some relief, while remaining generally within this model.

Given the generally negative public perception of the legal profession and lack of knowledge about legal problems and legal rights, it is safe to suggest that alternative mechanisms to the fee-for-service model may narrow the gap between the legal system and a large segment of the population which it attempts to serve. Most importantly,

---

[†]   Wydrzynski, C.J., "The Development of Prepaid Legal Services in Canada" in eds. R.G. Evans and M.J. Trebilcock, *Lawyers and the Consumer Interest* (Toronto: Butterworth & Co. (Canada) Ltd., 1982), 199–204. Reprinted by permission of Professors Robert G. Evans and Michael J. Trebilcock.

the prepaid model leaves the precise form of the remedy within the hands of those who are experiencing the problems. While proper regulation and ethical standards must be maintained, and political choices must also be made, it is not unwarranted to let the consumers have a large degree of independence in choosing an appropriate model to fit their needs.

THE PREPAID MODEL

Prepaid legal service plans relate directly to the cost of legal services because essentially they are a means to finance or budget legal service costs for the individual consumer. No precise definition can be formulated to illustrate the myriad forms of the model but the following can be helpful:

> ...any system or arrangement whereby payment is made in advance for legal services that may be needed later if such services are within the type of benefits provided by the plan.[12]

The many types of available financing for prepayment and intermarriage with a realistic scope of benefits provide flexibility in plan structure.

Prepayment of costs is a typical method for providing against future needs. The operative principle is group liability for individual costs: a spreading of the expense or cost of legal services over the members of the group. While the individual alone may be unable to sustain the costs of legal services because of limited financial resources, the enhanced power of a group of similarly interested individuals to finance individual members' costs is self-evident. Annual individual cost could be less than the cost of individual legal services used in any particular year. Of course, this assumption depends on annual utilization rates. Efficient funding of a plan makes such predictions essential.[13] Basically, simple principles of budgeting and insurance can be applied by middle-income persons to the legal services market.

A considerable and often excruciating debate has raged concerning whether prepaid legal service plans are really a form of insurance or prepayment. The mixture of fortuitous (insurance) and non-fortuitous (prepayment) events often covered by prepaid legal plans has caused this dilemma. In a practical sense, this debate is somewhat meaningless in that plans do in fact cover both types of activity. Whether the applicable principle is true risk-bearing or simple budgeting does not undermine the advantages of group affiliation for the average consumer.

Public funds need not be used directly to help solve this cost dilemma for the average citizen. While some governmental encouragement of plans might be induced by an equitable taxation format, basically, the mechanism is self-induced and self-funded. Unaided resources can command much greater influence and resolve common problems through group affiliation. Collective activity to resolve individual problems is a standard method of social organization. It is precisely the recognition of this fundamental principle that allowed the growth of prepaid plans in the United States.[14]

Sufficient group interest can be generated from commonly recognizable units or organizations within society. The union hall, the credit union, the church, a tenants' association, a co-operative and many others provide recognizable communities of interest which can provide the framework and administrative expertise necessary to operate a legal services plan for its members. The community of interest need not be narrow, although this adds an element of economic predictability as to the type of legal services a relatively homogenous group may require. On the other hand, insurance companies have shown an interest in circumscribing the parameters of a group simply on the basis of its desire to prepay for legal services. The community of interest is identified by a willingness to pay the premium cost, and individual policies might be sold to persons unattached to any group. However, the existence of a "group" is an obvious asset in plan administration.

There are many variations of prepaid legal services plan models. The models can vary on many levels: basic design and organizational features, how the plan is sponsored, who makes the administrative decisions, and how the service providers are regulated.[15] Creative planning can design a model which fits the cost and access needs of the member-clients with efficiency and quality, and which maintains the professional character of the services provided.

For example, the scope of available benefits can be relatively narrow or very extensive, depending on the commitment of available resources and the premium levels. Services which are covered by any particular plan will depend on the nature and character of the group to be served. Utilization rate would be an additional element in the cost calculus.[16] Costs can be estimated for each individual plan and reasonable predictions are possible.[17]

When there is a large enough subscription group, prepaid legal services compare favourably in cost to similar mechanisms used by other professions to deliver their services — for example, prepaid dental or optical plans.[18] The relatively low individual subscriber cost insures that those with unmet legal needs are provided with a reasonable method to meet those needs. At the least, prepaid legal plans should be attractive as a fringe benefit.

For those who are establishing Canada's first plans today, adoption of a meaningful schedule of benefits and exclusions can present serious problems of choice. Actuarial data relating to legal fees have not been developed with any degree of sophistication in this country. Appropriate financial levels of coverage for particular legal tasks have to be worked out through practical experience.

Since most plans are aimed at the middle-income individual, certain typical legal problems of such a group can be identified. These would include preparation of wills, uncontested divorces, landlord and tenant problems, real estate purchases, applications for various government benefits, consumer purchases, and general legal advice. Different types of coverage must be worked out for each group's needs.

In addition to the relatively predictable routinized services, plans can be structured to encompass problems which display greater elements of "risk". Criminal and civil defense as well as plaintiff civil actions, or total family law and estate planning services can be built into a specific plan. It would seem that plans can incorporate both the prepayment principle for routinized legal services and the traditional concept of insurance for protection against unforeseen risks which could lead to financial catastrophe.[19] On the whole, prepaid plans can be viewed as a financing or budgeting mechanism, rather than the traditional risk-spreading device. However, plans would seem to provide a genuine service that at least tends to bridge the gap toward traditional risk-spreading. For example, consumers may tend to doubt the need for insurance as protection against an unforeseen legal catastrophe, but may tend to see the value in a telephone advice service as part to the structure of their plan.

In addition, there are cost-saving mechanisms which can be used to tailor a plan further to available resources. These include maximum charges for services, deductibles, hourly rates and specific exclusions. For example, in some types of plans, "adverse selection", or inclusion of high risk individuals within the covered group, may present a threat to the financial stability of the plan. Exclusion of pre-existing legal problems or a time delay before the plan becomes effective may be used to counteract such difficulties.[20]

While the scope of coverage is a major problem to be resolved with any proposed plan, the method chosen to link the lawyer and client also presents a number of alternatives. Traditionally, the two basic structures are described as the open panel and the closed panel models. In open panel plans the beneficiary may choose any lawyer in the community to provide the services by his or her plan. The plan would eventually pay the lawyer directly for the services provided to the members, or allow the members to be reimbursed for their out-of-pocket expenses. Except for the fact that a third party — the plan — is paying the costs incurred, the traditional manner in which the client selects a lawyer and in which the lawyer's services are rendered remains largely undisturbed. Wide geographic distribution of a plan's members or a membership which experiences frequent interjurisdictional legal problems may make this type of access system desirable. In fact, many forms of regulation would make this system

mandatory. The thrust of this model is to indemnify member costs while remaining close to the fee-for-service mechanism.

At the opposite end of the spectrum is the closed panel model, in which the group retains one or more lawyers to represent, often exclusively, the members of the group. A staff of full-time salaried lawyers, members of a single law firm or a limited number of private practitioners might be chosen to provide the services. The member's freedom of choice of lawyer is limited by this type of structure, but it has been shown to be an efficient model in the union-sponsored, consumer group or co-operative setting. It is especially useful in controlling costs, due to the direct availability of price control, peer evaluation techniques, paraprofessional components and a centralized administration to standardize data collection and claims procedures. The approach is largely viewed as provision of a service rather than indemnification of costs.

Many variations of these open and closed panel models are possible. In fact, pure versions of either type are unusual in practice. For example, a partially open or partially closed system of lawyer selection might be used, in which lawyers participate in the plan if they agree to fee levels established by it. Only lawyers who agree to this condition would be eligible to provide services to plan members. The beneficiary would thus have a wider choice available than in the strict closed plan system, but would have less choice than a wholly open panel would provide. Even in open panel systems some form of informal referral system arises in practice.

It should be noted that the terms "open" and "closed" are not terms of art with specific meanings. The definitions vary with context and with need. Nor is the latter a limitation on "choice" and the former a protection of "free choice". When compared with the relevant choice available in the fee-for-service market, both improve access and the labels attached to relevant provider schemes tend to become less useful. The key issue should be to provide flexibility for the consumer.[21]

Endnotes

1.   Numerous methods of efficient law office management have been introduced into the modern law practice which might reduce the cost of legal services. Computers and word-processing machines are available to assist in time management and legal research. Use of paralegals, office administrators and management companies can improve the overall economy of a legal firm. These and many other ideas are discussed regularly in *Legal Economics* published bi-monthly by the Section of Economics of Law Practice of the American Bar Association. Canadian perspectives can be gained from Salzman, "Computers and the Legal Profession"; and Dokken, "An Efficient Law Office"; in *Cost of Justice* (Toronto: Carswell, 1980), 119 and 127.

2.   See generally, Cappelletti and Garth, "Access to Justice: The World-wide Movement to Rights Effective. A General Report" in *Access to*

Justice (Sijthoff, 1978), vol. 1; and Cooper and Kastner, "Access to Justice in Canada: The Economic Barriers and Some Promising Solutions", 247–346. General Canadian works include Friedland, *Access to the Law: A Study Conducted for the Law Reform Commission of Canada* (Toronto: Carswell, 1975); and Samek, "A Case for Social Law Reform" (1977), 60 *C.B.R.* 409.

3.   Examples include Ontario Law Reform Commission, *Report on the Administration of Ontario Courts* (Toronto: Ministry of the Attorney-General of Ontario, 1973), 3 vols.; Hugessen, "Are the Courts Cost-Efficient?"; and Howland, "Is the Appellate Court System Cost-Efficient?" both in *Cost of Justice, supra*, note 1, pp. 47 and 59.

4.   The literature is voluminous but for example see, Esau, "Specialization and the Legal Profession" (1979), 9 *Man. L.J.* 255; Graham, "Rejoice Bologna! A Study of Advertising By Lawyers From a Public Policy Perspective" (1978), 26 *Chitty's L.J.* 253; and Findlayson, "Professional Advertising — The Fine Line Between Informational and Promotional" (1979), 13 *Gazette* 93.

5.   See Roberts, *Anticombines and Antitrust*, (Toronto: Butterworths, 1980), 427–52.

6.   See Goodman, "The Trouble With Judicare" (1972), 48 *Amer. Bar. Assoc. J.* 476; and Brakel, *Judicare: Public Funds, Private Lawyers and Poor People* (Chicago: American Bar Foundation, 1974).

7.   Literature on legal aid in Canada is extensive. Many articles and citations can be found in the *Canadian Legal Aid Bulletin*, published by the National Legal Aid Research Centre of Montreal.

8.   The term "prepaid legal services" will be used throughout this article to describe the concept which is sometimes addressed as "group legal services", "legal expense insurance", or "fee indemnity insurance." It should be noted that none of these terms refers to schemes which would provide compensation for other than lawyers' fees. "Prepaid legal services" does not refer to compensation for fines, interest or other types of penalties. See generally, Wilson and Wydrzynski, "Prepaid Legal Services: Legal Representation for the Canadian Middle Class" (1978), 28 *U.T.L.J.* 25.

9.   The role which consumers should play in the delivery of legal services is still undetermined. However, consumer consciousness regarding legal services is increasing. Prepaid legal services is one system for delivery of legal services which depends on the consumer's input being functional. See Ralph Nader, "Consumerism and Legal Services: The Merging of Movements," speech at the Research Conference on the Delivery of Legal Services, December, 1975; published in L. Brickman and Richard Lempert, eds., *The Role of Research in the Delivery of Legal Services*, 97. Reprinted in (1976–77), 11 *Law & Society Rev.* 247.

10.   This attention is perhaps long overdue. "The middle classes lack the sentimental appeal of the poor, and they are unprofitable clients for the most successful members of the profession. Neither sentiment nor interest has led the profession to give to this largest part of our people the attention they merit"; Cheatham, "A Lawyer When Needed: Legal Services for the Middle Classes" (1963), 63 *Columbia L. Rev.* 973 at 974. See also, Calabresi, "Access To Justice and Substantive Law Reform: Legal Aid for the Lower Middle Class" in *Access to Justice, supra* note 2, vol. III, p. 169.

11.   It is not the object of this essay to address the issue of "legal need" directly. Numerous American studies demonstrate the unmet legal needs of the middle-income earner. It is sufficient to say that this portion of the population constitutes from 60–80%. However, problems of definition, the meaning of behavioural research, the reasons for unmet legal needs and the means to rectify this problem do not allow for determinative conclusions to be drawn. Frequently cited American studies relating legal need to prepaid legal services include the following: Stolz, "Insurance for Legal Services: A Preliminary Study of Feasibility" (1968), 35 *U. Chic. L. Rev.* 417; Christensen, *Lawyers for People of Moderate Means* (Chicago: American Bar Foundation, 1970); Curran and Spalding, *The Legal Needs of the Public* (Chicago: American Bar Foundation, 1974); and B. Curran, *The Legal Needs of the Public: The Final Report of a National Survey* (Chicago: American Bar Foundation, 1977). Reflective criticisms of these and other empirical studies can be found in Marks, "Some Research Perspectives for Looking at Legal Need and Legal Delivery Systems: Old Forms or New?" published in *The Role of Research*

in the Delivery of Legal Services, supra, note 9, p. 31. Reprinted in (1976–77), 10 *Law & Society Rev.* 191. Canadian studies are referred to *infra* under V. Experience to date. An excellent comparison can be found in Griffiths, "The Distribution of Legal Services in the Netherlands" (1977), 4 *Brit. J. of Law and Society* 260.

12.   Murphy, "Prepaid Legal Services: Development and Problems" (1978), 20 *Arizona L. Rev.* 485 at 488.

13.   See *infra*, note 16.

14.   See *United Transportation v. State Bar of Michigan* (1971), 401 U.S. 576 at 585 *per* Mr. Justice Black: "[C]ollective activity undertaken to obtain meaningful access to the courts is a fundamental right within the protection of the First Amendment".

15.   Alec M. Schwartz, Executive Director of the American Prepaid Legal Services Institute, at a Conference entitled High Intensity Workshop for Prepaid Legal Plan Administrators, Atlanta, Georgia, Nov. 15–17, 1979 (see Program and Materials, American Prepaid Legal Services Institute, Chicago) outlined 12 different models currently in operation in the United States. Obviously, cost and access can vary greatly within the prepaid model.

16.   Prepaid plans in the United States show an annual mid-range utilization rate of 10–20%. See Deitch and Weinstein, *Prepaid Legal Services, Socioeconomic Impacts* (San Diego: Lexington Book Co., 1976), p. 181. On the basis of this and other factors the authors demonstrate that "two-thirds of plan utilization would represent new business".

17.   The United States' experience has become quite sophisticated. Start-up costs, operational costs, necessary reserves and overheads can demonstrate a reasonable economic picture for a group's finances. Frequency of claims combined with the average cost of claims will show what a group can afford in annual benefit costs *per* person. American figures show that 60–70% of funds should be reserved for claims and/or staff, but that plans actually operate at 38–80%: see Dennis Farnsworth, President, Group Fifty Corporation, Lansing, Michigan, at the 8th National Conference on Prepaid Legal Services, San Francisco, California, March 12–15, 1980 (Program and Materials, American Prepaid Legal Services Institute, Chicago), pp. E–1 to E–15.

18.   Costs in the United States vary between $12 and $400 *per* year *per* member. Obviously, benefits would vary greatly, and cost is also a function of group size. Commonly, average annual cost between $25 and $150 will provide for the legal needs of a majority of employee groups. See American Prepaid Legal Services Institute, *Prepaid Group Legal Service Plans: What They Are and How They Work* (July, 1979), p. 16.

19.   The question of what constitutes a "financial legal catastrophe" is subject to many interpretations. It is difficult to suggest what a middle-income consumer would view as a sufficient "risk" worth insuring. For the purpose of this paper, I am assuming that an immediate claim for over $1,000.00 would be a sufficient financial dilemma for a middle-income person.

20.   Other typical exclusions in existing plans include, for example, a prohibition against using plan services for business purposes rather than personal legal needs or use of the plan to sue a sponsoring company, union or insurance company. Most plans only provide coverage for one family member in disputes between family members. Exclusions may also include high volume problems like preparation of income tax returns. Of course, such services could be provided by calculating these into the premium cost.

21.   The "open versus closed" debate has had a long history in the United States, first as a dilemma of professional ethics and today as to which is more efficient and economical. Both lawyers' access models are generally permitted and currently in use in the United States. Both models have virtues for differing types of groups. See Fisher versus Baron and Cole, "Future Options of the Private Bar in the Field of Prepaid Legal Services" versus "Real Freedom of Choice for the Consumer of Legal Services" (1973–74), 53 *Mass. L.Q.* 243 and 253; and Fisher versus Bernstein, "The Advantages of an Open Plan" versus "The Advantages of a Closed Plan" (1972–73), 44 *Penn. Bar Assoc. Q.* 249 and 256. Canadian experiences to date indicate that the open-closed debate is no less volatile. See *infra*, note 33.

Plan For Contingency Fees in Ont. 'On Ice,' Says Law Society Bencher[†]

R. Haliechuk

A plan to introduce contingency fees in Ontario has been put on ice, according to a bencher of the Law Society of Upper Canada.

The moment simply isn't right to start such a system, Ian Outerbridge, chairman of the society's special committee on contingency fees, said in an interview.

Eighteen months ago, it appeared as if Ontario was on the verge of adopting the new fee system, which supporters claim will allow more people with valid damage claims to get into court.

In 1988, the benchers of the society meeting in Convocation voted in principle for contingency fees, and word of the society's approval was released soon after at the Access to Justice Conference sponsored by Attorney General Ian Scott (see: "Time for contingency fees in Ont., committee says," *Lawyers Weekly*, July 8, 1988, p. 9).

Mr. Scott said at the time he was receptive to the idea, if it could be shown contingency fees would broaden access to justice.

The idea is to permit litigants of modest financial means to retain the services of a lawyer without having to pay a retainer; instead, the parties would sign a contract, which would give the lawyer a fixed percentage of whatever damages awarded to the plaintiff in a successful lawsuit.

If the action were lost, the lawyer would not be paid.

Ontario remains the only Canadian province without some form of formal contingency fee arrangement, although it's believed that many lawyers do accept briefs without requiring litigants to provide a down payment.

Following Convocation's decision, Mr. Outerbridge's committee was instructed to draft proposals on how such a system would work. A report has been prepared but not yet submitted to Convocation, Mr. Outerbridge said.

However, the Toronto civil litigation lawyer left no doubt that the concept has been shunted aside, and he cited the legal profession's poor public image as the reason.

The law society is hesitant to proceed in the face of a public perception that contingency fees are simply another way for lawyers to line their pockets, he said.

"I had the distinct impression that the legal profession was under fire," Mr. Outerbridge said. The plan is "on ice, for the moment."

Mr. Outerbridge did not say so, but it appears his belief that the profession is held in low esteem among the public stems from the recent Lang Michener controversy.

The law society has been accused of favouritism in its decision to bring misconduct proceedings against only five members of Lang Michener Lawrence and Shaw — a big Bay St. law firm — despite a recommendation by the society's former chief discipline counsel that four others should also have been charged.

One of the other four was Burke Doran, until Feb. 1 a bencher and chairman of the society's professional conduct committee.

Contingency fees have always had its detractors, including the Consumers' Association of Canada.

Helen Anderson, who heads the insurance committee for the association's Ontario wing, says she's concerned that the United States experience will be repeated in Ontario.

"What has happened in the United States is the system of ambulance-chasers, where lawyers find people who might not sue," Ms. Anderson said.

The problem is particularly acute in the automobile insurance sector, she says, where insurance firms are trying to cope with many frivolous lawsuits.

"I look at it from the point of view of who pays for it, and who pays is the consumer, as the insurers just pass along their legal costs," she said.

Mr. Outerbridge said his committee's report will be made available to Mr. Scott, if the attorney general decides to proceed with legislation implementing contingency fees.

---

†   Haliechuk, Rick, "Plan For Contingency Fees in Ont. 'On Ice,' Says Law Society Bencher" *The Lawyer's Weekly*, March 9, 1990, 4. This article originally appeared in the Mar. 9, 1990 issue of *The Lawyers Weekly*. Reprinted by permission.

Naken, The Supreme Court and What Are Our Courts For?[†]

W.A. Bogart

CLASS actions are not a clarion call to reckless social change. Their effect is not nearly so dramatic as some on either side of the question would maintain. They are, nevertheless, a useful device for litigating issues which affect large numbers of people. Since the 1960s there has been pressure to use them for many reasons, but a dominant one is the simple fact that they mirror societal structure. As much as many of us may yearn for it, the day when we could conduct ourselves as fiercely independent atoms is gone. Large entities — corporations, government, unions — have seen to that. When these entities act, their conduct affects many people. When they act wrongly the question is what means should be available to obtain redress so that the remedy will be sufficient to counter the widespread injury that has been inflicted.[1] Class actions are no universal solution, but properly designed they can be an effective means to achieve redress for widespread harm by allowing access to the court for the many claims of those injured and by providing an efficient means to litigate so that related issues do not have to be decided repeatedly.

. . . .

THE FUNCTION OF OUR COURTS

Introduction

Classically, we have thought of civil litigation's prime function as dispute resolution. Private parties have a difference and come to court — to a neutral, passive, aloof judge — to have their differences resolved by a finding of liability or non-liability. The whole process is both initiated and controlled by the parties as the hallmark of the adversarial process.[2]

These essential characteristics determine the other attributes of the traditional lawsuit. First, it is bipolar — two parties, with one the winner, the other the loser — unless they choose to settle. Secondly, the process is retrospective since it focusses upon the past conduct of the parties as the factual basis of the suit. Thirdly, rights and remedies are closely connected. Fourthly, the lawsuit is self-contained; the judgment only affects the parties before the court other than through *stare decisis*.[3] The prototypical lawsuit may be between businessmen in a suit where damages are claimed.[4] But lawsuits for damages for a car accident or for a breach of trust would also conform to the traditional model.

True, the traditional lawsuit sometimes does not conform strictly to the model just described. Admittedly, rules relating to joinder of parties and claims, counterclaims and third party proceedings could serve to extend its range.[5] But this enlargement is confined to a limited number of parties and kinds of issues. Similarly, forms of equitable relief such as injunctions and specific performance require the presence of the court to ensure that there is continuing compliance with, for example, an injunction when its terms so require. But the courts' suspicion of these remedies is, in large part, due to their concern about being involved on an ongoing basis.[6] In any event the terms of these remedies are usually narrow and well defined. It is a comparatively easy task to know whether or not the court's orders are being carried out.[7]

. . . .

The New Model of Litigation

In the United States a new form of litigation with an altered role for the court is now widely recognized, though its desirability remains deeply controversial. These lawsuits have been given a variety of titles — "managerial",[8] "complex",[9] "structural",[10] "public law".[11] Nevertheless, while these descriptions are meant to convey differing emphasis and varying degrees of approval, there are common aspects which have emerged.

In essence the new model involves a challenge to the policy of some large entity — most frequently that of government but also of corporations.[12] This principal feature determines other attributes which, it will be noted, are in marked contrast to the features of the traditional model. Firstly, the party structure and the matter in controversy are much less well defined and can change throughout the litigation. Secondly, the orientation of the lawsuit is prospective, particularly in relation to non-monetary relief. Thirdly, the relief, as it is forward looking, is not necessarily logically derived from the right established and is often established on the basis of some negotiating process. Fourthly, the relief described in points two and three requires continuing, and active, judicial involvement and the relief, because it is against some policy, governmental or corporate, will have far-ranging impact. The vehicle for this kind of litigation is frequently the class action.[13]

It would be surprising if the new model did not spark debate centring upon the changed role of the judge. No longer neutral, passive, and aloof, he or she is, at least sometimes, the main player. Supporters of the model see

† Bogart, W.A., "Naken, The Supreme Court and What Are Our Courts For?" (1984), 9 *Canadian Business Law Journal* at 280–81, 299–308. Reprinted by permission of Professor W.A. Bogart and Canadian Business Law Journal.

it as "stirring the deep and durable demand for justice in our society".[14] Detractors see the judge reduced to little more than a broker and negotiator presiding over intractable tasks such as institutional reform "constantly descending to the level of the litigants, as an examiner, patient or hectoring, as counselor and advisor [and] as insistent promoter of settlements".[15]

As is often the case, the state of the law in Canada in this area trails significantly that of the United States. However, one can point to a number of developments which suggest that there are alterations being made to the traditional model of litigation. And, as with any situation of following rather than leading, there is the opportunity to examine what is occurring here and to influence its direction based on what has already happened to those who have gone before.

To some extent litigation is changing simply because it is becoming more complicated. These complications, while making the lawsuit more protracted and difficult (and more expensive), cause relatively limited departures from the traditional model. For example, commercial litigation is often now more complicated but the complexity arises from the highly technical issues in the dispute and the sometimes vast numbers of documents generated in the relationship between the parties, rather than the introduction of a multitude of parties and wide variation of interests within the litigation.

However, complexities in other forms of litigation do arise from the nature of the parties involved and the rights sought to be enforced. For example, in derivative suits a shareholder normally sues in respect of a wrong done to a corporation. But the interests of the other shareholders, aligned in interest with the suing shareholder, are affected by the suit, which cannot be initiated without the court's permission or settled without its consent.[16] Furthermore, the nature of wrongs done to corporations often involves complicated corporate transactions and this too can add an additional dimension to derivative suits.[17]

Litigation conducted by an individual suing to enforce a "public right", which arises from harm done that affects a large group of people and yet no one of them particularly, will also depart from the traditional model.[18] These cases, which have had a history as checkered as class actions,[19] are often referred to as standing cases since the plaintiff's right to bring these suits is often challenged precisely because he has been harmed to no greater extent than other members of the public. Here the interests of a large group, many of whom will not actually be parties to the litigation, will have to be asserted by individuals and these actions will have to be monitored to ensure that the group's interests are taken into account. In addition, apart from the complexity inherent in deciding liability issues, the courts and the parties will expend substantial effort in fashioning an appropriate remedy for the harm done on a mass scale. There may be a variety of representations made by the group in respect of the kind and scope of the remedy that should be fashioned.[20]

Nevertheless, it is the class action which represents the greatest departure from the traditional model of litigation. The nature of the right asserted based upon a mass harm, the representation of absentee members whose interests may not coincide in all respects and the need to protect those interests, the assessment and distribution of monetary relief in innovative ways as well as the fashioning of other relief, sometimes on the basis of competing representations within the class, and the procedural aspects of class actions such as the motion for certification, are all factors which can make the class action, both in appearance and performance, a clear departure from the traditional model of litigation.[21]

Defining the Role of the Court in the New Litigation

If one accepts the basic proposition that we need a mechanism to challenge the actions of large entities, then it follows that we must be prepared to accept procedural changes that will allow such challenges to be made effectively. Unless one is prepared to create a totally new adjudicative body or adopt some other far-ranging solution, it seems to follow that the court's role will be altered as it begins to deal with this new form of litigation.

In contrast, to reject the need for effective challenge to the activities of large entities would, it seems to me, only breed confusion and frustration in a citizenry which already feels hopelessly at odds with much of the workings of society during the last part of the 20th century.[22] Even if such frustration is not the stuff of revolutions, at a minimum the widely held perception of our courts as anachronistic and unresponsive may spread.[23] More damaging may be the belief that the rules of litigation really do favour institutions and are less concerned with the enforcement of rights by individuals.[24]

To me the only realistic alternative is to develop new rules and standards which will allow this new form of litigation to proceed. In this Estey J.'s judgment in *Naken* is disappointing because it displays so little interest in the problems and issues raised by cases like *Naken*. Such an attitude does little to deflect the trenchant criticisms about the Supreme Court's lack of capacity or willingness to engage in far-ranging analysis of difficult problems.[25] Nevertheless, one clear effect of the Supreme Court's decision in *Naken* is to signal the Legislatures that change, if it is to come, must come through them.

In attempting to define the role of the court in class action litigation the recommendations of the Ontario Law Reform Commission in its *Report on Class Actions* offers a significant basis for discussion. The commission has attempted to steer a middle course between, on the one hand, a passive court that does little to control litigation and, on the other hand, an active court which, in perception at least, dominates it.

The key to its recommendations is to give the court a more developed role but one which is defined by specific guidelines. For example, a critical stage of the class action is the certification hearing during which the court decides whether or not the action should proceed as a class action. In Chapter 10 of the report, the commission makes recommendations about the certification hearing, the timing of it, the means by which evidence is placed before the court in the hearing and the powers of the court when it hears the certification application.[26] In addition, the court would be empowered to allow or refuse certification and to make all amendments to the proceedings required by its order.[27] The court could also amend a certification order and, subsequently, set the order aside if satisfied that the action was no longer one which should be a class action.[28]

In order to control the class action during and from certification to trial of the common questions general management powers are recommended for the court. These powers most closely resemble some of the pre-trial powers exercised by "activist" judges in the United States. While there are many differences, the vital one is that in the commission's model one judge would take all pre-trial motions and interlocutory proceedings, including the certification hearing, but another judge would preside at the trial of the common questions. The trial judge would also supervise any proceedings after the hearing of the common questions, for example, if the class were successful but hearings were necessary to determine individual questions.[29] Thus the function of "managing" the litigation during the pre-trial phase and actually adjudicating the merits of the action at trial would be separated. The lack of separation of these functions is a main criticism of those concerned with the activist stance of courts in the United States.[31] Central to this potential for greater involvement by the court is a provision which states:[31]

15. The court, upon the application of a party or upon its own motion, may make any order under this Act and all appropriate orders determining the course of the action for the purpose of ensuring the fair and expeditious determination thereof, including an order to prevent undue repetition or complication in the action, and the court may impose such terms and conditions upon the parties as it considers proper.

In making the recommendation concerning broader management powers the commission recognized the dual rationale of the need to protect the interest of absentees[32] and to deal with the complexity inherent in many class actions.[33] However, the commission was careful to point out that its guiding philosophy was not to depart from the adversarial model of litigation. It simply wished to equip the court with sufficient power to allow it to deal properly with this new form of expanded and complex litigation while, at the same time, permitting as much independence and freedom to the parties as possible.[34]

CONCLUSION

For those who see the potential of class actions there is clearly an agenda of issues to be discussed concerning their structure so that their intended purposes are achieved and abuses avoided. Issues such as design of a certification mechanism, whether class actions should play a deterrence function, calculation and distribution of monetary claims, the role of class members, and costs, are only a selection of issues which merit reflection. For me the effect of class actions upon the court and how we should design the mechanism both to allow the court to adjust to this new form of litigation and to be sufficiently innovative in managing it is the most fascinating aspect. To what extent will we need to become part of the debate about the appropriate function of courts in the new litigation which now seems so much a part of the American legal culture and how will we solve the issue to which this debate gives rise?[35]

Notwithstanding the complexities and controversies surrounding them, I believe those who reject class actions will have a hard road. If the basis of rejection is the lack of need for such a procedure, I think they will have a difficult time demonstrating that there are not widespread harms that require a means of redress. If they acknowledge these harms but simply object to class actions as the means of redress they will then have to suggest a suitable and adequate alternative. Thinking about such alternatives will be a fascinating exercise and we should not hesitate to do so. However, in the end I believe it is the class action — the *ad hoc* collectivity which organizes its members for a specific purpose and limited time — which will best answer the needs of group action at the end of the 20th century.

Endnotes

1. See The Ontario Law Reform Commission, *Report on Class Actions* (1982), Vols. 1 to 3 (hereafter "1, 2 or 3 O.L.R.C., *Class Actions Report*"), at p. 3:

The mass production and sale of an inherently defective product has the potential to touch all consumers of that product. Misleading advertising by a large corporation can have province-wide or even national implications. Large scale pollution of rivers or the atmosphere can affect countless persons over a long period of time. Sophisticated securities frauds, discrimination in hiring, illegal strikes, and many other types of unlawful conduct have direct and indirect ramifications for all of society. And in the wake of such misconduct, the individual is very often unable or unwilling to stand alone in meaningful opposition.

2. The discussion contrasting the traditional and the new forms of litigation is indebted to two pieces by Chayes: Chayes (1976), *supra*, footnote 4, and "The Supreme Court, 1981 Term — Foreword: 'Public Law Litigation and The Burger Court'" (1982), 96 *Har. L. Rev.* 4, hereafter "Chayes (1982)").

3. Chayes (1982), at pp. 4–5.

4. Fuller, "The Forms and Limits of Adjudication" (1978), 92 *Har. L. Rev.* 353 at 386.

5. See, for example, a discussion of this point in respect of third party claims in Halfnight, *op. cit.*, footnote 5, at p. 87.

6. Edmund H.T. Snell, *Snell's Principles of Equity*, 28th ed. (Toronto: Carswell, 1982), 637; and Hanbury and Maudsley, *Modern Equity*, 11th ed. (Toronto: Carswell, 1981), 53, 95.

7. *Snell's Principles of Equity, ibid.*, at 650–51.

8. See Resnick, "Managerial Judges" (1982), 96 *Har. L. Rev.* 376 (hereafter "Resnick").

9. See *Manual for Complex Litigation*, 5th ed. (1982). The manual is a handbook edited by a committee of judges in the Federal Judicial Center, which contains a text together with recommended forms, orders, and rules for the purpose of suggesting both pre-trial and trial techniques for handling complex cases.

10. See Fiss, "The Supreme Court, 1978 Term — Foreword: 'The Forms of Justice'" (1979), 93 *Har. L. Rev.* 1 at 2.

11. Chayes (1976).

12. Chayes (1982), at p. 5.

13. *Ibid.*, and see Chayes (1976), at p. 1291.

14. Chayes (1976), at p. 316.

15. Resnick, at p. 386. And for an English view sounding a substantial note of caution see Jolowicz, "Protection of Diffuse, Fragmented and Collective Interests in Civil Litigation: English Law" (unpublished report) (Wurzburg: The Seventh International Congress on Procedural Law, 1983). Professor Jolowicz says, at p. 15: "through the development of the class action...a serious judicial usurpation of the functions of the Legislature may be brought about".

16. See, for example, the *Business Corporations Act*, S.O. 1982, c. 4, s. 245 (hereafter "B.C.A.").

17. For a discussion of the derivative suit see: Baxter, "The Derivative Action Under the *Ontario Business Corporations Act*: A Review of Section 97" (1981), 27 *McGill L.J.* 453.

18. For the literature on standing see, *supra*, footnote 27.

19. The Supreme Court of Canada's latest contribution is *Minister of Justice of Canada v. Borowski* (1981), 130 D.L.R. (3d) 588, [1981] 2 S.C.R. 575.

20. The British Columbia Law Reform Commission has now reported on such litigation: *Report on Civil Litigation in the Public Interest* (1980). For a review of the report suggesting some other complexities of this litigation that ought to have been dealt with see: Bogart, (1981), 59 *Can. Bar Rev.* 868. The Ontario Law Reform Commission is now at work on a project on the law of standing.

21. Chayes has stated, in Chayes (1976), at p. 1291:

> Whatever the resolution of the current controversies surrounding class actions, I think it unlikely that the class action will ever be taught to behave in accordance with the precepts of the traditional model of adjudication. The class suit is a reflection of our growing awareness that a host of important public and private interactions — perhaps the most important in defining the conditions and opportunities of life for most people — are conducted on a routine or bureaucratized basis and can no longer be visualized as bilateral transactions between private individuals. From another angle, the class action responds to the proliferation of more or less well-organized groups in our society and the tendency to perceive interests as group interests, at least in very important aspects.

The growth of complex litigation, present and potential, in Canada is discussed, in a different context, in Wildsmith, "An American Enforcement Model of Civil process in a Canadian Landscape" (1980), 15 *Dal. L.J.* 71.

22. See 1 O.L.R.C., *Class Actions Report*, at p. 3:

> In the past, we generally have accepted as fair and reasonable the often heavy burden of ultimately vindicating our rights by the commencement of individual legal proceedings. We place our faith in an impartial judiciary, and in those whom we retain to assert our claims, to safeguard our interests and obtain redress for wrongs suffered by us.
>
> To a considerable extent, however, this perspective of our place in society is today somewhat outdated — an anachronism often more a reflection of nostalgia than reality. Individualistic notions of our capacity to assert and protect our legal rights by acting alone were, of course, never entirely in accordance with the often harsh facts. Moreover, it is hardly revolutionary to suggest that we have never had such comprehensive legal protection as we enjoy today. But the mere cataloguing of legal rights reveals only one part of the story, and masks another. Social, economic, political, and other changes in our society — telescoped as they have been into a brief period of time — have radically affected our ability to pursue our goals in isolation.

23. For a judicial view concerning the outmoded aspects of our courts see Hugessen, "Are the Courts Cost-Efficient?" in *Cost of Justice* (Montreal: Canadian Institute for the Administration of Justice, 1980). In his analysis, Mr. Justice Hugessen uses strong language: for example he states, at p. 52:

> Even after allowances are made, however, for the irreducible minimum of griping and complaining about the system, the conclusion seems inescapable that the courts are not giving satisfaction to their clientele. This, I think, is the only explanation which can be given for the continuing and growing flood away from the courts as a means of dispute resolution for the last three-quarters of a century or so. Despite all the roadblocks which the courts themselves have thrown up to protect their monopolistic position, citizens, governments and legislatures have kept up a constant pressure to avoid having their problems go to court.

The inflexibility of the courts has often been discussed in the administrative law context. See for example, Arthurs, "Jonah and the Whale: The Appearance, Disappearance, and Reappearance of Administrative Law" (1980), 30 *U.T.L.J.* 225 at 225.

24. There is a substantial body of literature which has explored the question of whether litigation favours institutional parties. See, for example, Cappelletti and Garth, "Access to Justice: The Newest Wave in the World-Wide Movement to Make Rights Effective" (1977–78), 27 *Buff. L. Rev.* 18; and Galanter, "Why the 'Haves' Come Out Ahead: Speculations on the Limits of Legal Change" (1974), 9 *Law & Soc. Rev.* 95.

25. See, for example, Weiler, *In the Last Resort* (1974).

26. See, O.L.R.C. Draft Bill, ss. 3 to 9.

27. *Ibid.*, ss. 9, 10.

28. *Ibid.*, s. 10.

29. *Ibid.*, s. 51, and see s. 22 dealing with distribution of monetary relief and s. 31 dealing with individual proceedings.

30. See Resnick, *supra*, footnote 88, at 433–34.

31. O.L.R.C. Draft Bill, s. 15. The provision is not without some precedent in Canada. See Nova Scotia *Civil Procedure Rules and Related Rules*, Rule 25, which permits the court on its own motion to make a wide range of orders, including an order giving "directions as to the procedure to govern the future course of any proceeding, which directions shall govern the proceeding notwithstanding the provision of any rule to the contrary" (Rule 25.01(1)(d)). See also s. 246 of the B.C.A., which authorizes the court regarding derivative actions to make "at any time...any order it thinks fit including...an order giving directions for the conduct of the action".

32. 2 O.L.R.C., *Class Actions Report*, at p. 445.

33. *Ibid.*, at p. 446.

34. *Ibid.*, at p. 452, the commission stated:

> We recognize that the initial reaction of some judges and lawyers to the Commission's recommendation for a broad general management power may be a fear that the proposed changes may undermine the adversarial system. The term "adversarial system" is one that is often used without too much attention to its meaning; in our view, a thoughtful definition should focus upon the fact that such a system envisages the initiation and prosecution of lawsuits by the parties. If these are the two salient characteristics of the adversarial system, the recommendation made in this section should not threaten this system in the slightest.

35. For a discussion of these issues from a comparative viewpoint see Cappelletti and Garth, "The Protection of Diffuse, Fragmented and Collective Interests in Civil Litigation" in Habscheid, ed., *Effectiveness of Judicial Protection and Constitutional Order* (Wurzburg: The General Reports for the Seventh International Congress on Procedural Law, 1983).

9 | People in the Legal Process: The Personnel of Law

A. What do Lawyers Do? The Practice of Lawyering

Specialization and the Legal Profession[†]
A. Esau

INTRODUCTION

Pressures For Change

Lawyers have often reminded themselves of the need to be responsive to changing needs in fulfilling the self-regulating mandate of the legal profession to focus on the public interest. This challenge appears to have become particularly urgent in our time as increasing pressures for change from both inside and outside the profession are converging around a number of often interrelated and difficult issues which have found their way to the top of the profession's agenda for consideration.

INFORMED ACCESS TO LEGAL SERVICES

The increasing growth and complexity of the law in substance and range, coupled with the increasing demands made by people for participation, protection, and equal rights within the legal process has led to increasing demands for legal services. We have witnessed in response a growing emphasis on legal aid plans aimed at providing essential legal services for those who cannot afford to pay for them. The provision of legal aid is still a very live issue for the legal profession due to such continuing problems as funding and the formulation of the most appropriate form of delivery system. However, the pressure for change appears to have shifted now to the legal needs of the majority of the population, namely the middle income groups. There appears to be some evidence that the general public has difficulty knowing when a legal problem exists, or how to find a lawyer to help, and that a segment of the public fears the size of legal fees or has a general distrust or even fear of lawyers. A recent survey in the United States revealed that even though adult Americans experience an average of 3.3 "serious legal problems" during their lives, a third of the public has never used a lawyer and another 28.9% has used a lawyer only once. This survey also revealed that 79.2% of all respondents agreed that "[a] lot of people do not go to lawyers because they have no way of knowing which lawyer is competent to handle their particular problem". As well, the survey revealed that over 60% of the respondents, including both people who have used and those who have not used lawyers, thought that lawyers cost too much.

The middle income groups in Canada have difficulty making informed choices about legal services and how much they cost, given traditional professional advertising rules, was recently documented in the *Canadian Consumer*. From inside the profession, Stuart Thom, The Treasurer of the Law Society of Upper Canada, confirmed that the public needs more knowledge about the availability and kinds of the legal services:

> The large corporation or institution with sophisticated personnel in charge of its affairs usually has a well-established legal connection. The average man or woman who as a rule seeks legal assistance only occasionally and for some immediate specific reason such as buying a house, because of an accident, to get a divorce, is not so

---

† Esau, Alvin, "Specialization and the Legal Profession" (1979), 9 *Manitoba Law Journal* 255. Reprinted by permission of Professor Alvin Esau.

equipped. The questions the occasional clients have to ask and try to get answered are "How do I get in touch with a lawyer who will do the work I want done?", "How do I know he will be any good?", "How much will he charge me?". The legal profession hasn't done much, in fact it has done very little, to help people answer these questions.

At the same time that these claims are made about unmet needs for legal services there appears to be a serious and growing problem finding articling positions and jobs for the increasing number of law school graduates. Thus pressure for change to provide better access to legal services is increased by the perception that a "job gap" should not exist when there is a "need gap" to fill.

QUALITY OF LEGAL SERVICES

Delay and neglect continue to be frequent complaints lodged against lawyers by their clients, and there is a rise in the number of successful malpractice suits against lawyers. Much of the pressure which has made the competency issue of such current concern, however, has come from within the legal fraternity itself. For example, Chief Justice Warren Burger of the United States Supreme Court has expressed the opinion on several occasions that up to one-half of the attorneys practising before the courts are incompetent as trial advocates. Professor Irving Younger, a former New York State Court judge, has stated:

> Perhaps half of the lawyers who tried cases before me showed an inadequate grasp of the law of evidence, the law of procedure, and trial technique. Some — perhaps 10% — were total strangers to those interesting subjects. The remaining 40% did not know enough about them to do a workmanlike job. Usually they stumbled through somehow — because the lawyer on the other side was just as bad, or the judge helped, or the jury managed to figure the case out despite the lawyer. This state of affairs is inexcusable.

Chief Justice Irving Kaufman of the United States Court of Appeals has stated that many attorneys lack competency as well as integrity, and one judge went so far as to say that only two percent of the lawyers appearing before him were competent.

Whether or not incompetence has reached such a crisis proportion can certainly be debated with regard to trial skills, and in non-trial aspects of lawyering as well, but in this period of both rapid change and increased complexity within many areas of the law, the problem of what the profession's response to the incompetency problem should

be, is a current issue of utmost importance occupying a great deal of the profession's attention, not only in the United States but also in Canada.

THE DELIVERY AND COST OF LEGAL SERVICES

Related to the need for informed access to quality legal services, is the issue involving the method of delivering these services and their cost. The suitability of the traditional delivery system of the sole practitioner or small law firm has been challenged by demands for prepaid and group legal services plans, by demands for special community legal clinics utilizing a high degree of standardization procedures and paraprofessional services, and by "public interest" law firms. Furthermore, demands for change in the method of delivering legal services are related to concurrent demands for change in the legal process such as legalization of certain conduct, no-fault laws, law reform proposals aimed at simplified and understandable legal forms and procedures, and the utilization of less formal mechanisms of dispute resolution.

THE CONCEPT OF SPECIALIZATION

One of the most debated proposals aimed at responding to the challenge of providing more informed access to competently performed, efficiently delivered, reasonably priced legal services is the demand for some formal regulation of specialization within the legal profession. This paper will outline the developments on this front in the United States and Canada and raise some of the specific problems involved in the formal regulation of specialization. First, however, some comments on *de facto* specialization, and the assumed positive goals and possible negative effects of specialization must be presented as a background to understanding the developments taking place.

De Facto Specialization

Leaving aside for a moment the problems of defining what it means to be a "specialist", it is at least common knowledge within the legal profession that some lawyers only handle certain matters and not others, or spend most of their time on certain matters. It is also common knowledge in the profession that the growth of large law firms is often based on teamwork within the context of a high degree of individual specialization.

Generally, a poll of Wisconsin lawyers found that 55% of the respondents indicated that their practices were more than 50% in one given field. A random survey of 125 Toronto lawyers in 1971 found that 72% were restricting their practice and that 58% of the lawyers were spending more than 70% of their time in one field of law or spending their full time in one or two fields. On a provincial basis, the MacKinnon Committee in Ontario found that of 4,411 lawyers responding to a questionnaire in 1972, approximately 50% said they specialized rather than engaged in general practice. According to a 1969 California survey, two out of three lawyers in that State considered themselves specialists, and four out of five lawyers called themselves specialists. A 1975 Illinois State Bar Association survey found that 48% of the lawyers in that State said they engaged in specialized practice only, while 51% called themselves general practitioners who also had one or more specialties.

While surveys may not help establish the actual amount of *de facto* specialization that exists, and until there is a consensus as to what the definition of "specialization" is, one can conclude at least that many lawyers do not hold themselves out as willing to help every potential client who happens to call. Thus, the issue is not whether specialization should exist in the profession, since it already does; but rather the issue is whether it should be encouraged and formally regulated and what the approach to that regulation should be.

There are undoubtedly many factors leading to the *de facto* narrowing of legal practice. Commonly noted is that with the increasing complexity of society, there is an increasing complexity in the law and an increasing difficulty in keeping up with legal developments in many areas. Some typical expressions in favor of narrowing practice are as follows:

If a lawyer truly tries to be proficient in a great number of fields, he must necessarily spend a fantastic number of hours in understanding those fields before he can move forward in them. When he develops a particular subject as his field, he can much more expeditiously accomplish the work to his own benefit, as well as to the benefit of his client, so that his time is utilized in the most efficient manner.

Concentration of experience enables lawyers to provide better legal services in their specialty in less time with consequent savings to their clients.

New developments, procedures and problems in every field of practice are generated continuously by the courts, legislatures, administrative agencies and special bar groups. Many popular and active fields of legal practice did not even exist forty years ago. The volume of current material in the form of advance sheets, services, synopses, summaries, articles, journals and the like are so numerous and voluminous that no practitioner can possibly read it all. It is unrealistic to expect any modern lawyer to stay abreast of all the de-

velopments in all the areas of law or to be competent in all fields of general practice.

Since most lawyers simply cannot maintain more than a nodding acquaintance with most areas of the law, we have witnessed the growth of an informal system of legal specialization.

Few practitioners today can hope, claim, or even pretend to be master of every field of the law —the day of the true general practitioner who handles every matter himself without referring to or consulting with others who have more particularized knowledge and experience is a thing of the past.

The connection between competence and specialization, then, appears to be a leading factor in the development of *de facto* specialization. Competence, furthermore, is a dimension of professional ethics, and thus to some degree *de facto* narrowing of practice is encouraged by our Code of Professional Conduct. Even the general practitioner may not be so "general" after all. Chapter II of the Code dealing with "Competency and Quality of Service" has the following rule:

(a) The lawyer owes a duty to his client to be competent to perform the legal services which the lawyer undertakes on his behalf.

(b) The lawyer should serve his client in a conscientious, diligent and efficient manner and he should provide a quality of service at least equal to that which lawyers generally would expect of a competent lawyer in a like situation.

The commentary after the rule includes the following provision:

It follows that the lawyer should not undertake a matter unless he honestly believes that he is competent to handle it or that he can become competent without undue delay, risk or expense to his client. If the lawyer proceeds on any other basis he is not being honest with his client. This is an ethical consideration and is to be distinguished from the standard of care which a court would invoke for purposes of determining negligence.

If becoming competent in a matter without undue delay, risk, or expense is an increasingly difficult problem, then one may conclude that *de facto* specialization is not only a present reality but may well substantially increase in the future.

One factor, however, which may be pointing away from a substantial increase in *de facto* specialization is the greater number of lawyers who are not able to stay with the law firms they articled in or find jobs with established law firms and thus move immediately into setting up their own independent practices, alone or in association with lawyers in the same position. This growth of independent practice by very recently licensed lawyers may lead to a greater number of general practitioners, unable economically to restrict their practices to a few fields, at least for many years. How are the Code provisions noted above accepted by these lawyers who may have a considerable lack of confidence and experience in many areas of the law, but who must nevertheless gain experience and confidence by taking cases if their independent practices are going to survive? What reforms, if any, should be undertaken by the legal profession to be fair both to young lawyers caught in a "job squeeze" and to the public who deserve high quality legal services?

Aside from the difficulty of being "omnicompetent" as one factor leading to *de facto* specialization, a variety of other factors could be cited, including a lawyer's own special interests in certain fields; or a lawyer's innate aptitude, or lack thereof, in particular skills like advocacy or negotiation; or the lawyer's sensitivity to perceived economic, political, or moral status attributed to certain kinds of firm or being employed for the particular needs of a certain group or individual, in government or industry.

The Definitional Problem

Any movement from the existence of *de facto* specialization to some formal regulation of specialization, including the provision for advertising to the public of the availability of specialists, must first deal with the fact that no consensus appears to exist as to what "specialization" really means.

How one chooses to define specialization — as expertise or concentration, in specialized areas or in all areas — may depend on the goal to be accomplished by the regulatory scheme.

Assumed Positive Goals of Specialization

While the existence, and perhaps increase, of *de facto* specialization may by itself further certain sought-after goals, the formal regulation of specialization may both accelerate the movement toward these goals as well as add to or modify them. At this stage, however, one must still make assumptions and speculate about the effects of formal regulation schemes because sophisticated evaluations of existing formal regulation programs have not been completed. The most recent report of the A.B.A. Committee on Specialization stated: "No data exists now, or will exist in the foreseeable future, which provides definitive answers to the access, quality and cost implications of specialization regulation." Until we have more data on the effects of formal regulation we are left with a number of

assumed effects which may be considered worthwhile if achieved by regulation. These assumed effects are related directly to the demands for change cited earlier.

IMPROVED QUALITY OF LEGAL SERVICE

The A.B.A. Committee on Specialization formulated a list of possible "pros and cons" of specialization. Of the sixteen items on the "pro" list, at least eight items related to the argument that specialization improves the quality of legal services:

1. The certified specialist will become more proficient in solving problems in his specialized field.
2. Other lawyers will become more proficient in solving legal problems.
3. The overall quality of legal services to the public will improve.

. . . .

6. The quality of solutions to legal problems on an individual basis will improve.
7. Specialized services will be made available to the general practitioner.

. . . .

14. Specialists will recognize a legal problem or solution overlooked by a general practitioner.
15. Law schools will be encouraged to offer in depth courses in the areas of specialization certification.
16. Because quality of legal work will be improved, there will be less load on court dockets.

How could a formal regulation scheme arguably lead to this effect of increased quality of service and competency of lawyers, individually and generally? As noted earlier, incentives to narrow practice may help lawyers to keep up with developments in their chosen areas and help lawyers gain substantial experience in certain matters which should lead to increased skill and familiarity in handling them. The primary function of a formal regulation scheme should be to encourage greater numbers of lawyers to move from generalist practice and thus generally raise the level of competence in the profession.

With the advertising of the availability of specialized legal services, matters calling for special expertise will more likely be channelled away from nonspecialists to the specialists and thus these matters will be better handled and the overall quality of legal services will be higher than in the present situation where some of these matters would be handled by generalists wanting work. Setting high standards and testing for experience, skill, and knowledge as entrance requirements for the formal certification or recognition of specialists may serve to weed out those who do not deserve to be called specialists and generally encourage achievement to reach the standards set, all of which may serve to improve standards of legal practice. Furthermore, periodic mandatory recertification requirements may serve to maintain high standards of competence over time. The formal regulation of specialization may encourage development and utilization of specialized C.L.E. programs and special post-graduate university educational programs all of which would help lawyers become more competent and maintain such competency. The formal regulation of specialization may provide general practitioners with more knowledge about the availability of specialists than they now have, and thus, a greater number of referrals may result with a consequent rise in the general quality of legal service.

These propositions about increased competency depend obviously on what form the scheme of regulation would take. As well, the effects of specialization on competency must be taken together with the effects of the many other factors bearing on the competency issue.

INFORMED ACCESS TO LEGAL SERVICES

Professor Reed, commenting on the view that formal regulation of specialization coupled with informational advertising, might increase informed rather than random access to legal services, noted that: "If I've got trouble with my head and I want to see a psychiatrist, I can find out who one is. I don't have to call some doctor and say, 'Do you know anything about psychiatry, Doctor?'" Similarly, demands for the formal regulation of specialization in California arose originally, not out of a perceived competency problem, but out of the suggestion of a Committee on Group Legal Services which urged the certification of specialists as a possible alternative or adjunct to meeting the needs of the public for informed access to legal services.

More informed access is accomplished through a formal regulation scheme providing some method whereby lawyers who meet certain standards can hold themselves out to the public as specialists in a certain field or fields of law. Again the achievement of this goal will depend on what form the specialization scheme takes, what fields of law are chosen, how many lawyers will meet the standards set or attempt to meet them and thus be able to participate in the program, how quickly the program can be implemented, and so forth.

The definitional problem of what it means to be a "specialist" may well depend on which goal is primarily pursued, increased access to legal services or increased quality. Whether the focus is, or should be primarily on access, may depend on the policies adopted or lacking regarding other factors that aim at public knowledge of the availability and kind of legal services.

EFFICIENT DELIVERY AND LOWER COST OF LEGAL SERVICES

Another assumed positive goal of the regulation of specialization is that the specialist can spend much less time on matters because the substantial experience gained by concentration should lead to increased efficiency. Decreased costs should also result because the client would not have to pay for as many research hours and perhaps in some situations with high volume, the lawyer may even have standardized procedures and paralegal services, which will lower the cost for the client. Of course, in all of this, the specialist, it is argued, will still be able to earn more than the generalist.

PUBLIC TRUST AND LEGAL ETHICS IMPROVED

Clients generally may be more satisfied with results achieved when specialists are used, so the public image of the legal profession may improve. The formulation of special standards of ethics and increased discussion of the special ethical problems encountered within certain areas of practice may lead to heightened sensitivity toward ethical dimensions of practice.

CONTROLLED ADVERTISING

While the formal regulation of specialization may *encourage* advertising to achieve the goal of informed access to legal services, the formal regulation of specialization may also serve to *control* advertising. If lawyers will be allowed to advertise fields of law in which they are willing to accept cases, then some formal regulation of specialization may serve to minimize the problem of misrepresentation to consumers of implied special expertise that results from such advertising in the absence of a specialization scheme. The most recent report of the A.B.A. Committee on Specialization noted that the changes made in advertising policy have resulted in an increased demand for regulation of specialization as "One step toward increasing the accuracy of information which the public and the bar will have about the lawyers who have appropriate qualifications to help with particular problems." Such regulation, of course, requires the formulation of generally accepted labels, definitions and quality standards if it is going to be successful in providing accurate information to the public. Specialization regulation might have the effect of allowing only those who are likely to be *able* to take problems in certain fields and not just *willing* to take them, to advertise such actual or implied competence.

LESS "UNAUTHORIZED PRACTICE"

The Alberta Law Society Committee reporting on specialization noted:

> If the public does not have specialist legal assistance available, there is a likelihood it will turn to other professions and groups for assistance in some fields. An example given is that a great deal of the work in tax matters formerly done by the legal profession is now done by chartered accountants. Similarly, in real estate transactions the parties may not use a lawyer at all or, at any event only in a late stage of the transaction. The specialist doing a volume of such work as a routine, can offer superior service at a lower fee.

Possible Negative Effects of Specialization

The formal regulation of specialization may be criticized without necessarily pointing to a list of possible negative effects that must be balanced against the assumed positive effects listed above. Rather the criticism can proceed by asserting that the positive effects cannot be attained by formal regulation anyway. For example, it may be argued that setting standards and testing for competency cannot achieve a measure of quality assurance because standards cannot be formulated that objectively measure competence in any case, and that furthermore, the cost to the consumer of legal services will rise with specialization, not fall.

The criticism of formal regulation might proceed as well with the assertion that the need to examine possible positive and negative effects is unnecessary because there is no public demand for specialized legal services in the first place. Those groups in need of specialized service have the legal connections to serve them in the present situation, and the public simply needs competent generalists and more information about their services. This, of course, begs the question again as to what the definition of a "specialist" should be.

If a critic, however, does accept that positive goals may be furthered by formal regulation, the argument may be made that the negative effects may outweigh the positive effects. What these negative effects are will depend on what form the regulation takes in the light of what priority of goals is emphasized and what concept of specialization is adopted.

OVERSPECIALIZATION DANGERS

Beneath the surface of the pressures for change in the legal profession there appears to be a tension between two value clusters which might broadly be labelled "consumerism" and "humanism." While these two movements are certainly not opposing systems of thought, there are points of tension discernible between them. On one hand, the consumer movement appears to favor developments that provide legal services very much like the supply of goods in a supermarket. Standardization of forms and procedures, check-list interviews, pre-advertised fees, labelled services, and the like, are indicative of this consumer movement stressing efficiency, low cost, and accessibility. On the other hand, there is a movement, most visible in legal education, but also discernible from both within and without the profession, stressing the need for greater awareness and aptitude on the part of lawyers in handling the relational aspects of legal practice. Legal educators stress the need to be sensitive to the whole person, to see the client as a person not simply as a problem, to have greater sensitivity to the interaction of nonlegal aspects with the legal aspects of a client's problems, to be sensitive to feelings in the interviewing and counselling process, and generally to concentrate on the lawyer-client relationship rather than on commercial dimensions of law practice. These humanistic values may be difficult to pursue within the delivery systems arising out of the consumer movement.

Perhaps a third force, partly related to humanism, might be labelled "traditionalism" which views many of the proposed changes in the legal profession with scepticism. Related to both the humanistic and traditionalistic forces are criticisms of the formal regulation of specialization focusing on a series of dangers brought about by over-specialization. The bad joke is told about the old doctor who was talking to the young doctor, who was just going into a specialty. The old doctor said, "I hear you are not going to be an ear, nose, and throat doctor like your daddy. You are just going to take the nose?" "Oh no," said the young man, "just the left nostril." The legal profession has traditionally viewed itself as being the architect of democracy, a prime source of wise leadership at all levels of policy making, with the capacity for a broad vision applied to human problems. Thus, a mass movement toward narrow practice is feared by some lawyers. The following comments are indicative:

> In some ways, it seems that as we get better and better at more restricted assignments, we are valued less and less on matters of general importance.
>
> A specialist loses touch with the many problems which present themselves in the general practice of law; specialists are generally ignorant of matters outside their specialty; a narrow and

confined approach to overall problems tends to hasten the disintegration of a free society which needs generalists as well as specialists; and, the well-rounded lawyer can more easily see the interrelated problems of a client and can thus better serve him.

The principal and overriding defect of most certification/recognition proposals is their acceptance of the theory of *expertise*. That concept is delusive because technical experts tend to destroy the integrity of any discipline of which they are a part. In the legal profession, more likely than not, they will substitute the ways of the expert for the traditional qualities of the generalist lawyer: reflection, comprehension, discrimination, imagination, inspiration, wisdom, fortitude and tenacity.

[S]pecialization, of necessity, tends to segmentize the law and, to some extent, emphasizes the mechanics of law as distinguished from a broad sense of justice acquired from familiarity with the legal problems of people of different walks of life in a variety of situations.

While some specialization of the "specialist area" or "specialist problem" variety giving rise to a number of "lawyer's lawyers" might be acceptable to these critics, any movement in the direction of full scale encouragement of narrow practice is viewed as leading to a dehumanized, less creative, overly technical profession. As one commentator, speaking about the virtues of a country lawyer, expressed it, "He will sometimes sacrifice efficiency to solve individual problems individually."

Is this just naive, romantic traditionalism or is there something here which must be taken seriously? After all, legal education continues to be based on a broad exposure to many doctrinal fields and some orientation to the "seamless web" view of law. Is it really true, however, that most general practitioners perform such a variety of work that their skill of legal analysis is particularly creative and that their understanding of legal principles is likely to be sharper than that of the lawyer concentrating on a few areas? Or is broad perspective more likely to result from a willingness to study with focused intensity the policies, practices, theories, and principles both legal and non-legal interacting on a particular area of practice? How can we have omnicompetent judges, however, if they are to be picked from a profession which will be largely specialized? Must we have a great number of specialized courts as well? Our perception of the importance of these questions may depend partly on how narrow or broad the recognized specialty fields will be. A formal regulation scheme which encourages very wide participation by formulating attainable standards, and allowing lawyers a number of specialty designations from many broadly de-

fined fields, including perhaps even a catch-all "general practice" field, would hardly mean a mass movement away from generalist practice, even if lawyers called themselves specialists. But, how meaningful would such a scheme be? Similarly, support for such a scheme might affect our perception of the importance of possible negative effects on those who choose to remain nonspecialists.

GENERAL PRACTITIONERS MAY BE HURT

The formal regulation of specialization may accelerate the movement of business from the sole practitioners and small firms to the large law firms. Even if specialists do not have a monopoly in their field, and lawyers are allowed to take on whatever they feel willing to do, in reality the market forces with formal regulation may result in an inability to practice in as broad a way as one might prefer. It has been suggested that the regulation of specialization will tend inevitably to the next step of a monopoly. Professor Mindes writes:

The desire of specialists to distinguish themselves from other less "professional" practitioners is the key to the internal processes that lead a group to want to separate itself from the rest and also to its subsequent course after separation is achieved.

. . . .

A distinctive identity increases the feeling of commonality with others in the specialty and increases the psychological, social, and professional distance from other members of the bar. Contacts within the group increase, and those with other lawyers decrease. A special language develops by stages, as do special techniques and attitudes. The in-group feeling of "we" against "they" grows, and this in turn leads to more isolation of the specialty group.

Professor Mindes suggests the final step would be a monopoly by specialists of the right to practice in their area.

A formal regulation scheme may have the further effect of implying to the public that a nonspecialist is not special and therefore not competent or important, and so public confidence in the nonspecialist may fall. Furthermore, a traditional concept is that law is a "seamless web" and that problems may result from clients self-diagnosing which specialist is needed. The validity and weight of some of these criticisms may depend on how generalists are related to the specialists in a formal regulation scheme.

The problem of possible negative effects on the nonspecialist is most often countered by the argument that formal regulation schemes include provisions relating to the referral of business from nonspecialist to specialist which protect the nonspecialist. "Anti-pirating" provisions could be formulated so that the specialist would be prevented from providing services to the referred client beyond the confines of the referral. The client would still "belong," as it were, to the generalist. This argument does not of course counter the argument that many clients will, or should, self-diagnose which lawyer they need, this being part of the goal of more informed access to legal services, which may lead to a movement of business from the generalist to the specialist.

The A.B.A. Committee on Specialization in 1969 suggested that formal regulation may, nevertheless, help rather than hinder the sole practitioner or small firm to compete with the large firm:

> The most frequently voiced objection to regulation of specialization presented to our committee was its supposed harmful effect upon the sole practitioner and the small partnership in rural areas. Everyone agrees that the big firm lawyer already has the benefits of specialized practice. It was argued that large law firms in general are not adversely affected by the failure of the bar to regulate specialization, because a large law firm usually has little difficulty in making the availability of the specialized services of its individual lawyers collectively known to its prospective clients, and that regulation would only encourage clients to leave general practitioners to go to those large conglomerates of legal specialists. The com-

mittee did not accept that argument as we believe that experimentation may demonstrate that regulation of legal specialization tends to equate the sole practitioner and small law firm with the large firm in making specialized services available to their respective clients.

> Realistically, one of the principal reasons for the success of large law firms is that they have had no difficulty in communicating to the public that they offer specialized services, and that the collective abilities of their lawyers enable them to be specialists in every field of the law. Many lawyers argue that the official recognition of specialists would enable general practitioners more easily to obtain qualified specialists to assist them in stiuations where they may occasionally need such specialized legal services. Certainly, the committee believes that it would aid those lawyers in informing the public that specialized legal services can be made available by general practitioners as well as by large law firms. If experimentation does show that it enables the small practitioner more effectively to compete with the large law firms, regulated specialization may be the means whereby the ultimate survival of the independent sole practitioner is insured.

That ever present ghost of definition haunts us again with the statement made above that "specialized legal services can be made available by general practitioners."

Styles of Legal Work[†]
E.M. Schur

ANOTHER avenue to an understanding of the law in action involves studying the organization and routine work patterns of the legal profession. As was mentioned earlier, some of the current sociological interest in the legal system developed out of research focused on the general analysis of occupations and professions. From this standpoint a broad array of sociological concepts my be applicable to analyzing the positions and work of the individuals who man the legal order — ranging from "professional self-image" to occupational "role set," from "recruitment" and "socialization" to colleague relation-

ships and possible "role conflicts." Similarly, at least for other than lone practitioners, organization theory may be relevant, with such concepts as "bureaucracy," organizational "commitment," and organizational "goals" coming into play.

It has been suggested, by at least one legal critic, that research along these lines may produce an overly narrow concentration on certain small-scale and mundane aspects of the realm of law. Thus, it is argued that law is much more than simply what lawyers do and further that the lawyer's role is, in some essential aspects, not at all like

---

†   Schur, Edwin M., "Styles of Legal Work" in ed. E. Schur, *Law and Society: A Sociological View* (New York: Random House, 1968), 163–71. Reprinted by permission of author.

other occupational and professional roles. Hazard states that "the term 'lawyer' refers less to a social function than to a type of training, a type which in fact is shared by people doing a bewildering variety of tasks." The same writer also insists that for full understanding of legal work one must recognize that with respect to any important legal problem "there is a long, a rich and a demanding intellectual culture." Certainly it is true, and most sociologists accept the fact, that lawyers operate in a great many different settings, that any conception of *the* lawyer (believed to apply to the entire profession) would be misleading. Likewise, sophisticated social analysts are aware of both the relevant heritage of legal philosophy and the significant technical formulations embodied in the legal system. Yet these factors do not vitiate an investigation of law as a profession. Such research represents one of a number of complementary, rather than mutually exclusive, approaches to the study of legal institutions. Nor is it an absolute prerequisite for such research that the sociologist have extensive training in the law. Clearly, some familiarity with legal substance and procedure will be of great help to the investigator. At the same time, it should be kept in mind that to require of the researcher lengthy formal and technical training in the discipline or occupational field to be investigated would greatly hamper sociological research in any number of fields, such as the sociology of science, of medicine, of religion, and indeed the social analysis of any occupation or profession. There is no greater need for specialized knowledge in studying the legal profession than in these other instances. Of course, a very good argument can be made for better communication and more cooperative interaction between sociologists and lawyers; cross-disciplinary team research will often provide a useful means of averting some of the problems just mentioned.

We have already seen that there is a very real social stratification within the legal profession, and that the lawyer's general standing and specific work patterns may be partly determined by his social background and type of legal education. The interplay between the numerous variables involved here is complex, but the overall relationship between recruitment and professional role is well summarized in the following statement: "Social background prescribes two major career contingencies: level of technical skill and access to clients." Whereas all lawyers theoretically share a common body of technical knowledge and special skills, as well as a dual commitment to serve the client (in a personal and confidential relationship) and the public (as "servant of the court"), in practice there is an enormous amount of variation not only in what particular types of lawyers do but also in how they relate to their clients and other individuals and agencies and in how they view their professional roles. If we examine actual work situations, a few dominant patterns emerge.

THE LARGE LAW FIRM

The major law firms maintain a position of considerable power in modern American society. They wield a substantial influence in the business community and on public policy in general. Members of such firms tend to be held in high social esteem. Under these circumstances, it is probably not surprising that the large, well-established firms tend to recruit as new members individuals of relatively high socioeconomic status. Members of large firms are much more likely than are members of small firms or individual practitioners to be Protestant; to have fathers who were in business, managerial or professional positions; to have attended an Ivy League or other high-quality college; and to have attended (and done well at) one of the major, nationally known law schools or at least some other full-time, university-connected and night law school (as compared with nonuniversity-connected law schools). In particular, a man who obtains top grades (and is on the "law review," the prestigeful and influential student-edited journal) at the top, nationally known schools (primarily Harvard, Yale, and Columbia) may be "ticketed for life as a first-class passenger on the escalator for talent." As David Riesman goes on to comment, there is a "self-confirming myth" in legal education, in which the law-review men get the top jobs, make the contacts, and gain the experience necessary for advancement, and hence attain a success that "proves" that the law-school marking system (which, in the first year, determines law-review membership) is an accurate indicator of talent. At an early point in their training, such men gain a high level of confidence and the conviction that they are destined for important jobs.

This conviction is usually upheld through their work experience in the large firms. As one observer puts it, "What the Wall Street lawyers do in their professional capacity is nothing less than to provide prudential and technical assistance in the management of the private sector of the world economy." Surveys reveal significant differences in work patterns and clientele between large-firm lawyers on the one hand and small-firm members and individual practitioners on the other. The former are more likely than the latter to serve business clients (mainly large corporations in the field of heavy industry and finance) and wealthy, Protestant, individual clients, to have an overwhelming concentration of work in the areas of business and probate law, to spend much less time in court, and to deal with federal and appellate courts (rather than local ones) when such contact does occur. There is also a pronounced pattern of higher income for lawyers in the larger firms.

At the very top of the bar's status hierarchy, in the major New York firms described in Smigel's *The Wall Street Lawyer*, the lawyer deals almost exclusively with the corporate and financial problems of big business. Here too, the incoming lawyer gains membership in a substantial organization, which is impressive is its own right. He finds himself part of an establishment that may occupy three or four floors of a downtown office building and that may comprise as many as 50 to 150 lawyers and up to 250 nonprofessional staff. The firm is likely to have a long and renowned history, an atmosphere all its own, and an almost tangible aura of importance. Lawyers in the firm hold positions within a well-elaborated hierarchy — as reflected in the distribution of income and general prestige and in the allocation of status symbols, such as office space, secretaries, and so forth, and of professional tasks and responsibilities. Although the young lawyer's initial work may be of a segmental or highly specialized variety, not involving direct contact with clients and perhaps dealing with only one small facet of a broader matter, he is likely at once to be impressed by the wealth and power of the clients and the sizable nature of their business transactions. Nor is he dealt with as a mere underling. He has been hired for his demonstrated competence and his potential for leadership in the profession and in many respects he is treated as a colleague, albeit a junior one.

Work in such a setting is not, of course, without its difficulties. Some lawyers feel that the firms engender too early and too great specialization; most of the large firms have separate departments, officially or unofficially, to deal with such areas of work as corporate law, tax law, litigation, and so on. Others find troublesome the very keen competition for advancement to full partnership. Then too, some lawyers may be concerned that the work in the impersonal, bureaucratic setting seems to have little relation to the ideal of the lawyer as a "free professional," as a free-wheeling and confidential advisor to trusting clients. A few of the lawyers may even be defensive about the close ties between Wall Street firms and big business and conscious of the fact that the bulk of their work contributes little to protecting the underdog, an important theme in popular conceptions of the lawyer's role. And notwithstanding the firms' attempts to maintain a spirit of colleagueship, the fact that they are salaried employees who must in the last analysis take orders is disturbing to some. Finally, the pervasive pressures to conform — personally, socially, and even politically — may cause irritation.

For most of its members most of the time, however, the large law firm provides good earnings, excellent experience, and satisfying work. The prospect of a partnership holds out the possibility of a really sizable income combined with enormous prestige and entrée to the inner circles of the corporate and financial worlds. And for those not destined to achieve partnership, or for those who may be dissatisfied with the firm for one reason or another, there is the possibility of using their positions in the large firm as a stepping stone to other favorable situations — in industry, government, teaching, or in somewhat smaller but still very successful law firms.

INDIVIDUAL PRACTICE

Sharply contrasting with the situation of the elite, large-firm lawyer, is that of the typical individual practitioner in a large city. As we have already seen, there are significant differences between lawyers in the two types of practice, both in social background and in the kinds of work they do and the success they achieve. The lone practitioner is likely to be the son of an immigrant, who has worked his way up; he is likely to have attended either a "proprietary" or a Catholic night law school and not to have completed college, which at one time was not always a requirement for admission to such law schools. At least at the lower levels of individual practice, he is earning a precarious living, and his clientele tends to be a transient one of lower-income individuals. His legal work involves mainly small-scale and routine business matters and litigation between individuals. His contact with agencies and courts (the latter being particularly frequent) tends to be at the local level. As Jerome Carlin points out in *Lawyers on Their Own*, an important study of individual practice in Chicago, these men constitute something like a "lower class" of the metropolitan bar. Their practice consists largely of "those residual matters (and clients) that the large firms have not pre-empted" — such as matters too inconsequential (financially or otherwise) for such firms to handle, and "the undesirable cases, the dirty work, those areas of practice that have associated with them an aura of influencing and fixing and that involve arrangements with clients and others that are felt by the large firms to be professionally damaging. The latter category includes local tax, municipal, personal injury, divorce, and criminal matters."

Carlin distinguishes between upper-level and lower-level individual practitioners; the former may have a more stable and secure small-business clientele for whom they perform a wider range of less routine services. It is primarily the lower-level, solo practitioners who are bogged down in the dirty work of the law, whose financial circumstances are perilous, and for whom getting business represents a continuous battle.

At the outset, many lawyers trying to establish practices of their own are closely tied to the local neighbourhood, a situation that few find satisfactory. As a fairly successful neighbourhood practitioner told Carlin:

> People don't look at the neighbourhood lawyer as on the same professional level as the lawyer in the Loop — but on the same level as service people, real estate and insurance brokers, and similar types of nonprofessional categories. He's looked at more as a neighbourhood businessman rather than as a professional. Doctors don't have that problem; you don't consider Loop doctors to be on a completely different level.

Going beyond the neighbourhood, the solo lawyer seeks contact with potential clients through membership in a range of communal organizations, which usually have an ethnic or religious basis. Politics is also seen as a useful means of extending one's clientele, as well as developing helpful court and other official contacts. But often these methods are insufficient, and it becomes necessary to rely on individuals who, for one reason or another may be in a position to channel legal business in his direction. As Carlin notes, such a "broker" (between lawyer and client) may be "another lawyer, an accountant, a real estate or insurance broker or agent, a building contractor, a doctor, a policeman, bondsman, precinct captain, garage mechanic, minister, undertaker, plant personnel director, foreman, etc." Personal injury cases often are referred by a variety of individuals who may serve as "runners"; waitresses and bar girls may refer divorce matters, policemen criminal matters. At the same time, and especially in connection with wills, business, and real-estate matters, these lawyers face continuous and increasingly strong competition from nonlegal sources, such as banks, real-estate brokers, and accountants. These competitors often have the edge both in specialized skill and visibility; and as Carlin points out, the lawyer cannot today claim exclusive access to the agencies that process the matters in question.

Apart from the sheer difficulty of earning a decent living under these circumstances, the less successful of the individual practitioners experience a generalized and severe status dilemma. Whereas "law appeared to provide the easiest and cheapest avenue to professional status...they find that access to the higher status positions is all but closed to them and that the positions they do manage to achieve are often marginal, their practice residual, and their foothold in the profession precarious." Not only is much of their work relatively insignificant by the dominant standards of the profession, but they have very little contact (and virtually no sense of real colleagueship) with the more successful, large-firm lawyers. Individual practitioners rarely attain positions of leadership in the bar, and in fact they are not even as likely as large-firm lawyers to maintain membership in the leading professional associations, often finding it more valuable to be active in the smaller, ethnic bar associations. While solo lawyers can at least pride themselves on being their own boss, most seem to recognize that this independence is a very mixed blessing.

Of course it must be kept in mind that the "Wall Street lawyer" and the lower-level individual practitioner represent the extreme points of a continuum along which legal practices vary. In between are numerous gradations involving membership in a variety of middle-sized and small firms, many of which are very successful and handle a considerable range of interesting legal work. Also, it should be noted that there certainly are some individuals who practice on their own and attain a high degree of success, both financially and in terms of professional standing. This attainment may occur particularly when a lawyer develops a reputation for great skill in a highly specialized field, such as patent law, literary property, civil liberties, or even matrimonial or criminal law. Indeed, all of the comments made thus far concerning stratification within the metropolitan bar must be recognized as reflecting statistical regularities only. They refer to large classes of individual instances, and to each generalization there are undoubtedly specific exceptions.

Furthermore, the major studies of legal practice have concentrated almost exclusively on lawyers in the largest metropolitan centers. As Carlin mentions, "In comparison with the highly stratified metropolitan bar, the smaller city bar has over the years remained a fairly homogeneous professional community." Attributing this homogeneity partly to the absence of huge "law factories," he noted that (in 1958) there were no firms with as many as fifteen lawyers in American cities of less than 200,000 population, and very few with more than five or six lawyers. Similarly, there has been virtually no sociological analysis of the position and functions of the small-town lawyer. Legal practice in such a setting undoubtedly varies a good deal from that of the lone practitioner in the metropolis. It is quite possible that some lawyers in small towns may be able satisfactorily to combine the independence of individual practice with a considerable measure of financial success and professional and social standing within the local community. Other varieties of legal work — including positions in government agencies, in prosecutor's and legal-aid offices, and as "house-counsel" on corporation staffs — also deserve further attention from researchers. Undoubtedly each type of legal practice has its peculiar recruitment and work patterns, compensations, drawbacks, strains, and dilemmas.

Law Firm Mergers: A Case of Greed or Survival?[†]
K. Makin

THE once-genteel pursuit of the law is running smack into the realities of the late twentieth century. Unbridled competition, globalization and the cult of greed have changed the face of law firms — and of the lawyers who work in them.

Professional courtesy and camaraderie are failing. Raiding and merger mania are replacing the old, relaxed atmosphere that was borne of a steady, reliable clientele.

"More than ever before, lawyers are working harder, getting richer, and enjoying it less," says Toronto lawyer Morris Gross. "I think the senior people in the profession have not done enough about it. You get lots of talk about fancy hardware or saving time and making money. But nobody is saying: 'What are we doing to ourselves?'"

The most dramatic sign is growth. Across the civil law landscape, firms are expanding almost uncontrollably. Suddenly, mega-firms dot the downtown centres. A significant proportion of the country's medium-sized firms — those with 10 to 70 lawyers — are gone.

"It is happening at a pace we cannot even keep track of," said Gerald Riskin, vice-president of Edmonton's Edge Consulting Associates.

The overhead for medium firms has proven too great and their range of services too limited to attract large clients. The result is the death of the firm or a merger into a mega-firm — usually involving 200 to 500 lawyers whose work is largely directed by rather anonymous management committees. Colleagues in the same firm barely recognize one another in the hallways.

"They have gotten bigger and they have gotten worse," said Mr. Gross, a senior partner in a mid-sized firm determined to survive. He said that mid-sized firms are obligated to find "niches" in which they can specialize.

Even large and venerable old firms such as Toronto's McCarthy and McCarthy have been erased by merger. The hybrid of that merger, McCarthy and Tetrault, had 450 lawyers. Fasken Martineau Walker is Canada's largest firm — for the moment. It boasts 480 lawyers. Yet even these numbers appear modest next to the grand-daddy of United States firms — 1,200-lawyer Baker & McKenzie.

Most self-respecting mega-firms now have branches not only in large Canadian cities, but also in New York and London. One has expanded into Moscow. The reasons that they need this enhanced flexibility to offer clients a full range of services. However, Mr. Riskin says many are doing it for strictly "defensive purposes."

The firms live in constant fear of being eclipsed. "People worried that if you do not follow along in expanding and growing, you will be seen as lagging behind other firms," said a partner in a mega-firm.

But there is a logic behind the fear. There is an increasing need to offer clients all services under one roof. These services might include active litigation and advice on taxation, real estate, competition law.

To be sure, the pool of clients is shrinking. More corporations are creating their own in-house counsel departments to deal with their legal needs. Para-legals and no-fault insurance schemes have also carved away some of their terrain.

Indeed, many observers think a vicious shakedown is bound to occur eventually, leaving a Big Eight of mega-firms.

Patrick McKenna, president of Edge Consulting, said the trend will only get worse. "Our fear is others may see it as a bandwagon to gang onto and that they are like sheep — following in the same footsteps without a client base to follow," he said.

Mega-firms are competing feverishly for clients with deep pockets. They compete just as hard when it comes to stocking their firms with fresh talent. Raiding has come into vogue, either directly or through head hunters. By attracting a leading light in a particular field of law, a firm can quickly become known as a specialist in that field.

There are about 37,000 lawyers in Canada. Still, firms compete furiously for the best young prospects coming out of law school. Like college athletes, the students are wooed and drafted before they can explain the difference between a tort and a torte.

The human factor is the great unknown in this rapid growth — from the perspective of both the client and the employee. Clients of large firms may feel they are being served by an anonymous monolith. They inevitably get less personal attention from senior partners.

Corporate clients may also become leery of going to a firm so large that it probably represents competitors.

The cost can be just as high on the other end — within the merging firms. "There is a cultural clash when two firms of professionals operate in very different ways," Mr. McKenna said. "Not everyone is willing to go along with the impersonalization of these large firms."

It all adds up to a profession-wide identity crisis. At law conferences and in the pages of legal journals, one frequently runs into lawyers anguishing over the evolution

---

†   Makin, Kirk, "Law Firm Mergers: A Case of Greed or Survival?" *Globe and Mail*, May 5, 1990, D1, D8. Reprinted by permission of The Globe and Mail.

of law from a calling to a cold-hearted, isolated business. Have they become overwhelmed by the "greed is good credo" that has swept other areas of business? Are they being carried along by forces beyond their control?

"I prefer to call it something other than greed," Mr. Gross said. "I think there is a status in making $350,000 per year. It filters down from the top. If you are a senior lawyer not making $350,000, you are made to feel somewhat inadequate."

The money and status-seeking leave them vulnerable to raiding. "You make them offers they simply can't refuse," Mr. Gross said.

A junior member of a large firm who asked for anonymity said: "More and more, the legal profession has become a competitive and cutthroat business. You have to spend more time on marketing and generating business than on practising law. The pressure is on to prove you can generate business for yourself and others in the firm."

The lawyer said that subtle pressure is usually applied to get lawyers in a firm to join business clubs, lunch with clients frequently, teach, and speak in seminars to get their names in front of the public.

In some firms, lawyers are expected to tabulate the time they spend on glad-handing. Their salaries may be docked if they do not do enough.

The supersonic pace is not appealing to everyone. Some fresh-faced young lawyers are burning out before they are 30, worn down by disillusionment, ridiculous demands and working hours. "We are finding that in the last year or two, some of the most promising lawyers have woken up and said: 'Gee, is this what I fought to get into law school for? I am just not going to sell my soul,'" said Mr. Gross.

In a recent paper prepared for the Canadian Bar Association (Ontario), lawyers Ronald Manes and Valerie Edwards spoke of this fear. Many lawyers practise in "a climate of anxiety," they said, worrying about making a costly mistake, losing an important client, being embarrassed in court, not being able to make ends meet "and, most ominously, about losing control and no longer being able to cope."

The starkest evidence of this is the sensitive issue of billable hours — the accumulation of work hours for which a client can actually be billed an hourly fee.

At some firms, each lawyer's billable hours are posted at the end of the month. "At the end of the year, you find out what everyone else made, which puts even greater pressure on you," said one lawyer.

Mr. Gross tells of a young lawyer at a mega-firm who had not been home for a weekday dinner in two years. His wife was distraught. Mr. Gross went to a senior partner he knew at the firm to suggest something was wrong. "His response was: 'What's wrong with that? If you want to make mega-bucks, the only way to do it is to put in mega-hours.'" He was, I think, rather proud of it.

"They are all aping what has gone on in New York," said Mr. Gross. "A few years ago in New York, they had 1,500 hours and people thought that was terrible. Now they have 2,500 hours and people think that is insanity."

"Large Toronto firms are making it clear that if you are not doing 2,000 hours, you are not going to make it here. This is an absolute outrage. You cannot do that without giving up a major portion of your private life."

In the past year, Canadian Bar Association President John Jennings and Supreme Court of Canada Judge John Sopinka have both publicly deplored the profession's obsession with increasing billable hours.

Mr. Justice Sopinka said many firms think nothing of demanding their lawyers work up to 10 hours a day, six days a week for 48 weeks of the year.

"I think it's time to send a warning," Mr. Jennings said in a speech. "I think the pressure of the bottom line has made us become legal technicians. The bottom line: how we worship it, how we pamper it, how we follow its every wish, its every demand, no matter how irrational or how unhealthy."

The concept of billable hours recognizes little but the ability to make money. It may actually discourage technological efficiency, experience and thoughtfulness. Indeed, some lawyers think straight fees per transaction or contingency fees will eventually replace the increasingly-ridiculous billing system.

'Invisible' Constraints on Lawyering and Leadership: The Case of Women Lawyers[†]
M.J. Mossman

INTRODUCTION

It has been a strength of patriarchy in all its historic forms to assimilate itself so perfectly to socioeconomic, political, and cultural structures as to be virtually invisible.[1]

This essay is an exploration of "invisible" constraints on ideas about the proper role for women in the legal profession. It focuses first on the historical struggle for women's admission as lawyers in Canada in the early part of this century (the issue of whether women could be lawyers at all), and secondly on the current status of women lawyers in Canada (the issue of whether women can become leaders in the legal profession). In both cases, there is some evidence that "invisible" ideas about the proper role for women, which prevented their acceptance as "lawyers" in the early years of this century, may impede their success in becoming "leaders" in the profession in the 1980s and beyond. For this reason, these invisible constraints have both historical and current significance for women, and men, who are lawyers.

This essay also represents an effort to bridge two separate parts of my research activity about women lawyers, one historical and one more current, and to examine the connections between them. For several years, I have been interested in the legal aspects of the history of the first Canadian women admitted to the legal profession. The types of legal arguments presented and usually rejected, the reasons given for negative court decisions on the question of women's admission to legal practice, and the content of statutory amendments to legislation about qualifications to practise law have provided a rich source of ideas about the role of such women in the early twentieth century. More recently, I have become interested in the social and cultural contexts of these legal decisions, and the significant extent to which reasons given by courts mirrored opinions and ideas expressed in secondary legal literature of the time. Indeed, the similarity between the views expressed in the law journals and in judicial decisions raises important questions about the contextual shaping of judicial decisions, both then and now.

The other part of my research has focused more specifically on the current status of women as lawyers in Canada, and the significance of the dramatic increase in the numbers of women entering the legal profession here since about 1970. In this context, issues about the structure and organization of the profession and of law firms, the professional ethos of law practice, and the roles expected of and accepted by lawyers in different kinds of law practices all have importance for women members of the profession now and for the future. Moreover, to the extent that these structures and ideas were designed and implemented by an exclusively male profession, it is important to determine whether a significant change in the gender composition of the profession may require changes of structures and ideas, and how such changes may occur. In this context, theoretical literature about the sociology of organizations and the nature of societal change provide interesting models for examining the potential for change in the legal profession.

Thus, in thinking about women lawyers, both in terms of historical and current struggles for acceptance, the issue is whether there are invisible ideas about the proper role for women which just as surely impede women's achievement of leadership roles in the profession now as once prevented them from being lawyers at all. Or, as Joan Kelly argues, are we now at a moment in history when we can not only "'see' how the patriarchal system works, but also...act with that vision — so as to put an end to it."[2]

· · · ·

WOMEN AND LEADERSHIP IN THE LEGAL PROFESSION

Despite these inauspicious beginnings for women lawyers, however, much had changed for women in the legal profession by the 1980s. By 1987, for example, there were over 3500 women who were current members of the legal profession in Ontario, representing about 18.6% of the total number of lawyers in the province.[3] Moreover, since law schools had experienced a significant increase in the number of women applicants over the preceding two decades, close to 50% of law school entry classes in Ontario in 1987 were women.[4] On the basis of such equality in numbers, most observers might readily agree with the optimism of a comment written several decades earlier:

† Mossman, Mary Jane, "'Invisible' Constraints on Lawyering and Leadership: The Case of Women Lawyers" (1988), 20 *The Ottawa Law Review* 569. Reprinted by permission of the author.

The time will come in the not too distant future when women will win equal distinction with men in every phase of the practice of law.[5]

The Current Status of Women Lawyers in Canada

Yet, there is already some evidence that this confident assertion may prove misleading. Both in Canada[6] and in the United States, women lawyers appear to be less well-represented in the prestigious and highly-paid sectors of the legal profession. In the hearings before the ABA Commission of Women in the Legal Profession in 1988, for example:

...several witnesses emphasized the great strides women have made in entering and succeeding in the profession, [but] most participants at the hearings expressed frustration and disillusionment that the barriers are still great and that progress has been far slower than expected. Witnesses cautioned that *we must not be lulled into complacency about the status of women in the profession simply because the numbers of women entering the profession continue to increase.*[7] (Emphasis added.)

Similarly, in their study of lawyers in Toronto, Hagan, Huxter and Parker concluded that women were disproportionately represented in the lower levels of the legal profession in subordinate positions with little autonomy in their work.[8] Although there is still relatively little data because of the recent entry of large numbers of women to the profession, the study concluded that women had almost as great a chance as men to reach the top of the profession but that there were significant disparities of representation by gender at the lower end of the profession.[9] Moreover, even for those women who reached the higher levels of the profession, the study results showed that they did "not benefit as much in their earnings as [did] men when they practise[d] in traditionally male areas, when they gain[ed] experience, or when they [became] partners in firms."[10]

These findings are similar to the results of a national study of lawyers' earnings in Canada.[11] Based on census figures of 1971 and 1981, the study showed that in 1981, female lawyers were five years younger, on average, than male lawyers, but that a much smaller percentage of female lawyers were married, with larger proportions either divorced, separated or single.[12] Over one-half of the female lawyers were salaried, compared with thirty per cent of the males, and a larger percentage of female lawyers practised in cities.[13]

In comparisons of earnings, moreover, the study found that male lawyers earned more than female lawyers: for 1980, female lawyers in private practice earned an average of $24,509 while male lawyers earned an average of $42,405.[14] These numbers must be further assessed, of course, to take account of the younger ages of female lawyers as a result of their more recent entry to the profession. However, even comparisons of lawyers by age groups in this study showed that the earnings of female lawyers started at a lower level ($22,000 at age 30 in 1980) and rose much more slowly than did the earnings of male lawyers:

Consequently, although female lawyers earn about 27 per cent ($8000) less than male lawyers at age 30, the differential increases to 37 per cent ($15,000) by age 40. The largest differential (about $23,000) occurs at age 50.[15]

The study attempted to account for a number of variables which might affect the differences in earnings of men and women lawyers, but concluded that there was an "earnings differential" of approximately $9,000 (in 1980) which was not explained by the variables in the model. The authors agreed with another commentator who had noted that:

...although this residual has traditionally been called discrimination, it is really "a measure of our ignorance", and that the male/female differential is "a complex matter that yields its secrets only grudgingly".[16]

The disadvantaged position of women lawyers in Canada is similar to that in other jurisdictions. In a comparative study of lawyers in several different countries,[17] Richard Abel found that there were cross-cultural similarities in the high rate of women's entry to the profession over the past two decades,[18] and also in the difficulties experienced in obtaining apprenticeship positions and permanent employment,[19] and in disparities in income.[20] After assessing the unequal position of women lawyers in a number of different jurisdictions, Abel concluded:

It seems to be true almost universally that once the legal and sociocultural barriers against women lawyers were removed, they entered the profession in numbers approximating those of men.... Yet once they leave the meritocratic arena of formal education and examinations, they once again encounter prejudice and role conflict. The result is that qualified women lawyers fail to enter practice, leave early, or accept less attractive positions. These forms of inequality will not change until there is a transformation of the sexual division of labor.[21]

This disquieting conclusion is echoed in the recent work of Carrie Menkle-Meadow, who has conducted cross-cultural research on women in the legal profession, concentrating primarily on western industrialized nations.[22] Significantly, she found that "women [were] disproportionately located in different spheres of the profession in virtually every country," but that they were uniformly found in the "lowest echelons" of the profession in each country (although what constituted the lowest echelons varied from one country to another).[23] In light of these findings, she warned that it is not appropriate to assume that increased numbers of women entering the profession will necessarily result in equality of opportunities for women; instead, she recommended that:

> ...we must examine the meaning of the entrance of women into the legal profession from more than the perspective of quantitative sociology. As we collect data and observe gender differences in location and type of practice, favoured tasks, and specialities, we should be prepared to examine the transformative potential of these social facts.[24]

Beyond Increased Numbers — "Invisible" Structural Barriers

In assessing the "transformative potential" of these social facts about women in the legal profession, it is helpful to consider recent literature which analyzes barriers to women's achievement of leadership roles in other societal contexts. In the context of theories about the sociology of organizations, for example, Rosabeth Moss Kanter has written extensively of the structural constraints within organizations which systematically exclude from promotion and advancement all those who are not "like" existing leaders in the organization.[25]

In her major study of the organizational structure of a large American corporation in the 1970s, Moss Kanter identified a number of features analogous to those of a modern law firm. For example, in her study of managerial roles in the corporation, she characterized tasks to be performed on the basis of whether they were "routine" or whether they required the exercise of discretion; as she reported, wherever discretionary decision-making was required within the corporate structure, the organizational response was to ensure homogeneity of personnel, in order to eliminate at least one aspect of uncertainty:[26]

> The uncertainty up the ranks...puts trust and homogeneity at a premium. The personal loyalty normally demanded of subordinates by officials is most intense at the highest levels of organizations.... The lack of structure in top jobs makes it very important for decision-makers to work together closely in at least the harmony of shared understanding and a degree of mutual trust.... [T]he solidarity that can be mustered through common membership in social networks, and the

social control this provides, is a helpful supplement for decision-makers....[27]

According to Moss Kanter, because the corporate response to discretionary decision-making was to choose new senior managers who were most "like" existing senior managers, the "more closed the circle, the more difficult it [was] for 'outsiders' to break in."[28]

Moss Kanter also examined the idea of power in the corporation and its effect on men and women.[29] She documented the expressed preferences of both men and women employees to work for male managers, rather than for female ones, because male managers were more readily perceived to be part of the power structure of the organization. "In the context of organizations where women do not have access to the same opportunities for power and efficacy through activities or alliances,"[30] the employees' expressed preference for men was clearly a preference for power. This structural barrier also affected women's abilities to achieve leadership roles within the organization.

Nonetheless, despite such barriers, a few women in Moss Kanter's study did succeed in becoming senior managers of the corporation. Her assessment of these "token" women of the corporation, numerically small by comparison with men who were senior managers, offers an interesting analogy to the position of those few women who are currently in senior positions within the legal profession. Moss Kanter identified the proportional representation of male and female workers in the corporation using a scale of participation rates from "dominant" to "token" representation. On this scale, she classified as "skewed" those groups with a large preponderance of one type over another, up to a ratio of about 85:15; in such a situation the numerically smaller group were likely to be "tokens" and the larger group "dominants". By comparison, in "tilted" groups with a ratio of about 65:35, dominants became just a "majority" while tokens became a "minority". Only at a ratio of 60:40 to 50:50 would a group be considered "balanced".

In Moss Kanter's analysis, the significance of different ratios for groups within organizations was their effect on the behaviour of individuals within the groups. In particular, Moss Kanter identified the serious effect on "tokens", the numerical minority within "skewed" groups, who suffered the double difficulty of invisibility in terms of their individual characteristics and at the same time the ascription of the general characteristics of "all women": "tokens [were] never really seen as they [were], always fighting stereotypes...."[31] As Moss Kanter concluded, "People's treatment, then, [was] not automatically fixed by inflexible characteristics but depend[ed] on their numbers in a particular situation."[32]

Thus, the structural constraints of roles, power and numbers significantly affected the position of men and women in the corporation. What appeared to be "sex differences" in the roles of men and women in the corporation were, according to Moss Kanter's analysis, the result of structural features of corporate organization. Concluding, moreover, that individual-based initiatives would never overcome these structural barriers, she recommended systematic structural change within the corporation: "batch" rather than one-by-one hiring of women managers; the deliberate creation of role models for women managers; opportunities for networking by women managers; more flexible organizational structures; better education of corporate leaders about tokenism; and support programs for women.[33]

The existence of structural, systemic barriers constraining women's opportunities for advancement within the corporation led Moss Kanter to conclude that such changes were likely to occur only as a result of "outside intervention".[34] This conclusion has frequently occurred in studies of women's roles in other contexts such as political activism. In a cross-cultural study of women in politics designed to analyze reasons for women's disproportionately small representation in the political process (relative to their numbers in the population), Cynthia Fuchs Epstein[35] identified a range of factors frequently cited to explain women's underrepresentation in "the ranks of the elite": women's "inherent incapacity" to be assertive and dominant; social factors which "direct women away from the public sphere to family-centred activities"; time problems and role strains flowing from "women's sex-role-associated duties"; the lack of "opportunity structures" for women to acquire appropriate skills; and others.[36]

For Epstein, these and other factors constitute a system for discouraging and disempowering women from seeking access to power and elites. Suggesting that positive intervention to assist women is necessary, she argued that the dominance of men in politics has remained essentially unchallenged because it has been regarded as "neutral":

> Some groups object to programs that guarantee women and other minorities a chance for better access to elite positions. Yet, in the past, elite gatekeepers were effective in maintaining existing hierarchies — in sifting and sorting out unwanted groups. These were seen as "natural" processes rather than as programs. Perhaps this is because the *maintenance* of systems, which require attention and input to keep them going, does not attract as much notice as the *alteration* of systems. Thus, because men have been successful in maintaining their domination of women, little notice has been taken of the methods used to maintain that dominance.[37] (Emphasis in original.)

Both the analysis of Moss Kanter and that of Epstein focus on "invisible" barriers which impede women's access to power and leadership roles. Despite some differences in their analyses, both studies identify systemic features in organizational structures which deter or prevent women from succeeding as men do. Such a structural analysis is helpful in understanding the current position of women as lawyers since their numbers in the practising legal profession are still small[38] and their numbers in the higher echelons of large law firms are even smaller. Visualizing the situation of women lawyers in structural terms has some potential to depersonalize the issue of sex discrimination in the profession, and to permit a clear focus on systematic efforts to overcome the problems of structural barriers to equality. As well, such an analysis recognizes the need for systemic change, rather than individualized efforts to assimilate to male standards; that is, while practising law like a man may be of some limited use to women, there is a need for change in the structure of law practice too.[39]

Particularly in the context of law, however, such a structural analysis also has some limitations. Because its solutions depend on outside intervention, it is unclear how such pressures will be forthcoming in a self-regulating profession. The assumption of a political will "outside" the profession which may demand such changes may be illusory at best. Second, the focus on barriers also seems to assume that they can be removed. In both cases, there is an underlying sense of rationality about the issue of appropriate sex role divisions in society and their reflection in the constraints experienced by women lawyers. In marked contrast to such rationality about existing "separate spheres" for men and women, however, it may be that there are less rational, but similarly "invisible", constraints on the idea of leadership which make it difficult (even impossible) for women to achieve positions of leadership in the legal profession.

Lawyers and Leadership — "Invisible" Barriers in Ideas

In the search for a rationale for "invisible" barriers for women in the legal profession, it is also important to focus on the significance of ideas about sex and sex roles in society. "Why...does one see the world in the way that one does; and what factors contribute to one's seeing it differently at another moment in time?"[40] How do our ideas about men and women (and prevailing notions of activities appropriate to each of them) affect our perceptions of their differences and potential abilities? In her study of the social reconstruction of "the feminine character", Sondra Farganis stated succinctly the view of those who assert that the male/female duality of our society operates negatively for women:

Certain terms in Western discourse...have been gendered: men have been seen as public persons, as reasonable, as persons of intellect and persons with a culture; women have been seen as private persons, irrational or passionate, as persons of the body and persons in line with nature, as persons in a culture. One must think past these false categories and begin to redefine terms like power and reason: one must conceptualize the former in terms that encourage persons to think in terms of power to not power over...[41]

If we regard sex roles as socially constructed by our experiences, rather than objective in their origins and formulations, it is possible to contemplate as well the idea of leadership as one defined by our experiences of those who have always been leaders: men.

In a number of recent studies of leadership, researchers have identified differences between men and women, both in their outward styles of leadership and in their self-perceptions as leaders.[42] Chapman reported, for example, on Megargee's study of the influence of sex roles on the manifestation of leadership.[43] In his study in 1969, Megargee paired persons who had previously been tested to determine their degree of dominance. When "high dominance" men and women were paired with persons of the same sex, 75% of high dominance men and 70% of high dominance women took the leadership role in the tasks assigned. When high dominance men were paired with low dominance women, 90% of the men assumed the leadership role, but when high dominance women were paired with low dominance men, only 20% of the women assumed a leadership role.[44]

As Chapman noted, the research results suggested that "...society does not expect women to express dominance, particularly in situations where women are required to interact with men in order to accomplish specified goals." Moreover, if women feel reluctance about expressing themselves as leaders, their default probably reinforces the assumptions (of both men and women) "that women are incapable of effective leadership within an organization".[45] The same conclusion appeared in a book published at about the same time, in which a leading management theorist described the model of the successful manager in our culture as "a masculine one", describing him as "agressive, [sic] competitive, firm and just" and not "feminine...soft and yielding or dependent or intuitive in the womanly sense".[46] Moreover, in such a context, women leaders may often face a "double bind":

...if the female manager adopts accommodative leadership behaviors...she will be criticized for being "motherly," indecisive, or weak. Conversely, if she adopts task-oriented behaviors, she will be criticized for being pushy, unfeminine and temperamental. Faced with this lose-lose conflict, the woman leader, in all likelihood, will experience extreme frustration and resort to a fairly passive existence in the organization, accepting her role as a mere transient in the mainstream of organizational leadership.[47]

Thus, the conflict for women between expectations based on their roles as women and those related to male models of leadership presents some difficulties for women seeking leadership roles within organizations. In the context of women lawyers, such conflicts were specifically identified in the hearings of the ABA Task Force on Women in the Legal Profession:

Witnesses expressed their belief that women must still work harder and be better than men in order to be recognized and succeed. Individuals also testified that women walk a fine line between being regarded as too feminine (and thus not tough, lawyerlike or smart) or too tough (and thus unfeminine or not the kind of woman male colleagues feel comfortable relating to).[48]

At the same time, however, the appropriateness of male models of leadership has also been increasingly challenged, particularly by feminists who suggest that there are more appropriate "female" qualities of leadership. In the work of Nancy Hartsock[49] and Carol Gilligan,[50] for example, women's knowledge and experiences are examined and legitimated as different from, and sometimes superior to, those of men: "[women's] ways are not only different but better...in the sense of liberating or negating a contrary male way of being that is competitive rather than cooperative, authoritative rather than democratic, life-denying rather than life-giving."[51] In such a context, the concept of leadership is dramatically transformed to one of "empowerment of others" rather than "power over others".

Regardless of the model of leadership that is adopted, however, societal ideas of appropriate sex roles for men and women present "invisible" constraints for women who aspire to leadership. Because most previous experience of leadership has been male, women who want to become leaders must often demonstrate both that they can provide leadership on the male model and also that they are able to offer leadership in ways which are different from, and superior to, the male model of leadership. In doing so, women must demonstrate their ability to "assimilate" the male model of leadership at the same time as they demonstrate how their own qualities of leadership are in fact preferable. In both cases, however, the existing male model remains the standard, either as the measure of women's conformity or the extent of their differences.

In the context of women in the legal profession, the importance of these comments is their implicit recognition of the maleness of societal ideas about leadership. Although women have finally succeeded in becoming lawyers in ever-increasing numbers, the "invisible" constraints of male leadership models have made them markedly less successful in becoming leaders in the profession. Because of the social construction of the idea of leadership on a male model, few women are perceived as leaders and those who achieve leadership do so only by accepting the male standard of leadership. In such a context, "thinking like a man" is a high compliment only if women lawyers deny that they have anything to offer as leaders in the profession which is different from the qualities of leadership offered by men.

What process is needed to transform the legal profession, only recently emerging from its male exclusivity, to a profession that welcomes and values essentially "female" qualities? If "[what] the feminine has come to mean is a result of a socially arrived at definition, made legitimate as a consequence of the power and influence of those in a position to define it",[52] what is needed to transform our ideas about female qualities of power and influence? As Menkle-Meadow has suggested, can we move beyond the question of increasing numbers of women lawyers — the question of quantitive sociology — to an exploration of "the transformative potential" of the social facts about women in the legal profession?[53]

WOMAN LAWYERS: TOWARD "TRANSFORMATIVE POTENTIAL"

I think all lawyers must agree
On keeping our profession free
From females whose admission would
Result in anything but good.
Because it yet has to be shown
That men are fit to hold their own
In such a contest, I've no doubt
We'd some of us be crowded out.[54]

When this verse was published almost one hundred years ago, women were not permitted to practise as lawyers anywhere in the British Empire. In less than one hundred years, women in Canada have successfully challenged the male exclusivity of the legal profession, losing initially in all three court cases but gaining the right to practise in all the provinces as a result of legislative action. Since 1970, moreover, increasing numbers of women have chosen to seek careers as lawyers so that, for the first time in history in Canada, the legal profession faces a problem — and an opportunity — because it is no longer an exclusively male profession, either in law or in terms of numbers.[55] Yet, the issue still to be resolved is the role for women in the profession: whether women will become leaders only by assimilation to male standards of lawyering, or whether, on the other hand, the nature of practice and of leadership will be transformed by their presence. In this sense, the moment of reckoning has arrived.

Both Moss Kanter's structural analysis of organizations and research on the social construction of sex roles offer useful ways of understanding the "invisible" barriers preventing women lawyers' achievement of leadership roles in the legal profession at the end of the twentieth century. Structural analysis suggests the need for systemic changes, "outside" intervention, and organizational strategies to increase the numbers of women in leadership roles and to ensure their access to power in such roles. Theories about the social construction of sex roles focus on the attitudes and behaviours of men and women in different situations, and suggest the need for education about stereotyping, and positive role models for both men and women in leadership positions.

While both these approaches offer assistance in understanding the barriers to women's achievements in the legal profession reflective of their increasing numbers, they differ in the extent to which they use male achievements as the target for women's leadership ambitions. Structural analysis suggests that an increase in the numbers of women exercising leadership and power will enhance opportunities for individual women but it does not necessarily challenge existing male models of leadership. Theories of the social construction of sex roles, by contrast, require some reflection about "inherent" and "learned" abilities, and permit some assessment of the extent to which leadership may be exercised in different ways by men and by women.[56]

This distinction is important, because it is fundamental to any strategy for increasing women's leadership to decide whether, on one hand, women must have opportunities to acquire male attributes of "leadership"; or whether, on the other hand, both men and women must learn to recognize "leadership" talents expressed by women which are currently invisible because they are different from expressions of leadership by men. In the first case, the strategy assumes that women and men exercise leadership in the same way, but women need to be assisted to learn the skills of leadership through training, opportunities, role models, mentoring, etc. In the second case, the strategy assumes that men and women exercise leadership in different ways and perhaps for different purposes, and that both individuals and organizations must be assisted to make better use of the leadership talents already being exercised but currently invisible.[57] The first strategy offers the possibility of increased opportunities and challenges for individual women in leadership positions, while the second promises a fundamental reconstruction of ideas about "success" and "leadership" and the potential for transforming societal values about them. As the report of the ABA Commission on Women in the Legal Profession stated:

> Several witnesses emphasized that the problems facing lawyers of both sexes, but especially women, in trying to combine professional demands with important human relationships and children, involve questioning the values and ethics of the profession. The concern is that, at a time when the pressures are growing for law firms to be successful businesses and for lawyers to produce even greater numbers of billable hours, lawyers are being dehumanized, unable to relate to clients and family members.
>
> Witnesses believe that lawyers will lose their sense of perspective and ethics under the weight of pressures to produce billable hours and the stress of cutting back on family involvement. These witnesses suggested that women, by raising the crucial issues of family and workplace, can take the lead in helping to restore sanity, balance, and respect to the profession.[58]

How will the "transformative potential of the social facts" about women lawyers be expressed? In the Canadian context, some women in the legal profession have achieved leadership positions by their (at least outward) assimilation to the male model.[59] Others have consciously chosen different paths of leadership, deciding to work more cooperatively and in less paternalistic relationships with clients, choices that represent decisions to express their talents for initiative and responsibility in ways which reflect female rather than male models of professional work.[60] For the present, however, it is women in the former group who are more often seen as leaders by the profession, and individual women continue to experience difficulties when they fail to conform, however understandably, to the male model of lawyering.[61]

At such a moment in the history of women lawyers, it is possible to assess both how much has been achieved and at the same time how much remains to be accomplished. For just as the concept of lawyer was male at the beginning of the twentieth century, preventing women from becoming lawyers at all, so the concept of leadership is male at the end of the century, preventing women from being recognized as leaders in their profession. Thus, the history of women in the legal profession is inextricably connected to their present concerns. As Gerda Lerner has suggested:

> History gives meaning to life and connects each life to immortality, but history has yet another function. In preserving the collective past and reinterpreting it to the present, human beings define their potential and explore the limits of their

possibilities. We learn from the past not only what people before us did and thought and intended, but we also learn how they failed and erred.[62]

In understanding the "invisible" constraints on those involved in the early cases concerning the admission of women to the legal profession, we can begin to appreciate the possibility of similar, equally "invisible", constraints on our understanding of the nature of leadership within the profession. And, as Joan Kelly has suggested, our recognition of such constraints means that we are now at a moment in history when we can not only "'see' how the patriarchal system works, but also...act with that vision — so as to put an end to it."[63]

Endnotes

1. Joan Kelly, "The Double Vision of Feminist Theory" in *Women, History and Theory: The Essays of Joan Kelly* (Univ. of Chicago Press: 1984) 51 at 61.

2. *Id.*, at 62.

3. According to the records of the Law Society of Upper Canada, there were 19,441 members in good standing (that is, excluding deceased, suspended, and disbarred members) on June 30, 1987, and 3625 of those were women. See LSUC computer printouts: analysis of members by sex and status.

4. In January 1986, the *Globe and Mail* reported that the first year class at the University of Windsor included more than 50% women for the first time, while the entrance rates for women at other common law schools in Canada hovered "around 35 to 45%". See *Globe and Mail*, January 29, 1986 at A16. The report also noted that the civil law universities had admitted more women than men to their first year programs for a number of years, Laval since 1979 and l'Universite de Montreal since 1981.

5. These words were written by Mary Appleby, then a student at Osgoode Hall Law School, in the student newspaper *Obiter Dicta* in 1934.

6. A recent poll of lawyers in Canada disclosed that 57% of lawyers believed that women were discriminated against in their law offices; and 71% believed that most allegations of discrimination in law offices are substantiated. See "Gender Discrimination: A Tricky Question" (*Canadian Lawyer Magazine*, March 1988) at 8. The report of the poll included comments from an Edmonton lawyer who stated that "an Alberta justice has been overheard as saying that the 'experiment' of having women in the profession was a failure and they should now return to the kitchen." *Ibid.*

7. "Summary of Hearings, ABA Commission on Women in the Profession" (February 1988) at 2. For further information on women in the legal profession in the United States, see the special report on "Women in Law: the Glass Ceiling" in *A.B.A.J.* (June 1988).

8. John Hagan, Marie Huxter and Patricia Parker, "Class Structure and Legal Practice: Inequality and Mobility among Toronto Lawyers" (Unpublished: 1897). This study characterized working conditions in terms of capitalists and working class categories. According to this characterization, the authors concluded:

> Women are significantly and disproportionately under-represented among the managerial bourgeoisie, and small employers, while they are significantly and disproportionately over-represented among semiautonomous employees, workers and the surplus population. If the latter three classes are combined, 61.8 per cent of the women are included, as compared to 32.5

per cent of the men. So women are about twice as likely as men to be found in this combined "underclass." *Id.*, at 23. This conclusion is not unlike that reached by Barry Adam and Kathleen Lahey in their earlier study of the graduates of Ontario law schools in 1974. See Barry Adam and Kathleen Lahey, "Professional Opportunities: A Survey of the Ontario Legal Profession" (1981), 59 *Can. Bar Rev.* 674. The demography of the Canadian legal profession is also reviewed in Harry Arthurs, Richard Weisman and Frederick Zemans, "Canadian Lawyers: A Peculiar Professionalism" in Richard Abel and Philip Lewis, eds., *Lawyers in Society, Vol. I: The Common Law World* (University of California Press: 1988) at 123; the authors briefly summarize some information about women in the profession, concluding that women are not found "in proportionate numbers in all types of practices". *Ibid.*, at 133.

9. The study measured the proportion of men and women in the "working class" of the profession from entry to six years, and then from six to eleven years of practice. Up to six years, 56.7% of women and 43.3% of men worked in the working class category; after six years of practice, 23.5% of women remained in the working class, compared to 13.5% of the men. As the study also demonstrated, "Women relative to men lawyers are significantly and disproportionately in the surplus population, both before (2.4 compared with 9.8%) and after (1.6 compared to 9.3%) the six year break-point." *Supra* fn. 80, at 24.

10. John Hagan, *Highlights from a Study of Toronto Lawyers* (CBAO Annual Institute, Program on Women in the Legal Profession: February 1988), at 2.

11. David A.A. Stager and David K. Foot, "Earnings and Employment of Female Lawyers" (Unpublished: 1987). An excellent summary of surveys and information sources on lawyers in Canada is found in David Stager, "Statistical Information on Lawyers in Canada"

12. *Id.*, at 6.

13. *Ibid.*

14. *Id.*, at 8.

15. *Id.*, at 8–9.

16. *Id.*, at 12, referring to R.K. Filer, "Sexual Differences in Earnings: The Role of Individual Personalities and Tastes" (1983), 19, *J. Human Resources* 408. In discussing this aspect of discrimination, Stager and Foot also acknowledged the homogeneity of legal education and training, and the possibility that such homogeneity may reduce other variables so as to permit the identification of sex discrimination in the legal profession more readily than in some other occupational groupings. As they stated:

> Because the professional education and training of lawyers
> is more homogeneous than for most other major occupations,
> it is possible to examine the male/female earnings differential
> for evidence of discrimination in a setting where the occupation,
> industry and education variables are so narrowly defined that
> sample heterogeneity can be greatly reduced.

Stager and Foot, *supra* fn. 83, at 11. The authors also suggested that hours worked and field of work may have some impact on the differential, although they were unable to be conclusive about this explanation. *Id.*, at 13.

17. Richard L. Abel, "Comparative Sociology of Legal Professions: An Exploratory Essay" (1985), 1. *Amer. Bar Found. Res. J.* 5.

18. According to Abel, "the number of male law students doubled between 1962/63 and 1980/81 while the number of female students increased 24 times" in the same period in Canada. The pattern of women's entry to the legal profession in Canada after 1970 occurred in a number of other western countries at the same time, in some cases even more dramatically. In the U.S.A., for example, Abel reported that "male enrollment in law school actually declined at an average rate of 0.1% a year in the 1970s, whereas female enrollment increased at an average annual rate of 41.4%. Male entry to the profession also declined after 1973, and *all* further increases in the rate of growth are attributable to new women lawyers." (Emphasis in original.). *Id.*, at 22–23. For details of similar statistics for other jurisdictions, see *ibid.*

19. The author reported difficulties in a number of jurisdictions, including Canada:

Decisions by lawyers to take on apprentices or hire new entrants are less visible and centralized, allowing greater scope for the expression of prejudice. The fragmentary evidence strongly suggests that women are becoming concentrated in positions that are less prestigious and remunerative, that deal with personal plight, and that can be held part time. *Id.*, at 39. For details of problems reported in other jurisdictions, see *id.*, at 39–40.

20. Abel attributed women lawyers' lower earnings to their lack of representation in the hierarchy of work in the legal profession, and provided statistics demonstrating the income differentials for a number of jurisdictions. As other commentators, however, he noted the need to adjust the data for age; see *id.*, at 40.

21. *Ibid.* Abel recommended cross-cultural research on the impact of a substantial minority of women in the profession for the first time in history. Indeed, in another article, he referred to the entry of women into the legal profession since 1970 as "nothing short of revolutionary". See Richard Abel, "The Contradictions of Professionalism" in Abel and Lewis, eds., *supra* fn. 80, at 202–203. For further consideration of these ideas, see also Carrie Menkle-Meadow, "Portia in a Different Voice: Speculations on a Woman's Lawyering Process" (1985), 1 *Berkeley Women's L. J.* 39; and "Excluded Voices: New Voices in the Legal Profession Making New Voices in the Law" (1987), 42 *U. Miami L. R.* 29.

Menkle-Meadow (and others) would, however, disagree with Abel's implicit suggestion that law schools offer a "meritocratic arena of formal education and examinations"; see Menkle-Meadow, "Feminist Legal Theory, Critical Legal Studies, and Legal Education or 'The Fem-Crits Go to Law School'" (1988), 38 *J. of Legal Ed.* 61, and other articles in this issue devoted to Women in Legal Education — Pedagogy, Law, Theory, and Practice. In Canada, see Christine Boyle, "Teaching Law as if Women Really Mattered, or, What About the Washrooms?" (1986), 2 *Can. J. of Women and the Law* 96; and Mary O'Brien and Sheila McIntyre, "Patriarchal Hegemony and Legal Education" (1986), 2 *Can. J. of Women and the Law* 69.

22. Carrie Menkle-Meadow, "The Comparative Sociology of Women Lawyers: The 'Feminization' of the Legal Profession" (1987), 24 *Osgoode Hall L.J.*, forthcoming; and (CBAO Annual Institute, Program on Women in the Legal Profession: February 1988). For information on lawyers in Third World nations, see Richard L. Abel, "Underdevelopment of Legal Professions: Review Article on Third World Lawyers", [1982] *Amer. Bar Res. Found. J.* 871.

23. Menkle-Meadow, *supra* fn. 94 (CBAO Annual Institute) at 15.

24. Menkle-Meadow, at *id.*, at 30. This conclusion mirrors that of the ABA Commission on Women in the Profession. In its Summary of Hearings, the Commission noted "the persistence of gender discrimination in the legal profession," and emphasized the need to recognize that the increased numbers of women entering the legal profession had not yet resulted in the removal of frustrations and barriers for women. See *supra* fn 79.

25. Rosabeth Moss Kanter, *Men and Women of the Corporation* (Basic Books: 1977). See also Moss Kanter, "Reflections on Women and the Legal Profession: A Sociological Perspective" (1978), 1 *Harv. Women's L.J.* 1; and Moss Kanter, "Structuring the Inside: The Impact of Organizations on Sex Differences" in Barbara Forisha and Barbara Goldman, *Outsiders on the Inside* (Prentice-Hall: 1981) at 75.

26. See *Men and Women of the Corporation*, *supra* fn. 97, at 47ff. As defined by Moss Kanter,

> Uncertainty can stem from either the time-span of decisions
> and the amount of information that must be collected, or from
> the frequency with which non-routine events occur and must
> be handled. The impossibility of specifying contingencies in
> advance, operating procedures for all possible events, leaves
> an organization to rely on personal discretion. (It is also this
> pressure that partly accounts for the desire to centralize responsibility in a few people who can be held accountable for
> discretionary decisions.)

Id., at 52.

27. *Id.*, at 53. Moss Kanter expressly noted the need for "homogeneity of class and ethnic background and prior social experiences" in relation to this comment; she applied it more specifically to women in Part III of her book.

28. *Id.*, at 68.

29. Her definition of power as "the ability to get things done, to mobilize resources, to get and use whatever it is that a person needs for the goals he or she is attempting to meet" is suggestive of power in a hierarchical setting. However, she also refers to power as a means of "empowering more people through generating more autonomy, more participation in decisions, and more access to resources", a definition which results in increasing the total capacity for effective action rather than for domination. *Id.*, at 166.

See also Rosabeth Moss Kanter, "Changing the Shape of Work: Reform in Academe" in *Perspectives on Leadership* (Current Issues examined by a number of feminists: see, for example, Jane Jaquette, "Power as Ideology: A Feminist Analysis" in Judith Stier, ed., *Women's Views of the Political World of Men* (Trasnational: 1982) at 9; Nancy Hartsock, "Political Change: Two Perspectives on Power" in *Building Feminist Theory: Essays for Quest* (Longman: 1981) at 3; Thelma McCormack, "Toward a Nonsexist Perspective on Social and Political Change" in Marcia Millman and Rosabeth Moss Kanter, eds., *Another Voice: Feminist Perspectives on Social Life and Social Sciences* (New York: 1975) at 1; Iva Ellen Deutchman, "Socialization to Power: Questions about Women and Politics" (1986), 5(4) *Women and Politics* 79; and Ann Duffy, "Reformulating Power for Women" (1986), 23 *Can. R. Soc. and Anth.* 22.

30. *Supra* fn. 91 199–200.

31. *Id.*, at 230.

32. *Id.*, at 241. For details of the stresses and costs to tokens, see 212–240 ff.

33. *Id.*, at 281–283.

34. *Id.*, at 260 ff. Moss Kanter was not overly optimistic about change occurring from within because of the structural features of the corporation itself:

> ...as long as the steep multi-leveled hierarchies that tend to accompany large size remain, it is impossible to remedy many inequities of compensation or opportunity, let alone empower more people or share decision-making more widely. When the model is hierarchical rather than collegial, there would also appear to be real limits on the extent to which it is possible to expand anyone's power, other than for those people who already have the managerial monopoly.

Id., at 286.

35. Cynthia Fuchs Epstein, "Women and Elites: A Cross-National Perspective" in Cynthia Fuchs Epstein and Rose Laub Coser, *Access to Power: Cross-National Studies of Women and Elites* (Allen and Unwin: 1981) at 3.

36. *Id.*, at 3–4. For further discussion, see *id.*, at 5–15.

37. *Id.*, at 6.

38. The 18.6% of the profession who were women in 1987 would represent Moss Kanter's "tilted" category; but it is only a few years since the percentage of women lawyers has been more than 15%, the ratio below which the category would have been "skewed". See *supra* fn. 75 and fn. 76, and text at fn. 104.

39. There is a rich literature about the roles of men and women in organizations, and the effects of socialization on their behaviour patterns: see, for example the bibliographical material in the section on organizations in Jarrard and Randall, *Woman Speaking: An Annotated Bibliography of Verbal and Non-Verbal Communication* (Garland, New York: 1982).

40. Sondra Farganis, *Social Reconstruction of the Feminine Character* (Rowman and Littlefield: 1986) at 193. Farganis offers an analysis of the sociology of knowledge focused on Viola Klein's *The Feminine Character*, a book concerned "with the relationship between writings about women and the social conditions out of which these writings are fashioned and within which they are placed." According to Farganis, "Perception, determined by the times in which one lives, changes as reality is reordered, which reordering is itself a consequence of the acceptance of new ideas."

Id., at 9. Farganis also considered the work of Mannheim, Kuhn, and Marx (among others) in relation to her thesis.

41. *Supra* fn. 112, at 193; Farganis attributed these ideas to Alison Jaggar, "Towards a More Integrated World", a paper presented to the Douglas College Women's Studies Seminar, January 1985.

42. M. Loden, *Feminine Leadership* (Times Books, New York: 1985); M. Maccoby, *The Leader* (Simon and Schuster: 1981); and J. Brad Chapman, "Male and Female Leadership Styles: The Double Bind" in Judith Ramaley, ed., *Covert Discrimination and Women in the Sciences* (Western Pres for Amer. Assoc. of Advancement of Sciences, Colorado: 1978) at 97. My special thanks to Cheryl Kristjanson for sharing with me her research and ideas on women and leadership.

43. Edwin I. Megargee, "Influence of Sex Roles on the Manifestation of Leadership" (1969), 53 *J. of Applied Psychology* 377; quoted by Chapman, *supra* fn. 114, at 102.

44. *Ibid.*

45. *Ibid.* In this article, Chapman reviewed a number of older studies about sex roles and behavior, including Virginia Ellen Schein, "The Relationship Between Sex Role Stereotypes and Requisite Management Characteristics" (1973), 57 *J. of Applied Psychology* 95; and Ivan D. Steiner and Evan D. Rogers, "Alternative Responses to Dissonance" (1963), 66 *J. of Abnormal and Social Psychology* 128. See also Nancy J. Adler and Dafna Izraeli, *Women in Management Worldwide* (M.E. Sharpe, New York: 1988).

46. D. McGregor, *The Professional Manager* (McGraw-Hill: 1967) at 23; quoted in Chapman, *supra* fn. 114 at 105. For a different perspective, see Adler and Izraeli, *supra* fn. 117.

47. Chapman, *supra* fn. 114, at 110.

48. "Summary of Hearings", *supra* fn. 79, at 3–4.

49. Nancy Hartsock, *Money, Sex and Power: Toward a Feminist Historical Materialism* (Longman: 1983).

50. Carol Gilligan, *In a Different Voice: Psychological Theory and Women's Development* (Harvard University Press: 1982).

51. Farganis, *supra* fn. 112, at 174; citing Nancy Hartsock, *supra* fn. 121 and Alison Jagger, *supra* fn. 113.

52. Farganis, *supra* fn. 112, at 196.

53. Menkle-Meadow, *supra* fn. 96.

54. As quoted by Christine Mullins, *supra* fn. 8, at 676; the author indicated that the poem first appeared in *Grip* in 1892, according to Ramsay Cook and Wendy Mitchison, eds., *The Proper Sphere: Women's Place in Canadian Society* (Oxford University Press: 1976) at 167.

55. Richard Abel has identified a number of demographic changes in the legal profession, resulting in younger average ages as well as increased numbers of women. He also has identified a "lag" in the numbers of ethnic law graduates, and has suggested that:

> These demographic shifts are of considerable importance. They reveal a profession that still does not reflect the class of ethnic composition of heterogeneous stratified societies. They reveal a substantial minority of women occupying inferior positions. And they reveal a youthful profession still governed almost exclusively by elderly males.... These tensions of class, ethnicity, gender, and age pose acute problems for professional associations.

Abel, *supra* fn. 89, at 41.

56. See, for example, Florence L. Denmark, "Styles of Leadership" (1977–78), 2 *Psych. of Women Q.* 99; and Anna R. Hauptman, "Styles of Leadership: Power and Feminine Values" in Forisha and Goldman, *supra* fn. 97 at 114.

57. In "The Death of Leadership or Educating People to Lead Themselves" (1978), 1 *Women's Studies Q.* 313, Margherita Rendel asserted that:

> We know that the achievements of men and women are perceived at different levels, those of women being rated as the lower even when the achievement is identical. This has been shown in a number of studies of the assessment of women's and men's work and *curricula vitae*.

Id., at 318. Rendel cited a number of studies, including Deaux and Emsmiller (1974); Fiddell (1970); Lewin and Duchan (1971); and Simpson (1969).

58. "Summary of Hearings", *supra* fn. 79, at 9.
59. In the context of Moss Kanter's structural analysis, it is logical that male hierarchies within the legal profession would choose to promote those women who are most "like" them, i.e., assimilated to the male model. There is all too little information about women who have achieved positions of leadership in the legal profession in Canada, but two comments might be made. First, the demographic information in Stager and Foot's research suggests that more women lawyers than men lawyers are unmarried, and this data might suggest that such women are more easily able to fit the male model of lawyer, i.e., a person without the significant family obligations which most women are assumed to have. See text at *supra* fn. 83.

Second, a recent article in the CBA *National* about women judges suggested their inability to identify with other women because "The very fact that these women are judges proves they have been professionally successful, and they may lack empathy with homemakers." More specifically, Louise Lamb's comment, quoted in the article, suggests the significance of the structural analysis in the contest of women judges:

> [Women judges] are drawn from a certain group, and feminist activity would possibly be held against them. The judiciary is still very much a kind of club.

National, October 1988, at 16.

For some information on the success of women in achieving positions of leadership in the profession, see Arthurs, Weisman, and Zemans, *supra* fn. 80, at 133. They reported, for example, that "Male judges and magistrates outnumbered female by more than eight to one in 1981 — more than nineteen to one on the federal bench." *Ibid.*
60. See, for example, the report on the eight-woman law firm in Toronto formed because "What we had in common is that we made similar decisions about how we want to practise and how we want to live our lives." See "How the Peanut Butter got on the Will," *Globe and Mail*, January 26, 1987, at B1, quoting Mary Dunbar.

61. Menkle-Meadow has suggested, for example, that many women lawyers who request maternity leave will receive it now, but that there is a sense in which most of them feel that thereafter they will never be "taken really seriously" by the firm. See Menkle-Meadow, "Women in Law? A Review of Cynthia Fuchs Epstein's *Women in Law*, [1983] *Amer. Bar Found. Res. J.* 189 at 197:

> Some law firms proudly proclaim their commitment to maternity leaves and "flexible" working arrangements for women lawyers with children, but many women who have availed themselves of such plans have quietly acknowledged that they are never again accepted as serious members of their firms...if women want to be successful in the corporate firm context they are going to have to do it by adopting the male work norms.

For some information about maternity leave arrangements in Canadian law firms, see Noelle Boughton, "Rock-a-Bye Lawyer", *Canadian Lawyer*, October 1988. Significantly, it is in the area of maternity leave that women experience the full effect of the social construction of sex roles; a pregnant lawyer will often be simultaneously valued and respected *as a woman* for her decision to make home life a priority on one hand and devalued *as a lawyer* for her failure to make work a priority on the other.
62. Gerda Lerner, *The Creation of Patriarchy* (Oxford: Oxford University Press, 1986) at 221.
63. *Supra* fn. 2, and text. Gerda Lerner has also commented in the same way:

> The system of patriarchy is a historic construct; it has a beginning; it will have an end. Its time seems to have nearly run its course — it no longer serves the needs of men or women...

Supra fn. 134, at 228–229.

Further Reading

Roy B. Flemming, "If You Pay the Piper, Do You Call the Tune? Public Defender in America's Criminal Courts" (1989), 14 *Law and Society Inquiry* 393–405.

C. Menkel-Meadow, "The Comparative Sociology of Women Lawyers: The Feminization of the Legal Profession" (1986), 24 *Osgoode Hall Law Journal* 901–18.

B. Legal Education

How to Become a Lawyer[†]
P. Fitzgerald and K. McShane

To become a lawyer involves basically four steps:

1. Obtaining a law degree — LL.B. or B.C.L.;
2. Completion of Articles;
3. Successful completion of *Bar Admission Course* and *Bar Examinations*; and
4. Admission to the Bar.

The first step falls under the jurisdiction of the law schools. The other three fall under the jurisdiction of the legal profession.

OBTAINING A LAW DEGREE

Law Schools

Today there are twenty law schools or Faculties of Law in Canada. Sixteen grant the common law Bachelor of Laws degree, LL.B., the language of instruction being English except at the University of Moncton which teaches common law in French. The University of Ottawa's Faculty of Law has a common law section and a civil law section, and McGill University's Law Faculty offers both the B.C.L. and LL.B. At these two universities it is possible to obtain both degrees through an extra year of study.

Admission to Law School

All Canadian Law schools require students to have completed at least two years of a recognized undergraduate degree programme. Because of the number of applicants for admission, however, the number of students admitted after two years only is small. Each law school has an Admissions Committee; and while standards for admission may vary slightly from school to school, they are pretty much the same. Factors considered are: (a) the student's academic record — while some law schools do not state a minimum requirement, admission statistics indicate the need for at least a good B+ average (75–79%), (b) letters of reference, and (c) results of the Law School Admission Test (LSAT). Information on admission standards, etc. may be obtained by writing directly to the particular law school.

Law School Admission Test

This is a general knowledge type of test administered by the Law Schools Admission Services in Newtown, Pennsyvania and is supposed to measure the candidate's aptitude for the study of law. Tests are held four times a year at various centres in Canada. A free booklet describing the test and containing an application form can be obtained from the Pre-Law Advisor (LSAT) at most Canadian Universities or by writing to: Law Services, Box 40, 661 Penn St., Newtown P.A. 18940–0998, U.S.A. As of June 1992 the LSAT is marked on a 120–180 point score scale with the mean score set at 150.

Notes

(a) The LSAT Registration and Information Book contains a limited amount of information on the programme and admission requirements of each Canadian Law School.

(b) If applicants do rather poorly on the LSAT it doesn't necessarily mean they will not be admitted to law school. They will, however need a much higher academic average. Conversely, a low academic standing could be offset by a very high LSAT. The weighting given to the LSAT, however, varies from one law school to another.

Letters of Reference

[These] are still required by most law schools. Such a letter is especially important if it serves to explain interruptions in an applicant's study programme (e.g., on account of illness), if the applicant has been in a field related to the study or practice of law and the letter comes from his or her employer, or it is comes from a former professor who can comment on the applicant's ability to do research, work under pressure, and speak out in seminar discussions. Given two candidates of equal academic records, a letter of reference may tip the scales.

Application Forms

[These] may be obtained by writing directly to the law schools. Each school has a deadline after which applications will not be considered. Most schools ask for a resume of the applicant's work, scholarships, prizes and extra-curricular activities. Some require an essay as to why

---

[†]   Fitzgerald, Patrick and McShane, King, "How to Become a Lawyer" in *Looking at Law — Canada's Legal System*, 4th ed. (Ottawa: Bybooks, 1994) at 119–22. Reprinted by permission of the authors and the publisher.

the applicant wants to study law. Many schools have a non-returnable application fee (approx. $40.00 to $50.00).

Quotas

Law schools in the Maritimes and Western Canada give priority to applicants from their own province by means of an out-of-province quota. There may also be quotas for native students and for mature students. To qualify as a mature student the applicants must be in their late twenties and have been in the work force for several years.

Pre-law Studies

Law Schools require applicants to have successfully completed two years of an undergraduate programme leading to a recognized degree. There is, however, no special programme of studies required for admission to law schools, but some courses may be particularly beneficial to a future lawyer. Since effective oral and written communication is essential for a successful lawyer, a course in English should be useful. Other recommended areas of study include history, political science, philosophy, and economics. Although these areas are in the Arts and Social Science Faculties, students graduating in science, engineering or business administration have just as much chance of being admitted to law school. Generally speaking, law students should obtain a good grounding in a variety of areas.

Undergraduate Courses in Law

A number of universities and colleges give courses in law at the undergraduate level as part of various programmes, and one Canadian university (Carleton) has a department of law. Such law courses provide no professional qualification, and no credit is given for them at any law school. Taking one or two such courses before going to law school has the following advantages. It gives the students a better idea of law and helps them decide whether they really want to be a lawyer. It familiarizes them with legal terminology, teaches them where to find the law, and lessens the strain of the first months of law school. At the same time, students not going on to law school can gain some knowledge of our legal system and its institutions.

The Law School Programme

Law schools offer three year courses leading to the LL.B. or B.C.L. degree. These contain certain compulsory courses and a limited number of optional courses, most of the courses in the first year being compulsory. Normally included are courses on contract, tort, property (real and personal), commercial law and criminal law. Courses on legal research and writing and legal institutions are usually included in the first year programme. In the second and third years there are various options, and a student wishing

to practise, say, in the corporate field may find sufficient courses to develop a specialty in that area. In most areas, however, specialization requires the student to go on to a Master of Laws degree.

THE PROFESSIONAL STEPS

After receiving a law degree the would-be lawyers still have a long way to go. They must article and pass the bar admission course. This part of the programme is controlled by the Law Society of the particular province in which the candidate wishes to practise. Since the requirements vary considerably from province to province, the following paragraphs only set out the general pattern.

Articles of Clerkship

This involves working in a law office under the supervision of an experienced practitioner for a certain period of time, between eight and twelve months depending on the province. The large number of law students graduating each year makes articling positions difficult to obtain. Students usually start looking for positions in the summer after their second year at law school.

While most students take articles with private law firms, there are many other openings. These include the Federal Department of Justice, which provides legal officers for all government departments, Provincial Attorneys-General or Departments of Justice, the Supreme Court of Canada (each of the nine justices has an articling student), some provincial Supreme Courts and the legal departments of many large corporations.

Bar Admission Course

These courses are administered by the law society of the province, are practice-oriented and are normally taught by practising lawyers. Their length, scope and content varies from province to province. They run from six to eight weeks to six to eight months. They may be conducted in conjunction with the articling programme, or they may be independent of articling, as in Ontario. At the end of the course, or of sections thereof, there are compulsory examinations.

Admission to the Bar

Having successfully completed the law degree, articles and bar admission course, the law student may now apply for admission to the bar. If the applicant meets the requirements as to age and residence, he will be sworn in at a meeting of the Law Society (called a Convocation in Ontario) or at a special sitting of the Supreme Court of the province. On being admitted to the bar in the Common Law provinces, a person becomes both a barrister and a solicitor, there being no divided profession in Canada. In the province of Quebec applicants are admitted to the bar as advocates or notaries depending upon the professional training which they have received.

CAREERS OPEN TO LAWYERS

While the great majority (over 80%) of those admitted to the bar in Canada go into private practice, some prefer to use their legal training in other areas of employment. They can use such training: (a) in federal, provincial and municipal government; (b) as legal counsel with boards, tribunals and regulating agencies; (c) as legal officers with the Armed Forces or RCMP; (d) in the legal sections of large corporations, e.g., insurance companies, Bell Canada, CPR; (e) in Law Reform Commissions; (f) in Human Rights Commissions; (g) working for the ombudsmen; (h) in the law teaching profession.

A recent publication, which should be available in most libraries, is *How to Become a Lawyer* by Duncan C. Thompson, published by Acorn Book Ltd., Edmonton, Alberta. This contains a host of information on Canadian law schools, admission requirements, and requirements for admission to the bar in all provinces.

Legal Education as Training for Hierarchy[†]
D. Kennedy

L AW schools are intensely political places despite the fact that the modern law school seems intellectually unpretentious, barren of theoretical ambition or practical vision of what social life might be. The trade-school mentality, the endless attention to trees at the expense of forests, the alternating grimness and chumminess of focus on the limited task at hand, all these are only a part of what is going on. The other part is ideological training for willing service in the hierarchies of the corporate welfare state.

To say law school is ideological is to say that what teachers teach along with the basic skills is wrong, is nonsense about what law is and how it works; that the message about the nature of legal competence, and its distribution among students, is wrong, is nonsense; that the ideas about the possibilities of life as a lawyer that students pick up from legal education are wrong, are nonsense. But all this is nonsense with a tilt; it is biased and motivated rather than random error. What it says is that it is natural, efficient and fair for law firms, the bar as a whole, and the society the bar services to be organized in their actual patterns of hierarchy and domination.

Because students believe what they are told, explicitly and implicitly, about the world they are entering, they behave in ways that fulfil the prophecies the system makes about them and about that world. This is the link-back that completes the system: students do more than accept the way things are, and ideology does more than damp opposition. Students act affirmatively within the channels cut for them, cutting deeper, giving the whole a patina of consent, and weaving complicity into everyone's life story.

．　．　．　．

The Formal Curriculum: Legal Rules and Legal Reasoning

The intellectual core of the ideology is the distinction between law and policy. Teachers convince students that legal reasoning exists, and is different from policy analysis, by bullying them into accepting as valid in particular cases arguments about legal correctness that are circular, question-begging, incoherent, or so vague as to be meaningless. Sometimes these are just arguments from authority, with the validity of the authoritative premise put outside discussion by professional fiat. Sometimes they are policy arguments (e.g., security of transaction, business certainty) that are treated in a particular situation as though they were rules that everyone accepts but that will be ignored in the next case when they would suggest that the decision was wrong. Sometimes they are exercises in formal logic that wouldn't stand up for a minute in a discussion between equals (e.g., the small print in a form contract represents the "will of the parties").

[†]   From David Kairys, ed. *The Politics of Law: A Progressive Critique* (New York: Pantheon Books, 1982), 40–41, 46–53, 60–61. Copyright © 1982 by Duncan Kennedy. Reprinted by permission.

Within a given subfield, the teacher is likely to treat cases in three different ways. There are the cases that present and justify the basic rules and basic ideas of the field. These are treated as cursory exercises in legal logic. Then there are cases that are anomalous — "outdated" or "wrongly decided" because they don't follow the supposed inner logic of the area. There won't be many of these, but they are important because their treatment persuades students that the technique of legal reasoning is at least minimally independent of the results reached by particular judges and is therefore capable of criticizing as well as legitimating. Finally, there will be an equally small number of peripheral or "cutting-edge" cases the teacher sees as raising policy issues about growth or change in the law. Whereas in discussing the first two kinds of cases the teacher behaves in an authoritarian way supposedly based on his objective knowledge of the technique of legal reasoning, here everything is different. Because we are dealing with "value judgements" that have "political" overtones, the discussion will be much more freewheeling. Rather than every student comment being right or wrong, all student comments get a pluralist acceptance and the teacher will reveal himself to be either a liberal or a conservative rather than merely a legal technician.

The curriculum as a whole has a rather similar structure. It is not really a random assortment of tubs on their own bottoms, a forest of tubs. First, there are contracts, torts, property, criminal law, and civil procedure. The rules in these courses are the ground rules of late-nineteenth-century laissez-faire capitalism. Teachers teach them as though they had an inner logic, as an exercise in legal reasoning, with policy (e.g., commercial certainty in the contracts course) playing a relatively minor role. Then there are second- and third-year courses that expound the moderate reformist program of the New Deal and the administrative structure of the modern regulatory state (with passing reference to the racial egalitarianism of the Warren Court). These courses are more policy oriented than first-year courses, and also much more ad hoc. Teachers teach students that limited interference with the market makes sense and is as authoritatively grounded in statutes as the ground rules of laissez-faire are grounded in natural law. But each problem is discrete, enormously complicated, and understood in a way that guarantees the practical impotence of the reform program. Finally, there are peripheral subjects, like legal philosophy or legal history, legal process, clinical legal education. These are presented as not truly relevant to the "hard" objective, serious, rigorous analytical core of law; they are a kind of playground or finishing school for learning the social art of self-presentation as a lawyer.

This whole body of implicit messages is nonsense. Teachers teach nonsense when they persuade students that legal reasoning is distinct, *as a method for reaching correct results*, from ethical and political discourse in general

(i.e., from policy analysis). It is true that there is a distinctive lawyers' body of knowledge of the rules in force. It is true that there are distinctive lawyers' argumentative techniques for spotting gaps, conflicts, and ambiguities in the rules, for arguing broad and narrow holdings of cases, and for generating pro and con policy arguments. But these are *only* argumentative techniques. There is never a "correct legal solution" that is other than the correct ethical and political solution to that legal problem. Put another way, everything taught, except the formal rules themselves and the argumentative techniques for manipulating them, is policy and nothing more. It follows that the classroom distinction between the unproblematic, legal case and the policy-oriented case is a mere artifact: each could as well be taught in the opposite way. And the curricular distinction between the "nature" of contract law as a highly legal and technical by contrast, say, with environmental law is equally a mystification.

These errors have a bias in favor of the center liberal program of limited reform of the market economy and pro forma gestures toward racial and sexual equality. The bias arises because law school teaching makes the choice of hierarchy and domination, which is implicit in the adoption of the rules of property, contract, and tort, look as though it flows from and is required by legal reasoning rather than being a matter of politics and economics. The bias is reinforced when the center liberal reformist program of regulation is presented as equally authoritative but somehow more policy oriented, and therefore less fundamental. The message is that the system is basically OK, since we have patched up the few areas open to abuse, and that it has a limited but important place for value-oriented debate about further change and improvement. If there is to be more fundamental questioning, it is relegated to the periphery of history or philosophy. The real world is kept at bay by treating clinical legal education, which might bring in a lot of information threatening to the cozy liberal consensus, as free legal drudge work for the local bar or as mere skills training.

It would be an extraordinary first-year student who could, on his own, develop a theoretically critical attitude towards this system. Entering students just don't know enough to figure out where the teacher is fudging, misrepresenting, or otherwise distorting legal thinking and legal reality. To make matters worse, the two most common kinds of left thinking the student is likely to bring with her are likely to hinder rather than assist in the struggle to maintain some intellectual autonomy from the experience. Most liberal students believe that the left program can be reduced to guaranteeing people their rights and to bringing about the triumph of human rights over mere property rights. In this picture, the trouble with the legal system is that it fails to put the state behind the rights of the oppressed, or that the system fails to enforce the rights formally recognized. If one thinks about law this way, one is inescapably dependent on the very techniques of legal reasoning that are being marshalled in defense of the status quo.

This wouldn't be so bad if the problem with legal education were that the teachers *misused* rights reasoning to restrict the range of the rights of the oppressed. But the problem is much deeper than that. Rights discourse is internally inconsistent, vacuous, or circular. Legal thought can generate equally plausible rights justifications for almost any result. Moreover, the discourse of rights imposes constraints on those who use it that make it almost impossible for it to function effectively as a tool of radical transformation. Rights are by their nature "formal," meaning that they secure to individuals legal protection for as well as from arbitrariness — to speak of rights is precisely *not* to speak of justice between social classes, races, or sexes. Rights discourse, moreover, simply presupposes or takes for granted that the world is and should be divided between a state sector that enforces rights and a private world of "civil society" in which atomized individuals pursue their diverse goals. This framework is, *in itself*, a part of the problem rather than of the solution. It makes it difficult even to conceptualize radical proposals such as, for example, decentralized democratic worker control of factories.

Because it is logically incoherent and manipulable, traditionally individualist, and wilfully blind to the realities of *substantive* inequality, rights discourse is a trap. As long as one stays within it, one can produce good pieces of argument about the occasional case on the periphery where everyone recognizes value judgments have to be made. But one is without guidance in deciding what to do about fundamental questions and fated to the gradual loss of confidence in the convincingness of what one has to say in favor of the very results one believes in most passionately.

The alternative left stance is to undertake the Procrustean task of reinterpreting every judicial action as the expression of class interest. One may adopt a conspiracy theory in which judges deliberately subordinate "justice" (usually just a left liberal rights theory) to the short-run financial interests of the ruling class, or a much more subtle thesis about the "logic" or "needs" or "structural prerequisites" of a particular "stage of monopoly capitalism." But however one sets out to do it, there are two difficulties. The first is that there is just too much drek, too much raw matter of the legal system, and too little time to give everything you have to study a sinister significance. It would be a full-time job just to give instrumental Marxist accounts of the cases on consideration doctrine in first-year contracts. Just exactly why it was that late-nineteenth-century capitalism needed to render an uncle's promise to pay his nephew a handsome sum if he didn't smoke till age twenty-one, a legal nullity? Or was it the other way around: that capitalism *needed* such promises to be enforceable?

The second difficulty is that there is no "logic" to monopoly capitalism, and law cannot be usefully understood, by someone who has to deal with it in all its complexity, as "superstructural." Legal rules the state enforces and legal concepts that permeate all aspects of social thought constitute capitalism as well as responding to the interests that operate within it. Law is an aspect of the social totality, not just the tail of the dog. The rules in force are a factor in the power or the impotence of all social actors (though they certainly do not determine outcomes in the way liberal legalists sometimes suggest they do). Because it is part of the equation of power rather than simply a function of it, people struggle for power through law, constrained by their limited understanding and limited ability to predict the consequences of their maneuvers. To understand law is to understand this struggle as an aspect of class struggle *and* as an aspect of the human struggle to grasp the conditions of social justice. The outcomes of struggle are not preordained by any aspect of the social totality, and the outcomes within law have no "inherent logic" that would allow one to predict outcomes "scientifically" or to reject in advance specific attempts by judges and lawyers to work limited transformations of the system.

Left liberal rights analysis submerges the student in legal rhetoric but, because of its inherent vacuousness, can provide no more than an emotional stance against the legal order. The instrumental Marxist approach is highly critical of law but also dismissive. It is no help in coming to grips with the particularity of rules and rhetoric because it treats them, a priori, as mere window dressing. These theories fail left students because they offer no base for the mastery of ambivalence. What is needed is to think about law in a way that will allow one to enter into it, to criticize it without utterly rejecting it, and to manipulate it without self-abandonment to *their* system of thinking and doing.

· · · ·

Incapacitation for Alternative Practice

Law schools channel their students into jobs in the hierarchy of the bar according to their own standing in the hierarchy of schools. Students confronted with the choice of what to do after they graduate experience themselves as largely helpless: they have no "real" alternative to taking a job in one of the conventional firms that hires from their school. Partly, faculties generate this sense of student helplessness by propagating myths about the character of the different kinds of practice. They extol the forms that are accessible to their students; they subtly denigrate or express envy about the jobs that will be beyond their students' reach; they dismiss as ethically and socially suspect the jobs their students won't have to take.

As for any form of work outside the established system — for example, legal services for the poor and neighbourhood law practice — they convey to students that, although morally exalted, the work is hopelessly dull and unchallenging, and that the possibilities of reaching a standard of living appropriate to a lawyer are slim or nonexistent. These messages are just nonsense — the rationalizations of law teachers who long upward, fear status degradation, and above all hate the idea of risk. Legal services practice, for example, is far more intellectually stimulating and demanding, even with a high case load, than most of what corporate lawyers do. It is also more fun.

Beyond this dimension of professional mythology, law schools act in more concrete ways to guarantee that their students will fit themselves into their appropriate niches in the existing system of practice. First, the actual content of what is taught in a given school will incapacitate students from any other form of practice than that allotted graduates of that institution. This looks superficially like a rational adaptation to the needs of the market, but it is in fact almost entirely unnecessary. Law schools teach so little, and that so incompetently, that they cannot, as now constituted, prepare students for more than one career at the bar. But the reason for this is that they embed skills training in mystificatory nonsense and devote more of the teaching time to transmitting masses of ill-digested rules. A more rational system would emphasize the way to learn law rather than rules, and skills rather than answers. Student capacities would be more equal as a result, but students would also be radically more flexible in what they could do in practice.

A second incapacitating device is the teaching of doctrine in isolation from practice skills. Students who have no practice skills tend to exaggerate how difficult it is to acquire them. There is a distinct lawyers' mystique of the irrelevance of the "theoretical" material learned in school, and of the crucial importance of abilities that cannot be known or developed until one is out in the "real world" and "in the trenches." Students have little alternative to getting training in this dimension of things after law school. It therefore seems hopelessly impractical to think about setting up your own law firm, and only a little less impractical to go to a small or political or unconventional firm rather than to one of those that offer the standard package of postgraduate education. Law schools are wholly responsible for this situation. They could quite easily revamp their curricula so that any student who wanted it would have a meaningful choice between independence and servility.

A third form of incapacitation is more subtle. Law school, as an extension of the educational system as a whole, teaches students that they are weak, lazy, incompetent, and insecure. And it also teaches them that if they are willing to accept dependency, large institutions will

take care of them almost no matter what. The terms of the bargain are relatively clear. The institution will set limited, clearly defined tasks and specify minimum requirements in their performance. The student/associate has no other responsibilities than performance of those tasks. The institution takes care of all the contingencies of life, both within the law (supervision and backup from other firm members; firm resources and prestige to bail you out if you make a mistake) and in private life (firms offer money but also long-term job security and delicious benefits packages aimed to reduce risks of disaster). In exchange, you renounce any claim to control your work setting or the actual content of what you do, and agree to show the appropriate form of deference to those above and condescension to those below.

By comparison, the alternatives are risky. Law school does not train you to run a small law business, to realistically assess the outcome of a complex process involving many different actors, or to enjoy the feeling of independence and moral integrity that comes of creating your own job to serve your own goals. It tries to persuade you that you are barely competent to perform the much more limited roles it allows you, and strongly suggests that it is more prudent to kiss the lash than to strike out on your own.

· · · ·

For progressive and left students, there is another possibility, which might be called the denunciatory mode. One can take law school work seriously as time serving and do it coldly in that spirit, hate one's fellow students for their surrenders, and focus one's hopes on "not being a lawyer" or on a fantasy of an unproblematically leftist legal job on graduation. This response is hard from the very beginning. If you reject what teachers and the student culture tell you about what the first-year curriculum means and how to enter into learning it, you are adrift as to how to go about becoming minimally competent. You have to develop a theory on your own of what is valid skills training and what is merely indoctrination, and your ambivalent desire to be successful in spite of all is likely to sabotage your independence. As graduation approaches, it becomes clearer that there are precious few unambiguously virtuous law jobs even to apply for, and your situation begins to look more like everyone else's, though perhaps more extreme. Most (by no means all) students who begin with denunciation end by settling for some version of the bargain of public against private life.

I am a good deal more confident about the patterns that I have just described than about the attitudes toward hierarchy that go along with them. My own position in the system of class, sex and race (as an upper-middle class white male) and my rank in the professional hierarchy (as a Harvard professor) give me an interest in the perception that hierarchy is both omnipresent and enormously important, even while I am busy condemning it. And there is a problem of imagination that goes beyond that of interest. It is hard for me to know whether I even understand the attitudes toward hierarchy of women and blacks, for example, or of children of working-class parents, or of solo practitioners eking out a living from residential real-estate closings. Members of those groups sometimes suggest that the particularity of their experience of oppression cannot be grasped by outsiders, but sometimes that the failure to grasp it is personal rather than inevitable. Often it seems to me that all people have at least analogous experiences of the oppressive reality of hierarchy, even those who seem most favored by the system — that the collar feels the same when you get to end of the rope, whether the rope is ten feet long or fifty. On the other hand, it seems clear that hierarchy creates distances that are never bridged.

It is not uncommon for a person to answer a description of the hierarchy of law firms with a flat denial that the bar is really ranked. Lawyers of lower middle-class background tend to have far more direct political power in the state governments than "elite" lawyers, even under Republican administrations. Furthermore, every lawyer knows of instances of real friendship, seemingly outside and beyond the distinctions that are supposed to be so important, and can cite examples of lower-middle-class lawyers in upper-middle-class law firms, and vice versa.

There are many lawyers who seem to defy hierarchical classification, and law firms and law schools that do likewise, so that one can argue that the hierarchy claim that everyone and everything is ranked breaks down the minute you try to give concrete examples. I have been told often enough that I *may* be right about the pervasiveness of ranking, but that the speaker has never noticed it himself, himself treats all lawyers in the same way, regardless of their class or professional standing, and has never, except in an occasional very bizarre case, found lawyers violating the egalitarian norm.

When the person making these claims is a rich corporate lawyer who was my prep school classmate, I tend to interpret them as a wilful denial of the way he is treated and treats others. When the person speaking is someone I perceive as less favored by the system (say, a woman of lower-middle-class origin who went to Brooklyn Law School and now works for a small, struggling downtown law firm), it is harder to know how to react. Maybe I'm just wrong about what it's like out there. Maybe my preoccupation with the horrors of hierarchy is just a way to wring the last ironic drop of pleasure from my own hierarchical superiority. But I don't interpret it that way. The denial of hierarchy is false consciousness. The problem is not whether hierarchy is there, but how to understand it, and what its implications are for political action.

Task Force Reports on Women in the Courts: The Challenge for Legal Education[†]
E.M. Schneider

THE ROLE OF THE LAW SCHOOLS

Law schools play a critical role in shaping and socializing our attitudes toward the law, the legal profession generally, and appropriate styles of lawyering. Law schools transmit out first messages about what is permissible in the law. Many present law school faculty members went to law school when there were few women students and almost no women faculty — when law school was a largely male institution. Only in the last fifteen years have women been in law schools in significant numbers. Women law teachers are still a minority on the faculty of many law schools. However, at schools such as Brooklyn Law School and a few others there are a sufficient number of

women law teachers (more than twenty at Brooklyn) to constitute a real critical mass, and many of the women play leadership roles within the law school community.[1]

The inclusion of women as law students and the presence of women on law school faculties have been important in many ways. In particular, women law faculty are important role models who send the message that women are a serious and important part of the profession. There are too few women faculty members at most schools and many who are on law faculties are not in tenure-track positions. They are clustered in clinical or legal writing jobs that frequently demand the most challenging work, but for less pay, long-term security, or status than other

† Schneider, Elizabeth M., "Task Force Reports on Women in the Courts: The Challenge for Legal Education" (1988), 38 *Journal of Legal Education* at 88–95. Copyright by the Association of American Law Schools. Reprinted by permission.

faculty members receive.[2] Yet the numbers have had an impact. Last year, for example, some first-year students in my section of Civil Procedure had three or four women teachers in their first year. Many told me how important it was for them to see women teaching the basic first-year courses. They understood the positive message that the law school was sending.

To acknowledge that increasing numbers of women in law schools is important in shaping attitudes toward the profession is not to suggest that numbers alone are sufficient. Numbers are only a start; they are *necessary* to begin to affect attitudes, but they are not *sufficient*. The task force reports dramatically document that numbers alone cannot change attitudes. The increasing numbers of women have had little impact on the pervasiveness of gender bias in the profession. And despite the statistical increase in women students and faculty, gender bias in legal education persists.

The increasing numbers of women law students and law teachers and their developing sensitivity to issues of concern to women stimulated the process of examination of gender bias in legal education that began while I was a student at NYU Law School. In 1972 I attended a historic conference, the Symposium on the Law School Curriculum and the Legal Rights of Women sponsored by the AALS, the first that I am aware of on gender bias in legal education. Presentations were made on many traditional areas of the law.[3] The focus was on the need to integrate issues concerning women within the basic structure of American legal education, rather than simply relying on the Women and the Law courses that were then developing to remedy serious omissions in the curriculum as a whole. Until a few years ago, however, the effort begun in 1972 to integrate women's issues into the curriculum had not developed very far.

Recently, law teachers around the country, mostly women, have begun to address these issues. Much of the most exciting work in legal education is now focusing on the problem of how to remedy gender bias in its many forms. The New York Task Force urges education in all the areas of inequity that it documents.[4] The education that many law students now receive in law schools still omits many of these areas. Women and men in legal education concerned with these issues are beginning to meet the challenge of the task force reports, although we are still largely talking to each other. Work is now focusing on analysis of curriculum content and on casebooks in traditional, particularly first-year courses. We are beginning not only to examine overt bias and omission of women's issues in courses but to explore the traditional pedagogy of legal education that leaves many women students feeling alienated and devalued. We are now also studying what actually goes on in the classroom — all the explicit and implicit ways that women are told that their ideas and perspectives are not equally valuable, but that the law is for men. Some have begun to examine the impact of gender on career choices, profes-

sional development, and professional socialization, and are urging law schools to address the issues raised, for example, by recent articles documenting the fact that women are leaving the legal profession.[5] In continuing legal education programs and the judicial education programs that schools such as CUNY Law School have developed, these issues are also being addressed. Let us look at some of these areas more closely.

CURRICULUM AND CASEBOOKS

In a number of substantive areas women in legal education have begun to explore gender bias in curriculum and casebooks, both biased coverage and omission of issues of concern to women. This work was begun at the 1972 AALS Conference and has now focused on the first-year curriculum. In 1983 Professors Nancy Erickson of Ohio State Law School and Nadine Taub of Rutgers Law School-Newark initiated a project on sex bias in the teaching of criminal law, responding to complaints by students in many law schools concerning the treatment of women's issues in criminal law. Their study analyzes the leading casebooks used in the field and surveys curriculum coverage. When completed, the report will be widely circulated to criminal law teachers and will provide supplementary course materials and suggestions for remedying gender bias.[6] Similar work is going on in torts, property, and contracts. A developing literature is analyzing gender bias in doctrine, casebooks and curriculum content.[7] For example, the Torts section of the AALS and the Women in Legal Education section jointly sponsored a program at the AALS Annual Meeting in 1987 on gender bias in Torts. The Women and the Law Project at American University Law School is dedicated to examining the problem of gender bias in the law school curriculum, particularly the first-year curriculum, and to coordinate these efforts.[8] The efforts are just beginning — much more needs to be done to ensure that the entire range of issues raised in the New York Task Force Report is included within curricula and course materials in all law school courses.

THE CLASSROOM

Course materials are not the only focus. Classroom dynamics are an additional area of study. A special workshop at the 1986 AALS Annual Meeting, sponsored by the Society of American Law Teachers (SALT) and various AALS sections, focused on Racism, Sexism, and Heterosexism in the Classroom. Women, minority, and gay students spoke movingly of the way in which they were made to feel unwelcome and were ignored or demeaned in the classroom. These students experienced legal education as excluding their own distinctive voices. Women students at Harvard and Yale Law Schools, for example, have written open letters to their faculties to confront and correct classroom attitudes and behaviours that they believe make women feel like outsiders in the classroom and ultimately in the legal profession.[9]

I certainly remember this from my own law school experience. In my first year another women student and I made a presentation to the NYU Law School faculty, on behalf of NYU Law Women, to complain of gender bias in the classroom. A study undertaken by faculty members at Yale Law School is examining this problem and analyzing its impact on professional socialization of women into law.[10] Many students recount that they perceive a difference in the reception of their concerns in classes taught by women or minorities. For example, some of my third-year students in Women and the Law say it is the first class in which they have spoken. The burden for eliminating these problems must not be left for women and minorities to carry alone.

LEGAL EDUCATION, LAWYERING, AND PROFESSIONAL DEVELOPMENT

Recent efforts to consider gender bias also look at the traditional structure of legal education and its impact on women. Many women students complain that traditional modes of legal education and models of lawyering are inappropriate, adversarial, and incorporate stereotypes of male aggressiveness as the norm. The New York Task Force Report documents the dilemma that these stereotypes pose for women lawyers when they do attempt to represent clients vigorously — they are punished for being too aggressive. Research is being undertaken to investigate whether women's lawyering styles have a different cast, modeled after Carol Gilligan's well-known work in differences in male and female moral development, In a Different Voice.[11] Many law teachers concerned with these issues are exploring the possibility of more dialogic, collaborative, and experiential educational approaches that attempt to empower and activate students rather than break and destroy them. These concerns intersect with modern efforts in legal education to include more experiential learning, clinical teaching, and simulation.[12] Our work seeks to help students integrate both heart and mind in addressing legal problems and to encourage the possibility of more self-critical and self-reflective styles of lawyering, sensitive to the dilemma of stereotyped roles.

LEGAL EDUCATION AND SCHOLARSHIP

The New York Task Force Report documents that judges and legal decision-makers have not been sufficiently educated on issues of concern to women, such as gender bias in family law, criminal law, and other areas of the law. There is a clear need for law schools to encourage faculty

to do more scholarly work on gender bias, not just in traditional women's rights areas or family law, but in the law broadly. This need contrasts with the implicit or explicit message which many women law faculty members have been given by deans and other members of their faculties: "Don't write on women's issues or soft topics like family law." Documentation by the task force reports of the way in which legal education has not been sufficiently responsive to women also suggests the need to recognize feminist jurisprudence as an important topic of scholarship generally. Feminist jurisprudence began with feminist legal scholars addressing issues that have largely been of concern to women. However, feminist legal theory has now been recognized as a significant approach to legal analysis and legal problem solving in general.[13]

LEGAL PROFESSION

In addition, the New York Task Force Report documents the need to investigate the impact on the profession and on women of the increasing numbers of women moving into the legal profession. The section of the Report which documents the problems which women attorneys face in practice has important implications for the legal profession generally, and for legal education. It suggests that it is important for the law schools to integrate discussion of gender bias in practice into clinical courses, trial advocacy courses, and into general discussion of ethics and strategy in more traditional courses as well. In addition it suggests that placement officers study the career paths of both men and women graduates and provide programs that are sensitive to issues which women may face in practice.

THE CHALLENGE OF THE TASK FORCE REPORTS: THE WORK AHEAD FOR LEGAL EDUCATION

The task force reports place the burden on the law schools. The devastating picture of treatment of women in the courts that the New York Task Force paints requires that the legal education community respond. In response to the New York Task Force Report, there have been some beginning efforts. In October 1986 the Metropolitan Women Law Teachers Association, an organization of women law teachers in the New York area, held a program addressing a range of issues on gender bias in legal education. In December of that year, the New York State Department of Education sent a letter to the deans of all New York state law schools asking for information concerning the implementation of the Report. The letter received a range of responses from law school deans. The Department of Education report summarizing these responses was issued in July 1987.[14] This report has been circulated to the deans of all New York State law schools, but no further action has been taken.

The New York Task Force Report demonstrates that law schools must deal affirmatively with issues of gender bias within their own institutions. Professional development workshops and faculty fora should be instituted by deans and given institutional priority. Gender bias should be a topic of serious attention and discussion within law schools. It is an important issue that should be addressed by the AALS. The AALS should provide leadership to stimulate law school deans to take more institutional initiative. The publication of the present symposium issue of the *Journal of Legal Education* can assist in these efforts.

The task force reports present an important challenge for legal education. Law schools can play a central role in changing gender bias. The question is whether they will meet the challenge. Legal education must be reconstructed to remedy the problems discussed in the task force reports. The law schools will be successful only when all law school graduates are not only knowledgeable about and sensitive to women's concerns in the law but have eradicated gender bias in their own practice.

Endnotes

1. At Brooklyn Law School, 15 of 41 tenured or tenure-track faculty are women, and there are 9 women clinical or legal writing instructors of law. According to figures compiled by the American Bar Association, Brooklyn Law School leads the nation in the number of women who serve on the full-time faculty. See "Brooklyn Leads Nation in Women Faculty Members" (Fall 1987), 1 *Brooklyn Law School News.*
2. For example, the preliminary results of a Society of American Law Teachers (SALT) 1986–87 law school national faculty composition study that Professor Richard Chused of Georgetown University Law School is presently completing indicate that women hold approximately 15.9% of all tenured or tenure-track positions but hold approximately 70% of all legal-writing positions.
3. The materials developed for the AALS Symposium on the Law School Curriculum and the Legal Rights of Women October 20–21, 1972, included the following unpublished materials: Babette Barton, Grace Blumberg and Carlyn McCaffrey, "Tax Law Materials"; Kenneth Davidson, "Cases and Materials on the Equal Pay Act of 1963", "Cases and Materials on Executive Order 12246"; and "Women in Unions: The LMRA, The LMRDA and Associated Problems: Cases and Materials"; Ruth Bader Ginsberg, "Toward Elimination of Sex-biased Discrimination: Constitutional Aspects"; Leo Kanowitz, "The Law School Curriculum and the Legal Rights of Women: Property"; Herma Hill Kay, Robert Levy, Cynthia Atwood and Kathryn Gehrels, "Family Law Materials"; Susan Ross, "Cases and Materials and Title VII of the 1964 Civil Rights Act"; Linda Singer, "Women in the Criminal Justice System." These materials are available in the bound volume, *AALS, Symposium on Law School Curriculum and Women's Rights* (1972).

   See also John Johnston, "Sex and Property: The Common Law Tradition, The Law School Curriculum, and Developments Toward Equality" (1972), 47 *N.Y.U. L. Rev.* 1033; Judith Younger, "Community Property, Women and the Law School Curriculum" (1973), 48 *N.Y.U. L. Rev.* 211 (both prepared for the AALS Symposium).
4. In addition to the suggestions already noted *supra* p. 88, the *New York Task Force Report, supra* note 2, recommends that law schools

ensure that criminal justice courses provide accurate information about rape, including substantial current data about the nature of the crime of rape, the psychology of offenders, the prevalence and seriousness of acquaintance rape, and the long-term psychic injury to rape victims. *Id.* at 64. The report also recommends that family law courses contain information about the hardship to children and custodial parents when awards are insufficient and unenforced. *Id.* at 100.
5. See, for example, Judy Klemesrud, "Women in the Law: Many Are Getting Out", *N.Y. Times*, Aug. 9, 1985, at A14, col. 2.
6. For a preliminary report of the project see Nancy S. Erickson, "Legal Education: The Last Academic Bastion of Sex Bias?" (1986), 10 *Nova L.J.* 457.
7. See Mary Joe Frug, "Re-Reading Contracts: A Feminist Analysis of a Contracts Casebook" (1985), 34 *A. U.L. Rev.* 1065; Lucinda Finley, "Laying Down the Masters Tools: A Feminist Re-Vision of Torts" (unpublished draft on file with author), and "Including Women's Issues in a Torts Course" (unpublished manuscript); Margaret Radin, "Market-Inalienability" (1987), 100 *Harv. L. Rev.* 1849. See also materials developed for the Women and Law Project's program on gender bias in the first-year curriculum, AALS Annual Meeting, January 1986 (available from Professor Ann Shalleck, Washington College of Law, American University), and materials on gender-bias in torts, prepared for the program, Torts: A New Perspective, jointly sponsored by the AALS Torts Section and the Section on Women in Legal Education at the AALS Annual Meeting, January 1987 (available from Professor Jean Love, University of California — Davis Law School).
8. The project has held meetings on gender bias in the curriculum at AALS Annual Meetings for the last four years. The first, in January 1985, was on teaching Women and the Law courses. The second, Integrating Issues Concerning Women into the First-Year Curriculum, was held in January 1986, the third, and informal meeting of people working on gender bias in legal education, was held in January 1987, and the fourth, Different Approaches to Integrating Women's Issues in the Classroom: The Many Forms of Feminist Teaching, was held in January 1988. See Ann Shalleck, "Report of the Women and the Law Project: Gender bias and the Law School Curriculum" (1988), 38 *J. Legal Educ.* 97.
9. See generally *Five Easy Steps Toward a Non-Sexist Classroom Environment* and other materials distributed by the Harvard Women's Law Association, April 1985; *Open Letter to the Law School Community from Minorities and Women at Yale Law School* (on file with author).
10. Project on Gender and Professional Socialization: Issues in Law and Legal Education, Yale Law School, coordinated by Professors Lucinda Finley, Robert Burt, and former Dean Jamienne Studley.
11. See Carol Gilligan, *In a Different Voice: Psychological Theory and Women's Development* (Cambridge, 1982). See generally Carrie Menkel-Meadow, "Portia in a Different Voice: Reflections on a Woman's Lawyering Process" (1985), 1 *Berk. Women's L.J.* 39.
12. For a fuller discussion of these issues in the context of the first-year course in Civil Procedure, see Elizabeth M. Schneider, "Rethinking the Teaching of Civil Procedure" (1987), 37 *J. Legal Educ.* 41.
13. A panel on Feminist Jurisprudence was included in the AALS Mini-Workshop on Emerging Traditions in Legal Education and Legal Scholarship at the AALS Annual Meeting, January 1987.
14. The report, entitled *Law School Response to the Task Force Report on Gender Bias in the Courts* (1987), included the following description of its mandate and findings:

> Responding to a request from the Education Commissioner's Statewide Advisory Council on Equal Opportunity for Women, the State Education Department's Office of Higher Education Academic Review sent letters in November 1986 to the deans of New York State's 15 law schools requesting information concerning their institutions' reactions to the Task Force Report. Without being issue or recommendation-specific, the letter inquired about the effects of the report on both required and elective courses within the law curricula, and it invited information concerning other institutional initiatives — formal and informal — which promote the elimination of gender bias in the courts.
>
> SUMMARY OF INITIATIVES:

Ten of the New York State's fifteen law schools replied to the State Education Department inquiry. Synopses of the replies are listed below by institution.

Any interpretation of these summaries must be tempered by at least two factors. The first of these is the open-ended nature of the survey. Consequently, while several law schools provided detailed and extensive reports of their efforts to eliminate gender bias in the courts, other institutions suggested that their replies were intended to serve only as examples of the manner in which they address gender bias issues in general and the Task Force Report in particular. Second, the following make no attempt to cite every activity mentioned in each institution's response. They are intended to perform the two-fold purpose of illustrating the reactions of New York's schools of law to the specific findings of the Task Force on Women in the Courts and of highlighting some of the known features and initiatives within each institution's response to the general issue of gender bias.

Id. at 1–2.

The report concludes:

On the basis of their replies to the State Education Department inquiry, reactions of the Task Force Report range from no specified activity to formal action initiated under the leadership of the dean. Eight of the ten respondents report that their curricula comply with at least some of the Task Force recommendations. However, this represents only slightly more than half of New York's fifteen law schools. Moreover, commentaries from two of the responding institutions suggest that law schools may encounter difficulty implementing certain Task Force recommendations.

Id. at 4.

The law schools that responded were New York Law School, Cornell University Law School, Brooklyn Law School, Albany Law School, Fordham University Law School, New York University Law School, SUNY — Buffalo Law School, Syracuse University College of Law, Touro Law School, Cardozo Law School.

The Report is available from the Office of Higher Education Academic Review of the New York State Department of Education, Albany, N.Y. 12230.

Further Reading

L. Hellman "Considering the Future of Legal Education: Law Schools and Social Justice" (1978), 29 *Journal of Legal Education* 170–93.

A. Hunt "The Case for Critical Legal Education" (1986), 20 *The Law Teacher* 10–20.

C. Control Over the Profession

Ontario Law Society v. Harry Kopyto: The Next Instalment[†]
R. Haliechuk

LIKE modern-day feuding Hatfields and McCoys, Toronto lawyer Harry Kopyto and the Law Society of Upper Canada have recently fired several more salvos in their long-standing war of words.

For its part, the Law Society has refined a complaint of professional misconduct brought against Mr. Kopyto, alleging, among other things, that he billed the Ontario Legal Aid Plan for more than 24 hours' work on a single day and billed for more than 1,000 phone calls on behalf of the same client during a 15-month period.

The Law Society alleges he is guilty of professional misconduct for deliberately submitting inflated accounts to Legal Aid during 1984, 1985 and 1986.

In response, Mr. Kopyto, the pit bull terrier of the legal profession, assailed the society for indulging in a public campaign to slander him.

Mr. Kopyto also faces a complaint of professional misconduct and conduct unbecoming a solicitor for saying in 1985 that the courts and police are so close, one would think they were "stuck together with Krazy glue."

The recent events at the front can be summarized as follows:

☐ On Jan. 30, a three-member discipline committee panel agreed with Mr. Kopyto's contention that it was a "court of competent jurisdiction" within the meaning of the Charter of Rights, to entertain a motion to strike down a Law Society rule.

The Law Society claims Mr. Kopyto's "Krazy Glue" and other comments violate Rule 11 of the rules of professional conduct.

Known as Rule 12 at the time of Mr. Kopyto's statements, the rule says a lawyer should encourage public respect for and try to improve the administration of justice.

The Law Society has retained Frank Marrocco of the Toronto firm of Marrocco, David and Trudell, to prosecute the complaint.

Mr. Marrocco argued that since the rule in question was passed by Convocation, only Convocation could rescind it.

Mr. Kopyto was represented at this hearing by Peter Rosenthal, a University of Toronto mathematics professor, who urged the committee to find that the rule has a "chilling effect" on free speech and is unconstitutional.

"This is the kind of political speech that has been of the gravest concern to those concerned about freedom of expression," Mr. Rosenthal maintained.

Other comments about a court decision made by Mr. Kopyto which the Law Society alleges to be contrary to the rule include:

- "This is a mockery of justice";
- "It stinks to high hell";
- "We're wondering what is the point of appealing and continuing this charade of the courts in this country which are warped in favour of protecting the police."

Mr. Kopyto had delivered his critique after Toronto Provincial Court Judge Marvin Zuker had tossed out a lawsuit he brought against the RCMP on behalf of a client.

The Crown then laid a contempt court charge against Mr. Kopyto, who was convicted at trial; but on appeal the conviction was quashed, with three of five Court of Appeal judges ruling that Mr. Kopyto's comments were constitutionally protected.

☐ On Feb. 10, Mr. Marrocco served notice that he was seeking judicial review in the Divisional Court of the Committee's conclusion it can deal with the Charter arguments. This development did not appear to sit well with Mr. Kopyto.

"I think the Law Society is leaving no stone unturned to rid the world of Harry Kopyto," he charged.

Asked if the judicial review application appears to be a case of one arm of the Law Society battling with another, Mr. Kopyto would only say that "there are cracks in the edifice."

But Mr. Marrocco defended his decision to go to court.

[†] Haliechuk, Rick, "Ontario Law Society v. Harry Kopyto: The Next Instalment" *The Lawyers Weekly*, February 24, 1989, 31. This article originally appeared in the Feb. 24, 1989 issue of *The Lawyers Weekly*. Reprinted by permission.

"I think the Law Society needs to know whether a discipline committee can use the Charter to declare a rule passed by Convocation to be unconstitutional," he said.

☐ On Feb. 3, it was revealed that the society has withdrawn a previous complaint against Mr. Kopyto about overbilling Legal Aid and replaced it with a new one containing three cases of alleged professional misconduct.

In addition to the allegation that he deliberately submitted inflated account to Legal Aid, the Law Society also says Mr. Kopyto used the research of two Toronto lawyers for a court motion, after telling them he would use it to write an article for the *Globe and Mail*, and then tried to mislead the Law Society when it was investigating this allegation.

The Law Society provided 11 particulars to the Legal Aid overbilling complaint, including that Mr. Kopyto:

* billed Legal Aid for more than 24 billable hours on Dec. 4, 1986, excluding time billed for phone calls;
* billed the plan for more than 12 billable hours per day on 87 separate days between 1984 and 1986 excluding time billed for phone calls;
* repeatedly billed the plan for performing more than one task at the same time between 1984 and 1986;
* billed the plan for an average of 2 hours and 40 minutes of phone calls per day between 1984 and 1986;
* billed the plan for 9 days spent at court, court offices and government offices on Saturdays and Sundays, with none of the time being spent on Saturday appearances at bail hearings on criminal matters;
* submitted accounts to the plan for 1,092 phone calls for one client made between March 3, 1985 and May 21, 1986.

Details of this complaint appeared in Toronto newspapers on Feb. 4 and Feb. 5, in advance of a hearing before another Law Society discipline committee on Feb. 7.

☐ On Feb. 7, Mr. Kopyto lashed out at Mr. Marrocco and the Law Society, accusing them of trying to slander him publicly.

As for the allegations, Mr. Kopyto said the complaint merely showed that he works very hard for his clients.

"It seems to me there's nothing that says a lawyer can't work more than 12 hours a day," an angry Mr. Kopyto charged. "Some of us take our clients more seriously than others, some of us have more energy."

He said that several of the particulars of the society's complaint do not disclose any conduct contrary to the rules, and he demanded he be provided with more precise particulars.

"If the accusation is that I work too hard, I want to know that," he said. "Give me a charge that I can face."

Mr. Kopyto and Mr. Marrocco leaked details of the complaint to the media before it was presented to the committee.

"They're facts Mr. Marrocco has designed to put into a press release, designed to slander me," he charged.

Charles Roach, counsel for Mr. Kopyto, said while it's true his client likes to be open about things, that was still not reason for the Law Society to disseminate information which suggests Mr. Kopyto is guilty of fraud or embezzlement.

Mr. Roach urged the committee to censure the Law Society's conduct.

The panel — comprised of lawyers Helen MacLeod of Kingston and Rino Bragagnolo of Timmins, and lay bencher June Callwood — questioned Mr. Marrocco about how the material came to find its way into the media first.

Mr. Marrocco said that since it was merely a revision of a complaint that had been earlier tendered at a public discipline committee hearing, the new complaint was a public document.

He said that it was not unusual for details of a complaint to be published before a hearing, although it depends "on how interested the media are in a particular case."

Mr. Marrocco said the Law Society had no interest in conducting a witch hunt against Mr. Kopyto.

"We're not harbouring any grudges against anyone," he said.

The committee decided it couldn't censure Mr. Marrocco or anyone else at the Law Society.

And it also declined to deal with Mr. Kopyto's demand that some of the particulars be tossed out, ruling that would be dealt with by the committee which becomes seized with hearing the complaint, on the basis of evidence presented to it.

This decision further angered Mr. Kopyto.

"Save me the hassles, save me the headache, save me calling dozens of witnesses," he implored.

In an interview, Mr. Kopyto characterized the complaint as the "fantasy of a demented mind."

"You can't make a living off Legal Aid, never mind rip it off," he said.

☐ On March 6, the protagonists are next scheduled to do battle and Mr. Kopyto is expected to present his argument that the Law Society cannot both prosecute and try lawyers accused of violating rules of conduct.

Paralegals Fill Gaps in Legal Service Delivery Ontario Task Force Discussion Paper Argues[†]

D. Brillinger

EVIDENCE gathered by Ontario's special task force on paralegals during the past 10 months suggests that independent paralegals should be allowed to operate "in some fashion with appropriate safeguards for the public interest."

In a discussion paper released last month, the task force says research indicates that Ontario's growing paralegal industry seems to be filling "some gaps in the system of legal service delivery" in the province and appears "to be filling an important public need."

"Most consumers seem to be satisfied with the quality of service they have obtained through independent paralegals. There is also some evidence that the fees charged by independent paralegals are lower than those charged by the legal profession for comparable work," the discussion paper says.

It adds that, "[o]n the whole, while there have been some inappropriate acts carried out by paralegals, the perception of the level of complaints has been exaggerated."

But while the task force says it recognizes independent paralegals should be subject to some form of regulation, it suggests that such controls should be implemented cautiously.

"We are mindful that to establish a costly and cumbersome regulatory scheme would be to defeat some of the potential benefits of greater access to legal services at a reasonable cost which would be possible through the recognition of independent paralegals.

"We think that the regulatory system chosen should be the least intrusive necessary to ensure a consistent and competent level of services being offered to the public," the paper says.

"Independent paralegals should be viewed as legal technicians provided with the capacity to service the public in a very specific manner in areas of lesser complexity and lower risk. The independent paralegal must also be educated to have the ability to recognize when a particular legal problem must be referred to a fully qualified lawyer," the paper adds.

The task force was created last summer by Attorney General Ian Scott to study the role of paralegals in Ontario and to recommend whether or not paralegals should be able to provide legal services to the public.

Chaired by University of Windsor president Ronald Ianni, it has spent the past 10 months gathering empirical research about the scope of paralegal activity in the province. It also has received more than 60 written submissions from paralegal organizations, law societies and other parties, and has met privately with legal and paralegal groups to explain its mandate and procedures.

The discussion paper outlines some of the task force's preliminary findings, and is intended to focus proceedings at a series of public hearings the group began holding across Ontario earlier this month.

The paper says the "phenomenon" of independent paralegals — those who work without direct supervision by lawyers — "is widespread throughout the province and is continuing to grow and attract new members to its ranks."

Consumers appear to be satisfied with paralegals, whose fees seem to be lower than those charged by lawyers "for comparable work," the discussion paper notes.

"...Members of the public are using the services of independent paralegals, especially with regard to the more routine and 'lower risk' legal services where form filling or minimal expertise is necessary."

Overall, the "perception" of the number of complaints about paralegals appears to be "exaggerated," the paper says, adding that the task force has "uncovered no generalized abuse of clients by independent paralegals."

Still, "there are definite concerns about the lack of education and training of most independent paralegals," of whom "very few have been operating for more than a couple of years."

Turning to the various options it could recommend to the attorney general, the task force says it does not favour retaining the *status quo*, "whereby independent paralegals are allowed to be gainfully employed as agents before some minor courts and administrative agencies, but not to provide any other legal services.

"Because of the concern expressed about the competence of the service being provided by independent paralegal agents, almost no individual or group which has made its views known to the task force has argued for retention of the present state of affairs. At the very least, independent paralegal agents should be trained and minimally regulated in some fashion.

"The task force is in agreement with these basic sentiments," the paper says, "and cannot see how the people of Ontario would be served by continuing on the current path. There is much confusion in the minds of the public concerning the legitimate role of paralegals in the legal services marketplace. Retaining the *status quo* would only perpetuate the present confused state."

[†]   Brillinger, Don, "Paralegals Fill Gaps in Legal Service Delivery Ontario Task Force Discussion Paper Argues" *The Lawyer's Weekly*, June 30, 1989. This article originally appeared in the Jun. 30, 1989 issue of *The Lawyers Weekly*. Reprinted by permission.

The task force also does not favour allowing paralegals to operate *only* under lawyers' supervision.

"This, in effect, would be to retain the legal status of the present situation, without expanding the range of services available to the public through independent paralegals."

Similarly, it is "not inclined to recommend the abolition of those agents currently appearing within minor courts and tribunals that have received the approval of the Court of Appeal in the *POINTTS* decision. Indeed, these activities appear to be filling an important public need."

(In *R. v. Lawrie and POINTTS Ltd.*, the Ontario Court of Appeal said paralegals may act as paid agents in traffic law prosecutions and certain other minor proceedings without violating *Law Society Act* prohibitions against the unauthorized practice of law. See: *Lawyers Weekly*, March 27, 1987.)

"Furthermore," says the paper, "should such agents and paralegals be allowed to carry out these limited activities, subject to some form of educational requirements and regulation, it would appear illogical to preclude paralegals from carrying out other technical tasks with similar or lesser skill requirements.

"This would involve setting out specific areas of practice, and establishing education and training programs relevant to these areas of practice. It would be necessary to appoint an individual with the responsibility of overseeing the activities of independent paralegals generally, and managing a regulatory scheme," the paper points out.

Finally, the task force warns that enacting a "costly and cumbersome" regulatory scheme could defeat the benefits of allowing paralegals to provide the public with legal services at a reasonable cost.

Regina v. Lawrie and POINTTS Ltd.[†]

THE judgement of the court was delivered by

BLAIR J.A.: — The question in this case is whether a paid agent acting for persons charged with traffic offences under the *Highway Traffic Act*, R.S.O. 1980, c. 198, pursuant to s. 51(1) of the *Provincial Offences Act*, R.S.O. 1980, c. 400, can be prosecuted for acting as a barrister or solicitor under s. 50(2) of the *Law Society Act*, R.S.O. 1980, c. 233.

The respondents, Brian Lawrie (Lawrie) and Pointts Limited (the Company) were separately charged in a private prosecution initiated by the Law Society of Upper Canada with unlawfully acting as barristers or solicitors contrary to s. 50 of the *Law Society Act*. (Pointts is an acronym for Provincial Offences Information and Traffic Ticket Service.) The charges were dismissed by His Honour Judge Kerr of the Provincial Court whose decision was affirmed on appeal by the Honourable Judge Moore of the District Court [58 O.R. (2d) 535, 29 C.C.C. (3d) 160]. This appeal is brought pursuant to leave granted by a judge of this court under s. 114 of the *Provincial Offences Act*.

Lawrie is not a barrister or solicitor. He is a retired policeman with considerable experience in the conduct of traffic cases under the *Provincial Offences Act*. He incorporated the company for the purpose of representing persons charged with traffic offences under the *Highway Traffic Act*. Each customer or client is required to sign a

form appointing the company as agent to act on his or her behalf "within the meaning of the *Provincial Offences Act*". Lawrie controls the company. At the time of trial, two former police officers were also employed by the company and represented its clients in proceedings under the *Provincial Offences Act*.

The relevant provisions in the *Law Society Act* are:

> **50.**(1) *Except where otherwise provided by law*, no person, other than a member whose rights and privileges are not suspended, shall act as a barrister or solicitor or hold himself out as or represent himself to be a barrister or solicitor or practise as a barrister or solicitor.
>
> (2) Every person who contravenes any provision of subsection (1) is guilty of an offence and on conviction is liable to a fine of not more than $1,000. (Emphasis added.)

The prosecution was conducted under the *Provincial Offences Act*, which provides:

> **51.**(1) A defendant may appear and act personally or by counsel or *agent*.

. . . .

---

† *Regina v. Lawrie and POINTTS Ltd.* (1987), 32 C.C.C. (3d) 549 (Ont. C.A.).

(3) The court may bar any person from appearing as an agent who is not a barrister and solicitor entitled to practise in Ontario if the court finds that the person is not competent properly to represent or advise the person for whom he appears as agent or does not understand and comply with the duties and responsibilities of an agent. (Emphasis added.)

The learned trial judge found that both respondents had acted as barristers or solicitors within the meaning of s. 50(1) of the *Law Society Act*. This finding was challenged by the respondents in this appeal but, since it is amply supported by the evidence, it should not be disturbed. The respondents were charged only with acting as barristers or solicitors and not with holding themselves out or practising as barristers or solicitors which are the other activities prohibited by s. 50(1).

Nevertheless, the trial judge acquitted both respondents. He held that the *Provincial Offences Act* permitted them to act as agents and that, consequently, they fell within the exceptions that were "otherwise provided by law" in s. 50(1) of the *Law Society Act*. He said [at p. 537 O.R., p. 162 C.C.C.]:

on all the evidence, bearing in mind that in the opinion of this court s. 48(1) of the *Provincial Offences Act*, that is, the burden section, means the burden is only upon the defence to satisfy a court on the balance of probabilities that an authorization, exception, exemption, or qualification operates in his favour, that Mr. Lawrie has done that in this case as has Pointts Limited. They have satisfied the burden cast upon them of showing that this exemption is provided for by the various sections of the *Provincial Offences Act*, certainly not expressly, but impliedly, and as a result, the defendant Lawrie and the defendant Pointts Limited must receive the benefit of the doubt on these informations, and the charges will be dismissed.

Judge Moore, affirming the trial judge's decision, went further and concluded that a new trade or profession of paralegals had been created by the *Provincial Offences Act*. After reviewing a number of statutes, which authorized the appearance of agents, he had this to say [at pp. 542–3 O.R., pp. 167–8 C.C.C.]:

[T]he Legislature...has provided a number of exceptions to the long-standing prohibition of...others acting and practising as lawyers. In saying that, I mean that the various Acts of Legislature I have referred to above permits agents to appear and act and represent others in provincial court,

and in some cases surrogate and district court. This legislation does not just permit an appearance in place of a defendant. It also permits an appearance with and for a defendant. No prohibition or restriction was brought to my attention which prevents the same person appearing as agent for a different person on numerous occasions or even receiving renumeration for so doing.

The Legislature has thus created a new trade or calling, that is to say, the calling of para-legals.

. . . .

Appearances through agents, who are not barristers or solicitors, are permitted by other statutes. These include the *Landlord and Tenant Act*, R.S.O. 1980, c. 232, s. 118(1), dealing with residential tenancies; the *Courts of Justice Act*, 1984 (Ont.), c. 11, s. 79, dealing with the Provincial Court (Civil Division) which is now responsible for small claims; the *Construction Lien Act*, 1983 (Ont.), c. 6, s. 69(5), dealing with lien claims not exceeding $200; the *Coroners Act*, R.S.O. 1980, c. 93, s. 41(2), dealing with coroners' inquests; and the *Statutory Powers Procedure Act*, R.S.O. 1980, c. 484, s. 23(3), dealing with appearances before administrative tribunals. With the exception of the *Statutory Powers Procedure Act*, these statutes permit the employment of agents only in relatively minor matters. All the statutes except the *Construction Lien Act, 1983* and the *Coroners Act* contain a provision similar to s. 51(3) of the *Provincial Offences Act* empowering the court or tribunal to bar any agent who is found not competent to represent or advise the person for whom the agent appears or who does not understand and comply with the duties and responsibilities of an agent.

There are other cases where persons, who are not qualified lawyers, are authorized by statute or permitted in practice to act as counsel or solicitors. The Crown makes use of agent under the *Crown Attorneys Act*, R.S.O. 1980, c. 107, s. 7, which provides for the appointment of provincial prosecutors under the *Provincial Offences Act* who are not members of the bar. The *Police Act*, R.S.O. 1980, c. 381, s. 57, enables police officers to act as prosecutors and they are considered agents under s. 1(h) of the *Provincial Offences Act*. Students are employed by the Ministry of the Attorney-General primarily to prosecute traffic offences under the *Provincial Offences Act*, as are students-at-law articled with the Attorney-General's office. Law students, who have completed one year of their law course, may appear in some legal aid matters handled by Student Legal Aid Societies: R.R.O. 1980, Reg. 575, s. 80, under the *Legal Aid Act*, R.S.O. 1980, c. 234. Under para. 12 of the rules of the law society made pursuant to s. 62(1) of the *Law Society Act*, articled students-at-law are permitted to appear in various proceedings.

Rule 20 of the Law Society's Rules of Professional Conduct permits delegation of many tasks by lawyers to employees who are not lawyers or articled students. The delegable tasks include conveyancing, drafting corporate and commercial documents, administration of estates and trusts, and research and preparation of documents in litigation. The rule states that "[g]enerally speaking a non-lawyer shall not attend on examinations or in court except in support of a lawyer also in attendance". The rule makes an exception for appearances by law clerks employed by only one lawyer or law firm in a variety of cases. These include appearances as agents where statutes or regulations permit non-lawyers to appear and on routine adjournments in Provincial Court. Law clerks may also attend on routine examinations in uncontested matters, *ex parte* or consent orders before a master and the taxation of costs.

The common thread that runs through these examples of employment of law students and non-lawyers is that their work is done under the direction and supervision of lawyers who are responsible to clients and the public for the work's proper performance. Moreover, the work is done by salaried employees whose renumeration, unlike that of lawyers, is fixed and not related to fees charged for specific services.

The position of the respondents in this case is different. They operate their own business independent of any direction or supervision by qualified lawyers. The respondents, when acting as agents under the *Provincial Offences Act*, perform the same services as lawyers and, like them, are paid on a fee-for-service basis. They are not barred, as the legal profession is, from carrying on their business through corporations. As recently as 1980 "The Report of the Professional Organizations Committee", April, 1980, at p. 69, reported that law clerks appearing before the committee did not seek independent status: see also "The Market for Legal Services: Paraprofessionals and Specialists", Working Paper No. 10 of the Professional Organizations Committee. It is the growth since that report of the independent paralegal business carrying on lawyer-like activities free from the direction and supervision of the legal profession that elevates the public importance of this case.

Agents have been authorized to act in some proceedings for more than a century. They were first permitted in small claims matters before Division Courts in 1872: "An Act to empower all persons to appear on behalf of others in the Divisional Courts in the Province of Ontario", 1872 (Ont.), c. 8, s. 1, and in mechanics' lien proceedings in 1910: *Mechanics and Wage-Earners Lien Act*, 1910 (Ont.), c. 69, s. 37(7). As previously mentioned they have acted in summary conviction proceedings under the *Criminal Code* since 1906. Their appearances before coroners' inquests was authorized by the *Coroners Act*, 1972 (Ont.), c. 98, s. 33, and their limited participation in proceedings in the *Landlord and Tenant Act* dates from 1975: *Landlord*

and Tenant Amendment Act, 1975 (Ont.) (2nd Sess.), c. 13, s. 6. The first statutory reference to their appearance before administrative tribunals was in the *Statutory Powers Procedure Act*, 1971 (Ont.), c. 47, s. 23(3), but it is known that laymen appeared as advocates before such tribunals prior to that date.

Despite the long participation of agents in judicial proceedings, they have been the subject of only one reported decision and little has been written about them. In *R. v. Duggan* (1976), 31 C.C.C. (2d) 167, this court held that right of audience of an agent was confined to the court which was specifically authorized by statute. Thus an agent authorized by s. 735(2) of the *Criminal Code* to appear in a summary conviction court was not entitled to appear on an appeal from conviction before the County Court. MacKinnon A.C.J.O. stated at p. 169:

It is clear that s. 50 does not allow, unless otherwise provided, non-barristers or solicitors to practise in the Courts, and non-barristers have not been permitted over the years to represent parties in either civil or criminal proceedings in the County or Supreme Court. When the Legislature, which is competent in this field, wished to make exceptions to s. 50 they did so in clear terms, as for example, s. 100 of the *Small Claims Courts Act*, R.S.O. 1970, c. 439:

"**100.** A barrister of solicitor, or any other person not prohibited by the judge, may appear at the trial or hearing of an action as agent for a party thereto."

(see also: the *Mechanics' Lien Act*, R.S.O. 1970, c. 267, s. 38(8).) It is of some historical interest to note that over a hundred years ago, in considering the predecessor section of s. 50(1) it was held that it was contrary to law and public policy to permit a person who was not a barrister to appear as an advocate in a County Court: *Re Brooke* (1864), 10 *U.C.L.J.* 49.

One is entitled, in my opinion, to take judicial notice of the extent of the business carried on in this province by persons acting as agents under the *Provincial Offences Act* quite apart from those performing other paralegal services. While it is the view of the law society that agents are not entitled to operate a business for reward, the obvious fact is that they do and have done so for many years. Writing in 1971 about the encroachment on the legal profession, Mark M. Orkin observed: "[T]he 'small claims' field of practice is no longer financially attractive for most lawyers, hence the emergence of division court 'agents', non-lawyers who openly carry on this type of business." (Orkin, Mark M. "Professional Autonomy and the Public Interest: A Study of the Law Society of Upper Canada", D.Jur. dissertation, York University, 1971 at p. 182.)

The hiring of agents as a common practice in provincial offence proceedings is acknowledged in the leading text-book on the *Provincial Offences Act*: see Drinkwater and Ewart, *Ontario Provincial Offences Procedure* (1980), note 46 at p. 57. It is beyond dispute that paid agents are employed in proceedings before administrative tribunals or under the *Construction Lien Act*. The fact that agents do carry on business for reward does not, of course, determine the legal question whether they are authorized to do so under the *Law Society Act*. It does, however, place this case in its proper context. It is not an isolated occurrence but appears rather to be an example of a reasonably common practice.

It is not the role of this court to determine whether, as a matter of policy, the operations of the respondents serve the public interest. It is obvious from the business they have attracted that they are providing an unmet need for service to the public. While no reflection of any kind was made in this case on the respondents, there must be concern about the absence of any control over the education, qualification, competence and probity of all agents. They deal with serious matters because penalties of up to six months imprisonment apply to some offences under the *Highway Traffic Act*. No provision exists for disciplining or supervising agents and protecting the public from financial loss arising from improper performance of their responsibilities by way of an insurance scheme like that of the law society.

It has been observed many times that the prohibition against the unauthorized practice of law is not merely to protect qualified lawyers from infringement of their right to practise their profession. Its primary purpose is to protect the public as Robertson C.J.O. stated in *R. ex rel. Smith v. Ott*, [1950] O.R. 493 at p. 496, 97 C.C.C. 302 at p. 302, [1950] 4 D.L.R. 426 at p. 426:

> To protect the public against persons who, for their own gain, set themselves up as competent to perform services that imperatively require the training and learning of a solicitor, although such persons are without either learning or experience to qualify them, is an urgent public service.

See also *R. ex rel. Smith v. Mitchell*, [1952] O.R. 896 at p. 903, 104 C.C.C. 247 at p. 250, [1953] 1 D.L.R. 700 at p. 703, *per* Laidlaw J.A. It is the responsibility of the Legislature to resolve these issues of policy. The task of this court is to determine whether, on a proper construction of the relevant statutes, they prohibit what the respondents were doing.

If only s. 50 of the *Law Society Act* had to be considered, there would be little difficulty in deciding that the respondents are not prohibited from carrying on the business of acting as agents for a fee under the *Provincial Offences Act*. I can find nothing in the Act that limits the exception in s. 50 of the *Law Society Act* of persons "otherwise authorized" to friends and relatives acting as agents without renumeration. Absent a specific limitation to this effect in the *Law Society Act*, the court could not read such a restriction into the statute.

. . . .

It is ironic that there is lack of clarity in the statutes governing the legal profession and their application to the respondents. I commend for the Legislature's attention to the clarification of this legislation and also the status of agents and other paralegals which is now a matter of considerable public discussion.

For the foregoing reasons, I would dismiss the appeals with costs.

Appeal dismissed.

Franchising Paralegals[†]

I. McGugan

After the appeal court decided *Law Society of Upper Canada v. Brian Lawrie*, the pricetag for a POINTTS franchise went from $2,000–$10,000 to $30,000–$50,000

ONE morning as he waited to present evidence in traffic court, Constable Brian Lawrie had a moment of insight. Presiding over the court was a non-lawyer who had been appointed a justice of the peace.

† McGugan, Ian, "Franchising Paralegals" *Lawyer's Weekly*, June 30, 1989, 17, 31. Reprinted by permission of the author.

The prosecutor, like Const. Lawrie, was a Metro Toronto police officer. "Since no-one else in the courtroom was a lawyer," he recalls, "I began to wonder why lawyers were the only ones to defend a case."

With that question, Mr. Lawrie, 39, launched himself on a collision course with the Canadian legal establishment. Tired of the regimented life of a police officer, he had been contemplating a career in business.

After quitting the force in February 1983, and spending several unsatisfying months as an executive with a family-owned bakery, he remembered this courtroom inspiration.

In a city where about 3,500 policemen hand out 1,650 traffic tickets every day, why not defend people accused of traffic offences?

Mr. Lawrie believed there had to be room for a paralegal service that could offer drivers a cheaper alternative to lawyers.

He knew that many lawyers were reluctant to handle traffic cases, regarding them as time-wasting, unprofitable nuisance. Given their lack of interest and his own wealth of police experience as a witness, Mr. Lawrie felt well qualified to be a courtroom defender.

Five years as a policeman in his native England, followed by another 10 years in Toronto, provided him with a detailed knowledge of the ins and outs of traffic law.

He quickly found, however, that banks weren't interested in lending money to an untried business with no tangible assets.

Undaunted, he raised $15,000 from relatives, and in May 1984, launched POINTTS Ltd. — a name derived from **P**rovincial **O**ffences **I**nformation and **T**raffic **T**icket **S**ervice.

Mr. Lawrie's formula remains as it was then. Potential clients pay nothing for an opinion on the merits of their case. If a client chooses to go to court, POINTTS charged a flat fee of $225 to represent those accused of minor offences, such as failing to halt at a stop sign, driving without a seatbelt or a minor speeding infraction.

The charge jumps to $375 for major offences, including careless driving, driving while under suspension or any incident involving an accident.

Mr. Lawrie estimates his fee to be one-third of what most lawyers charge. And, unlike lawyers' hourly billing, POINTTS's one-time fee covers any number of court appearances.

But how do you promote a business that doesn't already exist? A classified ad in the tabloid *Toronto Sun* brought two clients, Mr. Lawrie says.

Aware that he couldn't explain his concept in the short glib manner of advertisers, he "bugged the life out of the city staffs" of the three Toronto Daily newspapers to do a feature story on his innovative new business.

One day in July, a reporter bit: the article appeared in the Sunday business section. "That really ignited a booster rocket under this thing," Mr. Lawrie says.

Other newspapers called to get matching stories, as did interviewers from the CBC and local television and radio stations. And, at last, clients flooded in.

Nevertheless, Mr. Lawrie worried about his acceptance by the judiciary.

"My first court appearance was in the same court I used to appear in as a witness," he recalls.

Former police colleagues were friendly but sceptical. "When the justice of the peace came in, I was really nervous, and he had a quizzical look on his face when he saw me on the other side [opposite the prosecution]," Mr. Lawrie says.

"I went through the whole thing dry-mouthed, but I won the case."

At first, Mr. Lawrie represented clients himself. But by November, he had more cases than he could handle.

The enthusiastic response convinced him he could franchise the idea to other former police officers across the country.

He established POINTTS Advisory Ltd. as the franchisor and, after selling his first franchise for $2,000 in January 1985, he appeared well on his way. First-year revenues were $36,000, and because he was working from his home, he had few expenses.

Then came an unexpected blow. The Law Society of Upper Canada accused him, early in 1985, of unlawfully acting as a barrister and solicitor.

Mr. Lawrie found himself in a legal battle he had not anticipated. He won the initial case, then had to fight on as the law society appealed to the District Court and then to the Ontario Court of Appeal. Both decided in Mr. Lawrie's favour.

The two-year battle left Mr. Lawrie with a $120,000 legal bill, but failed to stop new POINTTS offices from popping up across Ontario.

The company grew from two franchises at the end of 1985 to 14 in 1986, generating franchise fees and royalties of $160,000 — 75 per cent of which went to pay Mr. Lawrie's legal bills.

Franchises now pay $30,000–$50,000 for an outlet ($2,000–$10,000 before the Ontario Court of Appeal decision), depending on the size of their territory.

All are former police officers with at least 10 years' experience, a prerequisite Mr. Lawrie uses to market the reliability of his service.

Once in business, they pay a nine per cent royalty on gross revenues and contribute five per cent to co-operative advertising expenses.

POINTTS guarantees them exclusive rights to their franchise territory and provides start-up expertise, management advice, on-going educational seminars and a computerized accounting service.

While Mr. Lawrie declines to reveal average franchise profits, he does say "no-one is earning less than he did as a policeman." (The Ontario Provincial Police force pays

$41,300 annually to constables with three years or more of experience.)

As POINTTS gained in visibility and reputation, imitators set up similar operations. To maintain his edge, Mr. Lawrie expanded.

He opened company-owned offices in Vancouver at the end of 1986 and in Alberta in May 1987. By the end of 1987, 24 POINTTS franchises raked in a total of $1.4 million in revenues and paid $200,000 in fees and royalties to their franchiser, POINTTS Advisory.

But legal societies continued to resist. In January 1988, B.C.'s law society won an injunction to close POINTTS's Vancouver office on the familiar ground that POINTTS agents were unlawfully acting as lawyers.

In Alberta, the provincial law society recently asked the attorney general to ban paralegals like POINTTS from representing drivers accused of traffic offences.

Mr. Lawrie believes he will emerge victorious in both provinces. Some members of the Alberta legislature hint that they will introduce a Bill to regulate (but not ban) paralegals, a proposal Mr. Lawrie welcomes.

Indeed, because of the standards he applies to his own franchises, POINTTS has obtained "errors and omissions" insurance — the equivalent of malpractice insurance in the medical profession — similar to that carried by lawyers.

By the end of 1988, the POINTTS network grew to 34 franchisees, who collectively made $2.5 million in revenues.

POINTTS Advisory earned fees and royalties of $340,000, but again legal costs and expenditures related to the development of the franchise network cancelled out profit.

"You have to invest a tremendous amount of time and money in making it a secure business that will be around in a few years," explains Mr. Lawrie.

"Even more so because of the natural scepticism of policemen, who come in with one eyebrow raised asking what kind of scam this guy is running."

Mr. Lawrie's battle with the Law Society of Upper Canada also continues: He is suing the society for malicious prosecution. The case is still before the courts.

POINTTS's growing ranks of competitors share Mr. Lawrie's belief that the market for traffic ticket defenders is still largely untapped, and that paralegals are here to stay.

"I think there's room for all of us," says Brain Stanley, a partner in Not Guilty, a Brampton, Ont.-based company that has been offering services similar to POINTTS's for the past two years.

"The industry is growing quickly as consumers become more aware, and it's only going to grow more in the future."

The question is how much of the market POINTTS will be able to claim.

Mr. Stanley and partner John Burd, both former police officers, give high marks to Mr. Lawrie's operation. But they rejected the idea of running a POINTTS franchise, largely because they didn't want to be limited to one franchise area.

Mr. Lawrie is counting on his company's marketing clout and size to help him fend off rivals. His current strategy emphasizes keeping ahead of the competition with aggressive expansion over the next few years through the western and Maritime provinces.

He opened a Winnipeg office in March and plans a Nova Scotia office later in the year. While the Manitoba Law Society has already made efforts to block his way, he's confident he can carry the day in court.

But one of his most significant claims to legitimacy is success. After representing more than 20,000 Ontario drivers over the past five years, POINTTS claims an impressive record.

In four out of five speeding cases, for example, the company has won an acquittal or succeeded in having the charge withdrawn or reduced.

"That's really not that surprising," says Mr. Lawrie. "There's no one who is likely to know the traffic code better than a former police officer who's had to deal with it day in and day out for years."

D. Juries

Justice and the Jury[†]
W.N. Brooks and A.N. Doob

The jury has been described as serving one of two separate functions. It can be seen as an institution designed to ensure the accuracy of fact finding in the adjudication of disputes, applying to the facts of the dispute the law as given by the judge; or it can be seen as an institution which has the right to construe or ignore a relevant rule of law in a case in which its application would not be in accord with the notions of justice and fairness prevailing in the community. After a short review of some of the views taken on each of these sides, we consider the kinds of extra-legal factors that appear to influence jury decisions.

AN important function of the legal process is settling controversies by adjudicating competing claims. Characteristically, judicial dispute resolution involves the application of a relevant and fixed rule of law to the factual conflict situation that is found to exist between two contesting parties. To be an effective means of social ordering in a democratic society the application of rules of law must obviously result in decisions that are morally acceptable to the community at large. That is to say, the outcome of adjudication must correspond with shared notions of what is equitable and fair between the parties to the dispute, whether one party is the state and the other a private person, or whether both are private parties.

Rules of law, however, have another important function. They permit social intercourse by serving as guidelines on the basis of which people may plan their affairs, knowing the consequence of different courses of action. To achieve this purpose, rules of law must be formulated at a level of generality that permits each rule to govern the consequence of recurrent factual situations. The necessity on the one hand for general fixed rules of law to regulate social action and the necessity on the other hand for rules that will result in the just resolution of all disputes poses a dilemma for the legal system. A general rule can be formulated that guides behavior and that results in the just resolution of most disputes controlled by it. However, a fact situation will inevitably arise in which, because of the particular equities between the parties to the dispute, a disposition of the case in accord with the relevant rule of law will result in an outcome that does not correspond with the community's notion of fairness, since a judge's decision in a particular case gives rise to a precedent that controls the disposition of all similar cases. Attempts by judges to interpret a general rule of law to reach a just decision in a case in which the equities between the parties are peculiar might cause injustices in future cases: "Hard cases make bad law" is a well known legal adage. A judicial institution that is capable, at least in theory, of resolving the tension between the need for general rules of law and the need to resolve each dispute equitably is the jury.

The proper role of the jury has been the subject of extended and often vigorous debate in legal and political literature. The jury may be seen and defended as fundamentally a political institution which has the right to construe or ignore a relevant rule of law in a case in which its application would not be in accord with the notions of justice and fairness prevailing in the community. This view has been advocated by a number of eminent legal scholars.

Wigmore, the great evidence scholar, urged that the jury's role was to supply "that flexibility of legal rules which is essential to justice and popular contentment" (1929, p. 170). Justice Holmes suggested:

> One reason why I believe in our practice of leaving questions of negligence to the jury is that jurors will introduce into their verdict a certain amount — a very large amount, so far as I have observed — of popular prejudice, and thus keep the administration of the law in accord with the wishes and feelings of the community. (1889, pp. 459–460)

Dean Pound noted that "Jury lawlessness is the great corrective of law in its actual administration" (1910, p. 36). As stated in a Columbia Law Review paper: "Respect for the law is increased when law operates with scrupulous firmness, but with the leaven of charity that is added when the jury acts as the conscience of the community" ("Trial by Jury," 1969, p. 471). The relative importance that is often placed on the jury's role in construing

---

[†] Brooks, W.N., and Doob, A.N., "Justice and the Jury" (1975), 31 *Journal of Social Issues* at 171–82. Reprinted by permission of the Society for the Psychological Study of Social Issues (SPSSI), Ann Arbour, MI.

the law in a particular case is illustrated by a statement made in 1789 by Thomas Jefferson: "Were I called upon to decide whether the people had best be omitted in the legislative or judicial departments, I would say it is better to leave them out of the legislative. The execution of the laws is more important than the making of them" (cited in Howe, 1939). Indeed Lord Devlin went so far as to declare: "Each jury is a little parliament. The jury sense is the parliamentary sense" (1956, p. 114).

On the other hand, the jury may be viewed simply as an institution designed to ensure the accuracy of fact finding in the adjudication of disputes, its task being to apply to the facts of the dispute before it, as the jurors find them, the law as given to them by the judge in his instructions. If the general rule of law they are asked to apply appears to result in a harsh or unjust decision in the particular case, that is of no consequence to them in reaching their verdict. Indeed the United States Supreme Court in a case in 1895 (*Sparf & Hansen v. United States*) expressly held that the jury was bound to follow the judge's instructions on the law. The court reasoned that certainty and uniformity in the application of the law was more important than flexibility in individual cases.

Throughout history the legal system has been ambivalent about which of these two roles the jury should assume. When jury trials first emerged in England in the twelfth century, juries were required to apply the law to the facts of the dispute, of which they were assumed to have personal knowledge. If a jury returned a verdict that was found to be wrong they were subject to punishment (Thayer, 1898). However, by the seventeenth century the prevailing view appeared to be that the jury could consider in reaching their verdict the peculiar equities in the case before them. Lord Hale, discussing the function of the jury in 1665, stated, "It is the conscience of the jury that must pronounce the prisoner guilty or not guilty" (cited in Scheflin, 1972). Five years later the judges in Bushnell's Case (1670) held that there was no recourse against the jury for acquitting a person even though the judge or a subsequent jury concluded that the jury's decision was not decided according to the law. Even though it was taken as established that the jury was not accountable for its verdict, and that a verdict of acquittal by the jury was final, several American judges in the middle and late nineteenth century returned to the theoretical position that the jury's only role was to determine the propositions of fact in dispute. The jury, they argued, had no right to refuse to apply the strict letter of the law. These cases are discussed in Howe (1939), in the *Yale Law Journal* ("The Changing Role," 1964) and in Scheflin (1972). Within the past five years, however, there appears to have been a return to the common law position of the sixteenth century. The decisions in a number of cases, including several Supreme Court of United States decisions have assumed, and several judges have noted, that an important function of the jury is to

consider the conscience of the community in reaching its verdict ("Trial by Jury," 1969).

In two states, Indiana and Maryland, the jury's right to nullify the law is given constitutional status, and juries in those states are instructed that they may ignore the strict application of the law. The state of Kansas was considering a constitutional amendment requiring that the following instruction be given to juries:

It is difficult to draft legal statements that are so exact that they are right for all conceivable circumstances. Accordingly, you are entitled to act upon your conscientious feelings about what is a fair result in this case. (Scheflin, 1972, p. 206)

Whatever role the jury has in theory, in practice it is clear that the jury can ignore the strict application of the law and respond to the unique aspects of each case that comes before it. The jury deliberates in secrecy, they do not give reasons for their verdict, they are in no way accountable for their verdict, their decisions do not establish a precedent that is binding on future cases, and in criminal cases if the jury acquits the accused their decision is final. Indeed the jury's right to determine the facts gives them an almost unlimited discretion in returning whatever verdict they choose. As chief Justice Hughes (cited in Broeder, 1954) in 1931 remarked, "An unscrupulous administrator might be tempted to say, 'Let me find the facts for the people of my country and I care little who lays down the general principles'." Lord Devlin has observed, "I do not mean that they [the jury] often deliberately disregard the law. But if they think it is too stringent, they sometimes take a merciful view of the facts" (1959, p. 21). Indeed the jury's power to ignore the strict application of a relevant rule of law in itself has been construed as the right to do so in certain cases (Kadish and Kadish, 1971).

The jury's right to ignore the law may be supported as an effective means of protecting individuals from the oppressive or unjust use of governmental power. However, whether the rules controlling the jury should permit it wide latitude in deciding a particular case, or indeed if we should retain the jury, because of the need for the exercise of an equitable jurisdiction to mitigate rigid rules in particular cases, depends upon how the jury exercises that function. This empirical question is of overriding importance in the debate on the jury in general. Kalven, co-author of one of the most definitive studies done to date on the jury, has remarked, "Debate about the merits of the jury system should center far more on the value and propriety of the jury's sense of equity, of its modest war with the law, than on its sheer competence" (1964, p. 1702).

Those who oppose the jury on the ground that it is lawless contend that the jury exercises its "equitable" jurisdiction on the basis of prejudices and biases, such as race or physical attractiveness, that are not in accord with acceptable community notions of equity. They argue that jury verdicts result not only in a lack of uniformity in the law but also in malicious decisions and invidious discrimination (Frank, 1949). Those who support the jury and the exercise by it of an equitable jurisdiction, argue that the extra-legal factors that might influence it in reaching its verdict are factors that should be considered by a rational decision maker in reaching a just decision.

STUDIES OF JURY DECISION-MAKING

A few years ago if disputants over the jury were to join on this issue their supporting arguments could only be based on conjecture and isolated personal experiences. In 1954 Broeder observed with respect to the jury's law dispensing function that "we do not know how well it works; the verdict is a seal of secrecy which the law has thus far refused to open" (p. 412). Although the jury's deliberations are still shrouded in secrecy, the use of various methods of empirical research has yielded some data on the extra-legal variables that influence the jury's decision-making process. These studies permit us to draw some tentative conclusions about the basis upon which the jury exercises its equitable jurisdiction.

In the remainder of this paper we will review a few recent studies which illustrate the kinds of extra-legal factors that appear to influence jury decisions. Even this impressionistic review should reveal the direction in which the jury appears to exercise its equitable jurisdiction and thus enable us to draw a tentative conclusion about whether it is a useful social institution for imparting justice into one aspect of societal decision making. But more importantly, it will hopefully illustrate the importance of research on jury decision-making in studying the justice motive (Lerner, 1970; Mysliwiec, 1974).

Common experience suggests that the jury's verdict is likely to be influenced by the personal characteristics of the parties in the dispute, such as their physical attractiveness, character, and race. Empirical studies tend to confirm this commonsense judgment. Efran (1974) found that when subjects were asked to judge a student who was accused of cheating, physically attractive defendants were less likely to be seen as guilty than were unattractive defendants. In this case, attractiveness was manipulated by giving subjects a picture of the hypothetical defendant, one group receiving a photo of an attractive person, the other receiving a photo of an unattractive person. Efran found that students drawn from a similar population generally reported that they did not feel that the defendant's physical attractiveness should influence such decisions. This same bias in favor of physically attractive persons was reflected in a study done by Dion (1972). She found that a transgression by an unattractive child was seen by

adults as more serious than was an identical transgression committed by an attractive child.

The attractiveness of a person's personality also affects decisions made by laymen about another's culpability. In a jury simulation experiment, Landy and Aronson (1969) found that on a charge of causing death by criminal negligence the jury recommended a shorter prison term for a defendant who was described as being happily married, regularly employed, and friendly with everyone than they did for a person described as being a janitor, a two-time divorcé, and an ex-convict. Although this was a study in which the simulated jurors were asked to give a judgment about sentencing, it seems likely that the jurors would also consider such facts in deciding on the guilt or innocence of the defendant. Indeed, in view of the danger that if the jury hears about the "bad" character of the accused they might be less careful about determining the certainty of his guilt before convicting, the law tries to keep this information from them. In no Anglo-American jurisdiction can evidence of the accused's bad character be led by the prosecution for the purpose of tending to prove that the accused committed the crime with which he is charged, even though it is sometimes undoubtedly relevant for that purpose.

In apparent conflict with the concern reflected by this rule is the rule whereby if an accused takes the witness stand in his own defense, evidence of his previous criminal convictions can be led by the prosecution. In such a situation, the judge must instruct the jury that this evidence of bad character can be used by them only in evaluating the accused's credibility as a witness. The jury must expressly be told not to infer from the criminal record that the accused is a bad person and therefore is more likely to have committed the crime with which he is charged. Simulations (Doob and Kirshenbaum, 1972; Hans, 1974) and correlational findings from reports of cases (Kalven and Zeisel, 1966) support the conclusion that such instruction is futile. An accused person with previous criminal convictions stands a much greater chance of being convicted of a crime than does a person with no such history.

Race is another personal characteristic that in some jurisdictions has clearly influenced juries in reaching their verdicts. Studies have demonstrated that it is a factor taken into account by the jury in the sentencing process (Bullock, 1961; Thornberry, 1973), and interviews with actual jurors reveal that it is a recurrent topic of conversation throughout their deliberations (Broeder, 1965a).

In criminal cases, the personal characteristics of the victim as well as the accused appear to influence the jury in reaching their verdict. Brooks, Doob, and Kirshenbaum (Note 1), in a jury simulation of a rape case, showed that jurors thought that it was less justified to convict a man of raping a woman who had a history of prostitution than it was to convict a man (on identical evidence) of raping a woman of chaste character. There was no evidence whatsoever that people thought that the defendant who was accused of raping the prostitute was less likely to have done it; rather it seemed that they simply felt that, given the amount of evidence that existed and the circumstances surrounding the rape, the person ought not to be convicted if the victim were "only" a prostitute. Similarly, Landy and Aronson (1969) found that people recommended longer sentences for someone who had been found guilty of killing (through criminal negligence) a "good" person than they did if the victim were a "bad" person.

The consequence of their decision, although in law irrelevant, is another factor which the jury considers in doing individual justice. In a criminal case, the consequence might be that the defendant will be incarcerated as a result of the decision or, in a few cases, could be executed. Vidmar (1972) and Hester and Smith (1973) have both shown that these consequences do indeed affect jury decision making. Where a jury sees that a consequence might be very severe, they seem less likely to come to a decision that might lead to such a severe result. Similarly, in civil actions the relative ability of the parties to absorb a financial loss is considered by the jury. In cases in which a simulated jury was told that the defendant had liability insurance, the average damages awarded rose considerably. Correspondingly, the jury takes into account any collateral benefits mitigating the loss (Kalven, 1958).

A study based on personal interviews with actual jurors about the deliberation in the jury room revealed that in a civil suit the plaintiff's family responsibilities influenced the jury both in finding liability and in awarding damages (Broeder, 1965b). The government of the province of Prince Edward Island, sensitive to the "deep pocket" philosophy sometimes adopted by jurors in doing individual justice, has recently moved to abolish the jury in civil suits where the government is the defendant (Charlottetown *Guardian*, 1973).

In criminal cases such as assault or various sexual offences, the victim though legally blameless may be partially responsible for the criminal act. The jury, however, is likely to consider the whole situation surrounding the particular crime in coming to a "just" (though not strictly legal) decision. Kalven and Zeisel (1966) found that in cases in which there was some degree of victim precipitation the jury was less likely to convict the accused or at least more likely to convict him of a lesser offense. In the past, a similar result was often revealed by juries in civil cases. Until recently, in many jurisdictions, if the plaintiff contributed to an accident to any degree, he was completely barred from any recovery no matter how negligent the defendant had been in causing the damages. In such cases, rather than bar the plaintiff completely, the jury would take a "merciful view of the facts," and adjust the size of their verdict to correspond to the comparative negligence of the parties (Ulman, 1933).

Kalven and Zeisel (1966) also cite a number of cases where the jury seemed to acquit the defendant because he had suffered enough, even though he might technically be guilty. Thus, for example, it would seem that a jury is less likely to convict a man on a charge of causing death by criminal negligence when it was the defendant's wife who was killed (through his negligence) and the defendant himself was permanently and totally paralyzed in the accident.

Finally, in criminal cases, although only the accused is on trial, the jury in reaching a decision appears to consider whether the state "deserves" to win. If the police have used grossly unfair methods in obtaining evidence against the accused, or if the accused is being singled out for prosecution among many who appear to be equally guilty of the crime, the jury is less likely to convict (Kalven and Zeisel, 1966).

DISCRETION AND EXTRA-LEGAL FACTORS

The argument is often made that to ensure certainty and equal treatment there should be no discretion in the legal process. If injustices result from decisions in particular kinds of cases, then it is the rules of substantive law that should be changed. The rules should not be subverted by ignoring them or by applying them liberally. While many rules of law are in need of reform, it is doubtful whether any system in which fixed rules were applied rigidly, untempered by considerations of justice and fairness in individual cases, could maintain its legitimacy. Kalven has asserted that "we have a sense that many of the jury's most interesting deviations would be exceedingly hard to codify and incorporate by rule" (1964, p. 1071).

The legal system recognizes this need to take into account the peculiar facts of each case. Prosecutors have a broad and largely unreviewable discretion in deciding whether to prosecute a suspected offender. In exercising their discretion, they undoubtedly consider many of the factors reviewed above. Another place in the criminal justice system where most of this kind of information can legally affect the court's decisions is in the sentencing of a convicted defendant. Indeed, many of the factors that are specifically excluded from the trial of an accused are to be taken into account in determining the proper disposition for a convicted person. Thus such factors as the defendant's criminal record, his standing in the community, his occupational status, etc., often form a critical part of the presentence report on which the judge bases his sentencing decision. The American Law Institute's Model Penal Code states:

> The presentence investigation shall include an analysis of the circumstances attending the commission of the crime, the defendant's history of delinquency or criminality, physical and mental

condition, family status and background, economic status, education, occupation and personal habits and any other matters that the probation officer deems relevant or the Court directs to be included. (American Law Institute, 1962, p. 118)

In Canada, recent legislation has given further recognition to the fact that these extra-legal factors should be considered in "doing justice." Where the maximum penalty for a crime is imprisonment of ten years or less, the judge can avoid some of the effects of a guilty verdict by granting an absolute or conditional discharge. The effect of this is that even though the man has been found guilty of a crime, a conviction is not registered. The intent behind the legislation appears to be to encourage a judge to find the defendant guilty or not guilty on the basis of the relevant facts, and then allow himself to be influenced by the totality of the circumstances surrounding the case in his decision to grant or not grant a discharge. (For a more complete description see Greenspan, 1973).

THE JURY'S FUNCTION

The question of whether we should retain the jury because of its ability to dispense justice in individual cases thus depends on the answer to two distinct questions: (a) does the jury exercise discretion in ways that are considered to be just, and (b) in view of the other stages in the legal process where such discretion can be exercised by both the prosecutor and the judge, is there any need for the additional institution of the jury. With respect to the first question, it appears, for instance, that in a shoplifting case, if the defendant is a person of some stature and will lose his job if convicted, the jury is likely to find that he has learned his lesson and that the consequences are too seri-

ous to warrant conviction. If the prosecutor does not prosecute the ringleader of a gang, but instead calls him as a witness against his underlings, the jury is likely to protest that this is unfair and acquit the accused. If the accused was seriously injured in an accident in which his beloved wife was killed because of his criminal negligence, the jury is likely to find that he has suffered enough. But law dispensing by the jury appears to cut both ways. The fact that minority groups have historically been unfairly subjected to jury lawlessness cannot be doubted. Furthermore, many people would argue that the fact that the accused is a nice fellow, a good looking woman, a cripple, or employed, or that his or her victim is insufferable, should not affect the disposition of the case.

It would appear, not surprisingly, that the jury injects into the legal process notions of fairness that are shared by the average person. However, they are not able to rise above the prejudices and biases held by the same people. Although empirical research is important in demonstrating the subtleties of jury equity, even when all of the evidence has been collected an important value judgment remains.

If the jury, however, is to perform a function different from that of the prosecutor in exercising his discretion to charge and the judge in exercising his discretion on sentencing, it would appear essential that the jury be representative of the community so that the breadth of community values be represented on the jury. Indeed if the juries were truly representative of the community, perhaps many of the present prejudices that influence the jury would be removed from their deliberations. In this regard, it is interesting that at present a heated battle is being fought over whether the jury should be reduced from the traditional twelve members to six (Note 2). If the jury is reduced in size legal process of community values would appear to be greatly weakened.

Are Selection Experts Stacking Juries?[†]
M. Crawford

CHOOSING JURIES NOW A SCIENTIFIC EXERCISE

On November 8, 1984, a jury of 12 people in Toronto acquitted Dr. Henry Morgentaler and two other doctors of criminal charges of conspiracy to procure a miscarriage.

As controversial as the verdict was the way in which the jury was chosen. Helping defence lawyer Morris Man-

ning eliminate potentially biased jurors were two American jury selection experts who used body language and verbal cues to detect prejudice.

As in any jury trial, the jurors had been chosen from a panel of citizens drawn at random from the community. But, the use of jury consultants in this explosively controversial case prompted anti-abortion lobbyists to cry "the jury was stacked."

---

† Crawford, Michael, "Are Selection Experts Stacking Juries?" *National*, February 1985, 30. Reprinted by permission of the Canadian Bar Association.

Scientific jury selection experts are a new breed of psychologists and sociologists who are bringing the behavioral sciences into the courtroom. The Morgentaler case has brought the infant profession of scientific jury selection under the scrutiny of the Canadian public for the first time.

While jury selection experts are becoming commonplace in many American courtrooms, they have been used only rarely in Canadian cases. Some people say they are not better than witch-doctors when it comes to picking juries, while others claim they can turn a losing case into a winner. The truth likely lies somewhere in between.

Scientific jury selection techniques grew out of the trials of American radicals and Vietnam war protestors in the early 1970's. Young, radical social scientists wanted to ensure their colleagues had a fair trial. The list of those early cases reads like a history of radical causes of the last decade, including the trials of black rights activist Angela Davis, militant Indians at Wounded Knee and the prisoners at riot-torn Attica prison.

There were many wins in the early cases. The granddaddy of scientific jury selection, who played a role in most of those cases, was New York Sociologist Jay Schulman. Said Schulman: "I would say in these major political cases or quasi-political cases in America we have won seven out of 10, and the usual batting average in a Federal court in America is you lose eight or nine out of 10."

Schulman was brought to Canada in 1983 for the trial of the Squamish Five, a group of terrorists accused of planting bombs in British Columbia. A community opinion survey in Vancouver was used to convince the judge that massive pre-trial publicity had created prejudices among potential jurors in the community and extensive questioning of prospective jurors was permitted.

The techniques of the jury selection consultants were eventually applied to other types of cases. By the mid-seventies, the techniques had captivated the interest of large American corporate law firms. The techniques which had been used in criminal trials of radicals could be applied just as easily in civil cases, particularly those involving millions of dollars. For highly complex cases, such as the anti-trust lawsuit involving International Business Machines in 1978, the jury selection experts offered invaluable advice on how the jury would interpret legal arguments.

Said Schulman: "Almost no important civil case in this country goes to trial without the use of jury work, and only 14 years after it began."

There are three main techniques used by jury selection experts. The first and most powerful is the community opinion poll. Prior to the trial, the jury selection consultant surveys a random sample of citizens to detect attitudes or prejudices which might somehow affect the case. The survey results can be used to change the lawyer's trial tactics and also to design a profile of the "ideal juror" for the case at hand.

In one American murder trial involving millionaire T. Cullen Davis, the researchers not only surveyed the community by telephone, they also checked car bumper stickers, the upkeep of yards and steel bars on home windows to draw conclusions about community attitudes and prospective jurors.

The second technique is the pre-trial simulation or mock jury. The lawyer presents his evidence and witnesses before a number of mock juries chosen by the consultant as being representative of the community where the trial will be held. The deliberation of each jury is video-taped for later consideration by the consultant and the lawyer. Weak arguments are dropped and complex points are simplified before the case actually goes to trial.

In one U.S. case, a railroad company being sued for the wrongful death of a young boy, found through mock juries that the verdict could go either way. Rather than risk a larger court-imposed settlement, the company settled before trial.

The third technique involves the jury selection expert sitting beside the lawyer in court, observing the verbal and non-verbal behaviour of each prospective juror. A rigid posture, folded arms or lack of eye contact are all cues to beliefs and attitudes.

An offshoot of the in-court technique, known as the "shadow jury," was used in the IBM case. After the jury was chosen, the consultants hired people who were demographically representative to the real jury to sit in the courtroom and give daily feedback on who was winning and what arguments they did or did not understand. The shadow jury allowed the IBM lawyers to change their strategies throughout the trial, always having some idea what jurors were thinking.

Lawyers in both the United States and Canada can use these techniques in the jury selection process by rejecting jurors in either of two ways. If a prospective juror displays obvious bias or is unable to deliver a fair verdict for some other reason, such as not understanding the language of the trial, a "challenge for cause" can be used to eliminate potential jurors. The Canadian jury selection system is unique in that a challenge for cause is decided by two potential jurors who are selected by the judge from the jury panel. In a sense, the jury selects itself when a challenge for cause is prompted.

In addition, each lawyer has a very limited number of "peremptory challenges" which can be used to reject a potential juror without giving any reasons. In Canada, peremptory challenges can number from four to 20 for each defendant in a criminal trial. The number of peremptory challenges vary in civil trials from province to province.

In criminal cases in Canada, the Crown also has up to 48 "stand-asides," which place prospective jurors in limbo.

The differences in the Canadian jury selection process have slowed the introduction of the scientific selection methods here. In Canada, the questioning of prospective jurors is not a right and the judge has to be convinced there is widespread prejudice in order to ask questions. In most trials, if bias isn't obvious or readily admitted by a prospective juror, a lawyer has few chances to discover otherwise.

The first use of any sort of modern jury selection techniques in Canada occurred in London, Ontario in 1979. A widely-publicized fraud trial involving a building products company which had cheated little old ladies upset the community. The defendant in that same trial was coming up in court on subsequent charges and the lawyer wanted a change of venue. He asked Neil Vidmar, a psychology professor at the University of Western Ontario, to perform a community opinion survey.

Said Vidmar of that first case: "We learned that large numbers of people had knowledge about the case, detailed knowledge; large numbers of people said any defendant that had any connection with that prior case they would automatically find guilty."

Vidmar has since become one of Canada's most prominent experts on jury selection techniques. He is also an unrelenting critic and realist about what jury selection experts can do.

Said Vidmar: "It's not really a question of what does not work, but what claims are made for it. For example, much claim has gone for the body language research. There are certain linguistic or kinesetic cues, body posture, that show some rough indications, but it does not tell much about personality, and in fact, is much over-rated. I think that the polling is the most useful technique. I think that the jury simulation is probably the second most useful."

However, Vidmar notes that a combination of all of the techniques together can be a powerful tool for a lawyer, sharpening his presentation skills and helping him understand the type of people sitting on the jury. But, Vidmar says these techniques are really only useful in certain types of trials.

"Where there's massive pre-trial publicity, where there are emotional issues, where there are political issues, or where one has a reason to believe that the evidence is so close that the jury could go either way, that is the instance where we find that the jury selection technique would be most useful" said Vidmar.

Even in those cases which are perfectly suited to sophisticated selection techniques, all of the experts agree the methods are only one factor in the outcome of the case. The nature of the evidence presented, the lawyer's presentation of the case or the lack of proof presented by the other lawyer, can all affect the verdict.

Vidmar says they cannot stack juries: "The jury selection experts are not that good. What they do is eliminate the most prejudiced persons from the jury." He notes the other side in the case would most likely reject jurors favoring the opposition.

In the Morgentaler case, Vidmar said: "I would point out something. Dr. Morgentaler was acquitted three times in Quebec in 1973, 1974 and 1975 by juries that had not in any way been selected by jury selection experts...should the jury selection experts get all of the credit for the acquittal or is it something about the nature of the law itself and the way juries respond?"

Canadian lawyers will, no doubt, consider using the techniques more often now. While the Canadian legal system is, in many ways, vastly different from the American system, there are similarities and modified versions of jury selection techniques which would work well in Canada.

At this moment, Canada is at crossroads. Before Canadians decide whether to follow the American example, Osgoode Hall law professor Louise Arbour suggests two questions must be dealt with. Prof. Arbour says there must be in-depth research into the way jurors make their decisions, whether they are influenced by their personalities and prejudices or if they decide on the evidence and law.

But more importantly, Arbour says we have to decide if we want juries to merely be a fact-finding neutral process or if we expect them to be the ultimate democratic test of the wisdom and the fairness of legislation.

Said Arbour: "If that's the function we want them to perform, to prevent convictions that would be harsh and unjust, then I think maybe our selection process is no longer adequate, maybe we'd have to know about who they are, the people who will pass that judgment."

Further Reading

Peter H. Russell, "The Declining Role of the Jury", in *The Judiciary in Canada: The Third Branch of Government*, (Toronto: McGraw-Hill Ryerson, 1987), 274–77.

E.P. Thompson, "Subduing the Jury" in *London Review of Books*, December 1987.

E. The Judges: Appointment and Accountability

The Meaning and Scope of Judicial Independence[†]
Justice B. Laskin

I hope I do not abuse this privilege if I strike a serious note in this address. It would please me better if I could banter and amuse, which I may assure you is not beyond my capacity. But special reasons, to which I will come shortly, impel me to speak more soberly on a subject of fundamental importance to the judicial office. That subject is the meaning and scope of judicial independence. I would have thought that its meaning would have been well understood over the years in which the Judges have exercised their judicial roles. I would have thought that there was a clear public understanding that Judges cannot be measured in the same way as other holders of public office or any members of the public. In my understanding, and in that of most of the members of the legal profession and members of the Bench, Judges are expected to abstain from participation in political controversy. Obviously, considering the storm that has brewed early this year on the Berger affair, I was somewhat mistaken. The limited public role of the Judge, one perfectly clear to me, seems to have been misunderstood or forgotten, even by lawyers, let alone by members of the press and of the public.

A fundamental principle has pervaded the judicial role since it took root in the reign of Queen Anne. It was established not without fits and starts that Judges would no longer hold office at the pleasure of the Crown, at the pleasure of the government. They would have the security of tenure, once assigned to their position, and would hold office during good behaviour to the age of retirement. Their duration in judicial office would no longer depend on governmental whim, and they could be removed only for judicial misbehaviour.

What this imported, as it evolved over the years, was the separation of the executive and the judiciary; no admixture of the one with the other; no mixture of the judiciary in politics or political controversy; correspondingly, no intermeddling of the executive with the judiciary; each branch was to be independent of the other, left alone to carry on its separate duties. For the Judges, they had utmost freedom of speech in the discharge of their judicial functions. Unbelievably, some members of the press and some in public office in this country, seem to think that freedom of speech for the Judges gave them the full scope of participation and comment on current political contro-

versies, on current social and political issues. Was there ever such ignorance if history and of principle?

A Judge, upon appointment and I am speaking here of appointments which cover all members of our provincial and federal superior courts as well as the Supreme Court of Canada takes a prescribed oath of office. It is a short oath which is common to all superior court Judges, being as follows:

> I do solemnly and sincerely promise and swear that I will duly and faithfully, and to the best of my skill and knowledge, execute the powers and trust reposed in me as...
> So help me God.

But it is invested with all the authority and surrounded by all the limitations that are imported by the principle of judicial independence and that are spelled out in the *Judges Act*, the federal statute which defines the judicial office.

What does the *Judges Act* say about the judicial office? It says quite clearly that a Judge may not, directly or indirectly, engage in any occupation or business other than his judicial duties. There is a limited exception for him or her to act as commissioner or arbitrator or adjudicator or referee or conciliator or mediator, if so appointed in respect of a federal matter by the federal Government; and similarly, if so appointed by the provincial government in respect of a provincial matter. These are short-term, temporary assignments not intended to give a Judge a regular assignment to carry out a non-judicial role. Two recent illustrations of the distinction may be mentioned. A few years ago, the Government of Canada wished to appoint a Judge as Deputy Minister of an executive department. He was unwilling to accept unless he retained his security as Judge. The Government was prepared to go along. I felt it my duty as Chief Justice to protest and did so vigorously, pointing out that it was either the one position or the other, but not both.

A Judge who wishes to accept an executive appointment could not remain a Judge at the same time. In the case I mentioned, the Judge put more store on his judicial position than on the proposed executive position. The

† Laskin, Bora, "The Meaning and Scope of Judicial Independence" in ed. F.L. Morton, *Law, Politics and the Judicial Process in Canada* (Calgary: University of Calgary Press, 1985), 115–20. Reprinted by permission of Professor F.L. Morton.

matter was accordingly dropped. The same thing happened a little later in Ontario when the provincial government wished to appoint an Ontario Supreme Court Judge as Chairman of the provincial Workman's Compensation Board. Again, I protested; if the Judge wished to accept the provincial appointment, he should resign from the Bench; he could not be both Judge and non-judicial or executive functionary. The principle was accepted and the matter was abandoned.

These instances concerned permanent appointments to governmental positions. The authorized exceptions to allow governments to appoint Judges to special assignments as, for example, by order-in-council or by a limited inquiry, do not involve Judges in executive government or in governmental operations. They are asked to perform a particular service, with generally a short-term duration, although some inquiries like the MacKenzie Valley Pipeline and the McDonald Inquiry in to the R.C.M.P. did go on for some years.

I am myself not a great supporter of the use of Judges to carry out short-term assignments at the behest of a government, federal or provincial. Apart from anything else, it is not always convenient to spare a particular Judge, given the ever increasing workload of all Courts. Moreover, there is always the likelihood that the Judge will be required to pass on policy, which is not within the scope of the regular judicial function. But I recognize that governments will continue to ask Judges (generally with the consent of their Chief Justice) to perform these limited tasks. The important thing to remember is that these short-term assignments are not intended to establish a career for the Judge in the work he or she carried out. The Judge is expected to make his or her report to the particular government and to regard the assignment as completed without any supplementary comment. Any comment or action is for the government; the Judge himself or herself is *functus*, done with the matter. This has been the general behaviour of Judges who have accepted and carried out special or particular government assignments. Whatever has been the value of the inquiry must rest in what it says the Judge is certainly not intended to be a protagonist, however enamored he or she may become of the work. Nor is the Judge intended to make a career of the special assignment.

There has been a large increase in the number of federally-appointed Judges in the last decade. Indeed, there are now 466 superior court Judges throughout Canada and 232 county and district court Judges. I do not take account of provincial court Judges who are appointed by provincial governments. The increase in the number of federally-appointed Judges increased the burden of judicial administration, the need to monitor complaints (which are inevitable, even if in most cases misconceived) and the need also to provide outlets for judicial conferences. It was beyond the capacity of Parliament to provide for

these matters and they also raised sensitive matters engaging the independent position of the Judges.

In 1971, a new policy was introduced by Parliament to govern supervision of judicial behaviour or, I should say, alleged misbehaviour....

...The Canadian Judicial Council came into being in October, 1971 and has had a considerable amount of business in the past decade. It has exercised its powers of inquiry and investigation with great care, seeking on the one hand to satisfy complaints against alleged judicial misbehaviour and on the other hand to protect the reputation of the Judge against unfounded allegations. The most common type of complaint received against Judges has to do with objections to their judgments. Laymen have misconceived the role of the Council: it is not a court of appeal to rectify decisions alleged to be in error; for that there are established appeal courts, and the Council repeatedly has to tell complainants that the recourse is an appeal, not an invocation of the powers of the Canadian Judicial Council.

Since the Canadian Judicial Council has a statutory mandate to conduct inquiries into alleged judicial misbehaviour, it can hardly ignore a responsible complaint. In the Berger case, the complaint was made by a long-serving superior court Judge. Was the Canadian Judicial Council to ignore it? At least, it had the obligation to consider whether the complaint merited investigation, that it was not merely frivolous. Those members of the press who became engaged with the complaint in Justice Berger's support seemed entirely ignorant of the mandate of the Canadian Judicial Council. They appeared to be of the view that a Judge's behaviour was for him to measure, that it was not open to the Canadian Judicial Council to investigate, let alone admonish a Judge in respect of a complaint against objectionable behaviour. This was clearly wrong and could have been established by some modest inquiry.

My mention of the Berger case is not to reopen an issue which is closed. It is only to set the record straight on the statutory function and duty of the Canadian Judicial Council, whoever be the subject of a complaint to it. In view of the obvious misunderstanding to which the Berger incident gave rise, it seemed important to me that I, as Chairman, should underline the role and duty of the Canadian Judicial Council, however distasteful it may seem to be to assess the behaviour of a fellow Judge. I would have welcomed, as I always do, the balance provided by the media, by the press, and I regret that it was unfortunate that they did not discharge that responsibility on this occasion.

There was one respect in which members of the press, and indeed some public "bodies" and members of Parliament, showed their ignorance of judicial propriety. It was said that pursuit of the complaint against Justice Berger was an interference with his freedom of speech. Plain nonsense! A Judge has no freedom of speech to address political issues which have nothing to do with his judicial duties. His abstention from political involvement is one of the guarantees of his impartiality, his integrity, his independence. Does it matter that his political intervention supports what many, including the press, think is a desirable stance? Would the same support be offered to a Judge who intervenes in a political matter in an opposite way? Surely there must be one standard, and that is absolute abstention, except possibly where the role of a Court is itself brought into question. Otherwise, a Judge who feels so strongly on political issues that he must speak out is best advised to resign from the Bench. He cannot be allowed to speak from the shelter of a Judgeship.

In the Berger case, the Judge's intervention was on a critical political and constitutional issues then under examination by the entire Canadian ministerial establishment. No Judge had a warrant to interfere, in a public way, and his conviction, however well intended, could not justify political intervention simply because he felt himself impelled to speak. To a large degree, Judge Berger was reactivating his McKenzie Valley Pipeline inquiry, a matter which was years behind him and should properly be left dormant for a political decision, if any, and not for his initiative in the midst of a sensitive political controversy.

The Canadian Judicial Council — one member of parliament accused us of being engaged in a witch hunt — was badly served by those who, obviously, did no homework on the Council's role and on its obligation. There was another matter which seemed rather shabby, also the result of failure to do any homework. It was indicated, quite explicitly in some news quarters, that the Canadian Judicial Council acted because the Prime Minister had complained of the Judge's intrusion into the political sphere when the Prime Minister was giving a press interview in Vancouver. The record on this matter is quite clear. The written complaint against Judge Berger was addressed to me under dates of November 18 and 19, 1981, and delivered to me, from Ottawa, on those days. The next day, November 20, 1981, I sent a memorandum to the Executive Secretary of Council asking that the complaints there were two successive ones be referred for consideration by the Executive Committee. So far as the Canadian Judicial Council was concerned, the complaint had become part of our agenda. The interview of the Prime Minister did not take place until November 24, 1981. It is therefore mere mischief making to suggest that the Canadian Judicial Council was moved to action by the Prime Minister.

The Berger inquiry, as I have said, is behind us, and I regret that I found it necessary to say as much as I did about it. However, the Canadian Judicial Council, which does not and cannot reach out publicly to the media,

deserves to have its record cleared. This would not have been necessary if we had been better served by the press throughout the whole affair. A matter like the Berger case is not likely to recur; the Canadian Judicial Council has signalled the danger of recommended removal from office if it should recur. As it was, the Council took a placating view and administered an admonishment in the following terms:

1. The judicial Council is of the opinion that it was an indiscretion on the part of Mr. Justice Berger to express his views as to matters of a political nature, when such matters were in controversy.
2. While the Judicial Council is of the opinion the Mr. Justice Berger's actions were indiscreet, they constitute no basis for a recommendation that he be removed from office.
3. The Judicial Council is of the opinion that members of the judiciary should avoid taking part in the controversial political discussions except only in respect of matters that directly affect the operation of the Courts.

In view of the obfuscation that surrounded the Berger case, there are a number of propositions that must be plainly stated. First, however personally compelled a Judge may feel to speak on a political issue, however knowledgeable the Judge may be or think he or she be on such an issue, it is forbidden territory. The Judge must remain and be seen to remain impartial. Compromise which would impair judicial independence and integrity is out, if the Judge is to remain in judicial office. Second, no federally-appointed Judge can claim immunity from examination by the Canadian Judicial Council of complaints (unless obviously frivolous) lodged against the Judge; nor against the decision of the Canadian Judicial Council to investigate the complaints through a formal inquiry. Third, the Canadian Judicial Council is not limited to recommending removal or dismissal; it may attach a reprimand or admonishment without either recommending removal or abandoning the complaint. Only if it gets to removal does it become necessary, in the case of a superior court Judge, to engage the Minister of Justice and Parliament, whose approval on a recommended removal must be sought. Fourth, Judges who are objects or subjects of a complaint are entitled to a fair hearing, to appear before the Council or before an appointed committee or to refuse to appear (as Justice Berger did refuse). Refusal to appear does not paralyse the Council, and did not in the Case under discussion....

Judicial Inquiries[†]
S. Bindman

Should judges be removed from their normal duties to investigate social ills?

SEX. Drugs. Free refrigerators. Hardly the stuff of which a typical day on the bench is made, yet Canada's most senior judges are being called upon more than ever to investigate these and other pressing social crises.

There are now seven judicial inquiries at work across the country, probing everything from drugs in amateur sports to sexual abuse in a Newfoundland orphanage to the problems of natives in the justice system.

And that has rekindled debate about whether it is proper for judges to be taken away from their ordinary duties to head royal commissions of inquiry into controversial political and social questions.

The advocates say no one is better suited for the job — judges are excellent fact finders, totally independent and generally respected in the community.

The critics, including the Canadian Bar Association, say appointments to royal commissions compromise the independence of judges and leave already overburdened courts even more shorthanded.

"You have to use judges because nobody else will do. Judges are the only figures in our society who command that kind of public respect," says Toronto civil rights lawyer Clayton Ruby, who is representing Donald Marshall at a Nova Scotia inquiry into his 11-year wrongful imprisonment.

"But they're overused. Governments are using judges to solve difficult problems that they ought to be taking direct responsibility for. They want to be seen to be doing something but clearly want to put an issue off for a year. That's the classic use of royal commissions and it's wrong."

Calling on judges to at least temporarily take the heat off the politicians is nothing new.

Between Confederation and 1982, almost 800 separate inquiries were called by provincial governments — on everything from public accountancy in Saskatchewan (1953) to tree farm licenses in British Columbia (1960) to lunatic asylums in Quebec (1888) to suspicious baby deaths at Toronto's Hospital for Sick Children (1984).

There have also been 446 royal commissions appointed by the federal government since 1867 — though not all were headed by sitting judges.

"Scandals aren't unusual in Canadian politics and using a judicial inquiry to deal with a scandal is almost the norm rather than the exception," said University of Toronto political science professor Peter Russell.

"You've got the opposition crying for it and I think the government finds it reasonably convenient if the scandal can't be swept under the rug."

Royal commissions are also costly.

The Parker commission, which investigated conflict-of-interest allegations against former industry minister Sinclair Stevens, cost the Canadian taxpayer more than $3 million. The budget for the Dubin drug probe has been set at about $3.7 million.

But some observers say the costs are even greater — the independence of the judiciary.

In 1985, a study by the Canadian Bar Association recommended judges not be allowed to sit on most commissions unless the subject matter makes the choice of a judge "particularly appropriate."

"When judges are too frequently seen to be working with the government, even if merely as commissioners, there will be a natural tendency for the public to see judges as not completely independent of the government," said the study, headed by former Supreme Court of Canada justice Louis-Philippe de Grandpré.

Two years later, a second bar report recommended Supreme Court justices not be allowed to sit on commissions because of the potential disruption to the country's top court.

In their response, all of the Supreme Court justices of the day agreed, except Willard Estey who left the bench for more than a year in 1985 when he headed a one-man inquiry into the collapse of two western banks.

However, in a recent speech, Mr. Justice John Sopinka, a newcomer to the country's highest court but a frequent commission participant as a lawyer, said judges shouldn't necessarily turn down inquiry appointments.

Sopinka noted there is some room for concern "because of the potential for conflict between policy-making functions" and a judge's future responsibilities.

(Since 1793, the U.S. Supreme Court has refused all extra-judicial assignments.)

Russell said it is particularly inappropriate for judges to be dragged into inquiries into purely political matters, such as reviewing the behaviour of cabinet ministers.

The political scientist also said most courts are already backlogged and "I resent the judgement of politicians that these scandals are more important things for judges to work on than the cases the judges have."

---

† Bindman, Stephen, (Southam News), "Judicial Inquiries" *Ottawa Citizen*, July 8, 1989. Reprinted by permission of Southam News.

"I also don't buy the theory that only judges have public respect. I think there are people in other walks of life, including such things as chartered accountancy, the business world, universities, who have equal credentials."

But Mr. Justice David Marshall, head of the new Canadian Judicial Centre at the University of Ottawa, said judges should accept appointments to royal commissions.

"Who else is going to do it? When you look around in our society, there aren't very many independent adjudicators. Judges are in a unique position. We're paid to be independent, we're not allowed to accept money from any other source."

"There really isn't anybody else in society that has that independence. They're men and women who presumably will not be turned by future promise of office or money. They should be the least corruptible."

Ottawa lawyer David Scott, who was counsel to the inquiry examining the Sinclair Stevens controversy, said the work a judge does while a commissioner isn't really that much different from regular judging.

"Most of these things are basically fact-finding exercises and there is no one better equipped to find facts than a judge. That's what they do every day of their life."

Former justice minister Ray Hnatyshyn said the "political realities" of the Canadian parliamentary system require that in most cases a judge be appointed.

Judges are so appealing because they have secure tenure and they must sever all their political connections when they are appointed to the bench, Hnatyshyn said.

Queen's University law professor Gordon Bale says judges who become commissioners should also be able to lobby for the changes they suggest in their reports.

"I don't think it should be a one-way street. If the politicians involve the judges in inquiries and the judges acquire expertise in this particular area, I think the country deserves to have the benefit of this even after their report is submitted."

Canada would probably not have a national health scheme today had former Supreme Court Justice Emmett Hall not been such an outspoken advocate after he headed a 1961 royal commission into health services, the professor said.

Panel of Chief Justices Expresses Disapproval of Judge's Conduct in Criticising Proposals for Firearms Legislation[†]
Canadian Judicial Council

OTTAWA, April 12, 1995 — A five-member Panel of members of the Canadian Judicial Council's Judicial Conduct Committee has strongly disapproved the conduct of Mr. Justice Jean-Claude Angers of New Brunswick for an open letter commenting critically on proposed federal firearms legislation. The Panel judged the open letter to be "highly partisan".

The disapproval was expressed in a letter from the chairman of the Panel, Chief Justice Allan McEachern, Chief Justice of British Columbia, to Mr. Justice Angers.

Mr. Justice Angers wrote the open letter to the Prime Minister and Members of Parliament in January, distributed it to newspapers, and agreed to an interview with Radio-Canada. At the time he was a judge on the Court of Appeal of New Brunswick. In December 1994, at his request, the Cabinet had appointed him a judge of the Court of Queen's Bench of New Brunswick, effective March 1, 1995.

The letter and relevant background material was made public today by Jeannie Thomas, Executive Director of the Canadian Judicial Council because of public interest in the matter.

The Panel states that, notwithstanding the *Charter of Rights and Freedoms*, judges should conform to a higher standard of conduct than other citizens in expressing themselves publicly. This is because of their institutional responsibility to fairly and impartially judge the issues that come before them for decision.

The Judicial Council Panel did not recommend a formal investigation of Mr. Justice Angers' conduct. A formal investigation would be required under the *Judges Act* before a recommendation could be made to the Minister of Justice that a judge be removed from office by Parliament.

The Panel concluded that, while regrettable, Judge Angers' conduct could not properly lead to a recommendation for his removal from office and had not seriously

† Canadian Judicial Council, "Panel of Chief Justices Expresses Disapproval of Judge's Conduct in Criticising Proposals for Firearms Legislation", April 12, 1995, File 94–147, letter of disapproval. Reprinted by permission of the Canadian Judicial Council, Ottawa, Ontario.

prejudiced the political process. As well, the letter to Mr. Justice Angers said "you should be able to put your partisan feelings aside and judge matters that come before you fairly and impartially."

A copy of the [judge's letter and the] Panel's letter to the judge is attached.

·　·　·　·

GUN CONTROLS AND DEMOCRACY

To the Prime Minister and Members of Parliament,

Although it is unusual for a member of the Judiciary to comment on Government policies, where they involve breaches of fundamental freedoms, including my own, my intervention is warranted. Thirty years of practice in criminal law as prosecutor, defence counsel and judge and forty years of using guns for recreation, perhaps, give me a realistic perspective.

The Gun Control proposals of our government purport to restrict the criminal use of firearms, a laudable purpose. In fact though, they restrict the lawful use and users of firearms. That is where they conflict with fundamental freedoms. Surely that conflict should be avoided. It is a wasted and expensive effort to control users of firearms who obey the law.

I would guess that more than 98% of firearms used in this country are used legally and for some enjoyable purpose. They provide safe and healthy recreation to millions of people in target shooting sports and hunting. They enable Canadian shooters to excel in competition. Let us remember Myriam Bédard, our famous Canadian gold medalist. The gun proposals would require, amongst other things, the testing of the skills of users and retesting every five years. Does Myriam Bédard need all this testing to shoot her rifle? Guns provide Canadians with a means of self-defence. Many rural citizens feel more secure with a gun at their side when their neighbourhood is threatened by an escaped murderer as was the case in N.B. a few years back.

Unfortunately, too many people have obtained their information about guns from television and that is an unrealistic and distorted view. I, for one, would support every effort to reduce violence on television. As the present proposals stand, it will be the honest law abiding citizens whose rights will be abridged by our government's gun laws.

The proposals abolish property rights without trial, hearing or compensation. That is the effect of the declaration that handguns of certain calibers are illegal. Moreover, that declaration is made retroactive, a move normally used by governments only in emergencies. There is no such emergency with guns of that calibre. There is no

justification to forfeit or render useless property which was obtained, possessed and used legally until now.

Property and civil rights are, under our Constitution, matters for the Provinces. Because the situation is different from region to region, perhaps the Provinces should deal with gun controls as they do with automobiles.

It seems to me that those who devised these proposals overlooked the serious infringements of the rights to security and enjoyment of the person and to own property. In that sense, the proposals are oppressive to the vast number of respectable Canadians who own or intend to own a gun. Oppressive laws, as we know, have the effect of turning many honest citizens into law breakers. We do not want that.

It is not my intention, at this time, to comment on the various proposals of our government's action plan, my sole purpose is to suggest a delay. There is no emergency, there is not even a serious gun problem in Canada. There is, however, a lot of misunderstanding and misinformation about the use of guns. Better and more effective schemes exist to prevent the criminal use of firearms.

Let us not, at this time, penalize the law abiding gun users by hastily enacted legislation promoted at times not by reason and common sense but by emotional reactions to abhorrent crimes. The program can be made more efficient against criminals and less oppressive to conscientious gun users. In this great democracy of ours, should we not pause and strive to attain this ideal?

J.-C. Angers, Justice of the Court of
Appeal of New Brunswick

·　·　·　·

By Courier
April 10, 1995

The Honourable Mr. Justice Jean-Claude Angers
Court of Queen's Bench of New Brunswick
Law Courts
P.O. Box 5001
Edmundston, New Brunswick
E3V 3L3

Dear Mr. Justice Angers:

Our File: 94–147

I write as Chairman of a Panel of Members of the Judicial Conduct Committee of the Canadian Judicial Council, established under its By-Laws, to consider two complaints made against you. The other members of the Panel are the Honourable Pierre Michaud, Chief Justice of Quebec, the Honourable Donald MacPherson, Chief Justice of the Court of Queen's Bench of Saskatchewan, the

Honourable Roy McMurtry, Chief Justice of the Ontario Court of Justice (General Division), and the Honourable Claude Couture, Chief Judge of the Tax Court of Canada.

As you know, in January 1995, it was the policy of the Government of Canada, as announced by the Honourable Minister of Justice, to amend the Criminal Code of Canada to provide for the registration of certain firearms in Canada. Legislation for this purpose was introduced into the House of Commons in February 1995.

As you also know, this was a controversial proposal approved by some, but disapproved by others. The traditional Canadian view is clearly that judges should refrain from controversial, partisan, out of court statements or comments, particularly criticism of government policy. This is because the interpretation of enactment, particularly new legislation, is an important judicial function, and matters relating to both the enforcement of the law, and about firearms generally, often come before the courts for decision.

We note, for example, that Chief Justice Wilson, in *A Book for Judges*, written at the request of the Canadian Judicial Council in 1980, recognized that judges could comment freely on the law as it is, but "less freely on the law as [they] think it should be." He suggested judges should avoid statements made off the bench about current legislation "lest [your] hearers infer criticism of a legislature, federal or provincial." The author's meaning is clear that out of court judicial criticism of proposed legislation should be avoided.

In 1982, this Council criticized the conduct of Mr. Justice Berger, as he then was, for having criticized omissions in the recently settled constitutional accord that led to the patriation of constitution. The language of this Council on that occasion was that "it was an indiscretion on the part of Mr. Justice Berger to express his views as to matters of a political nature when such matters were in controversy."

It is not our role to review the decision of the Council in the *Berger* case. In fact, it has been criticized by a number of legal commentators. However, we note that even the most severe critics of the decision in the *Berger* case continue to believe that there should be limits on the freedom of a judge to participate in political discussion. For example, in his text "The Limits to Judges' Free Speech: A Comment on the Report of the Committee of Investigation into the Conduct of the Honourable Mr. Justice Berger" (1984), 29 *McGill L.J.* 369, Professor Jeremy Webber concludes his analysis of that case at pp. 384–85:

> The line is crossed, I believe, when the judge identifies himself closely with a particular faction in the legislature or executive, or when he lobbies consistently and forcefully for a specific political goal — in short, when his activities become partisan in nature. When this occurs, many of the

considerations which lead the legislature or the executive to pay insufficient attention to individual interests begin to operate on the judge. If he joins the day-to-day struggle for a particular policy outcome, he may increasingly be tempted to decide matters solely on the basis of whether they conduce to that end, taking insufficient account of other interests involved in the decision. And in order to muster popular support for the desired policy or party, the judge may, in his adjudication of controversial disputes, be eager to appease public opinion.

Another commentator, Professor Peter Russell, in *The Judiciary in Canada: The Third Branch of Government* (Toronto: McGraw-Hill Ryerson, 1987) at p. 87, agrees that Mr. Justice Berger was indeed indiscreet "in permitting his views to be published in a leading national newspaper at the very time when this was the hottest political issue in the country."

Dean Russell Osgood of Cornell Law School said in the course of a seminar at that Law School in 1994 that, "I do not think a sitting judge should engage in overt political discussion." (See "Judicial Independence," a paper presented at the Cornell Lectures 10–16 July 1994, at p. 87 soon to be published in the *University of Toronto Law Journal*).

Even Mr. Justice Sopinka, the most outspoken of all Canadian judges, agrees in a paper he delivered to the Canadian Bar Association that there must be limits, as suggested by Professor Webber, on out of court statements by judges. (See "Must a Judge be a Monk?" Toronto, 3 March 1989, quoted in McKay, "Judicial Free Speech and Accountability: Should Judges Be Seen and Not Heard" (1993), 3 *N.J.C.L.* 159 at p. 159.)

Since the *Berger* case, Canada has adopted the *Canadian Charter of Rights and Freedoms*, which guarantees freedom of speech to all Canadians. Notwithstanding this important declaration of individual rights, Canadian judges have largely continued to confine their out of court statements and comments to questions about the work or management of their courts, or about the administration of justice. Indeed, it may fairly be said that ever since the *Charter*, judges have entirely refrained from out of court, partisan political comments. This Panel therefore concludes that the adoption of the *Charter* has not changed the traditional view described above.

Subsequent to the adoption of the *Charter*, this Council has published *Commentaries on Judicial Conduct* which you say is inconclusive. While the editors of *Commentaries* were unable to pronounce authoritatively on this question, the text strongly recommends a restrained approach. This is because there is no law that says a judge may or may not make controversial, political statements. Standards of judicial conduct, however, are surely different and much, much higher in these matters than for other citizens.

Notwithstanding this history and tradition, you have seen fit to comment publicly upon the proposed firearms legislation. You wrote an "open letter" signed as a Justice of Appeal, to the Prime Minister of Canada, copies of which you sent to the Minister of Justice and to the Members of Parliament from your Province of New Brunswick. You also sent copies to local and national newspapers, and the letter was published in New Brunswick. Lastly, you consented to be interviewed in the French language by a representative of Radio Canada. Your letter and interview criticized the Government's proposal for what it called "gun control". Attached is a copy of your letter. We pause to say, that unlike Mr. Justice Berger, who was commenting on matters of high constitutional importance that would rarely come before him as a judge, yours is a highly partisan attack upon a proposal which, if carried forward into legislation, could well come frequently before you for interpretation or enforcement.

This Council has a responsibility under the *Judges Act* to deal with complaints against federally appointed judges. As you have been informed, two complaints against you arising from your out of court statements have been received.

Pursuant to Council By-Laws, these complaints were referred to a Vice-Chairman of the Judicial Conduct Committee, Chief Justice Lorne Clarke of Nova Scotia, who asked for and received your comments. (We are honouring your request that your letter to the Council not be released to the complainants).

Due to the seriousness of this matter, and pursuant to the By-Laws, Chief Justice Lorne Clarke referred the complaints and your reply to this Panel which has given careful consideration to them.

We do not consider it necessary to decide the question of whether, because of the *Charter* or otherwise, a Canadian federally appointed judge may have a legal defence to formal proceedings brought in consequence of controversial, public statements. That is a matter that is yet to be resolved. However, proper judicial conduct cannot be measured only in terms of strict, individual, legal rights.

While recognizing a possible exception with relation to matters which might affect the proper administration of justice, there can be no doubt that the great majority of Canadian judges, and indeed most members of the public, do not believe that it is proper, or appropriate, for Canadian judges to make partisan, controversial, out of court statements or comments to the public, which criticize proposals that may be enacted into legislation. We test this against your institutional function. To some, your impartially may seem to have been compromised.

Accordingly, we must strongly disapprove your conduct in this connection.

Having thus expressed our disapproval of your conduct, we have considered whether we should go further and recommend the initiation of a formal investigation under sections 63–65 of the *Judges Act* to determine whether a recommendation should be made that you be removed from office on any of the grounds specified in s. 65 of the *Act*.

We have concluded that the grounds upon which we have expressed our disapproval, although regrettable, are not sufficiently serious to warrant a formal investigation by an Inquiry Committee. We say this because we do not think the result of such an investigation into facts and circumstances already known, could properly lead to a recommendation that you be removed from your office as a federally appointed judge. In addition, we believe your conduct has not seriously prejudiced the political process and that you should be able to put your partisan feelings aside and judge matters that come before you fairly and impartially.

For these reasons, no further action will be taken in this matter except that a copy of this letter will be sent to the complainants.

Yours sincerely,

Allan McEachern
Chief Justice of British Columbia
Chairman of the Panel

CBA President Calls for Change in Method of Appointing Judges[†]
K. Makin

THE federal government still has too much influence in appointing judges despite a new appointment process created a year ago, Canadian Bar Association president Patrick Peacock says.

Mr. Peacock said in an interview yesterday that he will be privately pushing Justice Minister Douglas Lewis to allow judicial appointment committees in each province to rank candidates when openings arise. Currently, the committees can do little more than assess whether candidates whose names are forwarded to them are qualified or unqualified.

"The change we want would put the committee in a position to bank all of these names and, if an appointment comes up, it could recommend three or four of these candidates. It would not be just blanketly designating them as qualified or unqualified. The minister (of justice) would be receiving a recommendation saying, 'These are the three best guys out of the group.'"

Mr. Peacock stressed that the new process has worked in many other ways. "We are not being critical just to be critical," he said. "It has been a step in the right direction to de-politicize the process. On the whole, it takes the appointment process out of the political arena. But now that it is in play, we think there can be improvements."

Names currently come to the committee from all manner of sources: job applications sent by lawyers themselves, or names forwarded by lawyers or citizens.

Each provincial assessment committee is made up of a representative from the CBA, the provincial judiciary, the province's law society, the attorney-general of the province and the federal justice minister.

Several reports from subcommittees were released at the association's general meeting yesterday, including one which would provide a position on the controversial paralegal issue for the 35,000-member association.

The brief report ended with one overriding recommendation — that paralegals be rejected from all areas of practice unless they are working for a lawyer.

"In order to qualify properly in...competence and thorough training, it is the committee's belief that paralegals, without the extensive training afforded to lawyers in the law schools and in bar admission courses, can never achieve the degree of competence required to properly counsel the public even in the simplest retainer," it concluded.

Paralegals ought to be able to continue working in law offices, the committee said, but "the buck must stop with a properly trained lawyer in all instances."

Will Women Judges Really Make a Difference?[††]
Justice B. Wilson

WHEN I was appointed to the Supreme Court of Canada in the Spring of 1982 a great many women from all across the country telephoned, cabled or wrote to me rejoicing in my appointment. "Now", they said, "we are represented on Canada's highest court. This is the beginning of a new era for women." So why was I not rejoicing? Why did I not share the tremendous confidence of these women? The reasons form the theme of my lecture this evening.

First of all, of course, came the realization that no-one could live up to the expectations of my well-wishers. I had the sense of being doomed to failure, not because of any

excess of humility on my part or any desire to shirk the responsibility of the office, but because I knew from hard experience that the law does not work that way. Change in the law comes slowly and incrementally; that is its nature. It responds to changes in society; it seldom initiates them. And while I was prepared — and, indeed, as a woman judge anxious — to respond to these changes, I wondered to what extent I would be constrained in my attempts to do so by the nature of judicial office itself.

In the literature which is required reading for every newly appointed judge it is repeatedly stated that judges must be both independent and impartial, that these quali-

† Makin, Kirk, "CBA President Calls for Change in Method of Appointing Judges" *The Globe and Mail*, August 21, 1989, A4. Reprinted by permission of The Globe and Mail.

†† Wilson, Bertha, "Will Women Judges Really Make a Difference?", The Fourth Annual Barbara Betcherman Memorial Lecture, Osgoode Hall Law School, February 8, 1990. Reprinted by permission of the author.

ties are basic to the proper administration of justice and fundamental to the legitimacy of the judicial role. The judge must not approach his or her task with pre-conceived notions about law or policy, with personal prejudice against parties or issues, or with bias toward a particular outcome of a case. Socrates defined the essential qualities of a judge in the following manner. "Four things belong to a judge; to hear courteously; to answer wisely; to consider soberly and to decide impartially."[1]

In Winters' *Handbook for Judges*,[2] there is a section devoted to the essential qualities of a judge and these are defined as integrity and independence, impartiality, flexibility, creativity, responsibility and common sense. The late Justice Frankfurter was quoted as stating:

> To practise the requisite detachment and to achieve sufficient objectivity no doubt demands of judges the habit of self-discipline and self-criticism, incertitude that one's own views are incontestable and alert tolerance toward views not shared. But these are precisely the presuppositions of our judicial process. They are precisely the qualities society has a right to expect from those entrusted with...judicial power.[3]

In an article entitled "The Virtue of Impartiality" the late Judge Shientag of the Appellate Division of the New York Supreme Court discusses the difficulty in attaining impartiality and states that the term implies an appreciation and understanding of the differing attitudes and viewpoints of those involved in a controversy.[4] He quotes Lord MacMillan's description of the difficulty judges face in this regard:

> The judicial oath of office imposes on the judge a lofty duty of impartiality. But impartiality is not easy of attainment. For a judge does not shed the attributes of common humanity when he assumes the ermine. The ordinary human mind is a mass of prepossessions inherited and acquired, often none the less dangerous because unrecognized by their possessor. Few minds are as neutral as a sheet of plate glass, and indeed a mind of that quality may actually fail in judicial efficiency, for the warmer tints of imagination and sympathy are needed to temper the cold light of reason if human justice is to be done.[5]

And later Lord MacMillan issues the following warning:

> [The judge] must purge his mind not only of partiality to persons, but of partiality to arguments, a much more subtle matter, for every legal mind is apt to have an innate susceptibility to particular classes of arguments.[6]

Many have criticized as totally unreal the concept that judges are somehow super-human, neutral, above politics and unbiased, and are able to completely separate themselves from their personal opinions and pre-dispositions when exercising their judicial function. For example, Lord Justice Scrutton doubted that complete impartiality was possible. He said:

> This is rather difficult to attain in any system. I am not speaking of conscious impartiality; but the habits you are trained in, the people with whom you mix, lead to your having a certain class of ideas of such a nature that, when you have to deal with other ideas, you do not give as sound and accurate judgments as you would wish. This is one of the great difficulties at present with Labour. Labour says: "Where are your impartial Judges? They all move in the same circle as the employers, and they are all educated and nursed in the same ideas as the employers. How can a labour man or a trade unionist get impartial justice?" It is very difficult sometimes to be sure that you have put yourself into a thoroughly impartial position between two disputants, one of your own class and one not of your class. Even in matters outside trade-unionist cases...it is sometimes difficult to be sure, hard as you have tried, that you have put yourself in a perfectly impartial position between the two litigants.[7]

In his text on *The Politics of the Judiciary*,[8] Professor Griffith caused a furore in legal and judicial circles in the United Kingdom when he questioned whether the English judiciary were capable of impartiality. He stated that for a judge to be completely impartial he or she would have to be like a political, economic and social eunuch and have no interests in the world outside the court. Because this is impossible, Griffith concludes that impartiality is an ideal incapable of realization.[9] He says of the English judiciary:

> These judges have by their education and training and the pursuit of their profession as barristers acquired a strikingly homogeneous collection of attitudes, beliefs, and principles which to them represents the public interest.[10]

The public interest, in other words, is perceived from the viewpoint of their own class. Chief Justice Nemetz has suggested that the views of Professor Griffith may have some validity in Canada too, more particularly, Professor Griffith's view that judicial attitudes towards political and social issues reflect the lack of a proper understanding of the views of labour unions, minorities and the under-privileged.[11]

Judge Rosalie Abella, Chair of the Ontario Law Reform Commission, also doubts that judicial impartiality is a realistic requirement. She emphasizes in her article ''The Dynamic Nature of Equality'' that ''every decision-maker who walks into a court room to hear a case is armed not only with the relevant legal texts but with a set of values, experiences and assumptions that are thoroughly embedded.''[12]

Judge Shientag refers to the fact that many judges believe that they have acted with the cold neutrality of an impartial judge when in fact they have completely failed to examine their prejudices and biases. He points out that the partiality and prejudice with which we are concerned is not overt, not something tangible on which the judge can put his or her finger. Yet many judges by failing to appreciate this are lulled into a false sense of security.[13] Judge Shientag emphasizes that progress will only be made when judges recognize this condition as part of the weakness of human nature and then ''[h]aving admitted the liability to prejudice, unconscious for the most part, subtle and nebulous at times, the next step is to determine what the judge, with his trained mind, can do to neutralize the incessant play of these obscure yet potent influences.''[14] Judge Shientag concludes that ''the judge who realizes, before listening to a case, that all men have a natural bias of mind and that thought is apt to be coloured by predilection, is more likely to make a conscientious effort at impartiality and dispassionateness than one who believes that his elevation to the bench makes him at once the dehumanized instrument of infallible logical truth.''[15]

But what, you may be asking, has all this got to do with my subject: ''Will women judges really make a difference?'' Well, I think it has a great deal to do with it and whether you agree with me or not will probably depend on your perception of the degree to which the existing law reflects the judicial neutrality or impartiality we have been discussing. If the existing law can be viewed as the product of judicial neutrality or impartiality, even although the judiciary has been very substantially male, then you may conclude that the advent of increased numbers of women judges should make no difference, assuming, that is, that these women judges will bring to bear the same neutrality and impartiality. However, if you conclude that the existing law, in some areas at least, cannot be viewed as the product of judicial neutrality, then your answer may be very different.

Two law professors at New York University, Professor John Johnston and Professor Charles Knapp, have concluded, as a result of their studies of judicial attitudes reflected in the decisions of judges in the United States, that United States judges have succeeded in their conscious efforts to free themselves from habits of stereotypical thought with regard to discrimination based on colour.[16] However, they were unable to reach a similar conclusion with respect to discrimination based on sex and found that American judges had failed to bring to sex discrimination the judicial virtues of detachment, reflection and critical analysis which had served them so well with respect to other areas of discrimination. They state:

> ''Sexism'' — the making of unjustified (or at least unsupported) assumptions about individual capabilities, interests, goals and social roles solely on the basis of sex differences — is as easily discernible in contemporary judicial opinions as racism ever was.[17]

Professor Norma Wikler, a sociologist at the University of California, has reviewed a number of other studies of judicial attitudes by legal researchers and social scientists and states that these confirm that male judges tend to adhere to traditional values and beliefs about the ''natures'' of men and women and their proper roles in society. They have found overwhelming evidence that gender-based myths, biases and stereotypes are deeply embedded in the attitudes of many male judges as well as in the law itself. They have concluded that particularly in areas of tort law, criminal law and family law, gender difference has been a significant factor in judicial decision-making. Many have concluded that sexism is the unarticulated underlying premise of many judgments in these areas and that this is not really surprising having regard to the nature of the society in which the judges themselves have been socialized.[18]

A number of strategies have been tried in the United States for the elimination of gender bias from the courts — legislative reform, enhanced legal representation of women litigants, increased numbers of women lawyers and judges. These measures have been accompanied by an intensive educational program aimed at judges right across the country. Women judges and women lawyers in the United States played a very active role in the creation of this program. They were able to persuade substantial numbers of their male peers that gender bias, like all other forms of bias they had worked so hard to eradicate, violated the core principle of judicial impartiality and neutrality and posed an increasing threat in the seventies and eighties to the maintenance of public confidence in the judiciary.

As might be anticipated, a direct frontal attack on gender bias in the courts and especially the institution of an educational program for judges on this subject, was highly controversial and would probably have died on the vine but for the support of a substantial number of the country's leading male judges and educators who recognized the profound changes that were taking place in the society including a major redefinition of the roles of men and women.

Professor Wikler has been one of the moving forces behind the United States program to sensitize judges to the problem of gender bias. She reports some modest indicators of success of the program, although she ac-knowledges that it is too early to assess the long term effects. She reports that requests for speakers and material generated from courses and workshops indicate a growing interest as does also the positive evaluation by judges themselves of the courses presented. Even more gratifying, attorneys practising in States where the program has been actively promoted report a noticeable increase in judicial sensitivity to gender bias. Program materials have been cited in the courts and quoted in the judgments. Judicial Conduct Commissions are disciplining judges for gender biased behaviour such as sexist remarks to women lawyers and litigants and inappropriate comments in rape cases. Professor Wikler concludes that one very important goal has been achieved: gender bias is now a subject which judges and judicial educators think and care about.[19]

Another development in the United States has been the establishment of judicially appointed Task Forces to investigate the extent to which gender bias exists in the judiciary. The first of these Task Forces was created in New Jersey in 1982 and, as stated by Chief Justice Wilentz, was mandated to "investigate the extent to which gender bias exists in the New Jersey judicial branch, and to develop an educational program to eliminate any such bias".[20] Since 1982 over twenty other States have created Task Forces. Lynn Hecht Schafran, in her article "The Success of the American Program", reports that the Task Forces have significantly enhanced judicial education pro-grams and have created a level of public awareness that generates its own pressures for reform.[21]

Schafran identifies four reasons why a judicially ap-pointed Task Force is important as opposed to other groups outside the court system focussing on particular concerns. The first is that a gender bias Task Force is able to look at a broad range of issues and demonstrate a pattern of gender bias that manifests itself throughout the judicial system. The second reason is credibility. She explains this critical reason in the following manner:

> When a coalition of rape crisis counsellors asserts that rape victims are ill-treated in court, or a women's bar association claims that women at-torneys are denied a fair share of appointments to challenging and lucrative civil and criminal cases, these charges are heard as the claims of special interest groups. When a blue ribbon panel ap-pointed by a state's chief justice makes these same charges, people listen. There was little in what the New Jersey and New York Task Forces reported that numerous women's rights organiza-tions and feminists' legal commentators have not been saying for years, but the task force reports twice made the front page of the New York Times.[22]

The third reason relates to the administration of the Task Force. The Chief Justice of the State is in a position to authorize funds, compel co-operation, endorse and pro-pose reforms and ensure their implementation, and support judicial education on the subject. A final reason in favour of the Task Force route to reform is that such a task force brings together judges, lawyers, law professors, and com-munity activists to study an issue which many of them do not initially appreciate is an issue at all. Schafran reports that Task Force members from New Jersey and New York "who start out with no knowledge of gender bias in the courts, or even a conviction that the idea is nonsense, emerge from the data collection process convinced that the problem is real and has deeply serious implications for the administration of justice."[23]

So, where do we stand in Canada on this matter? Well, as you might expect, feminist scholars in Canada have over the past two decades produced a vast quantity of literature on the subject, some of it, in my view, very insightful, very balanced and very useful, and some of it very radical, quite provocative and probably less useful as a result. But all of it, it seems to me, is premised, at least as far as judicial decision-making is concerned, on two basic propositions, one that women view the world and what goes on in it from a different perspective from men, and two that women judges, by bringing to bear that perspec-tive on the cases on which they sit, can play a major role in introducing judicial neutrality and impartiality into the justice system.

Let me say right away from my own experience as a judge of fourteen years' standing, working closely with my male colleagues on the bench, that in my view there are probably whole areas of the law on which there is no uniquely feminine perspective. This is not to say that the development of the law in these areas has not been influ-enced by the fact that the lawyers and the judges have all been men. But rather that the principles and the underlying premises are so firmly entrenched and, in my opinion, so fundamentally sound that no good would be achieved by attempting to re-invent the wheel, even if the revised ver-sion did have a few more spokes in it. I have in mind areas such as the law of contract, the law of real property and the law applicable to corporations. In some other areas of the law, however, I think that a distinctly male perspective is clearly discernible and has resulted in legal principles that are not fundamentally sound and should be revisited as and when the opportunity presents itself. Canadian feminist scholarship has, in my view, done an excellent job of identifying those areas and making suggestions for reform. Some aspects of the criminal law in particular cry out for change since they are based on presuppositions about the nature of women and women's sexuality that in this day and age are little short of ludicrous.

But how do we handle the problem that women judges, just as much as their male counterparts, are subject to the duty of impartiality? As we said at the outset, judges must not approach their task with pre-conceived notions about law and policy. They must approach it with detachment and, as Lord MacMillan said, purge their minds "not only of partiality to persons but of partiality to arguments."[24] Does this then foreclose any kind of "judicial affirmative action" to counteract the influence of the dominant male perspective of the past and establish judicial neutrality through a countervailing female perspective? Is Karen Selick, writing recently in the Lawyers Weekly, correct when she argues that offsetting male bias with female bias would only be compounding the injustice?[25] Does the nature of the judicial process itself present an insuperable hurdle so that the legislatures rather than the courts must be looked to for any significant legal change?

I think in part this may be so. Certainly, the legislature is the more effective instrument for rapid or radical change. But I see no reason why the judiciary cannot exercise some modest degree of creativity in areas where modern insights and life's experience have indicated that the law has gone awry. However, and I think this is extremely important, it will be a Pyrrhic victory for women and for the justice system as a whole if changes in the law come only through the efforts of women lawyers and women judges. The Americans were smart to realize that courses and workshops on gender bias for judges male and female are an essential follow-up to scholarly research and learned writing. In Canada we are just beginning to touch the fringes.

The first national, interdisciplinary conference on the relationship between judicial neutrality and gender equality was held in Banff, Alberta, in May of 1986. At the conference judges, academics, practising lawyers and experts in anthropology, political science, sociology and social welfare examined judicial behaviour in equality related matters. The judicial acceptance of traditional stereotypes concerning women was noted as well as its impact in Canada on important areas of constitutional equality litigation, family law, criminal law, tort law and human rights.[26]

Mr. Justice Rothman of the Quebec Court of Appeal, one of the speakers at the conference, endorsed the approach adopted in the United States to counteract gender bias through nation-wide educational programs for judges and the creation of judicial task forces. In his perception, women face the same kind of discrimination in Canada as they do in the United States and we should be working to change the old attitudes *now*. He suggested that conferences and seminars for newly appointed judges would be a good place to start but, in addition, courses on gender bias should be part of the continuing education programs for judges at all stages of their careers. Justice Rothman added that it is not, however, going to be enough to sen-

sitize judges to equality issues if lawyers are not sensitized to them as well![27]

The Canadian Judicial Council and the Canadian Judicial Centre have both recognized the need for judicial education in this area and will include gender issues in their summer seminars for judges this year. I understand that the Centre hopes to subsequently present the program in a number of locations across the country and the course materials will be available to all Canadian judges. I heartily endorse this initiative. It is, in my view, a significant first step towards the achievement of true judicial neutrality. But it is only a first step and there is a long way to go.

Coming back then to the question whether the appointment of more women judges will make a difference. Because the entry of women into the judiciary is so recent, few studies have been done on the subject. Current statistics, however, show that just over nine percent of federally appointed judges are women[28] and it is reasonable to assume that more and more women will be appointed to the Bench as more and more women become licensed to practise law. Will this growing number of women judges by itself make a difference?

The expectation is that it will; that the mere presence of women on the bench will make a difference. In an article entitled "The Gender of Judges", Suzanna Sherry, an Associate Law Professor at the University of Minnesota, suggests that the mere fact that women are judges serves an educative function and helps to shatter stereotypes about the role of women in society that are held by male judges and lawyers as well as by litigants, jurors and witnesses.[29]

Judge Gladys Kessler, former President of the National Association of Women Judges in the United States, defends the search for competent women appointees to the bench. She says:

> But the ultimate justification for deliberately seeking judges of both sexes and all colors and backgrounds is to keep the public's trust. The public must perceive its judges as fair, impartial and representative of the diversity of those who are being judged.[30]

Justice Wald has expressed similar sentiments. She believes that women judges are indispensable to the public's confidence in the ability of the courts to respond to the legal problems of all classes of citizens.[31]

Diane Martin, a criminal lawyer writing in the Lawyers Weekly, sees another way in which the presence of women on the bench is helpful and constructive. It is easier, she says, for women lawyers to appear as counsel before a woman judge. She says the "difference is that you are 'normal' — you and the judge have certain shared experiences and a shared reality that removes, to a certain extent, the need to 'translate' your submissions into 'man talk' or a context that a male judge will understand."[32] The woman judge does not see you as "out of place" or having "something to prove by appearing in a courtroom arguing a case before her."[33]

For women counsel, appearing in front of a woman judge also decreases the risk of sexist comments and inappropriate efforts at humour. The courtroom treatment of women litigants, witnesses and lawyers was examined by the New Jersey and New York task forces. The New York Task Force found that "[w]omen uniquely, disproportionately, and with unacceptable frequency must endure a climate of condescension, indifference, and hostility".[34] The New Jersey Task Force found strong evidence that women are often treated differently in courtrooms, in judges' chambers and at professional gatherings.[35] As Justice Rothman pointed out at the Banff conference, there is no excuse for a judge allowing himself or anyone else in his courtroom to make unprofessional or inappropriate references to gender. He saw as a possible solution the appointment of more women judges and more courteous and sensitive male judges![36]

Some feminist writers are persuaded that the appointment of more women judges will have an impact on the process of judicial decision-making itself and on the development of the substantive law. As I mentioned earlier, this flows from the belief that women view the world and what goes on in it from a different perspective from men. Some define the difference in perspective solely in terms that women do not accept male perceptions and interpretations of events as the norm or as objective reality. Carol Gilligan, a Professor of Education at Harvard University, sees the difference as going much deeper than that. In her view women think differently from men, particularly in responding to moral dilemmas. They have, she says, different ways of thinking about themselves and their relationships to others.[37]

In her book, *In a Different Voice*,[38] Gilligan analyses data she collected in the form of responses from male and female participants in a number of different studies. These responses, she submits, support her central thesis that women see themselves as essentially connected to others and as members of a community while men see themselves as essentially autonomous and independent of others. Gilligan makes no claim about the origins of the differences she describes. She does, however, use the psychoanalytical work of Dr. Nancy Chodorow as a starting point.[39] Chodorow postulates that gender differences arise from the fact that women do the mothering of children. Because the gender identity of male children is not the same as their mothers, they tend to distance and separate themselves from their mothers' female characteristics in order to develop their masculinity. Female children, on the other hand, define themselves through attachment to their mothers.[40] Masculinity is therefore, according to Gilligan, defined through separation and individualism while femininity is defined

through attachment and the formation of relationships. The gender identity of the male, she submits, is threatened by relationships while the gender identity of the female is threatened by separation.[41]

Gilligan's work on conceptions of morality among adults suggests that women's ethical sense is significantly different from men's. Men see moral problems as arising from competing rights; the adversarial process comes easily to them. Women see moral problems as arising from competing obligations, the one to the other, because the important thing is to preserve relationships, to develop an ethic of caring. The goal, according to women's ethical sense, is not seen in terms of winning or losing but rather in terms of achieving an optimum outcome for all individuals involved in the moral dilemma.[42] It is not difficult to see how this contrast in thinking might form the basis of different perceptions of justice.

I think there is merit in Gilligan's analysis. I think it may in part explain the traditional reluctance of courts to get too deeply into the circumstances of a case, their anxiety to reduce the context of the dispute to its bare bones through a complex system of exclusionary evidentiary rules. This is, it seems to me, one of the characteristic features of the adversarial process. We are all familiar with the witness on cross-examination who wants to explain his or her answer, who feels that a simple yes or no is not an adequate response, and who is frustrated and angry at being cut off with a half truth. It is so much easier to come up with a black and white answer if you are unencumbered by a broader context which might prompt you, in Lord MacMillan's words, to temper the cold light of reason with the warmer tints of imagination and sympathy.[43]

It may explain also the hostility of some male judges to permitting intervenors in human rights cases. The main purpose of having intervenors is to broaden the context of the dispute, to show the issue in a larger perspective or as impacting on other groups not directly involved in the litigation at all. But it certainly does complicate the issues to have them presented in polycentric terms.

Professor Patricia Cain of the University of Texas in an article entitled "Good and Bad Bias: A Comment on Feminist Theory and Judging" says:

> What we want, it seems to me, are lawyers who can tell their client's story, lawyers who can help judges to see the parties as human beings, and who can help remove the separation between judge and litigant. And, then, what we want from our judges is a special ability to listen with connection before engaging in the separation that accompanies judgment.[44]

Obviously, this is not an easy role for the judge — to enter into the skin of the litigant and make his or her experience part of your experience and only when you have done that, to judge. But I think we have to do it; or at least make an earnest attempt to do it. Whether the criticism of the justice system comes to us through Royal Commissions, through the media or just through our own personal friends, we cannot escape the conclusion that in some respects our existing system of justice has been found wanting. And as Mr. Justice Rothman says — the time to do something about it is *now*.

One of the important conclusions emerging from the Council of Europe's Seminar on Equality between Men and Women held in Strasbourg last November is that the universalist doctrine of Human Rights must include a realistic concept of masculine and feminine humanity regarded as a whole, that human kind *is* dual and must be represented in its dual form if the trap of an asexual abstraction in which "human being" is always declined in the masculine is to be avoided.[45] If women lawyers and women judges through their differing perspectives on life can bring a new humanity to bear on the decision-making process, perhaps they *will* make a difference. Perhaps they will succeed in infusing the law with an understanding of what it means to be fully human.

Endnotes

1. As given in F.P.A., *Book of Quotations* (1952) at p. 466.
2. G. Winters, ed., *Handbook for Judges* (Chicago: The American Judicature Society, 1975).
3. As quoted in L. Yankwich, "The Art of Being a Judge", in Winters, *supra*, note 2, pp. 3–17 at p. 4.
4. B. Shientag, "The Virtue of Impartiality", in Winters, *supra*, note 2, pp. 57–64.
5. *Supra*, note 4 at p. 62.
6. *Supra*, note 4 at p. 62.
7. Lord Justice Scrutton, "The Work of the Commercial Courts" (1921), 1 *Cambridge L.J.* 6 at 8.
8. J. Griffith, *The Politics of the Judiciary* (Manchester: Manchester University Press, 1977).
9. *Supra*, note 8 at pp. 209–215.
10. *Supra*, note 8 at p. 213.
11. Nemetz C.J.B.C., "The Concept of an Independent Judiciary" (1986), 20 *U.B.C. Law Rev.* 286 at 290.
12. R. Abella, "The Dynamic Nature of Equality" in S. Martin and K. Mahoney, eds., *Equality and Judicial Neutrality* (Toronto: Carswell, 1987), 3 at 8–9.
13. *Supra*, note 4 at p. 57.
14. *Supra*, note 4 at p. 58.
15. *Supra*, note 4 at p. 58.
16. J. Johnston and C. Knapp, "Sex Discrimination by Law: A Study in Judicial Perspective" (1976), 46 *N.Y.U. L.Rev.* 675.
17. *Supra*, note 16 at p. 676.
18. N. Wikler, "On the Judicial Agenda for the 80's: Equal Treatment for Men and Women in the Courts" (1980), 64 *Judicature* 202.
19. N. Wikler, "Identifying and Correcting Judicial Gender Bias" in Martin and Mahoney, *supra*, note 12, pp. 12–21.
20. As quoted in L. Schafran, "The Success of the American Program" in Martin and Mahoney, *supra*, note 12, pp. 412–420 at p. 412.
21. *Supra*, note 20 at pp. 412–13.
22. *Supra*, note 20 at pp. 413–14.
23. *Supra*, note 20 at p. 414.
24. *Supra*, note 4 at p. 62.
25. K. Selick, "Adding More Women Won't End Bias in Justice System" (1990), 9:35 *Lawyers Weekly* 7 at 7.
26. Preface to Martin and Mahoney, *Equality and Judicial Neutrality, supra*, note 12 at pp. iii–iv.
27. M. Rothman, "Prospects for Change in Canada: Education for Judges and Lawyers" in Martin and Mahoney, *supra*, note 12, 421–27.
28. Canadian Centre for Justice Statistics, April 1989.
29. S. Sherry, "The Gender of Judges" (1986), 4 *Law and Inequality* 159 at 160.
30. As quoted in J. Scott, "Women on the Illinois State Court Bench" (1986), 74 *Illinois Bar Journal* 436 at 438.
31. P. Wald, "Women in the Law — Despite Progress, Much Still Needs to be Done" (1988), 24:11 *Trial* 75 at 80.
32. D. Martin, "Have Women Judges Really Made a Difference?" (1986), 6:14 *The Lawyers Weekly* 5 at 5.
33. *Supra*, note 32 at p. 5.
34. *Supra*, note 20 at p. 419.
35. *Supra*, note 20 at p. 415.
36. *Supra*, note 27 at p. 427.
37. See C. Gilligan, *In a Different Voice — Psychological Theory and Women's Development*, (Cambridge: Harvard University Press, 1982).
38. *Supra*, note 37.
39. *Supra*, note 37 at p. 8.
40. N. Chodorow, *The Reproduction of Mothering — Psychoanalysis and the Sociology of Gender* (Berkeley: University of California Press, 1978), 91 and 167–70.
41. *Supra*, note 37 at p. 8.
42. *Supra*, note 37, see for example, pp. 16–18, 24–32 and 163–165.
43. *Supra*, note 4 at p. 62.
44. P. Cain, "Good and Bad Bias: A Comment on Feminist Theory and Judging" (1988), 61 *Southern California Law Rev.* 1945 at 1954.
45. Council of Europe Committee on Equality between Men and Women. Seminar on "The Democratic Principle of Equal Representation — Forty Years of Council of Europe Activity", Strasbourg, 6–7 November, 1989.

S.C.C. Judge Supports Task Forces to Probe Gender Bias in Courts[†]
C. Schmitz

ONE of Canada's top judges supports the creation of national and provincial judicial task forces to investigate gender bias in Canadian courts.

In an historic Feb. 8 address entitled "Will Women Judges Really Make a Difference?" Supreme Court of Canada Justice Bertha Wilson said a male bias in the legal system has resulted in some unsound legal principles which should be reformed as soon as there is an opportunity.

Madam Justice Wilson endorsed U.S. efforts to counter gender bias through judicial task forces and judicial education as "eminently sound," adding "I wish we would do it here. I wish that we would approach the subject with the seriousness that I think it deserves."

Since 1982, more than 20 American states have set up judicially appointed task forces to inquire into the extent of gender bias in the judiciary, and to develop educational programs to eliminate any such bias.

These panels of distinguished judges, lawyers, academics and lay people have concluded that gender bias is real, and that it profoundly affects the administration of justice in the United States.

This recognition has given a credibility and prominence to the problem of gender bias which years of feminist lobbying and scholarship were unable to accomplish.

When asked by *The Lawyers Weekly* whether Canada needs a judicially appointed task force on gender bias, the country's most senior woman judge replied: "Yes, I think we do, and I'm sure it's coming."

Asked whether such task forces should be national, or on a province-by-province basis, the judge shot back: "All of them!" Her remarks were applauded by several hundred law students and legal luminaries who packed the moot courtroom of Osgoode Hall Law School in Downsview, Ont.

A recurring theme of Madam Justice Wilson's address was that true judicial neutrality and impartiality can only be achieved in Canada when the law and the justice system reflect female, as well as male, perspectives on the world.

Criticism of the justice system through royal commissions, the media, "or just through our own personal friends," lead to the inescapable conclusion that the existing system has been found wanting in some respects and "the time to do something about it is *now*" the judge urged.

Madam Justice Wilson cited contract, real property and corporate law as areas of the law where the principles and underlying premises are "fundamentally sound," and where there is probably no uniquely feminine perspective.

"In some other areas of the law, however, I think that a distinctly male perspective is clearly discernible and has resulted in legal principles that are not fundamentally sound and should be revisited as and when the opportunity presents itself," she said.

The judge refused to elaborate, noting that "the last thing I would like to do would be disqualify myself from sitting on cases."

In her speech, however, Madam Justice Wilson did explain that "Canadian feminist scholarship has, in my view, done an excellent job" of making suggestions for reform.

"Some aspects of the criminal law, in particular, cry out for change since they are based on presuppositions about the nature of women and women's sexuality that in this day and age are little short of ludicrous."

The judge cited studies which showed that American judges failed to bring to sex discrimination the judicial virtues of detachment, reflection and critical analysis that had served them so well with respect to other areas of discrimination.

Gender difference was a significant factor in judicial decision-making, particularly in the areas of tort, criminal and family law.

Those studies confirmed that male judges tend to adhere to traditional values and beliefs about the natures of men and women and their proper roles in society, and that gender-based myths, biases and stereotypes are deeply embedded in the attitudes of many male judges, as well as in the law itself.

While feminist legal scholars have produced a vast amount of literature on the subject, the U.S. experience suggests that recommendations made by independent panels appointed by chief justices have greater credibility and carry more weight in reforming the law.

For example the first gender bias task force, created in New Jersey in 1982, significantly improved judicial education programs and heightened the public's awareness of gender bias, thereby generating its own pressures for reform.

Madam Justice Wilson quoted from one U.S. commentator who observed that "when a coalition of rape crisis counsellors asserts that rape victims are ill-treated in court, or a women's Bar association claims that women attorneys are denied a fair share of appointments to chal-

---

[†] Schmitz, Cristin, "S.C.C. Judge Supports Task Forces to Probe Gender Bias in Courts" *The Lawyers Weekly*, February 23, 1990, 1, 19. This article originally appeared in the Feb. 23, 1990 issue of *The Lawyers Weekly*. Reprinted by permission.

lenging and lucrative civil and criminal cases, these charges are heard as the claims of special interest groups.

"When a blue-ribbon panel appointed by a state's chief justice makes these same charges, people listen. There was little in what the New Jersey and New York Task Forces reported that numerous women's rights organizations and feminist legal commentators have not been saying for years, but the task force reports twice made the front page of the *New York Times*."

Madam Justice Wilson pointed out that judicially appointed task forces are also able to canvass a broad range of issues, as well as authorize funds, compel co-operation, endorse, propose and ensure implementation of reforms, and support judicial education on the subject.

Task forces also bring together judges, lawyers, law professors and community activists to study an issue which many of them do not initially consider to be an issue at all.

Madam Justice Wilson acknowledged that gender bias will be "a very sensitive and difficult subject to deal with" and that legal change is, by nature, slow and incremental.

But "in areas where it would appear that the principles that have been enunciated may not be sound, it is also our job to have a second look at those and try to do something about it," the judge explained.

"This is not something that is going to bring about revolutionary change in the law, but one has to make a start somewhere. And I think it is possible that we can take another look at some of the principles which more clearly indicate a masculine bias, or a perception of life that doesn't accord with the other half of the population's perception.

"Their has to be something wrong [there]. And what I suggest is that we focus on these areas where that seems to have happened and try to do something about it."

The judge added that where the law is coloured by the male perspective on the issues and is not the result of the application of judicial impartiality, "I can see no reason why it shouldn't be corrected. It seems to me that that's the role of an appellate court."

She went on to stress that "offsetting male bias with female bias is most definitely *not* the way to go.

"And that's why I opened in the beginning by pointing out that judicial impartiality and neutrality on the part of male or female judges is absolutely vital if the judiciary is going to get the respect that it has to have from the public."

However, the judge suggested that women judges can play an important role in introducing judicial neutrality and impartiality into the justice system.

"If women lawyers and women judges, through their differing perspectives on life, can bring a new humanity to bear on the decision-making process, perhaps they *will* make a difference. Perhaps they will succeed in infusing the law with an understanding of what it means to be fully human," she said.

Madam Justice Wilson said she favours an approach to judging which sees the parties as human beings, and which begins by removing the separation between the judge and the judged.

"Obviously, this is not an easy role for the judge — to enter into the skin of the litigant and make his or her experience part of your experience, and only when you have done that, to judge.

"But I think we have to do it; or at least make an earnest attempt to do it."

Madam Justice Wilson said there is "merit" to academic studies which suggest that men and women think differently about themselves, and their relationships to others.

While women view themselves as essentially connected to others and as members of a community, men see themselves as essentially autonomous, and independent of others.

One theory is that these differences arise from the fact that women do the mothering of children. In order to develop their masculinity, male children tend to distance and separate themselves from their mothers' female characteristics, while female children define themselves through their attachment to their mothers.

Thus masculinity is defined through separation and individualism, and femininity is defined through attachment and the formation of relationships. The gender identity of the male is threatened by relationships, while the gender identity of the female is threatened by separation.

According to this theory, men see moral problems as arising from competing rights; the adversarial process comes easily to them.

Women, on the other hand, see moral problems as arising from competing obligations, the one to the other, because the important thing is to preserve relationships, to develop an ethic of caring.

The goal is not seen in terms of winning or losing, but rather in terms of achieving an optimum outcome for all individuals involved in the moral dilemma.

"It is not difficult to see how this contrast in thinking might form the basis of very different perceptions of justice," Madam Justice Wilson observed.

The judge added that this analysis may partly explain the traditional reluctance of courts to get too deeply into the circumstances of the case, and their anxiety to reduce the context of the dispute to its bare bones through complex exclusionary rules of evidence.

"We are all familiar with the witness on crossexamination who wants to explain his or her answer, who feels that a simple 'yes' or 'no' is not an adequate response, and who is frustrated and angry at being cut off with a half truth," Madam Justice Wilson said.

"It is so much easier, you see, to come up with a black and white answer if you are unencumbered by a broader context which might prompt you, in Lord MacMillan's words, to temper the cold light of reason with the warmer tints of imagination and sympathy.

"It may explain also the hostility of many male judges to permitting intervenors in human rights cases. The main purpose of having intervenors is to broaden the context of the dispute, to show the issue in a larger perspective or as impacting on other groups not directly involved in the litigation at all.

Madam Justice Wilson said she feels that in general "women judges are much more comfortable in areas where they are dealing with conciliation or with things like pre-hearing conferences, where there is scope for a larger context — [to] put the dispute into a larger context and try to mediate it, and to achieve some kind of conciliation process.

"It's very hard to do that in the context of the usual adversarial process in a courtroom."

Madam Justice Wilson said the legislature remains a more effective instrument than courts for rapid or radical legal change, "but I see no reason why the judiciary cannot exercise some modest degree of creativity in areas where modern insights and life's experience have indicated that the law has gone awry.

"However, and I think this is extremely important, it will be a Pyrrhic victory for women and for the justice system as a whole if changes in the law come only through the efforts of women lawyers and women judges.

"The Americans were smart to realize that courses and workshops on gender bias for judges, male and female, are an essential follow-up to scholarly research and learned writing. In Canada we are just beginning to touch the fringes."

Madam Justice Wilson's address was the fourth annual Barbara Betcherman Memorial Lecture. Ms. Betcherman, an Osgoode graduate, was a dynamic feminist activist who died in a car accident at age 35.

Law and Social Transformation

A. The Institutional Framework of Law Reform

Law for the Seventies: A Manifesto for Law Reform[†]
Hon. John N. Turner

This address was delivered as the Inaugural Lecture in the George M. Duck Lecture Series at the University of Windsor in 1970. This address is printed here with the hope that the points discussed therein will suggest to our readers, much more effectively and successfully than an editorial could have, the directions which legal thought and action should be taking at present and in the immediate future.

IT has been said that the greatest achievement of the Sixties is that we survived them. Things that were thought impossible not only happened but have been already forgotten. A decade which dawned with such hope, which spawned such expectation, and which had been heralded as the Age of Achievement, culminated in the Age of Confrontation.

Assassination became a fact of political life. President Kennedy proclaimed "that the torch has been passed to a new generation of Americans"; but some of that flame died with him. Martin Luther King had a bold vision for black and white together; but some of that dream died with him. Robert Kennedy held forth a promise of a newer world; but some of that promise died with him. Tom Mboya was charting a new hope for Africans; but some of that hope died with him.

The full impact of these assassinations is yet to be appreciated. The shock waves are still reverberating internationally. But it is clear that those most cruelly disinherited or orphaned were the young. The politics of hope became the politics of despair. The promise *of* values became the crisis *in* values.

It is not surprising, then, that some have even called the Sixties the Age of the Apocalypse. Nations stockpiled weapons in the name of peace. Political leaders yawned the rhetoric of brotherhood while waging war. Governments destroyed cities in order to save them. Economies accumulated wealth and distributed poverty. Technology controlled man rather than released him. Corporate bureaucracies denied individuality while proclaiming it. The gross national product became Marcuse's One Dimensional Man.

And so the paradigm model for the relationship between man and society became the conflict between freedom and authority. Freud referred to this once as the major "discontent" of civilization. Indeed, authority and freedom seem now to be on a collision course everywhere. This conflict has become the brooding concern of the political commonwealth. The law is caught in the crunch. For, on the one hand, the law represents itself as the symbol of authority. On the other hand, it holds out the promise of freedom. And so this discontent, haunting our civilization, disturbs the roots of the law.

We are witnessing today what has been called a "crisis of legitimacy", or as some would have it, a "crisis of authority". All our institutions — the state, the university, the family, and, of particular concern to us tonight, the law — are being challenged. The challenge reaches not only the laws but those who make the laws. It strikes at the very legitimacy of the legal order itself. In a revolutionary climate, the law is considered the antithesis of revolution. In a mood of alienation, the law is regarded as

†   Turner, John N., "Law for the Seventies: A Manifesto for Law Reform" (1971), 17 *McGill Law Journal* 1. Reprinted by permission of the author.

a false consciousness. In an impatient world, the law is perceived as the curator of reaction.

I believe, however, that the law is *still relevant* — and can be made more relevant in contemporary terms; that authority and freedom are not contradictory but complementary; that they need not be opposed but juxtaposed; that law is not the enemy of revolution, but that "revolution" can be made possible through law. Indeed, in an age of confrontation our social problems become our legal problems. The problems of the Sixties are now the legal challenges of the Seventies. Society itself has become the lawyer's client, and society will hold the law to account.

OBJECTIVES FOR THE SEVENTIES

The faith that must move us, then, is the creative and even revolutionary role that law can play in the building and restructuring of a new society. For law is not just a "technical body of rules"; it is the organizing principle for the reconfiguration of society. Law is not just an agency of social control; it articulates the values by which men seek to live. The business of government, then, is the making of laws, and the process of law reform goes to the core of defining the kind of society we will have as a Canadian people and the kinds of rights which we will enjoy as individuals.

Here is the philosophic thrust and conceptual framework which I shall try to apply to what I understand to be the challenges and opportunities for the Seventies. As I see it, our objectives at the federal source of law must be four-fold:

The Administrative Process — The Individual and the State

First, we must redress the imbalance in the relationship between the individual and the state. The bigness and remoteness of government must not be allowed further to obscure or dwarf individual rights.

This is the rationale of the present Expropriation Bill now before Parliament. The Bill strikes a blow for individual rights against the arbitrariness of state power. It declares that the Canadian citizen will have the right to participate in the process by which he has been too often victimized. It provides that the expropriating authority must be a legal adversary rather than a clandestine arbiter. The Bill, with its guarantees of prior notice, of right to hearing, negotiation, appeal and fair compensation, enhances the scope of the individual. It is a citizen's bill.

But the administrative process still remains largely an unexplored labyrinth. We are concerned, for example, about the difficulty of challenging regulations that may well have gone beyond statutory limits or the scrutiny of Parliament; and we are concerned with controlling the breadth of the enabling powers that authorize these regulations.

We are concerned as well about the judicial powers exercised by administrative tribunals. We have introduced a Federal Court Bill to broaden the scope of judicial review of these powers by the courts, while making federal tribunals, boards and commissions more responsive to citizens' rights. This Bill is the beginning — and only the beginning — of the "civilizing" of the administrative process in the service of the individual. We will have to inquire into the complete workings of the public administrative law process, including the organization, administration, operation and procedure of these federal tribunals, boards and commissions. Also, we will have to probe the vast area of administrative discretion, or "discretionary justice" as Professor Kenneth Culp Davis has called it — that amorphous minefield of administrative decision-making which falls neither under the head of regulation-making nor within the scope of judicial review.

The federal Department of Justice will continue to define and create new remedies and new processes of review for the average Canadian against the state.

Towards a Humanistic Criminal Law

Secondly, Canada needs a more contemporary criminal law — credible, enforceable, flexible and compassionate. If we are to have a just society, we must begin with just laws; and nowhere is this more important than in the realm of criminal law; for it is here that the most fundamental values of life, liberty, property and dignity are to be protected and sanctioned, and it is here that the measure of our commitment to these values will be tested.

It is with this in mind that the Department of Justice will be submitting legislation in the form of a Right to Privacy Bill (to be part of the Criminal Code) to restrict electronic eavesdropping and wiretapping. The right to privacy, as Louis Brandeis once observed, is the most comprehensive of all the human freedoms, and the right most valued by civilized men.

We intend to introduce a Bail Reform Bill (also to be part of the Criminal Code) which will eliminate the criterion of money as the prerequisite for release. The practical result of the present system is that persons with money, or access to money, are often able to obtain release on bail, while poor people, who often cannot even meet the bondsman's fee, remain incarcerated. Empirical studies have demonstrated that persons released on bail are less likely to be convicted, and if convicted, are more likely to receive shorter or suspended sentences than are those who are preventively detained.

The Criminal Code amendments last year were predicated on the principle that private morality is the concern of the individual and not the province of a country's criminal law. Not everything that is immoral will be made illegal, just as not everything that is illegal is immoral.

The circles may at times intersect, but they need not inevitably be entwined.

We must also recognize that the criminal law sanction is the paradigm case of the controlled use of power in society. As Professor Herbert Packer of the Stanford Law School has remarked, it is both uniquely coercive as well as uniquely hazardous. There are limits to the use of the criminal sanction.

Accordingly, if we are to have any appreciation of the impact on society of the criminal law and the administration of criminal justice, we must begin by disabusing ourselves of some of the time-worn mythology that has served as a kind of self-protective mechanism for the perpetuation of the myths themselves:

1. We must disabuse ourselves of the myth that the criminal law process can be understood within the contours of the adversary system; for the criminal law process can only be understood by threading its impact from the initial phase of the "low visibility" discretionary decisions to invoke the criminal law process to the final disposition at time of sentencing.
2. We must disabuse ourselves of the myth that there is indeed an adversary system of criminal justice at all; for the criminal justice system is more administrative than adversarial; and at times more non-system than system.
3. We must disabuse ourselves of the myth that the criminal law sanction falls with equal impact on all segments of society. Indeed, it may well be — as some studies have pointed out — that our laws, such as vagrancy and public drunkenness — and our courts that administer them — have made it virtually a crime to be poor in public. And so it is that the *condition* of poverty may become the rationale for criminalization.
4. As a corollary, it may well be necessary for us to begin to question our self-appointed role as "moral entrepreneurs" of criminality, particularly where the decision to criminalize may be one of aesthetics — i.e., "the unattractive public poor" — rather than actual criminality.
5. Finally, it may well be that our decision-making about the orbit and impact of the criminal sanction is predicated on certain assumptions about man and the social order which may not be demonstrable empirically or even valid scientifically.

Law and Poverty: Justice for the Poor

Third, we must promote equality of access and equality of treatment before the law for rich and poor, young and old, alike. The adversary process before the courts must become a more meaningful, and less of a mythical, operation, particularly as it relates to the young, the dispossessed, the disenchanted, and the urban poor.

Few problems are more menacing than the presence of pervasive, life-long, grinding poverty. That we should have poverty in Canada is, as the Economic Council has reported, a disgrace. You don't have to tell the poor what poverty is; they know. They *feel* — very painfully — the sense of hopelessness and helplessness. They *understand* the deprivation of denial. They *know* what it is like to live in decrepit housing, to have the cracked pavements of the streets as their only parks, and to share their space with rodents — the only wildlife they see. The poor know what it means to live lives blighted by poor health, broken families, interrupted schooling, and frequent joblessness. They know what it means to be prey to debt, despair, dependence and crime.

And it is the poor who suffer most from society masked in the trappings of the law. For it is they who are victimized when urban renewal arbitrarily disrupts a neighbourhood; it is the poor who are hurt when creditors garnishee wages or repossess furniture; it is the poor who are deprived when welfare agencies deny, reduce or terminate welfare benefits on vague, unarticulated or clearly illegal grounds; it is the poor who are penalized when Draconian clauses permit landlords to withhold repairs or capriciously evict them into the street; it is the poor who are hit by bail procedures linked to financial means; it is the poor whose privacy is invaded and whose dignity is denied.

The poor do not use lawyers. They are often thought of as having no need of lawyers. Too many of us think of lawyers as counsellors to corporations, drafters of estate plans or wills, advisors on creditors' rights. But if the poor are rarely plaintiffs they are often defendants. They are bewildered and bemused by legalities they face daily as parents, consumers, tenants, recipients of public assistance and accused offenders. Too often the poor see the law not as a friend but as an enemy, not as an aid but as an adversary, not as a remedy but as an obstacle.

Justice in a society such as ours, a society marked by wide differences in wealth and power, demands a legal system that compensates for these differences. The law is above all a means of creating and protecting rights. What is so necessary is an enlarged conception of the rights of the poor and a changing conception of the role of law in establishing, protecting and implementing these rights. We must disabuse ourselves of the myth that poverty is somehow caused by the poor. We must recognize that the law itself often contributes to poverty. We must understand that, whereas the law for most of us is a source of rights, for the poor the law appears always to be taking something away. That we have to change.

And in this connection, I have been exploring for some time now the availability of the right to counsel and the alternative mechanisms for guaranteeing it in our law. As you know, one of the proposals has been to entrench it in a constitutional Charter of Human Rights. It is clear to me that the fundamental principle of due process must somehow be recognized in our law and before our courts. Those of us who have been given the temporary custody of our laws by the people must ensure that those laws and our courts treat all equally — rich and poor alike.

Technology and Environment: Ecology and the Law

We will have to harness technology in the service of the law rather than leave law at the mercy of technology. It will be necessary, then, to explore initiatives in the whole area of environmental control and probe the questions of interactive dynamics between science, technology and the law. For while technology races, the law lags; and once again the scientists are beating the lawyers.

Pollution is a good example of this. Rachel Carson's "Fable for Tomorrow" in *The Silent Spring* has now become today's painful reality. The Fifth Horseman of the Apocalypse — pollution — is riding towards us. We are choking our environment and being choked in return.

Water, as you know, is our greatest national resource; yet one hundred yards from the House of Commons the Ottawa River — one of the largest in the world — is dying. The Quebec Water Board has described this stretch of the river from the Rideau Rapids near Ottawa to Lake of Two Mountains fifty miles down-stream as "nothing but a vast bubbling swamp". A few years ago — nobody was paying close enough attention to know exactly when — Lake Erie died. Acidic wastes have strained its water of virtually every form of life except a mutant of the carp that has adjusted to living off poison.

Clean air is a precious, indispensable, life-giving nutriment; but it has all but disappeared. Recent air pollution readings in our major cities have approached critical health hazard. Scientists at the "Atmospheric Sciences Research Centre" in Scotia, New York, have predicted that in ten to fifteen years from now every man, woman and child in the Northern Hemisphere will have to wear a breathing helmet to survive outdoors. Streets for the most part will be deserted, and most animals and plant life already dead.

Unspoiled land ought to abound in Canada; but it is becoming an increasingly rare resource; and land, unlike air or water, has no "antibodies" to dillute pollutants. Soil once polluted stays polluted. Canadian women will carry in their breasts — and may already be carrying — milk that has anywhere from three to ten times more of the pesticide DDT than the government allows in dairy milk meant for human consumption.

The threshold of noise safety is 85 decibels. Yet the level is regularly exceeded in all major cities in Canada. Nor is deafness the only danger. Empirical studies have already shown noise to cause physiological changes of a cardiovascular, glandular and respiratory nature.

There are few among us who have not been exposed to noxious doses of chemicals, wastes, fumes, noise, sewage and heat. In the words of Tom Lehrer:

Just go out for a breath of air,
And you will be ready for medicare.
Fish gotta swim and birds gotta fly,
But they won't last long if they try.
Pollution! Pollution! You can use the latest
  toothpaste,
And then rinse your mouth with industrial
  waste.

Pollution, then, haunts us everywhere; and suddenly in this cause-conscious world everyone is against pollution. But as Mark Twain used to complain, everyone talked about the weather but nobody did anything about it; and so it is with pollution. Rhetoric is a blind alley. Indeed, we could do without a smog of words. And there is where the law comes in. For if the War on Pollution is to be won — indeed, if it is to be fought at all — a comprehensive national and international legal regime will have to be developed and applied. For what is needed is a hybrid "prevention-control" strategy. It would reflect the following imperatives:

1. We must create new regulatory institutions with alternative regulatory controls, i.e., penal, taxing, injunctive, etc. The Canada Water Bill is but a beginning.
2. We must deal with vested economic and community interests and the pressures they generate.
3. We may have to re-analyze the legal notion of the right of a person to use his own property as he sees fit.
4. We must translate our strategy for the War On Pollution into recognition of the individual and collective rights of ordinary citizens to a clean environment. These rights should be made actionable against polluters before the courts.
5. We must co-operate in developing an international legal regime to deal with pollution on a global scale.

Also, if the War on Pollution is to be won, we must abandon our "vandal ideology" which has permitted us to ravage our environment:

1. We must recognize that man is not the source of all value.
2. We must recognize that the universe does not exist for exploitation solely by man.
3. We must recognize that finite earth does not have infinite resources.
4. We must recognize that we cannot always remake the natural environment to suit a special interest.

5. Man must realize that his *actions* on the environment result in ecological *reactions*. He cannot punish the environment without being punished in return.

Ecology is the relationship between man and his environment; and law is the ordering of the relationships between man and his environment — the organizing principle of society. Pollution, then, is not only a problem of ecology; it is a problem for the law. Environment cannot only be the concern of ecologists; it must be the concern of lawyers and legislators and of ordinary citizens everywhere.

Give earth a chance. If we do, we may find that the environment will give us a chance.

IMPLEMENTATION OF OBJECTIVES

National Law Reform Commission

It is somewhat commonplace to say that legislatures are continually engaged in law reform; indeed, the very business of government is the making of laws. However, such law-making tends to be organized around reports of Parliamentary Committees, Task Forces or Royal Commission reports, and Bills which have come forward as a result of work in government departments. What is needed, however, is an institution uniquely dedicated to the process of law reform. In the words of Judge Cardozo, one of the early prime movers for the creation of a law reform commission in the United States:

> The inn that shelters for the night is not the journey's end. The law, like the traveller, must be ready for the morrow. It must have the principle of growth.

Accordingly, with this in mind, we have introduced a Bill establishing a federal Law Reform Commission, to give us a continuous, rather than episodic, review and reform of the law and the administration of justice in our country. This review will embrace the removal of anachronisms and anomalies in the law; relate and reconcile in our federal statutes the distinctive concepts and institutions of our civil and common law systems; eliminate obsolete laws; and develop and explore new approaches to, and new concepts of, the law to keep it alive and moving in a changing society. The law must never stand still again.

Research Planning Section in the Department of Justice

The creation of a Law Reform Commission for Canada in no way implies that the Department of Justice is abdicating its role in legal reform. There are changes that cannot await the critical and reasoned judgments of a Law Reform Commission. The federal Department of Justice has recently established a Research Planning Section. This section will serve as an investigative mechanism for short and long-run planning to ensure that the necessary data is gathered for the development of new legislation and the appraisal of present legislation. Hopefully, too, it will allow the Department of Justice to function more from the "justice" side as well as from the law enforcement or "attorney general" side. We want to act as counsel to the people, not just as lawyer to the Government.

CONCLUSION

This, then, is our manifesto for the law as we enter the Seventies. This is the nature of the advocacy we shall attempt to exercise to meet the challenges of the decade ahead.

For we are witnessing what has been described as a "new search for human values and relationships — relationships between man, and between men and government — that have meaning in the technological and psychological context of our age".

"What this search and the accompanying changes demand is not a law and order that freezes man into predetermined patterns, but a law and order of change, of movement, of options. Yesterday's order, if it is unresponsive, becomes tomorrow's oppression." We want a law in motion — a law that will never stand still again.

The Job of Law Reform[†]
P. Fitzgerald

BECAUSE societies change, their laws have to adjust to meet new problems (how is death to be defined?), new needs (how shall we protect the environment?), and new attitudes (how is women's equality best guaranteed?). Hence the need, in an era of accelerating change, for continuous law reform and permanent reform commissions like those set up in England, Australia, Canada, and elsewhere.

The job of law reform involves three stages: ascertaining the existing law, discovering its shortcomings, and recommending improvements. Reform commissions tend to overemphasize the first and last of these stages. A typical commission report carefully examines the law to be found emerging from the cases, draws a detailed comparison with the corresponding law in other countries, and concludes with a set of meticulously drafted recommendations for improvement. Any sustained discussion of principle, policy and values is usually missing.

Perhaps this is only natural. After all, both legal research and drafting are highly specialized activities involving primarily legal expertise. So it is not surprising that law reform commissions consist mostly of judges, legal practitioners, and academic lawyers.

Naturally such lawyers do what they are best equipped to do. They comb statutes and regulations, interpret legislation, and analyse case law — in short, they do legal research, concentrating on the law as it is. They are, however, much less at home with law as it ought to be. Their training, tradition, and experience provide no special skills to help them evaluate existing law and recommend improvements. Furthermore, conventional wisdom has it that evaluation and improvement of the law is a question of policy and should be left to legislators. And even when lawyers advise legislators, they are typically more concerned with precise legal drafting than law reform. Consequently, reported judgments, statutes, academic articles, and law reform reports often combine a mastery of authority and detail with a dearth of principle.

In the process, we may well lose sight of certain basic questions. What, after all, is the law that is to be reformed? What is to count as reform of that law? And what is the best way of engineering that reform?

WHAT IS LAW?

Though this is not the place for a discussion of the meaning of law, that question does have relevance for law reform. If we see law as the command of the sovereign, we will naturally stress the need for statutory amendments. If we see it, instead, as a prophecy of what the courts will do, we will emphasize the need for alteration of judicial practice. If we see it as an ongoing enterprise consisting of the activities of a wide variety of officials, policemen, prison officers, tax inspectors and other bureaucrats, we will concentrate on trying to change official attitudes and behaviour patterns.

Without adjudicating among these approaches, we can admit that for the law reformer all three have significance. Legislation that is unduly vague, ambiguous or otherwise unsatisfactory will obviously need improving. Judicial practice that is inconsistent or in conflict with legislative changes will clearly need to alter. And insofar as a law is what it actually does, activities in police stations, in prisons, in administrative offices and even in the street will need to change.

Law reformers, then, can't rest content with looking up the law in the books; they must go further and ascertain the living law, the law to be found in the real world. If, for example, we are concerned with the problem of strict liability in criminal law, we can't stop short at an examination of the case law; we must inquire how many offences of strict liability exist in our laws, how many such offences come to the notice of the prosecuting agencies, how many are and are not prosecuted and for what reasons, how many are convicted and what sentences are imposed. Likewise, if our concern is with the law relating to arrest, search and seizure, we have to find out how many warrants are issued, how many applications for warrants are rejected and for what reasons, how many arrests, searches and seizures are made without warrants and under what circumstances — in short, we have to investigate the whole law enforcement practice in this area.

Unfortunately, this kind of investigation falls outside the ambit of traditional legal research. It calls for skills conventionally exercised, not by lawyers, but by econometricians, sociologists, criminologists, and other social scientists and empirical researchers. Today such scientists and researchers are slowly becoming more active in the field of law reform.

WHAT COUNTS AS LAW REFORM?

Regardless of the view taken about the meaning of law, two questions arise about the meaning of law reform itself. One has to do with terms of reference, and the other with criteria for evaluation.

---

† Fitzgerald, Patrick, "The Job of Law Reform" (1981), 1:2 *Westminster Institute Review* 10 at 10–11. Reprinted by permission of the author and the Westminster Institute for Ethics and Human Values, London, Ontario.

With respect to the first of these, it is important to ask both what a law reformer is meant to reform, and how far he is supposed to go? Much law reform has been severely criticized in certain quarters as being mere tinkering with the existing system.[1] According to this view, there is a stark difference between legal law reform and real, or social, law reform. For example, redrafting the laws on theft and fraud, reducing sixty or more statutory sections to a mere half dozen, replacing of a wealth of detail by a handful of broad principles, and substituting simple formulae for complex expressions is seen as insignificant legal law reform so long as theft and fraud remains predicated on inequitable division of property. Real law reform, it is argued, must recognize criminal law for what it is, an instrument of class oppression, and seek to alter the basic system of property distribution.[2]

Without taking sides in this controversy, we can advance three propositions. First, in so far as the citizen has a right to know his law, clarification and improvement in the form of law is a significant part of law reform. Second, improvement in form is less significant than improvement in content — clarification of the laws relating, say, to disabilities of women is far less important than their abolition. But third, a law reformer requested to recommend improvements in the law relating to an institution like property, the family, or the criminal justice system, is hardly authorized to recommend the total abolition of that institution. Asked to reform the law concerning theft of property, a law reformer goes beyond his brief by recommending abolition of private property or a complete restructuring of the distribution system. Such abolition or restructuring may or may not be desirable, but it falls outside the scope of law reform commissions, and should be left to bodies with a broader social base.

Reform means change, but presumably only change for the better. This brings us to the second of our two questions: what shall be our criteria for evaluating change? In law reform, improvements are usually measured along three dimensions: logic, expedience and ethics.

The dimension most obvious to the lawyer is that of logic. As mentioned earlier, deleting ambiguities, discrepancies, inconsistencies, and what Bentham termed over-bulkiness, is one obvious method of legal improvement.[3] Replacing a multitude of conflicting provisions by a Napoleonic Code is clearly an advance which makes for easier administration. Harmonizing the laws of various jurisdictions by means of uniform codes, model codes, and restatements of the law is plainly an amelioration. Finally, rationalizing and systematizing the law through codification brings greater understanding, manageability and efficiency.

More difficult for the law reformer is the dimension of expedience, or what has been termed in law cases social convenience. However expedient is strict tort liability for defective products? How does it affect the industry in question, the consumer price index, the rate of unemployment — the whole economy? Such questions were answered by 19th century judges, if at all, by common sense and native intuition. It was automatically accepted that strict criminal liability for regulatory or welfare offences would serve to decrease negligence on the part of manufacturers, wholesalers, retailers and others governed by regulatory offences.

Today we are less unsophisticated. We realize that there are questions to which empirical research is relevant. Take strict liability and regulatory offences: manufacturers and others might be more anxious to maintain high standards if exposed, not to a strict liability conviction where carelessness is legally irrelevant, but to a negligence conviction where the judicial searchlight is focused on the degree to which their practice lives up to the requisite standard of care. So, as to expedience, law reform must place extensive reliance on social science investigations. Much useful work has been done in this regard by economists, and more recently by philosophers of law and others working in the area of economics of law.

Far and away the hardest dimension for the law reformer is that of ethics. Would such and such a change make this or that particular area of law more just, and bring it more into harmony with moral values? And, the question is, *whose* values? If it is argued that there can be no real objectivity in ethics and no objective values, a law reformer may be tempted to forward his own personal preferences. Alternatively, he may try to ascertain the values held by most members of society through market research techniques.

Neither approach is wholly satisfactory. A personal preference standpoint is obviously inadequate; we want reformers to tell us what is wrong with existing law, not just to tell us they don't like it. A social head-count strategy is equally inadequate: apart from other considerations, society may be totally divided on the issue in question, as it is, for example, on abortion.

Clearly a third approach is necessary. The law reformer should begin with the basic moral values essential for the survival of any society, e.g., respect for human life. He should also, as law reformer rather than revolutionary, work from such nonessential values as are accepted as necessary for his own particular society, e.g., freedom and privacy, in most Western democracies. These two types of values can be listed without empirical investigation.[4]

Reflection on such basic values must be the law reformer's starting point. From these, he must spell out all their various implications. These implications will guide him in determining the directions the law should take. In criminal law, for example, they will help him to work out how far society is entitled to use the law to counter certain kinds of behaviour, how much the use of criminal law may have to be restrained in the interests of liberty and privacy, and when there must be safeguards for the sake of defendants. Criminal law reform, like all law reform, must start with basic and social moral theory.

What about "tragic case" situations which admit of no obvious answer? What, for example, about abortion, about which good sense, it seems, can be put forward on both sides? How are we to decide, in this case, between the competing values, i.e., the mother's right to self-determination and the fetus' right to life?

There is, of course, no easy way. What is called for is a process, possibly a very long drawn-out process, of values clarification. It must also be one involving a variety of participants: medical and social scientists must contribute factual information, ethicists must bring insights on human values, philosophers must import conceptual clarification, and finally the concerned lay public must bring to bear community feelings, common sense and ordinary notions of morality.

There is a particular problem concerning participation by the public. The average citizen isn't overly concerned with law reform in general, although he may, from time to time, evince strong feelings over a particular issue. Also, it isn't easy for the average citizen to speak except through representatives. As an unfortunate result, professional administrators, lawyers, and law reformers either exclude members of the ordinary public from their inquiry process or, at most, find a limited role for them in the system. But surely it shouldn't be incumbent on the citizen to find his place within the system of legal reform, but rather on the system to accommodate itself within the general community.

HOW CAN WE BEST ENGINEER REFORM?

Law improvement is of course beyond the power of the law reformer to provide; he proposes, someone else disposes. Changes in written law must be made by legislators. Change in judicial practice must be brought about by judges. And change in police or other behaviour must be implemented by the agencies in question. In other words, the job of the reformer is to recommend better ways of doing things, and then get people to adopt them. To this extent, it is a job of education.

First, though, the reformer has to educate himself. This means he has to learn that the most obvious strategy for improvement is not necessarily the most effective. After all, the most obvious reaction to any social evil is to pass a law against it. But laws may pass and not result

in much real change. It may do little good, for instance, to try statutorily to increase the incidence of pre-trial bail without first winning over police and prosecutors to this new approach. Otherwise they may adapt their practice so as to thwart the wishes of the legislature. Conversely, laws may quite often be improved without involving legislation. Well argued reports, well run conferences and careful consultations with the judges may lead courts to change their interpretation of statutes. Similarly, discussion with prosecutors and others may result, without one bit of legislation, in a noteworthy alternation in practice.

THE FUTURE OF LAW REFORM

Law reform, then, is ultimately an exercise in changing people's attitudes. Accordingly, reformers must come out of their libraries and enter the field with judges, practitioners, police, and others. They must sit down together, discuss the problems with existing modes of operation, and suggest new strategies for solving them. Social scientists and philosophers also need to be involved. Perhaps in the long run, what may be most important for this enterprise is not the official agencies of law reform, but the various centres and institutes established in recent years for the continuous study of values. For while law has to be dynamic and open to change, reforming the law is not an instant process to be done overnight with a mere stroke of the lawyer's pen. Rather, it is a gradual process requiring close attention to legal theory, actual practice, and ethical principle.

Endnotes

1. See R.A. Samik, "A Case for Social Law Reform" (1977), 55 *Canadian Bar Review* 409–35.
2. See Ian Taylor, Paul Walton, and Jock Young, *Critical Criminology* (Boston: Routledge and Kegan Paul, 1975); and M.R. Goode, "Law Reform Commission of Canada — Political Ideology of Criminal Process Reform" (1976), 54 *Canadian Bar Review* 653–74.
3. Most of the 19th century reforms advocated by Jeremy Bentham fell into the categories of simplification, clarification, and rationalization of the law.
4. This approach is much the same as that of Hart's minimum content of natural law. See H.L.A. Hart, *Concept of Law* (Oxford: Clarendon Press, 1961): 189–95. See also John Finnis, *Natural Law and Natural Rights* (Oxford: Clarendon Press, 1980).

Social Control, State Autonomy and Legal Reform:
The Law Reform Commission of Canada[†]

R. Hastings and R.P. Saunders

THERE is a general agreement among social scientists that law serves a strategic purpose as a formal expression of the dominant values of a society, as a mechanism for the resolution of conflicts and the coercion of rule-breakers, or as a tool in the education or "civilizing" of the general public. In this sense, it is impossible to study the forms and uses of law apart from the wider social relations and structural arrangements from within which it emerges. However, this notion can be operationalized in very different ways. On the one hand, functionalists are more likely to view law as expressing the outcome of a relatively open negotiation process between competing interest groups and to focus their analysis on the consequences of law for the overall welfare of a given social system. On the other hand, Marxists emphasize the class-based material and ideological interests which are served by the law at a given social and political conjuncture. The common thread in these otherwise incompatible positions is a view of the law as emerging within current social relations and social structures and as contributing to their preservation or transformation.

. . . .

The present paper focuses on an aspect of the specific case of the reform of criminal law in Canada. The process, content, and consequences of legal reform can only be adequately understood in the context of the wider role of the state in general and of the issues of ideology and social control in particular. Our focus will be on the work of the Law Reform Commission of Canada (LRCC), which is one of the key state agencies involved in the current project of the Canadian government to rewrite the Canadian Criminal Code. We wish to establish the LRCC's contribution to this process and the degree to which this is related to the relative autonomy of the LRCC in particular and the criminal justice system in general.

The movement of the Canadian state towards the creation of a law reform agency began in the late 1960's, culminating in 1971 with the formation of the Law Reform Commission of Canada. The commission was intended to be a response, and in part a solution, to the conflict and social disjunctures which marked the 1960's. According to John Turner, Minister of Justice at the time, this period was an "age of confrontation": "we are witnessing today

what has been called a 'crisis of legitimacy' or as some would have it a 'crisis of authority.' All our institutions ...are being challenged" (1971, p. 2). In the face of this crisis, Turner nevertheless argued that "revolution" can be made possible through law, and that "law is not just a 'technical body' of rules; it is the organizing principle for the reconfiguration of society. Law is not just an agency of social control; it articulates the values by which men seek to live" (*ibid.*).

The LRCC was thus designed to contribute to the challenge of coming to grips with social conflict and social change. There was a recognition that the old order was giving way to a new, more heterogeneous and more fragmented society, one in which the law would be called upon to provide "the means by which multiple sets of values can co-exist and develop" (Burke, 1971; p. 5). The goal was to codify, rationalize, and rethink the law in order to adapt our legal instruments to the task of constructing a more harmonious world.

The formal mandate of the LRCC directed it to engage in both the technical task of systematizing and rationalizing the law and the broader sociopolitical task of reform. More specifically, the LRCC was authorized to make recommendations on:

1. the removal of anachronisms and anomalies in the law;
2. the reflection in and by the law of the distinctive concepts and institutions of the common and civil law systems in Canada and the reconciliation of differences and discrepancies in the expression and application of the law arising out of differences in these concepts and institutions;
3. the elimination of obsolete laws; and
4. the development of new approaches to and new concepts of the law in keeping with and responsive to the changing needs of modern Canadian society and individual members of that society (Law Reform Commission Act, 1970, s. 11).

This mandate, particularly in its directive to develop new orientations to the law, justifies an analysis of the results of over a decade of LRCC work.

. . . .

[†] This article is reprinted with permission of the publisher from *State Control: Criminal Justice Politics in Canada* by R.S. Ratner and J.I. McMillan eds. at pp. 126–131, 146. © University of British Columbia Press 1987. All rights reserved by the Publisher.

In order to accomplish this analysis, we will discuss the contributions of the LRCC to the current project of revising and rewriting the Canadian Criminal Code, focusing on three major issues. First, we will discuss the internal division of labour and the working process adopted by the LRCC in its attempt to accomplish its mandate. This general description will permit an appreciation of the broad scope of the task assigned to the LRCC, and will allow us to identify some of the main groups who participate in the work of legal reform.

. . . .

THE LRCC AND THE WORK OF REFORM

Despite its high level of funding and its original intentions to engage in fundamental research and consult broadly during the process of legal reform, the LRCC is relatively little known outside the legal profession. For this reason, a brief description of the organization and its working procedures is useful.

In order to fulfill its mandate, the LRCC has structured its tasks so as to best reflect the various potential areas of law reform within the federal jurisdiction.[1] This had led to a division of the work of the LRCC into four major research projects:

1. the Substantive Criminal Law Project, which is responsible for the writing of a new code of substantive criminal law;
2. the Criminal Procedure Project, which is involved in the production of a code of criminal procedure;
3. the Protection of Life Project, which is engaged in the examination of a broad range of medico-legal matters, including issues relating to pollution, the environment, and consumer products; and
4. the Administrative Law Project, which is concerned with research into the general relationship between law and administrative agencies. (LRCC, 1984, pp. 17–18)

Each project is headed by a project co-ordinator and is under the overall direction of an individual commissioner (*ibid.*, p. 5). For the purposes of our study, we have focused our attention solely on the work of the Substantive Criminal Law Project. There are two reasons for this. First, it is this project which is most directly responsible for the production of the *content* of criminal law within the law reform process. As such, its work will best illustrate the positions adopted by the LRCC on both the general aims of criminal law in Canadian society and the process of criminal law reform. Second, the government of Canada is currently engaged in a long-term project of rewriting the Criminal Code.[2] The Department of Justice has placed a high priority on the production of this code; as a result, the work of the LRCC has taken on an increased importance.

During its first years of operation, the LRCC produced its work in several stages:

First, the publication by a project group of a study paper (which does not express the views of the commission) inviting comments, then, of a commission working paper, written in the light of public reaction to the study paper and again inviting comment, and, finally, publication of a report to the Minister of Justice of his consideration and for tabling in Parliament. (Barnes, 1975, p. 84)

The working procedure of the LRCC changed, however, with more emphasis placed on the working paper itself. Moreover, in practice, the direction and spirit of the criminal law working papers have been substantially the same as those of the reports which followed them.[3]

In the actual preparation and production of its paper and reports, the LRCC and, more particularly, the Criminal Law Project, uses various research techniques. Four methods have been identified: 1) philosophical enquiry; 2) the comparative method; 3) empirical research; and 4) consultation (*ibid.*, p. 72). The first, philosophical enquiry, is a "search for values." We will focus on this issue later in this chapter, for it is the discussions of values and the purpose of criminal law which we find the most illustrative of the orientation of the LRCC. Using the comparative method, the LRCC has focused on the bi-jural nature of the Canadian system and has examined other common law and civil law systems (*ibid.*, p. 76). The goal of the LRCC in its empirical research is to "discover the actual living law, the law that really governs Canadian people." Even from a conventional perspective, however, this research has been found to be "sporadic" at best (*ibid.*, pp. 76–77). But a more fundamental criticism can be made of the type of empirical research into criminal law in which the LRCC engages. This criticism relates to the restricted methodology which the LRCC uses and is discussed later in this chapter. The consultation process of the LRCC in the production of its working papers and reports is a relatively narrow one. While the LRCC has at times attempted to involve the wider public in the law reform process, the response has been generally unsatisfying. An early example of the failure of an attempt at broad-based public involvement is the Ottawa Pilot Project (which was basically a series of public information meetings in 1974) which excited little public response (*ibid.*, pp. 85–85). In contrast, the regular consultations in which the LRCC engages are much more important and influential. They involve representatives of five groups: judges, defence lawyers, police chiefs, law teachers, and crown counsel (LRCC, 1984; pp. 19–20). It is evident from this list that the consultation process is a relatively closed one, involving as it does only certain (usually legal) professionals in the criminal justice system. This bias towards the legal profession is evident as well in the background of the majority of the members of the Substantive Criminal Law Project.[4] Not surprisingly, this restricted participation is not without consequence for the findings or recommendations of the LRCC.

．　．　．　．

In the long run, however, this may not be too important. The new Canadian Constitution and the emerging tendency for key political and legal issues to be resolved in the courts will probably shift the real axis of legal reform from the LRCC to the Supreme Court. Time goes on — the LRCC probably will not.

Endnotes

1.   For the structure and personnel of the LRCC, see LRCC, 1984B, pp. 1–5. It should also be noted that there are provincial law reform agencies which focus on areas of law within provincial jurisdiction.
2.   See Department of Justice, 1982.
3.   For a complete list of the LRCC's working papers and reports, see LRCC, 1984: Appendices A and B.
4.   For a complete list of the research personnel and their qualifications, see LRCC, 1984: Appendices I.

Responses to Elimination of the Law Reform Commission[†]
B. Cox

OTTAWA (CP) — The federal government's decision to eliminate the Law Reform Commission of Canada won't save money and could hamper efforts to change the country's laws, say legal experts and politicians.

The commission which has advised Ottawa on law reform since 1971, was among several government bodies cut in the federal budget on Tuesday.

"I think it's a great tragedy, really, because we need a body to look at our laws in a sort of comprehensive and detailed and in-depth manner and unfortunately the parliamentary process doesn't always lend itself to that," said University of Ottawa law professor Ed Ratushny.

"Law reform usually follows political agendas and often much-needed reforms can be ignored because of those agendas."

The commission and the government have often been at odds, though several commission reports have produced legislative changes.

A recent commission report recommended that Ottawa create a separate native-controlled criminal justice system.

Justice Minister Kim Campbell has said she does not favor a separate system for natives.

NO SAVINGS

Ian Waddell, the New Democrat justice critic, said such disagreements provide a better explanation than cost-cutting for getting rid of the commission.

Waddell said that no money will be saved because the Justice Department will still have to study legal issues that the commission studied in the past.

"It doesn't make sense to me," said Waddell. "Perhaps the commission just became too independent from the government."

J.J. Camp, president of the Canadian Bar Association, said the government may save some money by shutting down the commission, but the cost will be greater in the long run.

"You can't put a price on justice" he said. "There is an endless stream of improvement (to the justice system) that could have been affected by the commission."

Camp said there is little evidence to suggest the government cut the commission because it had become too critical of government policy.

---

†   Cox, Bob, "Responses to Elimination of the Law Reform Commission," *Canadian Newswire*, February 22, 1992. Reprinted by permission of the Canadian Press, Toronto, Ontario.

Former commission member Joe Maingot said the commission cost little, considering the use that lawyers, courts, governments and others made of its research.

"I think it's a question of penny-wise and pound-foolish," said Maingot.

Maingot said the commission functioned as an independent thinker on the law and "unfortunately there is no one there to fill that void."

The commission published almost 170 studies on issues ranging from theft and fraud to biomedical experiments on human subjects.

It had wide influence and its reports were often cited by the Supreme Court of Canada in its decisions.

Last year the Supreme Court overturned archaic Criminal Code provisions that automatically incarcerated anybody acquitted of a crime by reason of insanity.

The judgment was written by Chief Justice Antonio Lamer, who was vice-chairman of the commission when it first recommended changing the law 16 years ago. Lamer later served three years as chairman.

In recent years the commission's work was hampered because the government was not quick to replace departing commissioners.

Further Reading

Andrew Petter, "The Politics of the Charter" (1986), 8 *Supreme Court L.R.* 473.

Strangton Lynd, "The Genesis of the Idea of a Community Right to Industrial Property in Youngstown & Pittsburgh 1977–87" (1987), 74 *Journal of American History*.

Michael Mandel, *The Charter of Rights and the Legalizations of Politics in Canada*, 2nd ed. (Toronto: Wall & Thompson, 1994).

B. Social Movements and Rights Struggles

Doing Justice to 'British Justice': Law, Ideology and Canadian Historiography[†]
G. Marquis

In days of yore, from Britain's shore,
Wolfe, the dauntless hero came,
And planted firm Britannia's flag
On Canada's fair domain.
Here may it wave, our boast, our pride;
And joined in love together
The Thistle, Shamrock, Rose entwine,
The Maple Leaf forever!

Maple Leaf, our emblem dear, the Maple Leaf
forever!
God save our Queen, and heaven bless, the
Maple leaf forever!

At Queenston's Heights and Lundy's Lane
Our brave forefathers, side by side,
For freedom, homes and loved ones dear,
Firmly stood and nobly died;
And those dear rights which they maintained
We swear to yield them never;
Our watchword ever more shall be
The Maple Leaf forever!

— Alexander Muir, "The Maple Leaf Forever"

IN an era when Canada had only a handful of progressive labour lawyers and no mainstream national civil liberties organization, the Communist-organized Canadian Labour Defence League raised funds, attracted thousands of members and defended trade unionists and leftists in the courts. In 1933 the CLDL held a convention in Toronto to discuss matters such as the recent Red Scare. The convention's report attempted to explain the League's failure to exploit local issues such as police corruption, political scandals and the notorious section 98 of the Criminal Code, on the basis of radical organizers' distaste for "humanitarianism" or "sentimentalism":

For instance, many workers still believe in 'British justice' and 'Democratic rights.' We should

make effective use of demands on these very questions, thus drawing the workers into the struggle against the [police] terror.

The report was addressing a thorny issue for early twentieth-century Canadian socialists, the popular legitimacy of the rule of law, which was an important, if often latent and ambiguous dimension of political culture. The standard sloganeering of the *Worker* and the *Young Worker*, organs of the Communist Party, was that legal rights were a bourgeois sham. Hence workers arrested on picket lines or at public meetings were considered political prisoners, and the police, the judiciary and the bar were enforcers of class justice. The treatment of elements of the Toronto labour and socialist movements by the police and courts in the 1920s and 1930s lent credibility to such an instrumentalist view of the legal order. The CLDL 1933 report nonetheless advised organizers to remain sensitive to the superstitions of the masses regarding the rule of law:

Often, because we feel we are 'advanced', 'people on a higher level', etc., we do not take into account the moods, sentiments, and traditions of the workers, and arguing that they are 'bad' traditions, we therefore either ignore them or evoke resentment through tactics sneering at these traditions.

The CLDL anecdote serves as the springboard for this paper, which will discuss Canadian Criminal justice historiography and research possibilities. Two major suggestions are made. First, that historians in a number of fields would benefit from examining popular attitudes towards and expectations of legal authority. The second point is that much of the "new history" of the last fifteen years, particularly social and working-class history in the process of reinterpreting or rejecting liberal historiography, has emphasized coercion and control by the dominant classes and ignored or neglected the question of the popular legitimacy of state institutions. According to an influential interpretation in legal history, the dominant classes, acting

† Marquis, Greg, "Doing Justice to 'British Justice': Law, Ideology and Canadian Historiography", excerpt from speech given at the Canadian Law in History Conference, Carleton University, June, 1987. Reprinted by permission of the author.

through the state, with varying degrees of success, have indoctrinated the masses with these "moods, sentiments and traditions." This interpretation must yield to a more sophisticated approach sensitive to the complexities and ambiguities of popular attitudes towards the law.

Perhaps because intellectual history, which traditionally relies on elite sources, is not currently fashionable, we rely on assumptions, rather than systematic examination of popular ideologies in Canada's past. The law and its administration were not remote for nineteenth-century British North Americans, but part of their orientation towards local affairs, government and the Empire. Justice, in the form of the constable, the alderman, the justice of the peace or the stipendiary magistrate, was a highly visible if decentralized sign of the state. The law was viewed as an instrument of control as well as a vehicle for political and social change — not merely by great men, but by much of the ignorant populace. It is significant, for example, that the Patriote Party of Lower Canada responded to popular rural demands by advocating magistrates appointed by the people. Lloyd Kramer, in a recent article that attempts to find common ground between social and intellectual history, suggests one solution in the mentalité methodology developed by French historians who explore "the unconscious, deep structural aspects of human thought and behaviour" found "in popular culture, beliefs, ritual and ideologies." In like manner Robert Gordon has suggested that legal historians should

> treat legal forms as ideologies and rituals whose 'effects' — effects that include people's ways of sorting out social experience, giving it meaning, grading it as natural, just and necessary, or as contrived, unjust and subject to alteration — are in the realm of consciousness.

The challenge is to reconstruct a "demotic intellectual history" to complement the institutional approach of much criminal justice historiography. I have adopted the nineteenth-century term "British justice," which links law and legal institutions to political culture, to suggest a promising category of analysis for such inquiries.

THE ENGLISH INHERITANCE

Any study of Canadian attitudes towards the law and uses of the legal system must begin with the English cultural heritage, particularly the powerful view of British institutions as the bulwark of liberty. An 1880 Ontario government publication, for example, promised prospective immigrants from the old country no less than "All the protection and safety that British law can ensure." One has but to recall former generations of Canadian school textbooks for a glimpse of these Whiggish ideals. To date

these sentiments have been explored mainly by intellectual historians, in their most exaggerated form, in the writings and speeches of late nineteenth- and early twentieth-century Canadian imperialists. According to Carl Berger, Canadian imperialism combined an awareness of Canadian nationality and "an equally decided desire to unify and transform the British Empire so that this nationality could attain a position of equality within it." Historians should now turn to the hypothesis that emotional attachment to British institutions, which included a particular view of history, was not confined to the middle and upper classes but influenced the social experience of the urban and rural masses.

In the British constitutionalist tradition legal rights were not separated from political rights; both had been wrested from a tyrannical monarchy. Although these ancient rights and privileges were for most of British history ignored or honoured selectively, the culture of constitutionalism stressing the benefits of English law was an important ideological force in the eighteenth- and nineteenth-century British world. As Anne Pallister has demonstrated, the key to this tradition was veneration of an idealized past that included emotive symbols such as Magna Carta:

> The equation of law and liberty, the belief that the law of England protects rather than restricts the freedom of the individual, which is the central feature of the Charter, still lies at the heart of English political and legal thought and practice; and the Charter provides a standard of political ethos against which official action in its effects upon the individual can be measured.

Magna Carta and other symbols, moreover, became "the property of both conservative constitutionalists and radical agitators." These traditions were evident in the independence movements of Britain's rebellious eighteenth-century North American colonies, whose leaders were well versed in Whig history and ritualistic invocations of freedom as the birthright of Englishmen. By 1760, American Whigs were reaching back into history, appropriating national myths such as the Norman Yoke, Magna Carta and the Glorious Revolution, to legitimize their constitutional dispute with Britain. Similarly, despite national differences among Great Britain, the United States and Canada, the Victorians praised the spirit of Magna Carta as the heritage of all English-speaking peoples.

The rhetoric of British liberty can be interpreted in more than one way. A Marxist might explain that the great constitutional struggles that captivated Whig historians represented a debate of limited parameters, involving factions of the dominant classes, one representing landed property, the other commercial and industrial capitalism. That legal ideology can be used to buttress the status quo should come as no surprise. Douglas Hay, in an influential article, has argued that the law replaced monarchy as the principal ideology legitimizing the eighteenth-century English state. In Hay's functionalist interpretation, elite management of ideology is the key to state power. An earlier article, "Patrician Society, Plebeian Culture", by E.P. Thompson examined eighteenth-century paternalist relations and the importance of law as "public theatre" in maintaining the hegemony of the state. Although the law was used as an ideological weapon to reinforce class relations, it was not, in the opinion of Thompson, merely an instrument for maintaining control and consent. The ideology of the dominant classes could also become the rallying cry of popular resistance:

> And finally, far from the ruled shrugging off this rhetoric as hypocrisy, some part of at least was taken over by the plebeian crowd, of the 'free-born Englishman', with his inviolable privacy, his *habeas corpus*, his equality before the law.

Thus various social groups could combine self-interest with a vision of constitutional rights, often in a utopian frame of reference.

. . . .

CONCLUSION

How then, should we do justice to British justice? First, by attempting to recover a potentially rich and complex symbolic tradition that linked law to political culture. Second, by recognizing that the law's class instrumentality co-existed with a degree of popular legitimacy. The interaction of state ideology and institutions on the one hand and popular attitudes and responses on the other is a promising research area. Historians must develop strategies for evaluating both popular resistance to and the popular legitimacy of the legal order. This will not be *the way* to do legal history or a new organizing principle for social history, but a possible corrective to the internal focus of legal historiography and the great man focus of intellectual historiography. Legal historians cannot afford to ignore the legal consciousness of the masses, however vulgarized it may be. British justice and its meanings may also prove useful in social history where there will be increasing interest in ambiguity and less in conflict and control. Working-class historians, if they are to retain their claim of being on the cutting edge, must come to grips with these traditions. Inquiries along these lines will face methodological obstacles, notably the challenge of gauging the opinions of the common people, but they will broaden our conception of law, society and the state.

Citizenship and Social Class[†]
T.H. Marshall

THE sociological hypothesis latent in Alfred Marshall's essay postulates that there is a kind of basic human equality associated with the concept of full membership of a community — or, as I should say, of citizenship — which is not inconsistent with the inequalities which distinguish the various economic levels in the society. In other words, the inequality of the social class system may be acceptable provided the equality of citizenship is recognized. [...]

He recognizes only one definite right, the right of children to be educated, and in this case alone does he approve the use of compulsory powers by the state to achieve his object. He could hardly go further without imperilling his own criterion for distinguishing his system

from socialism in any form — the preservation of the freedom of the competitive market. [...] His sociological hypothesis lies as near to the heart of our problem today as it did three-quarters of a century ago — in fact nearer. The basic human equality of membership [...] has been enriched with new substance and invested with a formidable array of rights. It has developed far beyond what he foresaw, or would have wished. It has been clearly identified with the status of citizenship. [...]

Is it still true that basic equality, when enriched in substance and embodied in the formal rights of citizenship, is consistent with the inequalities of social class? I shall suggest that our society today assumes that the two are still compatible: so much so that citizenship has itself

---

† Marshall, T.H., "Citizenship and Social Class" in eds. D. Held et al., *States and Societies* (Oxford: Martin Robertson & Company Ltd., 1985), 248–60. Reprinted by permission of Basil Blackwell Ltd., Oxford, U.K.

become, in certain respects, the architect of legitimate social inequality. Is it still true that the basic equality can be created and preserved without invading the freedom of the competitive market? Obviously it is not true. Our modern system is frankly a socialist system not one whose authors are, as Marshall was, eager to distinguish it from socialism. But it is equally obvious that the market still functions — within limits. Here is another possible conflict of principles which demands examination. And thirdly, what is the effect of the marked shift of emphasis from duties to rights? Is this an inevitable feature of modern citizenship — inevitable and irreversible? [...]

I shall ask whether there appear to be limits beyond which the modern drive towards social equality cannot, or is unlikely to pass, and I shall be thinking, not of the economic cost (I leave that vital question to the economists), but of the limits inherent in the principles that inspire the drive. But the modern drive towards social equality is, I believe, the latest phase of an evolution of citizenship which has been in continuous progress for some 250 years. [...]

THE DEVELOPMENT OF CITIZENSHIP TO THE END OF THE NINETEENTH CENTURY

[...] I shall be running true to type as a sociologist if I begin by saying that I propose to divide citizenship into three parts. But the analysis is, in this case, dictated by history even more clearly than by logic. I shall call these three parts, or elements, civil, political and social. The civil element is composed of the rights necessary for individual freedom — liberty of the person, freedom of speech, thought and faith, the right to own property and to conclude valid contracts, and the right to justice. The last is of a different order from the others, because it is the right to defend and assert all one's rights on terms of equality with others and by due process of law. This shows us that the institutions most directly associated with civil rights are the courts of justice. By the political element I mean the right to participate in the exercise of political power, as a member of a body invested with political authority or as an elector of the members of such a body. The corresponding institutions are Parliament and councils of local government. By the social element I mean the whole range from the right to a modicum of economic welfare and security to the right to share to the full in the social heritage and to live the life of a civilized being according to the standards prevailing in the society. The institutions most closely connected with it are the educational system and the social services. [...]

By 1832 when political rights made their first infantile attempt to walk, civil rights had come to man's estate and bore, in most essentials, the appearance that they have today. 'The specific work of the earlier Hanoverian

epoch', writes Trevelyan, 'was the establishment of the rule of law; and that law, with all its grave faults, was at least a law of freedom. On that solid foundation all our subsequent reforms were built'. This eighteenth-century achievement, interrupted by the French Revolution and completed after it, was in large measure the work of the courts both in their daily practice and also in a series of famous cases in some of which they were fighting against Parliament in defence of individual liberty. The most celebrated actor in this drama was, I suppose, John Wilkes, and, although we may deplore the absence in him of those noble and saintly qualities which we should like to find in our national heroes, we cannot complain if the cause of liberty is sometimes championed by a libertine.

In the economic field the basic civil right is the right to work, that is to say the right to follow the occupation of one's choice in the place of one's choice, subject only to legitimate demands for preliminary technical training. This right had been denied by both statute and custom; on the one hand by the Elizabethan *Statute of Artificers*, who confined certain occupations to certain social classes, and on the other by local regulations reserving employment in a town to its own members and by the use of apprenticeship as an instrument of exclusion rather than of recruitment. The recognition of the right involved the formal acceptance of a fundamental change of attitude. The old assumption that local and group monopolies were in the public interest, because 'trade and traffic cannot be maintained or increased without order and government', was replaced by the new assumption that such restrictions were an offence against the liberty of the subject and a menace to the prosperity of the nation. [...]

By the beginning of the nineteenth century this principle of individual economic freedom was accepted as axiomatic. You are probably familiar with the passage quoted by the Webbs from the report of the Select Committee of 1811, which states that:

> no interference of the legislature with the freedom of trade, or with the perfect liberty of every individual to dispose of his time and of his labour in the way and on the terms which he may judge most conducive to his own interest, can take place without violating general principles of the first importance to the prosperity and happiness of the community. [...]

The story of civil rights in their formative period is one of the gradual addition of new rights to a status that already existed and was held to appertain to all adult members of the community — or perhaps one should say to all male members, since the status of women, or at least of married women, was in some important respects peculiar. This democratic, or universal, character of the status arose naturally from the fact that it was essentially the status of freedom, and in seventeenth-century England all men were free. Servile status, or villeinage by blood, had lingered on as a patent anachronism in the days of Elizabeth, but vanished soon afterwards. This change from servile to free labour has been described by Professor Tawney as 'a high landmark in the development both of economic and political society', and as 'the final triumph of the common law' in regions from which it had been excluded for four centuries. Henceforth the English peasant 'is a member of a society in which there is, nominally at least, one law for all men'. The liberty which his predecessors had won by fleeing into the free towns had become his by right. In the towns the terms 'freedom' and 'citizenship' were interchangeable. When freedom became universal, citizenship grew from a local into a national institution.

The story of political rights is different both in time and in character. The formative period began, as I have said, in the early nineteenth century, where the civil rights attached to the status of freedom had already acquired sufficient substance to justify us in speaking of a general status of citizenship. And, when it began, it consisted, not in the creation of new rights to enrich a status already enjoyed by all, but in the granting of old rights to new sections of the population. [...]

It is clear that, if we maintain that in the nineteenth century citizenship in the form of civil rights was universal, the political franchise was not one of the rights of citizenship. It was the privilege of a limited economic class, whose limits were extended by each successive Reform Act. [...]

It was, as we shall see, appropriate that nineteenth-century capitalist society should treat political rights as a secondary product of civil rights. It was equally appropriate that the twentieth century should abandon this position and attach political rights directly and independently to citizenship as such. This vital change of principle was put into effect when the Act of 1918, by adopting manhood suffrage, shifted the basis of political rights from economic substance to personal status. I say 'manhood' deliberately in order to emphasize the great significance of this reform quite apart from the second, and no less important, reform introduced at the same time — namely the enfranchisement of women. [...]

The original source of social rights was membership of local communities and functional associations. This source was supplemented and progressively replaced by a *Poor Law* and a system of wage regulation which were nationally conceived and locally administered. [...]

As the pattern of the old order dissolved under the blows of a competitive economy, and the plan disintegrated, the Poor Law was left high and dry as an isolated survival from which the idea of social rights was gradually drained away. But at the very end of the eighteenth century there occurred a final struggle between the old and the

new, between the planned (or patterned) society and the competitive economy. And in this battle citizenship was divided against itself; social rights sided with the old and civil with the new. [...]

In this brief episode of our history we see the *Poor Law* as the aggressive champion of the social rights of citizenship. In the succeeding phase we find the attacker driven back far behind his original position. By the Act of 1834 the *Poor Law* renounced all claim to trespass on the territory of the wages system, or to interfere with the forces of the free market. It offered relief only to those who, through age or sickness, were incapable of continuing the battle, and to those other weaklings who gave up the struggle, admitted defeat, and cried for mercy. The tentative move towards the concept of social security was reversed. But more than that, the minimal social rights that remained were detached from the status of citizenship. The *Poor Law* treated the claims of the poor, not as an integral part of the rights of the citizen, but as an alternative to them — as claims which could be met only if the claimants ceased to be citizens in any true sense of the word. For paupers forfeited in practice the civil right of personal liberty, by internment in the workhouse, and they forfeited by law any political rights they might possess. This disability of defranchisement remained in being until 1918, and the significance of its final removal has, perhaps, not been fully appreciated. The stigma which clung to poor relief expressed the deep feelings of a people who understood that those who accepted relief must cross the road that separated the community of citizens from the outcast company of the destitute.

The *Poor Law* is not an isolated example of this divorce of social rights from the status of citizenship. The early *Factory Acts* show the same tendency. Although in fact they led to an improvement of working conditions and a reduction of working hours to the benefit of all employed in the industries to which they applied, they meticulously refrained from giving this protection directly to the adult male — the citizen *par excellence*. And they did so out of respect for his status as a citizen, on the grounds that enforced protective measures curtailed the civil right to conclude a free contract of employment. Protection was confined to women and children, and champions of women's rights were quick to detect the implied insult. Women were protected because they were not citizens. If they wished to enjoy full and responsible citizenship, they must forgo protection. By the end of the nineteenth century such arguments had become obsolete, and the factory code had become one of the pillars in the edifice of social rights. [...]

By the end of the nineteenth century, elementary education was not only free, it was compulsory. This signal [*sic*] departure from *laissez faire* could, of course, be justified on the grounds that free choice is a right only for mature minds, that children are naturally subject to discipline, and that parents cannot be trusted to do what is in the best interests of their children. But the principle goes deeper than that. We have here a personal right combined with a public duty to exercise the right. Is the public duty imposed merely for the benefit of the individual — because children cannot fully appreciate their own interests and parents may be unfit to enlighten them? I hardly think that this can be an adequate explanation. It was increasingly recognized, as the nineteenth century wore on, that political democracy needed an educated electorate, and that scientific manufacture needed educated workers and technicians. The duty to improve and civilize oneself is therefore a social duty, and not merely a personal one, because the social health of a society depends upon the civilization of its members. And a community that enforces this duty has begun to realize that its culture is an organic unity and its civilization a national heritage. It follows that the growth of public elementary education during the nineteenth century was the first decisive step on the road to the reestablishment of the social rights of citizenship in the twentieth. [...]

THE IMPACT OF CITIZENSHIP ON SOCIAL CLASS

Citizenship is a status bestowed on those who are full members of a community. All who possess the status are equal with respect to the rights and duties with which the status is endowed. There is no universal principle that determines what those rights and duties shall be, but societies in which citizenship is a developing institution create an image of an ideal citizenship against which achievement can be measured and towards which aspiration can be directed. The urge forward along the path thus plotted is an urge towards a fuller measure of equality, an enrichment of the stuff of which the status is made and an increase in the number of those on whom the status is bestowed. Social class, on the other hand, is a system of inequality. And it too, like citizenship, can be based on a set of ideals, beliefs and values. It is therefore reasonable to expect that the impact of citizenship on social class should take the form of a conflict between opposing principles. If I am right in my contention that citizenship has been a developing institution in England at least since the latter part of the seventeenth century, then it is clear that its growth coincides with the rise of capitalism, which is a system, not of equality, but of inequality. Here is something that needs explaining. How is it that these two opposing principles could grow and flourish side by side in the same soil? What made it possible for them to be reconciled with one another and to become, for a time at least, allies instead of antagonists? The question is a pertinent one, for it is clear that, in the twentieth century, citizenship and the capitalist class system have been at war. [...]

It is true that class still functions. Social inequality is regarded as necessary and purposeful. It provides the in-

centive to effort and designs the distribution of power. But there is no overall pattern of inequality, in which an appropriate value is attached, *a priori*, to each social level. Inequality, therefore, though necessary, may become excessive. As Patrick Colquhoun said, in a much-quoted passage: 'Without a large proportion of poverty there could be no riches, since riches are the offspring of labour, while labour can result only from a state of poverty.... Poverty therefore is a most necessary and indispensable ingredient in society, without which nations and communities could not exist in a state of civilization. [...]

The more you look on wealth as conclusive proof of merit, the more you incline to regard poverty as evidence of failure — but the penalty for failure may seem to be greater than the offence warrants. In such circumstances it is natural that the more unpleasant features of inequality should be treated, rather irresponsibly, as a nuisance, like the black smoke that used to pour unchecked from our factory chimneys. And so in time, as the social conscience stirs to life, class-abatement, like smoke-abatement, becomes a desirable aim to be pursued as far as is compatible with the continued efficiency of the social machine.

But class-abatement in this form was not an attack on the class system. On the contrary it aimed, often quite consciously, at making the class system less vulnerable to attack by alleviating its less defensible consequences. It raised the floor-level in the basement of the social edifice, and perhaps made it rather more hygienic than it was before. But it remained a basement, and the upper stories of the building were unaffected. [...]

There developed, in the latter part of the nineteenth century, a growing interest in equality as a principle of social justice and an appreciation of the fact that the formal recognition of an equal capacity for rights was not enough. In theory even the complete removal of all the barriers that separated civil rights from their remedies would not have interfered with the principles or the class structure of the capitalist system. It would, in fact, have created a situation which many supporters of the competitive market economy falsely assumed to be already in existence. But in practice the attitude of mind which inspired the efforts to remove these barriers grew out of a conception of equality which overstepped these narrow limits, the conception of equal social worth, not merely of equal natural rights. Thus although citizenship, even by the end of the nineteenth century, had done little to reduce social inequality, it had helped to guide progress into the path which led directly to the egalitarian policies of the twentieth century. [...]

This growing national consciousness, this awakening public opinion, and these first stirrings of a sense of community membership and common heritage did not have any material effect on class structure and social inequality for the simple and obvious reason that, even at the end of the nineteenth century, the mass of the working people did not wield effective political power. By that time the franchise was fairly wide, but those who had recently received the vote had not yet learned how to use it. The political rights of citizenship, unlike the civil rights, were full of potential danger to the capitalist system, although those who were cautiously extending them down the social scale probably did not realize quite how great the danger was. They could hardly be expected to foresee what vast changes could be brought about by the peaceful use of political power, without a violent and bloody revolution. The 'planned society' and the welfare state had not yet risen over the horizon or come within the view of the practical politician. The foundations of the market economy and the contractual system seemed strong enough to stand against any probable assault. In fact, there were some grounds for expecting that the working classes, as they became educated, would accept the basic principles of the system and be content to rely for their protection and progress on the civil rights of citizenship, which contained no obvious menace to competitive capitalism. Such a view was encouraged by the fact that one of the main achievements of political power in the later nineteenth century was the recognition of the right of collective bargaining. This meant that social progress was being sought by strengthening civil rights, not by creating social rights; through the use of contract in the open market, not through a minimum wage and social security.

But this interpretation underrates the significance of this extension of civil rights in the economic sphere. For civil rights were in origin intensely individual, and that is why they harmonized with the individualistic phase of capitalism. By the device of incorporation groups were enabled to act legally as individuals. This important development did not go unchallenged, and limited liability was widely denounced as an infringement of individual responsibility. But the position of trade unions was even more anomalous, because they did not seek or obtain incorporation. They can, therefore, exercise vital civil rights collectively on behalf of their members without formal collective responsibility, while the individual responsibility of the workers in relation to contract is largely unenforceable. These civil rights became, for the workers, an instrument for raising their social and economic status, that is to say, for establishing the claim that they, as citizens, were entitled to certain social rights. But the normal method of establishing social rights is by the exercise of political power, for social rights imply an absolute right to a certain standard of civilization which is conditional only on the discharge of the general duties of citizenship. Their content does not depend on the economic value of the individual claimant. There is therefore a significant difference between a genuine collective bargain through which economic forces in a free market seek to achieve equilibrium and the use of collective civil rights to assert basic claims to the elements of social justice. Thus the acceptance of collective bargaining was not sim-

ply a natural extension of civil rights; it represented the transfer of an important process from the political to the civil sphere of citizenship. But 'transfer' is, perhaps, a misleading term, for at the time when this happened the workers either did not possess, or had not yet learned to use, the political right of the franchise. Since then they have obtained and made full use of that right. Trade unionism has, therefore, created a secondary system of industrial citizenship parallel with and supplementary to the system of political citizenship. [...]

A new period opened at the end of the nineteenth century, conveniently marked by Booth's survey of Life and Labour of the People in London and the Royal Commission on the Aged Poor. It saw the first big advance in social rights, and this involved significant changes in the egalitarian principle as expressed in citizenship. But there were other forces at work as well. A rise of money incomes unevenly distributed over the social classes altered the economic distance which separated these classes from one another, diminishing the gap between skilled and unskilled labour and between skilled labour and non-manual workers, while the steady increase in small savings blurred the class distinction between the capitalist and the property-less proletarian. Secondly, a system of direct taxation, ever more steeply graduated, compressed the whole scale of disposable incomes. Thirdly, mass production for the home market and a growing interest on the part of industry in the needs and tastes of the common people enabled the less well-to-do to enjoy a material civilization which differed less markedly in quality from that of the rich than it had ever done before. All this profoundly altered the setting in which the progress of citizenship took place. Social integration spread from the sphere of sentiment and patriotism into that of material enjoyment. The components of a civilized and cultured life, formerly the monopoly of the few, were brought progressively within reach of the many, who were encouraged thereby to stretch out their hands towards those that still eluded their grasp. The diminution of inequality strengthened the demand for its abolition, at least with regard to the essentials of social welfare.

These aspirations have in part been met by incorporating social rights in the status of citizenship and thus creating a universal right to real income which is not proportionate to the market value of the claimant. Class-abatement is still the aim of social rights, but it has acquired a new meaning. It is no longer merely an attempt to abate the obvious nuisance of destitution in the lowest ranks of society. It has assumed the guise of action modifying the whole pattern of social inequality. It is no longer content to raise the floor-level in the basement of the social edifice, leaving the superstructure as it was. It has begun to remodel the whole building, and it might even end by converting a skyscraper into a bungalow. It is therefore important to consider whether any such ultimate aim is implicit in the nature of this development, or whether, as

I put it at the outset, there are natural limits to the contemporary drive towards greater social and economic equality. [...]

The degree of equalization achieved [by the modern system of welfare benefits] depends on four things; whether the benefit is offered to all or to a limited class; whether it takes the form of money payment or service rendered; whether the minimum is high or low; and how the money to pay for the benefit is raised. Cash benefits subject to income limit and means test had a simple and obvious equalizing effect. They achieved class-abatement in the early and limited sense of the term. The aim was to ensure that all citizens should attain at least to the prescribed minimum, either by their own resources or with assistance if they could not do it without. The benefit was given only to those who needed it, and thus inequalities at the bottom of the scale were ironed out. The system operated in its simplest and most unadulterated form in the case of the *Poor Law* and old age pensions. But economic equalization might be accompanied by psychological class discrimination. The stigma which attached to the *Poor Law* made 'pauper' a derogatory term defining a class. 'Old age pensioner' may have had a little of the same flavour, but without the taint of shame. [...]

The extension of the social services is not primarily a means of equalizing incomes. In some cases it may, in others it may not. The question is relatively unimportant; it belongs to a different department of social policy. What matters is that there is a general enrichment of the concrete substance of civilized life, a general reduction of risk and insecurity, an equalization between the more and the less fortunate at all levels — between the healthy and the sick, the employed and the unemployed, the old and the active, the bachelor and the father of a large family. Equalization is not so much between classes as between individuals within a population which is now treated for this purpose as though it were one class. Equality of status is more important than equality of income. [...]

I said earlier that in the twentieth century citizenship and the capitalist class system have been at war. Perhaps the phrase is rather too strong, but it is quite clear that the former has imposed modifications on the latter. But we should not be justified in assuming that, although status is a principle that conflicts with contract, the stratified status system which is creeping into citizenship is an alien element in the economic world outside. Social rights in their modern form imply an invasion of contract by status, the subordination of market price to social justice, the replacement of the free bargain by the declaration of rights. But are these principles quite foreign to the practice of the market today, or are they there already, entrenched within the contract system itself? I think it is clear that they are. [...]

CONCLUSIONS

I have tried to show how citizenship, and other forces outside it, have been altering the pattern of social inequality. [...] We have to look, here, for the combined effects of three factors. First, the compression, at both ends, of the scale of income distribution. Second, the great extension of the area of common culture and common experience. And third, the enrichment of the universal status of citizenship, combined with the recognition and stabilization of certain status differences chiefly through the linked systems of education and occupation. [...]

I asked, at the beginning, whether there was any limit to the present drive towards social equality inherent in the principles governing the movement. My answer is that the preservation of economic inequalities has been made more difficult by the enrichment of the status of citizenship. There is less room for them, and there is more and more likelihood of their being challenged. But we are certainly proceeding at present on the assumption that the hypothesis is valid. And this assumption provides the answer to the second question. We are not aiming at absolute equality. There are limits inherent in the egalitarian movement. But the movement is a double one. It operates partly through citizenship and partly through the economic system. In both cases the aim is to remove inequalities which cannot be regarded as legitimate, but the standard of legitimacy is different. In the former it is the standard of social justice, in the latter it is social justice combined with economic necessity. It is possible, therefore, that the inequalities permitted by the two halves of the movement will not coincide. Class distinctions may survive which have no appropriate economic function, and economic differences which do not correspond with accepted class distinctions. [...]

Left and Rights[†]
S. Hall and D. Held

'CITIZENSHIP' has been largely absent from political discussion and debate for more than two decades. Only in relation to questions of race and immigration did it carry a deep political charge. Were the boundaries of citizenship to be redrawn with the end of empire? Could there be more than one class of citizenship for people of different ethnic backgrounds? The debate, crowned by the intervention of Enoch Powell in the late 1960s, marked a high point in the political currency of this dimension of citizenship. Elsewhere, the concept seemed rather out-of-date. Suddenly, however, citizenship is once more on the lips of politicians, academics and commentators of all political complexions. Why this renewed concern? What is at stake in this debate about citizenship between Right and Left?

A number of different factors seem to be responsible for the return of citizenship to the political agenda. Some derive from the experience of Thatcherism itself: the dismantling of the welfare state, the growing centralisation of power, the erosion of local democracy, of free speech, trade-union and other civil rights.

Some have a wider, more 'global', context: the growth of regional nationalism in Scotland and elsewhere; the prospects for greater European integration; the weakening of the old East-West frontiers under the Gorbachev offensive; the growing pace of international interdependence and globalisation — all, in one way or another, exposing and eroding the sovereignty of the nation-state, the entity to which, until now, the modern language of citizenship primarily referred.

These changes have been accompanied by shifts in attitude towards the idea of citizenship on both the Right and the Left. It used to be fashionable in some sections of the Left to dismiss the question of 'rights' as, largely, a bourgeois fraud. But the experience of Thatcherism in the West and of stalinism in the East has gradually shifted the Left's thinking on this question. The shift on the Right is more complex and uncertain. Thatcherism's drive towards unrestricted private accumulation, its attack on public expenditure, collectivism and the 'dependency culture' made it the natural enemy of citizenship in its modern, welfare-state form. As the prime minister put it: 'There is no such thing as society, only individual men and women and their families.'

However, this unswerving commitment to individualism and the competitive ethic has awakened, in its turn, the spectre of Hobbes' 'war of all against all': the breakdown of a sense of community and interdependence, the weakening of the social fabric and the loosening of the bounds of social violence — so often features of a society dedicated exclusively to competitive self-interest. Thatcherism has therefore rediscovered the need for some concept to help integrate and 'bind' society and has come up with the idea of the 'active citizen', who engages in 'doing good' but in a purely private capacity. In this discourse, citizenship is detached from its modern roots in institutional reform, in the welfare state and community struggles, and rearticulated with the more Victorian concepts of charity, philanthropy and self-help. In more recent versions, the 'active citizen' is decked out in the pious homilies of Thatcherism's version of the New Testament.

Clearly, we need a framework for thinking about citizenship and its place in the agenda of the Left which sets it in the context of recent developments. Far from simply returning us to the old language of citizenship, such an exercise requires us to confront new questions and to rethink the concept itself in the light of a new historical situation.

Does 'citizenship' belong, naturally and exclusively, to the Left? It has been part of what can broadly be identified as a variety of progressive historical movements — from older ideas of a just moral order to Paine's *Rights of Man* and Chartism. Nevertheless, it seems to be the case that citizenship belongs *exclusively* to neither Right nor Left, nor indeed to centre-ground. Like all the key contested political concepts of our time, it can be appropriated within very different political discourses and articulated to very different political positions — as its recuperation by the new Right clearly shows. The concept can only mean something decisive for the Left if we are prepared to do some theoretical and political work around it, actively integrating it within a whole set of related political ideas.

While there is no 'essence' to citizenship, it does have a long and rich history with which any new conception must come to terms. From the ancient world to the present day, citizenship has entailed a discussion of, and a struggle over, the meaning and scope of membership of the community in which one lives. Who belongs and what does 'belonging' mean in practice? Membership, here, is not conditional: it is a matter of right and entitlement. But it is two-sided, reciprocal: rights in, but also responsibilities towards, the community. These rights have to be defined and specified, because otherwise their loss cannot be chal-

---

† Hall, Stuart, and Held, David, "Left and Rights" (June, 1989), 33(b) *Marxism Today* 16–23. Reprinted by permission of the Statesman Newspaper and Society, U.K.

lenged, and may even go undetected. But formal definition alone will not suffice. Rights can be mere paper claims unless they can be practically enacted and realised, through actual participation in the community. These then are citizenship's three leading notions: membership; rights and duties in reciprocity; real participation in practice.

The issues around membership — who does and who does not belong — is where the *politics* of citizenship begins. It is impossible to chart the history of the concept very far without coming sharply up against successive attempts to restrict citizenship to certain groups and to exclude others. In different historical periods, different groups have led, and profited from this 'politics of closure': property-owners, men, white people, the educated, those in particular occupations or with particular skills, adults. However, as the struggles against exclusion have developed and broadened across history, so those stemming from the exclusive enjoyment of the advantages of property, ownership, wealth and privilege — in short, questions of *class* — have come to dominate the 'politics of citizenship', absorbing a wide variety of different struggles against different forms of exclusion under their rubric.

Certainly, class has constituted, historically, one of the most powerful and ramified of barriers to membership and participation by the majority. But this has also set up a tension within the idea of citizenship itself. For, as the politics of citizenship has been absorbed into class politics, so the citizenship idea has lost something of its specific force.

However, this exclusive reference to class is one of the things which is changing with the renewed interest in citizenship. In reality, attempts to restrict membership and participation take many different forms, involving different practices of exclusion and affecting different groups. This should be enough to convince us that questions of citizenship, though bound to place the issues of class at their centre, cannot simply be absorbed into class politics, or thought of exclusively in class terms, and in relation to capitalist relations of production.

A contemporary 'politics of citizenship' must take into account the role which the social movements have played in *expanding* the claims to rights and entitlements to new areas. It must address not only issues of class and inequality, but also questions of membership posed by feminism, the black and ethnic movements, ecology (including the moral claims of the animal species and of Nature itself) and vulnerable minorities, like children. But it must also come to terms with the problems posed by 'difference' in a deeper sense: for example, the diverse communities to which we belong, the complex interplay of identity and identification in modern society, and the differentiated ways in which people now participate in social life. The diversity of arenas in which citizenship is being claimed and contested today is essential to any mod-

ern conception of it because it is inscribed in the very logic of modern society itself.

However, this expansion of the idea of citizenship may run counter to the logic of citizenship, which has tended to absorb 'differences' into one common universal status — the citizen. In the year of the anniversary of the French Revolution, it is worth recalling that its three cardinal principles — liberty, equality and fraternity — formed a matrix within which the citizens of the new Republic claimed *universal* recognition on the basis of a common *equality*. This language of theoretical universality and equality is what distinguished this moment — the moment of the 'Rights of Man' — from earlier phases in the long march of citizenship. But in the light of the expansion and diversity of claims discussed above, the question must be posed as to whether the variety and range of entitlements can be adequately expressed through or represented by a single, universal status like 'citizenship'. Is there now an irreconcilable tension between the thrust to equality and universality entailed in the very idea of the 'citizen', and the variety of particular and specific needs, of diverse sites and practices which constitute the modern political subject?

We will come back to this question of 'difference' later — it is, in some ways, the joker in the citizenship pack. However, what the previous discussion makes clear is that contemporary claims to citizenship are interrelated with a range of other political questions. What we think about this range of political questions will inevitably affect what we think about citizenship itself.

What does the language of citizenship rights really mean in contemporary society? And who are the subjects of such rights? Citizenship rights are *entitlements*. Such entitlements are public and social (hence Mrs. Thatcher's difficulties with them). They are 'of right' and can only be abrogated by the state under clearly delimited circumstances (e.g., in the case of imprisonment, which curtails liberties which all citizens should otherwise enjoy). However, though citizenship is a social status, its rights are entitlements to individuals. Individual citizens enjoy such entitlements on the basis of a fundamental equality of condition — i.e., their membership of the community.

Citizenship rights establish a legitimate sphere for *all* individuals to pursue their actions and activities without risk of arbitrary or unjust political interference. Early attempts to achieve citizenship involved a struggle for the autonomy or independence of individuals from the locale in which they were born and from prescribed occupations. Later struggles have involved such things as individual entitlement to freedom of speech, expression, belief, information, as well as the freedom of association on which trade-union rights depend, and freedom of women in relation to marriage and property. Citizenship rights can therefore be thought of as a measure of the autonomy an individual citizen enjoys as a result of his or her status as 'free and equal' members of a society. The other important feature is that, though they are guaranteed to citizens by the state, they are also, in an important sense, guaranteed *against* the arbitrary exercise of state power. Citizenship in its full sense therefore combines, in rather unusual ways, the public and the social with the individual aspects of political life.

The left critique of this position is by now quite familiar, and carries considerable weight. It centres on the emphasis, in the language of rights, on *individual* entitlement. There are really three strands to this critique. First, the degree to which individuals really are 'free' in capitalist democracies is open to question. Second, everything depends on how freedom is defined. The rights and freedoms which interest the new Right refer to a very narrow arena of social action, and are constructed around a very limited conception of individual needs and desires. Largely, these are restricted to individuals as isolated atoms, acting in their own interests, maximised through exchange in the marketplace. Rights are not considered to have a social dimension or an interdependent character. Third, citizenship rights, particularly in Britain, are largely defined negatively. There are no laws preventing you entering the Ritz or buying property in Docklands or applying for most jobs. Whether in fact you have the means or the capacity to do or achieve any of those things, positively, is a quite different matter. In the famous words of Anatole France: 'The law in its majestic equality gives every man (prince and pauper alike) an equal right to sleep under a bridge or eat at the Ritz.'

This is really another way of restating the Left's critique of classic liberalism in terms of the tension between 'formal' and 'substantive' rights. The citizen may formally enjoy 'equality before the law'. But, important though this unquestionably is, does he or she *also* have the material and cultural resources to choose between different courses of action in practice? The 'free and equal individual', as one commentator suggests, is a person found more rarely in practice, than liberal theory suggests. What liberal theory, in both its classic and contemporary forms, takes for granted has, in fact, to be seriously questioned. Namely, whether the existing relations between men and women, between employers and employees, between the social classes, or blacks, whites and other ethnic groups, allow citizenship to become a reality in practice.

This question lies at the centre of the 'politics of citizenship' today. Any current assessment of citizenship must be made on the basis of liberties and rights which are tangible, capable of being enjoyed, in both the state and civil society. If it is not given concrete and practical content, liberty as an abstract principle can scarcely be said to have any very profound consequences for everyday life. It is difficult to hymn the praises of liberty, when massive numbers of actual individuals are systematically restricted — for want of a complex mix of resources and opportunities — from participating actively in political and civil life. Gross inequality of class, sex and race substantively hinder the

extent to which it can legitimately be claimed that individuals are really 'free and equal' in contemporary society.

There is therefore, much of substance to the Left's critique of the liberal conception of citizenship. On the other hand, this may have led us to go too far in the opposite direction. We must test every 'formal' right we are supposed to enjoy against its substance in practice. But this does not mean that the formal definition of rights — for example, in a constitution or bill of rights — is unimportant, or a matter of 'mere form'. Until rights have been specified, there is no way of monitoring their infringement or of calling to account their practical implementation.

In general, what this discussion suggests is that the 'politics of citizenship' today must come to terms with, and attempt to strike a new balance between, the individual and the social dimensions of citizenship rights. These two aspects are interdependent and cannot be separated. Neither, on its own, will suffice. On the other hand, there is no *necessary* contradiction between them.

The new Right would argue exactly the opposite, and this is one reason why the relationship between the individual and the social dimensions of rights becomes one of the key issues at stake in exchanges between the new Right and its left critics. The new Right has a very clear and consistent position on the question and the related issues of freedom and equality.

The new Right is committed to the classic liberal doctrine that the collective good can be properly realised in most cases *only* by private individuals acting in competitive isolation, pursuing their interests with minimal state interference. At root, the new Right is concerned with how to advance the cause of 'liberalism' against 'democracy' (or, as they put it, 'freedom' against 'equality') by limiting the possible uses of state power. On this view, the government can only legitimately intervene in society to enforce *general rules* — formal rules which broadly protect, in John Locke's works, the 'life, liberty and estate' of the citizen. Hayek, a leading advocate of these ideas, argues that a free liberal order is incompatible with rules which specify how people should use the means at their disposal. Governments become coercive if they interfere with people's capacity to determine their own objectives. Hence the reliance in Hayek's work on 'law', his critique of the so-called 'totalitarianism' involved in social planning and rejection of the idea that the state can represent the 'public interest'.

Hayek's prime example of coercive government is legislation which attempts to alter the 'material position of particular people or enforce distributive or "social" justice'. Distributive justice, he argues, always imposes on some person or group someone else's conception of merit or desert. It requires the allocation of resources by a central authority acting as *if* it knew what people should receive for their efforts or how to behave. In this view, there is only one mechanism sufficiently sensitive to determine collective choice on an individual basis without such imposition —

the free market. When protected by a constitutional state and a framework of law, it is argued, no system provides a mechanism of collective choice as dynamic, innovative and responsive. The free market is, for the new Right, the key condition of the liberty of citizens. When operating within the framework of a minimal state, it thus becomes constitutive of the nature of citizenship itself.

The Left has always taken issue with this line of argument. The free market, it has argued, produces and reinforces those very forms of exclusion and 'closure' associated with private property and wealth, against which the idea of citizenship was directed. Hence, through the redistributive welfare state, the prerogatives of property and wealth had to be cross-cut, modified or, in T.H. Marshall's famous phrase, 'abated', by the countervailing rights of citizenship. In practice, the only force of sufficiently compelling weight to bring to bear against the powers of property and capital was that of the state. Hence, for the Left, the state was not inimical but essential to the very idea of citizenship.

It is indeed difficult to see how a proper conception of citizenship could be established or effectively secured without the intervention of the state. On the other hand, it is not necessary to accept Hayek's line of reasoning to see that citizenship also entails the protection of the citizen *against* the arbitrary overweening exercise of state power. The weaknesses and limitations of a purely 'statist' conception of citizenship have become much more obvious in the light of recent history.

There is, then, an inevitable tension in the Left's position on citizenship, since it both requires and can be threatened by the state. One tendency of the Left has been to resolve or bypass this difficulty by, so to speak, dissolving the whole question into that of democracy itself. The extension of popular democracy, it is thought, will resolve all these knotty problems. Hence the Left's advocacy of collective participation as a resolution to all the problems of citizenship. Why bother to define and entrench specific rights if, in an expanded democracy, every individual is destined to become 'fully sovereign'? Thus, by focusing squarely on the extension of democracy, the Left has tended to leave any further specification of particular citizenship rights, and the complex relations between liberty, social justice and democratic processes, to the ebb and flow of democratic negotiation. From Karl Marx to Lenin to Roy Hattersley (in his recent defence of Labour Party policy against Charter 88) this is a constant and recurring theme. 'The people' are to become sovereign (via, respectively, the Commune, Soviets, Parliament). 'The people' are to become governors of their own affairs — without limit; so the argument runs. Within this broad democratic advance, the specific questions of citizenship and the difficulty of defining particular rights will take care of themselves.

This 'democratic' solution is in many ways an attractive argument. But it presents certain real difficulties. It is vulnerable to the charge of having failed to address the highly complex relations in modern societies between individual liberty, distributional questions of social justice, and democratic processes. It does not really resolve the question of who 'the people' are whose democratic sovereignty and enfranchisement is supposed to settle at a single stroke so many questions about particular rights. And it poses the extremely awkward issue of whether there are to be any specifiable limits to democracy. In short, is 'democracy' alone, unsupplemented and unmodified by any concept of citizenship any longer enough?

Should there be any limits on the power of 'the people' to change or alter political circumstances? The experience of 10 years of 'elective dictatorship' under Mrs. Thatcher may have changed the Left's thinking on this question. For example, should the winning of a majority vote at an election constitute a mandate to destroy parts of the system of local government which has been so important a counterweight to the encroaching powers of a centralising state — especially if achieved under our highly lopsided, first-past-the-post electoral system? Should the nature and scope of the liberty of individuals be left entirely to the 'play' of democratic decision? Don't individuals need to have their rights to freedom of speech, thought and expression protected? Must minorities conform, simply because they are minorities?

By answering questions about the necessary limits to democracy in the affirmative, the new Right at least recognises the possibility of real tensions between individual liberty, collective decision-making and the institutions and processes of democracy. By not systematically addressing these issues, the Left, in contrast, has perhaps too hastily put aside the problems. In making democracy, at all levels, the primary social objective to be achieved, the Left has relied on 'democratic reason' — a wise and good democratic will — for the determination of all just and positive social outcomes. But can 'the people' always be relied upon to be just to minorities or to marginal and so-called 'unpopular' interests? Can one assume that the democratic will will always be wise and good?

This is not a matter of abstract theoretical debate. It is around some of these tensions that the new Right generated so much political capital against the Left. It forced the Left to acknowledge the uncertain outcomes of democratic life: the ambiguous results of the welfare state, for example. It highlighted the fact that distributive justice can also lead to bureaucracy, surveillance and the excessive infringement of individual options (and not only in Eastern Europe). It represented the reallocation of resources by the local state (for example, in the form of 'equal opportunities' and 'anti-racist programmes') as an imposition of minority interests on the majority! These experiences have not necessarily made people more optimistic about collective democratic decision-making or more ready to fight to defend it.

Take the question of 'popular sovereignty'. Will the fact that we are all members of the great, collective democratic subject — 'the people' — provide a guarantee of the rights and the liberties of the individual citizen? Not necessarily. 'The people' is, after all, also a discursive figure, a rhetorical device, a mode of address. It is open to constant negotiation, contestation and redefinition. It represents, as a 'unity', what are in fact a diversity of different positions and interests. In its populist form — 'giving the people what they want' — it has been exploited by Thatcherism as a form of populist mobilisation against a range of different minorities who are 'not one of us'.

'The people' has also functioned so as to silence or marginalise the conflicts of interest which it claims to represent. Thatcherism has operated within a narrow and exclusive definition of 'the people'. It defines 'the people' as those who identify with or have done well out of the enterprise culture. But since, in reality, only a small number of prosperous people, mainly living in parts of the south east, can be represented in this figure, it is in effect a way of suppressing the rights, marginalising the needs and denying the identities of large numbers of other 'people' — including the Scots, the poor, the unemployed, the homeless, the underclasses, black people, many women, single-parent mothers, gay and lesbian people, and so on. Far from resolving anything, it is a highly-contested and contestable idea, around which a great deal of 'ideological work' is constantly going on.

Then there is the problem of what political entity the citizen is a citizen *of*. Everywhere, the nation-state itself — the entity to which the language of political citizenship refers — is eroded and challenged. The processes of economic, political, military and ecological interdependence are beginning to undermine it as a sovereign, self-contained entity from above. The rise of regional and local 'nationalisms' are beginning to erode it from below. In certain respects, this may have negative consequences for citizenship: how to give effect to the 'rights' of the citizens of Bhopal against chemical pollution caused by a multinational company registered in New York and operating worldwide? In other respects, its consequences for citizenship may be positive. The European Court has certainly provided a critical bulwark for the citizen of the UK against the steady erosion of civil liberties under Thatcherism. But whether these processes work to the advantage or disadvantage of citizenship, the question remains: is this the right moment, historically, to be trying to define claims and entitlements made in terms of membership of the nation-state?

There are then all kinds of problems which undermine any certainty that greater democracy will, in and of itself, resolve the dilemmas of citizenship. Is there any way through this impasse?

One point which does follow directly from the foregoing discussion can be stated clearly, and provides us with a fresh start. There is a need to think through, and

give institutional expression to the demands of citizenship and democracy as closely-related issues: but it is important to keep these questions distinct. Democracy can only really exist on the basis of 'free and equal citizens'. But citizenship requires some specification, and some institutional and political protection, separate from and beyond the extension of democracy. In short, in the relationship between citizenship and democracy is entailed a new balance — a new settlement — between liberty and equality.

Can the parameters of such a 'new settlement' be further specified? It appears that a plausible resolution of some of the dilemmas of contemporary politics can only be provided if enhanced political participation is embedded in a legal and constitutional framework that protects and nurtures individuals and other social categories as 'free and equal citizens'. However, to go down that road has some real political consequences. It requires us, for example, to recognise the importance of a number of fundamental tenets, often dismissed because of their association with liberalism; for example, the centrality, in principle of an 'impersonal' structure of public power; to guarantee and protect rights; a diversity of power centres, both within the state and outside it, in civil society; mechanisms to promote open debate between alternative political platforms; an institutional framework of enforceable and challengeable rights.

In many countries, West and East, the limits of 'government' are explicitly defined in constitutions and bill of rights which are subject to public scrutiny, parliamentary review and judicial process. The Left has sometimes been impatient with this procedural approach — and it is certainly true that no written constitution or judicial review, alone, has been able to guarantee the rights of the citizen against a state which is determined to abolish or reduce them. Nevertheless, the experience of recent history suggests that this idea is fundamental to democracy, conceived as a process which bites deep into the structure of state and society. Constitutional entrenchment, however, is not enough. Any conception of democracy which seeks to elaborate it as a form of 'socialist pluralism' requires the limits on the 'public power' to be reassessed in relation to a far broader range of issues than had been hitherto commonly presupposed.

What would be included in such an expanded system of rights? A constitution or bill of rights which enshrined the idea of the 'double focus' of citizenship — equal rights and equal practices — would have to specify rights with respect to the *processes* that determine outcomes. Thus, not only equal rights to cast a vote, but also to enjoy the conditions of political understanding, involvement in collective decision-making and setting of the political agenda which make the vote meaningful. These conditions for real political participation include, rights with respect to information, education, the 'right to know', including the defence of the right to make public things which governments prefer to keep under official restriction. There would have to be a bundle of social rights linked to reproduction, childcare and health; and economic rights to ensure adequate economic and financial resources for a citizen's autonomy. Without tough social and economic rights, rights with respect to the state could not be enjoyed in practice; and without rights in respect of the state, new forms of inequality of power, wealth and status could systematically disrupt the implementation of social and economic liberties.

For example, a right to reproductive freedom for women entails making public authorities responsible not only for medical and social facilities to prevent or assist pregnancy, but also for providing the material conditions which help to make the choice to have a child a genuinely free one. A right to the capacity really to choose between courses of action obliges the state to implement ways of distributing wealth and income much more equitably. One way of making such resources available may be a guaranteed minimum income for all adults, irrespective of whether they are engaged in wage or household-labour. Strategies of this type have to be treated with caution since their implications for collective or societal wealth-creation are complex and not fully clear. However, without a minimum guaranteed resource-base, many people will remain highly vulnerable and dependent on the charity or goodwill of others — a condition which, despite Mrs. Thatcher's passion for replacing welfare rights with private philanthropy, is in contradiction with the very idea of citizenship.

Such a system of rights must specify certain responsibilities of the state to groups of citizens which particular governments could not (unless permitted by an explicit process of constitutional amendment) override. The authority of the state — even of a much more democratic one than we enjoy at the moment — would thus, in principle, be clearly circumscribed; its capacity for freedom of action to a certain degree bounded. This challenges some fundamental assumptions still widely held on the Left.

We would go further. The important point about such a constitution or bill of rights would be that it radically enhances the ability of citizens to take action *against* the state (including a socialist state) to redress unreasonable encroachments on liberties. This would help tip the balance from state to parliament and from parliament to citizens. It would be an 'empowering' system, breaking with any assumption that the state can successfully define citizens' wants and needs for them, and become the 'caretaker of existence'. It would redefine the balance between state and civil society, which is at the heart of so much rethinking, from Left and Right alike.

Of course, empowerment would not thereby be guaranteed. But rights could be fought for by individuals, groups and movements and could be tested in, among other places, open court. The American system makes it clear that this can lead to interminable wrangles, social change getting delayed and bogged down in 'due process' within

the system. On the other hand, the *European Convention on Human Rights* has been a better defence of civil liberties than Britain's more venerable, customary arrangements. On balance, the gains from going in this direction are preferable to the present situation where it is extremely difficult to bring our archaic state system, operating so much of the time on the basis of undefined 'club' rules, to any open accountability.

Enter Charter 88. Charter 88 is rightly concerned with enshrining the rights and liberties of British subjects in a bill of rights and a constitution — and thereby making them 'citizens' for the first time in their history. The Charter is an immediate and practical intervention in current political discussion of the first importance and, as such, is to be welcomed and endorsed. But, if the argument above is correct, then it is a necessary but not a sufficient means for people to establish themselves in their capacity as citizens. In the contexts of the long-term struggle for socialism, it can be seen as one, but only one, essential moment in the elaboration of a diverse range of new rights and their conditions of existence.

The question of difference, however, which we discussed earlier, raises much deeper, more troubling issues, which are not easily resolved in the short term. Older European ideas of citizenship assumed a more culturally-homogeneous population, within the framework of a strong and unitary national state. It seemed appropriate, therefore, to believe that widening the democratic franchise and participation of all citizens would naturally enlarge the freedoms, rights and liberties of everyone.

But social and cultural identities have become more diversified and 'pluralised' in modern society. The modern nation-state is increasingly composed of groups with very different ethnic and cultural identities. Many of these groups belong to other histories, cultures and traditions very different from those of the indigenous people. These cultural differences are crucial to their sense of identity, identification and 'belongingness'. Similar differences are also beginning to show through in the communities and regions which originally constituted the United Kingdom. These differences present new challenges to, and produce new tensions within, what we called earlier the 'universalising' thrust in the idea of citizenship.

Of course, permanent residents in the society, whatever their differences of origin, history and culture, must be able to claim common rights and entitlements, as full members of the political community, without giving up their cultural identities. This is a key entitlement in any modern conception of citizenship — especially in societies whose populations are increasingly culturally and ethnically diverse. But this may not resolve all the problems. Differences of all kinds will continue to create *special and particular* needs, over and above those which can be addressed within a universalistic conception of citizenship. As the Rushdie affair demonstrates, it is not always possible to keep universal political claims and particularly cultural ones in separate compartments. They keep overlapping and invading each other's territory.

The politics of citizenship, in sum, throws us into the deep end of some very profound, general, theoretical concerns about politics as well as posing a set of complex organisational issues. To think it through — a project only just beginning — we need to attend to both dimensions. The elements of equality and universality associated with the idea of 'the citizen', and the diverse and particular requirements of different groups which have to be met if they are to enjoy 'free and equal' status, demand that the Left clarify, more profoundly than it has so far, both the principles of the politics of citizenship and their institutional requirements. What is at stake is nothing less than reformulating socialism to take better account of 'citizenship' and the conditions and limits this imposes on state action and political strategy.

The Legalisation of Politics in Advanced Capitalism: The Canadian Charter of Rights and Freedoms[†]
H.J. Glasbeek and M. Mandel

THE ENTRENCHMENT OF THE CHARTER AND THE EMERGENCE OF THE COURT

As recently as 1977, the leading Canadian constitutional law treatise stated that, despite the lack of entrenched guarantees,

...[i]t is a fact, however, that in Canada — as in the United Kingdom, Australia and New Zealand — civil liberties are better respected than in most other countries.[1]

This opinion was echoed by constitutional lawyers and civil libertarians up to and before that time.[2] While this does not prove that Canadians did have all the rights and freedoms they might have wanted, it does demonstrate that conventional wisdom sensed no serious lack of protection for individuals in Canada. Yet, a mere five years later, a *Charter of Rights and Freedoms* was entrenched in the Canadian *Constitution* to the applause of most of the same conventional wisdomeers.

The entrenchment is supposed to ensure that certain rights and freedoms will not be taken from individuals by acts of government. This is to be provided by giving the judiciary the power to disallow government action which infringes the rights and freedoms entrenched. Thus, the judiciary has been given a central role to play in Canadian socio-political affairs, beyond the role of umpire between the two levels of government. It has become a recognised participant. There had been no public demand for this change. Indeed, the process of constitutional rearrangement was remarkable for the lack of popular participation.[3] Given that the entrenchment of rights and freedoms was not a response to either a series of triggering events or to a palpable public demand, we may search for its origins in political economy.

. . . .

This is of interest because the judiciary has always had implicit opportunities and, with the *Bill of Rights*, was given some encouragement to enforce human rights and freedoms in Canada well before the entrenchment of the *Charter*. The inhibition demonstrated by the courts raises two issues. First, why would it ever be thought useful to make that very judiciary, whose record on human rights and freedoms was anything but progressive, the dominant means of safe-guarding civil liberties? Second, why would an historically reluctant judiciary play a major role in the creation of this very situation, one in which it would be asked to play a role it had up to then abjured?

. . . .

THE LEGALISATION OF POLITICS

The *Charter of Rights and Freedoms* grants to the judiciary a supervisory role over legislation and government activity in general. It constitutes a substantial step in a modern trend towards giving the judiciary a central role in Canadian politics. What view should socialists take of

† Glasbeek, Harry J., and Mandel, Michael, "The Legalisation of Politics in Advanced Capitalism: The Canadian Charter of Rights and Freedoms" (1984), 2 *Socialist Studies* at 84, 88, 95–101, 103–04, 106–09, 115 and footnotes in 119–24. Reprinted by permission of Society for Socialist Studies, Economics, Labour Studies, University of Manitoba.

this development? Two possible criteria for appraisal suggest themselves, analogous to Wright's distinction between immediate and fundamental interests of the working class.[4] While it is notorious that these interests may conflict, in that reform in the immediate interests of working people may indeed prolong the existence of capitalism, this is not always the case. Marx argued convincingly that legislative limitations on the hours of work were both in workers' immediate and fundamental interests.[5] Is the *Charter* such a "reform"? What, if anything, does it do for workers, either in the long or the short run? We want briefly to review a number of traditional approaches to *Bills of Rights* which can be adapted to this perspective, before coming to what we believe to be the main point.

The "Content" of Judicial Review

One approach is to analyse judicial review in terms of the "content" of court decisions. Are the courts likely to make more or less progressive decisions than legislatures? Are they likely to cause legislatures to make more or less progressive laws? One way of answering these questions is to look at the historical record. As we have seen, the Canadian Supreme Court's record under the *Canadian Bill of Rights* is one of deference to the federal Parliament. On the other hand, it might be argued that decisions concerning the *Bill of Rights* are not a good test because of the *Bill's* "non-constitutional" nature. To this it could be said that the courts had power to give it much more reach than they did. Such arguments are inconclusive.

The long experience in the United States with an entrenched *Bill of Rights* provides a richer testing ground. But the record there is, at the very best, equivocal. Proponents of the *Charter* as a potentially progressive tool might cite the desegregation decisions, starting with *Brown v. Board of Education of Topeka* in 1954,[6] and the pro-abortion decision of *Roe v. Wade* in 1973.[7] On the other hand, the period of time which elapsed between these two cases seems to be the only really progressive one in the Supreme Court's entire 200 year history. Its most active period other than that one (that is to say, active in the enforcement of the *Bill of Rights* against legislation, as opposed to activism in respect of issues of federalism) was one in which it fought a vigorous rear-guard action on behalf of laissez-faire capitalism against the regulation of business between 1900 and 1937. The Court struck down hard-fought-for maximum hours, minimum wage, child labour and anti-trust legislation, and so on, until the confrontation with Roosevelt in 1937, after it had "cut the heart from the New Deal Program":[8]

> There is no way of estimating reliably the restraining effect of this cloud of negativisms on state legislators and congressmen who might otherwise have made haste more speedily along the

road to the welfare state. No doubt the pace of social change was moderated; a respectable number of "excesses" were prevented; a respectable amount of money was saved for the businessmen; a good many labourers were left a little hungrier than they might have been if the Court had not been there to defend economic liberty.[9]

More recently, the Supreme Court of the United States has invalidated legislation limiting corporate spending in political campaigns as an infringement on "freedom of speech"[10] and local affirmative action programmes intended to benefit historically deprived racial minorities as an infringement of "equal protection of the law".[11] Then, there have been numerous instances throughout its history when the Supreme Court has merely sanctioned reactionary legislation. Famous examples include *Plessy v. Ferguson*,[12] which upheld legislation requiring blacks to ride in separate railway cars, the genesis of the "separate but equal doctrine" that stood for sixty years until Brown;[13] the *Korematsu* case[14] in 1945, sustaining removal of Japanese-Americans from their homes to internment camps without proof of anti-government activity by them; and, more recently, decisions sustaining legislation withholding medicare for abortions[15] even where medically necessary.[16] These are all examples of how weak a protector of even "bourgeois" liberty a judicially enforced *Bill of Rights* is. To suppose, on the basis of this record, that a court administering the *Charter* would be likely to launch an attack on the dominant relations of production, even without "property" enshrined therein (for now), would be naive. Moreover, there is nothing in the historical record to indicate that courts will protect those crucial political rights of criticism and dissent to which we are theoretically entitled, even under capitalism. During the prelude to the McCarthy period the *Bill of Rights* did not prevent the Supreme Court of the United States from upholding criminal convictions against Communists because they were Communists.[17] And when, during the same period, an otherwise qualified Canadian candidate was refused admission to the Bar on the sole ground that he was a Communist, none other than Judge C.H. O'Halloran, the Canadian advocate of an entrenched *Bill of Rights* mentioned earlier, approved of the action, notwithstanding the value he put on the principle (entrenched or not) of freedom of speech, thought or opinion:

> Freedom of expression cannot be given to Communists to permit them to use it to destroy our constitutional liberties, by first poisoning the minds of the young, the impressionable, and the irresponsible.

. . . .

408

[I]n Canada the accepted and non-technical use of the term "political opinions" is not related to the philosophies underlying different systems of Government, but is directed to adherence to or acceptance of the policies of a political party that upholds the constitution and is not subversive in its programme and tendencies.[18]

Nor did the freedom of speech clause in the American *Constitution* prevent the United States from denying the Marxist Ernest Mandel admission to the country for a speaking engagement, long after the McCarthy period had ended.[19]

Horrible though these decisions may seem, they are in no sense aberrations, though there are counter-examples in very different circumstances (besides cases like *Buckley*) where the courts have defended species of political freedom.[20]

The Enforceability of Judicial Decisions

There is also the problem of what one wins when one wins progressive court decisions, since they do not, after all, enforce themselves:

In 1955, the U.S. Supreme Court, in "Brown II", ordered that Topeka's schools racially desegregate "with all deliberate speed". Presently a federal district court judge is examining Topeka's schools to determine if they are in compliance with that original 1955 decision. Yet this remarkable fact should not surprise us, for in substantive areas as diverse as desegregation, school prayer, and criminal procedure, voluminous impact studies consistently informed us throughout this twenty-five year period of the difficulties encountered in implementing judicial decisions that mandate policy reform and social change.[21]

Enforcement depends on the alignment of real flesh-and-blood social forces, which are much more likely to be in favour of the overruled legislation than vice-versa. Indeed, more than one commentator has noticed that the abortion victories in the American courts in the seventies did more for the "pro-life" movement than for the pro-choice movement. While the legal victories "did not significantly move public opinion toward greater acceptance of abortion", they "triggered almost immediately a strong counterreaction, and the generation of a broad-based, well-organized right-to-life movement" which "gained political momentum throughout the 1970s and now threatens to recriminalize abortion at the level of a constitutional amendment or a human life statute".[22] This may be too sanguine a view of the pro-life movement's chances of success. It may be as hard to *reverse* progressive decisions

such as *Roe v. Wade* (not to mention reactionary decisions) as it is to *enforce* progressive decisions such as *Brown*. But the argument, that a preferable strategy would have consisted of ordinary political efforts to repeal abortion laws on a state by state basis, seems sound. At least this would have avoided confusing the abortion issue with the different one of democracy versus "government by judiciary" (of which more later).

The Forum of Judicial Review

Disappointment with the "content" of judicial review of legislation, and with the enforceability and impact of even successful litigation, has led some of its supporters to take a different tack altogether, one which emphasizes the political value of the litigation process itself, win or lose.

. . . .

In other words, litigation provides a forum with special, mostly attention-getting, features for causes that are politically weak or unpopular, as progressive causes frequently are. Why should these features inhere in the judicial process and not in the legislative one? Why should the media pay more attention when interests or positions with minority support are advanced in court than when they are advanced out of court? Assuming that this is the case, we think that the answer has to do with the special nature of legal argument which seems to many to be capable of leading to a special sort of result. In legal argument, the ordinary indicia of political power (for example degree of mass support, wealth) are not supposed to count, and "reason" is supposed to prevail. So, win or lose, the judicial forum provides an opportunity to advance the superior reasoning supporting progressive causes, to challenge laws, to raise consciousness, etc., in a setting where one is likely to be listened to no matter how weak one's political support is. We think that this is an important point — for different reasons — and we return to it shortly. For now, we want to reiterate what we suggested in Part I in connection with the constitutional reference cases, namely that it is a specific kind of "reason" that prevails in court, specifically the kind in which numbers or, to be more precise, *classes* do not count. In other words, you cannot say anything you want in court. Argument must take a particular form. Furthermore, not anyone can speak in court. In most courts, particularly the ones in which these kinds of issues are decided, only lawyers do the actual debating. This may be why lawyers find this forum so appealing.[23] But the problem is not that it is lawyers who do the speaking; it is the language they speak.

Democracy and Judicial Review

. . . .

For all their faults, modern bourgeois legal systems, such as Canada's, do contain substantive and procedural legal rights in many realms of life which are not only of great value to workers, but which are the product of many years of working class struggle. Thus, many Marxists have greeted with approval E.P. Thompson's celebration of "the rule of law" as an "unqualified human good".[24] But the *rule of law* must be sharply distinguished from the *legalisation of politics*. The rule of law is a democratic ideal under which the judicial function is impartially to apply the law to the facts of each case. The ideal of the rule of law is most closely approached when laws are specific and leave little room for personal discretion. It is most democratic when there is popular participation in law making. But the rights in the *Charter* differ from the ordinary legal rights evoked by the notion of the rule of law in both of these respects. In the first place, most of them are entirely *abstract*. The *Charter* does not spell out with precision the nature of these rights. For example, instead of the right to strike in specified circumstances, the *Charter* enshrines "freedom of association" and the "right to liberty". Do these include the right to strike? If so, when? As the American legal philosopher, Ronald Dworkin, has pointed out, rights such as those in the *Charter*, are "appeals to moral *concepts*", not "attempts to lay down particular *conceptions*".[25] They remain to be worked out. Worked out by whom, though? By the courts, of course. The government, on the other hand, has tried to give the impression that the rights in the *Charter* are as precise as can be, that indeed the *Charter* is meant to "clarify" as well as to "strengthen" them,[26] and that the judges have merely to apply them:

> Now, these rights *are* written into the *Constitution* so that you will know exactly where you stand.... The courts are there as an impartial referee to correct injustices in the event that you find that your constitutional rights are being denied.[27]

This is an attempt to conceal the basic democratic dilemma. Whereas without the *Charter*, the nature of rights can be, and is, largely worked out and made concrete by legislatures, with the *Charter*, a more or less substantial chunk of this job is handed over to the courts. The task is taken from people who must be elected on the basis of universal adult suffrage in constituencies all over the country, and who must face re-election on the basis of decisions they or their party have made, and handed over to a handful of lawyers appointed once and for all. Though these lawyers are appointed by the government of the day, their tenure typically outlasts that of their appointers and a relatively rigid hierarchy of judicial authority reposes the ultimate say in nine persons (to paraphrase Marx, nine "kings in the shape of irremovable inquisitors of legality"),[28] all appointed by the federal government. Not only are these people not responsible to any constituency, it is an offence even to criticise their decisions (disrespectfully at least), unless *they* should decide the contempt power is an infringement on "freedom of expression"![29]

. . . .

What is presented by the government as a strengthening of popular power, turns out to be a restriction on the universal suffrage for which so many bloody struggles were fought over so many bitter years. (Viewed in this light, the absence of the holding of a referendum or the creation of a deliberative constituent assembly in the patriation process seems almost to have been a matter of principle!)

. . . .

Then there is the mystique surrounding the *Charter* itself, deliberately cultivated by such schemes as Ed Broadbent's to hang it "on the wall of every classroom in every school in every region of Canada",[30] which makes *Charter* interpretation a rather awesome process. So, a court administering the *Charter* is a force to be reckoned with by elected representatives. This means, in addition, that political activists must devote enormous resources to litigation which, besides promoting the direct extraction of surplus value in favour of the legal profession, is a drain on the reservoir of energy and material available for direct participation in the political process. The last several years have seen the energies of the Native peoples and the women's movement consumed in the process of constitution-making, the end-result of which is to entrench a series of concepts to be worked out by judges (mostly male and all non-native). Constitutionalism has reached such proportions that, in the case of aboriginal rights, the right to discuss the issues is being entrenched!

. . . .

The Legalisation of Political Discourse

We are concerned here with a change in discourse , not in the linguistic sense, but in the sense of the structure of discussion, the way in which political issues are categorised and dealt with and, most important, the way in which political decisions are justified. It is the *form of legitimation* which concerns us here. Naturally, a legalisation of political discourse involves a concomitant increment in the peculiar legalese spoken by lawyers, the acquisition of which comprises almost all of their training and which is largely incomprehensible to ordinary human beings. We are concerned that political debate will henceforth have to take this form and be that much more removed from ordinary language. But this is an effect, not the essence, of the phenomenon we seek to identify. Nor are we suggesting that the discourse peculiar to courts imposes significant restraints on them, which force them to come to results very different from those reached by politicians who use a different from of discourse. We accept what the so-called "legal realists" established long ago and what is demonstrated in every courtroom every day, namely that enormous "leeway" exists within judicial reasoning which enables judges to reach conclusions consistent with prevailing interests and values.[31]

Any alternative hypothesis requires (for example) that we believe that differences of judicial opinion such as those in *Re Resolution to Amend the Constitution* are based on profound stupidity on somebody's part (because neither majority nor dissent express any doubt about their positions) and that these differences are uninfluenced by consideration of the social impact of the decision. In other words, judges seem to be no more restrained by their rhetoric than politicians are by theirs. They too can, and do, choose between competing policies and interests, and they too legitimate such choices by reference to reasons which may not reflect their real thinking and motivation. In this they are like legislative politicians. Judges may occasionally support different interests or values than do legislators, reflecting their particular personal biases and the judiciary's separate institutional needs. That they do so is shown by those instances, mentioned earlier, when courts administering Bills of Rights have invalidated legislation. But the evidence also indicates that courts and legislatures generally agree. In other words, legal discourse legitimates decisions necessitated on other grounds, as do other forms of political discourse. Thus, the legalisation of political discourse is a change in the nature of legitimation, not in what is legitimated (though it may *signify* a change in what is legitimated, a point we will pursue later). We should now indicate what we mean by a legal form of discourse.

. . . .

The work of the Soviet legal scholar E.B. Pashukanis is of assistance here. In the 1920s Pashukanis attempted to develop a Marxist theory of law on the basis of the commodity form. His point of departure was the fully developed legal subject of jurisprudence which differed greatly from the zoological human being, in that the legal subject was private, isolated, autonomous, egoistic and possessed of a free will. "Idealist" and "dogmatic" jurisprudence "explained" these strange attributes as innate eternal qualities of human personality: "from this point of view, being a legal subject is a quality inherent in man as

an animate being graced with a rational will".[32] And the legal powers of legal subjects were "explained" as emanations from these capacities. This, argued Pashukanis, was completely upside-down:

> In the logical system of judicial concepts, the contract is merely a form of legal transaction in the abstract, that is, merely one of the will's concrete means of expression which enable the subject to affect the legal sphere surrounding him. Historically speaking, and in real terms, the concept of the legal transaction arose in quite the opposite way, namely from the contract. Outside of the contract, the concepts of the subject and of will only exist, in the legal sense, as lifeless abstractions. These concepts first come to life in the contract. At the same time, the legal form too, in its purest and simplest form, acquires a material basis in the act of exchange.[33]

So, according to Pashukanis, it was the social practice of the contract that gave birth to all these innate qualities, which had no existence in the feudal world of serfdom and Guilds which lacked "any notion of a formal legal status common to all citizens",[34] especially one which included the freedom to contract. In fact, it was the requirements of capitalist exchange relations, especially in labour, first developed in practice and then in theory, that gave birth to the legal subject:

> After he has become slavishly dependent on economic relations, which arise behind his back in the shape of the law of value, the economically active subject — now as a legal subject — acquires, in compensation as it were, a rare gift: a will, juridically constituted, which makes him absolutely free and equal to other owners of commodities like himself.[35]

Anyone who doubts this should ask why the notion of free will demands that there be a total absence of all forms of coercion, *except those of history and class*. In other words, why is the concept of freedom so limited that a bargain entered into under *normal* economic pressure is nevertheless considered to be "free"? The answer is because it is precisely the real compulsions of class which are the essential preconditions for the unequal bargains between capitalist and worker being entered into it all. The notion of freedom is limited, that is determined, by its concrete role of legitimating the acute unfreedom of the status quo. According to Pashukanis, then, the juridical approach requires that class and history be denied and rendered irrelevant:

The free and equal owners of commodities who meet in the market are free and equal only in the abstract relation of appropriation and alienation. In real life, they are bound by various ties of mutual dependence. Examples of this are the retailer and the wholesaler, the peasant and the landowner, the ruined debtor and his creditor, the proletarian and the capitalist. All these innumerable relationships of actual dependence form the real basis of state structure, whereas for the juridical theory of the state it is as if they did not exist.[36]

A good example of the juridical approach is the treatment of abortion by the Supreme Court of the United States. The decriminalisation of abortion in the United States was achieved, almost single-handedly, by the six judges of the majority in the 1973 decision of *Roe v. Wade*. In that case it was held that the Due Process clause of the *Bill of Rights* implicitly included "a freedom of personal choice in certain matters", including "the freedom of a woman to decide whether to terminate a pregnancy". Consequently, a Texas statute making abortion a crime (except where there was medical evidence that it was necessary to save the potential mother's life) was unconstitutional, as would be any statute preventing any abortion during the first trimester of pregnancy or preventing one during the second trimester, unless it could be shown that the mother's health would be adversely affected. We have already mentioned the reaction that this decision engendered. Whether or not this reaction influenced the subsequent decisions on the availability of financial assistance to indigents wanting abortions is neither here nor there. Nevertheless, various statutes were subsequently enacted by federal and state legislatures severely limiting the availability of "medicaid" funds for the abortions which had been legalised by the *Roe v. Wade* decision. In 1976, the Supreme Court upheld a Connecticut regulation restricting such funds to abortions that were "medically necessary".[37] In 1980, it upheld the federal "Hyde Amendment" which restricted funding to abortions "where the life of the mother would be endangered if the fetus were carried to term" or "for the victims of rape or incest when such rape or incest has been reported promptly to a law enforcement agency or public health service".[38] The reasoning in *Harris v. McRae* is a classic illustration of the judicial approach which holds class entirely irrelevant and no obstacle to "freedom by choice". Here we find the fundamental and rigid distinction made by judicial reasoning between the public sphere of "Freedom, Equality, Property and Bentham"[39] and the private sphere of despotism and dependence:

But, regardless of whether the freedom of a woman to choose to terminate her pregnancy for health reasons lies at the core or the periphery of the due process liberty recognized in *Wade*, it simply does not follow that a woman's freedom of choice carries with it a constitutional entitlement to the financial resources to avail herself of the full range of protected choices. The reason why was explained in *Maher*; although government may not place obstacles in the path of a woman's exercise of her freedom of choice, it need not remove those not of its own creation. Indigency falls in the latter category. The financial constraints that restrict an indigent woman's ability to enjoy the full range of constitutionally protected freedom of choice are the product not of government restrictions on access to abortions, but rather of her indigency. Although Congress has opted to subsidize medically necessary services generally, but not certain medially necessary abortions, the fact remains that the Hyde Amendment leaves an indigent woman with at least the same range of choice in deciding whether to obtain a medically necessary abortion as she would have had if Congress had chosen to subsidize no health care costs at all. We are thus not persuaded that the Hyde Amendment impinges on the constitutionally protected freedom or choice recognized in *Wade*".[40]

Another example of the quintessential judicial approach can be found in *Buckley v. Valeo*[41] where the Supreme court of the United States struck down a federal law imposing serious limitations on private campaign expenditures in the wake of the Watergate controversy. The court held that this was an infringement on freedom of speech, thereby denying the relevance of class to political influence or, in other words, denying that limitations of class (*viz.* lack of wealth) could adversely affect people's right to participate in politics.[42]

Yet another example of the "principled" approach characteristic of judicial reasoning is the famous decision of the Supreme Court of the United States in *Regents of the University of California v. Bakke*.[43] In this case, a California medical school's affirmative action programme, which gave preferential admission to members of historically disadvantaged minority groups (blacks, Chicanos, Asians, American Natives) who were also "economically and/or educationally disadvantaged", was ruled unconstitutional on the basis that it offended the Equal Protection clause. The decision embraces several classic elements including the preference of individual rights over collective interests and the requirement of individual blame as a justification for a deprivation ("a classification that imposes disadvantages upon persons like the respondent, who bear no responsibility for whatever harm the beneficiaries of the special admissions programme are thought to have suffered").[44] But the most significant aspect of the decision is its denial of the relevance of history. When the majority held that "[t]here is no principled basis for deciding which groups would merit 'heightened judicial solicitude' and which would not",[45] it was ignoring the historical and concrete fact of racism in the United States, as well as the fact that the specific clause under which it struck down the programme was supposed to have been enacted for the benefit of blacks. As the dissent pointed out, "during most of the past 200 years, the *Constitution* as interpreted by this Court did not prohibit the most ingenious and pervasive forms of discrimination against the Negro. Now, when a state acts to remedy the effects of that legacy of discrimination...this same *Constitution* stands as a barrier".[46]

. . . .

No doubt, some of the concrete rights that might be comprehended by the abstract formulations in the *Charter of Rights and Freedoms* are rights that socialists should fight for. Others, however, are rights that we should fight against. As we noted earlier, given that the interest, points of view and strategic judgments of courts sometimes diverge from those of the legislators, and even from those of the bourgeoisie, victory in the courts is sometimes possible. But history tells us that there will be many more losses than victories. And, for judicial victories to become concrete gains, legitimacy must be accorded to the judicial process *in general*. Thus, each isolated victory legitimates the inevitably greater number of losses which will be suffered by the working class. We should not be seduced or forced to do our fighting in courts according to rules devised for capitalism's maintenance and survival. We should not do our fighting by *pleading*. We should not do our fighting in a form that presupposes that what rights we have depends on something other than what we have won by our struggles; that they fell from the sky to be interpreted by wise, rich men. But, most important, we should not do our fighting by denying the existence of class. To the contrary: it is at this moment that we should be doing our fighting on the basis of class. Collaboration in the legalisation of politics will prevent us from doing this.[47]

Endnotes

1.   P.W. Hogg, *Constitutional Law of Canada* (1977) at 118.
2.   Laskin, "An Inquiry into the Diefenbaker Bill of Rights" (1959), 37 *Can. Bar Rev.* 77; D.A. Schmeiser, *Civil Liberties in Canada* (1964); W.S. Tarnopolsky, *The Canadian Bill of Rights* (2nd ed., 1975).
3.   S. Rush, "Collective Rights and Collective Process: Missing Ingredients in the Canadian Constitution" (1983) in this volume.

4.   E.O. Wright, *Class, Crisis and the State* (1978) at 88.
5.   K. Marx, *Capital: A Critique of Political Economy*, trans. B. Fowkes (1976) at 411–416.
6.   347 U.S. 483 (1954); 349 U.S. 294 (1955).
7.   410 U.S. 113 (1973).
8.   R.G. McCloskey, *The American Supreme Court* (1960) at 14.
9.   *Ibid.* at 151.
10. *Buckley v. Valeo*, 424 U.S. 1 (1976).
11. *Regents of the University of California v. Bakke*, 438 U.S. 265 (1978).
12. *Plessy v. Ferguson*, 163 U.S. 537 (1896).
13. See note 60.
14. *Korematsu v. U.S.*, 323 U.S. 214 (1945).
15. *Beal v. Doe*, 432 U.S. 438 (1977); *Maher v. Roe*, 432 U.S. 464 (1977).
16. *Harris v. McRae*, 448 U.S. 297 (1980).
17. *Dennis v. U.S.*, 341 U.S. 494 (1951).
18. *Martin v. Law Society of B.C.* (1950), 3 D.L.R. 173 (B.C.C.A.) at 183 and 187.
19. *Kleindienst v. Mandel*, 408 U.S. 753 (1972).
20. L.H. Tribe, *American Constitutional Law* (1978) at 580ff.
21. R.A.L. Gambitta, "Litigation, Judicial Deference, and Policy Change" in R.A.L. Gambitta, M.L. May, and J.C. Foster, eds., *Governing Through Courts* (1981) 259 at 261.
22. M.C. Segers, "Governing Abortion Policy" in R.A.L. Gambitta et al., note 75, 283 at 295.
23. MacDonald, "Postscript and Prelude — The Jurisprudence of the Charter: Eight Theses" (1982), 4 *Supreme Court L.R.* 321. At 340–341:
     The thoughtful observer of events leading up to the entrenchment exercise could not help but notice the predominant role played by the legal profession in selling the country on the idea of a *Charter*. From the lobbying of the Canadian Bar Association, to the carping of criminal lawyers and the lawyer-dominated Canadian Civil Liberties Association about gaps and loopholes in need of closing, Canadians have been treated to the rare spectacle of juridical unanimity.
24. E.P. Thompson, *Whigs and Hunters* (1975) at 266.
25. R. Dworkin, *Taking Rights Seriously* (1977) at 136.
26. Can. *The Charter of Rights and Freedoms: A Guide for Canadians* (1982) at 2.
27. See note 79 at 7.
28. K. Marx, "The Class Struggles in France, 1848–1850" in *Collected Works*, vol. 10, (1976) at 45.
29. Martin, "Criticising the Judges" (1982), 28 *McGill L.J.* 1.
30. See note 83 at 15.
31. Holmes, "The Path of Law" (1897), 10 *Harvard L. Rev.* 457; J. Stone, *Legal Systems and Lawyers' Reasoning* (1964); J. Frank, *Courts on Trial* (1949).
32. Pashukanis, note 108 at 117.
33. *Ibid.* at 121.
34. *Ibid.* at 119.
35. *Ibid.* at 114.
36. *Ibid.* at 147.
37. *Maher v. Roe*, note 69.
38. *Harris v. McRae*, note 70 at 302.
39. Marx, note 59 at 280.
40. *Harris v. McRae*, note 70 at 316–317.
41. See note 64.
42. *Ibid.* at 48 and 57.
43. See note 65.
44. *Ibid.* at 310
45. *Ibid.* at 296.
46. *Ibid.* at 387.
47. It is not for us to pontificate on the forms our struggle must take. From our point of view, however, the object of struggle must be the widest and deepest democratization of both the so-called "private" and "public" spheres. Among other things (see note 95) this must include a restriction of judicial power to the narrow confines which enable the attainment of the ideal of the "rule of law".

The Role of Law in Social Transformation: Is a Jurisprudence of Insurgency Possible?[†]

S. Brickey and E. Comack

CONTEMPORARY Marxist theorizing on law has produced a number of different ways of conceptualizing the class character of law within a capitalist society. The main focus of these approaches has largely been on the role of law in maintaining and reproducing an unequal, exploitative system. As a consequence, the issue, even the possibility of using law as a mechanism for securing substantial social change has been downplayed and, in some cases, precluded.

The purpose of this paper is to argue for a rethinking of law, especially in terms of its potential as an agent for social transformation. The discussion will be divided into two main sections. The first involves theoretical considerations. Problems encountered with existing approaches to law *vis-à-vis* their implications for change will be examined and the direction in which a theoretical reformulation might proceed will be outlined. The second involves practical considerations. Here the focus will be on the kinds of legal strategies and particular forms and conditions of law that could be extended or developed in order to move in the direction of a socialist society.

. . . .

Toward a Theoretical Reformulation

It is not our intention to deny the insights to be gained from current Marxist theorizing on law. Much has been accomplished, for example, in the way of clarifying the class character of law under capitalism. Nor is it our intention to deny the significance of law as a mechanism of class domination. In this regard, we would agree with writers like Picciotto that the rule of law — to the extent that it has bourgeois limitations and characteristics — must and should be transcended. The question remains, however, as to *how* that is to be accomplished. Neither instrumentalism nor structuralism offers much hope for law as a mechanism for social transformation. Even those writers who are sensitive to the changing forms of state and law under advanced capitalism offer little guidance in the way of concrete strategies or proposals for bringing about substantive change.[1] As a result, we are left with the uneasy feeling that social transformation must await the 'revolution,' but are given no real indication as to how that will be possible.

In contrast, we would argue that law offers an important (although by no means the sole) source for realizing substantive social change. Implicit in this position is a particular conception of law. As opposed to instrumentalism, we take law to have a distinctly social character; that is, more than just a 'tool' or an external set of rules imposed on individuals, law emerges out of distinct social and historical conditions. In contrast to the structuralist tendency toward 'overdetermination,' we would suggest that emphasis be placed on the role of social actors in the constitution and reproduction of legal order. Following this, the legal sphere can be viewed as an arena of struggle which engages individuals of different classes and political positions.

We would also argue that there are some very good reasons for not abandoning the law. First, if we turn our backs on law, then, as Young suggests, we are left in a position whereby we are denied *any* of the protections afforded by the law — however limited they may be.[2]

Second, although several writers have objected to the discourse of rights as an inappropriate form for generating liberating practices,[3] the fact remains that the very terms of political argument and debate in advanced capitalist societies are unavoidably legalistic. As Hunt remarks:

> All political issues involve, usually quite directly, appeals to rights; whether it be the 'right to work' or 'the right to a fair profit,' 'a woman's right to choose' or 'the right to life,' politics and political demands invoke appeals to rights, or to the analogous language or 'freedom.' So persistent is this appeal to rights that it makes little or no sense to dismiss this reality as some on the left seek to do, by arguing that "rights" are merely ideological masks disguising naked interests.[4]

In this respect, despite its 'bourgeois character,' rights discourse at the very least offers the potential of facilitating the mobilization of political action among subordinate groups.

Third, the tendency for those on the left to deny the possibility of 'legal justice' has left the door wide open for other interpretations. As a result, the right has been given relatively free reign in defining the terms and parameters of 'law and order' issues. The increasing prominence of right wing law and order campaigns, coupled with

---

† Brickey, Stephen, and Comack, Elizabeth, "The Role of Law in Social Transformation: Is a Jurisprudence of Insurgency Possible?" (1987), 2 *Revue canadienne droit et société/Canadian Journal of Law and Society* at 97, 102–14. Reprinted by permission of the publisher.

the emergence of the new law and order state,[5] with its reduction of welfare services and legal encroachments on civil liberties and legal rights, only showcases the need to mount a defense and extension of existing rights and liberties.[6] Indeed, if (as the structuralists suggest) 'crime control' and related issues are an important source of legitimation for the status quo, then there is all the more reason to formulate a Marxist dialectical position which justifies the defense of legal rights and civil liberties.

Finally, to view the law as irrelevant in the attempt to secure social transformation denies the significance of the rights struggles of women, Natives, youth, prisoners and other subordinated segments of society. It promotes a narrow conception of class struggle in that, as Sumner notes, it excises the class character of these conflicts and reduces the struggle of the working class to the economic claims of an urban, white, male labour aristocracy.[7] In effect, it amounts to the 'colonization' of subordinate fractions of the working class by a dominant fraction. Not to give significance to these types of rights struggles also suggests that social transformation may result in a classless society, but it would still be sexist, racist and ageist.[8]

The question remains, then, as to what direction theoretical reformulation should proceed in order to fashion an approach which incorporates, rather than abandons, law as a potential agent for social transformation?

If the law is too narrowly conceived as simply a mechanism of class rule, then it can be easily dismissed as a 'fraud'; as an empty set of guarantees of equity and fairness that have somehow been sold to an unwitting public. Such a narrow conception of law misses some important considerations, not the least of which is that justice *is* often seen to be done. In order to maintain the appearance of equity and fairness, the law must live up to its own claims. As Thompson notes:

> If the law is evidently partial and unjust, then it will mask nothing, legitimate nothing, contribute nothing to any class's hegemony. The essential precondition for the effectiveness of law, in its function as ideology, is that it shall display an independence from gross manipulation and shall seem to be just. It cannot seem to be so without upholding its own logic and criteria of equity; indeed, on occasion, by actually *being* just.[9]

Mandel offers further clarification in the distinction he makes between two opposing senses of the rule of law. The first, which he labels 'democratic,' is essentially the one invoked by Thompson. It "stresses the inhibitions placed on official power...by clear rules strictly adhered to...[rules which] contribute in content to real equality and freedom."[10] The second, which Mandel labels the "juridical," is best described by Pashukanis's analysis of the legal form under capitalism.[11] It "stresses those charac-

teristic features which work to strengthen the *status quo* of unequal social power...."[12] One of the main insights to be gained from this distinction is that there is an inherent *tension* built into the law. This tension is further reflected in the fact that law is *both* a means of coercive and ideological domination; of force *and* consent. As an ideological form, the law acts as a legitimizer of capitalist social relations — it presents those relations in a certain light. Yet, at one and the same time, it too must be legitimized. The law requires an ideological base without which it is simply 'naked power.'[13]

In order to win the consent of the dominated classes to the capitalist order — in order to mediate class relations — the law has to take into account interests other than those of the dominant class. In this sense, "law is not simply imposed upon people, but is also a *product* and *object of* and provides an arena which circumscribes class (and other types of) struggle."[14] Indeed, the rights enshrined in law (universal suffrage, right to form a union, right to strike and so on) were not simply handed down by a benevolent state, but were the outcome of progressive struggles by the subordinate classes.

Thus, as Thompson and others have shown, if the law is to be a legitimizer of capitalist social relations, then the rhetoric and rules of law must be more than 'sham.' Law must provide some protection against the arbitrary use of state power. It must live up to its own claims of equity and fairness. While one need not go so far as to suggest, as Thompson does,[15] that the rule of law is an 'unqualified good' that should be defended at all costs (especially given its 'juridical' sense), the recognition of the tension built into law does open up a number of theoretical possibilities concerning its implications for social transformation. Specifically, law is no longer viewed exclusively as a weapon of class rule, as an abstract, homogeneous entity whose functions can be generalized across different historical periods and circumstances. Instead, the function of law can differ, depending upon the relative strength of social forces that struggle around and within the legal order. Such an assertion involves working at a different level of abstraction that most structuralist accounts.

As Hall and Scraton note, if we rely on Marx's writings in *Capital*, which discuss the 'laws of motion' of a capitalist economy at a very high and abstract level (generalizing these laws across historical periods and societies), then law will be assigned a more 'fixed' and determined role within capitalism.[16] If, however, we rely on the more historical writings of Marx, in which he takes account of the whole social formation — including its political, legal and ideological aspects — then the role of law is treated more problematically.[17] This latter viewpoint allows us to break with the notion of a 'necessary' or 'functional' fit between law and the economic interests of capital. Instead we are left with a very contradictory picture. To quote Hall and Scraton:

There is no historical guarantee that capital must prevail, and no certainty that it can prevail on its own terms, outside the limits imposed by contestation and struggle. The outcomes of particular struggles, sometimes waged within and about the law, sometimes against it, will have real and pertinent effects on how particular historical struggles develop. Law, in this sense, is constitutive of (i.e., it creates) the very conditions of historical development and struggle, and does not merely reflect them.[18]

What we would advocate, therefore, is a theoretical approach to law that moves beyond both a narrow conception of the relations between base and superstructure, and the more fixed and deterministic view of law as operating to the permanent advantage of capital. Such an approach must be materialist and dialectical. It must also be sensitive to the historically specific and contradictory nature of the bourgeois legal form and the system in which it operates.

An appropriate starting point for such an approach is the Marxist conception of social formation. 'Social formation' connotes that certain elements and forms of politics, culture and law are organic to a particular mode of production at a given phase of its development. Without their establishment and maintenance, such a mode of production cannot survive.[19] Once established, however, a capitalist mode of production generates its own internal contradictions. These contradictions will be expressed not only in the economic form (at the point of production), but also in the forms of politics, culture and law which correspond to it. Moreover, these internal contradictions will generate particular legal forms of resistance, which will emerge alongside economic, political and cultural forms. To quote Sumner: "Like feudalism, capitalism must breed its successor in legal forms...before it leaves the scene."[20] As such, the task — both theoretical and practical — is to determine what forms and principles of law we should develop and extend *now* as a precondition for a socialist transformation.

A general strategy for realizing this task is the development of what Tigar and Levy refer to as a "jurisprudence of insurgency."[21] Jurisprudence can be defined as a "process by which legal ideology is created and elaborated." Following this, "jurisprudence of insurgency" can be used to refer to "a certain kind of jurisprudential activity in which a group challenging the prevailing system of social relations no longer seeks to reform it but rather to overthrow it and replace it with another."[22]

If capitalist legality contains the seeds of a socialist legality, then one step toward the development of a jurisprudence of insurgency would be to explore the limits of the dominant legal ideology in order to gauge how much can be accomplished within those limits.[23] This would involve, as Tigar and Levy note, the use of the assumptions

of the governing class to one's own advantage. In short, given the tension built into law, the aim would be to grasp the contradictions inherent in the bourgeois legal form — to work *through* law — in order to alter the very nature of that legal form. Rather than dismissing the rule of law, therefore, we need to consider what effect pushing the 'democratic' sense of the rule of law to its full limit and extent would have on undermining the social relations of capitalism. It is this kind of strategy that we will explore in the remainder of this paper.

. . . .

PRACTICAL CONSIDERATIONS

In approaching the task of assessing the role of law in social transformation, we start from the premise, documented in Tigar and Levy's analysis of European society between the eleventh and nineteenth centuries, that legal change did not simply go through a single stage of transformation in the movement from feudalism to capitalism. Rather, the process was one of an increasing number of small, incremental legal changes that gave increasing power and legitimacy to the fledgling capitalist class. Consistent with this premise, we do not expect law to be either the vanguard or the consequence of the transformation from capitalist to socialist society. We would argue, instead, that it will be one of many strategic areas where existing tension within the system can be used to push the contradictions that result from the structure of capitalism.

Before delineating those legal activities that best represent a jurisprudence of insurgency, we readily admit the difficulty in attempting to predict what will be the most 'progressive' avenues of legal reform. The advantage of retrospective analysis — like that conducted by Tigar and Levy — is that one can discern the significance of small legal changes over historical periods by examining the diverse consequences these changes had over time. When trying to forecast how current legal changes may facilitate future substantive changes in society, one is blind to all of the potential consequences these changes may produce. If, however, historical analysis has any value, it is in the extent to which it enables us to make prescriptive statements, even tentative ones, on how to transform the existing system.

The central issue to be addressed is one of specifying the criteria by which legal reforms are to be evaluated. More specifically, what kinds of legal reform could be defined as insurgent in terms of their orientation or consequence? How do we distinguish, for example, between reforms which aim only for a greater participation of individuals within the capitalist order (i.e., demanding a "bigger share" of the capitalist pie) from those which aim to transform the very basis of that order?[24]

Structuralists have premised their scepticism about law on the observation that equality is limited to the legal sphere (i.e., it does not extend to the economic sphere of capitalist society). It is in this respect that principles like "equality of all before the law" or "blind justice" are viewed as a major source of legitimation for the system of structured or economic inequality. However, several writers have argued that this position with its ritual invocation of the Anatole France quote, lets the law off too lightly since the law is applied in anything but an equal manner.[25] This recognition of the inequalities in the legal order has led to a number of suggestions for reform.

Mandel, for example, in his analysis of Canadian sentencing law, notes that a central feature of sentencing practices is the recognition of varying punishment according to the offender's 'character,' in particular, the offender's relation to the productive apparatus.[26] By taking into account such factors as educational attainment, employment record and one's "good standing in the community" in the determination of sentence, the law operates to the advantage of one class over another. High status offenders, by virtue of their class position, are perceived as requiring (even deserving) less punishment to ensure their continued conformity. Hence, by varying punishment according to class, the law has the net effect of preserving the status quo of inequality, dominance and subordination. In light of this analysis, Mandel suggests that if sentencing was based solely on the utilitarian principle of general deterrence, that is, the protection of individuals from the harmful effects of crime at the least social cost, punishment would then be based entirely on the conduct sought to be prevented, and not on the "character" (i.e., class) of the offender.

What would be the effect of such a reform? Mandel suggests that it would represent a move in the direction of the 'neutral' state which liberals claim exists in modern democratic societies, that is, the system would be more 'just' in the sense that punishment would no longer vary by class. In this respect, such a reform strategy is laudable to the extent that it would mitigate the unequal treatment to which members of the subordinate classes are subjected by the legal system.

Yet, what of the structuralist argument that equality in sentencing practices would only reinforce the system of economic inequality and hence further legitimate that system? On the one hand, removing the class-based nature of punishment (i.e., viewing dominant class members as 'deserving' of lesser punishment) would eliminate one of the means by which class relations are strengthened and reinforced by the legal order. On the other hand, not taking class differences into account could be viewed as a way of ignoring and/or denying the class differences that do exist.[27] Although punishment would no longer vary by class, crime would continue to vary by class. In this respect Mandel's reform proposal has its advantages, but it is

limited.[28] It would only take us part way toward the development of a 'jurisprudence of insurgency.' Such a reform is not insurgent to the extent that it fails to call into question class relations.

Other writers have focused their attention on the content of law.[29] While the criminal law defines certain acts as 'socially injurious' or 'harmful,' it does not tend to define other acts — which are potentially more serious and harmful — as criminal and hence worthy of severe sanctions. For instance, violence against individuals occurs regularly in the workplace of capitalist societies. This typically takes the form of unsafe or hazardous working conditions, exposure to carcinogenic substances and the like. The result has been the loss of life and health for a substantial number of workers. Yet, while such occurrences meet the requirements normally associated with crime (for example, the intentional failure to provide safety equipment or the flagrant violation of safety regulations by owners in order to cut costs and increase profits), they are seldom defined or sanctioned as such. Reiman, therefore, has suggested that the criminal law be redrawn to more accurately reflect the real dangers that individuals pose to society:

> Avoidable acts where the actor had reason to know that his or her acts were likely to lead to someone's death should be counted as forms of murder. Avoidable acts where the actor had reason to believe that his or her acts were likely to lead to someone's injury should be counted as forms of assault and battery. Acts that illegitimately deprive people of their money or possessions should be treated as forms of theft regardless of the color of the thief's collar. Crime in the suites should be prosecuted and punished as vigorously as crime in the streets.[30]

Glasbeek and Rowland have taken this issue one step further.[31] They suggest that there already exist provisions in the criminal law which, although not initially designed for the purpose, could be applied to employer violations of workplace health and safety.[32] This approach is essentially one which advocates the use of criminal law as a vehicle for highlighting the class conflicts inherent in the productive process. By criminalizing employer practices which result in worker injury and death, the severity of the problem would be reinforced. In effect, the strategy proposed by Glasbeek and Rowland is one which aims at using the assumptions of the governing class to the advantage of the working class. To quote the authors:

> Because of the assumptions of the liberal state, the ideology of law requires it to claim that it punishes behaviour which has been judged unacceptable by society no matter who the perpetrator of the offensive behaviour is. It will be interesting

to see how the administrators of the legal justice system respond when it is argued that entrepreneurs offend against the criminal process in much the same way as do robbers of private property and people.[33]

In this respect, such a reform strategy would advance the development of a jurisprudence of insurgency in that it endeavours to push the rule of law to its full limit and extent. Defining the violence which occurs in the workplace of capitalist societies as criminal would have the potential of not only holding employers more accountable for their actions but raising the consciousness of workers as well.

On another level a jurisprudence of insurgency must also be capable of addressing the *manner* in which legal issues are handled by the courts. To elaborate, the law adheres to the principle of 'blind justice.' In so doing, it responds not to the "why" of an act, but to whether or not the act was committed. The race, class or sex of the accused is deemed irrelevant, as the primary criterion for judging cases is the empirical question of whether a formally proscribed act was committed. In short, the issue becomes a matter of "legally relevant facts" and, in the process of resolving this issue, the case is both *individualized* and *depoliticized*. As Grau explains:

> Cases are tried only between legal parties with defined legal interests that conflict over narrowly drawn legal issues. Collective needs are denied. The specificity of the rights and the narrowness of the legal issues combine to preclude the introduction of broader, though relevant, social questions. This restriction effectively depoliticizes the case.[34]

This feature of the legal order contributes to one of the main legitimizing effects of the rule of law, that is, the idea that society is composed, almost exclusively, of individuals and not groups, aggregates or classes. Equally significant is the related belief that legal struggles and political struggles are separate and distinct activities. We would argue, therefore, that a jurisprudence of insurgency must alter this artificial distinction between legal and political issues. This will encompass a two-sided dialectical process. The one side involves attempting to bring the collective nature of the problem into the legal arena while the other side involves broadening the definition of the situation to encompass the political nature of the problem.

"Collectivizing" and "Politicizing" Legal Battles

One way in which the law is being pushed to deal with problems that are more than individual concerns is the strategic use of law by groups to address collective problems. Historically, the labour movement was one of the

first to view the problems of workers as a condition common to all individuals whose work placed them in a subordinated position to capital. Because of the blatant nature of this subordination and the fact that workers could readily interact with other co-workers who were experiencing the same consequences of subordination, craft workers were quicker than other groups to approach their problems as collective in nature.

Before describing how some collectivities are currently attempting to use the law and assessing the insurgent nature of these efforts, it is important to note the dynamic interplay that appears to exist between groups defining their problems as collective problems and the concomitant recognition of the political nature of their problems. The consistency with which groups redefine their problems as political issues suggests that politicization is a typical — if not inevitable — consequence of recognizing the collective nature of the problem. By the very act of sharing their problem with others in a similar condition, people come to realize that approaching the problem as a narrow legal issue is unrealistic and often ineffective.

Of greater significance, however, is the tendency for groups not to rely solely on the courts to resolve their problems. By recognizing the political nature of their problems, activist groups also attempt to put pressure directly on the state by engaging in legislative and lobbying activities, which has traditionally been the almost exclusive domain of the major economic interests in society. The use of lobbying by farmworkers, tenants, environmental groups, women, Indians, the handicapped and the elderly is an indication of the extent to which collectivities are broadening the scope of their struggles beyond the traditional locus of the courts.

Although the lobbying efforts of the above groups may not be successful, they are an indication of how the groups view their difficulties as political problems and not simply legal problems. Billings describes this difference in her assessment on the use of advocacy by women's organizations:

> More and more, therefore, lobbying...has become a familiar tool of the women's movement. Although largely unproductive in proportion to the amount of energy expanded, *lobbying has at least familiarized women with the corridors of power*, created networks across the country and...created lengthy policy agendas that are agreed to nationwide as the action priorities.[35]

Although we will argue that the strategies utilized by some groups are more "insurgent" than other strategies, it is important to recognize that the very act of subordinate groups approaching the law as a collective is of value to the extent that it results in politicizing the manner in which the problem is defined.

Collectivities Using the Law

There appears to be a growing awareness among activist groups of the limitations and constraints of approaching the law as individuals. One way in which groups have attempted to increase their power in using the law is to develop strategies that increase the chances that cases heard before the courts represent the collective interests of the group (given the structural limitation that these collective interests must be fought on an individual basis since collectivities are not recognized as legal actors). Some of these strategies continue to use the courts as the arena for battle but expand the techniques by which groups gain access to the courts. The methods used include class action suits, test cases, judicial reviews, standing as *amicus curiae* and private prosecutions.[36]

There are a number of current examples of individuals in Canada forming groups with the sole purpose of fighting legal issues from a collective rather than an individual base. One of the most recent examples of this is the organization of women fighting for a range of issues that address the many consequences of the systemic subordination of women in capitalist society. These issues include affirmative action, equal pay for work of equal value, the handling of sexual offenses by the criminal justice system and the way in which wife battering is dealt with by the police and the courts. One of the consequences of women defining the legal battle as a collective battle is the shift in strategies that will increase the ability of women to influence the types of cases that should be emphasized in the legal arena. A report by the Canadian Advisory Council on the Status of Women, for example, suggests taking a systematic approach to litigation that would further the collective interests of women. The approach would involve the following four steps:

1. defining a goal in terms of the desired principle of law to be established;
2. plotting how the principle of law can be established from case to case in incremental, logical and clear steps;
3. selecting winnable cases suitable for each stage taken to achieve the goal;
4. consolidating wins at each stage by bringing similar cases to create a cluster of cases in support of the principle established.[37]

It is true that some of the above issues (such as affirmative action) simply strive for women to gain a larger piece of the pie within the existing system. Nonetheless, their importance is in the fact that the state is being asked to recognize that it is *not* the problem of a few individuals but a condition of a large segment of the population that has been adversely affected by the economic system. This demand for the recognition of problems as more than individual problems is also evident in the development of anti-poverty organizations, Indian groups fighting for aboriginal land claims and victims' groups demanding greater participation in the criminal justice system. The presumption that legal battles, particularly those in the area of civil law, are exclusively conflicts between individuals and the state or individuals against corporations is becoming less and less tenable.

Although the above strategies used by groups in approaching the law have a number of advantages over traditional approaches, the fact that the law forces these groups to fight their battles through cases of specific individuals in court limits the ability to use the law to redress collective problems. As long as the state is allowed to approach problems of inequality on an individual, case by case basis, there is little likelihood of the law being an effective tool for redressing the collective problems of subordinate groups.

Collective Rights

We would argue that one way in which the law could be used to promote substantive change is to have collectivities recognized as legal actors in society. In other words, to establish the legal principle that, in addition to individual rights in law, there are or should be collective rights that would acknowledge the existence of subordinate groups and provide them, analogically, with the same rights and freedoms that individuals currently have, in principle if not in practice. The recognition of collective rights enables groups to move away from the narrowly defined manner in which current legal ideology defines conflicts in society.

One subject which immediately comes to mind when discussing collective rights is the *Canadian Charter of Rights and Freedoms*. The passage of the *Constitution Act, 1982* has been lauded by some commentators as a means of providing the legal rights and guarantees that would mitigate against the discrimination of minorities in Canada. However, as Rush[38] has argued, while the *Charter* protects individual rights, collective rights are either ill-protected or disregarded altogether.[39] Rush suggests two ways in which collective rights can be perceived constitutionally:

First, collective rights are those rights which accrue to individuals because of their placement or membership in an identifiable group. In this sense, the realization of the right for each individual depends on its realisation for everyone in the group. These are the rights of cultural communities, ethnic and minority groups.... Second, collective rights are also rights which accrue to groups as groups. These include: the right of Indian people to title to and jurisdiction over their aboriginal land; and the right of women to affirmative action programmes in the workplace.[40]

Following this, Rush notes that "workingclass rights," full aboriginal rights and the rights of women have not been recognized.[41] In this regard, we would argue, alongside Rush, that continued pressure from working people, women, and ethnic and minority groups for greater recognition of collective rights in the *Charter* is needed.

It should be noted that not every instance of the demand for, or recognition of, collective rights represents explicit insurgent activity. For example, the current legislation in Canada regarding hate literature gives groups the legal ability to prohibit the broadcast or publication of material that has the express purpose of producing hatred toward the group. It is the collective analogy to the law of libel that affords an individual the right to protection from malicious material. While this law recognizes the existence of groups as legal actors, there is nothing within the law that directly addresses the relationship of groups to the state or to the economic base of the system. Similarly, what has historically been recognized as the collective right of management to determine the conditions of work, rates of productivity and the like would obviously fall outside the boundaries of a jurisprudence of insurgency. What this highlights is the need to question "collective right to what?" and establish the criteria and principles on which collective rights should be based.

Legal Recognition of Structural Inequality

To what extent is the demand for collective rights and the politicization of collectivities in their legal struggles indicative of a jurisprudence of insurgency? We would argue that, in addition to the obvious value of individuals no longer viewing their problems as isolated, non-political problems, there has been limited success by collectivities in demanding that the legal system *not* approach all citizens as equals. That is, groups are contending that it is unjust to start from the premise that all individuals are equal legally.

The current emphasis on affirmative action programs by the government could be interpreted as a recognition by the state that there is *structural* and *systemic* inequality in capitalist society. Women, minority groups, the handicapped and other groups who have been at the economic margins have been successful in getting the state at least to acknowledge the problem (even if the remedies to the problem have not been forthcoming). In a similar manner, the current efforts to establish the principle of equal-pay-for-work-of-equal-value is an attempt to pressure the government to acknowledge the structural inequality that has resulted from a segmented labour market.

Both affirmative action and the principle of equal-pay-for-work-of-equal-value are *potentially* insurgent because they use a contradiction within legal ideology to push the law and the state past the limits established by the legal system. By groups bringing public attention to the inconsistency that the law is premised on all citizens being equal, yet large segments of the society have been placed in a position of structural inequality, the state is placed in a position of either admitting that all citizens are not equal or making adjustments to provide greater equality. Although the state may attempt to coopt movement toward greater equality, the public focus on the contradiction requires that the state take some form of ameliorative action.

CONCLUSION

The purpose of this paper has been to open up debate on and interest in the role of law in social transformation. If one accepts that a socialist society is not going to emerge in a full-blown manner, then one must assess how the existing system — including law — can be used to push capitalist society along the path toward socialism. The jurisprudence of insurgency is based on the idea that to abandon law as an agent of change is to negate one method that can be used to challenge the present system. The insurgent role of law is to identify the existing contradictions within legal ideology and to use those contradictions to pit that ideology against itself.

Although it has been argued in this paper that the area of collective rights is one avenue that has the potential of bringing the issue of systemic inequality to the forefront, it must also be admitted that the demand for collective rights has the potential of producing divisions within the working class. These divisions are most likely to occur where some segments of the working class perceive a threat from the collective rights won by other segments of that class. A current example of this is affirmative action policy and the negative reaction to this initiative by individuals who do not fit into one of the target groups identified in the policy. The nature of this conflict is often expressed in the form of collective rights versus individual rights. While there will undoubtedly be instances where collective and individual rights will come into conflict, one should also note that capitalists have in the past facilitated this view of the inherent incompatibility of collective rights and individual rights to suit their own interests.[42]

It must also be admitted that there is a danger in groups using the law in the attempt to achieve their aims. Chief among these dangers is the likelihood that groups will start to define their struggles as ones to be fought exclusively within the legal arena. The consequence of this is that a loss in the courts is seen as the end of the struggle.[43] Several authors have written on the difficulties encountered when a group places all of its energies in legal struggles. In fact, Glasbeek has taken the position that groups should avoid using the *Charter* as a political tool.[44] While recognizing the difficulties in using law in a progressive manner, we would continue to argue, for the reasons stated earlier, that the law should not be abandoned as an arena for social struggle.[45]

Finally, a jurisprudence of insurgency has implications for the role that social scientists and legal practitioners play in legal struggles. For the social scientist, perhaps the most important role is to perform the task originally explicated by C. Wright Mills: to demonstrate the linkage between private troubles and public issues.[46] Applying Mills's dictum to the area of law, the task of the social scientist is to show the commonality of individuals' legal problems and the commonality of interests individuals have in collectively addressing these problems.

For the legal practitioner, the traditional approach to the practice of law and the lawyer-client relationship would be inadequate in developing collective struggles in law. In an article written on the subject of poverty law, Wexler describes the inadequacies of approaching social problems from a narrow legal perspective and suggests that conventional legal training does not equip lawyers for the problems that are systemic in nature:

Traditional practice hurts poor people by isolating them from each other, and fails to meet their need for a lawyer by completely misunderstanding that need. Poor people have few individual legal problems in the traditional sense; their problems are the product of poverty, and are common to all poor people.... In this setting the object of practicing poverty law must be to organize poor people, rather than to solve their legal problems. The proper job for a poor people's lawyer is helping poor people to organize themselves to change things so that either no one is poor or (less radically) so that poverty does not entail misery.[47]

By defining legal problems in a larger economic and social context, the lawyer is more likely to adopt an approach to litigation and other legal activities that would best benefit the group. Just as importantly, a lawyer who views the problem in the above manner will, one hopes, also see the value of other kinds of insurgent activities that fall outside of the traditional boundaries of adversarial law, such as confrontations, rent strikes, boycotts and other actions that, while not always legal, can produce effective results for economically subordinate groups.

Endnotes

1. Fraser, "The Legal Theory We Need Now," and Picciotto, "The Theory of the State, Class Struggle and the Rule of Law."
2. Jock Young, "Left Idealism, Reformism and Beyond: From New Criminology to Marxism," in B. Fine, ed., *Capitalism and the Rule of Law* (London: Hutchinson, 1979).
3. See, for example, Valerie Kerruish and Ian Duncanson, "The Regulation of Civil Liberty?" *Law in Context* 4 (1986).
4. Alan Hunt, "The Politics of Law and Justice," in Hunt, ed., *Politics and Power IV* (London: Routledge and Keagan Paul, 1981), 14.
5. Ian Taylor, *Crime, Capitalism and Community: Three Essays in Socialist Criminology* (Toronto: Butterworths, 1983).
6. See, for example, the discussion of the 'right to work' and how it has been appropriated by the right in its attack on organized labour in R.D. White, *Law, Capitalism and the Right to Work* (Toronto: Garamond Press, 1986).
7. Colin Sumner, "The Rule of Law and Civil Rights in Contemporary Marxist Theory" (1981), 9 *Kapitalistate* 65.
8. In this regard, although discussions such as Arthurs's on the emergence of industrial citizenship and the changing legal relations between the state, big business and organized labour, indicate a significant development (Harry Arthurs, "Developing Industrial Citizenship: A Challenge for Canada's Second Century" (1967), *Canadian Bar Review* 45), it is important to note that only about 40 percent of full time workers in Canada (most of whom are male) are unionized. See, for example, White, *Law, Capitalism and the Right to Work*, 73.
9. E.P. Thompson, *Whigs and Hunters* (Harmondsworth: Peregrine, 1975), 263.
10. Michael Mandel, "Marxism and the Rule of Law" (1986), 35 *UNB Law Journal* 20.
11. E. Pashukanis, *Law and Marxism: A General Theory*, C. Arthur, ed., (London: Ink Links Ltd., 1978).
12. Mandel, "Marxism and the Rule of Law," 21.
13. Colin Sumner, *Reading Ideologies: An Investigation into the Marxist Theory of Ideology and Law* (London: Academic Press, 1979).
14. R. Weitzer, "Law and Legal Ideology: Contributions to the Genesis and Reproduction of Capitalism" (1980), 24 *Berkeley Journal of Sociology* 138.
15. Thompson, *Whigs and Hunters*.
16. Stuart Hall and Phil Scraton, "Law, Class and Control" in M. Fitzgerald et al., eds., *Crime and Society: Readings in Theory and History* (London: Routledge and Keagan Paul, 1981).
17. This is the case, for example, in Marx's analysis of the Factory Acts. Workers won a legal victory in that law was used to set restrictions on capital.
18. Hall and Scraton, "Law, Class and Control," 493.
19. See Sumner, "The Rule of Law and Civil Rights in Contemporary Marxist Theory"; and Sumner, *Reading Ideologies: An Investigation into the Marxist Theory of Ideology and Law.*
20. Sumner, "The Rule of Law and Civil Rights in Contemporary Marxist Theory," 87.
21. M. Tigar and M. Levy, *Law and the Rise of Capitalism* (New York: Monthly Review Press, 1977).
22. *Ibid.*, 285–286.
23. In some respects, this is similar to the Gramscian notion of a 'counter hegemony.' See A. Gramsci, *Selections From the Prison Notebooks* (New York: International Publishers, 1971).
24. The difference between a Marxist and a Weberian or liberal orientation should be clear here. Whereas liberals are intent on improving the 'life chances' of disadvantaged groups and hence their ability to compete for scarce resources of an economic, social and political nature (equality of opportunity), Marxists aim for a more complete restructuring of the social order whereby the relations of productions would not be based upon force and coercion (equality of condition).
25. See, for example, Michael Mandel, "Democracy, Class and Canadian Sentencing Law" in Brickey and Comack, eds., *The Social Basis of Law*; and Jock Young, "Left Idealism, Reformism and Beyond: From New Criminology to Marxism."
26. Mandel, "Democracy, Class and Canadian Sentencing Law."
27. For a more thorough discussion of this idea, see Isaac Balbus, "Commodity Form and Legal Form: An Essay on the 'Relative' Autonomy of the Law" in Reasons and Rich, eds., *The Sociology of Law* (Toronto: Butterworths, 1978).
28. Mandel is aware of the limited nature of such a reform. He states: "(A) system based on utilitarian general deterrence...would thus fulfill

as closely as class society permits the democratic ideals of equality before the law and the separation of the public and private spheres" (emphasis added), Michael Mandel, "Democracy, Class and Canadian Sentencing Law," 152.

29.   See, for example, C. Reasons, L. Ross and C. Patterson, *Assault on the Worker: Occupational Health and Safety in Canada* (Toronto: Butterworths, 1981); and Jeffrey H. Reiman, *The Rich Get Richer and The Poor Get Prison*, 2nd ed., (New York: John Wiley & Sons, 1984).

30.   Reiman, *The Rich Get Richer and The Poor Get Prison*, 156.

31.   H. Glasbeek and S. Rowland, "Are Injuring and Killing at Work Crimes?" (1979), *Osgoode Hall Law Journal*.

32.   For example, criminal negligence, assault, criminal breach of contract, conspiracy and common nuisance.

33.   Glasbeek and Rowland, "Are Injuring and Killing at Work Crimes?" 523.

34.   C.W. Grau, "Whatever Happened to Politics? A Critique of Structuralist and Marxist Accounts of State and Law" in Bierne and Quinney, eds., *Marxism and Law* (New York: John Wiley & Sons, 1982), 205.

35.   Billings as quoted in Kim Roberts, *Public Interest Advocacy in Canada* (Ottawa: Department of Justice Canada, 1984), 58. Emphasis added.

36.   It should be emphasized that the claim is not being made that any of these legal techniques are inherently progressive. Although there are obvious advantages, for example, in individuals pooling their resources in class action suits, often the nature of the aggregate formed in these suits is based on a narrow issue and the individuals may share little beyond a common claim against another party. On the advantages that an organization has over an individual when dealing with legal disputes, see M. Galanter, "Delivering Legality: Some Proposals For the Direction of Research" (1976), II *Law and Society Review*. Because of their limited common interest, these aggregates are unlikely to remain a collective force beyond the life of a specific legal dispute. This does not mean, however, that groups fighting for progressive change cannot use class action suits as one method of achieving this change, although it is recognized that the courts are highly restrictive in their willingness to recognize these cases. For a discussion on the restrictive nature of class action suits in the U.S., see J. Handler, "Social Movements and the Legal System: A Theoretical Perspective" in E. Blankenberg, ed., *Innovations in the Legal Service* (Cambridge: Gunn and Hain, 1980).

37.   M.E. Atcheson, M. Eberts and B. Symes, *Women and Legal Action: Precedents, Resources and Strategies for the Future* (Ottawa: Canadian Council on Social Development, 1984), 167–68.

38.   Stuart Rush, "Collective Rights and Collective Process: Missing Ingredients in the Canadian Constitution" (1984), 2 *Socialist Studies: A Canadian Annual*.

39.   The two exceptions are the added protection for women in section 15, and Section 35, which confirms "existing" aboriginal rights.

40.   Rush, "Collective Rights and Collective Process: Missing Ingredients in the Canadian Constitution," 18.

41.   Working class rights include the right to employment, the right to the full enjoyment of the product of one's labour, the right to the enjoyment of just, safe and favourable working conditions and the right to collective bargaining. Aboriginal rights include the right to self-government and the right to title of land. Examples of women's rights are the right to full participation in the economic and political affairs of the country and the right of equal pay for work of equal value.

42.   One example is the frequent attempt by owners to assert that a closed union shop is a violation of the individual worker's freedom of choice to be a non-union employee.

43.   Mandel, "Marxism and the Rule of Law," 26–29.

44.   Harry Glasbeek, "Workers of the World, Avoid the Charter of Rights" (1987), 21 *Canadian Dimension*.

45.   For a discussion on how the Green Party of West Germany is attempting to deal with the dilemma of working within the system while simultaneously attempting to radically transform that same system, see Carl Boggs, "The Greens" (1986), 18 *Our Generation*.

46.   C. Wright Mills, *The Sociological Imagination* (New York: Oxford University Press, 1959).

47.   Stephen Wexler, "Practicing Law for Poor People" (1970), 79 *Yale Law Journal* 1053.

Toward a Political Economy of Law[†]

A. Bartholomew and S. Boyd

JURIDICAL FREEDOM AND FORMAL LEGAL EQUALITY

Perhaps the most fundamental and problematic basis for the ideological aspect of law in organizing consent, legitimating oppressive social and material relations, and fragmenting collective endeavours emanates from the construction of "free" and "equal" subjects through juridical categories. Central premises of law in liberal democratic capitalism are that individuals are "free" in the economic realm, insofar as they may strike their own bargains and dispose of their labour and property "freely,"[1] and free from the juridical inequality and dependence present in pre-capitalist modes of production. The ideological impor-

tance of these premises is found in the way they may obscure and justify unequal and oppressive class, gender, and other relations. As many commentators note, "economic freedom" within capitalism is a particularly cramped notion of freedom. Moreover, as both Leo Panitch and Ellen Meiksins Wood have emphasized, because classes are constituted by the relations of production rather than directly by the state and law, the coercion that obtains within capitalist systems tends to be obscured.[2]

Formal juridical freedom and equality may thus obscure the fact that capitalist relations of production are neither free nor equal. By treating unequally situated individuals and groups as if they were equal at least some of the time, formal juridical equality also perpetuates un-

†   Bartholomew, Amy, and Boyd, Susan, "Toward a Political Economy of Law" in eds. W. Clement and G. Williams, *The New Canadian Political Economy* (Kingston: McGill-Queen's University Press, 1989), 229–33. Reprinted by permission of McGill-Queen's University Press.

equal relations between classes, sexes, and races more directly. Rights are mediated by social, historical, political, and economic contexts which may be "invisible" to the law, a point illustrated by reference to struggles for formal equality rights. For instance, although obtaining the right to own property in the name of formal juridical equality with men was a significant victory for married women, other material and ideological constraints limited access by women to waged labour and the ability to acquire property in their own right. Similarly, capital and labour bargain collectively under conditions of structural inequality that include capital's greater material resources, greater "organizational and ideological resources," and "greater access to the state." Yet, in crucial respects, capital and labour are treated in collective bargaining law as if they meet on an equal footing.[3] Those who are "more equal" in reality are thereby favoured by the "neutrality" of law implicit in the concept of formal juridical equality, thus reinforcing the "net transfer" of power from those who do not own and control the means of production to those who do.[4]

Further, the discretion present in the law, operating against the backdrop of the presumed universal, neutral application of the law to "free and equal" individuals, simultaneously permits disparate and unequal treatment.[5] As Mandel points out, research into the invocation of criminal sanctions by courts demonstrates that "criminal law is applied in anything but an equal manner."[6] In labour law, the discretionary imposition of penalties by courts may be, and often is, particularly harsh when dealing with labour, as in the jailing of Jean-Claude Parrot in the last decade for refusing to order his workers back to work[7] and the recent jailing of Newfoundland labour leaders. The symbolic effects of such harsh example-setting should not be underestimated.

The juridical concepts of free and equal individuals are extended in capitalist democracies to the "interpellation" of people as free and equal citizens. Individual citizenship rights tend to both disarticulate classes and to rearticulate individual citizenship interests as the "national interest." In one fell swoop, classes are thereby fractured at the political level insofar as liberal democracies typically represent citizens, rather than classes, in the state. And political parties tend — at least in Canadian liberal democracy — to represent and articulate the "national interest," while the "national interest" represents pre-eminently the interests of capital. Hence, while subordinate classes may be disorganized by the categories of "free and equal," the capitalist class is brought together and represented broadly as if its interests truly expressed the common good. Thus, despite the fact that the franchise constituted a genuine victory for subordinate classes, oppressed races, and women, the exclusiveness of this mode of representation — the absence of class representation

mechanisms, workplace democracy, and the like — may curtail genuine participatory possibilities.[8]

Predicated on the core concepts of "free" and "equal" individuals, and contingent on historical resistances and struggles, is the constitution of state subjects as bearing other, predominantly individual-based civil liberties and rights in liberal democracies. The presumed atomizing consequences of these configurations are often commented on in the literature. However, the law does not only atomize. Vera Chouinard has provided an important corrective in the Canadian literature by arguing that historical and concrete class antagonisms and struggles may prey on systemic contradictions in particular conjunctures, thus creating possibilities for struggles to resist the logic of atomization. Chouinard indicates that concrete struggles may achieve both legal restrictions on the "degree and manner" of subjection to the logic of production and legal recognition as collectivities. She further argues that precisely to the extent that struggles achieve collectivized class-specific rights and recognition, class capacities may thereby be enhanced.[9]

It seems clear that political struggles often revolve around rights claims in liberal democracies partly because of the cultural and historical commitment to at least some rights in such societies. But the pre-eminence of formal juridical equality may facilitate the appropriation of rights discourse by any political group, progressive or otherwise. Jenson has argued, for example, that instead of the abortion issue being seen as a debate between women and men as groups divided by sex, women's "right" to choose abortion has been pitted against pro-life arguments for foetal rights, thereby obscuring the gendered nature of the issue: "In such a discourse, women disappear as a group and reappear as individuals with needs which can only be assessed against those of all other persons, including foetuses."[10] These sorts of struggles are implicitly, if not explicitly, premised on formal juridical equality — positing equality of "access" to the enormously important claim to "right."

The concepts of atomization, freedom, formal legal equality, individual civil liberties, and political and citizenship rights may currently constitute the most complex and pressing "'problem of legality' in historical materialism." The concepts of "free" and "equal" legal subjects do appear to fracture the subordinate classes, and the "centrality of a private isolated, autonomous, egoistic legal subject possessed above all of a freewill" *may* "enforce... and legitimate...oppressive class relations."[11] At the same time, insofar as the ideological role of law requires some kernel of truth to its claims, individual civil liberties may help protect us against at least the most direct and obvious state coercion and intrusions — a not unimportant point in the era of Thatcher, Reagan, and Vander Zalm. Moreover, citizenship and political rights, as limited as they are in Canada, are valuable and were bestowed on us by neither a beneficent nor a cunning state, but rather were won through struggle. And the importance to disadvantaged groups of legal instruments acquired through struggles for formal legal equality should not be underestimated.

Much work in political economy of law in Canada does not adequately address these important and complex contradictions and problems. Indeed, an unmitigated hostility is displayed toward individual rights, most especially in the work emanating from legally trained scholars.[12] Glasbeek and Mandel, for example, undervalue individual constitutional rights, while some work in administrative law also denigrates the importance of individual claims against the state.[13] These approaches fail to seriously investigate the admittedly problematic but potentially emancipatory status of the individual legal subject endowed with free will and deserving of respect. An unexplored assumption that notions of "autonomy" and "community" are necessarily antithetical also abounds in both the work of Glasbeek and Mandel and in the critical legal studies — inspired work of Hutchinson and Monahan. Hutchinson and Monahan claim, in fact, that "rights-based theories have corrosive implications for communal aspirations."[14]

The complexity of formal legal equality, the importance of civil and political rights against and within the capitalist state, and notions of individualism and citizenship must be explored much more seriously in a developed political economy of law.[15] This task does not require us to concede significant ground to liberal approaches to law. It means simply refusing to throw the baby out with the bathwater. Ian Taylor has aptly criticized those who imply that we can simply take notice of the bourgeois form of law and then go home:

> The danger...is that they frequently present law and legal institutions as an impenetrable and secure element in the apparatus of class domination, and that thereby they discourage the use of legal interventions as a useful move in political struggles. To say this is not, of course, to deny that one of the achievements of bourgeois law *is* to displace the *class* struggles that are constantly occurring in capitalist societies over commodities into disputes between *individual legal subjects*...legal discourse is a mystification of the true character of social relations in a propertied, unequal society, but it is none the less an important (imperfect) instrument in the defence of the liberties of the classes and the sexes.[16]

We would add that the new political economy of law could do worse than to recall the work of some of the "old" political economists, including that of Macpherson and F.R. Scott in their defence of "liberties."[17] Finally, work such as Chouinard's, which begins to theorize how the construction of legal subjects and rights can be challenged,

how class-specific, collective rights may be secured in particular capitalist conjunctures, and how collective constructions may enhance the potential for transformative politics, constitutes an important challenge for the new Canadian political economy. While the questions surrounding appropriate forms of socialist legality have not even been broached in the Canadian literature, commentators have begun to consider the nature of collective and "activist" rights and progressive rights strategies.[18] Even this work, however, is all too sparse and limited in Canada.

. . . .

Law, legal institutions, and rights represent both spaces and tensions, contradictions and possibilities, limitations and potential. We must, therefore, be cognizant of the ways in which law and legal institutions may contribute to the reconstitution and reproduction of existing relations of power. We must simultaneously begin to explore seriously what it means to say that law is embedded within struggle and is an arena of struggle itself; how and to what extent the discourse of rights and the forms of law may contribute to or detract from our struggles; how law, legal institutions, and rights may be used in strategic ways while minimizing the potentially demobilizing and integrative effects of participating within legal forms and legal arenas. If the new Canadian political economy meets these challenges, we will be that much better equipped to assess which strategies advance transformative and socialist politics.

Endnotes

1. See Macpherson, "Capitalism and the Changing Concept of Property"; Wood, *The Retreat from Class*; White, *Law, Capitalism and the Right to Work.*
2. See Wood, *The Retreat from Class*; Panitch, "Elites, Classes and Power."
3. See Panitch and Swartz, *From Consent to Coercion*, 20; see also Warskett, "Bank Worker Unionization." Family law too is now based on market assumptions, masking the gendered nature and disparate impact of the division of domestic responsibilities: Klein, "Individualism."
4. See Macpherson, *The Real World of Democracy*, 42–50.
5. On discretion, see Hay, "Property," and J.B. Wright, *Ideological Dimensions*. Also see Mandel, "Democracy, Class, and Canadian Sentencing Law"; Tucker, "The Law of Employers' Liability"; Warskett, "Bank Worker Unionization"; and Craven, "The Law of Master and Servant."
6. See Mandel, "Democracy, Class and Canadian Sentencing Law."
7. See Glasbeek and Mandel, "Crime and Punishment."
8. See Boyle, "Home Rule for Women."
9. Chouinard, "Class Formation," 12.
10. Jenson, "A False Victory," 36; see also Smart, "Feminism and Law," 120–1.
11. Mandel, "The Rule of Law," 279.
12. See, for example, Glasbeek and Mandel, "The Legalisation of Politics"; Mandel, "The Rule of Law"; Ison, "Sovereignty"; Pue, "The Law Reform Commission"; Arthurs, "Rethinking Administrative Law";

Hutchinson and Monahan, "The Rule of Law"; and Hutchinson, "Part of an Essay."

13. See Glasbeek and Mandel, "The Legislation of Politics."

14. Hutchinson and Monahan, "The Rule of Law," 114; also see 121.

15. See, for example, Panitch, "Liberal Democracy"; Wood, "Liberal Democracy" and *The Retreat from Class*. Also see Hunt, "The Politics of Law and Justice."

16. Taylor, *Law and Order*, 180, first emphasis added.

17. See, for example, Macpherson, *Democratic Theory* and *The Rise and Fall of Economic Justice*; Scott, *Essays on the Constitution*, especially "Freedom of Speech in Canada," 60–75.

18. See Miliband, "Activism"; White, *Law*; and Charles Campbell, "The Canadian Left."

The Politics of the Charter[†]

A. Petter

INTRODUCTION

When the *Canadian Charter of Rights and Freedoms* was proclaimed into law on April 17, 1982, it was an occasion of much rejoicing. Across the country, politicians, judges, civil servants, academics, lawyers, and earnest civil libertarians gathered together to celebrate the advent of the new Charter. At long last, Canadians were told, their rights and freedoms were constitutionally protected from government encroachment, never again to be subject to the vagaries of the political process.

Far away from the ceremonies, beyond the sound of the champagne bottles being popped and the clinking of glasses, the news of their new rights and freedoms may have struck a strange note to some Canadians. To the single mother depending upon government subsidized daycare and the laid-off steelworker collecting unemployment insurance, to the pensioner cashing her guaranteed income supplement and the hospital patient receiving public health care, the suggestion that government was the major adversary of rights and freedoms must surely have sounded peculiar. Some may also have been surprised to learn that the institution responsible for protecting their rights and freedoms from government encroachment was the courts, an institution that has traditionally shown little enthusiasm for the "eccentric principles of socialist philanthropy" upon which such benefits are founded.

Still, while some may have been surprised, relatively few seemed perturbed. No matter what one thought about the role of governments and of courts in our society, surely there was nothing to lose in having more rights and more freedoms. And, if there were smouldering doubts, they were quenched by the support that the Charter received from the federal New Democratic Party, from anti-poverty groups and from numerous other agencies who purported to speak on behalf of the socially and economically disadvantaged. Surely these agencies could not be mistaken as to the Charter's political impact?

The purpose of this essay, put bluntly, is to argue not only that these agencies could have been mistaken as to the Charter's political impact, but that they were mistaken. Far from advancing the interests of disadvantaged Canadians, the Charter is much more likely to work to the detriment of those interests. The reasons for this lie partly in the nature of the rights themselves but, more fundamentally, in the nature of the judicial system charged with their interpretation and enforcement.

Many of the groups that supported the Charter seem to have viewed it as a distributive instrument that would give to everyone without taking from anyone. Thus, while they contemplated how the Charter might promote interests that they favoured, they gave relatively little consideration to the ways in which the Charter could harm those same interests. Furthermore, to the extent that they did consider such harm, they assumed that it could be minimized by expanding some rights, such as equality rights, with which they identified, and by omitting others, such as property rights, to which they were ideologically opposed.

These groups fundamentally misconceived the nature of a charter of rights and of its impact upon society. First, it simply is not accurate to view a charter as being distributive in nature. This is because rights are not commodities that can be given away; they are entitlements governing the relationships among people within a community. The extent to which one person's rights and entitlements are expanded is the extent to which the rights and entitlements of others are contracted. In other words, the conferral of rights under a charter is a zero-sum rather than a positive-sum game.

The 1976 decision of the Supreme Court of Canada in *Harrison v. Carswell* provides a good illustration of this point. In that case, the owner of the shopping centre brought charges under the *Petty Trespasses Act* against a person who sought to picket her employer, a tenant of the

---

† Petter, Andrew, "The Politics of the Charter" (1986), 8 *Supreme Court Law Review* at 473–79. Reprinted by permission of Professor Petter.

centre. The question for the Court was whether the property rights of the owner with respect to the common area of the centre were sufficient to enable him to sustain an action in trespass. The majority decided that they were. By protecting the owner's property rights, however, the Court simultaneously limited the ability of employees and others to exercise their rights to free speech and assembly.

The view of a charter of rights as a distributive document is wrong not only because it fails to take account of the interrelationship amongst rights and entitlements. It is also wrong because it fails to take account of the true function of a charter in a liberal democracy. A charter distributes nothing because it has nothing to distribute. When we say that a person has rights and freedoms under a charter what we really mean is that government must not interfere with that person in particular ways. Thus a Charter gives to citizens only insofar as it takes from government. Governments, however, do not act in vain. Through redistribution of economic resources and regulation of private conduct, governments seek to pursue political purposes that benefit particular social interests. Viewed in this light, one can see that the function of a charter of rights is not to distribute or even to redistribute — it is to regulate the way in which governments go about distributing and redistributing.

The irony, of course, is that the very groups who supported the Charter in the name of disadvantaged Canadians are those who advocate greater intervention by government as means of achieving social justice. By bringing about the enactment of the Charter, they have inhibited the ability of government to engage in the very activities that they espouse.

But what of the rights themselves? Does not the broad guarantee of equality rights and the absence of property rights ensure that the Charter cannot be used in socially or economically regressive ways? Those who believe so misunderstand the nature of a rights document and the role of the judicial system in relation to that document. First, we must bear in mind what has just been said about the function of a charter of rights: it gives to citizens only insofar as it takes from government. For example, the guarantee of equality rights in the Charter does not give people a guarantee of social equality; it does not even commit the government to guaranteeing social equality. Its role is much more limited. What it does is to inhibit government from implementing measures that would bring about or perpetuate inequality.

Still, what can be wrong with preventing government from treating people unequally? In the abstract, of course, there is nothing wrong. We can all agree that people ought to be treated equally. The problem comes when we try to define what is meant by equality. As Justice Frankfurter once observed, "classification is inherent in legislation." We tax the rich to fund programs for the poor. We impose special obligations upon employers. We give special benefits to senior citizens. Most governmental measures treat one person or group differently from another. Thus, a commitment to some abstract notion of equality is not particularly useful. The idea of equality only becomes meaningful when it is animated by a particular social or political idea. A person who regards markets as fair allocators of wealth, for example, will likely view a system of taxation that imposes higher rates of taxation upon higher income earners as a denial of equality. A person who believes that markets do not allocate wealth fairly, on the other hand, will view such a system of taxation as an instrument for promoting equality.

Other rights in the Charter are no different. Rights to freedom of expression, freedom of conscience, freedom of association, liberty, and fundamental justice are just as amorphous unless and until they are infused with political content. Furthermore, the Charter leaves open for interpretation not only the scope of rights and freedoms, but how they interact with each other and with other societal values. As was stated by Jacques J. in a recent decision of the Quebec Court of Appeal:

> The power to determine the constitutionality of the legislation [under the Charter] imposes on the judge the obligation to "fill in the gaps in the law, to resolve potential contradictions, to choose one or the other interpretation of the legal text"...and finally to rank the various rules which come into play.

. . . .

The Statistical Protection of Minorities: Affirmative Action Policy in Canada[†]

R. Knopff

INTRODUCTION

The age of affirmative action in Canada is upon us. It is fast becoming one of the leading policy responses to the political claims of Canadian women and minorities. In June of 1983, Treasury Board President Herb Gray "announced that an affirmative action program, under the direction of the Treasury Board, is being implemented across the Public Service of Canada."[1] Many provincial governments have similar programs, as do a number of municipalities. While these public sector programs are mandatory, affirmative action in the private sector remains largely voluntary.[2] Governments are actively promoting private sector affirmative action, however. In 1979 the Affirmative Action Directorate of the Canada Employment and Immigration Commission (CEIC) was established to act as a consultant to private industry in the creation and implementation of affirmative programs; it does this for businesses under both federal and provincial jurisdiction. Some of the provincial human rights commissions have been doing the same thing. The response to these initiatives has not been overwhelming: from 1979 to 1983 only 49 of the 1130 firms approached by CEIC entered into agreements to establish affirmative action programs, a fact that led the Special House of Commons Committee on Visible Minorities to recommend the imposition of mandatory affirmative action in five years "if insufficient progress is detected under voluntary programs." (Daudlin, 1984:35)

The first affirmative action program in Canada, although it was not then known by that name, was the federal government's effort, beginning in the late 1960s, to increase the proportion of Francophones in the public service. The "target groups" benefitting from the most recent wave of affirmative action are women, indigenous people, the handicapped and blacks (in Nova Scotia). In March of 1984 the Commons Committee on Visible Minorities recommended extension of the policy to racial minorities in general.

In light of these developments, affirmative action becomes an important subject for a volume on minorities in Canada. Since the policy, in most of its current applications, has been borrowed somewhat uncritically from the United States, it is especially important for Canadians to assess its theoretical and practical validity.

. . . .

AFFIRMATIVE ACTION AND SYSTEMIC DISCRIMINATION

Advocates of affirmative action typically describe its purpose as the achievement of a more proportional representation of groups than currently exists. According to one formulation,

> Affirmative Action is a comprehensive planning process designed to ensure not only an equality of opportunity but also an equality of results. Its primary objective is to ensure the Canadian workforce is an accurate reflection of the composition of the Canadian population given the availability of required skills. (Phillips, 1981:2)

Depending on how one defines discrimination, this policy can be understood either as a remedial response to discrimination or as something separate from and additional to an anti-discrimination policy. In the early days of anti-discrimination legislation, when it was generally thought that the legal prohibition extended only to direct and intentional discrimination "because of"[3] an individual's group affiliation, affirmative action was understood in the latter sense. Since not all group underrepresentation could be attributed to direct discrimination, the prohibition of such discrimination could be expected to have a less than adequate impact on the problem of disproportionality. A policy designed to bring about proportional representation had therefore to be understood as overcoming factors other than legally prohibited discrimination, not as a remedy to such discrimination. It followed that the enforcers of anti-discrimination legislation had no authority to compel affirmative action; at best, they could recommend voluntary implementation. Peter Robertson, now a consultant to CEIC, recalls that this was the understanding with which he began his career in the enforcement of anti-discrimination legislation. Upon his appointment as Executive Director of the Missouri Human Rights Commission, he was briefed by a group of experts, one of whom told him, "If *all* you do is remedy discrimination, you will fail. The wave of the future is *affirmative action*." Says Robertson,

† Knopff, Rainer, "The Statistical Protection of Minorities: Affirmative Action Policy in Canada" in eds. N. Neville and A. Kornberg, *Minorities and the Canadian State* (Oakville: Mosaic Press, 1985), 87, 88–90. Copyright © 1985 by Mosaic Press. Reprinted by permission of Neil Neville, Allan Kornberg and Mosaic Press.

Thus, I started out in this field with the idea that affirmative action was entirely different from remedying discrimination and that it was really a sort of quasi-charitable activity which I would ask employers to engage in — out of the kindness of their hearts; but which I could not insist that they implement to comply with the law. (Robertson, 1980:4)

The second way of understanding affirmative action — as a remedy for discrimination — requires an expanded definition of discrimination. One must include in the concept those factors other than direct intentional discrimination that contribute to the underrepresentation affirmative action is designed to overcome. Proponents of affirmative action argue that such a transformation of the definition is logically required by the purpose to which anti-discrimination policy is directed. In this view, the legislation was enacted precisely to bring about greater proportionality, and the discrimination it prohibits must therefore be defined in a manner adequate to this end. Again, Peter Robertson summarizes this thinking:

...when we in the U.S. initially confronted the different unemployment rates, occupational distribution, and disparate income levels of minorities and women we attempted to change the situation by making it illegal to discriminate. When we discovered that eliminating discrimination (as it was then defined) was having no impact on the problem we began to talk about affirmative action and to perceive that action as something above and beyond eliminating discrimination. [However] that failure to change the underlying facts which had confronted Congress was not a failure of the anti-discrimination legislation but was, instead, a failure to understand the real nature of discrimination. It was only when we began to perceive discrimination in a totally different fashion that we began to have a real impact on the problem...on the facts. (Robertson, 1980:4–5)

The main way in which the concept of discrimination was expanded was by including in it neutral rules, procedures or requirements that are not implemented in order to exclude members of a group — and thus escape a prohibition of direct, intentional discrimination — but that

have an "adverse impact" on the group nevertheless. A common example is a height and weight requirement for police work, which, while neutral on its face, excludes many more women than men, thereby contributing to the underrepresentation of women in the police force. In Canada such barriers have come to be known as "systemic discrimination." Other, less common labels include "adverse effect discrimination," "indirect discrimination," and "constructive discrimination." Affirmative action, understood as a policy of increasing the proportional representation of groups, is generally described as a response to this kind of discrimination. One CEIC report, for example, defines affirmative action as "a comprehensive result-oriented plan adopted by an employer as a remedy for employment discrimination with special emphasis on systemic discrimination." (CEIC, 1979:1) Another states that

The affirmative action approach to the problem of inequity and inefficient utilization of target group workers is based on the concept of systemic discrimination. That is, this approach identifies discrimination in the workplace in terms of the impact of employment practices on the employment of target group members. (CEIC, 1982:41)

The prohibition of systemic discrimination is said to make it possible to conceive of affirmative action not only as a policy response to underrepresentation, but also, in appropriate circumstances, as a legal, and hence obligatory, remedy.

Endnotes

1. Treasury Board of Canada, News Release, June 27, 1983, 1.
2. Human Rights Commissions generally have the power only to approve affirmative action programs, not to impose them. A possible exception is the Saskatchewan commission, which, under section 47 of its Act, appears to have the power to order such programs. In some cases boards of inquiry or tribunals engaged in the quasi-judicial resolution of cases that cannot be settled by the commission have the power to order an affirmative action remedy.
3. In 1982, Ontario's Divisional Court interpreted these words in the province's Code as limiting the prohibition to intentional discrimination. *Theresa O'Malley v. Simpson-Sears Ltd.* III C.H.R.R.D./796 at D/799. At the time of writing this case is before the Supreme Court of Canada.

Canadian Charter Equality Rights for Women: One Step Forward or Two Steps Back?[†]

G. Brodsky and S. Day

THREE YEARS LATER

Women have invested hard work and important hopes in Canada's new Constitution and the guarantees of equality in the *Charter of Rights and Freedoms*. Now that the equality guarantees have been in effect for more than three years, some basic questions can be asked and answered. Are women using the Charter? How are the courts interpreting the equality guarantees? Are the guarantees helping women? What factors will determine whether women are helped by the Charter in the long run?

To answer these questions and many others, the authors of this study collected and analysed the 591 reported and unreported decisions handed down by courts at all levels during the first three years that section 15 of the Charter was in effect. Information about the decisions was consolidated in a computerized database. This has made it possible to identify patterns in the cases and to provide statistics about who is using the equality guarantees, and to what ends. By focussing particularly on the cases in which sex equality arguments were made, while considering *all* the decisions handed down, this study sets women's sex equality litigation in its full context.

The news is not good. Women are initiating few cases, and men are using the Charter to strike back at women's hard-won protections and benefits. At the time of writing, the Supreme Court of Canada had not delivered its first judgement concerning the equality guarantees. But the theories of equality and interpretive tests that, to date, have been applied by other courts in Canada will not improve women's condition.

This means that there is much more work to be done. The barriers to women's access to the courts must be removed, and interpretations of equality which are meaningful to women must be advanced more often in the courts. In addition, women must be actively concerned about judicial appointments as well as the education of lawyers and judges.

Recently some commentators have questioned the wisdom of investing work and hope in the Charter. These critics of entrenched rights argue that disadvantaged groups should not look to the courts for assistance with their equality problems because the courts are, by nature, undemocratic and elitist. By and large, judges are white, middle-aged, middle-class men with no direct experience of disadvantage. And the courts, it has been argued, are not known to be agents of change. These commentators contend that women and other disadvantaged groups would be wiser to put their efforts into the democratic system, trying to change conditions of disadvantage through political rather than legal means.

This position is not without justification. Indeed, this study appears to support the views of these critics to the extent that its findings give reason for concern about the efficacy of seeking redress for equality problems in the courts.

However, women have not chosen the courts as the sole forum in which to seek advancement of their equality. Women are pressing governments actively and continually for improvements in laws and programs. Nor can women conclude from their experience that governments provide a better forum for their concerns; after all, governments, like the courts, are unrepresentative and too often unresponsive to women's needs. Because women's disadvantage is so entrenched, women do not have the luxury of choosing one forum over the other. The full support of both governments and the courts is needed for women to take their rightful place in Canadian society. Women must press for changes in both arenas.

It is our hope that the information provided in this study will draw new attention to the importance of access to the courts and of interpretations of equality that will positively affect the lives of women in Canada. If the Charter's guarantees are to be meaningful, governments must make them truly accessible to women and other disadvantaged groups; they cannot be available only to the rich. Also, governments must argue *for* women's interests in court, not against them. For their part, courts must be willing to listen, learn, and give the law its full effect.

The entrenchment of newly framed equality guarantees in the Constitution should be a positive step towards addressing the real conditions of inequality in Canada. However, if this positive step forward is to be taken, equality litigation cannot proceed as it has begun. A question is posed inescapably by the information revealed in this study: How real is Canada's commitment to equality for women?

. . . .

[†]   Brodsky, Gwen, and Day, Shelagh, *Canadian Charter Equality Rights for Women: One Step Forward or Two Steps Back?* (Ottawa: Canadian Advisory Council on the Status of Women, 1989), 3–4, 49–50, 56, 59–67. Reprinted by permission of the Canadian Advisory Council on the Status of Women (CACSW), Ottawa, Ontario.

INTRODUCTION

Three years of constitutional equality litigation in Canada have produced a body of 591 decisions. Of these 591 decisions, 52 are concerned with sex as a ground of discrimination. The number drops to 44 when appeals and other additional proceedings related to any one case are discounted. This means that, in less than 10 per cent of the equality rights decisions, a challenge has been made on the basis that a rule or practice infringes the sex equality guarantee of section 15 of the Charter. This percentage of sex equality challenges is small, considering the interest women have shown in Charter litigation, the range of inequalities they experience, and the fact that women make up a majority of Canada's population.

The fact that the number of challenges is small would be less important if the challenges were ones that significantly promoted the equality of women. However, this is not the case. Ironically, women's sex equality challenges are significantly underrepresented among the sex equality decisions. Only nine of the sex equality challenges were made by or on behalf of women. The other 35 challenges were made by or on behalf of men. If men's "fetal rights" challenges to women's reproductive autonomy and men's challenges to sexual assault legislation (based on age equality, freedom of expression, liberty, and fair trial rights) were added to the tally, the picture would look even worse. (The 44 sex equality decisions are listed and categorized in Appendix C.)

To analyse the sex equality challenges we begin by describing the women's challenges and then we examine the cases in which the sex equality guarantee has been invoked to further the interests of men. The purpose of this overview is to show what types of claims are being brought by women and men and their outcomes. We also hope to familiarize readers with the facts of cases that now form part of Canada's Charter sex equality jurisprudence and to introduce certain interpretive issues.

The chapter concludes with an examination of selected cases that illustrate trends in the equality rights arguments being advanced by litigants.

THE WOMEN'S CHALLENGES

Women's sex equality challenges have been divided evenly between the areas of family law, employment law, and personal injury law, with a smattering of challenges in the areas of human rights law, prison law, and laws concerning women's reproductive autonomy. To date, most of women's sex equality challenges have been directed at longstanding rules and practices that are overtly discriminatory.

The women's challenges have generally been made in the context of civil litigation initiated by them, such as maintenance proceedings or a human rights complaint.

However, the initiator of a legal case and the party that raises the Charter challenge are not necessarily one and the same person. Therefore, some clarification of terminology is required. When we refer to "women's cases", we mean cases in which sex equality challenges have been raised to further women's interests, regardless of who commenced the litigation. Accordingly, *Wallace* and *Morgentaler*, both criminal cases, are included in the women's challenges. Correspondingly, when we refer to "men's cases" we mean cases in which sex equality challenges have been raised to further men's interests, regardless of who commenced the litigation. So, for example, a host of other criminal cases, mainly concerning sexual assault, are included in the men's challenges because, even though the cases were initiated by Attorneys General, these are cases in which the Charter has been invoked by men to further their interests in maintaining power over women.

The results of the women's cases have been mixed. The success rate of the women's initiatives stands at about 50 per cent, lower if one takes into account cases of marital status discrimination, lesbian rights cases, and lower court decisions that were reversed on appeal. However, because the number of women's cases is so small, this percentage may not be a reliable indication of the success rate of women's challenges over the longer term.

. . . .

MEN'S USE OF THE EQUALITY GUARANTEE

Earlier, we said that approximately half of women's sex equality challenges had met with success. The success rate for men's challenges is somewhat lower. However, because there are more men's sex equality challenges (in fact, there were more than three times as many), men's successes have been more than double those of women. Men have succeeded in 13 challenges in the areas of family, employment, prison, and criminal law. The greatest concentration of men's sex equality challenges is in the area of criminal law, with family law challenges in second place.

. . . .

Placing Men's Sex Equality Litigation in a Social Context

Looking at the body of men's cases as a whole, it is apparent that men are using the Charter's guarantees to strike back at certain of the law reforms that women fought for in the 1960s and 1970s. There may be some exceptions, but this is definitely the pattern. Their efforts do not appear to be co-ordinated or part of any conscious political strategy — indeed, there are few signs that men are even aware of a broad social context for their sex equality challenges.

However, most often, the targets of men applicants in sex equality cases are legislative protections and benefits that women have acquired in the last ten or twenty years as a result of intensive lobbying efforts. As the decided cases show, these protections and benefits include recent legislation concerning sexual assault, welfare benefits for single mothers, and unemployment insurance pregnancy benefits.

Whereas most women's challenges have been made in cases initiated by them, the pattern in the men's cases is quite different. Men's sex equality challenges have been made most often in the context of litigation in which they are on the defensive, either as accused persons in criminal cases or as respondents in civil cases. Some cases convey an impression that sex equality arguments are being made without a great deal of forethought, quite often in combination with other arguments, simply to help extricate men from uncomfortable legal predicaments.

The family law case of *Hommel v. Hommel* provides a good illustration. Mr. Hommel sought to reduce a monthly maintenance order for his former wife, Ms. Hommel, and their three children, contending that she had a "duty" to accept a marriage offer she had received from another man and, further, that she was keeping his maintenance payments artificially high by staying at home to care for the children rather than going out to work. The Nova Scotia Supreme Court noted that even though Ms. Hommel was caring for the three children of the marriage, the youngest of whom was under six years, Mr. Hommel took particular exception to her caring for a fourth "illegitimate" child who was not his. Mr. Hommel's Charter argument, which the Court rejected, was that he was being discriminated against because if he fathered another child, the courts would not consider the resulting added financial burden to him. This was plainly wrong, because the Court would have been required to consider a change in his ability to pay maintenance. The application for a reduction in maintenance was denied, and the Court had this to say about the equality argument:

Counsel should not be quick to allege discrimination merely because a judicial determination does not favour counsel's client.

Some may imagine that litigation to secure more benefits for men also may assist women. This is the implication of a statement by Shalom Schachter quoted in a major article in *The Lawyers Weekly* following the Federal Court decision on his successful challenge to unemployment insurance pregnancy benefits:

"I see this case as sort of opening the doors of fathers' consciousness that it is possible for them, it's appropriate for them [to care for their children]," he told *The Lawyers Weekly*. (words in square brackets added by *The Lawyers Weekly*)

One reason Mr. Schachter took on the government was his firm conviction that men must play a greater role in child-rearing if women are to achieve their full potential in the workplace.

"I felt it was ridiculous to expect women to take full advantage of the great opportunities outside the home if they then had to return to the house afterwards and shoulder all of the household responsibilities," he explained.

"I see fathers taking a greater share of household responsibilities as being an assist to women."

We do not take issue with Mr. Schachter's social objectives. Increased public financial support for all his parents has long been a goal of the Canadian feminist movement. The problem with the *Schachter* case is not its goal but the means of pursuing the goal. There is every reason to think that litigation of this sort, initiated by men, seriously endangers the minimal and fragile recognition that women's interests have received in the legislative arena. Indeed, Schachter proposed as a possible solution that biological fathers should be entitled to a share of the biological mother's pregnancy benefits. The Attorney General for Canada argued, moreover, that if any of the benefits provisions violated section 15, the Court should strike them down. Only the Women's Legal Education and Action Fund (LEAF), an intervenor in the case, argued consistently against reducing or eliminating pregnancy benefits.

The possibility that a court could strike down or reduce pregnancy benefits in response to the *Schachter* challenge was and still is a very real risk. Nobody could have predicted with confidence that Justice Strayer would extend the legislation as he did. There are numerous Charter precedents in which courts have specifically stated that the courts cannot fill in "legislative lacunae". Fortunately, Justice Strayer of the Trial Division of the Federal Court accepted the arguments of the intervenor (LEAF) and did, in fact, both protect pregnancy benefits and expand parental benefits for biological mothers and fathers. It is notable that, in *Schachter*, Justice Strayer not only accepted the arguments of the intervenor, but also explicitly acknowledged the assistance that the intervenor had provided, saying, "Through its counsel it played a very helpful role during these proceedings."

The outcome of *Schachter* in the Federal Court Trial Division creates an initial impression that the case has made a positive contribution to women's equality. However, it is far from clear that this will be the final result. The battle to protect pregnancy benefits has probably just begun. The federal government is appealing the Federal Court decision, and Justice Strayer's judgement is suspended, pending the outcome of the appeal.

Given the fact that women are initiating few challenges and men are attacking women's hard-won protections and benefits, the ability to intervene in cases initiated by men is extremely important. In the cases where men are attacking women's protections, the respondents are rarely women. The parties are usually a male applicant or male accused and one or more governments. Women require intervenor status in these circumstances in order to provide women's perspective on the equality issues that directly affect them and to defend the protections they have acquired. There is a great deal to say about women's inequality, little of which has ever been heard in Canadian courts.

EQUALITY CONCEPTS ADVANCED BY LITIGANTS

The underrepresentation of women in sex equality litigation is reflected in the equality concepts being advanced in the courts. In a majority of cases, these equality rights concepts are not in the best interests of women. The theory of equality consistently advanced by male applicants' lawyers is that men have the right to be treated the same as women. This formal equality theory is relied upon repeatedly, even in the face of the most obvious sex-based differences.

For example, in the case of *Re Getty and Crow*, an estates case concerning title to land, a lawyer representing an elderly man was required to persuade the court that his client would probably not have any more children. The man wanted to sell his land but there was a question about whether he might become a father to children who would have claims against the land. The lawyer sought to rely on an evidentiary presumption that women of an advanced age are incapable of having children. The client being male and the presumption applying only to females, the lawyer argued that his client was being discriminated against. He contended that section 15 of the Charter means that the presumption about childbearing capacities should be applied identically to men and women, notwithstanding biological differences between men and women.

In the *Re Getty and Crow* example, the concept of formal equality, or same treatment, is at odds with the biological differences between men and women. Whereas reproductive senescence in women is absolute once menstruation ceases, men's loss of reproductive capacity is relatively gradual, and sperm production can occur in men of very advanced years. However, not even in *Re Getty and Crow*, where one might have seen the absurdity of pretending that men and women are identical, did the Court say that it rejected the equality rights model put forward on behalf of the applicant. What District Court Judge Clements said was that he did not have to decide the "vexing problem" of the application of the Charter to men's and women's reproductive capacities.

The argument that equality requires the courts to ignore differences between men and women is prevalent not just in cases involving biological differences between men and women, but also in cases concerning facets of life in which women are socially or economically disadvantaged relative to men. These are the cases in which judicial endorsement of formal equality has its most devastating effects on women because the courts' decisions stand to legitimize real inequality.

For example, in the *Vincer* case, it was contended on behalf of the male applicant, who was a separated father with joint custody of his children, that the provisions of and regulations under the *Family Allowance Act* discriminate against men because they require that the family allowance cheque be paid to the mother, unless the father has sole custody of the children. In the Federal Court of Appeal, a central argument advanced on behalf of David Vincer was that "the mere fact" that a piece of legislation makes a distinction based on sex constitutes an "unreasonable classification". This argument was reinforced by reference to section 28 which states:

> **28.** Notwithstanding anything in this Charter, the rights and freedoms referred to in it are guaranteed equally to male and female persons.

On behalf of Vincer, it was contended that section 28 strengthens men's claim to be treated the same as women.

Although it is well documented that the negative financial consequences of marriage breakdown are experienced by women primarily, and that the financial position of divorced and separated men often improves, only one judge out of three indicated that he rejected the equality model put forward by the applicant. Justice Pratte noted that the legislation makes a distinction between men and women but said that the distinction is fully justified by the obvious disparity of income between husbands and wives. Justice Marceau and Stone offered no comment on the merits of the case.

The contention that section 28 requires courts to ignore the realities of women's inequality is a cruel twist on the use for which section 28 was intended. Although it may be noted that its gender-neutral wording belies its purpose (as outlined in the previous two chapters), section 28 was included by the Charter's drafters in response to women's lobby for its inclusion in the Charter. Women wanted to reinforce the section 15 promise of assistance to women in overcoming their position of disadvantage in society.

Unfortunately, Attorneys General have not shown themselves to be vigorous advocates for women's rights either, and often they are no better than advocates for men, in terms of the arguments they place before the courts. In most cases, Attorneys General assume the responsibility for defending impugned legislation. The characteristic posture of the Attorneys General is to defend challenged legislation, even if it is legislation that impinges on the

Charter rights of women. There is no shortage of reports concerning cases in which Attorneys General have defended legislation that threatens women's interests.

For example, the party defending the abortion provisions of the *Criminal Code*, in the case of *Morgentaler*, was the Attorney General for Ontario. The government's position on the abortion question was opposed to women's equality. The interpretive arguments put forward in that case by the government lawyers were actually hostile to women's interests. Morgentaler's counsel argued that section 251 of the Code violated women's right to equal benefit of the law. Counsel for the Attorney General for Ontario attacked the sex equality arguments saying:

> ...for section 251 to be decreed invalid as discriminatory on the basis of sex, it would have to be established that a man seeking an abortion would be required to comply with section 251. Clearly this is an impossibility, and therefore section 251 by its very nature cannot be attacked as discriminatory on the basis of sex, *per se.*

This argument that women's experiences are inconsequential unless comparable to an experience known to men is a corollary of the requirement that like be treated alike. It is a mirror image of the arguments put forward by the applicant in *Vincer*. Whereas in *Vincer* it was argued that equality requires that courts pretend that there are no differences between men and women, in *Morgentaler* it was contended by government that the differences can be so significant that no comparison is possible.

Williams v. Haugen is another case in which government lawyers argued that if there is no male group available for comparison, the distinction in question cannot possibly constitute discrimination. In *Williams*, the Saskatchewan Department of Justice argued that a one-year limitation period for women's child support claims could not discriminate on the basis of sex because the entire legislative scheme applied to women only.

Although the Attorneys General usually defend challenged legislation, they are apt to do so in a way that either ignores or undermines the substantive equality content of section 15. The position of most Attorneys General is that section 15 is essentially a guarantee of procedural equality. Counsel for Attorneys General frequently urge the courts to reaffirm a doctrine of judicial defence articulated by the Supreme Court of Canada in relation to the *Canadian Bill of Rights*. With the possible exception of the Attorney General of Ontario, Attorneys General in Canada do not accept the concept that the Charter imposes positive obligations in governments to assist disadvantaged groups in achieving equality. It should come as no surprise, therefore, that counsel for Attorneys General do not support the remedy of extension in equality cases involving under-in-

clusive benefits programs. The example of the *Schachter* case has already been mentioned.

In *Schachter*, although the Attorney General for Canada defended the two-part pregnancy and parental benefits scheme, he submitted that, if the Court found the scheme unconstitutional, it should strike down parental benefits. The position of the Attorney General for Canada then was that it would rather see adoptive parents' benefits eliminated than see parental benefits extended to biological parents.

Attorneys General are not even consistently strong advocates for the legislation of their own legislatures or parliament. For example, counsel for Attorneys General typically do not put forward constitutional sex equality arguments to defend law promulgated because of women's political actions. The case of *Canadian Newspapers Co. v. A.G. Canada* is illustrative.

In *Canadian Newspapers*, the company asserted the right to publish the name of a sexual assault victim, against her will. Section 442(3) of the *Criminal Code* protects sexual assault victims against involuntary publication of their names. The newspaper company applied under section 24 of the Charter for an order declaring that section 442(3) of the *Criminal Code* violates the freedom of the press guaranteed in section 2(b) of the Charter. Justice Osborne of the Supreme Court of Ontario upheld the provision under section 1 of the Charter, as a reasonable limit on freedom of the press.

Canadian Newspapers Co. appealed to the Ontario Court of Appeal, adding fair trial rights to its cache of legal arguments. The government lawyers who defended the legislation did not even mention the right of women to freedom from sexual assault or freedom to speak about sexual assault without fear of forced publication of their names. Instead, the legislation was defended solely under section 1 of the Charter as a reasonable limit, intended to facilitate the reporting of crime. In the result, the Ontario Court of Appeal weakened section 442(3), giving courts discretion to deny victims' requests for protection under section 442(3).

It was not until the Supreme Court of Canada level that the importance of section 442(3) for women's rights as distinct from government rights became a part of the case. On October 26, 1987, a coalition of feminist and community service organizations was granted leave to intervene in the case to argue the sex equality issues.

To ears that have not heard women talk about the experience of sexual assault or the fear of being sexually assaulted, the goal of facilitating the reporting of crime (by publishing the names of sexual assault victims) can sound as though it is the same thing as the goal of women's equality, making women's equality arguments redundant. But there is a difference. The following excerpts from the intervenor's *factum* illustrate concretely that difference:

32. Victims of sexual assault are, overwhelmingly, women; perpetrators of sexual assault are, overwhelmingly, men. Sexual violation of women by men is both an indication and a practice of inequality between the sexes, specifically of the low status of women relative to men.

33. Only a fraction of rapes are reported. Only a fraction of reported rapes are prosecuted. Only a fraction of prosecuted rapes result in convictions. Rape sentences are often short. Most rapists, therefore, continue to live in society either undetected or unpunished and unrehabilitated.

34. In sum, victims of sex crimes, largely women, are comparatively disadvantaged relative to the perpetrators of sex crimes, largely men. A systemic situation of inequality between the sexes thus exists in the social practice of sexual violence, the victims of which are women and in the operation of the criminal justice system, which *de jure* outlaws sexual violence but *de facto* permits men to engage in it on a wide scale.

Seaboyer is another case where constitutional sex equality arguments could have been made by the Attorneys General but were not. In that case, two male accused challenged section 246(6) of the *Criminal Code* on the basis that it violated their rights to a fair trial. Section 246(6) limits the ability of the defence to canvas the past sexual history of a sexual assault victim with anyone other than the accused. Like the provision protecting sexual assault victims against involuntary publication of their names, section 246(6) is a protection for which women's groups lobbied to improve the treatment of women who report sexual assault. Despite this, counsel for the Attorneys General in that case made no reference to the competing constitutional sex equality rights of women.

Further, in the *Borowski* "fetal rights" challenge, the Attorney General for Canada neglected even to mention in its *factum* the negative implications that Borowski's position poses for women's section 15 sex equality rights.

Some of the factums filed by counsel for Attorneys General convey an impression that counsel may not understand that women's inequality problem is not that they are different from men, but that they are disadvantaged relative to men. In *Reference Re Family Benefits Act*, counsel for the Attorney General of Nova Scotia attempted to defend legislation that benefits women, but relied on the same formal equality arguments that are used to undermine women's claims to access to male privileges: "women are differently situated", and therefore can be treated differently. Instead of rejecting the formal model of equality and concentrating on the amelioration of dis-

advantage as a Charter goal, the Attorney General's counsel supported it in order to justify the benefits for single mothers.

In *Reference Re Family Benefits Act*, Counsel's authority for the proposition that persons who are differently situated may be treated differently was the decision of the Ontario Court of Appeal in *R. v. Swain*. In *Swain*, the finding that mentally disordered accused persons are "differently situated" from other accused persons operated as a blanket justification for the automatic incarceration of mentally disordered accused persons. The *Swain* case is inimical to the rights of persons with mental disabilities, a group that includes women. It is also a threat to women as women. What women have in common with other equality-seekers is disadvantage, not difference, and it is because of their disadvantage that women and other equality-seekers need legal advocates who can direct the attention of judges to the concept of disadvantage and away from the concept of difference.

Evidence of women's disadvantage from counsel representing Attorneys General in cases involving challenges to laws that benefit or protect women is typically very sparse. This is particularly striking in the case where section 146 of the *Criminal Code*, which prohibited sexual intercourse with a girl under 14 years of age (statutory rape), was challenged by the accused. For example, in *Lucas*, the Court commented on the lack of evidence from the Crown, saying that no psychological of sociological evidence had been presented to demonstrate the differences "if any" in the sexuality of young teenagers that would justify a different protection for females than males. The Court declared the offence of statutory rape unconstitutional and dismissed the charges against the accused. This decision was overturned on appeal on the grounds that section 15 could not be used because the charges were laid prior to its coming into force.

It must be acknowledged that, in some cases, women's rights advocates have also advanced formal equality arguments, saying that men and women should be treated the same. For example, in *Shewchuk*, a coalition of intervenors, including the West Coast Women's Legal Education and Action Fund, supported the view that special treatment of single mothers was unwarranted and argued in favour of extending the benefit in question to single fathers. Presented with the risk of losing the special programs completely — and the reality of extremely few precedents to support alternatives to formal equality — it is not surprising that women have tried to make the best of formal equality arguments.

However, feminist organizations are attempting increasingly to present substantive equality arguments to the courts and to provide judges with information concerning the realities of women's inequality. One example is the women-run defence in the *Federation of Women Teachers* case. The defence in this case consisted of in-depth argument and extensive expert evidence concerning the unequal position of women teachers in the teaching profession and of women in the work force generally. It also documented the silence of the men's federation concerning discrimination against women teachers, the improvements in conditions for women teachers brought about by the women teachers' federation, the historical failure of mixed organizations to recognize and represent women's interests, the capacity of women's organizations to address women's distinctive priorities effectively, the positive recognition that women's advocacy groups have achieved in other societies such as Norway, Sweden, Denmark, and the United States, and the inability of the same-treatment model of equality to rectify existing social imbalances among groups.

The defence in the *Federation of Women Teachers* case was not conducted by counsel for Attorneys General and demonstrated a very different appearance from those cases conducted by them. The *factum* and the evidence were developed over a two-year period by a team of privately retained feminist lawyers and scholars. The resources and role of women advocates in this case were exceptional. Unfortunately, as a rule, women's organizations have neither the resources nor the standing to be the primary parties in sex equality challenges.

CONCLUSION

Women have initiated very little sex equality litigation. Men have initiated more than three times as many sex equality challenges as women have. Many of the men's challenges are to legislated protections and benefits such as rape law reforms and unemployment insurance pregnancy benefits, which women fought for in the political arena. To defend their few hard-won gains against men's equality challenges, and to establish a voice for women in the courts, women have been forced to seek the courts' leave to participate in equality litigation as intervenors.

In order to better assess the impact of sex equality litigation, Chapter Four will provide a closer look at the judges' decisions to determine what equality concepts are being adopted by the courts in sex equality cases, and how other important interpretive issues are being resolved.

Judging and Equality: For Whom Does the Charter Toll?[†]
A.W. Mackay

THE PROMISE OF JUDGES AND THE CHARTER

Unless this Court is willing to say that the condition of Duncan's (the accused) purse is no ground upon which to qualify or limit his rights as a citizen of the United States...then our heritage of constitutional privileges and immunities is only a promise to the ear to be broken to the hope, a teasing illusion like a munificent bequest in a pauper's will.

Canada's *Charter* has real potential in its broad and open-ended language and invites lawyers and judges to engage in a debate about basic values in Canadian society. The critical question raised by the opening quotation is whether the promise of the *Charter* is only a "promise to the ear to be broken to the hope." If the *Charter* creates an illusion of rights that cannot in fact be enforced, it is a bad thing for Canadians. Not only will raised expectations be dashed, but the limited energy for reform will have been diverted from more useful channels. After four years it is far from clear whether the *Charter* is a good or bad thing for the real protection of rights in Canada.

Legal academics are divided on the potential of the *Charter*. There are the *Charter* optimists, who, either as a matter of prediction or advocacy, make broad claims about the *Charter* as a vehicle for change. Another group of academics might be labelled as the *Charter* skeptics. A third group is the *Charter* pessimists. This latter group views the *Charter* as an obstacle to real change in society. If the *Charter* can be analogized to a religion, as Professor McBride does in his article, the optimists are the true believers, the skeptics are the agnostics and the pessimists are the atheists or heretics. Heretics may be the better term for the last group as they reject the *Charter* but embrace other religions. Practising lawyers and judges would also divide along similar lines.

[†]   Mackay, A. Wayne, "Judging and Equality: For Whom Does the Charter Toll?" (1986), 10:2 *Dalhousie Law Journal* at pp. 39–51. Reprinted by permission of Dalhousie Law Journal.

Assessment of the *Charter* and its implications for change may, for sake of clarity, be considered at three separate levels:

1. the choice of the rights paradigm as the central means of addressing the relationships amongst individuals and between individuals and the state;
2. the judicial treatment of the *Charter*;
3. the content of the *Charter* itself.

Most of what follows this part of the article will be concerned with the first two levels of analysis. This part of the article examines the *Charter* as a document. Since the words of the *Charter* only gain life from judicial interpretation, it is impossible to totally ignore the second level analysis but it will be kept to a minimum. I shall begin by considering the positive side of the *Charter* — its potential.

Broad Potential

The *Charter* contains broad and ringing phrases that invite creative arguments from lawyers and innovative responses from judges. While the catalogue of rights and their expression is not ideal, the wording is broad enough to encompass most of the important value disputes in Canadian society. Sections 7 and 15 are prime examples. The former has already been used on both sides of the abortion debate and in respect to the testing of cruise missiles in Canada. Out of section 7 there have also been claims of a right to die, a right to an education and a right to basic social security, to name but a few. The equality guarantees in section 15 offer an even broader scope and the kind of issues that will arise under it will be discussed in Part 2 of this article.

Implicit in the *Charter* is a balancing of interests that moves judges to a more overt policy-making role. This balancing will involve not only a weighing of individual rights against societal claims to reasonable limits in section 1 but also the weighing of one individual right against another. Often an equality right will be on one side of the scale and one of the liberty rights on the other. Thus the structure of the *Charter* may force judges to be more overtly political than they have been in the past. Patrick Monahan views this interest balancing role with some alarm:

> Even a cursory analysis of the language and structure of the *Charter* indicates that most *Charter* litigation may well turn on the issue of the "wisdom" of legislative choices. In part, this is a product of the abstract and generalized nature of the rights protected by the *Charter*. The very process of defining the content of the rights protected by the *Charter* seems inherently political. Many of these rights — most notably the right to

"equality" and "liberty" — contain little or no substantive criteria; they resemble blank slates on which the judiciary can scrawl the imagery of their choice. But there is a second problem. Having given content to these open-ended rights, the judiciary must then "balance" these rights against considerations of the general welfare under section one. This process of "interest balancing" seems just another way of asking the fundamental legislative questions; "is this worth what it costs?" The process of balancing individual against collective interests is a calculation which would have already been made by the legislature when it passed the statute under review. Since the government passed the statute, it must have calculated that the interests to be served outweigh those to be sacrificed. Section one of the *Charter* appears to invite the Court to assess and second-guess the "wisdom" of the balance struck by the legislature.

In response to his concern about courts that may become too actively involved in assessing the wisdom of government action, Professor Monahan articulates a theory of judicial review based upon the promotion of democratic values; these include the rights to participate in decision-making, equality of access and fair distribution of benefits. He goes beyond a strict process standard of review but stops short of having the judges evaluate outcomes. Monahan's touchstone is the democratic values implicit in Canadian society, which are distinct from those in the United States. This evolution of a distinct Canadian jurisprudence is one of the promising features of the *Charter*.

W.R. Lederman has also fixed his attention on the phrase "free and democratic society" in section 1 of the *Charter*, but to a rather different purpose than that of Monahan. Professor Lederman predicts that independent courts and democratic legislatures will both pursue the goals of the *Charter* in a spirit of partnership. The re-thinking of the comparative roles of legislators, administrators and courts is another promising feature of the *Charter* that is likely to be realized.

Part of the above reconsideration of institutional roles is a concern about the best way to protect minorities, defined as those who have been excluded from power; this includes all the groups specified in section 15 of the *Charter* and many more as well. Courts may offer minorities a shield against the majority, and this may be particularly important in times of political conservatism and economic restraint. Even those who are *Charter* skeptics see a useful role for the courts in relation to minorities.

Nevertheless, we should also see the *Charter* as a brave and necessary step in enhancing the civility of the Canadian state. The diversity of Canada has made it a polity with many minorities, which are everywhere vulnerable to the passing whims of majorities. Our history is full of instances where a national majority has imposed its will on local minorities, as in the imposition of the tariff or conscription in a way that created deeply-rooted resentments which lasted for generations, or where local majorities in particular provinces or regions abused the rights of their own minorities, such as Japanese-Canadians in British Columbia, Jehovah's Witnesses in Quebec and francophones in Manitoba. The *Charter* as it stands might not have been strong enough to protect or help them, but its ultimate object was to nourish an atmosphere of civility which will act as a restraint on the old Adam in us all. A truly civil polity is a very fragile thing, as it is, as Frank Scott said, a work of art that is never finished. It is very easy to destroy or damage it. It requires restraint and discipline to preserve it.

Another promising aspect of the *Charter* is the opening up of legal discourse to a wider range of sources and influences. Courts will have to reconsider what sources to use in resolving a *Charter* question and how they can become informed on matters beyond the law. Mr Justice Gerald La Forest made the following encouraging statement about *Charter* sources before being appointed to the Supreme Court of Canada and it appears to be a view shared by many of his present colleagues on the Court:

> the *Charter* forces us to look at questions differently than before. However clear a statute or its purposes may be, courts will be asked to make a value judgment about it, a duty that is very different from the traditional role of the court. This should profoundly affect the sources on which courts must rely for guidance.... Our courts must be guided by the felt needs and traditions of our own society. But they will be invaluable in raising the issues that must be considered. So often we fail to see that a course of action may unnecessarily infringe on the rights of the individual because we have simply become accustomed to that way of doing things.
>
> I hope, too, that our search will also lead us to seek light from disciplines other than the law, for many of the questions we will have to consider transcend the legal system. Rights continue to emerge from the human experience.

Perhaps the greatest potential for the *Charter* lies in its use outside the courtrooms, but it has important uses within too. While the judges play a crucial role in interpreting the *Charter*, it is the front-line lawyers who must take the lead in this new constitutional dance. Lawyers must be open to representing a wider range of clients and be prepared to raise innovative arguments, supporting alternative versions of reality. Judges, particularly those at the lower levels, are likely to resist such creative advocacy but there will be judges willing to break new ground. Furthermore, the polycentric nature of issues that arise under the *Charter* beg a larger role for intervenors and Brandeis style briefs in the litigation process. This opening up of the adjudicative process will have a positive effect even beyond *Charter* cases.

The growing media interest in *Charter* litigation also invites the use of the *Charter* as a political tool. This was high on the agenda of Operation Dismantle when they challenged the testing of cruise missiles in Canada on the basis of the *Charter*. Such litigation is expensive but for the amount of media exposure it may be a bargain. Some groups, however, cannot afford to litigate even if it offers an opportunity for political education. For such groups, the *Charter* may be used as part of the public debate about the issue, which may result in concessions in order to avoid bad press or possible litigation.

Whether Canadians like it or not, courts will become a more overt political forum under the *Charter*. As J.R. Mallory observes, this has been the situation in the United States for many decades:

> The *Charter* opens up a new avenue — one which has for a long time been available to interest groups in the United States. Attempts to extend civil rights to blacks could never succeed as long as there were powerful veto groups in the Congress which could stop any law on the subject. Accordingly, the strategy of shifting the action to the courts not only prodded the courts into interpreting the law and the constitution in a more liberal way, but also created a great deal of publicity which helped to mobilize public opinion and thus encourage legislative and executive compliance. In the past there were slight prospects for this strategy to succeed in Canada. Now that the *Charter* is part of the constitution we may expect a substantial number of issue-groups, from environmentalists to pro- and anti-abortion groups, to fight their battles in the courts, which will greatly enhance their capacity to mobilize public opinion.

The new political use of courts is not as novel as many people suggest. What may be new is the extent to which courts can now provide a forum for a wider range of political views. If minority interests will have as much chance to state their case in court as large corporate interests, that would be a promising step towards equality. I shall explore in the next part of the paper whose voices have been heard in the courts during the first four years of the *Charter*.

Some writers would dispute the distinction between the legal and political uses of the courts. As Professor McBride suggests in the preceding article in this volume, there is politics at some level in all adjudication. It is really a question of kind and degree. Mark Gold has argued that judges are advocates in rendering a decision and aware of the value of rhetorical devices. In some senses, judges are political actors in the adjudicative process, but they are restrained by training and institutional structures in ways that distinguish them from naked legislators. I shall return to this theme in the concluding part of this article.

A final promising feature of the *Charter* is its value as an educational tool. The role of the judge as teacher and expositor of the law was recognized before the *Charter*. As McBride indicates in the preceding article, this role is extended to broader audiences by the *Charter*. To a significant extent, the Supreme Court of Canada has become the leader of a national symposium on fundamental rights and values. While education in itself offers no panacea, the value of raising a "rights consciousness" should not be discounted. There is a potential in the *Charter* that suggests that it may be more than "a promise to the ear," but there are also limitations.

Charter Limitations

Section 52 of the *Constitution Act, 1982* declares that the *Charter*, as part of the Canadian Constitution, is the supreme law of the land and any conflicting policy is void. In spite of this declaration of judicial supremacy, there are limitations in the *Charter* as a document that make the label "judicial primacy" more applicable to the Canadian scene. While some lament the dilution of judicial power, others argue that the "joint primacy" of judicial and legislative institutions is both desirable and appropriate in the Canadian context. Supremacy of parliament as inherited from the United Kingdom has been qualified but not discarded. Whether this is a strength or limitation is a matter of opinion, but in terms of what judges can do with the *Charter* it is a limitation.

The clearest indication that supremacy of parliament is still alive is section 33 of the *Charter*. This section allows legislators to over-ride sections 2 and 7–15 of the *Charter* for a five-year period, which can then be renewed. It is significant that both sections 7 and 15, which are the broadest ones in the *Charter* with respect to equality, are included. Interestingly, section 28, dealing with sex discrimination, is outside the scope of the over-ride clause. On most important issues the legislators can still have the final say.

During the patriation process, the *Charter* sales people (mostly at the federal level) argued that it would be politically unpopular to use section 33 and it would thus have little impact. That has not been the case. In Quebec, under René Lèvesque's Parti Québecois, every Quebec statute contained a section 33 over-ride clause. In early 1986, the province of Saskatchewan became the first province outside of Quebec to use section 33. It was used in the context of back-to-work legislation to end rotating strikes by the Saskatchewan Government Employees Union. These uses were not overwhelmingly unpopular and other such uses will emerge in the future.

Section 33 represents a political limit on the use of the *Charter* and is a reaffirmation of majority rule. Whatever the courts say about what rights should be protected in Canadian society, these same rights can be over-ridden if there is the political will to do so. This has led some critics of the *Charter* to question the value of a document that only protects politically acceptable rights. Dean Rod MacDonald of McGill Law School is one such critic, and he argues that a proper analysis of the *Charter* requires an examination and justification of the basic tenets of liberal political theory. An attempt will be made in Part 4 of this article to assess the *Charter* in its legal and political context. Only when painting on this broader canvas will the strengths and limitations of the *Charter* appear.

MacDonald asserts that history teaches that charters of rights are ineffective in intolerant societies and unnecessary in tolerant ones. I would question the historical accuracy of this generalization, but even if it is true in most cases, does this undercut the value of the *Charter*? Surely there will be a few victories under the *Charter* that would not otherwise have occurred, and these will have some effect on unlitigated claims and administrative practices. Furthermore, the *Charter* itself and the litigation and debate that emerges from it has an educational component that can change social attitudes about rights.

There will be cases where political actors are more progressive than their judicial counterparts. In such cases, judges may use the *Charter* to impede rather than promote change. This is a limitation on the *Charter* but not a case for discarding it. When there is no political will to uphold civil liberties a judicial entrenchment of rights can buffer the effect of this absence. When there is such a political will the existence of the *Charter* may expedite the judicial acceptance of a similar view. The approach to the *Canadian Bill of Rights* offers some evidence of the value of a *Charter* as an education for judges. In an increasingly conservative political climate there is also some solace in the fact that even a conservative judiciary can hold the fort against an extreme shift away from human rights.

Many of MacDonald's complaints, and he is typical of many of the *Charter* skeptics, are against what judges will do with the *Charter* rather than the *Charter* itself. It is difficult to distinguish judicial interpretation from the words of the *Charter* as they converge to give meaning to the guaranteed rights. Whether the *Charter* should be read expansively or narrowly depends on assumptions about whether judges are promoters or inhibitors of rights. I shall return to the role of judges as protectors of equality in the latter parts of this article.

Section 1 of the *Charter* is the vehicle by which judges can limit the rights guaranteed in the document:

> *The Canadian Charter of Rights and Freedoms* guarantees the rights and freedoms set out in it subject only to such reasonable limits prescribed by law as can be demonstrably justified in a free and democratic society.

What are the reasonable limits on broad rights such as equality, that judges will find acceptable? The burden of demonstrable justification rests with the state but judges will be the final arbiters of what limitations are reasonable in "a free and democratic society." To put the question in the present context, what reasonable limitations on equality will be tolerated in Canada, as a free and democratic society? Judges will claim to reflect broader social values in making such judgment but they will inevitably impose their own values as well. Thus, the extent to which section 1 limits the impact of the *Charter* depends on the value structure implicit in both the judicial and the larger political process. These values will be examined later.

A significant limitation on the reach of the *Charter* is the application of section 32. The majority view on this section is that the *Charter* will encompass legislative and government action, broadly defined, but will not be extended to the private sector. There is a minority view that section 32 can be read to include the private sector and thus extend the *Charter* to all activity. Many violations of equality do occur in the private sector, and if it is immune from the *Charter*, the *Charter* will be blunted as an instrument of equality. Hester Lessard's article in this volume emphasizes the negative impact that a state action interpretation of the *Charter* would have on combating discrimination against women. The division of the world into public and private spheres has been identified by others as a limitation on legal reform generally.

Perhaps the most important limitation on the *Charter* is in the form of things that were omitted from the document. One such omission is a guarantee of the funding necessary to pursue a *Charter* challenge. This limits the real access to the *Charter*, as is discussed in the next part of this article. Limitations are also inherent in the choice of rights for inclusion in the *Charter* and the inferential exclusion of others.

One of the best critiques of the *Charter* on a philosophical basis is that presented by Robert Samek. He argues that the rights protected in the *Charter* are the predictable legal and political rights that characterize the liberal state. They are aimed at removing the negative constraint of the state on individual freedom of choice. There is a notable absence of social and economic rights

that would require a more positive intervention on the part of the courts.

As the title of his article suggests, Professor Samek is concerned about "untrenching" fundamental rights. In his view, real fundamental rights have a dynamism that denies a specific ideological content and precludes a static articulation and interpretation by the courts. Furthermore, he argues that most of the rights protected by the *Charter* are not fundamental. Samek takes the word "fundamental" in the term "fundamental rights" very seriously. He states that fundamental rights are rights that inhere in us *qua* human beings and not as participants in a particular political and social mix. Thus, the equality provision comes closest to capturing what Samek feels is a fundamental right. Language rights and mobility rights may be rights, but they are not fundamental rights, in Samek's view. Rights that are fundamental do not arise from conferral by the state. Neither can they be removed by the state. This is clearly a philosopher's objection to the *Charter*.

While I am in general agreement with the Samek critique and particularly like his link between rights and needs, there are also some problems with his analysis. Even if rights do inhere in people, the regulation of their exercise must involve the state. Another philosopher, Jacques Maritain, has argued that while fundamental rights are possessed by people and not conferred by the state, their exercise is a function of being recognized or limited by the state. Petter makes the perceptive comment that the *Charter* is not a distributive document but represents a "zero sum" game in which rights are given to citizens at the expense of governments.

The argument about what rights should be included in the *Charter* presupposes an assumption about the value of courts as protectors of fundamental rights. Since Samek is opposed to the entrenchment of fundamental rights, it appears that he is skeptical about the role of courts as a protector. Thus, one would expect him to be happy with the fact that social and economic rights, which he regards as real fundamental rights, are outside the *Charter*. This is not the case. Indeed section 7 and 15 could be broadly interpreted to encompass social and economic rights. A more difficult question is whether this would be a good thing.

When dealing with the issue of entrenchment of economic rights, *Charter* critics are as blind and legalistic as the objects of their scorn. More would be required than the simple entrenchment of an economic or social right. Such a move would give the *Charter* more clout, but entrenchment is only the legal act. What would this entail in terms of an egalitarian redistribution of wealth in our society? Would those from whom this wealth would be taken remain in Canada? Would the capital flight from a country contemplating such a move result in an economy that could not maintain its present standards of welfare or jobs, let alone give effect to the legal right to a job or a guaranteed minimum income? Failure by legal commentators to recognize and address such concerns gives real meaning to the term disciplinary blindness. MacDonald appears blind to this, while Samek says only that we must be willing to pay the price for economic rights; on what that price is, he is conspicuously silent.

Is the *Charter* negative, positive or neutral as a means of promoting equality? The answer to this question has less to do with the document itself than how it is used. If the *Charter* will be used negatively, then the limitations on it are positive for equality. If the *Charter* will be used positively, then the opposite is true. The *Charter* has the potential for positive use, although such use is limited. Whether this potential will be realized depends on the political and judicial context. The rest of this article turns to these matters.

I have identified myself as a *Charter* skeptic or agnostic, rather than a true believer. The basis for my skepticism is not the *Charter* document itself but rather the limits that are inherent in the ideology of the liberal state and the process of judging. While the *Charter* is not self-enforcing, it offers the potential for significant change. There will be no revolution in Canadian society and none was intended by its drafters. The *Charter* will, however, change the lot of some Canadians. Whether the protection of fundamental rights will be extended to those with fundamental needs will be the true test of the *Charter*.

Further Reading

Stuart Hall "Drifting into a Law and Order Society" (Amersham, Berkshire, U.K.: The Cobden Trust, 1980), 1–10, 17.

Bertha Wilson "Judicial Decision-Making in the Supreme Court" (1986), 36 *University of Toronto Law Journal* 227–38.

Barry Wright, "Criminal Proceedings and the Transformative Potential of Law: Taking Historical Experiences Seriously" (1991), 3 *Journal of Human Justice* 7.